Programming Windows 95

UNLEASHED

SAMS
PUBLISHING

201 West 103rd Street
Indianapolis, IN 46290

Copyright © 1995 by Sams Publishing

FIRST EDITION

International Standard Book Number: 0-672-30602-6

Library of Congress Catalog Card Number: 94-67092

98 97 96 95   4 3 2 1

Interpretation of the printing code: the rightmost double-digit number is the year of the book's printing; the rightmost single-digit, the number of the book's printing. For example, a printing code of 95-1 shows that the first printing of the book occurred in 1995.

Composed in AGaramond and MCPdigital by Macmillan Computer Publishing

Printed in the United States of America

Trademarks

Publisher and President	*Richard K. Swadley*
Acquisitions Manager	*Greg Weigand*
Development Manager	*Dean Miller*
Managing Editor	*Cindy Morrow*
Marketing Manager	*Gregg Bushyeager*
Assistant Marketing Manager	*Michelle Milner*

Acquisitions Editor
Grace M. Buechlein

Development Editors
Dean Miller
Phillip W. Paxton
Randall Tamura

Software Development Specialists
Steve Flatt
Timothy Wilson

Production Editor
Deborah Frisby

Copy Editors
Kimberly K. Hannel
Ryan Rader
Bart Reed
Kris Simmons
Tonya R. Simpson

Technical Reviewers
Robert L. Bogue
Randall Tamura

Editorial Coordinator
Bill Whitmer

Technical Edit Coordinator
Lynette Quinn

Formatter
Frank Sinclair

Editorial Assistant
Sharon Cox

Cover Designer
Tim Amrhein

Book Designer
Alyssa Yesh

Production Team Supervisor
Brad Chinn

Production
Carol Bowers, Georgiana Briggs,
Mona Brown, Michael Brumitt,
Greg Eldred, Ayanna Lacey,
Kevin Laseau, Paula Lowell,
Brian-Kent Proffitt,
SA Springer, Mark Walchle

Overview

Contents

Part II The Windows 95 User Interface

Part III User Interface Applications

Part IV Windows 95 Multimedia Programming

Part V   The Windows 95 Common Controls

About the Authors

Randall A. Tamura

Randall Tamura is President of the Graphware Corporation, a consulting company specializing in Windows and C++ development. He has over twenty years experience in the computer field, and before founding Graphware, he was the General Manager of Engineering Systems Development in the Application Solutions Division at IBM. Randy has been working with Windows 95 for over a year and is working with advanced copies of software from Microsoft, Borland, Lotus, and Symantec.

Randy has experience in helping both small and large companies with software development and strategies. Working with object-oriented technologies, he has helped his clients plan, implement, and deploy applications. He has taught at UCLA and other colleges in the Los Angeles area and is currently a member of the American Management Association, IEEE, and the Association for Computing Machinery (ACM). You can contact Randy through CompuServe at 70731,1630 or by phone at (310) 649-0310.

Peter Belew

Peter Belew was born in San Francisco and grew up in the Bay area. He earned a B.S. in Mathematics from Stanford University where he began programming in the early 60s, working with the biophysics department and a computer-based teaching project. After he made a cross-country bicycle trip from Holland to Sarajevo in the mid-60s, Peter worked for Stanford and various Silicon Valley firms, including Xerox PARC. He spent most of the 80s working at Olivetti Advanced Technology Center in Cupertino, California before moving on to Microsoft, where he spent a couple of years working on Windows 3.0 core code. Since 1990, Peter has been working independently under the company name Analy, Branciforte & Co. (the name is based on early Irish and Spanish roots in Central California), creating software for foreign language support under Windows and doing a bit of consulting. Peter lives near the beach close to Santa Cruz, California.

James M. Blakely

Jim is a Microsoft Certified Systems Engineer, Microsoft Certified Trainer, and a Microsoft Certified Product Specialist (Windows 3.1, Windows for Workgroups 3.11, Windows NT, and Windows NT Server). He has been designing and installing network-based computer systems for the last ten years. Since 1988, he has been the principal consultant for Blakely-Signature Associates, a Microsoft Solution Provider specializing in the design, installation, and support of local and wide area network-based computer systems. Jim currently consults with

IAR, Inc., a Microsoft Authorized Technical Education Center in Newark, Delaware. There he teaches courses covering Microsoft Operating Systems and Enterprise Strategies.

Orin Eman

Orin Eman has worked with Microsoft Windows since 1986 and has been a systems level programmer and software engineer for over 12 years. He has worked with Windows NT since 1992 and with Windows 95 from the early prereleases, using Remote Procedure Calls to help porting from Windows 3.X to Win32. He currently works in Bothell, Washington, as a Senior Software Engineer on Windows remote computing products.

Ewan Grantham

Ewan Grantham has been involved with microcomputers since the days of the Apple II and the TRS-80. He now runs an independent consulting firm that specializes in the design and creation of electronic documentation and multimedia presentations. In addition to his programming and writing, he teaches classes on related subjects and publishes an almost-monthly electronic magazine, *RADIUS*. Ewan can be reached on CompuServe at 74123,2232.

Robert Griswold

Robert M. Griswold, Jr. received his B.S. in Electrical and Electronic Engineering from California State University, Sacramento, in December 1990. After graduation, Robert worked as a SCSI hardware and software design engineer, joining Adaptec of Milpitas, California, in September 1992. As a Product Support Specialist for Adaptec, Robert led the Hardware Team in the diagnosis of end-user issues involving SCSI, RLL, and ESDI controllers. As an Applications Engineer for Adaptec's SPO and PI units, Robert supported Adaptec's engineering role in Plug and Play and Windows 95, in addition to supporting important customer designs with Adaptec's low-cost SCSI solutions. Currently, as Customer Engineering Manager, Robert directs Applications Engineers in the solution of large and small customer design needs with Adaptec's high-performance SCSI and RAID products.

William S. Hall

Bill Hall is a Software Consultant at Novell, Inc., with a strong interest in software internationalization, especially on Windows and Win32 platforms. Formerly a university mathematics professor, he changed careers at age 50 and joined AT&T Information Systems, where his first assignment was to port Windows 1.0 to AT&T hardware. In 1990, he developed a package for the Defense Language Institute that enables Microsoft Windows to work with the languages of Central Europe. A year later he oversaw the localization of Novell's Lantern Service Manager into French and German, and in 1994 he began the enabling and localization of Novell's

Network Management Products into Japanese. Holding a Ph.D. in mathematics from Brown University, Bill is also very interested in languages and their realizations on computers. Although making no claims to fluency, he has a working knowledge of French, Czech, and Japanese, and some background in Russian and Polish.

Lawrence Harris

Lawrence Harris is the author of *Teach Yourself OLE in 21 Days* (Sams Publishing) and the forthcoming *OLE Developer's Guide* (Sams Publishing). He is the President of Beacontree Software, which specializes in OLE applications. A member of the ANSI C++ Standards Committee and the WOSA Real-Time Market Data Committee, Harris also serves as a beta tester for various Windows products.

Peter Hipson

Peter Hipson is a developer, consultant, and author. His work is mostly in the Windows arena, but he also pursues work in ODBC, database, and GIS applications. He was a member of the Microsoft beta-test team for QuickC for Windows; Visual C++ 1.0, 1.5, and 2.0; Windows 3.0 and 3.1; Windows for Workgroups 3.1 and 3.11; Windows 95; and Windows NT 3.5 Workgroup and Windows NT 3.5 Server. Hipson is the author of Sams Publishing's *Database Developer's Guide with Visual C++*, *Advanced C*, *What Every Visual C++ 2 Programmer Should Know*, *Visual C++ Developer's Guide*, and Que's *Using QuickC for Windows*. He also writes from time to time for the *Windows Technical Journal*.

Hipson has been working with microcomputers since the mid-70s. He also has many years of experience with IBM mainframe computers. He is the author of STARmanager, a GIS-type application that assists sales and marketing managers in managing their resources. You may contact Peter Hipson via CompuServe (70444,52) or Internet (`phipson@darkstar.mv.com`).

Bethany Kenner

Bethany Kenner is cofounder of Smith, Kenner Consulting, specializing in Windows NT and Windows 95 software development with an emphasis on device drivers. She is based in New Orleans, Louisiana, and can be reached via the Internet at `71732.2571@compuserve.com`.

John J. Kottler

John J. Kottler has been programming for 14 years and has spent the past 5 years developing applications for the Windows platform. His knowledge includes programming in C, C++, Visual Basic, PowerBuilder, Lotus Notes, and Assembly. In the past, he has published numerous articles in a computer magazine in which he wrote original programs and instructed other developers on programming techniques. John was also a codeveloper of the shareware application Virtual Monitors. His more recent endeavors have included message-enabling applications and extensions, multimedia and digital video production, and Internet Web page development. In his spare time, John enjoys playing digital music on synthesizers and roller-blading. He is a graduate of Rutgers University with a degree in Computer Science and may be found in the *Who's Who Among Students in American Universities and Colleges.* John may currently be reached at one of the following Internet addresses: `73157,335@compuserve.com`, `jkottler@aol.com`, or `jay_kottler@msn.com`.

Ronald Laeremans

When not helping out fellow developers on CompuServe, Ronald is the lead consultant of his company, Tools and Solutions, which provides development consultancy and technical help to Win32 developers, mainly on the server side of the client/server arena. He can be reached via CompuServe at 100142,747.

Patrick L. Lujan

Patrick L. Lujan is a freelance graphic designer and programmer specializing in 32-bit Windows multimedia and graphics applications. Patrick has worked for Los Alamos National Laboratory, New Mexico Highlands University, and the National Institutes of Health, among his many projects. He is currently working on game development tools for Windows. He can be reached on the Internet at `luhan@merlin.nmhu.edu`.

Bill Montemer

Bill Montemer is a multimedia producer and programmer. Specializing in new media in all its forms, Bill is currently developing software engines and children's educational content to drive them.

Timothy Parker

Timothy Parker, Ph.D., is an internationally recognized writer, programmer, and systems analyst who has published more than 500 articles in various computer industry magazines. He is a contributing author to *The Internet Unleashed* (Sams Publishing) and has written two highly successful books on UNIX. Currently he is the President of Timothy Parker Consulting, Inc. (TPCI), a consulting company with a wide range of services, including technical writing, programming, systems analysis, and training.

Daryl Pietrocarlo

Daryl Pietrocarlo is the cofounder and President of Sof Tech Multimedia, Inc., in Rochester, New York. He is also the author of Piano Professor for Windows. Daryl has a degree in Computer Engineering from Rochester Institute of Technology. He has worked for Eastman Kodak, Northern Telecom, and Information View. Daryl has been involved in the development of Windows applications for ten years.

James Thayer

James Thayer graduated from UC Santa Barbara with a degree in Electrical and Computer Engineering. Since that time, he has been involved in a wide range of different projects, including work on intrusion detection sensors; control systems for hydraulic guillotines used in high volume production of electronic assemblies; data collection platforms for environmental, seismic, and geomagnetic monitoring; laser printer controllers; and network fax servers. For the last two years, he has worked to develop desktop telephony applications for OCTuS, Inc. Now with Qualcomm Inc., James is helping to develop CDMA cellular network base stations.

When not working, James enjoys dancing with Moreton Bay Fig Morris and riding on a tandem bicycle named Godot with his wife Marieke. James and Marieke share their home with two cats named Chaos and Entropy. James can be reached at `71360.62@compuserve.com`.

Viktor Toth

Viktor Toth is a Hungarian-born author and self-employed software developer. His professional career started in 1979 when he wrote his first Hungarian-language book on Ernö Rubik's Magic Cube. Between 1979 and 1986, he developed a variety of microcomputer and mainframe software applications for clients in Hungary, in Austria, in Germany, and in the United Kingdom. During this time, he became thoroughly familiar with techniques for scientific computing, real-time processing, and building database applications. He wrote applications in Fortran, a variety of assemblers, Simula-67, C, and Pascal, to name a few languages. In 1986, he authored his second book, a technical reference for programmers of the Commodore 16 home computer.

Mr. Toth became a resident of Canada in 1987 where he continued his self-employed career. He coauthored several studies as a consultant for the Canadian government and wrote applications in C, assembler, dBASE, and other environments. After briefly experimenting with other graphical systems such as the long-forgotten GEM, he eventually wrote his first Windows application in 1990. Coauthoring *Programming Windows 95 Unleashed* represents his first opportunity to be published in English and present some of his experience to a wider audience.

Mr. Toth lives with his wife in their ever-too-small apartment in Ottawa, surrounded by several hundred pounds of computing equipment (his), knitting yarn (hers), and books. They hope to move soon to a house where they can add some cats to the family inventory.

Stan Trujillo

Stan Trujillo specializes in interactive graphics and C++ but has also worked in areas such as parallel processing, neural networks, and application development. Stan has worked at Cal Tech and Los Alamos National Labs and consulted for the Department of Energy. More recently, he coauthored *C++ Games Programming* (M&T Books) with Al Stevens and is currently working on a similar book for Windows 95. Stan can be reached on CompuServe at 75233,1506.

Thomas Woelfer

Thomas Woelfer's first contact with computers was playing Lander on a PDP-8 when he was a boy. He began real-world programming in 1980 when he joined a company producing CAD systems.

Currently, Thomas runs a software development shop with his brother. They specialize in civil and building engineering software, finite element systems, and specialized CAD engines. Thomas runs the new interface development and tech writers group. Apart from that, he takes care of class library maintenance.

In his free time, Thomas writes for several programming related magazines (or pub crawl) in Munich.

Introduction

Beyond the hoopla and hyperbole, Windows 95 represents a real opportunity. Windows 95 represents an opportunity for developers because, say predications, tens of millions of people will upgrade to this new version of Windows within its first year. All of the people upgrading to Windows 95 will desire applications that take advantage of the new features Windows 95 brings with it. You have the opportunity to fulfill these expectations.

Windows 95 represents an opportunity for in-house developers because Windows 95 will enable you to write for this environment new applications that operate more smoothly, are easier to administer and use, and take advantage of the many new built-in communications features.

End-users will find the features in Windows 95 compelling enough to encourage them to upgrade. This is their opportunity to take advantage of a user interface that is much easier to use than Windows 3.1. Just about every aspect of Windows has been improved for end users in the transition from Windows 3.1 to Windows 95.

A Short Trip from Chicago

As an early beta tester for Windows 95, or *Chicago* as it was known originally, I have been using versions of the system since the end of 1993. I can tell you that the system has genuinely and dramatically improved over the testing period. Originally, at the beginning of 1994, I was using Windows for Workgroups 3.11 as my base system. At that time, Chicago was just becoming available and wasn't really useable. In about April of 1994, Chicago became stable enough that I could use it and have it coexist on my system with my other operating system, but I continued to work primarily in Windows for Workgroups 3.11. During the summer of 1994, as Chicago improved, I gradually shifted more of my work to it from Windows for Workgroups 3.11.

By the end of 1994, I was using Chicago more and returning to Windows for Workgroups 3.11 only when a particular program would not work, which was fairly rare. In 1995, we saw the maturing of the product and its final preparation for release. The final beta release came out in March, and I'm sure that, with a beta test group of tens of thousands of people, Microsoft was busy fixing and testing the remaining bugs.

That brings us to the present. What is Windows 95 like now? What's new in Windows 95? How can you exploit some of these new features in Windows 95? These are some of the questions that this book will answer for you.

Who Should Use This Book?

This book is intended primarily, but not exclusively, for people in a software development organization. For example, you may be one of the following types of readers:

- Current Windows 3.1 commercial application developers—you really need to know all about the new features in Windows 95, such as the new user interface, common controls, OLE 2.0 programming, and the networking and communications features.

- Corporate application developers—your applications help your company's operations by providing key operational programs or productivity tools. Your end users will soon be asking you to incorporate the new Windows 95 features. You need to be ready.

- Information developers—you could be developing manuals for commercial or corporate use. You'll need to know how to develop online help files and get ready for multimedia, if you're not already there.

- Commercial software development management—you need to know what's in Windows 95 so you can make better judgments about what new features to include in your software development projects. If you are not developing Windows 95 applications soon, you'll face the consequences. Time is money.

- Corporate information systems management—you need to develop applications for your end users. You need to know what's in Windows 95 to better plan, develop, and deploy the system and your applications.

Of course, you might not fit into any one of these categories at all. You might just like to write programs for the fun of it. You might not have any responsibility to anyone else. You might just be interested in how Windows 95 works and does its magic. Well, this book is for you.

How This Book Is Organized

A major theme of this book is the importance of the new user interface in Windows 95. This is the most visible aspect of the system, and it is the part that most users will associate with the new system. This book will give you the knowledge to understand how Windows 95 works and how to exploit the new user interface to make your programs easier for your users to use.

The book is organized into seven parts. Each part covers a major aspect of Windows 95, but as mentioned, I have placed a special emphasis on what your users will see.

Part I: What's New in the Windows 95 Architecture

Part I is designed to give you an overview of major components in Windows 95 with an emphasis on what is new and what has changed since Windows 3.1. This part has nine chapters, beginning with a discussion of the Windows 95 architecture. Chapter 1 highlights the architectural features of Windows 95 and provides you with a background for the rest of Part I. Chapter 2, "Memory Management and the Windows 95 32-Bit Environment," covers how memory is allocated and used. Chapter 3, "Multitasking, Processes, and Threads," covers the multitasking aspects of Windows 95.

Chapter 4, "File Management and Long Filenames," covers the new long filename API (Application Programming Interface) and provides you with a sample application that you can use and modify. Chapter 5, "Fundamentals of the Windows 95 Registry," tells you about this important Windows repository for information about software and hardware configuration. Chapter 6, "Programming for Plug and Play Devices," discusses how hardware devices are detected and managed as well as how Plug and Play affects device drivers. Chapter 7, "Win32 API for Windows 3.1 Programmers: Moving Windows 3.1 Applications to Windows 95," and Chapter 8, "Win32 API for Windows NT Programmers," are for experienced Windows 3.1 and Windows NT programmers. These two chapters will tell you what to watch out for in your transition from these existing systems. Finally, Chapter 9, "Database Support and ODBC," discusses important aspects of database programming for the Windows environment.

Part II: The Windows 95 User Interface

The user interface in many ways is the most important part of your application. It is what the user will see, so even if you have the fanciest algorithm for sorting and searching data, if your user cannot easily access it, he or she will be disappointed.

Part II consists of two chapters that are aimed at helping you understand the design aspects of your application and how to (and how not to) design for usability. Chapter 10, "Windows 95 User Interface Basics," covers the basic principles involved. Chapter 11, "Stepping Through Essential User Interface Design," shows you many of the user interface elements and covers practical tips on how and when these elements should be used.

Part III: User Interface Applications

Part III is meant to give you practical information on specific applications where the user interface is important. You can use the information provided in this part along with the actual code from the CD-ROM to incorporate in your own applications.

You must have a help system for your application. It is no longer optional, if it ever was, because users have come to expect this information online. Chapter 12, "Creating a Windows 95 Help System," provides you with the information you need to start creating a help system for your application now.

You might think you are already overworked just trying to get your application finished. You might not even be thinking about an installation program for your application. Don't make this mistake. Installation programs are the first thing your user will see, and a good installation program, like a first impression, will make either a lasting good impression or a lasting bad impression on your user. These days you'll also need to include a uninstall program if you want Microsoft to allow you to use the Windows logo. Even if you're not a commercial developer, users will soon come to expect a uninstall program. Don't disappoint them. Chapter 13, "Designing a Smart Install and Uninstall," will help you with many aspects of the installation process.

The software market outside the U.S. is larger than it is inside the U.S. Let me say that again: the U.S. market makes up less than 50 percent of the world's software marketplace. Users outside the U.S. that don't natively speak English expect their software to speak their language. If your software does not support internationalization, you're limiting your marketplace. This is a shame, and it doesn't have to be this way. Chapter 14, "Internationalization Support in Win32," tells you about the National Language Support (NLS) in Windows 95 and will help you teach your programs to speak other languages. Olé!

Part IV: Windows 95 Multimedia Programming

Multimedia is one of the biggest buzzwords in the industry today. In Part IV, we cover the basics to get you started. Chapter 15, "DIBs: High-Performance Bitmaps in Windows 95," covers the device-independent bitmap of Windows 95. It covers the bitmap file format and then discusses animation techniques using bitmaps.

Chapter 16, "Multimedia Extensions," covers the Windows 95 multimedia interface and how to write a program using it.

Part V: The Windows 95 Common Controls

The common controls represent one of the new, exciting features of the Windows 95 interface. Actually, there was a common control DLL in Windows for Workgroups 3.11. This DLL was used by some of the system components and was not documented fully. In Windows 95, documentation has been provided for the common controls, and in Part V we show you how to take advantage of them.

The first chapter in this Part, Chapter 17, "Common Controls, Property Sheets, and MFC with Visual C++ 2.x," gives you an overview of all of the common controls and enough information to start coding. The next five chapters give you more details about each of the controls and provide you with sample code. Chapter 18, "Toolbars and Status Bars," covers the bars typically at the top and bottom of your application window. Chapter 19, "Trackbars, Progressbars, Spinbuttons, and Hotkey Controls," covers those bars that tell you how much progress your program is making. Spinbuttons are a pair of up and down arrows associated with a box that contains (usually) a number. As you press the arrows, the number in the box increases or decreases.

Chapter 20, "Listview and Treeview Controls," covers information necessary about controls that are similar to those found in Windows 3.1 File Manager and Windows 95 Explorer. Chapter 21, "Property Sheets and Tab Controls," helps you to create tabbed property dialog boxes. These types of controls are becoming more common and are found throughout the Windows 95 user interface. Chapter 22, "The RichText Control and the Animation Control," covers information about the important new control that handles fonts and greatly enhances the current Windows 3.1 text edit control. Animation is becoming more important because multimedia is a hot topic.

Part VI: OLE 2.0 Programming

OLE 2.0 involves many new concepts, and to master programming for Windows 95, you'll need to start learning the OLE lingo. OLE, like Windows 95, is layered, and many of the upper layers build upon lower layers. We describe many of these layers in this part.

We start Part VI with Chapter 23, "OLE 2.0 for the First-Timer," in which OLE's general concepts are described. Chapter 24, "Component Object Model (COM)," describes one of the basic building blocks for OLE, the Component Object Model. This model provides a framework for the rest of OLE and describes the architectural framework for building binary, reusable objects. OLE describes a standard way for defining interfaces, and this method is the primary characteristic of the COM.

Chapter 25, "Windows Objects and Compound Documents," describes what additional interfaces must be implemented on top of COM to become a full-fledged Windows object. A compound document is a fancy term for the combination of several types of data such as a Lotus 1-2-3 spreadsheet inside of a Microsoft Word document. Chapter 26, "Visual Editing," covers the editing process for a document that is embedded (or linked) within another. Chapter 27, "Drag and Drop," discusses the standardized OLE drag-and-drop interface that is pervasive in the Windows 95 user interface for working in and among various applications.

OLE automation, described in Chapter 28, is an impressive new method for enabling one program to control (or automate) another application. OLE automation essentially enables your application to be controlled by (or to control other applications by) a generalized macro or scripting language facility. One of the most familiar scripting languages is Visual Basic, which you can use as an OLE automation controller, and you can write applications that can be controlled by Visual Basic. Chapter 29, "OLE 2.0 as a DDE Replacement," covers the features of OLE 2.0 that replace DDE functions. Chapter 30, "OLE Control Development Kit," covers the information you need to create these new OLE controls, sometimes called OCXs. OCXs will be 16- or 32-bit replacements for the 16-bit-only VBXs. Chapter 30 also gives you information on how to upgrade your current VBXs to OCXs. Chapter 31, "Providing File Viewers for the Windows 95 Explorer," covers shell extensions and file viewers. This feature of Windows 95 enables you to write extensions that hook into the Windows 95 Explorer.

Part VII: Windows 95 Networking and Communications

Networking and communications are areas that have been greatly enhanced in Windows 95. As a user of Windows 95, you can use NetWare as well as Microsoft and other networking systems. Built-in client software improves the performance and reliability of the networking software. In addition, e-mail and Computer-Telephone Integration (CTI) are becoming more important.

Part VII examines some of the networking aspects of Windows 95. In Chapter 32, we cover "Programming for Windows 95 in a Network Environment," which essentially presents an overview and introduction to network programming. Chapter 33, "Remote Procedure Calls (RPC)," covers the client/server concept of a program that is distributed over a network between two computers. The chapter describes how you can call a function from one machine, receive and process the call on another machine, and then return to the original machine. Chapter 34, "Winsock," covers Windows Sockets, which are an implementation of a standard so that Windows programs could use TCP/IP. Chapter 35, "Microsoft Exchange for the Programmer," covers this on the Microsoft Mail and provides some information on the Microsoft Network, fax support, and the Internet. Chapter 36, "The Messaging System—Extended MAPI," provides information and examples on the Messaging API (MAPI) provided with Windows 95. Finally, in Chapter 37, "TAPI," we cover the basics of the exciting new topic of TAPI, or Telephony API. This API enables you to write programs that control a telephone. In the future, with TAPI and telephone features such as Caller ID applications, you can find out who is calling and customize your actions accordingly. Imagine an application that shows a customer service representative the customer record, enables him to address the customer by name, and provides previous transaction histories all before the representative has even answered the phone. You'll soon be able to write that application yourself.

Tools You Need to Use This Book

This book is accompanied by a CD-ROM that includes many of the sample programs found in this book. In addition, there are several bonus applications you can try. In order to compile the sample application programs, you should have a copy of the Microsoft Visual C++ compiler, version 2.0 or 2.1. Although it might be possible to use other compilers such as the Borland or Watcom compilers, the programs in this book have not been tested with them.

In addition to the compiler, for some of the examples, you will need a copy of the Microsoft Windows 95 SDK. The examples here were tested with various prerelease builds of Windows 95. Every effort has been made to ensure that the programs will work with the final release of Windows 95, but as you might imagine, there may be changes made to Windows 95 after this book goes to press. If you choose to include the code from this book in any of your projects, be sure to test it in your own environment and make any changes necessary.

Chapter 13, "Designing a Smart Install and Uninstall," refers to several installation generation packages. The setup program comes from Microsoft with the SDK. A special version of

InstallShield from Sterling also comes with the Microsoft SDK. On the CD-ROM that comes with this book, we have included a special version of Installigence. You will need one of these or another tool to develop your install and uninstall programs.

You can manage the generation of help files with the SDK and a word processor that is capable of generating Rich Text Files (RTF). However, there are also several good third-party programs for creating help files. If you are generating many help files, you would probably benefit by using one of the commercially available tools.

Typographical Conventions Used in This Book

This book has a number of typographical conventions to make reading it easier and more enjoyable. The following conventions are used:

- `monospace`   Listings, code segments, commands, options, functions, and other elements of code appear in a special monospace font.
- `italic monospace`   Placeholders in code appear in an italic monospace typeface.
- *italics*   Plain italics are used to introduce new terms or emphasize important points.

When a code line is too long to appear in this book as a single line, the ➡ symbol is used to indicate that the two "lines" should be considered as one. If the ➡ symbol appears before a "line," you should read that line as a continuation of the preceding line.

> **NOTE**
>
> The Microsoft Network information in this book is based on information on Windows 95 made public by Microsoft as of July 1995. Because this information was made public before the release of the product, there may be some differences between the information in this book and the final packaging of Microsoft Network as it relates to Windows 95.

We've Left Chicago; Let's Go

I mentioned the opportunities provided by the introduction of Windows 95. This book will help you to capitalize on those opportunities by providing you with the information you need to get started now. Whether you're a professional developer, a corporate developer, or just a curious home-brew programmer, take advantage now. Let's go!

—Randy Tamura

PART

I

What's New in the Windows 95 Architecture

Windows 95 Architecture

1

by Randy Tamura

The Windows 95 architecture represents an evolution, not a revolution, from the enhanced mode of Windows for Workgroups 3.11. Although many of the aspects of Windows 95 are new, many concepts have been carried forward from existing Windows programs, as you will see in this chapter. Nevertheless, Windows 95 represents a huge upgrade from Windows 3.1; nearly everything has changed in some way.

Microsoft had to meet many design goals in order to develop a successful Windows 95 product. Of course, one of the most important design goals was for Windows 95 to be compatible with Windows 3.1, Windows for Workgroups 3.11, and even DOS applications. Maintaining compatibility while changing nearly everything is one of the reasons why it has taken so long for Windows 95 to be released.

The compatibility that Windows 95 achieves is quite good, and one of the reasons for this is an architecture that combines the new 32-bit code with a solid, production-tested 16-bit core. In this case, the core is made up of some of the code previously packaged as DOS and some from the 16-bit parts of Windows 3.x.

There have been various opinions on whether the inclusion of the DOS code has been a good idea or a bad idea. Technically, of course, it makes sense to reuse working, stable code. There is probably no controversy on this aspect. From a business and packaging perspective, however, Microsoft probably had several options, including the separate packaging of a DOS version 7.0. By packaging Windows and DOS together, Microsoft becomes freed of having to document DOS interfaces as they do today. This has various business advantages for Microsoft, but for the end user the major advantage is in the ease of installation and use of the product.

One of the striking characteristics of the Windows 95 architecture is its layered nature. *Layering* is a key feature that enables Windows 95 to support the multitude of computers and devices in the marketplace today. At the Windows API level, the familiar USER, GDI, and KERNEL service most application programs as they do today in Windows 3.11, but underneath is a wealth of 32-bit components for handling files, networking, communication, and multitasking.

This chapter provides an overview of the Windows 95 architecture and covers the main Windows 95 components. The purpose of this chapter is to give you an idea of the breadth and depth of Windows 95. The rest of Part I, "What's New in the Windows 95 Architecture," gives you the background you need to effectively write programs for this exciting new environment.

I start by exploring the privilege levels supported in Windows 95. The separation of Windows 95 into privilege levels improves the robustness of the system.

Privilege Levels in Windows 95

Intel processors since the 386 have four privilege levels, 0–3. Level 0 is the most privileged, and Level 3 is the least privileged. These four levels can be visualized as four concentric circles, or rings. For performance reasons, Windows 95 (and Windows NT and OS/2) uses only two of these levels: Ring 0, the most privileged, and Ring 3, the least privileged. Although Intel originally envisioned an operating system providing several levels of protection, only two are really implemented in practice.

In the Intel hardware architecture, when the processor is running in Ring 0, essentially all of the capabilities and resources of the processor are available. This level is reserved for critical operating system components such as memory management, paging, and low-level input/output operations.

Ring 3 is reserved for applications and higher-level operating system functions. When programs operate in Ring 3, they are given a *virtual environment*. This virtual environment is set up by the operating system and enables isolation of the programs; therefore, there is less likelihood that one program will cause problems for another program.

Components of Windows 95

The components of Windows 95 can be categorized into two broad groups of programs, based upon the privilege level in which they operate. In Figure 1.1, you can see that the Ring 0 components form the foundation of the operating system. These components provide a virtual machine environment, preemptive multitasking, paging memory management, file system services, networking, and configuration management.

There are three major areas of change in the Ring 0 components from Windows 3.1 to Windows 95. The first is the support for preemptive multitasking and multiple threads, the second is the protected 32-bit file management subsystem, and the third is the support for Plug and Play devices.

In Ring 3, Windows 95 has also added support for multiple, preemptively scheduled 32-bit applications. Probably the most notable characteristic of the Ring 3 programs is the new user interface, which should make Windows 95 much easier to use for both experienced and novice users. Refer to Figure 1.1 for the overall architecture for Windows 95.

In this discussion, I first look at all of the Ring 0 components and then examine the Ring 3 components. I start with the Virtual Machine Manager, one of the most important components of Windows 95.

FIGURE 1.1.

Windows 95 architectural components.

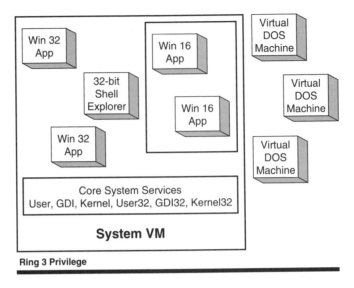

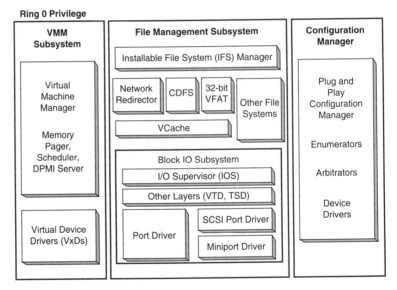

Virtual Machine Manager

The Virtual Machine Manager (VMM) provides a virtual machine environment that includes all of the characteristics of a real computer, including the CPU, memory, and I/O devices. In fact, the VMM provides for many simultaneous virtual machines (each capable of running DOS) and one special virtual machine called the system VM.

The VMM provides a virtual environment by either sharing time on the real devices or by simulating characteristics that do not actually exist. One of the most common simulations is for virtual memory. In this case, the VMM can provide an environment that seems to the program as if more (or less) memory exists than is actually present on the machine.

The memory management in the VMM has two parts: one aspect controls virtual memory and the other provides extended memory to DOS virtual machines. This second aspect is called the DOS protected mode interface (DPMI) server.

For Windows programs, the VMM provides an environment that typically has more memory available for allocation than is actually present on the machine. Sometimes, though not necessarily, the VMM gives DOS virtual machines an environment that seems as if it has less memory available to it than actually exists. In other words, the virtual environment for DOS does not have to match the environment of the real machine. The amount of memory for DOS programs can be specified by the user in the Properties tab for the DOS session. This is equivalent to the PIF files found in Windows 3.1.

The VMM is also the component responsible for the preemptive timeslice scheduling of multiple threads within Windows 95. The *scheduler* has a rather sophisticated algorithm that also takes into account priorities and temporary boosting of priorities.

The last set of programs packaged with the VMM is a set of device drivers, or VxD files. These VxD files make devices virtual for virtual machines. For example, there are virtual keyboard, mouse, and display devices. The device drivers as a group are called VxD devices because they have names such as *VKD* (Virtual Keyboard Device), *VMD* (Mouse), *VDD* (Display), *VTD* (Timer), and so on. The VxD files included in the VMM are the basic support for these devices; however, the VxD files may be overridden if necessary when Windows 95 is running by dynamic loading and unloading of different device drivers.

NOTE

The following are the primary differences between the Windows 3.1 VMM and the Windows 95 VMM:

■ Windows 3.1 VxDs must be loaded at initialization time and are specified in SYSTEM.INI. Windows 95 can dynamically load and unload VxD files. You'll see this in more detail in Chapter 6, "Programming for Plug and Play Devices."

■ Windows 3.1 VMM can schedule only virtual machines, not threads. In Windows 95, each 32-bit thread, each 16-bit Windows application, and each DOS virtual machine can be scheduled by the VMM scheduler.

Paging and Virtual Memory

Unlike memory allocation in a C or C++ program, virtual memory is usually implemented by the allocation of fixed-size blocks. In the case of Windows 95, these blocks, called *pages*, are 4096 bytes each. In the Intel CPU architecture, paging is enabled by setting a bit in one of the control registers. When enabled, the CPU does not access memory directly. It goes through a translation process for each address, translating the virtual memory address to a real memory address through a series of lookup tables called *page tables.*

By using the hardware address translation process and page tables, Windows 95 is able to implement virtual memory with both performance and protection. Performance is achieved because the translation is done by the hardware. Protection is achieved because, when an errant program tries to access memory that is not allocated to it, a protection exception is issued by the hardware and is handled by the operating system.

In Windows 95, the complete address space is 4 GB, which is the amount of memory that can be addressed with 32 bits. Each process running under Windows 95 has its own 4 GB space. Of this 4 GB, an application can address the lower 2 GB; the upper 2 GB is reserved for Windows 95 system usage, and parts are shared among all running processes. This 32-bit address space is one of the features of the 386 processor (and above). It is not available on the 286. Thus, Windows 95 will have a prerequisite of at least a 386-class CPU.

DOS Protected Mode Interface Server

DOS protected mode interface (DPMI) is a specification and a service that has been around for many years. This is the specification that enables DOS programs to take advantage of memory above the 1 MB line by using extended memory. The DPMI server in Windows 95 is available to give DOS programs an extended memory environment.

DPMI is a follow-on of sorts to the virtual control program interface (VCPI) developed for DOS in the 1980s. DPMI has been implemented by several third-party vendors in products such as QEMM and 386Max; however, with DPMI's inclusion in both Windows 3.1 and Windows 95, and with the decline of native DOS applications, the need for third-party products is diminishing.

DPMI provides the basic services of allocating and freeing extended memory in an application-independent manner, so that several applications can share extended memory. If applications did not use the DPMI services and conventions, then one application's use of extended memory could potentially clobber another application's data.

Virtual Device Drivers

The virtual device driver (VxD) concept has been in Windows since 386 enhanced mode began. This mechanism enables Microsoft, as well as third parties, to write device drivers for particular hardware devices so that many different types of devices can be handled in a standardized way.

In 16-bit versions of Windows prior to Windows 95, device drivers had to be loaded at system initialization time. An application or user would create entries in the SYSTEM.INI file such as

```
device=MYDEV.386
```

under the [386enh] section of the file. Windows would find the file and initialize it when the system started. There are several problems with this approach.

- All device drivers are loaded at initialization whether they are needed or not.
- Because the line in SYSTEM.INI is not tied to actual hardware, a user might change the hardware configuration and remove the hardware and forget to remove the line in SYSTEM.INI.
- A device driver cannot be unloaded once it has been loaded at the initialization. This uses up valuable system memory and resources.

The VxD concept has been enhanced in Windows 95 with the addition of Plug and Play. Essentially, the above restrictions have been removed. Windows 95 now dynamically checks the hardware configuration and dynamically loads the appropriate device drivers. Only those drivers actually required are loaded. Once loaded, a driver can be dynamically removed as well if it makes sense to do so. A commonly cited example is a notebook computer that docks and undocks with a docking station. When docked, the list of hardware available might be different than when the notebook computer is running as a stand-alone computer. We'll discuss Plug and Play in more detail in Chapter 6.

Scheduling and Multiple Threads

The VMM is responsible for scheduling separate processes and threads in a timeslicing, preemptive nature. A *process* is a running instance of a program. In Windows 95, each virtual machine and each 16-bit Windows program is essentially a single process. A *thread* shares a memory and execution context with a process and can be considered subsidiary to a process. If the process has a single thread, then that single thread is the unit of scheduling. In Windows 95, VxDs and 32-bit applications can create additional threads, which can then be scheduled separately from the process that created them.

As an example, a 32-bit Windows program (process) may have one thread to handle user input from the screen, another thread for doing I/O to a disk, and a third thread for handling a communication port. Each of these separate threads are scheduled separately.

Each thread can have a priority that ranges from 0 to 31. Priority 0 is the lowest and is reserved for system use. Priorities 1 to 31 are divided into four categories: Idle (1–6), Normal (5–11), High (11–15), and Real Time (16–31). The Normal category is further divided into two subranges: Background (5–9) and Foreground (6–11). You'll notice that the ranges overlap. This has been done to allow flexibility in scheduling and to allow, for example, some background tasks to be more important than some foreground tasks, even though in normal circumstances foreground ought to be the higher priority.

> **TIP**
>
> You should be very careful when using the Real Time priority. If you set the priority of a task too high, you could lose effective control of your machine. This is because the priority of the task will be so high that it will not allow other tasks in the system to run at all.

The VMM contains services to create, manage, and destroy threads and for thread scheduling. There are two schedulers in the VMM: the primary scheduler and the timeslice scheduler. The *primary scheduler* has the responsibility for determining the highest priority thread or threads. Only the highest priority thread will run—all other threads of lower priority will be blocked. The *timeslice scheduler* is responsible for timeslicing all runable tasks that have priority equal to the highest.

During the course of a running system, the priority of threads can be changed by the system or the device drivers (or both). For example, when an interrupt occurs, a thread to handle the interrupt might have its priority temporarily boosted so that it can get immediate time to handle the interrupt. Once completed, the priority may be lowered again.

File Management Subsystem

The major enhancement to the file management subsystem that is visible to users is the addition of long filenames. This feature will enable users to name their files with meaningful names of up to 255 characters rather than the old 8.3 file naming convention that has been used for over a decade.

Long filenames promise to be a great help to end users. Users will find it easier to remember and use the files if they can refer to both files and directories (folders) using long filenames. For example, it will be much easier for users to identify and use a file named "4th Quarter Sales Report" instead of "Q4SLSRPT."

In implementing the new file management subsystem, Microsoft has used the concept of an installable file system, which was already present in both OS/2 and Windows for Workgroups.

Installable File System Manager

The purpose of the Installable File System (IFS) Manager (see Figure 1.1) is to control access to the multiple types of file system implementations that might be present on a Windows 95 computer. It is likely, for example, that the computer will need to access a local disk, a CD-ROM, and a network drive. Each of these separate file systems may have a different implementation, and the IFS Manager is responsible for selecting the appropriate method, depending upon the device being accessed.

VCACHE

VCACHE (virtual cache) is a 32-bit protected mode cache driver. It replaces SMARTDRV and provides a common pool of memory for use by the VFAT (32-bit virtual file allocation table) driver, the network redirector, and CDFS (CD-ROM file system) driver. In contrast to the fixed-size buffer used by SMARTDRV, the pool of memory managed by VCACHE is dynamic and can expand or shrink depending on system loading. Because the memory is a common pool and is shared by VFAT, CDFS, and the network redirector, memory utilization is better than if separate areas of memory were allocated for each type of file system access.

VFAT

The FAT (File Allocation Table) file system has been with us since the original version of DOS 1.0 more than 10 years ago. As new versions of DOS came out, the FAT system has been enhanced, but newer versions have always been backward-compatible and have been able to read disks formatted by previous versions of DOS. VFAT (Virtual File Allocation Table) is a 32-bit DOS-compatible file system that was introduced in Windows for Workgroups, and has been enhanced for Windows 95. Because it is implemented in protected mode and is multithreaded, VFAT provides better performance than previous versions of the file system implemented by either DOS or Windows for Workgroups.

The VFAT system does not actually change the on-disk structure. Compatibility on the disk needs to be retained because there are hundreds of utilities that depend on the current FAT structure that is used by previous versions of DOS and Windows.

The majority of hard disks on the market today will be supported in native mode by the VFAT subsystem. Because it is implemented in protected mode, 32-bit code, VFAT will be much more efficient than 16-bit I/O implementations. Each transition from 32-bit protected mode to 16-bit real mode (and vice versa) incurs overhead; because fewer transitions are required, much less overhead is incurred.

Network Redirector

The network redirector layer in Windows 95 takes the place of the real-mode redirectors used in DOS. This is a welcome addition to Windows because, traditionally, real-mode redirectors in DOS are implemented as TSRs and use real memory below the 1 MB line. In contrast, the Windows 95 network redirectors are implemented as drivers that are part of the installable file system.

Also, because the network redirectors are part of the IFS, Windows 95 supports multiple protocols at the same time. A Windows 95 machine can, for example, communicate using the IPX/SPX, NetBEUI, and TCP/IP protocols all at once. IPX/SPX is typically used for NetWare networks, and TCP/IP is commonly associated with wide area networks (WANs) and UNIX.

CDFS

The CD-ROM file system (CDFS) is a replacement for the real-mode MSCDEX and provides support for ISO 9660 formatted CD-ROMs. CDFS provides the same logical type of support for CD-ROMs that the VFAT component provides for hard disks.

In Windows 3.1, most CD-ROM support consists of two pieces. One piece is a TSR program called MSCDEX, which is device-independent. The second piece is usually loaded as a device driver in CONFIG.SYS, provided by the hardware vendor, and is usually device (CD-ROM) dependent. The device-dependent portion is covered in the section called "Block I/O Subsystem."

In Windows 3.1, MSCDEX and the device driver do not provide much buffering for the CD-ROM. Although some third-party disk-cache software came on the market with the capability to cache both hard disk and CD-ROMs, they typically used additional low memory (that is, memory below 640 KB). CD-ROM support in Windows 3.1 usually consumes a significant amount of memory below the 1 MB line.

In Windows 95, the CDFS is built into Windows itself and does not take additional real memory to load. In addition, because CDFS shares the VCACHE along with the networking and VFAT support, there is much more efficient usage of cache memory.

Long Filenames

In order to implement long filenames, Microsoft has added a new set of INT 21 codes. These interrupt codes are similar to the existing file manipulation codes that are currently in DOS 6.2. New codes are introduced so that the operating system can tell whether an application has been "long filename enabled." The assumption is that any program that uses the new codes is aware of long filenames, while any program that uses the old interrupt codes is a legacy application and will not be aware of long filenames.

To implement long filenames in a way that is both upward- and downward-compatible was a challenge. A particular problem was that existing DOS applications, such as disk defragmenters and disk repair utilities, look at the on-disk data structures and manipulate them; therefore, great care was taken to make sure that utilities meant to optimize and repair disks don't inadvertently trash the data they are trying to enhance.

The fundamental trick in implementing long filenames relies on a bit in the directory that up until now has been fairly rare. In fact, it would be used in at most one directory entry per logical disk in systems up through DOS 6.2. This bit is the *label* bit of the directory entry. Its usage indicates that the directory entry is the disk volume label and should occur once, at most, in the directory if the disk has a label.

When the label bit is on, the fields in the directory entry, other than the name, are ignored because the label entry does not point to any actual disk file. To implement long filenames, a combination of bits, previously illegal, was used. This combination is *read only, hidden, system file,* and *volume label.* These four bits are located in the low-order bits of the attribute byte; therefore, the bit combination is 0FH.

Block I/O Subsystem

The block I/O subsystem is another example of the layered Windows 95 architecture. At the head of the block I/O subsystem is the IOS, or I/O supervisor. There are 32 predefined layers in the I/O architecture; Layer 31 is the bottom layer and Layer 0 is the top layer.

Device drivers are loaded and initialized from the bottom up; that is, Layer 31 drivers, which correspond to Windows NT miniport drivers, are initialized first. If there are several drivers at the same layer, the order of initialization among them is not defined. After all drivers at Layer 31 are initialized, Layer 30 drivers are initialized, and so on up to Layer 0.

Drivers also have the capability to respond to more than one layer if they are performing tasks on two logical layers. In this case, the IOS will initialize the driver on both layers, although the driver code itself will be loaded only once.

In Figure 1.2 you can see several of the most important layers. In addition, there can be other layers, such as disk compression layers (DriveSpace and Stacker, for example).

FIGURE 1.2.

Block I/O subsystem.

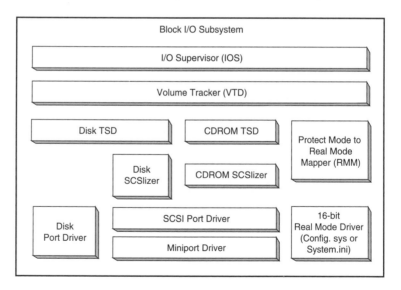

Just below the IOS (see Figure 1.2) are two layers called the volume tracking driver (VTD), and the type-specific driver (TSD). The VTD is responsible for tracking the current volume inserted in removable media devices. Keeping track of the current volume is important for removable devices because if the user asynchronously changes the removable volume without informing an application program accessing the disk, the disk could become corrupted.

The type-specific driver (TSD) is responsible for code that is common to all devices of a specific type. For example, there is a CD-ROM TSD responsible for all functions that are common to CD-ROM drives, and a Disk TSD that is responsible for all hard disks, regardless of the specific model. This mechanism enables the actual device drivers to be more compact and to use common code, which has been tested and debugged by Microsoft.

Port Drivers

As you can see in Figure 1.2, Port Drivers and SCSI Port Drivers provide equivalent logical support to the layers above them. A port driver provides support for a specific device, such as a hard disk controller. This type of driver is aware of the specific protocols for the controller. For example, there is a port driver for IDE/ESDI hard disks.

The port driver detects and initializes the adapter, sends I/O requests, handles interrupts from the device, and is responsible for error recovery and logging.

SCSI Layer

SCSI support begins when a type-specific driver (TSD) needs to send a command to a SCSI device. The TSD sends the command to a component called the *SCSI-izer*, which is responsible for converting the generic command to a device-type specific SCSI command. For example, there is a disk SCSI-izer and a CD-ROM SCSI-izer.

After the SCSI-izer has finished, it sends the command to the SCSI port driver. This layer has the responsibility of sending the command to the SCSI port using the Windows NT miniport architecture. The use of Windows NT miniport drivers should, in principle, make it easy for Windows 95 to quickly and automatically support many of the devices already supported by Windows NT.

Although Windows NT miniport drivers are unmodified, they may be used with Windows 95; however, it is not necessarily recommended. There are several extensions to the miniport drivers that are specific to Windows 95. Once these additional modifications have been made, however, the new driver will also work in Windows NT. In particular, the need to be able to support legacy real-mode SCSI drivers is a requirement for Windows 95, but the code is ignored if executed under Windows NT.

Real-Mode Mapper

An interesting component of the block I/O subsystem is the *real mode mapper* (RMM). This component enables backward compatibility with devices that do not have native support in Windows 95. Essentially, the RMM takes the 32-bit calls that come from IOS, translates them back to 16-bit requests, and then sends them on to a 16-bit real-mode DOS device driver. When the result comes back from the 16-bit real-mode driver, it is converted and sent back to the IOS in the standard 32-bit format. This RMM technology is available as a part of Windows for Workgroups, and is located in the device driver named RMM.D32.

The Registry

The registry is an extremely important part of Windows 95. Although it is present in Windows 3.1, it does not play a critical role to the operation of the system. In Windows 95, if you don't have a registry, you don't have a system.

The registry in Windows 95 is used to store hardware configurations, software configurations, performance data, and user preferences for one or more users. In addition, the registry has been reorganized into several, separate files that make management of network installations easier. For example, wouldn't it be nice if whenever you logged onto a network version of Windows, the system knew your preferences for your Desktop and Wallpaper? With the newly reconfigured registry, it's now possible.

The registry hardware section is used to support the Plug and Play features of Windows 95. When Windows 95 detects various devices on your machine, it stores the results in the registry. This normally occurs during setup, but detection also occurs when Windows is started and whenever there is a change in the configuration.

The registry is also used to store information formerly stored in the hundreds of INI files used by Windows and application programs. For example, file associations, program configurations, and setup data are stored in the registry. OLE 2.0 also makes heavy use of the registry for storing information about the various OLE classes.

The registry can be accessed via a set of calls in the VMM. These calls are located in the VMM so that VxD files, as well as Windows applications and system components, can access the registry. We'll discuss the Windows 95 registry in much more detail in Chapter 5, "Fundamentals of the Windows 95 Registry."

Plug and Play

The implementation of Plug and Play technology is a major industry-wide effort to make IBM-compatible PCs easier to use. This effort includes many hardware, software, ROM-BIOS, and operating-system vendors. Installing a SCSI adapter or a multimedia sound board might cause even an electrical engineer to scratch his or her head. With the variety of dip switches, jumpers, CONFIG.SYS settings, AUTOEXEC.BAT file commands, and environment variables, a typical user can become very frustrated.

In addition to making installation and setup easier for users, Plug and Play technology also strives for compatibility with existing legacy hardware devices. Without this type of compatibility, Plug and Play would have a hard time succeeding because of the tremendous cost to users for upgrading entire systems.

Basically, Plug and Play works by changing how adapter boards and devices are configured. Rather than placing the responsibility on the user, the operating system, hardware, and BIOS cooperate to provide an environment that assumes responsibility for the configuration. Rather than requiring the user to set configuration settings on the device, the device is configurable on the command of the operating system.

We'll discuss Plug and Play in more detail in Chapter 6, "Programming for Plug and Play Devices," but in essence, Plug and Play support requires the following changes in hardware devices and the operating system:

- Devices must be able to identify themselves.
- Devices must have several configurable options for IRQ, DMA, and memory ranges.
- The operating system must be able to enumerate all devices.
- The operating system must be able to resolve conflicts that arise.
- The devices must be able to respond to commands by the operating system to reconfigure themselves.

Configuration Manager

The Configuration Manager is the primary component for Plug and Play. It is responsible for maintaining the database of information in the registry, which describes the current configuration, and for notifying the device drivers of their assigned resources.

To accomplish its task, the Configuration Manager relies on two other types of programs: enumerators and arbitrators. *Enumerators* are responsible for a collection of devices on a bus. There can be several buses in one machine; for example, the machine might have an ISA bus and a PCI bus. Also, system devices, such as the timer, the numeric data processor (floating-point processor), as well as other devices on the motherboard, are considered to be on a bus. The enumerator is able to call device routines for each of the devices on its bus.

Enumerators, as you might imagine from the name, are responsible for sequencing through each device asking each one in turn about its characteristics. The enumerator saves these characteristics, and after it has cycled through all of the devices, bus arbitrators are called.

Arbitrators are responsible for handling the assignment of resources and for resolving conflicts between devices. When assigning resources, legacy devices with fixed resource requirements are always assigned first; these resources are removed from the available pool. Then, tentative assignments are made for each device. If a conflict occurs, a Plug and Play device might be asked to relinquish its previously assigned resources. It is then reassigned new resources. We'll go into more depth about the Configuration Manager in Chapter 6, with the rest of Plug and Play.

> **NOTE**
>
> The Configuration Manager and Plug and Play components are used very heavily during the Windows 95 setup procedure. The setup procedure's initial phase consists of detecting the hardware present on the machine. A great deal of testing went into this phase because the mere act of trying to detect certain hardware can cause other hardware or adapter cards to lock up the system. Even though thousands of hours went into the testing, a unique combination of legacy devices might still cause a lockup. If this happens to you during setup, just reboot. The recovery procedures should enable you to proceed.

Ring 3

The Ring 3 protection level in the Intel x86 architecture is the least privileged. This does not mean that this level is restricted to Windows application code, however. In fact, the core system services of USER, GDI, and KERNEL run in Ring 3. DOS virtual machines also run in Ring 3, and when they perform privileged operations such as I/O, the requests are captured and serviced by the Ring 0 components of Windows 95.

Running applications and operating system components at Ring 3 enables the operating system to do a better job of isolating the various components from one another. The purpose of this isolation is to improve the robustness of the system as a whole. Therefore, a failure in one component, whether an application or part of Windows itself, will not bring down the entire system.

Virtual Machines

The VMM component in Ring 0 provides a virtual machine environment for the programs running in Ring 3. In Windows 95, as in Windows 3.1, there may be multiple DOS virtual machines and a single, special virtual machine called the system VM. Each of the virtual machines provides a complete virtual context in which applications run.

Each of the virtual machines has virtual memory, virtual I/O ports, and a virtual CPU. The isolation provided by the separation of the virtual machines means that if one virtual machine crashes, it will not affect other virtual machines. However, this level of protection (protecting one virtual DOS machine from another) does not create a completely crash-proof system for Windows 95. Because all Windows applications run in the single system VM, one application can potentially affect the others within the system VM.

Virtual DOS Machines

When Windows 95 first starts up, it internally processes the CONFIG.SYS and AUTOEXEC.BAT files if they exist. After these files have been processed, Windows 95 takes a snapshot of the real-mode DOS environment. This environment includes all of the real-mode device drivers and any Terminate and Stay Resident (TSR) programs that have been loaded.

Whenever a virtual DOS machine is started, it inherits the environment just as it was after the start-up. In essence, the inherited environment is a "clone" of the environment that exists just after the system is booted. Once the DOS VM is up and running, however, the memory and environment are separated from other running virtual machines. Therefore, you can change characteristics, load programs, and so on within one DOS VM, and it will not affect other running VMs.

An interesting difference between Windows 95 and the Windows 3.1/DOS 6.2 combination is in the area of file I/O. In Windows 3.1 with DOS, a file I/O request is issued via an INT 21H interrupt. When Windows 3.1 encounters this interrupt, it switches context to virtual 8086 mode and then calls upon DOS to actually perform the I/O. This approach has the advantage of all I/O going through common code, and therefore compatibility with the rest of the DOS files is guaranteed. The approach has the disadvantage, however, of being much slower than staying in protected mode. Context switching between protected mode and virtual 8086 mode, used by Windows 3.1, is much more complicated and probably results in hundreds of more instructions being executed than the Windows 95 approach.

In Windows 95, the file system is written in 32-bit protected-mode code. Thus, when an I/O operation is encountered in Windows 95 via the INT 21H in a DOS virtual machine, the system passes the request on to the protected mode file management subsystem and remains in protected mode. In Windows 95, DOS programs running in a virtual machine actually call Windows Ring 0 components for I/O operations, so in some sense DOS is actually running on Windows rather than vice versa!

System VM

The system VM is a special virtual machine in which all Windows programs run. This includes both 16-bit Windows 3.1-type programs as well as new 32-bit programs. There are some differences in how memory is allocated and used in a Win32 application from a Windows 3.1 program. I explain how this works in the next section.

There is only one system VM; it is the only virtual machine enabled to have multiple threads in Windows 95. Several of the new desktop utilities, such as the shell (Explorer), are written as 32-bit applications to take advantage of the performance improvements of 32-bit programs.

Also running within the system VM are the traditional USER, GDI, and KERNEL modules, which perform the same functions as they did in Windows 3.1. I examine them in more detail in the section entitled "System VM Core Components."

Memory Management

The memory map for Windows 95 is shown in Figure 1.3.

FIGURE 1.3.

The memory map of Windows 95.

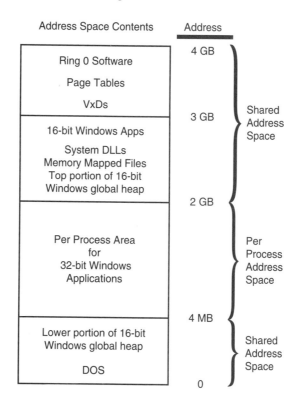

Address Space Contents

Address Space Contents	Address
Ring 0 Software / Page Tables / VxDs	4 GB — Shared Address Space
16-bit Windows Apps / System DLLs / Memory Mapped Files / Top portion of 16-bit Windows global heap	3 GB
Per Process Area for 32-bit Windows Applications	2 GB — Per Process Address Space
Lower portion of 16-bit Windows global heap / DOS	4 MB — Shared Address Space / 0

The designers of Windows 95 had much more elbow room when laying out the memory map than was available when Windows 3.x was originally designed. For Windows 95, a full 4 GB of virtual memory is available. Remarkably, the designers use all of it!

Starting from the top of the memory map, the first gigabyte (Addresses 3 GB–4 GB) is reserved for Ring 0 components, such as the VMM and VxDs. Although one gigabyte is reserved, only a small fraction of it is actually used. Stored in this area are the page tables used by the operating system to map virtual memory to real memory. Although visible to all programs, it is marked read-only to programs other than the Ring 0 components.

The second gigabyte (Addresses 2 GB–3 GB) is used to share information among 16-bit and some 32-bit components, such as USER, GDI, and KERNEL, in the system VM. This area also is the home for memory mapped files. *Memory mapped* files enable an application to allocate a block of memory and treat this block of memory as if it were a file. By using this method, one process can share a large amount of data with another process with relatively little overhead. Although I/O is still occurring, it is performed by the paging mechanism, which is an optimized high-performance method, rather than the file management subsystem, which has relatively more overhead.

The third area is actually nearly 2 GB large (Addresses 4 MB–2 GB) and is reserved for 32-bit applications (processes). Each process gets its own copy of this address space and is protected from other applications. All threads spawned by the 32-bit process share this address space. The 16-bit applications cannot address this area.

The space from 0 to 4 MB is shared and is visible to all processes running in the system VM. A memory image of DOS as it was loaded prior to Windows 95 start-up is included in this region.

Chapter 2, "Memory Management and the Windows 95 32-Bit Environment," discusses memory in much more detail.

Multiple Threads and Input Queues

Windows 95 introduces preemptive multitasking to the Windows 3.1 world. However, as in many areas of Windows 95, it is not a pure implementation but rather a hybrid of some of the characteristics in Windows 3.1 with some new features. This hybrid implementation enables old programs, and even the Windows core USER and GDI, to run cooperatively while enabling new programs to run preemptively.

Windows 3.1, of course, has always had cooperative multitasking, which requires each process to yield (through GetMessage, PeekMessage, or Yield) to other processes. If a process in Windows 3.1 misbehaved, it could bring user input to a halt and lock up the system. There was a single message queue in Windows 3.1, and all processes shared input from that queue.

In Windows 95, there are multiple input queues, one for each 32-bit thread, and one shared by all of the 16-bit processes, as in the Windows 3.1 implementation. In addition, there is a single system input queue, called the raw input queue, to which device drivers deliver their messages from devices. A VMM task monitors the raw input queue and delivers the messages to the input queue of the appropriate process. See Figure 1.4 for a pictorial representation of the input queues.

In Windows 95, there is a distinction between processes and threads. A *process* is essentially an EXE program and is used for the cooperative multitasking of Windows 3.1. In Windows 3.1, a process is sometimes called a *task*. Windows 95 moves away from this terminology.

FIGURE 1.4.

Windows 95 input queues.

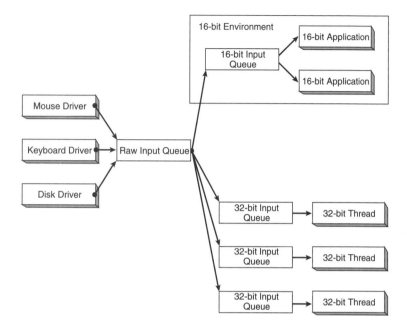

A *thread* is a unit of code and can be considered subsidiary to a process. A process, then, can spawn several threads, each executing asynchronously to one another. All threads spawned by a process share its address space. We'll examine multitasking (that is, multithreading) in more detail in Chapter 3, "Multitasking, Processes, and Threads."

Windows 95 provides preemptive multitasking among each of the DOS virtual machines and the 32-bit processes and threads within the system virtual machine (refer to Figure 1.1). However, inside the system virtual machine, for compatibility reasons, the 16-bit applications cooperatively multitask and still must yield as they do in Windows 3.1.

System VM Core Components

There are three major components in Windows 3.1: USER, GDI, and KERNEL. These components run in the system VM, as they do in Windows 95. USER is responsible for the majority of what you see on the screen. It handles Windows, dialog boxes, menus, and so on. GDI is the graphics device interface and is responsible for the graphical components you see. For example, GDI handles line drawing, icons, and bitmap images (BMP files) on your screen. KERNEL controls the system-related tasks of memory management, as well as the handling of input messages and queuing, communication, and so on.

Some of the characteristics of the environment that influenced the initial design of Windows many years ago have now changed. For example, originally, a decision was made to code much of the Windows core in x86 assembler language. Although probably necessary to make Windows run on an 8086, today it makes upgrading components more difficult and is prone to introducing bugs. Furthermore, many current Windows applications depend on the exact operation of the current versions of USER, GDI, and KERNEL.

This leads to one of the design decisions for Windows 95—namely, to reuse the 16-bit code in Windows 95. The following are some sound reasons for doing this:

- To help ensure compatibility by using current code
- To speed development time by utilizing existing code
- To keep the size of the core components small
- To reduce bugs (the current code has been thoroughly tested by millions of users)

Thunking

Using the existing code of Windows 3.1 while trying to upgrade many key components to 32-bit technology requires a mechanism to transfer control back and forth between 16-bit and 32-bit components. Simple calls cannot be made because there is an underlying difference in the memory referencing model used by 16-bit and 32-bit code; that is, 16-bit code fundamentally addresses memory by using a 16-bit selector and a 16-bit offset (this is sometimes denoted as 16:16), whereas 32-bit code can use a flat memory addressing model, which amounts to a 32-bit offset (sometimes denoted as 0:32).

Thunking is the name for the mechanism used by Windows 95 to transfer control between the 16-bit and 32-bit worlds. Thunking is also required in Windows NT and required in Windows 3.1 if Win32s has been installed. Writing code that uses thunking is complicated by the fact that Win32s, Windows NT, and Windows 95 all use different thunking models.

Win32s uses a thunking model with *universal thunks*, which is not supported by either Windows NT or Windows 95. Windows NT supports *generic thunks*, which are one-way thunks from 16 to 32 bits. Windows 95 supports a new thunking model called flat thunks. *Flat thunks* enable transitions from either 16 to 32 bits or vice versa, but requires the use of a tool called the thunk compiler.

If you use flat thunks in Windows 95, your code cannot be ported to Windows NT, and it will not work on any architecture other than the x86 family of processors. These flat thunks are used heavily in Windows 95 among the core components (USER, GDI, KERNEL). The primary reason Windows 95 uses a flat thunking model is that the design team felt it provided the best performance of the methods available.

USER, GDI, KERNEL, and Their 32-Bit Counterparts

USER, GDI, and KERNEL have both a 16-bit and a 32-bit component. In some cases, most of the work is done on the 16-bit side; in other cases, more work is done on the 32-bit side. Figure 1.5 shows that the size of the various components indicates that there is relatively more code in some components than in others.

FIGURE 1.5.

*The relationship between
16-bit and 32-bit
Windows components.*

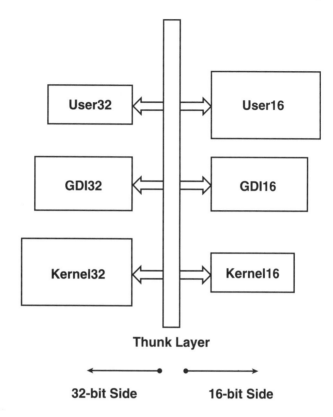

Thunk Layer

32-bit Side   **16-bit Side**

The 16-Bit and 32-Bit Versions of USER

Windows 95 retains much of the 16-bit USER module. In fact, it has been enhanced with new features, such as a new look for the Windows user interface. The 32-bit version of USER, which services 32-bit applications, actually thunks to the 16-bit version to obtain window and menu support from USER16.

This method of implementation means that the thousands of application programs currently running on Windows 3.1 will benefit from the new Windows 95 look and feel. It should be noted that in addition to the USER module, there are many other helper modules invoked to complete the user interface. For example, the new common controls, which have tabbed dialog boxes, tree views, toolbars, as well as many other features, are implemented in DLLs. Although not part of the Windows core, the common controls are crucial to the task of completing the user interface implementation. We'll cover the common controls in much greater detail in Part V, "The Windows 95 Common Controls," later in this book.

The 16-Bit and 32-Bit Versions of GDI

GDI has been enhanced on both sides. The 16-bit version includes support for a new type of object, called a *bezier*. The bezier, which is named after the French mathematician who invented it, is a compact method for representing curves. The mathematical representation of the bezier is called a *spline*. The 16-bit GDI also has support for enhanced metafiles, or EMFs.

The TrueType rasterizer, which is responsible for converting TrueType fonts to a displayable format, has been moved from the 16-bit side to the 32-bit side. The 32-bit GDI has new support for the enhanced subsystem, called the DIB engine. Also included in the 32-bit GDI are printing and spooling enhancements.

Probably the biggest disappointment to graphics programmers is that the interface to the GDI is still 16 bits, which makes the interface harder to program because each coordinate is still limited to 64 KB. This was a very tough design decision because changing the interface to 32 bits would have added code and degraded performance for small machines.

A welcome relief to all Windows programmers (as well as the millions of users) is that much of the data for USER and GDI has been moved out of the 64 KB segments. This means that users should now only rarely run into the limitations imposed by "system resources."

The 16-Bit and 32-Bit Versions of KERNEL

KERNEL32 is a major upgrade from KERNEL16. Included in KERNEL32 is new support for threads, memory management, file I/O, synchronization objects, and many other facilities. Virtually all of this code is new or enhanced from the 16-bit version.

A rewrite was necessary for KERNEL because it was important that this component make use of multitasking and multithreading. Also, by enhancing KERNEL, a performance boost could be accomplished.

Synchronization

When Windows was originally written, multithreading was not included in the programming model. Thus, USER16 and GDI16 are not reentrant and cannot be entered by two different threads simultaneously. This lack of reentrancy is a major problem in a multithreaded environment and must be solved for the system to work at all.

If a non-reentrant piece of code is reentered (that is, is called by a separate, independent thread or process), it will only be a short time before the system issues a general protection fault, or GPF. In order to prevent this from happening, Windows 95 has introduced `Win16Mutex`. This is essentially a lock that prevents more than one program from entering the 16-bit USER and GDI code at any one time. If a program has acquired `Win16Mutex`, and another thread wants to enter the 16-bit USER module, the second thread will be blocked until `Win16Mutex` is released.

`Win16Mutex` will be released whenever the thread that holds it enters one of the standard yielding functions, such as `GetMessage` or `PeekMessage`. It is important to note that if an errant 16-bit application does not yield by calling `GetMessage`, for instance, it can prevent the user interfaces of other applications from running.

The Shell

The shell in Windows 95 is also called the Windows Explorer. It has a familiar, yet new look to it. It is customizable and is aptly named: You can use it to explore your personal computer as well as other attached servers, disks, and printers.

The Explorer can have one or two panes. When it has only a single pane with large icons, it resembles the current Windows 3.1 Program Manager. You can add a toolbar and change the view to one of four modes: Large Icons, Small Icons, List, and Details. Small Icons and List mode provide a filename and a small icon. Detail mode provides a list of files with the name, size, type, and date modified for each file. An interesting feature of the Explorer is that the viewing configuration you set is remembered separately for each directory.

Explorer can also have a double-pane configuration, where on the left pane there is a tree structure and on the right pane can be one of the four modes discussed above. You can switch the mode either by using the menus or by enabling the toolbar and pressing one of the view mode buttons. The dual pane configuration with details resembles the current Windows 3.1 File Manager.

Users should easily become familiar with the Explorer. Anyone familiar with the Program Manager and the File Manager should have no problems. One difference between the File Manager and the Explorer, though, is that the Explorer only has one pair of panes; to look at two directories you must open two copies of the Explorer. The File Manager of Windows 3.1 uses the multiple document interface (MDI) to implement this same feature.

You can sort files while in Details mode by clicking the header of the section on which you want to sort. For example, to sort by modification date, you can click the "Modified" header. This will sort the files in descending order by date. By double-clicking the header, you can re-sort in ascending order by date. Similar sorting can be accomplished for the file and directory names, sizes, and types.

Windows 95 Architecture Summary

Windows 95 represents the results of thousands of design decisions—what to change and what to keep the same from Windows 3.1. Virtual machines still run DOS. The system VM still runs 16-bit and even 32-bit Windows programs. And there is still cooperative multitasking of 16-bit applications. However, there is so much that's new in Windows 95 that it's hard to identify the highlights.

New in Windows 95 is a 32-bit protected-mode file system, which takes the place of the primary usage of DOS in Windows 3.1. Support for multiple threads and preemptive multitasking enable new applications to run more smoothly than Windows 3.1. Plug and Play promises to make all of our lives easier by making it a snap to install and configure new hardware for our machines.

On top of all of this, Windows 95 has a slick, new user interface that's much easier to use than before; networking support that works pretty much out of the box; and some new administration utilities that enable easier network administration in larger enterprises.

Windows 95 has a firm architectural foundation that will enable us to enjoy its many benefits for many years to come. This architecture, with Plug and Play, allows support of new hardware devices as they come out. In the future, we'll see a migration of Windows 95 towards Windows NT. It's expected that sometime within the next year, the Windows 95 user interface will appear on Windows NT. Some of the function that is currently in Windows NT, such as 3-D graphics, will begin to appear on Windows 95. The object-oriented file system being developed for CAIRO (the next version of Windows NT) may eventually be merged with some future version of Windows 95. These are just a few of the possibilities for future directions for Windows 95.

You'll want to learn how to exploit the current features of Windows 95 to prepare you for this future. The rest of this book gives you the tools to create great applications for Windows 95 to take advantage of this important programming platform.

Memory Management and the Windows 95 32-Bit Environment

2

by Viktor T. Toth

One of the most distinguishing features of Windows 95 is that it is a 32-bit operating system. Memory management in the 32-bit environment presents some significant differences when compared to the segmented address model employed in MS-DOS and Windows 3.1. Most aspects of memory management are greatly simplified; it is no longer necessary to perform an elaborate dance with far and near addresses, nonstandard keywords in C and C++ programs, or various memory model options during program compilation. On the other hand, the new environment burdens the programmer with a set of new responsibilities. There are also some less-than-obvious differences between 16-bit and 32-bit code, which can trap the unwary when 16-bit programs are ported to the new 32-bit environment.

In the new environment, many of the earlier limitations of Windows have been lifted. However, unlike Windows NT, Windows 95 leaves some limitations in place; one of the first surprises I had after installing Windows 95 was the dreaded message from Notepad, shown in Figure 2.1.

FIGURE 2.1.

A Notepad error message.

Initially, I was hoping that what I encountered was merely a limitation of the beta Windows 95 release I was using; unfortunately, this turned out not to be the case. In this chapter, you will learn about this and other limitations inherent in the Windows 95 architecture. The experienced Windows NT programmer needs to know what these limitations are, in order to ensure that programs run flawlessly under both operating systems.

This chapter provides an overview of 32-bit programming, with special emphasis on the difference between 16-bit and 32-bit techniques. Some subtle but dangerous differences between Windows NT and Windows 95 are also mentioned.

Does the transition to the new 32-bit environment mean that it is no longer possible to develop 16-bit programs in Windows 95? Certainly not; 16-bit development tools, such as Microsoft's Visual C++ Version 1.5, continue to function well under this operating system. However, it is not possible to use the 32-bit compiler included in Visual C++ 2.0 or later to develop 16-bit code for MS-DOS or Windows 3.1.

Good-bye Segments, Hello Flat Addresses

In order to understand the differences between 16-bit and 32-bit programming on Intel-based computers, it is necessary to delve into the historical evolution of the 80x86 family of microprocessors in some detail.

With its 8086 microprocessor, Intel introduced the concept of segmented addressing. Segmented addressing enabled a 16-bit processor to address more than 64 KB of memory; it also made the life of many machine-language programmers miserable for years to come. In the segmented address model, a physical address was computed as the sum of two values: a segment base and a 16-bit offset value. The segment base, also 16 bits wide, was shifted to the left by 4 bits, yielding a total address width of 20 bits; thus, the 8086 was capable of addressing, at most, 2^{20} bytes, or 1 MB of physical memory. This addressing mechanism is illustrated in Figure 2.2.

FIGURE 2.2.

Segmented addressing of the 8086 microprocessor.

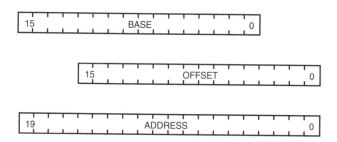

The 80286 microprocessor introduced a different programming model. In *real mode*, it continued to operate like a fast 8086; however, in *protected mode*, shown in Figure 2.3, segment base addresses were replaced by *selectors*. Selectors offered somewhat better control over memory for multitasking environments by hiding physical addresses from application programs. This made it possible for operating systems to move blocks of memory around as necessary, making the task of memory management easier and less dependent on the cooperation of application programs. The new architecture also enabled addresses to be 24 bits wide (for an effective address space of up to 2^{24} bytes, or 16 MB). Nevertheless, most of the limitations inherent to a fundamentally 16-bit design remained in place.

This was all changed with the introduction of the 80386 processor family. At last, this processor offered 32-bit registers and addresses, as seen in Figure 2.4. Finally, applications were able to address a 4 GB virtual memory space without resorting to segment manipulation.

It is important to emphasize that the 32-bit virtual address space seen by tasks on an 80386 processor does not necessarily correspond to the 32-bit physical address space of the computer. Through the processor's multitasking and page mapping functions, operating systems can configure tasks to have completely private virtual address spaces. The address that marks the beginning of code for one task might represent part of a data area for the second, and an invalid address for the third. In other words, the private address space of one task is typically completely invisible to other tasks. The chances that an application would overwrite another application's code or data are therefore much more remote than before.

FIGURE 2.3.

80286 protected mode addressing.

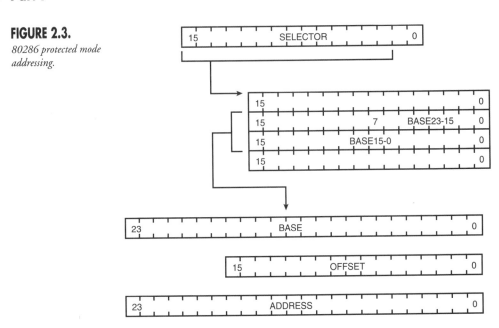

The great irony in all this is that although the 80386 architecture has been around for roughly a decade, very few programs utilize its capabilities. The limitations of 16-bit operating systems, the lack of 32-bit programming tools, and the need to remain compatible with legacy hardware forced programmers to continue writing 16-bit applications. Today's typical program written for MS-DOS or Windows is thus littered with countless occurrences of the _near and _far type modifier keywords, segment directives and pragmas, and

FIGURE 2.4.

32-bit protected mode addressing.

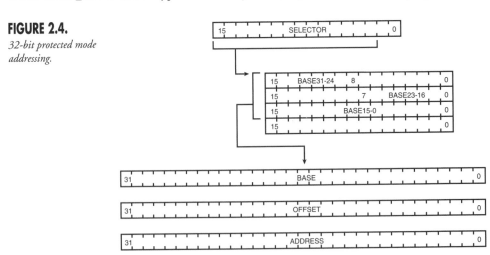

is subject to irritating errors due to incorrect address manipulations. Hopefully, this will change with Windows 95. If this operating system gains the massive customer acceptance Microsoft expects, together with Windows NT and the Win32 extensions for Windows 3.1, it will provide the necessary encouragement to developers. Finally, implementing new applications using 32-bit techniques will become commonplace.

The Basics of Writing 32-Bit Programs

In this section, you will learn the key differences between 16-bit and 32-bit programming.

Integer Size

One of the most striking differences between the 16-bit and 32-bit environments can be demonstrated by the following simple example:

```
#include <stdio.h>
void main(void)
{
    printf("sizeof(int)=%d\n", sizeof(int));
}
```

Compile this code from the Windows 95 command line using the Visual C++ 2.0 or 2.1 compiler. (You might have to first run the VCVARS32.BAT file, generated during Visual C++ installation, to set up the required environment variables for the compiler. It might also be necessary to change the environment space settings for your MS-DOS command window.) When you run this program, it will print the following result:

```
sizeof(int)=4
```

The sigh of relief heaved by UNIX programmers at this point is almost audible. Gone is the nightmare of trying to port UNIX programs that followed the deplorable practice of assuming that integers and pointers are of the same size; namely, four bytes. Many Windows programmers, on the other hand, are probably in a frenzy trying to assess how many times their programs relied implicitly on the 16-bit width of integers.

> **TIP**
>
> To ensure portability between the 16- and 32-bit APIs, use the `sizeof` operator instead of hard-coding the sizes of data types.

Note that the size of the short type remains 2 bytes; this type can be used when it is necessary to employ variables that are exactly 16 bits wide (for example, if you are reading binary data files created by older, 16-bit applications).

Type Modifiers and Macros

An obvious consequence of 32-bit addressing is that you no longer need to use type modifiers to distinguish between near and far pointers or to specify huge data. Does this mean that existing programs must be modified and all references to the _near, _far, or _huge keywords must be removed? Fortunately not; the 32-bit C/C++ compiler simply ignores these keywords to ensure backward compatibility.

Similarly, all the types that used to be defined in the windows.h header file, such as LPSTR for a far pointer to characters or LPVOID for a far pointer to a void type, still remain available. In the 32-bit environment, these types are simply defined to be equivalent to their near counterparts; thus, LPSTR is the same as PSTR, and LPVOID is the same as PVOID.

Address Calculations

Naturally, if your program performs address calculations specific to the segmented Intel architecture, it needs to be modified. (Such calculations would also be in violation of the platform-independent philosophy of the Win32 API, making it difficult to compile your program under Windows NT on the MIPS, Alpha, or other platforms.)

A particular case concerns the use of the LOWORD macro. In Windows 3.1, memory allocated with GlobalAlloc was aligned on a segment boundary, with the offset set to 0. This enabled code such as the following to work:

```
HGLOBAL hBuf;
LPSTR lpszBuf;

hBuf = GlobalAlloc(GPTR, 1024);
lpszBuf = (LPSTR)GlobalLock(hBuf);
LOWORD(lpszBuf) = 100;
*lpszBuf = 'X';      /* Set character 100 to 'X' */
```

Under the Win32 API, the assumption that an allocated memory block starts on a segment boundary is no longer valid. Instead of the preceding code, standard pointer constructs can (and should) be used.

```
LPSTR lpszBuf;
lpszBuf = malloc(1024);
lpszBuf[100] = 'X'; /* Set character 100 to 'X' */
```

Library Functions

In the 16-bit environment, many functions had two versions: one for near addresses and one for far addresses. It was often necessary to use both. For example, in medium model programs, one frequently had to use _fstrcpy to copy characters from or to a far memory location. In the 32-bit environment, these functions are obsolete.

GDI Limitations

There are also significant 16-bit limitations in the Graphics Device Interface (GDI) module. The GDI under Windows NT uses a 32-bit coordinate system; Windows 95 limits world coordinates to 16 bits. If your application passes 32-bit coordinates to GDI functions, the upper 16 bits will simply be truncated. Applications that rely on a 32-bit coordinate space (for example, if they use the MM_HIMETRIC mapping mode for lengths exceeding 32.767 centimeters) will fail under Windows 95.

Under Windows 95, logical objects such as bitmaps, brushes, pens, device contexts, or fonts share a single 64 KB heap (although at the time of this writing, there have been some unconfirmed reports that due to some changes since the final beta, fewer objects remain in this heap than originally planned). The standard practice of deleting these objects to ensure that adequate space is maintained in this heap should be continued.

Simple Memory Management

Memory allocation in the 32-bit environment is greatly simplified. It is no longer necessary to separately allocate memory and lock it for use. The distinction between global and local heaps has disappeared. On the other hand, the 32-bit environment presents a set of new challenges.

Memory Allocation via *malloc*

The venerable set of memory management functions in Windows versions prior to 3.1, such as GlobalAlloc and GlobalLock, addressed a problem specific to real mode programming of the 80x86 processor family. Because applications used actual physical addresses to access objects in memory, there was no other way for the operating system to perform memory management functions. It was necessary for applications to abide by a convoluted mechanism by which they regularly relinquished control of these objects. This enabled the operating system to move these objects around as necessary. In other words, applications had to actively take part in memory management and cooperate with the operating system. Because malloc not only allocated memory but also locked it in place, use of this function caused dangerous fragmentation of available memory.

In protected mode, applications no longer have access to physical addresses. The operating system is able to move a memory block around even while applications hold valid addresses to it that they obtained through a call to GlobalLock or LocalLock. Using malloc not only became safe, it became the recommended practice. Several implementations of this function (such as those in Microsoft C/C++ Version 7 and later) also solved another problem. Because of a system-wide limit of 8,192 selectors, the number of times applications could call memory allocation functions without subsequently freeing up memory was limited. By providing a suballocation scheme, the newer malloc implementations greatly helped applications that routinely allocated a large number of small memory blocks.

The 32-bit environment further simplifies memory allocation by eliminating the difference between global and local heaps (it is actually possible, although definitely not recommended, to allocate memory with `GlobalAlloc` and free it using `LocalFree`).

The bottom line? In Windows 95, allocate memory with `malloc`, release it with `free`, and let the operating system worry about all other aspects of memory management. For most applications, this approach is perfectly sufficient.

Using the C++ *new* and *delete* Operators

In the new environment, using `new` and `delete` is as dependable as using `malloc` and `free`. C++ programs can safely rely on these operators for most of their memory allocation needs.

The Problem of Stray Pointers

Working with a 32-bit linear address space has one unexpected consequence. In the 16-bit environment, every call to `GlobalAlloc` reserved a new selector. Attempting to address memory outside the allocated limits of that selector resulted in a protection violation.

In the 32-bit environment, automatic and static objects, global and local dynamically allocated memory, the stack, and everything else belonging to the same application share the application's heap and are accessed through flat 32-bit addresses. The operating system is less likely to catch stray pointers. The possibility of memory corruption through such pointers is greater, increasing the programmer's responsibility in ensuring that pointers stay within their intended bounds.

Consider, for example, the following code fragment:

```
HGLOBAL hBuf1, hBuf2;
LPSTR lpszBuf1, lpszBuf2;

hBuf1 = GlobalAlloc(GPTR, 1024);
hBuf2 = GlobalAlloc(GPTR, 1024);
lpszBuf1 = GlobalLock(hBuf1);
lpszBuf2 = GlobalLock(hBuf2);
lpszBuf1[2000] = 'X';   /* Error! */
```

In this code fragment, an attempt is made to write past the boundaries of the first buffer allocated via `GlobalAlloc`. In the 16-bit environment, this will result in a protection violation when the attempt is made to address a memory location outside the limits of the selector reserved by the first `GlobalAlloc` call. In the 32-bit environment, however, the memory location referenced by `lpszBuf1[2000]` is probably valid, pointing to somewhere inside the second buffer. An attempt to write to this address will succeed and corrupt the contents of the second buffer.

On the bright side, it is practically impossible for an application to corrupt another application's memory space through stray pointers. This increases the overall stability of the operating system.

Sharing Memory Between Applications

Because 32-bit applications each have a private virtual address space, it is no longer possible for them to share memory. The GMEM_DDESHARE flag is no longer functional. Passing the handle of a 32-bit memory block to another application is meaningless and futile; the handle will only refer to a random spot in the private virtual address space of the recipient program.

If it is necessary for two applications to communicate using shared memory, they can do this by using the DDEML library or by using memory-mapped files, which are described later in this chapter.

Virtual Memory and Advanced Memory Management

The concept of virtual memory is not new to Windows 95; ever since Version 3.1, Windows provided virtual memory management services. Through the memory management functions of 80386 processors, the operating system maps logical pages of memory in a variety of ways. They can be mapped to physical memory, to a swapping file on disk, or marked as invalid. When an application refers to an address location that is not mapped to physical memory, an exception is generated. In response, the operating system can either fetch the requested page from the swapping file (possibly swapping out other pages), or generate an invalid address condition.

In the Win32 programming environment, applications have improved control over how they allocate and use memory. An extended set of memory management functions is provided. Figure 2.6 shows the different levels of memory management functions available to Win32 applications.

FIGURE 2.6.

*Memory management
functions in the 32-bit
environment.*

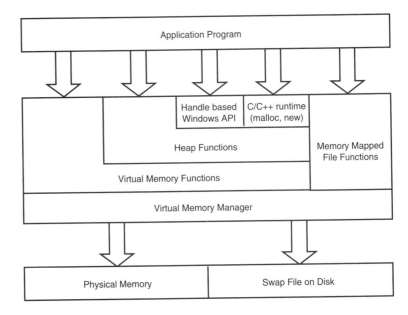

Windows 95 Virtual Memory Management

In Windows 95, every application sees a 4 GB linear address space. Of these 4 GB, the first 4 MB and the upper 2 GB are reserved by the operating system, whereas the lower 2 GB are available as the application's private address space.

It cannot be stressed strongly enough that the non-reserved address spaces of processes between 4 MB and 2 GB are completely private. Every process has its own private address space, which is completely independent of the address spaces of other processes. One process might have code at address 0x10000000; another might have allocated that address as a data area; for a third, it could be an invalid address. Using the processor's page mapping capabilities, the operating system provides a separate mapping of logical addresses to physical storage (RAM or paging file) for each process, making the address space of one process completely invisible to another.

Although the reserved areas below 4 MB and above 2 GB are actually shared among processes in Windows 95, this fact is specific to the Windows 95 implementation of Win32. Under Windows NT, none of these areas are shared unless explicitly marked by cooperating applications. In order to remain compatible with Windows NT (and compliant with the Windows 95 Logo requirements), applications should not rely on the fact that these regions are shared in Windows 95.

Figure 2.7 provides a schematic depiction of how the virtual address spaces of applications are mapped to addresses in physical memory or pages swapped to disk.

FIGURE 2.7.

Mapping of virtual addresses to physical devices.

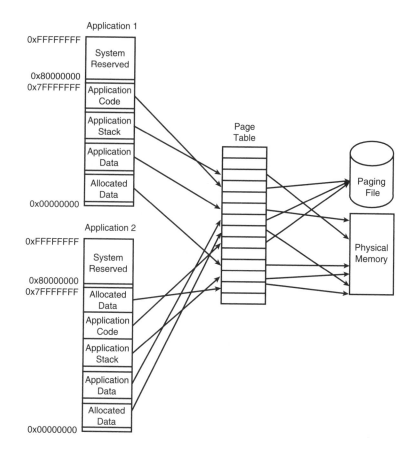

When a virtual memory location is referenced by an application, the processor checks whether the referred page is in memory; if not, it signals the operating system. The operating system can then fetch the required page from the paging file.

Figure 2.7 might appear to suggest that pages of virtual memory must always be mapped to either physical memory or a paging file. This is not the case; Windows 95's memory management makes a distinction between reserved pages and committed pages. A *committed page* of virtual memory is a page that is backed by physical storage, either in physical memory or in the paging file. In contrast, a *reserved page* is not backed by physical storage at all.

Why would you want to reserve addresses without allocating corresponding physical storage? One possibility is that you might not know in advance how much space is needed for a certain operation. This mechanism enables you to reserve a contiguous range of addresses in the virtual memory space of your process, without actually committing physical resources to it until such resources are actually needed. When a reference to an uncommitted page is made, the operating system generates an exception that your program can catch through structured exception handling. In turn, your program can instruct the operating system to commit the page, and then it can continue the processing that was interrupted by the exception. Incidentally, this is how Windows 95 performs many of its own memory management functions, such as stack allocation or manipulating the page table itself.

One real-life example concerns sparse matrices, which are two-dimensional arrays that have most of their array elements equal to zero. It is possible to reserve memory for the entire matrix but commit only those pages that contain nonzero elements, thus reducing the consumption of physical resources significantly while still keeping the application code simple.

Virtual Memory Functions

An application can reserve memory through the `VirtualAlloc` function. With this function, the application can explicitly specify the address and the size of the memory block about to be reserved. Additional parameters specify the type of the allocation (committed or reserved) and access protection flags. For example, the following code reserves 1 MB of memory, starting at address `0x10000000`, for reading and writing:

```
VirtualAlloc(0x10000000, 0x00100000, MEM_RESERVE, PAGE_READWRITE);
```

Later, the application can commit pages of memory by repeated calls to the `VirtualAlloc` function. Memory (reserved or committed) can be freed using `VirtualFree`.

A special use of `VirtualAlloc` concerns the establishment of *guard pages*. Guard pages act as one-shot alarms, raising an exception when the application attempts to access them. Guard pages can thus be used to protect against stray pointers that point past array boundaries, for example.

`VirtualLock` can be used to lock a memory block in physical memory (RAM), preventing the system from swapping out the block to the paging file on disk. This can be used to ensure that critical data can be accessed without disk I/O. This function should be used sparingly, because it can severely degrade system performance by restricting the operating system's capability to manage memory. Memory that was locked through `VirtualLock` can be unlocked using the `VirtualUnlock` function.

An application can change the protection flags of committed pages of memory using the `VirtualProtect` function. `VirtualProtectEx` can be used to change the protection flags of a block of memory belonging to another process. Finally, `VirtualQuery` can be used to obtain information about pages of memory; `VirtualQueryEx` obtains information about memory owned by another process.

Listing 2.1, written for the Windows 95 or Windows NT command line, demonstrates the use of virtual memory functions.

Listing 2.1. Handling sparse matrices using virtual memory management.

```c
#include <stdio.h>
#include <windows.h>

#define PAGESIZE 0x1000 /* Should really use GetSystemInfo */

/*
 * Exception filter function
 * Returns EXCEPTION_EXECUTE_HANDLER on page fault exceptions
 * Returns EXCEPTION_CONTINUE_SEARCH otherwise
 */

INT PageFault(DWORD dwCode)
{
    if (dwCode != EXCEPTION_ACCESS_VIOLATION)
    {
        printf("Unexpected exception code %d\n", dwCode);
        return EXCEPTION_CONTINUE_SEARCH;
    }
    return EXCEPTION_EXECUTE_HANDLER;
}

void main(void)
{
    double (*pdMatrix)[10000];
    double dTemp;
    LPVOID lpvResult;
    int x, y, i, n;

    /* Reserve memory for a matrix of 100,000,000 doubles */
    pdMatrix = VirtualAlloc(
               NULL,
               100000000 * sizeof(double),
               MEM_RESERVE,
               PAGE_NOACCESS);
    if (pdMatrix == NULL)
    {
        printf("Failed to reserve memory.\n");
        exit(1);
    }

    /* Populate matrix with 10 elements */
    n = 0;
    for (i = 0; i < 10; i++)
    {
        x = rand() % 10000;
        y = rand() % 10000;
        dTemp = (double)rand();
        printf("Setting MATRIX[%d,%d] = %f\n", x, y, dTemp);
        __try
        {
            pdMatrix[x][y] = dTemp;
        }
        __except (PageFault(GetExceptionCode()))
        {
            /* Only commit memory if value is non-zero */
            if (dTemp != 0.0)
```

continues

Listing 2.1. continued

```
            {
                n++;
                lpvResult = VirtualAlloc(
                            (LPVOID)(&pdMatrix[x][y]),
                            PAGESIZE,
                            MEM_COMMIT,
                            PAGE_READWRITE);
                if (lpvResult == NULL)
                {
                    printf("Cannot commit memory.\n");
                    exit(1);
                }
                pdMatrix[x][y] = dTemp;
            }
        }
    }
    printf("Matrix populated, %d pages used.\n", n);
    printf("Total memory committed: %d bytes.\n", n * PAGESIZE);

    /* 'User interface' loop */
    for(;;)
    {
        /* Input row and column values (terminate with ^C) */
        printf("  Enter row: ");
        scanf("%d", &x);
        printf("Enter column: ");
        scanf("%d", &y);

        /* Attempt to read matrix element */
        __try
        {
            dTemp = pdMatrix[x][y];
        }
        __except (PageFault(GetExceptionCode()))
        {
            /* An exception means the element is zero */
            printf("Exception handler was invoked.\n");
            dTemp = 0.0;
        }
        printf("MATRIX[%d,%d] = %f\n", x, y, dTemp);
    }
}
```

This program creates a 10000×10000 double-precision matrix. However, instead of allocating a whopping 800,000,000 bytes of memory, it only allocates memory on an as-needed basis. This mechanism is especially suitable for matrices that have very few nonzero elements; in this example, only 10 out of 100,000,000 elements are set to random nonzero values.

The program first reserves, but does not commit, 800,000,000 bytes of memory for the matrix. Next, it assigns random values to 10 randomly selected elements. If the element falls on a page of virtual memory that is not yet committed (has no backing in physical memory or in the paging file), an exception is raised. The exception is caught using the Microsoft try-select mechanism. The type of the exception is tested in the PageFault function. The exception handler checks whether the value to be assigned is nonzero; if so, it commits the page in question and repeats the assignment.

In the last part of the program, the user is invited to enter row and column indexes. The program then attempts to retrieve the value of the specified matrix element. If the element falls on a page that has not been committed, an exception is raised; this time, it is interpreted as an indication that the selected matrix element is zero.

The rudimentary user interface loop of this program does not include a halting condition; the program can be stopped using Ctrl+C.

The program's output looks similar to the following:

```
Setting MATRIX[41,8467] = 6334.000000
Setting MATRIX[6500,9169] = 15724.000000
Setting MATRIX[1478,9358] = 26962.000000
Setting MATRIX[4464,5705] = 28145.000000
Setting MATRIX[3281,6827] = 9961.000000
Setting MATRIX[491,2995] = 11942.000000
Setting MATRIX[4827,5436] = 32391.000000
Setting MATRIX[4604,3902] = 153.000000
Setting MATRIX[292,2382] = 17421.000000
Setting MATRIX[8716,9718] = 19895.000000
Matrix populated, 10 pages used.
Total memory committed: 40960 bytes.
   Enter row: 41
Enter column: 8467
MATRIX[41,8467] = 6334.000000
   Enter row: 41
Enter column: 8400
MATRIX[41,8100] = 0.000000
   Enter row: 1
Enter column: 1
Exception handler was invoked.
MATRIX[1,1] = 0.000000
   Enter row:^C
```

This program can be compiled and executed from the Windows 95 command line.

Heap Functions

In addition to their default heap, processes can create additional heaps using the HeapCreate function. Heap management functions can then be used to allocate and free memory blocks in the newly created private heap. A possible use of this mechanism involves the creation of a private heap at startup, specifying a size that is sufficient for the application's memory allocation needs. Failure to create the heap using HeapCreate can cause the process to terminate; however, if HeapCreate succeeds, the process is assured that the memory it requires is present and available.

After a heap is created via HeapCreate, processes can allocate memory from it using HeapAlloc. HeapRealloc can be used to change the size of a previously allocated memory block, and HeapFree deallocates memory blocks and returns them to the heap. The size of a previously allocated block can be obtained using HeapSize.

It is important to note that the memory allocated by HeapAlloc is no different from memory obtained using the standard memory allocation functions such as GlobalAlloc, GlobalLock, or malloc.

Heap management functions can also be used on the default heap of the process. A handle to the default heap can be obtained using GetProcessHeap. The function GetProcessHeaps returns a list of all heap handles owned by the process.

A heap can be destroyed using the function HeapDestroy. This function should not be used on the default heap handle of the process that is returned by GetProcessHeap. (Destroying the default heap would mean destroying the application's stack, global and automatic variables, and so on, with obviously disastrous consequences.)

The function HeapCompact attempts to compact the specified heap by coalescing adjacent free blocks of memory and decommitting large free blocks. Note that objects allocated on the heap by HeapAlloc are not movable, so the heap can easily become fragmented. HeapCompact will not unfragment a badly fragmented heap.

Windows API and C Runtime Memory Management

On top of the hierarchy of memory management functions are the standard Windows and C runtime memory management functions. As noted earlier, these functions are likely to prove adequate for the memory management requirements of most applications. Handle-based memory management functions provided in the Windows API include GlobalAlloc and LocalAlloc, GlobalLock and LocalLock, GlobalFree and LocalFree. The C/C++ runtime library contains the malloc family of functions (malloc, realloc, calloc, free, and other functions). These functions are safe to use and provide compatibility with the 16-bit environment should it become necessary to build applications that can be compiled as both 16-bit and 32-bit programs.

Miscellaneous and Obsolete Functions

In addition to the API functions described previously, a number of miscellaneous functions are also available to the Windows 95 programmer. Several other functions that were available under Windows 3.1 have been deleted or become obsolete.

Memory manipulation functions include CopyMemory, FillMemory, MoveMemory, and ZeroMemory. These functions are equivalent to their C runtime counterparts such as memcpy, memmove, or memset.

A set of Windows API functions is provided to verify whether a given pointer provides a specific type of access to an address or range of addresses. These functions are `IsBadCodePtr`, `IsBadStringPtr`, `IsBadReadPtr`, and `IsBadWritePtr`. For the latter pair, huge versions (`IsBadHugeReadPtr`, `IsBadHugeWritePtr`) are also provided for backward compatibility with Windows 3.1.

Information about available memory can be obtained using `GlobalMemoryStatus`. This function replaces the obsolete `GetFreeSpace` function.

Other obsolete functions include all functions that manipulate selectors (for example, `AllocSelector`, `ChangeSelector`, `FreeSelector`); manipulate the processor's stack (`SwitchStackBack`, `SwitchStackTo`); manipulate segments (`LockSegment`, `UnlockSegment`); or manipulate MS-DOS memory (`GlobalDOSAlloc`, `GlobalDOSFree`).

Memory-Mapped Files and Shared Memory

Earlier in this chapter, I mentioned that applications no longer are capable of communicating using global memory created with the `GMEM_DDESHARE` flag. Instead, they must use memory-mapped files to share memory. What are memory-mapped files?

Normally, the virtual memory mechanism enables an operating system to map nonexistent memory to a disk file, called the paging file. It is possible to look at this the other way around and see the virtual memory mechanism as a method of referring to the contents of a file, namely the paging file, through pointers as if the paging file were a memory object. In other words, the mechanism maps the contents of the paging file to memory addresses. If this can be done with the paging file, why not with other files? Memory-mapped files represent this natural extension to the virtual memory management mechanism.

You can create a file mapping by using the `CreateFileMapping` function. You can also use the `OpenFileMapping` function to enable an application to open an existing named mapping. The `MapViewOfFile` function will map a portion of the file to a block of virtual memory.

The special thing about memory-mapped files is that they are shared between applications. That is, if two applications open the same named file mapping, they will, in effect, create a block of shared memory.

Isn't it a bit of an overkill to be forced to use a disk file when the objective is merely to share a few bytes between two applications? Actually, it is not necessary to explicitly open and use a disk file in order to obtain a mapping in memory. Applications can submit the special handle value of `0xFFFFFFFF` to `CreateFileMapping` in order to obtain a mapping to the system paging file itself. This, in effect, creates a block of shared memory.

Listings 2.2 and 2.3 demonstrate the use of shared memory objects for intertask communication. They implement a very simple mechanism where one program, the client, deposits a simple message (a null-terminated string) in shared memory for the other program. This other program, the server, receives the message and displays it. These are Windows 95 command-line applications; they can be compiled and executed from the command line. To see how they work, start two MS-DOS windows, start the server program first in one of the windows, and then start the client program in the other. You will see the client send its message to the server; the server, in turn, displays the message it receives and then terminates.

Listing 2.2. Intertask communication using shared memory: the server.

```c
#include <stdio.h>
#include <windows.h>

void main(void)
{
    HANDLE hmmf;
    LPSTR lpMessage;

    hmmf = CreateFileMapping(  (HANDLE)0xFFFFFFFF,
                               NULL,
                               PAGE_READWRITE,
                               0,
                               0x1000,
                               "MMFDEMO"
                            );
    if (hmmf == NULL)
    {
        printf("Failed to allocated shared memory.\n");
        exit(1);
    }
    lpMessage = MapViewOfFile(hmmf, FILE_MAP_WRITE, 0, 0, 0);
    if (lpMessage == NULL)
    {
        printf("Failed to map shared memory.\n");
        exit(1);
    }
    lpMessage[0] = '\0';
    while (lpMessage[0] == '\0') Sleep(1000);
    printf("Message received: %s\n", lpMessage);
    UnmapViewOfFile(lpMessage);
}
```

Listing 2.3. Intertask communication using shared memory: the client.

```c
#include <stdio.h>
#include <windows.h>

void main(void)
{
    HANDLE hmmf;
    LPSTR lpMessage;
```

```
    hmmf = CreateFileMapping(   (HANDLE)0xFFFFFFFF,
                                NULL,
                                PAGE_READWRITE,
                                0,
                                0x1000,
                                "MMFDEMO"
                            );
    if (hmmf == NULL)
    {
        printf("Failed to allocated shared memory.\n");
        exit(1);
    }
    lpMessage = MapViewOfFile(hmmf, FILE_MAP_WRITE, 0, 0, 0);
    if (lpMessage == NULL)
    {
        printf("Failed to map shared memory.\n");
        exit(1);
    }
    strcpy(lpMessage, "This is my message.");
    printf("Message sent: %s\n", lpMessage);
    UnmapViewOfFile(lpMessage);
}
```

These two programs are nearly identical. They both start by creating a file mapping of the system paging file with the name MMFDEMO. After the mapping is successfully created, the server sets the first byte of the mapping to zero and enters a wait loop, checking once a second to see whether the first byte is nonzero. The client, in turn, deposits a message string at the same location and exits. When the server notices that the data is present, it prints the result and also exits.

NOTE

Shared memory-mapped file objects do not share the same addresses. In other words, the file will likely be mapped to different virtual memory addresses in different applications. This can be a problem if applications want to include pointers in the shared data. One solution to this problem is to use based pointers and set them to be relative to the start of the mapping area.

Summary

The Windows 3.1 programmer needs to know the following to make the transition to the 32-bit environment:

- Segments are gone, so are memory models; everything is "small model" (32-bit small model) programming.
- The size of integers changes from 16 to 32 bits.

■ Memory model-related keywords are still recognized but have no effect.

■ Address calculations involving segments or selectors are invalid.

■ Library functions no longer have far or near versions, although old-style function names are still defined in windowsx.h.

■ Selector-related functions are no longer available; programs cannot directly access physical memory.

■ Memory models are no more.

■ Using `malloc` for memory allocation is suitable in most cases.

■ The Win32 API provides advanced memory management functions.

■ Files can be accessed as memory-mapped files.

■ Shared memory can be implemented using memory-mapped files.

The Windows NT programmer, on the other hand, might get caught by the following 16-bit limitations, which are not lifted under Windows 95:

■ Edit controls are still limited to 64 KB.

■ The parameter `wParam` is limited to 16 bits for list box messages.

■ The parameter `wParam` is limited to 16 bits for certain message management functions.

■ Some User and GDI heap limitations are still present.

■ GDI world coordinates are 16-bit.

Multitasking, Processes, and Threads

3

by Viktor T. Toth

Although Windows has always been a multitasking operating system, in the past its nonpreemptive multitasking mechanism relied on the cooperation of applications for this capability. The first preemptive multitasking version of Windows was introduced with Windows NT. Now Windows 95 brings preemptive multitasking to the masses, by implementing a similarly powerful capability that runs on lower-cost hardware.

This chapter provides a comprehensive review of these new capabilities. Methods for managing processes and threads are introduced, and the subject of synchronization between threads and processes is reviewed. The second half of this chapter contains a complete example: a simple communication program written using the MFC library. This program utilizes a secondary thread to handle the communication port and demonstrates some of the other techniques presented in this chapter, such as using overlapped input and output, and thread synchronization.

Cooperative and Preemptive Multitasking

To begin the tour of the multitasking capabilities of Windows 95, let's first review the fundamentals.

> **NOTE**
>
> In the following text, I sometimes use the terms *task, process, application,* and *program* interchangeably. These terms really refer to the same thing: namely, one of the many concurrently running programs in the operating system. In the Windows 3.1 SDK documentation, Microsoft preferred the term *task*; in the Win32 SDK, the term *process* is used more often.

Cooperative Multitasking in Windows

In cooperative multitasking environments, processes must explicitly relinquish control to the operating system by calling a specified set of system functions before other tasks can gain control of the processor. Specifically, Windows applications have to call one of the following functions: GetMessage, PeekMessage, WaitMessage, or Yield. If an application fails to call one of these functions for an extended period of time, the system will appear hung, unable to accept user input.

To avoid hanging the system, applications must periodically call one of these functions (shown in Figure 3.1) even when they are busy doing some complicated processing that does not require user interaction (for example, printing a document or performing a lengthy calculation). The recommended method of doing this is to display a dialog box, which indicates to the user the nature of the processing that is taking place. The dialog box can contain a Cancel button, which enables the user to interrupt the lengthy process. Consider, for example, the code segment in Listing 3.1, taken from the very first Windows application I wrote about five years ago.

FIGURE 3.1.

Cooperative multitasking requires calls to functions that yield control.

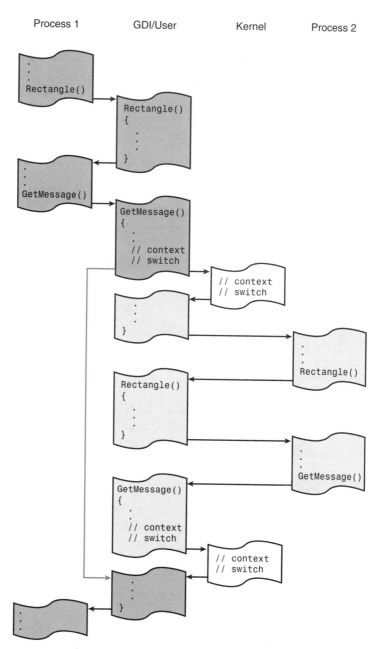

Listing 3.1. Code fragment that demonstrates yielding during lengthy processing.

```
DoAbort = FALSE;
lpProcAbort = MakeProcInstance(AbortDlg, hInst);
hAbortDlgWnd = CreateDialog(hInst, "AbortBox", hWnd, lpProcAbort);
ShowWindow(hAbortDlgWnd, SW_NORMAL);
UpdateWindow(hAbortDlgWnd);
EnableWindow(hWnd, FALSE);
/* ...
 * Prepare for processing
 */
while (!DoAbort)
{
    /* ...
     * Perform iterative processing
     */
    while (PeekMessage((LPMSG)&msg, NULL, NULL, NULL, PM_REMOVE))
    {
        if (!IsDialogMessage(hAbortDlgWnd,(LPMSG)&msg))
        {
            TranslateMessage((LPMSG)&msg);
            DispatchMessage((LPMSG)&msg);
        }
    }
}
EnableWindow(hWnd, TRUE);
DestroyWindow(hAbortDlgWnd);
FreeProcInstance(lpProcAbort);
```

The lengthy processing performed in the outer `while` loop (in this case, the calculation of iterative functions for the generation of fractal images) had to be regularly interrupted with calls to `PeekMessage`. This enabled the Windows message processing mechanism to do its task, making it possible to switch to and use other applications. Another beneficial side effect of this solution was that the application remained responsive. Not only were users able to interact with its Abort dialog box, but the application also processed `WM_PAINT` and other messages, responding correctly when parts of its window were uncovered, for example.

Preemptive Multitasking

In contrast to cooperative multitasking, in a preemptive multitasking environment the operating system is capable of interrupting the application at any time (see Figure 3.2). The application is no longer required to perform explicit calls to a function that yields control. Applications can contain loops that take a long time to execute but do not call any yielding function. In the example in Listing 3.1, preemptive multitasking eliminates the need for the regular calls to `PeekMessage` inside the iteration loop (although later you'll see why this is not such a good idea after all).

Preemptive multitasking is usually implemented using a regularly occurring hardware-generated interrupt (for example, a timer interrupt). When the processor receives the interrupt, it passes control to the operating system. Depending on its scheduling priorities, the operating system might then perform a *context switch*, suspending the process that was interrupted and returning control to another executing application.

Reentrancy and Process Synchronization

Sounds simple, doesn't it? Unfortunately, preemptive multitasking leaves the door open for a whole new set of problems, some of which are completely unheard of in nonpreemptive environments.

The first problem is *reentrancy*. In nonpreemptive environments, processes have to explicitly yield control; they are never interrupted by the operating system. This means that they yield control at well-defined points during their execution, which is no longer true in preemptive environments. It is important to recognize that the interrupt can occur at any time, even when the process is executing an operating system function.

What happens if the first process is suspended in the middle of an operating system function and a second process, which is now active, calls the same function? In many cases, this destroys any data pertinent to the first execution of the function. The result is, at the very least, a minor disaster; most likely, it is an operating system crash.

Figure 3.2 demonstrates such a scenario. In this scenario, Process 1 calls the GDI `Rectangle` function only to be interrupted in the middle of executing that function. A context switch takes place and Process 2 takes over; it then also makes a call to `Rectangle`. If the `Rectangle` function stores any data in global or static variables, those will be overwritten during this second call, even though processing of the first call is not yet complete.

To show how dangerous this problem can be, let's look at a simple, admittedly contrived, example. Consider the following naive implementation of the `Rectangle` function, which is part of someone's simplistic idea of a graphics library:

```
int i, j;
extern BYTE *screenbase;    /* video RAM (640x480x256 mode) */
extern BYTE currentcolor;   /* current 8-bit color setting */

BOOL Rectangle(HDC hdc, int nLeftRect, int nTopRect,
                        int nRightRect, int nBottomRect)
{
    i = nLeftRect;
    while (i != nRightRect)
    {
        j = nTopRect;
        while (j != nBottomRect)
        {
            _screenbase[i * 640 + y] = _currentcolor;
            j++;
        }
        i++;
    }
}
```

FIGURE 3.2.

Preemptive multitasking and reentrancy.

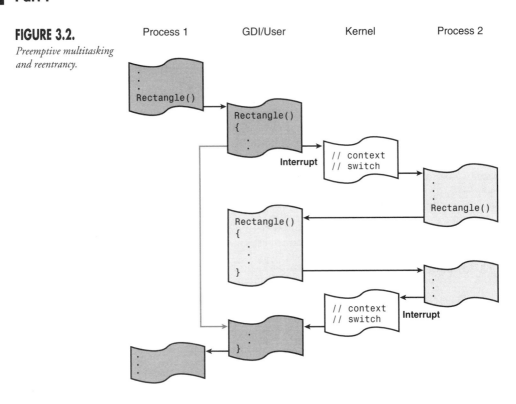

Now consider the scenario shown in Figure 3.2 with both processes making calls to the Rectangle function. Let us suppose that the following series of events takes place: first, process 1 calls the Rectangle function with the following coordinates: [(5,5),(25,25)]. The execution of the function is interrupted by a context switch, at which time process 2 takes over and also calls the Rectangle function—this time, with the coordinates [(10,10),(40,40)]. The function executes without interruption this time, leaving the value of both i and j at 40. Process 1 then regains control and attempts to continue executing the function. Because its parameters were passed on the processor stack, they remain unaffected; however, the global variables i and j are not preserved. Therefore, because the values of i and j are already greater than the values of nRightRect and nBottomRect, respectively, the two while loops continue executing indefinitely (until i and j wrap around). They overwrite the rest of the video RAM, other memory areas, code, and data, until the system crashes or an exception is raised because an invalid address is reached.

Those who wrote Terminate and Stay Resident (TSR) utilities under MS-DOS have firsthand exposure to this problem. TSRs that perform background processing typically hook themselves to the system's timer interrupt. The possibility exists that the interrupt occurs while the foreground application is executing an MS-DOS call. MS-DOS is fundamentally nonreentrant; it places the responsibility of preventing reentrant calls upon the shoulders of the TSR programmer. TSR applications rely on a special MS-DOS flag, the InDOS flag, to determine whether the interrupt occurs while an MS-DOS function is executing. If the flag is set, these TSRs typically give up and wait until the next interrupt, rather than risking reentrant calls to the same MS-DOS function.

Reentrancy can be viewed as a special case of a more general family of problems that concern process synchronization. Sometimes it is important to be able to suspend execution of one process until another process accomplishes a certain task. Sometimes it is important to prevent a critical section of program code from being executed reentrantly. Sometimes a process must suspend execution until the operating system completes a lengthy transaction.

Windows 95 provides a wide variety of synchronization objects and functions for these purposes. These are discussed in detail later in this chapter, in the section entitled "Programming with Processes, Threads, and Synchronization Objects."

Threads

Occasionally, utilizing the multitasking capabilities of the operating system seems beneficial, but it is either an overkill to spawn another task or it is impractical. After all, spawning a new task is a resource-consuming exercise that might also take a long time to complete. Moreover, the new task will have its own private data areas; it will no longer have access to the data areas of the first task. Communication between the two becomes cumbersome.

For situations like this, Windows 95 provides *threads*. Basically, threads enable several concurrent paths of execution within the same program. Switching between threads is usually less expensive than switching between processes; setting up a new thread typically involves very little overhead. Threads of the same program share the same virtual address space so that they can access the same set of variables.

NOTE

Every process has at least one thread, its *primary thread*. When that thread terminates, the entire process is terminated.

A typical area of application for multiple threads is communication programs. Instead of employing a convoluted algorithm, which simultaneously checks the keyboard and the communication port for input, the program can split itself into two threads. One thread can be responsible for handling the communication port and writing everything received to the screen. The other thread can manage the user interface and write everything typed by the user out to the port. This is the approach implemented by the sample TTY application presented later in this chapter.

Multitasking in Windows 95

Let's turn our attention now to how multitasking, threads, and synchronization are actually implemented in Windows 95.

Windows 95 and Windows NT

First, it should be noted that from a functional point of view, there is very little difference between the multitasking and multithreading capabilities of Windows 95 and Windows NT. Both operating systems provide the same programming interface and execute processes and threads in a similar fashion. The only notable differences between the two operating systems concern the lack of Windows NT's security features in Windows 95, and the constraints imposed by an underlying nonreentrant 16-bit system. In all other aspects, the discussion presented in this chapter is applicable to both systems.

Preemptive Multitasking in Windows 3.1

Although Windows 3.1 is characterized as a nonpreemptive operating system, it already implemented preemptive multitasking between *virtual machines*. Virtual machines are a concept specific to the 80386 microprocessor. This processor can operate in a *virtual 8086 mode*. Virtual 8086 mode enables an 80386 or better processor to emulate one or more real-mode 8086 processors. Windows 3.1 uses this capability to run multiple simultaneous MS-DOS sessions (windowed or full-screen).

Because DOS programs do not participate in the cooperative multitasking regime (they do not have message processing loops with calls to `GetMessage`), it was necessary to provide another multitasking mechanism to enable these programs to execute. Windows 3.1 employs a preemptive multitasking mechanism to switch between MS-DOS sessions and Windows itself, which is treated as yet another virtual machine.

32-Bit and 16-Bit Processes

Windows 95 expands and refines the rudimentary preemptive capabilities of Windows 3.1. It provides fully preemptive multitasking for all 32-bit processes. Like Windows NT, Windows 95 treats all 16-bit processes as a single entity for multitasking purposes and does not provide preemptive multitasking among 16-bit tasks. Unlike Windows NT 3.5 or later versions, Windows 95 does not provide the option to run 16-bit tasks in separate virtual machines.

How is preemptive multitasking for 32-bit processes implemented? Specifically, how do the concepts of preemptive multitasking coexist with Windows messaging and 16-bit applications that perform cooperative multitasking? To what extent is the multitasking architecture of Windows 95 similar to that of Windows NT?

I discovered one obvious difference between the two operating systems not more than a few hours after I first installed Windows 95. I use an application called the CompuServe Navigator (CSNav) as my offline reader for CompuServe. Unfortunately, CSNav occasionally corrupts the indexes of its message base. To resolve this problem, I must use CSNav's Rebuild Indexes option. This option displays a warning message before going about its task, informing the user that the operation will be lengthy. And lengthy it is. Rebuilding indexes usually takes several minutes to complete, during which time CSNav displays the ubiquitous hourglass cursor and does not yield to other applications at all. Windows 3.1 effectively hangs until CSNav completes this function.

Under Windows NT, this was not a problem. Although CSNav itself became unresponsive—and so did some other 16-bit applications if I was careless enough not to start CSNav in its own virtual machine—the overall system remained functional. I was able to switch to the Program Manager, work with other 32-bit applications, or work with 16-bit applications that were in different virtual machines. It was only natural for me to expect the same thing under Windows 95. What a disappointment! CSNav's lengthy operation froze the system completely. Other applications didn't respond; the taskbar didn't respond. Nothing happened, just like under Windows 3.1.

This behavior of CSNav provides some insight into how preemptive multitasking is implemented in Windows 95. At the heart of the problem is the fact that much of the core of Windows 95 is code inherited from Windows 3.1. As you probably know, Windows 3.1 was never intended to be a preemptive operating system; hence, its core components were not written with the reentrancy problem in mind.

This is not a problem when 16-bit applications are running; they participate in the cooperative multitasking scheme that prevents reentrant calls to Windows. Unfortunately, calls to Windows by 32-bit applications are also often transferred to the underlying 16-bit system. Unlike 16-bit programs, 32-bit applications can make system calls synchronously, and reentrancy becomes possible. With nonreentrant functions at its core, Windows 95 has to do something to prevent this.

Although there are many possible solutions for this problem, the requirement for small memory footprint (so that Windows 95 remains operational on "legacy" low-end computers with as little as 4 MB of memory), as well as the need to remain as compatible as possible with Windows 3.1, limits the number of options. Rewriting core functions of Windows in 32 bits (the NT way) is not an option because of the increased memory requirements and the resulting compatibility problems. Revising the vulnerable areas of core functions for reentrancy would be a monumental task, subject to numerous errors. And even if one of these solutions proved to be viable, it would still not address the reentrancy problem for the thousands of third-party 16-bit DLLs that are out there.

The name of the solution that Microsoft selected is *Win16Mutex*. This mutual exclusion mechanism essentially prevents the simultaneous execution of 16-bit code by two or more threads.

Threads of 32-bit applications "own" this Win16Mutex only when they execute 16-bit Windows functions. In contrast, 16-bit applications own the Win16Mutex whenever they are executing. Those 16-bit applications that do not yield for an extended period of time will therefore effectively hang the system by preventing other applications from calling 16-bit functions. As 32-bit applications implement their user interface with calls to Windows, which are eventually passed to the 16-bit system, these applications will become unresponsive as well. (32-bit threads that operate in the background and do not call Windows functions will continue to execute.)

Herein lies the explanation for my problems with CSNav. For reasons of their own, CSNav's implementers decided not to yield during the execution of its lengthy reindexing operation. Because it is a 16-bit application, it owns the Win16Mutex the entire time. As a result, Windows 95 freezes and becomes unresponsive until, several minutes later, CSNav finishes its task and yields.

This situation is noticeably similar to the behavior of MS-DOS windows under Windows 3.1. As I mentioned earlier, Windows 3.1 provides preemptive multitasking for MS-DOS sessions. However, an unresponsive Windows program also effectively hangs all running MS-DOS programs. This is due to the fact that MS-DOS sessions also rely on Windows for user interface events (keyboard, mouse). If Windows is in a hung state, the MS-DOS window never has a chance to receive user interface messages that it would then communicate to the MS-DOS program currently executing in that window. Similarly, the output of the MS-DOS program will never be displayed if the MS-DOS window never receives `WM_PAINT` messages.

Message Queues and Threads

In Windows 3.1, there is a single thread of execution and a single system-wide message queue. Windows 95, on the other hand, implements a separate message queue for each executing thread. This is necessary in order to ensure that concurrently executing threads properly receive messages sent to them and can process them simultaneously.

Another important thing to consider is how the `SendMessage` function is implemented in the multithreaded environment. In Windows 3.1, `SendMessage` simply calls the recipient window's message function. In the multithreaded environment, this mechanism would be insufficient; instead, the call must take place in the context of the thread that created the window, not in the context of the calling thread. Windows 95 provides the necessary mechanisms for suspending the calling thread until the called thread completes execution of the `SendMessage` call.

Is Yielding No Longer Necessary for 32-Bit Programs?

Does preemptive multitasking mean that it is no longer necessary to perform message dispatching during a lengthy operation? The answer is a resounding NO, and in this section, you'll see the reasons why.

Consider, for example, the code fragment I presented earlier in Listing 3.1. What would happen if the inner `while` loop, the one that contains the call to `PeekMessage`, was eliminated from this program?

Because of preemptive multitasking, Windows 95 remains responsive. You can switch away from this application at will, start additional programs, and interact with others. You can't cancel the lengthy operation, but perhaps the nature of the operation is such that it should not be canceled anyway. Is there anything wrong with this approach, then?

How about trying to switch back to the application? How will it respond to `WM_PAINT` messages when parts of its window are uncovered as other windows are moved around or closed? The answer is that it will not; it will no longer process any messages sent to it, which means it will no longer respond to any user interface events.

In other words, although preemptive multitasking prevents badly written applications from hanging the system, it does not provide a magic solution for applications that are not responsive.

Programming with Processes, Threads, and Synchronization Objects

Windows 95 provides separate sets of functions for the management of processes and threads. Additional sets of functions are available to control process scheduling and manage synchronization objects. Figure 3.3 provides a schematic overview of the relationship among these families of functions.

FIGURE 3.3.
*Process and thread
management functions.*

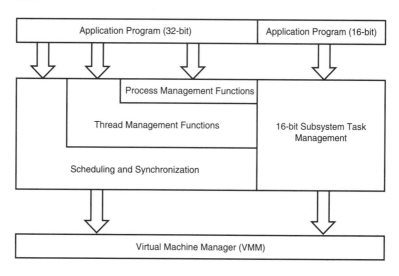

Managing Processes

In the old days, Windows 3.1 programmers did not give much thought to process (or, as it is called in the Windows 3.1 SDK documentation, *task*) management. There was WinExec; there was, for the more sophisticated, LoadModule; there were a few additional functions (mostly MS-DOS specific) that served to obtain information about tasks in the system; and that was that.

Windows 95 offers a whole new set of functions for process management. Gone are some of the MS-DOS specific functions (remember, the Win32 API is platform-independent, so MS-DOS specific features are no longer part of it). On the other hand, several new functions are available to create and manage processes in the system.

Although WinExec and LoadModule are still provided for compatibility with Windows 3.1, 32-bit Windows 95 applications should use the CreateProcess function to start another application. CreateProcess creates the new process and its primary thread. It also returns a process identifier that is unique throughout the system. This process identifier can be used to obtain a handle to the process via OpenProcess. The handle then can be used in subsequent calls to functions that require a process handle as a parameter. One such function is WaitForInputIdle. This function can be used to wait until a spawned process completes its initialization and begins waiting for user input.

> **WARNING**
>
> UNIX programmers are used to seeing processes organized into a hierarchy of parent and child tasks. This hierarchy does not exist in Win32; a process does not know about its parents or siblings. There is also no mechanism through which exceptions would be propagated from child to parent. This makes it difficult to implement a reliable cleanup mechanism for programs that regularly spawn other tasks (for example, a telnet service).

CreateProcess can also be used to control what is inherited by child processes from the parent process. Processes can inherit handles to files, the console, communication devices, or pipes; processes, threads, and synchronization objects; and file mapping objects. They can also inherit environment variables, the default directory, and the console of the parent process in the case of console applications. Handle inheritance is controlled by the *fInheritHandles* parameter of CreateProcess; the inheritance of the environment and the current directory are controlled by *lpvEnvironment* and *lpszCurDir*, respectively.

Child processes do not inherit the priority class of the parent process, memory handles, pseudohandles (such as handles returned by GetCurrentProcess or GetCurrentThread), DLL module handles, and handles to GDI and User objects (such as HWND and HDC).

The preferred way to terminate a process is with a call to ExitProcess. If the primary thread of a process returns, it is equivalent to an implicit call to ExitProcess. In this regard, the primary thread differs from other threads (a return from another thread is equivalent to an implicit call to ExitThread). A process also terminates if its last thread terminates, or if the TerminateProcess function is called and passed a handle to the process.

When a process terminates, all its handles are closed. Note that the objects referred to by those handles might remain valid if other processes have open handles to them.

ExitProcess is implicitly invoked by the system for most unhandled exceptions.

GetExitCodeProcess can be used to determine the exit status of a process. While the process is still active, this function returns the constant STILL_ACTIVE. When the process terminates, its exit status changes to the value passed to the ExitProcess or TerminateProcess function, or it becomes the return value of the primary thread.

A process can obtain its own process identifier using GetCurrentProcessId. Another function, GetCurrentProcess, returns a *pseudohandle* to the current process. This handle is called a pseudohandle because it is only valid in the context of the current process; the value cannot be passed on to other processes and expected to work. If a "real" handle is needed, one can be obtained using the DuplicateHandle function. Alternatively, a process can open its own process object using OpenProcess.

Using Threads

A process can create a new thread by calling CreateThread. When creating a new thread, the starting address of the code that the new thread is to execute must be specified. Note that CreateThread might succeed even if the address passed to it is invalid; however, when the operating system attempts to execute code at that address, an exception might occur.

CreateThread returns a handle to a thread object, which is maintained by the operating system. This handle can be used in subsequent calls to functions that expect a thread handle as their parameter, such as GetExitCodeThread or GetThreadPriority. The thread object remains valid until the thread itself terminates and all handles to the object are closed.

A thread is closed when it makes a call to ExitThread. Returning from the thread function is equivalent to an implicit call to ExitThread (except in the case of the primary thread, when it is equivalent to a call to ExitProcess). Threads are also terminated if a call is made to TerminateThread using the thread's handle.

How would an application use threads efficiently? Consider the example I presented in Listing 3.1. In this example, the application performed a lengthy calculation; in order to remain responsive, it had to periodically check its message queue. In the multithreaded environment, this code can be rewritten; the message loop and the iteration loop can be separated, as demonstrated in Listing 3.2.

Listing 3.2. Code fragment demonstrating the use of a secondary thread to perform lengthy processing.

```
    DoAbort = FALSE;
    lpProcAbort = MakeProcInstance(AbortDlg, hInst);
    hAbortDlgWnd = CreateDialog(hInst, "AbortBox", hWnd,
                                          lpProcAbort);

    ShowWindow(hAbortDlgWnd, SW_NORMAL);
    UpdateWindow(hAbortDlgWnd);
    EnableWindow(hWnd, FALSE);
    hThread = CreateThread(NULL, 0,
                          (LPTHREAD_START_ROUTINE)Iterate,
                          NULL, 0, &dwThread);
    while ((!DoAbort) && GetMessage((LPMSG)&msg, NULL, NULL, NULL))
    {
        if (!IsDialogMessage(hAbortDlgWnd,(LPMSG)&msg))
        {
            TranslateMessage((LPMSG)&msg);
            DispatchMessage((LPMSG)&msg);
        }
    }
    WaitForSingleObject(hThread, INFINITE);
    EnableWindow(hWnd, TRUE);
    DestroyWindow(hAbortDlgWnd);

    .
    .
    .


DWORD Iterate(LPDWORD lpdwParm)
{
    /* ...
     * Prepare for processing
     */
    while (!DoAbort)
    {
        /* ...
         * Perform iterative processing
         */
    }
    /*
     * Perform cleanup
     */
    return 0
}
```

When looking at this code, it is important to keep in mind that two loops are executing in parallel: the `while` loop that calls `GetMessage` in the main program function, and the `while` loop in the `Iterate` function.

The advantages of this approach are obvious. First of all, separating the dialog message loop and the iteration results in cleaner code. It is also slightly more efficient. Because `GetMessage` does not return until a message is placed in the application's message queue, the application's primary thread remains essentially suspended until the user actually interacts with the application's window.

The thread function's `while` loop is terminated when the value of the global `DoAbort` variable changes to `FALSE`. This variable is modified in the dialog box procedure for the Abort dialog box. The primary thread waits for the termination of the secondary thread using the `WaitForSingleObject` function, the use of which is explained in the next section, "Synchronization Objects."

Although it is not shown in the previous code fragment, it is important to note that `DoAbort` must be declared `volatile`. This ensures that any changes to its value will actually be written out to memory, thus enabling the secondary thread to read the proper value. Otherwise, compiler optimizations might prevent proper communication of this value between the two threads.

A thread can obtain its own thread identifier using the `GetCurrentThreadId` function. A pseudohandle to the current thread can be obtained using `GetCurrentThread`. This pseudohandle is only valid in the context of the current process; if it is necessary to create a "real" handle, the `DuplicateHandle` function can be used. Alternatively, the `OpenThread` function can also be used to obtain a handle.

It is also possible to suspend a thread's execution using `SuspendThread`. Execution can be resumed by a call to `ResumeThread`.

Synchronization Objects

In multithreaded programs, it is often necessary to provide some method to synchronize the execution of threads. There are numerous synchronization mechanisms in Windows 95—ranging from the trivial to the complex—that are available for applications.

The simplest method of synchronization can be achieved without any operating system support. Threads can communicate their state to each other using status variables. This is exactly how, in the example presented in Listing 3.2, the secondary thread was notified when the user clicked the button in the Abort dialog box.

What is wrong with this approach? There is one important problem. In order for the second thread to find out that the value of the status variable has changed, it has to regularly check the value of that variable. If the thread has nothing else to do—for example, if it is waiting for another thread to complete a lengthy operation—the `while` loop in which the status variable's value is checked will consume a lot of processor time, which slows down the system significantly. The problem can be alleviated somewhat if you add a delay between subsequent checks.

```
while (!bStatus) Sleep(1000);
```

Unfortunately, this is not always a satisfactory solution either. Often, you cannot afford to wait hundreds of milliseconds before a thread becomes responsive again. What you really need is a mechanism that would enable a thread to suspend its execution indefinitely but reawaken immediately when a specific event occurs.

Windows 95 provides a set of functions that can be used to wait until a specific object or set of objects becomes *signaled*. There are several types of objects to which these functions apply. Some are dedicated *synchronization objects*, and others are objects for other purposes that nevertheless have signaled and nonsignaled states. Synchronization objects include *semaphores*, *events*, and *mutexes*.

Semaphore objects can be used to limit the number of concurrent accesses to a shared resource. When a semaphore object is created using the `CreateSemaphore` function, a maximum count is specified. Each time a thread that is waiting for the semaphore is released, the semaphore's count is decreased by one. The count can be increased again using the `ReleaseSemaphore` function.

The state of an event object can be explicitly set to signaled or nonsignaled. When an event is created using the `CreateEvent` function, its initial state is specified, and so is its type. A manual-reset event must be reset to nonsignaled explicitly using the `ResetEvent` function; an auto-reset event is reset to the nonsignaled state every time a waiting thread is released. The event's state can be set to signaled using the `SetEvent` function.

A mutex (*mut*ual *ex*clusion) object is nonsignaled when it is owned by a thread. A thread obtains ownership of a mutex object when it specifies the object's handle in a wait function. The mutex object can be released using the `ReleaseMutex` function.

Threads wait for a single object using the functions `WaitForSingleObject` or `WaitForSingleObjectEx`; or for multiple objects, using `WaitForMultipleObjects`, `WaitForMultipleObjectsEx`, or `MsgWaitForMultipleObjects`.

Synchronization objects can also be used for interprocess synchronization. Semaphores, events, and mutexes can be named when they are created using the appropriate creation function; another process can then open a handle to these objects using `OpenSemaphore`, `OpenEvent`, and `OpenMutex`.

Critical section objects represent a variation of the mutex object. Critical section objects can only be used by threads of the same process, but they provide a more efficient mutual exclusion mechanism. These objects are typically used to protect critical sections of program code. A thread acquires ownership of the critical section object by calling `EnterCriticalSection` and releases ownership using `LeaveCriticalSection`. If the critical section object is owned by another thread at the time `EnterCriticalSection` is called, this function waits indefinitely until the critical section object is released.

Another simple yet efficient synchronization mechanism is *interlocked variable access*. Using the functions `InterlockedIncrement` or `InterlockedDecrement`, a thread can increment or decrement a variable and check the result for zero without fear of being interrupted by another thread (which might also increment or decrement the same variable before the first thread has a chance to check its value). These functions can also be used for interprocess synchronization if the variable is in shared memory.

In addition to dedicated synchronization objects, threads can also wait on certain other objects. The state of a process object becomes signaled when the process terminates; similarly, the state of a thread object becomes signaled when the thread terminates. A *change notification* object, created by FindFirstChangeNotification, becomes signaled when a specified change occurs in the file system. The state of a *console input* object becomes signaled when there is unread input waiting in the console's input buffer.

Overlapped Input

Input and output operations can be time consuming. Synchronous input and output operations can block the calling thread indefinitely. As an alternative, Windows 95 provides asynchronous input and output for files, communication devices, and named pipes.

When a file, communication device, or named pipe is opened for *overlapped* operations, input and output functions can return immediately, even when the operation has not yet been completed. Time-consuming operations can thus be relegated to the background, without blocking the execution of the calling thread.

A file, communication device, or named pipe can be opened for overlapped operations by specifying the FILE_FLAG_OVERLAPPED flag when calling CreateFile. To actually perform an operation synchronously, threads must specify an OVERLAPPED structure when calling input or output functions. To obtain the status of an overlapped operation, threads can use the GetOverlappedResult function or one of the wait functions.

It is possible to perform multiple asynchronous input and output operations simultaneously. In this case, threads can call the WaitForMultipleObjects function to wait for the completion of one of the operations.

Multithreading and the Microsoft Foundation Classes

Version 3.0 and later versions of the Microsoft Foundation Classes support multithreaded applications. Threads in MFC applications are represented by CWinThread objects. CWinApp is a class derived from CWinThread; additional CWinThread objects can be created, for example, by calls to AfxBeginThread.

The Microsoft Foundation Classes provide a distinction between *user interface threads* and *worker threads*. This distinction is specific to the MFC and is not reflected in the Win32 API or at the operating system level. These two types of threads will be discussed shortly.

The Microsoft Visual C++ documentation states that "MFC objects are not thread safe at the object level, only at the class level." I found that it is important to correctly interpret this statement. The Visual C++ documentation mentions that two threads can both use CString objects, but they cannot use the same CString object without appropriate precautions being taken (such as using a critical section object). Does this mean that your own CDocument derived class cannot have an integer member variable that is accessed by two threads simultaneously? No, it does not; it is the MFC class member functions that are not thread-safe on the object level. Anything that invokes a member function (such as assigning a value to a CString object, which invokes the overloaded assignment operator) is thus suspect. However, assigning a value to a variable of a built-in type does not invoke any member functions and should be considered safe, provided all other precautions applicable to using variables in multiple threads are taken.

The CWinThread class does not provide an interface for all thread-related functions. Many functions (such as the wait functions) must be used directly from the Win32 API.

User Interface Threads

A user interface thread is a thread that has its own message pump and processes user interface messages. The first step in creating a user interface thread is to derive a class from CWinThread. The class must be derived and implemented using the DECLARE_DYNCREATE and IMPLEMENT_DYNCREATE macros. It should override the InitInstance function and can provide overrides for others such as ExitInstance.

AfxBeginThread can be used to create a user interface thread object when passed a pointer to a CRuntimeClass object as its first parameter. The CRuntimeClass object can be created from the class derived from CWinThread using the RUNTIME_CLASS macro.

Worker Threads

In contrast to user interface threads, worker threads do not have a message pump and do not generally handle user input. These threads are typically used to perform background processing.

A worker thread is started by calling AfxBeginThread and passing the starting address of the thread function. AfxBeginThread creates and initializes a CWinThread object. Worker threads are not usually created using classes derived from CWinThread.

The thread function is declared as follows:

```
UINT ThreadFunction(LPVOID pParam);
```

The parameter *pParam*, a 32-bit value, is passed to the AfxBeginThread function. If you do not want to use this parameter, use NULL.

Working Example: A Simple Communications Program

The subjects of threads and synchronization are complex. Not only do they require the programmer to learn a whole new set of functions, the very concepts are new and have not been seen before in the Windows environment. It is very difficult to understand such fundamentally new concepts through abstract discussion. For this reason, I decided to include a real-life example that demonstrates many of the principles discussed in this chapter.

It is not necessary to walk through all the steps provided in this section. The complete set of source files and the executable for this example are included on the CD-ROM that accompanies this book.

The program you will build is a simple communication program, capable of performing the barest essentials: namely, transmitting and receiving characters on a communication port, and providing an ASCII terminal interface for the user.

This application, shown in Figure 3.4, is built using the Microsoft Foundation Classes. It also gives me a chance to demonstrate some of the techniques by using C++ and MFC, as opposed to the C language and Windows API examples that I used earlier.

The application is based in part upon sample code provided by Microsoft as part of Visual C++ 2.0. The code has been ported to the MFC and extensively modified.

FIGURE 3.4.
The TTY application.

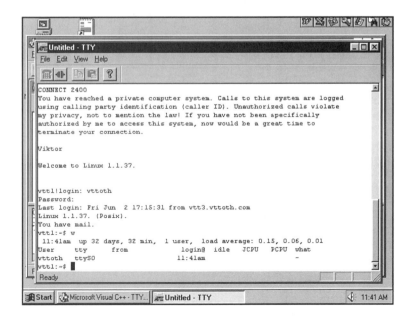

The TTY application has been built and tested under Windows 95 build 347, using the Visual C++ 2.1 compiler.

Creating the Project

This application, which I decided to simply and unimaginatively call TTY, is created like any regular MFC project using the Visual C++ AppWizard. Create a project named TTY.MAK using AppWizard with the following settings: single document interface, no database support, no OLE compound document support, no printing or print preview. All other AppWizard options should be left at their default settings.

Dialog Boxes and Resources

The TTY application will have two dialog boxes. One—its About dialog box—has been supplied by the MFC; you must build the other. The second dialog box, identified as IDD_TTYSETTINGS, contains the controls necessary to set communication parameters. The dialog box is shown in Figure 3.5.

FIGURE 3.5.

The TTY Settings dialog box.

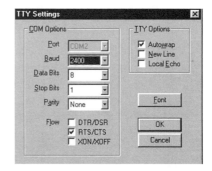

This dialog box contains controls corresponding to all communication port parameters. Some of the controls are combo boxes, with the list of choices preinitialized through the integrated resource editor. The controls, their types, and the initialization settings are as follows:

Control	Identifier	Type	Initialization
Port	IDC_PORTCB	combo box	COM1
			COM2
			COM3
			COM4

Control	Identifier	Type	Initialization
Baud Rate	IDC_BAUDCB	combo box	300
			1200
			2400
			9600
			14400
			19200
			38400
			57600
Data Bits	IDC_DATABITSCB	combo box	5
			6
			7
			8
Parity	IDC_PARITYCB	combo box	None
			Even
			Odd
			Mark
			Space
Stop Bits	IDC_STOPBITSCB	combo box	1
			1.5
			2
DTR/DSR	IDC_DTRDSR	checkbox	
RTS/CTS	IDC_RTSCTS	checkbox	
XON/XOFF	IDC_XONXOFF	checkbox	
Autowrap	IDC_AUTOWRAP	checkbox	
New Line	IDC_NEWLINE	checkbox	
Local Echo	IDC_LOCALECHO	checkbox	
Font	IDC_FONT	button	

Note that all the combo boxes in this dialog box should have their types set to Drop List and should be marked as unsorted.

Create this dialog box in `TTY.rc` using the integrated dialog box editor. While the dialog box editor is open, also create a class corresponding to the new dialog box. The name of the class is `CTTYSettingsDlg`, and its header and implementation files should be set to `ttyset.h` and `ttyset.cpp`, respectively. You can create this class by activating the Visual C++ ClassWizard while the dialog box editor is active and filling in the appropriate fields in the Add Class dialog box.

After the dialog box class has been created, the application's menu should be modified. From its File menu, all options created by AppWizard (except the Exit command and the separator bar above it) should be removed. Two new options should then be added: Connect (ID_FILE_CONNECT) and Disconnect (ID_FILE_DISCONNECT). From the Edit menu, all options except Copy and Paste should be removed. (Note that this example does not actually implement any clipboard operations.) A new option, TTY Settings... (ID_EDIT_TTYSETTINGS), should then be added at the bottom. Also, insert a separator bar above this option. You might also want to add prompt strings to the new menu items that will be displayed in the status bar and in tooltips.

The application's toolbar should also be modified. Many of the standard options are gone, so their corresponding toolbar buttons should also be removed. Two new buttons are added, which correspond to the Connect and Disconnect functions. The resulting toolbar bitmap is shown in Figure 3.6.

FIGURE 3.6.

The TTY application toolbar.

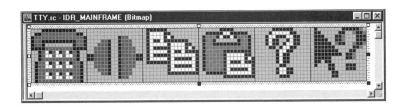

Three new strings should also be added to the resource file. These strings are used to warn the user of specific error conditions. The strings that should be added are as follows:

Identifier	String
IDS_CONNECTION_FAILED	Connection failed!
IDS_NOTHREAD	Failed to create secondary thread!
IDS_BADSETUP	Setup failed!

The new toolbar should be correctly reflected in mainfrm.cpp. Open this file and edit the initialization of the buttons array.

```
static UINT BASED_CODE buttons[] =
{
    // same order as in the bitmap 'toolbar.bmp'
    ID_FILE_CONNECT,
    ID_FILE_DISCONNECT,
        ID_SEPARATOR,
    ID_EDIT_COPY,
    ID_EDIT_PASTE,
        ID_SEPARATOR,
    ID_APP_ABOUT,
};
```

At this point, you might want to compile the application to see whether its user interface elements work as expected.

The View and Document Classes

The division of labor between TTY's view and document classes is as follows. The document class buffers all data, holds communication settings, and does the actual work of transmitting and receiving characters. The view class is responsible for the presentation of a scrollable terminal window and for handling event messages.

The principal function of the CTTYView class, which is derived from CScrollView, is redrawing the terminal screen as necessary. When the view has the focus, this class displays a blinking block cursor at the current character position and offers a few helper functions to move the cursor, set the terminal font, and reset the view's scrollbars. This class has message handlers for WM_CHAR (user input), WM_KILLFOCUS, and WM_SETFOCUS messages (to disable and re-enable the block cursor), and for WM_SIZE messages. One additional message handler function processes WM_COMMNOTIFY messages. This message type was borrowed from Windows 3.1 (it is not implemented in Win32) and is used by the secondary thread to notify the primary thread of incoming characters on the communication port.

The majority of the work is done by the CTTYDoc class. This class maintains a set of variables that reflect the settings of the communication port. These variables are updated via the CTTYSettings dialog box, which is itself implemented in the files ttyset.h and ttyset.cpp.

The serious work begins in the function CTTYDoc::OpenConnection. This function initializes the view, and then opens the communication port for overlapped input and output. After configuring the port, it starts a secondary worker thread using a call to AfxBeginThread.

The secondary thread monitors the communication port using the WaitCommEvent function. When this thread receives an event indicating incoming characters, it notifies the primary thread by sending a WM_COMMNOTIFY message. After doing so, it first verifies that the WM_COMMNOTIFY message has been processed by waiting for the m_hPostEvent event, which is declared as a member of CTTYDoc. Then it continues waiting for additional port events.

WM_COMMNOTIFY messages are handled by the OnCommNotify member function of CTTYView. When such a message is received, this function reads any available data on the communications port using CTTYDoc::ReadCommBlock and writes the result to the terminal buffer using CTTYDoc::WriteTTYBlock. When the input buffer becomes empty, CTTYView::OnCommNotify sets CTTYDoc::m_hPostEvent so that the secondary thread can send additional WM_COMMNOTIFY messages if necessary. This mechanism ensures that the secondary thread does not keep sending additional WM_COMMNOTIFY messages when the primary thread is already processing one.

CTTYView::OnCommNotify also checks the message queue and dispatches any pending messages using PumpMessage. This ensures that the application remains responsive while large blocks of data are read from the port.

CTTYView also handles WM_CHAR messages. When any user input is received, it is written to the communication port using CTTYDoc::WriteCommByte. If the local echo setting is on, the data is also written to the terminal buffer using `CTTYDoc::WriteTTYBlock`. This function also invalidates the appropriate portion of the application's view, causing the view class member function `CTTYView::OnDraw` to redraw the display.

The remaining member functions of these classes manage the terminal buffer and ensure that its contents are properly displayed in the application's view. The `CTTYDoc` class maintains a buffer of 100 rows by 80 columns. This buffer is used as a circular scrollback buffer; `CTTYDoc` also maintains member variables that keep track of the number of lines buffered, the current top of the buffer, and the current cursor position. The `CTTYView` class uses these variables when it redraws the application's view.

Building the *CTTYView* Class

As the first step in building the view class, you need a few message handlers. Using ClassWizard, add functions to handle the following messages: `OnInitialUpdate`, `WM_CHAR`, `WM_KILLFOCUS`, `WM_SETFOCUS`, and `WM_SIZE`. Next, edit the header file `TTYview.h`. At the top of the file, add the following definitions:

```
#define WM_COMMNOTIFY 0x0044
#define CN_EVENT 0x04
#define MAXBLOCK 80
```

The declaration of the `CTTYView` class should also be changed to be derived from `CScrollView` (as opposed to `CView`).

Next, add the following member variables and member functions:

```
// Attributes
protected:
    BOOL    m_bHasCaret;
    CFont   *m_pFont;


    .
    .
    .


// Operations
public:
    void MoveTTYCursor(BOOL bScroll = FALSE);
    void SetFont(LOGFONT *lf);
    void SetSizes();
```

Finally, the following message handler should be added after the ClassWizard-generated message map functions (make sure you add this after the `//}}AFX_MSG` comment line):

```
afx_msg LRESULT OnCommNotify(WPARAM wParam, LPARAM lParam);
```

`TTYview.h` can now be saved to disk.

The file `TTYview.cpp` contains the implementation of the view class. Open this file for editing. First, a message map entry must be added for the `OnCommNotify` function (make sure you enter this line after the `//}}AFX_MSG_MAP` comment line):

```
ON_MESSAGE(WM_COMMNOTIFY, OnCommNotify)
```

Next, change all occurrences of CView throughout this file to CScrollView because the view class is derived from that class.

The constructor CTTYView::CTTYView should contain lines that initialize member variables.

```
CTTYView::CTTYView()
{
    m_bHasCaret = FALSE;
    m_pFont = NULL;
}
```

The member variable m_pFont points to a CFont object that contains the font used for displaying the terminal screen. The member variable m_bHasCaret indicates whether there is a text cursor displayed in the view. The destructor code ensures that the font and the caret are properly destroyed.

```
CTTYView::~CTTYView()
{
    if (m_bHasCaret)
    {
        HideCaret();
        DestroyCaret();
        m_bHasCaret = FALSE;
    }
    if (m_pFont != NULL)
    {
        delete m_pFont;
        m_pFont = NULL;
    }
}
```

The CTTYView::OnDraw member function, shown in Listing 3.3, is responsible for redrawing the terminal screen. It also takes into account the current scrolling position. It only redraws the invalidated rectangle of the view.

Listing 3.3. CTTYView::OnDraw **member function.**

```
void CTTYView::OnDraw(CDC* pDC)
{
    RECT rect;
    CPoint scrollPos;
    int nRow, nCol, nEndRow, nEndCol, nCount, nHorzPos, nVertPos;
    CFont *pOldFont;
    CTTYDoc* pDoc = GetDocument();
    ASSERT_VALID(pDoc);

    rect = ((CPaintDC *)pDC)->m_ps.rcPaint;
    pOldFont = pDC->SelectObject(m_pFont);
    pDC->SetTextColor(RGB(0, 0, 0));
    pDC->SetBkColor(GetSysColor(COLOR_WINDOW));
    scrollPos = GetScrollPosition();
    rect.left += scrollPos.x;
    rect.top += scrollPos.y;
```

continues

Listing 3.3. continued

```
    rect.right += scrollPos.x;
    rect.bottom += scrollPos.y;
    nRow =
        min(MAXROW - 1, max(0, rect.top / pDoc->m_charSize.cy));
    nEndRow =
        min(MAXROW - 1, (rect.bottom - 1) / pDoc->m_charSize.cy);
    nCol =
        min(MAXCOL - 1, max(0, rect.left / pDoc->m_charSize.cx));
    nEndCol =
        min(MAXCOL - 1, (rect.right - 1) / pDoc->m_charSize.cx);
    nCount = nEndCol - nCol + 1;
    for (; nRow <= nEndRow; nRow++)
    {
        nVertPos = nRow * pDoc->m_charSize.cy;
        nHorzPos = nCol * pDoc->m_charSize.cx;
        rect.top = nVertPos;
        rect.bottom = nVertPos + pDoc->m_charSize.cy;
        rect.left = nHorzPos;
        rect.right = nHorzPos + pDoc->m_charSize.cx * nCount;
        pDC->SetBkMode(OPAQUE);
        pDC->ExtTextOut(nHorzPos, nVertPos,
          ETO_OPAQUE | ETO_CLIPPED, &rect,
          (LPSTR)(&(pDoc->m_pScreen[(nRow + pDoc->m_nTopRow) %
                    MAXROW][nCol])), nCount, NULL);
    }

    MoveTTYCursor();
    pDC->SelectObject(pOldFont);
}
```

The `CTTYView::OnInitialUpdate` function should include a call to the `CTTYView::SetSizes` helper function to ensure that the scrollbars are properly updated when the view is initialized.

```
void CTTYView::OnInitialUpdate()
{
    CScrollView::OnInitialUpdate();
    SetSizes();
}
```

`CTTYView::OnChar` calls `CTTYDoc::WriteCommByte` to ensure that anything the user types is sent to the communication port. This function also takes care of local echo.

```
void CTTYView::OnChar(UINT nChar, UINT nRepCnt, UINT nFlags)
{
    char cChar;
    CTTYDoc* pDoc = GetDocument();
    ASSERT_VALID(pDoc);

    cChar = (char)nChar;
    if (pDoc->m_bConnected)
```

```
    {
        pDoc->WriteCommByte(cChar);
        if (pDoc->m_bLocalEcho) pDoc->WriteTTYBlock(&cChar, 1);
        UpdateWindow();
    }
    else CScrollView::OnChar(nChar, nRepCnt, nFlags);
}
```

Because the application displays a text cursor (a caret), it must respond to WM_KILLFOCUS (Listing 3.4) and WM_SETFOCUS (Listing 3.5) messages to properly display and remove the caret.

Listing 3.4. `CTTYView::OnKillFocus` member function.

```
void CTTYView::OnKillFocus(CWnd* pNewWnd)
{
    CScrollView::OnKillFocus(pNewWnd);

    if (m_bHasCaret)
    {
        HideCaret();
        DestroyCaret();
        m_bHasCaret = FALSE;
    }
}
```

Listing 3.5. `CTTYView::OnSetFocus` member function.

```
void CTTYView::OnSetFocus(CWnd* pOldWnd)
{
    CTTYDoc* pDoc = GetDocument();
    ASSERT_VALID(pDoc);

    CScrollView::OnSetFocus(pOldWnd);

    if (pDoc->m_bConnected)
    {
        ::CreateCaret(m_hWnd, NULL,
                      pDoc->m_charSize.cx, pDoc->m_charSize.cy);
        ShowCaret();
        m_bHasCaret = TRUE;
        MoveTTYCursor();
    }
}
```

In response to WM_SIZE messages, the helper function CTTYView::SetSizes is called to ensure that the scrollbars are correctly updated.

```
void CTTYView::OnSize(UINT nType, int cx, int cy)
{
    CScrollView::OnSize(nType, cx, cy);
    SetSizes();
}
```

The last message handler function is for WM_COMMNOTIFY messages. These messages are posted by the application's secondary thread in response to incoming characters on the communication port. The handler in the following code fragment reads any waiting characters from the port, writes them to the terminal buffer using CTTYDoc::WriteTTYBlock, and finally notifies the secondary thread by setting the event CTTYDoc::m_hPostEvent. It also checks the application's message queue in order to ensure that the application remains responsive to the user while large blocks of data are received at high speed.

And yes, CTTYView::OnCommNotify also contains two goto instructions!

```
LRESULT CTTYView::OnCommNotify(WPARAM wParam, LPARAM lParam)
{
    int nLength;
    BYTE abIn[MAXBLOCK + 1];
    CTTYDoc* pDoc = GetDocument();
    ASSERT_VALID(pDoc);
    MSG msg;

    if (!(pDoc->m_bConnected)) goto CN_Done;
    if (CN_EVENT & LOWORD(lParam) != CN_EVENT) goto CN_Done;
    do
    {
        while (PeekMessage(&msg, NULL, 0, 0, PM_NOREMOVE))
            AfxGetApp()->PumpMessage();
        if (nLength = pDoc->ReadCommBlock((LPSTR)abIn, MAXBLOCK))
        {
            pDoc->WriteTTYBlock((LPSTR)abIn, nLength);
            UpdateWindow();
        }
    }
    while (nLength > 0);

CN_Done:
    SetEvent(pDoc->m_hPostEvent);
    return NULL;
}
```

Finally, there are some helper functions. CTTYView::MoveTTYCursor (Listing 3.6) moves the terminal cursor to its new position and optionally scrolls the view to make the cursor visible; CTTYView::SetFont (Listing 3.7) sets a new font and updates the terminal window as appropriate; and CTTYView::SetSizes (Listing 3.8) resets the scrollbars to reflect the window's current size and position.

Listing 3.6. CTTYView::MoveTTYCursor **member function.**

```
void CTTYView::MoveTTYCursor(BOOL bScroll /* = FALSE */)
{
    POINT scrollPos;
    POINT newPos;
    POINT toPos;
    BOOL needScroll;
```

```
    RECT clientRect;
    CTTYDoc* pDoc = GetDocument();
    ASSERT_VALID(pDoc);

    scrollPos = GetScrollPosition();
    newPos.x = pDoc->m_nColumn * pDoc->m_charSize.cx - scrollPos.x;
    newPos.y =
      ((pDoc->m_nRow + MAXROW - pDoc->m_nTopRow) % MAXROW) *
        pDoc->m_charSize.cy
          - scrollPos.y;
    if (m_bHasCaret) SetCaretPos(newPos);
    if (bScroll)
    {
        toPos.x = scrollPos.x;
        toPos.y = scrollPos.y;
        needScroll = FALSE;
        GetClientRect(&clientRect);
        if (newPos.x < 0)
        {
            toPos.x += newPos.x;
            needScroll = TRUE;
        }
        if (newPos.y < 0)
        {
            toPos.y += newPos.y;
            needScroll = TRUE;
        }
        if (newPos.x + pDoc->m_charSize.cx > clientRect.right)
        {
            toPos.x += newPos.x + pDoc->m_charSize.cx -
                        clientRect.right;
            needScroll = TRUE;
        }
        if (newPos.y + pDoc->m_charSize.cy > clientRect.bottom)
        {
            toPos.y += newPos.y + pDoc->m_charSize.cy -
                        clientRect.bottom;
            needScroll = TRUE;
        }
        if (pDoc->m_nScrolled > 0)
        {
            toPos.y += pDoc->m_nScrolled * pDoc->m_charSize.cy;
            if (m_nMapMode != MM_TEXT)
            {
                CWindowDC dc(NULL);
                dc.SetMapMode(m_nMapMode);
                dc.LPtoDP((LPPOINT)&toPos);
            }
            ScrollToDevicePosition(toPos);
            pDoc->m_nScrolled = 0;
        }
        else if (needScroll) ScrollToPosition(toPos);
    }
}
```

Listing 3.7. `CTTYView::SetFont` **member function.**

```
void CTTYView::SetFont(LOGFONT *lf)
{
    if (m_pFont)
    {
        delete m_pFont;
        m_pFont = NULL;
    }
    m_pFont = new CFont;
    m_pFont->CreateFontIndirect(lf);
    SetSizes();
    Invalidate();
    MoveTTYCursor(TRUE);
}
```

Listing 3.8. `CTTYView::SetSizes` **member function.**

```
void CTTYView::SetSizes()
{
    SIZE sizeTotal;
    SIZE sizePage;
    SIZE sizeLine;
    RECT clientRect;
    CTTYDoc* pDoc = GetDocument();
    ASSERT_VALID(pDoc);

    GetClientRect(&clientRect);
    sizeTotal.cx = pDoc->m_charSize.cx * MAXCOL;
    sizeTotal.cy = pDoc->m_charSize.cy *
        ((pDoc->m_nRow + MAXROW - pDoc->m_nTopRow) % MAXROW + 1);
    sizePage.cx = clientRect.right -
        clientRect.right % pDoc->m_charSize.cx;
    sizePage.cy = clientRect.bottom -
        clientRect.bottom % pDoc->m_charSize.cy;
    sizeLine.cx = pDoc->m_charSize.cx;
    sizeLine.cy = pDoc->m_charSize.cy;
    SetScrollSizes(MM_TEXT, sizeTotal, sizePage, sizeLine);
}
```

The *CTTYDoc* class

The document class contains command and command update message handlers for the new menu items Connect and Disconnect. It also contains a command handler (no update handler necessary) for the TTY Settings menu item. Add these five functions using ClassWizard. When that is done, open the file TTYdoc.h for editing.

At the top of the file, add the following definitions, which will be used later when handling the terminal buffer:

```
#define MAXROW 100
#define MAXCOL 80
#define TABSTOP 8

#define ASCII_BEL  0x07
#define ASCII_BS   0x08
#define ASCII_TAB  0x09
#define ASCII_LF   0x0A
#define ASCII_CR   0x0D
#define ASCII_XON  0x11
#define ASCII_XOFF 0x13

UINT CommWatchProc(LPVOID lpParam);
```

Next, a set of member variables should be added. These variables reflect communication port settings, the state of the application, the contents of the terminal buffer, and objects relating to the secondary thread and synchronization. The use of these variables is discussed later in this section.

Notice that some variables are marked `volatile`. Because these variables are accessed from the secondary thread, it is essential not to let the compiler's optimization features take over and prevent these variables from being written to memory. Otherwise, execution of the secondary thread will fail unpredictably.

Without declaring these variables `volatile`, it is possible that the optimizing compiler reuses their values that are already stored in the processor's registers, without bothering to reload them first from memory. Thus, if another thread changes their values, it is possible that the first thread will never become aware of that change. Similarly, it is possible that the optimizing compiler will prevent the value from being updated in memory in a timely manner. Using the `volatile` keyword helps avoid this problem.

```
//Attributes
public:
    volatile BOOL m_bConnected;

    BOOL m_bAutoWrap;
    long m_nBaud;
    int m_nDataBits;
    BOOL m_bDTRDSR;
    BOOL m_bLocalEcho;
    BOOL m_bNewLine;
    int m_nParity;
    Cstring m_sPort;
    BOOL m_bRTSCTS;
    int m_nStopBits;
    BOOL m_bXONXOFF;
    LOGFONT m_lfFont;
    CSize m_charSize;
    volatile HANDLE m_idComDev;
    volatile CWnd *m_pTermWnd;
    volatile HANDLE m_hPostEvent;
    CWinThread *m_pThread;
    OVERLAPPED m_osWrite, m_osRead;
    BYTE m_pScreen[MAXROW][MAXCOL];
```

```
int m_nRow;
int m_nColumn;
int m_nTopRow;
int m_nScrolled;
```

Declaration of several helper functions must also be added, as follows:

```
//Operations
public:
    BOOL WriteCommByte(char cChar);
    BOOL WriteTTYBlock(LPSTR lpBlock, int nLength);
    int ReadCommBlock(LPSTR lpBlock, int nMaxLength);
    void SetFontSize();
    BOOL SetupConnection();
    .
    .
    .
//Implementation
    .
    .
    .
protected:
    BOOL OpenConnection();
    void CloseConnection();
```

After these additions, the file TTYdoc.h can be saved. Next, open the file TTYdoc.cpp for editing.

The first things to be added are references to header files. Add the following lines at the top of the file following the #include directives already present:

```
#include "TTYview.h"
#include "ttyset.h"
```

The CTTYDoc constructor function in the following code fragment contains initializations for all member variables.

```
CTTYDoc::CTTYDoc()
{
    m_bConnected = FALSE;

    m_bAutoWrap = TRUE;
    m_nBaud = 2400;
    m_nDataBits = 8;
    m_bDTRDSR = FALSE;
    m_bLocalEcho = FALSE;
    m_bNewLine = FALSE;
    m_nParity = 0;
    m_sPort = "COM1";
    m_bRTSCTS = TRUE;
    m_nStopBits = 0;
    m_bXONXOFF = FALSE;
    memset(&m_lfFont, 0, sizeof(m_lfFont));
    m_lfFont.lfHeight = -9;
    m_lfFont.lfWeight = FW_DONTCARE;
```

```
    m_lfFont.lfPitchAndFamily = FIXED_PITCH | FF_DONTCARE;
    strcpy(m_lfFont.lfFaceName, "FixedSys");

    memset(&m_osRead, 0, sizeof(OVERLAPPED));
    memset(&m_osWrite, 0, sizeof(OVERLAPPED));
    m_hPostEvent = NULL;
    m_pThread = NULL;
    m_pTermWnd = NULL;

    memset(m_pScreen, ' ', MAXROW * MAXCOL);
    m_nRow = 0;
    m_nColumn = 0;
    m_nTopRow = 0;
    m_charSize.cx = 8;
    m_charSize.cy = 15;
    m_nScrolled = 0;
}
```

The destructor of CTTYDoc ensures that the communication port is properly closed and closes all event handles.

```
CTTYDoc::~CTTYDoc()
{
    if (m_bConnected) CloseConnection();
    if (m_osRead.hEvent)
    {
        CloseHandle(m_osRead.hEvent);
        m_osRead.hEvent = NULL;
    }
    if (m_osWrite.hEvent)
    {
        CloseHandle(m_osWrite.hEvent);
        m_osWrite.hEvent = NULL;
    }
    if (m_hPostEvent)
    {
        CloseHandle(m_hPostEvent);
        m_hPostEvent = NULL;
    }
}
```

Those event handles are obtained when the events are created in CTTYDoc::OnNewDocument. The following three CreateEvent calls should be added to that function:

```
if ((m_osRead.hEvent = CreateEvent(NULL, TRUE, FALSE, NULL))
        == NULL) return FALSE;
if ((m_osWrite.hEvent = CreateEvent(NULL, TRUE, FALSE, NULL))
        == NULL) return FALSE;
if ((m_hPostEvent = CreateEvent(NULL, TRUE, TRUE, NULL))
        == NULL) return FALSE;
```

Next, you should add the functions handling the TTY Settings (Listing 3.9), Connect (Listing 3.10), and Disconnect (Listing 3.12) menu commands, and command update handlers for the Connect (Listing 3.11) and Disconnect (Listing 3.13) menu commands.

Listing 3.9. `CTTYDoc::OnEditTtysettings` function.

```
void CTTYDoc::OnEditTtysettings()
{
    char buf[34];
    POSITION firstViewPos;
    CTTYView *pView;
    CTTYSettingsDlg TTYSettingsDlg;

    TTYSettingsDlg.m_bAutoWrap = m_bAutoWrap;
    TTYSettingsDlg.m_sBaud = itoa(m_nBaud, buf, 10);
    TTYSettingsDlg.m_sDataBits = itoa(m_nDataBits, buf, 10);
    TTYSettingsDlg.m_bDTRDSR = m_bDTRDSR;
    TTYSettingsDlg.m_bLocalEcho = m_bLocalEcho;
    TTYSettingsDlg.m_bNewLine = m_bNewLine;
    TTYSettingsDlg.m_nParity = m_nParity;
    TTYSettingsDlg.m_sPort = m_sPort;
    TTYSettingsDlg.m_bRTSCTS = m_bRTSCTS;
    TTYSettingsDlg.m_nStopBits = m_nStopBits;
    TTYSettingsDlg.m_bXONXOFF = m_bXONXOFF;
    TTYSettingsDlg.m_lfFont = m_lfFont;
    TTYSettingsDlg.m_bConnected = m_bConnected;

    if (TTYSettingsDlg.DoModal() == IDOK)
    {
        m_bAutoWrap = TTYSettingsDlg.m_bAutoWrap;
        m_nBaud = atoi(TTYSettingsDlg.m_sBaud);
        m_nDataBits = atoi(TTYSettingsDlg.m_sDataBits);
        m_bDTRDSR = TTYSettingsDlg.m_bDTRDSR;
        m_bLocalEcho = TTYSettingsDlg.m_bLocalEcho;
        m_bNewLine = TTYSettingsDlg.m_bNewLine;
        m_nParity = TTYSettingsDlg.m_nParity;
        if (!m_bConnected) m_sPort = TTYSettingsDlg.m_sPort;
        m_bRTSCTS = TTYSettingsDlg.m_bRTSCTS;
        m_nStopBits = TTYSettingsDlg.m_nStopBits;
        m_bXONXOFF = TTYSettingsDlg.m_bXONXOFF;
        m_lfFont = TTYSettingsDlg.m_lfFont;
        SetFontSize();
        firstViewPos = GetFirstViewPosition();
        pView = (CTTYView *)GetNextView(firstViewPos);
        pView->SetFont(&m_lfFont);
        if (m_bConnected)
        {
            if (!SetupConnection())
            {
                AfxMessageBox(IDS_BADSETUP);
            }
        }
    }
}
```

Listing 3.10. `CTTYDoc::OnFileConnect` function.

```
void CTTYDoc::OnFileConnect()
{
    if (!OpenConnection())
        AfxMessageBox(IDS_CONNECTION_FAILED, MB_OK |
                                             MB_ICONEXCLAMATION);
    else m_bConnected = TRUE;
}
```

Listing 3.11. `CTTYDoc::OnUpdateFileConnect` function.

```
void CTTYDoc::OnUpdateFileConnect(CCmdUI* pCmdUI)
{
    pCmdUI->Enable(!m_bConnected);
}
```

Listing 3.12. `CTTYDoc::OnFileDisconnect` function.

```
void CTTYDoc::OnFileDisconnect()
{
    POSITION firstViewPos;
    CTTYView *pView;

    firstViewPos = GetFirstViewPosition();
    pView = (CTTYView *)GetNextView(firstViewPos);
    pView->SendMessage(WM_KILLFOCUS);
    CloseConnection();
    m_bConnected = FALSE;
}
```

Listing 3.13. `CTTYDoc::OnUpdateFileDisconnect` function.

```
void CTTYDoc::OnUpdateFileDisconnect(CCmdUI* pCmdUI)
{
    pCmdUI->Enable(m_bConnected);
}
```

Finally, several helper functions need to be added. `CTTYDoc::OpenConnection` in Listing 3.14 opens the communication port. It also sets up port parameters and starts the secondary thread that monitors the port for incoming data. This function is called when the user selects the Connect command from the File menu.

Listing 3.14. CTTYDoc::OpenConnection function.

```
BOOL CTTYDoc::OpenConnection()
{
    POSITION firstViewPos;
    CTTYView *pView;
    HCURSOR hOldCursor;
    BOOL fRetVal;
    COMMTIMEOUTS CommTimeOuts;

    if (m_bConnected) return FALSE;
    SetFontSize();
    firstViewPos = GetFirstViewPosition();
    pView = (CTTYView *)GetNextView(firstViewPos);
    pView->SetFont(&m_lfFont);

    hOldCursor = ::SetCursor(::LoadCursor(NULL, IDC_WAIT));

    if ((m_idComDev = CreateFile(m_sPort,
            GENERIC_READ | GENERIC_WRITE, 0, NULL,
            OPEN_EXISTING,
            FILE_ATTRIBUTE_NORMAL | FILE_FLAG_OVERLAPPED,
            NULL)) == (HANDLE)-1)
        return FALSE;
    SetCommMask(m_idComDev, EV_RXCHAR);
    SetupComm(m_idComDev, 4096, 4096);
    CommTimeOuts.ReadIntervalTimeout = 0xFFFFFFFF;
    CommTimeOuts.ReadTotalTimeoutMultiplier = 0;
    CommTimeOuts.ReadTotalTimeoutConstant = 0;
    CommTimeOuts.WriteTotalTimeoutMultiplier = 0;
    CommTimeOuts.WriteTotalTimeoutConstant = 5000;
    SetCommTimeouts(m_idComDev, &CommTimeOuts);
    fRetVal = SetupConnection();

    if (fRetVal)
    {
        m_bConnected = TRUE;

        m_pTermWnd = pView;
        if ((m_pThread = AfxBeginThread(CommWatchProc, this))
            == NULL)
        {
            m_bConnected = FALSE;
            CloseHandle(m_idComDev);
            fRetVal = FALSE;
        }
        else
        {
            m_pThread->SetThreadPriority(
                    THREAD_PRIORITY_BELOW_NORMAL);
            m_pThread->ResumeThread();
            EscapeCommFunction(m_idComDev, SETDTR);
        }
    }
    else
    {
        m_bConnected = FALSE;
        CloseHandle(m_idComDev);
    }
```

```
    ::SetCursor(hOldCursor);
    if (fRetVal) pView->SendMessage(WM_SETFOCUS);
    return fRetVal;
}
```

`CTTYDoc::CloseConnection` in the following code segment closes an established connection, shuts down the secondary thread, and purges the communication buffers. This function is called in response to the user selecting the Disconnect command from the File menu.

```
void CTTYDoc::CloseConnection()
{
    if (!m_bConnected) return;
    m_bConnected = FALSE;
    SetCommMask(m_idComDev, 0);
    SetEvent(m_hPostEvent);
    WaitForSingleObject(m_pThread->m_hThread, INFINITE);
    m_pThread = NULL;

    EscapeCommFunction(m_idComDev, CLRDTR);

    PurgeComm(m_idComDev, PURGE_TXABORT | PURGE_RXABORT |
                          PURGE_TXCLEAR | PURGE_RXCLEAR);
    CloseHandle(m_idComDev);
}
```

`CTTYDoc::SetFontSize` is called when the user selects a new font.

```
void CTTYDoc::SetFontSize()
{
    CDC *pDC;
    TEXTMETRIC tm;
    CFont *pOldFont;
    CFont font;

    font.CreateFontIndirect(&m_lfFont);
    pDC = AfxGetMainWnd()->GetDC();
    pOldFont = pDC->SelectObject(&font);
    pDC->GetTextMetrics(&tm);
    m_charSize.cx = tm.tmAveCharWidth;
    m_charSize.cy = tm.tmHeight + tm.tmExternalLeading;
    if (pOldFont) pDC->SelectObject(pOldFont);
}
```

`CTTYDoc::WriteCommByte` is called to write a single byte to the communication port.

```
BOOL CTTYDoc::WriteCommByte(char cChar)
{
    BOOL fWriteStat;
    DWORD dwBytesWritten;

    if (!m_bConnected) return FALSE;
    fWriteStat = WriteFile(m_idComDev, &cChar, 1,
                           &dwBytesWritten, &m_osWrite);
    if (!fWriteStat && (GetLastError() == ERROR_IO_PENDING))
    {
```

```
        if (WaitForSingleObject(m_osWrite.hEvent, 1000))
            dwBytesWritten = 0;
        else
        {
            GetOverlappedResult(m_idComDev, &m_osWrite,
                                &dwBytesWritten, FALSE);
            m_osWrite.Offset += dwBytesWritten;
        }
    }
    return TRUE;
}
```

`CTTYDoc::ReadCommBlock` reads a block of characters from the communication port.

```
int CTTYDoc::ReadCommBlock(LPSTR lpBlock, int nMaxLength)
{
    BOOL fReadStat;
    COMSTAT ComStat;
    DWORD dwErrorFlags, dwLength;

    if (!m_bConnected) return 0;
    ClearCommError(m_idComDev, &dwErrorFlags, &ComStat);
    dwLength = min((DWORD)nMaxLength, ComStat.cbInQue);
    if (dwLength > 0)
    {
        fReadStat = ReadFile(m_idComDev, lpBlock, dwLength,
                             &dwLength, &m_osRead);
        if (!fReadStat)
        {
            if (GetLastError() == ERROR_IO_PENDING)
            {
                if (WaitForSingleObject(m_osRead.hEvent, 1000))
                    dwLength = 0;
                else
                {
                    GetOverlappedResult(m_idComDev, &m_osRead,
                                        &dwLength, FALSE);
                    m_osRead.Offset += dwLength;
                }
            }
            else dwLength = 0;
        }
    }
    return dwLength;
}
```

`CTTYDoc::WriteTTYBlock` in Listing 3.15 writes a block of characters to the terminal window. It also provides special handling for certain control characters, such as carriage returns or line feeds.

Listing 3.15. `CTTYDoc::WriteTTYBlock` function.

```
BOOL CTTYDoc::WriteTTYBlock(LPSTR lpBlock, int nLength)
{
    int i;
    RECT rect;
    POSITION firstViewPos;
    CTTYView *pView;
```

```
firstViewPos = GetFirstViewPosition();
pView = (CTTYView *)GetNextView(firstViewPos);

if (!m_bConnected) return FALSE;
for (i = 0; i < nLength; i++)
{
    switch (lpBlock[i])
    {
        case ASCII_BEL:
            MessageBeep(0);
            break;
        case ASCII_BS:
            if (m_nColumn > 0)
            {
                m_nColumn—;
            }
            break;
        case ASCII_TAB:
            if ((m_nColumn/TABSTOP) < ((MAXCOL-1)/ TABSTOP))
            {
                m_nColumn += TABSTOP - m_nColumn % TABSTOP;
                pView->MoveTTYCursor(TRUE);
            }
            break;
        case ASCII_CR:
            m_nColumn = 0;
            if (!m_bNewLine) break;
        case ASCII_LF:
            if (++m_nRow >= MAXROW) m_nRow = 0;
            if (m_nRow == m_nTopRow)
            {
                memset(m_pScreen[m_nTopRow], ' ', MAXCOL);
                m_nTopRow++;
                m_nScrolled++;
                if (m_nTopRow >= MAXROW) m_nTopRow = 0;
            }
            pView->SetSizes();
            break;
        default:
            m_pScreen[m_nRow][m_nColumn] = lpBlock[i];
            rect.left = m_nColumn * m_charSize.cx -
                        pView->GetScrollPosition().x;
            rect.top = ((m_nRow + MAXROW - m_nTopRow)
                        % MAXROW) * m_charSize.cy -
                        pView->GetScrollPosition().y;
            rect.right = rect.left + m_charSize.cx;
            rect.bottom = rect.top + m_charSize.cy;
            pView->InvalidateRect(&rect, FALSE);
            if (++m_nColumn >= MAXCOL)
            {
                if (m_bAutoWrap)
                {
                    if (m_bNewLine) WriteTTYBlock("\r", 1);
                    else WriteTTYBlock("\r\n", 2);
                }
                else m_nColumn—;
            }
    }
```

continues

Listing 3.15. continued

```
                break;
        }
    }
    pView->MoveTTYCursor(TRUE);
    return TRUE;
}
```

CTTYDoc::SetupConnection in Listing 3.16 is called when a connection is established, or when the user changes the connection parameters of an open connection using the TTY Settings dialog box.

Listing 3.16. CTTYDoc::SetupConnection function.

```
BOOL CTTYDoc::SetupConnection()
{
    BOOL fRetVal;
    DCB dcb;

    dcb.DCBlength = sizeof(DCB);
    GetCommState(m_idComDev, &dcb);
    dcb.BaudRate = m_nBaud;
    dcb.ByteSize = m_nDataBits;
    switch (m_nParity)
    {
        case 0: dcb.Parity = NOPARITY; break;
        case 1: dcb.Parity = EVENPARITY; break;
        case 2: dcb.Parity = ODDPARITY; break;
        case 3: dcb.Parity = MARKPARITY; break;
        case 4: dcb.Parity = SPACEPARITY; break;
        default: ASSERT(FALSE);
    }
    switch (m_nStopBits)
    {
        case 0: dcb.StopBits = ONESTOPBIT; break;
        case 1: dcb.StopBits = ONE5STOPBITS; break;
        case 2: dcb.StopBits = TWOSTOPBITS; break;
        default: ASSERT(FALSE);
    }
    dcb.fOutxDsrFlow = m_bDTRDSR;
    dcb.fOutxCtsFlow = m_bRTSCTS;
    dcb.fDtrControl = m_bDTRDSR ?
                DTR_CONTROL_HANDSHAKE : DTR_CONTROL_ENABLE;
    dcb.fRtsControl = m_bRTSCTS ?
                RTS_CONTROL_HANDSHAKE : RTS_CONTROL_ENABLE;
    dcb.fInX = dcb.fOutX = m_bXONXOFF;
    dcb.XonChar = ASCII_XON;
    dcb.XoffChar = ASCII_XOFF;
    dcb.XonLim = 100;
    dcb.XoffLim = 100;
    dcb.fBinary = TRUE;
    dcb.fParity = TRUE;
    fRetVal = SetCommState(m_idComDev, &dcb);
    return fRetVal;
}
```

The last function in this file is `CommWatchProc`, the secondary worker thread responsible for monitoring the communication port. This function, shown in Listing 3.17, waits for communication port events in a loop, which is terminated if the connection is shut down, as indicated by the variable `CTTYDoc::m_bConnected`. If characters are received, the worker thread notifies the primary thread by sending a `WM_COMMNOTIFY` message. It then waits for the primary thread to process this message before continuing with the monitoring loop.

Listing 3.17. `CTTYDoc::CommWatchProc` **function.**

```
UINT CommWatchProc(LPVOID lpParam)
{
    CTTYDoc *pDoc = (CTTYDoc *)lpParam;
    OVERLAPPED os;
    DWORD dwEventMask, dwTransfer;

    memset(&os, 0, sizeof(OVERLAPPED));
    os.hEvent = CreateEvent(NULL, TRUE, FALSE, NULL);
    if (os.hEvent == NULL)
    {
        AfxMessageBox(IDS_NOTHREAD, MB_OK | MB_ICONEXCLAMATION);
        return FALSE;
    }
    if (!SetCommMask(pDoc->m_idComDev, EV_RXCHAR)) return FALSE;
    while (pDoc->m_bConnected)
    {
        dwEventMask = 0;
        if (!WaitCommEvent(pDoc->m_idComDev, &dwEventMask, &os))
        {
            if (ERROR_IO_PENDING == GetLastError())
            {
                GetOverlappedResult(pDoc->m_idComDev, &os,
                                    &dwTransfer, TRUE);
                os.Offset += dwTransfer;
            }
        }
        if ((dwEventMask & EV_RXCHAR) == EV_RXCHAR)
        {
            ResetEvent(pDoc->m_hPostEvent);
            ((CWnd *)(pDoc->m_pTermWnd))->PostMessage(
                WM_COMMNOTIFY, (WPARAM)pDoc->m_idComDev,
                MAKELONG(CN_EVENT, 0));
            WaitForSingleObject(pDoc->m_hPostEvent, 0xFFFFFFFF);
        }
    }
    CloseHandle(os.hEvent);
    return TRUE;
}
```

Settings Dialog Box Implementation

To implement the settings dialog box, member variables that correspond with the dialog box's controls should first be added. The controls, variables, and their types are as follows:

Control	Variable Name	Type
IDC_AUTOWRAP	m_bAutoWrap	BOOL
IDC_BAUDCB	m_sBaud	CString
IDC_DATABITSCB	m_sDataBits	CString
IDC_DTRDSR	m_bDTRDSR	BOOL
IDC_LOCALECHO	m_bLocalEcho	BOOL
IDC_NEWLINE	m_bNewLine	BOOL
IDC_PARITYCB	m_nParity	int
IDC_PORTCB	m_sPort	CString
IDC_RTSCTS	m_bRTSCTS	BOOL
IDC_STOPBITSCB	m_nStopBits	int
IDC_XONXOFF	m_bXONXOFF	BOOL

These member variables can be added using ClassWizard. While ClassWizard is running, you can also add message handler functions for the message WM_INITDIALOG (OnInitDialog) and for BN_CLICKED messages for the control IDC_FONT (the Font button).

Next, edit the file ttyset.h. In addition to the member variables created by ClassWizard, two more variables should be added to the CTTYSettingsDlg class. Add these variables following the //}}AFX_DATA comment line:

```
LOGFONT m_lfFont;
BOOL m_bConnected;
```

Next, edit ttyset.cpp. First, additional initialization code should be added to the MFC-supplied member variable initializations in the constructor.

```
memset(&m_lfFont, 0, sizeof(m_lfFont));
m_lfFont.lfHeight = -9;
m_lfFont.lfWeight = FW_DONTCARE;
m_lfFont.lfPitchAndFamily = FIXED_PITCH | FF_DONTCARE;
strcpy(m_lfFont.lfFaceName, "FixedSys");
m_bConnected = FALSE;
```

Next, the CTTYSettingsDlg::OnFont (Listing 3.18) and CTTYSettingsDlg::OnInitDialog (Listing 3.19) functions should be supplied.

Listing 3.18. CTTYSettingsDlg::OnFont function.

```
void CTTYSettingsDlg::OnFont()
{
    LOGFONT newlf;

    newlf = m_lfFont;
    CFontDialog fontDialog(&newlf, CF_SCREENFONTS |
        CF_INITTOLOGFONTSTRUCT | CF_FIXEDPITCHONLY);
    if (fontDialog.DoModal() == IDOK)
```

```
    {
        m_lfFont = newlf;
    }
}
```

Listing 3.19. `CTTYSettingsDlg::OnInitDialog` **function.**

```
BOOL CTTYSettingsDlg::OnInitDialog()
{
    CDialog::OnInitDialog();

    ((CComboBox *)GetDlgItem(IDC_PORTCB))->EnableWindow(!m_bConnected);
    return TRUE;
}
```

With this step, construction of the TTY application is complete. Save all open files and recompile the application.

Summary

Windows 95 implements preemptive multitasking of 32-bit applications and offers a rich set of programming features, comparable to that found in Windows NT, in support of multiple processes, threads, and synchronization.

On the other hand, the Windows 95 programmer should still adhere to old programming conventions and yield explicitly to the operating system whenever possible. This ensures not only easy portability to older versions of Windows, but also ensures that the application remains responsive.

Preemptive multitasking introduces the problem of reentrancy; it is possible that while execution of a function is suspended due to task switching, the same function gets called again from another executing thread. Not only did this issue affect the design of Windows 95, application programmers should also be aware of it when writing multithreaded code. In particular, avoid using global and static variables if possible.

Windows 95 offers a series of synchronization mechanisms that aid in writing cooperating threads and processes. Events, semaphores, mutexes, and other objects can be used to suspend execution of threads based on externally controlled conditions.

Toward the end of this chapter, a simple, but functional, communication program was presented, demonstrating many of the techniques outlined here. The TTY application uses multithreading techniques to process communication port events. I hope this example proves useful in demonstrating how easy it is to employ secondary threads and provide a simple and elegant solution to many real-world problems.

File Management and Long Filenames

4

by Lawrence Harris

I have recently spent time teaching new PC owners how to use Windows. One problem seems to come up time and time again: whenever saving a file, the new users want to give the file a descriptive name, usually longer than the 8.3 characters allowed. New PC owners typically want to know why they cannot use more descriptive names—my only answer is to say, "Because." In Windows 95, long filenames are possible, but only if an application supports them. This chapter shows you how to implement long filenames into existing and new applications.

FAT and VFAT

In the days of DOS 1.0, files were written to disk using a file allocation table (FAT), which contained information about directories and files. All file access went through FAT (unless the application used its own disk I/O, especially popular in copy-protected software). When Windows for Workgroups 3.11 was made available, a new type of file system, called virtual file allocation table (VFAT), was introduced. VFAT is a 32-bit disk access system built into Windows for Workgroups that does not rely on DOS to perform disk access: VFAT is optimized for use with Windows. Other than these features, VFAT in Windows for Workgroups 3.11 does not make a significant or perceivable change for users or application programmers.

VFAT in Windows 95, however, does make significant and perceivable changes for users and application programmers. In Windows 95, users are now able to use long filenames. The characters allowed in filenames have also changed. From a programmer's standpoint, applications can no longer allocate buffers that expect 8.3-format filenames. But these changes do not necessarily come free. In fact, Windows 95 does not always return or support long filenames. For example, Windows 95 does not support or allow long filenames if configured for Windows 3.1 compatibility mode (during setup or from the System icon in the Control Panel). In fact, if you change a system that has Windows 95 installed to support long filenames and you go to the System Folder in the Control Panel to configure the system for Windows 3.1 compatibility, any long filenames previously stored by Windows 95 are discarded. Although the long filename is discarded, Windows 95 still maintains the *alias name*, a synthesized 8.3 filename based on the long filename. Windows 95 always creates an alias name in the 8.3 format so that applications that only support the 8.3 format can still operate.

When synthesizing a long filename, Windows 95 follows a few rules in order to create an alias name (8.3 filename). Here is a list of the rules:

1. If the long filename fits in the 8.3 format, Windows 95 uses the long filename as the alias name, converting any lowercase characters to uppercase characters.

2. If the long filename does not have an extension, the first eight characters of the long filename are used.

3. If the long filename has an extension of three characters or less, the long filename is truncated to eight characters and the extension from the long filename is used in the alias name.

4. If the long filename has an extension greater than three characters, the long filename is truncated to eight characters (the first eight characters) and the extension from the long filename is used in the alias name.

5. If the alias name already exists, only the first six characters of the long filename are used and ~1 is appended to the filename. If the long filename has an extension, then the extension is also used (or truncated to three characters and used).

6. If the generated name already exists, ~1 is changed to ~2, an so on, until a unique name is generated. If the unique name cannot be generated using a single digit, additional characters are dropped from the long filename until a unique name with a number can be generated.

All the rules mentioned in the previous list for long filenames also apply to long directory names. In addition, because VFAT is part of Windows 95 and not part of DOS, applications that run in DOS need to check to see if they are running under Windows 95 as a DOS box or in Windows 95 real mode, which does not support VFAT. Additionally, applications that update CONFIG.SYS must not use long filenames in entries in CONFIG.SYS because VFAT is not available until Windows 95 is running (CONFIG.SYS runs in DOS real mode before Windows 95 runs).

Windows 3.1 Compatibility Mode

As previously mentioned, if Windows 95 is running in Windows 3.1 compatibility mode, long filenames are not supported. To determine whether it is running in Windows 95 mode or in Windows 3.1 compatibility mode, an application can check the registration database. In the registration database is the entry HKEY_LOCAL_MACHINE\SYSTEM\CurrentControlSet\Control\FileSystem. If the value for this entry is Win31FileSystem=1, the application is running in Windows 3.1 compatibility mode and long filenames are not supported. If the value is Win31FileSystem=0, the application is using the native Windows 95 VFAT system and supports long filenames.

Long Filenames for 16-Bit Applications

If you currently have a 16-bit application, you might not need to recompile it to support long filenames. If your 16-bit application is marked as a Windows 4.0 application, Windows 95 automatically allows the 16-bit application to use long filenames. A 16-bit application, called Mark95, has been included with this book. Mark95 marks your application as a Windows 4.0 application, enabling your application to use long filenames. In addition, applications marked as Windows 4.0 will have their look and feel changed to a Windows 95 look and feel.

If your application expects the 8.3 format for the filename, performs its own validation for filenames, or is written in MFC or OWL, you need to make changes in your application. First of all, if your application expects the 8.3 format for the filename, you need to change the application to support 256 characters (including the trailing null) for the filename. Second, if your application performs custom name validation, you need to change the validation routine to expect not only 256 characters for the filename but also additional types of characters. Long filenames support all letters and numbers, as well as spaces and characters above 128 in the ASCII table. If your application is written in MFC or OWL, you need to recompile your application using the 32-bit version of MFC or OWL. The problem with the 16-bit version of MFC and OWL is that the common dialog boxes (File Open and File Save) only support the 8.3 format.

Long Filenames for 32-Bit Applications

Long filenames are automatically supported in 32-bit applications running under Windows 95. If your application can run under Windows NT or Win32s, you might need to perform additional work in your application. Windows NT supports long filenames in directories that are formatted for NTFS (NT file system) or HPFS (high-performance OS/2-compatible file system).

New File APIs

A few new APIs have been added to support long filenames and their aliases. `GetShortPathName` is used to change and obtain the alias name from long filename. Do not assume that `GetShortPathName` will succeed: if the volume on which the file resides does not support aliases, `GetShortPathName` returns an error because there is no alias. Table 4.1 shows the parameters for `GetShortPathName`.

Table 4.1. The `GetShortPathName` parameters.

Type	Name	Description
LPCTSTR	lpszLongPathname	The long pathname
LPTSTR	lpszShortPathname	The returned alias short pathname
DWORD	cchBuffer	The size of the `lpszShortPathname` buffer

When calling `GetShortPathName`, your application places the long pathname into `lpszLongPathname` and assigns a pointer to a buffer to `lpszShortPathname`. `cchBuffer` is assigned the size of the `lpszShortPathname` buffer. When `GetShortPathName` returns, `lpszShortPathname` contains the alias name. `GetShortPathName` is not available to 16-bit applications.

GetVolumeInformation is a useful API for determining if a particular volume supports long filenames. Table 4.2 shows the parameters for GetVolumeInformation.

Table 4.2. The GetVolumeInformation parameters.

Type	Name	Description
LPCTSTR	lpRootPathName	The root directory used to obtain the volume information
LPTSTR	lpVolumeNameBuffer	The name of the volume
DWORD	nVolumeNameSize	The length of lpVolumeNameBuffer
LPDWORD	lpVolumeSerialNumber	The serial number of the volume (may be NULL if you don't need the serial number)
LPDWORD	lpMaximumComponentLength	The maximum filename length supported by the volume
LPDWORD	lpFileSystemFlags	The file system flags (see Table 4.3)
LPTSTR	lpFileSystemNameBuffer	The name of the file system
DWORD	nFileSystemNameSize	The length of the buffer for the file system name

Table 4.3. File system flags.

Flag	Meaning
FS_CASE_IS_PRESERVED	The file system preserves the case of the filenames.
FS_CASE_SENSITIVE	The file system supports case-sensitive filenames.
FS_UNICODE_STORED_ON_DISK	The file system supports Unicode filenames.
FS_PERSISTENT_ACLS	The file system supports ACLs.
FS_FILE_COMPRESSION	The file system supports file-based compression (such as available in NT 3.51).
FS_VOL_IS_COMPRESSED	The volume is a compressed volume.

Sample Applications

Two sample applications are included with this book to demonstrate long filename support. Mark95 is a simple windows application that reads a 16-bit Windows executable and marks it as a Windows 95 executable. Once a 16-bit Windows executable is marked for Windows 95,

98

it automatically is able to use long filenames. In addition, any resources used by a marked 16-bit application are automatically freed—if the application does not free the resources itself.

The second sample application is VolInfo, which looks at all drives that are listed as part of My Computer and uses `GetVolumeInformation` to display information about each volume. VolInfo is especially useful if you want to determine which volumes on your computer support long filenames.

Fundamentals of the Windows 95 Registry

by
Daryl Pietrocarlo
and
Patrick L. Lujan

5

IN THIS CHAPTER

In previous versions of Windows, when an application, device driver, or hardware adapter found it necessary to access or write information pertaining to itself, a configuration file of some sort was used. A hardware adapter would use a configuration file such as an .INI, CONFIG.SYS, or AUTOEXEC.BAT file. This method, although adequate, was prolific and yielded many configuration files in many different locations across the platform.

The purpose of the Registry is to store this configuration information in one centralized repository. The Registry is a database of information that Windows 95 programs, hardware, and administrators use to identify themselves to the system, as well as to retrieve information on startup or during the runtime execution of the program. Where a Windows 3.1 program would use an .INI file to obtain a user's name, for example, it should now obtain that information from the Registry.

The Registry goes above and beyond the capabilities of the .INI file by allowing the following:

- Binary data (rather than simple text entries, as in Windows 3.x .INI files).
- Preferences for each individual user. (This only applies to a multiple user computer.)
- Subkeys (analogous to nested headings in an .INI file, which are not supported under Windows 3.x).

Here are some of the advantages introduced by the Registry:

- Allows tracking and configuration of the hardware, certain operating system parameters, applications, and device drivers.
- Enables configuration of the system by using the built-in Windows 95 tools such as the Control Panel, thereby virtually eliminating user entry errors.
- Provides a level of backup that enables the user or administrator to restore the Registry to the state it was in before the last series of changes. Each time Windows 95 is started, a backup copy of the Registry is saved.
- Allows different users to maintain their own personal preferences, such as desktop settings (cursors, color, icon arrangement) and application settings.
- Enables an administrator or user to examine system settings and configuration over a network, thus expediting the job of MIS and system support technicians by allowing remote system administration.

It should be noted that the AUTOEXEC.BAT and CONFIG.SYS files still exist in order to provide for backward compatibility. However, applications written for Windows 95 are discouraged from using these files and should now use the Registry.

Upgrading to Windows 95 from Windows 3.x

If you have installed Windows 95 as an upgrade to Windows 3.x, the installation program copies some of the .INI information to the Registry. The setup program is cognizant that some of the programs in Windows 95 are capable of using the Registry and copies those entries from the old WIN.INI, SYSTEM.INI, and other system files to the Registry. It doesn't copy entries that it does not know to be compatible with the Registry. For example, a 16-bit application that has its own .INI file will not be copied to the Registry. For backward compatibility, Windows 95 maintains the .INI files so that applications can still obtain their setup information and integrate seamlessly into Windows 95.

Starting and Navigating the Registry Editor

The Registry is located in your Windows directory:

```
c:\windows\regedit.exe
```

You can start the Registry by double-clicking the Registry Editor icon (from the Windows 95 directory in the Explorer or the My Computer window). Or, from the Start menu, you can select Run and type `regedit`.

As stated previously, the Registry is a database, although it might look much more like something you would see in the Windows Explorer or the File Manager. The six file folder icons seen below the My Computer icon in Figure 5.1 are called subtrees, and they represent the Registry keys. Individual keys can contain data items called value entries, or they can contain additional subkeys. Although their values differ significantly, these entries are analogous in structure to the files and directories (respectively) that are displayed in the Windows Explorer or the File Manager. How these components relate and interact with Windows 95 is covered in subsequent sections.

You can navigate through the Registry by double-clicking on the file folders. Depending on your choice, you will be presented with yet another subkey or perhaps the value entry for that particular key. A plus sign (+) next to the folder indicates the presence of additional subkeys, which expand or collapse upon double-clicking. The absence of a plus sign indicates that you have reached the value entry for that key. As you might have figured out by now, the value entry can be edited by double-clicking on the entry in the right pane of the Registry Editor window. This action presents you with a dialog box in which you can make changes to the value entry.

FIGURE 5.1.
The Registry Editor.

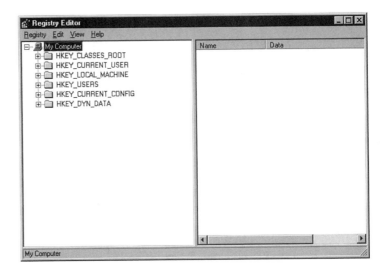

In addition to the editing features just mentioned, the Registry also allows several other features of interest. Under the Edit menu option, you find choices to perform the standard edit operations of Modify and Delete, as well as Find, which enables you to search for a particular value entry or key.

INI Files and the Registry

The Registry keys are analogous to the bracketed headings in .INI files, while the value entries are analogous to the entries between the bracketed headings. The following is an example of a few of the old entries in the WIN.INI file that Windows 95 will map to the Registry upon installation:

```
[Desktop]
Pattern=(None)
Wallpaper=leaves.bmp
IconSpacing=75
GridGranularity=0
TileWallPaper=1
```

The bracketed item [Desktop] is mapped to the Registry key:

```
HKey_Current_User\Control Panel\Desktop
```

This key contains the following value entry names and their data:

Value Entries	Data
Pattern	"(None)"
Wallpaper	"(None)"
GridGranularity	"0"
TileWallPaper	"1"

You might have noticed that the IconSpacing value entry is missing from this section of the Registry. Notice that the HKey_Current_User\Control Panel\Desktop key has two subkeys: HKey_Current_User\Control Panel\Desktop\ResourceLocale and HKey_Current_User\ Control Panel\Desktop\WindowMetrics. Some of the values from the WIN.INI file are mapped into one of these two subkeys. For example, the IconSpacing entry can be found under the HKey_Current_User\Control Panel\Desktop\WindowMetrics key.

If you wonder where your old WIN.INI entries can be found in the Registry, use the Find option under the Edit menu. If you cannot find the entry, remember that Windows 95 only maps the entries that can be used by the Windows 95 system and its applications. Some of the older Windows 3.x applications do not know how to use the Registry; therefore, these values are not mapped to the Registry. The INI files still exist under Windows 95 for just that reason. Applications that expect entries in the INI file will still find them there under Windows 95.

Using the Registry Editor

The Registry editor allows direct interaction with the Registry. In most instances, users or administrators use the tools provided with Windows 95 to automatically update and change Registry entries. For more advanced users, there might be times when editing the Registry is the fastest and easiest way to get their hardware and applications working properly. Application developers use the Registry API to interact with the Registry.

NOTE

Values in the Registry should not be changed via the Registry Editor until the user fully understands the Registry and the ramifications of changing Registry entries. Most of the entries can be changed through the use of standard tools such as those found in the Control Panel shown in Figure 5.2.

FIGURE 5.2.

The Windows 95 Control Panel tools.

Although the Registry appears as a single repository to the user, it is physically made up of two separate files:

SYSTEM.DAT contains information that is specific to the machine (such as installed hardware and device driver information). This file must be stored locally on the machine containing Windows 95.

USER.DAT contains information specific to each individual user (such as desktop wallpaper and window colors). This file can be stored in a local or network location.

The Registry has no notion of syntax checking and allows you to enter data that could potentially make Windows 95 unbootable. Fortunately, Windows 95 has a policy of backing up these files. Every time Windows 95 is started, the system makes backups of the two Registry files and names them like so:

```
\windows\system\SYSTEM.DA0
```

and

```
\windows\USER.DA0
```

Exporting the Registry

The Registry allows exporting of its entire contents or a subset of its contents. To export, choose Export Registry File from the Registry menu option. The export option defaults to exporting the currently selected branch of the Registry. For example, if you have HKEY_CURRENT_USER selected, the Export Registry File dialog box shows that it is prepared to export that branch of the Registry. In order to export the entire Registry, select All in the lower section of the dialog box. A file containing the exported information is saved with a name and location of your choice. If necessary, this file can be used to import back into the Registry. Exporting the Registry is a good habit to get into if you plan to change its values.

Importing Into the Registry

To import a Registry file, choose Import Registry File from the Registry menu option. At this time, you can choose the Registry file that you want to import into the Registry. The file you choose to import must be a valid Registry file (the default file extension for Registry files is .reg). The Registry file contains the information necessary to import the information into the correct location. Therefore, if a particular branch such as HKEY_CURRENT_USER was exported earlier and then imported, the entire HKEY_CURRENT_USER branch is replaced with the information contained in that file. Importing a particular branch leaves the other Registry sections unaffected.

> **NOTE**
>
> Importing a Registry overwrites the current contents without warning. Be certain of the information contained in the Registry file before performing an import.

Adding a Key or Value Entry

Before performing any of the following operations, position the cursor where you want the key added to the Registry. For example, if you want to add a key under HKEY_CURRENT_USER\ Software, double-click on HKEY_CURRENT_USER and then click once on Software. Follow the instructions under the "Adding a Key" heading. When you choose the type of entry you want to add, the entry is added and the Registry defaults the name to New [Key¦Value] #N (in which N is a unique number). This entry is then added and highlighted in the Registry editor. While it is highlighted, you can change the name by typing a new name at the highlighted position.

From the Edit menu, scroll to the New command. This opens a submenu consisting of the following options: Adding a Key, Adding a String Value, and Adding Binary and DWORD Values.

Adding a Key

Use this command to add a new key at the present position in the hierarchy. Type the name you want in the highlighted entry. In order to change this value after it has been saved to the Registry, use the Modify command (explained in the next section).

Adding a String Value

You can use this command to add new text information to the value entry. Select the key for which you want to add a value entry, and then choose Edit | New | String Value from the menu. You will then be presented with a dialog box in which you can edit the Registry information. Notice that a single key can have multiple entries.

Adding Binary and DWORD Values

Adding binary and DWORD values is similar to adding a String value. Many times, these values are entered by installation programs or tools such as those found in the Control Panel. If you need to add these values manually, the dialog box presented by the Registry automatically formats how the data is entered. The DWORD dialog box contains choices for entering the data in either decimal or hexadecimal format, while binary data can only be entered in hexadecimal format.

Deleting a Key or Value Entry

To delete a key or value entry, either select the item you want to delete and press the Delete key or choose Delete from the Edit menu. This will delete the key and any of its subkeys and value entries. You cannot delete or rename any of the predefined keys.

> **CAUTION**
>
> Deleting entries in the Registry is a volatile process. There is no undo operation; however, a confirmation dialog box is presented before completing the operation. Before deleting entries, you should save the Registry by using the Export Registry File option. This can be found under the Registry menu.

Renaming a Key or Value Entry

Select the item you want to rename and choose Rename from the Edit menu. The Registry will highlight the entry, and you can enter the information directly.

Modifying a Key or Value Entry

Keys are modified by selecting the key to modify and choosing Modify from the Edit menu. Your selection is highlighted and you can edit the name directly.

To modify values in the Registry, double-click the value entry in the right pane of the Registry window or select the entry you want to modify and choose Modify from the Edit menu. You are presented with a dialog box in which you can edit the information.

How Windows 95 Interacts with the Registry

Under Windows 95, checking hardware, application, or network settings takes place in one central repository called the Registry. Whether you are connecting to a network, starting the system, or changing your computer's configuration, the Registry is being consulted. The Windows 95 operating system uses the Registry efficiently to obtain this information. This is especially true in comparison to the method employed in Windows 3.x: using CONFIG.SYS, AUTOEXEC.BAT, and a plethora of INI files located in the Windows and individual application directories. The Registry frees the user and administrators from worrying about and tracking down these files.

As stated earlier, the Registry is comprised of two physical files: USER.DAT and SYSTEM.DAT. This separation of files allows the system administrator to keep a copy of the USER.DAT file in a central location (such as a server directory). This enables the administrator to import that file into the Registry of any computer on the network from a remote location. Also, in a networked environment, a copy of the user's USER.DAT file can be put in the user's network logon directory. By doing this, a user can log onto any machine on the network, obtain his user specific Registry information, and see a consistent desktop.

Software Applications

Software applications should use the Registry API to perform the necessary operations. The API contains all the functionality necessary to integrate your application with the Windows 95 Registry.

Plug and Play Devices

In order for your system to fully utilize Plug and Play, your computer needs to have the following: a Plug and Play BIOS, Plug and Play cards, and of course Windows 95.

Plug and Play devices will interact automatically with the Registry. Installing or removing a Plug and Play device from the system notifies the Registry that the system configuration has changed. The entries within the Registry are then changed accordingly. Note that this is only true of Plug and Play-compliant devices, and not necessarily true of devices that do not have the Plug and Play features. For Plug and Play-compliant devices, Windows 95 can use the information in the Registry to configure these devices automatically. This includes the resolution of conflicts such as IRQ, DMA, and address settings that had to be manually configured in previous versions of Windows. For non-Plug and Play devices, Windows 95 attempts to detect and automatically configure the Registry appropriately. Microsoft claims that if conflicts arise, the Device Manager should help to guide you through the process of resolving these conflicts.

Plug and Play introduces a new service called the Configuration Manager. This utility interacts with a number of other system components to extract the appropriate information from the system and configure the machine properly.

For more information, see Chapter 6, "Programming for Plug and Play Devices."

Legacy Devices and the Registry

For non-Plug and Play devices (also known as *legacy devices*), the configuration information is stored statically in the Registry. Thus, any changes to these values require a reboot of the operating system in order to take effect. Windows 95 cannot configure a legacy type card, but during the detection phase of installation or add-in/removal, it might be able to recognize the card and even suggest a setting. It might go even further and load the appropriate drivers.

Overview of the Predefined Registry Keys

The Registry contains six separate predefined subkeys. The individual subkeys are distinct enough in their duties to warrant separate descriptions. Don't be alarmed by the leading Hkey that prefixes all of the key names. This is a convention to inform application programmers that this key is a handle and can be used as such within their programs when using the Registry API.

Hkey_Local_Machine

The information contained in this section of the Registry is used by all the users that logon to the system. This is where the information for the local machine (this computer) is stored. It has information regarding the device, hardware and software installations, and configurations. Configuration of the ports such as the COM and Printer can also be found here.

Hkey_Current_Config

This key is really a pointer to a branch of the Hkey_Local_Machine\Config structure. It contains information regarding the current configuration of the machine and the hardware attached to it. For any type of computer, this configuration could change depending on the type of network to which it is currently connected or a change in hardware or application installations. For a docking station that is used for laptop computers, this information will change each time a new machine is docked.

`Hkey_Classes_Root`

This key contains information that allows Windows 95 to support the drag and drop capabilities of the desktop. It also contains information on file extensions. These keys and their definitions determine how file types and their icons will be displayed in the Windows Explorer and the Windows 95 desktop.

`Hkey_Users`

Each user on a computer has his own key and subkeys in this section. Depending on who is currently logged on, this key points to different sections of the `Hkey_Users` branch. When you log onto a computer running Windows 95, you should expect to get your own personal desktop and preferences. This information can be found under the `Hkey_Current_User` key. Information such as your desktop settings, background bitmaps, start menu entries, application shortcuts, display fonts, and so on are contained here. Note that many of these settings are changed through the various tools included in Windows 95. For example, to change your video resolution, you open the Control Panel, click the Display icon, and then proceed to change the display settings. The display tool automatically updates the Registry with the correct values. For a user who logs onto the computer and who does not have a profile, the `.Default` subkey is used.

`HKey_Current_User`

This key, like `Hkey_Current_Config`, is really a pointer to a branch of the `Hkey_Users` structure. The current user of the machine has his information mapped into the `HKey_Current_User` section.

`Hkey_Dyn_data`

It might seem that once changes are made to the Registry, they are immediately written to disk. The truth is that due to improved caching and other operating system features, the data might not get flushed out to disk immediately. Also, compared to RAM, disk is still slow by orders of magnitude. The `Hkey_Dyn_data` key is stored in RAM, and for this reason certain data that needs to be updated or retrieved quickly is stored here. This key is created every time Windows 95 is started. It contains the current hardware status of the system. The configuration data here is dynamic and changes as updates are made to the system. Therefore, this information is always up-to-date.

Overview of the Value Entries

As stated earlier, the Registry allows not only text strings, but also binary datatypes, as value entries.

String data: This type of data was of the type found in Windows 3.x INI files.

Binary data: This data can be displayed in either decimal or hexadecimal format. This type of data is typically used by device drivers or application code.

Figure 5.3 shows examples of both types of value entries. The values enclosed by double quotes are examples of string value entries, while the entries shown in hexadecimal format are binary value entries.

FIGURE 5.3.

Examples of String and Binary data within the Registry.

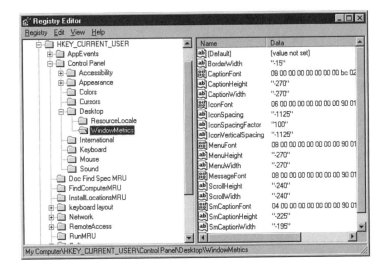

Software Written for Windows 95

Software written for Windows 95 should use the standard API functions discussed later in this chapter to add, modify, query, and delete Registry entries. By using this API, new applications can dismiss the .INI files that they have come to rely on.

Entering Your Application into the Registry

The information that used to be in .INI files for Windows 3.x applications is now stored under the HKEY_LOCAL_MACHINE\SOFTWARE and HKEY_CURRENT_USER\Software keys. Your application program should use the Registry API to implement these entries. If you are entering new information to the Registry for a new product, use the following form:

HKEY_LOCAL_MACHINE\SOFTWARE\YourCompanyName\YourProductName

and

HKEY_CURRENT_USER\Software\YourCompanyName\YourProductName

Under these keys, you can create any additional subkeys and value entries that are necessary for your application. Enter value entries under HKEY_CURRENT_USER\Software\

`YourCompanyName\YourProductName` to store information specific to the user and
`HKEY_LOCAL_MACHINE\SOFTWARE\YourCompanyName\YourProductName` to store computer-specific
information.

> **NOTE**
>
> It is wise to include yet another subkey containing the product version number. For
> the sake of brevity, it is not shown in this example.

Reserved Subkeys For Your Application

There are a few subkeys that can be added to the `HKEY_LOCAL_MACHINE\SOFTWARE\`
`YourCompanyName\YourProductName` structure that can benefit your application.

Application Startup

A user might shut down the system while using your application. In order for your application to be automatically started when Windows 95 is booted, a special key called `RunOnce` is
used. The location of this key is `HKEY_LOCAL_MACHINE\SOFTWARE\Microsoft\Windows\`
`CurrentVersion\RunOnce`. You add a key with any name (the name should be a logical one to
you) and the value entry should contain a command line for your application. Upon system
startup, Windows 95 attempts to run the text in the value entries under this key (there can
be more than one value entry for multiple instances).

> **NOTE**
>
> It is completely up to your application to maintain the values under this key. Upon
> receiving a shutdown message from Windows 95, your application must write out the
> pertinent information to this key!

The name of the value entry is up to you; the entry itself must contain a valid command
line. Any arguments on this command line must be valid for your application. The data in
the value entries will be removed automatically by the system when Windows 95 is started.

If the `RunOnce` key is added under the `HKEY_LOCAL_MACHINE` structure, applications will be run
before Windows 95 is started and will affect all users. This might be used to ask the user
specific questions before Windows 95 is started.

Windows 95 also supports `Run` key value entries containing commands similar to those under the RunOnce key. Unlike the RunOnce key, the value entries under the Run key are persistent. Therefore, these commands are run every time the system is started.

Path Information

The following hierarchy can be used to enter important path information:

```
HKEY_LOCAL_MACHINE
  SOFTWARE
  YourCompanyName
  YourProductName
    App Paths
      YourApplicationExecutableName
        Default = The path where the executable resides
        Path = Location of your applications DLL files
```

The Default entry is used to obtain the path if your application cannot be found in the standard system path. The Path entry is used to locate any DLLs used by your application.

Registering New File Extensions

Windows 95 supports the notion of file extension identifiers. For example, when you run the Windows Explorer, you will notice that most files have an icon and type associated with them (as shown in Figure 5.4).

The Registry information for these file extensions is found under the HKEY_CLASSES_ROOT

FIGURE 5.4.

How Windows 95 uses the file extension properties.

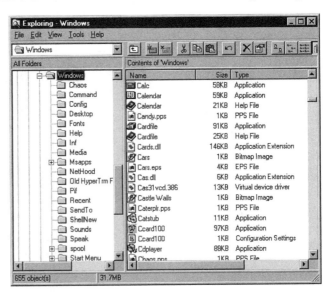

key. In order to add this capability, you have to perform the following steps:

1. Make sure that your extensions do not conflict with one that is already defined in the Registry.

2. Enter a new key with your extension. For example, to register files with the extension .xyz, it is necessary to qualify the extension with an application identifier. The application identifier is a text string that has the same name as another key you will create in step 3. For this example, the application identifier will be called `xyzid`.

   ```
   HKEY_CLASSES_ROOT
       .xyz=xyzid
   ```

3. Next, add another key with the same name as the identifier just created. Enter the value entry as shown.

   ```
   HKEY_CLASSES_ROOT
       xyzid = "XYZ Application Document"
   ```

Now, when you create a file with a .xyz extension, it will appear in the Windows Explorer with a type of `XYZ Application Document`. By using this method, you make it clear to users what files belong to your application.

Registering the Icon

As seen in Figure 5.4, each file has an icon associated with it, helping users to easily identify a specific type of file. To register an icon, add the following (using the previous example):

```
HKEY_CLASSES_ROOT
        xyzid = "XYZ Application Document" (added earlier)
        DefaultIcon = IconPathandFileName, index
```

Here, `IconPathandFileName` is the fully qualified path and name of the file containing your icon (usually an .EXE or DLL file), and index is the offset at which your icon is located in the `IconPathandFileName`. For this example, the entry should look like this:

```
DefaultIcon = c:\xyzpath\xyzapp.exe,1
```

You should now see your files displayed correctly in the Windows Explorer. If you use the Registry Editor, remember that these changes might not be written to disk immediately, so you might have to close the Registry first to flush the changes.

The Registry and Initialization Functions

The following are the functions used with the Registry and initialization files. The functions are broken up into three sections: one for Windows 3.1 compatibility functions, one for Win32-supported functions, and one for Windows 95-specific functions. For reasons that will become evident later, knowing how the Windows 3.1 functions work is still important.

Windows 3.1 Compatibility Functions

The following functions are used mostly for backward compatability.

- `GetPrivateProfileInt`
- `GetPrivateProfileSection`
- `WritePrivateProfileSection`
- `GetPrivateProfileString`
- `WritePrivateProfileString`
- `GetProfileInt`
- `GetProfileSection`
- `WriteProfileSection`
- `GetProfileString`
- `WriteProfileString`
- `RegOpenKey`
- `RegCreateKey`
- `RegEnumKey`
- `RegQueryValue`
- `RegSetValue`

Win32 Supported Functions

The following are functions you should use in your new applications.

- `RegOpenKeyEx`
- `RegCloseKey`
- `RegCreateKeyEx`
- `RegDeleteValue`
- `RegDeleteKey`
- `RegEnumKeyEx`
- `RegEnumValue`
- `RegQueryInfoKey`
- `RegQueryValueEx`
- `RegSetValueEx`
- `RegFlushKey`

Windows 95 Functions

These are functions used for read-mode and protected-mode virtual device drivers.

- LDR_RegOpenKey
- LDR_RegCloseKey
- LDR_RegEnumKey
- LDR_RegQueryValue
- LDR_RegQueryValueEx
- VMM_RegOpenKey
- VMM_RegCloseKey
- VMM_RegEnumKey
- VMM_RegQueryValue
- VMM_RegQueryValueEx
- VMM_RegCreateKey
- VMM_RegDeleteKey
- VMM_RegEnumValue
- VMM_RegSetValueEx
- VMM_RegFlushKey

The next section is a brief description of each of these functions along with examples of how to use them in your programs. Both the SDK and MFC functions (if available) are shown. For a complete overview of the function, refer to the online help provided with Visual C++.

Windows 3.1 Compatibility Functions

You already know what an initialization file is and what it looks like, but to remind you, here are the contents of the winfile.ini file in the Windows directory on my computer:

```
[Settings]
AddOns=
DriveBar=0
Window=118,73,793,575, , ,1
dir2=0,0,392,481,-1,-1,1,62,201,1905,180,D:\GAMEDEV.95\BIN\*.*
dir1=392,0,784,481,-1,-1,1,62,201,1905,180,C:\MSDNCD\*.*
```

The text [Settings] is termed a section. The text DriveBar, on the left side of the =, is termed a key; and the text 0, on the right side of the =, is termed the value. It is important to remember these terms because they will be used throughout this chapter. I will use this example for some of the functions you will see.

> **NOTE**
>
> The `GetPrivate` and `SetPrivate` functions have as their last parameter the name of the initialization file. If the initialization file you are using is in the Windows directory, you can just specify the filename. If your .INI file is located anywhere else, you must specify the complete path, such as c:\myapp\myini.ini.

> **TIP**
>
> Visual C++ projects default to creating and using INI files in the Windows directory. You can change this default behavior by changing the value of the `CWinApp::m_pszProfileName` variable. The following code accomplishes this task:
>
> ```
> // move INI file location
> char name[260];
> GetModuleFileName
> ➥( AfxGetInstanceHandle(), (LPSTR)name, sizeof( name ) );
> name[strlen(name)-4]='\0';
> strcat( name, ".ini" );
>  free( (void*)m_pszProfileName );
> m_pszProfileName=strdup( name );
> ```

GetPrivateProfileInt

The `GetPrivateProfileInt` function retrieves an integer value associated with a key in the specified section of the given initialization file.

SDK

```
UINT GetPrivateProfileInt(
    LPCTSTR   SectionName,  // name of the section to look in
    LPCTSTR   KeyName,      // name of the key to look for
    INT       DefaultValue,
    ➥ // value returned if section/key is not found
    LPCTSTR   IniFilename   // location of the INI file
    );
```

MFC

No function is available. Use the SDK function.

How To Use

```
int DefaultValue=0; // this is the default value I want
int DriveBar=GetPrivateProfileInt( "Settings", "DriveBar", 0, "winfile.ini" );
```

Using the example, the value that will be placed into the variable `DriveBar` after your call to `GetPrivateProfileInt` is `0`.

GetPrivateProfileSection

The `GetPrivateProfileSection` function retrieves all of the keys and values for the specified section from an initialization file.

SDK

```
DWORD GetPrivateProfileSection(
    LPCTSTR   SectionName,  // name of the section to look in
    LPTSTR    ReturnBuffer, // character buffer to put results in
    DWORD     BufferSize,   // size of the return buffer
    LPCTSTR   IniFilename   // location of the INI file
    );
```

MFC

No function is available. Use the SDK function.

How To Use

```
char buff[512];
DWORD CharsCopied=GetPrivateProfileSection
➥("Settings",buff,512,"winfile.ini");
```

The following will be in the character string `Buffer` after your call:

```
Buffer=
"AddOns=\0DriveBar=0\0Window=118,73,793,575,,,1\0dir2=0,0,392,481,-1,
➥-1,1,62,201,1905,180,D:\GAMEDEV.95\BIN\*.*\0dir1=392,0,784,481,-1,-1,
➥1,62,01,1905,180,C:\MSDNCD\*.*\0\0"
```

As you can see, each key and its value is appended to the string and is separated from other key/value entries with a string terminator (\0). The variable `CharsCopied` tells you that 167 characters were copied. This value is useful to let you know how long the string is.

WritePrivateProfileSection

The WritePrivateProfileSection function replaces the keys and values under the specified section in an initialization file.

SDK

```
BOOL WritePrivateProfileSection(
    LPCTSTR  SectionName,           // name of the section to look in
    LPCTSTR  KeysAndValuesString,   // character array with keys and values
    LPCTSTR  IniFilename            // location of the INI file
    );
```

MFC

No function is available. Use the SDK function.

How To Use

```
char KeysAndValues[]="Setting1=3\0Setting2=2\0Setting3=1\0\0";
BOOL success=WritePrivateProfileSection("Settings",KeysAndValues,"test.ini");
```

After your call returns, you now have an .INI file in the Windows directory named TEST.INI, and its contents look like this:

```
[Settings]
Setting1=3
Setting2=2
Setting3=1
```

GetPrivateProfileString

The GetPrivateProfileString function retrieves a string from the specified section in an initialization file.

SDK

```
DWORD GetPrivateProfileString(
    LPCTSTR  SectionName,            // name of the section to look in
    LPCTSTR  Key,                    // name of the key to look for
    LPCTSTR  DefaultString,          // value returned if section/key is not found
    LPTSTR   DestinationBuffer,      // chacter array to put results in
    DWORD    DestinationBufferSize,  // size of the destination buffer
    LPCTSTR  IniFilename             // location of the Ini file
    );
```

MFC

No function is available. Use the SDK function.

How To Use

```
char WinSetup[50];
int CharsCopied=
  GetPrivateProfileString("Settings","Window","",WinSetup, 50,"winfile.ini");
```

After your call, the character array `WindowSettings` contains the value `118,73,793,575, , ,1`.

WritePrivateProfileString

The `WritePrivateProfileString` function copies a string into the specified section of the specified initialization file.

SDK

```
BOOL WritePrivateProfileString(
    LPCTSTR   SectionName, // name of the section to look for
    LPCTSTR   Key,         // name of the key to look for
    LPCTSTR   String,      // character string to write to the INI file
    LPCTSTR   IniFilename  // location of the INI file
    );
```

MFC

No function is available. Use the SDK function.

How To Use

```
BOOL success=
WritePrivateProfileString("Settings","Window", "0,0,0,0,0,0,0","winfile.ini");
```

When your call returns, you have changed the value of the key Window in your .INI file.

> **NOTE**
>
> The SDK function's `Get`... and `Set`... functions default to using the WIN.INI file in the Windows directory, and the Visual C++ functions default to writing to an .INI file in the Windows directory with the same filename as the application's .EXE filename.

GetProfileInt

The GetProfileInt function retrieves an integer from the specified key name in the given section of the WIN.INI file.

SDK

```
UINT GetProfileInt(
    LPCTSTR  SectionName,  // name of the section to look for
    LPCTSTR  KeyName,      // name of the key to look for
    INT      DefaultName   // value returned if section/value is not found
);
```

MFC

```
UINT CWinApp::GetProfileInt( LPCTSTR lpszSection, LPCTSTR lpszEntry, int nDefault);
```

How to Use with SDK

```
int Value=GetProfileInt( "Desktop", "TileWallpaper", 0 );
```

This retrieves the integer value of the key TileWallpaper of the section Desktop in the WIN.INI file in the Windows directory.

How to Use with MFC

```
int Value=GetProfileInt( "Desktop", "TileWallpaper", 0 );
```

This retrieves the integer value of the key TileWallpaper of the section Desktop in the .INI file with the same name as your application in the Windows directory.

> **NOTE**
>
> The GetProfileInt function is a member function of CWinApp. In order to use the GetProfileInt function outside your derived CWinApp class, you must call the function with AfxGetApp()->GetProfileInt.

GetProfileSection

The GetProfileSection function retrieves all of the keys and values for the specified section of the WIN.INI file.

SDK

```
DWORD GetProfileSection(
    LPCTSTR SectionName, // name of the section to look for
    LPTSTR  Buffer,      // name of the key to look for
    DWORD   BufferSize   // size of return buffer
    );
```

MFC

No function is available. Use the SDK function.

How To Use

Please refer to the example shown for the GetPrivateProfileSection(...) function. It is exactly the same, except that here the WIN.INI file is read for the information.

WriteProfileSection

The WriteProfileSection function replaces the contents of the specified section in the WIN.INI file with the specified keys and values.

SDK

```
BOOL WriteProfileSection(
    LPCTSTR  SectionName,  // name of the section to look for
    LPCTSTR  KeysAndValues // character array with keys and value to write
    );
```

MFC

No function is available. Use the SDK function.

How To Use

Please refer to the example shown for the WritePrivateProfileSection function. It is exactly the same, except that here the information is written to the WIN.INI file.

GetProfileString

The GetProfileString function retrieves the string associated with the specified key in the given section of the WIN.INI file.

SDK

```
DWORD GetProfileString(
   LPCTSTR  SectionName,    // name of the section to look in
   LPCTSTR  Key,            // name of the key to look for
   LPCTSTR  DefaultString,  // default string to use if section/key is not found
   LPTSTR   Buffer,         // character array to put results into
   DWORD    BufferSize      // size of destination buffer
);
```

MFC

```
CString CWinApp::GetProfileString(
➥ LPCTSTR lpszSection, LPCTSTR lpszEntry, LPCTSTR lpszDefault=NULL );
```

How to Use with SDK

```
char Buffer[100];
DWORD CharsCopied=GetProfileString( "mci extensions", "wav", "", Buffer, 100 );
```

This gets the string associated with the key wav in the section mci extensions in the WIN.INI file. If there is no entry, the character array Buffer will be empty.

How to Use with MFC

```
CString StartWav=GetProfileString( "Wavs", "Start" );
```

This gets the string value of the key Start in the section Wavs in the .INI file with the same name as your program in the Windows directory.

> **NOTE**
>
> The GetProfileString function is a member function of CWinApp. In order to use the GetProfileString function outside your derived CWinApp class, you must call the function with this line:
>
> ```
>     AfxGetApp()->GetProfileString(...).
> ```

WriteProfileString

The `WriteProfileString` function copies a string into the specified section of the WIN.INI file.

SDK

```
BOOL WriteProfileString(
    LPCTSTR  SectionName, // name of the section to look in
    LPCTSTR  Key,         // name of the key to look for
    LPCTSTR  String       // character array to put results into
);
```

MFC

```
BOOL CWinApp::WriteProfileString(
➥ LPCTSTR lpszSection, LPCTSTR lpszEntry, LPCTSTR lpszValue );
```

How to Use with SDK

```
BOOL success=WriteProfileString( "windows", "load", "c:\\win95\\explorer.exe" );
```

This places the value `c:\\win95\\explorer.exe` into the key `load` in the section `windows` in the WIN.INI file.

> **CAUTION**
>
> Be very careful when writing to WIN.INI sections that are Windows-specific. You can make Windows unstable, even unusable, if you don't know what you are doing. More important, why are you writing to WIN.INI? New Windows applications should not write to WIN.INI or SYSTEM.INI for any reason. You should be writing your information to the registry.

How to Use with MFC

```
BOOL success=WriteProfileString( "Settings", "AlwaysOnTop", "yes" );
```

This places the value yes in the key `AlwaysOnTop`, which is in the section `Settings` in the .INI file with the same name as your program in the Windows directory.

> **NOTE**
>
> The WriteProfileString function is a member function of CWinApp. In order to use the WriteProfileString function outside your derived CWinApp class, you must call the function with AfxGetApp()->WriteProfileString(...).

RegOpenKey

The RegOpenKey function opens the specified key.

```
LONG RegOpenKey(
    HKEY    key,        // handle of open key
    LPCTSTR SubKeyName, // name of the subkey to open
    PHKEY   KeyHandle   // the key handle you get
    );
```

How To Use

```
HKEY key;
if ( RegOpenKey( HKEY_CURRENT_USER,
        "Software\\Microsoft\\Multimedia\\Sound Mapper", &key )==
  ERROR_SUCCESS ) {
  ...}
```

If the function succeeds, you will have a handle to a key that you can use with other functions to get more information.

RegCreateKey

The RegCreateKey function creates the specified key. If the key already exists in the registry, the function opens it.

```
LONG RegCreateKey(
    HKEY    key,        // handle of open key
    LPCTSTR SubKeyName, // name of the subkey to open
    PHKEY   NewKeyHandle // the key handle you get
    );
```

How To Use

```
HKEY key;
if ( RegOpenKey( HKEY_CURRENT_USER,
        "Software\\Microsoft\\Multimedia\\Sound Mapper", &key )==
ERROR_SUCCESS ) {
  HKEY NewKey;
  if (RegCreateKey(key,"Software\\MyCompany\\MyApp",&key)==ERROR_SUCCESS) {
    ...
    RegCloseKey( NewKey );
  }
  RegCloseKey( key );
}
```

RegEnumKey

The RegEnumKey function enumerates subkeys of the specified open registry key. The function retrieves the name of one subkey each time it is called.

```
LONG RegEnumKey(
    HKEY    key,         // handle of key to query
    DWORD   SubKeyIndex, // index of subkey to query
    LPTSTR  KeyName,     // where to put the subkey's name
    DWORD   KeyNameSize  // size of subkey buffer
    );
```

How To Use

```
HKEY key;
if ( RegOpenKeyEx( HKEY_CURRENT_USER,
        "Software\\Microsoft",0,KEY_READ,&key)==ERROR_SUCCESS ) {
LONG retCode;
  char KeyName[50];
  int i;
  for( i=0, retCode=ERROR_SUCCESS; retCode==ERROR_SUCCESS; i++ ) {
    if ( (retCode=RegEnumKey( key, i, KeyName, 50 ))==ERROR_SUCCESS ) {
    ...
    }
  }
  RegCloseKey( key );
}
```

This gets you all the subkeys for the key Software\\Microsoft.

RegQueryValue

The RegQueryValue function retrieves the value associated with the unnamed value for a specified key in the registry. Values in the registry have name, type, and data components. This function retrieves the data for a key's first value that has a NULL name.

```
LONG RegQueryValue(
    HKEY     key,         // handle of key to query
    LPCTSTR  SubKeyName,  // name of subkey to query
    LPTSTR   Value,       // buffer for returned string
    PLONG    ValueSize    // where to put size of the returned value
    );
```

How To Use

```
HKEY key;
if( RegOpenKeyEx( HKEY_CURRENT_USER,
     "Software\\MyCompany\\MyApp",0,KEY_WRITE,&key)==ERROR_SUCCESS) {
  char Data[100];
  long DataSize=100;
  RegSetValue( key, "Options", REG_SZ, "AllowSave", 11 );
  RegCloseKey( key );
  if( RegOpenKeyEx(HKEY_CURRENT_USER,
   "Software\\MyCompany\\MyApp",0,KEY_READ,&key)==ERROR_SUCCESS) {
```

```
RetCode=RegQueryValue( key, "Options", Data, &DataSize );
    RegCloseKey( key );
  }
}
```

RegSetValue

The `RegSetValue` function associates a value with a specified key. This value must be a text string and cannot have a name.

```
LONG RegSetValue(
    HKEY     key,         // handle of key to set value for
    LPCTSTR  SubKeyName,  // name of the subkey to use
    DWORD    ValueType,   // type of value
    LPCTSTR  Data,        // value data
    DWORD    DataSize     // size of value data
  );
```

How To Use

```
HKEY key;
if( RegOpenKeyEx( HKEY_CURRENT_USER,
    "Software\\MyCompany\\MyApp",0,KEY_WRITE, &key)==ERROR_SUCCESS){
  RegSetValue( key, "Options", REG_SZ, "AlwaysWork", 11 );
  RegCloseKey( key );
}
```

This sets the value `AlwaysWork` for the subkey `Options` for the key `Software\\MyCompany\\MyApp`.

This concludes the section on the Windows 3.1 Compatibility functions. You might be wondering why I even bothered to go over them. I have a surprise for you, but you have to keep reading.

Win32 Supported Functions

When working with the registry, you can access any key and the following predefined reserved handle values:

```
HKEY_CLASSES_ROOT
HKEY_CURRENT_USER
HKEY_LOCAL_MACHINE
HKEY_USERS
```

For our purposes, we will be dealing mostly with the predefined reserved handle value `HKEY_CURRENT_USER`. As an application programmer, you will want to write all information into this key unless you are doing very advanced work. If you have taken a look at the registry using regedit.exe, you have seen that all Microsoft applications store their information here. You should, too.

RegOpenKeyEx

The `RegOpenKeyEx` function opens the specified key.

```
LONG RegOpenKeyEx(
    HKEY    key,            // handle of open key
    LPCTSTR SubKeyName,     // address of name of subkey to open
    DWORD   Reserved,       // reserved; must be zero
    REGSAM  SecurityMask,   // security access mask
    PHKEY   KeyHandle       // address of handle of open key
);
```

How To Use

```
HKEY key;
if ( RegOpenKeyEx( HKEY_CURRENT_USER,
     "Software\\Microsoft\Windows Help",0,KEY_READ,&key)==
  ERROR_SUCCESS ) {
  ...}
```

If the function succeeds, you'll have a handle to a key that you can use with other functions to get more information. Please refer to the online help for more information about this function and the possible parameters to pass to it.

RegCloseKey

The `RegCloseKey` function releases the handle of the specified key.

```
LONG RegCloseKey(
    HKEY  key // handle of key to close
);
```

How To Use

```
HKEY key;
if ( RegOpenKeyEx( HKEY_CURRENT_USER,
     "Software\\Microsoft\Windows Help",0,KEY_READ,&key)==
  ERROR_SUCCESS ) {
  ...
  RegCloseKey( key );
}
```

When you open a key, make sure that you close it. Failing to do so can cause problems with the system.

RegCreateKeyEx

The `RegCreateKeyEx` function creates the specified key. If the key already exists in the registry, the function opens it.

```
LONG RegCreateKeyEx(
    HKEY                  key,              // handle of an open key
    LPCTSTR               SubKeyName,       // address of subkey name
    DWORD                 Reserved,         // reserved
    LPTSTR                Class,            // address of class string
    DWORD                 Options,          // special options flag
    REGSAM                SecurityMask,     // desired security access
    LPSECURITY_ATTRIBUTES SecurityAttributes,
    ➥// address of key security structure
    PHKEY                 NewKey,
    ➥// address of buffer for opened handle
    LPDWORD                 DispositionBuffer
    ➥// address of disposition value buffer
    );
```

How To Use

```
HKEY key;
if (RegOpenKeyEx(HKEY_CURRENT_USER
    "Software\\MyCompany\\MyApp",0,KEY_READ,&key)==ERROR_SUCCESS) {
  HKEY NewKey;
  if ( RegCreateKeyEx( key, "Settings", 0, )==ERROR_SUCCESS ) {
    ...
    RegCloseKey( NewKey );
  }
  RegCloseKey( key );
}
```

RegDeleteValue

The RegDeleteValue function removes a named value from the specified registry key.

```
LONG RegDeleteValue(
    HKEY    key,        // handle of key
    LPTSTR  ValueName  // address of value name
    );
```

How To Use

```
HKEY key;
if( RegOpenKeyEx( HKEY_CURRENT_USER,
    "Software\\MyCompany\\MyApp\\Settings",0,KEY_READ,&key)==
  ERROR_SUCCESS ) {
  RegDeleteValue( key, "Positions" );
  RegCloseKey( key );
}
```

This deletes the value Positions from the key Software\\MyCompany\\MyApp\\Settings. This function and the next one are the functions to use when you need to take out your application's information from the registry. For example, use them in the uninstall program for your application.

RegDeleteKey

The `RegDeleteKey` function deletes the specified key. This function cannot delete a key that
has subkeys.

```
LONG RegDeleteKey(
    HKEY    key,         // handle of open key
    LPCTSTR SubKeyName   // address of name of subkey to delete
    );
```

How To Use

```
HKEY key;
if( RegOpenKeyEx( HKEY_CURRENT_USER,
     "Software\\MyCompany\\MyApp",0,KEY_READ,&key)==ERROR_SUCCESS){
  RegDeleteKey( key, "Settings" );
  RegCloseKey( key );
}
```

This deletes the subkey `Settings` from the key `Software\\MyCompany\\MyApp`.

RegEnumKeyEx

The `RegEnumKeyEx` function enumerates subkeys of the specified open registry key. The
function retrieves information about one subkey each time it is called. Unlike the
`RegEnumKey` function, `RegEnumKeyEx` retrieves the class name of the subkey and the time it was
last modified.

```
LONG RegEnumKeyEx(
    HKEY      key,           // handle of key to enumerate
    DWORD     SubKeyIndex,   // index of subkey to enumerate
    LPTSTR    SubKeyName,    // address of buffer for subkey name
    LPDWORD   SubKeyNameSize,// address for size of subkey buffer
    LPDWORD   Reserved,      // reserved; Must be NULL
    LPTSTR    Class,         // address of buffer for class string
    LPDWORD   ClassSize,     // address for size of class buffer
    PFILETIME KeyLastWritten // address for time key last written to
    );
```

How To Use

```
HKEY key;
if ( RegOpenKeyEx( HKEY_CURRENT_USER,
     "Software\\Microsoft",0,KEY_READ,&key)== ERROR_SUCCESS ) {
  LONG retCode;
  char KeyName[50], Class[50];
  DWORD KeyNameSize=50, ClassSize=50;
  FILETIME LastWrittenTo;
  int i;
  for( i=0, retCode=ERROR_SUCCESS; retCode==ERROR_SUCCESS; i++ ) {
    if ((retCode=RegEnumKeyEx(
        key,i,KeyName,&KeyNameSize,NULL,Class,&ClassSize,&LastWrittenTo))
      ==ERROR_SUCCESS){
    ...
```

```
      }
   }
   RegCloseKey( key );
}
```

This returns the same information that the function `RegEnumKey` does, plus the class name and the last time the key was written to.

EnumValue

The `RegEnumValue` function enumerates the values for the specified open registry key. The function copies one indexed value name and data block for the key each time it is called.

```
LONG RegEnumValue(
    HKEY     key,            // handle of key to query
    DWORD    ValueIndex,     // index of value to query
    LPTSTR   Value,          // address of buffer for value string
    LPDWORD  ValueSize,      // address for size of value buffer
    LPDWORD  Reserved,       // reserved; Must be NULL
    LPDWORD  TypeCode,       // address of buffer for type code
    LPBYTE   ValueData,      // address of buffer for value data
    LPDWORD  ValueDataSize   // address for size of data buffer
   );
```

How To Use

```
HKEY key;
if ( RegOpenKeyEx( HKEY_CURRENT_USER,
        "Software\\Microsoft\\Visual C++ 2.0\\Recent File List",0,
      KEY_READ,&key )==ERROR_SUCCESS ) {
  LONG retCode;
  char Value[100];
  LPBYTE ValueData;
  DWORD ValueBufferSize=100, TypeCode, ValueDataSize;
  int i;
  for( i=0, retCode=ERROR_SUCCESS; retCode==ERROR_SUCCESS; i++ ) {
    if ((retCode=RegEnumValue( key, i, Value, &ValueBufferSize, NULL,
          &TypeCode, ValueData,&ValueDataSize ))==ERROR_SUCCESS) {
      TRACE( "%s = %s\n", Value, ValueData );
    }
  }
  RegCloseKey( key );
}
```

This enumerates all the values for the key `Software\\Microsoft\\Visual C++ 2.0\\Recent File List`.

QueryInfoKey

The RegQueryInfoKey function retrieves information about a specified registry key.

```
LONG RegQueryInfoKey (
    HKEY       key,            // handle of key to query
    LPTSTR     Class,          // address of buffer for class string
    LPDWORD    ClassSize,      // address of size of class string buffer
    LPDWORD    Reserved,       // reserved; must be NULL
    LPDWORD    NumSubkeys,     // address of buffer for number of subkeys
    LPDWORD    MaxSubkey,      // address of buffer for longest subkey name length
    LPDWORD    MaxClass,       // address of buffer for longest class string length
    LPDWORD    NumValues,      // address of buffer for number of value entries
    LPDWORD    MaxValueName,   // address of buffer for longest value name length
    LPDWORD    MaxValueData,   // address of buffer for longest value data length
    LPDWORD    SecurityDescriptor,
    ➡ // address of buffer for security descriptor length
    PFILETIME  LastWriteTime   // address of buffer for last write time
    );
```

How To Use

```
HKEY key;
if ( RegOpenKeyEx( HKEY_CURRENT_USER,
       "Software\\Microsoft\\Visual C++ 2.0", 0, KEY_READ, &key)==ERROR_SUCCESS ) {
   char Class[100];
   DWORD ClassLength=100, NumSubkeys, MaxSubkey, MaxClass, NumValues,
     MaxValueName, MaxValueData,SecurityDescriptor;
   FILETIME LastWriteTime;
   if ( RegQueryInfoKey( key, Class, &ClassLength, NULL, &NumSubkeys,
       &MaxSubkey, &MaxClass, &NumValues, &MaxValueName, &MaxValueData,
       &SecurityDescriptor, &LastWriteTime )==ERROR_SUCCESS ) {
   ...
   }
   RegCloseKey( key );
}
```

This returns information concerning the key Software\\Microsoft\\Visual C++ 2.0. Many useful values are supplied from this function.

RegQueryValueEx

The RegQueryValueEx function retrieves the type and data for a specified value name associated with an open registry key.

```
LONG RegQueryValueEx(
    HKEY    key,        // handle of key to query
    LPTSTR  ValueName,  // address of name of value to query
    LPDWORD Reserved,   // reserved
    LPDWORD ValueType,  // address of buffer for value type
    LPBYTE  Data,       // address of data buffer
    LPDWORD DataSize    // address of data buffer size
    );
```

How To Use

```
HKEY key;
if ( RegOpenKeyEx( HKEY_CURRENT_USER,
      "Software\\Microsoft\\Visual C++ 2.0\\Dialog Editor",
      0, KEY_READ, &key)==ERROR_SUCCESS ) {
  DWORD ValueType, DataSize=50;
  LPBYTE Data;
  if ( RegQueryValueEx( key, "GridSize", NULL, &ValueType, Data, &DataSize )
    == ERROR_SUCCESS ){
    ...
  }
  RegCloseKey( key );
}
```

This retrieves the data, the size of the data, and the type of the data for the key GridSize.

RegSetValueEx

The RegSetValueEx function stores data in the value field of an open registry key. It can also set additional value and type information for the specified key.

```
LONG RegSetValueEx(
    HKEY        key,        // handle of key to set value for
    LPCTSTR     ValueName,  // address of value to set
    DWORD       Reserved,   // reserved
    DWORD       ValueType,  // flag for value type
    CONST BYTE* Data,       // address of value data
    DWORD       DataSize    // size of value data
  );
```

How To Use

```
HKEY key;
if( RegOpenKeyEx( HKEY_CURRENT_USER,
      "Software\\MyCompany\\MyApp", 0, KEY_WRITE, &key)==ERROR_SUCCESS){
  char* data="Jon Doe";
  long RetCode=RegSetValueEx( key,
  "Owner", 0, REG_SZ, (LPBYTE)data, strlen(data)+1 );
  RegCloseKey( key );
}
```

RegFlushKey

The RegFlushKey function writes all the attributes of the specified open key into the registry.

```
LONG RegFlushKey(
    HKEY  key                           // handle of key to write
  );
```

How To Use

```
HKEY key;
if( RegOpenKeyEx( HKEY_CURRENT_USER,
    "Software\\MyCompany\\MyApp", 0, KEY_WRITE, &key)==ERROR_SUCCESS){
  ...
  RegFlushKey( key );
  ...
  RegCloseKey( key );
}
```

`RegFlushKey` forces the registry to save all information to the disk immediately. The function does not return until the registry writes out all information. You should avoid using this function and use `RegCloseKey` instead.

Windows 95 Functions

The following functions are for read-mode and protected-mode virtual device drivers.

Real-Mode VxD Registry Functions

These functions are available to a real-mode VxD (virtual device driver) during load time. They can read information only from the `HKEY_LOCAL_MACHINE` tree. They cannot write information to this tree, and they cannot read from or write to any other tree. Here are the functions:

- `LDR_RegCloseKey`
- `LDR_RegEnumKey`
- `LDR_RegOpenKey`
- `LDR_RegQueryValue`
- `LDR_RegQueryValueEx`

Protected-Mode VxD Registry Functions

Restrictions for protected-mode VxD functions depend on the `DEVICE_INIT` phase of loading the VxD. Until the `DEVICE_INIT` phase is complete, these functions can only read information from the `HKEY_LOCAL_MACHINE` tree. When the `DEVICE_INIT` phase is complete, the VxD functions can read from and write to the whole registry. Here are the functions:

- `VMM_RegOpenKey`
- `VMM_RegCloseKey`
- `VMM_RegEnumKey`

■ VMM_RegQueryValue

■ VMM_RegQueryValueEx

■ VMM_RegCreateKey

■ VMM_RegDeleteKey

■ VMM_RegEnumValue

■ VMM_RegSetValueEx

■ VMM_RegFlushKey

Please see your documentation for more information on these functions. This concludes the section on the Windows 95 functions. Now you get your surprise.

Your Surprise

A reward is in order. Once again, MFC comes to the rescue and makes your programming to the registry easier. Enjoy!

```
CWinApp::SetRegistryKey
```

The SetRegistryKey function simplifies using the registry when you use MFC. It transparently reads and writes to the registry using either of the following CWinApp functions:

```
// Profile settings (to the app specific .INI file, or registry)

UINT GetProfileInt(LPCTSTR lpszSection, LPCTSTR lpszEntry, int Default);

BOOL WriteProfileInt(LPCTSTR lpszSection, LPCTSTR lpszEntry, int nValue);

CString GetProfileString( LPCTSTR lpszSection,
LPCTSTR lpszEntry,LPCTSTR lpszDefault=NULL);

BOOL WriteProfileString(LPCTSTR lpszSection, LPCTSTR lpszEntry,
```

If you were paying attention, you see that you can use these four functions just like you did before. However, now the information gets written to the registry. This is yet another awesome feature of MFC. Here are the declarations for the SetRegistryKey functions. One is for specifying a string resource as your registry key and the other is for specifying a string resouce as your registry key.

```
void SetRegistryKey( LPCTSTR lpszRegistryKey );
void SetRegistryKey( UINT nIDRegistryKey );
```

In order to get this trick to work, you must tell MFC that you want it to perform this trick. This is all the work you need to do:

```
BOOL CYour Win::InitInstance()
{
  SetDialogBkColor( );
  Enable3dControls( );
  SetRegistryKey( "MyCompanyName" );
```

```
LoadStdProfileSettings(5);   // Load standard INI file options (including MRU)
...
}
```

You simply call this function in your overridden `CWinApp::InitInstance` function before you call the `LoadStdProfileSettings` function. MFC creates the key `HKEY_CURRENT_USER\\Software\\MyCompanyName` if it does not exist. Then it creates a subkey with the name of your application. From then on, the other MFC functions write to the subkeys of the key `HKEY_CURRENT_USER\\Software\\MyCompanyName\\MyAppName`. To test this, create a new application in Visual C++ using the AppWizard. Then put the `SetRegistryKey` call in your `InitInstance` function, and compile your program. Run it, stop the application, and then run regedit.exe. Now look under the `HKEY_CURRENT_USER\\Software` key and you see your application in there. Voilà, MFC magic.

Summary

That wraps up the registry functions. Although there are many functions, you will find that you only use a few. Power users and hackers will use the more obscure functions, and if you use MFC, you will use the MFC functions mentioned in this chapter. The registry might seem intimidating to the uninitiated, but after reading this chapter you should be able to talk about programming for the registry with the best of them.

> **NOTE**
>
> All of the functions discussed in this chapter allow the adventurous programmer to write his or her own Registry Editor. For more information and programming examples, see the example in the MSVC20\EXAMPLES\WIN32\REGISTRY directory, and consult the Microsoft Developers Network CD.

Programming for Plug and Play Devices

6

by Robert M. Griswold, Jr.

IN THIS CHAPTER

In both beta and shipping form, Microsoft's Windows 95 is the first operating system to fully embrace and fully implement the industry's various Plug and Play specifications. As one of the founders of the Plug and Play effort, Microsoft is deservedly receiving praise for the wealth of functionality and ease of use that the operating system provides. In a Windows 95 environment, users benefit from the capability to install software and add-on peripherals with little or no intervention. Developers and system engineers finally are able to reliably manage device resource allocations and configurations using items such as enumerators, arbitrators, and device nodes.

Flexibility and progress do not, however, come without a price. Engineers that develop device drivers and applications to run within the Windows 95 Plug and Play environment inevitably will need to sharpen skills and learn new programming concepts and terminology. Following are some of the new terms that appear in this chapter:

Applet	A small application provided with Windows 95.
Devnode	This is a structure that describes a hardware device. When it appears in the runtime device node tree, a devnode structure describes a currently installed device. Devnode structures also appear in the OS registry, where they describe devices previously installed in the system.
INF files	INF files are device information files. These files describe the properties of devices to Windows 95 installers, configurators, arbitrators, and the Configuration Manager.
Key and Subkey	These are entries and sub-entries in the hardware tree of the registry. For example, \\HKEY_LOCAL_MACHINE\ENUM is both a key and subkey registry entry that describes the enumerator for the local machine.
Enumerator and Arbitrator	Enumerators identify devices on a bus, and arbitrators resolve conflicts among devices identified by the enumerators.
Configuration Manager	This is the runtime OS real and protected mode layer that directs all system device enumeration and configuration within Windows 95.
Device Manager	Device Manager is both a Control Panel applet and a set of API calls provided for Plug and Play applications running in Windows 95.
Class	A class is a definition of devices or Plug and Play resources that have common settings. MODEM, for example, is a class of devices.

VxD	A Virtual x Driver is a driver model that was defined for Windows 3.x, and is expanded to include dynamically loaded drivers for Windows 95.
Device node tree or hardware tree	This is the current state of the machine, as depicted in memory.
Plug and Play Association	A group of industry leaders that define the specifications for Plug and Play.

Plug and Play Association
P.O. Box 14070
Portland, OR 97124-9499
(503) 797-4244

The Windows 95 CD-ROM for software and device driver developers comes packed with useful utilities, sample code, and documentation. These are basic items for developers who want to get into the Windows 95 Plug and Play development cycle. This chapter builds on the concepts of the Plug and Play specifications, available from the Plug and Play Association. These same specifications are available on CompuServe, in the PC Plug and Play Forum. Therefore, this chapter focuses on how to put those concepts into use in Windows 95, and how the developer can more quickly get into the Plug and Play development cycle. Here are the five goals Microsoft has embraced for Plug and Play in Windows 95:

- Easy installation and configuration of new devices
- Seamless dynamic configuration changes
- Compatibility with installed base and old peripherals
- Operating system and hardware independence
- To reduce complexity and increase flexibility of hardware

Compatibility, the third item on the preceding list, is extremely important. In the long run, compatibility with the installed base of legacy devices will make or break the usability of Windows 95. You can bet end users who attempt to upgrade but cannot use their Jackson Peripherals turntable controller card are going to be upset. To this end, Microsoft has built a huge database of legacy detection routines. To see how this detection is carried out during installation, take a look at the MSDET.INF file. In this file, you will find entries that detail the steps Windows 95 takes to detect various legacy devices. Each of these entries instructs Windows 95 to detect by class which INF file to use while predicting the probability of failure when detecting such devices. This file resides in the WINDOWS\INF directory on the CD-ROM included with this book.

For developers of newer hardware and software, legacy detection is fast becoming less of an issue. Developers now can avoid the legacy detection process by making their newer hardware compliant with current Plug and Play specifications. By adhering to existing Plug and Play specifications, such as the *PCI Local Bus Specification* and the *Plug and Play ISA*

Specification, designers accomplish the goals outlined in the fourth and fifth items of the preceding list, operating system and hardware independence and increased flexibility of hardware. As mentioned previously, however, flexibility and progress do not come without a price. Microsoft's implementation of Plug and Play requires that designers and developers become familiar with the way in which Windows 95 handles issues such as product identification strings, resource allocation, and dynamic event handling. For example, Windows 95 requires that Plug and Play device drivers be dynamically loadable, and that some hardware vendors comply to ease-of-use guidelines put forth in Microsoft's *PC 95 Hardware Design Guide.*

To understand how Windows 95 behaves, it is important to remember who is in charge—the Configuration Manager (CM) is the boss. The Configuration Manager is the administrator of the device node tree (devnode tree), also called the hardware tree, by way of the OS registry.

The Configuration Manager is responsible for launching enumerators, which in turn invoke arbitrators, or call the Configuration Manager to invoke arbitrators. Device drivers and loaders ask for their device's attributes from the Configuration Manager. The Configuration Manager also interacts with the systemboard's Plug and Play BIOS to perform tasks such as systemboard device configuration, runtime event messaging (docking and undocking, for example), and legacy device resource enumeration. Figure 6.1 indicates the interaction between the Configuration Manager and the Windows 95 Plug and Play pieces.

FIGURE 6.1.

Windows 95 and the Plug and Play interaction.

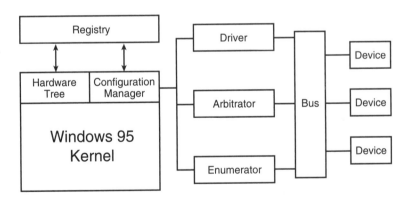

In order to keep things running smoothly, the Configuration Manager stores a comprehensive list of all system devices, enumerators, device drivers, and arbitrators in a structure called a device node tree (devnode tree).

Windows 95 employs the concept of the devnode tree structure in two separate places—in the system's disk-based registry and in the RAM-resident runtime hardware tree. Within the registry, the devnode tree stores the current hardware settings and configuration information for any hardware and software that has ever come in contact with the machine. When it appears in the runtime hardware tree, the device node tree contains an up-to-the-nanosecond snapshot of the machine's current operational state, including device ID, as well as driver and resource information.

If a runtime event occurs, such as the removal of a PCMCIA card, the hardware `devnode` tree is updated instantly to reflect the newly added or removed device. A partial `devnode` tree (taken from the Windows 95 Plug and Play DDK documentation) might look something like the following:

```
Htree\Root\0 - Root node of devnode tree
    \Root\*WPU0801\0 - Old-style Sound Blaster compatible sound device
    \Root\*WPU0C00\0 - Plug and Play BIOS
        \BIOS\*WPU0901\0 - Super VGA compatible display adapter
        \BIOS\*WPU0000\0 - AT Interrupt Controller
        \BIOS\*WPU0100\0 - AT Timer
        \BIOS\*WPU0200\0 - AT DMA Controller
        \BIOS\*WPU0301\0 - PS/2 Style Keyboard Controller
        \BIOS\*WPU0400\0 - Standard LPT printer port
        .
        .
```

Because the `devnode` tree is so critical to the operation of the Windows 95 machine, the Configuration Manager requires all Plug and Play enumerators and arbitrators that might have access to `devnode` tree contents to identify themselves. This is done through driver registration. The Configuration Manager has complete control over the current `devnode` tree.

Windows 95 enumerators and arbitrators are the same in concept as defined in the Plug and Play specifications. Generally speaking, the task of an enumerator is to identify and catalog system devices and device resource usage. Arbitrators, on the other hand, settle resource conflicts among devices that an enumerator, or series of enumerators have found to be in conflict. Windows 95 is structured in such a way that a single enumerator or arbitrator corresponds to a specific system bus, such as the ISA bus or PCI bus. Therefore, to settle a resource conflict between a PCI device and a Plug and Play ISA device, the Configuration Manager calls both the PCI and ISAWPU enumerators as well as the PCI and ISAWPU arbitrators.

Internally, the Configuration Manager holds many of the lowest level enumerators, including the root enumerator and the ISA bus enumerator. The Configuration Manager launches the system's enumeration process by invoking its internal low-level enumerators. When the Configuration Manager starts enumeration, with the root for example, it first identifies non-Plug and Play devices listed in the registry, and then arbitrates the resources for these devices. By doing this, the Configuration Manager masks the resources used by these devices as unavailable for Plug and Play devices.

Once the Configuration Manager has enumerated the system's non-Plug and Play or legacy devices, it then detects devices that respond to Plug and Play protocols, such as PCI and Plug and Play ISA plug-in adapters. In the case of the PCI and ISA buses, the Configuration Manager invokes enumerators to identify the installed devices, and then creates device nodes for them. Because this is done before the protected mode portion of Windows 95 is entered, the drivers are not yet loaded. The Configuration Manager identifies and resolves conflicts for any Plug and Play ISA or PCI bus devices and then loads any device drivers that correspond to those devices to which it has successfully assigned resources.

> **NOTE**
>
> To be fully compliant, Windows 95 device drivers must access Plug and Play information only through the Configuration Manager, and they must be dynamically loadable as well as loadable within protected mode. Unlike Windows 3.1 drivers, Windows 95 drivers do not appear in the SYSTEM.INI file, but instead are located and loaded in an "as needed" fashion, based on information contained in the registry.
>
> Windows 95 device drivers must be able to dynamically load and unload, based on Configuration Manager messages passed to their callback functions. Additionally, these device drivers should require a minimal amount of user intervention during user-oriented device installation, configuration, and selection processes. To achieve this type of fully featured Plug and Play support, Windows 95 device driver developers need to implement device installation routines, driver registration, and device information files.

In the following section I take a closer look at the Windows 95 process, starting with the Configuration Manager.

The Windows 95 Configuration Manager—The Boss

As mentioned previously, the Configuration Manager (CM) is the core of the Plug and Play environment in Windows 95. The Configuration Manager must handle all calls to the registry and allow device drivers to be loaded, unloaded, and executed. It also takes care of invoking enumerators and arbitrators so that the machine's platform remains stable. The Configuration Manager provides both real and protected mode Plug and Play support. Every Plug and Play operating system has some sort of configuration manager.

> **NOTE**
>
> All references in this chapter will refer to the Windows 95 Configuration Manager.

The Configuration Manager builds and maintains in memory the devnode tree, keeping track of all device nodes and how they interact with drivers and the registry. The fact that the Configuration Manager so tightly controls the interaction among device drivers and the registry is critical to the correct operation of a Plug and Play system. If the Configuration

Manager instead assigned this responsibility to the system's device drivers, the final state of the machine would be chaos. It would be utterly impossible to get one manufacturer after the next to comply with a certain procedure for loading, configuring, and identifying their hardware. The Windows 95 Configuration Manager device driver call interface provides a common structure for all device drivers and applications that need Plug and Play support.

The Configuration Manager has a vast pool of new Windows 95 calls. The following areas of functionality are provided by the Configuration Manager:

Device Node Services—Device node services are those services required by software wanting to access the devnode tree. The devnode tree exists in memory as a dynamically changing database. It cannot be accessed as a whole by any available Configuration Manager function call, but each node of the tree can be accessed and manipulated one at a time. The Configuration Manager provides this device node interface for drivers, specifically for access to the driver's nodes on the device node tree.

Logical Configuration Services—These services provide the means to determine the logical configuration of a certain device. These calls do not set the logical configurations. For a device, they allow the Configuration Manager to tell the requesting software what it can use. Typically, device drivers issue calls to logical device services to determine the current or possible settings for a particular hardware device. A logical configuration of a devnode is a set of resource descriptions for that devnode. For a modem, a valid logical configuration may describe the current COM port being used and the baud setting.

Resource Descriptor Services—This section of Configuration Manager calls allows the software to examine and change portions of the logical configuration. The calls allow changes to I/O ports, DMA channels, IRQ descriptors, memory ranges, and other resources as reported. These services also allow device drivers to assign I/O port aliases and I/O port decode ranges.

Device Loader Services—Device loader services allow device loaders to register with the Configuration Manager, perform their device driver load, and load device enumerators to manage the contents of the system's device nodes.

Enumerator Services—Enumeration services are provided so that an enumerator can register with the Configuration Manager as well as provide the Configuration Manager with information regarding the bus it enumerates.

Device Driver Services—Device driver services are similar to enumerator services. Device drivers register with the Configuration Manager and provide an interface for the Configuration Manager to call their specialized services. Importantly, a device driver invokes device driver services to supply Windows 95 with callback addresses, which point to callback functions within the driver. It is through the callback function mechanism that Windows 95 notifies the system's installed device drivers of runtime messages and events.

Arbitrator Services—Arbitrator services are provided as an add-on to the enumerator services. The resources associated with a particular bus must be arbitrated whenever a conflict occurs. Like enumerators, arbitrators must register with the Configuration Manager in order to be recognized. When the Configuration Manager needs a particular resource from a particular bus, it will call the appropriate registered arbitrator to provide the needed resource either by resolution or reassignment. Resource arbitration takes place during boot time or during the insertion of a new device. In the case of a PCMCIA device requesting ISA resources, the ISA bus arbitrator will be called during dynamic device driver loading.

Range List Services—Range lists are lists of consecutive I/O ports or memory addresses. These services exist so that arbitrators can determine whether a required range of I/O ports or memory addresses is available.

Registry Services—The all-inclusive registry needs services to get and receive information directly. These services allow device drivers and other elements to directly access and modify registry contents.

Hardware Profile Services—Hardware profiles define the current hardware present in the system. This usually is important in laptop and docking situations. These profiles carry a unique number that identifies the current profile; they can be read and changed with these services.

Miscellaneous Services—Some things just cannot be defined. The services defined here do everything from setting application execution parameters and checking the CRC of a buffer to locking or unlocking the Configuration Manager process.

The Configuration Manager's services are varied and in-depth. While an examination of all the Configuration Manager services could take up several chapters, this chapter examines a subset adequate for designing and implementing a compliant, working device driver. The calls outlined in this chapter also appear in the Win32 API DDK header file, CONFIGMG.H.

Configuration Manager Services Overview

The following is a complete list of function calls currently supported by the Configuration Manager in Windows 95 (compiled from the Windows 95 Plug and Play DDK documentation). The list is presented in such a way that the developer can get an understanding of how these calls are grouped.

Device Node Services

```
CONFIGMG_Create_DevNode
CONFIGMG_Disable_DevNode
CONFIGMG_Enable_DevNode
CONFIGMG_Get_Child
```

```
CONFIGMG_Get_Depth
CONFIGMG_Get_Device_ID
CONFIGMG_Get_Device_ID_Size
CONFIGMG_Get_DevNode_Status
CONFIGMG_Get_Parent
CONFIGMG_Get_Sibling
CONFIGMG_Locate_DevNode
CONFIGMG_Move_DevNode
CONFIGMG_Query_Remove_SubTree
CONFIGMG_Reenumerate_DevNode
CONFIGMG_Remove_SubTree
CONFIGMG_Remove_Unmarked_Children
CONFIGMG_Reset_Children_Marks
CONFIGMG_Setup_DevNode
```

Logical Configuration Services

```
CONFIGMG_Add_Empty_Log_Conf
CONFIGMG_Free_Log_Conf
CONFIGMG_Get_Alloc_Log_Conf
CONFIGMG_Get_First_Log_Conf
CONFIGMG_Get_Next_Log_Conf
CONFIGMG_ISAWPU_To_ CM
CONFIGMG_Read_Registry_Log_Confs
```

Resource Descriptor Services

```
CONFIGMG_Add_Res_Des
CONFIGMG_Free_Res_Des
CONFIGMG_Get_Next_Res_Des
CONFIGMG_Get_Res_Des_Data
CONFIGMG_Get_Res_Des_Data_Size
CONFIGMG_Modify_Res_Des
```

Device Loader Services

```
CONFIGMG_Get_DDBs
CONFIGMG_Get_Private_DWord
CONFIGMG_Load_DLVxD
CONFIGMG_Register_DevLoader
CONFIGMG_Set_Private_DWord
```

Enumerator Services

```
CONFIGMG_CallBack_Enumerator
CONFIGMG_Get_Bus_Info
CONFIGMG_Register_Enumerator
CONFIGMG_Set_Bus_Info
```

Device Driver Services

```
CONFIGMG_CallBack_Device_Driver
CONFIGMG_Get_Device_Driver_Private_DWord
CONFIGMG_Register_Device_Driver
CONFIGMG_Set_Device_Driver_Private_DWord
```

Enumerator and Device Driver Associated Messages

```
CONFIG_ENUMERATE
CONFIG_FILTER
CONFIG_REMOVE
CONFIG_START
CONFIG_STOP
CONFIG_TEST
```

Arbitrator Services

```
CONFIGMG_Deregister_Arbitrator
CONFIGMG_Query_Arbitrator_Free_Data
CONFIGMG_Query_Arbitrator_Free_Size
CONFIGMG_Register_Arbitrator
```

Arbitrator Associated Messages

```
ARB_FORCE_ALLOC
ARB_QUERY_FREE
ARB_RELEASE_ALLOC
ARB_REMOVE
ARB_RETEST_ALLOC
ARB_SET_ALLOC
ARB_TEST_ALLOC
```

Range List Services

CONFIGMG_Add_Range
CONFIGMG_Create_Range_List
CONFIGMG_Delete_Range
CONFIGMG_Dump_Range_List
CONFIGMG_Dup_Range_List
CONFIGMG_First_Range
CONFIGMG_Free_Range_List
CONFIGMG_Intersect_Range_List
CONFIGMG_Invert_Range_List
CONFIGMG_Next_Range
CONFIGMG_Test_Range_Available

Registry Services

CONFIGMG_Get_DevNode_Key
CONFIGMG_Get_DevNode_Key_Size
CONFIGMG_Read_Registry_Value
CONFIGMG_Write_Registry_Value

Hardware Profile Services

CONFIGMG_Fail_Change_HW_Prof
CONFIGMG_Get_HW_Prof_Flags
CONFIGMG_Query_Change_HW_Prof
CONFIGMG_Recompute_HW_Prof
CONFIGMG_Set_HW_Prof
CONFIGMG_Set_HW_Prof_Flags

Miscellaneous Services

CONFIGMG_Call_At_Appy_Time
CONFIGMG_Get_CRC_CheckSum
CONFIGMG_Get_Version
CONFIGMG_Lock
CONFIGMG_Process_Events_Now
CONFIGMG_Set_Private_Problem
CONFIGMG_Unlock
CONFIGMG_Yield

Specific Configuration Manager Functions

These Configuration Manager API functions (compiled from the Windows 95 Plug and Play DDK documentation), while they are not the only ones worth looking at, do hold value for the device driver writer. The enumeration, driver loader, and register functions should be understood by the developer for a complete understanding of Plug and Play in Windows 95.

All Configuration Manager calls outlined here return the type CONFIGRET, as defined in the header file CONFIGMG.H. The type definition of CONFIGRET is a "Standardized" return type, RETURN_TYPE, which is really just a double word (DWORD) type definition.

The following Configuration Manager call creates a new logical configuration entry with no resource descriptor.

```
CONFIGRET CONFIGMG_Add_Empty_Log_Conf(PLOG_CONF plcLogConf, DEVNODE dnDevNode,
PRIORITY Priority, ULONG ulFlags)
```

This call will return one of the following values:

```
CR_SUCCESS
CR_INVALID_FLAG
CR_INVALID_POINTER
CR_INVALID_DEVNODE
CR_INVALID_PRIORITY
CR_OUT_OF_MEMORY
```

plcLogConf	This address receives the handle of the created logical configuration.
dnDevNode	This is the address of the device node for which the logical configuration is being created.
Priority	This entry specifies the priority of the logical configuration as one of the following values:

LCPRI_FORCECONFIG	Specifies a forced configuration.
LCPRI_BOOTCONFIG	Specifies a boot configuration.
LCPRI_HARDWIRED	Specifies that the configuration is hardwired.
LCPRI_DESIRED	Specifies a desired configuration.
LCPRI_NORMAL	Specifies a functioning configuration.
LCPRI_SUBOPTIMAL	Specifies the least desired configuration or configurations.
LCPRI_RESTART	Indicates that Windows should restart.
LCPRI_REBOOT	Indicates that the machine should

	reboot.
LCPRI_POWEROFF	Indicates that a power cycle should take place.
LCPRI_HARDRECONFIG	Indicates that a hardware change is needed.

ulFlags	This entry is either BASIC_LOG_CONF or FILTERED_LOG_CONF, combined with either PRIORITY_EQUAL_FIRST or PRIORITY_EQUAL_LAST.
BASIC_LOG_CONF	Specifies that the supplied configuration is the basic logical configuration.
FILTERED_LOG_CONF	Specifies that the supplied configuration is a filtered logical configuration.
PRIORITY_EQUAL_FIRST	Specifies that the configuration is first and has the same priority.
PRIORITY_EQUAL_LAST	Specifies that the configuration is last and has the same priority.

The following Configuration Manager call adds a new resource descriptor to the specified logical configuration.

```
CONFIGRET CONFIGMG_Add_Res_Des(PRES_DES prdResDes, LOG_CONF lcLogConf,
RESOURCEID ResourceID, PFARVOID ResourceData, ULONG ResourceLen, ULONG ulFlags)
```

This call will return one of the following values:

```
CR_SUCCESS
CR_INVALID_FLAG
CR_INVALID_POINTER
CR_OUT_OF_MEMORY
CR_INVALID_LOG_CONF
CR_INVALID_RESOURCE_ID
```

plcLogConf	This is the address of the referenced logical configuration.
dnDevNode	This is the address of the device node for which the resource descriptor is being added.
ulFlags	These flags must be 0.

The following Configuration Manager call returns a handle to the first logical configuration of the device node's specified type.

```
CONFIGRET CONFIGMG_Get_First_Log_Conf(PLOG_CONF plcLogConf, DEVNODE dnDevNode,
ULONG ulFlags)
```

This call will return one of the following values:

```
CR_SUCCESS
CR_INVALID_FLAG
CR_INVALID_POINTER
```

```
CR_NO_MORE_LOG_CONF
```

plcLogConf   This address receives the handle of the retrieved logical configuration.

dnDevNode   This is the address of the device node for which the logical configuration is being retrieved.

ulFlags   These flags should represent one of the following values:

    ALLOC_LOG_CONF   Specifies the allocation element and can be used for the handling of dynamic configuration processing, such as `CONFIG_DYNAMIC_START`.

    BASIC_LOG_CONF   Requests the basic logical configuration.

    FILTERED_LOG_CONF   Requests the filtered logical configuration.

    BOOT_LOG_CONF   Requests the boot allocation element.

The following Configuration Manager call returns a handle to the next logical configuration, which follows the last configuration call.

```
CONFIGRET CONFIGMG_Get_Next_Log_Conf(PLOG_CONF plcLogConf, LOG_CONF lcLogConf,
ULONG ulFlags)
```

This call will return one of the following values:

```
CR_SUCCESS
CR_INVALID_FLAG
CR_INVALID_POINTER
CR_INVALID_DEVNODE
CR_NO_MORE_LOG_CONF
CR_INVALID_LOG_CONF
```

plcLogConf   This is the address of the next logical configuration.

lcLogConf   This is the current logical configuration. Remember, logical configurations are always retrieved in priority order.

ulFlags   These flags must be 0.

The following Configuration Manager call will invoke the `CONFIG_ENUMERATE` function of the specified device node's enumerator.

```
CONFIGRET CONFIGMG_Reenumerate_DevNode(DEVNODE dnDevNode, ULONG ulFlags)
```

This call will return one of the following values:

```
CR_SUCCESS
CR_INVALID_FLAG
```

dnDevNode   This is the address of the device node that will be re-enumerated.

ulFlags   These flags must be 0.

The following call is used to register a configuration handler for a device node. This typically is called after the `devnode` driver has registered the device loader, enumerator, and arbitrator, as needed.

```
CONFIGRET CONFIGMG_Register_Device_Driver(DEVNODE dnDevNode,
CMCONFIGHANDLER Handler, ULONG ulRefData, ULONG ulFlags)
```

This call will return one of the following values:

```
CR_SUCCESS
CR_INVALID_FLAG
CR_INVALID_DEVNODE
CR_NOT_SYSTEM_VM
```

dnDevNode	This is the devnode that will have the driver registered for it.
Handler	This is the device driver entry point that will handle all device driver configuration functions. This parameter can be NULL if the device driver either does not need to monitor or cannot handle configuration events. A static driver is an example of a driver that cannot handle configuration events.
ulRefData	This is the reference data that will be passed back to the handler.
ulFlags	STATIC indicates that the driver does not handle dynamic events. If the flag is set to either DISABLEABLE or REMOVABLE, then it will be alerted to events that require those actions. The flags can have one or more of the following settings:

```
        CM_REGISTER_DEVICE_DRIVER_STATIC

        CM_REGISTER_DEVICE_DRIVER_DISABLEABLE

        CM_REGISTER_DEVICE_DRIVER_REMOVABLE
```

The following Configuration Manager call is used to indicate that the calling VxD can be a device loader.

```
CONFIGRET CONFIGMG_Register_DevLoader(PVMMDDB pDDB, ULONG ulFlags)
```

This call will return one of the following values:

```
CR_SUCCESS
CR_INVALID_FLAG
CR_INVALID_API
```

pDDB	This represents the static VxD that is ready to be a device loader.
ulFlags	These flags must be 0.

Configuration events usually are posted to VxDs to tell them to perform some sort of action. The following are just a few of the call back messages that can be sent to registered VxDs:

CONFIG_REMOVE	Tells the called VxD that the indicated devnode should stop using its configuration.
CONFIG_START	Tells the VxD to start a new configuration process for the indicated devnode.
CONFIG_STOP	Results in the same action as CONFIG_REMOVE.

CONFIG_TEST   Instructs the VxD to check to see if the associated `devnode` can have its configuration changed.

The Registry Warehouse

No store of information is more critical to the operation of the Windows 95 machine than the registry. The *registry* is a hierarchical representation of the computer, its buses, device nodes, and associated software. This warehouse of information represents not only how the machine is operating right now, but also how it has operated in the past. Any device, device driver, or software ever presented to the machine is listed here. The registry can be accessed through the Configuration Manager, through drivers or VxDs that implement the registry services, or through utilities such as REGEDIT.EXE. The main purpose of the registry is to keep track of how the machine is currently set up and to provide a mechanism for all portions of the machine to exchange data.

The registry is constructed similar to the hardware or device node tree. It has a root, branches, and leaves or children. Figure 6.2 illustrates a typical registry listing, as seen in the program REGEDIT.EXE.

FIGURE 6.2.

REGEDIT.EXE display showing HKEY_CURRENT_CONFIG *branch.*

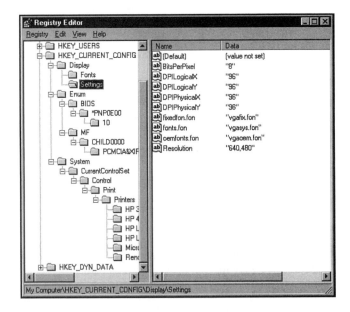

Figure 6.2 shows HKEY_CURRENT_CONFIG, but many other keys exist in the registry. The following are predefined keys defined for use by the registry:

HKEY_CLASSES_ROOT   Contains information about how files and documents can be accessed through OLE information.

HKEY_CURRENT_USER	Contains information about the current user's configuration. The HKEY_USERS key also represents this information.
HKEY_LOCAL_MACHINE	Holds information about any hardware and software ever used with the computer.
HKEY_USERS	Contains information about the users of the computer. Holds user-defined settings for specific hardware and software.
HKEY_CURRENT_CONFIG	Holds information about the hardware configuration of the computer.
HKEY_DYN_DATA	Contains dynamic data—that is, data about events that have occurred.

The registry implements this information for Plug and Play and non-Plug and Play elements of the system. In the Plug and Play world, the registry is where enumerators and arbitrators store the assigned values of the machine. These can be found in three places: HKEY_LOCAL_MACHINE, HKEY_CURRENT_USER, and HKEY_CURRENT_CONFIG. These keys store information regarding the global settings of the machine, the current user's preferences for the machine, and the machines current configuration. Any or all of these keys or their subkeys can be accessed through appropriate registry calls by using the Win32 APIs or by dynamic changes to the system and the invoking of enumerators.

Enumerators store their bus information in these keys. The subkey, or branch, used for this is the ENUM subkey. The \\HKEY_LOCAL_MACHINE\ENUM branch is the place in which the Windows 95 machine keeps most of the Plug and Play enumeration information. Each enumerator has its own appropriate entry, with each enumerated device appearing as a sub-branch or child to it. This hierarchical approach allows each associated enumerator and arbitrator to manage each of its own resources in the registry.

Entries for each child identify the child, how it is configured or can be configured, and which particular settings it should use. These entries are called *string values*, or *key values*. String values identify the manufacturer, the settings appropriate to the particular bus, the serial number, and vendor unique information. Here is where each particular device can be seen and has its settings added or changed. If a device requires settings not originally put in by the setup of the device, an experienced developer can go directly to the registry entry for that device and make the changes. By changing the settings of the device node through the editing of key values, a device driver developer is able to test the response of his or her driver to a battery of hypothetical settings.

The registry also keeps track of settings used for the interface, software installed, and reaction to events that can change the operation of the machine. Settings for the applets (mini-applications) that come with Windows 95 are kept in the HKEY_CURRENT_USER\Software\Microsoft\Windows\CurrentVersion\Applets branch of the registry. These settings are a good starting point for educating yourself on how changes to the registry are achieved when using a program.

For example, look at the entries for the Paint program. You will find a key setting called Text that holds all the settings for the last use of the Text tool. If the Text tool has never been used, the values in this key will be empty or null. Run the Paint applet, use the Text tool, and choose a font. The font registry setting for the Paint applet now reflects this selected font setting. Any changes made at the registry level will be reflected when the Paint applet starts up again.

The preceding Paint example helps illustrate the functionality of registry settings. When the user runs an application such as Paint, the application makes registry services calls during its load sequence to determine the user settings and preferences. This same concept is used when Windows 95 processes the registry for the loading of VxDs. The Configuration Manager finds entries for devices that need VxDs loaded, and calls these devices, whose resources are already set, and passes these to the drivers.

In the case of an ISA Plug and Play SCSI board, for example, the Configuration Manager first calls the ISAWPU enumerator, which verifies or gives the board resources. The SCSI board will have its driver initialized with a handle that points to the device node that caused it to load. This loads the associated SCSI Miniport driver with the right settings for the board it should control. All these calls are part of the registry services.

Buses, Nodes, and Enumeration

The hierarchical representation of the registry is the foundation on which the concepts of buses, nodes, and enumerators are built. The topics of buses, nodes, and enumerators go together because nodes cannot be seen on buses without enumerators. Even though the writing of an enumerator will not be covered in this chapter, understanding how enumerators are employed by Windows 95 is important.

The sample source code in this chapter does not include a sample enumerator because the sample driver deals with a Plug and Play ISA adapter, which resides on a bus that is supported by enumerators built into Windows 95. If you have devised a new bus that does not have an enumerator built into Windows 95, then your driver should provide an enumerator for that bus and a registration routine for that enumerator.

An example of a bus that does not currently have enumeration support via a built-in Windows 95 enumerator is the *infrared* (IR) bus. If it existed, the IR bus enumerator would be responsible for the identification of all IR devices attached to the system. When invoked by the Configuration Manager, the IR bus enumerator would supply a device node for each device it was able to identify on the IR bus.

The buses associated with a Windows 95 machine can be as varied as the number of users that can be expected to use the operating system. The following are some of the buses that will be on most Windows 95 machines:

`\Enum\Root`	The Root bus represents legacy-style devices that have been added to the registry. Systemboard devices, such as the DMA controller and the keyboard controller, exist here if no Plug and Play BIOS is installed in the machine.
`\Enum\BIOS`	The BIOS "bus" actually is the systemboard and associated systemboard devices that the Plug and Play BIOS identified.
`\Enum\ISAWPU`	The ISAWPU bus contains all of the devices that responded to the ISA Plug and Play isolation protocol.
`\Enum\PCI`	The PCI bus holds information regarding PCI devices that the OS was able to locate during its enumeration process and also includes a description of the system's PCI bus hierarchy.
`\Enum\PCMCIA`	The PCMCIA bus contains entries for each installed PCMCIA device from which Windows 95 was able to extract configuration tuples. Figure 6.3 shows an example of an attached PCMCIA device and the manufacturer's device settings.
`\Enum\EISA`	The EISA bus holds information, not only from the system's EISA cards, but from the EISA-style Extended System Configuration Data (ESCD), maintained in nonvolatile storage by the systemboard's BIOS.
`\Enum\COM`	The COM bus contains information identifying those devices attached to the system's COM ports, including those that adhere to the *Plug and Play External COM Port Specification.* Devices that adhere to this specification self identify by supplying the COM port enumerator with a serial device identification header whose format appears both in the *External COM Port Specification* and in the *Windows 95 Hardware Design Guide.*
`\Enum\SCSI`	The SCSI bus represents the devices found on an attached SCSI adapter. These devices may or may not be compliant with Plug and Play SCSI.
`\Enum\ESDI`	All standard hard drives (MFM, ESDI, IDE, EIDE) are identified on the ESDI bus, whether they actually exist on legacy-style controllers or on the systemboard.

In the future, designers will introduce to the Plug and Play system many new and dissimilar buses. As new bus standards emerge, manufacturers will be able to follow the rules of registration to dynamically add the definition of these newer buses to the registry. In the future, look for buses such as SSA, FIREWIRE, 1394, IR, as well as others to appear in the registry. The fact that the registry contains a particular bus entry does not guarantee that the bus is valid currently or even installed. Depending on how the driver or enumerator for a specific bus updates, its registry entry might indicate missing devices or resources that once belonged to devices on the bus but have been reallocated elsewhere. This is often the case if the bus does not support dynamic events—that is, the runtime insertion and removal of devices on a bus. The SCSI bus is an example of a bus that does not support dynamic event response. Because the definition for SCSI, even Plug and Play SCSI, does not allow for live insertion, activation, or removal of devices, the SCSI bus enumerator has no requirement to register itself into any dynamic reporting sequence.

FIGURE 6.3.

An example of an HKEY_LOCAL_MACHINE\ Enum\PCMCIA entry in the registry.

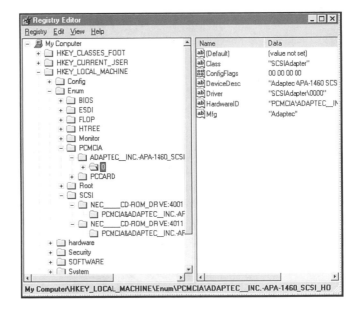

The Win32 APIs for registry services allow bus enumerators to add and delete nodes or subkeys from registry entries. Additionally, registry services allow applications to iteratively examine each node that belongs to a given bus or group of buses. When a device driver loads, the enumerator that corresponds to the driver's bus enumerates and identifies all devices on that bus. Once a device driver has loaded, it issues calls to the registry to add device nodes for each device it has located during its load sequence. Later, if the driver unloads or reloads, it can reissue calls to the OS registry services to again update the registry's device node contents.

Using the preceding example of the SCSI adapter, consider the user who switches on his or her external CD-ROM drive after the machine is up and running. After the user switches on the CD-ROM, the device will not necessarily appear on the bus. Why? Because the SCSI Miniport driver is not accustomed to late arriving devices; it never goes out to scan for devices on the bus after boot time. To see the new device, the driver needs to be told to enumerate the bus again. SCSI Miniport drivers only do this when they are called from the initial load.

The user can re-enumerate the devices on the SCSI bus by running System from the Control Panel, selecting Device Manager, and expanding the SCSI Adapters section. You can demonstrate this on your own system as well. After running System from the Control Panel as just described, select the appropriate SCSI adapter and choose Refresh. This forces the dynamically loaded Miniport driver to reinitialize, and dynamically reload.

If the new device attached to the bus, a CD-ROM in this case, has been seen before and is supported by the driver that enumerated the bus, it becomes an available device. In this case, the CD-ROM will appear as a useable device because at runtime the Device Manager calls the SCSI Miniport driver (via the registry) to re-enumerate the SCSI bus and each of its attached devices.

The following selected registry services calls are declared in the Win32 API DDK header file VMM.H.

The following call creates the specified key or opens the key if it already exists in the registry.

```
LONG RegCreateKey(HKEY hkey, LPTSTR lpszSubKey, LPHKEY lphkey)
```

This call may return one of the following values:

```
ERROR_SUCCESS
ERROR_CANNOT_OPEN_REGFILE
ERROR_INSUFFICIENT_MEMORY
ERROR_INVALID_PARAMETER
ERROR_REGFILE_READERROR
ERROR_REGFILE_WRITEERROR
ERROR_REGKEY_INVALIDKEY
ERROR_FILE_NOT_FOUND
ERROR_VALUE_NOT_FOUND
```

hkey
: Handle of the caller-selected key. If the key already exists, the registry will open it; otherwise, the registry will create the key using the caller's arguments.

lpszSubKey
: This string value specifies the subkey to be opened. If this is NULL, then the hkey must be one of the following predefined keys:

```
HKEY_CLASSES_ROOT
HKEY_CURRENT_USER
HKEY_LOCAL_MACHINE
HKEY_USERS
```

lphkey
: Holds the address of the HKEY returned for a create or open command that was successful.

The following call opens the subkey specified in the lpszSubKey variable.

```
LONG RegOpenKey(HKEY hkey, LPTSTR lpszSubKey, LPHKEY lphkey)
```

This call may return one of the following values:

```
ERROR_SUCCESS
ERROR_CANNOT_OPEN_REGFILE
ERROR_INSUFFICIENT_MEMORY
ERROR_INVALID_PARAMETER
ERROR_REGFILE_READERROR
ERROR_REGFILE_WRITEERROR
ERROR_REGKEY_INVALIDKEY
ERROR_FILE_NOT_FOUND
ERROR_VALUE_NOT_FOUND
```

`hkey`	This is the handle of the previously opened key and can specify one of the predefined key values. See `RegCreateKey`.
`lpszSubKey`	This null-terminated string specifies the subkey to be opened. If the subkey is not required, then the string can be `NULL`.
`lphkey`	Points to a variable that receives the handle of the opened or created key. The key opened by this service is a subkey of the key which `hkey` identifies. If `lpszSubKey` is either `NULL` or a pointer to an empty string, then the service returns `hkey`.

The following call closes the previously opened registry key.

```
LONG RegCloseKey(HKEY hkey)
```

This call may return one of the following values:

```
ERROR_SUCCESS
ERROR_BADKEY
ERROR_KEY_DELETED
ERROR_REGKEY_INVALIDKEY
```

`hkey`	This is the handle of the registry key to close.

The following registry call deletes the specified key that was previously opened. If the call is successful, then all other calls that have this key specified or opened will fail with the `ERROR_KEY_DELETED` error.

```
LONG RegDeleteKey(HKEY hkey, LPTSTR lpszSubKey)
```

This call may return one of the following values:

```
ERROR_SUCCESS
ERROR_CANNOT_OPEN_REGFILE
ERROR_INSUFFICIENT_MEMORY
ERROR_INVALID_PARAMETER
ERROR_REGFILE_READERROR
ERROR_REGFILE_WRITEERROR
ERROR_REGKEY_INVALIDKEY
ERROR_FILE_NOT_FOUND
ERROR_VALUE_NOT_FOUND
```

`hkey`	This is the handle of the previously opened key.
`lpszSubKey`	This null-terminated string specifies the subkey to be deleted.

The following call removes the named value from the given registry key.

```
LONG RegDeleteValue(HKEY hkey, LPTSTR lpszValue)
```

This call may return one of the following values:

```
ERROR_SUCCESS
ERROR_CANNOT_OPEN_REGFILE
ERROR_INSUFFICIENT_MEMORY
ERROR_INVALID_PARAMETER
ERROR_REGFILE_READERROR
ERROR_REGFILE_WRITEERROR
ERROR_REGKEY_INVALIDKEY
ERROR_FILE_NOT_FOUND
ERROR_VALUE_NOT_FOUND
```

hkey   This is the handle of the previously opened key. It can specify one of the predefined key values. See `RegCreateKey`.

lpszValue   This null-terminated string specifies the value in the named key to be deleted. If the value is NULL, then the specified key's NULL value is deleted.

The following call enumerates subkeys of the given open registry key, retrieving the name of one subkey each time the service is called.

```
LONG RegEnumKey(HKEY hkey, DWORD iSubKey, LPTSTR lpszName, DWORD cBuffer)
```

This call may return one of the following values:

```
ERROR_SUCCESS
ERROR_CANNOT_OPEN_REGFILE
ERROR_INSUFFICIENT_MEMORY
ERROR_INVALID_PARAMETER
ERROR_REGFILE_READERROR
ERROR_REGFILE_WRITEERROR
ERROR_REGKEY_INVALIDKEY
ERROR_FILE_NOT_FOUND
ERROR_VALUE_NOT_FOUND
```

hkey   This is the handle of the key to enumerate, as previously opened or created, and can specify one of the predefined key values. See `RegCreateKey`.

iSubKey   This is the index for the subkey to retrieve. On the first call this is 0, but it changes with each subsequent call.

lpszName   This is the address of the buffer that receives the subkey name.

cBuffer   This value holds the size, in bytes, of the specified subkey buffer.

The following call enumerates values for the given open registry key. The service copies one indexed value name and data block for the key each time it is called.

```
LONG RegEnumValue(HKEY hkey, DWORD iValue, LPTSTR lpszValue, LPDWORD
lpcbValueName, LPDWORD lpdwReserved, LPDWORD lpdwType, LPBYTE lpbData,
LPDWORD lpcbData)
```

This call may return one of the following values:

```
ERROR_SUCCESS
ERROR_CANNOT_OPEN_REGFILE
ERROR_INSUFFICIENT_MEMORY
ERROR_INVALID_PARAMETER
ERROR_REGFILE_READERROR
ERROR_REGFILE_WRITEERROR
ERROR_REGKEY_INVALIDKEY
ERROR_FILE_NOT_FOUND
ERROR_VALUE_NOT_FOUND
```

`hkey`	This is the handle of the key to enumerate, as previously opened or created, and can specify one of the predefined key values. See `RegCreateKey`.
`iValue`	Double that holds the index of value to be retrieved.
`lpszValue`	This is the address of the buffer that receives the name of the value enumerated. If no value name is returned, then this address can be `NULL`.
`lpcbValueName`	This double holds the address of a variable that contains the size of the `lpszValue` buffer. This represents the size of the retrieved value name. If `lpszValue` is `NULL`, then this also can be `NULL`.
`lpdwReserved`	This is reserved pointer. It must be `NULL`.
`lpdwType`	This is the address of the variable that receives the type code for the value data entry. It can be one of the following values:

`REG_BINARY`	Defines binary data, which can be in any form, and is a specific number of bytes.
`REG_SZ`	This defines a null-terminated UNICODE or ANSI string.
`NULL`	Defines that no data is required.

`lpbData`	Holds the address of buffer that receives the data for the value entry. If the value data is not required, then it can be `NULL`.
`lpcbData`	This holds the address of a variable that contains the size of the `lpbData` buffer.

Classes, Installers, and the Device Manager

Within the Windows 95 registry, a class is a group of similar logical devices, such as keyboards, SCSI controllers, and display controllers. The Windows 95 registry sorts devices by class in order to simplify and streamline the Device Manager's chore of finding, loading, and installing devices. Most manufacturers of mainstream products rely on classes already installed in the system. For example, manufacturers of IDE drives expect Windows 95 to maintain information for their devices in `HKEY_LOCAL_MACHINE\System\CurrentControlSet\Services\Class\hdc`, which is the built-in class for standard hard drives.

As Windows 95 enumerates the system, its enumerators locate and report devices to the Configuration Manager. Although Windows has located these devices, it has not yet loaded their corresponding device drivers.

Once an enumerator has reported a newly found device to the Configuration Manager, the Configuration Manager calls the Device Manager to load any device drivers associated with that device. The Device Manager, in turn, invokes the default installer for the class to which the new device belongs.

Each class within the registry has a default installer whose primary job is to locate and load device drivers for devices that belong to that class. Once the class installer has loaded a device driver, it calls the installer within that device driver, allowing the device driver to perform any device-specific startup operations.

The registry is structured in such a way that each class can support the installation of default devices, special devices, and devices that are not predefined. The installer associated with a class is the device, usually a dynamic link library, that is responsible for doing everything from adding the new class to loading the driver. The Device Manager provides API calls that allow the installer to configure device drivers, update INF files, and manipulate the registry. The installer can be a stand-alone module, or it can invoke Device Manager functions to assist in the installation sequence.

Figure 6.4 shows the Device Manager representation of an enumerated PCMCIA device.

FIGURE 6.4.

The same class entry from Figure 6.2, as shown by the Device Manager applet.

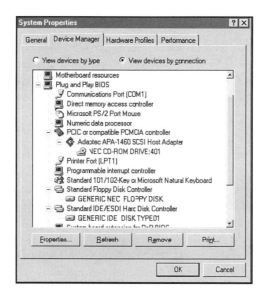

The following is a list of classes, taken from the registry editor of Windows 95, and the associated installer entry for each class:

Class	Installer
CDROM	IOSCLASS.DLL, `CDROMClassInstall`
Display adapters	SETUPX.DLL, `Display_ClassInstaller`
Sound, video and game controllers	MMCI.DLL
Modem	MODEM.CPL
Mouse	SETUPX.DLL, `Mouse_ClassInstaller`
Network adapters	NETDI.DLL
PCMCIA socket	MSPCIC.DLL
Printer	MSPRINT.DLL
System devices	SYSCLASS.DLL

These installers are used to install and load the listed devices. Some devices do not use these class installers. They rely on the system or use their own installer to detect them. For example, IDE hard drives do not have an Installer section listed; instead, they use a Loader section, `*IOS`. The preceding list shows that most of the installers are DLLs, but this is not the only way to perform installation. There is no requirement that a class or device must be installed using the Device Manager configuration–Manager Installer method. The Modem Installer has a .CPL extension, which means that it is a Control Panel device. To install a new modem, you run the Modem Tool applet in the Control Panel.

If a class does not already exist, the Device Manager must install it as a new class, in which case the Device Manager invokes the installer for the class to assist in performing the installation. Every installer is required to have a `ClassInstall` section that the Device Manager can call to ask the installer to carry out certain functions. When the Device Manager calls the `ClassInstall` function, which the installer has registered with the Device Manager, it will pass two arguments. One argument identifies what the Device Manager wants the installer to do, and the other argument indicates which `devnode` the installer should use. If the installer has not implemented the function for which the Device Manager is asking, then it returns `ERR_DI_DO_DEFAULT`. This return code instructs the Device Manager to perform the default action for the request it posted to the installer.

In the following code, the Device Manager makes requests to the installer by calling the Win32 API function `DiCallClassInstaller`.

The DiCallClassInstaller function forwards Device Manager messages to the current class installer call-back function. The format of the DICallClassInstaller function appears here:

```
RETERR DiCallClassInstaller(DI_FUNCTIONS diFctn, LPDEVICE_INFO lpdi)
```

This function returns one of the following values:

OK   The call to DiCallClassInstaller succeeded.

ERR_DI_*xxx*   DiCallClassInstaller returned an error.

Here is the argument for DiCallClassInstaller:

lpdi

Here is a pointer to a DEVICE_INFO struct for the device whose class installer is to be called:

diFctn

The following items are the defined Device Installer function messages:

DIF_SELECTDEVICE	This request asks the installer to choose a driver for a new device. If the installer can handle the request, then it prompts the user to select the device; otherwise, it asks the Device Manager to make the request of the user. Alternatively, it can ask for a new driver for an existing device.
DIF_INSTALLDEVICE	This request directs the installer to install the requested driver. When the installer can install the driver, it does; otherwise, it directs the Device Manager to install the driver. If the installer requires other files before continuing (such as dynamic link libraries), it directs the user for input regarding the source of these files and then returns to the Device Manager to complete the default action associated with this request.
DIF_PROPERTIES	This request prompts the installer to retrieve the appropriate property pages for the device or driver. If the installer does not implement this request, then the Device Manager uses the default property page for displaying the device's properties.
DIF_REMOVE	This request usually is implemented by all installers. The Device Manager makes this request of the installer to remove a specified device. For example, if the Device Manager Control Panel applet is running, then the deletion of a device listed prompts this request of the installer for the device.

DIF_FIRSTTIMESETUP	This request is only used with installers for first-time Windows 95 installation. This prompts the installer to take care of any special handling of the device or driver for the installation. For example, the installer might configure nonvolatile RAM on a device when the device is first installed.
DIF_CALCDISKSPACE	As its name implies, the DIF_CALCDISKSPACE message instructs the installer to calculate the disk space available for the installation. If the installer defers to the Device Manager for this, then the Device Manager will take the information out of the associated INF entry.
DIF_DESTROYPRIVATEDATA	This request tells the installer to free any memory associated with the device in its DEVICE_INFO structure. The Device Manager sends this function just before it deletes the DEVICE_INFO structure.
DIF_SELECTCLASSDRIVERS	This request, as well as the next two, are provided by the Device Manager for installers that need to manage or install multiple drivers for one device. For example, a SCSI board might have a secondary driver other than the Miniport driver installed. This request is a way for the Device Manager to ask the installer to find out. If any of these calls are passed back to the Device Manager for processing, then the default action "do nothing" is taken. This message enables the Device Manager to request that the installer locate and load the additional drivers.
DIF_VALIDATECLASSDRIVERS	This request prompts the installer to validate all the settings for the specified devices.
DIF_INSTALLCLASSDRIVERS	After the drivers have been selected and validated, this request is posted to prompt the installer to install the drivers.
DIF_MOVEDEVICE	This request tells the installer that the device specified is being moved to a different location in the registry structure.
DIF_DETECT	This request instructs the installer to detect any devices of its class. This request undoubtedly will cause the enumerator for the class to run.
DIF_INSTALLWIZARD	This request tells the installer to add pages to the Install Wizard for the class.

`DIF_DESTROYWIZARDDATA`	This request is posted to the installer following a wizard installation. The Device Manager instructs the installer to delete any private memory it requested for data during the installation.
`DIF_PROPERTYCHANGE`	This request instructs the installer to prepare for changes due to the disabling, enabling, or changing of resources.

The installer and Device Manager do more than just communicate through the `ClassInstall` function. The Device Manager supplies a full set of API calls that enable the installer to perform many different installation tasks. The majority of these tasks rely on the `DEVICE_INFO` structure that is defined for each class device being manipulated. To retrieve a list of the devices for a particular class in the `DEVICE_INFO` structure, the installer can call `DiGetClassDevs`. This function returns a linked list of all the individual devices.

The following structure and Table 6.1 are condensed from the Windows 95 Plug and Play DDK documentation. Together, they represent the `DEVICE_INFO` structure.

```
DEVICE_INFO
typedef struct {
    CHAR szDescription[LINE_LEN], szRegSubkey[MAX_DEVNODE_ID_LEN],
        szClassName[MAX_CLASS_NAME_LEN];
    DWORD dnDevnode, Flags, dwSetupReserved, dwClassInstallReserved, dwFlagsEx;
    UINT cbSize, InfType;
    ATOM atDriverPath, atTempInfFile;
    LPDRIVER_NODE lpCompatDrvList, lpClassDrvList, lpSelectedDriver;
    LPARAM gicplParam, lpClassInstallParams;
    LPDRIVER_INFO lpCompatDrvInfoList, lpClassDrvInfoList;
    HINSTANCE hinstClassInstaller, hinstClassPropProvidor,
hinstDevicePropProvidor,
hinstBasicPropProvidor, hinstPrivateProblemHandler;
    FARPROC fpClassInstaller, fpClassEnumPropPages, fpDeviceEnumPropPages,
        fpEnumBasicProperties, fpPrivateProblemHandler;
    struct _DEVICE_INFO FAR *lpNextDi;
    struct _DEVICE_INFO FAR *lpdiChildList;
    HKEY hRegKey;
    HWND hwndParent;
    GENCALLBACKPROC gicpGenInstallCallBack;
} DEVICE_INFO;
```

Table 6.1. The `DEVICE_INFO` structure members.

Members	*Description*
`szDescription[LINE_LEN]`	Character buffer for the name, or description, of the device in `dnDevnode`.
`szRegSubkey`	Character buffer for the `[MAX_DEVNODE_ID_LEN]` device's hardware registry subkey. This is the same key as `hRegKey`.

continues

Table 6.1. continued

Members	Description
szClassName	Character buffer for the MAX_CLASS_NAME_LEN] class name of the device in dnDevnode.
dnDevnode	When used, contains an address to the device node associated with the device.
Flags	These values are for setting installation options and for controlling the way the Device Manager displays and interacts with the user. Some values can be set before the use of the API, and others are set while the API processes.

	DI_SHOWOEM	Allows the use of an OEM disk for processing.
	DI_SHOWCOMPAT	This flag is set if the API function DiSelectDevice is displaying the compatible device list.
	DI_SHOWCLASS	This flag is set if the API function DiSelectDevice is displaying the class driver list.
	DI_SHOWALL	Used instead of setting both DI_SHOWCOMPAT and DI_SHOWCLASS members.
	DI_NOVCP	This flag is set if the API function DiInstallDevice does not require a virtual copy procedure (VCP).
	DI_DIDCOMPAT	This flag is set if the API function DiBuildCompatDrvList has completed and lpCompatDrvList points to a compatible driver list.
	DI_DIDCLASS	This flag is set if the API function DiBuildClassDrvList has completed and lpClassDrvList points to a class driver list.

Members	Description
DI_AUTOASSIGNRES	Not used.
DI_NEEDRESTART	This flag is set if Windows 95 needs to be restarted after installation or after changing a device's settings.
DI_NEEDREBOOT	This flag is set if the machine needs to be booted after installation or after changing a device's settings.
DI_NOBROWSE	When using an OEM disk, the Browse function is disabled.
DI_MULTMFGS	This flag is set if a class has multiple manufacturers associated with it.
DI_DISABLED	Not used.
DI_GENERALPAGE_ADDED	This flag is set if a property page provider or installer has added a general purpose property page to the device's property sheet.
DI_RESOURCEPAGE_ADDED	This flag is set if a property page provider or installer has added a resource properties page to the device's property sheet.
DI_PROPERTIES_CHANGE	This flag is set if the Device Manager's interface needs to be updated because of a change to the device's properties.
DI_INF_IS_SORTED	This flag is set if, after investigating the INF files, the provider or installer

continues

Table 6.1. continued

Members	*Description*
	reads that the INF files are in sorted order.
`DI_ENUMSINGLEINF`	This flag is set in order to keep the API functions `DiBuildCompatDrvList` and `DiBuildClassDrvList` searching only the INF file specified by `atDriverPath`.
`DI_DONOTCALLCONFIGMG`	While using the API function `DiInstallDevice`, this flag is set to keep the Configuration Manager from being called.
`DI_INSTALLDISABLED`	If this flag is set, it installs the device as disabled.
`DI_CLASSONLY`	This flag is set when the `DEVICE_INFO` structure has only a class name in it.
`DI_CLASSINSTALLPARAMS`	This flag is set if the `lpClassIntallParams` field is pointing to a class install parameter block.
`DI_NODI_DEFAULTACTION`	If this flag is set, the provider or installer is requesting that the API function `DiCallClassInstaller` not do any default actions if it returns `ERR_DI_DO_DEFAULT` or the class installer call fails.
`DI_QUIETINSTALL`	This flag is set if an API function installation should not display default choices.
`DI_NOFILECOPY`	This flag is set if the API function `DiInstallDevice`

Members	Description	
		should not perform file copying.
	DI_FORCECOPY	This flag is set if the API function DiInstallDevice should always copy files, whether or not they exist.
	DI_DRIVERPAGE_ADDED	This flag is set if a property page provider or installer has added a driver's property page to the device's property sheet.
	DI_USECI_SELECTSTRINGS	This flag is set if the API function DiSelectDevice should use string values provided by the installer.
	DI_OVERRIDE_INFFLAGS	Not used.
	DI_PROPS_NOCHANGEUSAGE	This flag is set to turn off the capability to disable the device in the device's general property page.
	DI_NOSELECTICONS	This flag is set if the API function DiSelectDevice should not use small icons while doing device selection.
	DI_NOWRITE_IDS	This flag is set if the API function DiSelectDevice should not write the device's hardware and compatible IDs to the device's entry in the registry.
dwSetupReserved	Reserved for setup.	
dwClassInstallReserved	Reserved for class installers.	
dwFlagsEx	Additional control flags.	
	DI_FLAGSEX_USEOLDINFSEARCH	This flag is set if search functions

continues

Table 6.1. continued

Members	Description
	should not use indexed searches.
`DI_FLAGSEX_AUTOSELECTRANK0`	This flag is set if the API function `DiInstallDevice` should automatically select rank 0 match drivers.
`DI_FLAGSEX_CI_FAILED`	This flag is set if a call to the `ClassInstaller` failed.
`DI_FLAGSEX_NOLOGCONFIGS`	This flag is set if the API function `DiSelectDevice` should not install a device's `LogConfigs`.
`DI_FLAGSEX_DIDINFOLIST`	This flag is set if the API function `DiBuildCompatDrvList` has completed, and the device's compatible driver information list has been built.
`DI_FLAGSEX_DIDCOMPATINFO`	This flag is set when the API function `DiBuildCompatDrvList` has completed, and the device's class driver information list has been built.
`cbSize`	The size of the `DEVICE_INFO` structure.
`InfType`	Identifies the type of INF file being used: `.INFTYPE_TEXT` or `.INFTYPE_EXECUTABLE`.
`atDriverPath`	A global `ATOM` containing the path to this device's INF file. A value of `zero` indicates that the INF file is a

Members	Description
	standard Windows 95 INF format. This is set when the driver comes from an OEM INF file.
atTempInfFile	A global ATOM containing the name of the temporary INF file. This is set when a driver comes from an old-style INF file and has been converted.
lpCompatDrvList	This is a pointer to a linked list of DRIVER_NODE structures representing compatible drivers for the devices.
lpClassDrvList	This is a pointer to a linked list of DRIVER_NODE structures representing all drivers of the device's class.
lpSelectedDriver	This is a pointer to a single DRIVER_NODE structure that has been selected as the required driver for the device.
lpClassInstallParams	This is a pointer to the class install parameter block.
lpCompatDrvInfoList	This is a pointer to a linked list of DRIVER_INFO structures that are compatible with the device.
lpClassDrvInfoList	This is a pointer to a linked list of DRIVER_INFO structures representing all drivers for the device's class.
hinstClassInstaller	This is a class installer for a module instance.
hinstClassPropProvider	This is a class property provider for a module instance.
hinstDevicePropProvider	This is a device property provider for a module instance.
hinstBasicPropProvider	This is a basic property provider for a module instance.
hinstPrivateProblemHandler	This is the module handle for the device's private problem procedure.
fpClassInstaller	This is the procedure address of the class install function.
fpClassEnumPropPages	This is the procedure address of the property provider page enumeration function for the class.
fpDeviceEnumPropPages	This is the procedure address of the property provider page enumeration function for the device.
fpEnumBasicProperties	This is the procedure address of the basic device property provider page enumeration function for the device.
fpPrivateProblemHandler	This is the procedure address of the device's private problem handler.
*lpNextDi	This is a pointer to the next DEVICE_INFO structure in a linked list that is compatible with the device.

continues

Table 6.1. continued

Members	Description
*lpdiChildList	This is a pointer to a linked list of DRIVER_INFO structures representing the children of the device.
hRegKey	This is the registry key that holds this device's registry subkey. Typically, this is HKEY_LOCAL_MACHINE.
hwndParent	This handle references the interface dialog boxes specific to the device.
gicpGenInstallCallBack	This is the procedure address of the GenInstall callback function. It is set if the class installer wants GenInstall callbacks during the API function DiInstallDevice.
gicplParam	lParam for the GenInstall callback function, needed by the DiInstallDevice call.

This by no means is a complete discussion of the Device Manager and the associated API functions. If you will be making full use of the Device Manager's functionality, you should be prepared to study this API set in its entirety.

Supporting Plug and Play Hardware

It's important to remember that, although it is a true Plug and Play operating system, Windows 95 supports a wide variety of legacy adapters as well. Vendors whose legacy devices (such as ST506-compatible ESDI controllers) adhere to established specifications are guaranteed support via the vast Windows 95 library of built-in legacy device detection and configuration algorithms.

Interestingly enough, Windows 95 usually requires additional, vendor-supplied support (in the form of an INF file and a device driver) for Plug and Play devices. For example, if you choose to add an ST506-compliant ESDI controller, Windows 95 can automatically install the device using its internal-disk-controller installer. If, on the other hand, you plug in a newer Plug and Play ISA device, Windows 95 will default to its unknown-hardware installer unless directed otherwise by a vendor-supplied INF file and device driver. Designers of Plug and Play-compliant hardware can avoid the unknown hardware installation route by mastering the INF file format.

INF files instruct various modules within Windows 95 about how to deal with newly introduced Plug and Play or legacy hardware. It is at the discretion of the hardware vendor to decide whether the device should ship with an INF file or should rely on the Windows 95 built-in device identification and configuration algorithms for installation. Normally, if you are producing a Plug and Play device, you should supply Microsoft with an INF file to guarantee that Windows 95 correctly installs the device and its associated drivers. If Windows 95 is not given an INF file to guide its Device Manager and Configuration Manager, then the default Unknown Hardware dialog box appears, which prompts the user to provide a device configuration diskette, to ignore the device, or to perform some other action to assist Windows 95 in dealing with the newly introduced hardware.

The structure of the INF file is well documented by Microsoft, and it is fairly easy to follow. Once you are familiar with which parts are required to support the hardware, then the file usually can be constructed from an existing INF file. You will rarely find that your device does not belong to an existing, built-in Windows 95 device category or that Windows 95 does not already provide an INF file similar to the one required by your new device.

You can find out if your hardware falls into an existing category by running the New Hardware applet from the Control Panel. This program lists all the available hardware categories. If your hardware falls into one of these categories, then your device has an INF file into which you can add information specific to your device.

Although INF files ship in ASCII text format, Windows 95 uses their contents in converted form. When it receives a new INF file, Windows 95 converts the file to binary form and appends its contents either to DRVDATA.BIN or DRVIDX.BIN. These two files reside in the hidden directory \Windows\INF and contain the binary data converted from the INF ASCII files.

Each time the user introduces a new or modified ASCII INF file during a device installation, Windows 95 converts the file's contents to binary form and appends the file to the binary DRVDATA.BIN and DRVIDX.BIN files. To force a total rebuild of these files, delete them and run Add New Hardware from the Control Panel.

The device driver and the INF file go hand-in-hand with Windows 95. When a device is enumerated on the bus, the INFs are investigated for the identifying manufacturer. After installation, the appropriate driver is called. The driver for any particular device might require an enumerator for its class. Here is the general sequence of events for loading a new device node:

1. A registry search identifies a dynamic VxD, and a `DevLoader` instance is called to initialize the VxD and register a `NewDevLoader` routine.
2. The Configuration Manager calls the registered `NewDevLoader` routine to register the enumerator and to configure the device driver.
3. The registered enumerator is called by the Configuration Manager.
4. If child devices are found, the device driver is called, and support is installed.

Windows 95 device interface provides a fully functional callback mechanism capable of invoking device-loader and driver-installation callback functions. Although not required by legacy devices, these functions allow for more robust installation and device driver identification.

To Plug and Play designers, however, the callback mechanism provides the opportunity to transparently install device drivers and install plug-in hardware without user intervention. The INF file guides Windows 95 through the installation of any new devices with which it is unfamiliar.

Device Information Files

INF files are ASCII text installation scripts that adhere to Microsoft's device information file format. This type of file comes from one of two sources—either it ships as a standard component of Windows 95, or it is supplied by hardware vendors in conjunction with a plug-in adapter.

Essentially, the INF file is an installation script. Both the Configuration Manager and Device Manager parse the contents of INF files to determine the correct method for installing and configuring newly introduced hardware devices.

The structure of the INF file is broken down into sections, which serve a particular purpose in directing the installation of hardware. Each section has entries, which are either pre-defined or can be defined by the writer of the INF file. Table 6.2 shows the sections and functions.

Table 6.2. A description of the INF file sections.

Section	Function
Version	This section contains a standard header that identifies the INF file for use with Windows 95 along with the class that the INF supports.
Class	This section usually is not used. Most classes are already defined in Windows 95.
Manufacturer	The Manufacturer section is used to declare the manufacturer of the hardware for the class. Many INF files contain multiple manufacturer identifiers and installation instructions.
Manufacturer Name	Each entry in the Manufacturer section has an appropriated Manufacturer Name section. This section is identified by the name string from the Manufacturer section.
Install	The Install section has the responsibility of defining other sections needed to complete the installation. Not all entries defined for the Install section are required; in fact, some are rarely used. These entries allow the INF writer to customize the installation process and to handle everything from temporary file creation to registry manipulation.
Strings	Strings are kept in this section for use throughout the rest of the INF file and in the installation of the devices supported.

The initial writing of an INF file usually can be done by copying an existing INF file and then making modifications to it so that it will work with your hardware. If you are manufacturing a SCSI host adapter, you can simply open the SCSI.INF file, see how the other manufacturers are using the entries, and then set up your entries to match your hardware. Figure 6.5 shows how an INF file looks as it is edited using a DOS-style editor.

FIGURE 6.5.

The MSFDC.INF file as viewed with the Windows 95 EDIT.COM DOS-style editor.

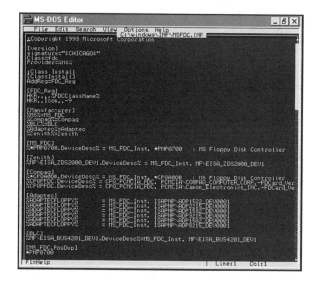

Simply put, INF files are macros that tell the service accessing them how to handle the installation of hardware and associated software. To aid in your understanding of INF files, I have dissected the following sample file for the sake of clarity:

```
; TEGPRNT.INF

[Version]
Signature="$CHICAGO$"    ; Signature is always ="$CHICAGO$", or $Windows 95$
Class=Printer            ; Class of the device is Printer
Provider=%MS%            ; The Provider is %MS%, as the writer of this .INF
LayoutFile=layout.inf    ; Defines the layout file to use. Layout.inf is the default

[Manufacturer]
"TEG Printers"           ; Manufacturer name points to [TEG Printers] section

              ; Each entry in the next section defines a section to execute for the
              ; installation of the device.  When the user picks a value from the
              ; Install Wizard that matches one of these, then that is the install
              ; section name is executed.  The entry after the install section name
              ; is the compatible device ID.  This is used for registry entries.
[TEG Printers]
"TEG Super PS 17/Plus" = TGSP_17.SPD, TEG_Super_PS_17/Plus
"TEG Color PS" = TGCR_MS.SPD, TEG_Color_PS
"TEG PrintServer Color 20" = TGV2_MS.SPD, TEG_PrintServer_Color_20
"TEG PS 11" = TEGPS11.SPD, TEG_ PS_11
```

```
                    ; Each Install section below has a CopyFiles entry.
                    ; This entry point to where the install provider
                    ; should go next for action.

[TGSP_17.SPD]        ; From the first entry in the [TEG Printers] section, above.
CopyFiles=@ TGSP_MS.SPD,@ TEGSPS17.SPD,TEGPRNT

 [TGCR_MS.SPD]        ; From the second entry in the [TEG Printers] section, above.
CopyFiles=@ TGCR_MS.SPD,@ TEGCLRPS.SPD,TEGPRNT

[TGV2_MS.SPD]           ; From the third entry in the [TEG Printers] section, above.
CopyFiles=@ TGV2_MS.SPD,@ TEGSVRC2.SPD, TEGPRNT

[TG11_MS.SPD]           ; From the fourth entry in the [TEG Printers] section, above.
CopyFiles=@ TG11_MS.SPD,@ TEGPS11.SPD, TEGPRNT

[TEGPRNT]            ; This section is called by all the Installer sections above.
PSCRIPT.DRV          ; Each Installer copies some individual files, then copies all of
PSCRIPT.HLP HLP      ; these common files.
TESTPS.TXT
APPLE380.SPD
FONTS.MFM
ICONLIB.DLL

[DestinationDirs] ; This section will tell the CopyFiles section where to copy the
DefaultDestDir=11    ; files.  11 = \Windows\System directory.

[Strings]  ; Localizable strings are stored here.  If for some reason the strings
MS="Microsoft"      ; needed to be changed or localized, this is where it is done.
```

The previous sample INF file contains only a basic subset of possible entries. For example, INF files also might contain a vendor-specific section whose content is understood only by the device's installer. Table 6.3 shows the major sections in an INF file that vendors can populate.

Table 6.3. Specific entries for INF file sections.

Section	Associated Entries
Version	[Version]
	Signature="$Chicago$"
	Class=*class-name*
	Provider=*INF-Creator*
	LayoutFile=*filename.inf*
Manufacturer	[Manufacturer]
	manufacturer-name ¦ *%strings-key%=manufacturer-name-section*
Manufacturer Name	[*manufacturer-name-section*]
	device-description=install-section-name,device-id[,compatible-device-id]…

Section	Associated Entries
Install	`[install-section-name]`
	`LogConfig=`*log-config-section-name[, log-config-section-name]*...
	`Copyfiles=`*file-list-section[,<file-list-section>]*...
	`Renfiles=`*file-list-section[,file-list-section]*...
	`Delfiles=`*file-list-section[,file-list-section]*...
	`UpdateInis=`*update-ini-section[,update-ini-section]*...
	`pdateIniFields=`*update-inifields-section[,update-inifields-section]*...
	`AddReg=`*add-registry-section[,add-registry-section]*...
	`DelReg=`*del-registry-section[,del-registry-section]*...
	`Ini2Reg=`*ini-to-registry-section[,ini-to-registry-section]*...
	`UpdateCfgSys=`*update-config-section*
	`UpdateAutoBat=`*update-autoexec-section*
	`Reboot ¦ Restart`
DestinationDirs	`[DestinationDirs]`
	file-list-section=`ldid[,`*subdir* `]`
	`.`
	`DefaultDestDir=`*ldid[,* *subdir* `]`
File-List	*[file-list-section]*
	destination-file-name,[source-file-name],[temporary-file-name]
SourceDisksFiles	`[SourceDisksFiles]`
	filename=disk-number
SourceDisksNames	`[SourceDisksNames]`
	disk-ordinal =`"`*disk-description*`",`*disk-label,disk-serial-number*
ControlFlags	`[ControlFlags]`
	`CopyfilesOnly=`*Device-id[,device-id]*...
	`ExcludeFromSelect=`*Device-id[,device-id]*...
PosDup	`[Device-id.posdup]`
	`Device-id[,device-id]`...

continues

Table 6.3. continued

Section	Associated Entries
NoResDup	[InstallSection.Noresdup]
	Device-id[,device-id]…
HW	[InstallSection.HW]
ClassInstall	[ClassInstall]
	Copyfiles=*file-list-section[,<file-list-section>]*…
	AddReg=*add-registry-section[,add-registry-section]*…
	Renfiles=*File-list-section>[,<File-list-section>]*…
	Delfiles=*File-list section[,<File-list-section>]*…
	UpdateInis=*Update-ini-section>[,<Update-ini-section>]*…
	UpdateIniFields=*Update-inifields-Section[,<Update-inifields-section>]*…
	AddReg=*Add-registry-section[,<Add-registry-section>]*…
	DelReg=*Del-registry-section[,<Del-registry-section>]*…
Strings	[Strings]
	strings-key=value

Device Driver Requirements

Windows 95 has redefined the role of the device driver to include dynamic VxD loading and unloading in addition to device-specific support. Compared to a fully featured Windows 95 VxD device driver, the real mode, hardware-specific, CONFIG.SYS-style device driver is a thing of the past. Interestingly enough, Windows 95 does not require that its Plug and Play device drivers work only in conjunction with Plug and Play hardware. As stated earlier, it is possible to write a dynamically loaded Windows 95 device driver that uses proprietary means to locate and configure its hardware.

Microsoft defines an ideal Plug and Play device driver as having the following characteristics:

- Dynamically reconfigurable
- Dynamically loaded and unloaded
- Interacts with the Configuration Manager to get device configuration information
- Requires little or no user interaction to load the proper driver
- Dynamically responds to messages regarding the removal of associated devices

■ Runs in different states based on machine configuration, such as being docked or undocked

Windows 95 Plug and Play support requires you to add new functions to device drivers, the most important of which is called the callback entry point. The *callback entry point* is used by the Configuration Manager and other providers to return to a device driver the logical configuration of the Plug and Play hardware that is currently being set up.

In addition to mastering new device driver features, you must become familiar with the Configuration Manager's calls and structures, the VMM libraries, and the registry. The Configuration Manager is used when loading device drivers because it is the Configuration Manager that is made aware of the new device found. The Configuration Manager also asks the new device, through its driver, to find all devices that are children to it. The VMM libraries define the Virtual Device services. This is where the developer learns about messages that initialize the device driver as a dynamic VxD. The registry is where the device driver adds new subkeys, or children, in the hardware tree.

In dynamically loaded device drivers, the callback function is used by an installer to pass the configuration information for the device being installed. The following paragraph outlines the steps taken by the Configuration Manager and the device driver to get the driver up and running.

When the device driver is identified, whether through the registry or an INF file, the Configuration Manager calls it with the VxD service VXDLDR_LoadDevice and sends the SYS_DYNAMIC_DEVICE_INIT message to the device driver. This message tells the driver to load dynamically and to register its DevLoader function. The driver needs to call the Configuration Manager using the CM_Register_Devloader function, which uses the VxD DeviceInfo structure to identify itself.

The Configuration Manager, with DevLoader registered, is now free to load other dynamic drivers or to call enumerators. When the Configuration Manager finds an acceptable configuration, the DevLoader function is called using the DLVXD_LOAD_DEVLOADER message.

The DLVXD_LOAD_DEVLOADER message instructs the driver to call its own enumerator and driver loader functions by passing the DLVXD_LOAD_ENUMERATOR and DLVXD_LOAD_DRIVER messages to the appropriate sections of the driver. Each VxD section, in turn, calls the appropriate registration function for that portion of code. In order to register itself, the enumerator portion of the device driver calls CONFIGMG_Register_Enumerator, whereas the actual driver registers itself via the function CONFIGMG_Register_Device.

Once all the parts of the driver are registered for use, the Configuration Manager calls the registered enumerator with the message CONFIG_ENUMERATE to ask it to enumerate any children of classes that exist on the enumerator's bus.

If the enumerator finds a valid device, it updates the devnode passed to it by the Configuration Manager and returns the value CR_SUCCESS. At this point, the Configuration Manager calls the registered driver loader with the CONFIG_START message. This message launches the device driver for the passed devnode that was previously given resources, and the device now has support.

The preceding procedure describes the process for not only the typical device driver but also for the device driver that provides its own enumerator and loader. This process assumes that the Configuration Manager is fully functional and is executing in its protected mode phase.

What about buses and devices that need resources before the system is fully functional? Suppose that the loader has not yet fully entered protected mode, and yet a device used to help load the OS requires resources in order for the OS load to proceed. The SCSI Miniport model is an appropriate example. The rule of dynamically loaded drivers says that any Ring 3 (protected mode) application or other VxD can load a dynamic driver using the VxD virtual services. In the case of a SCSI Plug and Play ISA adapter, the VxD IOS (a statically loaded VxD) loads SCSIPORT.VXD and SCSI Miniport driver dynamically. This process takes place like this: Because all dynamically loaded drivers require a device loader, the IOS acts as the loader for SCSI Miniport drivers. Remember, this driver will not implement its own enumerator because the card is an ISAWPU enumerated device. The ISAWPU enumeration takes place before the Configuration Manager starts to step through what is left of the registry. The VMM32 real mode loader ignores the SCSI card because it has no StaticVxD=yyy line in its registry entry. When the protected mode initialization begins, the IOS driver will get a Device_init message.

The IOS driver then uses the CONFIGMG_Register_DevLoader function to begin the hunt for devices in the registry that use the DevLoader=IOS entry. It passes the parameters IOS_DDB and 0, which are indicators to the Configuration Manager, to find any instances in the hardware tree that have corresponding matches in the registry of DevLoader=IOS.

For each device node found that has such an entry, the Configuration Manager calls back through a system control message to the IOS driver. This processes the devnode's device loader. The call to the IOS looks like this:

```
DirectedSysControl("IOS", WPU_NEW_DEVNODE, DLVXD_LOAD_DEVLOADER, LoadDevNode)
```

The call prompts IOS to find the device entry in the registry and to call the Miniport driver. The Miniport driver settings are passed to the registry by means of Configuration Manager calls that are initiated by the IOS driver.

Dynamic driver loading is probably the biggest ease-of-use gain for the Windows 95 end user. A current Windows 95 desktop machine should not have a CONFIG.SYS file. When using Windows 95, you will find that the use of drivers that do not conform to this standard provide nothing but headaches.

If you are a developer of dynamically loaded VxDs, you need to keep several guidelines in mind. If a dynamically loaded VxD also provides other VxD services, for example, then it forfeits the capability to be dynamically unloaded. The following are some other guidelines, as compiled from the Windows 95 Plug and Play DDK documentation:

■ VxDs that acquire resources while functioning must release those resources if the VxD receives a SYS_DYNAMIC_DEVICE_EXIT message. These resources are not deleted by the system.

■ Nonreleasable resources, such as break points, are not to be allocated every time the VxD is used. These resources should be allocated once during the VxD's initialization and reused if the VxD is reloaded for another instance.

■ The following services should only be used during the VxDs initialization:

```
Add_Global_V86_Data_Area
AddFreePhysPage
AddInstanceItem
Allocate_Global_V86_Data_Area
Allocate_Temp_V86_Data_Area
Free_Temp_V86_Data_Area
GetGlblRng0V86IntBase
SetFreePhysRegCalBk
SetLastV86Page
Allocate_PM_App_CB_Area
Convert_Boolean_String
Convert_Decimal_String
Convert_Fixed_Point_String
Convert_Hex_String
DOSMGR_BackFill_Allowed
DOSMGR_Enable_Indos_Polling
DOSMGR_Instance_Device
Get_Name_Of_Ugly_TSR
Get_Next_Arena
Get_Next_Profile_String
Get_Profile_Boolean
Get_Profile_Decimal_Int
Get_Profile_Fixed_Point
Get_Profile_Hex_Int
Get_Profile_String
GetDOSVectors
Locate_Byte_In_ROM
MMGR_SetNULPageAddr
OpenFile
PageFile_Init_File
Set_Physical_HMA_Alias
V86MMGR_NoUMBInitCalls
V86MMGR_Set_Mapping_Info
V86MMGR_SetAvailMapPgs
V86MMGR_SetLocalA20
VDMAD_Reserve_Buffer_Space
```

An ISA Plug and Play Example in Windows 95

Welcome to the meat of the chapter—a sample Windows 95 device driver. The example provided demonstrates the handling of a hypothetical Plug and Play ISA card. Because the driver supports a device that is enumerated by the Configuration Manager, it has no need to load its own enumerator. The device driver follows the same pattern of initialization as outlined in the first example, shown in the section "Device Driver Requirements," but will not use the `DLVXD_LOAD_ENUMERATOR` message.

The code that follows supports a Plug and Play ISA card produced by LP industries. This board's function is simply to consume ISA bus resources and to hold onto them as long as the machine is running. Because the board is not a boot device, the driver feasibly could implement the deactivation of the board using Configuration Manager calls and unload the device driver to free up resources; however, this device driver is not so polite. In place of politeness, this code focuses on the work necessary to get the VxD loaded, find the configuration of the board it is supposed to support, give the board the support it needs, and then unload the driver.

Sample Code Hardware Outline

The sample code functions on a board that was defined specifically for the purpose of this example. As a typical Plug and Play ISA card, the LP Industries adapter has preferred configurations and default values and can be dynamically activated and deactivated.

What's more important than the actual purpose of the LP Industries adapter is that you understand the process shown in the following sample code and that you understand the specific needs of your hardware.

The LP Industries board can use the following resources:

- IRQs 9, 10, 11, or 12
- DMA channels 0 or 5
- I/O Ports 120–127, 160–167, or 1A0–1A7

The machine in which the board is installed is a legacy BIOS machine, so no activation of the card takes place before Windows 95 loads. The card always comes up Plug and Play inactive and has the following preferred settings:

- IRQ 9
- DMA 0
- I/O Ports 160–167

The following is an INF file that can be used to load the device. Because the card is ISA Plug and Play, the INF file can describe the entire support needed with no user interaction. The class for the device is `Adapter`. Because the `Adapter` class already exists in Windows 95, the sample device driver does not need to create it.

```
; LPADAPT.INF  -- For Installing the LP Industries Plug and Play ISA Card

[Version]
signature="$CHICAGO$"
Class=Adapter
Provider=%Msft%
LayoutFile=LAYOUT.INF
```

```
[ClassInstall]
Addreg= AdapterReg

[AdapterReg]
HKR,,,,%AdapterClassName%
HKR,,Icon,,-9

 [Manufacturer]
%LPI%=LPI

[LPI]
%*LPI1020.DeviceDesc%=LPI1020

[LPI1020]
CopyFiles=@LPIDRIVR.VXD
AddReg=LPI1020.Reg
DevLoader= LPIDRIVR.VXD
LogConfig=*LPI1020.LogConfig.Best, *LPI1020.LogConfig.Ok

[*LPI1020.LogConfig.Best]
ConfigPriority= DESIRED
IOConfig=160-167(3FF::)
IRQConfig=9
DMAConfig=0

[*LPI1020.LogConfig.Ok]
ConfigPriority= NORMAL
IOConfig=8@120-1A7%FF0(3FF::)
IRQConfig=9,10,11,12
DMAConfig=0,5

[LPI1020.Reg]
HKR,,LPIDriver,, LPIDRIVR.VXD
HKR,,DevLoader,,LPIDRIVR.VXD

[DestinationDirs]
DefaultDestDir = 11

[Strings]
Msft="Microsoft"
*LPI1020.DeviceDesc ="LP Industries Famous ISA Plug and Play Adapter Board!"
```

Sample Code

The code presented here is for use as an example only. It will not provide any functionality for any known product available. The code was compiled using Microsoft Visual C++ Version 2.0 and Microsoft Assembler Version 6.11. The code might need some modifications to successfully compile on a different platform.

The sample code is in two parts. The first part is the ASM portion, which declares the VxD and the associated VxD messaging system. The second part is the C portion, which implements the calls to configure the board and install the device driver. The code is commented to help in the reading of it.

```
;---------------------------------------------------------------
TITLE TESTWPUA.ASM
;
; Robert M. Griswold, Jr.  TESTWPUA - Plug and Play VxD ASM File
; DLVxD Initialization
;
;---------------------------------------------------------------

    .386p

    .xlist
    include vmm.inc
    include configmg.inc
    .list


;---------------------------------------------------------------
;    VxD Declaration
;       WPUDRVS_Major_Ver      EQU    0004H        From configmg.inc
;       WPUDRVS_Minor_Ver      EQU    0000H        From configmg.inc
;       UNDEFINED_INIT_ORDER   EQU    080000000H   From vmm.inc
;
;    Declare_Virtual_Device  Name, MajorVer, MinorVer,
;                            CtrlProc, DeviceNum,
;                            InitOrder, V86Proc, PMProc
;
;       Name        Name of the virtual device
;       MajorVer    Value specifying the major version number
;                   for the virtual device
;       MinorVer    Value specifying the minor version number
;                   for the virtual device
;       CtrlProc    Name of the control procedure for the
;                   virtual device
;       DeviceNum   Device identifier for the virtual device
;       InitOrder   Value specifying the initialization order
;                   of the virtual device relative to other
;                   virtual device
;       V86Proc     Name of the V86-mode API procedure
;       PMProc      Name of the protected-mode API procedure
;
;---------------------------------------------------------------

DECLARE_VIRTUAL_DEVICE      TESTWPU,\
                            WPUDRVS_Major_Ver,\
                            WPUDRVS_Minor_Ver,\
                            TESTWPU_Dispatch,,UNDEFINED_INIT_ORDER

VXD_LOCKED_CODE_SEG         ; Control_Dispatch calls required
                           ; to take place from VXD_LOCKED_CODE_SEG


;---------------------------------------------------------------
;
;    TESTWPU_Dispatch
;
;       This test procedure will call the associated Initialization or
;       NewDevice procedure.  This is done by using the Control_Dispatch
;       MACRO from the VMM.INC inclusion file.  The structure of the
;       Control_Dispatch is as follows:
;
```

```
;                 Control_Dispatch Service, Procedure, callc, arglst
;
;          The call enters with the Control call ID in the EAX register,
;          exits with the carry flag cleared if the call was succesful,
;          else the call failed.  Refer to VMM.INC for register usage.
;
;              DEVICE_INIT              EQU     0001H       From vmm.inc
;              SYS_DYNAMIC_DEVICE_INIT  EQU     001BH       From vmm.inc
;              SYS_DYNAMIC_DEVICE_EXIT  EQU     001CH       From vmm.inc
;              WPU_NEW_DEVNODE          EQU     0022H       From vmm.inc
;--------------------------------------------------------------------

BeginProc TESTWPU_Dispatch

  Control_Dispatch SYS_DYNAMIC_DEVICE_INIT, TESTWPU_Init, sCall, <0>
      ; passed a null pointer for the VxD DeviceInfo structure
  Control_Dispatch WPU_NEW_DEVNODE, TESTWPU_NewDevice, sCall, <ebx, edx>
      ; ebx contains the DeviceNode instance
      ; edx contains the load type declaration
  Control_Dispatch SYS_DYNAMIC_DEVICE_EXIT, TESTWPU_Exit, sCall
    clc
    ret

EndProc     TESTWPU_Dispatch

VXD_LOCKED_CODE_ENDS

    end




//
// TESTWPU.H  Header File  3/7/95
// For TESTWPU.C Plug and Play VxD
//


//  BEGIN
//  Driver Control section, TESTWPU
//  Robert M. Griswold, Jr.

//
// TESTWPU_Exit

CM_VXD_RESULT CM_SYSCTRL
TESTWPU_Exit(struct DeviceInfo *DevInf, struct Vxd_Desc_Block *DDB);


//
// TESTWPU_Init

CM_VXD_RESULT CM_SYSCTRL
TESTWPU_Init(struct DeviceInfo *DevInf);


//
// TESTWPU_NewDevice
```

```
CONFIGRET CM_SYSCTRL
TESTWPU_NewDevice(DEVNODE DevInst, LOAD_TYPE DLVType);



//
//   BEGIN
//   Device Loader portion, TESTWPU
//   Robert M. Griswold, Jr.
//
//
// TESTWPU_NewDevLoader

CONFIGRET CM_INTERNAL
TESTWPU_NewDevLoader(DEVNODE DevInst);



//
//   BEGIN
//   Driver Loader and Installer portion, TESTWPU
//   Robert M. Griswold, Jr.
//

//
// TESTWPU_NewDriver

CONFIGRET CM_INTERNAL
TESTWPU_NewDriver(DEVNODE DevNode);




//
//   TESTWPU.C
//   Sample Source Code to support the LP Industries Device
//   Implements a dynamically loaded VxD for Windows 95
//   using Plug and Play.
//   Robert M. Griswold, Jr.   3/7/95
//
#include <basedef.h>
#include <vmm.h>
#include <debug.h>
#include <vmmreg.h>
#include <vxdwraps.h>
#include <configmg.h>
#include <testWPU.h>


//
//   BEGIN
//   Driver Control section, TESTWPU
//   Robert M. Griswold, Jr.
//
//

#pragma CM_PAGEABLE_DATA                    // configmg.h
#pragma CM_PAGEABLE_CODE                    // configmg.h

#pragma warning (disable:4026)  // Warning about parameter list
```

```
//
// TESTWPU_Exit
// This procedure is called when SYS_DYNAMIC_DEVICE_EXIT message
// is passed through the TESTWPUA.ASM file, using the
// Control_Dispatch.  The Exit procedure is in place to handle
// any static or global data areas that were created with the
// TESTWPU_Init call.
// Because nothing is created in the TESTWPU_Init call, the
// exit routine can simple return VXD_SUCCESS.
//

CM_VXD_RESULT CM_SYSCTRL
TESTWPU_Exit(VOID)
{
        return(VXD_SUCCESS);
}


#pragma warning (default:4026)


//
// TESTWPU_Init
// This procedure is called when SYS_DYNAMIC_DEVICE_INIT message
// is passed through the TESTWPUA.ASM file, using the
// Control_Dispatch.
// This message call passes in a null
// pointer to a VxD Virtual DeviceInfo Structure, PVMMDDB.
// The procedure returns to the installer, usually the CM,
// with a VXD_SUCCESS value, if all is well.
// The sole purpose of this call is to register the DevLoader
// portion of this driver, as the place were DLVXD messages can
// be sent from other install providers.
//
// CM_VXD_RESULT      int                    configmg.h
// CM_SYSCTRL         _stdcall               configmg.h
// PVMMDDB            VxD_Desc_Block struct  vmm.h
//

CM_VXD_RESULT CM_SYSCTRL
TESTWPU_Init(PVMMDDB ptrDDB)
{

        CONFIGRET    result;               // Local CM return value

        result = CM_Register_DevLoader(ptrDDB, 0);

        if (result==CR_SUCCESS)            // Coded this way, since
        return(VXD_SUCCESS);               // VXD_SUCCESS = 0 and
        else return(VXD_FAILURE);          // CR_SUCCESS = 1

}


//
// TESTWPU_NewDevice
// TESTWPU_NewDevice will process the Control_Dispatch message
// WPU_NEW_DEVICE.  This call will receive the message, then
```

```
// process the DevInst through the ebx register, and the DLVType
// through the edx register.  The DLVType is used to figure out
// what action to take.  This procedure only handles two choices,
// so an If-Else was used.
//
// CONFIGRET      // Std Return Value   configmg.h
// DEVNODE        DWORD                 configmg.h
// LOAD_TYPE      DWORD                 configmg.h
//

CONFIGRET CM_SYSCTRL
TESTWPU_NewDevice(DEVNODE DevInst, LOAD_TYPE DLVType)
{

      // DLVXD_LOAD_DEVLOADER    0x00000001   configmg.h
      //
      // This call to NewDevLoader will register the driver, and
      // return the standard return value of CR_SUCCESS.  If
      // the call was successful, the driver portion would
      // have initialized and registered the driver.
      // This call will also call the TESTWPU_NewDriver code for the
      // DevInst presented.

      if (DLVType == DLVXD_LOAD_DEVLOADER) {

          return(TESTWPU_NewDevLoader(DevInst));
      }

      // DLVXD_LOAD_DRIVER       0x00000002   configmg.h
      //
      // This call to NewDriver will register the driver for a
      // new DevInst.

      else if (DLVType == DLVXD_LOAD_DRIVER) {

          return(TESTWPU_NewDriver(DevInst));
      }
      else return(CR_DEFAULT);

}

//
//   END
//   Driver Control section, TESTWPU
//
//
//


//
//   BEGIN
//   Device Loader portion, TESTWPU
//   Robert M. Griswold, Jr.
//

//
// TESTWPU_NewDevLoader
// TESTWPU_NewDevLoader will be called by the _NewDevice call,
```

```
// from above.
// All this DevLoader does is register the driver.
//

CONFIGRET CM_INTERNAL
TESTWPU_NewDevLoader(DEVNODE DevInst)
{
        CONFIGRET      result;

        // This DevLoader only has to register the driver, because the
        // board is enumerated on the ISA bus by the CM.  This call
        // is actually to CONFIGMG_Load_DLVxDs.
        // The CM redefinition takes place in the VXDWRAPS.H file.
        // The DevInst is the DevNode created for the call.
        // testWPU.386 is a direction to the CM to call this exact
        // driver back again.
        // The CM calls with the DLVXD_LOAD_DRIVER message, and
        // TESTWPU_NewDriver is called.  This registers the driver
        // for the DevNode.

        result=CM_Load_DLVxDs( DevInst, "testWPU.386",\
                          DLVXD_LOAD_DRIVER, 0 );

        // The return value is most likely CR_SUCCESS.
        // This DevLoader does not do very much, because no enumerator
        // is needed.

        return(result);

}


//
//      END
//      Device Loader portion, TESTWPU
//
//


//
//      BEGIN
//      Driver Loader and Installer portion, TESTWPU
//      Robert M. Griswold, Jr.
//


//
// TESTWPU_ConfHandler
// TESTWPU_ConfHandler is where the configuration of the actual
// hardware support stuff takes place.  The card and its DevNode
// were created by the ISAWPU enumeration process, and the
// use of the .INF file.  Because of that, no enumerator is
// required, and no Resource Additions need to be made.
// Just set the driver and go.
//
// CM_HANDLER          _cdecl              configmg.h
//

CONFIGRET CM_HANDLER
```

```
TESTWPU_ConfHandler(CONFIGFUNC TESTFuncName, \
                    SUBCONFIGFUNC TESTSubFuncName,\
                    DEVNODE dnToDevInst, DWORD dwRefData, \
                    ULONG ulFlags)
{

  LOG_CONF  LogConf;
  RES_DES   ResIn;

      switch (TESTFuncName) {

          case CONFIG_START:

              // Here is where we begin the assigning of the
              // resources from the devnode to the driver
              // so that it will know where to get the board.
              // First, read in the first logical configuration
              // of the board.

                CM_Get_First_Log_Conf(&LogConf, dnToDevInst, \
                               ALLOC_LOG_CONF);

                CM_Get_Next_Res_Des(&ResIn, LogConf, ResType_IO, 0, 0);

              // Here is where the IO_RESOURCE structure would be
              // used to extract the I/O Port settings from ResIn.
              // Assign I/O port to driver variable.
              //
              // From here the programmer would continue on getting
              // the IRQ, then DMA settings using the same
              // CM_Get_Next_Res_Des call.  By changing the ResType
              // argument, all resources can be extracted for this
              // board.
              //
              // Again I will stress that because the devnode entered
              // this dynamically loaded driver in existence, no
              // assignment of resources from this level is needed,
              // the Configuration Manager did it all for us.


                  return(CR_SUCCESS);

          case CONFIG_TEST:
          case CONFIG_STOP:
          case CONFIG_REMOVE:         // CONFIG_REMOVE may need to
                  return(CR_SUCCESS); // remove memory structures
          default:                    // started for this DevNode.
                  return(CR_DEFAULT);
      }
}


//
// TESTWPU_NewDriver
// TESTWPU_NewDriver is where the driver's configuration handler
// actually gets registered.  Here is where non-Plug and Play
// devices would get their resource data added to a new
// logical configuration for the DevNode.  Because this is a
```

```
// Plug and Play ISA card, this DevNode already has logical
// configurations built by the .INF that was seen as the
// associated file for this hardware.
//
// CM_INTERNAL          _cdecl            configmg.h
//

CONFIGRET CM_INTERNAL
TESTWPU_NewDriver(DEVNODE DevNode)
{

    CM_Register_Device_Driver(DevNode, \
                        TESTWPU_ConfHandler, 0, 0);
    return(CR_SUCCESS);
}


//
//    END
//    Driver Loader and Installer portion, TESTWPU
//
```

Following are the files for the included sample code:

TESTWPUA.ASM	Intel 386-based assembly code
TESTWPU.C	C source code
TESTWPU.H	Header file for C code
MAKEFILE	NMAKE batch build file

You will need to change some parameters for MAKEFILE to run. Be sure all your binaries are in the path, as well as all applicable libraries and included files. These files were built and compiled using Microsoft's Visual C++ Version 2.0, Microsoft's MASM 6.11, and the Windows 95 SDK/DDK CD-ROM Build 347.

Good Luck!

Win32 API for Windows 3.1 Programmers: Moving Windows 3.1 Applications to Windows 95

7

by Bethany Kenner

IN THIS CHAPTER

There are two kinds of programmers in this world: Some are saying, "Oh boy, Windows 95 is here! Look at all the neat things I can do!" and others are groaning, "Oh no, it's a new operating system. Look at all the changes I have to make!" This chapter's first section, "Necessary Changes," aims to answer the fears of all programmers in the latter camp (the author included!). This section covers the bare-minimum changes that allow your program to run naked through a 32-bit operating system. (If you're really lazy, you can still send your app out clothed in a 16-bit shell; but it'll run like a depressed turtle.) This might turn out to be so easy, and the results so pleasing, that you suddenly find yourself jumping around with the former set, wondering what other nifty things can be done (the author herself confesses to a little jumping). The section on "Nice Changes" explains how to give your program a complete Windows 95 look and feel; "Improving Performance" shows you how to take advantage of Windows 95's underlying architecture.

Necessary Changes

What must you absolutely, positively do to your Windows 3.1 application? Not as much as you might think! Only a handful of the Visual C++ functions has been radically changed or deleted, such as those involving com port I/O and direct DOS access. The others have merely been altered to pass 32-bit parameters instead of 16-bit parameters. A few elementary function changes might be all your application needs. These changes can be made almost painlessly by using PORTTOOL. PORTTOOL.EXE scans your source code one file at a time, looking for obsolete and altered functions and tokens. Wherever it finds something obsolete, it inserts a comment such as `FlushComm: Replaced by PurgeComm`, which enables you to easily update your source code. PORTTOOL comes with Microsoft Visual C and MSDN (Microsoft Developer's Network). It may also be obtained from CompuServe or the Internet. More information is available in the accompanying article on MSDN: "Porting 16-Bit Windows-Based Applications to Win32," by Randy Kath.

More difficult porting problems may result from dependence on short filenames, shared memory across processes, and explicit dependence on 16-bit data type sizes. Let's go over the major porting issues in more detail.

Long Filenames

Filenames are no longer limited to 8.3 characters but can be up to 255 characters in length. They can include such characters as

.~'!@#$%^&()_-+={}[];'

and spaces. Although you may still find a .3 extension at the end of the filename, you could just as easily find a .22 extension. Because there can be multiple periods, a filename might look like

filename.old.Additional information from 1995.text

All kinds of assumptions about filenames have suddenly become obsolete. Directories can have long filenames as well, and Figure 7.1 shows a sample Win95 directory structure with both long file and directory names. Actually, a single file cannot use the entire 255 characters, because this limit applies to the entire path. A file off the root could have 252 characters in its name, with C:\ taking the first three positions. Also, if a file is nested within 50 directory folders, there may only be space for 1 or 2 more characters, or none.

FIGURE 7.1.

Long file and directory names.

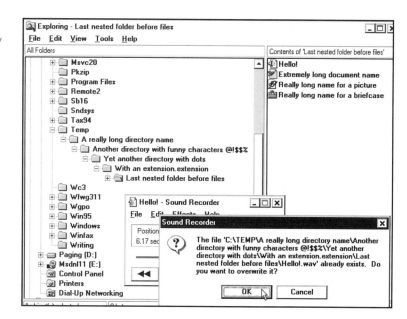

Consider the following:

- Your application should be able to display a reasonable amount of the filename in its user interface. Users should be able to scroll the filename horizontally, in case it won't fit on the display.

- Buffers for filenames should allocate space for 256 characters (255 and the trailing NULL). Better yet, allocate space for _MAX_PATH + 1 characters. That way, when Microsoft changes the path length, you won't have to change your code again.

- File extension parsing routines should look for the .3 extension at the end of the name, instead of looking at the ninth character or searching for the first period.

- Filename comparison routines may need altering.

Many of these changes are automatic with the use of common dialog boxes. The File | Open and File | Save dialog boxes can be accessed with the functions GetOpenFileName and GetSaveFileName. These dialog boxes display and abbreviate the filenames properly, provide proper scrolling, and use the Win95 user interface. GetOpenFileName and GetSaveFileName require an OPENFILENAME struct, with a preallocated buffer (lpstrFile) to contain the return path and filename. You should preallocate at least _MAX_PATH + 1 characters to lpstrFile.

32-Bit Everything

Most data types have become 32-bit, including ints, BOOLs, and HANDLEs. FAR pointers have become NEAR pointers. The only data types that have not become 32-bit are BYTE and char (8-bits), and short and WORD (16-bits). There is also a wide character type, WCHAR, which is 16-bits. The types to watch out for are outlined in the following sections.

Handles

All handle types are 32-bit (HWND, HANDLE, HGDIOBJECT, HDC, and so on). This might cause problems if your old program stores handles in a WORD or short. An example of this problem is shown below.

16-bit code:

```
DrawWindow( WORD hWnd ) {
    WORD hDC = GetDC( hWnd );
```

32-bit code:

```
DrawWindow( HWND hWnd ) {
    HDC hDC = GetDC( hWnd );
```

The 32-bit version in this example will compile properly for both 16-bit and 32-bit windows, because the compiler will use the appropriate HANDLE type.

GetWindowWord and GetClassWord are commonly used to obtain handles. Because handles are now 32-bit, you will need to use GetWindowLong and GetClassLong to obtain the entire handle.

Pointers

All pointers are 32-bit. If you've stored pointers in WORD or short types, they will need to be changed as well.

16-bit pointer:

```
short pWindowPos;
```

32-bit pointer:

```
LPWINDOWPOS pWindowPos;
```

16- or 32-bit pointer:

```
WINDOWPOS* pWindowPos;
```

The third declaration will produce a pointer whose size depends on the compiler and memory model.

Because FAR and NEAR pointers are now both 32-bit, these directives may be removed as well.

Graphics Coordinates

All graphics coordinates are 32-bit. This has necessitated some changes in several GDI functions, which formerly returned a DWORD containing the previous current position in the HIWORD and LOWORD. Because returning a position would now require passing 64 bits instead of 32, the functions have been altered. They return a BOOL indicating success or failure, and the previous current position is placed in an additional parameter. You will have to alter any GDI functions your application uses to accept an additional parameter, and retrieve the previous current position from that parameter when the function returns. An example of this problem is given below.

16-bit code:

```
MoveToCenter( HDC hDC, short left, short top ) {
    DWORD dwSize;
    short x,y;

    dwSize = GetWindowExt( hDC );
    MoveTo( hDC, left + LOWORD( dwSize ),
                top + HIWORD( dwSize ));
}
```

32-bit code:

```
MoveToCenter( HDC hDC, int left, int top ) {
    BOOL bSuccess;
    LPSIZE pSize;
    LPPOINT pPoint;

    bSuccess = GetWindowExtEx( hDC, pSize );
    if( bSuccess ) {
        MoveToEx( hDC, left + pSize->cx/2,
                    top + pSize->cy/2, pPoint );
    }
}
```

A complete list of altered functions can be found in the MSDN article "Porting 16-Bit Windows-Based Applications to Win32."

Message Parameters

Message IDs, WPARAM, and LPARAM are all 32-bit parameters. Many Windows 95 messages have been rearranged to accommodate handles in the lParam. Because these handles now take up the entire 32 bits, the remaining information in the lParam has been squeezed out. Where to put it? In the wParam!

Unfortunately, this change will affect almost every Windows 3.x program. If you have no other porting issues, you will still need to alter your message dispatching routines. An example for WM_COMMAND, WM_VSCROLL, and WM_HSCROLL follows. You should check the Win95 API help for each WM_ message your application handles.

16-bit code:

```
LRESULT MyWindow::WndProc( UINT uMsg, WPARAM wParam, LPARAM lParam ) {

    switch( uMsg ) {
        case WM_COMMAND: return OnCommand( wParam, LOWORD( lParam ),
                                                    HIWORD( lParam ) );
        case WM_VSCROLL: return OnVScroll( wParam, LOWORD( lParam ),
                                                    HIWORD( lParam ) );
        case WM_HSCROLL: return OnHScroll( wParam, LOWORD( lParam ),
                                                    HIWORD( lParam ) );
    }
}

LRESULT MyWindow::OnCommand( WORD idItem, HWND hwndCtl, WORD wNotifyCode ) {...
LRESULT MyWindow::OnVScroll( WORD wScrollCode, int nPos, HWND hwndCtl ) {...
LRESULT MyWindow::OnHScroll( WORD wScrollCode, int nPos, HWND hwndCtl ) {...
```

32-bit code:

```
LRESULT MyWindow::WndProc( UINT uMsg, WPARAM wParam, LPARAM lParam ) {

    switch( uMsg ) {
        case WM_COMMAND: return OnCommand( LOWORD( wParam ),
                                            HIWORD( wParam ), lParam );
        case WM_VSCROLL: return OnVScroll( LOWORD( wParam ),
                                            HIWORD( wParam ), lParam );
        case WM_HSCROLL: return OnHScroll( LOWORD( wParam ),
                                            HIWORD( wParam ), lParam );
    }
}

LRESULT MyWindow::OnCommand( WORD wID, WORD wNotifyCode, HWND hwndCtl ) {...
LRESULT MyWindow::OnVScroll( WORD wScrollCode, short nPos, HWND hwndCtl ) {...
LRESULT MyWindow::OnHScroll( WORD wScrollCode, short nPos, HWND hwndCtl ) {...
```

A few messages have changed (or haven't changed) in unexpected ways.

■ In dealing with mouse messages, note that mouse screen positions are not 32-bit. The LOWORD of lParam contains the x position, and the HIWORD contains the y position. It's often necessary to convert these to 32-bit integers during calculations with other integers. Unfortunately, the wrong cast might yield the unsigned value of the position. In order to preserve the sign, first cast the position to a short, and then to an int.

Unsigned integer:

```
(int) xPos
```

Signed integer:

```
(int) (short) xPos
```

- The WM_CTLCOLOR message no longer exists. It has been broken into WM_CTLCOLORBTN, WM_CTLCOLORDLG, WM_CTLEDIT, WM_CTLLISTBOX, WM_CTLMSGBOX, WM_CTLSCROLLBAR, and WM_CTLSTATIC. If your application processes WM_CTLCOLOR and nCtlType, you should rearrange the dispatch routing.

In addition to the above 32-bit considerations, it would be a good idea to search through your source files for all explicit casts and declarations of types WORD and short. Give them a once-over to ensure that no data is being lost because of truncation. Your Visual C++ compiler should warn you about most of these cases.

Shared Memory

Every process in Windows 95 runs in its own memory space. Not only can processes no longer corrupt each other's memory, but also processes can no longer share memory. For applications with multiple instances accustomed to sharing common memory, this could be a big problem; the applications probably require some redesigning. Here are two common methods for sharing memory between processes under Windows 95.

- Share memory with memory-mapped files. Memory-mapped files enable you to access file data as though it were memory. The file's contents are mapped into the process's virtual memory space. It is intended to provide fast file access for applications. When an application reads a 200 byte record from a file using standard file access, it makes a system call to ReadFile; the system swaps 4 KB of the file from the hard disk into actual memory, and then copies the 200 byte record into your application's space in actual memory. When that same 200 bytes is read from a memory-mapped file, 4 KB of the virtual memory is swapped from the hard disk into actual memory, and your application reads it right where it is. There are no system calls, and the 200 bytes are not copied into your application's memory space. Avoiding the system call and the additional 200 byte copying reduces the overhead and speeds up the access time. This is the primary purpose of memory-mapped files. They can also be used to share memory across processes.

  A process maps a file into memory with CreateFileMapping, assigning it a name as it does so. Subsequent processes can obtain a handle to the file mapping by using OpenFileMapping or CreateFileMapping with the same name. Both processes can read the same file mapping, using it as shared memory.

- Another way to share memory is to store common data in a DLL. Each process can query the same DLL for information.

If your application doesn't absolutely need to have multiple instances running, you can cop out and disallow it. In order to find out whether or not the application is already running, you'll need to call FindWindow. hPrevInstance is no longer passed to applications, so you can no longer use it to determine whether the application is running. The parameter is still there; but it's always NULL. FindWindow searches for a particular class and window name, and it returns NULL if the class is not running.

Plug and Play

Most external devices are handled automatically by the Windows 95 operating system. Devices can be plugged into and pulled out of a computer, and the system automatically searches for the correct device driver and allocates resources. What this means for your application is that it cannot rely on any device remaining available. Your application may be printing when suddenly a different printer is attached. Of course, that sort of thing has always happened; but under Win95 you will receive messages telling you about it. Your application can handle such events gracefully just by intercepting a few messages. WM_DEVICECHANGE comes through the LOWORD of WM_COMMAND. Its parameters tell you when a new device is detected, when a device is removed or about to be removed, and when the system configuration changes. WM_DISPLAYCHANGE is sent whenever the display resolution is changing. These are the only messages you need to handle in order to support Plug and Play. You can then reconfigure your application to use another device, ask the user to politely give the device back, perform an orderly shutdown, or handle the event in any number of ways other than simply crashing.

If You Use...

A few features have changed radically. If your application uses COM port I/O, sound, Dos3Call, or customized icon painting, you will have to make some special changes:

- The communications port has become just another file, accessible through functions such as CreateFile, ReadFile, and WriteFile. PORTTOOL, mentioned earlier, will suggest the appropriate replacement functions.

- Most of the functions used to manipulate sound have been replaced by PlaySound. PORTTOOL will also mark these functions.

- If your application uses any calls to Dos3Call, the calls will have to be replaced by file I/O functions from the Win32 API. Again, PORTTOOL will suggest the appropriate replacements.

- If your program depends in any way on performing its own customized icon painting, you will need to remove that dependency. Under Windows 95, a minimized application will never receive a WM_PAINTICON message. There are no icons sitting on the bottom of a Windows 95 screen—only a sometimes-visible status bar. Minimizing an application banishes it to the status bar, where only the program title and 16×16 icon are displayed.

Make Files

Don't forget to change the make file before recompiling your application. The changes listed in this section should enable you to compile and run under Windows 95, but you can't use your old make file. You can construct a make file by examining a new one from an SDK sample. If you are using Visual C++, it should convert the make file for you. If not, you can do what I always do: create a brand new project, add your source files, and let Visual C++ create the new make file from there.

Nice Changes

Now that your program runs under Windows 95, there are a number of things you should do so that it won't appear broken. Let's go over some of the major items.

OLE

Every Windows 95 application should support drag-and-drop OLE, if it is at all feasible that anyone would want to drag and drop it somewhere. Everything in Windows 95 is an object. And every object can be embedded in every other object. Windows 95 users will quickly become accustomed to dragging objects around and dropping them into documents and folders. If they try to grab your application and it doesn't do anything at all, it will look dysfunctional to them. If your application already supports cut-and-paste, this won't be a very difficult step. If not, you may have some work ahead of you.

At the very least, your application should either:

- Allow objects to be embedded and linked within it, and embed objects dropped over it; or...

- Be capable of embedding itself in another application, and recognize when it is being dropped on something.

The first kind of application is a container; the second is an object.

Most OLE objects allow visual editing: double-clicking on the object brings up the appropriate menu and toolbar in the same container (see Figure 7.2). A container should also store its data as an OLE compound file and provide file summary information. Implementing OLE will involve exposing a number of common functions for an object or calling those functions for a container. The OLE SDK contains sample code for a container, Cl2Test, and an object, Sr2Test.

FIGURE 7.2.
Visual editing of a picture embedded in WordPad.

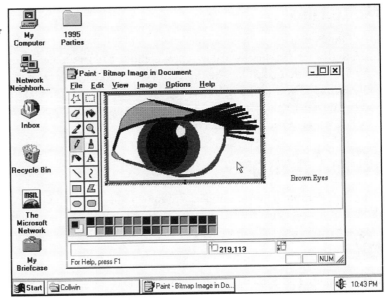

The Registry

The Windows 95 registry manages an enormous amount of application-specific, user-specific, and machine-specific data. It holds data for hardware configurations, devices, software initializations, user preferences—you name it. It holds everything found in Windows 3.x under the files autoexec.bat, config.sys, system.ini, and win.ini, all of which are now obsolete. Your application can and should store all its initialization data in the registry as well. The registry is quite large, so it's a good idea to store it in a logical place.

The registry stores its data in a hierarchy of keys and subkeys and allows each subkey to store multiple values. The major keys of interest are HKEY_LOCAL_MACHINE and HKEY_CURRENT_USER. Let's say your company, Good Software, needs to store both general and user-specific information for a word processor called Good Word Processor. A good place to store the user-specific information is under the HKEY_CURRENT_USER/Software key. The rest might go under HKEY_LOCAL_MACHINE/Software (see Figure 7.3).

Several functions are available to enable you to interact with the registry. A registry entry is stored as a particular type: REG_SZ is a string, REG_DWORD is a 32-bit number, and so on. The type must be specified in order to query the registry.

FIGURE 7.3.

Windows 95 registry entries.

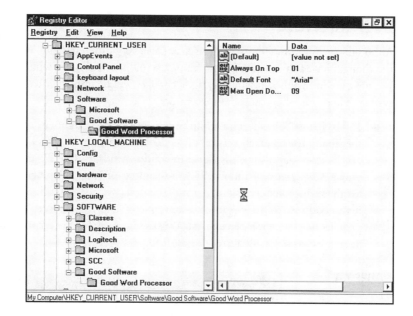

Retrieving Registry Information

Your application can read the registry using the RegQueryValueEx function. To store a value in the registry, use the RegSetValueEx function. The following code snippet reads the contents of the value name "Font" in the subkey HKEY_CURRENT_USER\Software\Good Software\Good Word Processor and then replaces it with "Arial".

```
HKEY hKey;
DWORD fontNameLength;

// Obtain a handle to the key
RegOpenKeyEx( HKEY_CURRENT_USER,
              "Software\\Good Software\\Good Word Processor",
              NULL, NULL, &hKey );

// Obtain the length of the key
RegQueryValueEx( hKey, "Font", NULL, REG_SZ, NULL, &fontNameLength );

// Create a string of the proper length
char fontName[ fontNameLength ];

// Retrieve the string
RegQueryValueEx( hKey, "Font", NULL, REG_SZ, fontName, &fontNameLength );

// Replace the font name with "Arial"
RegSetValueEx( hKey, "Font", 0, REG_SZ, "Arial", 6 );
```

User Interface

Although the Windows 95 user interface appears very different from Windows 3.x, most of the changes have to do with window frames, scrollbars, and other window elements. Unless you are drawing your own window, these changes will be implemented automatically by the system. There are, of course, a few exceptions.

■ 16×16 icons: Whenever an application is minimized, it goes to the status bar, where the small (16×16 pixel) version of the icon and the application title are displayed. The 16×16 icon may also be displayed in window title bars (see Figure 7.4). If you have only a 32×32 icon, Windows 95 will shrink it for you. The descriptions I have heard for these shrunken icons range from "unattractive" to "looks like a squashed bug." So it's a good idea to draw your own 16×16 icon, and register both the 16×16 and 32×32 pixel icons. There is a place in WNDCLASSEX, hIconSm, for the second icon. RegisterClassEx will register the WNDCLASSEX structure.

FIGURE 7.4.

Small icons.

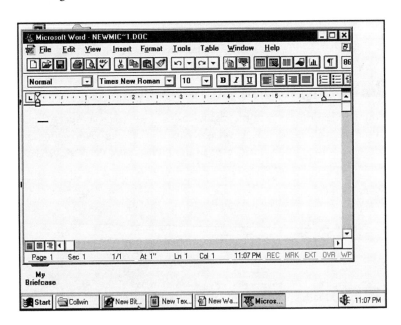

■ GetSysMetrics and GetSysColor: Thoughtful applications have always asked the system for the preferred color scheme and the current resolution. Windows 95 users will be accustomed to having their personal environment show up. At times, when trying to fix a bug on my neighbor's lime green, fluorescent orange, and yellow screen, I've questioned the wisdom of user-determined color schemes. But who am I to stand in the way of progress? Besides, if I hard-code my window text black, and the user's window background is black... More critical is the question of system font sizes, border widths, title bar heights, and so on. Your application can quickly become illegible if there is no room for titles, text, or even window space. Not only should your application obtain the system's metrics and user settings from the registry when initializing; it should also respond to WM_WININICHANGED, WM_FONTCHANGED, and WM_SYSCOLORCHANGE. (Although win.ini is no longer used, WM_WININICHANGED is still sent when parameters formerly found in win.ini change.)

Setup Guidelines

To encourage conformity among installation programs, Microsoft has issued a set of standard setup guidelines. They include methods of avoiding file clutter, using the registry rather than INI files, and uninstalling programs. These guidelines may be found in the Windows SDK or MSDN. For even more consistency in the appearance of your setup program, you may want to use the GUI Setup Toolkit provided in the SDK.

Help

Help files in Windows 95 have a different appearance and greater functionality than Windows 3.1 help files. No more confusing submenu items; help contents, index, and search are now together in one main window, separated by tabs. Even better, the help compiler does this part for you. The main change that might interest you is the new capability to launch applications from help. Your help topic on configuring your application could contain a button that brings up the configuration program (see Figures 7.5 and 7.6). Also, you might want to rearrange your help file tasks so that they are displayed in secondary windows.

FIGURE 7.5.

Launching a program from Windows 95 Help.

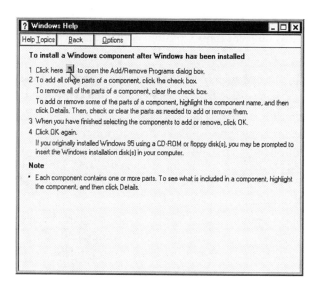

FIGURE 7.6.

Launched (Windows 95 Help remains open).

Common Dialog Boxes

Several common dialog box classes have been added to the Win32 API. Using these could save you a lot of trouble. For one thing, they already conform to the Win95 user interface; they accept long filenames; and they are aware of metrics and color options. Also, they can be compiled for Windows 95, Windows NT, and Win32s without any changes in code. The available dialog boxes are ChooseColor, ChooseFont, FindText, GetFileTitle, GetOpenFileName, GetSaveFileName, PrintDlg, and ReplaceText. All of them provide hooks so that you can add additional controls. For minor alterations (additional text, reduced functionality, different control placement) you won't even need the hooks. Just follow these three steps:

1. Copy the dialog box entry from cmndlg.rc in the SDK samples into your application's .rc file. The dialog box names are somewhat cryptic, but it's not too hard to figure out which one is which.

2. Open the dialog box and add text, move controls around, and change control properties as desired. To remove a control, turn on disabled and turn off visible (NOT WS_VISIBLE | WS_DISABLED for raw text file fans). Do not delete the control! The dialog box procedure in the library is depending on that control's existence and will not run without it.

3. Call the common dialog box from your program. Enable the use of templates and set your template name into the appropriate structure. File | Open and Save, for example, use an OPENFILENAME struct with an lpTemplateName member.

Voilà—a personalized common dialog box. Windows 95 templates are different from NT and 3.x templates, so if you're planning to run your application outside Windows 95, you'll need two templates. Then you can check the version (`GetVersionEx`) to determine which one to use.

Right Mouse Button

Windows 95 applications should use the right mouse button to bring up contextual pop-up menus. The right mouse button should not be used for anything else. `TrackPopupMenu` will display a pop-up menu at the coordinates you give it. It takes screen coordinates, so if you intercept `WM_RBUTTONDOWN` or `WM_RBUTTONUP`, first convert the mouse coordinates with `ClientToScreen`. The menu displayed should only show actions available to the object clicked. Right-clicking on an embedded sound in a text document, for example, should yield menu items like Play and Record, not Print or Spell Check.

Windows 95 Logo

If you've gotten this far, you might want to consider qualifying for the Windows 95 Logo. To qualify, your application must:

- Be a portable Win32 executable compiled with a 32-bit compiler.
- Run on both Windows 95 and Windows NT.
- Use long filenames.
- Follow the Microsoft Windows 95 User Interface Design Guide.

To fulfill the last requirement, your application should:

- Register 16×16 and 32×32 pixel icons for itself and each file type it supports.
- Use `GetSystemMetric` and `GetSysColor` to determine sizing and coloration.
- Use the right mouse button for contextual menus and not for anything else.
- Use the registry and not use win.ini or system.ini.
- Automatically install and be able to completely uninstall.

If your application uses files, you will also need to:

- Support Universal Naming Convention (UNC) pathnames. (Specify the server and share name before the path and filename.)
- Provide OLE container or object support and drag-and-drop support.
- Include Send Mail functionality through MAPI.

As you can see, the only requirements are Windows NT compatibility, UNC, and MAPI. The first should be automatic as long as you don't change your application too much. There are a number of API function calls available only in Windows 95. UNC support will require obtaining server and share names before using file access. MAPI will require adding Send File to your File menu and using MAPI function calls. Of course, if your application doesn't handle files, you have only NT compatibility to worry about.

Maintaining Backwards Compatibility

If an application must run on both Windows 95 and Windows 3.1, it should not take advantage of certain Windows 95 features. A subset of the Win32 functions are supported on all three platforms: Win32s on Windows 3.x, Windows 95, and Windows NT. If your application stays within this subset, the same executable will run on all three platforms. PORTTOOL can be used to scan your source code for all Win32 functions not supported on Win32s. PORTTOOL uses a data file, PORT.INI, to identify its porting issues and provide comments. To convert PORTTOOL to a Win32s scanning tool, rename WIN32S.DAT to PORT.INI. (Save PORT.INI somewhere else first.) Now PORTTOOL will search for Win32s-incompatible functions.

To take advantage of more Windows 95 features and still maintain backwards compatibility, you can use GetVersionEx to determine which platform you are running on and call different procedures depending on the result. You might want to use something like this in your winMain:

```
DWORD version = GetVersion();
enum {WINNT, WIN32s, WIN95, WIN3x};

#ifdef _WIN32
    if( version < 0x80000000 )
        version = WINNT;
    else if( LOBYTE( LOWORD( version ) ) < 4 )
        version = WIN32s;
    else
        version = WIN95;
#else
    version = WIN3x;
#endif
```

Then wherever you need to implement platform-dependent code, you can use something like this:

```
switch( version ) {
    case WINNT: // Windows NT functions
    case WIN32s: // Win32s functions
    case WIN95:  // Windows 95 functions
    case WIN3x:  // Windows 3.x functions
    }
```

Improving Performance

The Windows 95 operating system offers a number of powerful tools that can greatly enhance performance. There are also many powerful changes in functionality you can take advantage of.

Flat Memory Model

Applications are no longer confined to a 64KB memory segment. Instead, each process has its own 4 GB of virtual memory address space. If your application has been constrained by segment boundaries, this is the time to free it.

Multithreading

It's finally possible to do two things at once, given at least two processors. But Win95's multithreading capabilities give even a single processor machine a pretty good appearance of doing several things at the same time. It's not a good idea to use more threads than you really need because they consume system resources. And for most operations, additional threads will not significantly speed up the process. But if your application performs time-consuming operations such as printing or talking to the modem while maintaining an interactive user interface, having an extra thread or two could be a godsend (at least from the user's point of view). Threads can get tricky, though.

First, there's the timing. A parent thread, for example, can kill a child thread; but first it will want to make sure that the child thread has released any resources or memory it has allocated. The parent may decide to check a flag first, and then destroy the child. But because the threads are both active at the same time, the child may reallocate memory before the parent manages to call the `TerminateThread` function. Even if the parent does not explicitly stop the child thread, the parent's destructor must not complete until the child's resources are released.

Then there's the simple problem of communicating from one thread to another. For example, a background thread may finish printing a document and would like to tell the main thread it is ready for more.

There are a few objects available that enable threads to synchronize themselves.

- Very often one thread will, after completing its chores, have nothing further to do at the moment. It might have just finished a printing job, for example, and won't need to run again until it has something else to print.

  The thread can go into an idle state by waiting on an *event*. When another thread is ready to tell it something, it can wake it by setting the event. The idle thread does absolutely nothing while it is sleeping. The system doesn't even check on it. This provides an incredible performance advantage over the old method of waiting, which was to loop until something changed. An event is created with `CreateEvent`, and its handle can be passed to `CreateThread` so the new thread will know about it. The thread then goes to sleep on `WaitForSingleObject` or `WaitForMultipleObjects`. When the event is triggered, waiting stops, and the thread goes on to the next instruction.

- A *critical section* is an object that can only be held by one thread in a process. It can prevent threads from accessing the same thing at the same time. Before accessing a shared member variable, for example, a thread requests the critical section. If no other thread has the critical section, the first thread gains control immediately and proceeds to its tasks. However, if the critical section is currently owned, the first thread goes into a wait state until the critical section is released.

- A *mutex*, like a critical section, can only be held by one thread. But the mutex is shared across processes, whereas a critical section is only exclusive within its own process. If an application may have multiple instances of itself running, it may need a mutex to guarantee exclusive access. Because of the cross-process checking, mutexes are not as efficient as critical sections.

- *Semaphores* can be owned by a fixed number of threads at the same time. A semaphore is useful in limiting the usage of a resource. For example, to allow a process to use no more than three of the available timers, create a semaphore with a count of three and have each thread wait on the semaphore before obtaining a timer.

Overlapped I/O

Applications that spend much of their time accessing files will benefit greatly from overlapped I/O. ReadFile and WriteFile now accept a pointer to an OVERLAPPED structure. In the overlapped structure, you place a handle to an event. When your program issues a ReadFile or WriteFile, it immediately continues on the next instruction. When the read or write has completed, the event is set and can wake a waiting thread with the information. Your program can read and write at the same time, or perform multiple reads and writes at the same time. Think what that can do for your file access routines!

Structured Exception Handling

The ability to raise exceptions from anywhere within your code is a great time saver. When an exception is raised, it passes to the nearest exception handler or the system exception handler if no other handler is found. This means that instead of checking the same return value over and over again, you can check it once and raise an exception. You then enclose your main routine in a __try __except clause, and if anything goes wrong you will catch it there. Most of the Windows API functions unfortunately do not take advantage of exceptions, so you will still have to check the return value. But at least you only have to check it once.

Suppose your program calls a routine that reads a header, body, and footer from a file. You must check the return value for error after you read the header. After you read the body, you check the return values for both the header and the body. After you read the footer, you check all three return values and return whether the routine succeeded. At each error check, you must determine the cause of any error and handle it appropriately. When the routine returns, you must check the return value of the routine.

With exceptions, you check the return value once after each read and raise an exception if something has gone wrong. In the exception handler, you check the type of error and handle it there. That's all. When the routine returns, you know that no exception was raised; or at least if one was raised, it has already been handled. You don't need to put __try __except everywhere either. Just one set around your main will catch any exceptions in your application. However, if you spawn threads, each thread will need a set around its main procedure.

Unicode

The Unicode standard was designed to aid in making programs accessible internationally. At this writing, there is limited support for Unicode in the Windows 95 operating system. If your application is likely to be translated into other languages, using Unicode will enable you to easily replace your English text with Japanese text. If your code is full of one byte characters, and you need to represent several hundred or several thousand characters, translation will not be easy. Making all your character two bytes instead of one leaves room for any language. If you keep all your data in a string table, you can even port your application just by changing all the strings. You won't even need to recompile. There are a few things you should know about using Unicode.

- To specify that a string is a Unicode string, prefix an L to the left quotation.
  ANSI string:
  ```
  char myString[6] = "Hello";
  ```
  Unicode string:
  ```
  WCHAR myString[6] = L"Hello";
  ```

- Specify the Unicode versions of a function with W. Most character functions have both ANSI and Unicode versions. Although Visual C++ Help shows you only one version of TextOut, there are actually two versions.
  ANSI function:
  ```
  TextOutA( hDC, xPos, yPos, "Hello", 6 );
  ```
  Unicode function:
  ```
  TextOutW( hDC, xPos, yPos, L"Hello", 6 );
  ```
  Notice that the Unicode string L"Hello" is 12 bytes long; but the function has been passed a 6. TextOut requires the number of *characters* as the last parameter. This is always interpreted as the number of Unicode characters, not the number of bytes.

- Define _UNICODE in the Compiler Options. By default, the compiler chooses the ANSI versions of functions. If you add _UNICODE to the Preprocessor Definitions on the C/C++ tab of Project Settings, the compiler will choose the Unicode versions by default. However, the Unicode strings must still be specified with an L.
  ```
  TextOut( hDC, xPos, yPos, L"Hello", 6 );
  ```

Resources in Memory

Resources no longer need to be unlocked when you are finished using them. Memory allocation for them is handled automatically. Because they're unnecessary, these functions should be removed to speed up the application. Just scan your source code for UnlockResource commands and kill them.

Memory Usage Profilers

There are a number of utilities that will assist you in tuning your application. WSTUNE and CAP are among the most popular. Currently, these only tune for Windows NT, but that's still better than no tuning at all. These and several other tuners can be found in MSDN and in the Windows NT 3.5 Resource Kit, if you have Windows NT. These utilities help you to link your routines in the order they are most frequently called, saving lookup time.

Global Variables Allocation

Although each process is allocated 4GB of virtual memory, actual memory is paged in 4 KB at a time. In order to avoid excessive paging, it is wise to group global and main variables by function (for example, variables used in printing, variables used in screen drawing, and so on). That way, all the printing variables will already be in memory when you are printing.

Well, that's an overview of porting. Get your application running by using 32-bit parameters, making minor changes to the window message parameters, and making room for long filenames. Then intercept WM_DEVICECHANGE, WM_DISPLAYCHANGE, WM_WININICHANGED, WM_FONTCHANGED, and WM_SYSCOLORCHANGE and register a 16×16 pixel icon. Alter your setup routine to use the registry. Implement OLE (easy if you can already cut and paste) and enough MAPI to export your documents to Mail. Speed up your operations with multithreading and overlapped I/O.

OK, it's easier said than done. But Microsoft has tried hard to make porting applications from Windows 3.x to Windows 95 an easy task. They've left most of the API calls unchanged and provided PORTTOOL to quickly identify all the other ones. Happy porting.

Win32 API for Windows NT Programmers

8

by Viktor T. Toth

IN THIS CHAPTER

Windows 95 is not Win32s. Unlike its predecessor, if Win32s can be called that at all, Windows 95 delivers a rich implementation of the Win32 API, including support for preemptive multitasking, threads, virtual memory management, long filenames, structured exception handling, synchronization objects, asynchronous operations on serial devices, and many other features you have come to like in 32-bit programming. In fact, many Windows NT programs will run under Windows 95 without any changes. For example, I am writing this text using Microsoft Word 6.0 for Windows NT, running under Windows 95.

There are, however, some features and libraries missing, not implemented in the current release of Windows 95. On the other hand, Windows 95 provides some new services, some of which Microsoft has since made available in the Windows NT 3.51 interim release, some of which are not likely to be available before NT Cairo. Finally, there are some architectural and implementation differences between the two operating systems; examples that come to mind include nationalization support and 16-bit architectural limitations in Windows 95.

In this chapter, I'll review the Win32 API as implemented in Windows 95, from the perspective of a Windows NT programmer.

NT-Specific Functionality in the Win32 API

First, let's start by reviewing API elements that are NT-specific and not available in the present release of Windows 95.

How does Windows 95 handle unimplemented functions? It provides *stub functions,* functions that do nothing but return an error code. This enables Windows 95 to properly load programs that reference such functions. Otherwise, these programs would not load; it would not be possible to write applications that selectively call API functions depending on which operating system they run under.

One interesting situation concerns a specific DLL. If you ever looked at the contents of the SYSTEM subdirectory in your Windows 95 directory, you may have wondered what a file with the name NTDLL.DLL is doing there. Under Windows NT, this DLL contains several undocumented functions of the NT kernel. Unfortunately, many applications make calls to these functions. In order to ensure that these applications load correctly, the designers of Windows 95 were forced to include a file containing equivalent stub functions.

Object-Level Security

Windows 95 does not implement the object-level security found in Windows NT. Security-related parameters in functions such as CreateFile are ignored. It is safe to pass NULL whenever Win32 expects a value of type LPSECURITY_ATTRIBUTES, for example.

Unicode Support

Windows 95 does not provide Unicode support. Unicode versions of functions are merely stub functions. Windows 95 does provide international support in terms of its capability to load and handle multiple character sets. This capability is discussed in the next section.

Windows 95 does provide a Unicode implementation for the following functions: `ExtTextOut`, `GetCharWidth`, `GetTextExtentExPoint`, `GetTextExtentPoint`, `MessageBoxEx`, `MessageBox`, `TextOut`. In addition, the Unicode to ASCII conversion functions `MultiByteToWideChar` and `WideCharToMultiByte` are also implemented.

OpenGL

The OpenGL 3-D graphics rendering library is not available in Windows 95. Documents released by Microsoft (for example, documents in the Microsoft Developer Network Library) indicate that OpenGL might be part of the next release of Windows 95.

NTFS

Although Windows 95 supports (finally!) long filenames on FAT file systems, it does not at present provide support for the NT File System. On dual-boot systems, it is important to continue using FAT file systems in order to ensure that both operating systems can read disk partitions.

Tape Backup Functions

The tape backup functions of Windows NT (for example, `BackupRead`, `EraseTape`) are not available in Windows 95.

New Functionality in Windows 95

Although it lacks NT's functionality in certain areas, Windows 95 offers several new features. These include the new common dialog boxes and common controls, multiple character set support, Plug and Play, the new help system, the new MAPI, auto-run CD-ROM volumes, and a compressed file system.

Window Management

The change in window appearance is one of the most striking differences between Windows 95 and Windows NT. Windows 95 gives applications a new look by providing a new frame window with a close icon, new 3-D dialog boxes, a new appearance for menus, and a scrollbar that indicates the relative size of the visible region. Although these changes are the most visible, they basically require no changes in application programs. Menus continue to send the same WM_COMMAND messages as before, the new close icon sends a WM_CLOSE message, and the management of scrollbar sizes is automatic.

Common Dialog Boxes

Windows 95 offers a new implementation of the well-known set of common dialog boxes for opening and closing files, printing, color and font selection, and text find and replace.

In their simple form, the dialog boxes work exactly the way they do under Windows NT. However, they also offer extended functionality.

The File | Open and File | Save dialog boxes provide support for long filenames. They also present a new, Explorer-like look and feel to the user.

The Font Selection dialog box offers support for multiple character sets.

Printing is controlled through three common dialog boxes in Windows 95. The Printer Selection dialog box is nearly identical to its older version. The Printer Properties dialog box offers a choice of printer settings (depending on the printer selected) in the form of a property sheet. A new common dialog box in Windows 95 is Page Setup, which enables the user to select paper size, source, and orientation.

Finally, the Color Selection and the Find/Replace dialog boxes remain basically identical to their older counterparts.

Common Controls

Windows 95 supports a rich new set of common controls. Visual C++ programmers are already familiar with many of them, such as toolbars and status bars. Others are new to Windows 95. Support for the new common controls is initialized using the InitCommonControls function; the controls themselves can be created using the CreateWindowEx function and specifying the appropriate control style. Alternatively, the built-in Visual C++ dialog box editor and the Microsoft Foundation Classes (MFC) provide support for many of the new common controls.

As with common controls that existed in earlier versions of Microsoft Windows, the new common controls respond to standard messages (for example, WM_SETTEXT) as well as control-specific messages. Common controls send notifications to the application in the form of WM_NOTIFY messages.

The new common controls are summarized in Table 8.1.

Table 8.1. The new common controls.

Control Name	Messages	Notification	MFC 3.1
Animation	ACM_...	ACN_...	CAnimateCtrl
Header	HDM_...	HDN_...	CHeaderCtrl
Hotkey	HKM_...	N/A	CHotkeyCtrl
Image list	N/A	N/A	CImageList
List view	LVM_...	LVN_...	CListViewCtrl
Progress bar	PBM_...	N/A	CProgressCtrl
Property page	N/A	N/A	CPropertyPage
Property sheet	N/A	N/A	CPropertySheet
RTF edit	EM_...	ENM_...	N/A
Slider	TBM_...	TBN_...	CSliderCtrl
Spin	UDM_...	UDN_...	CSpinButtonCtrl
Status bar	SB_...	N/A	CStatusBarCtrl
Tab	TCM_...	TCN_...	CTabCtrl
Toolbar	TB_...	TBN_...	CToolBarCtrl
Tooltip	TTM_...	TTN_...	CToolTipCtrl
Tree view	TVM_...	TVN_...	CTreeCtrl

Animation controls can be used to play simple AVI video files. Certain restrictions apply to the contents of the AVI file (at the time of writing, it is unclear which of these restrictions, if any, will remain in force when the Windows 95 production version is released). Support for animation controls in MFC 3.1 is available through the CAnimateCtrl class. Animation controls respond to messages such as ACM_OPEN; they send notification messages such as ACN_START.

Header controls provide column headers. They are typically used in list view controls. MFC 3.1 provides support for header controls with the CHeaderCtrl class. Header controls respond to messages such as HDM_GETITEMCOUNT; they notify the application using messages such as HDN_ITEMCLICK.

Hotkey controls enable the user to specify a hotkey for a window. When the hotkey is subsequently used, the application receives a WM_SYSCOMMAND message. Hotkey controls respond to messages such as HKM_SETHOTKEY. In MFC 3.1, support for hotkey controls is available via the CHotkeyCtrl class.

Image lists are used to manage a large collection of bitmaps or icons that are of identical size. For example, a list view control uses image lists, which hold all the different icons that the control displays for its items. In MFC 3.1, image lists are supported via the `CImageList` class.

List view controls display a list of items in one of several view formats. List items can be displayed as large icons, or as lists of small icons and columnized text. List views respond to list view messages such as `LVM_SETBKCOLOR` or `LVM_GETIMAGELIST`. List views send list view notification messages, such as `LVN_ITEMCHANGED` or `LVN_ENDDRAG`, to the application. Figure 8.1 shows an example of a list view control in report view.

FIGURE 8.1.

List view control in report view.

List views are supported in MFC 3.1 via the `CListCtrl` class.

Progress bars provide a standardized way of tracking the progress of a lengthy process, such as a file download or scanning a hard disk. A sample progress bar is shown in Figure 8.2.

FIGURE 8.2.

Progress bar.

Progress bars are supported in MFC 3.1 or above via the `CProgressCtrl` class.

Property pages are overlapping child windows that together comprise a property sheet. Windows 95 now provides built-in support for applications that use this interface method. Property pages are actually application-defined modeless dialog boxes. Property pages are created using the `CreatePropertySheetPage` function. There is support for property pages in MFC 3.1 in the form of the `CPropertyPage` class.

Property sheets are system-defined dialog boxes that contain up to four buttons (OK, Cancel, Apply, and Help) and one or more application-supplied property pages. Property sheets are created using the `CreatePropertySheet` function. MFC 3.1 supports property sheets via the `CPropertySheet` class.

Rich-text edit controls provide extended text-editing functionality. RTF edit controls respond to an extended set of edit control messages and communicate with the application through an extended set of edit control notification messages. Note that Visual C++ version 2.1 or MFC version 3.1 do not provide support for RTF edit controls; in order to use these controls, you must include the `richedit.h` header file, available only as part of the Win32 SDK. Undoubtedly, later versions of Visual C++ will provide full support for this control.

Slider controls, also known as trackbar controls, can best be likened to the volume control on a stereo. They provide a much more convenient way to implement this functionality than the prior practice of using scrollbars for this purpose. Slider controls send WM_HSCROLL or WM_VSCROLL messages, depending on their orientation, to their parent window when the user interacts with them. Slider controls respond to messages such as TBM_GETPOS, and notify the application through messages like TBN_RESET. Figure 8.3 shows a sample slider control.

FIGURE 8.3.
Slider control.

MFC 3.1 or above supports slider controls via the CSliderCtrl class.

Spin controls, also known as updown controls, are similar to the Visual Basic spin control VBX. They are usually used in conjunction with edit controls and provide a convenient way to implement or decrement a setting using the mouse. The "buddy" edit control is specified by sending a UDM_SETBUDDY message to the control, which is one example of the kinds of messages spin controls respond to. An example for using spin controls without a buddy control is how property sheets handle many property page tabs in a single line. If the combined width of all tabs exceeds the width available in the property sheet, a horizontal spin control is used to enable the user to browse the tabs.

Spin controls notify the application via UDN_DELTAPOS messages. A spin control, together with its buddy edit control, is shown in Figure 8.4.

FIGURE 8.4.
Spin control with its buddy edit control.

MFC 3.1 or above supports spin controls via the CSpinButtonCtrl class.

Status bars are used to display the status of an application at the bottom of the window. A status bar may consist of several sections. Status bars respond to status bar messages such as SB_SETBORDERS or SB_SETTEXT. In MFC 3.1 or later, status bar controls are supported via the CStatusBarCtrl class.

Tab controls are used in conjunction with property sheets and provide a means for selecting a property page. Tab controls respond to tab control messages such as TCM_SETITEM. Tab controls notify the application via tab control notification messages such as TCN_SELCHANGE. Tab controls can also be configured to support tooltips. In MFC 3.1, support for tab controls is available via the CTabCtrl class. A sample tab control is shown in Figure 8.5.

FIGURE 8.5.
Tab control.

Toolbars are used to provide quick and easy access to an application's functions. A toolbar typically consists of buttons, but may contain other controls such as drop-down lists. Toolbars respond to toolbar messages such as TB_ADDSTRING or TB_DELETEBUTTON. Toolbars send toolbar notification messages, such as TBN_BEGINDRAG or TBN_RESET, to the application. MFC 3.1 or above supports toolbar controls via the CToolBarCtrl class.

Tooltip controls are small rectangular pop-up windows that can be used to display a single line of text describing a control. Tooltips are typically displayed for toolbar controls. Tooltips respond to messages such as TTM_ACTIVATE; they notify the application through messages such as TTN_NEEDTEXT. MFC 3.1 or above provides tooltip control support via the CToolTipCtrl class.

Tree view controls display items in a hierarchical arrangement. These controls can be used to represent a directory structure, documentation contents, or index entries. Tree view controls are used throughout the Windows 95 Explorer. Tree view controls respond to messages such as TVM_INSERTITEM; they communicate with the application using notification messages such as TVN_SELCHANGED. In MFC 3.1, support is available for tree view controls via the CTreeCtrl class. A sample tree view control is shown in Figure 8.6.

FIGURE 8.6.

Tree view control.

International Support with Multiple Character Sets

Although Unicode support is not available in Windows 95, the operating system provides a rather flexible approach for supporting multiple languages. Although Microsoft intends to release versions for over 30 languages, there will be only 3 different code bases for Windows 95: Western (SBCS, single-byte character set), Far-East (DBCS, double-byte character set), and Mid-East (bidirectional). In fact, the Microsoft Developer Network News joked about the ease with which international versions can be released by presenting a screenshot from the Klingon version of Windows 95 (not currently scheduled, unfortunately).

One reason why it is relatively easy to generate these versions is the support of multiple character sets. During installation of Windows 95, you might have noticed that it installed multiple versions for its common fonts, Arial, Courier, and Times New Roman. Applications that were not written for Windows 95 (such as the version of Word I am currently using) see these as separate fonts. Applications that use the new common dialog box for font selection offer an extra field, Script, which can be used to select a specific version of a font. Incidentally, older applications that were written to use the unmodified, "stock" font selection dialog box will also display the new dialog box automatically. For example, you will see this new common dialog box if you select the Fonts option in the Windows 3.1 version of Write, running under Windows 95.

Plug and Play

Windows 95 is Microsoft's first operating system that supports the new Plug and Play device standard. Plug and Play-aware applications must process a new message, WM_DEVICECHANGE. This message informs applications when a Plug and Play device is added to or removed from the system.

The New Help System

The new Windows 95 help system, apart from sporting a different appearance, also supports many new capabilities that authors of help files can take advantage of. These include, for example, support for shortcut buttons in the help text and built-in support for training cards.

The New MAPI

With Windows 95, Microsoft's new mail product, Microsoft Exchange, also debuts. More properly speaking, with Windows 95 Microsoft ships the Microsoft Exchange client, its first client implementation that conforms to the new MAPI, version 1.0.

It is important for application developers to be familiar with the basics of MAPI; Microsoft's Windows 95 logo program requires that applications provide at least basic messaging support in the form of a Send File command.

Applications can support the new MAPI through a choice of APIs. Simple MAPI is provided for backward compatibility for *mail-aware* applications—that is, applications that provide simple messaging services. Newer mail-aware applications should preferably use CMC, the Common Messaging Calls API, for cross-platform compatibility. Sophisticated applications that handle large or complex messages, complex information, or a large message volume (*mail-enabled* applications) can use the Extended MAPI API.

The Extended MAPI API can also be used to create custom extensions to the Microsoft Exchange client and to develop MAPI service providers, such as address book providers, message store providers, or transport providers.

Auto-Run CD-ROMs

Windows 95 supports the auto-run feature for CD-ROMs. In order to take advantage of this feature, the CD-ROM must contain the file AUTORUN.INF in its root directory. This file should contain an entry similar to the following:

```
 [AutoRun]
OPEN=MYAPP.EXE
```

The auto-run feature should not be used to automatically install applications to the user's hard disk.

Compressed Volumes

Having been introduced with MS-DOS 6.0, support for compressed disk volumes is not really a new feature. Windows 95 provides support for compressed disk volumes via its built-in DriveSpace compression. Support for DriveSpace compressed volumes is not presently available in Windows NT.

Other Extensions

In addition to the extensions listed previously, Windows 95 provides several other APIs to extend specific features.

Applications can extend the *shell name space* to create additional folders and objects visible from the desktop. Examples include folders representing remote computers, hardware devices, or fonts.

Applications can extend the shell's capabilities by providing *shell extensions*, which provide additional ways to manipulate file objects. Examples include context menu handlers, which provide new context menus when the right mouse button is used, or icon handlers, which provide a different icon display for each file. Applications can also create and manage *shell links*, or shortcuts.

Windows 95 provides an API to build *access bars*. Access bars are similar in function and appearance to the Windows 95 Taskbar.

Windows 95 provides an API to build file viewers. File viewers are used when the user selects the Quick View command from a file object's context menu.

Windows 95 provides a low-level interface for applications to directly communicate with virtual device drivers (VxDs) through the DeviceIoControl function.

Other Differences

In addition to major areas of functionality not implemented in Windows 95, such as Unicode support or the OpenGL graphics library, there are also other, more subtle differences, which are mostly due to architectural or implementation issues. These differences are mostly limitations of Windows 95 as compared with Windows NT.

The description of differences and limitations in this section is admittedly incomplete. It is based on information released by Microsoft in late spring 1995 and may be subject to change.

Window Management

Because of an internal 16-bit implementation, some limitations are imposed on window management. For example, the standard edit control remains limited to 64 kilobytes of text, in contrast to Windows NT's 32-bit implementation.

The number of window handles and menu handles is limited to 16,364 each. (No, not 16,384, this is not a typo; this is the number published by Microsoft.)

The wParam parameter is limited to 16 bits in calls to SendMessageCallback, SendMessageTimeout, and SendNotifyMessage.

The wParam parameter is limited to 16 bits in listbox messages. This effectively limits the number of listbox items to 32,767.

Keyboard layout functions (for example, ActivateKeyboardLayout) do not support extended error codes through GetLastError.

Windows 95 only supports a single desktop.

The values of IDC_STYLE and IDC_ICON are obsolete for the LoadCursor function.

For message box functions, the values of MB_ICONQUESTION, MB_ICONASTERISK, and MB_ICONHAND are obsolete; applications should use instead the values of MB_ICONEXCLAMATION, MB_ICONINFORMATION, and MB_ICONSTOP, respectively.

Graphics Device Interface

The most notable difference between the Windows NT and Windows 95 GDI implementations is that Windows 95 supports 16-bit world coordinates. When 32-bit coordinates are passed to GDI functions, the upper 16 bits are simply ignored. Specifically, this 16-bit limitation is applicable to bounding rectangles for arcs and other primitive objects, and it also affects metafile playback.

Certain logical objects are still stored in the 64-kilobyte GDI local heap. It is therefore important that applications continue to delete objects such as pens, brushes, or bitmaps that are no longer in use.

Specific limitations affect pens and brushes. For example, Windows 95 only supports dashed or dotted pen styles for thin lines.

World coordinate transforms that include shearing and rotation are not supported. If such a transformation matrix is specified, this will cause an error.

Certain functions (for example, `GetDIBits`) that previously returned the constant `TRUE` to indicate success may now return another non-zero value.

`DeleteObject` behaves differently when an attempt is made to delete a GDI object that is currently selected into a device context. Under Windows NT, the call fails; under Windows 95, it succeeds but results in what is described as a nonfunctioning object, which is automatically deleted when the device context is destroyed.

When a path is constructed under Windows 95 using `BeginPath` and `EndPath`, only the following functions are recorded: `ExtTextOut`, `LineTo`, `MoveToEx`, `PolyBezier`, `PolyBezierTo`, `Polygon`, `Polyline`, `PolylineTo`, `PolyPolygon`, `PolyPolyline`, and `TextOut`.

`SetGraphicsMode` under Windows 95 does not support the advanced graphics mode specified by the `GM_ADVANCED` flag.

`DeviceCapabilities` under Windows 95 does not support `DC_FILEDEPENDENCIES`. It does, however, support the new constants `DC_EMF_COMPLIANT` (to query printer drivers that support enhanced metafiles) and `DC_DATATYPE_PRODUCED` (to retrieve an array of strings indicating the data types supported by printer drivers).

Certain members of the `DEVMODE` structure are not supported under Windows 95 and are provided for compatibility only (for example, `dmFormName`).

Windows 95 does not support print monitors written for Windows NT. Only print monitors written specifically for Windows 95 can be installed using the `AddMonitor` function.

Some printer functions are not available under Windows 95. There are specific limitations in the implementation of some of the remaining printing and print spooling functions.

Kernel

Windows 95 does not support multiple processors and symmetric multiprocessing.

Extended error codes retrieved by `GetLastError` might be different under Windows NT and Windows 95 because of differences in the underlying implementation.

Windows 95 supports asynchronous (overlapped) input and output for serial communication devices only. Overlapped operations are not supported for files and named pipes.

The functions `FileTimeToDosDateTime` and `DosDateTimeToFileTime` are limited to dates up to December 31, 2099. Under Windows NT, these functions allowed dates up to December 31, 2107.

An attempt to use `DeleteFile` to delete a file that is open for normal input and output may succeed. Deleting open files can cause loss of data.

`GlobalRealloc` and `LocalRealloc` cannot be used to change the allocation of a memory block from fixed to moveable.

Guard pages cannot be allocated using the `PAGE_GUARD` attribute. Applications should use instead `PAGE_NOACCESS` and handle `EXCEPTION_ACCESS_VIOLATION` exceptions.

Under Windows 95, shared memory mapped files appear at the same address for all active applications. Also, `CreateFileMapping` does not support the `SEC_IMAGE` and `SEC_NOCACHE` attributes.

The `CreateFile` function does not support access to physical devices using Windows NT naming conventions (for example, `\\.\C:` or `\\.\PhysicalDrive0`).

The `DuplicateHandle` function cannot be used to duplicate handles to registry keys. Also, registry key names cannot contain control characters.

`LoadLibrary` cannot be used to load 16-bit DLLs.

Loaded resources must be freed using `FreeResource`.

Footnote for Developers: Memory Requirements

The difference between development system memory requirements under Windows NT and Windows 95 is not really a design issue. Nevertheless, I feel compelled to tell about my delightful experience concerning the memory requirements of the Visual C++ development system under Windows 95, as compared to Windows NT.

When version 2.0 of Visual C++ was released, the manual stated that the minimum memory requirement to run this system (under Windows NT, of course) is 16M, with 20M recommended. This meant the end of useful life for my notebook computer; with "only" 8M of RAM and a 120M hard drive, installing Windows NT alone seemed like a ridiculous idea, and setting up Visual C++ was not even worth thinking about. A pity—it had been less than two years since I'd bought the machine. Although it was still good enough to run a word processor, my notebook computer was no longer capable of serving as a portable development platform.

When I received my first copy of Windows 95, I decided to do a seemingly hopeless experiment. I emptied my notebook's hard drive and installed Windows 95 on it. I used DriveSpace for disk compression, and once Windows 95 was up and running, I ran the Visual C++ 2.1 installation program from the CD-ROM across the network. Visual C++ installed without a hitch; it also loaded fine and appeared to function normally, despite the small amount of RAM in the machine. So next I loaded a fairly large project (about 230 .CPP and .H files for a total of 3M of source code). Although it certainly cannot be accused of warp speed, my portable happily chugged along and in less than 2.5 hours recompiled the entire project flawlessly. I had a useful, functional Visual C++ installation on this machine! With disk compression, after installing Word for Windows NT and the Visual C++ Quick Reference help files, I still had about 60M of disk space free.

If I had to use this system every day, I would probably curse it for its slowness. On the other hand, this performance is adequate for my infrequent travels. Thanks to Windows 95, my portable now has another lease on life for development work, and I can put off a new purchase for at least another year. I am a convert.

Shared Features

Up to this point, we have enumerated those areas of functionality where Windows 95 differs slightly, or perhaps not so slightly, from Windows NT. Before we conclude this chapter, it is perhaps useful to summarize those areas that are supported by Windows 95 just as well as under Windows NT; in other words, there are key sets of features and services that programmers can depend on with both operating systems. The features mentioned here are those that most characteristically distinguish Windows 95 and Windows NT from Windows 3.1.

Preemptive Multitasking and Threads

Windows 95 supports the same level of preemptive multitasking as Windows NT. There are subtle differences when it comes to 16-bit applications, but 32-bit programmers essentially see the same API for process and thread control and for synchronization objects. Like Windows NT and unlike its predecessor, Windows 3.1, Windows 95 also implements per-thread message queues.

32-Bit Addressing

Windows 95 provides the same flat 32-bit addressing model for 32-bit applications as Windows NT. Applications can use the same family of virtual memory management functions and expect identical behavior. Minor differences exist when it comes to passing 32-bit parameters to the Windows 95 versions of some system functions. Because of an internal 16-bit implementation, Windows 95 might only interpret the lower 16-bit word of these parameters, whereas Windows NT interprets the full 32-bit word.

Exceptions

Structured exception handling is available under Windows 95. Application programs can expect identical behavior on behalf of system functions when it comes to raising exceptions.

For example, an application that relies on an access violation exception to allocate virtual memory on demand will work identically under Windows 95 and Windows NT.

Long Filename Support

Windows 95 supports the long filename FAT file system; this is the same file system that is supported by Windows NT version 3.5 and later. Applications that support long filenames behave identically under Windows NT and Windows 95. Obviously, under Windows NT these applications can also access files on NTFS volumes.

MS-DOS and Console Support

Windows 95 provides support for both 16-bit MS-DOS programs and NT console applications. Console applications can be run from the MS-DOS command prompt. Note that console applications are only supported in MS-DOS sessions started from within Windows 95; if Windows 95 is restarted in MS-DOS mode, console applications cannot be run.

Porting NT Applications to Windows 95

I can almost hear you scream, "What? I spent months developing for Win32 under Windows NT, and now this guy is telling me that my application has to be *ported* to Windows 95?" Calm down; most Windows NT applications run under Windows 95 perfectly fine. Examples that I use include the NT version of Microsoft Word and Excel, the Visual C++ compiler, and NCSA Mosaic, the World Wide Web browser.

Then why do several applications have separate 32-bit versions for Windows NT and Windows 95? For one thing, the Windows 95 version might have been designed to take advantage of the new user interface and its features. The subtle differences between the two operating systems might also be the cause of some minor compatibility problems that the Windows 95 version is designed to address.

Is Porting Necessary?

The first step when porting an NT application to Windows 95 is deciding whether porting is necessary at all. The questions to be asked are as follows:

- Does the application run under Windows 95?
- Does it have any features that are incompatible with Windows 95?
- Is it affected by any of Windows 95's limitations?
- Are any NT-specific features of the Win32 API used?
- Can the application take advantage of the new GUI?

The answer to the first question can be obtained by thoroughly testing the application under Windows 95. The answer to the second question can be found by reviewing the application's design for any feature set that is not supported under Windows 95. For example, if your application depends on the presence of security attributes, it might not run correctly under Windows 95, which does not support the security model of Windows NT.

Answering the third question might prove trickier. For example, your application might use a standard edit control to handle large text files; if you are not aware of the control's limitations under Windows 95, it might never occur to you to test the control with files that are sufficiently large to cause the application to malfunction.

The fourth question relates to implementation. For example, if your application relies on the OpenGL graphics library to implement its graphical functions, it will obviously not be compatible with Windows 95. By reviewing the application's design and the source code, these problem areas can be identified.

The fifth question represents a design decision. Does your application have features that can be improved by using a new common control? Can a custom implementation be replaced to provide a look and feel that is more consistent with Windows 95? Would your application benefit from using the new common dialog boxes? If the answer is yes to any of these questions, it might be worthwhile to consider upgrading your application to use the new common dialog boxes and common controls.

Using a Common Executable

As I mentioned before, Windows 95 provides stub functions in place of Win32 API functions it does not implement. Thus, applications written to take advantage of NT-specific features of the Win32 API will load correctly. It is therefore possible to create a single executable that uses a different feature set depending on which operating system it is loaded under: Windows 95, Windows NT, or possibly Win32s.

Specifically, an application can check which operating system it is running under and execute different code depending on the result. For example, an application may use the new, Explorer-like file management dialog boxes while it is running under Windows 95 and revert back to the old ones under Windows NT. This solution makes it possible to build a single executable that runs on all 32-bit platforms, as opposed to being forced to maintain separate versions.

Version information can be obtained using the `GetVersionEx` function (which supersedes `GetVersion`). For example, an application can determine which operating system it is running under and perform version specific operations with the following code.

```
OSVERSIONINFO versionInfo;
...
    GetVersionEx(&versionInfo);
    switch (versionInfo.dwPlatformId)
```

```
    {
        case VER_PLATFORM_WIN32s:
            // Do things the Win32s way
            ...
            break;
        case VER_PLATFORM_WIN32_NT:
            // Do things the NT way
            ...
            break;
        case VER_PLATFORM_WIN32_WINDOWS:
            // Do things the Windows 95 way
            ...
            break;
        default:
            // Report error: unknown OS version
    }
    ...
```

> **NOTE**
>
> The version information constants used above are defined in `winbase.h`. However, it appears that the version of `winbase.h` supplied with Visual C++ version 2.1 does not contain the definition for `VER_PLATFORM_WIN32_WINDOWS`. In order to use this constant, you either have to define it yourself (it should be defined as 1) or use the version of `winbase.h` that comes with the Win32 SDK for Windows 95. Presumably, later versions of Visual C++ will correct this problem.

The New GUI

There are two reasons for converting an existing application to the new GUI. The first reason is to conform to the Windows 95 look and feel; the second is to take advantage of the new features.

Applications can take advantage of the new GUI by utilizing the new common dialog boxes and by making use of the new common controls.

Applications that use common dialog boxes in their unaltered form are easily upgraded to the new look. In most cases, nothing needs to be done; sometimes, as in the case of the File | Open and Save dialog boxes, the application must explicitly specify a flag to indicate that it wishes to use the new version of the dialog box.

In the case of applications that use custom dialog box templates, it might become necessary to upgrade the templates to reflect the new common dialog boxes. If the application is to remain compatible with older versions of Windows, such as Windows NT 3.5 or earlier, it might be necessary to supply two sets of templates.

The new common controls can enhance, and often simplify, an application's dialog boxes. For example, if the application relied on a custom implementation of a list control, it might be worthwhile to consider replacing that with the new list view control. (Or maybe not; fixing something that works just fine is not always a great idea.)

Using the new common controls in place of private implementations also ensures a more consistent look and feel for the application with respect to the rest of the Windows 95 environment.

Database Support and ODBC

9

by Ronald Laeremans

IN THIS CHAPTER

Accessing Databases in Your Application: A Fresh Start

How you look at database access in an application and with what mindset you approach ODBC are likely to be different depending on whether you are upsizing from ISAM-type databases such as FoxPro or downsizing from mainframe, mini, or UNIX-based relational databases. ODBC will be more of a culture shock if you belong to the upsizing group.

Databases: ISAM and Relational/SQL

ISAM (Indexed Sequential Access Method) is the term used to describe most of the databases the majority of us have been working with for most of the PC era. They have the following main characteristics:

- One-record-at-a-time access
- Explicit use of access paths (that is, indexes)
- An absence of mechanisms to look at anything other than one base table at a time

The inability to use joins, derived tables, relations, or any other mechanism that is on a higher level than accessing just one base table means quite simply that you have to write all of the database navigation code yourself.

Databases: File- and Server-Based

Both relational and nonrelational databases can exist in two forms: file-based and server- or engine-based. For single-user access it can be argued that file-based databases and server-based databases are identical, but in general they have very little in common from a design viewpoint.

File-based databases (see Figure 9.1) share only one thing: the actual disk files where the data, indexes, and (possibly) lock files are stored. The server on which the files are stored is only accessed using the normal file-sharing protocols. It does not play any active role in managing the database or the clients. The client-side ODBC drivers in this type of database talk to the physical files directly—that is, using _open, _read, _write, and similar operations. Locking of data is performed by either locking byte ranges in the files (or entire files) or by a shared lock file in which each driver writes a record specifying what its client has locked in the database files.

FIGURE 9.1.
File-based database.

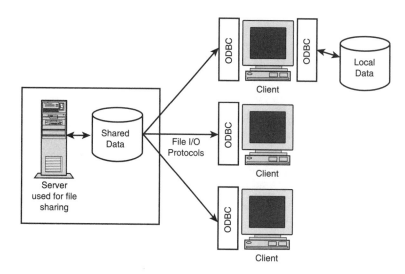

Server-based databases (see Figure 9.2) don't share the physical files themselves. They have a dedicated server process running on the server machine that accesses the physical data files. Clients connect to that engine using any mechanism of *IPC* (Inter-Process Communications) that the server and client both understand. For example, in the case of SQL Server, the ODBC driver communicates over named pipes, sockets, or one of the other transport protocols using the TDS (Tabular Data Stream) protocol that is proprietary to SQL Server.

FIGURE 9.2.
Server-based databases.

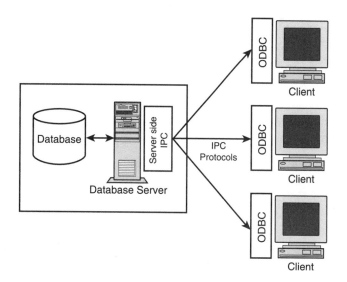

Server-based databases have several inherent advantages, detailed in the following list. These advantages become more significant when the number of clients using the data increases. Most of these advantages are a direct result of the fact that one process (that is, the server) has full control over all physical data access.

- Locking can be much more efficient. Locked tables are mostly held in RAM for rapid access in server databases. This is, of course, impossible with file sharing because in that case there is no single process that has the "total picture" of what all the users are doing.

- Online backup (that is, backup without taking down the database), commit/rollback, and concurrency are easier to achieve with good performance.

- Database caching is much more efficient when done by the server process than is the file system-based caching that could conceivably be used by file-sharing databases.

- You can get good leverage from using a high-end server platform.

- There is less network loading if you write your ODBC code correctly. You will see how to do this later in the chapter.

- Database recovery in the case of hardware or software failures is much more robust and usually automatic upon restarting the server engine.

ODBC

To understand ODBC, you have to isolate the language it uses to access databases from the mechanics it employs. I will discuss both aspects in the following sections.

What Is SQL?

Structured Query Language, or SQL, was designed as a *lingua franca* to speak to relational databases. From its mainly IBM origins it has evolved into a range of ANSI standards. It has commands both for defining the structure of the data (Data Definition Language, or DDL) and for manipulating the actual data (Data Manipulation Language, or DML).

Although SQL is *the* language to access relational databases and is often talked about as being synonymous with relational databases, it is not held in high esteem by most relational-model theorists. Indeed, SQL violates most of the basic tenets of how a true relational database should behave.

> **NOTE**
>
> Chris Date, one of the fathers of relational theory, makes the following comments in his classic tome *An Introduction to Database Systems*, 6th edition, page xii:

> *"Unfortunately, however, the gulf between SQL and the relational model has grown so wide that I now feel it would be actively misleading to treat SQL first. In fact, SQL in its present form is so far from being a true embodiment of relational principles—it suffers from so many sins of both omission and commission—that I would have preferred to relate it to an appendix in this edition."*

SQL is not a complete programming language in itself. It is usually used with a traditional programming language, most frequently a 3GL or 4GL. ODBC is one of the methods that provides this coupling between SQL and the host programming language.

What Is ODBC?

ODBC permits applications to access data in database-management systems (DBMS) that don't use SQL. Unlike proprietary mechanisms for accessing a DBMS, ODBC provides a mechanism that permits a single application to access many different database-management systems without massive code duplication. This enables an application developer to create an application without targeting a specific DBMS. Users can then add modules called *database drivers* that link the application to their choice of database-management systems.

ODBC is defined in the *ODBC Programmer's Reference* as

- A library of ODBC function calls that permit an application to connect to a DBMS, execute SQL statements, and retrieve results.
- SQL syntax based on the X/Open and SQL Access Group (SAG) SQL CAE specification (1992).
- A standard set of error codes.
- A standard way to connect and log on to a DBMS.
- A standard representation for data types.

In fact, ODBC belongs in the category of CLIs, or *Call Level Interfaces*, to SQL. This means you write function calls in your application to call into the database-management system. The main alternative method of using SQL is *embedded SQL*. Using embedded SQL consists of writing SQL code in your source, indicated by special markers, and then preprocessing the source files with a SQL preprocessor. In other words, when using embedded SQL, your source files only become legal .c or .cpp files after this preprocessing.

The glue in ODBC is provided by the *ODBC Driver Manager*, a component written by Microsoft. This layer of software (ODBC32.DLL) passes the ODBC API calls your program makes to the correct, database-specific ODBC driver.

If the database you want to connect to already uses the relational model and SQL as its access method, the driver only has to translate your calls into the appropriate SQL dialect and submit them to the database server. Such drivers are called *multi-tier* drivers. Prime examples of these are the SQL Server and Oracle drivers included with Visual C++.

However, if the database you want to use is file based, the ODBC driver will have a lot more work to do. These single-tier drivers must

- Parse the SQL command you give it
- Figure out an access plan (in what order to execute joins, what indexes—if any—to use, and so on)
- Translate the access plan to record-oriented ISAM commands
- Execute the ISAM commands against the database files

The Microsoft Desktop Databases Drivers 1.x were single-tier drivers. The current 2.x versions, however, are two-tier drivers that talk to the JET engine using OLE 2 protocols. In other words, the new drivers are two-tier, local engine, shared file drivers.

Should You Use ODBC?

This question encompasses the following:

- Is it reliable?
- Does it expose the backend features I need?
- Is it fast enough?
- Does it offer significant benefits to the alternatives?

The answer is a resounding yes to all questions if you are using a multi-tier driver to access a database server or engine. My own informal benchmarks and those done by Microsoft and by Q&E Software (now part of Intersolv) indicate that performance using these drivers with SQL Server is within a few percent of using the native dblib interface for SQL Server. In fact, for SQL Server 6 (the upcoming version), Microsoft has stated that ODBC will be the fastest and preferred API. These drivers have been very stable and there are precious few areas where they lack functionality compared to the native API. In short, you get a fair amount of portability practically for free.

Almost all of the comments you read on CompuServe in the MSMFC and WINEXT forums about problems with ODBC concern the single-tier drivers. Some of these problems are actually just an incorrect perception that stems from a misunderstanding of what ODBC is and what it does; other problems were very real, and in some instances crippling, with the old 1.x drivers. Most of these have been eliminated or are much less serious with the new drivers. Some of the problems, however, are aggravated by the way MFC implements ODBC, as you'll see in the next section.

Does ODBC Have a Future?

There is much confusion and speculation about the future of ODBC, so maybe it's time just to enumerate the facts:

- Fact 1. Microsoft is working on the ODBC 3.0 spec, due out in beta by autumn 1995 and released somewhere near the end of the year. This spec will be fully aligned with the SAG spec; or to put it differently, the SAG spec will be ODBC 3.0 barring a standards upheaval.

- Fact 2. Microsoft is also working on a product known as *Nile*. This is indeed a new data-access spec that is technologically a merger of OLE and ODBC. ODBC is expected to be a subset of Nile, and ODBC tools should be able to work with Nile tools and data and vice versa.

- Fact 3. Microsoft also has stated that it will be publishing a native interface to the JET engine that is the basis of the Access, Visual Basic, and ODBC desktop database drivers. This interface is going to be called DAO for *Data Access Objects*. It is, in fact, the interface ODBC drivers now use to talk to the engine.

I would not hesitate going the ODBC route, nor panic if already committed to ODBC. The simple truth is that there are entire issues unaddressed by ODBC or, for that matter, by almost any existing data-access standard and tool.

Server discovery—that is, "where the heck is my data stored?"—is one of these. But I think the major issue is the number of new data types we are seeing right now: audio, video, e-mail messages with embedded and linked attachments, and so on. The best illustration of the fact that these data types are not supported by current databases and tools is that such data is most commonly referred to as BLOB or *Binary Large Object*. In reality, however, this data is not a BLOB or an unstructured data element; it does have structure, be it frames for video or the message structure itself for e-mail objects. We really need tools to get to the richness of this data without having to parse the binary information ourselves. Because this is the task of OLE in Microsoft's grand vision of the world, it is fairly logical that a marriage between OLE and ODBC is a major point on the agenda.

Whether the DAO interface is going to be an alternative to ODBC access to the JET engine or will totally replace it, or whether it will offer significant performance benefits, currently is just speculation. Because ODBC doesn't impose a major performance hit on other engine-based backends, I personally doubt whether using DAO will be such an obvious choice—especially if you want to keep your backend options open.

Lowest Common Denominator?

That ODBC is a lowest-common-denominator approach to database access is one of the criticisms most often levied against it. To put it simply, ODBC *can be* that if you use it that way, but it *doesn't have to be*. Of course, the difference between good ODBC applications and bad ones is just code—either your code or third-party code such as an ODBC class library.

ODBC can be called a lowest-common-denominator solution because it doesn't force a driver to support all functions, all data types, and all of the SQL syntax. This means that your code must behave in one of several ways when you would like to use a feature that the specific driver doesn't support:

- Don't take notice, just try and use the feature; don't even check the error return and just crash.
- Check the error return and give up at that time.
- At the start of the application, after connecting to the driver but before doing anything else, check for the availability of the feature and bow down gracefully at that time before storming ahead.
- Do the same check as in the previous option, but work around the nonexistent feature by using an alternative feature that might be slower or have some other disadvantages (for example, more network traffic, less scaleable, more database contention, and so on).

    or

- Don't use *any* feature that might not be supported by each and every driver. Do everything in your code yourself, using only a minimal ODBC subset.

For me, applications that use the first option are totally unacceptable and those that use the second option only marginally more acceptable than the first. The third option, though, sometimes is the only solution. As an example, if your application requires transaction support (more about that later) and the driver doesn't support transactions, there really is no reasonable workaround and you'd better give up before running the risk of wrecking your user's or organization's data.

Applications that are written according to the fifth method are truly lowest-common-denominator users of ODBC, and it usually shows in very slow execution and high network loading when run against a server database. Naturally, the difficulty in writing a truly great ODBC application is that to support the fourth method, you *do* have to write the code for the fifth method as well if you want to be able to run against less-powerful drivers. This brings us to the tools that can help you achieve this.

Ways to Use ODBC

If you have decided to use ODBC, you still have several alternatives:

- Write directly to the ODBC API
- Use the MFC database classes
- Use a third-party ODBC class library

You really have to be rather masochistic to write directly to the API. Although ODBC is not a very complex API at first sight, it does contain some pitfalls for the unwary. In addition, it is extremely tedious to write all those lines of boilerplate code for something such as parameter and variable binding—especially when you know the tools exist to take that work off your hands.

The MFC database classes do a reasonable job for applications that are not extremely database-intensive, and good alternative class libraries are available (from Intersolv, for example) for applications that require ODBC functionality not wrapped by MFC or that require better-implemented support for backend independence.

The main shortcomings of MFC are

- No real support for the ODBC catalog functions.
- Limited support for backend-variable native data types for a particular schema.
- No support for dynamically determined schema. For example, the MFC database classes would not help you a great deal if you were developing a general report writer.
- A possible performance-hindering double-buffer copy of all data on `AddNew()` or `Update()`. That is, all of the rows that you want to change first get duplicated to a `CMemFile` to enable MFC to determine what fields you changed.

Unless one of these weaknesses hurts your application specifically, however, the database classes are a safe bet.

The MFC Database Classes

The MFC database classes were developed as a way to ease traditional database developers into using ODBC and relational database engines. They have evolved quite a bit in their successive versions by bundling more intelligence into the framework—for example, deciding autonomously which of several alternative ODBC methods to use, depending on the backend, to give you the best performance possible.

The JET/Access/VB Paradigm

The MFC database classes try to meet ISAM developers halfway by presenting an ISAM-ish model of ODBC. This has both advantages and disadvantages.

The following paragraph is from the Visual C++ documentation on the database classes:

> *"The goal of the Microsoft Foundation Database Classes is to provide programmers a high-level C++ and Microsoft Windows API for accessing ODBC data sources. These high-level abstractions are the C++ equivalent of the Microsoft Access and Microsoft Visual Basic data-access objects, so the programming model is simple and familiar for programmers who have used either of those products but who want to work in C++."*

This is probably the most important paragraph in the materials and helps you to understand a lot of decisions and tradeoffs the MFC designers made. This fundamental design decision is at the same time the greatest strength and the greatest weakness of the MFC database classes.

It's all well and good that SQL is a set-based language that handles the entire result set at the same time. Our program still has to work with one record (in ISAM-speak) or one row (in relational-speak) at a time. The construct that provides this translation is called a *cursor*. A cursor provides you with a scrolling window on the result set that the database returns in response to a query.

MFC tries to emulate JET's (the Access/VB database engine) cursor handling. When you get a result set, it becomes in essence an ISAM table you can work with one record at a time. You have a *first record*, a *current record*, and a *last record*. You can move the current record pointer forward and backward, and you can read and update the field values of the current record. The strength of this approach is that it provides a familiar model for those of us accustomed to the ISAM model.

This model was a very bad fit with the version 1.*x* desktop databases drivers. If you coded as if you were really working with an ISAM database, performance tended to be horrific in many circumstances. Because the new drivers export engine-based cursors, the match between the model and the actual drivers is now much better.

But one of the major sources of disappointment with ODBC and SQL for ISAM-trained developers is that coding the way you used to will still work, for the most part, but will be extremely inefficient. To illustrate, say that you want to increase prices of all red items by 10 percent.

The most naive approach would be to create a recordset containing all of the items and then go through them, checking each record to see if it is red. If so, you then update the price and update the record in the database.

A slightly better approach would be to use a filter to limit the recordset to the red items in the first place, and then go through the items in the recordset and update the price and the record in the database.

But by far the most efficient way would be to forego the use of a recordset altogether and use the `CDatabase.ExecuteSQL()` method directly to do a *searched update* as follows:

```
MyDatabase.ExecuteSQL("UPDATE ItemTable
                SET Price = Price * 1.1
                WHERE ItemColor = 'Red'");
```

Depending on what driver you are using, the direct SQL method can be more than an order of magnitude faster. It will also generate almost no network traffic for a remote database, whereas the first alternative could swamp the network if `ItemTable` is large.

The Database Classes Hierarchy

MFC lends a big hand in dealing with ODBC. It has several thousand lines of prewritten code to present you with an ODBC framework on which you can layer your code. Figure 9.3 illustrates the MFC database classes hierarchy.

FIGURE 9.3.

The MFC database classes hierarchy.

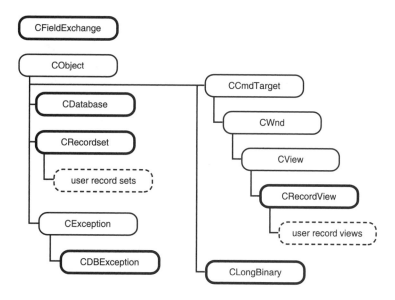

CDatabase is a repository for the connection with the database object (a hdbc in ODBC parlance). You use it to set options for the database as a whole (R/O, time-outs, and so on) and for transactions.

CRecordset, or more exactly, the classes ClassWizard or AppWizard help you derive from it are usually the main focus of the database code you write yourself. These classes encapsulate a set of records selected from the database. Here you specify what tables or views to select from, which fields (columns) to include, and what filter or sort order to use. CRecordset also defines the member functions to scroll through the records (MoveFirst, MoveLast, MoveNext, and MovePrevious) and to update, add, and delete records.

CRecordView derived classes are used to display and possibly edit the records in a record-at-a-time, dialog-resource-based view. The DDX mechanism is modified in working with this class so that data is exchanged *from* the dialog box fields *through* the recordview object *to* the field data members of the associated recordset object, thus involving three parties instead of two.

CFieldExchange is a helper class for the *Record Field Exchange* (RFX) mechanism that exchanges data between the recordset class and the actual database. It is to RFX what the CDataExchange class is to DDX.

CLongBinary is a class used for working with large fields. It is needed for fields greater than 64 KB and is more efficient than the normal binding method for object of greater than a few KB. It uses the ODBC **SQLGetData** and **SQLPutData** methods instead of **SQLBindParam**.

CDBException is the database-specific exception class. Although you might have been able to avoid exceptions in most of your MFC work, this is no longer the case when you use the database classes. If you don't catch exceptions, you will get unhandled exceptions, your users will get incomprehensible error messages or unexpected application exits, and your clients or boss will definitely not be very happy. The database classes throw exceptions to signal unexpected events in many places and you will simply have to respond.

For many developers coming from an Access or VB background, there seems to be one class missing: **CTableView**. This would provide a table-based (spreadsheet-like) view of the recordset, with in-place editing. Well, it ain't there! The class designers probably found that low-level components were more important for C++ developers and they decided to leave this class to third-party developers. I am sorry to say that so far, I haven't found a good table browser implemented as an MFC class library.

ClassWizard Comes to the Rescue

The major drudgery in using ODBC is all the parameter and result-column binding. This is exactly the task that ClassWizard helps you accomplish. It can retrieve a table description from the resultset and then write the code to do all the parameter binding for you.

But note the word *table* in the previous sentence. It hits on ClassWizard's major weakness: It can only give you this binding for a table, not for a view or stored query, and certainly not for the absolutely general case—an arbitrary resultset. Many large-scale databases prohibit access to the base tables to general users, reserving this access for the database administrator. If your end users should access views and other derived tables only, this can really make ClassWizard fairly useless for you as a developer. The only workaround is to copy your view to a dummy table (for example, using INSERT INTO) and then have ClassWizard bind to that table. After it has done its deed, you can drop the dummy table and alter the table name in the ClassWizard-generated code. If you are using aggregate functions such as SUM() or COUNT() in your SELECT, you will have to adjust the code manually as described in the database classes documentation.

If you are still using Visual C++ version 2.1 or lower, another major weakness in the RFX mechanism itself is that it can only use the natural C language type that goes with the SQL data type to which you are binding. It doesn't support the data type translations that the ODBC drivers can do for you; for example, most drivers can translate from SQL char data type to a C long or float. You could, for example, store your floating-point values as text in the database to avoid being dependent on the binary representation backends use. But

ClassWizard will not let you select a C/C++ data type other than CString for a SQL char data type, and if you try to change the generated code yourself, you will hit an ASSERT in the RFX code. In version 2.2, the framework will permit the conversion but will still output a trace message informing you about the conversion in a debug build.

> **NOTE**
>
> I would like to add that I think getting an edition of Visual C++ other than the subscription edition just doesn't make good sense. For a fairly nominal amount (about $100 extra) you get updates on roughly a four-month cycle. These updates offer new functionality, but even more importantly, in my opinion, lots of bug fixes.

...And Beyond

The next few sections will deal with using the new features available in the updated Microsoft ODBC drivers and preparing for new versions of ODBC.

The Microsoft ODBC Drivers: New and Improved!

Figure 9.4 illustrates the basic structure of the Microsoft Desktop Databases drivers version 2.x. OLE 2 is an operative word for these drivers. Most of the complaints developers voice against the new drivers are directly related to the use of OLE by the drivers:

- **The drivers take a long time to load.** The OLE 2 libraries are fairly large, so they do take quite a long time to load. If no other application in the system is using OLE, you will incur that load time at the time of SQLConnect—that is, when you connect to a DSN. You should make a concerted effort to not let your application disconnect and reconnect all the time when using the new drivers. If you can't stay connected to the drivers, however, you should take advantage of the recent driver-manager enhancement: ODBC.DLL no longer unloads the driver DLLs when you do a SQLDisconnect. It waits until you either do a SQLFreeConnect or a new SQLConnect to another driver. To use this optimization with MFC, however, you will have to override at least CDatabase::Close() and CDatabase::Open().

- **OLE 2 exacts quite a performance overhead on memory-constrained machines.** You will not get much joy from running your application against the drivers on a 4MB machine, even less so if that machine has a very slow disk or is running a shared Windows install over a slow network.

But the features and performance of the new drivers by far outweigh the few disadvantages. The new drivers are much faster than the old drivers, and they support quite a bit more SQL and many more ODBC functions. They are also much more stable and fully suited for moderate multiuser access.

FIGURE 9.4.

Using a JET-engine driver.

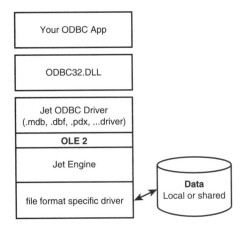

ODBC Versionitis

When you get to writing the install for your application: *Use version checking!* If you use the ODBC setup toolkit correctly, you are almost there. You do, however, have to remember to install both ODBC32.DLL and ODBCCR32.DLL as a matched set (that is, don't update just one of them, even if your application doesn't use the cursor library). Also, never install any shared component in a private directory.

Failure to do proper version checking *is* a major support headache for ODBC applications. You can be 100-percent sure that you will get support calls from users whose ODBC setup was trashed by a lousy install program. According to my last informal tally, at least 25 percent of all programs that install ODBC components get it wrong—including some prominent Microsoft products.

If you want to gain some friends in your tech-support department, you can score a big bonus with them if you do version checking for the version of ODBC your application is confronted with at startup. That way you could, for example, give an error message if your application depends on ODBC 2.10 or later being installed and you are faced with a system that only has version 2.0 installed. The alternative is probably a mysterious crash a good deal later in your application. If you require specific driver features in your application (that is, you need the Access 2.00.2317 or later drivers), you could also check for specific driver-name and driver-version combinations.

The ODBC function you use for this is SQLGetInfo. This function is not wrapped by MFC, so you need to call it yourself, passing it the m_hdbc public data member of your CDatabase. The most relevant fInfoTypes that you could check are:

- SQL_ODBC_VER: A character string with the version of ODBC to which the driver manager conforms. The version is of the form ##.##, where the first two digits are the major version and the next two digits are the minor version. This is implemented solely in the driver manager and has nothing to do with the driver to which you are connected. Use this to check whether the user has the correct version of ODBC32.DLL installed. If you anticipate having problems even on the connect because of really ancient ODBC versions, you have to use a more roundabout way of finding out the version of the driver manager.

- SQL_DRIVER_VER: A character string with the version of the driver and, optionally, a description of the driver. At a minimum, the version is of the form ##.##.####, where the first two digits are the major version, the next two digits are the minor version, and the last four digits are the release version.

- SQL_DRIVER_ODBC_VER: A character string with the version of ODBC that the driver supports. The version is of the form ##.##, where the first two digits are the major version and the next two digits are the minor version. SQL_SPEC_MAJOR and SQL_SPEC_MINOR define the major and minor version numbers.

- SQL_DRIVER_NAME: A character string with the filename of the driver used to access the data source.

Besides the ODBC version crisis, your application might also face nasty surprises with the c runtime library and the MFC libraries if you are using them in shared (that is, DLL) form. With the subscription edition's incremental releases, the Microsoft Visual C++ team made the decision to ship backward-compatible versions of the shared libraries instead of shipping renamed versions. This decision was implemented to avoid cluttering the windows\system32 directories of all users with about 10 MB of DLLs every four months.

For example, Visual C++ 2.0, 2.1, and 2.2 contain MSVCRT20.DLL (the c runtime library) and MFC30.DLL (the main MFC DLL) and similar files for the MFC database and OLE support. Thus, if you have compiled your application with Visual C++ 2.2 and shared DLLs and your user installs an older version of one of these files over the new version, you will again be in trouble. Sadly enough, the only totally safe option is using the static versions of the libraries, thus wasting precious disk space. A quite revealing example of this problem is that the ODBC 2.10 SDK on MSDN Level 2, issues 10 and 11, installs 2.0 versions of these files over newer versions.

I really can't stress the version-checking enough. It is simply not a question of whether your application will hit version problems in the field, but one of what percent of your users will be hit. My estimate would be to expect a number somewhere in the high single digits.

ODBC 2.5

Concurrent with the release of Windows 95, Microsoft is releasing a new version of ODBC to address some of the issues that have come up with previous versions of ODBC on Windows 95 and Windows NT. Microsoft has made only two major additions to ODBC with version 2.5.

■ **Uninstall support.** Because it is a Windows logo flag requirement for applications to have uninstall support, ODBC has to provide the needed plumbing to make this possible. With version 2.5 the ODBC installer keeps a tally of how many applications have installed ODBC and specific drivers.

This component usage count is incremented each time an application install routine installs a new component by calling the ODBC installer functions `SQLInstallDriverManager`, `SQLInstallDriver`, or `SQLInstallTranslator` and gets decremented when an application uninstall routine uninstalls a component by calling the ODBC installer functions `SQLRemoveDriverManager`, `SQLRemoveDriver`, or `SQLRemoveTranslator`.

When the usage count for any component goes to zero, the uninstall that causes this should remove the files comprising that component. It is very important that all applications follow the rules; you can imagine scenarios in which needed files vanish suddenly because a rogue application didn't use the correct installer functions, but just copied the files over and wrote to the registry manually.

■ **System DSNs.** On Windows 95 and Windows NT, the ODBC data set setup is normally done on a per-user basis and consequently stored in the registry under the `HKEY_CURRENT_USER` key. This is normally what you would want; that is, the database access is set up per user. However, if you are, for example, installing a server-type application that is not really dependent on who is actually logged on, then you don't want to require that each user do the same install. For that case, ODBC 2.5 offers the capability to create ODBC data sets on a system-wide basis, that is, with registry information stored under the `HKEY_LOCAL_MACHINE` key.

Dynasets and Snapshots

FROM THE VISUAL C++ 1.5X "DATABASE ENCYCLOPEDIA"

"A snapshot is a recordset that reflects a static view of the data as it existed at the time the snapshot was created. Once you open the snapshot, the set of records it contains and their values don't change until you rebuild the snapshot by calling Requery. You can create updatable or read-only snapshots with the database classes. Unlike a dynaset, an updatable snapshot doesn't reflect changes to record values made by other users but does reflect updates and deletions made by your program. Records added to a snapshot don't become visible to the snapshot until you call Requery.

"Unlike dynasets, snapshots are always available when you use the Microsoft Foundation Database Classes, regardless of the capabilities of the ODBC driver you're using. By default, when you open a recordset object, it is an updatable snapshot.

"A 'dynaset' is a recordset with dynamic properties. During its lifetime, a recordset object in dynaset mode (usually called simply a "dynaset") stays synchronized with the data source in

> *the following way. In a multi-user environment, other users might edit or delete records that are in your dynaset or add records to the table your dynaset represents. Records your application adds to or deletes from the recordset are reflected in your dynaset. Records that other users add to the table will not be reflected in your dynaset until you rebuild the dynaset by calling its Requery member function. When other users delete records, MFC code skips over the deletions in your recordset. Other users' editing changes to existing records are reflected in your dynaset as soon as you scroll to the affected record.*
>
> *"Similarly, edits you make to records in a dynaset are reflected in dynasets in use by other users. Records you add are not reflected in other users' dynasets until they requery their dynasets. Records you delete are marked as "deleted" in other users' recordsets. If you have multiple connections to the same database (multiple CDatabase objects), recordsets associated with those connections have the same status as the recordsets of other users."*

So, snapshots are what you get by default with MFC. Snapshots, however, probably are not what you want. In general, you want the most recent data and you would also like to get the performance benefits that dynasets can bring.

To get dynasets, you must

- Pass FALSE as the bUseCursorLib (fifth) argument to CDatabase::Open() to disable the loading of the cursor library. (If you forget this, you will get errors about dynasets not being supported later on.)
- Pass CRecordSet::dynaset as the nOpenType (first) argument to CRecordSet::Open().

Furthermore, you can only get dynasets with drivers that *natively* support positioned updates or that support SQLSetPos. The cursor library does not count here. If you are loading the cursor library, you will not be able to use dynasets with any driver.

It is important to realize that with the new Microsoft drivers you can have either

- Dynasets, but not updatable snapshots, by not loading the cursor library
- Updatable snapshots, but not dynasets, by loading the cursor library

If you need both in the same application, the trick is to open two connections; that is, use two database objects and load the cursor library on one and not on the other Open().

For we poor souls who mainly develop to the SQL Server backend, the SQL Server 4.2xx drivers don't support dynasets via any method known to man. SQL 6 will solve this unfortunate situation. In that product there will be a true smorgasbord of cursor types from which to choose.

The Cursor Library

In the previous section's quote, the MFC documentation is a bit deceiving when it states that you can get updatable snapshots with all drivers. This is only true if you use the cursor library embodied in ODBCCR32.DLL. This library will create a local snapshot; in other words, it will copy all the records from your recordset to the local drive and then use that copy to scroll. In the course of building this local copy, the cursor library will generate a lot of network traffic and disk I/O.

The cursor library also plays a major role in helping MFC with its `CRecordset::Update` and `CRecordset::Delete` member functions for drivers that do not support `SQLSetPos`. These functions update and delete the current record. The SQL syntax they use is `UPDATE TableName SET ColumnIdentifier = Value WHERE CURRENT OF CursorName`. The cursor library comes to the rescue of drivers that don't support this syntax. It simulates the positioned update by gathering together all of the columns in the recordset and turning the positioned update into a SQL-searched update that all drivers should support.

As an example, say you are updating the following record of the `CCourseSet`, based on the ENROLL sample's Course table of the Student Registration database.

```
CourseID = 'MATH101'; CourseTitle ='Algebra'; Hours = 4
```

If you change `Hours` to `5` and call `Update`, the cursor library will translate the statement

```
"UPDATE Course SET Hours = 5 WHERE CURRENT OF xxxx"
```

to

```
"UPDATE Course SET Hours =  5
WHERE CourseID = 'MATH101' AND
                 CourseTitle = 'Algebra' AND
                 Hours = 4"
```

thus opening another cursor with all the resulting overhead.

This explains why the earlier example about increasing the price of red items had such major performance problems when we used the normal MFC update loop and snapshots. It also demonstrates a very important caveat when doing updates and deletes with the help of the cursor library: "Thou shalt always include all of thy primary key columns in thy recordset." If you don't, the cursor library will not have these fields available to generate the searched update and delete statements and you can end up updating or deleting many more records than you bargained for. In that case, MFC will throw an exception, but the damage will have been done.

Engine-Based Cursors

So what is the alternative to using the cursor library for those less-anemic drivers for which you have an alternative, like the Microsoft 2.x drivers? The alternative is using an engine-based cursor—that is, a cursor that is fully implemented in the backend and not via some magical piece of software on the client side. This does give a major performance advantage for local engines like the 2.x drivers, but it will be even more important for SQL Server 6 and other server databases because transferring data over the network is still slower than getting it from a local disk. As mentioned before, the 2.x drivers have engine support for dynasets only, not for snapshots.

Microsoft did something that served its corporate agenda more than ODBC portability when it exposed the JET engine cursors in the new drivers: It used a formerly obscure ODBC Level 2 function, `SQLSetPos`, to do so instead of going native with the mechanism the cursor library already emulated—the WHERE CURRENT OF SQL syntax.

This syntax also has been used for engine-cursor support long before the ODBC standard came into existence, so abandoning this and forcing all frontend ODBC tools and applications to use the `SQLSetPos` functionality where available was certainly not expected. South Wind Designs, Inc. was in beta with a new version of their odbc/Classlib ODBC library when the Microsoft drivers 2.0 beta came out. They were just as surprised as anyone else about this Microsoft implementation and had to rewrite parts of their library in a hurry to take advantage of this functionality.

MFC checks to see what a driver returns to `SQLGetInfo(hdbc, SQL_POS_OPERATIONS)` and uses `SQLSetPos` if it is supported. If you are writing an application that should have driver independence and that has to work well with the Microsoft drivers, you should really do the same if you are not using a class library. Look at the MFC `CRecordSet::OnSetOptions` code to see how to do this.

Transact Your Way Out of Trouble

Transaction support is one of the distinguishing factors in determining whether a database engine is production quality or just a toy. Simply put, a *transaction* is a bunch of operations on the database that either fail or succeed *as a whole.* That is, they either all succeed or all fail (rollback). The classic example is a debit/credit transaction: You transfer $100 from your checking account to your savings account. Including the debit of your checking account and the credit of your savings account in a transaction ensures that you are never out of your $100, no matter what happens with the database. If there were no transactions and something (the frontend, the LAN, the WAN, the communications server, the transaction monitor, the database…) in the system failed between the first and the second operation, you would probably be switching financial institutions.

The SQL Server driver supports transactions and so does the Access 2.x driver. The other JET-engine drivers do not. However, if you call `CDatabase::CanTransact()` or `CRecordSet::CanTransact`, *all* of the drivers will return FALSE. The problem is that MFC requires that the driver preserve cursors after a commit and after a rollback. That means you still have all of the results and your position in that result set after you have finished the transaction. If the driver doesn't preserve cursors, the database classes would have to re-execute and possibly reprepare all SQL statements after each commit or rollback.

It is unclear if the MFC class designers made the decision to require cursor preservation in the driver to enable transactions because of performance implications. In any case, if you can live with the performance hit, you can do the following:

- Derive a `CTransactDatabase` from `CDatabase`. You need to do this because the `CDatabase m_bTransactions` member is protected, so you can only change it from a derived class.
- Create a public member function `SetTransactions()` of this derived class that can set the `m_bTransactions` flag.
- Check if the database supports transactions with the `SQL_TXN_CAPABLE` parameter.
- If the result is positive, call `SetTransactions()`.
- Check the `SQLGetInfo` return value with `fInfoTypes SQL_CURSOR_COMMIT_BEHAVIOR` and `SQL_CURSOR_ROLLBACK_BEHAVIOR`.
- If you get `SQL_CB_PRESERVE`, you don't have to do anything special; with `SQL_CB_CLOSE`, you have to do a `Requery` on all the recordsets after a commit and/or rollback and with `SQL_CB_DELETE`, you have to close and reopen all recordsets.

```
class CTransactDatabase : public CDatabase
{
public:
    void SetTransactions()) { m_bTransactions = TRUE; }
};
```

You can find more information on MFC support for transactions in MFC Technote 47.

CAUTION

If you are using transactions with the Access driver, you have to be aware that this driver has a major deficiency in its transaction support: You can only start a transaction if you don't have an open cursor. In other words, you can only do a `CDatabase::BeginTrans()` if you do not have any recordsets open on that `CDatabase`.

Where to Go for Help

This chapter has only skimmed the surface of the large number of issues that make up ODBC and MFC support for ODBC. Based on the information here, you should be able to decide whether ODBC can meet your data-access requirements. You should also have a good idea of where you are likely to run into problems. For specific information on implementing ODBC support in your application, however, you'll need some additional sources.

For me, three sources have been instrumental in getting a grasp on the database classes, on ODBC, and on MFC in general:

- The documentation included with MFC has improved a lot with the introduction of the Encyclopedia sections of Books Online. Working through the enroll tutorial, looking at the catalog and dynabind samples, and reading the Database Classes Encyclopedia should be your first priority. You will also find more material on the MSDN CD, including the KnowledgeBase (KB) that contains bug lists and clarifications. Due to the publishing and production schedules, the KnowledgeBase is of course already at least six weeks out of date by the time you get your CD. So if you don't find it there, please try the KB on CIS; or if you have World Wide Web or Microsoft Network access, the Microsoft WWW server, which has a much nicer search engine than CIS. All of the online KB versions are updated on a nightly basis.

- Hang out on CompuServe. Both the Database Classes section in the MSMFC forum section and the ODBC and Desktop Databases Drivers section in the WINEXT forum are monitored by a lot of knowledgeable folks willing to help. Do note that these and all other Microsoft CIS forums are peer-support forums. Although Microsoft does monitor the forums and participates in them with great regularity, the company doesn't commit itself to answering any questions in any time frame. If you require a support commitment from Microsoft, you *will* have to pay them for Priority, Premier, or per-incident support if you have used up your 30 days from first call support included with the purchase of Visual C++, or if the question pertains to ODBC and not to MFC's use of it.

- "Use the Source, Luke" has been traditional advice given to UNIX developers. It is no less valid to users of the MFC framework. The source is the definitive judge on what MFC does. Having it also enables you to correct the most serious bugs while waiting for a corrected version.

The Windows 95 User Interface

PART

II

Windows 95 User Interface Basics

10

by William A. Montemer

IN THIS CHAPTER

When people think of PC user interfaces, sooner or later they think of DOS, character mode I/O, and the infamous c:\ command prompt. Even with the overwhelming success of Windows 3.1 and its Mac-like graphical interface, both novice and "power" users complete at least a few tasks by directly entering DOS command lines—whether it's listing a directory with DIR, formatting a floppy with FORMAT a:, or even creating havoc with the dangerous DEL *.*. Although DOS and command line entry is unfriendly, unintuitive, and almost totally obsolete, we use it because it helps us get work done. We've learned to live with it, however uncomfortably, because there hasn't really been another option—until now.

With the introduction of Windows 95, we at last have an alternative to DOS. Of course, even Windows 95 can be run in a nongraphical MS-DOS mode, complete with command line entry and the familiar DOS prompt as shown in Figure 10.1. But rather than existing on top of DOS like Windows 3.1, the Windows 95 command prompt mode is a virtual DOS mode. It looks like DOS and acts like DOS, but it isn't DOS.

FIGURE 10.1.

The Windows 95 user interface can hold a variety of objects, including the venerable DOS prompt.

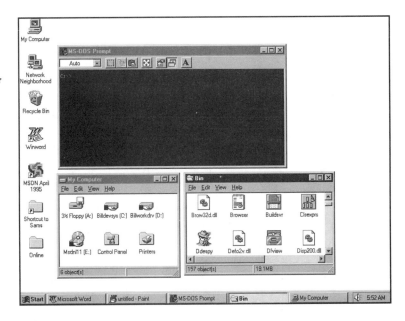

From the first bootup, Windows 95 presents to the user a clean new look. In order to use and develop applications for Windows 95, both users and developers will have to learn about the new look. Fortunately, the Windows 95 user interface continues what Windows 3.1 began and takes it closer to the ultimate goal of Windows: making computers easy for everyone.

What's New with the Windows 95 Interface?

The Windows 95 user interface represents a design evolution from a basic graphical user interface to a new, more object-oriented one. But the new UI is more than just an updated 3-D look or a collection of recast custom controls and designer widgets. The UI reflects a new way of thinking about how people use the computer and how people work. Now, as the Windows 95 operating system gains exposure and acceptance, developers and designers need to rethink what the application interface represents from a long underappreciated user's perspective.

In its design manifesto for Windows 95, Microsoft set the following goal: to make using the computer easy for all people.

Although such a broad goal seems to be the stuff of poets and philosophers, it is not as unreachable as you might think. At least one other computer system, the Macintosh, had taken this long forgotten road more than a decade ago. The Mac's ease-of-use philosophy of computer system design, which was itself an adaptation of the pioneering work done at Xerox's Palo Alto Research Center, has been a time-honored success. In fact, there are many who believe that Microsoft merely stole Apple's best ideas. In reality (as Xerox PARC might attest), where the ideas come from and their implementation are two very different things.

Another influential operating system that we can guess played a role in Windows 95 is IBM's OS/2. Parts of its object-oriented interface can be seen in the Windows 95 UI, and many of its design fundamentals—which are based on IBM's Common User Access design guidelines—undoubtedly found their way into the new operating system (in spirit, if not in actuality).

The success of Windows 3.1 also played a role in Windows 95's design. With a wealth of information about Windows 3.1 and what would make it better, Windows 95 set about deconstructing what worked in Windows 3.1, what it attempted to do, and what it failed to accomplish. Also, as a matter of practical economics, backwards compatibility with the previous Windows version must have been a sizable influence. As an upgrade from Windows 3.1, Windows 95 had to allow 3.1 users to make the transition to the new operating system without throwing out all they had already learned.

With such a rich background and heritage, the Windows 95 user interface does not attempt to be new, unique, or different for its own sake. Instead, showing surprising maturity for a new operating system, it attempts something that is novel and very refreshing for PC users. It wants to help users get their work done.

What Is User Interface Design in Windows 95?

A user interface is the first thing a user sees upon starting an application. More than anything else, the user interface (UI) sets the tone for the user's experience of working in and with an application.

The function of a UI is essentially to act as an intermediary between a user and an application. In an event-driven system such as Windows 95, the UI communicates the user's wishes and intentions to the powerful 32-bit operating system and relays its results and system states back. Like the proverbial iceberg, the UI sits on top while the unseen application engine underneath runs multiple processes, performs high-resolution updates, or fetches massive amounts of data.

But, although the UI might take a subservient role to the application engine it services, a well-designed UI is vitally important to a program's acceptance and ultimate success. If the UI is confusing and unclear, the application will be fatally flawed. But if the UI is well-designed, easy to learn, and easy to use, the application has a good chance to succeed both technically and in the marketplace.

There is one thing that characterizes a well-designed interface, however. A well-designed user interface is almost transparent to the people who use it. In other words, a good user interface requires little conscious thought from the user.

At this point, it might be enlightening to turn the question around. Instead of asking, "What is UI design?" you might ask, "What is UI design not?"

- ■ UI design is not putting menus and buttons on an application program to access all of a program's features.

  Getting to a program's functional parts has never been a problem. Even in its most raw form, a user interface provides access to a program's functionality. In the days of mainframes and early PCs, it was acceptable to start and control a program with a string of words entered at the command line. When programmers started using menus, users immediately saw the benefits and wanted more. When graphical user interfaces (GUIs) came into vogue, some developers put a set of picture buttons on a menu and called it a user interface. But there is more to UI design than that.

- ■ UI design is not something programmers and engineers do just before an application is released.

  Although there is a tendency in software development to finish the UI last, user interface design should be integral to the entire development process from the first conceptual specification to the last beta test and sign-off. When the development team decides what a product should do, a UI designer should be considering what the user wants to do. And while a quality assurance team looks at test reports to find bugs and defects, the UI design team should be looking at usability reports to locate UI inconsistencies and confusion.

■ UI design is not having a graphics designer create a polished look for an application.

Another tendency in the software development cycle is to bring in visual designers toward the end of a project. After the functional design has been completed, and even prototyped, the graphics designers are supposed to make things more attractive. At this point, they can choose colors, use drop shading, and add nice bitmaps to an application, but these are all external embellishments. The area in which UI designers need to function most is in the unseen internal aspects of an application.

■ UI design is not a one-person job.

It is widely accepted that software development is a team activity because no one individual has the ability to function in all the areas required by modern application development. In the same way, it is necessary to have a balanced approach to user interface design with influence from visual designers, programmers, human-factors design specialists, and users. Each group has its own point of view, and giving one primacy over the others is a mistake.

■ UI design is not a cookbook task with fully prescribed practices and guidelines.

User interface design is a domain with many guidelines but few rules. As such, it is a perfect playing field for both creative and more structured designers. On one side, the human/computer interaction people from the traditional engineering and scientific fields value measurement, quantification, and scientific method. On the other side, free-wheeling creative designers who love to break rules and explore new territory experiment with new paradigms and metaphors.

Most of the time, the discussions in this chapter will move freely between both camps. Using a solid scientific approach will help you develop a mental checklist to make sure you've covered everything. Looking for new ways to do things will keep you open to new ways of helping the user and your application become more productive and successful.

As stated earlier, there are few rules in UI design but many guidelines. This chapter will cover some of these guidelines and principles; in the next chapter, you'll see more specific examples that illustrate these concepts as we move more freely through UI development.

Task-Oriented Design

In Windows 95, the success or failure of a user interface depends on whether it helps users accomplish their tasks. How a user works with an application—whether the steps are straightforward or convoluted—is more important than giving the user access to a wide range of features.

But you might wonder, "Hasn't application software always been developed around a specific task?" The answer is yes, of course. But too often the application required the user to focus on something other than getting the task done. For example, if the task was writing a letter, the user had to focus on opening a word processing program, opening a new file, selecting a style for the document, and then refocus on writing the letter. Even in this case, all the little distractions from writing the letter make the user less productive.

The goal of a Windows 95 user interface is to make the application less distracting and more productive. The UI does this by focusing the user's attention on the task. The UI provides tools and functions to help the user perform tasks, but the tools themselves should not require the user's attention.

Think of the difference between tool and task like this: A baseball player uses a tool—a bat—to hit the ball. He does not (and, in fact, should not) think about the bat at all. His total concentration is on the ball. In the same way, a user interface should not require any conscious thought from the user.

To carry this line of thought even further, the goal of the application itself is to become transparent, so that users can focus on what they are doing without worrying about what application they are using. Transparency is a very important technique in UI design and can be used effectively to focus the user's attention, as the following example demonstrates.

Task Orientation: Dialing a Number

Dialing a phone number is a very common task and one that most people can handle quite easily. The Windows 3.1 applet CardFile provided a very rudimentary function that dialed a phone number through a connected modem. Figure 10.2 shows the Autodial dialog box from the CardFile app.

FIGURE 10.2.

The Autodial dialog box from the Windows 3.1 CardFile applet can be used to dial the phone through a modem.

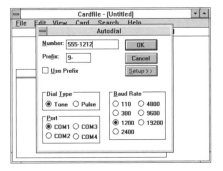

If the user is familiar with Windows 3.1, dialing a number with this applet is fairly straightforward. If you are entering a number and dialing on the fly, the required steps are as follows: move the mouse to the top edit box; click the left mouse button; enter the number on the keyboard; click the OK button. Notice also that you had to move from the mouse to the keyboard and back again within this procedure.

Windows 95 supplies a separate applet for dialing, called Phone Dialer. The Phone Dialer (shown in Figure 10.3) resembles a modern telephone with large number buttons and a programmable speed dialer. Performing the same dialing task on this applet requires the following steps: click on a number button; repeat the first step six more times for the full number; click on the Dial button. To be fair, these two applets are not designed to be alike, and the Phone Dialer requires more steps than the CardFile, but the task you performed is the same. To do the task in the Windows 95 applet, the user could simply point and click, instead of thinking about where to enter the number and what input device to use. In other words, the Phone Dialer UI helps the user concentrate on the user's task—dialing a phone number.

FIGURE 10.3.

The Phone Dialer from Windows 95 resembles a speed-dial phone in both look and function.

This simple task comparison demonstrates how task orientation works in a user interface. It also shows one way to achieve transparency. Because the pushbutton telephone is a common device, using the speed-dial telephone as a metaphor makes the applet seem more natural and intuitive. The user does not have to spend much conscious effort understanding how to use a telephone and transfers this understanding to the Phone Dialer applet.

User-Centered Design

A related goal of Windows 95 user interface design is to make the interface user-centered. In a user-centered design, information about users—who the users are, what they want to do, their backgrounds, and their skill levels—is an important influence on the final design.

The designer must get this user information from research, surveys, observations, and usability tests. The designer must also involve the user throughout the development process—in design and test, and in redesign and retest. In addition to learning as much as possible about the user, the designer must listen to whatever the user has to say.

Although it may appear that only well-supported, large development companies have the resources to do this type of R-and-D work, ingenuity and insight cannot be bought for any price. For individuals or small entrepreneurial teams, the extra attention and time spent with a variety of computer users—and even non-users—will help make the end-product more professional and will separate it from some of the "hobby programming" shareware efforts. Also, because Windows 95 supplies many built-in visual interface controls, it is now even easier to produce a UI that is both attractive and useful.

But what's the reason for all this attention? What's so special about the user? It's really quite simple: The user is never wrong.

Design for Skill Levels

Sooner or later, everyone is a novice. You cannot and should not assume that users have a certain level of understanding when they purchase your product. But this doesn't mean that the UI has to be a mid-grade design for the least common denominator. It means that the UI designers have to work harder in order to make the UI workable for novice and power users alike.

Most often that involves providing different strokes for different folks. For instance, because novice Windows users often have difficulty with the mouse, a user-centered design must provide clearly defined keyboard alternatives for performing the basic tasks that novices do most often.

And, just as often, what was good in the beginning gets old fast. An experienced or aggressive user tires of the simplistic step-by-step approach designed for a novice and wants a more straight-ahead approach. For these users, providing keyboard accelerators and user-customizable menus and toolbars is a must (see Figure 10.4).

FIGURE 10.4.

A customizable toolbar is a standard user interface component for power users.

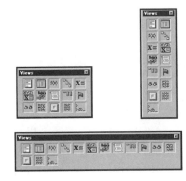

Design to Put the User in Control

Another aspect of user-centered design is placing the user in control. In Windows 95, the user should feel empowered and able to do anything at any time. Rather than reacting to prompts and dialog boxes generated by the computer, the user should be able to initiate and control the computer's actions.

Sometimes the question of who is in control (the user or the app?) is subtle, because applications already possess so much automation and functionality that the user never sees. Still, it is important to make the user feel as though he's in control by implementing methods that provide the user with choices, thus making the UI more interactive.

Of course, providing more interactivity means that the application must also be more responsive. For Windows programming in particular, this means that modes must be used carefully. A mode is a state in an application in which only certain actions are possible. Basically, a mode limits a user's options.

There are times when using a mode is the only technical alternative, although modes have been historically overused by program designers. If using a mode is unavoidable, the mode should be implemented intelligently by informing the user of what to expect and providing a way to cancel the action. Failure to provide appropriate alternatives is a sure way to frustrate the user.

Design for Feedback

For the user to feel comfortable and in control of the computer and the application, the user needs to know what is happening at all times. In a user interface, feedback provides this application-user connection. Status bars, progress indicators, and visual and audio cues all help to orient the user.

Also, feedback should be timely to be effective. Immediate feedback makes the user feel that the application is responsive and under user control, but often this is not practical. For instance, in applications that involve network access, the network server might control when a data request is processed and the application might lose sync. In this situation, providing the user with a manual update control helps to alleviate the impression that the user is on the reactive end of the process.

Sometimes, especially in lengthy CPU-intensive processes, the application might seem to lock out user commands or responses. In this situation, a progress indication and some estimate of the process completion will keep the user updated and keep the user from rebooting the computer.

One final type of feedback that must be considered by an effective UI design is using messages. Often, message boxes appear after a fatal system error. At this time, the user probably needs the most help and reassurance. Concise and intelligent messages explaining the error, or how to recover from it, will be the most appropriate response.

The Windows 95 taskbar shown Figure 10.5 exemplifies a user-centered design that succeeds at ease of use and is easy to learn. In spite of its simple design and appearance, it provides a wealth of functionality.

FIGURE 10.5.

The Windows 95 taskbar succeeds admirably at ease of use and is easy to learn.

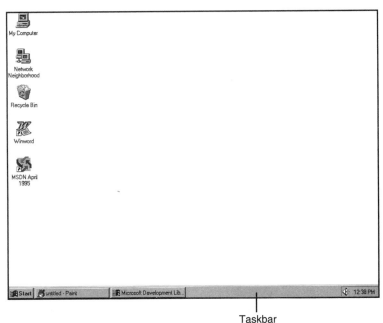

Taskbar

For example, the taskbar functions as a program launcher and a single-click task switcher, and it provides access to all of Windows 95's configuration and setup programs. It is also a pop-up menu for a recently opened document list, a customizable Program menu, the Windows 95 Help Engine, a command-line Run item, a system Shutdown item, and a hardware monitor/access window.

In particular, let's look at some features implemented by the taskbar to provide ease-of-use, and what motivated their inclusion.

The Start button shown in Figure 10.6 is large and clearly labeled. It responds to a single-click, because double-clicks were difficult for novice users to perform. At the single-click, a pop-up menu appears, which acts as a program launcher.

FIGURE 10.6.

The Windows 95 Start button enables experienced users to start programs quickly, and novices to explore easily.

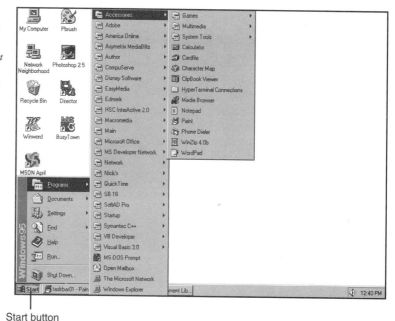

Start button

To launch programs, users can move the mouse through the cascading menus, exploring what's on the computer and discovering how the menus and submenus work. Single-clicking on an item launches the desired program, something that users discover very quickly after launching their first Windows 95 programs.

Document-Centered Computing

In continuing the direction set by Microsoft's OLE (Object Linking and Embedding) technology, applications running under Windows 95 become less application-centered and more data- or document-centered. In a document-centered approach, the file containing data also contains the "embedded-intelligence" to connect to all the applications that created it.

OLE in-place activation is an example of this type of document-centered implementation. An OLE document is called a compound document. To edit a compound document, a user opens it with an OLE-enabled word processor such as Microsoft Word. The compound document can contain other OLE-enabled applications, such as the embedded Excel worksheet shown in Figure 10.7.

FIGURE 10.7.

This Microsoft Word document contains an embedded Excel worksheet. OLE enables the user to change the work environment without leaving the document.

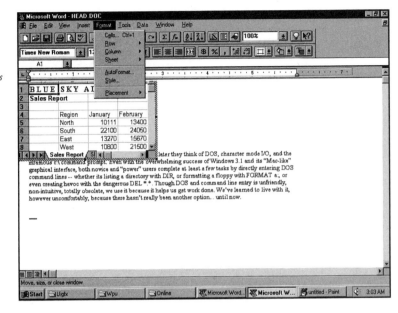

When you double-click an OLE object, the word-processing application interface changes to display the Excel menus within the Word environment. In the older application-centered paradigm, to edit the worksheet linked to the Word document, the user would have to switch to the Excel app. Obviously this type of application integration, called in-place editing, is more direct and easier for the user. But the advantages are even more subtle than that. With document-centered computing, the computer begins to work the way users do, by switching the context around a particular document while keeping the document in focus.

Power and Functionality

As computers and operating systems become more powerful, there is always the temptation to "take the technology to the limit." Windows 95 is no exception to this rule, and its powerful multitasking and multithreading technology could take complexity to record limits.

It is up to developers and designers to balance and constrain the technology so that added functionality does not necessarily mean added confusion for users. In Windows 95, it is the user interface designer's challenge to manage complexity. There are several ways to accomplish this in UI design.

By controlling the amount of information that a user must absorb at any one time, the UI designer can keep the user from being unnecessarily preoccupied by the app. By analyzing the presented information and determining the minimum necessary to communicate a task's intentions or progress, the UI designer can plan how and when the information is displayed. In cases in which there is simply too much information, the designer can consult with the program developers and try to find a solution.

Visual organizational methods can also lend clarity to the presented information. Separating information into appropriate groups can make that information easy to recognize and remember. And if the designer combines the visual organization and information control techniques, it is possible to mask the complexity and make even complex functionality appear simple.

But you might wonder why you shouldn't just build simpler apps without all the added functionality. This might not be as easy as it seems. Even a simple app might not be easy to use, and making an application easy to use usually makes it more complex.

Wizards are proven tools that were originally developed for the Microsoft Office applications (see Figure 10.8). They are designed to help all users take advantage of powerful but complex functionality. With a Wizard, the UI designer uses a simple series of questions to lead the user through a complex process.

FIGURE 10.8.

Wizards are proven Microsoft tools that enable any user to take advantage of powerful but complex functionality.

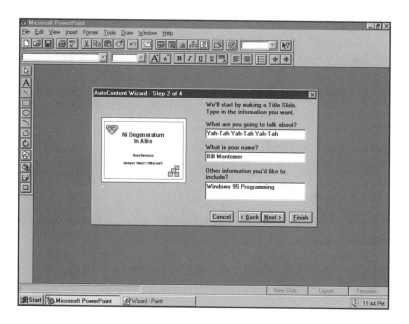

In a typical Wizard, such as the Setup Wizard, information gathering takes place in the first phase and user confirmation is done next, followed by a final confirmation and chance to Cancel before the actual work is done. This uniform approach gives the programmer all the necessary data, lets the UI designer create a simple set of instructions, and makes the user feel well-oriented and in control—all UI design goals.

Object-Oriented Design

Although Windows 95 is not a true object-oriented interface, it borrows from an object-oriented programming (OOP) approach in order to present an understandable, consistent framework to users. The object metaphor provides a natural and intuitive way for users to interact with information on the computer, while shielding them from details of the underlying technology. Also in an object-oriented interface, as OLE and other intelligent object applications are developed, the boundary between the application and the operating system will continue to disappear.

What Is an Object?

In a task-oriented approach, an object is an item that is used to do work. In terms of an interface, an object is any visual component that the user can work with as a unit. In Windows 3.1, objects were identified by graphical icons, but it was just as possible to have an icon from one application identify the binary executable from another. These icons were no more than graphical name tags that had little meaning on their own.

In Windows 95, visual objects and their binary components are basically the same thing to the user. To copy an object from your PC onto a floppy, you simply drag the object from a folder object on the hard disk to the floppy disk object. The desired object is then copied from the hard disk to the target floppy. As the operation continues, an icon animation of the copy process appears, letting the user know graphically just what is happening.

An object in an object-oriented interface possesses attributes similar to those of its OOP counterpart. The interface objects contain properties that identify particular characteristics. In a manner similar to OOP methods, objects support operations such as move or copy. Finally, the idea of containment—in which one object can be held or contained by another—rounds out the object metaphor.

Although most user interaction occurs with icon objects, a user can also interact with an object by opening a window. For instance, in Windows 95 all objects have property sheets, which provide UI designers with a uniform access point to examine or change specific object properties or attributes. As anyone familiar with OOP can see, the object metaphor provides a convenient description for both UI designers and application programmers.

Browsing Between Directories

As shown in Figure 10.9, the Windows 95 object metaphor is particularly strong in file management. Here, an audio file object has been dragged from one directory window and dropped into another. Immediately, the user interface responds with a dialog box animation showing sheets of paper flying from one folder to the next. Notice also that the animation dialog box contains a Cancel button. Even the small details such as immediate feedback and user cancel control make this UI very intuitive and pleasant to use.

FIGURE 10.9.

File management in Windows 95 benefits greatly from the object interface metaphor.

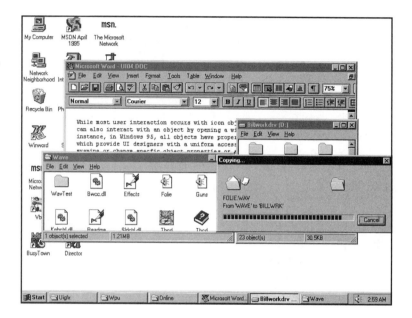

Team Design: Users, Programmers, and Interface Designers

As stated earlier, effective user interface design is a team activity. It should begin early in the development cycle and finish only as the final release nears. In a balanced team, several disciplines need to be represented: programmers, visual designers, human factors people, users, and more. For purposes here, however, you can identify three primary perspectives that conveniently break into three group activities. Together, these three areas cover the essentials of user interface design (see Figure 10.10).

FIGURE 10.10.

The user interface design triad is made up of users, programmers, and designers.

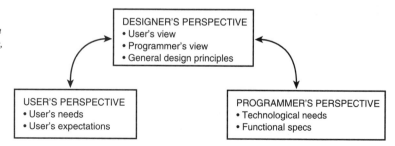

Users

In user-centered, task-oriented UI design, it is necessary to have users (or someone who knows and understands the user's point of view) involved. The problem is that the user's perspective is not usually easy to define. As far as user interface work goes, it can be thought of as the way a user understands a task. In the language of cognitive psychology, this can be referred to as a conceptual model.

Most often, a user's conceptual model cannot be described or drawn concretely. Just as often, the user is not even aware that there is a model. A person uses this mental model, however, to explain how elements of any given situation relate. For instance, given a softball, a tennis racket, and a bowling ball, your mind might imagine a gym or an athletic club. Toss in a cash register, and right away you might see a sporting goods shop. In the same way, a user sees objects and perceives relationships between them.

The user conceptual model has several interesting aspects that relate to UI design. First, the user develops these models based on experience, including experience with computers and other application programs. Second, the user develops expectations based on this model. Third, when confronted with a new situation or program, the user compares it to some existing model and transfers concepts from that model to the new situation. Finally, if the model does not work in the new situation, the user becomes hesitant and confused and possibly gives up.

From this point of view, how well an application lives up to this mental model determines to a large extent how a user will react to the application. But what happens if the user can't come up with a good model to base expectations on? According to this way of thinking, a user's model can change over time with more experience.

Before throwing all of this out as psychobabble, think about how a child learns new things. Children first relate the unknown to what they already know and tend to try to use similar devices and objects in the same way. Obviously, if a UI designer could define a user's conceptual model, satisfying it would be straightforward.

That's what you would like to do, but there are other considerations.

Programmers

Programmers need to be involved in UI design because they have to write the actual code that creates and implements the application and the UI. Just like the user, the programmer has a model of the task and how to do it. And also like the user, the programmer sees objects and defines relationships between them. But the programmer has consciously created the model. It can be diagrammed and described in almost cookbook detail, because the programmer possesses a thorough understanding of the target hardware and operating system.

In essence, there is a wide gap between the user's mental model of a task and the programmer's explicit model. Without someone to build a bridge between the two under-standings, we might still be at the mercy of strict procedural programming—standing in long lines outside centralized computer centers, handing punch cards to faceless operators. Instead, thanks to the insight of a few bright PC pioneers and insightful designers, we use computers on our desktops, on airplanes, and even on our laps. As you can see, a lot of our modern approach to computers and computing can be traced to a new way of thinking about them, something we might call a UI designer's model.

Designers

A designer who is aware of what the users want and what the programmer must work with is the final piece in the UI design pyramid. The designer must specify, visualize, and design an interface that satisfies the needs of both users and programmers, and also satisfies general user interface design principles and guidelines.

The designer also has a model, which not surprisingly involves both of the user's and programmer's models. In fact, because there is usually no direct connection between a user's mental model and a programmer's explicit model, the task of the designer's model is to bridge them both. The designer must understand the user's conceptual framework and the programmer's functional model. The designer must also account for the functionality that is required by the product specification and determine how much of that functionality to expose to the user, and when to expose it.

Like the user and the programmer, a designer is concerned with objects. In fact, a large part of the designer's effort should be spent specifying and defining objects and how to commu-nicate them to the user. If there is no existing model to satisfy the user's needs, the designer must try to help the user build one. Once again, using object metaphors will help the user extend his or her model.

Another important part of the designer's role is defining how the user interacts with the objects in the interface, and what kind of application-user feedback and response is possible and necessary. In software development terms, this feedback and response is commonly known as the "feel" of the application.

Finally, because visual design is usually the UI designer's forte, the designer must be concerned with what the user interface looks like (also known as the "look"). Working on both the look and feel and balancing the user's and the programmer's models, the UI designer has a lot to consider.

Summary

Obviously, I can't cover the subject of user interface design in a few chapters. It is a relatively new field, beginning in the early 1980s, and there are relatively few major working models to learn from. At the same time, however, the relative newness of the field and the new Windows 95 operating system make UI design a promising and exciting opportunity.

In the next chapter, you will see more specific scenarios that illustrate the team design approach, what factors influence UI design and how applying UI design principles is often a matter of compromise. In the end, you will understand the essentials of user interface design, what makes a user interface work, and why.

Stepping Through Essential User Interface Design

11

by William A. Montemer

In the last chapter you learned about the fundamentals of user interface design. You examined task-oriented, user-centered design principles, managed complexity with simplicity, and saw how team design functioned in the ideal world. Hopefully, these theoretical basics will give you something to think about as you develop wonderful, useful, and easy-to-learn user interfaces.

In the real world, things are not so cut and dried. For instance, although listening to what users say about using your software is a necessity (after all, I have said users are never wrong), reality shows that if you try to satisfy everybody, you end up pleasing nobody. In the same vein, if you spend too much time alone, designing the ultimate interface according to the guidelines and principles directly from the book of Microsoft (see the *Windows 95 User Interface Design Guidelines*), history shows that you can be sure no one will like it.

There are problems with working in the real world and there are solutions; sometimes you can't see one without the other. But that's what this chapter is about. You will look at some of the basic design principles again, but this time in a more realistic context. By stepping through the design process and putting user interface design on a timeline, you'll get another view of the kinds of development scenarios UI designers and programmers face. Before launching into this user interface reality check, let's review some of the basics of the Windows 95 environment and its interface resources as they pertain to UI design.

The Windows 95 Environment

One of the subtle things that differentiates Windows 95 from previous versions of Windows is how people work with data. Windows 3.1 was basically an application-oriented environment. To perform a task in an application-oriented system, the user first opened the application, and then used the application to open a document. To open the application, the user located the application icon and clicked it.

In contrast, Windows 95 is an object-oriented environment. To perform the same task in an object-oriented system, the user simply opens the document by clicking its document icon. The operating system takes care of opening the application without any further user intervention.

Although the difference between the two environments may seem trivial—in Windows 3.1, the user could associate an application with a file extension that Windows would then open and use to process the selected file—there is a world of difference, especially in terms of user interface design. Basically, in Windows 95, the operating system does all the work for you. As an interface designer, you can use the extra power in the Windows 95 environment to create elegant document-manipulation schemes and simple-to-use, yet powerful, applications. Or you can continue to use the application-oriented methodology, and gradually move your application to the newer paradigm. Let's see what makes up this new Windows environment.

The Desktop

The desktop in Windows 95 is the background for all tasks, as well as a container for all objects. As the desktop metaphor aptly points out, most of a user's work is done here.

Icons

Although icons in Windows 3.1 represented application and file objects, manipulating an icon did not directly correspond to manipulating its binary object. For instance, deleting an application icon in Program Manager did not delete the application. In Windows 95, icons are equivalent to objects; there is a one-to-one correspondence between icons and their objects. This means that deleting an icon in the Explorer effectively deletes its binary counterpart.

Icons can appear on the desktop and in various windows. An *icon* is a pictorial representation of an object; an *object* is a data file, a device, a container, or an application. Windows 95 supplies basic icons for system resources and operations, and the developer provides a set of icons for each application.

In the Windows 95 interface, icons represent objects that a user manipulates to perform tasks; therefore, it is important that icons clearly communicate their purpose. Application icons should represent their tasks, and data icons should represent their contents. Icons that are designed effectively increase the visual communications character of Windows and aid in user recognition. Because recognizing objects is easier for users than recalling procedures, designing icons that represent particular tasks or types of data files is invaluable in creating intuitive user interfaces.

Icons should be designed not only for the application, but also for all the types of data supported by the application. For instance, an accounting program might need icons that represent and display the chart of accounts, individual invoices, transaction records, and so on. In the same way, a multimedia interface might contain separate icons for various multimedia elements—sound, video, and graphics.

Icons should also be designed as a set according to what the objects represent to the user and how each object relates to the other objects. Icons for documents and data files should be different from the icon used by the application, although for consistency, some repeating element in the icon design is helpful. Finally, to be sure that the icons communicate the purpose of both the program and the design team, the set of icons should be tested and refined in usability studies.

ICON DESIGN

As shown in Figure 11.1, Windows 95 icons are required in three standard sizes: 16×16-pixel, 32×32-pixel, and 48×48-pixel. To make them easy to recognize and recall, design icons should be simple and distinct. Sets of icons should be similar in shape and repeat any distinctive markings.

FIGURE 11.1.

Windows 95 icons are required in three standard sizes.

ICON DESIGN

As shown in Figure 11.2, large icons are used to represent application objects, and the small icons appear in title bars and in the taskbar task-switching buttons for minimized applications. The developer should always supply the new small icons. Icons can be rendered in 256 colors to provide more realism, but be sure to use a system identity palette to avoid unpleasant discoloration.

FIGURE 11.2.

To aid user recognition, make the small icons as similar as possible to their larger counterparts.

Windows

In Windows 95, icons open into windows. A *window* is a fundamental interface object that is used to display and organize data, commands, and controls. A window provides a way to view and edit information in an object or to display an object's properties—all objects in Windows 95 possess properties. Windows are also used to display dialog boxes, message boxes, toolbars, and resource palettes.

NOTE

Windows can be classified by use. Depending on the type, windows may perform some or all of the following operations: activation and deactivation, opening and closing, moving and sizing, and scrolling and splitting.

Primary windows—Primary windows are used to display most of an application's data and commands. A typical primary window contains a sizable frame and a title bar. The content viewed in a primary window is not directly tied to the window. If the display area of the information exceeds the window size, horizontal and vertical scrollbars can be included to control the information view. The window can also include other components such as menu bars, toolbars, and status bars.

Secondary windows—Secondary, or child, windows can be included in the primary window. These supplementary windows provide extra views of the data object and can be used to supply other application information. A child window usually contains a sizable frame but cannot extend beyond the parent window. In fact, a child window cannot exist without its parent window; closing the parent window also closes the child window.

Dialog Box windows—A dialog box window contains controls that are used to collect additional information from the user. Windows supplies many common dialog boxes that provide a standardized method of interaction and execution across all Windows 95 applications. Among the common dialogs are the Save As common dialog box, the Open common dialog box, and the Property sheet dialog box.

Windows 95 Interface Elements

Windows supplies a set of preconstructed elements or controls to build Windows applications that look and act alike. This approach builds familiarity into Windows and enables users to easily transfer knowledge from a familiar product to a new unfamiliar one. Applications can also define custom controls and styles, giving interface designers the freedom to develop and use completely new paradigms and metaphors.

As shown in Table 11.1, Windows 95 supports all the basic interface controls supplied in Windows 3.1. These standard elements have been enhanced and improved in Windows 95.

Table 11.1. Windows 95 supports all the standard controls available in Windows 3.1.

Standard Control	Description
Button	Graphical control used to start actions or change properties
Dialog box	Used to obtain information from the user; can also contain other controls
Group box	Visual control used to organize other controls

continues

Table 11.1. continued

Standard Control	Description
List box	Used to display lists of items; can be combined with buttons and text boxes
Scrollbar	Used to scroll a window horizontally or vertically
Static control	Used to display text or graphic elements
Edit box	Used to display and edit text

Windows 95 has new enhanced controls that are specially designed to offer the user and the programmer more functionality, built-in interactivity, and a much more up-to-date look. Table 11.2 lists these new controls, along with a brief description of each control. Many of these new common controls may seem familiar, because most had been implemented by Microsoft and other software developers in Windows 3.1. As standard elements in Windows 95, these are easy to implement and they are included free.

Table 11.2. Windows 95 provides new common controls that offer improved user accessibility and consistency across applications.

New Control	Description
Heading control	Adds column heading to a view
Image list	List of graphical images
List view	List of icons and labels
Progress indicator	Visual gauge of task completion
Rich edit box	Font-formattable edit box
Status bar	A bar that displays status information
Tab control	File folder tabs
Toolbar	Graphics-based menu
Tooltip	Small pop-up label for added description
Slider	Slider control similar to a scrollbar
Tree view	Tree-structured display

Buttons

A button control is used to start an action or change a property (see Figure 11.3). The three types of buttons are command buttons, option buttons, and checkboxes. In Windows 95, the highlighting and light sourcing (light sourcing involves the direction light appears to be coming from) of a button simulates turning a physical pushbutton on and off.

FIGURE 11.3.

A button control is used to start an action or change a property.

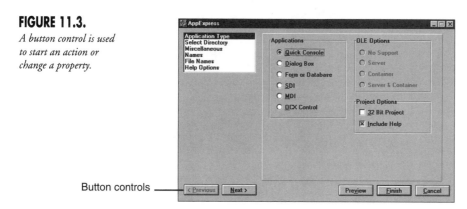

Button controls

A checkbox contains items that may or may not be checked (see Figure 11.4). If an item is checked, it is selected. If there is more than one checkbox, more than one item may be selected.

FIGURE 11.4.

If there is more than one checkbox, more than one item may be selected.

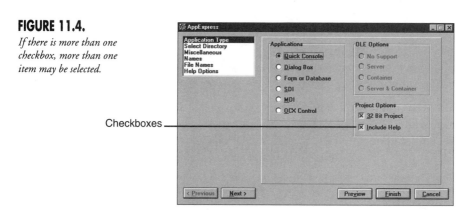

Checkboxes

An option or radio button is similar to a checkbox, but it is used to make mutually exclusive choices (see Figure 11.5). The selected option contains a black dot, and the unselected items are empty.

These controls can be used separately or together to create highly accessible user-preference, configuration, or setup dialog boxes.

FIGURE 11.5.

An option button is used to make mutually exclusive choices.

Option buttons

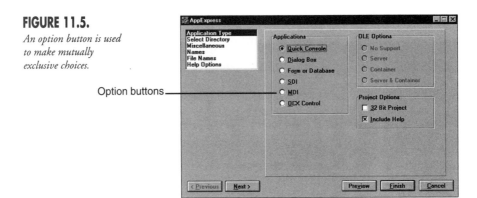

List Box

A *list box* is a preconstructed control used to display a large list of choices—text, color, icons, or other graphics—for the user. The attached scrollbar comes into play automatically if the number of items exceeds the box display capacity. In most cases, only a single option can be selected. Figure 11.6 shows a single selection list box.

FIGURE 11.6.

A list box is used to display a large list of choices.

If the screen area is limited and you still want to show a list of items, the drop-down list box might prove useful (see Figure 11.7). The drop-down list box holds a current value for the control and a list of optional values. By clicking the small downward-pointing triangle, the list box expands to display the other options and enables the user to make a new selection.

FIGURE 11.7.

The drop-down list box is useful if the screen area is limited and a list of items is still desired.

Some applications need the user to make multiple selections from a list box. The multiple selection list box shown in Figure 11.8 uses checkboxes to keep track of selected items.

FIGURE 11.8.

The multiple selection list box enables the user to make multiple selections.

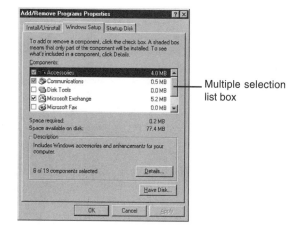

Multiple selection list box

List View

A list view control is a list box that displays a collection of items and enables the user to select one of them (see Figure 11.9). An icon and label for each item is displayed in the initial view, and four other views are available: full-sized icon and label; small icon and label; small icon and label in column format; and small icon, label, and report in column format.

FIGURE 11.9.

A list view control displays a collection of items and enables users to select one.

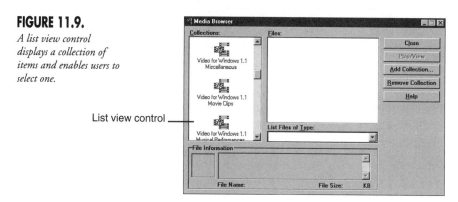

List view control

Tree View

The tree view control displays a list of information as an indented outline based on the list's hierarchical relationships (see Figure 11.10). The user can expand or collapse the outline to reveal or hide information.

FIGURE 11.10.

The tree view control displays a list of information as an indented outline.

Tree view control

Text or edit boxes enable the user to enter a string (see Figure 11.11). Edit boxes provide built-in Windows editing features including full clipboard text support.

FIGURE 11.11.

Text or edit boxes provide built-in Windows editing features.

Rich text boxes (see Figure 11.12) provide the same functionality as standard text boxes but also support the font properties of the current text including typeface, size, color, bold, and italic.

FIGURE 11.12.

Rich text boxes provide Windows editing functionality plus support of font properties.

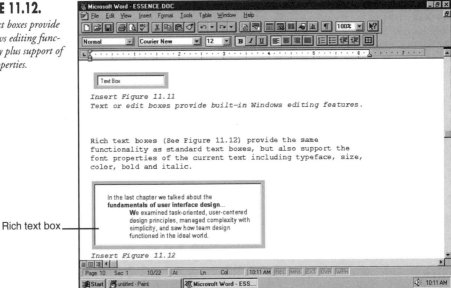

Rich text box

A combo box, shown in Figure 11.13, combines a list box with an edit control. This combination enables the user to enter text directly or select it from the provided list. Figure 11.14 shows a further refinement of the combo box, the drop-down combo control.

FIGURE 11.13.

A combo box combines a list box with an edit control.

FIGURE 11.14.

A drop-down combo box combines a combo box with a drop-down box control.

The spin box is another combination control that combines a text box and a special up-down construction called a spin control (see Figure 11.15). The up-down control works like a tiny scrollbar without anything in the middle. The text box displays a set of discrete ordered numbers that create a circular loop.

FIGURE 11.15.

The spin box combines a text box and a special spin control.

Spin box

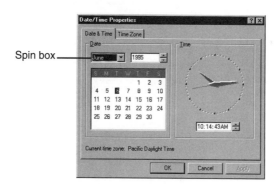

A group box is a static control that is used to visually group checkboxes and option controls. Static controls such as the group box do not receive focus from Windows and cannot receive event messages. Adding visual organization to an "information-dense" application makes the interface less distracting and easier to use.

Another control that helps visual organization is the heading control (see Figure 11.16). With this control, you can display program-definable headings above multiple columns of text or numbers.

FIGURE 11.16.

The heading control displays program-definable headings above multiple columns of text or numbers.

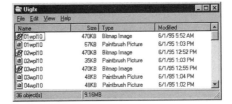

A tab control looks like the tab on a notebook or file folder, as shown in Figure 11.17. This control helps the UI designer manage the complexity of an application. The tab control conserves on-screen space required by seldom-used functions of an application.

FIGURE 11.17.

A tab control looks like the tab on a notebook or file folder.

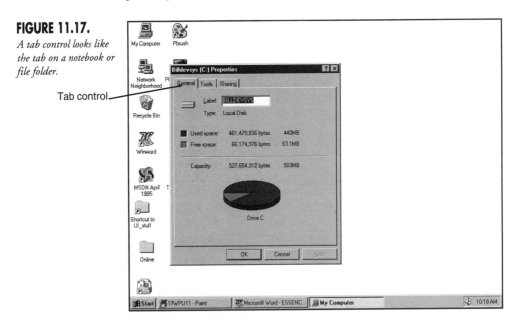

A Property Sheet Control

Because all objects in Windows 95 have property sheets, the system provides an easy-to-use control for defining a property sheet (see Figure 11.18). It provides the common controls used in a basic property sheet and provides modeless dialog box layout definitions to create tabbed property pages.

FIGURE 11.18.

The property sheet control provides a modeless dialog box to create tabbed property pages.

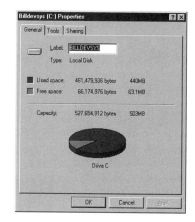

Scrollbars (see Figure 11.19) are horizontal or vertical scrolling controls used to control the view of the content in a window frame or list box.

FIGURE 11.19.

Scrollbars are horizontal or vertical scrolling controls that control the view of the content in a window frame or list box.

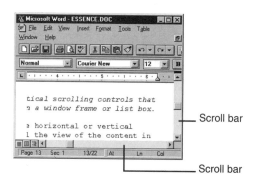

A slider (see Figure 11.20), or trackbar, is similar in operation to a scrollbar but resembles a sliding volume or tone control on a modern consumer stereo.

FIGURE 11.20.

A slider resembles a sliding volume or tone control on a modern consumer stereo.

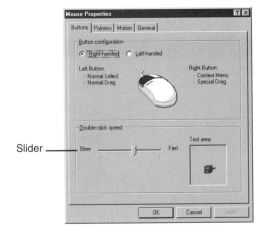

Slider

A progress indicator, or progress bar control (see Figure 11.21), shows the percentage of completion of a lengthy operation.

FIGURE 11.21.

A progress indicator shows the percentage of completion of an operation.

A tooltip control (see Figure 11.22) is a small pop-up window that displays a descriptive label of a control whenever the user moves the pointer over the control.

FIGURE 11.22.

A tooltip is a small pop-up window that displays a descriptive label of a control.

A well control (see Figure 11.23) provides a visual container for graphic resource items and operates much like a mutually exclusive group of option buttons. A well is useful to display sets of graphic values such as color, pattern, or images.

FIGURE 11.23.

A well provides a visual container for graphic resource items.

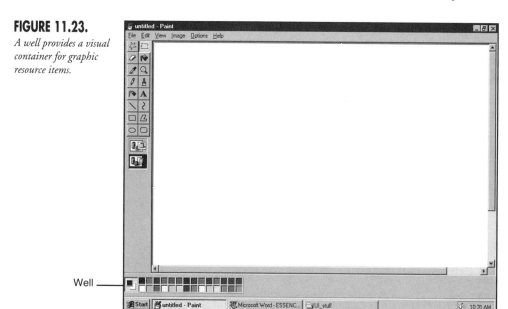

Well

Let's Return to UI Design

Now that you've seen most of the common interface devices available in Windows 95, you can look at the user interface design process, step-by-step. At each step, you'll learn some of the problems that occur in real development and look at some solutions.

An actual development occurs in an iterative cycle. First, the product is defined and specifications are written. Next, the product is designed and a prototype is made. The next step is testing, including both quality assurance and usability testing.

In UI design, the results of usability tests are used to refine the product design. After the prototype is revised, usability testing is repeated. The test-redesign-retest process continues until a final UI design that meets all product specifications is developed.

Specifying

Developing an application begins with deciding what to do. In a real development scenario, there are at least two major groups of people who help to define an application—the people you do work for, and the people you sell work to. The first group, the people you do work for, determines your product's budget and delivery schedule. These are the constraints within which you must work. The second group—the people you sell work to—are your customers or users.

Obviously, the first constraints a developer must account for are time and budget. If there is a rush to get a product out by a certain calendar date, lower-priority design goals as the date approaches. Also, as the budget allotted to a project begins to disappear, less primary issues such as extra usability testing and redesign cycles also vanish.

Other factors that influence UI design are platform and hardware issues. If the product must also support Windows 3.1, then the new system-supported interface controls will be unavailable. If the application supports different color depths—for instance, graphics packages typically support 256, 65,000, and 16 million colors—the UI must be designed accordingly. Most basic Windows 95 installations support 256 colors, and Windows will "dither down" to create the illusion of more colors. In a user interface, however, dithered colors are unacceptable. It is better to work within a standard identity palette and control precisely what the user will see.

Another factor influencing UI design is the scope of the new product. To begin with, there's a big difference between reworking a user interface for an existing product and designing one for a new product. If a product exists and has a reasonably sized installed base, you can't change the UI too much or current users will get angry. The current users want the software to improve, perform better, and cost less. They also want to be able to use it the first time they see it, without requiring any extra training or orientation. Therefore, one very large constraint in developing new revisions for existing software is maintaining some continuity with a previous version.

Users also think they know what will make your software better, and most likely they do. The problem is that they usually cannot verbalize this information; it is up to the development team to extract it from whatever the users say. So, rather than disregard the complaints and suggestions, the developer must listen to them very closely. For instance, if users always seem to say things such as, "Your program should allow me to this and that... just like your competitor's application!" then they are probably basing their understanding on a mental conceptual model that is very different from the one your program uses. The UI designer's task then becomes modifying the model to provide a similar point of view, or introducing a metaphor to help the users extend their mental model. Be careful, however, because by changing your model, you may create inconsistency in how your UI works, or even lose your product identity completely.

This points out another problem about listening to users: No one knows your software better than you. The user doesn't have detailed knowledge of a program's interior design and capabilities. It is therefore up to the developer to know what makes the product different from the other products on the market. If you don't know, or you sense a change in focus is due, get the team together and write a white paper about the product. Documenting what you see—especially at the beginning of the design cycle—will help you evaluate your product better at the end. Often, as you get deeper into development and new technologies, the development team loses sight of the original goal. Once again, good documentation will help re-orient your team and your efforts.

Besides defining the objectives and features of your product, you must have a clear understanding of who your users are, what they want to do, and what their intentions and goals are. You need to know everything you can about your target users—including their age and their experience with computers. Understanding who the user is and approaching even simple user interface tasks with creativity can be the difference between a stroke of genius and a dull interface.

Because Windows provides a built-in graphical user interface, there is a tendency among developers to think that any graphical method is intuitive for everyone. Figure 11.24 shows an Exit dialog box for an application designed for children. It is self-explanatory to users who have experience using Windows; however, it is debatable whether child users fit this criteria. The next illustration, Figure 11.25, shows an Exit dialog box for another application aimed at roughly the same age group. Besides being more fun—and undoubtedly more expensive—the second application does not assume the user has any prior experience with computers.

FIGURE 11.24.

This Exit dialog box is from an application designed for children.

Storybook Weaver	☒

Save Changes to Untitled?

| Yes | No | Cancel |

FIGURE 11.25.

This is a more creative Exit dialog box for an application aimed at roughly the same age group. When the child clicks the exit sign, the animated YES/NO sign drops down from the top with a "thud."

Although most development projects do not have the large budgets that Disney Software allots, in these two examples the main difference still lies in the creative application of user interface design techniques—not in the art.

Designing

By now, you understand your users and you also have defined what your product will do functionally. Now it's time to give the user interface a good think.

As the program development team begins to think about functionality and what to put into the product, the user interface designers should be asking similar questions. For instance, the UI designer might imagine a new user sitting at the program, wanting to perform a special task. If the program is powerful, as most Windows 95 applications are sure to be, a new user might look at the UI and wonder, "Before I can do this task, do I have to learn everything about the program and all its functionality first?"

Answering this simple question should put the UI designer in the right frame of mind to manage the complexity of the new application. Other similar questions might be: "Is the software accessible or frightening?" or, "If it's powerful, is it at least digestible?" The UI designer's response to all these questions is the same—keep it simple.

User interface designers use the idea of progressive disclosure when they talk about making a complex program seem simple. By determining what the user has to know and when, the UI designer can mask the overall complexity and reveal it to the user in smaller, digestible chunks. This is not unlike teaching someone to drive a car. First, you introduce the obvious—the key, the starter, the steering wheel, the brake. You do not discuss the electronic ignition or the anti-lock brake system because the driver usually does not need to know about those items. In exactly the same way, the UI designer shows the user only what applies to the task at hand.

However, the UI designer is not just limited to covering up complexity. By understanding how a user performs a task, the UI designer can reveal new options and commands as they become appropriate. For example, in one application, as the user moves the mouse around, the UI designer calls attention to new options by changing the option command highlight level—a technique called backlighting. When the mouse leaves the hotspot, the option is subdued once more.

Letting the mouse position control whether or not an option is active is an example of smart programming. Strangely enough, many user interfaces do not take advantage of the computer's capability to make intelligent decisions. The software should be smart—but not too smart. If the programmer knows what steps have to be done to do something, and it's obvious that the user intends to do just that, the computer should do it. Instead, most programs throw up a dialog box asking the user if they intend to do something. In life, we consider a person who has to ask for confirmation every step of the way a dullard. It's odd that we sometimes write programs that way.

Another example of smart programming involves a concept called embedded power. In this approach, a program tracks a user's usage patterns and if they reflect a certain understanding, the program opens up new, more complex features. Once you've given the UI design sufficient thought and devised a strategy for managing the application's complexity, you can start mapping your user's desires to your product's functions. Ideally, your functional model should account for whatever the programmer and the user consider important. Now it's time to start putting the design on paper and begin the process of fleshing it out.

Prototyping

Prototyping an interface begins with working on a sketchpad. You can use a pencil and paper to draw some pictures. Imagine using the program, one screen at a time, and sketch out your progress. Play them back to yourself, and try rearranging their order to see if that makes a difference. By the way, don't put too much emphasis on the quality of your sketches; let the critic inside you take some time off. There will be plenty of opportunity for that later.

Laying the foundation of your application's user interface is a very important stage in the design process. Ideas can be developed quickly, and scrapping one approach for another does not cost much—maybe a new notepad and a pencil. Revamping an approach after prototyping or coding is decidedly more expensive. The sketchpad stage is the best time for the designer to experiment and to incorporate some new user interface paradigms or emulate a new favorite technique. In Windows 95, a favorite word that user interface designers use a lot is "exploration."

Exploration means that the user can move around the program, trying out different options and settings and learning by trial and error. Of course, in a true Explorer mode there is no concept called error. Instead, UI designers offer up another concept called "forgiveness." (This, of course, implies that exploring means learning by trial and forgiveness!)

Forgiveness, in the UI sense, means that an application does not die a sudden, unexpected death or "paint the user into a corner" by providing no way for the user to back out of a set of choices or cancel a process. By designing error protection and exception handling into an application, developers can warn the user before they make a drastic or fatal mistake. To do even better than a warning, UI designers can make the potentially fatal actions reversible. In this more complete context, making a user interface explorable means that the application contains a virtual safety net to keep the user from damaging the system or important data files. With this sort of bullet-proofing, the user can experiment and learn how a program works without trepidation.

After the sketchpad stage, you might have an artist storyboard the user interface with better pictures to help you visualize it. Again, each successive step forces you to look deeper into your model than you had before. A final visualization step involves creating the more operational prototype with a Rapid Application Development (RAD) tool like Visual Basic. Using a RAD tool enables you to model a user interface that looks and acts like the actual executable version, right in Windows itself.

This prototype is invaluable for many reasons. Because it looks and acts like the application, it can communicate the final design and implementation to management, corporate backers, or customers. It can also enable the developer and UI designers to define the actual task flow, and can be altered or adjusted very quickly. Finally, it gives the UI designer a low-cost working model to use for usability testing. At this point in the design process, the operational prototype is ready for the user. Here, the design of the user interface undergoes the first of many usability tests.

Usability Testing

Usability testing differs from QA (quality assurance) or defect and reliability testing. Rather than finding defects and errors in what the software does, usability testing looks for inconsistency and operational mistakes in how a person uses the software. Also, to be valid, the profile of usability test participants must match that of your application's target audience.

Usability testing provides comparisons of task efficiency with previous versions or competing products, and success-or-failure data on what tasks users attempted and completed. It also gives you information about the user's perception of your application, how the user feels about it, and what kinds of problems the user has with it.

You might be wondering what "how a user feels" has to do with interface design. UI design is more of a holistic than a technical discipline. Factors such as how much confidence a user has in a program affects a user's performance. One factor that influences how a user feels is whether the user feels in control or not. For instance, if the UI is sluggish to respond to clicks on a certain menu choice or hotspot, an impatient user may repeatedly click it before moving on. By the time the system then responds, the user will be unable to identify which click came from where.

Another factor related to how a user feels is user feedback. When a user performs an action on an object, the object needs to return feedback in a timely manner. Without this feedback, the user can't tell if the action had any effect. Before long, the user will become disoriented and confused.

Also, the feedback should have a one-to-one correspondence with the action. This means that every user action should have one visible result. If actions a user takes appear to generate illogical or inconsistent results, the user will become unsure of what to expect.

Iterating

Testing often reveals design weaknesses. At the very least, it provides information you can use in a redesign phase. After you redesign the UI, rebuild the prototype and test it again. Successive trips through this design cycle will make the final UI design polished and refined.

During the iterative cycles, you can start substituting components of the actual application for the corresponding parts of the prototype. In this way, you can start gaining confidence in your final application and uncover any hidden dependencies that would plague the final binary executable.

The Ultimate Goal

As odd as it might sound, it is possible to summarize the essential goal of user interface design in a single, long-winded question: How can I couple the user's desires with a set of constraints that enables them to explore in a very forgiving way, enables them to see they are in control at all times, and is consistent, clear, and interesting?

In a nutshell—even if it's a very large one—this question touches on the ultimate goal of user interface design. And in a rather fancy way, we can use it to describe the basic Windows 95 UI development cycle. First, you must know and account for the user's desires while at the same time work within practical and economically feasible constraints. You then design a UI that enables users to explore your application and yet forgives their mistakes, while protecting them from program crashes and other disasters. Next, you build a responsive prototype that enables users to see what they are doing at all times so that they feel comfortable and in control of the application. Finally, in an series of usability tests, redesigns, and rebuilds, a clear and consistent UI design is refined. The result is an interesting and thoroughly enjoyable Windows 95 application!

PART

III

IN THIS PART

User Interface Applications

Creating a
Windows 95
Help System

Microsoft Windows Help (also known as WinHelp) is the standard program for the display of online Help files for programs that have been written for the Windows operating system. Because it is a standard piece of Windows, WinHelp has also emerged as a popular platform for delivering multimedia and hypertext titles. Along with making other improvements in Windows 95, Microsoft has reworked the Help engine to create WinHelp 4.0, which has been designed to make it easier to use for the end user, as well as have more flexibility for the developer. The following lists indicate the most significant changes between the Help engine in Windows 3.1 (also used in Windows for Workgroups and Windows NT versions prior to 3.51) and Windows 95. This same engine is also being used in the new Windows NT 3.51 release so that you can create one file for both platforms.

Product Changes

- Full-text search with phrase searching (similar to that in Multimedia Viewer 2).
- Graphics can have up to 16 million colors without an additional DLL.
- You can include AVI, WAV, and MIDI files without an additional DLL.
- Separate window with an expandable tree structure table of contents (like the MSDN CDs).
- Can display up to nine secondary windows at a time.
- Configurable button bars in secondary windows.
- Auto-sizable secondary windows to match the length of the topic text.
- Authorable buttons (the kind that depress when you click them).
- Can run macros when a user selects author-defined keywords from the index.
- Integrates multiple HLP files seamlessly.
- New training card feature for running things step-by-step.

Programming Changes

- The Help compiler (HCW) is now a Windows application—no more shelling to DOS to compile.
- Provides 26 new macros.
- Supports curly quotation marks, em and en dashes, and em and en spaces.
- Number of permitted build tags is now 16,383.
- Number of permitted entries in [MAP] section of the HPJ file is now 16,000.
- The size limitation for a hotspot has been raised to 4095 characters.
- The [WINDOWS] section of the HPJ file can have 255 window definitions.
- All limits for macro length and nesting have been removed. Macro length is limited only by the amount of local memory available at the time the macro is invoked (typically 10 to 20KB), and nesting is limited to the stack size.

- A Help file can reference as many as 65,535 unique bitmaps.

- Font names can be as long as 31 characters (was limited to 20), and you can now use the Wingdings font as well as other fonts.

Many of these changes are optional. In other words, you can take advantage of them or not, depending on the needs of your users and your own preferences. To support all these changes, Microsoft has changed the tools that are used to create Help files, as well as added some files both to the creation process (CNT or CONTENTS file) and the runtime process (GID files).

To get an idea of what WinHelp 4.0 looks like, take a look at Figures 12.1, 12.2, and 12.3. Figure 12.1 is the opening screen of a small, sample WinHelp 4.0 file. At this point, there isn't much to indicate that this is not a WinHelp 3.1 file. Clicking on the Contents button shows the first major difference.

FIGURE 12.1.

A sample Help file.

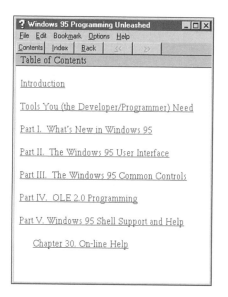

Figure 12.2 shows what the new Contents tab looks like. The Help file's first or "parent" topic is shown as a book. Topics that are "subordinate" to it are shown as pages with question marks. Notice that subtopics can also have subtopics, which is why the topic "Part V. Windows 95 Shell Support and Help" is shown as a book. You can expand or collapse headings by simply clicking on them. You can also use this to provide jumps to multiple WinHelp files in a way that is transparent to the user. If a particular component of the program and its assigned Help file haven't been installed on the system, WinHelp automatically drops all references to those topics in that Help file from the Contents tab.

Clicking on the Find tab brings up the next major difference.

FIGURE 12.2.

The sample Help file's Contents tab.

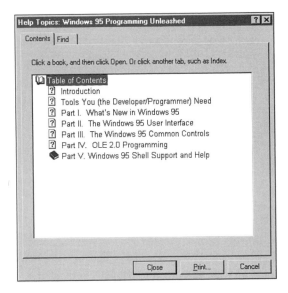

Full-text search was one of the most requested features for this version of WinHelp. Figure 12.3 shows how the tab appears that enables you or your user to find topics with specific words or phrases. This makes it much easier for the programmer—who doesn't have to remember to create an index or keyword for every possible combination of important terms—and for the user, who can find what he or she wants more directly.

FIGURE 12.3.

Our sample Help file's Full-Text Search tab.

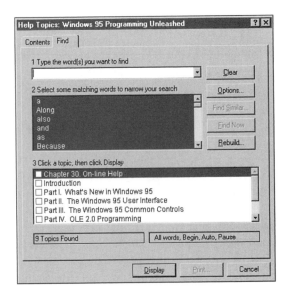

The rest of this chapter will address how to create these kinds of WinHelp 4.0 files, as well as provide some tips on design and delivery techniques. If you haven't created WinHelp files before, you might want to start thinking about something you can do as your own sample Help file. One idea a lot of folks use is setting up their resumes as WinHelp files. This can be as simple as creating topics for experience, education, and so on, or as complex as adding a spoken narrative or pictures of the family as pop-up topics.

Creating a WinHelp 4.0 Title

Now that we've looked at the basics of what a WinHelp 4.0 file looks like and the differences between it and WinHelp 3.1, it's time to look at the process of creating your own WinHelp 4.0 title.

Design Considerations

WinHelp presents online information using the following elements:

- Text with many fonts, type sizes, and colors
- Graphics, both for illustration and for serving as hotspot jumps
- Hypertext jumps for linking information
- Pop-up windows for presenting context-sensitive Help or additional text and graphics
- Secondary windows for presenting information in a controlled format
- Keyword-search capability for finding specific information
- Multimedia elements such as voice and video

When a user first starts WinHelp, the Help Topics dialog box is displayed. This dialog box stays open until the user selects a topic or closes it. Information appears within windows that can have all the standard window elements: a title bar, a menu bar, a button bar, a display area (with scrolling and nonscrolling regions), and scrollbars.

Because a WinHelp file is composed of all these diverse elements, you don't want to just jump into creating a file. You want to spend some time going through a design phase. This should include defining the contents and goals for the file. Here are a few questions you need to consider:

- Will this file be accompanying an application, or is it being used as a multimedia/ hypertext delivery platform? A WinHelp file that is part of an application will need a lot of screen shots, will need to be set up to handle context-sensitive calls as well as general browsing, and will need to be set up to open in a minimal configuration to allow the application to be visible at the same time. A hypertext or multimedia title that is being delivered as a stand-alone package will want to open initially in a full-screen (or close to it) mode to allow as much text, graphics, and so on, as possible to be shown at once. Such a title will probably have more and larger graphics, and may have to include a setup program as well.

■ Will the file normally be run from the user's hard drive or from a CD-ROM? How your GID file is set up will be affected by whether or not the Help file is on a writable drive. To a lesser extent, how the file is distributed may also affect your choices in compression of the Help file.

■ Will the title provide backward compatibility? If you are supporting users who are still on Windows 3.1, there are two ways that you can create one file for both platforms.

The first option is to also distribute a copy of Win32s—the 32-bit library for Windows 3.1—to your Windows 3.1 users and the WinHelp.exe from WinHelp 4.0. This will require multiple disks but gives you a better platform for future growth.

The second option is to create a WinHelp 3.1 file—but to get some of the WinHelp 4.0 functionality by providing a separate, non-compiled CNT file. This allows the file to run, as usual, on a Windows 3.1 platform and also provides the Contents facility of WinHelp 4.0 when the WinHelp file is run on either Windows 95 or Windows NT 3.51 machines.

The design phase is a good time to build an outline for the Help file so that you can determine what sort of material you will need and plan how you will link topics together. An example of an outline you might want to emulate is in Figure 12.4. In this example, you can see that the main topics are chapter topics, with jumps to the subtopics within each topic. Already we have some hard decisions to make: do we want each subtopic to be a separate topic (which would require that the user click to go to each one), or should each chapter be a topic with the subtopics as mid-topic jumps (in which case the user has to click to scroll down the page)?

FIGURE 12.4.

Outline for the sample Help file.

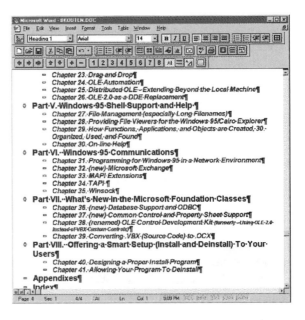

Creating the Base Files

Having done some preliminary planning, we can begin the actual construction of the Help file. The process for building a WinHelp 4.0 file can be broken into five steps:

1. Create the RTF and BMP/Segmented HyperGraphics (SHG) files with the text, graphics, and defined jumps.
2. Create the CNT file to describe the hierarchy of the file (optional, but you generally want it).
3. Create the HPJ file that directs the compiler in how to put all the files together.
4. Compile the project using HCW.
5. Test the compiled HLP file.

To build WinHelp 4.0 files, you will need the following software on your computer:

Microsoft Help Compiler version 4.0 (HCW.EXE and HCRTF.EXE)

Microsoft Hotspot Editor version 2.0 (SHED.EXE)

Microsoft Multi-Resolution Bitmap Compiler version 1.1 (MRBC.EXE)

Microsoft Windows Help version 4.0 (WINHELP.EXE)

A text-file editor that handles rich-text format (RTF)

The Microsoft files are included with the Win32 SDK for Windows 95 or Windows NT. Most third-party WinHelp authoring packages that support Windows 95 will also have the compiler and the other tools.

Topic files for WinHelp files must be created in RTF (rich-text format) to be properly compiled by the Help compiler (HCW). If you are familiar with RTF coding, you can prepare and save your topic file in any word processor or text editor that can create an RTF file. Coding RTF by hand, however, is time-consuming, and most WinHelp authors prefer to create the topic file within a word processor, format the topic text the way they want it to look, and then save the topic file as an RTF file. For this you need a word processor that can do the following:

Save files in rich-text format (RTF)
Insert custom footnotes
Support single and double underlining
Support hidden text

Microsoft Word for Windows (version 1.1 or later) and Microsoft Word (version 5.0 or later) can produce compatible RTF files. Also note that although you can author WinHelp files on any version of the Microsoft Windows NT operating system, WinHelp version 4.0 does not run on versions 3.11 and 3.5 and will only run on Windows NT 3.51 or later.

> **CAUTION**
>
> It is important to note that the Microsoft WordPad program that comes with Windows 95 does not create compatible RTF files.

Figure 12.5 shows our sample Help file as it appears in Microsoft Word. Notice the various formats of the text that are used to denote certain things to the Help compiler. Double-underlined text represents hypertext jumps. Text with a broken underline is a context string—in other words, a value telling the compiler where the jump is going to. Each page break represents the start of a new topic. Normally when you make a hypertext jump you are moving to a particular topic. However, you can also have mid-topic jumps with which you jump into the middle of a topic, then page up or down to see the rest of the topic as well. Also, you will probably define some pop-up topics where clicking on the hotspot brings up a small box with more information about the term or item.

FIGURE 12.5.

The sample Help file in RTF format. Notice the various styles used.

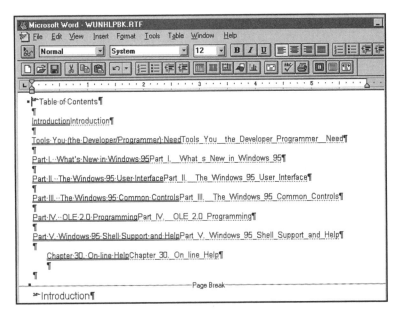

Once the RTF file has been created, you still need to build at least an HPJ file to direct the compiler in building the Help file. If you are using a third-party tool, the HPJ file should be automatically generated for you.

Figure 12.6 shows the HPJ file for the sample Help file. Each section is used to tell the Help compiler something about how the final file should be put together. If you are familiar with

C or C++ programming, you'll notice that the HPJ file bears a resemblance to a Make file. One of the important things that has changed in the HPJ file for WinHelp 4.0 is the addition of the FTS flag for indicating that the generated Help file will support a full-text search. For the FTS flag to actually take effect, however, you must also have specified a Compress flag greater than 0. Although the reason for this might not seem obvious, it is actually pretty clever. As in previous versions of WinHelp, Compress scans the RTF file that has been created and does some compression when it builds the final WinHelp file. In WinHelp 4.0, the scan for compression is also used to scan the included text to build the full-text search index.

FIGURE 12.6.

The Project (HPJ) file for our sample Help file.

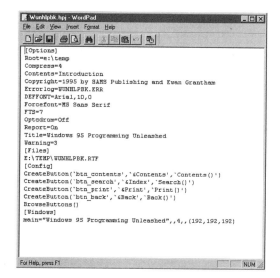

If you aren't using a third-party tool, you have two ways of creating the HPJ file. First, you could type it in using any ASCII editor. The other option is to use the Project File Editor built into HCW. Figure 12.7 shows what the screen looks like when you first start to build your HPJ file.

You enter this screen by selecting File | New from the HCW menu, then selecting Help Project from the list. From here, you can use the buttons on the side to bring up requesters, which ask you for the various pieces of information you need to build your project and then format them accordingly.

WinHelp 4.0 has a few changes in its HPJ file, including new values for some options. Here I've outlined what WinHelp 4.0 has changed for each section.

FIGURE 12.7.

A default beginning HPJ file using HCW's built-in Project editor.

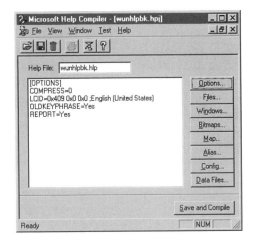

[OPTIONS] Section

CHARSET	Specifies the default character set for all fonts to be used in the WinHelp file.
CNT	Specifies the name of the Contents (CNT) file for this WinHelp (HLP) file.
DBCS	Specifies a double-byte character set for the topic (RTF) files.
DEFFONT	Specifies the default font to use in WinHelp text boxes.
FTS	Specifies the level of information to include in the full-text search index file.
HCW	Reserved for use by HCW. This line is always added by the Project File Editor, with a default value of 1.
HLP	Specifies the name of the WinHelp file to create.
INDEX_SEPARATORS	Identifies the characters used to denote separate keyword entries.
LCID	Specifies the locale identifier (used when translating Help files).
NOTES	Specifies whether or not the compiler will display any notes. The default is ON (display notes).
REPLACE	Specifies a path to replace and the new path.
TMPDIR	Specifies a folder for temporary files when compiling the Project file.

The COMPRESS option has new values (a combination of bit flags).

Hex Value	Meaning
0x00	No compression.
0x01	HCW determines the best possible compression for the current WinHelp file.
0x02	HCW uses phrase compression on text.
0x04	HCW uses Hall compression.
0x08	HCW uses Zeck compression.

[WINDOWS] Section

Instead of storing RGB values as three numbers, HCW saves this information as a lowercase letter r and the complete RGB number. If auto-sizing is specified, a lowercase letter f is placed at the end of the line before the optional number that is used to indicate the window state. The value used for indicating a maximized window is now always placed in the line and is actually a combination of the following bit flags:

0x0001	Maximizes the window and ignores the x-coordinate, y-coordinate, width, height, and on-top-state parameters given in the type definition.
0x0004	Turns off the default buttons on the button bar (used only for the main Help window).
0x0100	Adds the Options button to the button bar.
0x0200	Adds the Browse button to the button bar.
0x0400	Adds the Contents button to the button bar.
0x0800	Adds the Index button to the button bar.
0x1000	Adds the Help Topics button to the button bar.
0x2000	Adds the Print button to the button bar.
0x4000	Adds the Back button to the button bar.
0x8000	Adds the Find button to the button bar.

[MAP] Section

Files specified in an #include statement in the [MAP] section may contain // comment delimiters. Anything that comes after the // on the same line is ignored. Included files may be specified in angle brackets, quotation marks, or nothing at all.

[MACROS] Section

The optional [MACROS] section associates macros with keywords. The macros are run when the user selects the associated keyword from the index. This can be very powerful, enabling you to create WinHelp files that change to fit the user's preference.

[CONFIG:x] Section

The optional [CONFIG:x] section works much like the [CONFIG] section, except that the macros specified are run when a particular window (specified in the [WINDOWS] section) is opened. The Project File Editor automatically assigns a number to the section name, which associates that section to a particular window definition.

As we discussed earlier, you will probably want to create a special Contents (CNT) file. This is an ASCII-text file that specifies which topics appear in the Contents as well as which files should be included in the index. As with the HPJ file, the CNT file can be created from a third-party tool; created by typing in the proper codes and options using a text editor; or built using the Contents editor in the HCW program. Contents (CNT) files contain the following:

- Headings called books, which contain a group of related topics and other books in the Contents tab. End users view the contents of a book by double-clicking its icon.
- Topics, which include the text that appears in the Contents tab and the jump information, such as topic ID, WinHelp filename, and window name.
- Commands that specify the scope and appearance of your Contents and Index.
- Names of the default WinHelp file (and window).
- Title to display in the Help Topics dialog box.
- Names of WinHelp files to include in the index.
- Names of WinHelp files to search for keywords when the ALink and KLink macros are used in topics.
- Whether or not to display the Find tab (displaying is the default option, so you can leave this out most of the time).
- Names and locations of other tabs to display.

If you look at Figure 12.8, you can see what a simple CNT file looks like. In this example, we have specified only those items that aren't already default behavior (such as displaying the Find tab). You'll notice that each of the items in the Contents list starts with a number to indicate what level it is, followed by the title for that listing, and an = (equals sign), followed by the context string in the WinHelp file that is being mapped to that title.

FIGURE 12.8.

*The Contents (CNT) file
for our sample Help file.*

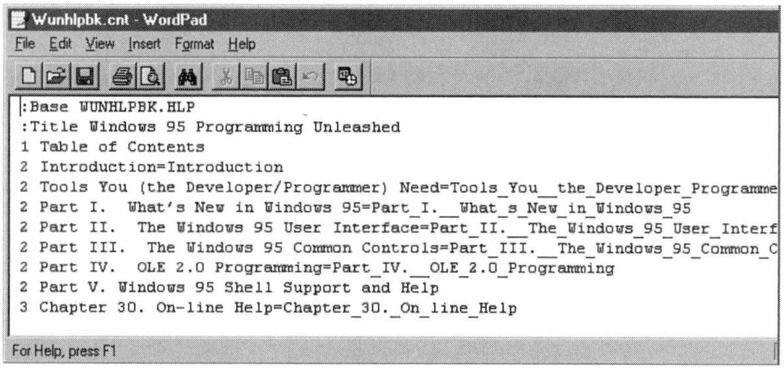

```
Wunhlpbk.cnt - WordPad
File   Edit   View   Insert   Format   Help

:Base WUNHLPBK.HLP
:Title Windows 95 Programming Unleashed
1 Table of Contents
2 Introduction=Introduction
2 Tools You (the Developer/Programmer) Need=Tools_You__the_Developer_Programme
2 Part I.    What's New in Windows 95=Part_I.__What_s_New_in_Windows_95
2 Part II.   The Windows 95 User Interface=Part_II.__The_Windows_95_User_Interf
2 Part III.  The Windows 95 Common Controls=Part_III.__The_Windows_95_Common_C
2 Part IV.   OLE 2.0 Programming=Part_IV.__OLE_2.0_Programming
2 Part V.  Windows 95 Shell Support and Help
3 Chapter 30. On-line Help=Chapter_30._On_line_Help

For Help, press F1
```

Note that the Contents tab will not appear in the Help Topics dialog box unless both of the
following conditions are met:

> The Contents file is specified in the Project file or a WinHelp file is specified in the
> Contents file.

> The Contents file contains topic jumps with defined context strings.

When designing a Contents file, keep the following in mind:

- Headings (represented by book icons) are containers of topics. Only topic entries
  actually link the user to a topic.

- A page icon usually jumps to a topic, but it can also be used to run a macro.

- A page icon can define a jump to a topic in another Help file and to a specific window
  definition.

- Users can print all topics in a book and any nested books by clicking the book icon
  and then clicking the Print button. This can be very handy but may also be worth
  warning your users about so they don't accidentally print out the complete collection
  of your company's manuals.

- Books that are nested beyond the third level will probably confuse your users.

- You can include other Contents files in your Contents file. But keep in mind the
  possibility of confusion.

A common item in any WinHelp file is a glossary. This is usually a single topic with an
alphabetical list of definitions or topics. In most cases it is implemented by having a graphic
image of a keyboard (or some other representation of the alphabet) where each letter is a
graphical hotspot. In order to do this we will need to set up each letter as a mid-topic jump,
and we will need to use the SHED editor to create a proper graphic. The same process that
is outlined here can be used for setting up any bitmap as a hotspot to jump to any topic,
such as a Continue button.

Loading SHED, we can pull in any BMP or SHG (Segmented HyperGraphics) file on the system to serve as the graphic hotspot. As you can see in Figure 12.9, I have a small keyboard with a letter on each key. You'll also notice that the letters are in alphabetical order rather than the order they appear on an actual keyboard. Once the bitmap is in SHED, you can click at the top left of the part of the bitmap where you want to start your hotspot, and drag the mouse toward the bottom right until the outline of the box completely surrounds the hotspot. In this example, we would need to do that for each of the letters and the question mark.

FIGURE 12.9.

An example of editing a bitmap for a WinHelp file.

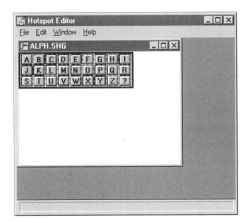

Once you have defined a hotspot, double-click inside the box to select the hotspot and bring up the Attributes requestor. The Attributes requestor enables you to set the topic to jump to. Figure 12.10 shows this dialog box. In this instance, all of our glossary topics have a context string that is simply an underscore and a letter. You can also set this up to have the name of the Help file first, followed by a period, and then the context string of the topic or mid-topic jump you want to have as the target. This is especially useful if you are working on multiple files at once and are worried about mixing and matching. Also notice that the Attribute has been set to invisible. If we wanted to have an outline (to emphasize that this is a hotspot), we could have selected Visible instead.

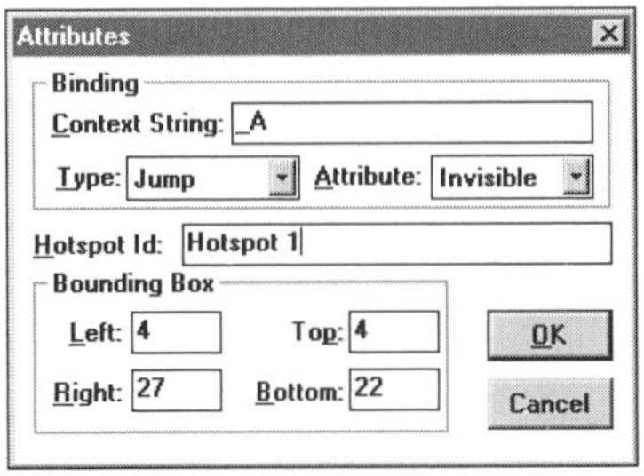

FIGURE 12.10.

The Attributes requestor in SHED. Notice the Context String.

One other option here is to choose a Type of Macro, in which case you would be asked for a Macro Name instead of the Context String. This can be useful if you want a button that causes another program to be run, or some text to be printed, for example.

Once you have defined all the hotspots on the graphic, select File | Exit. You'll be prompted to save your changes as an SHG file. This format stores the image and the hotspot definitions, and compresses the image.

It is important to realize that SHED saves a file by default in the same color resolution you used when you were editing the file. In other words, if you are running Windows in 16-color mode, you will get a 16-color graphic. On the other hand, if you are using a True Color mode (24-bit color), the SHG will be 24-bit as well. Depending on your user base this could be a good or a bad thing. In any case, SHED also performs some compression on the image, so that an SHG can be as small as 1/10th the size of the original bitmap, which is usually a good thing.

If you are creating a graphic without any hotspots and are concerned with how it will appear under different screen resolutions, there is one other tool you should be aware of—MRBC. The Multi-Resolution Bitmap Compiler (MRBC) is the one tool that still can be run only from the command line. Its purpose is to enable you to create a single file that has bitmaps in several resolutions so that you can compile this into your WinHelp file. This only helps, though, if the resolutions you are looking to support are CGA, EGA, VGA (Standard), and 8514.

Full documentation of the MRBC command can be found in the HCW.HLP file, but the basic command looks like:

```
MRBC [/S] name.vga [name.cga, name.ega, name.851]
```

where name would be replaced with the name of your bitmap file(s).

Using HCW and HCRTF

As mentioned before, HCW and HCRTF work together to create the final Help file from your base files. In fact, you should never need to call HCRTF directly because HCW should call it automatically. It is important to make sure you have it and that it is in your path, however, because HCW will call it.

Figure 12.11 shows the HCW requestor for compiling the Help file. Notice that you specify the HPJ file, which then tells the compiler how to construct the Help file. Also notice the three options that can make building and testing a help file a little easier.

Figure 12.12 shows the progress indicator for HCW. If you've programmed in Multimedia Viewer, this should look quite familiar. As the Help file is compiled, the crank turns, and the pages continue to feed in.

FIGURE 12.11.

HCW's compile requestor.

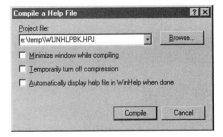

FIGURE 12.12.

HCW's progress indicator.

Finally, in Figure 12.13, we see the results of the compilation of the file. The important things to note after a compile are how many notes (Microsoft-speak for non-fatal errors) or errors (these cause an abort of the compile) were received, how much compression was actually achieved in the file, and whether the number of topics is what you expected. This last check is quite important because it's easy to accidentally delete a page break or change the formatting of a line to introduce or remove topics when you didn't want to.

FIGURE 12.13.

HCW output from compiling our sample Help file.

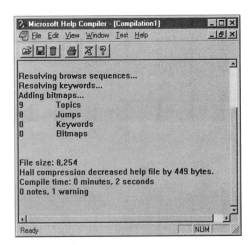

It's important to remember that each time HCW builds a Help file, it creates a temporary file of the same size. HCW gives this file a TMP extension and by default stores it in the topic file folder. If your WinHelp file is large and the space on your hard disk limited, you will want to specify a folder on a different drive.

In the examples above, HCW is being run interactively. However, you can also call HCW from the Windows 95 shell (the command line) by using : HCW *filename*, in which *filename* is the name of the Project (HPJ) file.

Once the WinHelp file has been created by HCW, you may want to run your WinHelp file in debug mode. To do this, select File | Help Author from within HCW, then run your WinHelp file by selecting File | Run WinHelp. You then are given a requestor, and you tell HCW which HLP file you want to run, where the HPJ file for the HLP file is, and how you want the WinHelp file to appear to have been invoked.

In this mode, you will notice the following:

Your topic titles in the title bars are replaced with their topic numbers.

Accelerator keys Ctrl+Shift+right arrow and Ctrl+Shift+left arrow are activated to enable you to display topics forward and backward by topic number.

The accelerator key Ctrl+Shift+J is activated to display the Jump dialog box. This enables you to jump to any topic based on its topic ID, topic number, or map number. You can also run a macro from the Jump dialog box by typing an exclamation mark (!) and the macro name and parameters in the Enter Topic Identifier box.

Accelerator keys Ctrl+Shift+Home and Ctrl+Shift+End are activated to enable you to display, at any time, the first topic in the WinHelp file, and the last topic in the WinHelp file, respectively.

The Topic Information command is added to the right-click menu. When you select this command, WinHelp displays for the current topic the text of the title ($) footnote, the macros specified in the entry macro (!) footnote, the current window name, and the WinHelp filename (including path).

The Ask on Hotspots command is added to the right-click menu. When this command is selected, WinHelp changes the effect of clicking on a hotspot. Instead of running the hotspot jump or macro when you click on a hotspot, WinHelp displays the text of the hotspot (topic jump or macro syntax) in a dialog box. You can then choose to run the jump or macro, or to return to the topic.

NOTE

When the debug mode is on, it is on for any or all Help files that you view.

The Ask on Hotspots command might not work correctly if there are no keywords in the Help file.

In addition to this debug mode, HCW also offers some other testing features. You can generate a report on various aspects of a WinHelp file by clicking the Report command on the File menu in the HCW program. For each WinHelp file you can request reports by topic titles, hash numbers, or keywords. You can also request a report containing all the ASCII text in the Help file.

The HCW program offers the following commands on the Test menu:

- CNT Item. The HCW program checks parameter limits, level coherence, nesting depth, duplicate elements, missing parameters, file availability, and other components of the Contents file. To test the topic jumps from Contents entries, use the Test(5) or Test(6) macro. The 5 and 6 here are the test numbers that are defined for the Test macro. Test(5) results in a jump to all topics listed in the CNT (Contents file), and Test(6) does the same jump, and then exits.

- WinHelp API Item. Enables you to launch a WinHelp API as if it were invoked from another program.

- Send a Macro Item. Enables you to see how a specific macro will perform in a Help file without having to run the entire Help file.

The new Test macro, which can be launched from the Jump dialog box, enables you to display the Help file in a number of specific ways. The new Compare macro, which can be run from a program, enables you to display the original and translated versions of a Help file.

When HCW cannot find a bitmap, it inserts its own placeholder bitmap and includes the name of the missing bitmap. This way, you can easily tell the difference between a missing bitmap and a bitmap that WinHelp cannot display. If you are in debug mode and a bitmap cannot be found, WinHelp provides information regarding the specific problem.

Third-Party Tools

At this point in time (mid-1995), there are only two commercial third-party tools that support the creation of WinHelp 4.0 titles. These are Blue Sky's WinHelp Office (which includes RoboHelp and a video on creating WinHelp files) and Olson Software's Help Writer's Assistant. What is unique about both of these tools is that not only can you build both WinHelp 3.1 and WinHelp 4.0 files with them, but they will also both enable you to import your old Help files into the tool so that you can add, change, or delete material and then build a new WinHelp file.

> Blue Sky Software
> WinHelp Office
> Price to Be Announced (U.S.)
> Toll Free 800-677-4WIN
> International 619-459-6365
> Fax 619-459-6366

Olson Software
Help Writer's Assistant (Professional)
$199 (U.S.)
Phone +64 6 359 1408
Fax +64 6 355 2775
CIS 100352,1315

Where tools like this really help is in complex environments where having to keep track of multiple jumps or building complex HPJ or CNT files would take a good bit of time. Also if you have to write Help files, but don't really want to have to do all the RTF codes and building of HPJ and CNT files by hand, a third-party tool will come in handy. Figure 12.14 is a screen shot of HWA, which gives you an idea of how such a tool works. What this doesn't show are all the options for specifying macros, having an H file built automatically for you to include in your C or C++ program, and so on. Basically, if you create help files, you really should consider a third-party authoring system.

FIGURE 12.14.

An example of using a third-party authoring kit to create our sample Help file.

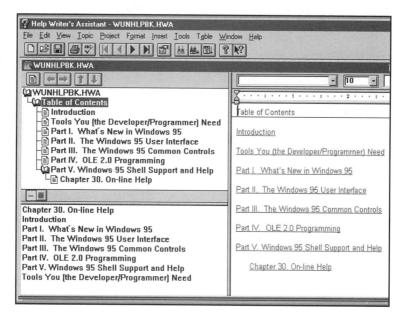

Using WinHelp for Context-Sensitive Help

Context-sensitive help is a way to help the user quickly understand your application and how it works. Under earlier versions of WinHelp, context-sensitive help was called using the F1 key. This method still works in WinHelp 4.0, along with the new methods of placing the cursor over the point to be queried and clicking What's This on the right-click menu, or pressing the ? button in the title bar and pulling the ? cursor to the field or dialog box in question. Also new in WinHelp 4.0 is that you can provide context-sensitive help for dialog boxes, menus, and commands, as well as other interface elements in your program. You can even create a Help button in a dialog box or window to serve as your context-sensitive help initiator.

Programming context-sensitive help requires coordination between the help files and the program itself. First, you write the relevant topics, and then modify the program to call the correct one. As part of this modification, you assign numeric values to objects that the end user is likely to query. You then map these numeric values to the appropriate topic IDs in your Help topics, which is done by using the Map dialog box in the Project File Editor to map topic IDs to the context numbers.

When you are assigning the topic IDs to your context-sensitive help topics, use IDH_ as the prefix for the topic ID. The Help compiler recognizes these topic IDs as identifiers a program will call, and allows HCW to recognize if any of these topic IDs are in your topic files but are not in the [MAP] section of your Project file. That way you are likely to find inconsistencies in naming, for example. HCW also lists identifiers that are in the [MAP] section but not in your topic files so you can check for mistakes in that direction, too.

The steps to follow once you have determined your numeric values for your objects are:

1. Start the HCW compiler.
2. Open your Project (HPJ) file.
3. Click on the Map button.
4. Click on the Add button.
5. Type the topic ID, the numeric value for the object, and any comments in the appropriate text boxes.
6. If you want to include a C header file, click the Include button.

Tips and Techniques for WinHelp 4.0

Now that you are familiar with the basics of creating a WinHelp 4.0 file, you are ready to look at some of the "extra effort" things you can do to make your WinHelp title stand out.

Macros

WinHelp provides a set of custom commands, or macros, that enable you to control and customize WinHelp's functionality. The available macros fall into six categories. These are:

Button macros

Menu macros

Linking macros

Window macros

Functionality macros (called Keyboard and Auxiliary macros in the MS documentation)

Text-Marker macros

The following section is a quick list of the macros available in each of these categories. More information can be found on each of these macros in the HCW.HLP file that comes with the HCW compiler.

Button Macros

Button macros enable you to access, create, or modify buttons.

`Back`	Displays the previous topic in the Back list.
`BrowseButtons`	Adds the Browse buttons to the Help button bar.
`ChangeButtonBinding`	Changes the assigned function of a Help button.
`ChangeEnable`	Assigns a macro to a navigation bar button and enables that button (equivalent to calling both ChangeButtonBinding and EnableButton).
`Contents`	Displays the Contents tab or default topic of the current Help file.
`CreateButton`	Creates a new button and adds it to the button bar.
`DestroyButton`	Removes a button from the button bar.
`DisableButton`	Disables a button on the button bar.
`EnableButton`	Enables a disabled button.
`EndMPrint`	Dismisses the printing message box and ends the printing of multiple topics.
`Finder`	Displays the Help Topics dialog box, in its last state.
`History`	Displays the history list.
`InitMPrint`	Begins printing multiple topics by presenting the Print dialog box.
`Menu`	Displays the context menu normally accessed by the right mouse button.
`Next`	Displays the next topic in a browse sequence.
`Prev`	Displays the previous topic in a browse sequence.
`Search`	Displays the Index.
`SetContents`	Designates a specific topic as the Contents topic.

Menu Macros

Menu macros enable you to access, create, or modify menus and menu items.

About	Displays the About dialog box.
Annotate	Displays the Annotate dialog box.
AppendItem	Appends a menu item to the end of a custom menu.
BookmarkDefine	Displays the Bookmark Define dialog box.
BookmarkMore	Displays the Bookmark dialog box.
ChangeItemBinding	Changes the assigned function of a menu item.
CheckItem	Displays a checkmark next to a menu item.
CopyTopic	Copies the current topic to the Clipboard.
DeleteItem	Removes a menu item from a menu.
DisableItem	Disables a menu item.
EnableItem	Enables a disabled menu item.
Exit	Exits the WinHelp program.
ExtAbleItem	Enables a custom menu item that was added with the ExtInsertItem macro.
ExtInsertItem	Inserts a menu item at a given position on a menu, in a given state.
ExtInsertMenu	Inserts a new menu to the WinHelp menu bar, in a given state.
FileOpen	Displays the Open dialog box.
FloatingMenu	Displays a floating menu with author-specified items at the current mouse position.
HelpOn	Displays the How To Use Help file.
InsertItem	Inserts a menu item at a given position within a menu.
InsertMenu	Adds a new menu to the WinHelp menu bar.
Print	Sends the current topic to the default printer.
ResetMenu	Resets the WinHelp menu bar and menus to their default states.
UncheckItem	Removes a checkmark from a menu item.

Linking Macros

Linking macros affect and define hypertext links.

ALink	Jumps to the topics containing the specified A-keywords.

JumpContents	Jumps to the contents topic of a specific WinHelp file.
JumpContext	Jumps to the topic with a specific context number.
JumpHash	Jumps to the topic with a specific topic hash number.
JumpHelpOn	Jumps to the contents topic of the How To Use Help file.
JumpId	Jumps to the topic with a specific topic ID.
JumpKeyword	Jumps to the first topic containing a specified K-keyword.
KLink	Jumps to the topics that contain the specified K-keywords.
PopupContext	Displays the topic with a specific context number in a pop-up window.
PopupHash	Displays the topic with a specific hash code in a pop-up window.
PopupId	Displays the topic with a specific topic ID in a pop-up window.
UpdateWindow	Jumps to the specified topic in the specified window, and then returns the focus to the window that called the macro.

Window Macros

Window macros enable you to control or modify the various WinHelp windows.

CloseSecondarys	Closes all but the current secondary WinHelp window.
CloseWindow	Closes the main or secondary WinHelp window.
FocusWindow	Changes the focus to a specific WinHelp window.
Generate	Sends a message to the currently active WinHelp window.
WinHelpOnTop	Places all WinHelp windows on top of other windows.
NoShow	Prevents the WinHelp window from appearing.
PositionWindow	Sets the size and position of a WinHelp window.
SetPopupColor	Sets the background color of pop-up windows.

Functionality Macros

Functionality macros add functionality to your WinHelp files.

AddAccelerator	Assigns an accelerator key to a WinHelp macro.
Compare	Runs a second instance of WinHelp next to the first.
ControlPanel	Opens a specific tab on a dialog box in the Control Panel program.
ExecFile	Opens a file and runs the program associated with that file.

ExecProgram	Starts a program.
FileExist	Checks to see whether the specified file exists on the user's computer.
Flush	Forces WinHelp to process any pending messages, including previously called macros.
IsBook	Determines if WinHelp is being run as a stand-alone system (as a book) or if it is being run from a program.
MPrintHash	Prints a topic, identified by a specific hash number.
MPrintID	Prints a topic, identified by a specific topic ID.
RegisterRoutine	Registers a function within a DLL as a WinHelp macro.
RemoveAccelerator	Removes an accelerator key from a WinHelp macro.
ShellExecute	Opens or prints the specified file.
ShortCut	Runs a program if it is not already running and sends it a WM_COMMAND message with the specified wParam and lParam values.
TCard	Sends a message to the program that is invoking WinHelp as a training card.
Test	Enables an author or a program to test a WinHelp file.
TestALink	Tests whether an ALink macro has an effective link to at least one topic.
TestKLink	Tests whether a KLink macro has an effective link to at least one topic.

Text-Marker Macros

Text-marker macros enable you to create and manipulate markers within a WinHelp file for navigation and other purposes.

DeleteMark	Removes a marker added by SaveMark.
GotoMark	Jumps to a marker set by SaveMark.
IfThen	Runs a Help macro if a given marker exists.
IfThenElse	Runs one of two macros if a given marker exists.
IsMark	Tests whether a marker set by SaveMark exists.
IsNotMark	Tests whether a marker set by SaveMark exists.
Not	Reverses the result returned by IsMark.
SaveMark	Saves a marker for the current topic and WinHelp file.

When creating Help files, you can make your macros run by:

- Placing macros in the Project (HPJ) file so that WinHelp runs the macros whenever the user opens the Help file or a particular window definition.

- Placing macros in a topic footnote so that the macros run when the user displays the topic.

- Placing macros in the Contents (CNT) file so that WinHelp runs the macros whenever the user clicks the page icon.

- Configuring the menu bar and button bar so that WinHelp runs a macro when the user chooses the menu item or button.

- Adding to your topic hotspots that run a macro when the user chooses the hotspot. This was discussed earlier in the section on the SHED editor.

- Using an external program to send to WinHelp a function call that requests a Help macro to be run.

WinHelp macros are designed to imitate standard C-language format. However, these macros do not support variables or expression evaluation. If you find that the standard set of WinHelp macros is not able to do the job, you can create your own WinHelp macros using DLL functions.

Converting Multimedia Viewer Files to WinHelp 4.0

To convert a Microsoft Multimedia Viewer 2 title to a WinHelp 4.0 file, do the following:

1. Update macro references in the topic (RTF) files.
2. Update multimedia references in all the source files.
3. Convert the Viewer Project file (MVP) to a WinHelp Project (HPJ) file.
4. Create a Contents (CNT) file.
5. Build the new Help (HLP) file.

The primary differences between WinHelp 4.0 and Multimedia Viewer 2 are:

WinHelp does not support panes, groups, or fields.

WinHelp has its own (optional) full-text search indexer and user interface.

WinHelp supports the `LDLLHandler` callback function but does not support other Viewer APIs.

The GID File

A GID file is a hidden file created by WinHelp when a Help file is first opened or updated. If you run a WinHelp 3.1 file using the WinHelp 4.0 engine, you still get a GID file, although it doesn't have all the elements of a WinHelp 4.0 GID file. A GID file contains various information about the Help file, including:

Binary representation of the Contents (CNT) file, including jumps and commands, after it has been processed. Only topics that were found during processing are stored.

The filenames and titles of all Help files included in the Contents file.

Keywords from other Help files, for the combined index (if :Index statements were used).

List of which files have full-text search index (FTS) files.

The size and location of Help windows and dialog boxes.

WinHelp creates a GID file for each Help file that does not have a Contents file, or one GID file for each Contents file (even if that Contents file includes a family of Help files). If a user deletes a GID file, WinHelp will create a new one the next time the user accesses the Help file.

If you are setting up a WinHelp file on a network or CD-ROM, you will usually want to provide a GID file in the same location as the Help file, particularly if your WinHelp file is large. In addition to giving you read-only control, this will save disk space on the user's computer. If you do not provide a GID file in such circumstances, WinHelp will try to create a GID file in that same location. If that location is read-only, WinHelp will then try to create the GID file in the \windows\HELP folder on the user's computer (or in the Windows folder if no Help folder exists). If WinHelp finds a GID file of the same name on the user's computer, it will use that file instead of creating a new one.

If you ship GID file(s) for a Help system that will not change, you do not need to ship the Contents file(s). However, it is probably a good idea to go ahead and do so anyway.

Updating a Help System

Whenever you release an updated Help system, your setup program should run the WINHELP -G command on the master (default) WinHelp file. This option forces WinHelp to create a new GID file for the master Contents file, which then ensures that the user can access the topics in the new or updated WinHelp and Contents files. Otherwise, strange things might happen when the user tries to access a topic that has been changed or removed.

Using Training Cards

Training Cards enable WinHelp to communicate with another program. WinHelp can send a message to the program, and then the program can send a message to WinHelp telling it which topic to display next.

This feature can be used to provide the steps of a procedure to a user one step at a time. For example, you could have a topic that contains only the first step of a procedure. When the user has successfully completed the first step, the program would tell WinHelp to display the topic containing the second step.

The Training Card feature can be used for many other powerful programs. For example, there may be cases when the WinHelp topic that should be displayed is dependent on some variable of the software program. If you set up Training Cards, the software program can query the user and act on the responses.

When you use the Training Card feature, you must work with a program developer to set it up in the program code. The process is similar to setting up context-sensitive help and makes use of the TCard macro to pass data to the other program.

Using DLLs

A dynamic-link library (DLL) is an executable module containing functions that programs such as WinHelp can call to perform useful tasks. WinHelp accesses DLLs in two ways:

- Through DLL functions registered as Help macros in a Project file. These functions can then be used in hotspots and macro footnotes in topic files.
- Through embedded window ({ewx}) references in topic files.

You can extend WinHelp by providing custom DLLs containing author-defined WinHelp macros and by providing DLL access through embedded-window references.

When creating DLLs for embedded windows, you must follow all the standard design requirements for Windows DLLs. These requirements are described in the Microsoft Win32 Software Developers' Kit (SDK).

To create DLLs for WinHelp, you need the Microsoft Win32 SDK and the Microsoft C/C++ development system , or the Microsoft QuickC graphical development environment.

As mentioned above, you can create embedded windows to extend the functionality of WinHelp by placing objects in a fixed-size window under the control of a DLL. For example, you could create a DLL to display custom animation sequences. However, you cannot create an embedded window that functions as a hotspot.

To create an embedded window, you would insert an embedded window reference, {ewx}, in the RTF source file. If you are using a third-party tool, you probably have an option for this.

WinHelp displays embedded windows within your topic windows. To WinHelp, an embedded window is simply a child window of the topic window. Users cannot minimize, maximize, or resize an embedded window. Embedded windows cannot be used as hotspots. However, you can include hotspots in an embedded window if they are controlled by the DLL. Your users will not be able to use the keyboard equivalents to access these hotspots, however, because embedded windows cannot receive the input focus, which means they cannot process keystrokes. So, don't place anything in an embedded window that requires keyboard input from users. Although embedded windows do not process keyboard input, their DLLs must be able to process the following messages, which are specifically defined for use with embedded windows:

```
EWM_RENDER (0x706A)
EWM_QUERYSIZE (0x706B)
EWM_ASKPALETTE (0x706C)
```

WinHelp positions the embedded window using the justification character (left, right, or character) specified by the author in the embedded window reference. In other words, you replace the x in ewx with either l, r, or c. The embedded window DLL is expected to display the information in the window and resize the window appropriately. Help expects the window size to remain fixed as long as the topic is displayed. The window element and DLL determine the size and content of the embedded window, and Help arranges the other elements of the topic around the embedded window.

WinHelp displays embedded windows only when necessary—while the topic containing the embedded window is being displayed. However, an embedded window may exist while it is not being displayed (if the user scrolls the topic past the embedded window, for example). Because it is part of a specific topic, an embedded window goes away when the user displays a different topic.

Using WinHelp as a Multimedia Engine

One of the increasingly popular uses for WinHelp is as a delivery platform for multimedia titles. As stated earlier, WinHelp 4.0 has the advantage of not requiring a separate reader program, and with a third-party authoring tool, it can be as easy to create with as any product on the market.

Earlier in the chapter you saw how to include graphics with or without hotspots into your title. You may also want to add elements such as animations or sounds to your WinHelp file. WinHelp 4.0 creates an embedded window for an included multimedia file and automatically sizes it for the display window and controller (if any) for AVI files, or for the size of the controller for WAV, MID, or CD audio files. If the window is not large enough to display the controller, WinHelp will crop the right and bottom edges of the window displaying the controller. WinHelp also will crop the controller if the window is not big enough to display it. However, the user can resize the window to show any part of the controller that does not initially appear in the window.

Multimedia files tend to be large and will increase a WinHelp file's size accordingly. If your Help file is likely to be copied to a user's hard disk (rather than run from a CD), file size might be a serious issue. If the total size of the Help file and multimedia components is over 8 MB, the Help compiler will automatically create a temporary file.

One thing to consider is that you can keep multimedia files outside a WinHelp file; you do not need to build them in. This can be helpful if you want to run sample files that are already included as part of the product, or that are known to exist on the user's computer. A good example would be if you wanted to play one of the WAV files that comes with Windows.

To add sound to one of your topics:

1. Place the insertion point at the line in your topics (RTF) file where you want the sound controller to be displayed.

2. Type the reference in the following syntax:

   ```
   {mci filename.wav}
   ```

   where `filename.wav` is the name of the sound file you want to add.

If the end user's computer has a sound card, WinHelp will play the recording when the user clicks on the sound icon.

You follow the same process to add animations or video to a title. Simply change the `filename.wav` to be `filename.avi`, or whatever extension indicates the type of file that is to be played. For this to work, the file to be played or displayed must be of a type that has been defined and available to the Media Player tool.

Other WinHelp Resources

In addition to what we have covered in this chapter, you may also find the following sources of information helpful:

- The HCW.HLP Help file—Goes into more detail on using HCW, as well as some of the overall features of WinHelp 4.0.

- *Programmer's Reference, Volume 6:* Chapter 2, "Help"—Discusses using the HELP_* constants of the WinHelp function.

- *Microsoft Windows User Interface Design Guide*—A book dedicated to the principles of user interface design and the specifics of how the principles tie into good Windows development.

Summary

In this chapter, we looked at the various ways you can create a WinHelp file to be used in Windows 95. Not only are there a large number of new features, but Microsoft has also improved the toolset used to take advantage of those features. The most notable features include:

- The addition of the Contents tab, which enables you to set up a visual table of contents for your file, or to link several files together
- The addition of the full-text search, or Find, tab, which provides your users more flexibility in searching for particular topics
- Making the Help compiler (HCW) a Windows program
- Making it easier to include higher resolution graphics

The WinHelp authoring process can be aided by a third-party authoring tool, but regardless of the tools used, the basic process is to design the flow of the file by deciding where you need hypertext jumps, what kind of graphics to use, and so on; create the base documents, both text and graphics; compile; and test.

With the information in this chapter and the Win32 SDK tools, you should have no problem helping your users to make the most of your program or your on-line documentation.

Designing a Smart Install and Uninstall

13

by Peter D. Hipson

Installing applications under Windows 95 is both easier and more complex than installing under earlier versions of Windows. If that sounds like a contradiction, read on.

With Windows 95, Microsoft has introduced a new feature: uninstall. With the uninstall capability of Windows 95 users can easily remove applications that they no longer wish to have installed on their computer. This means that the uninstall program must maintain a record of what files are installed by the application, and what changes (if any) are made to the system when the application is installed and used. The actual uninstall program is found in the Control Panel's applet: Add/Remove Programs. This applet, shown in Figure 13.1, enables the user to remove an application that has been properly installed.

FIGURE 13.1.

The Control Panel applet Add/Remove Programs.

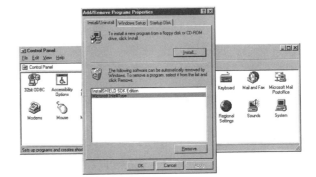

To remove a program, simply select it from the list of installed applications, and then select the Remove button.

> **NOTE**
>
> I've had to tell several users who had installed a substantial number of applications that the only foolproof way to remove applications under Windows 3.*x* was to reinstall Windows. This method of removing applications is somewhat like using a sledge hammer to push in a thumbtack.

Installations are easier under Windows 95 because Microsoft has included in the WIN32SDK not one, but two application installation programs. The first program is the old standby, Microsoft Setup. The Setup toolkit has been updated to 32 bits (necessary for Windows 95) and is now better documented.

In addition to Microsoft Setup, Microsoft has included a limited functionality version of Sterling Software's InstallSHIELD program, called InstallSHIELD SDK. This program can be used to install many simpler programs. The InstallSHIELD SDK program also introduces you to Sterling's other products.

Another Windows 95 installation program is Installigence from Instance Corporation. Installigence is not included with the WIN32SDK; however, the CD for this book contains a demo version of this program for you to try.

This chapter is divided into four parts.

- The first part of the chapter covers the Microsoft Setup program. You will create a simple dummy application (Visual C++'s AppWizard does this nicely), and then create the setup program for your dummy application.

- The second part covers Sterling's InstallSHIELD SDK program, because it is provided with the WIN32SDK. As with Microsoft's Setup program, you will create a dummy application, and then create the setup program for your dummy application.

- The third part of the chapter covers Instance's Installigence program, because it is provided with this book's CD. As with Microsoft's Setup program, you will create a dummy application, and then create the setup program for your dummy application.

- The final part of this chapter covers the CD-ROM AutoPlay features. These features enable a program to be executed each time the CD is inserted into the CD-ROM drive. This feature enables, for example, a game to be executed whenever the game's CD is inserted into the CD-ROM drive. This feature is not limited to running the actual program; you could execute the program's setup routine or take some other action as appropriate.

Most install programs take advantage of several standardized features. Often, these features are expected by users, and can be useful in providing information to the user. The following is a list of some standard features:

- Billboards. Billboards consist of graphical messages that perhaps coax the user to send in a registration card, tell about new program features, or perhaps just entertain the user as the program is being installed. You should never put critical information on billboards; they are displayed and removed without any interaction by the user, and it is quite possible that the user will never see them.

- Backgrounds. The background for the installation usually consists of a gradient blue background, often with a company logo superimposed, perhaps in the corner. Although blue is often used for setup program backgrounds, using this color is not necessary. Any other color could be used, and some setup programs allow the use of a bitmap for the background.

- Install disk branding. Most setup programs include a facility to brand the installation disk with information about the user, such as the user's name and company. A serial number can be saved on the installation disk as well. This is not viewed as a copy protection technique, but rather as a method in which the user might not have to reenter this information when doing re-installations. Whether you enable the user to edit the branded information is a policy decision that your organization will have to make.

■ Dialog and message boxes. The use of dialog boxes to get information from the user (such as the user's name and address and the desired installation configuration) and to provide information to the user (perhaps concerning the status of the installation).

NOTE

It is now considered good practice to make your setup program and the installation run off a hard disk. This enables users to copy the setup disks to a directory on a hard disk and perform the install using the copy, not the original disks. This is advantageous to users when they must install more than one copy of your product or when the product must be often re-installed.

TIP

As of mid-1995, the cost of producing a CD-ROM-based installation was continuing to fall. You can now create a CD-ROM-based installation package for a mastering charge of about $250, and a per-disk cost of about $.25, when the run is as small as 250 disks. That would bring the cost of producing a CD-ROM application to about $1.25 in quantities of 250, and that price would drop as the quantity increases.

All applications should be capable of determining whether Windows has been reinstalled, perhaps as a "clean" installation where any files that the application had installed in the Windows directory, folders and links to the Start menu, and any registration database entries may have been lost. If the application is able to recover gracefully from this situation, it should. The recovery probably would be capable to detect the fact that Windows was reinstalled and that the application's interface with Windows has been lost. When this situation has been detected, the application could either re-create this information (replace the lost files, folders, links, and registration database entries) or prompt the user to re-install the product.

NOTE

Windows 95 supports long filenames. Use them!

The Microsoft Setup Program

The Microsoft Setup program has been available for some time from Microsoft. It is the same program that many of the Microsoft applications use to do their own installations, and is a well-behaved program. One of the less attractive aspects of the Microsoft Setup program is that it needs you, the programmer, to actually write and build the setup program, using tools and a shell provided by Microsoft.

In this part of the chapter, we will examine the Microsoft Setup program and create an actual setup that can be used with almost any Visual C++ created application. First, to get started, use AppWizard to create a dummy application. The application needs only one known piece of information: its name. For the purposes of this chapter, the program that you are installing is called DUMMY. This is a program that does nothing, and that enables the user to do nothing well. In Visual C++'s AppWizard, create an application with any attributes you wish and call the project DUMMY. Save the project, and build the DUMMY program. You now have an application that you can distribute to purchasers.

Now you are ready to begin to develop your installation system.

Installing the Microsoft Setup Toolkit

The Microsoft Setup Toolkit is found in the WIN32SDK, in the directory \WIN32SDK\MSTOOLS\MSSETUP on the Windows SDK CD-ROM. Generally, it is advisable to simply copy the entire directory tree from this location to a directory on a local drive, perhaps called MSSETUP. By copying the files to a writable drive, you can modify them as required for your project.

To use Microsoft Setup to create a setup program, follow these steps:

1. Determine which files will be installed with your application. For simple applications, you probably will be installing all files, whereas more complex applications may have optional components so that the user can install only those parts of the program he or she wants. Divide your application files into the group that constitutes the minimum application, and into logical groups of optional components.

2. Design the application's directory structure. For simple applications, a single subdirectory may be sufficient. More complex applications need more complex subdirectory structures. Try to separate the application's files from the user's data.

3. Determine what parameters the user may want to define. For example, your application may keep a record of the user's name and address, and use that for a default report header. You should anticipate other information that may be needed.

4. Design whatever dialog boxes your application will need to display to either obtain information (such as the parameters described in step 3) or to provide information to the user (such as a product code or a generated parameter that the user may need to know).

5. Create your SETUP.EXE program, using the example code provided in the directory \WIN32SDK\MSTOOLS\MSSETUP\SAMPLE as a starting point. You can customize this example program from Microsoft for your own purposes, such as adding the dialog boxes described in step 4.

In your version of SETUP, you also can specify the background bitmap, title, and billboards (those messages that prompt the user to register the product and so on). Make sure that your presentation to the user is professional, and watch for spelling errors.

6. Layout of the files on the distribution media (usually disks, but now more commonly CD-ROMs). To lay out your application, use the DSKLAYT program, which is shown in Figure 13.2.

FIGURE 13.2.

The DSKLAYT program in action.

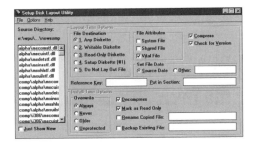

7. The final step is to create the SETUP.INF file and distribution disks. The SETUP.INF file is used by your setup program to control the installation of the application. The DSKLAYT2.EXE program takes the layout file created by DSKLAYT.EXE and the files included with your application, and creates the SETUP.INF file for you. DSKLAYT2.EXE also creates distribution media images, each in their own directory.

8. Test, test, and retest your installation. If the installation fails, the user will have little or no confidence in your application. First impressions are lasting impressions.

Selecting Files for Inclusion

For every installation of an application you will need to select a set of files to be included. These files usually will include some or all of the following files:

- The program's executable (.EXE) file. This file is necessary for all stand-alone windows applications. This is what is executed when your application is used.

- Any dynamic link library (.DLL) files that are called by your application and that are not included with Windows. When in doubt as to whether a file from Visual C++ 2 is needed, you should check the directory \MSVC20\REDIST on the Visual C++ CD. All of the files in this directory may be redistributed with your applications. Remember to implement version checking for all .DLL files that are installed outside your application's directory.

- Shared program files. Usually, a shared program file is placed in the WINDOWS directory so that it will be accessible to all applications that use it. Generally, shared program files should be used only with applications from a single source.

CAUTION

Resist the urge to use program files (DLLs or utilities) that are part of another application that you do not produce. You can cause yourself and your users considerable problems when your application uses files (such as DLL libraries) that are from other applications and these DLL files change without your knowledge. Of course, DLL files that are part of Windows (either the base Windows product or one of the redistributable components) and are documented by Microsoft can and should be used as appropriate.

- Initialization or registration files. Microsoft is working on making the use of INI files by applications unnecessary. Microsoft would prefer that applications use the Windows registry to save information about the application and other information that the application must retain between execution sessions. This makes application management easier for the user. For more information, see Chapter 5, "Fundamentals of the Windows 95 Registry."

- Data files. Many applications must use data files in order to work. For example, a GIS program would use cartographic files.

- Sample data and other sample files. For all but the most trivial applications, you should include either a sample project or sample data with which the user can experiment to gain experience working with your application. Tutorial files fit into this category, too.

- Documentation and help files. All programs must have online help. There is no excuse for not having a complete online help file. Use WinHelp—don't try to write your own help engine. You should also have whatever errata and other readme files on the first disk in the install set.

Writing Your Setup Program

You must "write" your setup program. This is not quite as difficult as it might seem, because Microsoft provides a shell setup program that you can customize and use. This shell is found in the directory MSSETUP\SAMPLE.

One (minor) problem is that Microsoft has only included a DOS command line-driven makefile. Hopefully, you are all developing using Visual C++ under Windows and don't want to bounce back and forth to a DOS command line. Building under the DOS command-line environment makes debugging much more difficult.

I created a project to enable the SETUP program to be built as a Visual C++ project. This was not very difficult. Although Microsoft Setup can be built for a number of different platforms (including Alpha, MIPS, PowerPC, and Intel), Windows 95 runs only on the Intel platform. Therefore, my Visual C++ project can be run only on the Intel.

To create the Setup project, you can follow these steps. I've included my SETUP.MAK file, which assumes that the files are resident in a directory structure of \WPU\MSSETUP\SAMPLE, on the sample source CD that is included with this book. You can either use that project (modifying the directories as needed) or follow these steps to create your own SETUP.MAK project file:

1. From Visual C++, select File | New | Project. Make the project type Application and specify the correct directories for your project. Name the project Setup, and select Create when you are satisfied that the dialog box has been filled in correctly.

2. From the Tools menu, select Options. Then select the Directories tab, and add another include path (..\include). This path is used to include the header files that are used by the sample application.

> **NOTE**
>
> Rather than modifying the Visual C++ environment, you could copy the header files from ..\include to the SAMPLE directory. This step would add more files to the SAMPLE directory as well.

3. When you select Create, you will be presented with the Project Files dialog box. Select the source files in the SAMPLE directory, (*.c, *.rc, and *.def), and select Close.

4. You must add the libraries to the project. You do this in the Project Setting's dialog box, in the Link tab. The following libraries must be added:

```
..\lib\i386\msuilstf.lib
..\lib\i386\msdetstf.lib
..\lib\i386\msinsstf.lib
..\lib\i386\msshlstf.lib
..\lib\i386\mscomstf.lib
```

Make these changes both to the debug version and the release version.

5. You must copy the correct DLL files for the setup program to the program's directory. The DLL files are found in SAMPLE\I386. Copy all the files found in this directory to your project directory.

6. You must set some defines for your Setup project. These includes are

```
DEBUG
_X86_=1
try=__try
except=__except
leave=__leave
finally=__finally
```

Make these changes both to the debug version and the release version.

7. You then can build the project. Test your SETUP program, and once you are satisfied with the program's performance and operation, you should rebuild it as a release build. Test your release build to make sure it works correctly.

Take a look at the sample .INF file that Microsoft provides. This file describes two optional sets of files. Listing 13.1 is the basic .INF file that is part of the SAMPLE application.

Listing 13.1. The SAMPLE.INF file from MS Setup (Source Media Descriptions).

```
    "1", "Disk 1", "", ""

[Minimum Files]
    1, setupapi.c,,,COPY,1992-01-30,,,,,,,,,,,52174,,999,,,

[Extra Files]
    1, sample.inf,,,!COPY,1992-01-30,,,,,,,,,,,10,,999,,,

[Default File Settings]
"STF_BACKUP"     = ""
"STF_COPY"       = "YES"
"STF_DECOMPRESS" = "YES"
"STF_OVERWRITE"  = "ALWAYS"
"STF_READONLY"   = "YES"
"STF_ROOT"       = ""
"STF_SETTIME"    = "YES"
"STF_TIME"       = "1"
"STF_VITAL"      = "YES"
```

There are four main parts of the .INF file shown in Listing 13.1. As in .INI files, these sections are titled, with the exception of the first section, which is an untitled section. These sections are

1. The untitled first section, which describes the overall environment. This section specifies that there is a single disk in this application.

2. The section [Minimum Files] is a file list section that specifies the minimum files that make up the application. Those files that are necessary for the application to be functional are specified in this section.

3. The section [Extra Files] is an optional file list section that lists file that are optional for this application. It is important to note that each application may have a [Minimum Files] section, but other file list sections are optional.

4. The section [Default File Settings] specifies defaults for the installation.

Listing 13.2 shows part of another SETUP.INF file, the one that is used to install Word 6 for Windows. This file is an example of a much more complex SETUP.INF file for a large, complex installation. To make this listing fit into this chapter, I've deleted about 75 percent of the listing, which was over 580 lines long.

Listing 13.2. The SETUP.INF file for Word for Windows 6.

```
[Source Media Descriptions]
    "1","Microsoft Word: Disk 1 - Setup","ACMSETUP.EX_","."
    "2","Microsoft Word: Disk 2","WINWORD.E1_","..\disk2"
```

continues

Listing 13.2. continued

```
      "3","Microsoft Word: Disk 3","WINWORD.E2_","..\disk3"
      "4","Microsoft Word: Disk 4","WINWORD.E3_","..\disk4"
      "5","Microsoft Word: Disk 5","WINWORD.HL_","..\disk5"
      "6","Microsoft Word: Disk 6","GR_AM.LE_","..\disk6"
      "7","Microsoft Word: Disk 7","MSTH_AM.LE_","..\disk7"
      "8","Microsoft Word: Disk 8","AGENDA.WI_","..\disk8"
      "9","Microsoft Word: Disk 9","WORDCBT.LE_","..\disk9"

[Default File Settings]
"STF_BACKUP" = ""
"STF_COPY" = "YES"
"STF_DATE" = "1993-09-27"
"STF_DECOMPRESS" = "YES"
"STF_OVERWRITE" = "ALWAYS"
"STF_READONLY" = ""
"STF_ROOT" = ""
"STF_SETTIME" = "YES"
"STF_TIME" = "0"
"STF_VITAL" = ""


;REMOVE FILES ****************************************************

[CleanGraph]
    1,graph.hlp,,,!COPY,,,,,,REMOVE,,,,,0,,,,,

[CleanWW1]
    1,adimport.flt,,,!COPY,,,,,,REMOVE,,,,,0,,,,,
    1,cgmmport.flt,,,!COPY,,,,,,REMOVE,,,,,0,,,,,
    1,draw.flt,,,!COPY,,,,,,REMOVE,,,,,0,,,,,
    1,epsimp.flt,,,!COPY,,,,,,REMOVE,,,,,0,,,,,
    1,hpglimp.flt,,,!COPY,,,,,,REMOVE,,,,,0,,,,,
    1,imamport.flt,,,!COPY,,,,,,REMOVE,,,,,0,,,,,
    1,lotuspic.flt,,,!COPY,,,,,,REMOVE,,,,,0,,,,,
    1,pcximp.flt,,,!COPY,,,,,,REMOVE,,,,,0,,,,,
    1,tiff.flt,,,!COPY,,,,,,REMOVE,,,,,0,,,,,
    1,vidmport.flt,,,!COPY,,,,,,REMOVE,,,,,0,,,,,
    1,wmf.flt,,,!COPY,,,,,,REMOVE,,,,,0,,,,,
    1,conv-dca.dll,,,!COPY,,,,,,REMOVE,,,,,0,,,,,
    1,conv-mcw.dll,,,!COPY,,,,,,REMOVE,,,,,0,,,,,
    1,conv-mm.dll,,,!COPY,,,,,,REMOVE,,,,,0,,,,,
    1,conv-tx8.dll,,,!COPY,,,,,,REMOVE,,,,,0,,,,,
    1,conv-txt.dll,,,!COPY,,,,,,REMOVE,,,,,0,,,,,
    1,conv-wp.dll,,,!COPY,,,,,,REMOVE,,,,,0,,,,,
    1,conv-wp5.dll,,,!COPY,,,,,,REMOVE,,,,,0,,,,,
    1,conv-wrd.dll,,,!COPY,,,,,,REMOVE,,,,,0,,,,,
    1,conv-wri.dll,,,!COPY,,,,,,REMOVE,,,,,0,,,,,
    1,conv-ws.dll,,,!COPY,,,,,,REMOVE,,,,,0,,,,,
    1,conv-wwp.dll,,,!COPY,,,,,,REMOVE,,,,,0,,,,,

[CleanWW2]
    1,setup.exe,,,!COPY,,,,,,REMOVE,,,,,0,,,,,
    1,winword.ini,,,!COPY,,,,,,REMOVE,,,,,0,,,,,
    1,thes.dll,,,!COPY,,,,,,REMOVE,,,,,0,,,,,
    1,macrocnv.doc,,,!COPY,,,,,,REMOVE,,,,,0,,,,,
    1,newmacro.doc,,,!COPY,,,,,,REMOVE,,,,,0,,,,,
```

```
1,wphelp.dll,,,!COPY,,,,,,REMOVE,,,,,0,,,,,
1,convinfo.doc,,,!COPY,,,,,,REMOVE,,,,,0,,,,,
1,graphics.doc,,,!COPY,,,,,,REMOVE,,,,,0,,,,,
1,printers.doc,,,!COPY,,,,,,REMOVE,,,,,0,,,,,
1,pss.doc,,,!COPY,,,,,,REMOVE,,,,,0,,,,,
1,wword20.inf,,,!COPY,,,,,,REMOVE,,,,,0,,,,,
1,ww20.reg,,,!COPY,,,,,,REMOVE,,,,,0,,,,,
1,readme.doc,,,!COPY,,,,,,REMOVE,,,,,0,,,,,
1,template.doc,,,!COPY,,,,,,REMOVE,,,,,0,,,,,
1,macrode.exe,,,!COPY,,,,,,REMOVE,,,,,0,,,,,
1,40convrt.gly,,,!COPY,,,,,,REMOVE,,,,,0,,,,,
1,50convrt.gly,,,!COPY,,,,,,REMOVE,,,,,0,,,,,
1,55convrt.gly,,,!COPY,,,,,,REMOVE,,,,,0,,,,,
1,winword.hlp,,,!COPY,,,,,,REMOVE,,,,,0,,,,,
1,gr_am.lex,,,!COPY,,,,,,REMOVE,,,,,0,,,,,
1,hy_am.lex,,,!COPY,,,,,,REMOVE,,,,,0,,,,,
1,sp_am.lex,,,!COPY,,,,,,REMOVE,,,,,0,,,,,
1,sp_br.lex,,,!COPY,,,,,,REMOVE,,,,,0,,,,,
1,th_am.lex,,,!COPY,,,,,,REMOVE,,,,,0,,,,,
1,ww20.reg,,,!COPY,,,,,,REMOVE,,,,,0,,,,,
1,dca_rtf.txt,,,!COPY,,,,,,REMOVE,,,,,0,,,,,
1,mw5_rtf.txt,,,!COPY,,,,,,REMOVE,,,,,0,,,,,
1,pcw_rtf.txt,,,!COPY,,,,,,REMOVE,,,,,0,,,,,
1,rtf_dca.txt,,,!COPY,,,,,,REMOVE,,,,,0,,,,,
1,rtf_mw5.txt,,,!COPY,,,,,,REMOVE,,,,,0,,,,,
1,rtf_pcw.txt,,,!COPY,,,,,,REMOVE,,,,,0,,,,,
1,rtf_wp5.txt,,,!COPY,,,,,,REMOVE,,,,,0,,,,,
1,wp5_rtf.txt,,,!COPY,,,,,,REMOVE,,,,,0,,,,,
1,rftdca.cnv,,,!COPY,,,,,,REMOVE,,,,,0,,,,,
1,txtwlyt.cnv,,,!COPY,,,,,,REMOVE,,,,,0,,,,,
1,worddos.cnv,,,!COPY,,,,,,REMOVE,,,,,0,,,,,
1,wordmac.cnv,,,!COPY,,,,,,REMOVE,,,,,0,,,,,
1,wordwin1.cnv,,,!COPY,,,,,,REMOVE,,,,,0,,,,,
1,wpft5.cnv,,,!COPY,,,,,,REMOVE,,,,,0,,,,,
1,writwin.cnv,,,!COPY,,,,,,REMOVE,,,,,0,,,,,
1,xlbiff.cnv,,,!COPY,,,,,,REMOVE,,,,,0,,,,,
1,grammar.dll,,,!COPY,,,,,,REMOVE,,,,,0,,,,,
1,hyph.dll,,,!COPY,,,,,,REMOVE,,,,,0,,,,,
1,winword.exe,,,!COPY,,,,,,REMOVE,,,,,0,,,,,
1,spell.dll,,,!COPY,,,,,,REMOVE,,,,,0,,,,,

(Lines deleted...)

[Printer Drivers]
"pscript" = 2,PSCRIPT.DRV,,,,1993-10-21,,1033,,,,,,,,314672,SYSTEM,,,3.10.0.110,
"unidrv" = 2,UNIDRV.DLL,,,,1993-10-21,,1033,,,,,,,,128432,SYSTEM,,,3.10.0.111,

[Winword Help]
"wordhelp" = 5,WINWORD.HLP,,,,1993-10-06,,,OLDER,,,,,,,1978729,,,,,
"readme" = 1,WDREADME.HLP,,,,1993-10-25,!DECOMPRESS,,,,,,,,,113913,,,,,
"wordpss" = 2,WORDPSS.HLP,,,,1993-09-23,,,OLDER,,,,,,,46118,,,,,

[WP Help]
    2,WPHELP.HLP,,,,1993-09-21,,,OLDER,,,,,,,164755,,,,,

[Help CBT Support]
"wordres" = 2,WORDRES.DLL,,,,1993-09-19,,1033,,,,,,,,72192,SYSTEM,,,1.10.9.0,
```

continues

Listing 13.2. continued

```
"wordcbt" = 1,WORDCBT.DLL,,,,1993-10-13,,1033,,,,,,,,12448,SYSTEM,,,1.5.0.0,
"shareres" = 1,SHARERES.DLL,,,,1993-10-06,,1033,,,,,,,,37888,SYSTEM,,,1.10.50.0,

[INI Files]
"msfntmapini" = 1,MSFNTMAP.INI,,,,1993-08-31,,,OLDER,,,,,,2041,,,,,
"ttembedini" = 1,TTEMBED.INI,,,,1993-04-23,,,OLDER,,,,,,280,,,,,

[WordBasic Help]
    4,WRDBASIC.HLP,,,,1993-10-13,,,OLDER,,,,,,1073317,,,,,

[Equation Editor]
"equation" = 2,EQNEDIT.EXE,,,,1993-10-25,,1033,,,,,,SHARED,434640,,,,2.0.0.20,
"help" = 2,EQNEDIT.HLP,,,,1993-10-13,,,OLDER,,,,,,137614,,,,,
"equationreg" = 1,EQNEDIT2.REG,,,,1993-09-21,,,,,,,,,,2239,,,,,

[Fonts]
"mtextratt" = 1,MTEXTRA.TTF,,,,1993-10-18,,,,,,,,,,7656,SYSTEM,,,3.1.0.0,

[Graphics Filters]
"cgmimp" = 2,CGMIMP.FLT,,,,1993-06-28,,1033,,,,,,SHARED,44912,,,,2.1.0.32783,
"drwimp" = 3,DRWIMP.FLT,,,,1993-09-14,,1033,,,,,,SHARED,226352,,,,1.9.7.27,
"epsimp" = 2,EPSIMP.FLT,,,,1993-06-28,,1033,,,,,,SHARED,71984,,,,2.1.0.32783,
"iffgif" = 2,IFFGIF.DLL,,,,1993-09-20,,1033,,,,,,SHARED,13008,,,,3.11.0.32768,
"iffpcx" = 3,IFFPCX.DLL,,,,1993-09-20,,1033,,,,,,SHARED,10160,,,,3.11.0.32768,
"ifftiff" = 3,IFFTIFF.DLL,,,,1993-09-20,,1033,,,,,,SHARED,32624,,,,3.11.0.32768,
"pictimp" = 3,PICTIMP.FLT,,,,1993-06-01,,1033,,,,,,SHARED,57600,,,,2.2.0.1,
"wpgexp" = 3,WPGEXP.FLT,,,,1993-10-19,,1033,,,,,,SHARED,111720,,,,93.10.19.1,
"wpgimp" = 3,WPGIMP.FLT,,,,1993-10-19,,1033,,,,,,SHARED,146632,,,,93.10.19.1,
"gifimp" = 3,GIFIMP.FLT,,,,1993-09-20,,1033,,,,,,SHARED,11728,,,,3.11.0.32783,
"tiffimp" = 3,TIFFIMP.FLT,,,,1993-09-20,,1033,,,,,,SHARED,11728,,,,3.11.0.32783,
"pcximp" = 3,PCXIMP.FLT,,,,1993-09-20,,1033,,,,,,SHARED,11728,,,,3.11.0.32783,
"wordcgm" = 1,MS.CGM,,,,1993-09-29,,,,,,,,,,1586,,,,,
"worddrw" = 3,MS.DRW,,,,1993-09-29,,,,,,,,,,3615,,,,,
"wordeps" = 3,MS.EPS,,,,1993-09-29,,,,,,,,,,12274,,,,,
"wordgif" = 1,MS.GIF,,,,1993-09-29,,,,,,,,,,1087,,,,,
"wordpct" = 3,MS.PCT,,,,1993-09-29,,,,,,,,,,3064,,,,,
"wordpcx" = 2,MSPCX.TMP,,,,1993-09-29,,,,,,MS.PCX,,,,1461,,,,,
"wordtif" = 3,MS.TIF,,,,1993-09-29,,,,,,,,,,2054,,,,,
"wordwpg" = 3,MS.WPG,,,,1993-09-29,,,,,,,,,,1390,,,,,

[MSGraph]
"msgraph" = 4,GRAPH.EXE,,,,1993-01-29,,1033,,,,,,SHARED,550400,,,,3.0.2.0,
"help" = 3,MSGRAPH.HLP,,,,1993-01-29,,,,,,,,,,297500,,,,,
"graphreg" = 3,MSGRAPH3.REG,,,,1993-08-31,,,,,,,,,,420,,,,,

[ODBC]
"odbcinstdll" = 1,ODBCINST.DLL,,,,1993-09-29,,1033,,,,,,,82704,SYSTEM,,,1.5.9.23,
"odbcdll" = 9,ODBC.DLL,,,,1993-09-20,,1033,,,,,,,49584,SYSTEM,,,1.5.9.16,
"odbcadm" = 8,ODBCADM.EXE,,,,1993-09-20,,1033,,,,,,,722272,SYSTEM,,,1.5.9.16,
"odbcinsthlp" = 9,ODBCINST.HLP,,,,1993-09-09,,,,,,,,,,17412,SYSTEM,,,,

[Access Files]
"Help" = 8,DRVACCSS.HLP,,,,1993-08-31,,,,,,,,,,50469,SYSTEM,,,,
"IsamDrv" = 9,MSJETDSP.DLL,,,,1993-08-31,,1033,,,,,,,0,SYSTEM,,,1.10.0.1,
"Isam" = 9,RED110.DLL,,,,1993-08-31,,1033,,,,,,,238416,SYSTEM,,,1.10.0.11,
"Setup" = 9,SIMADMIN.DLL,,,,1993-09-17,,1033,,,,,,,0,SYSTEM,,,1.1.21.15,
```

```
"Driver" = 9,SIMBA.DLL,,,,1993-09-17,,1033,,,,,,,,0,SYSTEM,,,1.1.21.15,

[dBase Files]
"Help" = 8,DRVDBASE.HLP,,,,1993-08-31,,,,,,,,,,54455,SYSTEM,,,,
"IsamDrv" = 9,MSJETDSP.DLL,,,,1993-08-31,,1033,,,,,,,,0,SYSTEM,,,1.10.0.1,
"Setup" = 9,SIMADMIN.DLL,,,,1993-09-17,,1033,,,,,,,,0,SYSTEM,,,1.1.21.15,
"Driver" = 9,SIMBA.DLL,,,,1993-09-17,,1033,,,,,,,,0,SYSTEM,,,1.1.21.15,
"Isam" = 9,XBS110.DLL,,,,1993-08-31,,1033,,,,,,,,263840,SYSTEM,,,1.10.0.11,

[Fox Files]
"Help" = 9,DRVFOX.HLP,,,,1993-08-31,,,,,,,,,,55004,SYSTEM,,,,
"IsamDrv" = 9,MSJETDSP.DLL,,,,1993-08-31,,1033,,,,,,,,0,SYSTEM,,,1.10.0.1,
"Setup" = 9,SIMADMIN.DLL,,,,1993-09-17,,1033,,,,,,,,0,SYSTEM,,,1.1.21.15,
"Driver" = 9,SIMBA.DLL,,,,1993-09-17,,1033,,,,,,,,0,SYSTEM,,,1.1.21.15,
"Isam" = 9,XBS110.DLL,,,,1993-08-31,,1033,,,,,,,,263840,SYSTEM,,,1.10.0.11,

[Paradox Files]
"Help" = 9,DRVPARDX.HLP,,,,1993-08-31,,,,,,,,,,54540,SYSTEM,,,,
"IsamDrv" = 9,MSJETDSP.DLL,,,,1993-08-31,,1033,,,,,,,,0,SYSTEM,,,1.10.0.1,
"Isam" = 9,PDX110.DLL,,,,1993-08-31,,1033,,,,,,,,189168,SYSTEM,,,1.10.0.11,
"Setup" = 9,SIMADMIN.DLL,,,,1993-09-17,,1033,,,,,,,,0,SYSTEM,,,1.1.21.15,
"Driver" = 9,SIMBA.DLL,,,,1993-09-17,,1033,,,,,,,,0,SYSTEM,,,1.1.21.15,

[Grammar]
     3,GRAM.DLL,,,,1993-08-26,,1033,,,,,,,SHARED,375808,,,,3.0.0.2024,
     6,GR_AM.LEX,,,,1993-09-03,,,,,,,,,,1193398,,,,,

[Hyphenation]
     3,HYPH.DLL,,,,1993-08-24,,0,,,,,,,SHARED,21680,,,,1.30.2.0,
     5,HY_EN.LEX,,,,1993-06-16,,,,,,,,,,45568,,,,,

[Spelling]
"mssp2_en" = 6,MSSP2_EN.LEX,,,,1993-08-26,,,,,,,,,,199680,,,,,
"msspel2" = 6,MSSPEL2.DLL,,,,1993-10-13,,0,,,,,,,SHARED,142288,,,,1.60.0.0,

[Thesaurus]
"msthes" = 3,MSTHES.DLL,,,,1993-09-02,,1033,,,,,,,SHARED,83868,,,,6.0.0.2030,
"msth_am" = 7,MSTH_AM.LEX,,,,1993-08-12,,,,,,,,,,670477,,,,,

[Macro Templates]
     4,CONVERT.DOT,,,,1993-09-28,,,,OLDER,,,,,,78848,,,,,
     4,LAYOUT.DOT,,,,1993-09-28,,,,OLDER,,,,,,67072,,,,,
     6,MACRO60.DOT,,,,1993-10-14,,,,OLDER,,,,,,180224,,,,,
     5,TABLES.DOT,,,,1993-09-23,,,,OLDER,,,,,,117248,,,,,

(Lines deleted...)

[WordArt]
"alger" = 8,ALGER.TTF,,,,1993-04-21,,,,,,,,,,69496,SYSTEM,,,1.0.0.0,
"arlrdbd" = 8,ARLRDBD.TTF,,,,1993-04-21,,,,,,,,,,39960,SYSTEM,,,1.0.0.0,
"bookosb" = 8,BOOKOSB.TTF,,,,1993-04-21,,,,,,,,,,68216,SYSTEM,,,1.1.0.0,
"bragga" = 8,BRAGGA.TTF,,,,1993-04-21,,,,,,,,,,33956,SYSTEM,,,1.10.0.0,
"britanic" = 8,BRITANIC.TTF,,,,1993-09-21,,,,,,,,,,35360,SYSTEM,,,1.11.0.0,
"brushsci" = 8,BRUSHSCI.TTF,,,,1993-09-21,,,,,,,,,,45728,SYSTEM,,,1.1.0.0,
"colonna" = 8,COLONNA.TTF,,,,1993-04-21,,,,,,,,,,49288,SYSTEM,,,1.0.0.0,
"desdemon" = 8,DESDEMON.TTF,,,,1993-04-21,,,,,,,,,,54468,SYSTEM,,,1.10.0.0,
"ftltlt" = 8,FTLTLT.TTF,,,,1993-04-21,,,,,,,,,,78096,SYSTEM,,,1.0.0.0,
```

continues

Listing 13.2. continued

```
"gothic" = 8,GOTHIC.TTF,,,,1993-09-21,,,,,,,,,,,61280,SYSTEM,,,1.27.0.0,
"impact" = 8,IMPACT.TTF,,,,1993-04-21,,,,,,,,,,,56936,SYSTEM,,,1.10.0.0,
"kino" = 8,KINO.TTF,,,,1993-04-21,,,,,,,,,,,28872,SYSTEM,,,1.0.0.0,
"latinwd" = 8,LATINWD.TTF,,,,1993-04-21,,,,,,,,,,,39188,SYSTEM,,,1.10.0.0,
"maturasc" = 8,MATURASC.TTF,,,,1993-04-21,,,,,,,,,,,46044,SYSTEM,,,1.0.0.0,
"playbill" = 8,PLAYBILL.TTF,,,,1993-04-21,,,,,,,,,,,40528,SYSTEM,,,1.10.0.0,
"pubole" = 8,PUBOLE.DLL,,,,1993-10-06,,1033,,,,,,,,,78928,SYSTEM,,,1.0.1.747,
"wordart2" = 8,WORDART2.EXE,,,,1993-09-22,,1033,,,,,,,SHARED,250000,,,,2.0.1.734,
"wahelp" = 8,WORDART2.HLP,,,,1993-07-07,,,,,,,,,,,58044,,,,,
"wordartreg" = 6,WORDART2.REG,,,,1993-07-19,,,,,,,,,,,1912,,,,,

[CBT]
    8,CBTLIB4.DLL,,,,1993-10-13,,1033,,,,,,,,17104,SYSTEM,,,1.22.0.0,
    8,CBTNORM.DOT,,,,1993-09-30,,,OLDER,,,,,,,42496,,,,,
    8,FX.DLL,,,,1993-09-29,,1033,,,,,,,,41382,SYSTEM,,,1.1.0.0,
    8,MOUSEMV.DEX,,,,1993-09-29,,1033,OLDER,,,,,,25568,SYSTEM,,,1.3.0.0,
    7,NEWDEMO.DOC,,,,1993-09-30,,,OLDER,,,,,,,13824,,,,,
    8,NEWS1.DOC,,,,1993-09-30,,,OLDER,,,,,,,34816,,,,,
    8,NEWS2.DOC,,,,1993-09-30,,,OLDER,,,,,,,38912,,,,,
    7,NEW_LILS.DOC,,,,1993-09-30,,,OLDER,,,,,,,10752,,,,,
    8,PAUSE.DEX,,,,1993-09-29,,1033,OLDER,,,,,,15312,SYSTEM,,,1.3.0.0,
    8,PREVIEW.LES,,,,1993-10-01,,,OLDER,,,,,,,158079,,,,,
    8,SAMPLE1.DOC,,,,1993-10-22,,,OLDER,,,,,,,26112,,,,,
    8,SAMPLE10.DOC,,,,1993-09-30,,,OLDER,,,,,,,12288,,,,,
    8,SAMPLE11.DOC,,,,1993-10-22,,,OLDER,,,,,,,13312,,,,,
    8,SAMPLE12.DOC,,,,1993-09-30,,,OLDER,,,,,,,10240,,,,,
    6,SAMPLE2.DOT,,,,1993-09-30,,,OLDER,,,,,,,7680,,,,,
    8,SAMPLE3.DOC,,,,1993-09-30,,,OLDER,,,,,,,11264,,,,,
    8,SAMPLE4.DOC,,,,1993-09-30,,,OLDER,,,,,,,11264,,,,,
    8,SAMPLE5.DOC,,,,1993-10-22,,,OLDER,,,,,,,29184,,,,,
    8,SAMPLE6.DOC,,,,1993-09-30,,,OLDER,,,,,,,26624,,,,,
    8,SAMPLE7.DOC,,,,1993-09-30,,,OLDER,,,,,,,12288,,,,,
    8,SAMPLE8.DOC,,,,1993-09-30,,,OLDER,,,,,,,13824,,,,,
    8,SAMPLE8A.DOT,,,,1993-09-30,,,OLDER,,,,,,,9728,,,,,
    8,SAMPLE9.DOC,,,,1993-09-30,,,OLDER,,,,,,,15872,,,,,
    8,TUTFX.DEX,,,,1993-09-29,,1033,OLDER,,,,,,,7440,SYSTEM,,,1.1.0.0,
    8,WDCBT.DEX,,,,1993-10-13,,1033,OLDER,,,,,,,8000,SYSTEM,,,1.5.0.0,
    8,WINNERS.DOC,,,,1993-09-30,,,OLDER,,,,,,,11264,,,,,
    8,WNFISH3.WMF,,,,1993-09-29,,,OLDER,,,,,,,17032,,,,,
    8,WNFISH4.WMF,,,,1993-09-29,,,OLDER,,,,,,,8182,,,,,
    8,WORDCBT.CBT,,,,1993-10-13,,,OLDER,,,,,,,108912,,,,,
    9,WORDCBT.LES,,,,1993-10-13,,,OLDER,,,,,,,597600,,,,,

[end-of-file]
```

How does one create an .INF file and the distribution disks? The answer is simple: you use the tools supplied with MSSETUP. The next section in this chapter describes the disk layout tools and takes you through a simple layout.

Disk Layout — What Goes Where?

The layout of your application's distribution disk set is rather flexible. The first disk should have all the files necessary to launch and initialize the SETUP program, and subsequent disks can hold other files as needed. Make sure that related files are kept on the same disk; this is always appreciated by the user, who may be installing portions of the application at different times. Nothing is more inconvenient than having to insert five or six disks to install an additional feature of an application.

> **NOTE**
>
> To use the disk layout tools, first set up a directory structure that will look like the final directory structure that would be installed by the setup program. The layout tools work by example.

Figure 13.3 shows the process of creating a distribution disk set using Microsoft's MSSETUP program.

FIGURE 13.3.

Creating a distribution disk set.

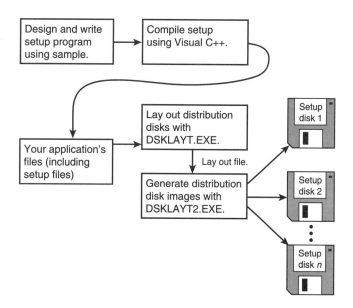

NOTES:
1. DSKLAYT2 creates a directory for each distribution disk.
2. DSKLAYT2 compresses files as necessary.

First, select the files that your application will need. Use directory listings, and separate them into groups (such as necessary files, files that are optional, and so on). Then run the DSKLAYT program (found in the MSSETUP\DISKLAY directory). This program will prompt you to either create a new layout file or open an existing layout file.

When a layout file has been opened, all the files in the directory will be displayed in the Source Directory window. You can choose to display only new files if you are updating an existing layout. Figure 13.2 shows the DSKLAYT program running on a sample application. In DSKLAYT, each file has a set of attributes, as listed in Table 13.1. Each of these attributes applies to the selected file(s). Each file in an installation can have a different set of attributes.

Table 13.1. DSKLAYT file options.

Category	Option	Description
File Destination		
	1. Any Disk	The file will be placed on any of the distribution disks, wherever there is room for it to fit.
	2. Writable Disk	The file will be placed on any distribution disk that will not be write-protected, wherever there is room for it to fit.
	3. Read-Only Disk	The file will be placed on any distribution disk that is write-protected, wherever there is room for it to fit.
	4. Setup Disk (#1)	The file will be placed on the first disk. Usually, files on the first disk are those used by the SETUP program, or are necessary for some other reason by SETUP.
	5. Do Not Lay Out File	The file will not be assigned to any disk.
File Attributes		
	System File	The file will be a Windows System file. Often, DLL files are marked as a system file.
	Shared File	The file may be opened by other applications and will need special processing when it is already open by other applications.

Category	Option	Description
	Vital File	The file is necessary for the SETUP to succeed.
(not grouped)	Compress	This checkbox controls whether the file is to be compressed or not. The file would not normally be compressed if it is a readme, or a file that the user or the setup program might need to access before installing the program for the user.
(not grouped)	Check for Version	The file's version information is to be checked. This option is useful for both .EXE and .DLL files, which have embedded version information.
(not grouped)	Reference Key	Sets the reference key for this file.
(not grouped)	Put in Section	Places the file in a specific section (such as tutorial, sample data, or other optional sections).
Set File Date		
	Source Date	The file will have the same date as the original source file.
	Other	The file will have the specified date. Useful where you use date information for support purposes.
Overwrite		
	Always	The new file will always overwrite an existing version of the file.
	Never	An existing file of the same name is always retained.
	Older	The newer file is retained.
	Unprotected	The new file will overwrite an existing copy of the file if the existing file is not write protected.
(not grouped)	Decompress	The source file will be decompressed if it was stored in a compressed format. Usually left checked, if the source file is not compressed no error occurs.

continues

Table 13.1. continued

Category	Option	Description
(not grouped)	Mark as Read Only	The new file will have the attribute of READONLY when it is installed on the user's drive.
(not grouped)	Rename Copied File	The new file will use the name that you specify in the edit box.
(not grouped)	Backup Existing File	If there is an existing file of the same name, the existing file will be renamed to the name you provide. Specifying an asterisk (*) for the name will cause SETUP to rename the file with the same name, and a .BAK extension.

After you have finished laying out the files and are satisfied with the layout and ready to create a trial install, you must save the layout. Select the File | Save option to save your layout. If this is a new layout, you must provide a filename to save as, preferably using an extension of .LYT.

After the layout has been saved, you can create your install disk images. This process is easy; you use the Microsoft-provided DOS command, DSKLAYT2. This command takes a number of parameters, as shown in Table 13.2. The command line for DSKLAYT2 is

```
Usage: DSKLAYT2 [drive:][path]LayoutFile [[drive:][path]InfFile] [options]
```

Table 13.2. The DSKLAYT2 options.

Option	Description
/c "<Compress Directory>"	This option specifies the location to store compressed files used for the installation.
/d "<Destination Directory>"	This option specifies the location where the installation's disk images are to be stored. Usually, the directory structure will be DISK1, DISK2, ..., depending on the number of disks needed to hold the installation.
/f	This option tells DSKLAYT2 to overwrite an existing INF file if one exists.
/k 360¦720¦12¦144¦N	This option specifies the installation's target media. The N parameter specifies a Network media, which may be used to create a CD-ROM based installation.

Option	Description
/k 0,<s>,<n>	This option is used to specify a special media. The two parameters specify the media's characteristics. The suboptions for this option are: **s** = cluster size, and **n** = number of clusters.
/v	This option tells DSKLAYT2 to display verbose progress information.
/w <Disk#>	For files that were specified as being on a writeable disk, this option specifies the disk that will be writable. If this option is not specified, the default is to use the last disk in the installation as the writeable disk.
/z "<Compress Executable>"	This option specifies the path for the compression utility that will be used to compress the files on the disks which are marked as compressed. Normally, you would use the default (which is to use the utility COMPRESS.EXE on the current path). If you choose to use a non-standard compression tool, then your SETUP program must have access to the decompression routine to perform the install.

Listing 13.3 is a sample run of DSKLAYT2. This run was done using the NEWLAY.LYT file found on the sample code CD-ROM. The command line for this run was

```
..\disklay\i386\dsklayt2 newlay.lyt newlay.inf /f
➥/K144 /v /d"temp" /c"comp" >layout.lst
```

Listing 13.3. The output from the DSKLAYT2 program (LAYOUT.LST).

```
Reading layout file
Warning: Could not get version attribute for e:\wpu\mssetup\newsamp\newlay.lyt
Starting layout: 04/28/95 19:33:18
Compressing files
Compressing file e:\wpu\mssetup\newsamp\compress.exe
System command: compress.exe \s3vv43jv. \s3vv43jv.1 > NUL
Compressing file e:\wpu\mssetup\newsamp\makefile
System command: compress.exe \s3vv43jv. \s3vv43jv.1 > NUL
Compressing file e:\wpu\mssetup\newsamp\msdetect.c
System command: compress.exe \s3vv43jv. \s3vv43jv.1 > NUL
Compressing file e:\wpu\mssetup\newsamp\msregdb.c
System command: compress.exe \s3vv43jv. \s3vv43jv.1 > NUL
Compressing file e:\wpu\mssetup\newsamp\msshared.c
System command: compress.exe \s3vv43jv. \s3vv43jv.1 > NUL
Compressing file e:\wpu\mssetup\newsamp\newlay.inf
System command: compress.exe \s3vv43jv. \s3vv43jv.1 > NUL
```

continues

Listing 13.3. continued

```
Compressing file e:\wpu\mssetup\newsamp\newlay.lyt
System command: compress.exe \s3vv43jv. \s3vv43jv.1 > NUL
Compressing file e:\wpu\mssetup\newsamp\windebug\mscomstf.dll
System command: compress.exe \s3vv43jv. \s3vv43jv.1 > NUL
Compressing file e:\wpu\mssetup\newsamp\windebug\mscuistf.dll
System command: compress.exe \s3vv43jv. \s3vv43jv.1 > NUL
Compressing file e:\wpu\mssetup\newsamp\windebug\msdetect.obj
System command: compress.exe \s3vv43jv. \s3vv43jv.1 > NUL
Compressing file e:\wpu\mssetup\newsamp\windebug\msdetect.sbr
System command: compress.exe \s3vv43jv. \s3vv43jv.1 > NUL
Compressing file e:\wpu\mssetup\newsamp\windebug\msdetstf.dll
System command: compress.exe \s3vv43jv. \s3vv43jv.1 > NUL
Compressing file e:\wpu\mssetup\newsamp\windebug\msinsstf.dll
System command: compress.exe \s3vv43jv. \s3vv43jv.1 > NUL
Compressing file e:\wpu\mssetup\newsamp\windebug\msregdb.obj
System command: compress.exe \s3vv43jv. \s3vv43jv.1 > NUL
Compressing file e:\wpu\mssetup\newsamp\windebug\msregdb.sbr
System command: compress.exe \s3vv43jv. \s3vv43jv.1 > NUL
Compressing file e:\wpu\mssetup\newsamp\windebug\msshared.obj
System command: compress.exe \s3vv43jv. \s3vv43jv.1 > NUL
Compressing file e:\wpu\mssetup\newsamp\windebug\msshared.sbr
System command: compress.exe \s3vv43jv. \s3vv43jv.1 > NUL
Compressing file e:\wpu\mssetup\newsamp\windebug\msshlstf.dll
System command: compress.exe \s3vv43jv. \s3vv43jv.1 > NUL
Compressing file e:\wpu\mssetup\newsamp\windebug\msuilstf.dll
System command: compress.exe \s3vv43jv. \s3vv43jv.1 > NUL
Compressing file e:\wpu\mssetup\newsamp\windebug\sample.bsc
System command: compress.exe \s3vv43jv. \s3vv43jv.1 > NUL
Compressing file e:\wpu\mssetup\newsamp\windebug\sample.exp
System command: compress.exe \s3vv43jv. \s3vv43jv.1 > NUL
Compressing file e:\wpu\mssetup\newsamp\windebug\sample.ilk
System command: compress.exe \s3vv43jv. \s3vv43jv.1 > NUL
Compressing file e:\wpu\mssetup\newsamp\windebug\sample.inf
System command: compress.exe \s3vv43jv. \s3vv43jv.1 > NUL
Compressing file e:\wpu\mssetup\newsamp\windebug\sample.lib
System command: compress.exe \s3vv43jv. \s3vv43jv.1 > NUL
Compressing file e:\wpu\mssetup\newsamp\windebug\sample.pch
System command: compress.exe \s3vv43jv. \s3vv43jv.1 > NUL
Compressing file e:\wpu\mssetup\newsamp\windebug\sample.pdb
System command: compress.exe \s3vv43jv. \s3vv43jv.1 > NUL
Compressing file e:\wpu\mssetup\newsamp\windebug\setup.obj
System command: compress.exe \s3vv43jv. \s3vv43jv.1 > NUL
Compressing file e:\wpu\mssetup\newsamp\windebug\setup.res
System command: compress.exe \s3vv43jv. \s3vv43jv.1 > NUL
Compressing file e:\wpu\mssetup\newsamp\windebug\setup.sbr
System command: compress.exe \s3vv43jv. \s3vv43jv.1 > NUL
Compressing file e:\wpu\mssetup\newsamp\windebug\setupapi.c
System command: compress.exe \s3vv43jv. \s3vv43jv.1 > NUL
Compressing file e:\wpu\mssetup\newsamp\windebug\setupapi.obj
System command: compress.exe \s3vv43jv. \s3vv43jv.1 > NUL
Compressing file e:\wpu\mssetup\newsamp\windebug\setupapi.sbr
System command: compress.exe \s3vv43jv. \s3vv43jv.1 > NUL
Laying out files
Laying out compress.exe
Laying out makefile
Laying out msdetect.c
```

```
Laying out msregdb.c
Laying out msshared.c
Laying out newlay.inf
Laying out newlay.lyt
Laying out windebug\mscomstf.dll
Laying out windebug\mscuistf.dll
Laying out windebug\msdetect.obj
Laying out windebug\msdetect.sbr
Laying out windebug\msdetstf.dll
Laying out windebug\msinsstf.dll
Laying out windebug\msregdb.obj
Laying out windebug\msregdb.sbr
Laying out windebug\msshared.obj
Laying out windebug\msshared.sbr
Laying out windebug\msshlstf.dll
Laying out windebug\msuilstf.dll
Laying out windebug\sample.bsc
Laying out windebug\sample.exe
Assigning windebug\sample.exe to disk with ID = 1
Laying out windebug\sample.exp
Laying out windebug\sample.ilk
Laying out windebug\sample.inf
Laying out windebug\sample.lib
Laying out windebug\sample.pch
Laying out windebug\sample.pdb
Laying out windebug\setup.obj
Laying out windebug\setup.res
Laying out windebug\setup.sbr
Laying out windebug\setupapi.c
Laying out windebug\setupapi.obj
Laying out windebug\setupapi.sbr
System command: compress.exe dummy.___ \s3vv43jv.1 > NUL
Compressed dummy INF file size is 703
Assigning windebug\msdetect.sbr to disk with ID = 2
Assigning windebug\msregdb.sbr to disk with ID = 2
Assigning windebug\msshared.sbr to disk with ID = 2
Assigning windebug\sample.exp to disk with ID = 2
Assigning windebug\sample.inf to disk with ID = 2
Assigning windebug\sample.lib to disk with ID = 2
Assigning windebug\setup.res to disk with ID = 2
Assigning windebug\setup.sbr to disk with ID = 2
Assigning windebug\setupapi.sbr to disk with ID = 2
Assigning makefile to disk with ID = 2
Assigning newlay.inf to disk with ID = 2
Assigning newlay.lyt to disk with ID = 2
Assigning msshared.c to disk with ID = 2
Assigning msdetect.c to disk with ID = 2
Assigning msregdb.c to disk with ID = 2
Assigning windebug\msshared.obj to disk with ID = 2
Assigning windebug\setup.obj to disk with ID = 2
Assigning windebug\msregdb.obj to disk with ID = 2
Assigning windebug\msdetstf.dll to disk with ID = 2
Assigning windebug\msshlstf.dll to disk with ID = 2
Assigning windebug\setupapi.c to disk with ID = 2
Assigning windebug\msdetect.obj to disk with ID = 2
Assigning windebug\mscuistf.dll to disk with ID = 2
Assigning windebug\msuilstf.dll to disk with ID = 2
Assigning windebug\msinsstf.dll to disk with ID = 2
```

continues

Listing 13.3. continued

```
Assigning compress.exe to disk with ID = 2
Assigning windebug\setupapi.obj to disk with ID = 2
Assigning windebug\mscomstf.dll to disk with ID = 2
Assigning windebug\sample.ilk to disk with ID = 2
Assigning windebug\sample.pdb to disk with ID = 2
Assigning windebug\sample.bsc to disk with ID = 2
Assigning windebug\sample.pch to disk with ID = 1
Creating destination files
System command: compress.exe newlay.inf temp\disk1\newlay.in_ > NUL
Ending layout: 04/28/95 19:36:18
```

In the output directory, TEMP, the following directories (and files) were created as shown in the following listing:

```
Volume in drive E is E-SHARE

Directory of E:\WPU\MSSETUP\NEWSAMP\TEMP

.                <DIR>        04-28-95   7:38p
..               <DIR>        04-28-95   7:38p
DISK1            <DIR>        04-28-95   7:38p
DISK2            <DIR>        04-28-95   7:38p
        0 file(s)              0 bytes

Directory of E:\WPU\MSSETUP\NEWSAMP\TEMP\DISK1

.                <DIR>        04-28-95   7:38p
..               <DIR>        04-28-95   7:38p
COMPRESS EX_        32,466    04-14-95  12:00p
MSCOMSTF DL_        37,964    04-14-95  12:00p
MSCUISTF DL_        22,809    04-14-95  12:00p
NEWLAY   IN_           714    04-22-95   6:52p
SAMPLE   EXE        74,752    04-22-95   6:53p
SAMPLE   IL_        53,421    04-22-95   6:53p
SAMPLE   PC_     1,143,436    04-22-95   6:52p
SAMPLE   PD_        88,639    04-22-95   6:53p
        8 file(s)      1,454,201 bytes

Directory of E:\WPU\MSSETUP\NEWSAMP\TEMP\DISK2

.                <DIR>        04-28-95   7:38p
..               <DIR>        04-28-95   7:38p
MAKEFILE _            543     04-14-95  12:00p
MSDETECT C_         4,058     04-14-95  12:00p
MSDETECT OB_       12,975     04-22-95   6:52p
MSDETECT SB_           16     04-22-95   6:55p
MSDETSTF DL_       10,909     04-14-95  12:00p
MSINSSTF DL_       31,079     04-14-95  12:00p
MSREGDB  C_         4,696     04-14-95  12:00p
MSREGDB  OB_       10,168     04-22-95   6:51p
MSREGDB  SB_           16     04-22-95   6:55p
MSSHARED C_         2,887     04-14-95  12:00p
MSSHARED OB_        8,348     04-22-95   6:51p
MSSHARED SB_           16     04-22-95   6:55p
```

```
MSSHLSTF DL_         11,232  04-14-95 12:00p
MSUILSTF DL_         25,392  04-14-95 12:00p
NEWLAY   IN_            756  04-28-95  7:29p
NEWLAY   LY_          1,862  04-28-95  7:32p
SAMPLE   BS_        404,911  04-22-95  6:53p
SAMPLE   EX_            296  04-22-95  6:53p
SAMPLE   IN_            317  04-14-95 12:00p
SAMPLE   LI_            480  04-22-95  6:53p
SETUP    OB_          9,621  04-22-95  6:52p
SETUP    RE_             26  04-22-95  6:50p
SETUP    SB_             16  04-22-95  6:55p
SETUPAPI C_          12,241  04-14-95 12:00p
SETUPAPI OB_         32,601  04-22-95  6:50p
SETUPAPI SB_             16  04-22-95  6:55p
          26 file(s)       585,478 bytes

Total files listed:
          34 file(s)     2,039,679 bytes
           8 dir(s)      67,911,680 bytes free
```

Note how the first disk (in the directory DISK1) is filled as full as possible. A total of 1,454,201 bytes were used out of a total of 1,457,644 bytes on a 1.44 disk. However, because of the use of clusters (the units on a disk that are allocated to a file), there are only 1024 bytes available on the disk. The second disk (in the directory DISK2) will only be about 35 percent full, enabling more files to be added to this product's installation without increasing the disk count.

The .INF File

The .INF file that the sample installation program created is shown in Listing 13.4. The .INF file is generated by DSKLAYT and does not need to be modified by the programmer. It is possible that the .INF file might need be modified, and the layout for this file is described in the *Setup Toolkit for Windows* manual, which is found on the WIN32SDK CD and also on the Microsoft Developer Network (MSDN) CD.

Listing 13.4. The NEWLAY.INF file.

```
[Source Media Descriptions]
    "1", "disk1", "sample.pc_", "..\disk1"
    "2", "write disk", "sample.bs_", "..\disk2"

[Default File Settings]
"STF_BACKUP"     = ""
"STF_COPY"       = "YES"
"STF_DECOMPRESS" = "YES"
"STF_OVERWRITE"  = "ALWAYS"
"STF_READONLY"   = "YES"
"STF_ROOT"       = ""
"STF_SETTIME"    = "YES"
"STF_TIME"       = "0"
"STF_VITAL"      = "YES"
```

continues

Listing 13.4. continued

```
[Files]
    2, msdetect.sbr,,,,,,,,,,,,,,, 0,,,,,
    2, msregdb.sbr,,,,,,,,,,,,,, 0,,,,,
    2, msshared.sbr,,,,,,,,,,,,,, 0,,,,,
    2, sample.exp,,,,,,,,,,,,,, 479,,,,,
    2, sample.inf,,,,,,,,,,,,,, 470,,,,,
    2, sample.lib,,,,,,,,,,,,,, 1378,,,,,
    2, setup.res,,,,,,,,,,,,,, 32,,,,,
    2, setup.sbr,,,,,,,,,,,,,, 0,,,,,
    2, setupapi.sbr,,,,,,,,,,,,,, 0,,,,,
    2, makefile,,,,,,,,,,,,,, 1281,,,,,
    2, newlay.inf,,,,,,,,,,,,,, 2054,,,,,
    2, newlay.lyt,,,,,,,,,,,,,, 10759,,,,,
    2, msshared.c,,,,,,,,,,,,,, 8199,,,,,
    2, msdetect.c,,,,,,,,,,,,,, 16564,,,,,
    2, msregdb.c,,,,,,,,,,,,,, 15842,,,,,
    2, msshared.obj,,,,,,,,,,,,,, 16316,,,,,
    2, setup.obj,,,,,,,,,,,,,, 19306,,,,,
    2, msregdb.obj,,,,,,,,,,,,,, 21396,,,,,
    2, msdetstf.dll,,,,,,,,,,,,,, 19968,,,,,
    2, msshlstf.dll,,,,,,,,,,,,,, 23040,,,,,
    2, setupapi.c,,,,,,,,,,,,,, 52174,,,,,
    2, msdetect.obj,,,,,,,,,,,,,, 29647,,,,,
    1, mscuistf.dll,,,,,,,,,,,,,, 65536,,,,,
    2, msuilstf.dll,,,,,,,,,,,,,, 146432,,,,,
    2, msinsstf.dll,,,,,,,,,,,,,, 55808,,,,,
    1, compress.exe,,,,,,,,,,,,,, 50240,,,, 3.51.1004.1,
    2, setupapi.obj,,,,,,,,,,,,,, 81311,,,,,
    1, mscomstf.dll,,,,,,,,,,,,,, 82944,,,,,
    1, sample.ilk,,,,,,,,,,,,,, 162244,,,,,
    1, sample.exe,,,,,,,,,,,,,, 74752,,,,,
    1, sample.pdb,,,,,,,,,,,,,, 233472,,,,,
    2, sample.bsc,,,,,,,,,,,,,, 776966,,,,,
    1, sample.pch,,,,,,,,,,,,,, 2634816,,,,,
```

Editing and changing an .INF file is difficult and should not be attempted unless you have no other choice. Instead, make your changes in the DSKLAYT program.

Making Your Distribution Disks

To make your distribution disks, simply copy the files from each of the disk image directories (DISK1, DISK2, and so on) to disks. Test and retest your installation. The following lists several things that all installations must be tested against:

■ The correct installation of the single components of your product. When your product has optional components, they must be installable without forcing the user to re-install the entire product.

■ Ease of use, where your product has more than one component. Issues to look out for include excessive disk swapping. (We've all seen this problem, haven't we?)

■ Error handling when something unexpected happens must be graceful; the install program should never just "crash and die." It is not acceptable to hang the user's computer when a disk file cannot be read. Your install should try to recover if at all possible. If a component cannot be installed for whatever reason, don't abort the entire installation. Install what you can, and skip the parts that have failed if possible.

■ Install the base product first and then any optional components.

■ Test an install from a local hard drive, where the disks are copied to a subdirectory with an arbitrary name. This is useful when users are forced to re-install the product often.

■ Wherever possible, test an installation from a networked drive. The installation should work as if the drive were a local drive.

■ Test an installation to a networked drive as well. It should work as if the drive were a local drive. Just because the directory to which your product is installed is a networked resource, don't assume that the user is violating a single user license. There are many diskless workstations in larger businesses. In many corporate environment, all software must be installed on a centrally located server, where only authorized users may access the installation directory.

Once you have tested your installation to the limit, give it to some users and have them try to install it. Make your first few test installations users who are nearby and are not expert computer users. Stand behind the subject, and if you must say anything to them to install your product, or you note any problems, you should correct the problem. If each user can install the program without any assistance from you, try a broader beta test, perhaps from outside your company.

We have now covered the Microsoft MSSETUP program. The next section in this chapter covers the problems that are presented by having to uninstall a Windows 95 application.

Uninstalling Under Windows 95

When you install an application under Windows 95 (and Windows NT, when it supports uninstalls), you must also plan for the eventual uninstallation of the program. Uninstallation of an application basically reverses the installation process.

Uninstalling applications is simple if the install program did a predictable job during the installation. Simple applications are simple to uninstall, more complex applications are more difficult to uninstall.

Each uninstall program must do the following (as applicable) to uninstall the application:

1. Remove any shared program files. These files must be removed only if they are not used by other applications. This means that as applications from your company that use a shared file are installed, a counter must be maintained by the uninstall program.

When this counter indicates that no other application uses the shared program file, the shared program file may be safely removed.

2. Remove all stand-alone program files. These files are usually in the application's subdirectory; however, sometimes these files must be installed in other locations. Regardless of where the file is located, make sure that your uninstall program removes all of the program files.

3. Remove all folder items. Folder items are usually shortcuts to the program, help or other files that the user might select to execute.

4. Remove all program folders. Program folders are generally found under the folder C:\WINDOWS\START MENU\PROGRAMS and are where the application's links would be stored.

5. Remove all program directories. The program directories are where the application and all support files (such as the help files) are stored. These directories should be empty, because the program files were deleted in step 2. If there are files in these directories that your uninstall cannot account for, then the directories (and the files contained within) should not be removed. A message box to the user would be appropriate, explaining that the directories were not removed and why.

6. Any registry entries made for the program (including the uninstall entries) must be removed. These registry entries include OLE information.

There are some issues that you must address with your uninstall program. The most important include the following:

■ The uninstall program must have access to a list of the files, directories, folders, shortcuts, and registry entries for the application.

■ The uninstall program must not be in the application's directory. Because the uninstall program will be open when the uninstall is being performed, it will not be possible to delete this file. There are several ways to solve this problem. First, you can locate the uninstall program in the Windows directory. A second solution would be to execute the uninstall as a two-part process; the first copies the uninstall program to either the Windows or the root directories, and the second executes the copy of the uninstall program.

NOTE

Microsoft recommends that you do not launch a second process when performing an uninstall. Windows 95 expects the application to have been uninstalled when the uninstall process exits.

This leaves the issue of how to get rid of the final remnants of the uninstall program; a program cannot delete itself while it is running. If you create a batch file with the name WINSTART.BAT, this file will be executed the next time Windows is started. This batch file can then be used to delete the uninstall program, and perhaps other files. The WINSTART.BAT file is covered later in this chapter in the section, "The WINSTART.BAT File."

NOTE

Microsoft recommends that the uninstall program directly carry out the uninstall process. It is recommended that the uninstall not use a batch program or a subprocess to perform the uninstall. This should be interpreted to mean that the uninstall program should not return until the uninstall has been completed.

There are two registry entries that control uninstallations. These are both found under the same key, as shown here:

```
HKEY_LOCAL_MACHINE
 SOFTWARE
  Microsoft
   Windows
    CurrentVersion
     Uninstall
      ApplicationName
       DisplayName = Application Name
       UninstallString = path [ switches ]
```

For example, on my computer I have two applications that can be uninstalled: the InstallSHIELD SDK product and the IntelliType program.

```
HKEY_LOCAL_MACHINE
 SOFTWARE
  Microsoft
   Windows
    CurrentVersion
     Uninstall
      IntelliType
       "DisplayName"="Microsoft IntelliType"
       "UninstallString"="C:\\MSINPUT\\KEYBOARD\\uninstal.exe -s"

HKEY_LOCAL_MACHINE
 SOFTWARE
  Microsoft
   Windows
    CurrentVersion
     Uninstall
      InstallSHIELD SDK Edition
       "UninstallString"="C:\\WINDOWS\\uninst.exe
       ➥ -f\"C:\\Program Files\\Stirling\\InstallSHIELD\\DeIsLog.1\""
       "DisplayName"="InstallSHIELD SDK Edition"
```

Notice that the IntelliType program is uninstalled by a program that has a simple command line: `C:\\MSINPUT\\KEYBOARD\\uninstal.exe -s`, where the only option passed to the uninstall program is the -s option (which is undocumented, and application-specific). The InstallSHIELD SDK program's uninstall program is passed a filename. This file probably contains the names of the files and directories that were installed with the original application. I'm guessing because when I looked at the file, it was simply binary data that could not be read.

The uninstall program could be extremely simple. It is good practice to request a confirmation from the user ("You are about to uninstall this application, do you really wish to do this?") so that if the uninstall were started inadvertently the user could abort the process.

You know the old saying: I have some good news and some bad news. First, the bad news: the Microsoft MSSETUP program doesn't support uninstalls automatically (InstallSHIELD SDK does). The good news is that an uninstall can be very simple for many applications: remove folders, files and directories, and then update the registry.

NOTE

Don't forget to remove the registry entries for the uninstall program.

WARNING

When you install your application you are adding entries to the registration database. Adding entries rarely causes problems. When you uninstall applications you are removing entries from the registration database; if you remove the wrong entries, you can cause serious problems, possibly necessitating that Windows be re-installed. Be very careful whenever you remove anything from the registration database.

Do not take this warning as permission to leave "trash" in the registration database. Make sure your uninstall cleans up properly.

When you are uninstalling, if you must use the WINSTART.BAT file to remove files, you should prompt the user to (optionally) restart Windows so that the WINSTART.BAT file is executed. If the user chooses to not restart Windows, then the next time Windows is restarted the WINSTART.BAT file will be executed.

The WINSTART.BAT File

The WINSTART.BAT file is a batch file that is executed when Windows is started. This file is executed as one of the first things that Windows does when starting, before opening any files. The WINSTART.BAT file can be used both for installations and uninstalls. I've listed here some of the usages for a WINSTART.BAT file:

- When installing, some files that you may wish to install (such as system files) may already be open by Windows. If the file is open, you cannot replace it. You can use WINSTART.BAT to replace these files at the next restart of Windows. Listing 13.5 shows an example of replacing an opened file.

- When uninstalling, it is not possible to delete the uninstall program, and perhaps some files that the application that is being uninstalled has open when the uninstall is taking place. With WINSTART.BAT, you can later delete the uninstall program, directories, and other files. Listing 13.6 shows the IntelliType uninstall's WINSTART.BAT file that was created when IntelliType was removed from the system.

Listing 13.5. A typical installation WINSTART.BAT file.

```
@ECHO OFF
copy C:\MSINPUT\KEYBOARD\TASKSW32.EXE C:\WINDOWS\TASKSW32.EXE
copy C:\MSINPUT\KEYBOARD\TSKLNG32.DLL C:\WINDOWS\SYSTEM\TSKLNG32.DLL
DEL C:\WINDOWS\WINSTART.BAT
```

Listing 13.6. The IntelliType WINSTART.BAT file from an uninstall.

```
@ECHO OFF
if exist C:\WINDOWS\TASKSW32.EXE del C:\WINDOWS\TASKSW32.EXE
if exist C:\WINDOWS\SYSTEM\TSKLNG32.DLL del C:\WINDOWS\SYSTEM\TSKLNG32.DLL
if exist C:\WINDOWS\SYSTEM\OEMKBD01.INF del C:\WINDOWS\SYSTEM\OEMKBD01.INF
if exist C:\MSINPUT\KEYBOARD\KEYBOARD.HLP del C:\MSINPUT\KEYBOARD\KEYBOARD.HLP
if exist C:\MSINPUT\KEYBOARD\KBDX32.EXE del C:\MSINPUT\KEYBOARD\KBDX32.EXE
if exist C:\MSINPUT\KEYBOARD\KBD32.CPL del C:\MSINPUT\KEYBOARD\KBD32.CPL
if exist C:\MSINPUT\KEYBOARD\PSS.HLP del C:\MSINPUT\KEYBOARD\PSS.HLP
if exist C:\MSINPUT\KEYBOARD\INFO.WRI del C:\MSINPUT\KEYBOARD\INFO.WRI
if exist C:\MSINPUT\KEYBOARD\INFO.TXT del C:\MSINPUT\KEYBOARD\INFO.TXT
if exist C:\MSINPUT\KEYBOARD\LISEZMOI.WRI del C:\MSINPUT\KEYBOARD\LISEZMOI.WRI
if exist C:\MSINPUT\KEYBOARD\LISEZMOI.TXT del C:\MSINPUT\KEYBOARD\LISEZMOI.TXT
if exist C:\MSINPUT\KEYBOARD\LEAME.WRI del C:\MSINPUT\KEYBOARD\LEAME.WRI
if exist C:\MSINPUT\KEYBOARD\LEAME.TXT del C:\MSINPUT\KEYBOARD\LEAME.TXT
if exist C:\MSINPUT\KEYBOARD\LEGGIMI.WRI del C:\MSINPUT\KEYBOARD\LEGGIMI.WRI
if exist C:\MSINPUT\KEYBOARD\LEGGIMI.TXT del C:\MSINPUT\KEYBOARD\LEGGIMI.TXT
if exist C:\MSINPUT\KEYBOARD\KBDCPL.EXE del C:\MSINPUT\KEYBOARD\KBDCPL.EXE
if exist C:\MSINPUT\KEYBOARD\KBDCPL.LAN del C:\MSINPUT\KEYBOARD\KBDCPL.LAN
if exist C:\MSINPUT\KEYBOARD\ITYPE.EXE del C:\MSINPUT\KEYBOARD\ITYPE.EXE
if exist C:\MSINPUT\KEYBOARD\ITYPE.LAN del C:\MSINPUT\KEYBOARD\ITYPE.LAN
if exist C:\MSINPUT\KEYBOARD\UNINSTAL.EXE del C:\MSINPUT\KEYBOARD\UNINSTAL.EXE
if exist C:\MSINPUT\KEYBOARD\NTFILE.EXE del C:\MSINPUT\KEYBOARD\NTFILE.EXE
if exist C:\MSINPUT\POINT32.EXE del C:\MSINPUT\POINT32.EXE
if exist C:\MSINPUT\POINT32.DLL del C:\MSINPUT\POINT32.DLL
if not exist C:\MSINPUT\KEYBOARD\*.* rmdir C:\MSINPUT\KEYBOARD
if not exist C:\MSINPUT\*.* rmdir C:\MSINPUT
DEL C:\WINDOWS\WINSTART.BAT
```

WINSTART.BAT files come in two flavors. The first is a temporary WINSTART.BAT file that deletes itself when done. With this type of a WINSTART.BAT file, your install or uninstall program could create a new WINSTART.BAT file, adding new lines, and then appending to the end the existing WINSTART.BAT. You would append so that the command that deletes the WINSTART.BAT file will remain the last line in the WINSTART.BAT file.

The second type of WINSTART.BAT file is permanent. In this case, your install or uninstall program take the following steps:

1. Rename the existing, permanent file (any WINSTART.BAT file that does not have a delete as the last line in the batch file), to a new, temporary name (for example, NEWSTART.BAT).

2. Create your WINSTART.BAT file, which then calls the renamed WINSTART.BAT file (NEWSTART.BAT) after performing whatever house cleaning is required.

3. For the last line in your WINSTART.BAT file, use the MOVE command with the /Y option to replace your WINSTART.BAT file with the existing, permanent one.

When using a WINSTART.BAT file, the programmer must do several things.

1. Make the last line in the WINSTART.BAT file a delete command to delete the WINSTART.BAT file, or a move command to copy the permanent WINSTART.BAT file over the current one. The trick is that this last line must be terminated by a Ctrl+Z, and not a CR/LF. If there is a CR/LF pair after the delete command, an error will be generated. If there is an end-of-file, the command processor will not look for further lines; if there is a CR/LF, the command processor will look for the next line, which—if the file has been deleted—causes a file-not-found error.

2. Before writing a WINSTART.BAT file, you must check to see if there is already a WINSTART.BAT file in existence. If there is, you must either add your commands to the WINSTART.BAT file that already exists (if the existing WINSTART.BAT file is not a permanent one) or rename the existing WINSTART.BAT file and call it from within your WINSTART.BAT file.

WARNING

If there is an existing WINSTART.BAT file, and you rename and then call it with its new name, you must make sure that the called file does not attempt to delete your WINSTART.BAT file. If you look at both of the previous examples, the delete command that is the last line in the WINSTART.BAT file is hard coded with the filename of WINSTART.BAT.

InstallSHIELD SDK from Sterling

Included with the WIN32SDK is a product called InstallSHIELD SDK. This is a limited feature version of Sterling's InstallSHIELD Pro product. This section covers the SDK version of InstallSHIELD (which, for the remainder of this chapter is referred to as InstallSHIELD SDK).

■ InstallSHIELD SDK install programs are equipped with a built-in uninstall program. This uninstall saves you the effort of writing your own uninstall program.

■ The InstallSHIELD SDK program, like the MSSETUP program, needs you to do considerable amounts of preparation work. However, you do not have to compile your SETUP program with InstallSHIELD SDK. The InstallSHIELD SDK setup script must be processed by the InstallSHIELD SDK "compiler," as shown in Figure 13.4.

FIGURE 13.4.

The InstallSHIELD SDK compiler in action.

Installing InstallSHIELD SDK

InstallSHIELD SDK is found in the directory \WIN32SDK\MSTOOLS\ISHIELD, on the WIN32SDK CD-ROM. The install is in disk image directories (DISK1 through DISK5). To install InstallSHIELD SDK, change to the directory \WIN32SDK\MSTOOLS\ISHIELD\DISK1, and run the SETUP program from that directory. The install runs fine from the WIN32SDK CD-ROM, and you do not have to copy these images to disks unless the target computer does not have a CD-ROM drive.

The default installation of InstallSHIELD SDK is acceptable to virtually all programmers. You should not have any reason to change the defaults unless you are installing to a different drive. A complete installation of InstallSHIELD SDK takes just under 15 MB of disk space, if that is a critical consideration.

> **NOTE**
>
> When this chapter was written, the InstallSHIELD SDK was still being finished. Therefore, some things, such as disk requirements, may be different when the final product is completed.

Once you have installed the InstallSHIELD SDK product, you can then proceed to create your own install programs. Several quick notes are in order here. In contrast to the MSSETUP program, the InstallSHIELD SDK program offers the ability to create an installation without having to write an actual program. As well, InstallSHIELD SDK provides support for uninstalling your application when used with Windows 95.

Using InstallSHIELD SDK

Creating an InstallSHIELD SDK installation takes a number of steps. First, you must plan your installation. This planning is the same planning that any installation (such as an installation using MSSETUP) requires.

- Planning the groups; placing a set of files into a logical group (such as the base product, tutorial, help, and support groups).
- Planning the installation's appearance, including billboards, banners, and backgrounds.
- Create the billboards, bitmaps, and dialog boxes that your installation will require. In many cases, if you need to create images you could create dummy graphics for testing, and once the setup code has been finalized, the final graphics can be created by an artist.

> **NOTE**
>
> The installation program is probably the user's first exposure to your company and its products. Amateur graphics, an install that fails, and other less-than-professional things in the installation will seriously undermine the user's confidence in your company.

- Planning for the media types, such as disks or CD-ROMS.

Once you have done the basic planning for your installation, you then can proceed to create the installation. The following steps can serve as a general guide for many installations.

Figure 13.5 shows the relationships between the InstallSHIELD SDK utilities, files, and your application when you are creating an installation. The steps following the listing also refer to these items in the figure.

FIGURE 13.5.

The InstallSHIELD SDK installation creation process.

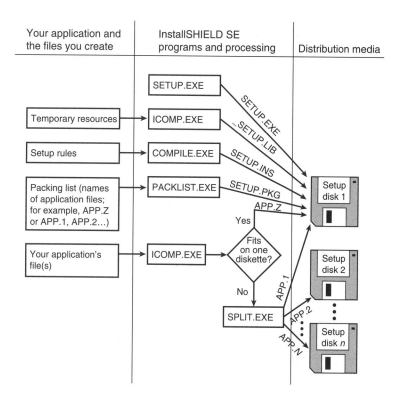

Listing 13.7 shows the sample script that comes with InstallSHIELD SDK. This script looks much like a C program, and follows the basic C syntax. Remember that InstallSHIELD SDK scripts are case-dependent, and not all C keywords are supported. An example of a non-supported keyword is the `switch()` statement's `case:` blocks, which do not end in a

`break;` statement. Also, the `switch()` statement is ended with an `endswitch;` statement, and `if(...)` blocks are ended with an `endif;` statement.

The file SETUP.RUL can be found in the InstallSHIELD SDK directory \template\one\setup.

Listing 13.7. The InstallSHIELD SDK sample script file SETUP.RUL.

```
/*--------------------------------------------------------------------*\
 *
 *   IIIIIII SSSSSS
 *      II   SS                          InstallSHIELD (R)
 *      II   SSSSSS          (c) 1990-1995, Stirling Technologies, Inc.
 *      II       SS                    All Rights Reserved.
 *   IIIIIII SSSSSS
 *
 *
 *   This source code is intended as a supplement to Stirling Technologies,
 *   Inc., product documentation.  Refer to your Stirling Technologies, Inc.,
 *   product documentation for more detailed information.
 *
 *
 *     File Name:   SETUP.RUL
 *
 *   Description:   InstallSHIELD SDK Edition Template One script.
 *
 *
 *
 *
 *       Author:   Stirling Technologies, Inc.      Date:  2-4-95
 *
 *     Comments:   This template script performs a basic installation to a
 *                 Windows 95 or Windows NT platform.  The installation
 *                 includes components: Application Program Files, Sample and
 *                 Template Files, Online Help Files, and Multimedia Tutorial
 *                 Files.  With minor modifications, this template can be
 *                 adapted to create new, customized installations.
 *
 *
 *
\*--------------------------------------------------------------------*/


// Size of components.
#define SIZE_REQ_SAMPLES           82000
#define SIZE_REQ_TEMPLATES          2000
#define SIZE_REQ_PROGRAM         1660000

#define APP_NAME                 "Sample App"
#define PROGRAM_GROUP_NAME       "Sample App Group"
#define APPBASE_PATH             "Company\\SampleApp\\"
#define COMPANY_NAME             "SampleCompany"
#define PRODUCT_NAME             "SampleApp"
#define PRODUCT_VERSION          "3.0"
#define PRODUCT_KEY              "designer.exe"
```

```
#define UNINSTALL_KEY          "SampleAppV3"
#define APPBASE_DIR95          "Program Files"
#define BASE_REGISTRYNT
        ➡ "Software\\Microsoft\\Windows NT\\CurrentVersion\\App Paths\\"
#define BASE_REGISTRY95
        ➡ "Software\\Microsoft\\Windows\\CurrentVersion\\App Paths\\"

#define SYS_BOOTMACHINE        3

#define STR_COMPLETE95
        ➡ "by selecting the program icon in the Programs menu.\n\n"
#define STR_COMPLETENT
        ➡ "by selecting the program icon in the program group.\n\n"

declare

        // Global variable declarations.
        STRING   svGrp, szMsg, szFileSet, szTitle, szAppPath, szAppSharedDir;
        STRING   szProgram, szTemp, svUninstLogFile, szRegKey;
        STRING   svMainDirectory[ _MAX_STRING ];
        BOOL     bSpaceOk, bReshowSetupType;
        NUMBER   nResult, nStatusId, nType;

        BOOL     bIncludeProgram, bIncludeSamples, bIncludeHelp;
        BOOL     bWinNT;

        // Function declarations.
        prototype SetupScreen();
        prototype CheckRequirements();
        prototype CheckSpaceRequirements( number, number, number, string );
        prototype CreateRegDBEntries();

program

StartHere:
        Disable( BACKGROUND );

        // Set up the installation screen.
        SetupScreen();

        // Set installation info., which is required for registry entries.
        InstallationInfo( COMPANY_NAME, PRODUCT_NAME,
                             ➡ PRODUCT_VERSION, PRODUCT_KEY );

// Create a Welcome dialog.
WelcomeDlg:
        Disable( BACKBUTTON );
        Welcome( "Welcome", 0 );
        Enable( BACKBUTTON );

        // Test target system proper configuration.
        CheckRequirements();

        // Ask user for a destination location for the installation.
GetTargetDirectory:

        svMainDirectory = TARGETDISK ^ APPBASE_DIR95 ^ APPBASE_PATH;
```

continues

Listing 13.7. continued

```
        szMsg = "";
        if ( AskDestPath( "Choose Destination Location", szMsg,
                          svMainDirectory, 0 ) = BACK ) then
            goto WelcomeDlg;
        endif;

        szAppSharedDir = svMainDirectory ^ "System";

        nType = TYPICAL;
DetermineUserSelection:

        nType = SetupType( "Setup Type", "", svMainDirectory, nType, 0 );
        if ( nType = BACK ) then goto GetTargetDirectory; endif;

        bReshowSetupType = FALSE;

        switch (nType)
        case TYPICAL:
            bIncludeSamples  = TRUE;
            bIncludeProgram  = TRUE;
            bIncludeHelp = TRUE;
        case COMPACT:
            bIncludeProgram  = TRUE;
        case CUSTOM:
            SetDialogTitle( DLG_ASK_OPTIONS, "Select Components" );
            bIncludeSamples  = TRUE;
            bIncludeProgram  = TRUE;
            bIncludeHelp     = TRUE;
            szMsg = "Select the components that you wish to install.\n"+
                    "If the check box is unchecked, that component "+
                    "will not be installed. Click Next to continue "+
                    "with the installation.";

            nResult = AskOptions( NONEXCLUSIVE, szMsg,
                        "Application Program Files", bIncludeProgram,
                        "Sample and Template Files", bIncludeSamples,
                        "On-Line Help Files", bIncludeHelp );

            if ( nResult = BACK ) then goto DetermineUserSelection; endif;

            // Handle user clicking Cancel button.
            if (nResult = CANCEL) then
                if (AskYesNo( "Are you sure you would like to exit setup?",
                              ➥ NO ) = YES) then
                    abort;
                else
                    bReshowSetupType = TRUE;
                endif;
            endif;
        endswitch;

        if (bReshowSetupType = TRUE) then goto DetermineUserSelection; endif;

        // Check to see if target system meets space requirements.
        bSpaceOk = CheckSpaceRequirements( bIncludeSamples,
                                           bIncludeProgram,
```

```
                           bIncludeHelp,
                           svMainDirectory );

    // Ask user to try again if not enough space available.
    if (bSpaceOk = FALSE) then goto DetermineUserSelection; endif;

FolderSelection:
        if ( bWinNT ) then
            svGrp = PROGRAM_GROUP_NAME;

            // Allow user to modify folder name.
            if ( SelectFolder( "Folder Selection", svGrp, svGrp ) = BACK ) then
                goto DetermineUserSelection;
            endif;
        endif;

FileTransferSetup:

        // Prepare InstallSHIELD to record deinstallation information.
        DeinstallStart( svMainDirectory, svUninstLogFile, UNINSTALL_KEY, 0 );
        RegDBSetItem( REGDB_UNINSTALL_NAME, APP_NAME );

        // Set registry App Paths key information for the main application.
        szAppPath = svMainDirectory ^ "PROGRAM" + ";" + szAppSharedDir;
        RegDBSetItem( REGDB_APPPATH, szAppPath );
        szProgram = svMainDirectory ^ "PROGRAM\\designer.exe";
        RegDBSetItem( REGDB_APPPATH_DEFAULT, szProgram );

        // Set registry  App Paths\demo.exe key information.
        if (bWinNT) then
            szRegKey = BASE_REGISTRYNT ^ "demo.exe";
        else
            szRegKey = BASE_REGISTRY95 ^ "demo.exe";
        endif;
        RegDBSetDefaultRoot( REGKEY_LOCAL_MACHINE );
        RegDBSetKeyValueEx( szRegKey, "Path", REGDB_STRING,  szAppPath, -1 );
        szProgram = svMainDirectory ^ "PROGRAM\\demo.exe";
        RegDBSetKeyValueEx( szRegKey, "", REGDB_STRING,  szProgram, -1 );

        // Define the "General" file set.
        szFileSet = "General";
        TARGETDIR = svMainDirectory;

        FileSetBeginDefine( szFileSet );

          SetStatusWindow( -1, "Copying program files..." );

          // Always copy README & related files, located at
          // the root level in the DATA.Z library file.
          CompressGet( "data.z", "*.*", COMP_NORMAL );

          if (bIncludeProgram) then
              TARGETDIR = svMainDirectory ^ "PROGRAM";
              CompressGet( "data.z", "program\\*.*", INCLUDE_SUBDIR );
              CompressGet( "data.z", "shared\\*.*", COMP_NORMAL );
              TARGETDIR = szAppSharedDir;
              CompressGet( "data.z", "shared\\*.*", SHAREDFILE | COMP_NORMAL );
```

continues

Listing 13.7. continued

```
        endif;

        if (bIncludeSamples) then
           TARGETDIR = svMainDirectory ^ "SAMPLES";
           CompressGet( "data.z", "samples\\*.*", INCLUDE_SUBDIR );
        endif;

        if (bIncludeHelp) then
           TARGETDIR = svMainDirectory ^ "TEMPLATE";
           CompressGet( "data.z", "template\\*.*", INCLUDE_SUBDIR );
        endif;

     FileSetEndDefine( szFileSet );

DoFileTransfer:
        // Set up progress indicator and information gauge.
        Enable( STATUSDLG );
        Enable( FEEDBACK_FULL );
        StatusUpdate( ON, 90 );

        // Perform the file set.
        nResult = FileSetPerformEz( szFileSet, 0 );

        switch (nResult)

        case FS_DONE: // Successful completion.

        case FS_CREATEDIR: // Create directory error.
          MessageBox( "Unable to create a directory under " + TARGETDIR + "."+
                     "Please check write access to this directory.", SEVERE );
             abort;

        default: // Group all other errors under default label.
             NumToStr( szTemp, nResult );
             MessageBox( "General file transfer error."+
                     "Please check your target location and try again."+
                     "\n\n Error Number:"+szTemp, SEVERE );

             abort;
        endswitch;

SetRegistryEntries:

        Disable( FEEDBACK_FULL );
        CreateRegDBEntries( );

        Delay(2);
        Disable( STATUSDLG );

        // Create program groups (folders) and icons.

CreateFolderIcons:
        SetStatusWindow( 95, "Creating Folder and Icons...." );

        if ( bWinNT ) then
           CreateProgramFolder( svGrp );
```

```
      ShowProgramFolder( svGrp, SW_SHOW );
      LongPathToShortPath( svMainDirectory );
      Delay(1);
   endif;

   TARGETDIR = svMainDirectory;

   if (bIncludeProgram) then
      szProgram = TARGETDIR ^ "PROGRAM\\DESIGNER.EXE";
      if ( bWinNT ) then
         AddFolderIcon( svGrp, APP_NAME, szProgram,
                        TARGETDIR ^ "PROGRAM",
                        "", 0, "", REPLACE );
      else
         LongPathToQuote( szProgram, TRUE );
         AddFolderIcon( "", APP_NAME, szProgram,
                        TARGETDIR ^ "PROGRAM",
                        "", 0, "", REPLACE );
      endif;
      Delay( 1 );
   endif;

   if ( bWinNT ) then
      if (bIncludeSamples) then
         szProgram = TARGETDIR ^ "PROGRAM\\DEMO.EXE ";
         AddFolderIcon( svGrp, "Example1",
                        szProgram + TARGETDIR ^ "PROGRAM\\MULTI.DBD",
                        TARGETDIR ^ "PROGRAM",
                        "", 0, "", REPLACE );
         Delay( 1 );
      endif;

      if (bIncludeSamples) then
         AddFolderIcon( svGrp, "Example2",
                        szProgram + TARGETDIR ^ "SAMPLES\\LAUNCHER.DBD",
                        TARGETDIR ^ "SAMPLES",
                        "", 0, "", REPLACE );
         Delay( 1 );
      endif;

      AddFolderIcon( svGrp, "ReadmeFile",
                     "NOTEPAD.EXE " + TARGETDIR ^ "README.TXT",
                     TARGETDIR,
                     "", 0, "", REPLACE );
      Delay( 1 );

      szProgram = WINDIR ^ "UNINST.EXE";
      LongPathToShortPath( szProgram );
      LongPathToShortPath( svUninstLogFile );
      AddFolderIcon( svGrp, "Uninstaller",
                     szProgram + " -f" + svUninstLogFile,
                     WINDIR,
                     "", 0, "", REPLACE );
      Delay( 1 );
   endif;

// Announce setup complete and offer to read README file.
```

continues

Listing 13.7. continued

```
        SetStatusWindow( 100, "Installation complete." );

        // If shared files could not be installed,
        //          then users must restart system.
        if (BATCH_INSTALL = TRUE) then
           szMsg = "Some files could not be installed because they are "+
                   "currently in use by other programs in the system.  "+
                   "To allow for proper operation of the new program you "+
                   "should restart your system at this time.";
          if (RebootDialog( "Restart Windows", szMsg, SYS_BOOTMACHINE ) = 0)
                ➥ then
                // Set up shared files to be installed
                //    after system is next rebooted.
                CommitSharedFiles(0);
          endif;
        else

           szMsg = "Setup is complete.  You may run the installed program ";
           if ( bWinNT ) then
              szMsg = szMsg + STR_COMPLETENT;
           else
              szMsg = szMsg + STR_COMPLETE95;
           endif;

           MessageBeep( 0 );
           MessageBox( szMsg, INFORMATION );
        endif;

        exit;


    /*-------------------------------------------------------------------------*\
     *
     *
     * Function:   SetupScreen
     *
     *
     *  Purpose:   This function will set up the screen look.  This includes
     *             colors, fonts, text to be displayed, etc.
     *
     *
     *
     *   Input:
     *
     *  Returns:
     *
     * Comments:
    \*-------------------------------------------------------------------------*/

    function SetupScreen()
          begin

             Enable( DEFWINDOWMODE );
             Enable( INDVFILESTATUS );

             SetTitle( APP_NAME + " Setup", 36, WHITE );

             SetTitle( "Setup", 0, BACKGROUNDCAPTION ); // Caption bar text.
```

```
            Enable( BACKGROUND );

        end;


/*-------------------------------------------------------------------------*\
 *
 * Function:   CheckRequirements
 *
 *  Purpose:   This function will check all minimum requirements for the
 *             application being installed.  If any fail, then the user
 *             is informed and the installation is terminated.
 *
 *
 *     Input:
 *
 *   Returns:
 *
 * Comments:
\*-------------------------------------------------------------------------*/

function CheckRequirements()
        number  nvDx, nvDy;
        number nvResult;
        STRING szResult;
    begin

        // Determine if target system uses NT or Windows 95.
        GetSystemInfo( WINMAJOR, nvResult, szResult );
        bWinNT = TRUE;
        if (nvResult = 4) then
            bWinNT = FALSE; // Running Windows 95.
        endif;

        // Check screen resolution.
        GetExtents( nvDx, nvDy );
        if (nvDy < 480) then
            MessageBox( "This program requires VGA or better resolution.",
                   ➥ WARNING );
            exit;
        endif;

    end;

/*-------------------------------------------------------------------------*\
 *
 * Function:   CheckSpaceRequirements
 *
 *  Purpose:   This function will check space requirements based on the
 *             elements being installed.
 *
 *     Input:
 *
 *   Returns:
 *
 * Comments:
\*-------------------------------------------------------------------------*/
```

continues

Listing 13.7. continued

```
function CheckSpaceRequirements( bIncludeSamples,
                                 bIncludeProgram,
                                 bIncludeHelp,
                                 szDir )
        number  nSizeRequired;
    begin

        nSizeRequired = 0;

        // Determine total size.
        if (bIncludeSamples) then
          nSizeRequired = nSizeRequired + SIZE_REQ_SAMPLES;
        endif;

        if (bIncludeHelp) then
          nSizeRequired = nSizeRequired + SIZE_REQ_TEMPLATES;
        endif;

        if (bIncludeProgram) then
          nSizeRequired = nSizeRequired + SIZE_REQ_PROGRAM;
        endif;

        // Check space on target drive.
        bSpaceOk = TRUE;
        if (GetDiskSpace( szDir ) < nSizeRequired) then
            szMsg = "There is not enough space available on the disk\n" +
                    "'" + svMainDirectory + "' \n" +
                    "Please free up some space or change the target location\n" +
                    "to a different disk";
          MessageBeep(0);
          MessageBox( szMsg, WARNING );
          bSpaceOk = FALSE;
        endif;

        return bSpaceOk;
    end;


/*-------------------------------------------------------------------------*\
 *
 * Function:  CreateRegDBEntries
 *
 * Purpose:   This function will create necessary keys and values for
 *            the sample program.
 *
 *    Input:
 *
 * Returns:
 *
 * Comments:
\*-------------------------------------------------------------------------*/

function CreateRegDBEntries()
        string szKey[255], szValue, szDemo, szProgram;
begin
        // Create PRODUCT_KEY key.
```

```
szKey = "SOFTWARE\\" + COMPANY_NAME + "\\" + PRODUCT_NAME + "\\" +
        PRODUCT_VERSION + "\\" + "DESIGNER";
RegDBCreateKeyEx( szKey, "" );

RegDBSetKeyValueEx( szKey, "Template", REGDB_STRING, "good.tpl", -1 );
RegDBSetKeyValueEx( szKey, "TemplatePath", REGDB_STRING,
            ➥ svMainDirectory ^ "TEMPLATE", -1 );

if (bIncludeSamples) then
    // Create "DEMOS" key.
    szKey = "SOFTWARE\\" + COMPANY_NAME + "\\" + PRODUCT_NAME + "\\" +
            PRODUCT_VERSION + "\\" + "DEMOS";
    RegDBCreateKeyEx( szKey, "" );

    szDemo    = svMainDirectory ^ "PROGRAM\\MULTI.DBD";
    szProgram = svMainDirectory ^ "PROGRAM\\DEMO.EXE";
    RegDBSetKeyValueEx( szKey, "path0", REGDB_STRING, szDemo, -1 );

    szDemo    = svMainDirectory ^ "SAMPLES\\LAUNCHER.DBD";
    szProgram = svMainDirectory ^ "PROGRAM\\DEMO.EXE";
    RegDBSetKeyValueEx( szKey, "path1", REGDB_STRING, szDemo, -1 );
    RegDBSetKeyValueEx( szKey, "exe", REGDB_STRING, szProgram, -1 );
    RegDBSetKeyValueEx( szKey, "active", REGDB_STRING, "Play", -1 );

endif;

// Create "HELPMENU" key.
szKey = "SOFTWARE\\" + COMPANY_NAME + "\\" + PRODUCT_NAME + "\\" +
        PRODUCT_VERSION + "\\" + "HELPMENU";
RegDBCreateKeyEx( szKey, "" );

RegDBSetKeyValueEx( szKey, "MaxNum", REGDB_NUMBER, "1", -1 );

RegDBSetKeyValueEx( szKey, "path0", REGDB_STRING, svMainDirectory ^
                    ➥ "README.TXT", -1 );
RegDBSetKeyValueEx( szKey, "exe0", REGDB_STRING, "NOTEPAD.EXE", -1 );
RegDBSetKeyValueEx( szKey, "active0", REGDB_STRING, "Read Me", -1 );

end;
```

As Listing 13.7 shows, the InstallSHIELD SDK script language looks very similar to C source code. However, InstallSHIELD SDK scripts don't use braces ({ and }) to delimit blocks. Instead, a block is created using a `switch()`-`endswitch`, `if()`-`endif`, `while()`-`endwhile`, and `repeat`-`until` to create a logical block of code. Also, the `exit` keyword can be used to unconditionally end the setup process, usually because there has been an error.

1. Copy the InstallSHIELD SDK directory

   ```
   C:\Program Files\Stirling\InstallSHIELD\TEMPLATE\ONE
   ```

   to a new directory. Name this new directory with the name of your installation project. Notice that the subdirectory `Program Files` is a Windows 95 long filename and has an embedded space. Remember, Windows 95 supports long filenames, so use them.

2. Using either Visual C++ 2.0 or your favorite program editor, open the file SETUP.RUL (found in the SETUP subdirectory). This file contains the basic setup script as supplied with InstallSHIELD SDK. Do a global search and replace, replacing the string `Sample App` with the name of your application.

3. Make any coding changes necessary to support your application. For example, if you add any new sections (such as help files, tutorial files, or so on), you will have to modify the supplied function `CheckSpaceRequirements(...)` function.

4. Modify the scripts to set up the folders and icons as needed. It will be some time before all programmers understand the difference between where an application is stored and where the shortcuts to the application are going to be found.

5. The supplied program COMPILE is a DOS-based application. You could start it from Visual C++, or you could start a DOS window. Options for the COMPILE command are shown in Table 13.3. If you are like me, you will probably always have a DOS window (or two) running in the background for just this reason. To get SETUP.INS, compile your completed SETUP.RUL file with the following command:

```
COMPILE SETUP.RUL
```

Table 13.3. COMPILE program options.

Option	Description
/N	Tells COMPILE not to generate a CRC.
/S	COMPILE will produce a line number status count on the screen.
/E*nn*	Used to limit the number of errors (*nn*) before COMPILE will abort because of excessive errors.
/W*n*	Used to set the warning level.
/D*id=nn*	A constant can be defined (like the C compiler's /D option) using this option.
/g	This option will tell COMPILE to generate a .DBG file.
/?	The /? option will display help on COMPILE's options.

6. If there is an output file (DATA.Z) in your installation directory (DISK1), delete it. Then use the ICOMP command (again, a DOS-based utility) to create your new DATA.Z file. Options for ICOMP are listed in Table 13.4. The DATA.Z file contains the files for your application. The DATA.Z file of larger applications will be too large for a single disk. If DATA.Z will not fit on the first disk (remember to first copy the SETUP program's files), use the InstallSHIELD SDK command SPLIT to split DATA.Z into several smaller files. The command line for ICOMP is shown

below, where *directory* is the directory that you are using to save your project's files in.

```
ICOMP directory\*.* DISK1\DATA.Z
```

Table 13.4. ICOMP program options.

Option	Description
-c	This is the default specification for compression, which will compress the source files.
-d	This option will decompress the files in the compressed library.
-dt	This option will execute the decompression test mode.
-h	Tells ICOMP to hide the percent complete bar.
-i	Searches will include all subdirectories.
-l	Provide a listing of the files being compressed in the output file.
-o	Tells ICOMP to overwrite the output file(s) without prompting.
-ox	Tells ICOMP to overwrite output file(s) based on newer date/time stamp information only.
-r	Tells ICOMP to remove files from the compressed library.
-sh	This is the default level of compression, which uses the highest level of compression.
-sl	This option tells ICOMP to use the lowest level of compression. This option sacrifices compression for speed.
-sm	Use a medium level of compression.
-sn	Do not compress the files.

7. If you are going to need more than one disk in your application's installation, then you must use the SPLIT program to split the DATA.Z file into smaller components. This SPLIT program has the options that are shown in Table 13.5. The following is a typical SPLIT command line:

```
SPLIT inputpath outputpath -options
```

Table 13.5. SPLIT command options.

Option	Description
-l	Tells SPLIT to list the split files that are split from the input file.
-c	SPLIT will split the input file contiguously (that is, split files will not cross disks). The default action is a non-contiguous split.

continues

Table 13.5. continued

Option	Description
-dN@*xxxx*	The maximum size for the split file, specified in *xxxx* KB.
-f*xxxx*	The maximum size of the resulting files, in *xxxx* KB. The default size is 1024 (1 MB).
-h	Tells SPLIT to hide the percent complete bar.

8. Make any changes necessary to the packing list, and compile it using the PACKLIST program. This program will create the .PKG file that must be on the first disk in the installation. The PACKLIST program has no options, and requires only an input filename.

```
PACKLIST SETUP.LST
```

9. Copy the SETUP.INS file (from step 5) and SETUP.PKG (from step 7) to the DISK1 subdirectory.

10. You can then test your application by changing to the DISK1 subdirectory and using the command SETUP. You should be able to do an installation.

Making Your Distribution Disks

After you have tested your installation script and are satisfied that it functions correctly, you should do your final disk creation. Again, test the installation, using the disks. You should not have any problems with your disk-based installation if the hard disk-based test works correctly.

An excellent example of a multidisk installation is the InstallSHIELD SDK installation itself. You can see the DISK1 through DISK5 directories in the \WIN32SDK\MSTOOLS\ISHIELD directory. Notice that the DATA.Z file was split into DATA.1, DATA.2, DATA.3, DATA.4, and DATA.5 files. Also notice that each installation disk has a file called DISK*n*.ID, where *n* is the disk number. The name of the disk ID files is the only significant thing—the contents of these files is ignored. The DISK*n*.ID file is used to ensure that the user has inserted the correct disk into the drive. Because an installation can be performed entirely from the hard disk, the use of a volume label is not practical.

Using the Instolligence Installation Program

Instance Corporation markets an application installation system called Installigence. This product was initially developed for Windows 3.*x*, and Windows NT and Windows 95 are also supported platforms.

Using Installigence is easy, and much simpler than using the MS Setup program. Installigence is a totally Windows-based installation program that offers extensive user feedback to assist the user in creating their installation disks. Installigence is capable of creating not only disk-based installs, but also installs for CD-ROM based products. This is very helpful, because the AutoRun facility (described later) can call the Installigence created setup program if needed.

Installigence is a single program and requires no additional scripts or other input from the user. This differs from both MS Setup and from InstallSHIELD, which both are multistep processes requiring some form of script from the user.

Installigence's main window is shown in Figure 13.6. This window shows Installigence before a project has been opened.

FIGURE 13.6.

*Installigence's main
window.*

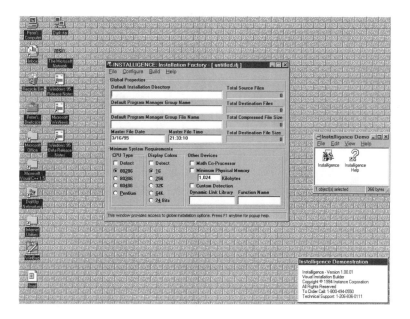

After a project has been opened, the values defined by the programmer are displayed in Installigence's main window. Figure 13.7 shows Installigence's main window with a sample project opened.

The main thing a user sees when installing applications is the install program's background. All installation programs enable you to configure the background, and Installigence is no different. With Installigence you can configure the shading (the trend for a gradient color in install programs has almost become the standard) or specify a bitmap that will be either tiled, centered, or stretched. Also, your application's title can be either text (two lines) or a bitmap. Finally, you can specify a startup and shutdown sound scheme (with the built-in sounds of Windows 95, this may not be an important option).

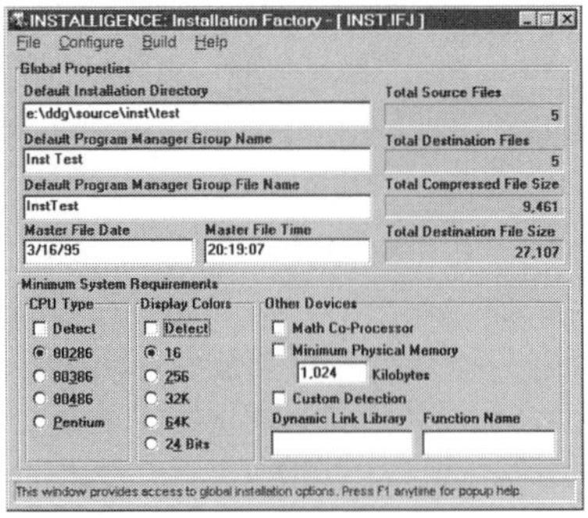

FIGURE 13.7.

*Installigence's main
window with a project
opened.*

Figure 13.8 shows Installigence's Background Window Properties dialog box.

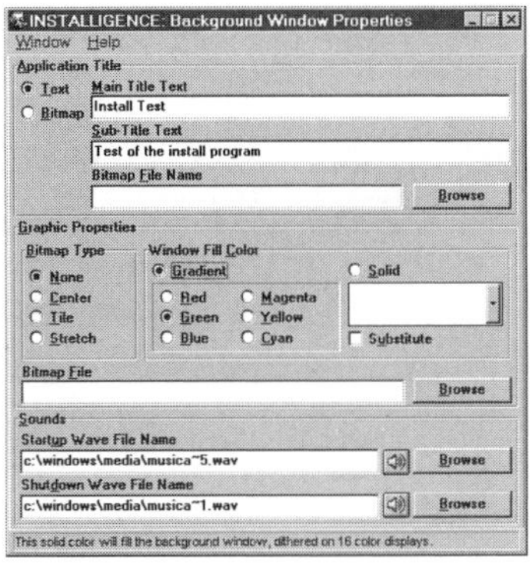

FIGURE 13.8.

*Installigence's Back-
ground Window
Properties dialog box.*

Building a distribution disk set is a simple process with Installigence. You can specify the destination (most of the time you will build to a directory on a hard disk) and the disk size (all the common sizes, and an unlimited size for CD distribution media).

After you have configured the distribution of your application and generated the disk images, you then can copy these images to disks and distribute your application.

The CD-ROM AutoPlay Facility

Microsoft has added a new feature to Windows 95 (and soon to Windows NT)—the capability to have a program run whenever an AutoPlay-enabled CD is inserted into the CD-ROM drive. This feature enables software developers who distribute by (or execute from) CD-ROM disks to have either the program or an installation routine start whenever the CD-DISK is inserted into the drive. The AutoPlay facility enables Plug and Play to extend into the software arena.

Users benefit from products that are easier to use and more user-friendly. Under Windows 95, you can select the property page for the current CD in the drive by clicking with the right button on the CD in Explorer, as shown in Figure 13.9 later in the chapter.

Many users (and developers) have decried the poor interface between CD-ROM based applications and Windows. In the past, the user had to insert a CD into the drive, and enter a command (often, but not always, called *setup*) to install the product. Although many setup programs ran well, the concept of many CD-ROM based applications is that the application (and much of its static data) need not always be copied to the computer's local hard disk but are usable from the CD-ROM. This permits a user to have a large library of CD-ROM based applications, without having to dedicate substantial portions of the hard disk to these applications.

To make it easier for users to utilize their CD-ROM based applications Microsoft has created the AutoPlay technology. This technology enables users to simply insert a CD and have a predefined action take place. Some of the features of Plug and Play are these:

- AutoPlay-enabled CD-ROMs will execute the designated program. This program will typically be either a setup program (less optimal) or will actually execute the CD-ROM's main program (more optimal).
- Audio CDs will automatically play the CD using the CD Player applet, which is a standard part of Windows 95. CD Player works very much like your home CD player and offers many of the options and features of a typical CD player.
- All other CDs will behave as they did under Windows 3.x; that is, they will do nothing special.

Sometimes users will not want to activate a program (or play an audio CD) automatically. In this case, the user can press the Shift key when the CD is inserted, and AutoPlay will be disabled. This enables the user to perhaps simply do a directory of the CD, run a different program from the CD, or to otherwise use the CD.

The AUTORUN.INF file, which is located in the CD's root directory, makes the AutoPlay CD work, as described in the following section.

Using AUTORUN.INF Files

To make AutoRun work, Windows 95 looks at the CD that has been inserted by the user. If the CD is an audio CD, then the CD Player applet is launched, and the CD is played. If the CD has an AUTORUN.INF file, then Windows 95 examines this file and takes the actions specified in the AUTORUN.INF file. The AUTORUN.INF file is stored in the root directory of the CD.

The minimum necessary AUTORUN.INF file is shown in Listing 13.8. This listing represents the minimum code necessary to create a functional AUTORUN.INF file. Later in this chapter, you will see the AUTORUN.INF file that is found on the CD that accompanies this book. The AUTORUN.INF file for this book shows a few other of the options allowed.

Listing 13.8. Minimal AUTORUN.INF file for AutoRun compliance.

```
[autorun]
open=filename.exe
icon=filename.ico
```

Even this minimal AUTORUN.INF file, with only three lines of information, can be expanded. Take a look at each of the basic options available, and what you can use in your AUTORUN.INF files.

- `open=` The `open=` line specifies what program is to be executed whenever the user inserts the CD. This program can either reside in the same directory as the AUTORUN.INF (the CD's root directory) or in any other directory. To specify a subdirectory, use the format

  ```
  open=subdir1\subdir2\filename.exe
  ```

  In the preceding example, Windows 95 will search the CD's directory structure, inserting the correct drive letter as necessary. When the program specified in the `open=` line is executed, the current directory is not changed. Microsoft recommends that you use the `open=` line to launch a "teaser" application. This teaser application might give the user an opportunity to execute the program or do an install. A more complex teaser program might check to see whether the application has been installed, and if so, launch the application rather than the install program.

- `icon=` The icon for the CD is contained in either an .ICO, .BMP, .EXE, or a .DLL file. If the file contains more than one icon (the STARmanager application has a number of different icons), you can specify the icon using the following syntax:

  ```
  icon=filename.exe,2
  ```

  In the preceding example, you have specified that the third (it's zero-based) icon will be used. Unlike the `open=` expression, the `icon=` line does not allow a path. To use a path, you should use the `defaulticon=` expression, which is documented next.

- `defaulticon=` The `defaulticon=` line specifies an icon path. This path is relative to the CD-ROM drive if no drive specification is provided. Microsoft recommends that you do not use a drive specification; you cannot dependably find any drive at a known location, nor can an application require drives be at specific places.

> **WARNING**
>
> Do not code your programs to expect a C drive to be present or writeable. There is
> nothing in the rule book that says a computer will have a C drive, or that it will be
> accessible to applications to write to. Diskless workstations may have drives that are
> found at different locations each time the system is started, and your application must
> take this into consideration.

When an AutoPlay-enabled CD is inserted into the CD-ROM drive, the user may click the
CD's icon with the right mouse button to get a menu of choices. If your AUTORUN.INF
file has an open= line, the menu that is displayed by Explorer includes the commands shown
in Figure 13.9.

FIGURE 13.9.

*An AutoRun-enabled
CD in Explorer.*

The AutoRun facility added the AutoPlay selection to the list of actions in the pop-up
properties menu. If you add the following lines to your AUTORUN.INF file, a new menu
item will be added to the properties menu with the text of Item For Menu:

```
shell\verb\command=filename.exe
shell\verb=Item For Menu
```

When this new menu item is selected, the program specified in the command line is
executed. For example, if you want the user to look at a readme file, you could add the
following to the AUTORUN.INF file:

```
shell\readme\command=notepad readme.txt
shell\readme=Read &Me
```

In the preceding example, the user's menu will include a selection called Read Me. When Read Me is selected, it will execute the Notepad program, loading and displaying the readme.txt file. Normally, the default menu selection for an AutoPlay-enabled CD is AutoPlay (as shown in Figure 13.9). You can change this default by adding

```
shell=verb
```

The `shell=` line specifies the action that will take place when the user selects the AutoPlay menu selection. For example, to activate the `readme` selection, you might include the following lines in your AUTORUN.INF file:

```
shell=readme
shell\readme\command=notepad readme.txt
shell\readme=Read &Me
```

In the preceding example, if the user selects AutoPlay from the menu the readme.txt file will be loaded in NOTEPAD.

Hints and Suggestions

Microsoft has several suggestions for developers who are creating AutoPlay CDs. The most important suggestion is that the application that is launched automatically be small. Microsoft recommends that you do not try to load a large application whenever the CD is inserted; instead, load the smaller teaser application that will enable the user to then load the larger application. The justification for this is that many CD-ROM drives are still slow devices (when this book was written, the 6X CD-ROM drives were just becoming available).

The teaser program on CD-ROMs that contain only data, and no executable program, can simply display a readme file. This enables the user to quickly determine the contents of the CD-ROM. Be sure to date the data on data CDs, using a date format that is easily understood. Don't use summer/winter/spring/fall designators—these seasons mean different things to people in different parts of the world. Also, don't use 1Q designators, because these terms are not always meaningful to all users. Instead, use months and years, such as January 1995 to date data. Spell out the month in characters, don't use 12/5, which in some countries is the fifth day of December, and in other countries is the 12th day of May. Your readme file should also indicate how often the data on the CD is updated. For example, for a database of company information that is updated on a quarterly basis, you will want to inform the user when the data has become "stale" so that they may get an update to the CD.

With applications in which the teaser or introduction program includes a button to enable the user to launch the full application, you can take advantage of the multithreaded processes of Windows 95 to begin the loading process as soon as the teaser program starts execution. That way, if the user decides to start the application, you are one step ahead of him or her and will be able to start the application without (hopefully) having to incur a long delay while the main program loads.

Whenever possible, try to create applications that run well from CDs. This enables the user to better manage his or her hard disk. Also, if you must install programs or other files on the hard disk, use a recognized install program (such as the InstallSHIELD SDK program,) to enable the user to easily de-install the program from his or her hard disk. There is nothing worse than having a CD-based application create a directory that contains virtually everything that is on the CD.

> **NOTE**
>
> Do not forget to clean up the registry when uninstalling. Your uninstall program should make sure that all registry entries for your application have been removed.

Demos and Shows

Being able to send a demonstration of your product (either a working version or a canned demo) to a prospective purchaser is always nice. It is now possible to publish the demonstration versions of your products either using traditional techniques (such as by itself or as part of a CD-ROM compilation with other products), or by using online publication techniques, including the Internet and CompuServe.

Using DemoSHIELD

There are a number of packages for creating demo programs. One such product is DemoSHIELD. The DemoSHIELD product enables the developer to create a professional demonstration of the product's capabilities, without having to resort to low-level programming to create the demo.

Using DemoSHIELD is simple and easy. The WIN32SDK has a working demo model of DemoSHIELD with which you can experiment. This version of the product is limited to three panels (or displays of information), but with this limitation you can still examine the product and see its capabilities.

Working Demos

Many programmers distribute their applications using the "working demo" technique. A working demo is a version of an application that has almost all the functionality of the product being sold. Often times, a working demo either will not support saves of documents or will have some other limitation so that you are not giving away a product that might compete with your product's sales. This enables the potential user to use the application, get a feel for the application's weaknesses and strengths, and see how well the application fills the projected needs.

There is a difference between using a working demo and using shareware to distribute your application. A working demo is (almost always) a copy of the product that has some limitation—usually, the save functionality is disabled. There is no way for most working demo programs to be upgraded without sending the user a new copy of the program. Shareware programs are usually either fully functional or they can be upgraded to full functionality by the user when the application is registered.

Distributing working demos and shareware applications is no different from distributing any other application. A smooth install of the demonstration version goes a long way in selling the potential user on your product. A poor install will convince users that your product is substandard regardless of how well the application has been written.

Summary

This chapter covered issues you may face when you plan and implement installations under Windows 95. Many of these problems are easy to solve, using tools available with the WIN32SDK or from third-party product suppliers. This chapter covered the following topics:

- The MSSETUP program, a program that is written in C and may be compiled using Visual C++. This setup program is used as the basis for the installation program that many of the Microsoft commercial applications use. To use MSSETUP you must write some C code; however, a good prototype program that may be modified to allow for your final installation program is supplied.

- The support that Windows 95 provides. Although Windows 95 itself does not offer an uninstall facility, Windows 95 supplies the interface to application-specific uninstall programs.

- The WINSTART.BAT file, which is useful for manipulating files when Windows is restarted. This file is often used to replace files that are open by Windows and therefore cannot be changed at the time of installation.

- The InstallSHIELD SDK program, which is supplied with the WIN32SDK. This program works by having the programmer write a script for the install. This script is written in a C-like language and is then compiled into a metafile format by the InstallSHIELD SDK supplied compiler program.

- The Installigence program. This third-party application does not require any programming to create an install. The entire installation process is defined using a Windows application interface, using point-and-click techniques.

- The Windows 95 CD-ROM AutoPlay facility. This facility is used to enable a specific action to take place whenever an AutoPlay CD is inserted in the CD-ROM drive of a Windows 95 system.

- Some of the issues regarding program demonstrations. The DemoSHIELD program is one of many demo programs available to software vendors.

Internationalization Support in Win32

by Peter Belew and William Hall

14

IN THIS CHAPTER

Today, it is not at all unusual to see this kind of advertisement in the Employment section of your newspaper:

> *Windows developer; Minimum 3 yrs. experience with Microsoft Windows, C++, OLE2. Knowledge of Internationalization, including DBCS, a must. Send resume to...*

Progressive companies now recognize that from the beginning of the software cycle, they must target their products for the global market. Part of that strategy is to ensure that designers, managers, and developers are competent to create products that respect a user's language and conform to local cultural conventions.

In the past, the typical methodology was to develop the product without regard to international considerations and then hand over the code base to an *internationalization* team to retrofit and translate. Often, this is how a company does its first internationalization. Most companies quickly realize that this approach is expensive, results in multiple code bases for the same product, generates new bugs, and can be extraordinarily slow in getting to market.

Fortunately, on Win32 operating platforms such as Windows NT and Windows 95, it has never been easier to design and code software that is globally enabled and can be easily localized. The reason is simple. Most of what is needed is already present in the operating system. As a developer, all you have to learn is what is available and how to use it. The same could be said for GDI, OLE, and MFC, so learning to add that extra layer of software engineering called internationalization requires some effort and practice on your part.

For a developer, a major part of mastering an operating platform is understanding the system's Application Programmer Interface or API. Anyone who has worked with Microsoft Windows in its various incarnations knows that the Windows API contains hundreds of functions in such categories as GDI, memory management, Resource retrieval, windows manipulation, data exchange, OLE, and so on. But did you know that there is also a subgroup of functions devoted to National Language Support (NLS)? Although it is a rather small set in Windows, it has grown in Win32 to a substantial part of the system. Understanding the available national language support is a large part of internationalizing software; in this chapter, we will spend most of our time presenting the current features of the Win32 NLS API.

To accomplish this, we will concentrate on four areas: character sets (including the Windows 95 WGL4 set), locale and language, Resource management, and keyboards. We suppose that you are already competent programmers with some Windows experience, and we will try to emphasize the practical aspects of internationalization. We also expect you to have some degree of international awareness. For example, we assume you know that natural languages are written in an amazing variety of symbols and directions; that date, time, currency, numbers, and calendars can be organized in an extraordinary number of ways; and that linguistic text can be ordered and categorized in several different manners, even within the same language. (There are many excellent references you can consult; at the end of the chapter, you'll find a list of books and articles to help you go as deeply as you like.) But, most of all, we presume that you realize that potential users of your software have an overwhelming preference for programs that run in their own language and employ culturally expected conventions for presenting information. If you are interested primarily in Windows 95, you might be interested to know that nearly all the Win32 NLS functions, as well as the important new definitions of language and locale, are functional on this platform. We point out the exceptions in this chapter, which are very few. As a result, if you master the information here, you will understand internationalization in Windows NT as well. There is one caveat regarding Windows 95: The system has not been released as of the time of this writing, so small changes might (and probably will) be made by the time the system is on the market. In particular, it is not yet clear exactly what languages will be supported in the U.S. version, and when and if add-ons will be available for additional languages.

It is always helpful to see sample programs and source code that illustrate the principles and provide practical examples. At the end of this chapter is a description of several programs that can be found on the book's CD-ROM. Also, later in this chapter, there is a detailed code listing on reading information from TrueType fonts used in Windows 95.

Will the knowledge of the NLS API help you to design, create, develop, and manage code that can be easily internationalized? No more than learning all MCI functions will help you to write a great multimedia application. But if you combine this knowledge with other sources of information, coding examples, and practice, you will develop those extra skills that contribute to your organization's effort to reach the world market in a timely fashion and at reasonable cost.

Terms and Definitions

A few terms are in common use in the area of software internationalization. The one that developers hear most often is *enabling*. For example, a manager might say to an engineer, "Your code is already enabled, right?" The engineer can answer yes if he or she has created a code base that is mostly independent of language and locale, and has placed any such dependencies in isolated subcomponents that can be generically accessed. In other words, most of the program will work in any world region and with any user interface language, and those parts that are language- and locale-dependent are isolated from the main body of code. A simple example from the Windows world is LoadString. The parameters are an instance handle, a string identifier, a buffer, and the desired length. The string itself resides in a language-dependent part of the module or in a separate component, but by simply varying the instance handle and the identifier, a string from any language can be retrieved.

A second term that is often used is *localization*, as in the statement "The localization language of the Windows you are using is Japanese." The art of localization is to convert the initial user interface language (in the U.S., usually English) of a product to a language that is usable in another world region. Generally, translation of the user interface to the appropriate language is the major effort in the localization, but there are other considerations as well.

For example, startup values in the system must also be adjusted to ensure that the locale defaults (date, time, currency, and so on) are the culturally expected forms for the target area. Occasionally, you see *localization* abbreviated as L10N (*L* + 10 letters + *N*).

Now we can give a more precise definition of internationalization, in the following manner:

internationalization = enabling + localization

The term *internationalization* is often abbreviated as I18N (*I* + 18 letters + *N*). Some experts prefer the term *globalization* to *internationalization*.

The internationalization life cycle of a software project ideally begins with the product itself. During the early part of development, enabling is the main effort. As the product approaches 80-percent completion, localizations can begin with translations into the various languages scheduled for simultaneous initial release. Later, additional localizations can be made concurrently with main line development and bug fixing. The result is the timely appearance of the product in markets around the world, while maintaining a single code base.

Many successful companies follow this development plan, but more often—especially where an enabling culture has not yet evolved—the software cycle involves a less desirable step, namely *retrofitting*. In this case, software has been written without regard to enabling and future localization, and in order to enter the world market arena, some major modifications are required. Retrofitting can be done in two ways: one is to simply change the code to work in a given target area; the other is to enable the code as an afterthought. The first method is frequently used when a company first tries to penetrate Far East markets, and one of the unpleasant side-effects is multiple code bases for the same product. It is much more cost effective to retrofit by enabling if several different languages will eventually be released. However, it takes longer and, when it is completed, the result is a product with no new features that still requires a complete quality assurance cycle. Either way, retrofitting may double initial development costs and cause fatal delays in entering the global market.

Win32 Internationalization Overview

International support in Win32 owes much to evolution. As in older systems such as Windows, DOS, and OS/2, Win32 supports code pages, language and locale, Resource files for isolating and retrieving the user interface, and an independent online help facility. However, the definition of locale has been tightened. Resources can be manipulated by language, and in a significant departure from the past, underneath is a character set with worldwide scope: Unicode. The presence of Unicode, which encompasses a significant portion of world scripts, introduces new considerations in programming for language independence. At the same time, the semantics of Unicode fix, once and for all, the characteristics of each of its members independently of language. Even if you fully understand the internationalization paradigm of Windows or DOS, you'll find that in order to use systems based on the Win32 API effectively, there is substantially more to learn.

Today, Win32 has been realized in two major operating platforms: Windows NT and Windows 95. The former is regarded as a Unicode-based system, whereas the latter is thought to be based on regional character sets (also called code pages). But the reality is that Unicode permeates both systems extensively. For example, in Windows 95 it is possible to render Unicode with a TextOutW call; in Windows NT, code pages are extensively supported for compatibility with non-Unicode clients; and both Win32 systems support data exchange among Unicode and non-Unicode applications.

The concept of locale has been greatly extended in Win32. Unlike Windows, which only remotely couples locale and language, Win32 has quantified both and tied the two together. Locale can be changed globally as well as at the thread level, and routines are available to assist in using locale for the display of certain kinds of information, as well as in manipulating linguistic text.

Win32 handles Resources somewhat differently than does Windows. The most notable changes are Unicode storage format and the introduction of the Language keyword, although there is still inadequate support for using Language tagged Resources in multilingual Resource files.

Keyboards, although similar in functionality to Windows and DOS, have been extended to work with Unicode (in Windows NT), and layouts can be changed programmatically. Thanks to a new set of keyboard APIs, it is possible to have layered keyboards that enable the user to work with several scripts simultaneously. In Windows 95, keyboard selection has been tied very tightly to locale, an unfortunate design decision in our opinion: a keyboard is constrained more by code page (which can support several locales) than locale. Also, Windows 95 keyboard drivers generate 8-bit characters in a particular code page, which can be translated to Unicode if desired.

Win32 Character Sets

It is the operating system's character set that determines its internationalization scope. After the character set is decided upon, the languages and world regions that the system can support become fixed. Windows NT uses Unicode as its main character set, so its scope is potentially worldwide. Unicode is used exclusively in its base and server layers. GDI text calls assume Unicode code points, fonts are Unicode encoded, Resource strings are compiled internally as Unicode, system information files are stored as Unicode, and the NTFS file system names are Unicode. However, a client (application) might be written to use Unicode or one of the Windows (ANSI) or DOS (OEM) code pages. Thus, in a single Windows NT session, it is possible to have a program mix consisting of non-Unicode Windows and DOS 16- and 32-bit programs, and Unicode-based Windows 32-bit programs.

Windows 95, like its Windows and DOS predecessors, is anchored to regional character sets; therefore, it does not support Unicode applications. However, Unicode lies quietly underneath. Exactly as in Windows NT, fonts and resources are based on Unicode, system information files are in Unicode, certain text display routines can handle Unicode strings, and Unicode is an ever-present reference for character semantics and as a conversion operational pivot. For example, character mappings from one code page to another are not direct but always pass through Unicode tables, and properties of a character (uppercase, lowercase, digit, punctuation, right-to-left, and so on) depend on the semantics assigned to it by the Unicode standard.

Therefore, in both systems, all the elements required to join environments having different character sets and coexisting in the same session are present. Such a mix adds to the complexity of the system and imposes the need for mutual data exchange among all classes of programs.

Unicode

Unicode is a fixed width, uniform text and character encoding standard. Containing characters from the world's writing systems and technical symbols, Unicode's 16-bit architecture extends the benefits of ASCII's 7-bit encoding scheme, while overcoming its inadequacies in representing multilingual text. Unicode treats all characters equally, and neither escape sequences nor control codes are required to represent any character from any language.

Content

To define the content of Unicode, the Unicode Consortium relied heavily on existing standards. Unicode Version 1.0 included the characters from all major standards published before December 31, 1990. Also included are characters from draft standards, such as ISO DIS 6861.2, and from various industry standards in common use, including code pages from Adobe, Apple, IBM, Lotus, Microsoft, Xerox, WordPerfect, and others. Not included are rare, obsolete, novel, and private-use characters; logos, graphics, and musical and dance notations; and Braille.

Unicode has been revised to Version 1.1, mainly to bring it into alignment with the more general 32-bit encoding standard ISO 10646. Thus, Unicode today has the status of an international standard. Viewing ISO 10646 as an array of 64 KB planes of characters, Unicode (designated officially as ISO 10646-1) occupies plane zero, which is called the Base Multilingual Plane (BMP).

It is expected that future additions will include less-common and archaic scripts such as Ethiopian, Burmese, Khmer, Sinhala, and Mongolian, pending reliable information. Others being considered include the Inuktitut/Cree syllabary, Egyptian Hieroglyphics, Cherokee, Cuneiform, Glagolitic, Maldivian, and Syriac. If you have trouble seeing an immediate value for being able to represent scripts that might seem to offer low market potential (at least for now), think about the overwhelming problem bibliographic services and libraries face in accurately representing information on a worldwide basis. It is a job ideally handled by computing machinery—provided that an adequate representation scheme, such as Unicode, is available and can be electronically realized.

Layout

The first page of Unicode is familiar. ASCII makes up the initial 128 elements, and the first 256 characters of Unicode are from the widely used character encoding standard ISO (International Standards Organization) 8859-1 (usually known as Latin I). However, the layout of Unicode is not a sequence of existing character set standards one after the other. Rather, the emphasis has been on encoding scripts and symbols in clearly defined blocks.

The main areas of Unicode are currently allocated into six major sections interspersed by unused areas. About 40 percent of the available space is unused in the Unicode 1.1 standard. Approximately the first 4000 entries are derived from a number of alphabetic and alphabetic-like writing systems including Latin, Greek, Cyrillic, Armenian, Hebrew, Arabic, Georgian, and several Indic blocks.

About 2,000 symbols (monetary signs, punctutation, superscripts, mathematical operators, and so on) are encoded, beginning at position 0x2000.

The next major block is the CJK Auxiliary, which includes the Japanese Katakana and Hiragana syllabaries, Korean Hangul, Chinese Bopomofo, and supporting special forms.

The largest section by far is devoted to Chinese, Japanese, and Korean logograms in the so-called CJK block. A decision was made to merge the largely common characters from these languages in order to provide for a more consistent and efficient data exchange, as well as to save code point space. The result is called Han Unification (because these symbols are called Hanzi in Chinese, Kanji in Japanese, and Hanja in Korean—each word means literally "Han character"), which has succeeded in reducing the main Far East character entries to about 20,000. Despite this, not all possible Han characters are encoded. Although many of the missing characters are of interest principally to scholars and historians, some of them are still used in names of people and places. For this and other reasons, mechanisms are provided in Unicode to extend its scope by using 4-byte representations. Toward the high end of the Unicode spectrum is the private use area. It is reserved for those who need a special set of characters. The region has no particular semantics except by private agreement. For example, the Lucida San Unicode font supplied with Windows NT uses this area to provide alternate glyphs for several European letters.

Near the top is the compatibility zone, which is provided for backward compatibility with existing standards. For example, in Japanese fonts for Windows, when viewed as a Unicode layout, one can find a second encoding of Roman letters and Katakana, mimicking a similar dual encoding in the Shift JIS character set normally used for representing Japanese on PCs. Thus, programs that must differentiate between the two encodings can still do so in Unicode-based applications.

The last 16 places from 0xFFF0 to 0xFFFF in the Unicode standard are reserved for special uses and *noncharacters*. For example, 0xFFFD is the general substitution character and can be used for an "unknown" character in another encoding, which cannot be mapped in terms of known Unicode values. Neither 0xFFFE nor 0xFFFF are Unicode characters. The latter might appear in an application as a noncharacter value.

The value 0xFFFE can be used with the Unicode character 0xFEFF, the Byte Order mark, to determine the byte storage order. For example, the Unipad editor of Windows NT saves its files prefaced with the byte order mark. Thus, a Unipad file that has 0xFF and 0xFE as its first two bytes, respectively, indicates that it was created on an Intel machine. If such a file is to be exported to a Motorola processor, the byte order mark signals the system that the bytes must be reversed before the file can be used. Later, you'll see that Win32 actually has an API, FoldString, that can be used (among other things) to reverse bytes in a Unicode string. Another use of 0xFEFF is as a nonbreaking, zero-width space.

Advantages of Unicode

Unicode offers a number of advantages over the familiar code pages of DOS and Windows. In the code page model, a limited number of code points represent a set of characters and symbols selected to cover a range of languages and locales. Alphabetic languages typically contain 256 code points, with each character requiring a single byte. Languages needing more than 256 symbols, such as those based on the Chinese characters, require more than one byte per character; code pages for such languages contain a mix of characters of varying byte widths, and mechanisms are needed to locate character boundaries. Altogether, therefore, many multibyte code pages are needed to cover the world. Across code pages, the same code point can represent several different characters, which greatly complicates the problem of document exchange and the movement of textual data across linguistic boundaries.

However, in the Unicode model, each code point has a unique interpretation and the character stream is of uniform width. Even if it is never displayed, the Unicode representation provides a universally available encoding scheme that can serve as a reference base and an operational pivot point. Indeed, this is Unicode's major role in Windows 95, where Unicode is not normally rendered.

Of course, at the same time that it solves many fundamental problems, the potential of Unicode introduces others. Fonts must contain many more glyphs. Files tend to increase in size. Language support grows from a few to dozens of languages on a given system, and locale information must be extended to include new regions and provide finer granularity. All of these needs greatly increase the complexity of internationalization support that a modern operating system must provide but present the developer and user with rich, new functionality. Indeed, the developer's enabling task becomes simpler because so much support now resides in the operating system; in applications that can depend exclusively on Unicode, the complexities of multibyte text handling disappear altogether.

Code Pages

A code page is simply a set of characters arranged in a given order and size and requiring a particular storage format. The characters themselves are usually selected for a particular purpose; those serving to express natural languages usually contain the letters and symbols required for a given world region. Individual elements are called code points. For example, the Windows code page for Western European is designated as 1252 and contains 256 elements, each of which requires 8 bits of storage (see Figure 14.1). Code page 1252 supports about a dozen languages including English, Dutch, French, German, Spanish, Italian, Portuguese, Danish, Norwegian, Swedish, Faroese, Irish, and Icelandic. Code page 850 plays a similar role in DOS and supports the same set of languages. Code page 932 covers Japanese, so it has several thousand members and requires two bytes to represent most of its elements.

Code pages used in DOS, Windows, and Win32 always contain ASCII as part of their first 128 elements, although there can be minor glyph differences (such as the currency sign for the backslash in Far East code pages). So, it is always possible to render English text in any code page.

In any Win32 session, at least two (and possibly three) character sets can be present. One is the so-called ANSI code page; the second is the OEM code page; and the third, in Windows NT, is Unicode. The first two names are traditional but rather misleading. The ANSI code page is the one you normally see in a non-Unicode windows program. The name *ANSI* comes from the original ANSI designation of the Windows 1.0 character set. The term *OEM* stands for original equipment manufacturer. In earlier times, the DOS character set was part of a PC's firmware; today it is the generic name for any of the various DOS code pages. These arcane terms can be viewed as part of Windows culture, if you believe such a thing is possible.

ANSI Code Pages

The original Windows code page was coincident with ISO 8859-1. Today, Windows ANSI code pages can be any one of a dozen different layouts encompassing European, Middle Eastern, and Far Eastern languages. Most Windows code pages are multilingual and can support more languages than are actually provided on the platform. For example, the Cyrillic code page can actually function with Ukrainian, Byelorus, Bulgarian, Serbian, Russian, and the Turkish code page also includes all the languages of the Western European set except for Icelandic. They all work adequately with English because ASCII is a subset.

A Win32 user can change code pages within certain limits and the platform's capability. From the Control Panel, the change is accomplished indirectly by selecting a language. If the language crosses a code page boundary, a new ANSI code page is installed along with its corresponding OEM companion. For example, if you choose Greek in Windows NT, your default ANSI code page becomes 1253 and the OEM code page becomes 737. (And, if the new language setting requires a different code page, you should reboot your system to complete the installation, although you will not be informed of this step.) However, on Far East platforms, you cannot select another European or Far East language. The capabilities of all versions of Windows 95 in terms of code page switching are somewhat uncertain at this writing. For now, you can assume that any regional version of Windows 95 is based on a single base code page with limited excursions into others. For example, with the multilingual extentions installed, you will be able to switch to certain other code pages from within an application if it so permits.

FIGURE 14.1.

Windows code page 1252.

	0	1	2	3	4	5	6	7	8	9	A	B	C	D	E	F
2		!	"	#	$	%	&	'	(	)	*	+	,	-	.	/
3	0	1	2	3	4	5	6	7	8	9	:	;	<	=	>	?
4	@	A	B	C	D	E	F	G	H	I	J	K	L	M	N	O
5	P	Q	R	S	T	U	V	W	X	Y	Z	[	\	]	^	_
6	`	a	b	c	d	e	f	g	h	i	j	k	l	m	n	o
7	p	q	r	s	t	u	v	w	x	y	z	{	|	}	~	•
8	•	•	,	ƒ	„	…	†	‡	^	‰	Š	‹	Œ	•	•	•
9	•	'	'	"	"	•	–	—	~	™	š	›	œ	•	•	Ÿ
A		¡	¢	£	¤	¥	¦	§	¨	©	ª	«	¬	-	®	¯
B	°	±	²	³	´	µ	¶	·	¸	¹	º	»	¼	½	¾	¿
C	À	Á	Â	Ã	Ä	Å	Æ	Ç	È	É	Ê	Ë	Ì	Í	Î	Ï
D	Ð	Ñ	Ò	Ó	Ô	Õ	Ö	×	Ø	Ù	Ú	Û	Ü	Ý	Þ	ß
E	à	á	â	ã	ä	å	æ	ç	è	é	ê	ë	ì	í	î	ï
F	ð	ñ	ò	ó	ô	õ	ö	÷	ø	ù	ú	û	ü	ý	þ	ÿ

OEM Code Pages

Both Windows NT and Windows 95 allow DOS sessions, and the code pages used there are the traditional ones defined by IBM. As in Windows, the DOS code pages are generally multilingual, even though they might have traditional names that indicate support for only one language. All contain ASCII as a subset. However, as you probably know, DOS and Windows code pages are laid out quite differently in the 8-bit range. These differences, by the way, complicate interactions between DOS and Windows clients in the areas of display, data exchange, and an underlying FAT file system; code conversions between them can result in loss of data. However, some DOS code pages are closely related in character content (but not in code point order) to particular Windows code pages, and conversions between them result in the least amount of character folding. The following are some Windows/ DOS pairings that result in the least loss of information when converting from one to another.

Windows code page	DOS code page
1252	850
1250	852
1251	855
1253	869
1254	857

Usually, if your Windows code page is one shown in the left column of the list, the DOS console will have the corresponding value from the right column. However, there are two important exceptions: in the U.S. the usual pairing is 1252 to 437, and for Russia the pairing is 1251 to 866. Code page 866 is known as the ALT character set in Russia, and it covers Ukrainian as well. There are also some special code pages for Portugal (860) and Nordic countries (865), which are used on some PCs sold in those countries. Win32 provides a command shell that emulates DOS. The default code page is one inherited from DOS, as discussed earlier. The shell also contains the equivalents of the MODE and CHCP commands for code page switching of the console. However, the printer code page support (which was originally provided exclusively for certain IBM printers) is not implemented.

Character Data Types

In Win32, the wchar_t (wide character) data type is used to contain a Unicode character. wchar_t is compiler-dependent; in the Microsoft Win32 compiler, wchar_t is typed as unsigned short. A wide character or string literal can be placed in a C or C++ program using the L operator:

```
wchar_t wc = L'a';
wchar_t *pwstr = L"ABC";
```

Not all operating systems use wchar_t for Unicode, so portability is always an issue. However, Microsoft has made some attempt to hide character type differences, at least among its own platforms, by the use of the generic character type TCHAR. TCHAR is defined in the C-header file tchar.h, which can be found in all Microsoft Win32 compilers, as well as in its 16-bit compiler that accompanies the Japanese version of Visual C++. In addition to TCHAR, tchar.h defines a number of generic ctype and string functions prefixed by _t. By defining the manifest _UNICODE, TCHAR becomes wchar_t, LPTSTR becomes LPWSTR (a pointer to wchar_t), and the generic string functions are mapped to those working with Unicode characters. Similarly, when _MBCS is defined (for multibyte characters), the basic data type becomes unsigned char and the string functions are mapped to those that know how to deal with multibyte character sets such as those found in Far East versions of DOS, Windows, and Win32. If neither _UNICODE nor _MBCS is defined, the standard character types and string functions are generated. For example, if _UNICODE is defined, then _tcstok is mapped to wcstok; if _MBCS is defined, then _tcstok becomes _mbstok; if neither _MBCS nor _UNICODE is specified, then _tcstok becomes the familiar strtok.

By using the generic functions, it becomes easier to have single-source modules that generate Unicode or ANSI single-byte or multibyte binaries. In addition, when _MBCS or _UNICODE is defined and MFC is being used, the CString class becomes, respectively, multibyte or Unicode enabled. This is quite a big benefit to a programmer, especially in dealing with multibyte strings. Many complexities of text handling can be hidden in well-written classes.

Actually, in Win32, defining _UNICODE has some additional effects. If it is defined, the
manifest UNICODE is also defined in most Win32 header files (but not all of them, so you
might have to do this yourself). After UNICODE is defined, a large number of Win32 APIs are
mapped by means of macros to their Unicode equivalents. Otherwise, the ANSI version is
obtained. The following header fragment is an example:

```
BOOL WINAPI OemToCharA(LPCSTR lpszSrc, LPSTR lpszDst);
BOOL WINAPI OemToCharW(LPCSTR lpszSrc, LPWSTR lpszDst);
#ifdef UNICODE
#define OemToChar   OemToCharW
#else
#define OemToChar   OemToCharA
#endif // !UNICODE
```

Thus, it becomes possible to maintain a single source that generates Unicode or ANSI
single- or multibyte binaries, which means a single source can be written for both Windows
NT and Windows 95.

Code Page APIs

Two functions return information about the current code page.

GetACP   Returns the current ANSI code page
GetOEMCP   Returns the current OEM code page

For a particular code page, you can call GetCPInfo to obtain information about any valid
code page in the system. The first parameter is the code page identifier and the second is a
CPINFO structure containing the following fields:

UINT MaxCharSize   Maximum length, in bytes, of a character
BYTE DefaultChar   Default character in the WideCharToMultiByte function
BYTE LeadByte   Table of lead byte for multibyte code pages

For European code pages, a character is 1 byte wide and the table of lead bytes is null. In Far
East code pages, the maximum byte width is 2 and the lead byte table has nonzero entries
(more about lead bytes later). You can also enumerate the system code pages with
EnumSystemCodePages to get information about the pages that are supported by the platform
as well as those currently installed. Either of two flags can be used: CP_INSTALLED or
CP_SUPPORTED. The latter returns all the code pages covered by a major Win32 platform,
whereas the former returns values supported on the particular system running at the time.
You can also check a given code page for validity by using IsValidCodePage. If you enumer-
ate the code pages using CP_SUPPORTED and then check each one found with
IsValidCodePage, you will generate the same list as returned by enumerating with the
CP_INSTALLED flag.

Win32 supplies a set of about 30 APIs for character-based applications, including provisions
to create a console containing a single input buffer and one or more screen buffers. The
following four APIs can be used to read and set the input and output console code pages.

GetConsoleCP	Gets the console's input code page
SetConsoleCP	Sets the console's input code page
GetConsoleOutputCP	Gets the console's output code page
SetConsoleOutputCP	Sets the console's output code page

Character Conversions

These are the transformations that map a string in one character set to another or fold a string within a character set.

Mapping to and from Unicode

One of the most important design decisions that must be made about an operating system or application program is how to store character information. Increasingly, Unicode, or one of its alternate encodings such as UTF-8, is becoming recognized as one of the most desirable means. Because of its universality, Unicode provides an accurate representation of text, especially of linguistic data. Win32 systems take advantage of this fact. For example, permanent information about various regions of the world (such as native spellings of country, language, names of the weekdays, and names of the months) is stored in files using Unicode format. Another important example is the use of Unicode to store strings in Resource files.

A second major consideration arises in the exchange of text data. How should textual data be transmitted between diverse systems in which the sending and receiving character sets are usually unknown to each other? Again Unicode provides a solution. By using a universal transmission scheme such as Unicode, neither side has to know about the other's local character set. Novell NetWare Version 4 uses Unicode in its Directory Services to maintain the integrity of names in its Enterprise Network model, although NetWare itself is not a Unicode system.

Clearly, then, there is a need to perform character mappings to and from Unicode. For example, the Resource compiler must convert a string resource from the code page of the source to Unicode. Similarly, a call to LoadString necessarily retrieves a string from Resources in Unicode format; before being returned to a non-Unicode program, it must be converted to the appropriate code page.

Conversions are also necessary between client code pages. Suppose, for instance, that DOS text is to be imported into a non-Unicode Windows program. Before the Windows program can use the information, the text must be converted from the DOS code page to the ANSI code page. Similarly, if a file whose name is given in characters from the ANSI character set is opened in a Windows program, the name might have to be converted to an OEM code page if the underlying storage media uses FAT rather than NTFS filenames.

Character set conversions in Win32 pivot around Unicode; two functions do most of the work, MultiByteToWideChar and WideCharToMultiByte (discussed in the next section).

(Here, `WideChar` refers to a Unicode character, and `MultiByte` means characters represented by single- or double-byte code pages.) Such a design reduces the number of tables required but increases the number of conversion steps. For example, to make all conversions in a single step among *N* code pages, $N \times (N - 1)$ tables are required; to convert in two steps through Unicode means that only $2 \times N$ tables are necessary. Thus, when *N* is greater than 3, substantially fewer tables are needed if Unicode is the pivot. However, the tables mapping from Unicode can be rather large, unless some sparse table techniques are used.

Multibyte to Wide Character Conversion

The basic function in Win32 is `MultiByteToWideChar`:

```
int MultiByteToWideChar(UINT CodePage, DWORD dwFlags,
                LPCSTR lpMultiByte, int cchMultiByte,
                LPWSTR lpWideChar, int cchWideChar);
```

Here, `LPWSTR` is a typedef for a (far) pointer to a wide (Unicode) character string. The return value is the number of characters (not bytes!) copied, or `0` if there is an error.

The flags are as follows:

`MB_PRECOMPOSED`	Map to precomposed forms
`MB_COMPOSITE`	Map to composite forms
`MB_USEGLYPHCHARS`	Use glyphs for control codes
`MB_ERR_INVALID_CHARS`	Return the error `ERROR_NO_UNICODE_TRANSLATION` if an invalid character is encountered

`MultiByteToWideChar` is used to transform a string from a particular code page to a Unicode string. The source string can be from any installed ANSI or OEM character set. Alternatively, the special values `CP_ACP`, `CP_OEMCP`, or `CP_MACCP` can be used to convert from the default ANSI, OEM, or Macintosh code page, respectively.

The mapping can be into precomposed or composite types, which requires some explanation. Many accented characters can be seen as consisting of a base letter and one or more diacritical marks. For example, À, which is normally viewed simply as the letter *A-grave* (precomposed), can also be regarded as *A* plus a nonspacing grave accent (composite). The first form has Unicode code point `0x00C0`; the second description consists of two Unicode characters `0x0041` and `0x0300`. The following table shows some typical forms when mapping precomposed accented characters from code page 1252 to composite Unicode representations.

Precomposed Character	Multibyte code point	Composite Representation	Unicode Code Points
À	00C0	A + `	0041 + 0300
Á	00C1	A + ´	0041 + 0301
Â	00C2	A + ^	0041 + 0302
Ã	00C3	A + ~	0041 + 0303
Ä	00C4	A + ¨	0041 + 0308
Å	00C5	A + °	0041 + 030A
Ç	00C7	C + ¸	0043 + 0327
Ñ	00D1	N + ~	004E + 0303
Ø	00D8	O + /	004F + 0338

Without delving into the merits of composite versus precomposed representations, it is clear that composition allows new letters to be formed in Unicode, even though their precomposed representations do not exist in the standard. Another important use of composite forms is to build sort keys from character strings. More about that later.

A mapping to composite form might generate a character string whose size is difficult to predict. Hence, if the destination string length is set to 0 in a call to MultiByteToWideChar, the number of characters required in the destination string is returned. This enables the programmer to dynamically allocate the required space before making the actual conversions. Also, if the source string is null terminated, its size can be set to -1 and the length will be calculated for you. These are typical size options in the various string mapping APIs of Win32.

The following code fragment maps all the characters in a single-byte code page to a Unicode array for eventual display in a Unicode window. OEM control character glyphs (the IBM-created smiley faces, and so on) are to be displayed instead of control codes (0x0000 to 0x0031). Note the use of the sizeof operator, especially with WCHAR (a typedef for wchar_t). This is a common programming oversight when porting code from an 8-bit environment, where sizeof(char) equals 1, to Unicode where sizeof(WCHAR) equals 2.

```
extern WCHAR display [256]; // Unicode array receiving the conversion
int SetDisplayToCP(UINT CodePage)
{
   register int i;
   char tbuf[sizeof(display) / sizeof(WCHAR)];

   /* generate an 8-bit code page */
   for (i = 0; i < sizeof(tbuf) / sizeof(char); i++)
        tbuf[i] = i;

   /* convert and fill the Unicode array */
   return MultiByteToWideChar(CodePage, MB_PRECOMPOSED | MB_USEGLYPHCHARS,
                             tbuf, sizeof(tbuf) / sizeof(char),
                             display, sizeof(display) / sizeof(TCHAR));
}
```

Wide to Multibyte Character Conversion

The WideCharToMultiByte function maps a wide character string to its multibyte character string counterpart. The result depends on the specified code page, and you should restrict usage to the values CP_ACP, CP_OEMCP, CP_MACCP, or one of the installed code pages.

```
int WideCharToMultiByte(UINT CodePage, DWORD dwFlags,
                __LPCWSTR pWideChar, int cchWideChar
                __LPSTR lpMultiByte, int cchMultiByte,
                __LPCSTR lpDefaultChar, LPBOOL lpUsedDefChar)
```

The return value is the number of characters copied or zero in case of an error. If the destination string count is zero, the required length is returned instead. If the Unicode string is null terminated (a wide character 0, not a single byte!), -1 can be substituted for the source's string size.

Naturally, when mapping from Unicode, some characters might not have a representation in the destination code page, and the programmer can decide to use the default character or specify a customized value with lpDefaultChar. At any rate, if the conversion requires one or more default insertions, the lpUsedDefChar value is set. Both pointers can be set to null for faster conversions.

The following list shows some interesting flags. The last three come into play only if the first is set. They determine how composite characters are handled.

WC_COMPOSITECHECK	Convert composite characters to precomposed
WC_DISCARDNS	Discard nonspacing characters
WC_SEPCHARS	Generate separate characters (default)
WC_DEFAULTCHAR	Replace exceptions with default character

For example, if the Unicode string consisting of *A* followed by a nonspacing grave accent, {0x0041, 0x0300}, is mapped back to code page 1252 without WC_COMPOSITECHECK, a string containing *A* and ` (ASCII grave) is returned. Otherwise, the result is a string containing the single (precomposed) character À (*A-grave*).

Mapping Within Unicode

The Win32 API has several functions that map one Unicode string to another, usually performing some transformations in the process, such as monocasing or building sort keys. Most functions depend on a locale identifier, which we have not yet defined, so we will postpone their discussion. However, it is appropriate now to look at one, FoldString, whose actions are related to character transformations.

FoldString

The FoldString function maps one wide character string to another while performing certain translations:

```
int FoldString(DWORD dwMapFlags, LPWSTR lpSrcStr,
          int cchSrc, LPWSTR lpDestStr, int cchDest)
```

The return value is the number of characters written to the destination, if successful; otherwise, it is 0. As expected, the source count can be set to -1 for null terminated strings, and if the destination count is 0, the required space for the conversion is returned. Again, this is a useful feature when folding strings from precomposed to composite forms because the final length is difficult to predict.

The flags are as follows:

MAP_PRECOMPOSED	Transform accented characters to precomposed
MAP_COMPOSITE	Transform accented characters to composite
MAP_FOLDDIGITS	Map native digits to Unicode 0–9
MAP_FOLDCZONE	Fold compatibility zone characters

We have already discussed the composite/precomposed representations, so let's look at the last two flags.

In many cultures, numbers have other shapes. For example, in the Arabic block of Unicode, two sets of numbers are shown: the Arabic-Indic digits beginning at `0x0660`, and the Eastern Arabic-Indic variants starting at `0x06F0`. Many of the same shapes exist in the Indic language blocks as well. If a string containing Indic digits is folded with the flag `MAP_FOLDDIGITS`, they are replaced with the ASCII digits beginning at `0x0030`. Additionally, some numeric symbols such as subscripts and superscripts are also remapped to ASCII digits when `MAP_FOLDDIGITS` is used.

Finally, compatibility zone characters can be folded to their Unicode equivalents with the flag `MB_FOLDCZONE`. An interesting example is the sets of Katakana and Roman letters in the Japanese Shift-JIS code page, which have both single- and double-byte forms. The double-byte Roman symbols and the single-byte Katakana symbols in a Unicode layout lie in the Compatibility zone. However, if they are mapped with `MB_FOLDCZONE`, they are replaced by their standard Unicode values.

As of this writing, `FoldString` is not implemented in Windows 95. By the way, if you are in doubt about the functionality of a Win32 API in Windows 95 or Win32s, check the return value. An easy way is to use an `ASSERT` statement that will also print the error string returned by the operating system.

Code Page Mappings

In Windows, several functions are provided for converting characters between Windows and DOS. These are used in many places, usually transparently, to handle file system interactions. For example, an 8-bit filename obtained from a Windows client is likely to be unusable unless it is massaged by conversion before calling the file system. Similarly, a DOS filename using 8-bit characters will not appear correctly on a Windows screen without being transformed to the Windows character set.

Because the need for these conversion routines has not disappeared in Win32—both for compatibility with old programs, as well as interactions with non-Unicode clients and FAT file systems—they are still around but with new names and enhancements to deal with Unicode strings (if applicable). Macros allow access to the old names. Here they are, along with a brief description of their functionality.

Windows names	*Win32 names*	*Purpose*
AnsiToOem	CharToOem	Maps a null-terminated Unicode or ANSI string to the current OEM character set
AnsiToOemBuf	CharToOemBuff	Maps an arbitrary Unicode or ANSI buffer to the current OEM character set

Windows names	Win32 names	Purpose
OemToAnsi	OemToCharBuff	Maps a null-terminated string of OEM characters to Unicode or the current ANSI character set
OemToAnsiBuff	OemToCharBuff	Maps an arbitrary buffer of OEM characters to Unicode or the current ANSI character set

The Char/Oem functions operate as in Windows, but whenever possible they have been extended in Win32 to handle strings from Unicode as well as ANSI character sets (hence the new names). These functions simply serve as front ends to calls to the MultiByte/WideChar conversion routines. For example, the following code shows one way CharToOem could be implemented when converting a null-terminated string from the current ANSI to the current OEM code page. Note how Unicode is the pivot and that the input and output buffers can be the same.

```
CharToOem(LPTSTR inbuf, LPSTR oubuf)
{
    LPWCHAR temp;
    int len = MultiByteToWideChar(CP_ACP,MB_PRECOMPOSED,inbuf, -1, NULL, 0);
    temp = (LPWCHAR)LocalAlloc(LPTR, sizeof(WCHAR) * len);
    if (temp) {
        len = MultiByteToWideChar(CP_ACP,MB_PRECOMPOSED,inbuf, -1,temp,len);
        if (len) {
            len = WideCharToMultibyte (CP_OEMCP,
            ➥WB_COMPOSITECHECK,temp,-1,outbuf, len);
            LocalFree((HANDLE)temp);
        }
        return len;
}
```

If the conversion is from a Unicode string, only MultiByteToWideChar needs to be called. In this case, the input and output buffers must differ.

It is important to recognize that when converting between character sets, information can readily be lost. In the figure, some accented characters from code page 1252 are followed by their mapping to the closest equivalents in DOS code page 437. Because many of the letters of 1252 don't exist in 437, much information has been discarded in the transformation.

```
À  →  A
Á  →  A
Â  →  A
Ã  →  A
Ä  →  Ä
```

Implicit Conversions

Many APIs in Windows and the C library take strings as parameters, but the programmer needs to read the fine print to discover in which character set the strings are expected to be located. Special care is required for those functions dealing with the file system. For example, passing a filename containing 8-bit characters from the Windows character set to the C-library functions `creat` and `open` without converting to the DOS character set will cause undesirable results. For this reason, Windows provides replacement functions, such as `_lcreate` and `OpenFile`, for the most frequently used C-library functions. The strings are expected to be in the Windows character set and undergo implicit conversion to the closest matching DOS characters before being passed on to the file system.

In Win32, the number of such functions has been substantially increased. Typical among them are several welcome additions, including `CreateDirectory`, `RemoveDirectory`, `FindFirstFile`, and `FindNextFile`. These functions can use strings from either the Unicode or current ANSI character sets, and both convert the strings according to the target device's character set.

However, if functions such as `CreateDirectory`, `OpenFile`, and so on, are used in a Win32 console program, the programmer must realize that implicit conversions can sometimes be undesirable if the program's character set is already the same as the file system's. For this reason, Win32 supports a new API, `SetFileApisToOEM`, which is mainly useful when working with console programs. `SetFileApisToANSI` has the opposite effect. In addition, the status can be checked with `AreFileApisANSI`. The following is a list of functions affected by the `FileApis` type functions:

`_hread`	`_lclose`
`_llseek`	`_lread`
`AreFileApisANSI`	`CopyFile`
`CreateDirectory`	`ExCreateIoCompletionPort`
`DeleteFile`	`FindClose`
`FindFirstChangeNotification`	`FindNextChangeNotification`
`FlushFileBuffers`	`GetCurrentDirectory`
`GetDriveType`	`GetFileInformationByHandle`
`GetFileType`	`GetLogicalDrives`
`GetQueuedCompletionStatus`	`GetTempDrive`
`GetTempPath`	`LockFile`
`MoveFile`	`OpenFile`
`ReadFile`	`RemoveDirectory`
`SetCurrentDirectory`	`SetFileApisToANSI`
`SetFileAttributes`	`SetHandleCount`
`UnlockFile`	`WriteFile`
`_lcreat`	`_hwrite`
`_lwrite`	`_lopen`

CreateDirectory	CloseHandle
DefineDosDevice	CreateFile
FindCloseChangeNotification	FileIOCompletionRoutine
FindNextFile	FindFirstFile
GetDiskFreeSpace	GetBinaryType
GetFileSize	GetFileAttributes
GetLogicalDriveStrings	GetFullPathName
GetTempFileName	GetShortPathName
LockFileEx	GetVolumeInformation
QueryDosDevice	MoveFileEx
SearchPath	ReadFileEx
SetFileApisToOEM	SetEndOfFile
SetVolumeLabel	SetFilePointer
WriteFileEx	UnlockFileEx

Implicit conversions can also occur during presentation. Suppose a client is entering a filename into an edit or combo box. The characters are those from the ANSI character set. But, you've already seen that the file system might not be able to support all the ANSI characters. To this end, Win32 (and Windows) provides a special windows style, ES_OEMCONVERT, and its combo box companion, CBS_OEMCONVERT, to ensure that the user sees only acceptable filename characters as they are being entered. Again, implicit conversions are being made. Clearly, you must know the character set in use and understand the conversion process, both implicitly and explicitly, whenever you program.

Character Width Independence

Although the European versions of released Win32 platforms do not contain multibyte code pages, the basic support for multibyte string processing is provided. A wise programmer will always use them to make his or her program independent of character width, especially if the application will eventually be targeted for the Far East. It is very easy to do these things up front and very hard to find and repair later.

As with the ANSI/OEM conversion functions, some name changes and extensions to wide character strings have occurred in moving from Windows to Win32.

Windows Functions	Win32	Purpose
AnsiNext	CharNext	Moves string pointer to next character
AnsiPrev	CharPrev	Moves string pointer to previous character

IsDBCSLeadByte, in both name and function, remains the same; it is useful only with ANSI and DOS character strings. Win32 also has an extended version, IsDBCSLeadByteEx, which allows a code page identifier as a parameter (because each Far East code page has a different lead byte range).

Figure 14.2 illustrates the basic facts about multibyte character sets. For example, when testing the bytes 0x8a and 0x8e, IsDBCSLeadByte returns TRUE on a Japanese system. It returns FALSE on any of the single-byte letters shown. CharNext will increment a character pointer two bytes over the Kanji characters but one byte along the Roman letters.

FIGURE 14.2.

A mixed-byte character string.

Note also that IsDBCSLeadByte returns TRUE on the trailing byte 0x9a of the second character, because that value also lies in the lead byte range for Japanese. This overlap of lead and trail byte ranges contributes to the problem of multibyte string manipulation.

Data Exchange

Naturally, with so many code pages in operation simultaneously, data exchange among the program mix becomes more complex. However, regardless of the type of program—whether it is ANSI, Unicode, or DOS—it is possible to exchange text data either through the Clipboard or via Dynamic Data Exchange. It is only necessary for the programmer to specify the nature of the underlying code page.

The following are some functions from the Win32 API for clipboard support:

```
EnumClipboardFormats(UINT wFormat);
GetClipboardData(UINT wFormat)
SetClipboardData(UINT wFormat, HANDLE hdata)
```

For text, the relevant flags are CF_TEXT (ANSI text), CF_UNICODETEXT (Unicode), and CF_OEMTEXT (DOS text). These three flags can also be used as the cfFormat parameter in the DDEADVISE, DDEDATA, and DDEPOKE data structures.

For DDE exchanges, the function

```
HSZ hsz = DdeCreateStringHandle(DWORD idInst,
    LPTSTR lpszString, int codepage)
```

is used to create a handle for a string. The codepage parameter is one of the two flags CP_WINANSI or CP_WINUNICODE. One or the other of the two functions is chosen depending on whether the ANSI or Unicode version of DdeInitialize was called by the client application.

After the handle is obtained, the function

```
DdeQueryString(DWORD idInst, HSC hsz, LPTSTR lpsz, DWORD cchMax, int codepage)
```

will copy the string. The code page flag is as in DdeQueryString.

Locale in Win32

In computer terminology, *locale* has come to mean a set of attributes describing a particular region of the world. To support a given locale means to meet the cultural expectations of that region's inhabitants. Locale support can include such diverse considerations as date, time-of-day, monetary, and numerical formats as well as calendars, measurement systems, page sizes, cardinal number shapes, sentence spacing, punctuation, and word breaking. A single application can contain its own locale information, but generally it is much better to depend on the operating environment and program accordingly. As a result, locale-dependent code moves from the program to the operating system itself, new locales can be easily accommodated, and consistency can be maintained among applications running on the same platform.

Both DOS and Windows supply a small set of items that provide guidelines on how to format date, time, currency, numbers, and lists. The information is indexed by country name in Windows and country code in DOS. The connection with a given language and the region in the world where it is spoken is only implicit.

By contrast, in Win32, locale is defined in terms of language, where the language is spoken, and how it is collated. In addition, the number of data items (locale types) has been extended to about a hundred. Best of all, support is provided for displaying date, time, currency (credit and debit), and numbers (positive and negative). Therefore, except in special applications, you no longer have to write the code that reads the appropriate parameters and shows the information in a culturally acceptable form.

Locale and Language IDs

The Win32 definition of locale combines a sort identifier (ID) with a language identifier into a 32-bit value called a locale ID (LCID). The upper 12 bits are reserved. The next 4 bits contain the Sort ID, which provides for alternate sorting methods in the same language. The lower 16 bits make up the Language ID. Although modeled on Posix, the Win32 locale ID does not contain a code page as part of its definition.

The Language ID itself is a 16-bit combination of primary and secondary language values.

Reserved	Sort ID	Language ID
31 20	19 16	15 0

The lower 10 bits make up the Primary Language ID and the upper 6 bits comprise the Sublanguage ID.

Sublanguage ID	Language ID
15 10	9 0

Here are some current Win32 primary languages. Many new ones are being added for Windows 95.

Primary language	ID
LANG_NEUTRAL	0x00
LANG_BULGARIAN	0x02
LANG_CHINESE	0x04
LANG_CROATIAN	0x1a
LANG_CZECH	0x05
LANG_DANISH	0x06
LANG_DUTCH	0x13
LANG_ENGLISH	0x09
LANG_FINNISH	0x0b
LANG_FRENCH	0x0c
LANG_GERMAN	0x07
LANG_GREEK	0x08
LANG_HUNGARIAN	0x0e
LANG_ICELANDIC	0x0f
LANG_ITALIAN	0x10
LANG_JAPANESE	0x11
LANG_KOREAN	0x12
LANG_NORWEGIAN	0x14
LANG_POLISH	0x15
LANG_PORTUGUESE	0x16
LANG_ROMANIAN	0x18
LANG_RUSSIAN	0x19
LANG_SLOVAK	0x1b
LANG_SLOVENIAN	0x24
LANG_SPANISH	0x0a
LANG_SWEDISH	0x1d
LANG_TURKISH	0x1f

Here are some Win32 sublanguages:

Sublanguage	ID
SUBLANG_NEUTRAL	0x00
SUBLANG_DEFAULT	0x01
SUBLANG_SYS_DEFAULT	0x02
SUBLANG_CHINESE_TRADITIONAL	0x01
SUBLANG_CHINESE_SIMPLIFIED	0x02
SUBLANG_CHINESE_HONGKONG	0x03
SUBLANG_CHINESE_SINGAPORE	0x04
SUBLANG_DUTCH	0x01

Sublanguage	*ID*
SUBLANG_DUTCH_BELGIAN	0x02
SUBLANG_ENGLISH_US	0x01
SUBLANG_ENGLISH_UK	0x02
SUBLANG_ENGLISH_AUS	0x03
SUBLANG_ENGLISH_CAN	0x04
SUBLANG_ENGLISH_NZ	0x05
SUBLANG_ENGLISH_EIRE	0x06
SUBLANG_FRENCH	0x01
SUBLANG_FRENCH_BELGIAN	0x02
SUBLANG_FRENCH_CANADIAN	0x03
SUBLANG_FRENCH_SWISS	0x04
SUBLANG_GERMAN	0x01
SUBLANG_GERMAN_SWISS	0x02
SUBLANG_GERMAN_AUSTRIAN	0x03
SUBLANG_ITALIAN	0x01
SUBLANG_ITALIAN_SWISS	0x02
SUBLANG_NORWEGIAN_BOKMAL	0x01
SUBLANG_NORWEGIAN_NYNORSK	0x02
SUBLANG_PORTUGUESE	0x02
SUBLANG_PORTUGUESE_BRAZILIAN	0x01
SUBLANG_SPANISH	0x01
SUBLANG_SPANISH_MEXICAN	0x02
SUBLANG_SPANISH_MODERN	0x03

For example, four language identifier pairs involving French are as follows:

```
LANG_FRENCH     SUBLANG_FRENCH
LANG_FRENCH     SUBLANG_FRENCH_BELGIAN
LANG_FRENCH     SUBLANG_FRENCH_CANADIAN
LANG_FRENCH     SUBLANG_FRENCH_SWISS
```

Thus, a language identifier—and hence a locale—contains information about a language as well as the place where it is spoken.

As of this writing, the following sort identifiers are defined:

```
SORT_DEFAULT
SORT_JAPANESE_XJIS
SORT_JAPANESE_UNICODE
SORT_CHINESE_BIG5
SORT_CHINESE_UNICODE
SORT_KOREAN_KSC
SORT_KOREAN_UNICODE
```

The Unicode sort orders have the value 1; the others are 0. In general, none of the sort values for the Far East languages are particularly interesting in the real world. They can be compared to an ASCII sort for English, which is quite far from an actual dictionary, telephone book, or encyclopedia sort order.

Both the language and locale identifiers (ID) serve as function parameters for a number of Win32 APIs. As a general rule, the language ID affects Resource manipulation functions and is a key word in Resource scripts. The locale ID appears in APIs that deal with the retrieval of locale information and operations on linguistic text.

Win32 provides several macros that can be used to create Locale or Language IDs or to extract component parts:

MAKELCID	Construct locale ID from language and sort IDs
LANGIDFROMLCID	Get the language ID from a locale ID
SORTIDFROMLCID	Extract the sorting ID from a locale ID
LOCALE_SYSTEM_DEFAULT	Get the system locale
LOCALE_USER_DEFAULT	Get the user's locale
MAKELANGID	Construct language ID from primary and sublanguage IDs
PRIMARYLANGID	Extract primary language ID from language ID
SUBLANGID	Extract secondary language from language ID

You can also retrieve information about the system and user locales, and you can enumerate both supported and installed locales, test a locale for validity, and convert certain special locale identifiers to actual locales. Here are the functions that perform these tasks.

GetSystemDefaultLCID	Returns the system default locale
GetUserDefaultLCID	Returns the user default locale
EnumSystemLocales	Enumerates the supported or installed locales
IsValidLocale	Tests a locale ID for validity
ConvertDefaultLocale	Converts special locale identifiers such as LOCALE_SYSTEM_DEFAULT or LOCALE_USER_DEFAULT into real locale IDs

Win32 Locale Types

The basic function for reading locale types is GetLocaleInfo. The value returned is always a string. Because the data is actually stored in Unicode format, the string might have been already converted according to the program's code page with the ever-present possible loss of information. If necessary, you can preserve the original data by using the Unicode version GetLocaleInfoW to retrieve a Unicode string. Such a string can actually be displayed with TextOutW, even in Windows 95, if a TrueType font is used.

The locale types available in Win32 can be divided into several categories. In the next few sections, you will see these categories along with some examples of the available information. Although most of the information is stored in read-only format in a Unicode file called locale.nls, some of the values (marked by an asterisk) can be customized by the user or even changed by a running program using SetLocaleInfo. Your program, therefore, might want to detect these changes and respond accordingly. You can monitor user alternations with WM_WININICHANGE. Even though variable internationalization information is no longer stored in win.ini but in the Registry, many changes to the Registry are still posted to programs under the WININICHANGE message.

Country and Language Information

This data provides essential information about each locale including associated code pages, country and language names in various formats, and measuring systems. The parameters and some examples are shown in Figure 14.3.

FIGURE 14.3.

Country and language information.

Locale Identifier	Hex value	Example (France)	Brief description
LOCALE_ILANGUAGE	0x00000001	040C	Language identifier
LOCALE_SLANGUAGE	0x00000002	French	Localized name of language
LOCALE_SENGLANGUAGE	0x00001001	French	English name of language
LOCALE_SABBREVLANGNAME*	0x00000003	FRA	Abbreviated language name
LOCALE_SNATIVELANGNAME	0x00000004	français	Native name of language
LOCALE_ICOUNTRY*	0x00000005	33	IBM Country code
LOCALE_SCOUNTRY*	0x00000006	France	Localized name of country
LOCALE_SENGCOUNTRY	0x00001002	France	English name of country
LOCALE_SABBREVCTRYNAME	0x00000007	FRA	Abbreviated country name
LOCALE_SNATIVECTRYNAME	0x00000008	France	Native name of country
LOCALE_IDEFAULTLANGUAGE	0x00000009	040C	Default language id
LOCALE_IDEFAULTCOUNTRY	0x0000000A	33	Default country code
LOCALE_IDEFAULTCODEPAGE	0x0000000B	850	Default code page
LOCALE_IDEFAULTANSICODEPAGE	0x00001004	1252	Default ANSI code page
LOCALE_IMEASURE*	0x0000000D	0	0 = metric system, 1 = imperial measure

Note that LOCALE_SLANGUAGE and LOCALE_SCOUNTRY vary according to the language of localization of the platform and thus are not constant across different Win32 language versions. Of course, LOCALE_SNATIVELANGNAME, LOCALE_SENGLANGUAGE, LOCALE_SENGCOUNTRY, and LOCALE_SNATIVECTRYNAME are the same across all Win32 platforms.

Numbers and Lists

These locale types (see Figure 14.4) control the formatting of numbers not used to represent currency, as well as lists of such numbers.

FIGURE 14.4.

Numbers and lists.

Locale Identifier	Hex value	Example (France)	Brief description
LOCALE_SDECIMAL*	0x0000000E	,	Decimal separator
LOCALE_STHOUSAND*	0x0000000F	(null)	Thousand separator
LOCALE_SGROUPING	0x00000010	3;0	Digit grouping
LOCALE_IDIGITS*	0x00000011	2	Number of fractional digits
LOCALE_ILZERO*	0x00000012	1	Leading zeros for decimal
LOCALE_SNATIVEDIGITS	0x00000013	0123456789	Native digits 0-9
LOCALE_INEGNUMBER	0x00001010	1	Negative number mode
LOCALE_SLIST*	0x0000000C	;	List item separator

Fortunately, you usually do not have to apply these types if you have to display numbers. Rather, you can rely on the function GetNumberFormat, which takes as parameters a locale ID, a return buffer and its length, and the desired number using a simplified C language-like syntax. The result is the number in a culturally acceptable form for the specified locale. Again, if you need the string in Unicode format, you can call the Unicode equivalent GetNumberFormatW.

Currency

These locale types (see Figure 14.5) control the display of currency in both credit and debit forms.

FIGURE 14.5.

Currency.

Locale Identifier	Hex value	Example (France)	Brief description
LOCALE_SCURRENCY*	0x00000014	F	Local monetary symbol
LOCALE_SINTLSYMBOL	0x00000015	FRF	International monetary symbol
LOCALE_SMONDECIMALSEP	0x00000016	,	Monetary decimal separator
LOCALE_SMONTHOUSANDSEP	0x00000017	(null)	Monetary thousand separator
LOCALE_SMONGROUPING	0x00000018	3;0	Monetary whole part grouping
LOCALE_ICURRDIGITS*	0x00000019	2	Monetary fractional digits
LOCALE_IINTLCURRDIGITS	0x0000001A	2	International monetary digits
LOCALE_ICURRENCY*	0x0000001B	3	Positive currency mode (0 - 4)
LOCALE_INEGCURR*	0x0000001C	8	Negative currency mode (0 - 15)
LOCALE_SPOSITIVESIGN	0x00000050	(null)	Positive sign
LOCALE_SNEGATIVESIGN	0x00000051	-	Negative sign
LOCALE_IPOSSIGNPOSN	0x00000052	1	Positive sign position
LOCALE_INEGSIGNPOSN	0x00000053	1	Negative sign position
LOCALE_IPOSSYMPRECEDES	0x00000054	0	Money symbol precedes positive value
LOCALE_IPOSSEPBYSPACE	0x00000055	1	Money symbol spaced from positive amount
LOCALE_INEGSYMPRECEDES	0x00000056	0	Money symbol precedes negative amount
LOCALE_INEGSEPBYSPACE	0x00000057	1	Money symbol spaced from negative amount

You can use the function GetCurrencyFormat to help you to display currency in the form suitable for a given locale.

Date and Time

Today, the tendency is to use a pattern string for formatting date and time. However, you can still read the individual types as well (see Figure 14.6).

FIGURE 14.6.

Date and time.

Locale Identifier	Hex value	Example (France)	Brief description
LOCALE_SDATE*	0x0000001D	/	Date separator
LOCALE_STIME*	0x0000001E	:	Time separator
LOCALE_SSHORTDATE*	0x0000001F	dd/MM/yy	Short date format string
LOCALE_SLONGDATE*	0x00000020	dddd d MMMM yyyy	Long date format string
LOCALE_STIMEFORMAT*	0x00001003	HH:mm:ss	Time format string
LOCALE_IDATE*	0x00000021	1	Short date format ordering
LOCALE_ILDATE	0x00000022	1	Long date format ordering
LOCALE_ITIME*	0x00000023	1	Time format specifier
LOCALE_ICENTURY	0x00000024	1	Century format specifier
LOCALE_ITLZERO*	0x00000025	1	Leading zeros in time field
LOCALE_IDAYLZERO	0x00000026	1	Leading zeros in day field
LOCALE_IMONLZERO	0x00000027	1	Leading zeros in month field
LOCALE_S1159*	0x00000028	(null)	AM designator
LOCALE_S2359*	0x00000029	(null)	PM designator

Time and date can be formatted using `GetTimeFormat` and `GetDateFormat`, respectively. You can also enumerate both time and date formats for a given locale with `EnumTimeFormats` and `EnumDateFormats`.

Calendar Information

Researching this kind of information can be quite difficult. Fortunately, Win32 provides it for every supported locale (see Figure 14.7).

FIGURE 14.7.

Calendar information.

Locale Identifier	Hex value	Example (France)	Brief description
LOCALE_ICALENDARTYPE	0x00001009	1	Calendar type (Gregorian, etc.)
LOCALE_IOPTIONALCALENDAR	0x0000100B	0	Optional calendar
LOCALE_IFIRSTDAYOFWEEK	0x0000100C	0	First day of the week
LOCALE_IFIRSTWEEKOFYEAR	0x0000100D	0	First week of the year
LOCALE_SDAYNAME1	0x0000002A	lundi	Long name for Monday
LOCALE_SDAYNAME2	0x0000002B	mardi	Long name for Tuesday
LOCALE_SDAYNAME3	0x0000002C	mercredi	Long name for Wednesday
LOCALE_SDAYNAME4	0x0000002D	jeudi	Long name for Thursday
LOCALE_SDAYNAME5	0x0000002E	vendredi	Long name for Friday
LOCALE_SDAYNAME6	0x0000002F	samedi	Long name for Saturday
LOCALE_SDAYNAME7	0x00000030	dimanche	Long name for Sunday
LOCALE_SABBREVDAYNAME1	0x00000031	lun.	Abbreviated name for Monday
LOCALE_SABBREVDAYNAME2	0x00000032	mar.	Abbreviated name for Tuesday
LOCALE_SABBREVDAYNAME3	0x00000033	mer.	Abbreviated name for Wednesday
LOCALE_SABBREVDAYNAME4	0x00000034	jeu.	Abbreviated name for Thursday
LOCALE_SABBREVDAYNAME5	0x00000035	ven.	Abbreviated name for Friday
LOCALE_SABBREVDAYNAME6	0x00000036	sam.	Abbreviated name for Saturday
LOCALE_SABBREVDAYNAME7	0x00000037	dim.	Abbreviated name for Sunday
LOCALE_SMONTHNAME1	0x00000038	janvier	Long name for January
LOCALE_SMONTHNAME2	0x00000039	février	Long name for February
LOCALE_SMONTHNAME3	0x0000003A	mars	Long name for March
LOCALE_SMONTHNAME4	0x0000003B	avril	Long name for April
LOCALE_SMONTHNAME5	0x0000003C	mai	Long name for May
LOCALE_SMONTHNAME6	0x0000003D	juin	Long name for June
LOCALE_SMONTHNAME7	0x0000003E	juillet	Long name for July
LOCALE_SMONTHNAME8	0x0000003F	août	Long name for August
LOCALE_SMONTHNAME9	0x00000040	septembre	Long name for September
LOCALE_SMONTHNAME10	0x00000041	octobre	Long name for October
LOCALE_SMONTHNAME11	0x00000042	novembre	Long name for November
LOCALE_SMONTHNAME12	0x00000043	décembre	Long name for December
LOCALE_SMONTHNAME13	0x0000100E	(null)	Long name for 13th month
LOCALE_SABBREVMONTHNAME1	0x00000044	janv.	Abbreviated name for January
LOCALE_SABBREVMONTHNAME2	0x00000045	févr.	Abbreviated name for February
LOCALE_SABBREVMONTHNAME3	0x00000046	mars	Abbreviated name for March
LOCALE_SABBREVMONTHNAME4	0x00000047	avr.	Abbreviated name for April
LOCALE_SABBREVMONTHNAME5	0x00000048	mai	Abbreviated name for May
LOCALE_SABBREVMONTHNAME6	0x00000049	juin	Abbreviated name for June
LOCALE_SABBREVMONTHNAME7	0x0000004A	juil.	Abbreviated name for July
LOCALE_SABBREVMONTHNAME8	0x0000004B	août	Abbreviated name for August
LOCALE_SABBREVMONTHNAME9	0x0000004C	sept.	Abbreviated name for September
LOCALE_SABBREVMONTHNAME10	0x0000004D	oct.	Abbreviated name for October
LOCALE_SABBREVMONTHNAME11	0x0000004E	nov.	Abbreviated name for November
LOCALE_SABBREVMONTHNAME12	0x0000004F	déc.	Abbreviated name for December
LOCALE_SABBREVMONTHNAME13	0x0000100F	(null)	Abbreviated name for 13th month

Of course, the information in Figure 14.7 is used in displaying date formats, but it can also be used in creating calendars. Although there are currently no convenient APIs in Win32 for doing so, it is possible to enumerate calendar types with `EnumCalendarInfo`. At this time, the possible types are these:

> Gregorian (localized)
> Gregorian (English strings always)
> Japanese Era
> Year of the Republic of China
> Tangun Era (Korea)

You probably noticed the locale types for short and long names for a thirteenth month. Several of the calendars used in the world today are based on lunar, rather than solar, cycles. Because a lunar calendar is shorter, in some cases an extra month is inserted from time to time to help resynchronize the lunar and solar years. The Hebrew calendar is an example of one having a thirteenth month. Other lunar calendars such as the Islamic have only 12 months; the Islamic and Gregorian calendars come into synchronization only after 32.5 Islamic years.

Getting and Setting Locale

In Win32, locale can be set and read down to the thread level.

`GetThreadLocale`	Returns the calling thread's current locale
`SetThreadLocale`	Sets the calling thread's current locale

However, at this writing, in Windows 95 `SetThreadLocale` seems to have no effect, which is an unfortunate defect if you want to write a single multilingual resource script.

Changing the locale of a running thread can affect its operation significantly. For example, in Win32 it is possible to have a single Resource file containing Resource types that have the same identifier but are stored under different Language identifiers. By setting the locale, the corresponding Resource can be fetched according to the language component of the current locale ID. In this way, a program's user interface language can be conveniently switched dynamically.

Several Win32 objects implicitly perform their functions according to locale or language. For example, if a string is added to a list box with `LB_SORT` as one of its styles, the order is determined by the control's current thread locale. If the current locale changes, so might the appearance of the list. In this context, the following messages are of interest:

`CB_ADDSTRING`	Adds a string to the list of a combo box and sorts the contents if `CBS_SORT` style is set
`CB_GETLOCALE`	Gets the current locale of a combo box
`CB_SETLOCALE`	Sets the locale of a combo box
`LB_ADDSTRING`	Adds a string to a list box and sorts the contents if `LBS_SORT` style is set
`LB_GETLOCALE`	Gets the current locale of a list box
`LB_SETLOCALE`	Sets the locale of a list box

Finally, locale has a profound effect on linguistic text, and we have devoted a separate section to examine this area.

Locale and Language

The individual shown in Figure 14.8 is commanding his machine to speak Polish (and is perhaps a bit exasperated that it does not!). Fortunately, this and many other languages besides English are possible on most modern operating systems including Win32. Naturally, a basic requirement is for the system to provide support for real languages.

FIGURE 14.8.

Speak Polish!

Language facilities in an operating system can generally be broken down into three categories: monocasing, character testing, and collation. Monocasing support provides the means for converting a character or string to upper- or lowercase when applicable (not all characters have case). Character testing provides information on whether a character is a letter, symbol, or digit, and whether it is in lower- or uppercase. Finally, collation provides the means for arranging characters and words into an acceptable order according to cultural and linguistic requirements. Monocasing and collation are language-dependent; all are dependent on the semantics of the underlying character set.

The language support APIs of Win32 substantially extend those of Windows. However, for compatibility you can find the old ones, sometimes renamed, but all augmented to handle both wide and multibyte characters when possible. For the renamed APIs, macros are provided for source code compatibility. As you might imagine, the Win32 versions are actually front ends to and special cases of a set of APIs that work exclusively with Unicode strings.

The language functions of Win32 are intended to replace their C-library counterparts, which are generally inadequate to handle the requirements of real languages and which work reliably only with ASCII characters. Thus, `CharLower` replaces the familiar C-library function `tolower`, `IsCharAlpha` substitutes for `isalpha`, `lstrcmp` replaces `strcmp`, and so on.

Character Testing

The Win32 character testing functions inherited from Windows are as follows:

`IsCharAlpha`	Returns TRUE if an alphabetic character
`IsCharAlphaNumeric`	Returns TRUE on an alphabetic character or numeric characters
`IsCharLower`	Returns TRUE on a lowercase character
`IsCharUpper`	Returns TRUE on an uppercase character

These are language-dependent replacements for the ctype functions `isalpha`, `isalnum`, `islower`, and `isupper`, which work only on ASCII characters. When dealing with real languages, however, text layout, analysis, and control require much more information. Supplying this information in Win32 is the function `GetStringTypeEx`. The functions in the previous table are just special cases of this more general one.

```
BOOL GetStringTypeEx(LCID lcid, DWORD fdwInfoType,
                     LPCTSTR lpSrcStr, int cchSrc, LPWORD lpCharType)
```

`GetStringTypeEx` examines each character in the input string and fills out an array of words that contain flags indicating the types. The information returned depends on three type classes, which must be named in the `fdwInfoType` parameter. Except for the second class, the results can be a combination of subtypes. Although the Windows compatible functions perform a limited number of tests—uppercase, lowercase, alphabetic, or alphabetic plus numeric—the Win32 function offers many more options.

`GetStringTypeEx` actually uses the semantics of Unicode to determine the nature of the elements being examined. Before the analysis takes place, the string is mapped to Unicode, if necessary, and the locale parameter helps only to identify the code page from which to convert. In general, character semantics are independent of a particular locale.

CTYPE1

The Type 1 group is useful for finding words and performing word breaks in text. Of course, such routines are highly language-dependent, although the `GetStringTypeEx` function itself is independent of language and locale and depends only on the character semantics of Unicode. Here are the current Type 1 parameters.

`C1_UPPER`	Uppercase
`C1_LOWER`	Lowercase
`C1_DIGIT`	Decimal digits
`C1_SPACE`	Space characters
`C1_PUNCT`	Punctuation
`C1_CNTRL`	Control characters
`C1_BLANK`	Blank characters
`C1_XDIGIT`	Hexadecimal digits
`C1_ALPHA`	Any letter

CTYPE2

This class (see Table 14.1) is used for Unicode text layout of bidirectional text. The various categories cannot be combined.

Table 14.1. Type 2 character parameters.

Parameters	Description
	Strong directionality
C2_LEFTTORIGHT	Left to right
C2_RIGHTTOLEFT	Right to left
	Weak directionality
C2_EUROPENUMBER	European number, European digit
C2_EUROPESEPARATOR	European numeric separator
C2_EUROPETERMINATOR	European numeric terminator
C2_ARABICNUMBER	Arabic number
C2_COMMONSEPARATOR	Common numeric separator
	Neutral directionality
C2_BLOCKSEPARATOR	Block separator
C2_SEGMENTSEPARATOR	Segment separator
C2_WHITESPACE	White space
C2_OTHERNEUTRAL	Other neutrals
	Not applicable
C2_NOTAPPLICABLE	No implicit directionality (for example, control codes)

The Hebrew characters are examples of strong right-to-left elements.

CTYPE3

The members of this class are placeholders for extensions to Posix or C-library functions.

C3_NONSPACING	Nonspacing mark
C3_DIACRITIC	Diacritic nonspacing mark
C3_VOWELMARK	Vowel nonspacing mark
C3_SYMBOL	Symbol
C3_KATAKANA	Katakana character
C3_HIRAGANA	Hiragana character
C3_HALFWIDTH	Half width character
C3_FULLWIDTH	Full width character

C3_IDEOGRAPH	Ideographic character
C3_KASHIDA	Arabic kashida character
C3_LEXICAL	Lexical character
C3_ALPHA	Any linguistic character
C3_NOTAPPLICABLE	Not applicable

Collation

Two functions were provided in Windows for comparing strings from the Windows character set, and they are still present in Win32:

lstrcmp   Case-sensitive string comparison

lstrcmpi   Case-independent string comparison

In Windows, these two functions are table driven and perform character comparisons from left to right. They are sensitive to language and can handle digraphs (such as *ch* and *ll* in Traditional Spanish), ligatures (such as æ and œ in French), and character expansion (such as β in German). However, they do not always provide culturally correct results.

In Win32, comparisons are supported by a pair of Unicode-based functions, CompareString and LCMapString, which provide more sophisticated comparison methods based on building sort keys. As a result, culturally correct lexical comparisons can be made. For example, in Win32 the dictionary order concerning capitalization for American English is being observed. Thus, although a straight ASCII comparison of the two words Polish and polish produces Polish < polish, CompareString returns polish < Polish. This is the order found in an American English dictionary. (By the way, these two words seem to be the only ones in English that change pronunciation with capitalization!)

Here is another example of a culturally correct comparison from Win32. First, note that in French the diacritics are ranked in this order (from lowest to highest): none, acute (´), grave (`), circumflex (^), diaeresis (¨). Now let's try to compare the two words *côte* and *coté* left to right, character by character.

c = c

o < ô

t = t

é > e

Clearly, the result is that *coté* comes before *côte* by this method, because *o* comes before *ô* at the first place where the two words differ. But the standard dictionary order and the result of CompareString are just the opposite. The reason is that in French, right-most diacritics take precedence. So the diacritic scan must be made from right to left in the word, a fact that is handled correctly by CompareString. Of course, the preceding results of comparing the words are highly language-dependent. The same words when compared in the American English locale give the opposite result.

CompareString

`CompareString` is the basis for lexical comparison and collation. It depends on locale.

```
int CompareStringW(LCID lcid, DWORD fdwStyle,
                LPCWSTR lpString1, int cch1,
                LPCWSTR lpString2, int cch2)
```

The return values are as follows :

3	String 1 is lexically greater than String 2
2	String 1 is lexically equivalent to String 2
1	String 1 is lexically less than String 2
0	An error has occurred

If the return value is greater than zero, it can be converted to the traditional values returned by the `strcmp` family (> 0, = 0, < 0) by subtracting 2.

Here are the flags:

`NORM_IGNORECASE`	Ignore case.
`NORM_IGNORENONSPACE`	Ignore nonspacing characters.
`NORM_IGNORESYMBOLS`	Ignore symbols.
`SORT_STRINGSORT`	Treat punctuation the same as symbols.
`NORM_IGNOREKANATYPE`	Do not differentiate between Hiragana and Katakana characters. Corresponding Hiragana and Katakana characters compare as equal.
`NORM_IGNOREWIDTH`	If set, do not differentiate between a single-byte character and the same character as a double-byte character.

Case-independent comparisons can be made by setting `NORM_IGNORECASE`. Symbols can be bypassed by using `NORM_IGNORESYMBOLS`. Letters that can be regarded as composite, either explicitly or implicitly, can be compared in base forms by adding the flag `NORM_IGNORENONSPACE`. Differences in single- and double-byte characters can be suppressed with `NORM_IGNOREWIDTH`, and Japanese Kana can be compared without regard to type with `NORM_IGNOREKANATYPE`.

`SORT_STRINGSORT` requires some additional explanation. If it is set, two special characters—the ASCII hyphen and apostrophe—are treated just as any other symbols and come before any letter. This is called a string sort. Otherwise, these two characters can appear as part of words (the so-called *word sort*). Thus, in a word sort, *sued* comes before *sues*, which comes before *sue's*, but in a string sort *sue's* comes first. For English, at least, the word sort is the better alternative. Note that the functions `lstrcmp` and `lstrcmpi`, which are special cases of `CompareString`, use a word sort. The following comparison table should clarify things. The test words *cöop* and *co-op* are equivalent, although the use of the diaeresis (¨) on the first *o* has largely given way to the hyphen in modern English.

Ignore Case	Ignore Nonspace	Ignore Symbols	String Sort	Word 1	Compare Result	Word 2
0	0	0	0	cöop	>	Co-op
1	0	0	0	cöop	>	Co-op
0	1	0	0	cöop	<	Co-op
0	0	1	0	cöop	>	Co-op
0	0	0	1	cöop	>	Co-op
1	1	0	0	cöop	<	Co-op
1	0	1	0	cöop	>	Co-op
1	0	0	1	cöop	>	Co-op
0	1	1	0	cöop	<	Co-op
0	1	0	1	cöop	>	Co-op
0	0	1	1	cöop	>	Co-op
1	1	1	0	cöop	=	Co-op
1	0	1	1	cöop	>	Co-op
1	1	0	1	cöop	>	Co-op
0	1	1	1	cöop	<	Co-op
1	1	1	1	cöop	=	Co-op

LCMapString

LCMapString provides the support for monocasing in Win32. It also performs some other operations such as reversing bytes and building sort keys. Like CompareString, this routine takes a locale ID.

```
int LCMapString(LCID lcid, DWORD fdwMap,
                LPCWSTR lpSrcStr, int cchSrc,
                LPWSTR lpDestStr, int cchDest)
```

The flags presented in Table 14.2 help to separate the various tasks performed by this function, which are generally mutually exclusive except for the byte reversal operation.

Table 14.2. Flags.

Flag	Description
	Monocasing
LCMAP_LOWERCASE	Map to lowercase
LCMAP_UPPERCASE	Map to uppercase
	Sort keys
LCMAP_SORTKEY	Create wide-character sort key (normalize)
NORM_XXX	Flags from CompareString

continues

Table 14.2. continued

Flag	Description
	Byte reversal
LCMAP_BYTEREV	Reverse bytes during the operation
	Japanese Kana
LCMAP_HIRAGANA	Map DBCS Katakana to DBCS Hiragana
LCMAP_KATAKANA	Map DBCS Hiragana to DBCS Katakana
	Double Byte
LCMAP_FULLWIDTH	Map single-byte characters to double-byte equivalents
LCMAP_HALFWIDTH	Map double-byte characters to single-byte equivalents

As is usual with such functions, if the source string has length -1, it is assumed to be null terminated and the length is computed automatically. And if the destination string has length 0, the number of characters required to hold the result is returned. This kind of information is especially helpful when building sort keys. Note that when a sort key is requested, the result is not actually a wide character string but rather an array of bytes.

Sort Keys

When strings are compared in Win32, a sort key is built to achieve culturally correct results. The need for such an approach was discussed quite nicely by Denis Garneau of IBM in a very readable monograph (see the References at the end of this chapter). Many of the ideas presented there seem to have been adapted to Win32. Here, we can present only a brief idea of how it works. At this time, Microsoft has not made public many details, which seem to always be changing and expanding.

Based on some research done when Windows NT 3.1 was released, here is the basic idea. Each component in a string is examined and assigned various weights. The basic elements considered are scripts, letters, diacritics, casing, and compression. Each part has an associated weight, and the sort key is the combination of all the weights. It is important to note that unless a particular feature such as a diacritic is discovered, it is omitted; but when it is found, each base letter in the remainder of the string must also be assigned a value for that feature. A 1 in the sort key acts as separator, and a 0 indicates the end of the key. When building the key, the string is parsed in the direction appropriate for the locale, usually left to right. One exception is French, in which we have already seen that the diacritics are examined in reverse order.

Consider the French words *côte* and *coté*, for which the locale is Standard French. First, note that the weights for the letters *c, o, t,* and *e* are 0x7, 0x31, 0x3f, and 0x15, respectively. The script weight is the hex number 0x0e. The sort keys for the two words under consideration are as follows (the byte values are in hex; we omit the 0x prefix for clarity):

cöte	e 7 e 31 e 3f e 15 1 17 2 1 1 0
coté	e 7 e 31 e 3f e 15 1 6 2 2 2 1 1 0

Thus, the combined letter and script weights of the two words are the same, and the first part of the sort key for both words is just e 7 e 31 e 3f e 15 (all values in hex). The 1 that follows separates this portion from the diacritical section.

Because this is French, let's scan backward on the first word. The letters *e* and *t* have no diacritics, but the *o* carries a circumflex (^), which has weight 0x17. Having found a diacritic, you must now put in diacritic weights for the remaining letters. Because *c* has no diacritic, the weight is 0x02. So the diacritic portion of the sort key for the first word is just 17 2 and is followed by the separator 1. No more fields are required, so a final 1 and 0 indicates the end of the string. Moving to the next word and going in the reverse direction for the diacritic scan, you immediately find an *e* with acute accent, which has diacritical weight 0x06. Now you have to add the diacritic weight for the remaining elements; because they have none, the diacritic weights of the last three letters are just 0x02. No more weights are required to complete the analysis. Clearly, the second string is lexically greater than the first, so *côte* is less than *coté* is the required order, which is correct for French.

Monocasing

Except for ASCII and Latin I, most character sets have no simple formula correlating lowercase characters and their uppercase equivalents. So, operating system support for monocasing is really necessary. Win32 inherits a set of functions from Windows that provides monocasing support.

Windows	*Win32*	*Purpose*
AnsiLower	CharLower	Maps null terminated string to lowercase
AnsiLowerBuff	CharLowerBuff	Maps buffer of specified size to lowercase
AnsiUpper	CharUpper	Maps null terminated string to uppercase
AnsiUpperBuff	CharUpperBuff	Maps buffer of specified size to uppercase

Working underneath these functions is LCMapString. Monocasing generally depends on character semantics, but occasionally it depends on locale. For example, accents are traditionally dropped when moving to uppercase in standard French but retained in French Canada. However, in Win32, accents are retained even for standard French. So when the word *salé* ("salted") is mapped entirely to uppercase, it remains *SALÉ* and keeps its meaning, rather than becoming *SALE* ("dirty"). (As you can see, accents can make a difference!). But, you can still find locale dependencies in monocasing. In most languages using Roman letters, the uppercase form of *i* is *I*. However, in Turkish, the uppercase form also has a dot. And, as you might expect, the uppercase form for the Turkish undotted *i* is just *I*.

Resource Management

In Windows, the user interface is placed in a Resource segment; access is by means of a set of APIs that can load and display the interface components as needed. In Win32, the concept remains the same but several new features have been added that are centered about the concept of the Language identifier.

A Resource is created by compiling a text description of its components called a Resource script (.RC file). The result of the compilation (the .RES file) is then attached to a module (.EXE or .DLL) by some means. A rich set of functions is then available to the program for accessing its Resources at runtime. For example, `DialogBox`, `DialogBoxIndirect`, `DialogBoxParam`, and `DialogBoxIndirectParam` can all be used with a dialog Resource to generate a modal dialog box. `LoadString` fetches a string from a String table. Other functions can access clip art in the form of icons, bitmaps, cursors, and metafiles. Because the Resource file contains the user interface, localization of a Win32 program is essentially one of translating the Resource components into the appropriate language and adding them back to the program.

A program can also use those resources known to it even if they are contained in another module. All that is required is an appropriate instance handle. For the program's own resources, the start-up instance handle suffices. For other modules, the handle returned by `LoadLibrary` will do. Thus, it is possible to build so-called language DLLs that can contain both language-specific routines as well as a translated version of the program's user interface. A vendor could, therefore, create a multilingual version of an application by shipping several of these language DLLs with the program. Even if a multilingual version of a program is not desired, the design itself is one that supports easy localization of the product to other languages.

In Windows, the Resource (RC) compiler reads the Resource script and generates the .RES file. The same utility is then used to add the compiled .RES file directly to the end of the executable module and to modify its header with a table describing the locations and sizes of each Resource type. Thus, it is possible to modify and replace the Resource component without having to relink the program. This is the method used to translate a Windows program to another language if the Resource script is available. On the other hand, if the Resource script is not available, it is still possible to extract the Resources using third-party tools. Alternatively, although there are no convenient Windows APIs for this purpose, you can write your own extractor using the published file formats found in the Windows SDK.

In contrast, in Win32, Resources are treated as just another component to be linked with the object files when the module is built. The Resources are compiled as in Windows with the RC compiler. The resulting output is then converted to .OBJ format and linked with the remaining object files making up the module. Thus, at first glance, it seems that one cannot modify Resources in Win32 programs and dynamic link libraries without access to the other object files. However, Win32 has a new set of APIs that can enumerate an executable module's Resources by types, names, and languages, as well as functions that are able to update those Resources in-place.

Format

If you use Debug to dump a .RES file created by the Win32 Resource compiler, you will see something quite interesting about the text: characters require a word to represent them. This is indeed the case because the strings—even identifier strings—are stored as Unicode text. A Resource source file itself is just a non-Unicode text description of its components; the Resource Compiler does the translation to internal format including the Unicode translation of strings. The user can select the source code page of the Resource file with the c switch; the default is from the current ANSI code page of the system. One consequence of the conversion method used by the RC compiler is that it is not possible to mix text from several code pages in the same Resource file. Hence, although the languages of a given code page can be placed in a single Win32 module, a multilingual application crossing several different code pages requires multiple language modules. (It would be helpful if the Resource compiler could deal with Unicode files!)

Hierarchy

The LANGUAGE keyword in Win32 Resource files has introduced a new level into the Resource hierarchy. Whereas in Windows, Resources are characterized by type and identifier, in Win32 an individual element, section, or even the entire file can also be characterized by a Language ID.

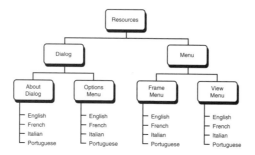

The new syntax is simple enough. Here is how a Resource file might appear when the LANGUAGE keyword is applied to multiple line statements. The language setting applies only to that particular Resource.

```
ABOUTBOX DIALOG 10, 10, 200, 100
STYLE DS_MODALFRAME ¦ WS_CAPTION ¦ WS_SYSMENU
LANGUAGE LANG_FRENCH, SUBLANG_FRENCH
CAPTION "About"
BEGIN
```

```
     DEFPUSHBUTTON    "OK", IDOK, 160, 80, 32, 14, WS_GROUP
END

STRINGTABLE
LANGUAGE LANG_ENGLISH, SUBLANG_ENGLISH_UK
BEGIN
     IDS_HELLO              "Hello, Windows"
END
```

In the case of single-line statements such as icons or bitmaps, the LANGUAGE statement must precede

```
LANGUAGE LANG_CZECH, SUBLANG_DEFAULT
ID_ICON1   ICON      icon1.ico
ID_BITMAP1           BITMAP    bitmap.ico
```

and remains in effect until the next LANGUAGE statement outside a block is encountered. The default is your current language, which is determined by the system's Language setting. Usually, Resource tools also use this setting, but it can be overridden. You can also specify the Language ID with the l switch on the Resource Compiler. You should review the Tools Documentation to sort out all the effects and priorities of the various ways the language can be set in Resource scripts.

One implication of the new Resource hierarchy is that a single Resource file can be multilingual. Here is an example of a script that has Resources in several languages:

```
LANGUAGE LANG_ENGLISH, SUBLANG_DEFAULT
STRINGTABLE
BEGIN
     IDS_HELLO      "Hello, Windows"
END

MT_MENU MENU
BEGIN
POPUP    "&File"
    BEGIN
         MENUITEM "E&xit", IDM_EXIT
    END
POPUP    "&Help"
    BEGIN
         MENUITEM "&About...", IDM_ABOUT
    END
END

LANGUAGE LANG_FRENCH, SUBLANG_DEFAULT
STRINGTABLE
BEGIN
     IDS_HELLO      "Salut, Windows"
END

MT_MENU MENU
BEGIN
POPUP    "&Fichier"
    BEGIN
         MENUITEM "E&xit", IDM_EXIT
    END
```

```
POPUP      "&?"
    BEGIN
        MENUITEM "&Apropos de...", IDM_ABOUT
    END
END
```

The key feature of this script is that the set of identifiers used in one language block is the same in the next. Thus, it is not necessary to use a different identifier to load a French or an English string or menu. The only requirement is to have a language identifier, a value that can be global to the program, set at start-up, and even be changed when the program is running. Currently, however, there is little direct API support in Win32 for this sort of thing. For example, if you compiled the file just shown and tried to use it in a program, the string or menu you would obtain by LoadString or LoadMenu depends on the thread locale. Change it and the appropriate Resource according to the locale's language ID component will be obtained. If you can change the locale with SetThreadLocale (possible in Windows NT but currently not possible in Windows 95), you can exercise more control on exactly which language you will retrieve.

For more complete control, you need to use a new API, FindResourceEx, which takes a language identifier as a parameter. If you don't mind doing the extra work to get to a particular Resource element by more primitive means, you can manage a multilingual script. By the way, lots of this kind of ugliness can be hidden in C++ classes.

A New Resource Type

Win32 has all the familiar Resource types of Windows. In addition, it has taken over a very convenient feature of OS/2 called the Message Table, which is for isolating strings from the main body of a program. Message files can be used in both Windows and DOS programs, are responsive to the LANGUAGE keyword, and offer many convenient formatting possibilities. All the system messages in Win32 are stored in Message Tables. A new function, FormatMessage (described in the next section), is required to obtain a string from a Message Table. One of the parameters of FormatMessage is a language identifier.

Message Tables have a somewhat arcane syntax, so it is helpful to see coding examples. Look for files having the extension .MC in the SAMPLES directories of the Win32 SDK. Most of them are in DOS applications. Also, don't overlook the SDKTOOLS sample code, where you can find examples of Message files in Windows programs as well as the source code for the message compiler itself.

The following code is a simple message file containing a single message in two languages, one a translation of the other. Because the message identifier is the same, only the language identifier has to change when the message is fetched for use in a program. If the language identifier is a global variable, the retrieval source code does not have to be modified at all to get the appropriate message for the current language.

```
LanguageNames=(GermanStandard=0x0407:msg00002)

MessageId=100
SymbolicName=MSG_ERROR
Language=English
The code %1!d! was returned by function %2!d!%0

.
Language=GermanStandard
Die Funktion %2!d! endete mit dem Fehlercode %1!d!%0
```

The parameter `English` is predefined by the message compiler as

```
MAKELANG(LANG_ENGLISH, SUBLANG_ENGLISH_US)
```

The name `GermanStandard` is ours, but the value is the same as

```
MAKELANG(LANG_GERMAN SUBLANG_GERMAN)
```

How do you attach a message file to your program? First, run the message compiler
MC.EXE. In the process, several binary files are created, one for each language. English
defaults to MSG00001.BIN; you must name the rest. In the preceding example, the
German messages end up in MSG00002.BIN. The compiler also creates a header file
containing `#define` statements for the message numbers and an .RC file that you can
include in the Resource script. The final step is to compile and link the Resources to your
application, which can be either a DOS or Windows program.

The previous Message Table example was chosen to illustrate a problem that occurs frequently when a format string has more than one replacement parameter of the same type.
Let's look at this message as it might be naively used in a C program to load a buffer for
subsequent output.

```
sprintf(buffer, "The code %d was returned by function %d", code_number,
function_number);
```

The German translation below requires that the replacement parameters be interchanged.
Hence, the source code must be rewritten as follows:

```
sprintf(buffer, "Die Funktion %d endete mit dem Fehlercode %d", function_number,
code_number);
```

Clearly this situation defeats several principles of software internationalization. First, the
string is embedded in the code—but that is only a side issue that can be easily corrected.
The main problem is that the order of the variables `code_number` and `function_number` has to
be interchanged to accommodate the translation. Hence, even if the string is loaded from
some other file, the underlying source code has to be altered to display the message. However, Message Tables offer a solution: namely, numbered replacement parameters %1, %2, and
so on, where the numbers refers to the positions of the substituted variables in the argument
list (reading from left to right). Up to 99 parameters are allowed. If no further information
is furnished, they are assumed to be strings. Otherwise, additional formatting information
must be supplied. In the messages of the previous slide, the numbered parameters %1 and %2

are integers, as indicated by the !d! qualifier. Message files have a number of additional formatting expressions. For example, the %0 at the end of the message signals suppression of an \n. Others are explained in the documentation or online help. By this means, in the source code, the original ordering of the variables can remain the same; the translator, if necessary, simply changes the parameter numbers to accommodate any changes in the word order. Of course, you have to tell the translator what these parameters represent in order to obtain a meaningful result.

New Resource Functions

Several new functions have been added to the Win32 API to deal with Message Tables, to locate resources by language as well as by name and type, and to extract and update resources in the executable modules.

FormatMessage

If you use Message Tables in your program, you must call FormatMessage to get the strings stored there. FormatMessage is also required to obtain system strings that are associated with the GetLastError function. Finally, the function can be used as a generalized sprintf function for any string. Especially powerful is the capability to change the order of replacement parameters in a format string without changing the code that uses them.

FormatMessage is one of those functions that tries to do everything. If you are using it a lot, you should consider wrapping it with some macros or inline functions for special purposes (such as showing a system string obtained with GetLastError()). It is a tiresome function to use because it takes a lot of parameters and has many flags. You almost need a wall chart to use it. The following is a brief description, but you'll have to read the Win32 SDK help or documentation to really appreciate what it can do.

FormatMessage takes a message definition from a buffer, a Message Table Resource, or the system's Message Table Resources; processes any embedded insert sequences in the message; and copies the resulting message to an output buffer.

```
DWORD FormatMessage(DWORD dwFlags, LPVOID lpSource,
                DWORD dwMessageId, DWORD dwLanguageId,
                LPTSTR lpBuffer, DWORD nSize,
                LPVOID lpArguments)
```

Here are some of the flags:

FORMAT_MESSAGE_ALLOCATE_BUFFER	Create a buffer and hand back a pointer.
FORMAT_MESSAGE_FROM_STRING	lpSource is a pointer to printf type statements along with insert sequences.
FORMAT_MESSAGE_IGNORE_INSERTS	Ignore insert sequences. Used to fetch a message for later formatting.
FORMAT_MESSAGE_FROM_HMODULE	Get lpSource from a message module.

FORMAT_MESSAGE_FROM_SYSTEM	Search system message file.
FORMAT_MESSAGE_ARGUMENT_ARRAY	Arguments parameter is not a va_list structure but a pointer to an array of 32-bit values that represent the arguments.

The format string, if used, has the form `%n!printf format string!`, in which n equals
`1 - 99`. `FormatMessage` returns the number of bytes copied or zero in case of an error. Note
that normally the argument list in `FormatMessage` is a `va_list` (see `stdarg.h`). However, a
simple array of 32-bit pointers can be supplied; in this case, the flag
`FORMAT_MESSAGE_ARGUMENT_ARRAY` is required.

An important use of `FormatMessage` is to obtain an error string from the system. The
following fragment illustrates its use. Note that the only consistently variable parameters are
the buffer and its size, so this usage is ideal for a macro or inline statement.

```
len = FormatMessage(FORMAT_MESSAGE_FROM_SYSTEM,
                    NULL, GetLastError(),
                    MAKELANGID(LANG_NEUTRAL, SUBLANG_DEFAULT),
                    buf, sizeof(buf), NULL);
```

Another really useful feature of this function is the replacement parameter feature of
`FormatMessage` with a string obtained from a source other than a message file. Here is a silly
example that you can extend to more serious ones:

```
LPTSTR args[] = {TEXT("I"),TEXT("love"),TEXT("New York"))};
fmt1 = TEXT("%1!ts! %2!ts! %3!ts!");
fmt2 = TEXT("%1!ts! %3!ts! %2!ts!");
TCHAR buf[100];

/* display the string "I love New York" */
FormatMessage(FORMAT_MESSAGE_FROM_STRING,fmt1,0,0,buf,sizeof(buf),args);

/* display the string "I New York love" */
FormatMessage(FORMAT_MESSAGE_FROM_STRING,fmt2,0,0,buf,sizeof(buf),args);
```

Note that the format and message strings could just as well have come from a String table or
Message Table in a Resource file. You can see how to make your source code quite independent of word order in strings by simply using `FormatMessage`. The order shown in the
second string (*subject + predicate + verb*) is quite common in many languages, including
Japanese.

FindResourceEx

In Windows, a Resource of a particular type is obtained by a call to a specialized function.
Thus, `LoadString` gets a string, `DialogBox` retrieves and creates a modal dialog, and so on.
Underpinning these functions is `FindResource`, which requires a Resource name and type, as
well as an instance handle. When combined with `LoadResource`, `LockResource`,
`UnlockResource`, and `FreeResource`, `FindResource` can be used to obtain any stored Resource
in a particular module.

In Win32, a new function FindResourceEx is available for obtaining Resources according to their language tag as well as name and type. But, as we have pointed out, in the current API there are no corresponding specialized functions such as LoadStringEx, DialogBoxEx, and so on. So a programmer who really wants to exploit the new Resource hierarchy must write his own version based on FindResourceEx. On the other hand, Win32 provides some very useful tools for dealing with Resources as entities to be manipulated. Combined with FindResourceEx, it is now possible to enumerate Resources by type, name, and language. In turn, the enumeration functions can be used to update Resources in a nonexecuting file without recompilation.

For example, to load a menu, a call to LoadMenuIndirect with the pointer obtained from LockResource returns the desired menu handle. If a modal dialog box is to be created, use DialogBoxIndirect with the handle returned by LoadResource. A string is a bit more trouble because the correct string block must be located and searched. If the program is not a Unicode application, the string must also be converted with a call to WideCharToMultiByte. The following is an example of how the MFC C++ menu class CMenu can be used to derive a new class, CMenuEx, so that a language-tagged menu can be loaded and used in a program.

```
class CMenuEx : public CMenu
{
    public:
        BOOL LoadMenuEx(UINT wID, LANGID langid);
};

BOOL CMenuEx::LoadMenuEx(UINT wID, LANGID langid)
{
    BOOL result = 0;
    HINSTANCE hInst = AfxGetResourceHandle();
    HRSRC hRC = FindResourceEx(hInst,RT_MENU,MAKEINTRESOURCE(wID),langid);
    if (hRC) {
        HGLOBAL hgl = LoadResource(hInst, hRC);
        if (hgl) {
            MENUTEMPLATE *lpTemplate = (MENUTEMPLATE *)LockResource(hgl);
            if (lpTemplate) {
                result = this->LoadMenuIndirect(lpTemplate);
                UnlockResource(hgl);
            }
            FreeResource(hgl);
        }
    }
    return result;
}
```

By the way, the Win32 API does not require you to unlock and free resources, but if you are trying to share code with Windows 3.x, you cannot be so cavalier with globally or locally allocated memory.

Resource Enumeration

Three functions are available in Win32 for enumerating a program's Resources according to the new hierarchy. To descend the hierarchy, begin with EnumResourceTypes; only a module handle (which can be obtained with a call to LoadLibrary, whether or not the application is a DLL or an EXE), and a callback function are required. With each type obtained, call EnumResourceNames to obtain the identifiers. Finally, use the type and identifier in EnumResourceLanguages. After that, you can use FindResourceEx to view, extract, or even update the Resources.

An important reason for having a set of Resource enumeration functions is to help in building Resource editing and management tools. Enumeration performs the extraction task. The task of updating the Resources is the other half of the problem. In Win32, a new function, UpdateResource, is available for adding and replacing a module's current set of Resources according to type, identifier, and language. UpdateResource has two companion functions: BeginUpdateResource and EndUpdateResource. BeginUpdateResource requires a module name and returns a handle needed by UpdateResource. EndUpdateResource terminates the update sequence by actually writing the Resources to the target file. The Resource update functions can be used as an aid to translating a module's user interface. As a preliminary to this discussion, let's look at how translation is done in Windows. For simplicity, imagine that you have a single Windows program, a Resource script in English, and a collection of header files needed to compile the script. To localize the program, you copy the program, the Resource file, and the headers to a new directory; translate the Resource file; and compile it with RC.EXE using the -r switch. A second use of the RC compiler without the -r switch removes the old Resources and attaches the new ones to the program. Note that the process of translation does not require having access to most of the original source, and the translation process can proceed in a series of incremental stages with the translator running the program to test the results of each step. Additionally, the methodology lends itself to building a localization kit—complete with appropriate directory structure, required sources, and tools—that can be installed by the translator.

Now, in Win32, Resources are bound to the program during the link phase. But it is still possible to emulate the approach from Windows. After translating the target Resource script, it is compiled, converted, and linked with a do-nothing dummy program. Then, using UpdateResource and its companion functions, a local copy of the affected module can be updated from the dummy program. As in the Windows case, the process is conducive to incremental translation and can be used as a basis for building a localization kit. Of course, you will have to write the tools that use the UpdateResource functions, or get them from the compiler package or third parties.

Keyboards in Win32

In Windows 3.0 and 3.1, keyboard support was divided into two modules: a separate driver portion handling the hardware, and a collection of layout DLLs providing national keyboard layout support. Similarly, in Win32, there is a single keyboard driver that can be customized for special hardware, but it is generally the same for all standard keyboards. The keyboard layout information is now in a data file with a .KBD extension, which is listed in the Registry and can be selected from the Control Panel.

Briefly, the driver transforms the scan code obtained at interrupt time from the physical keyboard to a virtual key code. A Windows application sees the virtual key code in the wParam of the WM_KEYDOWN and WM_KEYUP or WM_SYSKEYDOWN and WM_SYSKEYUP messages. Then the driver translates the key code into a character code, if one exists, and the application receives the result in wParam in a subsequent WM_CHAR, WM_SYSCHAR, or WM_DEADCHAR message. In Far East keyboards, the message flow differs somewhat, and a discussion requires a background in Far East character sets; so here we will confine our discussion to European keyboards and layouts.

Hardware

Although the keyboard driver module can support a range of keyboards, the general PC standard today is the IBM 101/102-key Enhanced keyboard. The 101-key version is found primarily in the United States, whereas in nearly every other part of the world the 102-key model is standard. (In the Far East, the popular keyboards have either 101 or 106 keys.) Key number 102 is found just to the right of the left shift key, which has itself been made narrower than its 101-key counterpart to accommodate the addition. Another difference between the two models is in the shape of the Enter key: On European keyboards, it is wider at the top and extends over two rows; on U.S. keyboards, the Enter key might be only one row high, or if it is two rows high, it has its wider portion on the bottom. This design causes other minor key displacements, and generally the number of keys on the second and third letter key rows tends to differ between 101 and 102 key models.

Two functions return information about the current keyboard. GetKBCodePage is supplied mostly for compatibility with Windows applications. The value returned is the same result as calling GetOEMCP. The second function, GetKeyboardType, obtains hardware features in terms of types, subtypes, and number of function keys. The subtype is OEM-dependent; usually it indicates a minor variation.

Some of the following types (particularly the Nokia and Olivetti keyboards) are mainly for out-of-date systems, using 8086/8088 or 80286 processors. However, these old keyboards are still being supported, because 80386 or 80486 upgrades might be available for some of the systems using them.

Type	*Keyboard*	*Function keys*
1	IBM PC/XT 83-key keyboard	10
2	Olivetti ICO 102-key keyboard	12 or 18
3	IBM AT 84-key keyboard	10
4	IBM Enhanced 101/102-key keyboard	12
5	Nokia 1050 and similar models	10

Type	Keyboard	Function keys
6	Nokia 9140 and similar models	24
7	Japanese keyboard	OEM-dependent

Layouts

Win32 is supplied with a large selection of keyboard layouts. The identifier numbers will look familiar: They are just the language IDs supplemented, when necessary, by an extra value if there is more than one keyboard layout for that language. For example, the standard U.S. keyboard has identifier `0x00000409` (U.S. English), but the Dvorak layout is named `0x00020409`. By the way, the identifier as a string is often called the keyboard name; the function `GetKeyboardLayoutName` can be used to return the identifier of the currently active keyboard layout.

The following is a current list of Win32 keyboards. Where applicable, a DOS ID is shown for the layout. The Windows 95 ID column shows the two-character identifier that will show up on the Windows 95 taskbar when a keyboard is selected; these identifiers are not unique, so a user can get more specific information about a keyboard selection by clicking on the ID on the taskbar.

Identifier	Name	DOS ID	Windows 95 ID
00000402	Bulgarian	-	Bg
00000403	Catalan (Spanish keyboard)	sp	Ca
00000405	Czech Republic	cz	Cz
00000406	Danish	dk	Da
00000407	German	gr	De
00000408	Greek	-	Gr
00000409	English (U.S.)	us	En
0000040A	Spanish (Traditional sort)	sp	Sp
0000040B	Finnish	su	Fi
0000040C	French (Standard)	fr	Fr
0000040E	Hungarian	hu	Hu
0000040F	Icelandic	-	Is
00000410	Italian (Standard)	it	It
00000413	Dutch (Standard)	nl	Nl
00000414	Norwegian (Bokmal)	no	No
00000415	Polish	pl	Pl
00000416	Portuguese (Brazilian standard)	br	Pt
00000419	Russian (Standard layout)	-	Ru
0000041D	Swedish	sv	Sv

00000421	Indonesian (U.S. keyboard)	us	Ba
00000423	Belarusian	-	Be
00000424	Slovenian (different kbds)	yu	Sl
0000042D	Basque (Spanish keyboard)	sp	Eu
00000436	Afrikaans (U.S. keyboard)	us	Af
00000807	Swiss German	sg	De
00000809	British	uk	En
0000080A	Latin American (Mexican)	la	Es
0000080C	Belgian French	be	Fr
00000813	Dutch (Belgian)	nl	Nl
00000814	Norwegian (Nynorsk)	-	No
00000816	Portuguese (Standard)	po	Pt
00000C07	German (Austrian)	gr	De
00000C09	English (Australian)	us	En
00000C0A	Spanish (Modern Sort)	sp	Es
00000C0C	French Canadian	cf	Fr
00001007	German (Luxembourg)	gr	De
00001009	Canadian English (Multiling.)	us	En
0000100A	Latin American (Guatemala)	la	Es
0000100C	Swiss French	sf	Fr
00001407	German (Liechtenstein)	gr	De
00001409	English (New Zealand)	us	En
0000140A	Latin American (Costa Rica)	la	Es
0000140C	French (Luxembourg)	fr	Fr
00001809	English (Irish keyboard)	uk	En
0000180A	Latin American (Panama)	la	Es
00001C09	English (South Africa)	us	En
00001C0A	Latin American (Dominican Rep.)	la	Es
00002009	English (Jamaica)	us	En
0000200A	Latin American (Venezuela)	la	Es
00002409	English (Caribbean) (U.S. keyboard)	us	En
0000240A	Latin American (Columbia)	la	Es
0000280A	Latin American (Peru)	la	Es
00002C0A	Latin American (Argentina)	la	Es
0000300A	Latin American (Ecuador)	la	Es
0000340A	Latin American (Chile)	la	Es
0000380A	Latin American (Uruguay)	la	Es
00003C0A	Latin American (Paraguay)	la	Es
00010402	Bulgarian (Latin)	-	Bg
00010405	Czech (Qwerty)	-	Cz

Identifier	Name	DOS ID	Windows 95 ID
00010407	German (IBM)	gr	De
00010408	Greek IBM 220	-	Gr
00010409	United States-International	-	En
0001040E	Hungarian (101 keys)	-	Hu
00010410	Italian 142	-	It
00010415	Polish (Programmers)	-	Po
00010416	Portuguese (Brazilian ABNT2)	-	Pt
00010419	Russian (Typewriter)	-	Ru
00020408	Greek IBM 319	-	Gr
00020409	United States-Dvorak	dv	En
00030408	Greek Latin IBM 220	-	Gr
00040408	Greek Latin IBM 319	-	Gr

Support for Slovak, Serbian, and Ukrainian might not be in the final release of Windows 95, but it will probably be available eventually as an add-on. Likewise, there is no support for the Baltic languages (Latvian, Lithuanian, and Estonian) in the keyboard layouts and locale tables, but the WGL4 fonts do seem to contain the needed characters, so one can presume that Baltic support is coming in the near future.

Let's use the Swiss-German keyboard to illustrate a typical Western European layout.

As you can see, the general organization of the keys is familiar to anyone familiar with the U.S. layout. Notable differences are the exchange of *Y* and *Z*, and the replacement of a number of symbols and punctuation by letters required in the languages of Switzerland. Several keys also have three characters; the ones shown on the right are accessed by using the right Alt key (Alt+gr, or alternate graphics). A few keys are so-called nonescaping or *dead* keys. They allow the entry of accented letters not directly accessible from the keyboard. For example, to enter ñ from the Swiss-German keyboard, the sequence Alt+gr+~+n will do the job. Alt+gr, by the way, is equivalent to Alt+Ctrl. So if you define a hot key in your application with Alt+Ctrl as a prefix, you can interfere with the proper operation of many European keyboards. Some famous programs written by those who should know better have made this mistake.

At the bottom left is key number 102 (just left of the *Y* key). Key 102 is actually an extra graphic key—that is, one that supports a character as opposed to a function (F1, F2, Home, End, and so on). European layouts have useful characters on key 102; on this one, \, <, and > are located there.

Although it is quite possible to use a European keyboard layout with a U.S. 101-key keyboard, it can be inconvenient not having the extra key, and one must resort to using the numeric pad to enter the missing characters. (For example, Alt+0244 generates the character at code point 244 in your current ANSI character set. Without the leading 0, you get the character at 244 from the OEM character set, or something similar if the conversion between ANSI and DOS is not 1:1). For reasons that remain obscure, practically no effort has ever been made in either DOS or Windows to add the characters found on key 102 in order to make a European keyboard easier to use with U.S. hardware. However, it is quite easy to add the extra code in the layout KBD files. A notable exception is in the keyboards for Eastern Europe, on which the characters on key 102 have also been placed in other locations that can be reached from a 101-key keyboard.

In addition to National Language keyboards, Windows and Win32 platforms also provide for handicapped users by means of special layouts based on the Dvorak model. There are three Dvorak layouts: one for two-handed users, one for people who type only with their left hand, and one for people who type only with their right hand. The left- or right-hand keyboard layouts can also be used by people who type with a single finger or a wand. You do not need to purchase any special equipment in order to use these features. The two-handed Dvorak is included with all versions of Windows and Win32 platforms, and the others can be downloaded from various bulletin boards or obtained directly from Microsoft.

Changing Layouts

Often a user needs to switch layouts rapidly from one to another, especially when working in a language with several scripts. For example, when typing Japanese, concurrent access to Katakana, Hiragana, and Roman letter input are indispensable. Users of Russian, Greek, Arabic, and Hebrew need to obtain access to Roman letters and to change layouts rapidly, preferably with a hot key toggle.

DOS has always provided keyboards with two layers. For example, if you install a French keyboard in DOS, you can quickly change between French (Alt+Ctrl+F2) and U.S. (Alt+Ctrl+F1) layouts. However, in Windows, except for certain special cases or when using special keyboard software from vendors other than Microsoft, the only way to change keyboard was through the Control Panel.

Now, in Win32 platforms, a number of new keyboard functions have been added to facilitate rapid keyboard switching. Although Windows NT and Windows 95 share the same keyboard APIs, the two platforms also differ in some behaviors. Windows 95 has two new messages that are sent to applications, which can affect keyboard switching. Here we shall concentrate mostly on Windows 95, with occasional comments on Windows NT.

User Layout Control

A user simply uses the Control Panel to change the default keyboard layout. If the required keyboard layout module is already in the system directory, it is activated and becomes the current keyboard. If the module is not present, it must be copied from the Setup CD-ROM or diskettes. This is done from the keyboard control panel, using the Language pane in Windows 95. Each new addition is added to a list maintained in the registry under the following key:

```
HKEY_LOCAL_MACHINE\SYSTEM\CurrentControlSet\Control\Keyboard\Layout
```

From this list, an application can dynamically load new keyboard layouts using a new set of APIs (described in the "Program Control" section later). The keyboard switcher that comes with Windows 95 does just this.

In Windows 95, from the Keyboard Control Panel, a user can load a number of different languages with associated keyboards. The user can switch among them by using a hotkey combination (Control+Shift or Shift+Alt) or by using the Control Panel. Note that this hotkey switching is between locales: the standard Windows 95 keyboard switcher doesn't allow a user to switch between two keyboards for the same locale with a hotkey. But there is nothing preventing a programmer from writing a replacement switcher that uses the APIs described here to change keyboards for the same locale (such as between the standard U.S. keyboard and the Dvorak layout) using a hot key.

Viewing Layout Information in the Registry

Win32 systems keep keyboard layout information in the Registry. The two views of the Windows 95 registry editor seen in Figure 14.9 show entries for two different Bulgarian layouts (both Cyrillic and Central European Latin support have been installed). The first view shows how to get through the tree of entries in the Registry to find the list of all keyboard layouts that the system has registered (whether they are actually installed or not).

The layout shown in Figure 14.9 is the standard Bulgarian Cyrillic layout. Note that the four leftmost digits of its key (00000402) are all 0. This means that it is the primary layout for this locale. Also, note that there are only three entries on the right side of the window, which is normal for the primary layout for a locale.

The layout selected in Figure 14.10 is another Bulgarian layout, with key 00010402. Notice that there is an additional entry in the right side of the window: Layout id. The layout ID field must exist whenever the leftmost four digits of the layout key are nonzero. Also, the layout ID must be unique if it exists in this list.

FIGURE 14.9.

Registry entries for standard Bulgarian layout.

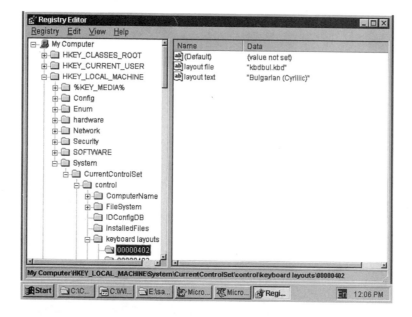

FIGURE 14.10.

Registry enteries for Latin Bulgarian keyboard layout.

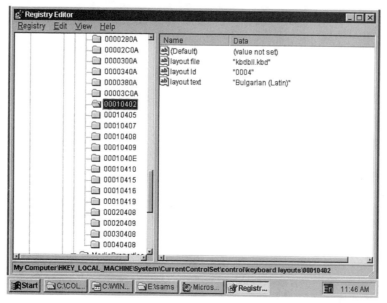

Note that an actual keyboard layout file can be used for a number of different locales, even though the keys, IDs, and layout text are all different. For example, the KBDUS.KBD layout is used not only for the United States and Canada, but also in Australia, New Zealand, Indonesia, and various other countries.

Changing DOS Keyboard Layouts

While running a DOS command shell, you can change the DOS keyboard layout by using the familiar KEYB command:

```
KEYB [xx[,[yyy][,[drive:][path]filename]]] [/E] [/ID:nnn]
```

Here, xx is one of the two-letter DOS keyboard IDs listed previously, and yyy is a console code page. The rest of the fields are present for compatibility with older systems and are ignored in Win32.

In Windows 95, unlike Windows NT, the DOS and Windows keyboard layouts are selected entirely independently. In addition, Windows 95 keyboard layouts are selected on a per-thread basis: two different 32-bit programs might have entirely different keyboard layouts. The Figure 14.11 shows two instances of WordPad running side-by side.

FIGURE 14.11.

Russian and English text in two instances of WordPad.

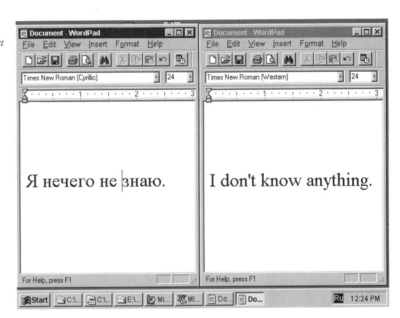

Note that the focus is on the left WordPad window, and the taskbar button shows *Ru*. The Russian layout is selected simply by clicking on the Cyrillic text in WordPad. Clicking on the text in the right window will select the U.S. layout, so the button will display *En* for English.

Program Control

Layouts can also be changed from a program; as we have noted, the change is global in Windows NT and local in Windows 95. Three APIs support this feature. The core function is `LoadKeyboardLayout`:

```
HKL LoadKeyboardLayout(LPCTSTR lpszKLName, UINT fuFlags)
```

This function takes an identifier string as described earlier. The flags describe how the layout is to be loaded.

Flag	Meaning
KLF_ACTIVATE	Load (if not already loaded) and activate the layout
KLF_REORDER	Place loaded layout at head of layout circular list
KLF_SUBSTITUTES_OK	Load substitute layout
KLF_UNLOADPREVIOUS	Unload the previously active layout

If the `KLF_ACTIVATE` flag is set and the layout is not already loaded, it becomes the active layout and is inserted into the system's circular list of loaded layouts ahead of the previously active layout. If the `KLF_ACTIVATE` flag is set and the layout is loaded, the arrangement of the circular list depends on the `KLF_REORDER` bit. If it is not set, the system's circular list of loaded layouts is simply rotated. Otherwise, the layout is removed from its position in the list and placed at the head as the active layout. The following table shows what happens when English is the currently active keyboard and German is next chosen from a list of four loaded keyboards.

Original List	English	French	German	Spanish
Reorder bit not set	German	Spanish	English	French
Reorder bit set	German	English	French	Spanish

If the `KLF_SUBSTITUTE_OK` flag is set, the Registry is consulted to find a preferred substitute. An example of a preferred substitute might be a Dvorak keyboard in place of the standard U.S. layout. Finally, the `KLF_UNLOADPREVIOUS` flag will unload the previously loaded active layout.

`LoadKeyboardLayout` returns a keyboard handle, which can then be used in other keyboard functions. Loading several keyboard layouts makes it relatively fast to switch among layouts. Such a feature is especially very useful in working with multiple scripts such as Russian and English or Greek and English.

After a keyboard handle is obtained, activation can more conveniently be changed with the following function:

```
BOOL ActivateKeyboardLayout(HKL hkl, UINT fuFlags)
```

This API can use only the two flags, `KLF_REORDER` and `KLF_UNLOADPREVIOUS`. Instead of specifying a keyboard handle, you can use `HLF_NEXT` and `HLF_PREVIOUS` to move through the list of loaded layouts.

HKL_NEXT   Selects the next layout in the system's circular list of loaded layouts.

HKL_PREV   Selects the previous layout in the system's circular list of loaded layouts.

Finally, the function

```
BOOL UnloadKeyboardLayout(HKL hkl)
```

can be used to remove a keyboard layout from the currently loaded list.

Windows 95 provides a means of changing the input language under user control. This can be accompanied by a keyboard change, because the user can associate one keyboard with each language identifier.

Two messages are sent to the program: WM_INPUTLANGCHANGEREQUEST is a request to change the language. lParam contains a handle to the new keyboard layout. By returning the message to DefWndProc, the next message (WM_INPUTLANGCHANGE) announcing the change will be received. For this message, lParam is the keyboard layout handle and wParam contains the base character set identifier. At this point, the application can change the current font, if necessary, so that the user can perform input in the new language.

Other Keyboard APIs

When TranslateMessage is called in the Windows message loop of a non-Unicode program, the virtual key obtained from WM_KEYDOWN and WM_KEYUP is translated to an ANSI character or characters by the function ToAscii. There is also a similar function ToUnicode for returning Unicode characters in Unicode applications.

Although it is not generally needed by applications, it is possible to use ToUnicode and ToAscii to read keyboard layouts according to the state of a local keyboard state buffer. As a loop is run through the various character scan codes supported by the keyboard, the MapVirtualKey function obtains the corresponding virtual key codes, and the state of the Shift, Control, and Alt keys are varied in the key state buffer to obtain the characters supported by the layout.

MapVirtualKey can also be used to obtain a scan code from a virtual key code. To go from character to virtual key code, VkKeyScan will do the job according to the shift state of the Shift, Control, and Alt keys. This function is used primarily to simulate keystrokes using WM_KEYUP and WM_KEYDOWN messages.

A related function is provided by keybd_event, which can be used to synthesize a keystroke. One interesting use is to have an application simulate the PrintScreen function to send a picture of the entire screen or the active window. The technique is explained in the Win32 SDK documentation.

An application can also read and set its own key state with GetKeyboardState and SetKeyboardState, or the status of an individual key with GetKeyState and

`GetAsyncKeyState`. These functions can also distinguish between left and right versions of the Control, Shift, and Alt keys by a new set of virtual key codes: `VK_LSHIFT`, `VK_RSHIFT`, `VK_LCONTROL`, `VK_RCONTROL`, `VK_LMENU`, and `VK_RMENU`.

If you must present a text representation of accelerator keys (hotkeys) to your user, you can use `GetKeyNameText` to obtain a string that names the key and has the proper language translation according to the keyboard. The PIF editor uses this feature.

TrueType Fonts in Windows 95

In the U.S. and European versions of Win32, applications normally use 8-bit (single-byte) characters that are selected from one of the ANSI code pages: 1250, 1251, 1252, 1253, and 1254. Additional code pages are defined or are in the process of being defined and approved by Microsoft and various national and international standards committees, but only these code pages are currently supported. Each of these code pages contains a maximum of 192 glyphs, including two space characters (one normal and the other a nonbreaking space used for text control and layout).

1250	Central European
1251	Cyrillic
1252	Western European
1253	Greek
1254	Turkish

Each code page contains the U.S. ASCII character set in code points 32 through 127 (decimal) and additional alphabetic characters and punctuation in the "high ASCII" range from 128 through 255. A number of characters in this range—such as the nonbreaking space, bullets, and smart quotes—are common to all of the code pages because various applications (such as Microsoft Word) assume they are at fixed code points. Earlier, in the section "Win32 Character Sets," you saw the layout for 1252, the so-called Western European code page.

Each of these code pages was derived from the famous ISO-8859 standard. For example, 1252 contains the well-known 8859-1(Latin I) standard as a subset. Similarly, 1254 is a superset of ISO-8859-9. Others, however, have been modified not only by additions but with some shifting of code points.

Although a Windows 95 application mainly uses only one 8-bit character set (such as one of the code pages just mentioned, or a special symbol set), a mechanism has been provided for using fonts that contain characters for all five of the code pages. These are special TrueType fonts, called *WGL4 fonts* by Microsoft, which use an expanded "PanEuropean" character set containing all the characters needed for these code pages. These fonts are actually Unicode fonts that have been marked to indicate which of the code pages are supported.

438

When WGL4 fonts are installed, they appear in the font selection dialog box of some word processors (such as Word for Windows 6.0), showing all the supported code pages of the fonts. For example, if a font supports code pages 1251 and 1252 (at least), and code page support for code page 1251 as well as the Western character set (code page 1252 or ANSI) has been installed, Times New Roman will appear in a font-selection list box as both "Times New Roman" and "Times New Roman Cyrillic." (In the case of Word 6.0 and other word processors written explicitly for Windows 3.1, it is necessary to select the keyboard independently of the font.) Figure 14.12 shows how the code-page variants for the New Times Roman font appear in the font-section combo box of Word for Windows.

However, in the case of word processors written with Windows 95 in mind (such as the WordPad applet provided with Windows 95), font code page selection is automatic when a keyboard selection is made if the current font is a WGL4 font. Thus, if a user has selected the Times New Roman (Western) font in WordPad and switches to a Russian keyboard layout with a hotkey, the font selection will change to Times New Roman (Cyrillic). (Note that the Western font is displayed a bit differently in the selection list box in WordPad.) In this case, a single hotkey changes both the keyboard layout and the font. An example of this is shown in Figure 14.13.

FIGURE 14.12.

Selection of Cyrillic font in Word for Windows.

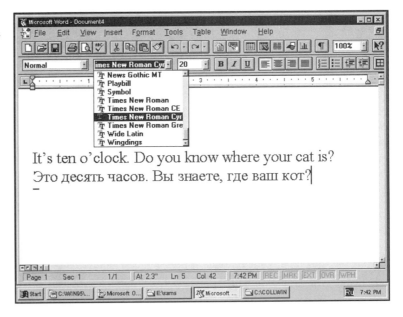

FIGURE 14.13.

Font codepage automatically selected in WordPad.

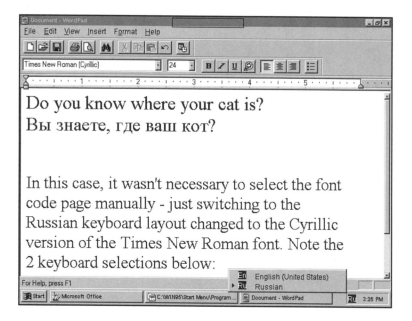

A number of sets of TrueType and Type 1 Postscript fonts are available from various vendors, which support the Cyrillic, Central European, Greek, or Turkish code pages. These existing fonts are 192-character fonts with the supported code page mapped from ASCII 32 decimal (space) through 255, and they are not marked (generally) as supporting any code page other than 1252. In this case, it is necessary to manually select the font as well as the keyboard layout when changing code pages. Thus, if one is using a Casady & Greene VremyaFWF font for Russian and a compatible Times font for French, it is necessary to explicitly select both the font and the keyboard layout when changing between the two languages.

WGL4 Information: Program Sample

The following DOS program provides an example of how to access the bit tables in the OS/2 table of a TrueType font in order to mark it as a WGL4 font for Windows 95. The program reads the header of the file, searches for the OS/2 table, reads the entire OS/2 table, and displays the bit table fields in it to indicate which Windows and MS-DOS (or IBM) code pages and which Unicode ranges are supported by the font. Note the somewhat peculiar bit ordering in the bit tables: in each doubleword, the bytes are numbered starting with the high-order byte ("big-endian"), but the bits are numbered starting with the low-order bit ("little-endian") in the specification. The Microsoft specification isn't too clear about this bit ordering, but the following program makes it clear that this is the format. The table is designated the "OS/2 Table" for historical reasons.

For font vendors who want to use existing font editors (such as Macromedia's Fontographer for Windows) to create WGL4 fonts for Windows 95, it is necessary to write a utility to set the code page and Unicode range bits in their fonts in order to indicate what their fonts support. This program should make the method of addressing these bits clear to the programmer.

```c
// READTT.C ======================================================
//
// This DOS program reads the header of a Microsoft TrueType
// file, and determines what code pages and Unicode character
// ranges it supports.
//
// This program is based on information in the Microsoft
// TrueType file spec, version 1.0, from the Microsoft Develop-
// ment library CDROM.
//
// Note that the Microsoft bit numbering with bytes is
// backwards for 'big-endian' byte and bit numbering, which
// makes the documentation confusing! Bytes are numbered left
// to right in a word or doubleword, but bits are numbered
// right to left (low-order bit is 0).
//
// Written by Peter L. Belew, Analy Branciforte & Co.
//   email: peterbe@netcom.com
//
// ==============================================================

#include <stdio.h>
#include <fcntl.h>
#include <sys\stat.h>
#include <io.h>
#include <string.h>

#define ULONG        unsigned long
#define USHORT       unsigned short int
#define SHORT        short int
#define UINT         unsigned short int

// swapping routines to make big-endian numbers little-endian

USHORT swapbytes( USHORT u );
ULONG revbytes( ULONG u );

// other subroutines
void DisplayCodepages();
void DisplayUnicoderanges();

// structure for the OS/2 table:

static struct _os2 {
        USHORT      version;
        SHORT       xAvgCharWidth;
        USHORT      usWeightClass;
        USHORT      usWidthClass;
        SHORT       fsType;
        SHORT       ySubscriptXSize;
        SHORT       ySubscriptYSize;
```

```
        SHORT       ySubscriptXOffset;
        SHORT       ySubscriptYOffset;
        SHORT       ySuperscriptXSize;
        SHORT       ySuperscriptYSize;
        SHORT       ySuperscriptXOffset;
        SHORT       ySuperscriptYOffset;
        SHORT       yStrikeoutSize;
        SHORT       yStrikeoutPosition;
        SHORT       sFamilyClass;
        char        panose[10];
        ULONG       ulUnicodeRange[4];   // interesting stuff
        char        achVendID[4];              // 4-character vendor ID
        USHORT      fsSelection;
        USHORT      usFirstCharIndex;
        USHORT      usLastCharIndex;
        USHORT      sTypoAscender;
        USHORT      sTypoDescender;
        USHORT      sTypoLineGap;
        USHORT      usWinAscent;
        USHORT      usWinDescent;
        ULONG       ulCodePageRange[2]; // code page flags
    } os2;


// code starts here ...
void main( int argc, char * argv[] )
{
int fh;
int len;
ULONG offset;
USHORT i;
int numTables;

// A TrueType file begins with this header ...

struct _directory {
    ULONG           version;
    USHORT          numTables;
    USHORT          searchRange;
    USHORT          entrySelector;
    USHORT          rangeShift;
    } directory;

// followed by numTable Table Directory entries:

struct _tabdir {
    char  tag[4];           // 4-byte tag
    ULONG checkSum;         //
    ULONG offset;           // file offset of table
    ULONG length;
} tabdir;

// CODE:

// check argument count

if (argc != 2)
    {
```

```
    printf( "\nUsage:\n\treadtt <file>\n" );
    exit( 1 );
    }

// open file.

fh = _open( argv[1], _O_RDONLY );
if (fh < 0)
    {
    printf( "\nFile %s not found", argv[1] );
    exit( 2 );
    }

// read in TrueType file directory

len = _read( fh, & directory, sizeof (directory) );

if ( ( len < sizeof (directory) ) ||
        ( directory.version != 0x00000101 ) )
    {
    printf("\nFile %s is not a version 1.0 TT file",
                argv[1] );
    _close( fh );
    exit( 3 );
    }

// find the OS/2 table directory entry; read table
// directory entries till we find it.

numTables = swapbytes( directory.numTables );

offset = 0l;
for (i = 0; i < numTables; i++)
    {
    // read a table directory entry
    len = _read( fh, & tabdir, sizeof( tabdir ));
    if ( len < sizeof( tabdir ) )
        {
        printf("\nIllegal table directory entry");
        _close( fh );
        exit( 4 );
        }

    if ( 0 == strncmp( "OS/2", tabdir.tag, 4 ) )
        {
        offset = revbytes (tabdir.offset);
        break;
        }
    }

if ( 0l == offset )
    {
    printf("\nNo OS/2 table in TT file.");
    _close( fh );
    exit( 5 );
    }

// seek to the offset we found, and read in the OS/2 header:
```

```
if ( offset != _lseek( fh, offset, SEEK_SET ) )
    {
    printf("\nCan't seek to OS/2 header");
    _close( fh );
    exit( 5 );
    }

len = _read( fh, & os2, sizeof( os2 ));
if ( len != sizeof( os2 ))
    {
    printf("\nCan't read all of OS/2 header");
    _close( fh );
    exit( 6 );
    }


// display the filename and font foundry ID:

{
char szbuf[5];

printf("\nTrueType font: %s", argv[1] );
strncpy( szbuf, os2.achVendID, 4 );
szbuf[4] = '\0';
printf("\nFont version = %d, vendor ID is <%s> ",
        swapbytes( os2.version ), szbuf );
}

// Show which codepages are supported.
DisplayCodepages();

// Show which Unicode ranges are supported.
DisplayUnicoderanges();

// finally, close the file

_close( fh );

printf("\n");

} // main()


// various subroutines

// swap bytes of a USHORT:

USHORT swapbytes( USHORT u )
{
char c;
union
    {
        USHORT              u;
        struct {
            char  lo;
            char  hi;
        } b;
    } un;
```

```
un.u = u;
c = un.b.lo;
un.b.lo = un.b.hi;
un.b.hi = c;
return un.u;

} // swapbytes()

// reverse bytes of a ULONG:

ULONG revbytes( ULONG u )
{
char c;
int i;
union
    {
        ULONG    u;
        char     c[4];
    } un;


un.u = u;

for (i = 0; i < 2; i++)
    {
    c = un.c[3 - i];
    un.c[3 - i] = un.c[i];
    un.c[i] = c;
    }
return un.u;

} // revbytes()

static char * pUnicode[128] =
    {
    // 0 - 7
    "Basic Latin", "Latin-1 Supplement",
    "Latin Extended-A", "Latin Extended-B",
    "IPA Extensions", "Spacing Modifier Letters",
    "Combining Diacritical Marks", "Basic Greek",
    // 8 - 15
    "Greek Symbols, Coptic", "Cyrillic",
    "Armenian", "Basic Hebrew",
    "Hebrew Extended (A+B)", "Basic Arabic",
    "Arabic Extended", "Devanagari",
    // 16 - 23
    "Bengali", "Gurmukhi", "Gujarati", "Oriya",
    "Tamil", "Telugu", "Kannada", "Malayalam",
    // 24 - 31
    "Thai", "Lao",
    "Basic Georgian", "Georgian Extended",
    "Hangul Jamo", "Latin Extended Additional",
    "Greek Extended", "General Punctuation",
    // 32 - 39
    "Superscripts & Subscripts", "Currency symbols",
    "Combining Diacritical Marks for Symbols",
    "Letterlike Symbols", "Number forms", "Arrows",
```

```
    "Math. operators", "Miscellaneous Technical",
    // 40 - 47
    "Control Pictures", "OCR",
    "Enclosed Alphanumerics", "Box Drawing",
    "Block Elements", "Geometric shapes",
    "Miscellaneous Symbols", "Dingbats",
    // 48 - 55
    "CJK Symbols and punctuation", "Hiragana",
    "Katakana", "Bopomofo",
    "Hangul Compatibility Jamo", "CJK Misc.",
    "Enclosed CJK Letters and Months",
    "CJK Compatibility",
    // 56 - 63
    "Hangul", "Hangul Supplementary-A",
    "Hangul Supplementary-B", "CJK Unified Ideographs",
    "Private Use Area", "CJK Compatibility Ideographs",
    "Alphabetic Presentation Forms",
    "Arabic Presentation Forms-A",
    // 64 - 71
    "Combining half marks", "CJK Compatibility Forms",
    "Small Form Variants", "Arabic Presentation Forms-B",
    "Halfwidth and Fullwidth Forms", "Specials",
    // The remainder of the SubRanges are reserved for
    // future definition.
    "", "",
    // 72 - 79
    "", "", "?", "", "", "", "", "",
    // 80 - 87
    "", "", "", "", "", "", "", "",
    // 88 - 95
    "", "", "", "", "", "", "", "",
    // 96 - 103
    "", "", "", "", "", "", "", "",
    // 104 - 111
    "", "", "", "", "", "", "", "",
    // 112 - 119
    "", "", "", "", "", "", "", "",
    // 120 - 127
    "", "", "", "", "", "", "", ""
    };

// list of Code pages in order specified by Microsoft
// for ulCodePageRange[] bits. Note comments below
// regarding the zigzag ordering of the bits!
// These code pages include both ANSI Windows code
// pages and OEM (PC) code pages

static char * pCodePage[64] =
    {
    // 0 - 7
    "1252: Latin 1 (ANSI)", "1250: Latin 2, Central Europe",
    "1251: Cyrillic", "1253: Greek", "1254: Turkish",
    "1255: Hebrew", "1256: Arabic", "1257: Windows Baltic",
    // 8 - 15
    "Reserved", "Reserved", "Reserved", "Reserved",
    "Reserved", "Reserved", "Reserved", "Reserved",
    // 16 - 23
    "Reserved", "874: Thai", "932: JIS/Japan",
```

```
            "936: Chinese simplified", "949: Korean Wansung",
            "950: Chinese Traditional", "Reserved", "Reserved",
            // 24 - 31
            "Reserved", "Reserved", "Reserved", "Reserved",
            "Reserved", "Reserved", "Macintosh (Roman)", "Symbol",
            // 32 - 39
            "Reserved (OEM)", "Reserved (OEM)", "Reserved (OEM)",
            "Reserved (OEM)", "Reserved (OEM)", "Reserved (OEM)",
            "Reserved (OEM)", "Reserved (OEM)",
            // 40 - 47
            "Reserved (OEM)", "Reserved (OEM)", "Reserved (OEM)",
            "Reserved (OEM)", "Reserved (OEM)", "Reserved (OEM)",
            "Reserved (OEM)", "Reserved (OEM)",
            // 48 - 55
            "869: IBM Greek", "866: MS-DOS Russian (ALT)",
            "865: MS-DOS Nordic", "864: Arabic",
            "863: MS-DOS Canadian French", "862: Hebrew",
            "861: MS-DOS Icelandic", "860: MS-DOS Portugese",
            // 56 - 63
            "857: IBM Turkish", "855: IBM Cyrillic",
            "852: IBM Latin 2", "775: MS-DOS Baltic",
            "737: Greek (437 G)", "708: Arabic (ASMO 708)",
            "850: WE/Latin 1", "437: IBM USA"
            };

// Display one of the bit tables in the OS/2 table.
// Long words are stored in increasing order.
// Bytes within them are stored in decreasing order
// (big-endian). But bits within the bytes are
// documented as being numbered right-to-left -
// little-endian!  Confused? You won't be after
// reading and understanding this code ...

void DisplayStuff(
        ULONG * pBits,              // OS/2 table
        char ** ppText,             // name array
        int icount )                // no. of ULONGS
{
int i;
int ibit;
ULONG ulmask;
ULONG u;
int iall;

iall = 0;

for ( i = 0; i < icount; i++ )
    {
    // get ULONG from table and reverse its
    // bytes, so it's all 'little-endian':
    u = revbytes( pBits[i] );

    // check the ULONG bit by bit:
    ulmask = 11;
    for ( ibit = 0; ibit < 32; ibit++ )
        {
        if ( ulmask & u )
            {
```

```
            printf( "\n%d\t%s", iall, ppText[iall] );
            }
        ulmask <<= 1;
        iall++;
        }
    }

} // DisplayStuff()

void DisplayCodepages()
{
printf("\n\nCode pages supported\n\n"
        "Bit     Code Page and name\n");

DisplayStuff( os2.ulCodePageRange, pCodePage, 2 );

} // DisplayCodepages()

void DisplayUnicoderanges()
{
printf("\n\nUnicode ranges supported\n\n"
        "Bit     Unicode range\n");
DisplayStuff( os2.ulUnicodeRange, pUnicode, 4 );

} // DisplayUnicoderanges()
```

References

Kano, Nadine. *Developing International Software for Windows 95 and Windows NT.* Redmond, WA: Microsoft Press, 1995.

Hall, W. S. "Adapt Your Program for Worldwide Use with Windows Internationalization Support." *Microsoft Systems Journal,* Vol. 6 No. 6 (1991), pp. 29-58.

Hall, W. S. "Internationalizing Applications," Windows 3.1 Developer's Workshop. Redmond, WA: Microsoft Press, 1993.

InternaX, Windows Internationalization Training Tape, 6 Johnston Way, Scotts Valley, CA, 408-438-2270.

Microsoft Windows International Handbook for Software Design. Redmond, WA: Microsoft Corporation, 1990.

Uren, E.; R. Howard; and T. Perinotti. *An Introduction to Software Internationalization and Localization.* New York: Van Nostrand Reinhold, 1993.

Taylor, D. *Global Software, Developing Applications for the International Market.* New York: Springer-Verlag, 1992.

The Unicode Consortium. *The Unicode Standard: Worldwide Character Encoding, Version 1.0.* Addison-Wesley, Vol. 1, 1991 and Vol. 2, 1992.

IBM Corporation. *National Language Design Guide Series, SE09 8001 - 8004.*

IBM Corporation. *Keys to Sort and Search for Culturally Expected Results.* Denis Garneau, Document Number GG24-3516.

Welch, Kevin P. "What's in There? Windows 3.0 Executable and Resource File Formats Revealed." *Microsoft Systems Journal,* Vol. 6 No. 5, Sep/Oct (1991), pp. 43-74.

Hall, B. "Exploring the Windows INTL Control Panel." Multilingual Computing, January/February, 1994, pp. 14-21.

Richter, J. "Simulating Keyboard Input Between Programs Requires a (Key) Stroke of Genius." *Microsoft Systems Journal,* Vol. 7 No. 8, 1992, pp. 43-58.

Hall, William S. "Internationalization in Windows NT, Part I: Programming with Unicode." *Microsoft Systems Journal,* Vol. 9 No. 6, 1994, pp. 57-71.

Hall, William S. "Internationalization in Windows NT, Part II: Locales, Languages, and Resources." *Microsoft Systems Journal,* Vol. 9, No. 7, 55-74.

The GUI Guide. Redmond, WA: Microsoft Press, 1993.

"TrueType 1.0 Font File Specification, v. 1.65," Microsoft Corporation (available on Microsoft Developer's Network CD-ROM).

Freytag, Asmus and Nadine Kano. "The International Character Set Conundrum: ANSI, Unicode, and Microsoft Windows." *Microsoft Systems Journal,* November 1994.

Freytag, Asmus, and Nadine Kano. "Internationalization of Win32 Software." *Microsoft Systems Journal,* December 1994.

Freytag, Asmus. "Build a Mulltilingual User Interface for your Application with Win32." *Microsoft Systems Journal,* Volume 10, No. 4, 61-80.

Ken Lunde, *Understanding Japanese Information Processing.* Sebastobol: O'Reilly and Associates, 1993.

Sample Programs

The following programs accompany this chapter and can be found on the CD included with this book. Most are completely documented with online help files.

Internat	A Windows NT Unicode/Windows 95 program demonstrating a variety of internationalization features and functions of the Win32 API.
Keymap	A Windows NT Unicode/Windows 95/Win32s/Windows 3.x program that reads and displays a keyboard layout.

Locale   A Windows NT Unicode/Windows 95/Win32s program that
                displays locale information for all supported locales in the Win32
                operating system. Users should have the Lucida Sans Unicode font
                installed for best results.

Hello   A Windows NT program written in C++ that uses multilingual
                resource files to run in three European languages. This program also
                runs in Windows 95 and Windows 3.1 with Win32s installed.

Textw   An example of a Windows 95 program that uses TextOutW.

ReadTT   A DOS program that shows codepage and Unicode-range bits in TT
                font (source included).

ShowTT   A Windows 95 program that shows the codepage and Unicoded-
                range bits in a TT font (source included).

Windows 95 Multimedia Programming

IV

PART

DIBs: High-Performance Bitmaps in Windows 95

15

by Stan Trujillo

IN THIS CHAPTER

DIB stands for *Device Independent Bitmap*, and, coupled with new WIN32 GDI functions, provides programmers with flexibility and performance previously unavailable under Windows. For the first time, Windows bitmap performance rivals that of DOS.

DOS: Dominant Operation System

DOS doesn't really stand for Dominant Operation System, but DOS sure has dominated Windows in the high-performance graphics market. Even after the huge success of Windows, after most word processors, spreadsheets, databases, and desktop publishing software had migrated to Windows, DOS still had all the graphics-intensive software, including games.

Why is this? What is it about DOS that has made it the Dominant Operating System when it comes to high-performance graphics?

DOS has been around for some time and was designed to run on processors that are very slow by today's standards. The PC of the time had at most 640 KB. For these reasons, DOS had to be both efficient and small. Its role was to provide minimal command support and a file system. Essentially, DOS is a thin software layer between the user and the BIOS. It was never intended to buffer developers from video cards, sound cards, and pointing devices.

DOS enabled developers to access video memory, interrupt vectors, and controllers directly. This made for good performance, but also created some problems. The PC industry was being bombarded with add-on cards of all sorts. Each of these new cards had a different interface, and soon developers were spending more time trying to figure out each interface than they were writing applications.

Windows 3.x

When Windows 3.0 came out, developers were ready for an operating system that came with drivers for all of the major devices. Users were ready for multitasking and GUI features. Windows 3.0 was a huge success.

Not everyone was happy, though. The developers who wrote games and animations found that porting their code to Windows meant a stiff drop in performance. The problem was that in order to support the various video cards, Windows used device drivers, and because all of the graphics had to go through these drivers, performance suffered. Although it was true that Windows applications could now use any device that Windows supported, the applications themselves were too slow to be of any use.

Windows 95

What about Windows 95? It also uses video drivers, so performance will still suffer, right? Not really. Microsoft noticed the lack of graphical Windows applications and decided to do something about it. First it released WinG, which enabled developers to get nearly the same performance from Windows 3.1 as they got from DOS. Windows 95 can use WinG too, but that isn't necessary because in Windows 95, WinG is nothing more than a portability layer. That is, in Windows 95, WinG uses functions in the WIN32 API that developers can use directly.

DIBs: Device-Independent Bitmaps

The DIB file format (Device-Independent Bitmap) is the heart of the speedy Windows 95 graphics for two reasons. First, the bitmap data can be accessed directly. This enables developers to write fast, customized drawing routines. Second, the DIB pixels are copied directly to video memory. Older Windows bitmaps are forced to undergo color evaluation routines, which slow each update.

We are going to limit our discussion to 256-color DIBs, but non-256-color DIBs can be converted with Paintbrush. DIB files still have the familiar .BMP extension, so it won't do any good to look for .DIB files.

Primary Components

DIB files contain three main components:

- Header data
- Palette data
- Pixel data

The header data falls into two categories: file data and bitmap data. It is advisable to read the file information, but it is rarely kept in memory. The bitmap information, however, is usually kept in memory along with the palette and pixel data.

The DIB File Format

Figure 15.1 illustrates the DIB file format.

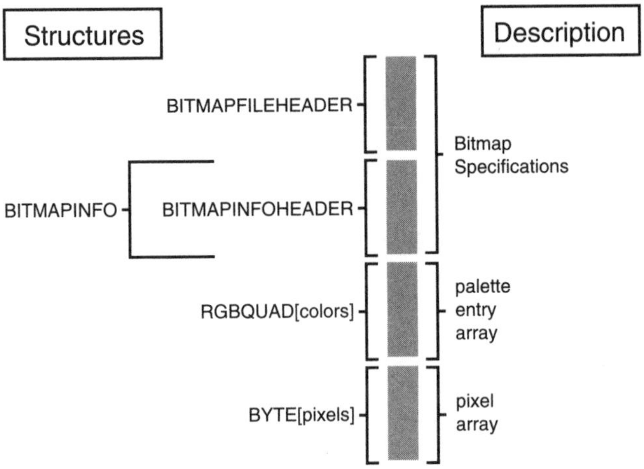

FIGURE 15.1.
The DIB file format.

An interesting facet of this format is that it contains nested structures. For example, the BITMAPINFOHEADER structure is completely contained within the BITMAPINFO structure. It is tempting at first to try to get away with using only one or the other, but that proves to be impractical. Also, the BITMAPINFO structure overlaps slightly into the RGBQUAD array. It isn't clear from looking at the figure, but the first RGBQUAD entry is part of the BITMAPINFO structure.

Another detail is that the image is stored upside down. Later, you take care of this detail by drawing the image starting at the bottom line and proceeding upward.

Let's look at the BITMAPFILEHEADER structure first:

```
typedef struct tagBITMAPFILEHEADER {
        WORD    bfType;
        DWORD   bfSize;
        WORD    bfReserved1;
        WORD    bfReserved2;
        DWORD   bfOffBits;
} BITMAPFILEHEADER, FAR *LPBITMAPFILEHEADER, *PBITMAPFILEHEADER;
```

This portion of the file is not usually kept in memory, but should be examined before reading the rest of the file.

The first field, bfType, contains the ASCII characters "BM" and serves as a file signature. That is, if you are reading a file, and this field does not contain the "BM" signature, the file is not a valid DIB file.

The second field, bfSize, contains the size of the file. This field is not usually used for two reasons: the size of the file can be determined by other means, and the field itself is said to be unreliable due to an error in documentation.

The following two fields, bfReserved1 and bfReserved2, are, as their names imply, not used for anything at this point. Both values should be zero.

Finally, `bfOffBits` is the distance, in bytes, from the `BITMAPFILEHEADER` structure to the bitmap bits, or *pixels*. This field might come in handy if you were interested in only the bitmap pixels and didn't want to read the rest of the data. In practice, however, this detail takes care of itself, because after you have read the two headers and the palette, the file pointer is automatically left at the bitmap data.

Next is the `BITMAPINFOHEADER` structure:

```
typedef struct tagBITMAPINFOHEADER{
        DWORD       biSize;
        LONG        biWidth;
        LONG        biHeight;
        WORD        biPlanes;
        WORD        biBitCount;
        DWORD       biCompression;
        DWORD       biSizeImage;
        LONG        biXPelsPerMeter;
        LONG        biYPelsPerMeter;
        DWORD       biClrUsed;
        DWORD       biClrImportant;
} BITMAPINFOHEADER, FAR *LPBITMAPINFOHEADER, *PBITMAPINFOHEADER;
```

The first field, `biSize`, is the size of the `BITMAPINFOHEADER` structure. This seems rather silly, because the same value can be calculated with the following code:

```
DWORD size=sizeof(BITMAPINFOHEADER);
```

The next two fields, `biWidth` and `biHeight`, are the width and height of the bitmap itself.

The `biPlanes` field is a remnant of the days when file formats stored images in bit planes because it was compatible with the VGA memory format (PCX files store bit planes this way). Because storing bitmaps in planes for the sake of VGA compatibility would violate the device independence of a device-independent bitmap format, this value is always 1.

The `biBitCount` field is the number of bits available to store each pixel. This is important because it determines the maximum number of colors used in the bitmap. Because this discussion is focusing on only 256-color bitmaps, this value should be 8.

The `biCompression` field is usually 0, which means that the bitmap is not compressed. DIBs do come in compressed varieties, but they are rare.

The `biSizeImage` field is the size in bytes of the pixel data. Usually, this field is only used for compressed bitmaps. For uncompressed bitmaps, it is set to zero.

The fields `biXPelsPerMeter` and `biYPelsPerMeter` can contain the horizontal and vertical number of pixels per meter, but both values are usually set to zero.

The `biClrUsed` field is the number of colors that the bitmap uses. Just because a bitmap has 8 bits per pixel doesn't mean that the image uses 256 colors, so `biClrUsed` can be set to a value that is less than the maximum colors possible. This value is often set to zero, but that usually means the bitmap uses all of the possible palette entries, not that the bitmap doesn't use colors.

The last field in the `BITMAPINFOHEADER` is the `biClrImportant` field. This field is meant to store how many of the colors in the bitmap are vital, but is usually set to zero.

Reading DIBs into Memory

Before you write any code to read a DIB into memory, let's talk about your options. You want to examine at least one field in the `BITMAPFILEHEADER` structure, but you won't need to keep it in memory, so it doesn't really matter how you perform the read. The `BITMAPFILEHEADER` structure, on the other hand, will be kept in memory. Because the size of the structure cannot change, you could simply declare an instance of the structure and then fill it with the data you read from a file. Then you could allocate two blocks of memory: one to store the palette data and one to store the actual image bits.

Alternatively, you could calculate the size of each block of data and then allocate one large block that you would then use to store the entire DIB. This second method has some advantages. First, because you are allocating one large block instead of multiple small blocks, you lessen the chance that you will fragment memory. More importantly, however, you need the palette to follow the header in memory, because otherwise your `BITMAPINFO` structure is invalid. Remember, the `BITMAPINFO` structure consists of the entire `BITMAPINFOHEADER` structure, along with the first `RGBQUAD` entry from the palette. If you stored this separately, `CreateDIBSection()`, which takes a pointer to a `BITMAPINFO` structure as a parameter, would be given fallacious palette data.

Now you are ready to write some code. Let's define a class called `CDib`, which will have a member function called `load()`. The load member will read a DIB from a file and store it in a single block of memory. In addition, `CDib` will provide a number of member functions that will return information about the DIB.

`CDib` is defined like this:

```
class CDib : public CObject
{
public:
  CDib(char* fname);
  ~CDib();
  int getx()             { return x; }
  int gety()             { return y; }
  void setxy(int xx,int yy)  { x=xx; y=yy; }
  int getwidth()         { return w; }
  int getheight()        { return h; }
  BITMAPINFOHEADER* getheader()    { return infohdr; }
  BYTE* getbits()        { return pixels; }
  RGBQUAD* getrgbinfo()  { return quads; }
  int getcolors()        { return colors; }
  virtual void draw(BYTE*,CDib*);
protected:
  void load(char*);
private:
```

```
    char* dibdata;
    BITMAPINFOHEADER* infohdr;
    BITMAPINFO* info;
    RGBQUAD* quads;
    BYTE* pixels;
    int colors;
    int w,h;
    int x,y;
};
```

Before you look at the constructor, let's talk about the private data members. You have declared a `char` pointer called `dibdata`, which you will use to point to the block of memory where your DIB is stored. Because this pointer is used to allocate the memory, it becomes a flag that, if set, tells you that you have a DIB in memory. If `dibdata` is equal to 0, no DIB has been loaded. Other member functions will test this member for this reason.

There are four more pointers in CDib: `infohdr`, `info`, `quads`, and `pixels`. Each points to a different type of structure. Figure 15.2 illustrates the purpose of each pointer.

FIGURE 15.2.

The role of the CDib member pointers.

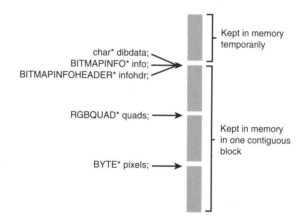

After you get the pointers in CDib to point to their respective sections, you can use the public member functions to retrieve pointers to specific portions of the DIB. According to pure object-oriented design, you shouldn't give the user of the class direct access to the data within. In reality, however, direct access enables users of the class to manipulate the bitmap in memory in the fastest and most flexible manner possible. They can't corrupt your pointers, as they are private, but they can easily corrupt the data to which the pointers point. This is a risk you are willing to take here for the sake of performance.

The rest of the CDib data members are integers that you will use to store basic information about the bitmap. The width, height, and number of colors, for example, are stored in private data members. Also, the `x` and `y` data members store the location of the bitmap within the application window.

The CDib constructor looks like this:

```
CDib::CDib(char* fname)
{
  dibdata=0;
  x=0,y=0;
  load(fname);
}
```

It is important that you initialize the dibdata member, because load() is going to assume that if it is not set to 0, it points at a bitmap already, and that the first bitmap should be deleted before another one is loaded. The x and y data members are initialized too, in case the user of the class draws the DIB without first assigning a location with a call to setxy(). The last thing that the constructor does is call load(), which is defined like this:

```
BOOL CDib::load(char* filename)
{
  TRACE("CDib::load(%s)\n",filename);
  delete dibdata; dibdata=0;

  BITMAPFILEHEADER tmpfilehdr;
  BITMAPINFOHEADER tmpinfohdr;
  ifstream bmpfile(filename,ios::binary);
  if (!bmpfile.is_open())
    throw NoSuchFile();
  bmpfile.read((char*)&tmpfilehdr,sizeof(tmpfilehdr));
  bmpfile.read((char*)&tmpinfohdr,sizeof(tmpinfohdr));

  char* ptr=(char*)&tmpfilehdr.bfType;
  if (*ptr!='B' || *++ptr!='M')
    throw InvalidDIBFile();

  if (tmpinfohdr.biBitCount!=8)
    throw Not256ColorDIB();

  if (tmpinfohdr.biClrUsed==0)
    colors=(1<<tmpinfohdr.biBitCount);
  else
    colors=tmpinfohdr.biClrUsed;

  int colorbytes=sizeof(RGBQUAD)*colors;
  int pixelbytes=((tmpinfohdr.biWidth+3)&~3)*tmpinfohdr.biHeight;
  int totalbytes=sizeof(BITMAPINFOHEADER)+colorbytes+pixelbytes;

  dibdata=new char[totalbytes];
  infohdr=(BITMAPINFOHEADER*)dibdata;
  info=(BITMAPINFO*)dibdata;
  quads=(RGBQUAD*)(dibdata+sizeof(BITMAPINFOHEADER));
  pixels=(BYTE*)quads+colorbytes;

  memcpy(infohdr,&tmpinfohdr,sizeof(tmpinfohdr));
  bmpfile.read((char*)quads,colorbytes);
  bmpfile.read((char*)pixels,pixelbytes);
  return 1;
}
```

There are several features about `load()` that you need to examine. The first line is a TRACE macro. The messages sent to TRACE appear in the output window of the debugger, and can be an essential part of debugging. Each TRACE macro is removed by the preprocessor when you compile a release version of the program, so there is no performance loss.

The next line passes `dibdata` to the `delete` operator. Notice that you don't check the value of `dibdata` before you call `delete`. It doesn't hurt to check, but it is unnecessary because `delete` checks the value, and ignores values of 0. As long as you assign 0 to `dibdata` when it is not in use, you're safe. For that reason, you assign it to zero immediately after you call `delete`.

Next you declare two local, and therefore temporary, structures, one of type `BITMAPFILEHEADER` and the other of type `BITMAPINFOHEADER`, which you then use to read in the header data from the file. The next step is to check the file signature. If the test fails, throw an `InvalidDIBFile` exception; otherwise, move on to check the bits per pixel. Throw a `Not256ColorDIB` exception if the `biBitCount` field is not set to 8. These exceptions are empty classes that you have defined in `stdafx.h`.

You determine the number of colors used by first checking the `biClrUsed` field. If it is set, use it; but otherwise assume that the DIB uses the maximum number of colors as determined by the `biBitCount` field. The reason you are concerned about the number of colors is because you need to know how many `RGBQUAD` structures to expect in the file.

The next step is to determine the size of the block needed to store the entire DIB. This is calculated by taking the sum of the size of the palette, the size of the pixel data, and the size of the `BITMAPINFOHEADER` structure. The `totalbytes` variable is used to store the result.

The rest is simple. Allocate the memory using `new`, and assign the pointers to point at the locations discussed previously. You then copy the `BITMAPINFOHEADER` structure from the temporary structure to the new memory block and read in the rest of the file. The file is closed automatically when the function ends, because the `ifstream` object was local to the `load()` function.

The `draw()` member function requires explanation as well, but I'll put that off until the section on animation.

Palettes

Programming for Windows should mean that things get simpler. It should mean that Microsoft has taken care of the details, and that you can get to work. For example, you don't need to worry about the keyboard or the mouse; you just let Windows notify you if a key has been pressed or if the mouse has been moved. Unfortunately, some things get worse. Because Windows supplies so much functionality, it can often get in your way. Managing the palette is one area that gets more complicated in Windows, but, as usual, there are ways to solve the problems that arise.

The Theory

A *palette* is a collection of colors you use to create or display an image. The reason it exists is because the VGA card, and other palletized display adapters, can display virtually any color, but only 256 at a time. In other words, the card can display 256 colors, each of which can be virtually any color. Your task is to install the colors you need into the VGA palette, so that your bitmaps appear as they are intended.

In DOS, this was fairly easy, because you had complete access to the palette. You could assign each palette entry to an RGB (red, green, blue) combination, and trust that the VGA card would display it when you assigned to a pixel the value associated with the palette entry. In Windows, it's not that simple.

The Windows Palette Manager

There are two reasons that palettes are more trouble in Windows than they are in DOS. First, Windows reserves 20 colors for itself. Although you are in 256-color mode, you can only pick and choose 236 of those colors. Second, Windows examines the palettes you install, and in some cases rearranges or removes colors.

In WIN32s, this was a serious problem, because to get the best performance out of Windows you had to ensure the system palette and the palette in your bitmap were identical. If they were, Windows could copy the bitmap pixels straight to video memory, without first examining each pixel value to determine the best color match.

New functions have been added to the WIN32 GDI that ensure the best performance and free you from worrying about whether the DIB palette and the system palette are identical.

What All of This Means to You

It isn't entirely true that palette management is more difficult in Windows than in DOS. MFC provides a `CPalette` class, which doesn't do everything you need but is quite useful. You will create a new class derived from `CPalette` and call it `CDibPalette`. `CDibPalette` is defined like this:

```
class CDibPalette : public CPalette
{
public:
  CDibPalette(CDib*);
};
```

Obviously `CDibPalette` is a simple class. In fact, it has no data members. The constructor looks like this:

```
CDibPalette::CDibPalette(CDib* dib)
{
  int colors=dib->getcolors();
  if (colors==0)  return;

  RGBQUAD* rgbquad=dib->getrgbinfo();

  LOGPALETTE* logpal=(LOGPALETTE*)
      new char[sizeof(LOGPALETTE)+sizeof(PALETTEENTRY)*colors];
  logpal->palVersion=0x300;
  logpal->palNumEntries=(WORD)colors;
  for (int i=0;i<colors;i++)
    {
    logpal->palPalEntry[i].peRed  =rgbquad[i].rgbRed;
    logpal->palPalEntry[i].peGreen=rgbquad[i].rgbGreen;
    logpal->palPalEntry[i].peBlue =rgbquad[i].rgbBlue;
    logpal->palPalEntry[i].peFlags=0;
    }
  CreatePalette(logpal);
  delete logpal;
}
```

Using a pointer to an instance of CDib, CDibPalette first gets the number of colors in the DIB. If this value is zero, constructing a palette makes little sense, so the constructor returns. Next a pointer to the RGBQUAD structures is acquired and used to construct a structure of type LOGPALETTE. The LOGPALETTE structure is followed in memory by a number of PALETTEENTRY structures, one for each color found in the DIB palette. The LOGPALETTE structure is recognized by CPalette, so this temporary structure is passed to CreatePalette() and then to the delete operator. At this point, your class is ready for use.

The ShowDIB Demo

Now that you have the DIB and its palette nicely wrapped up in classes, you can write a simple application. ShowDIB is a simple DIB viewer that is included on the CD-ROM along with the source code and project files.

The Application Architecture

Before you can write any code, you need to think about your design. You want an application architecture that will help you divide the code into logical components. Let's review MFC application architecture.

MFC provides support for applications that read, modify, and save documents. There are two types of MFC document-processing applications; *Single-Document Interface* (SDI) and *Multiple-Document Interface* (MDI). Figure 15.3 shows the two application architectures.

FIGURE 15.3.
The MFC application architectures.

SDI
single-document interface

MDI
multiple-document interface

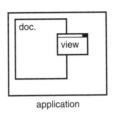

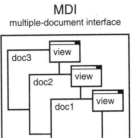

SDI applications can manipulate one document at a time, whereas MDI applications can handle more than one at a time. In either case, the CDocument class provides a basis for user-defined document classes, which, among other things, are responsible for reading and writing the document format in question. The CView class provides support for displaying the document in a window and interpreting the user's actions into commands that are meaningful to the document class.

The documents supported by a CDocument derived class can be of any type. Most frequently, the documents are textual, but there is no reason they can't be graphical documents. You can create a CDocument derived class to read your DIB into memory, and a CView derived class to display it on the screen. Your classes won't provide support for modifying or saving DIBs, because after all, ShowDIB is only a DIB viewer. Figure 15.4 illustrates the ShowDIB architecture.

FIGURE 15.4.
The ShowDIB application architecture.

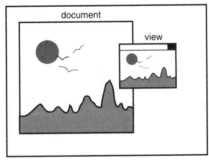

The *CDibDoc* Class

You've defined a DIB class already, and you'll use it for the second application, but for ShowDIB, you'll build the DIB support right into the document class. You'll call it CDibDoc, and it is defined like this:

```
class CDibDoc : public CDocument
{
protected:
  CDibDoc();
  DECLARE_DYNCREATE(CDibDoc)
public:
  int getwidth()      { return infohdr->biWidth; }
  int getheight()     { return infohdr->biHeight; }
  BITMAPINFOHEADER* getheader()     { return infohdr; }
  BYTE* getbits()     { return pixels; }
  int getcolors()     { return colors; }
  RGBQUAD* getrgbinfo()  { return quads; }
  Palette* getpalette()  { return palette; }
public:
  virtual BOOL OnOpenDocument(LPCTSTR lpszPathName);
  virtual ~CDibDoc();
protected:
  DECLARE_MESSAGE_MAP()
private:
  BOOL load(LPCTSTR);
private:
  char* dibdata;
  int colors;
  BITMAPINFOHEADER* infohdr;
  BITMAPINFO* info;
  RGBQUAD* quads;
  BYTE* pixels;
  Palette* palette;
};
```

Portions of the listing have been removed, such as the comments that Visual C++ adds for its own bookkeeping. Aside from some extra functions and macros, CDibDoc looks a lot like CDib. One difference is the OnOpenDocument() member function, which is called automatically by MFC whenever the user has selected a new filename.

The CDibDoc constructor looks like this:

```
CDibDoc::CDibDoc()
{
  dibdata=0;
  palette=0;
}
```

This is similar to the CDib constructor, except this one does not call the load() member function. That brings up an interesting issue. In SDI (single-document interface) applications, the document class is recycled. That is, MFC creates one instance of the document class, and that same object exists until the program is terminated. This means that you need to be able to restore your class to a state in which it is safe to read another DIB. If this were an MDI application, your document class would be created when a document was opened, and be destroyed as soon as the document was closed.

The constructor initializes CDibDoc so that the class is empty upon construction. Only after the user chooses File|Open from the menu and selects a filename will CDibDoc load a DIB. The OnOpenDocument() member function looks like this:

```
BOOL CDibDoc::OnOpenDocument(LPCTSTR lpszPathName)
{
  int ok=load(lpszPathName);
  POSITION first=GetFirstViewPosition();
  CDibView* view=(CDibView*)GetNextView(first);
  if (ok)
    view->update(this);
  else
    view->update(0);
  return TRUE;
}
```

MFC sends you the name of the file via the `lpszPathName` parameter, after which you simply call `load()` and save the outcome in `ok`. You then retrieve a pointer to the view class and notify the view that a change has occurred. (Sending zero to the view is a way of saying that something went wrong.) Finally you return `TRUE`, which tells MFC to notify the view to redraw itself. Even if the load failed, you want the view to redraw, because otherwise it might continue to display a previous bitmap.

The `load()` member function itself is the same as `CDib::load()`, which you learned about earlier.

The *CDibView* Class

From looking at the `CDibDoc::OnOpenDocument()` function, you already know a little about `CDibView`. You know that it has a member function called `update()` and that it is responsible for actually displaying the bitmap. `CDibView` looks like this:

```
class CDibView : public CView
{
protected:
  CDibView();
  DECLARE_DYNCREATE(CDibView)
public:
  CDibDoc* GetDocument();
  void update(CDibDoc* doc);
virtual void OnDraw(CDC* pDC);
public:
  virtual ~CDibView();
protected:
  afx_msg void OnPaletteChanged(CWnd* pFocusWnd);
  afx_msg BOOL OnQueryNewPalette();
  DECLARE_MESSAGE_MAP()
private:
  char* dibdata;
  BITMAPINFOHEADER* infohdr;
  BITMAPINFO* info;
  WORD* palette;
  BYTE* pixels;
  HBITMAP section;
  int width,height;
};
```

Again, this is a simplified version. The ClassWizard comments and debugging functions have been removed for readability.

The private data member section at the bottom of the definition looks much like the CDib and CDibDoc classes. The similarities are due to the fact that CDibView must create its own special DIB that it will use to copy to video memory. One difference is that instead of a pointer to the RGBQUAD structure, as with CDib and CDibDoc, CDibView has a pointer to the type WORD. This is because the palette of this DIB serves a different purpose than before. Instead of storing an array of RGB values, an identity palette is created that uses indexes instead of color values.

Another difference is the section data member, which is declared to be of type HBITMAP. You use this to store a handle to the DIB that CDibView will create.

The CDibView class definition looks like this:

```
void CDibView::update(CDibDoc* dib)
{
  delete dibdata;        dibdata=0;
  DeleteObject(section);  section=0;
  if (dib==NULL)  return;

  width=dib->getwidth();
  height=dib->getheight();
  int totalbytes=sizeof(BITMAPINFOHEADER)+sizeof(WORD)*256;

  dibdata=new char[totalbytes];
  infohdr=(BITMAPINFOHEADER*)dibdata;
  info=(BITMAPINFO*)dibdata;
  palette=(WORD*)(dibdata+sizeof(BITMAPINFOHEADER));

  memcpy(dibdata,dib->getheader(),sizeof(BITMAPINFOHEADER));
  info->bmiHeader.biClrUsed=0;

  for (WORD i=0;i<256;i++)
    palette[i]=i;

  CDibPalette* pal=dib->getpalette();
  CDC* dc=GetDC();
  CPalette* oldpal=dc->SelectPalette((CPalette*)pal,FALSE);
  dc->RealizePalette();
  section=CreateDIBSection(dc->GetSafeHdc(),
               info,DIB_PAL_COLORS,(VOID**)&pixels,0,0);
  dc->SelectPalette(oldpal,FALSE);
  ReleaseDC(dc);

  int pixelbytes=((width+3)&~3)*height;
  memcpy(pixels,dib->getbits(),pixelbytes);
}
```

Bear in mind that this member function is called whenever the CDibDoc class loads a new DIB. A pointer to the CDibDoc class is provided as a parameter. In the first two lines you are initializing the new section data member along with the familiar dibdata member. You then check the dib parameter. If it is NULL, the function returns.

Next you determine the dimensions of the new DIB with calls to getwidth() and getheight(). Store these values in the width and height data members.

You then calculate the size of part of a new DIB. Unlike CDibDoc, however, you are using WORD-sized palette entries, and you are not including the pixel data in your calculation because the memory for the pixel data will be supplied by the CreateDIBSection() function.

Your next move is to allocate the memory and assign the pointers in a manner that is similar to the procedure illustrated in Figure 15.2, except that you don't have any pixel data yet. Then you duplicate the BITMAPINFOHEADER portion of the newly loaded DIB, and force the biClrUsed field to 0. Next you create the identity palette, which is simply a list of WORD-sized integers, ranging in value from 0 to 255.

The next step is to acquire a pointer to the DIB's CDibPalette object and create a device context. You then select the palette into the device context and realize it, causing Windows to install the new palette. The next call is to CreateDIBSection(), which creates the DIB. CreateDIBSection() returns a handle to the new DIB and assigns the pixel argument to point at the bits that it will allocate. This new DIB can be written to with the traditional GDI routines via its handle, but also provides direct image access.

Select the old palette and release the device context. The last step is to copy the pixels from the DIB that were loaded by CDibDoc into the memory allocated by CreateDIBSection(). Now you are free to copy the new DIB to the screen. This is the job of CDibView::OnDraw(), which looks like this:

```
void CDibView::OnDraw(CDC*)
{
  if (!dibdata)  return;

  CClientDC dc(this);

  CDibDoc* doc=GetDocument();
  CDibPalette* pal=doc->getpalette();
  CPalette* oldpal=dc.SelectPalette((CPalette*)pal,FALSE);
  dc.RealizePalette();

  HDC dcmem=CreateCompatibleDC(dc.GetSafeHdc());
  HBITMAP old=(HBITMAP)SelectObject(dcmem,section);
  BitBlt(dc.GetSafeHdc(),0,0,width,height,dcmem,0,0,SRCCOPY);
  SelectObject(dcmem,old);
  DeleteDC(dcmem);

  dc.SelectPalette(oldpal,FALSE);
}
```

The first line checks if dibdata points to a DIB. If not, there is no bitmap to display, so the function returns. You then create a client device context, which will enable you to draw to the client area of the window. You acquire pointers to both the CDibDoc object and the CDibPalette object. As before, you select and realize the DIB palette. This ensures the system palette is compatible with the pixels you are about to display.

You then create a memory device context that is compatible with the client device context and select your section handle into it using the SelectObject() function. Then, using the BitBlt() function, you copy the DIB to video memory. BitBlt() copies the bitmap from the memory device context to the client area of the window. It is at this point that the DIB actually becomes visual on the screen. After that, you restore the state of the memory device context before deleting it. Finally, you select the old palette. The client device context is deleted automatically when the function returns.

Now you have a bitmap on the screen, in all the right colors, but you aren't quite finished. The DIB will display correctly, but several things could go wrong. What if, for example, you run another program next to ShowDIB, and the new application installs its own palette? How would your DIB look then? Not very good, because your bitmap won't be aware of the new palette. In reality, should this situation arise, your DIB is simply not going to look as good as it does with its own palette. But it will look terrible if you don't attempt to use the new palette.

When an application makes a palette change, Windows notifies other applications by sending messages. Your view responds to two such messages, with messages handlers that look like this:

```
void CDibView::OnPaletteChanged(CWnd* pFocusWnd)
{
  CView::OnPaletteChanged(pFocusWnd);
  if (pFocusWnd!=this)
  {
    CDC* pdc=GetDC();
    CDibDoc* pDoc=GetDocument();
    CPalette* poldpal=pdc->SelectPalette((CPalette*)pDoc->getpalette(),TRUE);
    pdc->RealizePalette();
    pdc->SelectPalette(poldpal, TRUE);
    pdc->RealizePalette();
    ReleaseDC(pdc);
    InvalidateRect(NULL, TRUE);
  }
}

BOOL CDibView::OnQueryNewPalette()
{
  CDC* pdc=GetDC();
  CDibDoc* pDoc=GetDocument();
  CPalette* poldpal=pdc->SelectPalette((CPalette*)pDoc->getpalette(),FALSE);
  UINT num_changes = pdc->RealizePalette();
  pdc->SelectPalette(poldpal, TRUE);
  pdc->RealizePalette();
  ReleaseDC(pdc);
  if (num_changes>0)
    InvalidateRect(NULL, TRUE);
  return (BOOL)num_changes;
}
```

If the application is in the background (if it does not have the input focus) and the palette changes, the bitmap is redrawn to conform to the new palette. Chances are the image won't look as good as it did before, but at least it won't look bizarre. If the application is in the foreground, its own palette will be installed and the bitmap will appear correctly.

The ShowDIB demo is on the CD-ROM. Try running two instances of ShowDIB and loading a different DIB into each. Unless the foreground image only uses colors reserved by Windows, the background image will look rough. Try commenting out one or both of the palette message handlers and performing the same test, and try this with other parts of the demo as well. This is a great way to learn about the purpose of each component.

Animation Techniques

High-performance graphics aren't very exciting without animation. Sure, your ShowDIB viewer is fast, but who cares? As long as it reads and displays the DIB in reasonable time, speed isn't an issue for a bitmap viewer. The next demo, AnimDIB, contains animation, and provides a much better idea of how fast DIBs are.

Types of Animation

Before you can write an animation demo, you need to learn a bit about animation itself. There are several different forms of animation, and they generally fall into one of the following two categories:

- Frame-based
- Sprite-based

Frame animation is familiar to most computer users in the form of video, which is usually stored in .FLI or .FLC files. Video is the mainstay of multimedia and can be used in games, but it has a serious drawback. Each frame of a video clip must be known in advance. This means that video can't be truly interactive.

Most video games employ sprite-based animation. A *sprite* is a shape that moves across a complex background without disturbing it. Sprite-based animation is more flexible than frame-based animation because each scene is constructed at runtime.

A number of games combine the two techniques—that is, a simple game is played on top of a video clip. This sounds silly, but the effect is impressive. Usually, the video is a quickly moving terrain. The game player tries to hit targets that are superimposed over the landscape. Of course, the scenery is the same each time you play the game. Some games let you decide between two paths at a specific point. This is implemented by starting one of two video clips depending on the user's choice.

You'll be implementing sprite-based animation in the AnimDIB demo.

Sprite-Based Animation

There are many different approaches to sprite-based animation. Some computers have hardware support for sprites, which makes animation as simple as loading the sprite and telling it where to go. The PC does not provide hardware support, so you have to write your own. There are many specific techniques for sprite animation, and no one technique is the best. Each has its strengths and limitations. Most approaches take steps to reduce flicker and optimize screen updates, so let's start there.

If you write code that draws a sprite on the screen and then erases it (by drawing the section of background that it covered), and then draws the sprite at a new location, you will discover that the sprite flickers and appears to be translucent, like a ghost. This is because for the brief period of time after the sprite has been erased and before it has been replaced, it is not on the screen at all. The only way to eliminate this effect is to prepare each scene in an off-screen buffer. The screen is then updated by copying portions of the buffer to video memory. In other words, the sprite must appear on the screen in some form at all times. Repairing the background can only be done off-screen.

Another issue involves optimization. Animation itself is very simple, but without optimization, performance is unacceptable. The following steps represent a brute-force (and easy to implement) form of animation:

1. Draw the entire background in an off-screen buffer.
2. Draw all of the sprites into the buffer.
3. Copy the entire off-screen buffer to the screen.
4. Repeat steps 1, 2, and 3.

This technique works—there is no sprite flicker—but it is slow because so much unnecessary work is being done. For example, why draw the whole background in step 1? Why not just draw the sections of the background that have been corrupted by sprites? Why copy the entire off-screen buffer to the screen in step 3? Again, only the areas affected by the sprites need to be copied.

There are some subtle details. For example, when you are copying the regions from the off-screen buffer to the screen, which regions should you copy? The areas where the sprite is now, or the area where the sprite used to be? If you only copy the area where the sprite is now, it will appear on the screen at its new location, but you can't be guaranteed that the old location will be completely erased. On the other hand, if you only copy the old area, the old instance will be erased but only a portion, if any, of the new instance will appear.

Clearly, you have to copy both areas to the screen. You could do this either by copying one area and then the other, or by taking the union of the area. That is, by calculating the smallest rectangle that contains both the old location and the new location, and copying it instead, you can save yourself one whole update. This technique assumes that you won't be drawing a sprite first on the left side of the screen and then, on the next update, on the right side of the screen. If you do, performance will degrade because you will be copying many more pixels than you need. As a sprite typically only moves a few pixels on each update, this optimization works well.

Buffered Output

Now turn your attention to the memory requirements of an application that performs animation. It is clear that you need an off-screen buffer. Its size will decide how much screen area you can animate. You also need a buffer to store your background image. This buffer will store a clean copy of the background at all times. Memory to store your sprites is also needed. Figure 15.5 illustrates the memory requirements.

FIGURE 15.5.

The ShowDIB memory requirements.

sprites

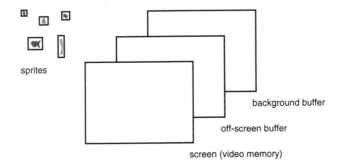

background buffer

off-screen buffer

screen (video memory)

The frontmost buffer is the actual screen. This isn't memory that you need to allocate because it exists on the video card. In this sense, it is not part of your application, but conceptually it is a memory buffer and has a place in your figure. Of course, the actual memory requirements depend on the number of sprites and the size of each DIB.

You already have a class called CDib, which you can use for your background buffer. You can also use it as a base class for your new sprite class, CSprite. You'll handle the off-screen buffer a little differently, storing it in a class you'll call CAnimWindow, which is a CView derivative. CAnimWindow will have the ability to write directly to video memory, as your CDibView class did in ShowDIB. Unlike CDibView, however, it needs the ability to write specific sub-rectangles to the screen.

Transparency

Up to this point, you have been avoiding the important issue of transparency. Sprites, because they are DIBs, are rectangular, but you don't want to animate a bunch of rectangles. You want to animate irregular, complicated sprites. To do this, you need a way to make parts of each sprite transparent. This way, only part of the sprite's rectangular region will appear when it is drawn.

Early in this chapter, you were promised a discussion of CDib::draw(). Because transparency is supported in Cdib::draw(), we'll discuss it now. The code is as follows:

```
void CDib::draw(BYTE* buffer,CDib* dib)
{
  int bw=dib->getwidth();
  int bh=dib->getheight();
  int w=infohdr->biWidth;
  int h=infohdr->biHeight;

  BYTE* ptr=buffer+bw*(bh-y-h)+x;
  BYTE transclr=*pixels;
  for (int i=0;i<h;i++)
    for (int j=0;j<w;j++)
    {
      BYTE clr=*(pixels+w*i+j);
      if (clr!=transclr)
      *(ptr+bw*i+j)=clr;
    }
}
```

The parameters provided to draw() are pointers to the off-screen buffer and to the background DIB. The CDib pointer is used to retrieve the dimensions of the buffer. The dimensions of the DIB to be drawn are extracted via CDib's infohdr data member.

Next, a pointer is assigned to point into the buffer. The pixel it points to in the buffer will be the bottom left corner of the DIB about to be drawn. A DIB's pixels start at the lower left corner, so the image is in effect stored upside down. The x and y data members of CDib, however, are based on an upper left-hand origin. An alternative would be to simply expect the user of the class to provide x and y in terms of a lower left origin.

The next line assigns the variable transclr to the color found in the first pixel of the DIB's buffer (the lower leftmost pixel). In this way, you are allowing each DIB to define its own transparent color. Usually sprites do not make use of their corner pixels, so this is a reasonable design. If you really to want to animate rectangles, you'll have to modify this function, or leave an empty column and row on the left and bottom edges of your bitmap.

What follows is a double loop. The loop variables i and j are used to iterate through each pixel in the DIB. The color at the i,j location in the DIB is extracted. If it is *not* the transparency color, it *is* copied into the off-screen buffer. This way, only the pixels that define the sprite are copied.

This is by no means an optimized function, but it should be scrutinized, because it is called once for each sprite on each update. We can use Visual C++'s profiler to determine how much time is being spent in this function. If it proves to be significant, then we know that optimization will pay off. The following code is output from a profiling session with the AnimDIB demo.

```
Module Statistics for animdib.exe
_ _ _ _ _ _ _ _ _ _ _ _ _ _ _ _
    Time in module: 6708.089 millisecond
    Percent of time in module: 100.0%
    Functions in module: 126
    Hits in module: 25175
    Module function coverage: 67.5%

        Func        Func+Child       Hit
        Time    %      Time      %   Count  Function
_ _ _ _ _ _ _ _ _ _ _ _ _ _ _ _ _ _ _ _ _ _ _ _
2998.084 44.7   3017.975 45.0   729 CAnimWindow::update_rect(class CRect &)
1736.382 25.9   1741.371 26.0   729   CDib::draw(unsigned char *,class CDib *)
 586.083  8.7   6610.839 98.6     1 _WinMain@16
 202.919  3.0    210.257  3.1   726 CAnimDoc::repair_rect(class CRect &)
 196.328  2.9    233.977  3.5     1 CAnimWindow::set_background(class CDib
*)
 181.462  2.7    181.462  2.7     4 CDib::load(char *)
 170.707  2.5    710.378 10.6     1 CAnimApp::InitInstance(void)
  93.689  1.4     93.915  1.4     1 CAnimWindow::OnQueryNewPalette(void)
  73.845  1.1     73.845  1.1  1302 CAnimWindow::AssertValid(void)
  62.553  0.9    128.877  1.9  1007 CAnimDoc::AssertValid(void)
  54.671  0.8   6707.815 100.0    1 _WinMainCRTStartup
  53.325  0.8   5061.439 75.5   242 CAnimDoc::on_timer(void)
  52.763  0.8     52.788  0.8     1 CAnimWindow::OnDraw(class CDC *)
  40.287  0.6     40.287  0.6     1 CAnimApp::CAnimApp(void)
  37.624  0.6     37.633  0.6     1
 ➥CDibPalette::CDibPalette(class CDib *)
 ...
```

The top portion of the output contains statistics concerning the entire application. The second portion is a table that lists the timing information for each function in the program (not all of the functions appear, since the listing is truncated).

The CAnimWindow::update_rect() function is taking 45 percent of the processor's time—more time than any other function. This isn't too surprising, because this function has the task of coping rectangular regions from the off-screen buffer to video memory. Video memory is typically slower than conventional memory, so this operation can take some time. As you will see later, there isn't much you can do to optimize this function, because each line is either trivial or a call to a function that you don't supply.

The CDib::draw() function is second in the list, with 26 percent of the time. This is significant, and would benefit from optimization. If you were to cut the time of the function in half, you could gain a 13-percent increase in speed.

The lesson here is that the profiler is a valuable tool because it not only indicates to you which functions should be rewritten, but also how much you stand to gain.

The AnimDIB Demo

The AnimDIB demo animates three textured spheres over a marble background. Multiple sprite animation brings with it the issue of *Z-order*, or the illusion that one sprite is in front of another. Z-order is determined by the order in which the sprites are drawn. Sprites drawn first appear to be farther away, or behind sprites drawn later. The last sprite drawn has the potential to appear above all of the other sprites. In the case of AnimDIB, an array is used to store the sprites, and the sprites are drawn starting at location zero of the array. Because the red sphere is created first, it appears to be the farthest away. The blue sphere seems to be somewhere in-between, and the green sphere appears to be the closest. To enhance this effect, the green sphere is the largest, followed by the blue sphere. It is possible to change the Z-order of a sprite at runtime by changing its location in the sprite array.

The Application Architecture

Like ShowDIB, AnimDIB is an SDI application. The document class contains the background buffer and a list of sprites. Although the view class creates the off-screen buffer, the document class has complete access and updates the buffer directly. As usual, the view does the actual screen updates.

The *CSprite* Class

The CSprite class is derived from CDib and overrides CDib::draw(). CSprite is defined like this:

```
class CSprite : public CDib
{
public:
  CSprite(char* fname);
  void draw(BYTE*,CDib*);
  void getrect(CRect& r);
private:
  int x,y;
  int xi,yi;
};
```

In addition to the x and y data members, CSprite includes xi and yi, which are used to increment the sprite's position on each update.

The CSprite constructor takes a DIB filename as a parameter and passes it to the CDib constructor. The data members are then initialized. The constructor looks like this:

```
CSprite::CSprite(char* fname) : CDib(fname)
{
  x=rand()%200+10;
  y=rand()%100+10;
  xi=rand()%8+2;
  yi=rand()%4+2;
};
```

The data members are all assigned on a semi-random basis. The x data member, for example, is assigned a value that can vary from 10 to 209. This is so each sprite will have a different starting location. The xi and yi data members are initialized in the same way, but with smaller ranges. The x coordinate of the sprite can be incremented by as little as 2 and as much as 9.

The `draw()` member function looks like this:

```
void CSprite::draw(BYTE* buffer,CDib* bg)
{
  x+=xi;
  y+=yi;
  if (x+getwidth()>=bg->getwidth() || x<0)
  {
    xi=-xi;
    x+=xi;
  }
  if (y+height()>=bg->getheight() || y<0)
  {
    yi=-yi;
    y+=yi;
  }
  setxy(x,y);
  CDib::draw(buffer,bg);
}
```

The first thing `draw()` does is increment the x and y data members. The range of the coordinates is then checked. The limits of the coordinates vary depending on the size of the bitmap and the size of the background buffer. If the limit of the sprite is encountered, the increment is negated, causing the sprite to reverse direction. It might seem wasteful to call `getwidth()` and `getheight()` each time this function is called, but because they are `inline` functions, you don't pay the price of a function call. After the ranges have been checked, a call to `setxy()` notifies the base class `CDib` of the location of the next draw. The last line is a call to `CDib`'s version of `draw()`, which performs the actual buffer manipulation.

The remaining member function in `CSprite` is `getrect()`, which looks like this:

```
void CSprite::getrect(CRect& rect)
{
  rect.left=x;
  rect.top=y;
  rect.right=x+getwidth()-1;
  rect.bottom=y+getheight()-1;
}
```

There isn't any mystery here. The `getrect()` member function is used by the `CAnimDoc` class to determine which parts of the off-screen buffer should be repaired and copied to the screen.

The CAnimWindow Class

The `CAnimWindow` class is defined like this:

```
class CAnimWindow : public CView
{
protected:
  CAnimWindow();
  DECLARE_DYNCREATE(CAnimWindow)
public:
  BYTE* set_background(CDib*);
  virtual void OnDraw(CDC* pDC);
```

```
  void update_rect(CRect&);
  virtual ~CAnimWindow();
protected:
  afx_msg void OnPaletteChanged(CWnd* pFocusWnd);
  afx_msg BOOL OnQueryNewPalette();
  DECLARE_MESSAGE_MAP()
private:
  char* dibdata;
  BITMAPINFOHEADER* infohdr;
  BITMAPINFO* info;
  WORD* palptr;
  BYTE* pixels;
  HBITMAP section;
  int width,height;
  CDibPalette* palette;
};
```

Let's examine the data members first. Most of the them are exactly the same as they were in CDibView, but there is one addition. The CDibPalette* member means the CAnimWindow class is going to create and maintain its own CDibPalette instance. This is appropriate, as CAnimWindow needs access to the palette in no less than five of its member functions.

The first member function of significance in the listing is set_background(), which is called by CAnimDoc after the background DIB is created. The set_background() member function is defined like this:

```
BYTE* CAnimWindow::set_background(CDib* dib)
{
  delete dibdata;
  DeleteObject(section);
  delete palette;

  width=dib->getwidth();
  height=dib->getheight();
  int totalbytes=sizeof(BITMAPINFOHEADER)+sizeof(WORD)*256;

  dibdata=new char[totalbytes];
  infohdr=(BITMAPINFOHEADER*)dibdata;
  info=(BITMAPINFO*)dibdata;
  palptr=(WORD*)(dibdata+sizeof(BITMAPINFOHEADER));

  memcpy(dibdata,dib->getheader(),sizeof(BITMAPINFOHEADER));
  info->bmiHeader.biClrUsed=0;
  for (WORD i=0;i<256;i++)
    palptr[i]=i;

  palette=new CDibPalette(dib);
  CDC* dc=GetDC();
  CPalette* oldpal=dc->SelectPalette((CPalette*)palette,FALSE);
  dc->RealizePalette();
  section=
  ➥CreateDIBSection(dc->GetSafeHdc(),info,DIB_PAL_COLORS,(VOID**)&pixels,0,0);
  dc->SelectPalette(oldpal,FALSE);
  ReleaseDC(dc);

  int pixelbytes=((width+3)&~3)*height;
  memcpy(pixels,dib->getbits(),pixelbytes);
```

```
  return pixels;
}
```

Because this is almost identical to `CDibView::update()`, which you used in ShowDIB, we won't go over every line. The task of `set_background()` is to create a DIB that you can copy directly to video memory. A complete copy of the background DIB is made. Remember, it is `CAnimDoc`'s job to create the background buffer, and it is `CAnimWindow`'s job to create the off-screen buffer. The DIB created here is the off-screen buffer previously discussed. Notice that on the last line, a pointer to the DIB's pixels is returned to the caller. This gives `CAnimDoc` direct access to the buffer.

The next member function worthy of note is `OnDraw()`, which looks like this:

```
void CAnimWindow::OnDraw(CDC*)
{
  if (!dibdata)  return;

  CClientDC dc(this);

  CAnimDoc* doc=GetDocument();
  CPalette* oldpal=dc.SelectPalette((CPalette*)palette,FALSE);
  dc.RealizePalette();

  HDC dcmem=CreateCompatibleDC(dc.GetSafeHdc());
  HBITMAP old=(HBITMAP)SelectObject(dcmem,section);
  BitBlt(dc.GetSafeHdc(),0,0,width,height,dcmem,0,0,SRCCOPY);
  SelectObject(dcmem,old);
  DeleteDC(dcmem);

  dc.SelectPalette(oldpal,FALSE);
}
```

Like `CDibView::OnDraw()`, the essence of the function is the call to `BitBlt()`, which performs the actual screen draw. Now compare this function with the next one, whose job it is to draw only certain portions of the off-screen buffer:

The `update_rect()` function looks like this:

```
void CAnimWindow::update_rect(CRect& draw)
{
  if (!dibdata)  return;

  CClientDC dc(this);

  int w=draw.right-draw.left+1;
  int h=draw.bottom-draw.top+1;
  int x=draw.left;
  int y=draw.top;

  CAnimDoc* doc=GetDocument();
  CPalette* oldpal=dc.SelectPalette((CPalette*)palette,FALSE);
  dc.RealizePalette();

  HDC dcmem=CreateCompatibleDC(dc.GetSafeHdc());
  HBITMAP old=(HBITMAP)SelectObject(dcmem,section);
  BitBlt(dc.GetSafeHdc(),x,y,w,h,dcmem,x,y,SRCCOPY);
  SelectObject(dcmem,old);
```

```
    DeleteDC(dcmem);

  dc.SelectPalette(oldpal,FALSE);
}
```

The two functions are very similar. The `update_rect()` member function is important because it is called so often. Unlike `OnDraw()`, which is called only for the initial display and after the application has been moved or minimized, `update_rect()` is called once for each sprite movement. It is just like `OnDraw()` except that it takes a `CRect` reference as a parameter, which is then used to define which portion of the off-screen buffer should be copied to the screen. Notice that you can use the same variable for both the source and destination coordinates in the call to `BitBlt()` because the same relative portion of both buffers is being accessed.

The remaining members—`CAnimWindow`, `OnPaletteChanged()`, and `OnQueryNewPalette()`—are identical to the message handlers you wrote for `CDibView`. Their purpose is to correct the image should the palette change due to another application's requests.

The *CAnimDoc* Class

Now it's time to look at `CAnimDoc`, which is where the interesting stuff is. The sprites are created by `CAnimDoc`, and the animation is performed by the `on_timer()` member function. The `CAnimDoc` class is defined like this:

```
class CAnimDoc : public CDocument
{
protected:
  CAnimDoc();
  DECLARE_DYNCREATE(CAnimDoc)
public:
  void on_timer();
  void repair_rect(CRect&);
public:
  virtual BOOL OnNewDocument();
public:
  virtual ~CAnimDoc();
protected:
  DECLARE_MESSAGE_MAP()
private:
  CDib* background;
  CSprite* sprite[SpriteLimit];
  int scount;
  CRect oldrect[SpriteLimit];
  CRect newrect[SpriteLimit];
  BYTE* buffer;
};
```

In the `private` section of the class definition, you see that there is a `CDib` pointer called `background`, which is your copy of the background that you'll use to repair the off-screen buffer. Next there is a list of `CSprite` pointers, which you'll use to store sprites. The `scount` integer is used to keep track of how many sprites are loaded. The two `CRect` arrays are used to track which areas of the off-screen buffer need to be repaired and copied to the screen. Finally, the `buffer` data member points to the off-screen buffer.

The first member function you need to examine is `OnNewDocument()` because it is where you perform your sprite creation and do the initial sprite draw. `OnNewDocument()`, which is called by the application class, looks like this:

```
BOOL CAnimDoc::OnNewDocument()
{
  try
  {
    background=new CDib("bg.bmp");
    sprite[scount++]=new CSprite("red.bmp");
    sprite[scount++]=new CSprite("blue.bmp");
    sprite[scount++]=new CSprite("jade.bmp");
  }
  catch (NoSuchFile)
  {
    AfxMessageBox("Can't find specified file");
    return 0;
  }
  catch (InvalidDIBFile)
  {
    AfxMessageBox("This is not a valid DIB file");
    return 0;
  }
  catch (Not256ColorDIB)
  {
    AfxMessageBox("Only 256 color DIBs are supported");
    return 0;
  }

  POSITION first=GetFirstViewPosition();
  CAnimWindow* window=(CAnimWindow*)GetNextView(first);
  buffer=window->set_background(background);

  int i;
  CRect r;
  for (i=0;i<scount;i++)
    sprite[i]->draw(buffer,background);
  for (i=0;i<scount;i++)
  {
    sprite[i]->getrect(r);
    window->update_rect(r);
  }

  return CDocument::OnNewDocument();
}
```

The first thing `OnNewDocument()` does is create the background DIB and the sprite DIBs. This section is in a `try` block because there are a number of exceptions that can be thrown during the creation of the DIBs. There is one `catch` block below the `try` block for each exception that might get thrown. Cases like invalid filenames and invalid file format result in your displaying a message box and then returning 0, which will cause the application to terminate.

If all goes well, `OnNewDocument()` retrieves a pointer to the `CAnimWindow` instance and calls the `set_background()` member function, which you looked at previously. The `buffer` data member now points to the off-screen buffer. At this point, you have the background bitmap loaded into the off-screen buffer and are ready to draw the sprites. This is done with two loops. The first loop instructs the sprites to draw themselves into the off-screen buffer. The second loop first asks the sprite where it drew itself, and then instructs the CAnimWindow instance to copy those rectangular regions from the off-screen buffer to the screen.

Now you have your sprites on the screen, and it's time to animate them. This is done in on_timer(), which looks like this:

```
void CAnimDoc::on_timer()
{
  int i;
  for (i=0;i<scount;i++)
    sprite[i]->getrect(oldrect[i]);      // store old locations
  for (i=0;i<scount;i++)
    repair_rect(oldrect[i]);             // restore work buffer
  for (i=0;i<scount;i++)
    sprite[i]->draw(buffer,background);  // draw at new locations
  for (i=0;i<scount;i++)
    sprite[i]->getrect(newrect[i]);      // store new locations

  POSITION first=GetFirstViewPosition();
  CAnimWindow* window=(CAnimWindow*)GetNextView(first);
  CRect unionrect;
  for (i=0;i<scount;i++)
  {
    unionrect = oldrect[i] | newrect[i];
    window->update_rect(unionrect);
  }
}
```

The first step is to store the current locations of the sprites in the oldrect array. This is simply a matter of iterating through the sprite list and calling getrect() for each sprite. Next, you repair the off-screen buffer: Erase all of the sprites from the buffer so the original background is restored. Next, you draw the sprites with the draw() member function. This accomplishes two tasks. First, the sprite updates its location, and then it draws itself into the off-screen buffer. Finally, store the new sprite locations in the same way you stored the old locations, but use the newrect array this time.

Now that you have a new scene built in the off-screen buffer, with all of the sprites in their new positions, you need to update the screen. Using the old and new rectangles for each sprite, you create a *union*—a rectangle that contains both rectangles. The union operator is defined by CRect. Using the update_rect() member of CAnimWindow, copy each union rectangle to video memory. The AnimDIB demo is on the CD-ROM.

Some Final Details

Before concluding this chapter, there are two issues you must address: message forwarding and sprite palettes.

Message Forwarding

Both ShowDIB and AnimDIB contain `CView` derivative classes that respond to palette messages in order to maintain image coherence. These messages, however, do not normally reach application views.

Our discussions of the MFC application architecture omitted the fact that in addition to application, document, and view components, MFC applications have a frame class. This `CFrameWnd` derived class receives a number of messages that do not reach the view unless they are forwarded.

A similar situation exists for `CDocument`. In AnimDIB, the document class receives a timer message from Windows. This message must also be forwarded by the `CFrameWnd` derivative.

By default, Visual C++ names the frame window class `CMainFrame`. The forwarding is performed by first adding message handlers to the frame window class. After the addition, the `CMainFrame` definition looks similar to this:

```
class CMainFrame : public CFrameWnd
{
protected:
  CMainFrame();
  DECLARE_DYNCREATE(CMainFrame)
public:
  virtual ~CMainFrame();
protected:
  afx_msg void OnPaletteChanged(CWnd* pFocusWnd);
  afx_msg BOOL OnQueryNewPalette();
  afx_msg void OnTimer(UINT nIDEvent);
  DECLARE_MESSAGE_MAP()
};
```

The palette message handlers are defined like this:

```
void CMainFrame::OnPaletteChanged(CWnd* pFocusWnd)
{
  SendMessageToDescendants(WM_PALETTECHANGED,
                           (WPARAM)(pFocusWnd->GetSafeHwnd()),
                           (LPARAM)0,
                           TRUE);
}

BOOL CMainFrame::OnQueryNewPalette()
{
  CView* pView = GetActiveView();
  if (!pView) return FALSE;
  int i = pView->SendMessage(WM_QUERYNEWPALETTE,
                           (WPARAM)0,
                           (LPARAM)0);
  return (BOOL)i;
}
```

In both cases the objective is simply to ensure that the view receives the message. The `CMainFrame::OnTimer()` handler is defined like this:

```
void CMainFrame::OnTimer(UINT)
{
  CAnimDoc* doc = (CAnimDoc*)GetActiveDocument();
  if (!doc) return;
  doc->on_timer();
}
```

The CDocument class does not have an OnTimer() member function to override, so you are forced to add a custom member function, which you'll call on_timer(). Because the CMainFrame class installs the timer, it decides the rate at which the animation is updated.

Sprite Palettes

You have learned about the issue of palettes, and resolved that Windows will evaluate palettes that you install and modify them if it sees fit. The details are taken care for you by CreateDIBSection(), and that is the extent to which you have had to worry.

How is it, then, that AnimDIB manages to display sprites that were never introduced to Windows via CreateDIBSection()? If you prepare a background and sprites, and use AnimDIB to animate them, you will find that the sprites do not appear correctly. This is because the AnimDIB sprites share the same palette as the AnimDIB background. If they did not, their colors would appear to be random.

Creating sprites and backgrounds that share the same palette can be accomplished in a number of ways. One way is to use a paint program to manipulate the palette of each DIB. A master palette can be constructed, and then the background and each sprite can be forced to use the new palette.

Another way is to write a utility that performs this task for you. Because you are already familiar with the DIB format, it is possible to read the DIBs into memory, create a master palette, convert the DIBs, and then save them back to disk.

Let's examine this alternative in more detail. The steps of the algorithm are outlined below.

1. Read the background and sprite DIBs into memory.
2. Create a master palette.
3. Convert the pixel data of each DIB to use the new palette.
4. Save each DIB.

You already know how to read the DIBs, so let's discuss creating a master palette. First, a large array is filled with the entries from each palette. Duplicate entries can be detected and eliminated during this step. You perform duplicate detection by testing two RGBQUAD structures for equivalent red, green, and blue values.

After this has been done, there is the possibility that the total number of colors will exceed 236 (remember, there are 256 colors, but 20 are reserved). If there are 236 colors or less, you are free to move on to step 3. If not, you need to perform a color reduction.

Reducing the number of colors involves more color comparison. Your task is to determine which colors can be eliminated from the palette without unduly compromising image quality. Some degree of image decay is inevitable at this point, but you can minimize this effect. You need to compare each color against every other color and determine which colors are the most alike. One color in a closely matching pair can be omitted safely from the master palette.

You can evaluate the similarity of two colors by treating their RGB values as indexes into a three-dimensional array. This places each color at a different location within a three-dimensional cube. Figure 15.6 illustrates this concept.

FIGURE 15.6.

The RGB cube.

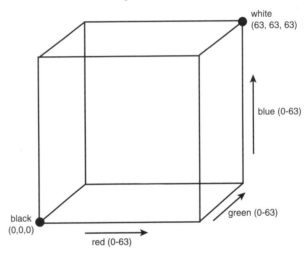

You can determine how alike the two colors are by measuring the distance between the two. The closer they reside in the cube, the more alike they are. The colors in the figure, black and white, are as far apart as two colors can get. You find the closest match and remove one of the entries until you have 236 entries left. Now your master palette is ready for use.

The next step involves updating the DIB's pixel data. Each pixel must be converted by finding the best match for each pixel's color in the new master palette. Again the color's distance in the RGB cube is used. Each pixel value indicates a palette entry in the DIB's original palette. This color is compared to each entry in the master palette. The index of the closest match is assigned to the pixel.

The last step is to save the DIBs. Don't forget to save each DIB with the master palette, though, and not with its original palette. The process of saving the DIB is trivial, because each DIB's BITMAPINFOHEADER structure will already be in memory.

Hardware-Assisted Graphics

One of the reasons that PC graphics have always been slow when compared to coin-operated arcade games and home entertainment systems is that the PC lacks graphics acceleration hardware. Recently, video cards have been appearing on the market that include graphics acceleration chips. In addition, Microsoft recently announced the Windows 95 Game SDK, which, among other things, allows developers to use the advanced features of these new video cards.

Because of these developments, Windows 95 will not be dominated by DOS when it comes to graphics.

For More Information

Here are some sources of additional information:

Thompson, Nigel. *Animation Techniques in Win32.* Microsoft Press, 1995.

Walnum, Clayton. *Dungeons of Discovery.* Que, 1995.

Multimedia
Extensions

by John J. Kottler

16

"Any sufficiently advanced technology is indistinguishable from magic."

—Arthur C. Clarke

Multimedia Magic

Multimedia is one of the biggest buzzwords in the computer industry today. It has revolutionized the way people think and has changed the expectations people have for the personal computer system. For the past several years a familiar question has been heard near the turn of each year: Will next year be the year of the multimedia PC? But because purchasing a new computer system that includes a CD-ROM, sound card, and video capabilities is the norm, it is hard to argue that we aren't already in the multimedia era.

Even with all of the improvements we have witnessed in multimedia technology, it still requires a little magic to make it work. Ask anyone who has installed individual multimedia components and has struggled with IRQs, DMAs, and countless jumpers before getting the system to work (or in some cases not work). For the multimedia developer, projects in the past were not friendly primarily because of the lack of support in the operating system. In the older versions of Windows, developers who wanted to add multimedia capability to their applications struggled not only with the APIs but also with the limitations of Windows graphics capabilities and video technology. The typical need to release software drivers with a product for supporting things such as Video for Windows (which every user *should* have but wasn't guaranteed to have) only compounded the frustration.

Windows 95 addresses these and other issues and helps relieve some of the stress multimedia developers encountered in the past. In this chapter I will examine a portion of the multimedia capabilities in Windows 95. With the vastness of multimedia and its associated technologies, it is impossible to discuss every nuance in this chapter and would clearly extend beyond the scope of this book. However, in this chapter, I will attempt to address in general the new multimedia features found in Windows 95.

What Is Multimedia?

If you ask three different people what they think multimedia is, you can be sure that you will hear three different answers. In its most general definition, multimedia is an application that incorporates not only text data, but also graphics, animation, sound, digital video, and CD-ROM technology. Not all of these technologies have to be included to form a multimedia application, but because video and sound information require much more storage space than conventional textual data, CD-ROM is the norm for multimedia applications.

As one of the answers to your question, you might hear the technical standards for multimedia as defined by the Multimedia PC Marketing Council. This group defined the basic requirements for equipment needed to run multimedia on a typical IBM-compatible PC.

To date, the group has established two levels of multimedia specifications: MPC-1 and MPC-2. These specifications define the basic requirements necessary for adding multimedia to PCs for minimal multimedia performance.

MPC-1 was defined in 1990 and established the basic hardware and software requirements a PC needed to be qualified as a multimedia PC. However, at that time, 386SX chips and 8-bit sound cards were the norm; it wasn't long before the standard was outgrown and required revision.

In 1993, the MPC standard was reviewed and enhanced to reflect the newer achievements in hardware and software technology. This standard, MPC-2, is still in use today. Some of the requirements in MPC-2 are still adequate for today's multimedia, but they will not be sufficient for tomorrow's multimedia. With so many advancements continuing in the computer industry, you can expect an MPC-3 level before long.

On the World Wide Web there is a site that thoroughly discusses the different MPC levels, including progress on MPC-3. The site is actually a part of the Software Publishers Association and can be found at this address: `http://www.spa.org/mpc/mpcqa.htm`.

Multimedia '95

Chances are that when asked to define multimedia, some people would say, "Isn't that when you see a tiny TV screen on your computer?"

Frustrating, but true. This definition is what most people think of when they think of multimedia. The biggest hurdle with which multimedia developers struggle, other than the technical challenges of multimedia, is dealing with the mind-set of end users who are used to the television and expect the same capabilities on their desktop PC.

So, what can you expect to see for multimedia in the future? With Windows 95 you can expect to see enhanced multimedia services. Windows 95 offers enhancements in every area, from the video subsystems, to CD-ROM drive access, and to sound card setup. In addition to these enhancements, increased processor performance will enable many users to view full-screen video on their PCs without dedicated hardware. However, Windows 95 will not ignore hardware improvements as it paves the way for DCI (Display Control Interface) and MPEG (Motion Picture Experts Group) hardware in the future.

The foremost improvement to multimedia is the sheer power that the Windows 95 operating system offers, a power that was never found in earlier versions of Windows. Here's a quick glance at the newest features added to Windows 95 and a description of what they mean to you:

■ **32-bit file system**—The new 32-bit file system is sure to stream data faster than ever from the source medium to the PC's memory. Also included in the 32-bit file system is disk-caching technology to help buffer frequently used data and avoid multiple-reads from files.

■ **32-bit video subsystem**—The 32-bit video subsystem, the new core of the video and graphics systems in Windows 95, is a vast improvement over the restricting 16-bit technology of Windows 3.x. With a faster video subsystem, graphics and video windows can be painted more quickly, and larger video windows can be drawn.

■ **32-bit system architecture**—The new 32-bit architecture found in Windows 95 is more robust than the 16-bit architecture found in previous versions of Windows. This architecture offers more stability as well as enhanced multitasking for multimedia developers.

■ **Plug and Play**—As mentioned earlier, the experience of mixing and matching multimedia hardware from different vendors can be stressful. To help alleviate this stress, Windows 95 supports Plug and Play-aware devices. This will help users configure their computers easily without any hair-raising encounters with interrupts, DMAs, or jumpers. For users who install devices that are not Plug and Play aware, Windows 95 offers enhanced methods for determining and resolving hardware conflicts.

■ **WinG**—Why haven't games been developed for Windows as they have been for DOS? One simple reason is speed. Many of today's games require fast microprocessors and complex routines for rendering complex graphics. The games also need to access the video card quickly, with as little interference as possible. In previous versions of Windows, this was impossible. The time required to pass a graphics command from the program through the hierarchy of Windows drivers made fast-paced action games unrealistic on the Windows platform. With the WinG engine, applications will have the opportunity to write directly to the video controller in a PC instead of stepping through the normal progression of Windows drivers.

■ **Built-in Video for Windows**—Almost every Windows multimedia title on the market today comes with an installation routine for either Video for Windows or QuickTime for Windows. This has been necessary because in the past developers had no way of being guaranteed a user had the appropriate video drivers for the application. Windows 95 is a little more considerate to developers than Windows 3.x. Windows 95 includes Video for Windows 1.1 and enhanced video subsystem drivers. Several familiar video codecs (COmpressor-DECompressors) are also included with Windows 95 such as Indeo, Cinepak, and Microsoft Video 1. This way, developers can be assured that if their application runs on Windows 95, they will never need to include the Video for Windows drivers again.

QUICK LESSON ON DIGITAL VIDEO

The term *codec* is short for COmpressor/DECompressor. Most digital video must be compressed in order to be stored with a reasonable amount of space. Then, when the stored video is played, the data must be decompressed in order to be displayed. For example, a 320x240-pixel video clip with 24-bit color depth and a frame rate of 15 frames per second (fps) would take up just less than 3.5 megabytes of space for just one second of video without compression!

Several companies, such as Intel, Cinepak, and Microsoft, have designed digital video compression technologies, each with varying quality and amount of storage space saved. These compression/decompression techniques are accomplished using software, but there are several hardware-based codecs as well. MPEG (Motion Pictures Expert Group) is an example of a hardware-based compression/decompression scheme.

■ **Built-in audio support and compression**—Windows 95 includes drivers for several popular sound cards and automatically detects them during installation. In addition, Windows 95 adds support for audio compressors, such as ADPCM (Adaptive Differential Pulse Code Modulation) and TrueSpeech, to reduce the size of digital wave files.

QUICK LESSON ON DIGITAL AUDIO

A sound wave can be recorded by measuring its amplitude over a series of time. In order to capture sound digitally, an infinite amount of time must be broken into a discrete number of points (this is referred to as the *sampling frequency* or *rate*). The amplitude of the waveform at each discrete point in time may then be measured and stored as a digital code. Actually, the measurement represents the amount of modulation necessary to modify a constant pulse. Thus, when the amount of modulation is indicated by a stored digital code, the term PCM (Pulse Code Modulation) is used. Adaptive Differential Pulse Code Modulation (ADPCM) is a compression technique where the differences between actual points on a sound wave and data points predicted mathematically by the compression algorithm are stored. By storing only these differences and not every data point, audio information can be stored using less space.

■ **Built-in CD-ROM support**—If you have ever struggled with obtaining and configuring the appropriate drivers for your PC when adding a CD-ROM drive, you'll be happy to learn that Windows 95 will take care of all of this for you. SCSI and IDE CD-ROM drives, as well as proprietary formats such as Mitsumi, Sony, and Panasonic, are all automatically supported by Windows 95. The Windows 95 operating system also recognizes and optimizes the performance of faster CD-ROM drives such as triple- and quad-speed readers. Caching is an automatic feature as well. There are even special services for playing audio CDs and running CD-ROMs automatically when inserted into the player (more on this later).

Windows 95 is also the first operating system to support the new Philips/Sony Enhanced CD format. This new format allows audio players and computers to use the same CD for music and data, respectively. The new "stamped multisession" format allows data and music tracks to exist anywhere on the CD and avoids the problems encountered when data could only reside on the first track. This allows a CD to be played on a computer as well as on an audio CD player without the audio CD player reading a data track of static noise.

■ **Built-in MIDI enhancements**—Typical MIDI capability is found in Windows 95. However, an additional new technology, called Polymessage MIDI Support, is found as well. This technology allows multiple MIDI instructions to be sent during a single interrupt. This lessens the load on the processor when handling MIDI music and gives Windows 95 and the CPU more time to work on graphics and other demanding procedures.

■ **Built-in joystick support**—Finally, a joystick will be recognized automatically under Windows 95. The biggest advantage to this feature is that once you calibrate the joystick, Windows 95 will remember the settings. A control panel is available for setting up the joystick.

Multimedia Programming in Windows 95

Anyone who has created multimedia applications using Video for Windows 1.1 for Windows 3.x should have an easy time adapting to Windows 95. As mentioned earlier, Windows 95 makes multimedia development a little easier by including Video for Windows 1.1 and additional drivers for CD-ROM, audio, and joystick support.

In this chapter, I discuss the various functions available in Windows 95 for C++ developers. Although the sample code is written in C++, the actual function calls to the respective Video for Windows and multimedia system libraries are typical C calls, which can be implemented easily in C programs.

Let's Make Some Noise

To begin, I'll discuss some simple ways to make sounds on a Windows 95 PC. There are two extremely simple commands that cause digital audio to play on an appropriately equipped PC: `MessageBeep()` and `PlaySound()`. These are the most basic functions for digital audio playback.

MessageBeep()

In Windows 95, it is easy to attach different sound effects to several key system events. Windows 95 offers ways to manage these groupings as schemes and has the capability to change the set of sounds easily. To access these simple system sounds from your program, use the `MessageBeep()` function. It is defined as follows:

```
void MessageBeep(UINT uAlert);
```

The `MessageBeep()` function plays a waveform audio sound based on the system event specified by the uAlert parameter. Table 16.1 lists the possible valid parameter values for the `MessageBeep()` function.

Table 16.1. A description of the valid uAlert parameters for `MessageBeep()`.

Constant	Description
-1	Plays a beep from the computer's speaker (no digital audio).
MB_ICONASTERISK	Plays the sound associated with the Asterisk system event.
MB_ICONEXCLAMATION	Plays the sound associated with the Exclamation system event.
MB_ICONHAND	Plays the sound associated with the Critical Stop system event.
MB_ICONQUESTION	Plays the sound associated with the Question system event.
MB_OK	Plays the default sound.

The sounds for each of these events are defined in the Sounds Properties control panel. The Sounds Properties control panel is displayed in Figure 16.1.

FIGURE 16.1.

The Sounds Properties control panel.

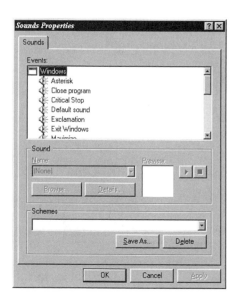

For example, here is a program that does error checking and posts a critical message when an error occurs:

```
if(MyError){
    MessageBeep(MB_ICONEXCLAMATION);
```

```
MessageBox("Sorry, this is a critical error.", "Title", MB_ICONEXCLAMATION |
       ➥MB_OK);
}
```

When the error condition in this example is TRUE, the specified sound for the exclamation system event will be played followed by the appropriate message box.

PlaySound()

As convenient as the MessageBeep() function is, it obviously was not designed for sounds other than those defined as key system sounds in the control panel. To play any digital audio file or resource in your application, you can use the PlaySound() or sndPlaySound() function. Although both of these functions work in Windows 95, you should use PlaySound(), where possible, to ensure portability across all Win32 platforms. PlaySound() has the following definition:

```
BOOL PlaySound(LPCSTR pszSound, HMODULE hmod, DWORD fdwSound);
```

This function returns the value of TRUE if the sound was successfully played; otherwise, it returns FALSE. PlaySound() expects three parameters: a string, a handle to an executable, and a bitmask of several flags. Here is a review of each parameter:

- pszSound—This string points to the sound file to be played. The actual information in this string can point to any of the following items: the filename for a sound file, the name of a resource in the application, or a system sound event registered in the system registry or identified in WIN.INI. The action taken depends on the fdwSound flags. If the string passed in this function is NULL, the currently playing sound is stopped.

- hmod—This is the current application's handle to the instance. You need this handle when playing resource sounds embedded in the application; otherwise, it must be set to NULL.

- fdwSound—Several different actions can be taken on the sound as specified by this parameter. The flags that may be passed into this parameter are described in Table 16.2.

Table 16.2. A description of PlaySound() flags.

Flag	Definition
SND_APPLICATION	The sound is played with an application-specific association.
SND_ALIAS	The pszSound parameter contains the name of a system event alias in either the registry or WIN.INI to play.
SND_ALIAS_ID	The pszSound parameter contains a predefined sound identifier.

Flag	Definition
SND_ASYNC	The sound is played asynchronously. The PlaySound() function returns immediately after starting a sound. The sound can be terminated prematurely by calling PlaySound() and setting pszSound to NULL.
SND_FILENAME	Plays the digital audio wave file specified by the pszSound parameter.
SND_LOOP	A sound is played repeatedly until terminated by a call to PlaySound() with the pszSound parameter set to NULL. You must also use the SND_ASYNC flag in order for the sound to loop in the background and your application to regain control. Otherwise, your application might never get the chance to call PlaySound() with the NULL parameter to stop the sound.
SND_MEMORY	Plays a sound file loaded into memory. In this case, pszSound must act as a pointer to the memory location of the sound data.
SND_NODEFAULT	Suppresses the default sound event. Typically, when a sound file cannot be found, the default sound found in either the registry or WIN.INI is played instead. To prevent this from happening, use the SND_NODEFAULT flag.
SND_NOWAIT	Instead of waiting for a busy sound driver to become available, SND_NOWAIT enables you to return immediately to your application and bypass playing the sound.
SND_PURGE	Stops all applications associated with the calling task. If the pszSound parameter is NULL, all sounds are stopped. Otherwise, sounds uniquely identified by the pszSound parameter can be stopped independently.
SND_RESOURCE	Use this flag to indicate that a resource associated with the application is to be played. To play a resource, the pszSound parameter must then contain the resource identifier of the sound wave, and the hmod parameter must contain the resource instance.
SND_SYNC	Enables synchronous playback of sounds. Your application regains control only after the sound event completes.

sndPlaySound()

The second function, sndPlaySound(), is very similar to PlaySound() but expects different parameters. Here is the definition for sndPlaySound():

```
BOOL sndPlaySound(LPCSTR lpszSound, UINT fuSound);
```

Like PlaySound(), sndPlaySound() returns TRUE if the sound played successfully; otherwise, it returns FALSE. However, unlike PlaySound(), sndPlaySound() only expects two parameters: lpszSound and fuSound. Here are the definitions for these two parameters:

■ lpszSound—This string contains any of the following items: the filename of the audio file to play, the name of the system event in either the system registry or WIN.INI, or a pointer to a block of memory. Again, the actual data needed in this parameter depends on the flags specified in the fuSound parameter.

■ fuSound—Contains flags for determining what to do with the sound to be played. The valid flags are shown in Table 16.3.

Table 16.3. A description of sndPlaySound() flags.

Flag	Description
SND_ASYNC	Plays a sound asynchronously. Control is returned to your application after the sound has started. To stop the sound, the sndPlaySound() function must be called with NULL passed to the lpszSound parameter.
SND_LOOP	Repeats a sound continuously until sndPlaySound() is called with NULL passed to the lpszSound parameter. You must specify the SND_ASYNC flag as well to allow control to return to your application.
SND_MEMORY	Plays a sound loaded in memory. When using the SND_MEMORY flag, you should make certain that the lpszSound parameter contains the address of the sound data.
SND_NODEFAULT	If the sndPlaySound() call cannot execute a sound, the function usually plays the default sound. To prevent this from occurring, enable the SND_NODEFAULT flag.
SND_NOSTOP	If another sound is playing, sndPlaySound() immediately returns without either interrupting the current sound or playing the requested sound. The function will set the return value to FALSE.
SND_SYNC	Plays a sound synchronously and does not return control to your application until the sound has finished playing.

The best place to see how these functions work is in a program. The MCIWnd sample application included in this book demonstrates some of the capabilities of the MCIWnd command set. I will discuss these commands shortly. Also included in this application is the PlaySound() command. (The MessageBeep command can be found in the joystick sample application later in this chapter.)

Let's assume that you want the TADA.WAV sound file to play every time you click the Play Sound button in your application. (TADA.WAV is located on your hard disk under the C:\WINDOWS\MEDIA directory.) The function for doing this is the following:

```
void CMyAppDlg::OnPlaysound()
{
    //This plays a sound file asynchronously
    PlaySound("c:\\windows\\media\\tada.wav", NULL, SND_FILENAME ¦ SND_ASYNC);
}
```

But what if you want to play a system sound, such as the one used when Windows 95 starts?

You could use the following code:

```
void CMyAppDlg::OnPlaysound()
{
    //This plays a system event registered in the registry
    //or found in the WIN.INI
    PlaySound("SystemStart", NULL, SND_ALIAS);
}
```

A final example would be to play a resource associated with your application, but this, however, is a little more complex than a single function call, unfortunately. Here are the steps involved in the process:

1. Find the resource by using the FindResource command.
2. Load the resource into memory from the executable by using LoadResource.
3. Lock the resource by using LockResource.
4. Play the resource by using sndPlaySound() or PlaySound().
5. Free the resource after playback by using the FreeResource function.

To add a digital audio sound wave to your application, you can add the following line of code to your application's .RC file. In this example, IDR_SOUND is the application's resource name, WAVE is the resource type, and "tada.wav" is the file to be imported. Here is the line of code:

```
IDR_SOUND WAVE DISCARDABLE "tada.wav"
```

Another way is to open your resource file in Visual C++ 2.0 and choose the Import option from the Resource menu. Then choose the resource you want to add to the file. You can rename the resource in the Properties window.

Listing 16.1 is sample code you can use to play a resource. In this example, a separate function, named PlayResource, was created. In order to play a resource identified by the function, another portion of the program needs to call PlayResource.

Listing 16.1. Sample code that uses `PlaySound()` to play audio resources.

```
static void PlayResource()
{
   //Handle to wave resource
   HRSRC hRes;
   HGLOBAL hData;
   //Playback result
   BOOL bResult = FALSE;

   //Find the resource in the application.  In this case, the
   //application has a resource called IDR_SOUND that is a
   //"WAVE" type.
   hRes = ::FindResource(AfxGetResourceHandle(),
                     (LPCTSTR)IDR_SOUND,
                     (LPCTSTR)("WAVE"));
   if(hRes==NULL){
      AfxMessageBox("Can't find resource");
      return;
   }

   //Load the resource now, using the handle we got from the
   //FindResource call above.
   hData = ::LoadResource(AfxGetResourceHandle(), hRes);
   if(hData==NULL){
      AfxMessageBox("Can't load resource");
      return;
   }

   //Play the sound, locking the resource at the same time.
   //Make sure that the flags include SND_MEMORY to indicate a
   //pointer to a memory location.
   bResult=PlaySound((LPCTSTR)::LockResource(hData),
                  NULL,
                  SND_MEMORY | SND_SYNC | SND_NODEFAULT);

   //That's it, clean up our mess.
   FreeResource(hData);

   if (!bResult)
      AfxMessageBox("Sound cannot be played");
}
```

Whenever your application calls the `PlayResource()` function, the TADA.WAV sound will be played from the resource embedded in the application.

MCIWnd

As convenient as the `MessageBeep()`, `sndPlaySound()`, and `PlaySound()` functions are, there are times when you will want to have more control over your sound or to control other media devices such as CD-ROM players, video windows, or MIDI files. Enter the `MCIWnd` command set.

If you worked with the Media Control Interface (MCI) in the past, you might be accustomed to issuing command strings to the interface. However, Video for Windows 1.1 includes a new set of functions in addition to the command string interface. MCIWnd is a set of functions that controls properties and functions of different media devices. It takes care of a lot of features automatically for you: for instance, playback windows, option menus, recording capabilities, Open and Save dialog boxes, and much more. In this section, I will show you some of the different functions and how they can be used in a Windows 95 program.

MCIWndCreate

Before you can do anything with MCIWnd, you must create a window. Creating a basic window automatically provides a lot of functionality. Take a look at the sample MCI window shown in Figure 16.2.

FIGURE 16.2.

An example of an MCI window.

You will notice several niceties the Video for Windows 1.1 interface gives you for free. First, you get a fully functional window. You can size it, minimize it, maximize it, or close it. You also get a title bar with the filename, mode, and position calculated automatically. At the bottom of the window, you'll find a toolbar with a play button on the far left, a pop-up menu button, and a position/seek play bar. If you click the pop-up menu button, a menu will appear with several additional options. These options enable you to adjust the volume and speed controls, to scale the playback window, to open additional files, and more. Figure 16.3 shows the MCI window with the pop-up menu opened.

Here is the definition of the MCIWndCreate function:

```
HWND MCIWndCreate(HWND hwndParent,
                  HINSTANCE hInstance,
                  DWORD dwStyle,
                  LPSTR szFile);
```

FIGURE 16.3.

The MCI window is shown with the menu options opened.

As you can see from the definition, the function returns a handle to a window similar to a typical CreateWindow call in the Windows API. Here is a list of the parameters accepted by MCIWnd:

- **hwndParent**—This is the handle to the window creating the MCI window. This association is optional. You can either pass the handle to a window to establish a parent/child relationship or pass NULL to create a new, stand-alone window.

- **hInstance**— Associates the MCI window with an application by passing the handle to the instance of the module calling the MCI window.

- **szFile**—This parameter is a string with the name of the media file or device to open. To open a file, you would set the szFile parameter to the file's name (WELCOME.AVI, for example). For a device such as the CD player, you would pass the device name (for example, "CDAudio") into the szFile parameter. A complete list of available devices available to Windows 95 can be found in either the MCI section of the WIN.INI file or the Windows 95 registry. To find the list in the registry, look under MyComputer\HKEY_LOCAL_MACHINE\System\CurrentControlSet\ Control\MediaResources\MCI.

- **dwStyle**—This parameter contains a set of flags that determine the overall appearance and style of the window. You can use the flags found in the CreateWindow and CreateWindowEx functions as well as the following MCIWnd style flags listed in Table 16.4.

Table 16.4. A list of valid `MCIWnd` style flags.

Style Flag	Description
`MCIWNDF_NOAUTOSIZEWINDOW`	Prevents the MCI window from changing size when the image changes size.
`MCIWNDF_NOAUTOSIZEMOVIE`	Prevents the image from changing size when the MCI window changes size.
`MCIWNDF_NOERRORDLG`	Suppresses error dialog boxes from appearing on the MCI window.
`MCIWNDF_NOMENU`	Disables the pop-up menu, which is normally accessible from the toolbar of the MCI window, and hides the pop-up menu's button.
`MCIWNDF_NOOPEN`	Disables the Open and Close options on the MCI window's pop-up menu.
`MCIWNDF_NOPLAYBAR`	Hides the MCI window's toolbar.
`MCIWNDF_NOTIFYMODE`	Forces `MCIWnd` to pass the `MCIWNDM_NOTIFYMODE` message back to the parent window. The `lParam` portion of the message identifies a new mode.
`MCIWNDF_NOTIFYPOS`	With this flag, `MCIWnd` sends a `MCIWNDM_NOTIFYPOS` message to the parent window. The `lParam` then holds the current playback or recording position.
`MCIWND_NOTIFYMEDIA`	When a new device is used or a file is opened or closed, the `MCIWNDM_NOTIFYMEDIA` message is posted to the parent window. The `lParam` then contains the pointer to a new filename.
`MCIWND_NOTIFYSIZE`	Sends a `MCIWNDM_NOTIFYSIZE` message to the parent window when the MCI window has changed its size.
`MCIWNDF_NOTIFYERROR`	Whenever there is an error in `MCIWnd`, the `MCIWNDM_NOTIFYERROR` message is posted to the parent window.
`MCIWNDF_NOTIFYALL`	Instead of combining the above `NOTIFY` codes all together yourself, you can simply set the `NOTIFYALL` flag.
`MCIWNDF_RECORD`	Shows the recording button if the device used by the MCI window has recording capability.
`MCIWNDF_SHOWMODE`	Displays the current mode of the MCI window in its title bar.

continues

Table 16.4. continued

Style Flag	Description
MCIWNDF_SHOWNAME	Instructs MCIWnd to display the name of the current file in the title bar of the MCI window. When a filename is not available, the device type will be displayed (for example, "CDAudio").
MCIWNDF_SHOWPOS	Causes MCIWnd to update the current playback or recording position in the window's title bar.
MCIWNDF_SHOWALL	If you want to activate all of the above SHOW-type flags, set the MCIWNDF_SHOWALL flag instead of manually combining them together with binary ORs.

Now I will discuss the code that creates an MCI window in C++. First, the following code shows you how to create a stand-alone window (it isn't a child of the parent window) by passing NULL to the hwndParent parameter:

```
hMCIWnd=MCIWndCreate(NULL, AfxGetInstanceHandle(), MCIWNDF_SHOWALL, NULL);
```

In this example, the filename or device name is also set to NULL. This creates a blank MCI window in which the user can click the pop-up menu button to choose files to open.

Now, what if you want to place the MCI window in your application's window? To do this, pass the handle to the parent window into the first parameter of the MCIWndCreate function. Here is the code:

```
hMCIWnd=MCIWndCreate(CWnd::m_hWnd,
                     AfxGetInstanceHandle(),
                     MCIWNDF_SHOWALL,
                     NULL);
//CWnd::m_hWnd is C++, pass hWnd from C.
```

Can't Cramp *MCIWnd's* Style

After you have created the MCI window, you can alter the style parameters associated with the window. To do this, you need to use the MCIWndChangeStyles function. Here is the definition of the MCIWndChangeStyles function:

```
LONG MCIWndChangeStyles(hwnd, mask, value);
```

As you may see from the code, the MCIWndChangeStyles function accepts three parameters:

hwnd—This function expects the handle to MCIWnd as the first parameter.

mask—This function identifies the styles to be changed. mask may be a combination of styles combined together with binary ORs.

value—Identifies the new style to be applied to the MCI window, depending on the mask. A value of 0 disables all MCIWnd styles.

Listing 16.2 is an example in which a checkbox control can enable or disable a particular style.

Listing 16.2. Sample source code that alters the styles for MCIWnd.

```
void CMyMCIDlg::OnOptPlaybar()
{
   UpdateData(TRUE);

   // If the "Show Playbar" check-box option is unchecked
   if(!m_Opt_Playbar)
      // Hide the playbar only
      MCIWndChangeStyles(hMCIWnd, MCIWNDF_NOPLAYBAR, MCIWNDF_NOPLAYBAR);
   else
      // Show the playbar, NULL indicates the opposite of NOPLAYBAR.
      MCIWndChangeStyles(hMCIWnd, MCIWNDF_NOPLAYBAR, NULL);
}
```

Moving and Sizing an MCI Window

Now that you've created an MCI window, you can reposition it or change its dimensions. The MCI window is a typical window and can be altered using the same Windows functions as those applied to regular windows. In this case, you use the MoveWindow function to move the window. However, in C++ this task is a little more daunting.

The difficulty lies in the fact that MCIWnd does not contain an object-oriented class. This is a problem except when you want to alter the window (moving the window's position, for example). Visual C++ uses the Microsoft Foundation Class Library in which MoveWindow is redefined as this:

```
CWnd::MoveWindow(int x,int y,int nWidth,int nHeight,BOOL bRepaint = TRUE);
```

Because MCIWnd is not object oriented, you cannot call MCIWnd::MoveWindow as you would expect. Therefore, to make changes to the MCI window, you must be hooked to a C++ CWnd structure. To do this in C++, you can use the Attach function to make a handle to a window a CWnd class and the Detach function to release the association. Listing 16.3 demonstrates how to successfully move an MCI window in Visual C++.

Listing 16.3. Sample code for moving and sizing an MCI window.

```
HWND    hMCIWnd;    //Handle to the MCIWnd
CWnd    CMCIWnd;    //Make a CWnd object

//Create the MCIWnd
hMCIWnd=MCIWndCreate(CWnd::m_hWnd,
                     AfxGetInstanceHandle(),
                     MCIWNDF_SHOWALL,
                     NULL);
```

continues

Listing 16.3. continued

```
//Attach the MCIWnd to the CMCIWnd object
CMCIWnd.Attach(hMCIWnd);

//Move the Window to its new x,y,width,height coordinates
CMCIWnd.MoveWindow(40,5,320,240,TRUE);

//Detach MCIWnd from CMCIWnd
CMCIWnd.Detach();
```

Of course, you do not have to attach and detach the MCI window every time you change an attribute. You could use the Attach function once during creation of the MCI window and then use the Detach function when you destroy the MCI window.

To resize a video window, simply alter the width and height of the MoveWindow function. You can double the size of a video window by multiplying both the width and height by 2 or halve it by dividing both by 2. You can specify any arbitrary size for the video window.

Opening Files and Devices in the MCI Window

When you create an MCI window, you can specify the name of the file or device you want to open and use in the MCI window. But what if you create an empty MCI window or wish to open different files or devices at a later time? MCIWnd provides the MCIWndOpen and MCIWndOpenDialog commands for this purpose. First, here is the MCIWndOpenDialog command:

```
LONG MCIWndOpenDialog(hwnd);
```

The function is easy to implement. It returns a value of 0 if the function was successful at opening the file or device; otherwise, the error code is returned. Like every additional command you will see in the MCIWnd command set, the handle to the MCI window must be passed to this function. This creates the association between the dialog box and the MCI window in which the device or file is loaded.

When you call this function, a window similar to the one shown in Figure 16.4 will appear.

The Open dialog box for the MCI window is robust and gives you several capabilities automatically. First, it uses the typical Explorer metaphor familiar in Windows 95. You are able to preview and even play the media file in a small window located on the right side of the dialog box.

As wonderful as the MCIWndOpenDialog function is, there are times when you will want to open a specific file without user intervention. In this case, you can use the MCIWndOpen command. Here is the definition for MCIWndOpen:

```
LONG MCIWndOpen(hwnd, szFile, wFlags);
```

FIGURE 16.4.

A sample of the Open dialog box provided by MCIWnd.

The value returned by this function is either 0 (for no errors) or the error ID number.

Like MCIWndOpenDialog, MCIWndOpen requires the MCI window's handle to be passed to the function. In addition, you may pass in two additional parameters:

- szFile—This is the name of the device or file you wish to open and associate with the MCI window. To open a file, you pass in the complete filename. If, however, you want to open a device, you specify the device name as defined in the MCI section of WIN.INI or as found in the registry (as discussed earlier in this chapter). If you pass a -1 value to this parameter, the Open dialog box will be displayed.

- wFlags—There is just a single flag associated with the MCIWndOpen function. You can use the MCIWndOpen command to specify a new file. To do this, you set the wFlags parameter to MCIWNDOPENF_NEW. Otherwise, to open a file or device, you pass in NULL to wFlags.

Controlling the MCI Window

After the MCI window has been created and a media file has been opened, you will have tremendous control over the media. The following is a list of MCIWnd commands that control the device or file currently loaded:

MCIWndPlay - LONG MCIWndPlay(hwnd);

Call MCIWndPlay to play the media currently loaded in the MCI window. You must pass the handle of the MCI window to this function. The function returns 0 if successful; otherwise, it returns an error.

MCIWndEnd - LONG MCIWndEnd(hwnd);

This causes the MCI window to seek the end of the media content. It returns 0 if successful; otherwise, it returns an error. You must specify the handle to the MCI window.

MCIWndEject - LONG MCIWndEject(hwnd);

Calling this function will eject the media of the current MCI device in the MCI window if the device is capable of being ejected.

MCIWndHome - `LONG MCIWndHome(hwnd);`

This function is the opposite of the `MCIWndEnd` function. Calling this function will cause the MCI window to seek to the beginning of the media content.

MCIWndPause - `LONG MCIWndPause(hwnd);`

Pauses the playback or recording process of the MCI window.

MCIWndResume - `LONG MCIWndResume(hwnd);`

Resumes playback or recording from the paused mode and continues from the current position in the content.

MCIWndPlayFrom - `LONG MCIWndPlayFrom(hwnd,lPos);`

Plays the media in the MCI window from a given position (`lPos`) to the end of the content or until another `MCIWnd` command interrupts the playback. The current position of the media may be determined using the `MCIWndGetPosition` function. Also, instead of passing in obscure long values to indicate a starting position, you may use the `MCIWndSetTimeFormat` function or the `MCIWndUseFrames` and `MCIWndUseTime` macros to specify formatting options for position information in the content. Then the value passed in as a position (`lPos`) is either a frame number or a time value in milliseconds, depending on the content.

The `MCIWndPlayFrom` function accepts both the handle to the MCI window and a long integer that specifies the position to begin playback.

MCIWndPlayFromTo - `LONG MCIWndPlayFromTo(hwnd,lStart,lEnd);`

Plays the media in the MCI window between two distinct positions in the content. The playback begins at the From point (`lStart`) and ends at the To point (`lEnd`) unless interrupted by another `MCIWnd` command.

MCIWndPlayTo - `LONG MCIWndPlayTo(hwnd,lPos);`

This function will play the content in the MCI window from the current position to a specified position (`lPos`).

MCIWndPlayReverse - `LONG MCIWndPlayReverse(hwnd);`

Content in the MCI window is played in reverse order, from the current position backwards to the beginning of the content.

MCIWndSeek - `LONG MCIWndSeek(hwnd, lPos);`

Moves the current playback position to a specified location (`lPos`) in the media. You may also specify the constant `MCIWND_START` to move to the beginning of the content or `MCIWND_END` to move to the end of the content.

MCIWndStep - `LONG MCIWndStep(hwnd,n);`

Steps forward or backward by a given increment through the media content. The amount to step (n) can be positive for forward movement or negative for backward movement.

MCIWndStop - `LONG MCIWndStop(hwnd);`

Halts playback or recording of the content in the MCI window.

MCIWndCan Do What?

Besides invoking commands to control an MCI window, you can also get information about the MCI window. `MCIWnd` offers a set of `MCIWndCan` commands that check for the capability of a particular function in the MCI window. The following is a list of the available functions:

MCIWndCanConfig - `BOOL MCIWndCanConfig(hwnd);`

This function returns `TRUE` if the device currently used in the MCI window is configurable through the Configuration dialog box. This function expects the handle to the MCI window.

MCIWndCanEject - `BOOL MCIWndCanEject(hwnd);`

Determines if the current device used by the MCI window can eject its media content. `TRUE` is returned if the media can be ejected; otherwise, `FALSE` is returned.

MCIWndCanPlay - `BOOL MCIWndCanPlay(hwnd);`

If the device or file opened in the MCI window is capable of playback, this function returns `TRUE`.

MCIWndCanRecord - `BOOL MCIWndCanRecord(hwnd);`

Returns `TRUE` if the device associated with the MCI window is capable of recording content.

MCIWndCanSave - `BOOL MCIWndCanSave(hwnd);`

If the device used by the MCI window can save data, this function returns `TRUE`.

MCIWndCanWindow - `BOOL MCIWndCanWindow(hwnd);`

If the device currently loaded by the MCI window can support window-oriented commands, this function returns `TRUE`.

MCIWndGet and *MCIWndSet* Commands

Just as there are several `MCIWnd` commands for determining the capabilities of the MCI window, there are several command groups for getting information about the MCI window or media and for setting this information. The following list shows some of the basic commands in pairs when applicable. The first half of a pair is the function for retrieving specific information, and the second half of the pair shows how to set the information.

MCIWndGetDevice - `LONG MCIWndGetDevice(hwnd,lp,len);`

This function retrieves the name of an open MCI device in the MCI window. It returns 0 if successful; otherwise, it returns an error code. It expects three parameters, the handle to the MCI window, a string buffer in which the device name is inserted, and the maximum length of characters to place in the string buffer. Here is an example:

```
long lResult;
char lpszDeviceName[128];

lResult=MCIWndGetDevice(hMyMCIWnd,lpszDeviceName,128);
```

MCIWndGetDeviceID - `UINT MCIWndGetDeviceID(hwnd);`

Sometimes you will need to use the `mciSendCommand` to control certain specific commands of `MCIWnd`, such as displaying the Configuration dialog box (I discuss this shortly). The `mciSendCommand` expects the device ID of the MCI window in order for the command to be executed properly. The `MCIWndGetDeviceID` function returns the device ID as an integer.

MCIWndGetEnd - `LONG MCIWndGetEnd(hwnd);`

If given a handle to an MCI window, this function returns the ending position of the content in an MCI device or file.

MCIWndGetError - `LONG MCIWndGetError(hwnd,lp,len);`

Retrieves the last MCI error and places it in a string buffer. This function returns the error number of the last `MCIWnd` error. Even if recent function calls were successful, `MCIWndGetError` returns information on the last error that did occur. Also, this function expects the handle to the MCI window, a string buffer to hold the error text, and the maximum length of the string buffer (similar to `MCIWndGetDevice`).

MCIWndGetFileName - `LONG MCIWndGetFileName(hwnd,lp,len);`

Retrieves the file or device name of the media currently in use in the MCI window. The function requires the handle to the MCI window, a string buffer for the file or device name, and a maximum string length for the buffer. If 0 is returned, the function is successful. A return value of 1 indicates an error.

MCIWndGetLength - `LONG MCIWndGetLength(hwnd);`

Returns the length of the content currently used in the MCI window. Do not confuse this with what `MCIWndGetEnd` returns. This value, if added to `MCIWndGetStart`, yields the same value returned by `MCIWndGetEnd`.

MCIWndGetMode - `LONG MCIWndGetMode(hwnd,lp,len);`

Returns the current mode of the MCI device. The function expects a handle to the MCI window, a string buffer to hold the mode, and the maximum length of the buffer. The value returned can be one of the following constants shown in Table 16.5.

Table 16.5. A list of return codes for `MCIWndGetMode`.

Constants	Definition
`MCI_MODE_NOT_READY`	Not ready
`MCI_MODE_OPEN`	Opened
`MCI_MODE_PAUSE`	Paused
`MCI_MODE_PLAY`	Playing
`MCI_MODE_RECORD`	Recording
`MCI_MODE_SEEK`	Seeking
`MCI_MODE_STOP`	Stopped

MCIWndGetPalette - `HPALETTE MCIWndGetPalette(hwnd);`
MCIWndSetPalette - `MCIWndSetPalette(hwnd,hpal);`

These two functions allow you to determine and control the palette for an MCI device, such as a video window. The `MCIWndGetPalette` function returns the handle of the palette in use by the MCI device. `MCIWndSetPalette` expects two parameters: the handle to the MCI window and a handle to a color palette. The second handle sends a palette to the MCI device.

MCIWndGetPosition - `LONG MCIWndGetPosition(hwnd);`
MCIWndGetPositionString - `LONG MCIWndGetPositionString(hwnd,lp,len);`

These two functions return the current playback or recording position of the content in the MCI window. `MCIWndGetPositionString` also copies the recording position as a string and places it in the string buffer passed to the function (`lp`).

MCIWndGetRepeat - `BOOL MCIWndGetRepeat(hwnd);`
MCIWndSetRepeat - `VOID MCIWndSetRepeat(hwnd,f);`

If the content in the MCI window is set to repeat continuously, the `MCIWndGetRepeat` function returns `TRUE`. You can also enable or disable media looping by calling the `MCIWndSetRepeat` function and setting the repeat flag (`f`) parameter to either `TRUE` or `FALSE`, respectively.

MCIWndGetSpeed - `LONG MCIWndGetSpeed(hwnd);`
MCIWndSetSpeed - `LONG MCIWndSetSpeed(hwnd,iSpeed);`

`MCIWndGetSpeed` returns the current speed setting for an MCI device. `MCIWndSetSpeed` allows you to set the playback speed of an MCI device. The `MCIWndSetSpeed` function expects the handle to an MCI window and the speed of the device as an unsigned integer in the second parameter. Larger numbers indicate faster speeds while smaller numbers indicate lower speeds. The normal playback speed is 1000.

MCIWndGetVolume - `LONG MCIWndGetVolume(hwnd);`
MCIWndSetVolume - `LONG MCIWndSetVolume(hwnd,iVol);`

These two functions allow you to access and set the volume for the MCI device. `MCIWndGetVolume` returns the current device's volume. `MCIWndSetVolume` expects an unsigned integer as the volume parameter (iVol) to set the volume. Normal volume is 1000. Larger numbers indicate louder volume, and smaller numbers represent softer volume.

`MCIWndGetZoom` - UINT MCIWndGetZoom(hwnd);
`MCIWndSetZoom` - VOID MCIWndSetZoom(hwnd,iZoom);

To control the zoom size of a video device while preserving the aspect ratio of the window, you use the `MCIWndSetZoom` command. The function expects the second parameter to be the zoom amount; 100 is the normal size, 200 is double the normal size, and 50 is half the normal size. `MCIWndGetZoom` returns the zoom amount (50, 100, or 200, for example).

Displaying the Configuration Window

To perform certain actions in MCI, you may need to revisit the more familiar `mciSendCommand` and `mciSendString` functions. For instance, invoking the Configuration dialog box for a window requires the use of `mciSendCommand`. In this case, the `MCIWndGetDeviceID` function is necessary in order to accomplish this task. Listing 16.4 is sample code for displaying the Configuration dialog box for a device.

Listing 16.4. Sample code for displaying the Configuration dialog box.

```
void CMCIAppDlg::OnConfigure()
{
    char buffer[128];
    MCIERROR error;

    // Check first to make sure the device can be configured
    if (MCIWndCanConfig(hMCIWnd)){
        // Call the configuration dialog box for the current device

        error=mciSendCommand(MCIWndGetDeviceID(hMCIWnd),
                         MCI_CONFIGURE,
                         MCI_WAIT,
                         NULL);
        if (error!=0){
            mciGetErrorString(error, buffer, 128);
            MessageBox(buffer);
        }
    }
}
```

When the above code executes, a configuration window will appear, depending on the device. For a video window, the configuration window will look similar to the one shown in Figure 16.5.

FIGURE 16.5.

The Video Properties configuration window.

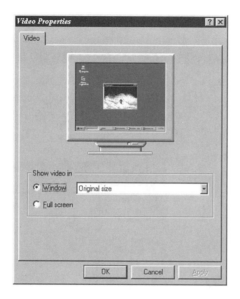

Recording with *MCIWnd*

So far, all of the commands for the MCI window have been related to playback or positioning. Fortunately, recording and saving media content is equally as easy with MCIWnd.

To perform basic recording to a device, MCIWnd provides the MCIWndRecord function. This function is defined as:

> **MCIWndRecord** - LONG MCIWndRecord(hwnd);
>
> MCIWndRecord accepts a handle to the MCI window and returns 0 if the recording process was successful; otherwise, it returns the error code.

The most important aspect to remember about the MCIWndRecord function is that it will begin recording at the current position of the current media file in the MCI window. It will *overwrite* all data already in the file, from the beginning; it will not insert new data after the current position of the file. Therefore, you may decide to create a new file and then save it separately. To do this procedure, you will need to know three more commands: MCIWndNew, MCIWndSave, and MCIWndSaveDialog.

> **MCIWndNew** - LONG MCIWndNew(hwnd, lp);
>
> This function requires two parameters, the handle to the MCI window (hwnd) and a string that contains the name of the MCI device to use for the file. This may be a device name found in either WIN.INI or the Windows 95 registry.

> **MCIWndSave** - LONG MCIWndSave(hwnd, szFile);
>
> MCIWndSave does exactly what its name implies; it saves the data in the MCI window as a file. It expects two parameters, the handle to the MCI window (hwnd), and a string

that identifies the filename (szFile) to use to save the content. Like MCIWndOpen, if you pass a -1 value to this parameter (szFile), a Save dialog box appears.

`MCIWndSaveDialog` - LONG MCIWndSaveDialog(hwnd);

If you want a dialog box to appear, which asks the user where to save the media content, use the MCIWndSaveDialog function. The function returns an error code; otherwise it returns 0 if there was no error while saving the content. Figure 16.6 shows a typical MCIWnd Save As dialog box.

FIGURE 16.6.

The typical Save As dialog box provided by MCIWnd.

Listing 16.5 is sample code that demonstrates how to use the MCIWndRecord function to record digital audio files. It is assumed that a Stop button is available to halt the recording process.

Listing 16.5. Sample source code used to record from an MCI device.

```
void MyRecordingDlg::OnRecord()
{
    hMCIWnd=MCIWndCreate(NULL, AfxGetInstanceHandle(), MCIWNDF_SHOWALL, NULL);

    //Create a new file type of WaveAudio(.WAV)
    MCIWndNew(hMCIWnd, "WAVEAudio");
    MessageBox("Click 'OK' to begin recording.\n
              Click on the 'Stop' button when finished.");

    //Begin the actual recording process.
    MCIWndRecord(hMCIWnd);
}
```

Listing 16.6 is additional code that may be added to a Save button or menu option to store the captured audio as a file.

Listing 16.6. Sample code used to save media content from an MCI window.

```
void CAvicppDlg::OnSave()
{
```

```
MCIWndSaveDialog(hMCIWnd);

//Or optionally, you could use MCIWndSave
//MCIWndSave(hMCIWnd,"TEST.WAV");
}
```

Avoiding Gotchas with *MCIWnd* and C++

While developing the sample application for the MCIWnd control interface included with this book, I encountered and resolved several difficulties before the application worked. Some of the trials, such as attaching the MCI window to a CWnd class so that the window can be positioned, I have already mentioned. At this point, I want to give you a few last words of advice for using MCIWnd.

- Remember to use #include *<afxole.h>* in your application. The best place to add it to is your STDAFX.H file. Although this is not necessary when writing MCIWnd commands in C, it is essential for Visual C++. If you don't do this, you can expect to get a C2371: 'BSTR' : redefinition; different basic types error when you attempt to compile because of the way VFW.H uses OLE.

- Remember to use CWnd::Attach and CWnd::Detach to make modifications, such as window placement, to your MCI window.

- Remember to use #include *<digitalv.h>* for lower-level driver functions such as displaying the Configuration dialog box for a device. Use to #include *<vfw.h>* for MCIWnd commands.

- When linking, remember to use libraries such as VFW32.LIB and WINMM.LIB. Make sure that they are included in your C++ project.

The *MCIWnd* Sample Application

This sample program was developed in Visual C++ to demonstrate some of the basic capabilities of the MCIWnd command set. It is found on the CD-ROM included with this book. It shows how to use many of the MCIWnd commands discussed earlier in this chapter.

Additional CD-ROM Capabilities in Windows 95

As mentioned earlier, MCIWnd is a complete set of functions for controlling media devices of any type: digital audio, video, MIDI, or CD-ROM audio tracks. However, there are additional features Windows 95 offers to the CD-ROM world.

On the user-interface side, Windows 95 reads a CD-ROM each time it is inserted into the computer. If it is an audio CD, the CD icon is updated with a musical note graphic in the My Computer window. If you double-click this icon, the CD Player program starts and plays the disc from the beginning. This same CD Player program (shown in Figure 16.7) also automatically appears whenever the disc is inserted into the system.

FIGURE 16.7.

The CD Player application that comes with Windows 95.

As appealing as this is for playing audio CDs, wouldn't it be nice to start program discs as well? Windows 95 gives you just that capability. Assume you are creating a program that you want to distribute on CD-ROM. With Windows 95 you can now create a CD that will automatically install or run your application whenever it is inserted into the PC. Because Windows 95 automatically supports CD-ROM drives from various manufacturers, your instructions for setting up a CD-based application could be as simple as "place the CD-ROM in your computer's CD-ROM player while running Windows 95."

If you create a CD-ROM, you only need one additional file to allow this capability. Windows 95 searches for the AUTORUN.INF file on the root directory of the CD when it is inserted into the drive. The following is a sample of an AUTORUN.INF file:

```
[AutoRun]
OPEN=myprog.exe
```

The content of the file is incredibly simple. However, there are a few things you should consider when making an autorunning CD.

- Make sure that when the program runs, it first checks to see if it has been properly installed. If it hasn't, then run the installation procedure, prompting the user to continue. Otherwise, just run the program.

- If your application creates shortcuts somewhere else on the Windows 95 desktop, make certain that the shortcut is linked to a real program that is installed on the hard disk. This program should instruct the user to do something like inserting the right CD, if it is not loaded. This way, users can avoid cryptic error messages from Windows 95 about missing files when the CD is not loaded.

- Don't assume that the autorun feature is always available. It may be disabled through SYSTEM.INI or the device manager in Windows 95. Make sure that you have an alternative method for running your application in the absence of the autorun feature.

No More Mousin' Around

Considering all of the sound cards that support a MIDI/Joystick connector, you might have found it surprising that, even though MIDI was supported in Windows 3.x, joystick support did not exist. Now game developers can take advantage of the new joystick capabilities that are standard with Windows 95. Windows 95 comes with a new Joystick Properties control panel, which is shown in Figure 16.8. This allows the gamer to test the joystick. A wizard is included to help calibrate it, which only needs to be done once. This means that games will not have to go through cumbersome calibration routines again and again. This is a friendly feature for the game player as well as the game developer.

FIGURE 16.8.

The Joystick Properties control panel and a test window.

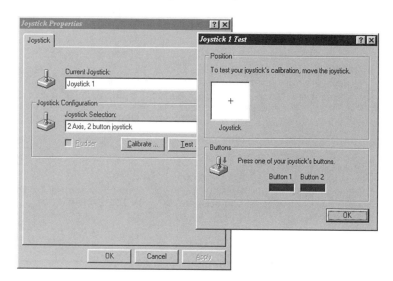

So, how do you use the joystick in Visual C++? First, you have to enable joystick capturing. To do this, you need to use the joySetCapture function. Here is the definition for the joySetCapture function, as well as a description of each of its parameters:

```
int joySetCapture(HWND hwnd,UINT uJoyID,UINT uPeriod,BOOL fChanged);
```

- hwnd—This parameter is the handle to the parent window.
- uJoyID—Specifies which joystick to poll. It can be JOYSTICKID1 or JOYSTICKID2.
- uPeriod—The information about the joystick can be sent back to your application on a given polling interval. This parameter controls the polling frequency in milliseconds.

Listing 16.7 is sample setup code used to enable a joystick on the application's Create event.

Listing 16.7. Setup code for capturing joystick messages.

```
int CJoystickDlg::OnCreate(LPCREATESTRUCT lpCreateStruct)
{
   int result;

   //This is the standard OnCreate call created by C++
   if (CDialog::OnCreate(lpCreateStruct) == -1)
      return -1;

   //Start capturing Joystick #1
   result=joySetCapture(CDialog::m_hWnd, JOYSTICKID1, 0, FALSE);

   if(result==MMSYSERR_NODRIVER){
      MessageBeep(MB_ICONEXCLAMATION);
      MessageBox("Cannot find the joystick driver.", NULL,
               MB_OK | MB_ICONEXCLAMATION);
      return -1;
   }

   if(result==JOYERR_NOCANDO){
      MessageBeep(MB_ICONEXCLAMATION);
      MessageBox("Cannot capture joystick input because a required
               service (such as a Windows timer) is unavailable.",
               NULL, MB_OK | MB_ICONEXCLAMATION);
      return -1;
   }

   if(result==JOYERR_UNPLUGGED){
      MessageBeep(MB_ICONEXCLAMATION);
      MessageBox("The specified joystick is not connected to the
               system.", NULL, MB_OK | MB_ICONEXCLAMATION);
      return -1;
   }
   return 0;
}
```

Once you have started capturing joystick messages, you can examine the messages that come back from the device. However, the joystick does not have a C++ class and cannot be added to the typical Visual C++ message maps. The best way to capture joystick messages is to add a separate WindowProc procedure as shown in Listing 16.8. The joystick device passes messages, such as MM_JOY1BUTTONDOWN, to the WindowProc procedure. The wParam parameter in WindowProc holds information on the joystick button status; the lParam parameter's top eight bits hold the y coordinate (0–65535) and the lower eight bits hold the x coordinate (0–65535). Position 0,0 indicates the top-left corner of the joystick and position 65535,65535 indicates the bottom-right corner of the joystick.

Listing 16.8. A code listing for a sample joystick application.

```
LRESULT CJoystickDlg::WindowProc(UINT message, WPARAM wParam, LPARAM lParam)
{
   switch(message){
      case MM_JOY1BUTTONDOWN:
         if (wParam & JOY_BUTTON1){
```

```
            MessageBeep(MB_ICONQUESTION);
            SetDlgItemText(IDC_BUTTON1, "Button 1: <<<PRESSED>>>");
        }

        if (wParam & JOY_BUTTON2){
            MessageBeep(MB_ICONEXCLAMATION);
            SetDlgItemText(IDC_BUTTON2, "Button 2: <<<PRESSED>>>");
        }
    break;

    case MM_JOY1BUTTONUP:
        if (wParam & JOY_BUTTON1){
            SetDlgItemText(IDC_BUTTON1, "Button 1: <<<PRESSED>>>");
            SetDlgItemText(IDC_BUTTON2, "Button 2:");
        }
        else if (wParam & JOY_BUTTON2){
            SetDlgItemText(IDC_BUTTON2, "Button 2: <<<PRESSED>>>");
            SetDlgItemText(IDC_BUTTON1, "Button 1:");
        }
        else{
            SetDlgItemText(IDC_BUTTON1, "Button 1:");
            SetDlgItemText(IDC_BUTTON2, "Button 2:");
        }
    break;

    case MM_JOY1MOVE:
        WORD x, y;
        POINT pt;

        UpdateData(TRUE);  //Get the Checkbox value.

        // Get the current cursor position in screen coordinates.
        GetCursorPos(&pt);

        // If we're talking about absolute values, make mouse cursor
        // on the screen represent the joystick position on a 1:1 ratio.
        // For example: top-left of joystick is top-left of screen,
        // bottom-right of joystick is bottom-right of screen.
        else{
            // We need to create a DC to get the screen's coordinates
            CDC* pDC = GetDC();

            // Read the x and y coordinates (0-65535)
            x=LOWORD(lParam);
            y=HIWORD(lParam);

            // Our screens are not that big (yet!), we have to scale down
            // to the physical pixels available.
            pt.x=(pDC->GetDeviceCaps(HORZRES)*x)/65536;
            pt.y=(pDC->GetDeviceCaps(VERTRES)*y)/65536;

            ReleaseDC(pDC);
        }

        // Update the mouse cursor position
        SetCursorPos(pt.x, pt.y);
    break;
}
```

continues

Listing 16.8. continued

```
    return CDialog::WindowProc(message, wParam, lParam);
}
```

When you have finished using the joystick, make sure that you release the capture. You can do this with the joyReleaseCapture function. Here is the definition for the function:

```
MMRESULT joyReleaseCapture(UINT uJoyID);
```

The uJoyID is either JOYSTICKID1 or JOYSTICKID2. Listing 16.9 shows how the joystick was released in the Destroy window event for the application.

Listing 16.9. Sample code that shows how a joystick is released.

```
void CJaystickDlg::OnDestroy()
{
    CDialog::OnDestroy();
    joyReleaseCapture(JOYSTICKID1);
}
```

The Joystick Sample Application

If you would like to try using a joystick in Windows 95, the sample code in Listings 16.7, 16.8, and 16.9 is used in an application available on the CD-ROM included with this book. The application creates a simple dialog window. Whenever a button is pressed on the joystick, <<<PRESSED>>> will appear next to the button's text. As you move the joystick, the mouse cursor will move on the screen. Typically, when you hold the joystick in one direction, the mouse will move in that direction. If you release the joystick, the mouse will remain motionless at its current position. You can also enable the Absolute Coordinates option to treat the screen like a calibration test tool. In this case, a motionless joystick places the mouse cursor in the center of the screen; if the joystick is moved to the top-left corner, the mouse moves to the top-left of the screen, and if the joystick is moved to the bottom-right corner, the mouse moves to the bottom-right of the screen.

MCIWndGetEnd

Multimedia is a wide and diverse universe. With new technology being introduced at a rapid pace, it is one of the most exciting areas of the computer industry. Although I could continue to examine the depths of Windows 95 support for multimedia, it would reach far beyond the scope of this book. But for now, you should be acquainted well enough with some of the new features found in Windows 95 to begin practicing some "magic" of your own.

V

The Windows 95 Common Controls

Common Controls, Property Sheets, and MFC with Visual C++ 2.x

17

by Thomas Woelfer

IN THIS CHAPTER

This chapter is about programming with the new common controls using the Microsoft Foundation Classes. To get the most out of this chapter, you should know how to use MFC and you should have created a dialog box using the DDX/DDV mechanisms as supplied by the framework. If you've never worked with MFC before or you've never heard of DDX/ DDV, I suggest you get a grip on these topics first.

After the release of Visual C++ 2.0, Microsoft continued to add support for the new Windows 95 common controls in the Foundation Classes. Some of the directly supplied classes rely on the common controls, so you can't use these classes when the common controls are not available. Other classes implement user interface features that provide a Windows 95 look but do not actually use Windows 95 controls internally.

You will find that the MFC wrapper classes only add a very thin layer to the direct API calls in most cases; in fact, support for common controls more or less boils down to a single include file containing inline functions. However, the dialog box editor in Visual C++ 2.x recognizes some of the common controls and you can assign member variables using ClassWizard—so there are some benefits to using the MFC wrappers.

Because other chapters cover the new controls from an API point of view, I won't go into detail for some of the classes. There is nothing to be gained from repeating here what possible bits can be set. Instead, I'll tell you about the things that are important about using the MFC in particular. When you finish this chapter, you should be able to use MFC with the common controls, as well as property sheets, without bothering about style bits. If you need more details than are provided here, you can refer to the online documentation.

To use the sample code, you will at least need Visual C++ 2.1 and a recent build of Windows 95 or NT 3.51. Please note, however, that some of the functionality MFC supplies has nothing to do with common controls and can be used in older versions of the compiler or other operating systems. The toolbars, for example, have been part of Visual C++ since Version 1.0 and will work under Windows 3.1.

At the time of this writing, Visual C++ as well as Windows 95 was still a moving target. New features have been added frequently to the compiler, the operating system, and the compiler IDE's support for the operating system. In Visual C++ 2.0, the following controls are supported in the dialog box editor:

Animation control—enables you to play .avi files.

Tab control—enables you to place tabs.

Tree view and list view—these two make up what you see in Explorer in the left and right panes, respectively. Both tree and list views support drag-and-drop operations, as well as in-place editing.

Hotkey control—enables your users to select hotkey combinations.

Trackbar control—normally referred to as a slider control.

Progress indicator—indicates, you guessed it, progress.

UpDown control—otherwise known as a spin button.

CToolBar, CStatusBar

Toolbars and statusbars are very common in Windows applications; there is nothing Windows 95-specific about these. However, you should make some special considerations when you're using the MFC implementation.

Support for toolbars and statusbars is directly implemented in AppWizard: When you tell AppWizard you want these in your application, everything is done automatically for you. The CToolBar and CStatusBar classes have some member functions that you can use to customize the appearance of toolbars as well as the way they are positioned in the client area of your window. However, because you probably won't want to do this, I won't go into detail.

The minimum you should know about toolbars and statusbars is the following: There are two sets of quite similar classes in MFC. There is a CToolBar as well as a CToolBarCtrl, and a CStatusBar as well as a CStatusBarCtrl.

The CToolBarCtrl and CStatusBarCtrl are not actually integral parts of the MFC architecture. Instead, these two are just thin wrappers around the common controls providing the toolbar and statusbar functionality. Currently, MFC is not using the Ctrl wrapper classes but its own implementations—and you should probably do the same, because all the functionality you get for free when using CToolBar instead of CToolBarCtrl is lost when you're using the Windows control instead of the MFC implementation.

Apart from some rare situations (that I doubt will ever come your way) where you want to use the CToolBarCtrl rather than the CToolBar class, there is one acceptable reason to use CToolBarCtrl—customization.

The CToolBarCtrl offers a much richer API than the CToolBar does, which means creating customizable toolbars is a lot easier with a CToolBarCtrl. However, you need to write a lot more code when using the control wrappers, and you can no longer use the AppWizard-provided functionality.

The documentation for CToolBars states that customization will be part of CToolBars in a later release of MFC, so I'll be talking about CToolBars and CStatusBars, not the Windows 95 wrapper classes. Your users surely will expect to get a toolbar in their Windows 95 applications, but I doubt they will care if the toolbar control was used to paint it.

To create an application with toolbars and statusbars, all you need to do is check the appropriate option when AppWizard is preparing your new project. If you did so, your application will have a dockable toolbar at the top of its client area, with some of the default commands already in place. These default commands will be based on other options you selected in AppWizard, but there will probably be at least the commands File | Open, File | Save, Print, and Help. All of the toolbar buttons will have tooltips.

You will also get a statusbar at the bottom of your main window. There'll be three panes in the statusbar, and the first pane will be used to display short help texts when you select a menu command.

Both the toolbar and statusbar are created in your `CMainFrame`'s `OnCreate()` method. If you want to configure the toolbar or statusbar, this is the place to go. You can easily change the number of panes in the statusbar, disable the docking feature of the toolbar, remove tooltip support, and so on. All of these possible actions are commented in the code if you asked AppWizard to comment the generated code.

Both classes are members of the `CMainFrame` (derived) class, so you can use the classes inside each member function of the main frame window. In the toolbar sample, I added to the default application a command that sets some text into one of the status panes. I also added a new button to the toolbar. These are the most important things you can do with these two classes, and both are archived quite easily.

To add a new button to a toolbar, do the following:

1. Implement the new command and the command handler, and add a menu entry for this command.
2. Edit the bitmap containing the toolbar buttons with the bitmap editor. You need to add a new bitmap that will be displayed in the toolbar. The framework will automatically do the shading and coloring for different button states, so you only need to supply one image.
3. Add the menu ID to the array of button commands in your `CMainFrame` implementation file. Everything else will be done automatically by MFC.

There is some more functionality you can use without much effort. Go to the menu editor and activate the property page for the new menu command you just added. At the bottom of the property page, there's an edit control. Text you enter into this control will be used as the small helper text that is displayed when the user is moving the highlight inside a menu. If you enter two lines of text, the second line will be used for the toolbar button's tooltip. You need to separate the two lines of text by adding a newline literal \n at the end of the first line.

The association between help text, tooltip text, button, and menu command is done via the resource IDs, which is why you don't need to do any special coding for this.

As you can see in the sample, it is quite easy to display text in the statusbar. The statusbar class provides you with a `SetPaneText()` method. The method expects you to provide a string to provide an index that tells it which pane to use and an optional flag that determines if the text is to be displayed immediately.

CSpinButtonCtrl

You will find the sample code to this part on the CD. Look for the file sample.zip.

Spin buttons, also known as UpDown controls, are most useful when you are querying your users for numerical input. Normally, you'll use the spin button in places where you also have an edit control. That is, your users will be able to enter text directly into the edit control or use the spin button to increase or decrease the numbers inside the edit control.

The edit control normally is referred to as the "buddy" of the spin button. There's not much work required to use the spin button in the way I have described. In AppStudio, go to the dialog box editor and place an edit control on your dialog box. Next, place a spin button close to the edit control that you want to be the buddy. You don't actually need to place the spin button close to the edit control because the alignment of the controls is handled at runtime, but it is always a good idea to keep the appearance of dialog boxes at design time close to their appearance at runtime. To choose an alignment for the controls, go to the property page of the spin button.

There are several ways you can make the spin button work. For example, you could go ahead and process all the spin button's messages yourself; however, in most cases it will be a lot more convenient to let the spin button take care of the messages itself. If you turn on the Set Buddy Integer checkmark in the spin button's property page, the spin button will set its buddy's text as the user chooses either of its arrow buttons.

There are other properties you can try as well, but most of these are obvious so I won't provide details here.

There is one detail that is not obvious. You will find that the spin button's default behavior is to decrement its buddy's integer when the user presses the up button and to increment the number upon a down event. This might have a logic of its own, but I doubt your users will easily adapt, so you should change this behavior. You should also change the spin button's range. For some reason, there is no range property exposed in AppStudio. This option may be provided in a later release of the dialog box editor, but for now you need to change the range programmatically. It turns out that changing the default behavior and the default range can be done with the same call to a spin button's member function.

1. In ClassWizard, add a variable of type CSpinCtrl to the dialog box.
2. Go to the dialog box's InitDialog() member and add a call to the spin class's SetRange() method. SetRange() requires two parameters—the smallest possible value and the largest possible value, respectively.
3. Don't forget to include afxcmn.h in your stdafx.h header file.

CSliderCtrl and CProgressCtrl

You will find the sample code to this part in the file slider.zip on the CD.

A slider control is similar to a spin control in that you can place both of them on your dialog boxes using AppStudio, and both can be used to select a value from a range of discrete values.

Most of the things you can do with slider controls are pretty obvious. You can define tickmarks, set ranges, and so on. What may not be obvious is the Autoclicks option on the property page: You need to make sure Autoclicks is turned on if you want to use the SetTicFreq() member function of the wrapper class.

To use a slider control in your application, do the following:

1. Place the slider control on your dialog box. You can specify the orientation (vertical or horizontal), as well as some other parameters that deal with layout (for example, which direction you want the slider to point). Make sure you don't forget to turn on the Autoclicks option.

2. In ClassWizard, add a member variable of type CSliderCtrl to your dialog box.

3. Don't forget to add afxcmn.h to your stdafx.h.

4. Go to the InitDialog() method and add the following lines of code:

```
m_slider.SetRange( 500, 5000);
m_slider.SetTicFreq( 500);
```

SetRange() obviously sets the range for the slider: The smallest possible value will be 500, the largest one 5000. SetTicFreq() defines the frequency at which tickmarks are displayed for the slider. That is, in this sample, a tickmark will be displayed every 500 units.

Well, that's about all there is to say about sliders. However, because the slider on its own is a little boring, let's add some more controls to the dialog box—introducing progress indicators.

As with the other controls, progress indicators can be placed on dialog boxes from inside the dialog box editor. You will usually use such indicators to show progress during a lengthy operation. In the sample code, that lengthy operation is supplied by a simple loop. The duration of the loop is determined by the current position of the slider control. The loop is started when you press the button labeled "Progress !". To use the progress indicator as in the sample code, do the following:

1. Add the progress indicator to the dialog box and assign a member variable of type CProgressCtrl to the control.

2. Add a button to the dialog box and create an event handler for the button click.

3. Add a static control and a member variable for this control. The sample program uses this static control in order to display the current loop range.

4. In the event handler to the click message, add the following code:

```
// display loop range
char szBuffer[ 128];
wsprintf( szBuffer, "0 to %d", m_slider.GetPos());
m_steps.SetWindowText( szBuffer);

// start the progress indication
m_progress.SetRange( 0, m_slider.GetPos());
m_progress.SetPos( 0);
m_progress.SetStep( 1);

// step it...
for( int i=0; i<m_slider.GetPos(); ++i)
    m_progress.StepIt();
```

There is more than one method to set the progress indicator's position. You can use the SetPos() method to set the control's position property to an absolute value. The OffsetPos() method can be used to move the position counter relative to the current position. The StepIt() method advances the current position of a progress bar by the increment defined in SetStep(), which is what the sample code is doing.

Most of the new controls have some style bits you can set to change the layout or behavior of the controls. Some of these aren't available in the dialog box editor, maybe because these style bits hadn't been defined when the dialog box editor was coded, or maybe because these style bits were thought to be not important enough to be exposed in dialog box editor.

I think that some of these will eventually turn up in later versions of the dialog box editor. As of now, there are two interesting bits you might want to use with progress indicators, that are currently not exposed in the dialog box editor: PBS_SHOWPERCENT and PBS_SHOWPOS.

You might have noticed that the sample progress indicator does not display any textual information about its current state. These two bits can be used to make a progress control display this information: PBS_SHOWPERCENT will display the percent of the range that has completed, and PBS_SHOWPOS will display the current position of the progress bar. However, when you attempt to set these bits at runtime, you will notice that currently Visual C++ does not come with the header files you need— you will need a copy of the SDK to set these bits. (This is why the sample doesn't really do anything when you change the progress label settings. I didn't want to use code that could not be compiled using the currently available versions of Visual C++.) I suggest that you ignore these styles until a future version of Visual C++ exposes these bits in the dialog box editor.

CAnimateCtrl

There isn't much to say about the animate control. The interface consists of a few functions you can use to open an .avi file, play it, seek to a position (a frame) within the file, and stop the playback. The .avi file will be played by Windows simultaneously with your application, so you can keep receiving messages while the video is playing. (A sample for the use of this control is the Find dialog box in the Windows 95 Start menu.)

All of CAnimateCtrl's methods are pretty obvious in their usage; however, note that there's a bug in the MFC wrapper to this control. The Play() method, which is used to start the video playback, expects two parameters of type UINT. Unfortunately, one of these must be set to -1 in order to play a video without explicitly giving the number of frames in the video. Well, I know I keep repeating myself, but I guess this is another case where a future version of Visual C++/MFC will bring some improvements.

CHotKeyCtrl

The CHotKeyCtrl wraps the common hotkey control. A hotkey control enables your user to enter a hotkey combination. The user's choice is displayed in the hotkey control's text pane. You can query this combination from the control and install a hotkey in the system using the WM_SETHOTKEY message.

Not much else is to be said about this class. I doubt you'll realize that you are using C++ when you're working with it because in this case, the C++ wrapper gets so thin, it can hardly be noticed.

CToolTipCtrl

In a way, the tooltip class is very similar to the hotkey class: The MFC wrapper is extremely thin, and there's no gain in functionality here. You cannot place or assign tooltip controls in the dialog box editor or at design time at all, which makes CToolTip controls not much easier to use than the Windows tooltip control itself.

As this time, there is nothing to say about the tooltip class that you cannot find in the chapter on common controls, and I won't repeat the information here.

You should note, however, that the MFC does have some tooltip support built right in. There are tooltips available for toolbars, and you can find more information in the section "CToolBar, CStatusBar" at the beginning at this chapter.

CListCtrl, CTreeCtrl, CImageList, and CHeaderCtrl

Again, these are extremely thin wrapper classes for the common controls. There is not much functional difference, and you can find all information you need in the chapter on common controls.

Property Sheets and Property Pages

You can find the sample code to this section in the file propsheet.zip on the CD.

Property sheets, otherwise known as tabbed dialog boxes, solve the common problem of having more options than would fit on a single dialog box. Without property sheets, your users could end up with a lot of dialog boxes, all accessible via different menu commands. With property sheets, this is different. A property sheet is a special kind of dialog box that contains several pages of information. The user can switch between these pages by using a tab that is attached to the top of each page.

There are three main parts to a property sheet: the framed dialog box containing the pages, one or more pages of information, and the tab at the top of each page.

MFC supports property sheets with the `CPropertySheet` and `CPropertyPage` classes. `CPropertySheet` is the container class, and `CPropertyPage` serves as a base class for the pages contained within. MFC takes care of all the glue logic. All you need to do is provide the dialog boxes. However, there are some things you need to set up correctly to provide the framework with the information needed.

To create a simple property sheet (such as in the propsheet sample), do the following:

1. Include afxdlgs.h in your stdafx.h.

2. In the dialog box editor, create a dialog resource for each individual page. Your users will be able to switch between the pages, so keep the layout as consistent as possible. The pages do not have to be the same size. The size of the property sheet is determined by the first page that is added to the property sheet.

   It's a good trick to create an empty dialog box in the dialog box editor and use this dialog box in copy and paste operations for each new page you create. This way, you will have consistent page sizes throughout your property sheets. You might want to add standard controls to that template, too. (A standard control is a control you expect to be needed on every page. For example, a Reset to Factory Defaults button would be useful to have.)

3. Make sure you use the following styles for all pages.

   The dialog style must be child.

   The border style must be thin.

   The Disabled and Titlebar checkboxes must be checked.

4. On the General page, enter the text you want to appear in the tab for the page you are working on.

5. Change to ClassWizard and create a `CPropertyPage`-derived class for each page you need by choosing `CPropertyPage` from the Base Class listbox.

6. Create member variables to hold values for each page just as you would for ordinary dialog boxes. The individual pages basically work the same as dialog boxes as far as ClassWizard is concerned.

7. In your source code, instantiate a CPropertySheet object. You will normally do this in the event handler function that is used to display the property dialog box. To create a CPropertySheet instance, you need to supply a string (or string ID) for the property sheet's caption bar. (The page's captions will be used for the tabs.) Optionally, you can supply a pointer to the parent window and to the index of the page you want initially to be displayed on top of the property sheet.

8. You need to instantiate an object of each page-derived class you want on your property sheet. If you derived a class from CPropertyPage, you could embed the objects in your sheet-derived class.

9. Add each page to the property sheet using the Add() method. If you derived a class from CPropertyPage, you could do this in your derived class's constructor.

10. You can now display the property sheet using DoModal(), just as you would with a dialog box.

```
CPropertySheet p;
CShapeDlg shape;
CColorDlg color;
p.AddPage( &shape);
p.AddPage( &color);
p.DoModal();
```

After you create the property sheet, you'll probably want to exchange data between the pages and the owner of the property sheet. This exchange is accomplished the same way as it is in ordinary dialog boxes; however, you need to exchange the data with every single page, not with the sheet itself.

If your user switches between the pages of the property sheet, you might want to update your views, or at least parts of them. In order to accomplish this, you need to prepare some things in your code:

1. For your individual pages, create constructors that take a pointer to your document as an argument.

2. When you instantiate your page objects, use GetDocument() to obtain a pointer to the document that is currently displayed in the view and pass that pointer to the page objects. The page objects must store this pointer for later use.

3. In the page's DoDataExchange() function, call UpdateAllViews() (or the appropriate function for your needs) to make sure everything that needs to be repainted gets repainted.

In the sample, you can see that if a new shape gets selected, it will be painted when the pages get switched.

OnOK() and other handling in the pages is identical to the handling in ordinary dialog boxes; the one main difference is the Apply button the framework supplies. When the user changes a setting on a page, you can enable this button by calling the SetModified() method. When the user presses this button, DoDataExchange() is called, and you can update your views. After this has been done, you can call SetModified(FALSE) and the Apply button will be disabled again.

Summary

In this chapter you learned how to use the MFC wrapper classes to the Windows 95 common controls. You also learned that some of the MFC classes don't actually use the common controls but only provide identical user interface features. As the MFC evolves, you will see better support for common controls, as well as added functionality not available with SDK-style common controls. A currently available example of added functionality is the dockable toolbars that were discussed at the beginning of this chapter.

Toolbars and Status Bars

18

by Peter D. Hipson

IN THIS CHAPTER

Windows 95 offers a new level of controls for the developer. These controls are part of the Win32 Common Controls and are supported by Visual C++ 2.x (and later). You can program these controls using either C code or the MFC classes. This chapter covers the toolbar and status bar controls that are part of the Win32 Common Controls.

Also covered in this chapter (briefly) are the MFC toolbar and status bar controls. I've covered these to enable you to compare the differences between the two different implementations.

It is usually easier to use the MFC-implemented classes for the Win32 Common Controls than to try and write the entire support code yourself. The toolbar control is managed with the CToolBarCtrl class, and the status bar control is managed with the CStatusBarCtrl class. In this chapter we look at these classes, then build an implementation of each control giving a practical example of how each control is used.

The MFC Toolbar and the *CToolBarCtrl* Toolbar

Visual C++ 2.x (and later) offer both toolbars and status bars. Now the logical question is: Why did Microsoft create a new set of toolbar and status bar objects? There are several reasons for Microsoft to have done this; however, for many programmers, there is a great deal of redundancy in having two sets of the toolbar and status bar objects.

In this section we look at toolbars.

First, let's look at the attributes for a MFC CToolBar toolbar:

- ■ CToolBar toolbars are dockable and floating. This feature enables the user to move the toolbar from the top of the application's window and place it at the bottom, or simply have it float as a modeless dialog box.

- ■ CToolBar toolbars offer tooltips. Tooltips provide quick feedback to the user regarding a toolbar button's function.

- ■ CToolBar works with the same ON_UPDATE_COMMAND_UI handlers that correspond to the menu items.

- ■ CToolBar works with MFC's document/view architecture, resizing the view as required to reflect changes in the toolbar's state.

- ■ CToolBar toolbars are simple to implement. (With AppWizard-created projects, you can have a default toolbar created for you.)

- ■ CToolBar toolbars support fixed buttons, which are difficult to modify at runtime. The button size can be controlled by the developer.

The most important feature of MFC toolbars is that they are very easy to implement and customize.

There are a number of reasons why a programmer would want to use a CToolBarCtrl object rather than a CToolBar object. These include:

- The CToolBarCtrl object can be attached to windows other than those derived from CFrameWnd. This enables you to have a dialog box with a toolbar. Our sample CToolBarCtrl program places a toolbar into a dialog box.

- The CToolBarCtrl can easily support other dialog box controls (such as a combo box) with a minimum amount of program coding. Our example, later in this chapter, has a combo box control as part of our toolbar example.

- A CToolBarCtrl is modifiable by the user at program runtime. A simple style selection enables the user to add, remove, and reorder toolbar buttons. However, the application must manage some of the customization features, such as non-shifted drag-and-drop.

- The CToolBarCtrl object is much more customizable than the CToolBar object. This will change as MFC becomes more mature. Microsoft expects to add more customization features to CToolBar in one of the future releases of MFC.

First, for our CToolBarCtrl example and for all the other Win32 Common Controls examples in this part of the book, we need a sample application. For this we use Visual C++'s AppWizard to create a dummy application that we'll call DUMMY. Great name, right? Next, we add a new menu selection called &Common Controls. This menu selection should be placed just after the View menu selection. Under Common Controls we place a selection called &ToolBar, which will call up a dialog box demonstrating our toolbar implementation. Figure 18.1 shows the new menu structure.

FIGURE 18.1.

The DUMMY program's menu structure in Visual C++ resource editor.

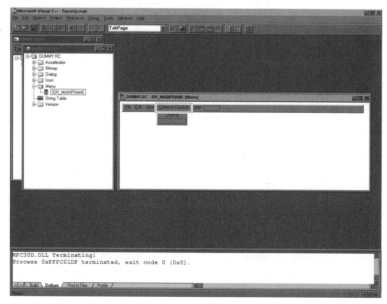

There is nothing special about DUMMY; virtually any MFC application could directly use the examples shown in these chapters.

The *CToolBarCtrl* Class

The CToolBarCtrl class has a number of functions to enable the programmer to create and manage an advanced toolbar. In this part of the chapter, we create a dialog box that has a toolbar in it. This toolbar will have both a set of standard buttons and a number of buttons that the user can add to the toolbar during program execution time.

The steps for adding a toolbar to a dialog box are similar to the steps for adding a toolbar to any other window. First, you need a dialog box. In our sample program, we've created a very simple dialog box with three controls: OK and Cancel buttons and a single checkbox control. Figure 18.2 shows this dialog box with each control labeled with its control ID.

FIGURE 18.2.

The ToolBar dialog box.

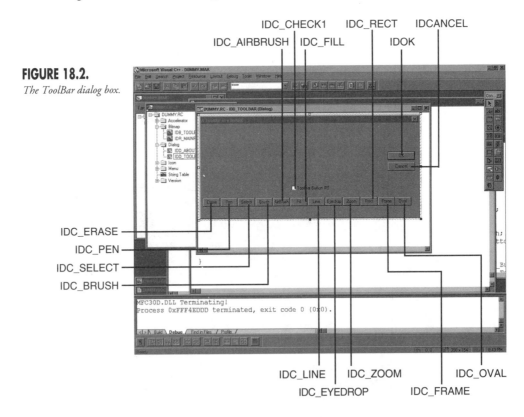

Notice how we have moved the OK and Cancel buttons down to leave room for our toolbar. This is necessary because a dialog box does not resize itself for a toolbar. Maybe right now I'm the only one who's putting toolbars in dialog boxes, but I suspect the technique will become popular as programmers see just how easy it is to add a toolbar to any window, even a dialog box!

In Figure 18.3, you see the bitmap that is used to create the toolbar buttons. All the toolbar buttons are kept in the single bitmap; however, it is possible to have one bitmap resource for each button or some other combination. Because the CToolBarCtrl class is efficient at managing the bitmap resources (it is happy with any combination), the choice of how to arrange your bitmaps is left to you. Many applications will have buttons grouped into classes (for example: edit, file, and window) that will correspond to functionality groupings within the application.

FIGURE 18.3.

The bitmap for our CToolBarCtrl toolbar.

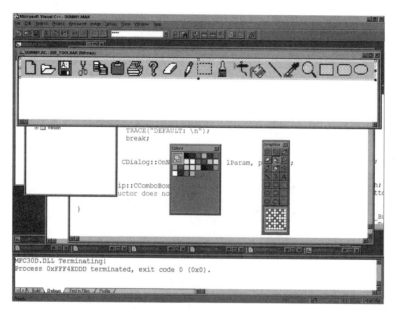

The sample toolbar that I've created for this chapter shows three features of the CToolBarCtrl toolbar. These features are:

■ The addition of a dialog box control (a CComboBox object) in our toolbar. Other dialog controls could be added using this example.

■ The use and activation of toolbar tooltips (those handy flags that pop up when the mouse cursor passes over a toolbar button).

■ User-configurable toolbar buttons. The user may remove or insert buttons on the toolbar. We have a group of 12 buttons that the user can add or remove.

The main code for our toolbar is found in Listing 18.1 and Listing 18.2. This listing is rather complex looking (actually it is not too difficult to follow, once you study it), so we cover implementing the three features and describe the necessary steps after the listings.

Listing 18.1. The TOOLBARD.CPP file, which implements a `CToolBarCtrl` toolbar.

```cpp
// toolbard.cpp : implementation file
//

#include "stdafx.h"
#include "Dummy.h"
#include "toolbard.h"

#ifdef _DEBUG
#undef THIS_FILE
static char BASED_CODE THIS_FILE[] = __FILE__;
#endif

/////////////////////////////////////////////////////////////////////////////
// CToolBarDlg dialog


CToolBarDlg::CToolBarDlg(CWnd* pParent /*=NULL*/)
    : CDialog(CToolBarDlg::IDD, pParent)
{
    //{{AFX_DATA_INIT(CToolBarDlg)
        // NOTE: the ClassWizard will add member initialization here
    //}}AFX_DATA_INIT

    m_ComboBox.m_hWndToolBar = m_ToolBarCtrl.m_hWnd;
}


void CToolBarDlg::DoDataExchange(CDataExchange* pDX)
{
    CDialog::DoDataExchange(pDX);
    //{{AFX_DATA_MAP(CToolBarDlg)
    DDX_Control(pDX, IDC_ZOOM, m_Zoom);
    DDX_Control(pDX, IDC_SELECT, m_Select);
    DDX_Control(pDX, IDC_RECT, m_Rect);
    DDX_Control(pDX, IDC_PEN, m_Pen);
    DDX_Control(pDX, IDC_OVAL, m_Oval);
    DDX_Control(pDX, IDC_LINE, m_Line);
    DDX_Control(pDX, IDC_FRAME, m_Frame);
    DDX_Control(pDX, IDC_FILL, m_Fill);
    DDX_Control(pDX, IDC_EYEDROP, m_Eyedrop);
    DDX_Control(pDX, IDC_ERASE, m_Erase);
    DDX_Control(pDX, IDC_BRUSH, m_Brush);
    DDX_Control(pDX, IDC_AIRBRUSH, m_AirBrush);
    DDX_Control(pDX, IDC_CHECK1, m_CheckButton);
    //}}AFX_DATA_MAP
}

BEGIN_MESSAGE_MAP(CToolBarDlg, CDialog)
    //{{AFX_MSG_MAP(CToolBarDlg)
    ON_BN_CLICKED(IDC_CHECK1, OnCheck1)
    //}}AFX_MSG_MAP

//    We add our own handlers for toolbar buttons also.
//    This is used where a button does not have a dialog control
```

```
//    (or menu item) to handle the button's actions.

    ON_BN_CLICKED(IDC_LAST_BUTTON, OnLastButton)
    ON_BN_CLICKED(IDC_OTHER_BUTTON, OnOtherButton)

//    Handlers for the 'optional' buttons:

    ON_BN_CLICKED(IDC_ERASE,    OnIDC_ERASE   )
    ON_BN_CLICKED(IDC_PEN,      OnIDC_PEN     )
    ON_BN_CLICKED(IDC_SELECT,   OnIDC_SELECT  )
    ON_BN_CLICKED(IDC_BRUSH,    OnIDC_BRUSH   )
    ON_BN_CLICKED(IDC_AIRBRUSH, OnIDC_AIRBRUSH)
    ON_BN_CLICKED(IDC_FILL,     OnIDC_FILL    )
    ON_BN_CLICKED(IDC_LINE,     OnIDC_LINE    )
    ON_BN_CLICKED(IDC_EYEDROP,  OnIDC_EYEDROP )
    ON_BN_CLICKED(IDC_ZOOM,     OnIDC_ZOOM    )
    ON_BN_CLICKED(IDC_RECT,   / OnIDC_RECT    )
    ON_BN_CLICKED(IDC_FRAME,    OnIDC_FRAME   )
    ON_BN_CLICKED(IDC_OVAL,     OnIDC_OVAL    )

END_MESSAGE_MAP()


/////////////////////////////////////////////////////////////////////////
// CToolBarDlg message handlers

// Default (addable) buttons:

TBBUTTON tbButtonNew[] =
{
    { 8,   IDC_ERASE,      TBSTATE_ENABLED, TBSTYLE_BUTTON, 0, 0},
    { 9,   IDC_PEN,        TBSTATE_ENABLED, TBSTYLE_BUTTON, 0, 0},
    {10,   IDC_SELECT,     TBSTATE_ENABLED, TBSTYLE_BUTTON, 0, 0},
    {11,   IDC_BRUSH,      TBSTATE_ENABLED, TBSTYLE_BUTTON, 0, 0},
    {12,   IDC_AIRBRUSH,   TBSTATE_ENABLED, TBSTYLE_BUTTON, 0, 0},
    {13,   IDC_FILL,       TBSTATE_ENABLED, TBSTYLE_BUTTON, 0, 0},
    {14,   IDC_LINE,       TBSTATE_ENABLED, TBSTYLE_BUTTON, 0, 0},
    {15,   IDC_EYEDROP,    TBSTATE_ENABLED, TBSTYLE_BUTTON, 0, 0},
    {16,   IDC_ZOOM,       TBSTATE_ENABLED, TBSTYLE_BUTTON, 0, 0},
    {17,   IDC_RECT,       TBSTATE_ENABLED, TBSTYLE_BUTTON, 0, 0},
    {18,   IDC_FRAME,      TBSTATE_ENABLED, TBSTYLE_BUTTON, 0, 0},
    {19,   IDC_OVAL,       TBSTATE_ENABLED, TBSTYLE_BUTTON, 0, 0},

};


BOOL CToolBarDlg::OnInitDialog()
{
    CDialog::OnInitDialog();

    // TODO: Add extra initialization here

//    We create our toolbar (this is in a standard dialog box)
//    with the CToolBarCtrl.Create() function. This function takes
//    a RECT structure as a parameter, but the RECT structure is ignored
//    and not used.

    int ButtonBitmap = 0;
```

continues

Listing 18.1. continued

```
        int ButtonString = 0;
        int ButtonCount = 0;

        RECT    rect;
        rect.top = 0;
        rect.left = 0;
        rect.bottom = 60;
        rect.right = 100;

        m_ToolBarCtrl.Create(
            WS_CHILD ¦ WS_VISIBLE ¦ CCS_TOP ¦ TBSTYLE_TOOLTIPS ¦ CCS_ADJUSTABLE,
            rect, this, 0);

        ButtonBitmap = m_ToolBarCtrl.AddBitmap(20, IDB_TOOLBAR);
        ButtonString = m_ToolBarCtrl.AddString(IDS_FIRST_BUTTON);

        m_Buttons[ButtonCount].iBitmap = NULL;
        m_Buttons[ButtonCount].idCommand = 0;
        m_Buttons[ButtonCount].fsState = TBSTATE_ENABLED;
        m_Buttons[ButtonCount].fsStyle = TBSTYLE_SEP;
        m_Buttons[ButtonCount].dwData = 0;
        m_Buttons[ButtonCount].iString = NULL;

        ++ButtonCount;

//      Move everything over to leave room for the ComboBox
//      that will be on the far left of the toolbar.
//      The ComboBox could be anywhere, but putting it on the
//      left is easier for the programmer. Most applications with
//      stock implementations of CToolBarCtrl do it this way.

        m_Buttons[ButtonCount] = m_Buttons[ButtonCount - 1];
        ++ButtonCount;
        m_Buttons[ButtonCount] = m_Buttons[ButtonCount - 1];
        ++ButtonCount;
        m_Buttons[ButtonCount] = m_Buttons[ButtonCount - 1];
        ++ButtonCount;
        m_Buttons[ButtonCount] = m_Buttons[ButtonCount - 1];
        ++ButtonCount;
        m_Buttons[ButtonCount] = m_Buttons[ButtonCount - 1];
        ++ButtonCount;
        m_Buttons[ButtonCount] = m_Buttons[ButtonCount - 1];
        ++ButtonCount;
        m_Buttons[ButtonCount] = m_Buttons[ButtonCount - 1];
        ++ButtonCount;
        m_Buttons[ButtonCount] = m_Buttons[ButtonCount - 1];
        ++ButtonCount;
        m_Buttons[ButtonCount] = m_Buttons[ButtonCount - 1];
        ++ButtonCount;
        m_Buttons[ButtonCount] = m_Buttons[ButtonCount - 1];
        ++ButtonCount;
        m_Buttons[ButtonCount] = m_Buttons[ButtonCount - 1];
        ++ButtonCount;
        m_Buttons[ButtonCount] = m_Buttons[ButtonCount - 1];
        ++ButtonCount;

        m_Buttons[ButtonCount].iBitmap = ButtonBitmap + 0;
```

```
m_Buttons[ButtonCount].idCommand = IDOK;
m_Buttons[ButtonCount].fsState = TBSTATE_ENABLED;
m_Buttons[ButtonCount].fsStyle = TBSTYLE_BUTTON;
m_Buttons[ButtonCount].dwData = 0;
m_Buttons[ButtonCount].iString = ButtonString;

++ButtonCount;

m_Buttons[ButtonCount].iBitmap = NULL;
m_Buttons[ButtonCount].idCommand = 0;
m_Buttons[ButtonCount].fsState = TBSTATE_ENABLED;
m_Buttons[ButtonCount].fsStyle = TBSTYLE_SEP;
m_Buttons[ButtonCount].dwData = 0;
m_Buttons[ButtonCount].iString = NULL;

++ButtonCount;

m_Buttons[ButtonCount].iBitmap = ButtonBitmap + 1;
m_Buttons[ButtonCount].idCommand = IDCANCEL;
m_Buttons[ButtonCount].fsState = TBSTATE_ENABLED;
m_Buttons[ButtonCount].fsStyle = TBSTYLE_BUTTON;
m_Buttons[ButtonCount].dwData = 0;
m_Buttons[ButtonCount].iString = NULL;

++ButtonCount;

m_Buttons[ButtonCount].iBitmap = ButtonBitmap + 2;
m_Buttons[ButtonCount].idCommand = IDC_CHECK1;
m_Buttons[ButtonCount].fsState = TBSTATE_ENABLED;
m_Buttons[ButtonCount].fsStyle = TBSTYLE_CHECK;
m_Buttons[ButtonCount].dwData = 0;
m_Buttons[ButtonCount].iString = NULL;

++ButtonCount;

m_Buttons[ButtonCount].iBitmap = ButtonBitmap + 3;
m_Buttons[ButtonCount].idCommand = IDC_OTHER_BUTTON;
m_Buttons[ButtonCount].fsState = TBSTATE_ENABLED;
m_Buttons[ButtonCount].fsStyle = TBSTYLE_BUTTON;
m_Buttons[ButtonCount].dwData = 0;
m_Buttons[ButtonCount].iString = NULL;

++ButtonCount;

m_Buttons[ButtonCount].iBitmap = ButtonBitmap + 4;
m_Buttons[ButtonCount].idCommand = 0;
m_Buttons[ButtonCount].fsState = TBSTATE_ENABLED;
m_Buttons[ButtonCount].fsStyle = TBSTYLE_SEP;
m_Buttons[ButtonCount].dwData = 0;
m_Buttons[ButtonCount].iString = NULL;

++ButtonCount;

m_Buttons[ButtonCount].iBitmap = ButtonBitmap + 5;
m_Buttons[ButtonCount].idCommand = IDC_LAST_BUTTON;
m_Buttons[ButtonCount].fsState = TBSTATE_ENABLED;
m_Buttons[ButtonCount].fsStyle = TBSTYLE_BUTTON;
```

continues

Listing 18.1. continued

```
      m_Buttons[ButtonCount].dwData = 0;
      m_Buttons[ButtonCount].iString = ButtonString;

      ++ButtonCount;

//    Once the m_Buttons[] array is filled in, then we add
//    the buttons to the toolbar.

      m_ToolBarCtrl.AddButtons(ButtonCount, m_Buttons);

//    Since our bitmaps are non-standard in size, we resize
//    the toolbar's buttons to fit the bitmaps:

      CSize sizeButtons(55, 65);

      m_ToolBarCtrl.SetButtonSize(sizeButtons);

//    Since our bitmaps are non-standard in size, we tell
//    the toolbar the real size of our images:

      CSize sizeBitmap(48, 45);

      m_ToolBarCtrl.SetBitmapSize(sizeBitmap);

//    Finally, we resize the toolbar for our non-standard
//    button sizes:

      m_ToolBarCtrl.AutoSize();

//    Finally, add our ComboBox to the toolbar. We add it to the
//    left edge to make things easy. The buttons are spaced over
//    using a bunch of TBSTYLE_SEP buttons.
//
//    The ComboBox will be created with a standard string height for the
//    visible portion. The rect.bottom specifies the dropdown part.
//    We set the height of the top part later...

      rect.top = 2; rect.left = 5; rect.bottom = 200; rect.right = 100;

      if (m_ComboBox.Create( WS_CHILD | WS_BORDER | WS_VISIBLE |
         CBS_HASSTRINGS | CBS_DROPDOWN, rect, (CWnd *)&m_ToolBarCtrl, 123) == 0)
      {// Real applications would have to perhaps recover from this error:
         TRACE("Could not create combobox\n");
      }
      else
      {
//       Set the ComboBox's edit area's height to the height of
//       the button's bitmap size!

         m_ComboBox.SetItemHeight(-1, 45);

//       Add (some dummy) strings to the ComboBox:

         m_ComboBox.AddString("asdf");
         m_ComboBox.AddString("qwer");
         m_ComboBox.AddString("zxcv");

//       Set the current selection to the (zero based) second item
```

```
            m_ComboBox.SetCurSel(1);
    }

    rect.top = 2; rect.left = 5; rect.bottom = 45; rect.right = 100;
    CToolTipCtrl * tt;
    tt = m_ToolBarCtrl.GetToolTips();

    if (tt->AddTool(&m_ComboBox, IDC_COMBO_BOX) == 0)
    {
        TRACE("AddTool() failed!!!!!\n");
    }


    return TRUE;   // return TRUE unless you set the focus to a control
                   // EXCEPTION: OCX Property Pages should return FALSE
}

void CToolBarDlg::OnCheck1()
{
//    Our pushbutton on the toolbar is at command index IDC_CHECK1.

//    Notice how the dialog's check feature now cannot be used directly,
//    that is, you must use the toolbar to check/uncheck the control!
//    Real applications would not use this type of control/toolbar connection
//    however, so this is not an issue.

    if (m_ToolBarCtrl.IsButtonChecked(IDC_CHECK1))
    {// Checked in toolbar
        m_CheckButton.SetCheck(1);
        TRACE("The CheckButton was checked!\n");
    }
    else
    {// Not checked in toolbar
        m_CheckButton.SetCheck(0);
        TRACE("The CheckButton was not checked!\n");
    }

    TRACE("Our Check button has been pressed!\n");
}

void CToolBarDlg::OnLastButton()
{
//    Toggle the third button on the toolbar!
//    Note: this changes the visual state, but does
//    not call the handler!  Notice that we use a really crude
//    index to determine the check box's state, and this
//    should not be used in 'real' programs!

//    Calling m_ToolBarCtrl.PressButton(IDC_CHECK1, TRUE);
//    would give the effect of a pressed button without
//    the 'checked' effect (which displays in a lighter background)

    static int j = 0;

    if (j == 0)
    {
```

continues

544

Listing 18.1. continued

```
        m_ToolBarCtrl.CheckButton(IDC_CHECK1, TRUE);
        j = 1;
    }
    else
    {
        m_ToolBarCtrl.CheckButton(IDC_CHECK1, FALSE);
        j = 0;
    }

    TRACE("The last button was pressed!\n");
}

void CToolBarDlg::OnOtherButton()
{
//    Toggle the third button on the toolbar!
//    Note: this changes the visual state, but does
//    not call the handler! Notice that we use a really crude
//    index to determine the check box's state, and this
//    should not be used in 'real' programs!

//    Calling m_ToolBarCtrl.PressButton(IDC_CHECK1, TRUE);
//    would give the effect of a pressed button without
//    the 'checked' effect (which displays in a lighter background)

    static int j = 0;

    if (j == 0)
    {
        m_ToolBarCtrl.CheckButton(IDC_CHECK1, TRUE);
        j = 1;
    }
    else
    {
        m_ToolBarCtrl.CheckButton(IDC_CHECK1, FALSE);
        j = 0;
    }

    TRACE("The other button was pressed!\n");
}
//--------------------

void CToolBarDlg::OnIDC_ZOOM()
{
//    Handles the optional toolbar button, if on the toolbar!

    static int j = 0;

    if (j == 0)
    {
        m_Zoom.SetState(TRUE);
        j = 1;
    }
    else
    {
```

```
            m_Zoom.SetState(FALSE);
            j = 0;
        }
}

void CToolBarDlg::OnIDC_SELECT()
{
//    Handles the optional toolbar button, if on the toolbar!

    static int j = 0;

    if (j == 0)
    {
        m_Select.SetState(TRUE);
        j = 1;
    }
    else
    {
        m_Select.SetState(FALSE);
        j = 0;
    }
}

void CToolBarDlg::OnIDC_RECT()
{
//    Handles the optional toolbar button, if on the toolbar!

    static int j = 0;

    if (j == 0)
    {
        m_Rect.SetState(TRUE);
        j = 1;
    }
    else
    {
        m_Rect.SetState(FALSE);
        j = 0;
    }
}

void CToolBarDlg::OnIDC_PEN()
{
//    Handles the optional toolbar button, if on the toolbar!

    static int j = 0;

    if (j == 0)
    {
        m_Pen.SetState(TRUE);
        j = 1;
    }
    else
    {
        m_Pen.SetState(FALSE);
```

continues

Listing 18.1. continued

```
        j = 0;
    }
}

void CToolBarDlg::OnIDC_OVAL()
{
//    Handles the optional toolbar button, if on the toolbar!

    static int j = 0;

    if (j == 0)
    {
        m_Oval.SetState(TRUE);
        j = 1;
    }
    else
    {
        m_Oval.SetState(FALSE);
        j = 0;
    }
}

void CToolBarDlg::OnIDC_LINE()
{
//    Handles the optional toolbar button, if on the toolbar!

    static int j = 0;

    if (j == 0)
    {
        m_Line.SetState(TRUE);
        j = 1;
    }
    else
    {
        m_Line.SetState(FALSE);
        j = 0;
    }
}

void CToolBarDlg::OnIDC_FRAME()
{
//    Handles the optional toolbar button, if on the toolbar!

    static int j = 0;

    if (j == 0)
    {
        m_Frame.SetState(TRUE);
        j = 1;
    }
    else
    {
```

```
        m_Frame.SetState(FALSE);
        j = 0;
    }
}

void CToolBarDlg::OnIDC_FILL()
{
//    Handles the optional toolbar button, if on the toolbar!


    static int j = 0;

    if (j == 0)
    {
        m_Fill.SetState(TRUE);
        j = 1;
    }
    else
    {
        m_Fill.SetState(FALSE);
        j = 0;
    }
}

void CToolBarDlg::OnIDC_EYEDROP()
{
//    Handles the optional toolbar button, if on the toolbar!


    static int j = 0;

    if (j == 0)
    {
        m_Eyedrop.SetState(TRUE);
        j = 1;
    }
    else
    {
        m_Eyedrop.SetState(FALSE);
        j = 0;
    }
}

void CToolBarDlg::OnIDC_ERASE()
{
//    Handles the optional toolbar button, if on the toolbar!

    static int j = 0;

    if (j == 0)
    {
        m_Erase.SetState(TRUE);
        j = 1;
    }
    else
    {
        m_Erase.SetState(FALSE);
        j = 0;
```

continues

Listing 18.1. continued

```
    }
}

void CToolBarDlg::OnIDC_BRUSH()
{
//    Handles the optional toolbar button, if on the toolbar!

    static int j = 0;

    if (j == 0)
    {
        m_Brush.SetState(TRUE);
        j = 1;
    }
    else
    {
        m_Brush.SetState(FALSE);
        j = 0;
    }
}

void CToolBarDlg::OnIDC_AIRBRUSH()
{
//    Handles the optional toolbar button, if on the toolbar!

    static int j = 0;

    if (j == 0)
    {
        m_AirBrush.SetState(TRUE);
        j = 1;
    }
    else
    {
        m_AirBrush.SetState(FALSE);
        j = 0;
    }
}


//--------------------
BOOL CToolBarDlg::OnNotify(WPARAM wParam, LPARAM lParam, LRESULT* pResult)
{
//    Our own OnNotify (ClassWizard does not create OnNotify, bummer)...
//    TRACE("OnNotify() called \n");

    TOOLTIPTEXT    * tt;
    NMHDR    *    hdr;
    tt = (TOOLTIPTEXT *)lParam;
    hdr = (NMHDR *)lParam;
    LPTBNOTIFY    lpTbNotify = (LPTBNOTIFY)lParam;

    CString        Tip;
```

```
    CString         String;

    switch(tt->hdr.code)
    {
        case TTN_NEEDTEXT:
//              TRACE("TTN_NEEDTEXT \n");
            Tip.LoadString(tt->hdr.idFrom);
            strcpy(tt->szText, (LPCSTR)Tip);
            break;

        case TBN_QUERYINSERT:
//              TRACE("TBN_QUERYINSERT \n");

            if (pResult != NULL)
                *pResult = TRUE;

            return(TRUE);
            break;

        case TBN_QUERYDELETE:
//              TRACE("TBN_QUERYDELETE \n");

            if (pResult != NULL)
                *pResult = TRUE;

            return(TRUE);
            break;

        case TBN_GETBUTTONINFO:
//              TRACE("TBN_GETBUTTONINFO \n");

            if (lpTbNotify->iItem < 12)
            {
//                  The below TRACE()'s allow you to peek at the passed structures!

//                      TRACE("lpTbNotify = %p \n", lpTbNotify);

//                      TRACE("lpTbNotify->hdr.hwndFrom = %d \n",
//                          lpTbNotify->hdr.hwndFrom);
//                      TRACE("lpTbNotify->hdr.idFrom = %p \n",
//                          lpTbNotify->hdr.idFrom);
//                      TRACE("lpTbNotify->hdr.code = %p \n",
//                          lpTbNotify->hdr.code);

//                      TRACE("lpTbNotify->iItem = %d \n", lpTbNotify->iItem);

//                      TRACE("lpTbNotify->tbButton.iBitmap = %d \n",
//                          lpTbNotify->tbButton.iBitmap);
//                      TRACE("lpTbNotify->tbButton.idCommand = %d \n",
//                          lpTbNotify->tbButton.idCommand);
//                      TRACE("lpTbNotify->cchText = %d \n",
//                          lpTbNotify->cchText);
//                      TRACE("lpTbNotify->tbButton.fsState = %d \n",
//                          lpTbNotify->tbButton.fsState);
//                      TRACE("lpTbNotify->tbButton.fsStyle = %d \n",
//                          lpTbNotify->tbButton.fsStyle);
//                      TRACE("lpTbNotify->tbButton.dwData = %d \n",
```

continues

Listing 18.1. continued

```
//                 lpTbNotify->tbButton.dwData);
//             TRACE("lpTbNotify->tbButton.iString = %d \n",
//                 lpTbNotify->tbButton.iString);

//           TRACE("lpTbNotify->pszText = %p \n",
//                 lpTbNotify->pszText);


           lpTbNotify->tbButton = tbButtonNew[lpTbNotify->iItem];

           if (lpTbNotify->pszText != NULL)
           {// Only return the string, if there is a buffer!
               String.LoadString(
                   tbButtonNew[lpTbNotify->iItem].idCommand);

               strcpy(lpTbNotify->pszText, (LPCSTR)String);
               lpTbNotify->cchText = strlen(lpTbNotify->pszText);
           }

           if (pResult != NULL)
               *pResult = TRUE;

           return(TRUE);
       }
       else
       {//    Not a valid button for the toolbar!
//             TRACE("Was not a valid selection!\n");
       }

       break;

   case TBN_BEGINDRAG:
//         Called when the user starts a drag (without using
//         the shift key). Your code must handle this
//         case.

//             TRACE("TBN_BEGINDRAG: \n");
           break;
   case TBN_ENDDRAG:
//         Called when the user ends a drag (without using
//         the shift key). Your code must handle this
//         case.

//             TRACE("TBN_ENDDRAG: \n");
           break;
   case TBN_BEGINADJUST:
//             TRACE("TBN_BEGINADJUST: \n");
           break;
   case TBN_ENDADJUST:
//             TRACE("TBN_ENDADJUST: \n");
           break;
   case TBN_RESET:
//             TRACE("TBN_RESET: \n");
           break;
   case TBN_TOOLBARCHANGE:
//             TRACE("TBN_TOOLBARCHANGE: \n");
```

```
            break;
        case TBN_CUSTHELP:
//             TRACE("TBN_CUSTHELP: \n");
            break;

        default: // Should never happen.
//             TRACE("DEFAULT: \n");
            break;
    }

    return CDialog::OnNotify(wParam, lParam, pResult);
}

CComboBoxTip::CComboBoxTip()
{// Constructor does nothing at all!


}
```

Listing 18.2 is the header file that accompanies Listing 18.1. This file is short and simple and requires no explanation.

Listing 18.2. The TOOLBARD.H header file.

```
// toolbard.h : header file
//

class    CComboBoxTip : public CComboBox
{
// Construction
public:
    CComboBoxTip();    // standard constructor

    HWND m_hWndToolBar;
};



/////////////////////////////////////////////////////////////////////////////
// CToolBarDlg dialog

class CToolBarDlg : public CDialog
{
// Construction
public:
    CToolBarDlg(CWnd* pParent = NULL);    // standard constructor

// Dialog Data
    //{{AFX_DATA(CToolBarDlg)
    enum { IDD = IDD_TOOLBAR };
    CButton    m_Zoom;
    CButton    m_Select;
    CButton    m_Rect;
    CButton    m_Pen;
    CButton    m_Oval;
```

continues

Listing 18.2. continued

```
    CButton     m_Line;
    CButton     m_Frame;
    CButton     m_Fill;
    CButton     m_Eyedrop;
    CButton     m_Erase;
    CButton     m_Brush;
    CButton     m_AirBrush;
    CButton     m_CheckButton;
    //}}AFX_DATA

    TBBUTTON        m_Buttons[25];
    CToolBarCtrl    m_ToolBarCtrl;
    CToolTipCtrl    m_ToolTipCtrl;
//    CComboBox        m_ComboBox;
    CComboBoxTip    m_ComboBox;

// Overrides
    // ClassWizard generated virtual function overrides
    //{{AFX_VIRTUAL(CToolBarDlg)
    public:
    virtual BOOL OnNotify(WPARAM wParam, LPARAM lParam, LRESULT* pResult);
    protected:
    virtual void DoDataExchange(CDataExchange* pDX);    // DDX/DDV support
    //}}AFX_VIRTUAL

// Implementation
protected:

    // Generated message map functions
    //{{AFX_MSG(CToolBarDlg)
    virtual BOOL OnInitDialog();
    afx_msg void OnCheck1();
    //}}AFX_MSG

//    Default toolbar button handlers:

    afx_msg void OnLastButton();
    afx_msg void OnOtherButton();

//    Optional toolbar button handlers:

    afx_msg void OnIDC_ERASE();
    afx_msg void OnIDC_PEN();
    afx_msg void OnIDC_SELECT();
    afx_msg void OnIDC_BRUSH();
    afx_msg void OnIDC_AIRBRUSH();
    afx_msg void OnIDC_FILL();
    afx_msg void OnIDC_LINE();
    afx_msg void OnIDC_EYEDROP();
    afx_msg void OnIDC_ZOOM();
    afx_msg void OnIDC_RECT();
    afx_msg void OnIDC_FRAME();
    afx_msg void OnIDC_OVAL();

    DECLARE_MESSAGE_MAP()
};
```

Implementing a *CToolBarCtrl* Toolbar

There is a minimum amount of code to implement the CToolBarCtrl object. You must complete the following steps at the time the parent window is created (the one that will have the toolbar in it):

1. Create your CToolBarCtrl object. Use the CToolBarCtrl::Create() function to do this. After creating the toolbar, you must attach the bitmaps (and strings, if applicable) to the toolbar.

2. Initialize your button structures. The button structures are used by CToolBarCtrl to obtain information about the button style, the image used to display the buttons, and the button's text (for tooltips).

3. Do final housekeeping tasks, such as setting the button size if your CToolBarCtrl object uses buttons that are not standard size.

Creating a *CToolBarCtrl* Object

First, create your CToolBarCtrl object:

```
m_ToolBarCtrl.Create(
    WS_CHILD | WS_VISIBLE | CCS_TOP | TBSTYLE_TOOLTIPS | CCS_ADJUSTABLE,
    rect, this, 0);
```

The styles used include those styles typical to almost all windows (WS_CHILD and WS_VISIBLE) and then styles that are unique to CToolBarCtrl objects. I chose to use the CCS_TOP style (toolbar is at the top of the parent window rather than at the bottom); TBSTYLE_TOOLTIPS, which specifies that I want tooltips; and CCS_ADJUSTABLE, which specifies that the user is able to add, remove, and reorder the toolbar's buttons.

Table 18.1 shows the styles that may be used when creating a CToolBarCtrl toolbar.

Table 18.1. Possible CToolBarCtrl window styles.

Style	Description
WS_CHILD	Always specified for a CToolBarCtrl toolbar.
WS_VISIBLE	Usually specified for a CToolBarCtrl toolbar.
WS_DISABLED	Rarely specified for a CToolBarCtrl toolbar, but can be used with the assumption that perhaps later the toolbar will be specifically enabled.
CCS_ADJUSTABLE	Specifying the CCS_ADJUSTABLE style allows the toolbar to be customized by the user. You must implement OnNotify() to manage the WM_NOTIFY messages generated by customization.

continues

Table 18.1. continued

Style	*Description*
CCS_BOTTOM	The converse of CCS_TOP, the CCS_BOTTOM style will have the CToolBarCtrl toolbar positioned at the bottom of the parent window's client area. The default width will be the same as the parent window's width.
CCS_NODIVIDER	When the CCS_BOTTOM style is specified, this style will prevent the two-pixel divider from being drawn at the top of the toolbar.
CCS_NOHILITE	When the CCS_BOTTOM style is specified, this style will prevent the one-pixel highlight from being drawn at the top of the toolbar.
CCS_NOMOVEY	Tells the CToolBarCtrl toolbar to resize and move the toolbar horizontally, but not vertically, when a WM_SIZE message is received. If the CCS_NORESIZE style is specified, this style has no effect.
CCS_NOPARENTALIGN	The CCS_NOPARENTALIGN style will prevent the toolbar from automatically moving to the top (or bottom) of the parent window. The toolbar will keep its position within the parent window regardless of changes to the size of the parent window. When this style is used with the CCS_TOP or CCS_BOTTOM styles, the height will be adjusted to the default height, but the toolbar's position and width will not change.
CCS_NORESIZE	This style will prevent the toolbar from using the default width and height when setting its initial size or a new size. Instead, the control uses the width and height specified in the *rect* parameter specified in the CToolBarCtrl::Create() call.
CCS_TOP	The converse of CCS_BOTTOM, the CCS_TOP style will have the CToolBarCtrl toolbar positioned at the top of the parent window's client area. The default width will be the same as the parent window's width. This is the default if CCS_BOTTOM is not specified.
TBSTYLE_TOOLTIPS	The TBSTYLE_TOOLTIPS style will cause the toolbar to create and manage a CToolTipCtrl tooltip control. If you use the TBSTYLE_TOOLTIPS style, you must handle tooltip notifications as described in the section on tooltips.

Style	Description
TBSTYLE_WRAPABLE	The TBSTYLE_WRAPABLE style is used to create a toolbar that can have more than one row of buttons. For example, our program's dialog box is rather narrow for our large buttons, and using more than one row of buttons would enable the user to have twice as many buttons in the toolbar. Wrapping is managed automatically by the CToolBarCtrl object.

The CToolBarCtrl's size (only if the CCS_NORESIZE style was specified) is specified with the *rect* parameter. If you have not specified the CCS_NORESIZE style, then the *rect* parameter is ignored.

The parent of the toolbar is specified in the *pParentWnd* parameter. With C++, you can simply use the *this* keyword.

The CToolBarCtrl ID is specified with the *nID* parameter. This identifier is passed to the CWnd::Create() function. It is the child window identifier value.

Once the toolbar has been created, then you must attach the bitmaps (and text strings, if used). You call CToolBarCtrl::AddBitmap() (and CToolBarCtrl::AddString()) to add the bitmaps. You can call these functions more than one time; however, you must keep the returned index to associate with the buttons in your toolbar. If you have only one bitmap, you can assume that the returned value for these two functions will be zero and code your program appropriately.

```
ButtonBitmap = m_ToolBarCtrl.AddBitmap(20, IDB_TOOLBAR);
ButtonString = m_ToolBarCtrl.AddString(IDS_FIRST_BUTTON);
```

Once you have added your bitmaps (and strings, if required), you can initialize your buttons.

Setting Up the *TBBUTTON* Structures

You must set up (initialize) the button structures. There are two ways to set up your buttons. First, if you decide that you want your button structures to be member variables within a class, you need to initialize each member, as the following code shows. You declare the button in the class's header file. Then, you initialize each button in the source file, using either a loop or simple in-line code:

```
m_Buttons[ButtonCount].iBitmap = ButtonBitmap + 0;
m_Buttons[ButtonCount].idCommand = IDOK;
m_Buttons[ButtonCount].fsState = TBSTATE_ENABLED;
m_Buttons[ButtonCount].fsStyle = TBSTYLE_BUTTON;
m_Buttons[ButtonCount].dwData = 0;
```

```
m_Buttons[ButtonCount].iString = ButtonString;

++ButtonCount;

m_Buttons[ButtonCount].iBitmap = ButtonBitmap + 1;
m_Buttons[ButtonCount].idCommand = 0;
m_Buttons[ButtonCount].fsState = TBSTATE_ENABLED;
m_Buttons[ButtonCount].fsStyle = TBSTYLE_SEP;
m_Buttons[ButtonCount].dwData = 0;
m_Buttons[ButtonCount].iString = NULL;

++ButtonCount;
```

The code fragment shows two buttons initialized. For each button, you must set the following member variables:

```
m_Buttons[ButtonCount].iBitmap = ButtonBitmap + 0;
```

The iBitmap member takes an index to your bitmap. This index is based on the value returned by the call to CToolBarCtrl::AddBitmap(), with an incremental index to the current button image. All button images must be the same size.

```
m_Buttons[ButtonCount].idCommand = IDOK;
```

The idCommand member holds the identifier for the button's command. This could be a menu item command identifier or perhaps a dialog box control. You can create command handlers that are independent of both the menu and any dialog box controls, as the sample program shows.

```
m_Buttons[ButtonCount].fsState = TBSTATE_ENABLED;
```

The fsState member holds the state for the button. Valid states are listed in Table 18.2.

Table 18.2. Valid TBBUTTON.fsState values.

Identifier	Description
TBSTATE_CHECKED	This button will initially be in the checked state. The style will be TBSTYLE_CHECKED (see Table 18.3).
TBSTATE_ENABLED	The button is enabled and is able to accept input from the user. A button that is not enabled will be grayed and cannot accept user input.
TBSTATE_HIDDEN	The button is neither visible nor can it receive any input from the user.
TBSTATE_INDETERMINATE	The button is grayed, and its state is undefined.
TBSTATE_PRESSED	The button is in the pressed state.
TBSTATE_WRAP	Following this button is a line break (that is, the next button will be on a new line). A button with this value must have the TBSTATE_ENABLED value as well.

```
m_Buttons[ButtonCount].fsStyle = TBSTYLE_BUTTON;
```

The fsStyle member holds the style for the button. Valid styles are listed in Table 18.3.

Table 18.3. Valid TBBUTTON.fsStyle values.

Identifier	Description
TBSTYLE_BUTTON	The button will be a standard toolbar pushbutton.
TBSTYLE_CHECK	The button will be able to show a pressed and unpressed state. The Project Build button in Visual C++ 2.x is a checkbutton—it stays pressed until the build has completed.
TBSTYLE_CHECKGROUP	The button will be part of a group. As an example, WordPad's paragraph justification buttons (which allow flush left, flush right, and centered text) are TBSTYLE_CHECKGROUP style buttons.
TBSTYLE_GROUP	The button will be part of a group. Only one member of a group will be selected at a time.
TBSTYLE_SEP	The TBSTYLE_SEP style creates a button separator, which allows separation between buttons that might be logically grouped. You can spread buttons out further using consecutive separators, if necessary.

```
m_Buttons[ButtonCount].dwData = 0;
```

The dwData member may be used to hold any data (32-bit) that you desire. You could store handles to structures, unique data values, or indexes in this member.

```
m_Buttons[ButtonCount].iString = ButtonString;
```

The iString member is the (zero-based) index to the string that is associated with this button. See the CToolBarCtrl::AddString() function for more information. Many toolbars will not use this member.

Telling the *CToolBarCtrl* About the Buttons

The final step in initializing your toolbar is to tell the CToolBarCtrl object about your buttons. You do this by passing a pointer to the first TBBUTTON array element and specifying how many buttons (elements) are in the TBBUTTON array:

```
m_ToolBarCtrl.AddButtons(ButtonCount, m_Buttons);
```

Many applications offer toolbar buttons in two kinds: the few, big, easy-to-see buttons; or the many, small, and difficult-to-see buttons. Our example uses large buttons (huge, really). Our button bitmaps are 45 pixels high and 48 pixels wide. The buttons must be a few pixels wider than the bitmaps to allow for the three-dimensional effect.

```
CSize sizeButtons(55, 65);

    m_ToolBarCtrl.SetButtonSize(sizeButtons);

//    Since our bitmaps are non-standard in size, we tell
//    the toolbar the real size of our images:

    CSize sizeBitmap(48, 45);

    m_ToolBarCtrl.SetBitmapSize(sizeBitmap);
```

Once you've set the buttons' size, you need to tell the toolbar to resize itself. The `CToolBarCtrl::AutoSize()` function will be called whenever anything causes the size of the toolbar to change, or when objects in the toolbar change in size (such as when the user elects to use differently sized buttons for applications that support such a functionality).

```
//    Finally, we resize the toolbar for our non-standard
//    button sizes:

    m_ToolBarCtrl.AutoSize();
```

Once you have done the preceding steps, you have a toolbar that the user can use. Not every toolbar has only buttons. Although buttons are the most common toolbar control, the combo box is the next most popular toolbar control. In the next part of this chapter, we cover how to add controls other than buttons to the toolbar.

Adding a *CComboBox* Control to a Toolbar

As we noted previously, combo boxes are the second most common toolbar control. It is rather easy to add a combo box to a toolbar and work with the combo box. First, to add your combo box, you must create a `CComboBox` object. For example, our dialog box has a `CComboBoxTip` member called `m_ComboBox` (`CComboBoxTip` is my class derived directly from `CComboBox`).

Our combo box is going to be located on the left end of our toolbar. To make room for the combo box, we force the normal toolbar buttons to the right by inserting a number of separators. The exact number of separators needed was determined by experiment and will vary depending on the size of the buttons.

To add a non-button control to the `CToolBarCtrl` toolbar, follow these steps:

1. Determine the new control's size. In our example, I've set the combo box's size to be 100 pixels wide and the drop-down box to be 200 pixels deep. Next, I moved the combo box down two pixels (to align it with the top edges of the buttons) and the left

edge over by five pixels, to give it some spacing from the left edge of the toolbar. These dimensions were placed in the *rect* structure.

2. The `CComboBox::Create()` function is then called. The parent of the combo box is the toolbar; the combo box's styles are standard for a text-based combo box control. The code fragment shows how the combo box was created.

```
rect.top = 2; rect.left = 5; rect.bottom = 200; rect.right = 100;

    if (m_ComboBox.Create( WS_CHILD ¦ WS_BORDER ¦ WS_VISIBLE ¦
        CBS_HASSTRINGS ¦ CBS_DROPDOWN, rect, (CWnd *)&m_ToolBarCtrl,
        123) == 0)
    {// Real applications would have to perhaps recover from this error:
        TRACE("Could not create combobox\n");
    }
    else
    {
```

Once you have created your control, it may be necessary to resize it. Combo box controls use the size specified in the call to `Create()` to size the drop-down box, not the edit box. To size the edit box, a call to `CComboBox::SetItemHeight()` is made.

```
//      Set the ComboBox's edit area's height to the height of
//      the button's bitmap size!

        m_ComboBox.SetItemHeight(-1, 45);
```

Once the combo box is created, it can be filled with the data. In our simple example, we just add three classic strings. Then we select the second string in the list (remember, the string's index is zero-based).

```
//      Add (some dummy) strings to the ComboBox:

        m_ComboBox.AddString("asdf");
        m_ComboBox.AddString("qwer");
        m_ComboBox.AddString("zxcv");

//      Set the current selection to the (zero based) second item

        m_ComboBox.SetCurSel(1);
    }
```

The combo box is now part of your toolbar. Using the `m_ComboBox` variable, you can determine what changes the user has made and update the program as necessary.

Adding Tooltip Support

Your toolbar is not complete until you have tooltip support built in. Tooltips are those little text windows that pop up when the mouse cursor is over a toolbar button and no mouse button has been pressed.

Users have become accustomed to having tooltips for toolbar controls. Although a picture is worth a thousand words, when that picture is a toolbar bitmap (usually only about 15 pixels square), those "thousand words" are very short words. A word or two in a tooltip can inform the user about a button's action (such as Save, Save As, or Open), especially when the picture in the button is a bit ambiguous.

With a `CToolBarCtrl` toolbar, you can implement tooltips by doing the following things:

1. You must specify the style `TBSTYLE_TOOLTIPS` when you create the toolbar, as the code example shows:

```
m_ToolBarCtrl.Create(
    WS_CHILD | WS_VISIBLE | CCS_TOP | TBSTYLE_TOOLTIPS | CCS_ADJUSTABLE,
    rect, this, 0);
```

2. You must handle the `WM_NOTIFY` case for `TTN_NEEDTEXT`. This can be done in several different ways. First, if you are writing an MFC application, you can code an `ON_NOTIFY(TTN_NEEDTEXT, idButton, memberFn)` macro in the owner window's message map. Or you can override the `OnNotify()` handler for the owner window, as I've done in my example. Either method is acceptable, but the `ON_NOTIFY()` macro in the message map is the more correct method.

   The handler for the case `TTN_NEEDTEXT` must return the text that is to be displayed in the tooltip window. Remember to keep this text short (one or two words is best).

The `OnNotify()` function to manage tooltip text retrieval is shown in the next code fragment. This handler allows the return of text based on a string resource that has the same identifier as the button's ID. Generally, most programs are able to base a string resource on the button's ID. It is possible to build string resources that contain multiple text items, such as AppWizard does when creating `CToolBar` toolbars. These string resources are broken using a newline character (`\n`); the first part of the string is the prompt that appears in the status bar (and is usually a full sentence), and the second part is a one- or two-word description for the tooltip.

This listing example shows an `OnNotify()` override that handles only tooltip notifications. Remember that `OnNotify()` handles other conditions than `TTN_NEEDTEXT`, so you will need to test the `hdr.code` parameter with either a `switch()` or an `if()` statement.

```
BOOL CToolBarDlg::OnNotify(WPARAM wParam, LPARAM lParam, LRESULT* pResult)
{
//    TRACE("OnNotify() called \n");

    TOOLTIPTEXT    * tt;
    tt = (TOOLTIPTEXT *)lParam;

    CString        Tip;

    switch(tt->hdr.code)
    {// There are other codes used other than TTN_NEEDTEXT!
        case TTN_NEEDTEXT:
//            TRACE("TTN_NEEDTEXT \n");
            Tip.LoadString(tt->hdr.idFrom);
            strcpy(tt->szText, (LPCSTR)Tip);
            break;
```

```
   }
   return CDialog::OnNotify(wParam, lParam, pResult);
}
```

Each time the mouse moves on top of a toolbar button, `OnNotify()` is called, and (if the `hdr.code` is `TTN_NEEDTEXT`) the application can return the text for the tooltip. Windows will then display the tooltip for the user.

Adding Toolbar Customization

Toolbars that may be customized by the user are a hot item today. Many users have come to expect the capability to customize the toolbar—adding, moving, and removing toolbar buttons with wild abandon. When I work with Word for Windows, I have two custom toolbars displayed at all times. I only wish that all applications enabled me to customize the toolbars!

Adding the capability to customize the toolbar is accomplished by specifying the `CCS_ADJUSTABLE` style when you create your toolbar. This style tells the `CToolBarCtrl` toolbar that the user may do the following:

- Move buttons to different places on the toolbar.
- Remove buttons from the toolbar by dragging them off the toolbar.
- Display the toolbar customization dialog box (see Figure 18.4 for an example). A toolbar customization dialog box enables users to add, remove, and reorder buttons on the toolbar.

FIGURE 18.4.

The `CToolBarCtrl`
Customize Toolbar
dialog box.

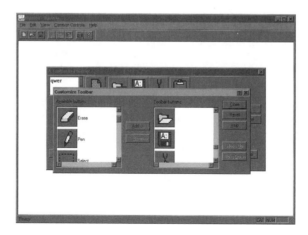

The following code example shows the use of the `CCS_ADJUSTABLE` style.

```
m_ToolBarCtrl.Create(
     WS_CHILD | WS_VISIBLE | CCS_TOP | TBSTYLE_TOOLTIPS | CCS_ADJUSTABLE,
     rect, this, 0);
```

Once you have created a toolbar with the CCS_ADJUSTABLE style, you must then have additional code in the OnNotify() handler to support the customization. These handlers are used by Windows to obtain information from the application, including:

- Whether the toolbar be customized. Even if the CCS_ADJUSTABLE style is specified at toolbar creation time, the toolbar may not be customizable.
- Information about buttons that are not currently located on the toolbar but may be added.
- Whether the toolbar supports drag-and-drop customization.

> **NOTE**
>
> Drag-and-drop customization for toolbars is done by two methods. The first is when the user presses the Shift key and then drags and drops buttons. This is managed by the CToolBarCtrl toolbar, not by your code. The second method is when the Shift key is not pressed by the user. In this situation the drag and drop is performed by code in your application. Generally the CToolBarCtrl-managed drag and drop is more generic and much easier to implement, whereas the application-managed drag and drop offers more power and flexibility to the user.

The OnNotify() function to support basic customization must handle a minimum of three different actions. Other notification codes are shown in Table 18.4. The minimum types of notifications are:

- TBN_QUERYINSERT—Sent to the OnNotify() handler when the user is going to customize the toolbar. This function should return TRUE to allow a button to be inserted in front of a specified button.
- TBN_QUERYDELETE—Sent to the OnNotify() handler to determine whether a button may be deleted from the toolbar.
- TBN_GETBUTTONINFO—Sent to the OnNotify() handler to add buttons to the right-side list of buttons that may be added to the toolbar. The OnNotify() function must fill in the provided TBNOTIFY structure and return a TRUE. If the structure could not be filled in, OnNotify() must return a FALSE.

Table 18.4. The toolbar TBN_ OnNotify() values.

Code	Description
TBN_BEGINADJUST	The TBN_BEGINADJUST will be sent to the OnNotify() function when the user begins to customize the toolbar. A pointer points to a NMHDR structure that will contain information about the customization. OnNotify() doesn't need to return any specific value.

Code	Description
TBN_BEGINDRAG	The TBN_BEGINDRAG will be sent to the OnNotify() function when the user starts to drag a button on the toolbar. A pointer points to a TBNOTIFY structure that will be passed to OnNotify(). The TBNOTIFY.iItem member will contain a zero-based index to the button that is being dragged. OnNotify() doesn't need to return any specific value.
TBN_CUSTHELP	The TBN_CUSTHELP will be sent to the OnNotify() function when the user selects the Help button in the Customize Toolbar dialog box. There is no return value for this code. A pointer points to a NMHDR structure that will contain information about the notification message. OnNotify() doesn't need to return any specific value.
TBN_ENDADJUST	The TBN_ENDADJUST will be sent to the OnNotify() function when the user finishes with the toolbar customization. A pointer points to a NMHDR structure that will contain information about the notification message. OnNotify() doesn't need to return any specific value.
TBN_ENDDRAG	The TBN_ENDDRAG will be sent to the OnNotify() function when the user finishes dragging a button in the toolbar. A pointer to a TBNOTIFY structure is provided, and the TBNOTIFY.iItem member will contain a zero-based index to the button that was being dragged. OnNotify() doesn't need to return any specific value.
TBN_GETBUTTONINFO	The TBN_GETBUTTONINFO will be sent to the OnNotify() function when the user begins to customize a toolbar control. The TBN_GETBUTTONINFO will also be sent as buttons are added to the toolbar. A pointer to a TBNOTIFY structure is passed, and the TBNOTIFY.iItem member will specify a zero-based index to a button. Your OnNotify() should use the pszText and cchText members provide the address and length, in characters, of the current button's text. The TBNOTIFY structure should be filled in as shown in our example program's OnNotify() handler. OnNotify() must return TRUE if button information was copied to the structure, or return FALSE otherwise.
TBN_QUERYDELETE	The TBN_QUERYDELETE will be sent to the OnNotify() function when a toolbar is being customized by the user to determine whether a button may be deleted from a toolbar control. A pointer to a TBNOTIFY structure is provided, and the

continues

Table 18.4. continued

Code	Description
	`TBNOTIFY.iItem` member will have a zero-based index of the button that is to be deleted. `OnNotify()` must return `TRUE` if the button may be deleted, or `FALSE` if the button is not to be deleted.
`TBN_QUERYINSERT`	The `TBN_QUERYINSERT` will be sent to the `OnNotify()` function when the user is customizing a toolbar to determine whether a button may be inserted to the left of the given button. A pointer to a `TBNOTIFY` structure is provided, and the `TBNOTIFY.iItem` member will contain a zero-based index to the button that is to be inserted. `OnNotify()` must return `TRUE` if the button may be inserted, or `FALSE` if the button may not be inserted.
`TBN_RESET`	The `TBN_RESET` will be sent to the `OnNotify()` function when the user chooses the Reset button in the Customize Toolbar dialog box. A pointer to a `NMHDR` structure will contain information about this notification message. `OnNotify()` doesn't need to return a specific value.
`TBN_TOOLBARCHANGE`	The `TBN_TOOLBARCHANGE` will be sent to the `OnNotify()` function after the user has completed the customization of the toolbar. A pointer points to a `NMHDR` structure that will contain information about the notification message. `OnNotify()` doesn't need to return a specific value.

The following code example shows a minimal implementation for an `OnNotify()` handler. This handler would also require code for the tooltips notification messages if your toolbar supported tooltips.

> **NOTE**
>
> To return `TRUE` or `FALSE` in your `OnNotify()`, use a `return(TRUE)` or a `return(FALSE)`. Don't call the default `OnNotify()` handler if a specific return value must be returned!

```
BOOL CToolBarDlg::OnNotify(WPARAM wParam, LPARAM lParam, LRESULT* pResult)
{
    TOOLTIPTEXT   * tt;
    NMHDR      *   hdr;
    tt = (TOOLTIPTEXT *)lParam;
    hdr = (NMHDR *)lParam;
    LPTBNOTIFY    lpTbNotify = (LPTBNOTIFY)lParam;
```

```
CString        Tip;
CString        String;

switch(tt->hdr.code)
{
    case TTN_NEEDTEXT:
        Tip.LoadString(tt->hdr.idFrom);
        strcpy(tt->szText, (LPCSTR)Tip);
        break;

    case TBN_QUERYINSERT:
        if (pResult != NULL)
            *pResult = TRUE;

        return(TRUE);
        break;

    case TBN_QUERYDELETE:
        if (pResult != NULL)
            *pResult = TRUE;

        return(TRUE);
        break;

    case TBN_GETBUTTONINFO:
        if (lpTbNotify->iItem < 12)
        {
            lpTbNotify->tbButton = tbButtonNew[lpTbNotify->iItem];

            if (lpTbNotify->pszText != NULL)
            {// Only return the string, if there is a buffer!
                String.LoadString(
                    tbButtonNew[lpTbNotify->iItem].idCommand);

                strcpy(lpTbNotify->pszText, (LPCSTR)String);
                lpTbNotify->cchText = strlen(lpTbNotify->pszText);
            }

            if (pResult != NULL)
                *pResult = TRUE;

            return(TRUE);
        }
        else
        {//    Not a valid button for the toolbar!
        }

        break;

    case TBN_BEGINDRAG:
        break;

    case TBN_ENDDRAG:
        break;

    case TBN_BEGINADJUST:
        break;

    case TBN_ENDADJUST:
```

```
            break;

        case TBN_RESET:
            break;

        case TBN_TOOLBARCHANGE:
            break;

        case TBN_CUSTHELP:
            break;

        default: // Should never happen.
            break;
    }
// Only call CDialog::OnNotify() if you don't handle the message!
    return CDialog::OnNotify(wParam, lParam, pResult);
}
```

As the previous sample program shows, a CToolBarCtrl toolbar can be a powerful and flexible addition to any Windows application. Although many applications are able to use the standard MFC toolbar (CToolBar), the CToolBarCtrl can offer just what the programmer needs for those applications that require more power or flexibility.

Figure 18.5 shows our final toolbar.

FIGURE 18.5.

The final CToolBarCtrl toolbar.

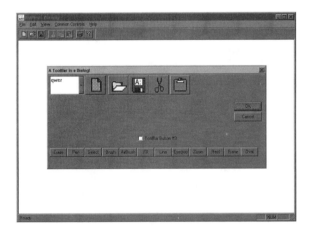

The MFC Status Bar and the *CStatusBarCtrl* Status Bar

The new Win32 Common Controls CStatusBarCtrl status bar control offers a degree of flexibility that the CStatusBar status bars don't have. The CStatusBarCtrl status bars offer a high degree of customizability and flexibility. Although a CStatusBar status bar has more standard features, it is much more difficult to customize.

First, let's look at the attributes for an MFC `CStatusBar` status bar:

- `CStatusBar` status bars have a set of predefined panes that are automatically updated. A `CStatusBar` status bar is fixed at the bottom of the frame window and is very difficult to implement in windows that are not derived from `CFrameView`.

- `CStatusBar` status bars have a message area that is updated whenever the user moves to a menu item (or a `CToolBar` button) and provides a simple message about the menu items' functions.

- `CStatusBar` status bars work with MFC's document/view architecture, resizing the view as required to reflect the addition of the status bar to a frame window.

- `CStatusBar` status bars are very easy to implement. The program simply specifies a status bar when creating the application with AppWizard. Usually the status bar's default implementation will be adequate for most applications' needs.

There are a number of reasons for a programmer to use a `CStatusBarCtrl` status bar in an application. These reasons include:

- A `CStatusBarCtrl` status bar can be attached to virtually any window type, including windows based on `CDialog`. This enables you to have a dialog box with a status bar.

- The `CStatusBarCtrl` status bar can be made to include other types of dialog controls, if necessary (although you would normally use a status bar for output to the user only).

- A `CStatusBarCtrl` status bar is easily modified at runtime.

- A `CStatusBarCtrl` status bar offers two modes: *simple* when only one part (or pane) is displayed, and *multiple* when all parts (panes) of the status bar are shown. The text strings and their attributes are kept separate for each of these modes.

We are going to use the same sample program that we created for our `CToolBarCtrl` example previously. This program has no functionality other than offering a number of menu selections for each of our Win32 Common Control examples. The creation of this program (which I've called DUMMY) is shown in text that follows Figure 18.1.

In the DUMMY program you need to add a new menu item called *Statusbar*. This menu item's handler should display the dialog box that we will create to demonstrate the `CStatusBarCtrl` status bar.

The *CStatusBarCtrl* Class

In the final part of this chapter we implement a `CStatusBarCtrl` status bar. As in our toolbar example that we created in the first part of this chapter, we implement our status bar in a dialog box. Don't take this implementation as the only way to implement a `CStatusBarCtrl` status bar; you can add this status bar to any window desired.

> **NOTE**
>
> Sometimes it is a pane! (Bad pun intended.) The `CStatusBar` documentation refers to each output area in a status bar as a *pane*. The `CStatusBarCtrl` documentation refers to these output areas as *parts*. Whether called parts or panes, they are the same: individual output areas on a status bar. I prefer panes (there is no confusion with that term) but will refer to them as parts in our `CStatusBarCtrl` status bar.

First, we need a dialog box for our status bar to live in. Create this dialog box like you would any other dialog box. I've shown the dialog box in Figure 18.6, and you can see the control IDs for each of the controls in the dialog box.

FIGURE 18.6.

The status bar dialog box.

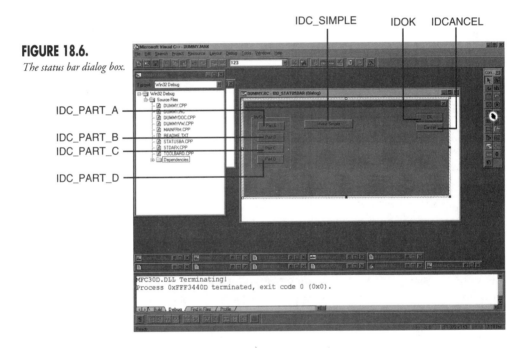

Notice in Figure 18.6 we have left room at the bottom of the dialog box for the status bar. Because the status bar is not being created in a frame window, we must manage the space for the status bar. Simply leave a small blank area (perhaps a bit taller than a simple push-button) at the bottom of the dialog box or window. If you are planning to place your status bar at the top of the dialog (or window), leave space there for it.

Once you have created the status bar dialog box and a menu item in the program's menu, you next need to use ClassWizard to create a class for the dialog box. I've called my dialog box class `CStatusBarDlg`. We will create a handler for the `WM_INITDIALOG`, which is where the status bar will be created and initialized.

The main part of our status bar is shown in Listings 18.3 and 18.4. They will be explained in detail following the listings.

Listing 18.3. The STATUSBA.CPP file, which implements a `CStatusBarCtrl` status bar.

```
// statusba.cpp : implementation file
//

#include "stdafx.h"
#include "Dummy.h"
#include "statusba.h"

#ifdef _DEBUG
#undef THIS_FILE
static char BASED_CODE THIS_FILE[] = __FILE__;
#endif


/////////////////////////////////////////////////////////////////////////////
// CStatusBarDlg dialog


CStatusBarDlg::CStatusBarDlg(CWnd* pParent /*=NULL*/)
    : CDialog(CStatusBarDlg::IDD, pParent)
{
    //{{AFX_DATA_INIT(CStatusBarDlg)
        // NOTE: the ClassWizard will add member initialization here
    //}}AFX_DATA_INIT
}


void CStatusBarDlg::DoDataExchange(CDataExchange* pDX)
{
    CDialog::DoDataExchange(pDX);
    //{{AFX_DATA_MAP(CStatusBarDlg)
    DDX_Control(pDX, IDC_PART_D, m_PartD);
    DDX_Control(pDX, IDC_PART_C, m_PartC);
    DDX_Control(pDX, IDC_PART_B, m_PartB);
    DDX_Control(pDX, IDC_PART_A, m_PartA);
    //}}AFX_DATA_MAP
}


BEGIN_MESSAGE_MAP(CStatusBarDlg, CDialog)
    //{{AFX_MSG_MAP(CStatusBarDlg)
    ON_BN_CLICKED(IDC_PART_B, OnPartB)
    ON_BN_CLICKED(IDC_PART_A, OnPartA)
    ON_BN_CLICKED(IDC_PART_C, OnPartC)
    ON_BN_CLICKED(IDC_PART_D, OnPartD)
    ON_BN_CLICKED(IDC_SIMPLE, OnSimple)
    //}}AFX_MSG_MAP
END_MESSAGE_MAP()


/////////////////////////////////////////////////////////////////////////////
```

continues

Listing 18.3. continued

```
// CStatusBarDlg message handlers

BOOL CStatusBarDlg::OnInitDialog()
{
    CDialog::OnInitDialog();

    // TODO: Add extra initialization here

    RECT    rect;

    rect.top = 0;
    rect.left = 0;
    rect.bottom = 20;
    rect.right = 100;

    m_StatusBar.Create(WS_CHILD | WS_VISIBLE | CCS_BOTTOM,
        rect, this, 123);

//    RIGHT edge location.
    int    nWidths[] = {100, 255, 450, -1};

//    Make four parts (panes) in the status bar.
    m_StatusBar.SetParts(4, nWidths);

//    We could have called SetPartA() through SetPartD()...

    Simple = "Simple - Good for prompts and the like.";
    A = "A-in";
    B = "B-in";
    C = "C-in";
    D = "D-in";

    m_StatusBar.SetText((LPCSTR)Simple, 255, 0);
    m_StatusBar.SetText((LPCSTR) A, 0, 0);
    m_StatusBar.SetText((LPCSTR) B, 1, 0);
    m_StatusBar.SetText((LPCSTR) C, 2, 0);
    m_StatusBar.SetText((LPCSTR) D, 3, 0);

    return TRUE;  // return TRUE unless you set the focus to a control
                  // EXCEPTION: OCX Property Pages should return FALSE
}

void    CStatusBarDlg::SetPartA(int nState)
{
    m_StatusBar.SetText((LPCSTR) A, 0, nState);
}

void    CStatusBarDlg::SetPartB(int nState)
{
    m_StatusBar.SetText((LPCSTR) B, 1, nState);
}

void    CStatusBarDlg::SetPartC(int nState)
{
    m_StatusBar.SetText((LPCSTR) C, 2, nState);
```

```
}

void     CStatusBarDlg::SetPartD(int nState)
{
    m_StatusBar.SetText((LPCSTR) D , 3, nState);
}

void CStatusBarDlg::OnPartA()
{
    // TODO: Add your control notification handler code here
    static    int    nState = 0;

    if (nState == SBT_POPOUT)
    {
        nState = 0; // Pop-in look;
        A = "A-in";
    }
    else
    {
        nState = SBT_POPOUT; // Pop-out look;
        A = "A-out";
    }
    SetPartA(nState);
}

void CStatusBarDlg::OnPartB()
{
    // TODO: Add your control notification handler code here
    static    int    nState = 0;

    if (nState == SBT_POPOUT)
    {
        nState = 0; // Pop-in look;
        B = "B-in";
    }
    else
    {
        nState = SBT_POPOUT; // Pop-out look;
        B = "B-out";
    }
    SetPartB(nState);
}

void CStatusBarDlg::OnPartC()
{
    // TODO: Add your control notification handler code here
    static    int    nState = 0;

    if (nState == SBT_POPOUT)
    {
        nState = 0; // Pop-in look;
        C = "C-in";
    }
    else
    {
        nState = SBT_POPOUT; // Pop-out look;
        C = "C-out";
    }
}
```

continues

Listing 18.3. continued

```
    SetPartC(nState);
}

void CStatusBarDlg::OnPartD()
{
    // TODO: Add your control notification handler code here
    static    int    nState = 0;

    if (nState == SBT_POPOUT)
    {
        nState = 0; // Pop-in look;
        D = "D-in";
    }
    else
    {
        nState = SBT_POPOUT; // Pop-out look;
        D = "D-out";
    }
    SetPartD(nState);
}

void CStatusBarDlg::OnSimple()
{
    // TODO: Add your control notification handler code here

    static    int    nState = 0;

    if (nState)
    {
        nState = 0; // Multi-part display
    }
    else
    {
        nState = 1; // Simple display, one part
    }
    m_StatusBar.SetSimple(nState);
}
```

Listing 18.4 is the header file that accompanies Listing 18.3. This file is short and simple and requires no explanation.

Listing 18.4. The STATUSBA.H header file.

```
// statusba.h : header file
//

/////////////////////////////////////////////////////////////////////////////
// CStatusBarDlg dialog

class CStatusBarDlg : public CDialog
{
// Construction
```

```
public:
    CStatusBarDlg(CWnd* pParent = NULL);   // standard constructor

    CStatusBarCtrl    m_StatusBar;

    CString    Simple;
    CString A;
    CString B;
    CString C;
    CString D;

    void SetPartA(int nState = SBT_POPOUT);
    void SetPartB(int nState = SBT_POPOUT);
    void SetPartC(int nState = SBT_POPOUT);
    void SetPartD(int nState = SBT_POPOUT);

// Dialog Data
    //{{AFX_DATA(CStatusBarDlg)
    enum { IDD = IDD_STATUSBAR };
    CButton    m_PartD;
    CButton    m_PartC;
    CButton    m_PartB;
    CButton    m_PartA;
    //}}AFX_DATA


// Overrides
    // ClassWizard generated virtual function overrides
    //{{AFX_VIRTUAL(CStatusBarDlg)
    protected:
    virtual void DoDataExchange(CDataExchange* pDX);   // DDX/DDV support
    //}}AFX_VIRTUAL

// Implementation
protected:

    // Generated message map functions
    //{{AFX_MSG(CStatusBarDlg)
    virtual BOOL OnInitDialog();
    afx_msg void OnPartB();
    afx_msg void OnPartA();
    afx_msg void OnPartC();
    afx_msg void OnPartD();
    afx_msg void OnSimple();
    //}}AFX_MSG
    DECLARE_MESSAGE_MAP()
};
```

Implementing a *CStatusBarCtrl* Status Bar

There is a minimum amount of code that is necessary to implement a CStatusBarCtrl status bar. You must do the following when the parent window is created (that is, the window that the status bar will be in):

1. Create your `CStatusBarCtrl` status bar. Use the `CStatusBarCtrl::Create()` function to do this. After creating your status bar, you then must define the parts of the status bar's display area and the parts' sizes.

2. Initialize any string (or better yet, `CString`) objects that will hold status bar text. Using a `CString` object makes modification of the displayed strings easier.

3. Do any final housekeeping tasks, such as setting border sizes.

Creating a *CStatusBarCtrl* Status Bar

First, create your `CStatusBarCtrl` status bar object:

```
m_StatusBar.Create(WS_CHILD ¦ WS_VISIBLE ¦ CCS_BOTTOM,
    rect, this, 123);
```

The styles used include those styles typical to almost all windows (`WS_CHILD` and `WS_VISIBLE`) and then a style that is unique to `CStatusBarCtrl` objects. I chose to use the `CCS_BOTTOM` style (toolbars are usually at the top of the parent window, status bars at the bottom). Table 18.5 shows the `CToolBarCtrl` window styles.

Table 18.5. Possible `CToolBarCtrl` window styles.

Style	Description
CCS_BOTTOM	Tells Windows to create the status bar at the bottom of the parent window. The width of the status bar will be equal to the width of the parent window's client area. This is the default for a status bar.
CCS_NODIVIDER	Tells Windows not to draw the two-pixel divider line between the top of the status bar and the window.
CCS_NOHILITE	Tells Windows not to draw the one-pixel highlight line at the top of the status bar.
CCS_NOMOVEY	Tells the status bar to resize itself horizontally (but not vertically) when a `WM_SIZE` message is received.
CCS_NOPARENTALIGN	Tells the status bar not to move to either the top or bottom of the parent window (provides a floating effect). When the parent window is resized, the status bar will not move. If `CCS_TOP` or `CCS_BOTTOM` is specified, then the height of the status bar will be adjusted, but the position and width of the status bar will remain unchanged.
CCS_NORESIZE	Tells the status bar not to change its size in response to any `WM_SIZE` messages. The size of the control will be the value specified in the *rect* parameter passed to the call to `CStatusBarCtrl::Create()`.

Style	Description
CCS_TOP	Tells Windows to create the status bar at the top of the parent window. The width of the status bar will be equal to the width of the parent window's client area.

The CStatusBarCtrl's size (only if the CCS_NORESIZE style was specified) is specified with the *rect* parameter. If you have not specified the CCS_NORESIZE style, then the *rect* parameter is ignored.

The parent of the toolbar is specified in the *pParentWnd* parameter. With C++, you can simply use the *this* keyword.

The CStatusBarCtrl ID is specified with the *nID* parameter. This identifier is passed to the CWnd::Create() function. It is the child window identifier value.

After creating your status bar, you then can create the status bar's parts. Although a CStatusBar object creates a default area on the left side of the status bar, the CStatusBarCtrl status bar has its default area on the right. This doesn't present a major problem. The following code could be used to determine the actual width of the status bar. Knowing the status bar's width allows the application to compute the border positions for each pane.

> **NOTE**
>
> Many applications (such as Word for Windows) assume a width for the status bar and simply leave the far right part unused if the window is wider than the assumed value, or truncate the status bar if the window is narrower than the assumed value. If you check the width and set the part's width based on the status bar width, you must have a plan for when the different parts will not all fit on the status bar!

```
rect.top = 0;
rect.left = 0;
rect.bottom = 0;
rect.right = 0;

m_StatusBar.GetWindowRect(&rect);

nWidth = rect.right - rect.left;
```

Setting Up the Pane Text

The text that each pane displays is provided by your application. Whenever you want to reset the pane's display attribute (such as displaying the text as drop-in or pop-out) you must resupply the text. In our sample program, I created a CString object for each status bar part. These CString objects are easy to work with because they can load a resource string using the CString::LoadString() member function.

In our sample program, we simply assign a string to our CString objects:

```
Simple = "Simple - Good for prompts and the like.";
A = "A-in";
B = "B-in";
C = "C-in";
D = "D-in";
```

Once you have created the text for each pane, you then can tell the status bar to display the part's text by calling CStatusBarCtrl::SetText(). This call will set a part's text and style in a single call:

```
m_StatusBar.SetText((LPCSTR)Simple, 255, 0);
m_StatusBar.SetText((LPCSTR) A, 0, 0);
m_StatusBar.SetText((LPCSTR) B, 1, 0);
m_StatusBar.SetText((LPCSTR) C, 2, 0);
m_StatusBar.SetText((LPCSTR) D, 3, 0);
```

The final parameter in the CStatusBarCtrl::SetText call is the style for the part. Valid styles are shown in Table 18.6. The SBT_NOBORDERS style may be specified with the other styles as appropriate. The SBT_POPOUT style overrides the pushed-in style (value 0, which has no predefined identifier).

Table 18.6. Part display styles.

Style	Description
0	The text will be displayed in a box that appears to be lower (pushed-in) than the status bar. There is no defined identifier for this value. This is the default style if SBT_POPOUT is not specified.
SBT_NOBORDERS	The text will be displayed without borders.
SBT_OWNERDRAW	The text will be drawn by the parent window. Using SBT_OWNERDRAW specifies that the parent window will draw the text using whatever styles that it is able to support.
SBT_POPOUT	The text will be displayed in a box that appears to be higher (popped-out) than the status bar.

Changing the Status Bar's Display

The purpose of a status bar is to display information that will be changing. This implies that either the part's text, style, or both will change from time to time. Your application can make calls to CStatusBarCtrl::SetText() to change both the text and the style at any time.

When calling CStatusBarCtrl::SetText(), you can either use the text that you saved or you can retrieve the current part's text using a call to CStatusBarCtrl::GetText(). The CStatusBarCtrl::GetText() function returns the current text, text length, and display style for any part in the status bar. For status bars where the text may toggle (like our example), the text may be stored either in the application (using CString objects, or strings) or as resource strings. Regardless of where or how the part's text is saved, changing a part's text or style simply requires a call to CStatusBarCtrl::SetText() with updated text and style parameters.

Switching Between Simple and Multiple Modes

A CStatusBarCtrl status bar can display in either simple or multiple part modes. In simple mode, only one pane (whose identifier is 255) is displayed. In multiple part mode all panes (other than 255) are displayed.

You can switch modes at any time. You do not have to update the parts or otherwise change any text. A call to CStatusBarCtrl::SetSimple() takes care of the details of the switch, as our sample program shows:

```
if (nState)
{
    nState = 0; // Multi-part display
}
else
{
    nState = 1; // Simple display, one part
}
m_StatusBar.SetSimple(nState);
```

As the sample program shows, a CStatusBarCtrl status bar can be a powerful and flexible addition to any Windows application. Although many applications are able to use the standard MFC status bar (CStatusBar), the CStatusBarCtrl can offer just what the programmer needs for those applications that require more power or flexibility.

> **NOTE**
>
> You can update part text and styles regardless of which mode the status bar is in. This allows the update code to disregard the current state of the status bar.
>
> To see this effect, try setting the status bar to simple, then click on a button to change a part's text and style. Then set the status bar back to multiple part mode.

578

Figure 18.7 shows our final status bar in the multiple part mode, and Figure 18.8 shows our final status bar in the simple mode.

FIGURE 18.7.

The status bar in multiple part mode.

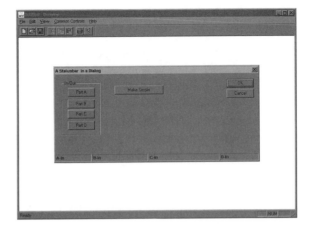

FIGURE 18.8.

The status bar in simple mode.

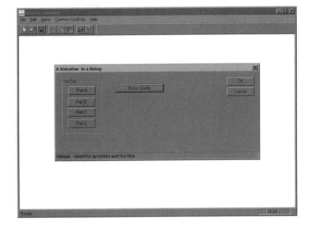

Summary

This chapter showed how to use both the CToolBarCtrl toolbar control and the CStatusBarCtrl status bar control. Both of these Win32 Common Controls are powerful additions to the Visual C++ programmer's toolkit.

It is possible to use the CToolBarCtrl and CStatusBarCtrl controls in windows other than frame windows. You can now have a dialog box with both a toolbar and a status bar. The CToolBarCtrl toolbar buttons can mimic dialog box controls and may be customized with other dialog controls, such as combo boxes.

Trackbars, Progressbars, Spinbuttons, and Hotkey Controls

19

by Peter D. Hipson

IN THIS CHAPTER

In this chapter I will introduce four more Win32 Common Controls. These controls are the Trackbar control, the Progress Indicator control, the Spinbox control, and the Hotkey control. There are MFC classes to manage each of these controls. In this chapter the MFC class name, in addition to the more proper name of the controls, will be used to refer to these controls.

- *The Trackbar (or Slider) control* This control enables the user to input a nonexact value within a predetermined range. This control is very useful where analogue values must be provided, such as for volume controls. This control is usually managed with the MFC class CSliderCtrl. Although this control is often referred to as a slider control, I refer to it as a *Trackbar control*, which is how Microsoft refers to this control. The button, the object that the user moves, is referred to as the Trackbar's *slider.*

- *The Progress indicator* This control provides the user a nonexact value within a predetermined range. This control is useful for informing users of the status of an operation that might take a long time, such as copying files from diskettes during installations. This control is normally managed with the MFC class CProgressCtrl.

- *The Spinbox control* This control enables the user to select from a predetermined set of values, either numeric or character-based. This control allows only one selection at a time, and selections are usually made sequentially from within the range of values. This control is normally managed with the MFC class CSpinButtonCtrl.

- *The Hotkey control* This control enables the user to select a hotkey that the application will then assign to an action. This allows the application to be able to configure the keyboard (much as does the Keyboard tab control *Press New Shortcut Key* in the Customize dialog box of Visual C++ 2.x). The dialog box is able to query the control to determine what hotkey the user wishes to use.

Although these controls will be used most often in dialog boxes, the programmer can (as with any Windows control) implement them in other types of windows. For example, the programmer can place one of these controls in a CToolBarCtrl toolbar window.

The CSliderCtrl Class

A Trackbar control enables a user to enter a nonexact value that will fall within a predetermined range. This control is modeled after a scrollbar control and actually sends many of the same messages that a scrollbar control would send. A scrollbar is usually used only to scroll the contents in a window, whereas a Trackbar control is used where there is no other feedback (like a window scrolling) to the user. Many of the differences between the two are cosmetic.

For the remainder of this chapter, I'll refer to this control as the *Trackbar control*, and the button that the user manipulates I'll refer to as the *slider.*

Figure 19.1 shows an example of a Trackbar control in a dialog box. This example is from our sample program (see Chapter 18, "Toolbars and Status Bars") and shows a typical implementation of the Trackbar control in a dialog box.

FIGURE 19.1.

A Trackbar control shown in a dialog box.

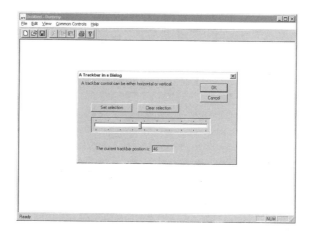

Your application, when using a CSliderCtrl class object, will need to do a minimal amount of management of the Trackbar control. The application must set the range, the initial value for the Trackbar control, and the frequency of the tickmarks (if any). A Trackbar control can have a number of attributes (all attributes may be set by using the resource editor in Visual C++). I've listed them in Table 19.1.

Table 19.1. The Trackbar control's attributes.

Attribute	Description
Pointer	The Pointer attribute specifies the shape of the slider in the control. It can point up/left, down/right, or both ways. The tickmarks, if used, will match the pointer; if the pointer is up, the tickmarks will be on the top.
Orientation	A Trackbar control can be either vertical or horizontal. The direction that the Pointer points is dependent on the control's orientation.
Tickmarks	The Trackbar control can have tickmarks that provide the user with some visual feedback when the user is positioning the pointer.
Autoticks	The tickmarks are added automatically when the range has been set.

continues

Table 19.1. continued

Attribute	Description
Enable Selection	The Trackbar control may have a selection range that provides the user with visual feedback. The selection range does not limit the Trackbar control in any way; it only provides a method to give output to the user.
Border	The Trackbar control can either have or not have a border. This style will be application-specific.

After you have added the Trackbar control to a dialog box, you then can use ClassWizard to bind a CSliderCtrl object to your Trackbar control. This CSliderCtrl object is your interface with the Trackbar control.

The Enable Selection style allows a subset of the Trackbar's range to be marked. The user is not restricted to the marked range, however, and may select any value in the Trackbar's range. In Figure 19.2, I've shown a Trackbar control with a range (30 to 70) set as the Enable Selection range. You can write code in your application to force the user to keep the slider within the range in the OnHScroll() or OnVScroll() handlers.

FIGURE 19.2.

A Trackbar control with a selection range set.

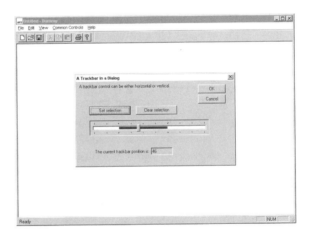

Implementing a *CSliderCtrl* Trackbar Control

If you are using a Trackbar control in a dialog box, you would use ClassWizard to bind a CSliderCtrl object to the control. Were you to be implementing a Trackbar control in a window that is not a dialog box, you would call the CSliderCtrl::Create() function to create the Trackbar control. You quite possibly might find a use for a Trackbar control in a normal window or perhaps as part of a toolbar.

Figure 19.3 shows our dialog box (in Visual C++'s resource editor) with the properties for the Trackbar shown. For Trackbar controls that are in dialog boxes, these properties can be set easily by use of the resource editor. When the Trackbar control is in a window other than a dialog box, the properties are set when the Trackbar control is created.

FIGURE 19.3.

The Trackbar and its properties in Visual C++'s resource editor.

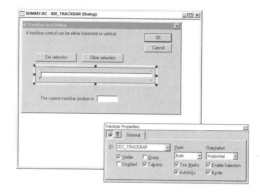

If you look at Figure 19.3, you will see that I've added two buttons to the dialog box. These two buttons are used to set (and clear) an Enable Selection range.

In Listing 19.1 is the code that manages our Trackbar sample dialog box. The base for this code was developed using ClassWizard; the base was then modified to add the necessary features.

Listing 19.1. The TRACKBAR.CPP file.

```
// trackbar.cpp : implementation file
//

#include "stdafx.h"
#include "Dummy.h"
#include "trackbar.h"

#ifdef _DEBUG
#undef THIS_FILE
static char BASED_CODE THIS_FILE[] = __FILE__;
#endif

/////////////////////////////////////////////////////////////////////////////
// CTrackBarDlg dialog


CTrackBarDlg::CTrackBarDlg(CWnd* pParent /*=NULL*/)
    : CDialog(CTrackBarDlg::IDD, pParent)
{
    //{{AFX_DATA_INIT(CTrackBarDlg)
```

continues

Listing 19.1. continued

```
        // NOTE: the ClassWizard will add member initialization here
    //}}AFX_DATA_INIT
}


void CTrackBarDlg::DoDataExchange(CDataExchange* pDX)
{
    CDialog::DoDataExchange(pDX);
    //{{AFX_DATA_MAP(CTrackBarDlg)
    DDX_Control(pDX, IDC_TRACKBAR, m_TrackBar);
    DDX_Control(pDX, IDC_EDIT1, m_EditControl);
    //}}AFX_DATA_MAP
}


BEGIN_MESSAGE_MAP(CTrackBarDlg, CDialog)
    //{{AFX_MSG_MAP(CTrackBarDlg)
    ON_WM_HSCROLL()
    ON_BN_CLICKED(IDC_CLEARSELECTION, OnClearselection)
    ON_BN_CLICKED(IDC_SETSELECTION, OnSetselection)
    //}}AFX_MSG_MAP
END_MESSAGE_MAP()


/////////////////////////////////////////////////////////////////////////
// CTrackBarDlg message handlers

BOOL CTrackBarDlg::OnInitDialog()
{
    CDialog::OnInitDialog();

    // TODO: Add extra initialization here

//    Initialize the Trackbar control range from 10 to 100:

    m_TrackBar.SetRange(10, 100);

//    Set the Trackbar tick marks to every tenth point:

    m_TrackBar.SetTicFreq(10);

//    Initialize trackbar position, and our output window:

    m_TrackBar.SetPos(10);

    char    szBuffer[81];
    sprintf(szBuffer, "10");
    m_EditControl.SetWindowText(szBuffer);


    return TRUE;  // return TRUE unless you set the focus to a control
                  // EXCEPTION: OCX Property Pages should return FALSE
}


void CTrackBarDlg::OnHScroll(UINT nSBCode, UINT nPos, CScrollBar* pScrollBar)
```

```
{
    // TODO: Add your message handler code here and/or call default

//   The trackbar sends an WM_HSCROLL (or WM_VSCROLL if the
//   trackbar is vertical) message telling the position of the
//   slider has changed!

//   This diagnostic message shows what parameters are passed to our
//   OnHScroll() handler!

//   TRACE("nSBCode = %d, nPos = %d, pScrollBar = %p &m_TrackBar = %p\n",
//       nSBCode, nPos, pScrollBar, &m_TrackBar);

    char    szBuffer[81];

    CSliderCtrl * pSlider = (CSliderCtrl *)pScrollBar;

//   First, check to see if the scrollbar is *really* our Trackbar control:

    if (pSlider == &m_TrackBar)
    {//    It's our trackbar! Do our thing, display the data returned:

//        If your application must work with the individual actions,
//        use a case such as shown below: (Uncomment the TRACE()
//        lines to see what messages are really sent).

        switch(nSBCode)
        {
            case TB_BOTTOM:              // User pressed END key.
//                TRACE("TB_BOTTOM \n");
                break;
            case TB_TOP:                 // User pressed HOME key.
//                TRACE("TB_TOP \n");
                break;
            case TB_ENDTRACK:            // Mouse released after drag.
//                TRACE("TB_ENDTRACK \n");
                break;
            case TB_LINEDOWN:            // DOWN ARROW or RIGHT ARROW pressed.
//                TRACE("TB_LINEDOWN \n");
                break;
            case TB_LINEUP:              // UP ARROW or LEFT ARROW pressed.
//                TRACE("TB_LINEUP \n");
                break;
            case TB_PAGEDOWN:            // Click rt of slider, or PAGEDOWN pressed.
//                TRACE("TB_PAGEDOWN \n");
                break;
            case TB_PAGEUP:              // Click lf of slider, or PAGEUP pressed.
//                TRACE("TB_PAGEUP \n");
                break;
            case TB_THUMBPOSITION:       // Trackbar move to nPos position.
//                TRACE("TB_THUMBPOSITION \n");
                break;
            case TB_THUMBTRACK:          // User dragging the slider!
//                TRACE("TB_THUMBTRACK \n");
                break;
            default: // Should never, ever happen.
//                TRACE("default: (error) \n");
```

continues

Listing 19.1. continued

```
                break;
        }

        sprintf(szBuffer, "%d", pSlider->GetPos());
        m_EditControl.SetWindowText(szBuffer);
    }
    else
    {//    It's some other scrollbar in the program!

    }

    CDialog::OnHScroll(nSBCode, nPos, pScrollBar);
}

void CTrackBarDlg::OnClearselection()
{
    // TODO: Add your control notification handler code here

    m_TrackBar.ClearSel(TRUE);
}

void CTrackBarDlg::OnSetselection()
{
    // TODO: Add your control notification handler code here

    m_TrackBar.SetSelection(30, 70);
    m_TrackBar.Invalidate();
}
```

In Listing 19.2 is the TRACKBAR.H header file that accompanies the TRACKBAR.CPP file shown in the preceding Listing 19.1. The TRACKBAR.H file was modified only by ClassWizard; no manual changes were necessary.

Listing 19.2. The TRACKBAR.H file.

```
// trackbar.h : header file
//

/////////////////////////////////////////////////////////////////////////////
// CTrackBarDlg dialog

class CTrackBarDlg : public CDialog
{
// Construction
public:
    CTrackBarDlg(CWnd* pParent = NULL);    // standard constructor

// Dialog Data
    //{{AFX_DATA(CTrackBarDlg)
    enum { IDD = IDD_TRACKBAR };
    CSliderCtrl    m_TrackBar;
    CEdit    m_EditControl;
    //}}AFX_DATA
```

```
// Overrides
    // ClassWizard generated virtual function overrides
    //{{AFX_VIRTUAL(CTrackBarDlg)
    protected:
    virtual void DoDataExchange(CDataExchange* pDX);    // DDX/DDV support
    //}}AFX_VIRTUAL

// Implementation
protected:

    // Generated message map functions
    //{{AFX_MSG(CTrackBarDlg)
    virtual BOOL OnInitDialog();
    afx_msg void OnHScroll(UINT nSBCode, UINT nPos, CScrollBar* pScrollBar);
    afx_msg void OnClearselection();
    afx_msg void OnSetselection();
    //}}AFX_MSG
    DECLARE_MESSAGE_MAP()
};
```

The *CSliderCtrl* Class in a Dialog Box

As stated previously, you would usually bind your CSliderCtrl object to a Trackbar control by using ClassWizard. After you have bound the CSliderCtrl object, you can then, in the OnInitDialog() function, initialize your Trackbar control.

Generally, you will want to set three attributes for your Trackbar:

- *The Trackbar's range* With Trackbars, both the lower and upper limits can be set. You may set the upper range, the lower range, or both ranges with a single function call.

- *The Trackbar's tick frequency* With a Trackbar, having about four to ten ticks is best. Generally, having more than ten tickmarks makes the control look too "busy" and is more difficult for the user to use it.

- *The Trackbar's initial position* Sometimes you will want the slider always to start at the minimum position. Most times, the application should set the slider to the current value.

The following code listing shows the three lines (in boldface) that initialize the sample Trackbar. The order of the calls to initialize the Trackbar is not critical, but setting the range first is a good practice.

```
BOOL CTrackBarDlg::OnInitDialog()
{
    CDialog::OnInitDialog();

    // TODO: Add extra initialization here

//    Initialize the Trackbar control range from 10 to 100:
```

```
    m_TrackBar.SetRange(10, 100);

//   Set the Trackbar tick marks to every tenth point:

    m_TrackBar.SetTicFreq(10);

//    Initialize trackbar position, and our output window:

    m_TrackBar.SetPos(10);

    char    szBuffer[81];
    sprintf(szBuffer, "10");
    m_EditControl.SetWindowText(szBuffer);

    return TRUE;  // return TRUE unless you set the focus to a control
                  // EXCEPTION: OCX Property Pages should return FALSE
}
```

Creating *CSliderCtrl* Objects in Nondialog Windows

To create a CSliderCtrl object in a window that is not a dialog box, you would call CSliderCtrl::Create(). The CSliderCtrl::Create() function takes four parameters, a style (see Table 19.2), a RECT structure specifying the Trackbar's location and size, a pointer to the parent window, and the control ID.

```
CSliderCtrl::Create(
    WS_CHILD | WS_VISIBLE | TBS_HORZ | TBS_AUTOTICKS | TBS_ENABLESELRANGE,
    rect, this, 0);
```

Table 19.2. Window styles for the CSliderCtrl::Create() function.

Identifier	Description
TBS_HORZ	A Trackbar control can be either vertical or horizontal. The direction to which the Pointer points is dependent on the control's orientation. This style creates a horizontal Trackbar and is the default.
TBS_VERT	A Trackbar control can be either vertical or horizontal. The direction to which the Pointer points is dependent on the control's orientation. This style creates a vertical Trackbar.
TBS_AUTOTICKS	The tickmarks are added automatically when the range has been set.
TBS_NOTICKS	The Trackbar has no tickmarks.
TBS_BOTTOM	The Trackbar displays tickmarks on the bottom of the horizontal slider. When used with TBS_TOP, this style is the same as TBS_BOTH.
TBS_TOP	The Trackbar displays tickmarks on the top of the horizontal slider. When used with TBS_BOTTOM, this style is the same as TBS_BOTH.

Identifier	Description
TBS_RIGHT	The Trackbar displays tickmarks on the right of the vertical slider. When used with TBS_LEFT, this style is the same as TBS_BOTH.
TBS_LEFT	The Trackbar displays tickmarks on the left of the vertical slider. When used with TBS_RIGHT, this style is the same as TBS_BOTH.
TBS_BOTH	The Trackbar displays tickmarks on both sides of the slider. This style applies both to vertical and horizontal Trackbars.
TBS_ENABLESELRANGE	The Trackbar control may have a selection range that provides the user with visual feedback. The selection range does not limit the Trackbar control in any way; it only provides a method to give output to the user.

In a number of situations a programmer might want to create a Trackbar control in a nondialog window. Using CSliderCtrl::Create() is an easy method to create a Trackbar control.

CSliderCtrl Options

The CSliderCtrl object allows setting a number of parameters (such as range and initial position as previously described). Other parameters that the application can set include the following:

- The amount that the slider moves when a lineup or linedown (such as pressing the right- or left-arrow keys) is requested. The default is 1. The CSliderCtrl::SetLineSize() member function is used to set this parameter.

- The amount that the slider moves when a pageup or pagedown (such as pressing the Page Up or Page Down keys) is requested. The default is set by Windows, based on the range provided. The CSliderCtrl::SetPageSize() member function is used to set this parameter.

- The tickmark positions. In a Trackbar you can have tickmarks arranged either automatically by Windows (where the tickmarks will be equally spaced) or by the application (where the tickmarks will be asymmetrically spaced). You can add a tickmark to show the original position of the slider or, if desired, some other value. The CSliderCtrl::SetTic() member function is used to set a tickmark.

- The frequency of tickmarks. The default frequency is to have one tickmark for each increment of the Trackbar. For trackbars that have a large range (perhaps a range of more than ten or so), you should limit the number of tickmarks to a reasonable count. The CSliderCtrl::SetTicFreq() member function is used to set the frequency of the tickmarks.

Using the *CSliderCtrl* Trackbar Object

The CSliderCtrl Trackbar object takes data input (the range and initial slider position) and provides output (the final slider position). As well, the Trackbar can provide input to the application in the form of scrollbar messages whenever the user changes the slider's position.

The *CSliderCtrl* Trackbar Input

The CSliderCtrl Trackbar can be initialized by using the CSliderCtrl::SetPos() member function. This function takes a single integer value that represents the initial position of the slider. This value should be within the range of the Trackbar control.

The *CSliderCtrl* Trackbar Interaction

The user interacts with a trackbar by repositioning the slider. Whenever the slider is moved, the control sends scrollbar messages to the parent window. These messages are either WM_HSCROLL or WM_VSCROLL (depending on whether the trackbar is a horizontal or a vertical control).

In MFC applications, you can have ClassWizard create an OnHScroll() or OnVScroll() handler. This handler then can, when it is called, determine that the Trackbar is the control that caused the message. It is generally necessary to check to see which control sent the message because other controls (including scrollbars) also send WM_HSCROLL and WM_VSCROLL messages.

The following code sample shows a simple handler that updates an edit window's contents based on the current position of the trackbar.

```
void CTrackBarDlg::OnHScroll(UINT nSBCode, UINT nPos, CScrollBar* pScrollBar)
{
    // TODO: Add your message handler code here and/or call default

    char    szBuffer[81];

    CSliderCtrl * pSlider = (CSliderCtrl *)pScrollBar;

    if (pSlider == &m_TrackBar)
    {//    It's our trackbar! Do our thing, display the data returned:
        sprintf(szBuffer, "%d", pSlider->GetPos());
        m_EditControl.SetWindowText(szBuffer);
    }

    CDialog::OnHScroll(nSBCode, nPos, pScrollBar);
}
```

Several items in this code sample need closer examination. First, to determine whether the control that caused the scroll message is the Trackbar control, you test the passed pScrollBar parameter with the CSliderCtrl object for the Trackbar. If they are identical, you know the control that caused the scroll message was the Trackbar control. If they are not the same, some other control (such as a scrollbar or perhaps a Spinbutton control) caused the scroll message.

After you have determined that the Trackbar control was responsible for the scroll message, you then can perform whatever action is appropriate. You might want to check the current position of the slider and perhaps provide some form of feedback to the user, based on the slider's position. In the example, you get the slider's position and update an edit control to display the slider's position. This updating is fast, as the sample program shows.

> **NOTE**
>
> Be careful to avoid trying to do too much in the processing of scroll messages. You can make the action of the Trackbar control choppy or irregular (no, Exlax won't help here). Try to keep the scroll-message processing at a reasonable level.

The *CProgressCtrl* Class

A Progressbar control allows the application to display progress, levels, or other nonexact data to a user. The display represents a nonexact value that will fall within a predetermined range. This control is simple, having only a few options.

Figure 19.4 shows an example of a Progressbar control in a dialog box. This example is from our sample program (see Chapter 18, "Toolbars and Status Bars") and shows a typical implementation of the Progressbar control in a dialog box. The Progressbar control shown in Figure 19.4 has its value set using a Trackbar control.

FIGURE 19.4.

A Progressbar control shown in a dialog box.

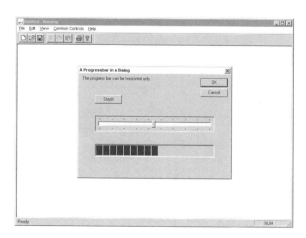

Your application, when using a `CProgressCtrl` class object, will need to do a minimal amount of management of the Progressbar control. The application must set the range and the incremental value.

After you have added the Progressbar control to a dialog box, you then can use ClassWizard to bind a `CProgressCtrl` object to your Progressbar control. This `CProgressCtrl` object is your interface with the Progressbar control.

Implementing a *CProgressCtrl* Progressbar Control

If you are using a Progressbar control in a dialog box, you would use ClassWizard to bind a `CProgressCtrl` object to the control. Were you to be implementing a Progressbar control in a window that is not a dialog box, you would call the `CProgressCtrl::Create()` function to create the Progressbar control. You quite possibly might find a use for a Progressbar control in a normal window or perhaps as part of a toolbar.

Figure 19.5 shows the dialog box (in Visual C++'s resource editor) with the properties for the Progressbar. These properties are generic attributes that apply to most windows. The Progressbar controls specific attributes can not be set using the resource editor. When the Progressbar control is in a window other than a dialog box, the properties are set when the Progressbar control is created.

FIGURE 19.5.

The Progressbar and its properties in Visual C++'s resource editor.

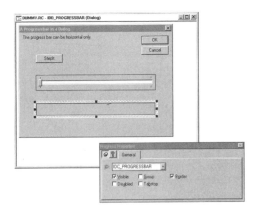

If you look at Figure 19.5, you will see that I've added a Trackbar control, which is used to provide the input to the Progressbar.

In Listing 19.3 is the code that manages the Progressbar sample dialog box. The base for this code was developed using ClassWizard and then modified to add the necessary features.

Listing 19.3. The PROGRESS.CPP file.

```cpp
// progress.cpp : implementation file
//

#include "stdafx.h"
#include "Dummy.h"

#include "progress.h"

#ifdef _DEBUG
#undef THIS_FILE
static char BASED_CODE THIS_FILE[] = __FILE__;
#endif

/////////////////////////////////////////////////////////////////////////////
// CProgressBarDlg dialog


CProgressBarDlg::CProgressBarDlg(CWnd* pParent /*=NULL*/)
    : CDialog(CProgressBarDlg::IDD, pParent)
{
    //{{AFX_DATA_INIT(CProgressBarDlg)
    //}}AFX_DATA_INIT
}


void CProgressBarDlg::DoDataExchange(CDataExchange* pDX)
{
    CDialog::DoDataExchange(pDX);
    //{{AFX_DATA_MAP(CProgressBarDlg)
    DDX_Control(pDX, IDC_TRACKBAR, m_TrackBar);
    DDX_Control(pDX, IDC_PROGRESSBAR, m_ProgressBar);
    //}}AFX_DATA_MAP
}


BEGIN_MESSAGE_MAP(CProgressBarDlg, CDialog)
    //{{AFX_MSG_MAP(CProgressBarDlg)
    ON_WM_HSCROLL()
    ON_BN_CLICKED(IDC_STEPIT, OnStepit)
    //}}AFX_MSG_MAP
END_MESSAGE_MAP()


/////////////////////////////////////////////////////////////////////////////
// CProgressBarDlg message handlers

BOOL CProgressBarDlg::OnInitDialog()
{
    CDialog::OnInitDialog();

    // TODO: Add extra initialization here

//    Initialize the Trackbar control:

    m_TrackBar.SetRange(10, 100);
```

continues

Listing 19.3. continued

```
    m_TrackBar.SetTicFreq(10);
    m_TrackBar.SetPos(10);

//    Initialize the Progressbar control to match the Trackbar:

    m_ProgressBar.SetRange(10, 100);

    m_ProgressBar.SetStep(1);  // Default is 10, chunky!

    m_ProgressBar.SetPos(10);    // Same position as the Trackbar!

    return TRUE;  // return TRUE unless you set the focus to a control
                  // EXCEPTION: OCX Property Pages should return FALSE
}

void CProgressBarDlg::OnHScroll(UINT nSBCode, UINT nPos, CScrollBar* pScrollBar)
{
    // TODO: Add your message handler code here and/or call default

    CSliderCtrl * pSlider = (CSliderCtrl *)pScrollBar;

//    First, check to see if the scrollbar is *really* our Trackbar control:

    if (pSlider == &m_TrackBar)
    {//    It's our trackbar! Do our thing, display the data returned:
//        Same position as the Trackbar!
        m_ProgressBar.SetPos(pSlider->GetPos());
    }

    CDialog::OnHScroll(nSBCode, nPos, pScrollBar);
}

void CProgressBarDlg::OnStepit()
{
    // TODO: Add your control notification handler code here

    m_ProgressBar.StepIt();
}
```

In Listing 19.4 is the PROGRESS.H header file that accompanies the PROGRESS.CPP file shown in the preceding Listing 19.3. The PROGRESS.H file was modified only by ClassWizard; no manual changes were necessary.

Listing 19.4. The PROGRESS.H file.

```
// progress.h : header file
//

/////////////////////////////////////////////////////////////////////////////
// CProgressBarDlg dialog

class CProgressBarDlg : public CDialog
```

```
{
// Construction
public:
    CProgressBarDlg(CWnd* pParent = NULL);    // standard constructor

// Dialog Data
    //{{AFX_DATA(CProgressBarDlg)
    enum { IDD = IDD_PROGRESSBAR };
    CSliderCtrl    m_TrackBar;
    CProgressCtrl    m_ProgressBar;
    //}}AFX_DATA


// Overrides
    // ClassWizard generated virtual function overrides
    //{{AFX_VIRTUAL(CProgressBarDlg)
    protected:
    virtual void DoDataExchange(CDataExchange* pDX);    // DDX/DDV support
    //}}AFX_VIRTUAL

// Implementation
protected:

    // Generated message map functions
    //{{AFX_MSG(CProgressBarDlg)
    virtual BOOL OnInitDialog();
    afx_msg void OnHScroll(UINT nSBCode, UINT nPos, CScrollBar* pScrollBar);
    afx_msg void OnStepit();
    //}}AFX_MSG
    DECLARE_MESSAGE_MAP()
};
```

The *CProgressCtrl* Class in a Dialog Box

As stated previously, you would usually bind your CProgressCtrl object to a Progressbar control using ClassWizard. After you have bound the CProgressCtrl object, you can then, in the OnInitDialog() function, initialize your Progressbar control.

Generally, you will want to set three attributes for your Progressbar:

- *The Progressbar's range*   With Progressbars, the lower and upper limits can be set. The default range is zero to 100, which is easily translated to percentages if desired.

- *The Progressbar's step value*   When using CProgressCtrl::SetStep(), you set the step value. This value is used when the CProgressCtrl::StepIt() member function is called to increment the Progressbar. When you set the Progressbar using the CProgressCtrl::SetPos() function, the step value is ignored. The default step value is 10.

- *The Progressbar's initial position*   The default initial position is 0; however, you can set whatever initial position your application needs.

The following code listing shows the three lines (in boldface) that initialize our Progressbar. The order of the calls to initialize the Progressbar is not critical; however, if you are using a nondefault range, it would be wise to set the range first.

```
BOOL CProgressBarDlg::OnInitDialog()
{
    CDialog::OnInitDialog();

    // TODO: Add extra initialization here

//    Initialize the Trackbar control:

    m_TrackBar.SetRange(10, 100);
    m_TrackBar.SetTicFreq(10);
    m_TrackBar.SetPos(10);

//    Initialize the Progressbar control to match the Trackbar:

    m_ProgressBar.SetRange(10, 100);

    m_ProgressBar.SetStep(1);  // Default is 10, chunky!

    m_ProgressBar.SetPos(10);     // Same position as the Trackbar!

    return TRUE;  // return TRUE unless you set the focus to a control
                  // EXCEPTION: OCX Property Pages should return FALSE
}
```

Creating *CProgressCtrl* Objects in Nondialog Windows

To create a CProgressCtrl object in a window that is not a dialog box, you would call CProgressCtrl::Create(). The CProgressCtrl::Create() function takes four parameters: a style, a RECT structure specifying the Progressbar's location and size, a pointer to the parent window, and the control ID.

```
CProgressCtrl::Create(
    WS_CHILD | WS_VISIBLE,
    rect, this, 0);
```

In a number of situations, a programmer might want to create a Progressbar control in a nondialog window. Using CProgressCtrl::Create() is an easy method of creating a Progressbar control.

Using the *CProgressCtrl* Progressbar Object

The CProgressCtrl Progressbar object takes data input (the range and initial slider position) and provides output (the position of the progress bar). There is no feedback from the Progressbar control to the application, for the Progressbar control does not take any input from the user.

The *CProgressCtrl* Progressbar Display

The CProgressCtrl Progressbar can be initialized by using the CProgressCtrl::SetPos() member function. This function takes a single integer value that represents the position of the slider. This value should be within the range of the Progressbar control.

The *CProgressCtrl* Progressbar Interaction

The application interacts with the Progressbar by repositioning the progress bar. Whenever the Progressbar's indicator is moved, the user will see the change in the Progressbar's display.

Your application can change the display of the Progressbar's indicator by using either of the following function calls:

- A call to CProgressCtrl::SetPos() allows the application to set the indicator to any position. You can increment or decrement the indicator as needed.

- A call to CProgressCtrl::StepIt() allows the application to increment the indicator to the next position. Your application must use care not to increment the position past the maximum value; if it does increment the position past the maximum value, the control will reset to zero. You can see the effects of stepping past the maximum value using the sample program's StepIt button.

The *CSpinButtonCtrl* Class

A Spinbutton control (often referred to as an UpDown control) enables a user to enter an exact value, usually sequentially, that will fall within a predetermined range or set of values. This control is modeled after the scrollbar control and actually sends many of the same messages that a scrollbar control would send.

The Spinbutton control usually is paired with an edit control to form a multipart control. The Spinbutton control is able, when the values being entered are numeric integers, to automatically update the buddy edit control's contents. For the remainder of this chapter, I'll refer to this control as the Spinbutton control; I'll refer to the buddy edit control as the buddy control.

In Figure 19.6 is an example of two Spinbutton controls in a dialog box. One control is a simple integer-only control that enables the user either to use the up and down selectors or to enter a numeric value into the buddy control. The other Spinbutton control enables the user to select a color from a list of colors. The user's only method of changing the color is to use the up and down buttons, for the buddy control in this example is read-only. This example is from our sample program and shows a typical implementation of the Spinbutton control in a dialog box.

FIGURE 19.6.

Two Spinbutton controls shown in a dialog box.

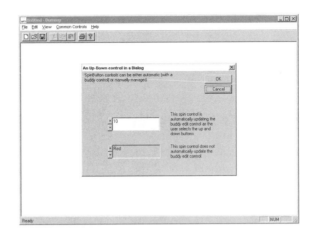

Your application, when using a CSpinButtonCtrl class object, will need to do a minimal amount of management of the Spinbutton control. The application must set the range, the initial value for the Spinbutton control, and—optionally—the accelerator table. A Spinbutton control can have a number of attributes (some attributes may be set by using the resource editor in Visual C++; other attributes must be set at execution time). I've listed the Spinbutton control's attributes in Table 19.3.

Table 19.3. The Spinbutton control's attributes.

Attribute	Description
Horizontal	The control is horizontal, with the arrows pointing right and left (rather than up and down).
Vertical	The control is vertical, with the arrows pointing up and down (rather than right and left).
Arrowkeys	The Spinbutton control responds to the up- and down-arrow keys by incrementing or decrementing the selection.
Wrap	When the Spinbutton control is incremented past the maximum value, it automatically resets to the minimum value. When the Spinbutton control is decremented below the minimum value, it automatically resets to the maximum value.
BuddyInt	The Spinbutton control updates the text in the buddy control using integers formatted in either decimal or hexadecimal (see CSpinButtonCtrl::SetBase()).
NoThousands	There will not be thousands separators between each three digits in the display when BuddyInt is specified.
AutoBuddy	An automatically updated edit control is logically attached to the Spinbutton control.

Attribute	Description
AlignLeft	The Spinbutton control is aligned to the right edge of the buddy control.
AlignRight	The Spinbutton control is aligned to the left edge of the buddy control.

After you have added the Spinbutton control to a dialog box, you then can use ClassWizard to bind a `CSpinButtonCtrl` object to your Spinbutton control. This `CSpinButtonCtrl` object is your interface with the Spinbutton control.

The BuddyInt style allows you to have the buddy control automatically updated with an integer value. The user is not restricted to using the up and down controls when BuddyInt is specified; if the buddy control is not read-only, the user may enter a valid integer and the Spinbutton will be correctly updated to the value entered. This enables the user to avoid having to scroll through perhaps thousands of values to get to the desired value.

Implementing a *CSpinButtonCtrl* Spinbutton Control

If you are using a Spinbutton control in a dialog box, you would use ClassWizard to bind a `CSpinButtonCtrl` object to the control. Were you to be implementing a Spinbutton control in a window that is not a dialog box, you would call the `CSpinButtonCtrl::Create()` function to create the Spinbutton control. It is quite possible that you might find a use for a Spinbutton control in a normal window or perhaps as part of a toolbar.

Figure 19.7 shows our dialog box (in Visual C++'s resource editor) with the properties for the Spinbutton shown. For Spinbutton controls that are in dialog boxes, these properties can be set easily using the resource editor. When the Spinbutton control is in a window other than a dialog box, the properties are set when the Spinbutton control is created.

FIGURE 19.7.

The Spinbutton with BuddyInt and AutoBuddy attributes set.

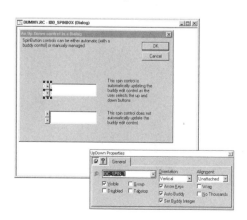

If you look at Figure 19.7, you will see that there are two Spinbutton controls. Figure 19.8 shows the second Spinbutton control, which does not have BuddyInt and AutoBuddy attributes set. The second SpinButton's buddy control is updated manually by the program.

FIGURE 19.8.

The Spinbutton without the BuddyInt and AutoBuddy attributes set.

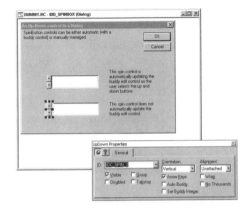

I have noticed that the Spinbutton controls are sensitive to the tab order of the dialog box controls. If you find that a control other than the correct buddy control is being updated when the buddy control should have been updated, try changing the tab order of the controls in the dialog box.

In Listing 19.5 is the code that manages our Spinbutton sample dialog box. The base for this code was developed using ClassWizard and then modified to add the features that were necessary.

Listing 19.5. The SPINBOXD.CPP file.

```
// spinboxd.cpp : implementation file
//

#include "stdafx.h"
#include "Dummy.h"
#include "spinboxd.h"

#ifdef _DEBUG
#undef THIS_FILE
static char BASED_CODE THIS_FILE[] = __FILE__;
#endif

/////////////////////////////////////////////////////////////////////////////
```

```
// CSpinBoxDlg dialog


CSpinBoxDlg::CSpinBoxDlg(CWnd* pParent /*=NULL*/)
    : CDialog(CSpinBoxDlg::IDD, pParent)
{
    //{{AFX_DATA_INIT(CSpinBoxDlg)
    //}}AFX_DATA_INIT
}


void CSpinBoxDlg::DoDataExchange(CDataExchange* pDX)
{
    CDialog::DoDataExchange(pDX);
    //{{AFX_DATA_MAP(CSpinBoxDlg)
    DDX_Control(pDX, IDC_SPIN_2, m_Spin2);
    DDX_Control(pDX, IDC_SPIN_1, m_Spin1);
    DDX_Control(pDX, IDC_BUDDY_2, m_Buddy2);
    DDX_Control(pDX, IDC_BUDDY_1, m_Buddy1);
    //}}AFX_DATA_MAP
}


BEGIN_MESSAGE_MAP(CSpinBoxDlg, CDialog)
    //{{AFX_MSG_MAP(CSpinBoxDlg)
    ON_WM_VSCROLL()
    //}}AFX_MSG_MAP
END_MESSAGE_MAP()

char    * szColors[] = {
    "Red",
    "Blue",
    "Green",
    "Yellow",
    "Cyan",
    "Magenta",
    "Black",
    "White",
    "Gold",
    "Silver"};



/////////////////////////////////////////////////////////////////////////
// CSpinBoxDlg message handlers

BOOL CSpinBoxDlg::OnInitDialog()
{
    CDialog::OnInitDialog();

    // TODO: Add extra initialization here

//    Spinbox 1 has an automatically updated buddy control.
//    Just setting the buddy takes care of the updating of the
//    buddy edit control.
    m_Spin1.SetRange(10, 100);
    m_Spin1.SetBuddy(&m_Buddy1);
```

continues

Listing 19.5. continued

```
    m_Spin1.SetPos(10);

//    Spinbox 2 DOES NOT have an automatically updated buddy control.
//    Setting the buddy links the two controls, but updating is
//    our program's responsibility.
    m_Spin2.SetRange(0, (sizeof(szColors) / sizeof(szColors[0])) - 1);
    m_Spin2.SetPos(0);
    m_Spin2.SetBuddy(&m_Buddy2);
    m_Buddy2.SetWindowText(szColors[0]);

    return TRUE;  // return TRUE unless you set the focus to a control
                  // EXCEPTION: OCX Property Pages should return FALSE
}

void CSpinBoxDlg::OnVScroll(UINT nSBCode, UINT nPos, CScrollBar* pScrollBar)
{
    // TODO: Add your message handler code here and/or call default

    CSpinButtonCtrl * pSpin = (CSpinButtonCtrl *)pScrollBar;

//    First, check to see if the scrollbar is *really* our Spinbox control:

    if (pSpin == &m_Spin2)
    {//    It's our second spinbox control!
//        Do our thing, display the data returned:
//        Same position as the Trackbar!
        m_Buddy2.SetWindowText(szColors[pSpin->GetPos()]);
    }

    CDialog::OnVScroll(nSBCode, nPos, pScrollBar);
}
```

In Listing 19.6 is the SPINBOXD.H header file that accompanies the SPINBOXD.CPP file shown in Listing 19.5. The SPINBOXD.H file was modified only by ClassWizard; no manual changes were necessary.

Listing 19.6. The SPINBOXD.H file.

```
// spinboxd.h : header file
//

/////////////////////////////////////////////////////////////////////////
// CSpinBoxDlg dialog

class CSpinBoxDlg : public CDialog
{
// Construction
public:
    CSpinBoxDlg(CWnd* pParent = NULL);   // standard constructor

// Dialog Data
    //{{AFX_DATA(CSpinBoxDlg)
```

```
    enum { IDD = IDD_SPINBOX };
    CSpinButtonCtrl    m_Spin2;
    CSpinButtonCtrl    m_Spin1;
    CEdit    m_Buddy2;
    CEdit    m_Buddy1;
    //}}AFX_DATA

// Overrides
    // ClassWizard generated virtual function overrides
    //{{AFX_VIRTUAL(CSpinBoxDlg)
    protected:
    virtual void DoDataExchange(CDataExchange* pDX);    // DDX/DDV support
    //}}AFX_VIRTUAL

// Implementation
protected:

    // Generated message map functions
    //{{AFX_MSG(CSpinBoxDlg)
    virtual BOOL OnInitDialog();
    afx_msg void OnVScroll(UINT nSBCode, UINT nPos, CScrollBar* pScrollBar);
    //}}AFX_MSG
    DECLARE_MESSAGE_MAP()
};
```

The *CSpinButtonCtrl* Class in a Dialog Box

As previously stated, you would usually bind your CSpinButtonCtrl object to a Spinbutton
control by using ClassWizard. After you have bound the CSpinButtonCtrl object, you can
then, in the OnInitDialog() function, initialize your Spinbutton control.

Generally, you will want to set a number of attributes for your Spinbutton:

- *The Spinbutton's range* With Spinbuttons, both the lower and upper limits can be
  set. The range must not be greater than UD_MAXVAL; the minimum must not be less
  than UD_MINVAL; and the maximum must not be greater than UD_MAXVAL.

- *The Spinbutton's initial position* Sometimes you will want the Spinbutton control to
  start at the minimum position. Most times, the application should set the Spinbutton
  control to the current value for whatever variable the Spinbutton control represents.

- *The Spinbutton's buddy control* The buddy control, if used, must be logically attached to the Spinbutton at initialization time. This is critical if the Spinbutton
  control has the buddy and BuddyInt attributes.

- *The Spinbutton's BuddyInt base* The integer value presented in a buddy control when
  BuddyInt is specified can be in base-10 (decimal) or base-16 (hex). Unless you are
  writing a technical application, don't use base-16 (hex)—only programmers and
  scientists understand base-16!

■ If you are using accelerator keys, set the accelerator values. This allows the accelerator key to have two "speeds." When initially pressed, the increment will be slow. After a predetermined time has elapsed, the increment speed will increase to higher value. There can be more than one set of increments (that is, you can have slow, fast, faster, and fastest — four levels of speed).

The following code listing shows the three lines (in boldface) that initialize our first Spinbutton, which has both the buddy and the BuddyInt attributes. The second set of four lines initializes the second Spinbutton control, which does not use the buddy and BuddyInt attributes. The order of the calls to initialize the Spinbutton is not critical, but setting the buddy control before setting the position is necessary to ensure that the buddy's contents reflect the correct value for the Spinbutton control.

> **NOTE**
>
> You need not specify the Buddy attribute to use the `CSpinButtonCtrl::SetBuddy()` function. A Spinbutton control where the buddy is always updated by the parent window (as our second example is) would not have the Buddy attribute set.

```
BOOL CSpinBoxDlg::OnInitDialog()
{
    CDialog::OnInitDialog();

    // TODO: Add extra initialization here

//    Spinbox 1 has an automatically updated buddy control.
//    Just setting the buddy takes care of the updating of the
//    buddy edit control.
    m_Spin1.SetRange(10, 100);
    m_Spin1.SetBuddy(&m_Buddy1);
    m_Spin1.SetPos(10);

//    Spinbox 2 DOES NOT have an automatically updated buddy control.
//    Setting the buddy links the two controls, but updating is
//    our program's responsibility.
    m_Spin2.SetRange(0, (sizeof(szColors) / sizeof(szColors[0])) - 1);
    m_Spin2.SetPos(0);
    m_Spin2.SetBuddy(&m_Buddy2);
    m_Buddy2.SetWindowText(szColors[0]);

    return TRUE;  // return TRUE unless you set the focus to a control
                  // EXCEPTION: OCX Property Pages should return FALSE
}
```

Creating *CSpinButtonCtrl* Objects in Nondialog Windows

To create a `CSpinButtonCtrl` object in a window that is not a dialog box, you would call `CSpinButtonCtrl::Create()`. The `CSpinButtonCtrl::Create()` function takes four parameters: a style (see Table 19.4), a RECT structure specifying the Spinbutton's location and size, a pointer to the parent window, and the control ID.

```
CSpinButtonCtrl::Create(
    WS_CHILD | WS_VISIBLE | UDS_HORZ | UDS_AUTOBUDDY | UDS_SETBUDDYINT,
    rect, this, 0);
```

Table 19.4. Window styles for the `CSpinButtonCtrl::Create()` function.

Identifier	Description
UDS_HORZ	A Spinbutton control can be either vertical or horizontal. The direction to which the Pointer points is dependent on the control's orientation. This style creates a horizontal (arrows point left and right) Spinbutton.
(default)	Not specifying UDS_HORZ creates a vertical Spinbutton. This is the default and has no identifier defined.
UDS_ARROWKEYS	The Spinbutton control is incremented and decremented when the user presses the up- and down-arrow keys.
UDS_SETBUDDYINT	The Spinbutton automatically updates the integer value displayed in the buddy control. If the buddy control is not read-only, the user is able also to enter a new value for the Spinbutton control using the buddy control.
UDS_NOTHOUSANDS	There will be no thousands separator between each three digits in the buddy control.
UDS_AUTOBUDDY	The Spinbutton control has a buddy control that is automatically updated with the value of the Spinbutton control.
UDS_ALIGNRIGHT	The Spinbutton control is aligned to the left edge of the buddy control.
UDS_ALIGNLEFT	The Spinbutton control is aligned to the right edge of the buddy control.

In several situations, a programmer might want to create a Spinbutton control in a nondialog window. Using `CSpinButtonCtrl::Create()` is an easy method of creating a Spinbutton control.

CSpinButtonCtrl Options

The `CSpinButtonCtrl` object allows setting the base parameter at program execution time. Other attributes are usually set at the time the application is created (using the resource editor for Spinbutton controls that are located in dialog boxes).

Using the *CSpinButtonCtrl* Spinbutton Object

The CSpinButtonCtrl Spinbutton object takes data input (the range and initial position) and provides output (the final position).

As well, the Spinbutton can provide input to the application in the form of scrollbar messages whenever the user changes the control's position. This allows the application to update the buddy control (or perform other application-specific computations) as needed.

The *CSpinButtonCtrl* Spinbutton Input

The CSpinButtonCtrl Spinbutton can be initialized by using the CSpinButtonCtrl::SetPos() member function. This function takes a single integer value that represents the initial position of the control. This value should be within the range of the Spinbutton control.

The *CSpinButtonCtrl* Spinbutton Interaction

The user interacts with the Spinbutton by repositioning the control using the up and down selectors. Whenever the slider is moved, the control will send scrollbar messages to the parent window. These messages are either WM_HSCROLL or WM_VSCROLL (depending on whether the Spinbutton is a horizontal or a vertical control).

In MFC applications, you can have ClassWizard create an OnHScroll() or OnVScroll() handler. This handler then can, when it is called, determine that the Spinbutton is the control that caused the message. It is generally necessary to check to see which control sent the message because other controls (including scrollbars) also send WM_HSCROLL and WM_VSCROLL messages.

The following code sample shows a simple handler that updates the buddy control's contents based on the current position of the Spinbutton. The buddy control is not updated automatically because I did not select AutoBuddy or BuddyInt when I created the Spinbutton control with the resource editor.

```
void CSpinBoxDlg::OnVScroll(UINT nSBCode, UINT nPos, CScrollBar* pScrollBar)
{
    // TODO: Add your message handler code here and/or call default

    CSpinButtonCtrl * pSpin = (CSpinButtonCtrl *)pScrollBar;

//    First, check to see if the scrollbar is *really* our Spinbox control:

    if (pSpin == &m_Spin2)
    {//    It's our second spinbox control!
//        Do our thing, display the data returned:
//        Same position as the Trackbar!
        m_Buddy2.SetWindowText(szColors[pSpin->GetPos()]);
```

```
    }

    CDialog::OnVScroll(nSBCode, nPos, pScrollBar);
}
```

Several items in this code sample need closer examination. First, to determine whether the control that caused the scroll message is the Spinbutton control, you test the passed `pScrollBar` parameter with the `CSpinButtonCtrl` object for the Spinbutton. If they are identical, you know the control that caused the scroll message was the Spinbutton control. If they are not the same, some other control (such as a scrollbar or perhaps a Slider control) caused the scroll message.

After you have determined that the Spinbutton control was responsible for the scroll message, you can perform whatever action is appropriate. You might want to check the current value of the Spinbutton and update the buddy control based on the slider's position. In the example, you get the Spinbutton's value and update the buddy control so that the correct color is displayed for the user. This updating is fast, as the sample program shows.

> **NOTE**
>
> Try to avoid doing too much in the processing of scroll messages. Otherwise, you may make the action of the Spinbutton control choppy or irregular. Try to keep the scroll-message processing reasonable.

The *CHotKeyCtrl* Class

A Hotkey control enables a user to enter a hotkey combination (usually a character key modified with Alt, Ctrl, or Shift) that the application may later assign to a specific action. This control is modeled after an edit control. For the remainder of this chapter, I'll refer to this control as the Hotkey control.

Figure 19.9 shows an example of a Hotkey control in a dialog box. This example is from the sample program and shows a typical implementation of the Hotkey control in a dialog box.

Your application, when using a `CHotKeyCtrl` class object, will need to do a minimum amount of management of the Hotkey control. The application should initialize the current hotkey that is being defined (if there is any) and may optionally set the rules for the hotkey (for example, not allowing Alt + hotkeys). A Hotkey control has no special attributes and uses only standard attributes for dialog box controls.

After you have added the Hotkey control to a dialog box, you then can use ClassWizard to bind a `CHotKeyCtrl` object to your Hotkey control. This `CHotKeyCtrl` object is your interface with the Hotkey control.

FIGURE 19.9.

A Hotkey control shown in a dialog box.

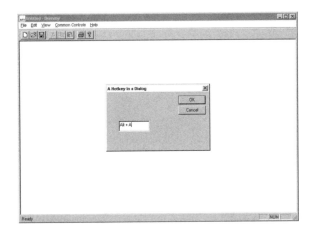

Implementing a *CHotKeyCtrl* Hotkey Control

If you are using a Hotkey control in a dialog box, you would use ClassWizard to bind a CHotKeyCtrl object to the control. Were you to be implementing a Hotkey control in a window that is not a dialog box, you would call the CHotKeyCtrl::Create() function to create the Hotkey control. You might find a use for a Hotkey control in a normal window or perhaps as part of a toolbar.

Figure 19.10 shows our dialog box (in Visual C++'s resource editor) with the properties for the Hotkey shown. For Hotkey controls that are in dialog boxes, these properties can be set easily by using the resource editor. When the Hotkey control is in a window other than a dialog box, the properties are set when the Hotkey control is created.

FIGURE 19.10.

The Hotkey and its properties in Visual C++'s resource editor.

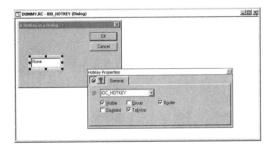

In Figure 19.10 you will see that I've not added any buttons other than the Hotkey control to the dialog box.

In Listing 19.7 is the code that manages the Hotkey sample dialog box. The base for this code was developed using ClassWizard and then modified to add the necessary features.

Listing 19.7. The HOTKEYDL.CPP file.

```cpp
// hotkeydl.cpp : implementation file
//

#include "stdafx.h"
#include "Dummy.h"
#include "hotkeydl.h"

#ifdef _DEBUG
#undef THIS_FILE
static char BASED_CODE THIS_FILE[] = __FILE__;
#endif

/////////////////////////////////////////////////////////////////////////////
// CHotKeyDlg dialog


CHotKeyDlg::CHotKeyDlg(CWnd* pParent /*=NULL*/)
    : CDialog(CHotKeyDlg::IDD, pParent)
{
    //{{AFX_DATA_INIT(CHotKeyDlg)
        // NOTE: the ClassWizard will add member initialization here
    //}}AFX_DATA_INIT
}


void CHotKeyDlg::DoDataExchange(CDataExchange* pDX)
{
    CDialog::DoDataExchange(pDX);
    //{{AFX_DATA_MAP(CHotKeyDlg)
    DDX_Control(pDX, IDC_HOTKEY, m_HotKey);
    //}}AFX_DATA_MAP
}


BEGIN_MESSAGE_MAP(CHotKeyDlg, CDialog)
    //{{AFX_MSG_MAP(CHotKeyDlg)
    //}}AFX_MSG_MAP
END_MESSAGE_MAP()


/////////////////////////////////////////////////////////////////////////////
// CHotKeyDlg message handlers

BOOL CHotKeyDlg::OnInitDialog()
{
    CDialog::OnInitDialog();

    // TODO: Add extra initialization here

//    SetRules() is optional:

    m_HotKey.SetRules(0, HOTKEYF_ALT);

/*
MFC's CHotKeyCtrl::GetHotKey() and CHotKeyCtrl::SetHotKey() both
get the parameters for the keycode and modifiers wrong! Someday maybe
```

continues

Listing 19.7. continued

```
MSFT will get these right, but for Visual C++ Versions 2.0 and 2.1
you must modify your code to make it work correctly!

From the documentation for the HKKM_SETHOTKEY message:

[new-Windows NT]

HKM_SETHOTKEY
wParam = MAKEWORD(bVKHotKey, bfMods);
lParam = 0;


The HKM_SETHOTKEY message sets the hot key combination for a
hot-key control.

Parameters

bVKHotKey

Virtual-key code of the hot key.

bfMods

Modifier flags indicating the keys that, when used in
combination with bVKHotKey, define a hot-key combination.
For a list of modifier flag values, see the description
of the HKM_GETHOTKEY message.

Return Value

No return value.

See Also

HKM_GETHOTKEY
*/
/*
    MFC's CHotKeyCtrl::SetHotKey() expects you to use:

    m_HotKey.SetHotKey('A', HOTKEYF_ALT);

    but as the note above shows, this doesn't work. Take a look at
    the MFC source code and you will see the problem!

    You must call SetHotKey() as shown below:
*/
    m_HotKey.SetHotKey(MAKEWORD('A', HOTKEYF_ALT), 0);

    return TRUE;  // return TRUE unless you set the focus to a control
                  // EXCEPTION: OCX Property Pages should return FALSE
}

void CHotKeyDlg::OnOK()
{
    // TODO: Add extra validation here

    WORD    wVirtualKeyCode = 0;
```

```
WORD    wModifiers = 0;
char    szString[80] = "Key is ";
char    szOutput[80] = "";
```

```
/*

MFC's CHotKeyCtrl::GetHotKey() and CHotKeyCtrl::SetHotKey() both
get the parameters for the keycode and modifiers wrong! Someday maybe
MSFT will get these right, but for Visual C++ Versions 2.0 and 2.1
you must modify your code to make it work correctly!

From the documentation for the HKKM_GETHOTKEY message:

- - - - - - - - - - - - - - - -
[new-Windows NT]

HKM_GETHOTKEY
wParam = 0;
lParam = 0;


The HKM_GETHOTKEY message retrieves the virtual-key code and
modifier flags of a hot key from a hot-key control.

Return Value

Returns the virtual-key code and modifier flags.
The virtual-key code is in the low-order byte,
and the modifier flags are in the high-order byte.

The modifier flags can be a combination of the following values:

Value    Meaning
HOTKEYF_ALT      ALT key
HOTKEYF_CONTROL     CTRL key
HOTKEYF_EXT     Extended key
HOTKEYF_SHIFT     SHIFT key
Remarks

The 16-bit value returned by this message can be used as the wParam
parameter in the WM_SETHOTKEY message.

See Also

WM_SETHOTKEY

*/

/*
    MFC's CHotKeyCtrl::GetHotKey() thinks it's is returning:

    m_HotKey.SetHotKey(WORD &wVirtualKeyCode, WORD &wModifiers);

    but as the note above shows, this doesn't work. Take a look at
    the MFC source code and you will see the problem!

    You must call GetHotKey() as shown below:
```

continues

Listing 19.7. continued

```
*/

    m_HotKey.GetHotKey(wVirtualKeyCode, wModifiers);

    wModifiers = HIBYTE(wVirtualKeyCode);
    wVirtualKeyCode = LOBYTE(wVirtualKeyCode);

/*
//   or you could code this function as:

    DWORD    dwModifierWithKey = m_HotKey.GetHotKey();

    wModifiers = HIBYTE(LOWORD(dwModifierWithKey));
    wVirtualKeyCode = LOBYTE(LOWORD(dwModifierWithKey));

//   But this method takes one more variable, and is more complex!
*/

    if (wModifiers & HOTKEYF_ALT)
       strcat(szString, "ALT + ");

    if (wModifiers & HOTKEYF_CONTROL)
       strcat(szString, "CTRL + ");

    if (wModifiers & HOTKEYF_EXT)
       strcat(szString, "EXTENDED + ");

    if (wModifiers & HOTKEYF_SHIFT)
       strcat(szString, "SHIFT + ");

    strcat(szString, " '%c' ");

    sprintf(szOutput, szString, wVirtualKeyCode);

    AfxMessageBox(szOutput);

    CDialog::OnOK();
}
```

CAUTION

There are two bugs in MFC 3.0. The CHotKeyCtrl::SetHotKey() and the
CHotKeyCtrl::GetHotKey() functions both have their passed parameters described
incorrectly. Notes in the listings describe how the parameters are really packed.
Basically, the *wModifiers* parameter is ignored, and the modifier key information is
packed in the high byte of the *wVirtualKeyCode* parameter.

I do not expect that Microsoft will change the existing function in the future, for this would break existing applications that are using the methods I've shown in this book. You should check, however, each time there is a new release of MFC (if you are using these functions) to see whether the `CHotKeyCtrl` class functions have been changed.

In Listing 19.8 is the HOTKEYDL.H header file that accompanies the HOTKEYDL.CPP file shown in Listing 19.7. The HOTKEY.H file was modified only by ClassWizard; no manual changes were necessary.

Listing 19.8. The HOTKEYDL.H file.

```
// hotkeydl.h : header file
//

///////////////////////////////////////////////////////////////////////////
// CHotKeyDlg dialog

class CHotKeyDlg : public CDialog
{
// Construction
public:
    CHotKeyDlg(CWnd* pParent = NULL);    // standard constructor

// Dialog Data
    //{{AFX_DATA(CHotKeyDlg)
    enum { IDD = IDD_HOTKEY };
    CHotKeyCtrl     m_HotKey;
    //}}AFX_DATA


// Overrides
    // ClassWizard generated virtual function overrides
    //{{AFX_VIRTUAL(CHotKeyDlg)
    protected:
    virtual void DoDataExchange(CDataExchange* pDX);    // DDX/DDV support
    //}}AFX_VIRTUAL

// Implementation
protected:

    // Generated message map functions
    //{{AFX_MSG(CHotKeyDlg)
    virtual BOOL OnInitDialog();
    virtual void OnOK();
    //}}AFX_MSG
    DECLARE_MESSAGE_MAP()
};
```

The *CHotKeyCtrl* Class in a Dialog Box

As stated previously, you would usually bind your CHotKeyCtrl object to a Hotkey control by using ClassWizard. After you have bound the CHotKeyCtrl object, you can then, in the OnInitDialog() function, initialize your Hotkey control.

Generally, you will want to set the rules (if you have rules) and initialize the Hotkey control with the current hotkey value (if there is a current hotkey defined).

- ■ *The Hotkey's rules* With Hotkeys you can choose not to allow the user to enter a certain type of hotkey, based on modifier keys. Modifier keys are Alt, Ctrl, and Shift. When the user selects a modifier key that you have chosen not to allow, the Hotkey control will substitute a modifier key that you specify.

- ■ *The Hotkey's initial value* When you use the Hotkey control to modify an existing hotkey, you should initialize the Hotkey control with the current hotkey value.

The following code listing shows the lines (in boldface) that initialize our Hotkey. The order of the calls to initialize the Hotkey is not critical, but setting the rules first is a good practice. In this example, I've eliminated many of my comments so that the code is more readable.

```
BOOL CHotKeyDlg::OnInitDialog()
{
    CDialog::OnInitDialog();

    // TODO: Add extra initialization here

//    SetRules() is optional:

    m_HotKey.SetRules(0, HOTKEYF_ALT);

    m_HotKey.SetHotKey(MAKEWORD('A', HOTKEYF_ALT), 0);

    return TRUE;  // return TRUE unless you set the focus to a control
                  // EXCEPTION: OCX Property Pages should return FALSE
}
```

Creating *CHotKeyCtrl* Objects in Nondialog Windows

To create a CHotKeyCtrl object in a window that is not a dialog box, you would call CHotKeyCtrl::Create(). The CHotKeyCtrl::Create() function takes four parameters: a style (only the standard dialog box control styles are supported by a Hotkey control), a RECT structure specifying the Hotkey's location and size, a pointer to the parent window, and the control ID.

```
CHotKeyCtrl::Create(
    WS_CHILD | WS_VISIBLE | WS_BORDER | WS_TABSTOP,
    rect, this, 0);
```

There are a number of situations in which a programmer might want to create a Hotkey control in a nondialog window. Using CHotKeyCtrl::Create() is an easy method of creating a Hotkey control.

CHotKeyCtrl Options

The CHotKeyCtrl object allows the setting of rules. These rules allow your application to reject certain modifier keys. When a modifier key that is not acceptable to your application is pressed, another modifier key will be substituted.

Using the CHotKeyCtrl Hotkey Object

The CHotKeyCtrl Hotkey object takes input from the user (a hotkey selection) and is also able to provide output (the currently defined hotkey).

The CHotKeyCtrl Hotkey Input

The CHotKeyCtrl Hotkey control can be initialized using the CHotKeyCtrl::SetHotKey() member function. This function takes two WORD values. Due to a serious bug in MFC (3.0), the action of these parameters is incorrectly documented. If you are using Visual C++ 2.1 (and later, until Microsoft fixes this problem), you should use the following information when you design your Hotkey control.

The CHotKeyCtrl::SetHotKey() function is shown as taking two parameters, as shown here:

```
CHotKeyCtrl::SetHotKey(WORD wVirtualKeyCode, WORD wModifier);
```

The *wModifier* parameter is ignored. The modifier information must instead be packed into the high order byte of the *wVirtualKeyCode* parameter using the MAKEWORD() macro:

```
m_HotKey.SetHotKey(MAKEWORD('A', HOTKEYF_ALT), 0);
```

This example sets the initial hotkey to be Alt+A.

The CHotKeyCtrl Hotkey Input

The CHotKeyCtrl Hotkey control's current value can be retrieved using the CHotKeyCtrl::GetHotKey() member function. This function takes two WORD values. Due to a serious bug in MFC (3.0), the action of these parameters is incorrectly documented. If you are using Visual C++ 2.1 (and later, until Microsoft fixes this problem), you should use the following information when you design your Hotkey control.

The CHotKeyCtrl::GetHotKey() function is shown as taking two parameters, as shown here:

```
CHotKeyCtrl::SetHotKey(WORD &wVirtualKeyCode, WORD &wModifier);
```

The *wModifier* parameter is ignored. The modifier information is actually packed into the high order byte of the *wVirtualKeyCode* parameter. You can retrieve the modifier by using the HIBYTE() and LOBYTE() macros:

```
m_HotKey.GetHotKey(wVirtualKeyCode, wModifiers);

wModifiers = HIBYTE(wVirtualKeyCode);
wVirtualKeyCode = LOBYTE(wVirtualKeyCode);
```

This example retrieves the keycode and the modifier and stores them in the correct parameters.

The *CHotKeyCtrl* Hotkey Interaction

The user interacts with a Hotkey by setting input focus to the Hotkey control (usually using the mouse or perhaps the tab key) and pressing the new hotkey combination. Whenever a modifier key is pressed, the Hotkey control expects that another key will be pressed at the same time. If a modifier key is pressed and then released, the current hotkey definition will be lost.

Summary

This chapter has shown four different Win32 Common Controls:

- The Trackbar control enables the user to enter a nonexact value from a predetermined range.
- The Progress control provides feedback to the user about the progress of a possibly time-consuming process.
- The Spinbutton control enables the user to select a specific value from a predetermined range of values.
- The Hotkey control enables the user to specify a hotkey combination to the application. This control is useful for customizing the keyboard interface of an application.

Listview and Treeview Controls

20

by Peter D. Hipson

In this chapter, I introduce two Win32 common controls: Listview and Treeview. These two controls contain some of the most useful data-output controls offered by the Win32 common controls. Also, there are Microsoft Foundation Class library (MFC) classes to manage the controls. In this chapter, the MFC class names are sometimes used to refer to these controls. The two controls covered in this chapter are the following:

■ The Listview control allows an application to display data to the user in any of these formats: list, small icon, large icon, and report. This control is very useful for dealing with columns of data.

■ The Treeview control allows an application and the application's user to manage hierarchical data. An example of hierarchical data is the structure of the directory and subdirectory files on your hard disk. The Windows 95 Explorer program makes extensive use of the Treeview control.

NOTE

The Windows 95 Explorer program uses an almost generic implementation of the Treeview control. Microsoft has modified Treeview to load only the minimum amount of data necessary. Whenever the Treeview control needs more information, it notifies Explorer. Explorer then supplies the necessary information.

This feature allows the Explorer program to provide good performance to the user regardless of the complexity of the directory structure or the number of files! I load Treeview with more than 750 folders and 15,000 files on my C drive!

Although these controls are most often used in dialog boxes, they can be implemented in other types of windows—the same as any other Windows control. For example, you can place one of these controls in a `CToolBarCtrl` toolbar window.

The *CListCtrl* Class

A Listview control allows data to be displayed in one of four different formats:

■ The large icon view presents the user with icons that have titles under them. The application determines the size of the icons. The example of this control in Figure 20.1 has 32×32 pixel icons. The title is the item's text. This view is the "classic" icon view: the icon and text represent an object. Figure 20.1 shows a Listview control displaying data in large icon mode.

■ The small icon view presents the user with smaller icons that have titles to the left of them. The application determines the size of the icons. The example of this control in Figure 20.2 has 16×16 pixel icons. The title is the item's text. There can be more than one column of icons if more than one column fits into the control. Figure 20.2 shows a Listview control displaying data in small icon mode.

■ The list view presents the user with smaller icons that have titles to the left of them. The application determines the size of the icons. The example of this control in Figure 20.3 has 16×16 pixel icons. The title is the item's text. Unlike the small icon view, there is only one column of icons in the list view. Figure 20.3 shows a Listview control displaying data in the list mode.

■ The report view presents the user with smaller icons and secondary subcolumns of additional information. This Listview control can be designed to support column sorting so that the user can sort on any subcolumn desired. The application determines the size of the icons. The example of this control in Figure 20.4 has 16×16 pixel icons. The title is the item's text. There can be more than one column of small icons if more than one column fits into the control. Figure 20.4 shows a Listview control displaying data in the report mode.

Figures 20.1 through 20.4 are examples of the Listview control in each of the four different display modes. Although the display mode is different, the data is the same in each control.

FIGURE 20.1.

A Listview control displaying data in the large icon view.

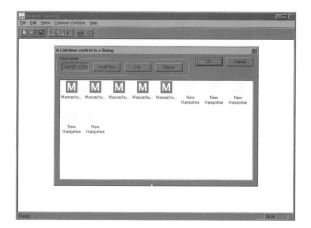

FIGURE 20.2.

A Listview control displaying data in the small icon view.

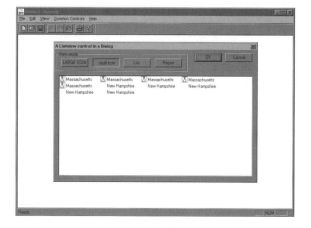

FIGURE 20.3.

A Listview control displaying data in the list view.

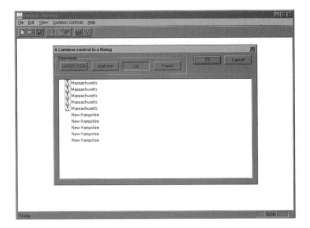

FIGURE 20.4.

A Listview control displaying data in the report view.

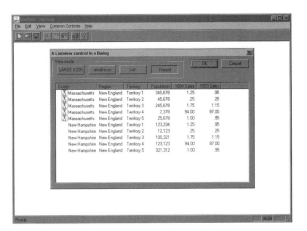

When using a `CListCtrl` class object, your application needs to do a minimal amount of management of the Listview control. The application must have data and a set of images to display with the data. A Listview control can have a number of attributes, which can be set using the resource editor in Visual C++ and then modified at runtime. Table 20.1 lists the attributes for the Listview control.

Table 20.1. The attributes for the Listview control.

Attribute	Description
Align top	The label's text is aligned to the top of the image when the display mode is either large icon or small icon view.
Align bottom	The label's text is aligned to the bottom of the image when the display mode is either large icon or small icon view. The align bottom mode is the default mode. It is the most commonly used alignment.

Attribute	Description
Align left	The label's text is aligned to the left of the image when the display mode is either large icon or small icon view.
Align right	The label's text is aligned to the right of the image when the display mode is either large icon or small icon view.
Auto arrange	The items in the Listview control are automatically arranged when in the large icon and small icon view modes.
Button	The large icon view has items that resemble buttons.
Edit labels	The labels can be modified by the user. The application must be able to process the LVN_ENDLABELEDIT message, sent when the user has completed the label edit.
Icon	The Listview control is displayed in the large icon view mode.
List	The Listview control is displayed in the list view mode.
No column headers	The report view of the control does not have column headers.
No label wrap	The labels do not wrap to multiple lines when the Listview control is in large icon view mode.
No scroll	The Listview control does not have scrollbars. All items must fit within the control's display area.
No sort header	The report view headers do not work as sort pushbuttons. Headers do not have to sort; you can connect a button to any functionality your program needs.
Owner draw fixed	The items are drawn by the control's owner.
Report	The Listview control is displayed in the report view mode.
Shared image lists	The Listview control does not take ownership of the image lists. This allows other Listview controls to access and use the image lists without having to create and destroy the lists on a constant basis.
Single selection	Only one item at a time can be selected in the Listview control.
Small icon	The Listview control is displayed in the small icon view.
Sort ascending	The Listview sorts the items as text in ascending order.
Sort descending	The Listview sorts the items as text in descending order.

Once you have added the Listview control to a dialog box, you can use the ClassWizard to bind a `CListCtrl` object to your Listview control. The `CListCtrl` object is your interface with the Listview control.

Implementing a *CListCtrl* Listview Control

If you are using a Listview control in a dialog box, use the ClassWizard to bind a CListCtrl object to the control. If you are implementing a Listview control in a window that is not a dialog box, call the CListCtrl::Create() function to create the Listview control. You might find a use for a Listview control in a normal window, perhaps as part of a toolbar.

Figure 20.5 shows a sample dialog box (in the Visual C++ resource editor) and the properties for the Listview control. These properties are easily modified using the resource editor for Listview controls in dialog boxes. When the Listview control is in a window other than a dialog box, the properties are set when the Listview control is created.

FIGURE 20.5.

A Listview control and its properties in the Visual C++ resource editor.

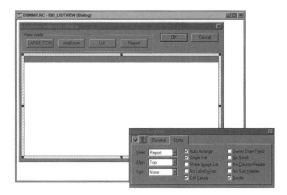

You can see in Figure 20.5 that I've added four buttons to the dialog box. These four buttons are used to set the four different view modes (large icon, small icon, list, and report). When the user presses these buttons, they work much like radio buttons; that is, they form a group. The method for making pushbuttons work in a group is shown in the program in Listing 20.1.

The code in Listing 20.1 manages a sample Listview dialog box. The base for this code was developed using the ClassWizard and was then modified to add the necessary features.

In Listing 20.1, code that I've modified or added manually is marked in boldface type. The changes I made using the ClassWizard are not marked but are described in the section following Listing 20.1. Basically, I used the ClassWizard to add variables for the controls in the dialog box, handlers for the dialog box controls, and the WM_INITDLG handler.

Listing 20.1. The LISTVIEW.CPP file.

```
// listview.cpp : implementation file
//

#include "stdafx.h"
#include "Dummy.h"
```

```
#include "listview.h"

#ifdef _DEBUG
#undef THIS_FILE
static char BASED_CODE THIS_FILE[] = __FILE__;
#endif

/////////////////////////////////////////////////////////////////////////////
// CListviewDlg dialog


CListviewDlg::CListviewDlg(CWnd* pParent /*=NULL*/)
    : CDialog(CListviewDlg::IDD, pParent)
{
    //{{AFX_DATA_INIT(CListviewDlg)
    //}}AFX_DATA_INIT
}


void CListviewDlg::DoDataExchange(CDataExchange* pDX)
{
    CDialog::DoDataExchange(pDX);
    //{{AFX_DATA_MAP(CListviewDlg)
    DDX_Control(pDX, IDC_SMALLICON, m_SmallIconButton);
    DDX_Control(pDX, IDC_LIST, m_ListButton);
    DDX_Control(pDX, IDC_LARGEICON, m_LargeIconButton);
    DDX_Control(pDX, IDC_REPORT, m_ReportButton);
    DDX_Control(pDX, IDC_LISTVIEW, m_Listview);
    //}}AFX_DATA_MAP
}


BEGIN_MESSAGE_MAP(CListviewDlg, CDialog)
    //{{AFX_MSG_MAP(CListviewDlg)
    ON_BN_CLICKED(IDC_LARGEICON, OnLargeicon)
    ON_BN_CLICKED(IDC_LIST, OnList)
    ON_BN_CLICKED(IDC_REPORT, OnReport)
    ON_BN_CLICKED(IDC_SMALLICON, OnSmallicon)
    ON_WM_DESTROY()
    ON_NOTIFY(LVN_COLUMNCLICK, IDC_LISTVIEW, OnColumnClick)
    //}}AFX_MSG_MAP
END_MESSAGE_MAP()


/////////////////////////////////////////////////////////////////////////////
// CListviewDlg message handlers

//    Below is some (dummy) data used to fill our ListView control:

//    Column headings for report view mode
char    *szColumn[6] =
 {"District     ", "Region         ", "Territory     ",
  "Population", "1994 Sales", "1993 Sales"};

//    Actual data, ten lines worth:
char    *szData[20][6] =
 {{
  "Massachusetts", "New England", "Territory 1", "345,678", " 1.25", "  .95"},
```

continues

Listing 20.1. continued

```
{"Massachusetts", "New England", "Territory 2", " 45,678", "  .25", "  .25"},
{"Massachusetts", "New England", "Territory 3", "245,678", " 1.75", " 1.15"},
{"Massachusetts", "New England", "Territory 4", "  2,378", "94.00", "87.00"},
{"Massachusetts", "New England", "Territory 5", " 25,678", " 1.00", "  .95"},
{"New Hampshire", "New England", "Territory 1", "123,234", " 2.25", " 2.95"},
{"New Hampshire", "New England", "Territory 2", " 12,123", " 3.25", " 3.25"},
{"New Hampshire", "New England", "Territory 3", "100,321", " 4.75", " 4.15"},
{"New Hampshire", "New England", "Territory 4", "123,123", "90.00", "80.00"},
{"New Hampshire", "New England", "Territory 5", "321,312", " 5.00", "23.95"},
{"Vermont      ", "New England", "Territory 1", "345,678", " 1.25", "  .95"},
{"Vermont      ", "New England", "Territory 2", " 45,678", "  .25", "  .25"},
{"Vermont      ", "New England", "Territory 3", "245,678", " 1.75", " 1.15"},
{"Vermont      ", "New England", "Territory 4", "  2,378", "94.00", "87.00"},
{"Vermont      ", "New England", "Territory 5", " 25,678", " 1.00", "  .95"},
{"Connecticut  ", "New England", "Territory 1", "123,234", " 2.25", " 2.95"},
{"Connecticut  ", "New England", "Territory 2", " 12,123", " 3.25", " 3.25"},
{"Connecticut  ", "New England", "Territory 3", "100,321", " 4.75", " 4.15"},
{"Connecticut  ", "New England", "Territory 4", "123,123", "90.00", "80.00"},
{"Connecticut  ", "New England", "Territory 5", "321,312", " 5.00", "23.95"}};

BOOL CListviewDlg::OnInitDialog()
{
    CDialog::OnInitDialog();

    // TODO: Add extra initialization here

//    Setup the image lists:

    if (m_ImageLarge.Create(IDB_LISTVIEW_LARGE, 32, 0, FALSE))
    {// Add error handler here, as needed:
        TRACE("Could not create the large images\n");
    }
    if (m_ImageSmall.Create(IDB_LISTVIEW_SMALL, 16, 0, FALSE))
    {// Add error handler here, as needed:
        TRACE("Could not create the small images\n");
    }
    if (m_ImageState.Create(IDB_LISTVIEW_STATE, 16, 0, FALSE))
    {// Add error handler here, as needed:
        TRACE("Could not create the state images\n");
    }

//    Add image lists to listview control:

    m_Listview.SetImageList(&m_ImageLarge, LVSIL_NORMAL);
    m_Listview.SetImageList(&m_ImageSmall, LVSIL_SMALL);
    m_Listview.SetImageList(&m_ImageState, LVSIL_STATE);

//    General purpose variables (loop counters and the like)

    int   i = 0;
    int j = 0;

//    First add columns:
```

```
//    To use columns in a listview control you need a LV_COLUMN structure:

     LV_COLUMN lvc;

     lvc.mask =
         LVCF_FMT      ¦ // The fmt member of LV_COLUMN is valid.
         LVCF_WIDTH    ¦ // The cx member of LV_COLUMN is valid.
         LVCF_TEXT     ¦ // The pszText member of LV_COLUMN is valid.
         LVCF_SUBITEM; // The iSubItem member of LV_COLUMN is valid.

     lvc.fmt = LVCFMT_LEFT;

     for (i = 0; i < sizeof(szColumn) / sizeof(szColumn[0]); i++)
     {// Insert each column in the list:
         if (i == 0)
         {//     First column, leave room for icon!
             lvc.cx = m_Listview.GetStringWidth(szColumn[i]) + 65;
         }
         else
         {
             lvc.cx = m_Listview.GetStringWidth(szColumn[i]) + 15;
         }

         lvc.pszText = szColumn[i];

         if (i > 2) // Format numbers in columns 3, 4, and 5  to right!
             lvc.fmt = LVCFMT_RIGHT;

         lvc.iSubItem = i;

         m_Listview.InsertColumn(i, &lvc);
     }

//    Add data to the listview control.

     LV_ITEM lvi;
     lvi.mask = LVIF_TEXT ¦ LVIF_IMAGE ¦ LVIF_PARAM;
     lvi.iSubItem = 0;

     for (i = 0; i < 20; i++)
     {
         lvi.iItem = i;
         lvi.pszText = szData[i][0];
         lvi.cchTextMax = 5;
         lvi.lParam = (LPARAM)i;

         if (i < 5)
             lvi.iImage = 0;
         else
             lvi.iImage = 1;

         m_Listview.InsertItem(&lvi);

         // Add subitems to each main item:
         for (int k = 1; k < 6; k++)
         {
             m_Listview.SetItemText(i, k, szData[i][k]);
```

continues

Listing 20.1. continued

```
        }
    }

//    default is report mode, press report button:

    m_ReportButton.SetState(TRUE);
    m_LargeIconButton.SetState(FALSE);
    m_SmallIconButton.SetState(FALSE);
    m_ListButton.SetState(FALSE);

    return TRUE;  // return TRUE unless you set the focus to a control
                  // EXCEPTION: OCX Property Pages should return FALSE
}

void CListviewDlg::OnLargeicon()
{
    // TODO: Add your control notification handler code here

    long    lStyle;

    lStyle = GetWindowLong(m_Listview.GetSafeHwnd(), GWL_STYLE);

    lStyle = (lStyle & 0xFFFF0000) |
        LVS_ICON |
        LVS_AUTOARRANGE | LVS_EDITLABELS | LVS_SINGLESEL;

    SetWindowLong(m_Listview.GetSafeHwnd(), GWL_STYLE, lStyle);
    m_Listview.Invalidate();

    m_ReportButton.SetState(FALSE);
    m_LargeIconButton.SetState(TRUE);
    m_SmallIconButton.SetState(FALSE);
    m_ListButton.SetState(FALSE);
}

void CListviewDlg::OnList()
{
    // TODO: Add your control notification handler code here

    long    lStyle;

    lStyle = GetWindowLong(m_Listview.GetSafeHwnd(), GWL_STYLE);

    lStyle = (lStyle & 0xFFFF0000) |
        LVS_LIST |
        LVS_AUTOARRANGE | LVS_EDITLABELS | LVS_SINGLESEL;

    SetWindowLong(m_Listview.GetSafeHwnd(), GWL_STYLE, lStyle);
    m_Listview.Invalidate();

    m_ReportButton.SetState(FALSE);
    m_LargeIconButton.SetState(FALSE);
    m_SmallIconButton.SetState(FALSE);
    m_ListButton.SetState(TRUE);
}

void CListviewDlg::OnReport()
```

```
{
    // TODO: Add your control notification handler code here

    long    lStyle;

    lStyle = GetWindowLong(m_Listview.GetSafeHwnd(), GWL_STYLE);

    lStyle = (lStyle & 0xFFFF0000) |
        LVS_REPORT |
        LVS_AUTOARRANGE | LVS_EDITLABELS | LVS_SINGLESEL;

    SetWindowLong(m_Listview.GetSafeHwnd(), GWL_STYLE, lStyle);
    m_Listview.Invalidate();

    m_ReportButton.SetState(TRUE);
    m_LargeIconButton.SetState(FALSE);
    m_SmallIconButton.SetState(FALSE);
    m_ListButton.SetState(FALSE);
}

void CListviewDlg::OnSmallicon()
{
    // TODO: Add your control notification handler code here

    long    lStyle;

    lStyle = GetWindowLong(m_Listview.GetSafeHwnd(), GWL_STYLE);

    lStyle = (lStyle & 0xFFFF0000) |
        LVS_SMALLICON |
        LVS_AUTOARRANGE | LVS_EDITLABELS | LVS_SINGLESEL;

    SetWindowLong(m_Listview.GetSafeHwnd(), GWL_STYLE, lStyle);
    m_Listview.Invalidate();

    m_ReportButton.SetState(FALSE);
    m_LargeIconButton.SetState(FALSE);
    m_SmallIconButton.SetState(TRUE);
    m_ListButton.SetState(FALSE);
}

void CListviewDlg::OnDestroy()
{
    CDialog::OnDestroy();

    // TODO: Add your message handler code here

}

int CALLBACK OurCompare(
    LPARAM lParam1, LPARAM lParam2, LPARAM dwData)
{
    char * p1 = (char *)szData[lParam1][dwData];
    char * p2 = (char *)szData[lParam2][dwData];

    return(stricmp(p1, p2));
}

void CListviewDlg::OnColumnClick(NMHDR* pNMHDR, LRESULT* pResult)
```

continues

Listing 20.1. continued

```
{
    NM_LISTVIEW* pNMListView = (NM_LISTVIEW*)pNMHDR;
    // TODO: Add your control notification handler code here

//    TRACE("OnColumnClick\n");

    m_Listview.SortItems(OurCompare, pNMListView->iSubItem);

    *pResult = 0;
}
```

Listing 20.2 contains the LISTVIEW.H header file that accompanies the LISTVIEW.CPP
file shown in Listing 20.1. I modified the LISTVIEW.H file with the ClassWizard and
added some variables as well as the prototype for the compare function OurCompare()
manually. The ClassWizard was unable to add an OnNotify() handler; I added this manually
also.

> **NOTE**
>
> Visual C++ 2.1 improves the functionality of the ClassWizard. However, some
> capabilities are still lacking. For example, the ClassWizard is not able to add an
> OnNotify handler, even though the code for managing OnNotify() is part of MFC.
> Fortunately, the ClassWizard is quite happy to let you add your own OnNotify handler,
> even if it is placed in the blocks normally reserved for the ClassWizard's own use.

Listing 20.2. The LISTVIEW.H file.

```
// listview.h : header file
//

/////////////////////////////////////////////////////////////////////////////
// CListviewDlg dialog

class CListviewDlg : public CDialog
{
// Construction
public:
    CListviewDlg(CWnd* pParent = NULL);    // standard constructor

// Dialog Data
    //{{AFX_DATA(CListviewDlg)
    enum { IDD = IDD_LISTVIEW };
    CButton    m_SmallIconButton;
    CButton    m_ListButton;
    CButton    m_LargeIconButton;
    CButton    m_ReportButton;
    CListCtrl    m_Listview;
```

```
    //}}AFX_DATA


    // Image list variables:
    CImageList m_ImageLarge;
    CImageList m_ImageSmall;
    CImageList m_ImageState;

// Overrides
    // ClassWizard generated virtual function overrides
    //{{AFX_VIRTUAL(CListviewDlg)
    protected:
    virtual void DoDataExchange(CDataExchange* pDX);    // DDX/DDV support
    //}}AFX_VIRTUAL

// Implementation
protected:

    // Generated message map functions
    //{{AFX_MSG(CListviewDlg)
    virtual BOOL OnInitDialog();
    afx_msg void OnLargeicon();
    afx_msg void OnList();
    afx_msg void OnReport();
    afx_msg void OnSmallicon();
    afx_msg void OnDestroy();
    afx_msg void OnColumnClick(NMHDR* pNMHDR, LRESULT* pResult);
    //}}AFX_MSG
    DECLARE_MESSAGE_MAP()
};

// Not a member function!
int CALLBACK OurCompare(LPARAM lParam1, LPARAM lParam2, LPARAM dwData);
```

The *CListCtrl* Class in a Dialog Box

You bind your CListCtrl object to a Listview control using the ClassWizard. After you have bound the CListCtrl object, you can initialize your Listview control in the OnInitDialog() function.

NOTE

You don't have to put a lot of items, such as image lists, icons, icon views, and list views, in your Listview control. You can have a simple Listview control that has a report view of the data and no images. This configuration produces a control that provides tabular data used for a database front-end program. Unlike editing data in a spreadsheet-type control, editing data in columns (other than the first column in this situation) is not trivial.

When initializing your Listview control, perform the following tasks:

- Set up the image lists. There are three image lists: the large icons (often 32×32 pixels, or larger), the small icons (typically 16×16 pixels), and the state images (application defined, such as opened or closed)(16×16 pixels in many applications). Image lists can be either shared between multiple Listview controls or private to a specific Listview control.

NOTE

Make sure that your application properly cleans up after itself. If the image lists are shared, you must destroy them when you are done with them. Also, don't try to reload the images twice without an intervening call to `DeleteImageList()`.

WARNING

At the time this book was written, the MSDN documentation was in error in describing the `CImageList` members. There is no `CImageList::DeleteObject()` member function. The `CImageList::DeleteImageList()` function performs the functionality of `CImageList::DeleteObject()`. `CImageList::DeleteImageList()` is called automatically by the `CImageList` destructor.

- Attach your image lists to the Listview control.
- Set up the column headings for the report view. If your control doesn't use the report view, column headings (and sub-item data) are not necessary.
- Add the items to your Listview control. Each item is added much like an item is added to a listbox control. After adding an item, your application should add any sub-items for the item. Sub-items are not necessary if the Listview control doesn't use the report view to display data.
- Mark the current selection in the Listview control. From the user's viewpoint, a Listview control is similar to a listbox-type control. Selection is controlled by an item's state, which is set either by calling `CListCtrl::SetItemState()` or when the item is added to the Listview control.

Listing 20.3 shows the initialization of the sample Listview control. The order of these steps should be followed for best results. In this listing, I use boldface type to indicate each step in the process for setting up the Listview control.

Listing 20.3. The Listview `OnInitIDialog()` handler.

```
BOOL CListviewDlg::OnInitDialog()
{
    CDialog::OnInitDialog();

    // TODO: Add extra initialization here

//    Setup the image lists:

    if (m_ImageLarge.Create(IDB_LISTVIEW_LARGE, 32, 0, FALSE))
    {// Add error handler here, as needed:
        TRACE("Could not create the large images\n");
    }
    if (m_ImageSmall.Create(IDB_LISTVIEW_SMALL, 16, 0, FALSE))
    {// Add error handler here, as needed:
        TRACE("Could not create the small images\n");
    }
    if (m_ImageState.Create(IDB_LISTVIEW_STATE, 16, 0, FALSE))
    {// Add error handler here, as needed:
        TRACE("Could not create the state images\n");
    }

//    Add image lists to listview control:

    m_Listview.SetImageList(&m_ImageLarge, LVSIL_NORMAL);
    m_Listview.SetImageList(&m_ImageSmall, LVSIL_SMALL);
    m_Listview.SetImageList(&m_ImageState, LVSIL_STATE);

//    General purpose variables (loop counters and the like)

    int   i = 0;
    int j = 0;

//    First add columns:
//    To use columns in a listview control you need a LV_COLUMN structure:

    LV_COLUMN lvc;

    lvc.mask =
        LVCF_FMT     ¦ // The fmt member of LV_COLUMN is valid.
        LVCF_WIDTH   ¦ // The cx member of LV_COLUMN is valid.
        LVCF_TEXT    ¦ // The pszText member of LV_COLUMN is valid.
        LVCF_SUBITEM; // The iSubItem member of LV_COLUMN is valid.

    lvc.fmt = LVCFMT_LEFT;

    for (i = 0; i < sizeof(szColumn) / sizeof(szColumn[0]); i++)
    {// Insert each column in the list:
        if (i == 0)
        {//    First column, leave room for icon!
            lvc.cx = m_Listview.GetStringWidth(szColumn[i]) + 65;
        }
        else
        {
            lvc.cx = m_Listview.GetStringWidth(szColumn[i]) + 15;
```

continues

Listing 20.3. continued

```
        }

        lvc.pszText = szColumn[i];

        if (i > 2) // Format numbers in columns 3, 4, and 5  to right!
            lvc.fmt = LVCFMT_RIGHT;

        lvc.iSubItem = i;

        m_Listview.InsertColumn(i, &lvc);
    }

//    Add data to the listview control.

    LV_ITEM lvi;
    lvi.mask = LVIF_TEXT | LVIF_IMAGE | LVIF_PARAM;
    lvi.iSubItem = 0;

    for (i = 0; i < 20; i++)
    {
        lvi.iItem = i;
        lvi.pszText = szData[i][0];
        lvi.cchTextMax = 5;
        lvi.lParam = (LPARAM)i;

        if (i < 5)
            lvi.iImage = 0;
        else
            lvi.iImage = 1;

        m_Listview.InsertItem(&lvi);

        // Add subitems to each main item:
        for (int k = 1; k < 6; k++)
        {
            m_Listview.SetItemText(i, k, szData[i][k]);
        }
    }

//    default is report mode, press report button:

    m_ReportButton.SetState(TRUE);
    m_LargeIconButton.SetState(FALSE);
    m_SmallIconButton.SetState(FALSE);
    m_ListButton.SetState(FALSE);

    return TRUE;  // return TRUE unless you set the focus to a control
                  // EXCEPTION: OCX Property Pages should return FALSE
}
```

Creating *CListCtrl* Objects in Nondialog Box Windows

To create a `CListCtrl` object in a window that is not a dialog box, you call
`CListCtrl::Create()`. The `CListCtrl::Create()` function takes four parameters: a style (see
Table 20.2); a `RECT` structure, which specifies the Listview control's location and size; a
pointer to the parent window; and the control ID.

```
CListCtrl::Create(
    WS_CHILD | WS_VISIBLE | TBS_HORZ | TBS_AUTOTICKS | TBS_ENABLESELRANGE,
    rect, this, 0);
```

Table 20.2. Window styles for the `CListCtrl::Create()` function.

Identifier	Description
LVS_ALIGNBOTTOM	The label text is aligned to the bottom of the image when the display mode is either large icon or small icon view. The align bottom mode is the default as well as the most commonly used alignment.
LVS_ALIGNLEFT	The label text is aligned to the left of the image when the display mode is either large icon or small icon view.
LVS_ALIGNRIGHT	The label text is aligned to the right of the image when the display mode is either large icon or small icon view.
LVS_ALIGNTOP	The label text is aligned to the top of the image when the display mode is either large icon or small icon view.
LVS_AUTOARRANGE	The items in the Listview control are automatically arranged when in the large icon and small icon views.
LVS_BUTTON	The large icon view has items that resemble buttons.
LVS_EDITLABELS	The labels can be modified by the user. The application must also be able to process the LVN_ENDLABELEDIT message that is sent when the user has completed the label edit.
LVS_ICON	The Listview control is displayed in the large icon view.
LVS_LIST	The Listview control is displayed in the list view.
LVS_NOCOLUMNHEADER	The report view of the control does not have column headers.
LVS_NOITEMDATA	There is only enough space allocated for the item's state. There will not be item data, labels, icons, or sub-item strings. The Listview control's parent window must process the LVN_GETDISPINFO message to provide information to the Listview control when needed.
LVS_NOLABELWRAP	The labels do not wrap to multiple lines when the Listview control is in large icon view mode.

continues

Table 20.2. continued

Identifier	Description
LVS_NOSCROLL	The Listview control doesn't have scrollbars. All items must fit within the control's display area.
LVS_NOSORTHEADER	The report view headers do not work as sort pushbuttons. Headers do not have to sort: You can connect the button to any functionality your program needs.
LVS_OWNERDRAWFIXED	The items are drawn by the control's owner.
LVS_REPORT	The Listview control is displayed in the report view.
LVS_SHAREIMAGELISTS	The Listview control doesn't take ownership of the image lists. This allows other Listview controls to access and use the images lists without having to create and destroy the lists on a constant basis.
LVS_SINGLESEL	Only one item at a time can be selected in the Listview control.
LVS_SMALLICON	The Listview control displays in the small icon view.
LVS_SORTASCENDING	The Listview control sorts items as text in ascending order.
LVS_SORTDESCENDING	The Listview control sorts items as text in descending order.

There are a number of situations in which a programmer might want to create a Listview control in a nondialog box window. Using CListCtrl::Create() is an easy way to create a Listview control.

Listview States

Items in a Listview control can have different states. The states are application-specific and are defined by the application. Table 20.3 shows a number of states defined by Windows.

Table 20.3. Listview system states.

State	Description
LVNI_DROPHILITED	The LVIS_DROPHILITED state flag is set for this item, and the item is selected as a drag-and-drop target.
LVNI_FOCUSED	The LVIS_FOCUSED state flag is set for this item, and the item has current focus.
LVNI_HIDDEN	The LVIS_HIDDEN state flag is set for this item, and the item is currently not visible.

State	Description
LVNI_MARKED	The LVIS_MARKED state flag is set for this item, and the item is currently marked.
LVNI_SELECTED	The LVIS_SELECTED state flag is set for this item, and the item is currently selected.

Using Listview State Images

The Listview control can have state images used to represent the various states that a user-defined item can take. State images are placed to the left of the items' main image; the size of the state image remains the same, regardless of the size of the image displayed in the Listview control.

The code in Listing 20.4 shows you how to test the various state combinations applied to a Listview object. This listing can be substituted for the OnInitDlg() handler from Listing 20.1. The significant changes are marked in boldface type in this listing.

Listing 20.4. The OnInitDlg() handler, which shows states in Listview controls.

```
BOOL CListviewDlg::OnInitDialog()
{
    CDialog::OnInitDialog();

    // TODO: Add extra initialization here

//   Setup the image lists:

    if (m_ImageLarge.Create(IDB_LISTVIEW_LARGE, 32, 0, FALSE))
    {// Add error handler here, as needed:
       TRACE("Could not create the large images\n");
    }
    if (m_ImageSmall.Create(IDB_LISTVIEW_SMALL, 16, 0, FALSE))
    {// Add error handler here, as needed:
       TRACE("Could not create the small images\n");
    }
    if (m_ImageState.Create(IDB_LISTVIEW_STATE, 16, 0, FALSE))
    {// Add error handler here, as needed:
       TRACE("Could not create the state images\n");
    }

//   Add image lists to listview control:

    m_Listview.SetImageList(&m_ImageLarge, LVSIL_NORMAL);
    m_Listview.SetImageList(&m_ImageSmall, LVSIL_SMALL);
    m_Listview.SetImageList(&m_ImageState, LVSIL_STATE);

//   General purpose variables (loop counters and the like)

    int   i = 0;
```

continues

Listing 20.4. continued

```
    int j = 0;

//   First add columns:
//   To use columns in a listview control you need a LV_COLUMN structure:

    LV_COLUMN lvc;

    lvc.mask =
        LVCF_FMT     | // The fmt member of LV_COLUMN is valid.
        LVCF_WIDTH   | // The cx member of LV_COLUMN is valid.
        LVCF_TEXT    | // The pszText member of LV_COLUMN is valid.
        LVCF_SUBITEM; // The iSubItem member of LV_COLUMN is valid.

    lvc.fmt = LVCFMT_LEFT;

    for (i = 0; i < sizeof(szColumn) / sizeof(szColumn[0]); i++)
    {// Insert each column in the list:
        if (i == 0)
        {//    First column, leave room for icon!
            lvc.cx = m_Listview.GetStringWidth(szColumn[i]) + 65;
        }
        else
        {
            lvc.cx = m_Listview.GetStringWidth(szColumn[i]) + 15;
        }

        lvc.pszText = szColumn[i];

        if (i > 2) // Format numbers in columns 3, 4, and 5  to right!
            lvc.fmt = LVCFMT_RIGHT;

        lvc.iSubItem = i;

        m_Listview.InsertColumn(i, &lvc);
    }

//   Add data to the listview control.

    LV_ITEM lvi;
    lvi.mask = LVIF_TEXT | LVIF_IMAGE | LVIF_PARAM | LVIF_STATE;
    lvi.iSubItem = 0;

    for (i = 0; i < 20; i++)
    {
        lvi.iItem = i;
        lvi.pszText = szData[i][0];
        lvi.cchTextMax = 5;
        lvi.lParam = (LPARAM)i;

        if (i < 5)
            lvi.iImage = 0;
        else
            lvi.iImage = 1;

        switch(i)
        {
```

```
case 0:
    lvi.state = LVIS_FOCUSED; // 0x0001
    lvi.pszText = "LVIS_FOCUSED";
    lvi.stateMask = lvi.state;
    break;
case 1:
    lvi.state =  LVIS_SELECTED; // 0x0002
    lvi.pszText = "LVIS_SELECTED";
    lvi.stateMask = lvi.state;
    break;
case 2:
    lvi.state =  LVIS_CUT; // 0x0004
    lvi.pszText = "LVIS_CUT";
    lvi.stateMask = lvi.state;
    break;
case 3:
    lvi.state = LVIS_DROPHILITED; // 0x0008
    lvi.pszText = "LVIS_DROPHILITED";
    lvi.stateMask = lvi.state;
    break;
case 4:
    lvi.state =  0x0040; //LVIS_LINK; // 0x0040
    lvi.pszText = "LVIS_LINK";
    lvi.stateMask = lvi.state;
    break;

case 5:
    lvi.state =  0x0100;
    lvi.pszText = "LVIS_OVERLAYMASK";
    lvi.stateMask =  LVIS_OVERLAYMASK; // 0x0F00
    break;
case 6:
    lvi.state =  0x1000;
    lvi.pszText = "LVIS_STATEIMAGEMASK";
    lvi.stateMask =  LVIS_STATEIMAGEMASK; //0xF000
    break;

case 7:
    lvi.state =  0x0200;
    lvi.pszText = "LVIS_OVERLAYMASK";
    lvi.stateMask =  LVIS_OVERLAYMASK; // 0x0F00
    break;

case 8:
    lvi.state =  0x2000;
    lvi.pszText = "LVIS_STATEIMAGEMASK";
    lvi.stateMask =  LVIS_STATEIMAGEMASK; //0xF000
    break;

case 9:
    lvi.state =  0x0300;
    lvi.pszText = "LVIS_OVERLAYMASK";
    lvi.stateMask =  LVIS_OVERLAYMASK; // 0x0F00
    break;

case 10:
    lvi.state =  0x3000;
    lvi.pszText = "LVIS_STATEIMAGEMASK";
```

continues

Listing 20.4. continued

```
                lvi.stateMask = LVIS_STATEIMAGEMASK; //0xF000
                break;

            case 11:
                lvi.state = 0x0400;
                lvi.pszText = "LVIS_OVERLAYMASK";
                lvi.stateMask = LVIS_OVERLAYMASK; // 0x0F00
                break;

            case 12:
                lvi.state = 0x4000;
                lvi.pszText = "LVIS_STATEIMAGEMASK";
                lvi.stateMask = LVIS_STATEIMAGEMASK; //0xF000
                break;

            case 13:
                lvi.state = 0x0500;
                lvi.pszText = "LVIS_OVERLAYMASK";
                lvi.stateMask = LVIS_OVERLAYMASK; // 0x0F00
                break;

            case 14:
                lvi.state = 0x5000;
                lvi.pszText = "LVIS_STATEIMAGEMASK";
                lvi.stateMask = LVIS_STATEIMAGEMASK; //0xF000
                break;

            case 15:
                lvi.state = 0x0600;
                lvi.pszText = "LVIS_OVERLAYMASK";
                lvi.stateMask = LVIS_OVERLAYMASK; // 0x0F00
                break;

            case 16:
                lvi.state = 0x6000;
                lvi.pszText = "LVIS_STATEIMAGEMASK";
                lvi.stateMask = LVIS_STATEIMAGEMASK; //0xF000
                break;

            default:
                lvi.state = 0;
                lvi.stateMask = lvi.state;
                break;
        }

        m_Listview.InsertItem(&lvi);

        // Add subitems to each main item:
        for (int k = 1; k < 6; k++)
        {
            m_Listview.SetItemText(i, k, szData[i][k]);
        }
    }

//    default is report mode, press report button:

    m_ReportButton.SetState(TRUE);
```

```
    m_LargeIconButton.SetState(FALSE);
    m_SmallIconButton.SetState(FALSE);
    m_ListButton.SetState(FALSE);

    return TRUE;   // return TRUE unless you set the focus to a control
                   // EXCEPTION: OCX Property Pages should return FALSE
}
```

The Listview control from Listing 20.4 looks like the example shown in Figure 20.6. The sample Listview control is in the report mode.

FIGURE 20.6.

*State images in a
Listview control in
report mode.*

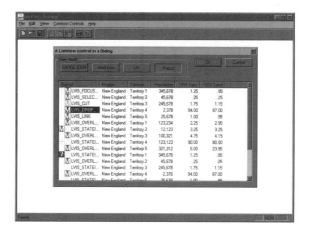

Using the *CListCtrl* Listview Object

The CListCtrl Listview object takes data input (items and, optionally, images) that is placed in the Listview control and displays this information in a number of formats for the user.

CListCtrl Listview Interaction

The user interacts with a Listview control by selecting objects in the control. It's possible to have both editing of labels and drag-and-drop support (an item can be dropped on another item). Most Listview controls are used for basic data output; the report mode effectively displays columnar data.

Sorting in a *CListCtrl* Listview Control

The contents of a Listview control, when displayed in report mode, can be sorted by the user based on any column available. For example, Figure 20.7 shows the default order for items in the sample Listview control, and Figure 20.8 shows the Listview control sorted on the 1994 Sales column.

FIGURE 20.7.

The Listview control in report mode with the default sort order.

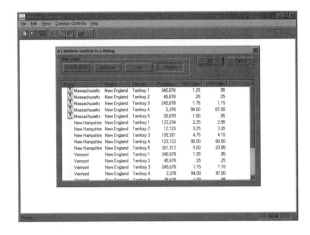

FIGURE 20.8.

The Listview control in report mode, sorted on the 1994 Sales column.

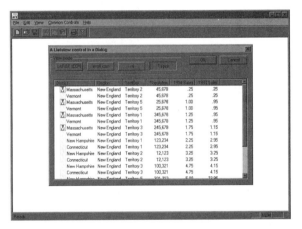

The support for sorting is done by creating an OnNotify() handler to the sample code. I created this handler by hand because Visual C++ 2.1 did not have ClassWizard support implemented for OnNotify. Here are the changes that must be performed to add the OnNotify handler:

1. In the header file (LISTVIEW.H in the sample program), the prototype for the handler must be added. I call this function OnColumnClick(). This line is in boldface type in the following listing fragment:

```
// Implementation
protected:

    // Generated message map functions
    //{{AFX_MSG(CListviewDlg)
    virtual BOOL OnInitDialog();
    afx_msg void OnLargeicon();
    afx_msg void OnList();
```

```
afx_msg void OnReport();
afx_msg void OnSmallicon();
afx_msg void OnDestroy();
afx_msg void OnColumnClick(NMHDR* pNMHDR, LRESULT* pResult);
//}}AFX_MSG
DECLARE_MESSAGE_MAP()
```

2. In the source file (LISTVIEW.CPP in the sample program), a macro in the message map must be added for the function `OnColumnClick()`. This line is in boldface type in the following listing fragment:

```
BEGIN_MESSAGE_MAP(CListviewDlg, CDialog)
    //{{AFX_MSG_MAP(CListviewDlg)
    ON_BN_CLICKED(IDC_LARGEICON, OnLargeicon)
    ON_BN_CLICKED(IDC_LIST, OnList)
    ON_BN_CLICKED(IDC_REPORT, OnReport)
    ON_BN_CLICKED(IDC_SMALLICON, OnSmallicon)
    ON_WM_DESTROY()
    ON_NOTIFY(LVN_COLUMNCLICK, IDC_LISTVIEW, OnColumnClick)
    //}}AFX_MSG_MAP
END_MESSAGE_MAP()
```

3. In the source file (LISTVIEW.CPP in the sample program), the actual `OnColumnClick()` function must be inserted. The following code fragment shows the sample `OnColumnClick()` function.

```
void CListviewDlg::OnColumnClick(NMHDR* pNMHDR, LRESULT* pResult)
{
    NM_LISTVIEW* pNMListView = (NM_LISTVIEW*)pNMHDR;
    // TODO: Add your control notification handler code here

//    TRACE("OnColumnClick\n");

    m_Listview.SortItems(OurCompare, pNMListView->iSubItem);

    *pResult = 0;
}
```

4. Notice that the `OnColumnClick()` function calls the `CListCtrl::SortItems()` function. The `SortItems()` function takes a parameter that is a compare function. It also takes a second application-specific LPARAM value. The compare function I use is shown in the following code:

```
int CALLBACK OurCompare(
    LPARAM lParam1, LPARAM lParam2, LPARAM dwData)
{
    char * p1 = (char *)szData[lParam1][dwData];
    char * p2 = (char *)szData[lParam2][dwData];

    return(stricmp(p1, p2));
}
```

Whenever the function `CListCtrl::SortItems()` is called, it sorts the items in the Listview control using the sort function provided. The second parameter passed to the `CListCtrl::SortItems()` function is passed directly to the compare function. In the sample program in Listing 20.1, I use this parameter to identify which column is being sorted.

> **WARNING**
>
> You might be tempted to make the compare function a member of the `CListCtrl` object. Don't! When `CListCtrl::SortItems()` calls the compare function, it expects a function that is not a member of a class. Because all class member functions expect to receive an implicit pointer to the class and because the `CListCtrl::SortItems()` call to the compare function does not provide this pointer, the call will fail.

In many cases, you can easily make your compare function by calling `stricmp()` or one of the other string compare functions in which the column's data is textual, or by using simple numeric comparisons.

The *CTreeCtrl* Class

A Treeview control allows the display of data to the user in a hierarchical format. The data is displayed as a tree structure that the user can expand or compress as needed. There are a number of different examples of the Treeview control in Windows 95. The most common is the Explorer application's left side pane (see Figure 20.9), which uses the Treeview control to display a disk drive's directory structure.

FIGURE 20.9.

The Windows 95 Explorer program with a Treeview control.

Figure 20.10 shows an example of the Treeview control from the sample program. This control uses the text mode to display the items in the list. There are no images for the items in the sample Treeview control.

FIGURE 20.10.

*A Treeview control
displaying data.*

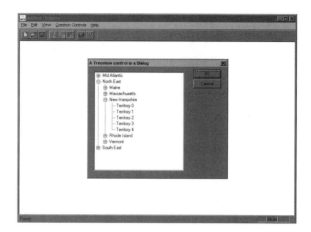

When using a `CTreeCtrl` class object, your application needs to do a minimum amount of management of the Treeview control. The application must have a set of images to display with the data if images are being used, and of course, it must have data to display. A Treeview control can have a number of attributes. All attributes can be set using the resource editor in Visual C++ and can be modified at runtime. Table 20.4 is a list of the attributes for a Treeview control.

Table 20.4. The attributes for a Treeview control.

Attribute	Description
Has buttons	The Treeview control has small boxes with [+] and [-] symbols to signify whether a node can be expanded or is already expanded.
Has lines	The Treeview control has lines drawn to show the structure.
Lines at root	There is a line at the root level of the Treeview control.
Border	Standard control border.
Edit labels	The labels can be modified by the user. The application must be able to process the `LVN_ENDLABELEDIT` message that is sent when the user has completed the label edit.
Disable drag drop	The Treeview can optionally support drag-and-drop operations. The user can disable drag-and-drop support if desired.
Show sel always	The selection can be hidden if desired, or the Treeview control can be forced to show the selection at all times.

After you have added the Treeview control to a dialog box, you can use the ClassWizard to bind a `CTreeCtrl` object to the Treeview control. The `CTreeCtrl` object is your interface with the Treeview control.

Implementing a *CTreeCtrl* Treeview Control

If you are using a Treeview control in a dialog box, you use the ClassWizard to bind a CTreeCtrl object to the control. If you are implementing a Treeview control in a window that is not a dialog box, you call the CTreeCtrl::Create() function to create the Treeview control. You might find a use for a Treeview control in a normal window (perhaps similar to how Explorer uses the Treeview control) or as part of a toolbar.

Figure 20.11 shows a sample dialog box in the Visual C++ resource editor with the properties for the Treeview control. These properties are easily modified using the resource editor for Treeview controls in dialog boxes. When the Treeview control is in a window other than a dialog box, the properties are set when the Treeview control is created.

FIGURE 20.11.

A Treeview control and its properties in the Visual C++ resource editor.

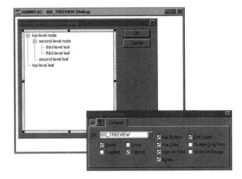

Listing 20.5 is the code that manages the sample Treeview dialog box. I developed the base for this code by using the ClassWizard, and then I added any needed features.

Code that was modified or added manually is marked in boldface type. The changes made using the ClassWizard are not marked but are described in the text following the listing. Basically, the ClassWizard was used to add the following features: variables for the controls in the dialog boxes, handlers for the dialog box controls, and the WM_INITDLG handler.

Listing 20.5. The TREEVIEW.CPP file.

```
// treeview.cpp : implementation file
//

#include "stdafx.h"
#include "Dummy.h"
#include "treeview.h"

#ifdef _DEBUG
#undef THIS_FILE
static char BASED_CODE THIS_FILE[] = __FILE__;
```

```
#endif

/////////////////////////////////////////////////////////////////////////
// CTreeviewDlg dialog


CTreeviewDlg::CTreeviewDlg(CWnd* pParent /*=NULL*/)
    : CDialog(CTreeviewDlg::IDD, pParent)
{
    //{{AFX_DATA_INIT(CTreeviewDlg)
        // NOTE: the ClassWizard will add member initialization here
    //}}AFX_DATA_INIT
}


void CTreeviewDlg::DoDataExchange(CDataExchange* pDX)
{
    CDialog::DoDataExchange(pDX);
    //{{AFX_DATA_MAP(CTreeviewDlg)
    DDX_Control(pDX, IDC_TREEVIEW, m_TreeView);
    //}}AFX_DATA_MAP
}


BEGIN_MESSAGE_MAP(CTreeviewDlg, CDialog)
    //{{AFX_MSG_MAP(CTreeviewDlg)
    //}}AFX_MSG_MAP
END_MESSAGE_MAP()


/////////////////////////////////////////////////////////////////////////
// CTreeviewDlg message handlers

BOOL CTreeviewDlg::OnInitDialog()
{
    CDialog::OnInitDialog();

    // TODO: Add extra initialization here

//--First the tree control:

    int              nRegion;
    int              nDistrict;
    int              nTerritory;
    HTREEITEM        RegionParent;
    HTREEITEM        DistrictParent;
    HTREEITEM        TerritoryParent;
    TV_INSERTSTRUCT  InsertItem;

    char    szBuffer[255];
    char    *szRegion[3] = {"North East", "Mid Atlantic", "South East"};
    char    *szDistrict[3][5] =
       {{"New Hampshire", "Massachusetts", "Vermont", "Maine", "Rhode Island"},
        {"New York", "New Jersey", "Delaware", "DC", "Maryland"},
        {"Virginia", "North Carolina", "South Carolina", "Georgia", "Florida"}};

    for (nRegion = 0; nRegion < 3; ++nRegion)
```

continues

Listing 20.5. continued

```
    {
        InsertItem.item.mask = TVIF_TEXT;
        InsertItem.item.pszText = szRegion[nRegion];
        InsertItem.item.cchTextMax = 15;
        InsertItem.hParent = NULL;
        InsertItem.hInsertAfter = TVI_SORT;

        RegionParent = m_TreeView.InsertItem(&InsertItem);

        for (nDistrict = 0; nDistrict < 5; ++nDistrict)
        {
            InsertItem.item.pszText = szDistrict[nRegion][nDistrict];
            InsertItem.item.cchTextMax = 20;
            InsertItem.hParent = RegionParent;
            InsertItem.hInsertAfter = TVI_SORT;

            DistrictParent = m_TreeView.InsertItem(&InsertItem);

            for (nTerritory = 0; nTerritory < 5; ++nTerritory)
            {
                sprintf(szBuffer, "Territory %d", nTerritory);
                InsertItem.item.pszText = szBuffer;
                InsertItem.item.cchTextMax = 20;
                InsertItem.hParent = DistrictParent;
                InsertItem.hInsertAfter = TVI_SORT;

                TerritoryParent = m_TreeView.InsertItem(&InsertItem);
            }
        }
    }

    return TRUE;  // return TRUE unless you set the focus to a control
                  // EXCEPTION: OCX Property Pages should return FALSE
}
```

Listing 20.6 is the TREEVIEW.H header file that accompanies the TREEVIEW.CPP file (shown in Listing 20.5). I modified the TREEVIEW.H file by using the ClassWizard; no manual modifications were needed.

Listing 20.6. The TREEVIEW.H file.

```
// treeview.h : header file
//

/////////////////////////////////////////////////////////////////////////
// CTreeviewDlg dialog

class CTreeviewDlg : public CDialog
{
// Construction
public:
    CTreeviewDlg(CWnd* pParent = NULL);   // standard constructor

// Dialog Data
```

```
    //{{AFX_DATA(CTreeviewDlg)
    enum { IDD = IDD_TREEVIEW };
    CTreeCtrl    m_TreeView;
    //}}AFX_DATA


// Overrides
    // ClassWizard generated virtual function overrides
    //{{AFX_VIRTUAL(CTreeviewDlg)
    protected:
    virtual void DoDataExchange(CDataExchange* pDX);    // DDX/DDV support
    //}}AFX_VIRTUAL

// Implementation
protected:

    // Generated message map functions
    //{{AFX_MSG(CTreeviewDlg)
    virtual BOOL OnInitDialog();
    //}}AFX_MSG
    DECLARE_MESSAGE_MAP()
};
```

The *CTreeCtrl* Class in a Dialog Box

As stated previously, you usually bind your CTreeCtrl object to a Treeview control using the ClassWizard. After you have bound the CTreeCtrl object, you can initialize your Treeview control in the OnInitDialog() function.

> **NOTE**
>
> You are not required to have image lists in your Treeview control. Many implementations of the Treeview control use text only. To use image lists with the Treeview control, simply create a CImageList object and then call CTreeCtrl::SetImageList() as shown in the Listview example in Listing 20.4. Then use the image indexes in the same manner. There is only one size for an image and two types of image lists (normal and state).
>
> The example shows the images in normal type. The state image techniques are identical to those found in the Listview control.

Generally, you perform the following steps when initializing your Treeview control:

- Set up the image lists if you are using them. There are two image lists: the icons (typically 16×16 pixels), and the state images (16×16 in many applications). Image lists can be shared between multiple Treeview controls or private to a specific Treeview control.

> **NOTE**
>
> Make sure that your application properly cleans up after itself. If the image lists are shared, they must be destroyed when the application is done with them. Also, don't try to reload the images twice without an intervening call to `DeleteImageList()`.

- Attach your image lists to the Treeview control by calling `CTreeCtrl::SetImageList()`.

> **NOTE**
>
> If some items in the Treeview control have images, all items in the Treeview control must have images. Any item in the Treeview you do not want to have an image is assigned a blank image.

- Add the items to your Treeview control. Each item should be added in the same order in which it appears in the hierarchy: start by selecting the highest level, and then select the next highest level, and so on. Nested loops work well for this purpose, as shown in the sample program for this chapter. Listing 20.5 shows the Treeview implementation.

- Mark the current selection in the Treeview control. Selection is controlled by an item's state. An item's state is set when `CTreeCtrl::SetItemState()` is called or when the item is added to the Treeview control.

Listing 20.7 shows the initialization of the sample Treeview control. The order of the steps should be followed for best results. Each step in the process of setting up the Treeview control is shown in boldface type.

Listing 20.7. The Treeview `OnInitIDialog()` handler.

```
BOOL CTreeviewDlg::OnInitDialog()
{
    CDialog::OnInitDialog();

    // TODO: Add extra initialization here


//--First the tree control:

    int             nRegion;
    int             nDistrict;
    int             nTerritory;
    HTREEITEM       RegionParent;
    HTREEITEM       DistrictParent;
    HTREEITEM       TerritoryParent;
    TV_INSERTSTRUCT InsertItem;
```

```
char    szBuffer[255];
char    *szRegion[3] = {"North East", "Mid Atlantic", "South East"};
char    *szDistrict[3][5] =
   {{"New Hampshire", "Massachusetts", "Vermont", "Maine", "Rhode Island"},
    {"New York", "New Jersey", "Delaware", "DC", "Maryland"},
    {"Virginia", "North Carolina", "South Carolina", "Georgia", "Florida"}};

for (nRegion = 0; nRegion < 3; ++nRegion)
{
    InsertItem.item.mask = TVIF_TEXT;
    InsertItem.item.pszText = szRegion[nRegion];
    InsertItem.item.cchTextMax = 15;
    InsertItem.item.iImage = 0;
    InsertItem.hParent = NULL;
    InsertItem.hInsertAfter = TVI_SORT;

    RegionParent = m_TreeView.InsertItem(&InsertItem);

    for (nDistrict = 0; nDistrict < 5; ++nDistrict)
    {
        InsertItem.item.pszText = szDistrict[nRegion][nDistrict];
        InsertItem.item.cchTextMax = 20;
        InsertItem.hParent = RegionParent;
        InsertItem.hInsertAfter = TVI_SORT;

        DistrictParent = m_TreeView.InsertItem(&InsertItem);

        for (nTerritory = 0; nTerritory < 5; ++nTerritory)
        {
            sprintf(szBuffer, "Territory %d", nTerritory);
            InsertItem.item.pszText = szBuffer;
            InsertItem.item.cchTextMax = 20;
            InsertItem.hParent = DistrictParent;
            InsertItem.hInsertAfter = TVI_SORT;

            TerritoryParent = m_TreeView.InsertItem(&InsertItem);
        }
    }
}

return TRUE;   // return TRUE unless you set the focus to a control
               // EXCEPTION: OCX Property Pages should return FALSE
}
```

Creating *CTreeCtrl* Objects in Nondialog Box Windows

To create a CTreeCtrl object in a window that is not a dialog box, you call
CTreeCtrl::Create(). The CTreeCtrl::Create() function takes four parameters: a style (see
Table 20.5), a RECT structure specifying the Treeview control's location and size, a pointer to
the parent window, and the control ID.

There are only four unique styles for a `CTreeCtrl` object. Below is a call to the `CTreeCtrl::Create()` function showing a typical Treeview control creation.

```
CTreeCtrl::Create(
    WS_CHILD | WS_VISIBLE | TBS_HORZ | TBS_AUTOTICKS | TBS_ENABLESELRANGE,
    rect, this, 0);
```

Table 20.5. Window styles for the `CTreeCtrl::Create()` function.

Identifier	Description
TVS_HASLINES	The Treeview control has lines drawn to show the structure.
TVS_LINESATROOT	There is a line at the root level of the Treeview control.
TVS_HASBUTTONS	The Treeview control has small boxes with [+] and [-] symbols that signify whether a node can be expanded or is already expanded.
TVS_EDITLABELS	The labels can be modified by the user. The application must also be able to process the LVN_ENDLABELEDIT message, sent when the user has completed the label edit.

There are a number of situations in which a programmer might want to create a Treeview control in a nondialog box window. Using `CTreeCtrl::Create()` is an easy method for creating a Treeview control.

Treeview States

Items in a Treeview control can have different states. The states are application-specific and are defined by the application. A number of states are defined by Windows. These states are shown in Table 20.6.

Table 20.6. Treeview system states.

State	Description
TVIS_DROPHILITED	The TVIS_DROPHILITED state flag is set for this item.
TVIS_SELECTED	The TVIS_SELECTED state flag is set for this item.
TVIS_CUT	The TVIS_CUT state flag is set for this item.
TVIS_EXPANDED	The TVIS_EXPANDED state flag is set for this item.
TVIS_EXPANDEDONCE	The TVIS_EXPANDEDONCE state flag is set for this item.
TVIS_BOLD	The TVIS_BOLD state flag is set for this item.

Using Treeview State Images

The Treeview control can have state images used to represent the various states that a user-defined item can take. The state image is placed to the left of the item's main image, and the size of the state image remains the same regardless of the size of the image displayed in the Treeview control.

The code in Listing 20.8 shows you how to test the various state combinations that can be applied to a Treeview object.

Listing 20.8. The `OnInitDlg()` handler, which shows the states in a Treeview control.

```
BOOL CTreeviewDlg::OnInitDialog()
{
    CDialog::OnInitDialog();

    // TODO: Add extra initialization here

//   Setup the image lists:

    if (m_ImageNormal.Create(IDB_TREEVIEW, 16, 0, FALSE))
    {// Add error handler here, as needed:
       TRACE("Could not create the normal images\n");
    }
    if (m_ImageState.Create(IDB_TREEVIEW_STATE, 16, 0, FALSE))
    {// Add error handler here, as needed:
       TRACE("Could not create the state images\n");
    }

//   Add image lists to Treeview control:

    m_Treeview.SetImageList(TVSIL_NORMAL, &m_ImageNormal);
    m_Treeview.SetImageList(TVSIL_STATE,  &m_ImageState);


//--First the tree control:

    int             nRegion;
    int             nDistrict;
    int             nTerritory;
    HTREEITEM       RegionParent;
    HTREEITEM       DistrictParent;
    HTREEITEM       TerritoryParent;
    TV_INSERTSTRUCT InsertItem;

    char    szBuffer[255];
    char    *szRegion[3] = {"North East", "Mid Atlantic", "South East"};
    char    *szDistrict[3][5] =
      {{"New Hampshire", "Massachusetts", "Vermont", "Maine", "Rhode Island"},
       {"New York", "New Jersey", "Delaware", "DC", "Maryland"},
       {"Virginia", "North Carolina", "South Carolina", "Georgia", "Florida"}};

    for (nRegion = 0; nRegion < 3; ++nRegion)
```

continues

Listing 20.8. continued

```
{
    InsertItem.item.mask = TVIF_TEXT | TVIF_STATE;
    InsertItem.item.pszText = szRegion[nRegion];
    InsertItem.item.cchTextMax = 15;
    InsertItem.item.iImage = 0;
    InsertItem.item.state = 0;     // SET WHAT STATE IS DESIRED
    InsertItem.item.stateMask = 0; // SET WHAT STATE MASK IS DESIRED
    InsertItem.hParent = NULL;
    InsertItem.hInsertAfter = TVI_SORT;

    RegionParent = m_TreeView.InsertItem(&InsertItem);

    for (nDistrict = 0; nDistrict < 5; ++nDistrict)
    {
        InsertItem.item.pszText = szDistrict[nRegion][nDistrict];
        InsertItem.item.cchTextMax = 20;
        InsertItem.hParent = RegionParent;
        InsertItem.hInsertAfter = TVI_SORT;
        InsertItem.item.state = 0;     // SET WHAT STATE IS DESIRED
        InsertItem.item.stateMask = 0; // SET WHAT STATE MASK IS DESIRED

        DistrictParent = m_TreeView.InsertItem(&InsertItem);

        for (nTerritory = 0; nTerritory < 5; ++nTerritory)
        {
            sprintf(szBuffer, "Territory %d", nTerritory);
            InsertItem.item.pszText = szBuffer;
            InsertItem.item.cchTextMax = 20;
            InsertItem.hParent = DistrictParent;
            InsertItem.hInsertAfter = TVI_SORT;
            InsertItem.item.state = 0;     // SET WHAT STATE IS DESIRED
            InsertItem.item.stateMask = 0; // SET WHAT STATE MASK DESIRED

            TerritoryParent = m_TreeView.InsertItem(&InsertItem);
        }
    }
}

return TRUE;  // return TRUE unless you set the focus to a control
              // EXCEPTION: OCX Property Pages should return FALSE
*}
```

Using the *CTreeCtrl* Treeview Object

The CTreeCtrl Treeview object takes data input (items and, optionally, images) that is placed in the Treeview control and displays this information in a number of formats for the user.

The *CTreeCtrl* Treeview Interaction

The user interacts with a Treeview control by selecting objects in the control. It's possible to have both editing of labels and drag-and-drop support. Most Listview controls are used for basic data output; the report mode effectively displays columnar data.

The final user input is often the "selected" item. This is returned using `CTreeCtrl::GetSelectedItem()`, which returns information about the selected item in the Treeview list.

Summary

This chapter details the use of two different Win32 common controls: the Listview control and the Treeview control. The Listview control displays data to the user in one of four formats (list, small icon, large icon, and report) and enables the user to select an item. When data is presented in the report mode, the user can perform a sorting operation based on the contents of a specified column. The Treeview control provides the user with a display of hierarchical data. Like the Listview control, the Treeview control enables the user to select an item.

Property Sheets and Tab Controls

21

by Peter D. Hipson

IN THIS CHAPTER

MFC offers property sheets similar to the ones offered by the Win32 Common Controls tab control. There are differences between the two implementations as I will show you in this chapter.

For many programs, you will find that MFC `CPropertyPage` and `CPropertySheet` objects are the most easily implemented. These two objects are very easy to work with because they have a simple dialog box design and are totally managed by the system. However, as is often the case, ease of use sacrifices flexibility: `CPropertySheet` doesn't easily allow for customization.

This chapter will be difficult to understand without the following definitions:

- `CPropertyPage`—A single tab (or page) in a property sheet dialog box. For example, in the Visual C++ ClassWizard dialog box (see Figure 21.1), the Message Maps tab is a `CPropertyPage` object. There is always more than one property page in a property sheet.

- `CPropertySheet`—The entire dialog box. A property sheet has more than one property page contained within it. `CPropertySheet` does not allow for any other controls to be placed within its dialog box. For example, the ClassWizard dialog box from Figure 21.1 can be produced with a `CPropertySheet` object.

- `CTabCtrl`—A dialog box control that may be located in a dialog box to allow a set of tabbed property pages (usually based on `CPropertyPage` objects containing other dialog controls) to exist in the dialog box. In Figure 21.2, the property pages are in fact arranged within a `CTabCtrl` object in the Visual C++ Project Settings dialog box. The other control is a `CTreeCtrl` object, described in Chapter 20, "Listview and Treeview Controls."

FIGURE 21.1.

ClassWizard, a
`CPropertySheet`
dialog box.

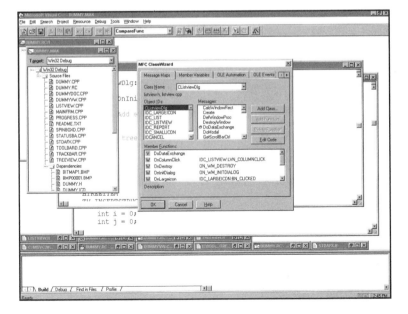

FIGURE 21.2.

Project Settings, a CTabCtrl object in a dialog box.

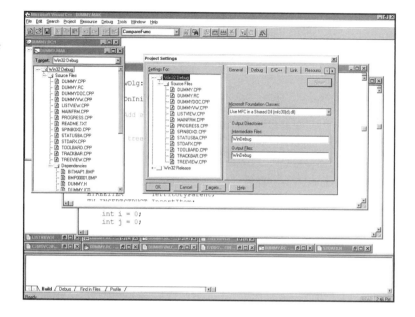

The CPropertyPage object is derived from the CDialog object. There are only a few new or overridden member functions in CPropertyPage. Generally, regardless of whether you are using CPropertySheet or CTabCtrl, you should have your pages use the CPropertyPage class rather than CDialog.

In the sample program for this chapter, I have examples of both CPropertySheet and CTabCtrl (in different dialog boxes). However, the four tab pages in both examples are the same. The examples show how easy it is to migrate between these two types of dialog boxes.

The MFC Property Sheet and the CPropertySheet Property Sheet

Visual C++ 2.x and later versions offer property sheets and property pages. You can choose to implement a CPropertySheet dialog box if the standard features of the CPropertySheet dialog box provide the functionality that you will need in your application. All controls—except for the supplied OK, Cancel, Help, and Apply buttons—must be on the CPropertyPage pages.

Here is a list of the attributes for an MFC CPropertySheet property sheet:

- CPropertySheet property sheets have default OK, Cancel, Help, and Apply buttons. No other controls may be located on the main CPropertySheet dialog box.

- CPropertySheet property sheets are easy to create and implement.

The CTabCtrl tab control offers you a fixed location on a dialog box where you can locate a set of CPropertyPage pages. Because a CTabCtrl tab control can be only one of many other dialog box controls in a single dialog box, you are not restricted to the four CPropertySheet default buttons.

The most important feature of MFC property sheets is that they are very easy to implement.

There are a number of reasons why a programmer would want to use a CTabCtrl object rather than a CPropertySheet object. Here are two of them:

1. The CTabCtrl object can be attached to windows other than those derived from CDialog. This allows you to have a special-purpose window with a property sheet.
2. Using CTabCtrl in a standard dialog box makes it easy to support other dialog box controls—something that CPropertySheet does not allow. The example I use later in this chapter has other controls in the main dialog box.

For the CPropertySheet and CTabCtrl examples, I use the sample application created in Chapter 18, "Toolbars and Status Bars." As well, the complete source for this program is found in Chapter 18.

The *CPropertySheet* Dialog Box

The CPropertySheet object is based on the CDialog dialog box class. You create the tab dialog boxes, and then CPropertySheet creates the final host dialog box. The CPropertySheet and CPropertyPage classes are not really part of the Win32 Common Controls; however, because I use CPropertyPage dialog boxes for the tabs in the tab control example, I include examples of the CPropertyPage and CPropertySheet property sheet dialog boxes as well.

To create a CPropertySheet dialog box, you must first create the property pages. Each property page takes the form of a dialog box. All dialog box controls are usable on a CPropertyPage property page. The title of the tabs for CPropertySheet are taken from the CPropertyPage dialog box titles. Figure 21.3 shows a CPropertyPage dialog box for the sample program. Actually, I have created four similar dialog boxes, differing only in name, to simulate a four-page property sheet dialog box.

NOTE

Although a CPropertyPage dialog box is essentially a standard dialog box, it never has an OK or Cancel button. These buttons are found on the parent dialog box (either the parent dialog box of the CTabCtrl control or the CPropertySheet dialog box).

FIGURE 21.3.

A CPropertyPage basic dialog box.

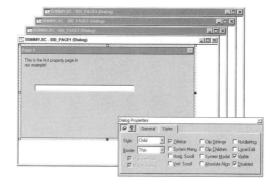

In Figure 21.3, you can see the attributes for the property sheet pages, which I refer to as simply *pages*. Here is a list of some of the critical attributes:

- Style must be set to Child, not to Popup (the default).
- Border must be set to Thin, not to Normal (the normal dialog box frame border).
- The Disabled option for the dialog box must be marked.
- The title of the dialog box is used for the text of the tab when used with the `CPropertySheet` property sheet dialog box. When used with a `CTabCtrl` tab control, the title of the dialog box is ignored unless you write code to retrieve the page's title and use the title in the tab.

NOTE

When creating a `CPropertySheet` dialog box, the size of the dialog box will be based on the first property page. You should either make all the pages the same size (the preferred method) or ensure that the first page is the largest one.

After you have created your pages, you then must bind a `CPropertyPage` handler class to each dialog box template using ClassWizard. ClassWizard, by default, uses the `CDialog` class; you must make a point of changing from `CDialog` to `CPropertyPage` when binding the page template to a class.

After you have created your page handlers using ClassWizard, you modify the `CPropertyPage` dialog handlers as needed. There is no difference between a `CPropertyPage`-managed dialog box and a `CDialog`-managed dialog box in this respect.

When the application needs to display a `CPropertySheet` dialog box, perhaps in response to a menu selection, it follows the steps shown in the code in Listing 21.1. This code is very simple and does reflect all that is necessary to create and display a `CPropertySheet` property sheet dialog box with four pages in it.

Listing 21.1. Sample code used to create a `CPropertySheet` dialog box.

```
void CDummyView::OnCommoncontrolsPropertysheet()
{
    // TODO: Add your command handler code here

    CPage1   pg1;
    CPage2   pg2;
    CPage3   pg3;
    CPage4   pg4;

    CPropertySheet PropertySheetDlg(IDS_PROPERTY_SHEET_TITLE);

    PropertySheetDlg.AddPage(&pg1);
    PropertySheetDlg.AddPage(&pg2);
    PropertySheetDlg.AddPage(&pg3);
    PropertySheetDlg.AddPage(&pg4);

    PropertySheetDlg.DoModal();
}
```

The final result of a call to the code from Listing 21.1 is shown in Figure 21.4. The pages in this dialog box are simple, but the effect is obvious.

FIGURE 21.4.

The CPropertySheet dialog box in action.

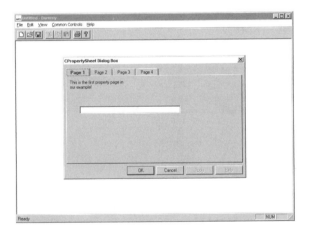

The *CTabCtrl* Class

The `CTabCtrl` class has a number of functions that allow you to create and manage a tab control in a dialog box. In this part of the chapter, I create a dialog box that has a tab control in it. This tab control has a total of four tabs (your program can have fewer or more tabs) that are used to display the four `CPropertyPage` dialog boxes created with the `CPropertySheet` example. There is no need to change any attributes of the `CPropertyPage` dialog boxes; you do not need to change the `CPropertyPage` handlers either.

NOTE

A `CTabCtrl`-based control may be located in any window that supports dialog box controls, not just a dialog box. However, I do refer to the `CTabCtrl` control as being in a dialog box in this chapter.

The steps for adding a tab control to a dialog box are much the same as adding any other control to a dialog box. First, you need a dialog box. In the sample program, I have created a very simple dialog box with four controls: an OK button, a Cancel button, a single text control, and a tab control (see Figure 21.5). The tab control occupies the majority of this dialog box and has been sized to be larger than any of the `CPropertyPage` property pages that are placed in it.

FIGURE 21.5.

A tab control in a simple dialog box.

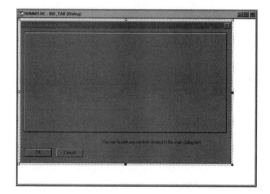

Notice that in Figure 21.5 I have moved the OK and Cancel buttons down to the bottom of the dialog box to leave room for the tab control. Placing the OK and Cancel buttons (as well as the Help and Apply buttons) at the bottom of the dialog box is recommended by Microsoft. Other controls can be placed where desired. For example, the Visual C++ Project Settings dialog box has a treeview control to the left of the tab control. I've also placed a simple text control below the tab control.

The sample tab control shows the following features of the `CTabCtrl` tab control:

1. The tab's text can set during or after tab creation.
2. The contents of the various pages in the tab control can be provided when the main dialog box is created. Note that the example dynamically creates the pages for the tab control. These pages can be kept as member variables as well.
3. The user's input can be recovered when the OK or Apply button has been selected.

The main code for the sample tab control dialog box is found in Listing 21.2 and Listing 21.3. These listings might look rather complex, but they are actually not too difficult to follow once you study them. I cover the implementation of the tab control in detail in the section after the listings.

Any changes done by hand to the code are shown in boldface type.

Listing 21.2. The TABDLG.CPP file, which implements a `CTabCtrl` tab control.

```cpp
// tabdlg.cpp : implementation file
//

#include "stdafx.h"
#include "Dummy.h"
#include "tabdlg.h"
#include "page1.h"
#include "page2.h"
#include "page3.h"
#include "page4.h"


#ifdef _DEBUG
#undef THIS_FILE
static char BASED_CODE THIS_FILE[] = __FILE__;
#endif


/////////////////////////////////////////////////////////////////////////////
// CTabDlg dialog


CTabDlg::CTabDlg(CWnd* pParent /*=NULL*/)
    : CDialog(CTabDlg::IDD, pParent)
{
    //{{AFX_DATA_INIT(CTabDlg)
        // NOTE: the ClassWizard will add member initialization here
    //}}AFX_DATA_INIT
}


void CTabDlg::DoDataExchange(CDataExchange* pDX)
{
    CDialog::DoDataExchange(pDX);
    //{{AFX_DATA_MAP(CTabDlg)
    DDX_Control(pDX, IDC_TAB, m_Tab);
    //}}AFX_DATA_MAP
}
```

```
BEGIN_MESSAGE_MAP(CTabDlg, CDialog)
    //{{AFX_MSG_MAP(CTabDlg)
    ON_NOTIFY(TCN_SELCHANGING, IDC_TAB, OnSelChangingTab)
    ON_NOTIFY(TCN_SELCHANGE,   IDC_TAB, OnSelChangeTab)
    ON_WM_DESTROY()
    //}}AFX_MSG_MAP
END_MESSAGE_MAP()


///////////////////////////////////////////////////////////////////
// CTabDlg message handlers

BOOL CTabDlg::OnInitDialog()
{
    CDialog::OnInitDialog();

    // TODO: Add extra initialization here


//    For the Tab control, we will add three tabs,
//        called 'Tab 1', 'Tab 2' and 'Tab 3'.

    TC_ITEM    TabItem;
    char       szTitle[80];

//    Method one: get title for tab from the property page
//    dialog box title:

    CPage1* pPage1;
    pPage1 = new CPage1;

    TabItem.mask = TCIF_PARAM | TCIF_TEXT;
    TabItem.lParam = (LPARAM)pPage1;
    VERIFY(pPage1->Create(CPage1::IDD, &m_Tab));
    pPage1->GetWindowText(szTitle, sizeof(szTitle));
    TabItem.pszText = szTitle;
    m_Tab.InsertItem(0, &TabItem);
    pPage1->SetWindowPos(NULL, 10, 30, 0, 0, SWP_NOSIZE | SWP_NOZORDER);
    pPage1->ShowWindow(SW_SHOW);
    pPage1->EnableWindow(TRUE);

//    Method two: get title for tab from a hard coded text string.

    TabItem.mask = TCIF_TEXT;
    TabItem.pszText = "Tab 2";
    m_Tab.InsertItem(1, &TabItem);

    CPage2* pPage2;
    pPage2 = new CPage2;
    TabItem.mask = TCIF_PARAM;
    TabItem.lParam = (LPARAM)pPage2;
    m_Tab.SetItem(1, &TabItem);
    VERIFY(pPage2->Create(CPage2::IDD, &m_Tab));
    pPage2->SetWindowPos(NULL, 10, 30, 0, 0, SWP_NOSIZE | SWP_NOZORDER);
    pPage2->ShowWindow(SW_HIDE);

    TabItem.mask = TCIF_TEXT;
    TabItem.pszText = "Tab 3";
    m_Tab.InsertItem(2, &TabItem);
```

continues

Listing 21.2. continued

```
    CPage3* pPage3;
    pPage3 = new CPage3;
    TabItem.mask = TCIF_PARAM;
    TabItem.lParam = (LPARAM)pPage3;
    m_Tab.SetItem(2, &TabItem);
    VERIFY(pPage3->Create(CPage3::IDD, &m_Tab));
    pPage3->SetWindowPos(NULL, 10, 30, 0, 0, SWP_NOSIZE ¦ SWP_NOZORDER);
    pPage3->ShowWindow(SW_HIDE);

    TabItem.mask = TCIF_TEXT;
    TabItem.pszText = "Tab 4";
    m_Tab.InsertItem(3, &TabItem);

    CPage4* pPage4;
    pPage4 = new CPage4;
    TabItem.mask = TCIF_PARAM;
    TabItem.lParam = (LPARAM)pPage4;
    m_Tab.SetItem(3, &TabItem);
    VERIFY(pPage4->Create(CPage4::IDD, &m_Tab));
    pPage4->SetWindowPos(NULL, 10, 30, 0, 0, SWP_NOSIZE ¦ SWP_NOZORDER);
    pPage4->ShowWindow(SW_HIDE);

//    Select the first tab:

    m_Tab.SetCurSel(0);

//    Finally, update the page's dialog controls:

    pPage1->m_Edit = "This is Page 1";
    pPage1->UpdateData(FALSE);

    pPage2->m_Edit = "This is Page 2";
    pPage2->UpdateData(FALSE);

    pPage3->m_Edit = "This is Page 3";
    pPage3->UpdateData(FALSE);

    pPage4->m_Edit = "This is Page 4";
    pPage4->UpdateData(FALSE);

    return TRUE;  // return TRUE unless you set the focus to a control
                  // EXCEPTION: OCX Property Pages should return FALSE
}
void CTabDlg::OnSelChangingTab(NMHDR* pNMHDR, LRESULT* pResult)
{
    // TODO: Add your control notification handler code here

    int      iTab = m_Tab.GetCurSel();
    TC_ITEM  tci;

    tci.mask = TCIF_PARAM;
    m_Tab.GetItem(iTab, &tci);
    ASSERT(tci.lParam);
```

```
        CWnd* pWnd = (CWnd *)tci.lParam;
        pWnd->ShowWindow(SW_HIDE);
        pWnd->EnableWindow(FALSE);

        *pResult = 0;
}

void CTabDlg::OnSelChangeTab(NMHDR* pNMHDR, LRESULT* pResult)
{
        // TODO: Add your control notification handler code here
        int        iTab = m_Tab.GetCurSel();
        TC_ITEM    tci;

        tci.mask = TCIF_PARAM;
        m_Tab.GetItem(iTab, &tci);
        ASSERT(tci.lParam);

        CWnd* pWnd = (CWnd *)tci.lParam;
        pWnd->ShowWindow(SW_SHOW);
        pWnd->EnableWindow(TRUE);

        *pResult = 0;
}

void CTabDlg::OnDestroy()
{
        int        iTab = 0;
        TC_ITEM tci;
        CPropertyPage * pWnd;

        tci.mask = TCIF_PARAM;

        for (iTab = 0; iTab < m_Tab.GetItemCount(); iTab++)
        {// Once for each tab that we have!
            m_Tab.GetItem(iTab, &tci);
            ASSERT(tci.lParam);
            pWnd = (CPropertyPage *)tci.lParam;

            pWnd->DestroyWindow();
            delete pWnd;
        }

        CDialog::OnDestroy();

        // TODO: Add your message handler code here
//  Kill the tab sheets first!
}

void CTabDlg::OnOK()
{
        // TODO: Add extra validation here

        int      iTab = 0;
        TC_ITEM tci;
        CPage1 * pWnd;

        tci.mask = TCIF_PARAM;
```

continues

Listing 21.2. continued

```
    for (iTab = 0; iTab < m_Tab.GetItemCount(); iTab++)
    {// Once for each tab that we have!
        m_Tab.GetItem(iTab, &tci);
        ASSERT(tci.lParam);
        pWnd = (CPage1 *)tci.lParam;

//      Get each page's data, and save as needed.
        pWnd->UpdateData(TRUE);
        AfxMessageBox(pWnd->m_Edit);
    }

    CDialog::OnOK();
}
```

Listing 21.3 is the header file that accompanies Listing 21.2. This file is short and simple and requires no explanation.

Listing 21.3. The TABDLG.H header file.

```
// tabdlg.h : header file
//

/////////////////////////////////////////////////////////////////////////////
// CTabDlg dialog

class CTabDlg : public CDialog
{
// Construction
public:
    CTabDlg(CWnd* pParent = NULL);   // standard constructor

// Dialog Data
    //{{AFX_DATA(CTabDlg)
    enum { IDD = IDD_TAB };
    CTabCtrl    m_Tab;
    //}}AFX_DATA


// Overrides
    // ClassWizard generated virtual function overrides
    //{{AFX_VIRTUAL(CTabDlg)
    protected:
    virtual void DoDataExchange(CDataExchange* pDX);     // DDX/DDV support
    //}}AFX_VIRTUAL

// Implementation
protected:

    // Generated message map functions
    //{{AFX_MSG(CTabDlg)
    virtual BOOL OnInitDialog();
    afx_msg void OnSelChangingTab(NMHDR* pNMHDR, LRESULT* pResult);
    afx_msg void OnSelChangeTab(NMHDR* pNMHDR, LRESULT* pResult);
```

```
afx_msg void OnDestroy();
virtual void OnOK();
//}}AFX_MSG
DECLARE_MESSAGE_MAP()
};
```

Implementing a *CTabCtrl* Tab Control

There is a minimal amount of code needed to implement the CTabCtrl object. You must, at the time the dialog box (the one that will have the tab control in it) is created, do the following:

1. Create a tab for each page in the tab control. Tabs may be created all at once or when adding the pages to the tab control. I chose the latter for the example because the code is better organized, keeping everything for a tab in one place.

2. Create each of the CPropertyPage dialog boxes that serve as the tab pages. If a tab will be filled using something other than dialog boxes, then create a window for the tab. Each of the CPropertyPage dialog boxes is created by allocating an object of the correct type and then calling the Create() function. After creating the property sheet, you must then attach it to the correct tab.

3. Initialize your pages. The pages should be initialized by the dialog box. Often, initialization is passed to the main dialog box, and the information is then passed to the pages as needed.

4. Do any final housekeeping tasks, such as setting the currently active tab (usually, but not always, the first tab), the text color, and the background color. You can also assign tooltips if desired.

> **NOTE**
>
> There is no rule that says you must have dialog boxes in every tab. A tab can contain any window desired; for example, you can have a tab control that shows charts with a tab for each chart type (bar chart, line graph chart, scatter chart, and so on).

Creating a *CTabCtrl* Object

When you are not using a dialog box to hold your CTabCtrl tab control, you must create your CTabCtrl object by calling the CTabCtrl::Create() member function. Here is an example:

```
m_Property sheetCtrl.Create(
    WS_CHILD | WS_VISIBLE | TCS_TABS | TCS_SINGLELINE,
    rect, this, 0);
```

The styles used include those typical to almost all windows (WS_CHILD and WS_VISIBLE) as well as styles unique to CTabCtrl objects. I chose to use the TCS_TABS style (the tab control has tabs, not buttons, and is outlined), and the TCS_SINGLELINE style, which specifies a single, scrollable (if there are too many) line of tabs.

Table 21.1 shows the styles that may be used when creating a CPropertySheet property sheet.

Table 21.1. Possible CPropertySheet window styles.

Style	Description
WS_CHILD	Always specified for a CTabCtrl tab control.
WS_VISIBLE	Usually specified for a CTabCtrl tab control.
WS_DISABLED	Rarely specified for a CTabCtrl tab control but can be used with the assumption that perhaps later the tab control will be specifically enabled.
WS_GROUP	Specifies that the tab control is the first control in a group.
WS_TABSTOP	Specifies that the control can be moved to when the user presses the Tab key.
TCS_BUTTONS	Specifies that the tab control's tabs look like buttons (not tabs).
TCS_FIXEDWIDTH	Specifies that the tabs will all be the same width.
TCS_FOCUSNEVER	Specifies that the tab never receives focus.
TCS_FOCUSONBUTTONDOWN	Specifies that the tab receives input focus when selected. This style is often used with the TCS_BUTTONS style.
TCS_FORCEICONLEFT	Forces the icon to the left, leaving the label centered.
TCS_FORCELABELLEFT	Forces the label and icon to the left.
TCS_MULTILINE	Specifies that there will be more than one line of tabs if there are more tabs than will fit on a single line. The Word for Windows property type dialog boxes have this style.
TCS_OWNERDRAWFIXED	Specifies that the tabs are drawn using the Owner Draw style.
TCS_RIGHTJUSTIFY	Specifies that the tabs are right justified.
TCS_SHAREIMAGELISTS	Specifies that the image list is shared by other controls.
TCS_TOOLTIPS	Specifies that the tab control supports tooltips.
TCS_TABS	Specifies that the tabs appear as tabs (not buttons) with a border drawn around the display area.

Style	Description
TCS_SINGLELINE	Specifies one, scrollable, line of tabs if there are more tabs than will fit on a single line. The Visual C++ property type dialog boxes have this style.
TCS_RAGGEDRIGHT	Specifies that the tabs are not stretched to fit the tab control. Generally, this leaves a gap between the last tab and the edge of the tab control.

The size of CTabCtrl is specified with the rect parameter.

The parent of the tab control is specified in the pParentWnd parameter. With C++, you can simply use the this keyword.

The CTabCtrl ID is specified with the nID parameter. This identifier is passed to the CWnd::Create() function, and it is the child window identifier value.

Once the tab control has been created, you must attach the page dialog boxes the same as you would if the tab control was located in a dialog box.

Defining the Tabs

To define and set up your tabs, you must specify the following information for the tab control:

- The handle of the CPropertyPage object for the dialog box, or the handle for the window if the tab is not being filled with a dialog box. This information is used by your application to manage the CPropertyPage objects when the user switches between different tabs.
- The text to place in the tab. Text is optional when you have an image but is highly recommended.
- The image (icon) for the tab. This is optional—tab controls seldom have images in the tabs.

Most tab controls have only text in the tabs. It is possible to have an image with the text (or just an image). The image should be sized so that it is not too large (perhaps the size of a small toolbar button) for the text or the dialog box.

The tab control is informed about each tab through the use of a TC_ITEM structure. This structure has a number of members, as shown in the following code:

```
typedef struct _TC_ITEM
{
    UINT mask;
    UINT lpReserved1;
    UINT lpReserved2;
    LPSTR pszText;
```

```
    int cchTextMax;
    int iImage;

    LPARAM lParam;
} TC_ITEM;
```

> **NOTE**
>
> The two fields marked `lpReserved1` and `lpReserved2` should not be used by your program.

The `lParam` member is usually used to point to the `CPropertyPage` object. The sample application works with the `CPropertyPage` page using this pointer. The `pszText` member is a pointer to the tab's text, and the `iImage` member is the image index from the image list.

> **NOTE**
>
> `CTabCtrl` does not control what is in a given tab. Your application must do all of the necessary management of the tabs and their contents.

You must specify for the `CTabCtrl` tab control which members are being used by supplying one or more of the flags shown in Table 21.2.

Table 21.2. The `TC_ITEM` mask values.

Value	Description
TCIF_TEXT	The `pszText` member is a pointer to the text for the tab.
TCIF_IMAGE	The `iImage` member is the index to the tab's image.
TCIF_PARAM	The `lParam` points to the `CPropertyPage` object.
TCIF_ALL	Signifies a combination of all `TCIF_` flags.
0	No members are valid.

Setting Tab Attributes

You can either create a tab and fill in the tab's attributes in one step, or you can create the tab and then, as a second step, fill in the tab's attributes. Either method is acceptable. The code fragment below shows how to create and fill in a tab in a single step:

```
CPage1* pPage1;
pPage1 = new CPage1;

TabItem.mask = TCIF_PARAM | TCIF_TEXT;
```

```
TabItem.lParam = (LPARAM)pPage1;
VERIFY(pPage1->Create(CPage1::IDD, &m_Tab));
pPage1->GetWindowText(szTitle, sizeof(szTitle));
TabItem.pszText = szTitle;
m_Tab.InsertItem(0, &TabItem);
```

Because this example does not use images, only the `lParam` and `pszText` members are assigned values. I retrieve the tab's text from the title of the dialog box template using a call to `GetWindowText()`. Remember to create the window for your page dialog box prior to calling `GetWindowText()`.

The second way to create a tab is to create an empty tab first and then fill in the tab's attributes as a second step. The code shown below illustrates this technique:

```
TabItem.mask = 0; // Nothing used here!
m_Tab.InsertItem(1, &TabItem);

CPage2* pPage2;
pPage2 = new CPage2;
TabItem.mask = TCIF_PARAM | TCIF_TEXT;
TabItem.pszText = "Tab 2";
TabItem.lParam = (LPARAM)pPage2;
m_Tab.SetItem(1, &TabItem);
```

There is a great deal of flexibility when creating the tabs in a tab control; you can add and remove tabs at any time while the tab control is in use. Of course, it is not acceptable to remove the current tab!

Once you have added your tabs, it is then necessary to manage them. The `CTabCtrl` tab control is meant to be flexible. There is no rule that says that each tab must contain a dialog box template. I put dialog box templates in the example because using dialog box templates is the most common implementation of a `CTabCtrl` tab control. The different ways to use the tabs for a `CTabCtrl` tab control is only limited by the programmer's imagination!

To provide this flexibility, the parent window (or dialog box) must handle the switching between different tabs. This is done by the tab control sending WM_NOTIFY messages to the parent window, and these messages are then processed by the window.

Unlike the dynamically created `CToolBarCtrl` control in Chapter 18, the handlers for the example in this chapter are created directly using the ClassWizard. There are three main messages sent by the `CTabCtrl` tab control. These messages are shown in Table 21.3.

Table 21.3. The `CTabCtrl` tab management WM_NOTIFY messages.

Message	Event
TCN_KEYDOWN	A key has been pressed while the control has input focus.
TCN_SELCHANGE	The current selection has changed. The `CTabCtrl` control enables and shows the new tab as needed.
TCN_SELCHANGING	The current selection will change. The `CTabCtrl` control will disable and hide the current tab as needed.

The TCN_SELCHANGING and TCN_SELCHANGE messages will always be sent in pairs. First, the TCN_SELCHANGING message is sent to allow the application to clean up, disable, and hide the old tab. Second, the TCN_SELCHANGE message is sent to allow the application to initialize, enable, and show the new tab. In both cases, the identifier of the tab is retrieved using the CTabCtrl::GetCurSel() function.

Here is the handler for the TCN_SELCHANGING message in the sample program:

```
void CTabDlg::OnSelChangingTab(NMHDR* pNMHDR, LRESULT* pResult)
{
    // TODO: Add your control notification handler code here

    int        iTab = m_Tab.GetCurSel();
    TC_ITEM    tci;

    tci.mask = TCIF_PARAM;
    m_Tab.GetItem(iTab, &tci);
    ASSERT(tci.lParam);

    CWnd* pWnd = (CWnd *)tci.lParam;
    pWnd->ShowWindow(SW_HIDE);
    pWnd->EnableWindow(FALSE);

    *pResult = 0;
}
```

The ShowWindow() and EnableWindow() functions are called in this handler to hide and disable the old tab's dialog box.

Here is the handler for the TCN_SELCHANGE message in the sample program:

```
void CTabDlg::OnSelChangeTab(NMHDR* pNMHDR, LRESULT* pResult)
{
    // TODO: Add your control notification handler code here
    int        iTab = m_Tab.GetCurSel();
    TC_ITEM    tci;

    tci.mask = TCIF_PARAM;
    m_Tab.GetItem(iTab, &tci);
    ASSERT(tci.lParam);

    CWnd* pWnd = (CWnd *)tci.lParam;
    pWnd->ShowWindow(SW_SHOW);
    pWnd->EnableWindow(TRUE);

    *pResult = 0;
}
```

The ShowWindow() and EnableWindow() functions are called in this handler to show and enable the new tab's dialog box.

Summary

In this chapter, I discussed the Win32 common controls tab control.

The tab control works very much like the property sheet dialog box object, which you create using the `CPropertySheet`. Tab controls allow the application to have a tabbed control as well as other controls in the same dialog box.

Also in this chapter, I introduced the `CPropertyPage` class, used to manage property pages for both `CTabCtrl` tab controls and the `CPropertySheet` property sheet dialog boxes.

The RichText Control and the Animation Control

by Peter D. Hipson

IN THIS CHAPTER

This final chapter on the Win32 Common Controls documents the RichText edit control and the Animation control. Both of these controls are very visual: the RichText edit control can be described (quite accurately) as a word processor in a control. The fact that there have already been several very powerful editors built using the RichText edit control shows the power of this specific control.

The RichText edit control has built-in input and output functionality. Reading an input file or writing an output file with the contents of the RichText edit control is very easy. Microsoft has given programmers easily available sample programs to do file I/O. The RichText edit control also has built-in printing support. Although print preview is limited (the MFC class that this chapter introduces does not support print preview), actual printer output is available using simple code that is easy to implement.

The Animation control provides a simple way for the user to display basic animation (but no audio). Of course, the first thing that comes to mind is now we can have cartoons in our dialog boxes! Actually, there are more serious uses for the Animation control, such as showing people, products, or properties. Imagine a real estate office being able to walk a potential customer through a house with a simple click of a button. The possibilities are endless!

This chapter is divided into three parts:

1. The RichText edit control is documented in the first part of this chapter. The example will use the CRTFEditCtrl class (which is based on CEdit) to support the RichText edit control.

2. The CRTFEditCtrl MFC class, which I wrote to support the RichText edit control. This class is not documented anywhere else, so I've added it to this chapter.

3. The Animation control and the CAnimateCtrl are documented in the final part of this chapter.

The RichText Edit Control

I can hear it now: "Hey, Peter" (that's me), "the RichText edit control is not part of the Win32 Common Controls." This is true, and I'll admit this right at the start. However, the RichText edit control is so important that I've decided to cover it as if it were a Win32 Common Control.

> **NOTE**
>
> At the time this book is written, the RichText edit control does not have MFC support. This makes it a bit difficult to use, especially for programmers who have jumped on the MFC bandwagon.

To make things a little less painful, I've written a basic MFC interface for the RichText edit control. Missing, but easy to add, is a print preview function. The WritePad example program is found on the WIN32SDK CD (from Microsoft) in the directory \WIN32SDK\MSTOOLS\SAMPLES\FRMWORK\WRITEPAD. This example shows a powerful program that uses the RTF control. The WRITEPAD program does not use MFC at all, but most of the RichText edit control code is found in one file, called RTF.C.

The RichText edit control enables a user to enter Rich Text Format (RTF) formatted text in a standard Windows edit control. The user can manipulate the text to create a document that can be as appealing as a document produced using a full-featured word processor by changing such attributes as font, color, style, and size. This control is modeled after the edit control. For the remainder of this chapter, this control is referred to as the RichText edit control.

Figure 22.1 shows an example of a RichText edit control in a dialog box. This example is from our sample program and shows a typical implementation of the RichText edit control in a dialog box. I've tried to show a number of different font attributes in this figure.

FIGURE 22.1.

A RichText edit control shown in a dialog box.

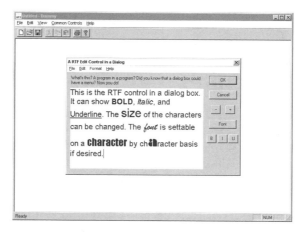

NOTE

There is a sample RTF file (called DOCUMENT.RTF) in the same directory as the DUMMY program. This sample was created using the WordPad program that comes with Windows 95. You can either type or edit the DOCUMENT.RTF file to see what native RTF documents look like. Unlike Word for Windows (and many of the newer

WYSIWYG word processors), RTF files contain only text, and can actually be modified by hand using a simple text editor. Of course, modifying an RTF document this way would be a bit tedious.

When you use a CRTFEditCtrl class object, your application will need to do a minimum amount of management of the RichText edit control. The application should initialize the current RichText edit control that is being defined (if there is any) and may optionally set the format for the RichText edit control (and if desired, read in a style document to initialize the RichText edit control). A RichText edit control has the same attributes as a regular edit control, and uses the standard attributes for dialog box controls as well.

Because there is no MFC support for the RichText edit control (as of Visual C++ 2.1), you cannot add a RichText edit control directly to a dialog box. Instead, you can create a frame control that has the size and placement of the RichText edit control. Then, you must set the frame control's attributes to hidden. Later, in your dialog box you can get the frame control's size and placement using a call to GetWindowPlacement(), and use these dimensions to locate your RichText edit control.

In the dialog box, you will have a CRTFEditCtrl class member variable (I named the CRTFEditCtrl in my example: m_RTFEdit). You can call the CRTFEditCtrl::Create() function to create the actual RichText edit control. Then use the CRTFEditCtrl object as your interface with the RichText edit control.

Implementing a RichText Edit Control

If you are using a RichText edit control in a dialog box, you must create your edit control by calling CRTFEditCtrl::Create(). Typically, because the RichText control is not supported by Visual C++, you would create a dummy frame control and then create your RichText control to the same size as the dummy frame control. If you implement a RichText edit control in a window that is not a dialog box, you need to call the CRTFEditCtrl::Create() function to create the RichText edit control. You might possibly find a use for a RichText edit control in a normal window, or perhaps as part of a toolbar.

NOTE

Most of this section assumes that Microsoft has not added the RichText edit control to MFC. If Microsoft has added a RichText edit control in MFC, then you should use its implementation rather than the one I have provided.

When Microsoft adds the RichText edit control to MFC, it will also add it to the resource editor so that you can locate a RichText edit control in a dialog box directly. You should be able to use ClassWizard to bind a RichText edit control MFC class directly to the control, instead of having to call CRTFEditCtrl::Create(), as my example shows.

Figure 22.2 shows our dialog box (in Visual C++'s resource editor), with the properties for the frame that holds the place where the RichText edit control will be located. The hidden property is easily set using the resource editor.

FIGURE 22.2.

The RichText edit control dialog box in Visual C++'s resource editor.

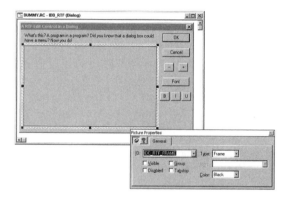

In the sample dialog box, I've done something that is rather nonstandard: I've added a menu to a dialog box. At the time this book was written, there were very few programs that sported menus in dialog boxes; in fact, it was just recently that the capability to have a menu in a dialog box was added to Windows. I have also placed a number of buttons to the right side of the dialog box. These are standard dialog box pushbuttons. The user may either use these buttons to modify the attributes of the RichText edit control's contents, or select from the menu.

When the RichText edit control is in a dialog box or in some other window, the properties for the RichEdit edit control are set when the RichText edit control is created. This is necessary because the RichText edit control is not yet supported by the resource editor, MFC, or ClassWizard.

If you look at Figure 22.2, you will see that I've added six buttons in addition to the frame that marks the spot where the RichText edit control will be placed in the dialog box.

Listing 22.1 shows the code that manages the RichText edit control sample dialog box. The base for this code was developed using ClassWizard and then modified to add the necessary features. The manual additions are marked in bold in this listing.

Listing 22.1. The RTFEDITD.CPP file.

```cpp
// rtfeditd.cpp : implementation file
//

#include "stdafx.h"
#include "Dummy.h"
#include "rtfeditd.h"

#ifdef _DEBUG
#undef THIS_FILE
static char BASED_CODE THIS_FILE[] = __FILE__;
#endif

/////////////////////////////////////////////////////////////////////////////
// CRTFEditDlg dialog


CRTFEditDlg::CRTFEditDlg(CWnd* pParent /*=NULL*/)
    : CDialog(CRTFEditDlg::IDD, pParent)
{
    //{{AFX_DATA_INIT(CRTFEditDlg)
    //}}AFX_DATA_INIT
}


void CRTFEditDlg::DoDataExchange(CDataExchange* pDX)
{
    CDialog::DoDataExchange(pDX);
    //{{AFX_DATA_MAP(CRTFEditDlg)
    DDX_Control(pDX, IDC_RTF_FRAME, m_RTF_Frame);
    //}}AFX_DATA_MAP
}


BEGIN_MESSAGE_MAP(CRTFEditDlg, CDialog)
    //{{AFX_MSG_MAP(CRTFEditDlg)
    ON_COMMAND(ID_FORMAT_BIGGER, OnFormatBigger)
    ON_COMMAND(ID_FORMAT_SMALLER, OnFormatSmaller)
    ON_COMMAND(ID_FORMAT_FONT, OnFormatFont)
    ON_COMMAND(ID_FORMAT_BOLD, OnFormatBold)
    ON_COMMAND(ID_FORMAT_ITALIC, OnFormatItalic)
    ON_COMMAND(ID_FORMAT_UNDERLINE, OnFormatUnderline)
    ON_COMMAND(ID_RTF_FILE_NEW, OnFileNew)
    ON_COMMAND(ID_RTF_FILE_OPEN, OnFileOpen)
    ON_COMMAND(ID_RTF_FILE_SAVE, OnFileSave)
    ON_COMMAND(ID_RTF_FILE_SAVE_AS, OnFileSaveAs)
    ON_COMMAND(ID_RTF_FILE_PRINT, OnFilePrint)
    ON_COMMAND(ID_RTF_FILE_PRINT_SETUP, OnFilePrintSetup)
    ON_BN_CLICKED(IDC_BIGGER, OnBigger)
    ON_BN_CLICKED(IDC_SMALLER, OnSmaller)
    ON_BN_CLICKED(IDC_FONT, OnFont)
    ON_BN_CLICKED(IDC_BOLD, OnBold)
    ON_BN_CLICKED(IDC_ITALIC, OnItalic)
    ON_BN_CLICKED(IDC_UNDERLINE, OnUnderline)
    //}}AFX_MSG_MAP
END_MESSAGE_MAP()
```

```
//////////////////////////////////////////////////////////////////////
// CRTFEditDlg message handlers

BOOL CRTFEditDlg::OnInitDialog()
{
    CDialog::OnInitDialog();

    // TODO: Add extra initialization here

//    This shows an alternative method to create our RTF edit
//    control:

    WINDOWPLACEMENT wp;
    wp.length = sizeof(wp);
    m_RTF_Frame.GetWindowPlacement(&wp);

    m_RTFEdit.Create(WS_CHILD | WS_VISIBLE |
        ES_NOHIDESEL | ES_AUTOHSCROLL | ES_AUTOVSCROLL |
        ES_MULTILINE | ES_WANTRETURN,
        wp.rcNormalPosition, this, IDC_RTFEDIT);

    return TRUE;  // return TRUE unless you set the focus to a control
                  // EXCEPTION: OCX Property Pages should return FALSE
}


void CRTFEditDlg::OnFileNew()
{
    // TODO: Add your command handler code here
    if (m_RTFEdit.CheckForDirtyContents())
    {
        m_RTFEdit.NewDocument();
    }
}

void CRTFEditDlg::OnFileOpen()
{
    // TODO: Add your command handler code here
    if (m_RTFEdit.CheckForDirtyContents())
    {
        m_RTFEdit.Open();
    }
}

void CRTFEditDlg::OnFileSave()
{
    // TODO: Add your command handler code here
    m_RTFEdit.Save();
}

void CRTFEditDlg::OnFileSaveAs()
{
    // TODO: Add your command handler code here
    // zap filename and do regular save:
    m_RTFEdit.SaveAs();
}
```

continues

Listing 22.1. continued

```
void CRTFEditDlg::OnFilePrint()
{
    // TODO: Add your command handler code here
    m_RTFEdit.Print();
}

void CRTFEditDlg::OnFilePrintSetup()
{
    // TODO: Add your command handler code here
    m_RTFEdit.SetupPrinter();
}

void CRTFEditDlg::OnFormatFont()
{
    m_RTFEdit.ChangeFont();
}

void CRTFEditDlg::OnFormatBold()
{
    // TODO: Add your command handler code here
    m_RTFEdit.ChangeCharAttribute(CFM_BOLD, CFE_BOLD);
}

void CRTFEditDlg::OnFormatItalic()
{
    // TODO: Add your command handler code here
    m_RTFEdit.ChangeCharAttribute(CFM_ITALIC, CFE_ITALIC);
}

void CRTFEditDlg::OnFormatUnderline()
{
    // TODO: Add your command handler code here
    m_RTFEdit.ChangeCharAttribute(CFM_UNDERLINE, CFE_UNDERLINE);
}

void CRTFEditDlg::OnFormatBigger()
{
    // TODO: Add your command handler code here
    m_RTFEdit.ChangeSizeAttribute(2);
}

void CRTFEditDlg::OnFormatSmaller()
{
    // TODO: Add your command handler code here
    m_RTFEdit.ChangeSizeAttribute(-2);
}

void CRTFEditDlg::OnBigger()
{
    // TODO: Add your control notification handler code here
    m_RTFEdit.ChangeSizeAttribute(2);
}

void CRTFEditDlg::OnSmaller()
{
    // TODO: Add your control notification handler code here
    m_RTFEdit.ChangeSizeAttribute(-2);
```

```
}

void CRTFEditDlg::OnBold()
{
    // TODO: Add your control notification handler code here
    m_RTFEdit.ChangeCharAttribute(CFM_BOLD, CFE_BOLD);
}

void CRTFEditDlg::OnFont()
{
    // TODO: Add your control notification handler code here
    m_RTFEdit.ChangeFont();
}

void CRTFEditDlg::OnItalic()
{
    // TODO: Add your control notification handler code here
    m_RTFEdit.ChangeCharAttribute(CFM_ITALIC, CFE_ITALIC);
}

void CRTFEditDlg::OnUnderline()
{
    // TODO: Add your control notification handler code here
    m_RTFEdit.ChangeCharAttribute(CFM_UNDERLINE, CFE_UNDERLINE);
}
```

CAUTION

You may be tempted to use the `CRTFEditCtrl` class with the standard `DDX_` dialog box control data exchange management routines. Don't do it! Although this will create the RichText edit control, the control will not work correctly.

After Microsoft has added a RichText edit control to MFC, it will make the necessary changes to the `DDX_` dialog box data exchange management routines.

Listing 22.2 shows the RTFEDITD.H header file that accompanies the RTFEDITD.CPP file shown in Listing 22.1. The RTFEDITD.H file was modified only by ClassWizard, and there were manual additions for the menu command handlers as well. The manual additions are marked in bold in this listing.

Listing 22.2. The RTFEDITD.H file.

```
// rtfeditd.h : header file
//

//////////////////////////////////////////////////////////////////////
// CRTFEditDlg dialog

class CRTFEditDlg : public CDialog
```

continues

Listing 22.2. continued

```
{
// Construction
public:
    CRTFEditDlg(CWnd* pParent = NULL);    // standard constructor

// Dialog Data
    //{{AFX_DATA(CRTFEditDlg)
    enum { IDD = IDD_RTF };
    CStatic    m_RTF_Frame;
    //}}AFX_DATA

    CRTFEditCtrl    m_RTFEdit;

// Overrides
    // ClassWizard generated virtual function overrides
    //{{AFX_VIRTUAL(CRTFEditDlg)
    protected:
    virtual void DoDataExchange(CDataExchange* pDX);    // DDX/DDV support
    //}}AFX_VIRTUAL

// Implementation
protected:

    // Generated message map functions
    //{{AFX_MSG(CRTFEditDlg)
    virtual BOOL OnInitDialog();
    afx_msg void OnFormatBigger();
    afx_msg void OnFormatSmaller();
    afx_msg void OnFormatFont();
    afx_msg void OnFormatBold();
    afx_msg void OnFormatItalic();
    afx_msg void OnFormatUnderline();
    afx_msg void OnFileNew();
    afx_msg void OnFileOpen();
    afx_msg void OnFileSave();
    afx_msg void OnFileSaveAs();
    afx_msg void OnFilePrint();
    afx_msg void OnFilePrintSetup();
    afx_msg void OnBigger();
    afx_msg void OnSmaller();
    afx_msg void OnFont();
    afx_msg void OnBold();
    afx_msg void OnItalic();
    afx_msg void OnUnderline();
    //}}AFX_MSG
    DECLARE_MESSAGE_MAP()
};
```

The *CRTFEditCtrl* Class in a Dialog Box

As stated earlier, as with other dialog box controls, you would usually bind an edit control to a CEdit class object. However, MFC does not support RichText edit controls. Therefore, you must write the code to create your RichText edit control. The following techniques could be used in any number of situations where you need to locate a special-purpose window (or dialog control) in a dialog box, and the window must be sized correctly.

To locate a RichText edit control or any other non-supported window in a dialog box, follow these steps:

1. First, create and locate a frame control where the RichText edit control will be located. Give this frame control its own identifier (don't use IDC_STATIC because ClassWizard will ignore controls with the IDC_STATIC identifier). Size the frame window to fill the area where you want your RichText edit control to be. When the dialog box is displayed on systems of different resolutions (or where there are other considerations that cause the absolute size of the dialog box to be changed), this frame control will also be resized proportionally. Mark this frame as hidden.

2. Use ClassWizard to bind a CStatic class object to your frame window.

3. In your WM_INITDIALOG handler, get the size of the frame window with a call to GetWindowPlacement(). This function is passed a single parameter, the pointer to a WINDOWPLACEMENT structure, which will be filled in.

   ```
   WINDOWPLACEMENT wp;
   wp.length = sizeof(wp);
   m_RTF_Frame.GetWindowPlacement(&wp);
   ```

4. The WINDOWPLACEMENT member rcNormalPosition will have the coordinates to the frame window. This member may then be passed directly to any CWnd::Create() call. Your CRTFEditCtrl class is derived from CEdit, and CEdit is in turn derived from CWnd.

After you have created your frame control (which is really only used to find the size for the RichText edit control), you can then create your CRTFEditCtrl object in the OnInitDialog() function.

```
BOOL CRTFEditDlg::OnInitDialog()
{
    CDialog::OnInitDialog();

    // TODO: Add extra initialization here

//    This shows an alternative method to create our RTF edit
//    control:

    WINDOWPLACEMENT wp;
    wp.length = sizeof(wp);
    m_RTF_Frame.GetWindowPlacement(&wp);

    m_RTFEdit.Create(WS_CHILD | WS_VISIBLE | ES_MULTILINE,
        wp.rcNormalPosition, this, IDC_RTFEDIT);

    return TRUE;   // return TRUE unless you set the focus to a control
                   // EXCEPTION: OCX Property Pages should return FALSE
}
```

A rather normal call to `CRTFEditCtrl::Create()` in your application does the work. (You will see the actual `Create()` function in the next part of this chapter.) When calling `Create()`, you can use the standard window styles and several styles that are unique to the RichText edit control. These styles are shown in Table 22.1.

Table 22.1. Styles for the RichText edit control.

Style	*Description*
ES_AUTOHSCROLL	This style will cause the RichText edit control to scroll automatically when the user tries to move beyond the visual area of the RichText edit control at the end of a line. The RichText edit control will not scroll past the end of the current line, or past the beginning of the current line. This style is recommended in any RichText edit control that is expected to have more characters than will fit within the width of the control. If you want to have a scrollbar, you should also specify the WS_HSCROLL style when creating your RichText edit control. Although a horizontal scrollbar is not required, if the control is expected to hold lines that are longer than the width of the RichText edit control, having a scrollbar may make the control more user friendly.
ES_AUTOVSCROLL	This style will cause the RichText edit control to scroll automatically when the user tries to move beyond the visual area of the RichText edit control at the top or bottom of the displayed text. The RichText edit control will not scroll past the top, or beyond the bottom of the text. This style is recommended in any multiline RichText edit control. To provide for a scrollbar, you should also specify the WS_VSCROLL style when you create your RichText edit control. Although a vertical scrollbar is not required, if the control is expected to hold a great deal of text, then having a scrollbar may make the control more user friendly.
ES_MULTILINE	This tells Windows to create a multiline RichText edit control. The default is to create a single-line RichText edit control. As with any other edit control, to use the Enter key as a carriage return you must specify the ES_WANTRETURN style.
ES_NOHIDESEL	The default for a RichText edit control is to hide the selection when any other control gets input focus. However, because your application will probably have buttons and menus to

Style	Description
	modify the attributes of the text in the RichText edit control, you will want to specify this flag. This flag tells Windows not to hide the current selection when another control gets the focus.
ES_WANTRETURN	The default action is to have the Enter key activate the default button (the OK button in most dialog boxes). The ES_WANTRETURN style specifies that the RichText edit control is to get the Enter key instead of the default button. This enables the user to simply press the Enter key, instead of having to specify Ctrl+Enter.

Although the preceding section covers the window options for the RichText edit control, the control lends itself to being initialized by the application. Most applications use an input stream (see the following section for more information about streaming) to initialize their RichText edit controls. You can use an initialization stream to set font, style, and other attributes.

Using the *CRTFEditCtrl* RichText Edit Control Object

The CRTFEditCtrl RichText edit control takes input from the user (typed text and text attributes) or from an RTF file that the user specifies and displays the user's input. The RichText edit control is also able to save the RichText edit control's contents to a file. Printed output is managed with only a minimum amount of programmer intervention (your application must be able to manage pages when a RTF document has more than one page of printed output).

However, the RichText edit control's entire management interface consists of Windows messages, which is not the most convenient interface for the programmer. To be fair, all dialog box controls are really managed using Windows messages. The rub is that the RichText edit control has not had an MFC class created for it (until now, because this chapter introduces a simple MFC class object to manage a RichText edit control).

Rather than creating a lengthy reference section in a chapter that is really tutorial, I list the RichText edit control messages in Table 22.2. Each message includes a brief description, but for further information you should refer to the Win32 help file.

Table 22.2. The RichText edit control messages.

Message	Description
EM_CANPASTE	This message determines whether your RichText edit control can paste a specified clipboard format or not.
EM_DISPLAYBAND	This message is used to display a portion of your RichText edit control's text. This text must have already been formatted for a device using a EM_FORMATRANGE message.
EM_EXGETSEL	This message retrieves the starting and ending character positions of the selection in your RichText edit control.
EM_EXLIMITTEXT	This message sets an upper limit to the amount of text in your RichText edit control.
EM_EXLINEFROMCHAR	This message determines which line contains a given character in your RichText edit control.
EM_EXSETSEL	This message selects a range of characters in your RichText edit control.
EM_FINDTEXT	This message finds a specified piece of text within your RichText edit control contents.
EM_FINDWORDBREAK	This message will find the next word break before or after the position specified, or retrieves information about the character at that position.
EM_FORMATRANGE	This message formats a range of text in your RichText edit control for a specific device.
EM_GETCHARFORMAT	This message determines the current character formatting in your RichText edit control.
EM_GETEVENTMASK	This message retrieves the event mask for a RichText edit control.
EM_GETOLEINTERFACE	This message retrieves an IRichEditOle object that a client can use to access your RichText edit control's OLE functionality.
EM_GETPARAFORMAT	This message retrieves the paragraph formatting of the currently selected text in your RichText edit control.
EM_GETSELTEXT	This message retrieves the currently selected text in your RichText edit control.
EM_GETTEXTRANGE	This message retrieves a specified range of characters from your RichText edit control.
EM_HIDESELECTION	This message hides or shows the selection in your RichText edit control.

Message	Description
EM_PASTESPECIAL	This message pastes a specific clipboard format in your RichText edit control.
EM_REQUESTRESIZE	This message forces your RichText edit control to send an EN_REQUESTRESIZE notification message to its parent window. The parent window must be able to respond to the EN_REQUESTRESIZE message.
EM_SELECTIONTYPE	This message determines the selection type for your RichText edit control.
EM_SETBKGNDCOLOR	This message sets the background color for your RichText edit control.
EM_SETCHARFORMAT	This message sets character formatting in your RichText edit control.
EM_SETEVENTMASK	This message sets the event mask for your RichText edit control.
EM_SETOLEINTERFACE	This message gives your RichText edit control an IRichEditOleCallback object that the control uses to get OLE-related resources and information from the client.
EM_SETPARAFORMAT	This message sets the paragraph formatting for the current selection in your RichText edit control.
EM_SETTARGETDEVICE	This message sets the target device and line width used for WYSIWYG formatting in your RichText edit control.
EM_STREAMIN	This message reads a RichText file and uses it to replace the contents of your RichText edit control.
EM_STREAMOUT	This message writes the contents of your RichText edit control to the specified data stream.

Differences Between RichText Edit Controls and Regular Edit Controls

There are some functions that regular edit controls support and RichText edit controls do not. The following list shows these differences, which are listed by standard edit control messages:

- EM_FMTLINES—This functionality is not supported.

- EM_GETHANDLE—Because a RichText edit control does not store its contents in a text array, there is no pointer to the control's contents.

- ▓ EM_GETMARGINS—This functionality is not supported.

- ▓ EM_GETPASSWORDCHAR—The password functionality is not supported.

- ▓ EM_SETHANDLE—Because a RichText edit control does not store its contents in a text array, there is no pointer to the control's contents.

- ▓ EM_SETMARGINS—This functionality is not supported.

- ▓ EM_SETPASSWORDCHAR—The password functionality is not supported.

- ▓ EM_SETRECTNP—This functionality is not supported.

- ▓ EM_SETTABSTOPS—The RichText edit control uses the EM_SETPARAFORMAT message.

- ▓ WM_CTLCOLOR—The RichText edit control uses the EM_SETBKGNDCOLOR message.

- ▓ WM_GETFONT—The RichText edit control uses the EM_GETCHARFORMAT message.

The following edit control window styles are not supported by the RichText edit control:

```
ES_LOWERCASE
ES_UPPERCASE
ES_PASSWORD
ES_OEMCONVERT
```

The RichText Edit Control Input and Output

The RichText edit control uses the two messages EM_STREAMIN and EM_STREAMOUT to perform file I/O. Most (but not all) of the file reading and writing is managed by the RichText edit control. However, your application must provide a callback routine that is used to read or write the text.

The application will pass a pointer to an EDITSTREAM structure when the application uses the EM_STREAMIN and EM_STREAMOUT messages. The structure's member pfnCallback will have a pointer to the function that is to be used to perform the necessary file manipulation. The dwCookie member may be used by the application (and its callback function) as needed. Most applications will use dwCookie to hold the handle for the file that is being used. The dwError member is non-zero if there were errors.

```
typedef struct _editstream {
    DWORD dwCookie;
    DWORD dwError;
    EDITSTREAMCALLBACK pfnCallback;
} EDITSTREAM;
```

The callback function to write the RichText edit control's contents to a file would typically look like the one shown in the following code fragment. Notice that there is minimal error checking used.

```
DWORD CALLBACK SaveCallback
    (DWORD dwCookie, LPCSTR pbBuff, LONG cb, LONG *pcb)
{
```

```
    _lwrite((HFILE)dwCookie, pbBuff, cb);
    return(0);
}
```

If the callback function (when writing the stream) returns a non-zero value, then the RichText edit control will continue to write output. If there is an error, or for some other reason no further output should be written to the file, then the callback function should return zero. In most situations the callback will be called only one time to write the RichText edit control contents.

The callback function to read the RichText edit control's contents from a file would typically look like the one shown in the following code fragment. Notice that there is minimal error checking used in this example as well.

```
DWORD CALLBACK OpenCallback
    (DWORD dwCookie, LPBYTE pbBuff, LONG cb, LONG *pcb)
{
// Read as much data as allowed in the cb variable
    *pcb = _lread((HFILE)dwCookie, pbBuff, cb);

    if(*pcb < cb)
    {// If done, say:
        return (0);     // All done!
    }

    return *pcb;  // Otherwise say: There is more to read!
}
```

The callback function (when reading from a stream) returns a count of the number of characters read. When a non-zero value is returned, then the RichText edit control will continue to read from the file. If there is an error, or for some other reason no further input should be read from the file, then the callback function should return zero. In most situations the callback will be called more than one time to read the RichText edit control contents. Calling the read callback function more than one time is necessary because the RichText edit control does not know how much text is present in the input file.

The RichText Edit Control Interaction

Typically, the user will interact with the RichText edit control by using accelerator keys (your application will define keys, for example, such as Ctrl+B, as bold), buttons (either dialog box or toolbar), or menu selections. Most applications will offer more than one way to interact because user preferences vary.

Our example program's RTF dialog box has a menu, and also offers dialog buttons to control basic character formatting. Because this was a dialog box, I chose to use dialog buttons rather than a toolbar because dialog buttons are easier to implement.

Generally, you will always want to implement the basic controls (font selection, bold, italic, underline, and resizing) for most RTF edit controls. After all, if you don't allow the user to set the control's contents, you may as well use a standard edit control.

In the next section of this chapter, you will review the CRTFEditCtrl class object that I've created to manage the RichText edit control.

The *CRTFEditCtrl* Class

When this book was written, Microsoft had not yet provided an MFC class to manage the RichText edit control. This is unfortunate. However, because you have purchased this book, you now have a basic RichText edit control management class, CRTFEditCtrl.

The CRTFEditCtrl class that I have written is basic—it represents only about two days of programming effort—and could be improved upon greatly. However, with the CRTFEditCtrl class you can utilize virtually all of the RichText edit control's features.

When you use CRTFEditCtrl, you should keep in mind that this class is derived from CEdit, which is in turn derived from CWnd. All the member functions of the CEdit and the CWnd classes are available. Not all CEdit member functions will function correctly with the RichText edit control. My CRTFEditCtrl class object does not attempt to mask off any CEdit member function that could cause problems or simply is not useful.

What Is the *CRTFEditCtrl* Class Object

The CRTFEditCtrl class object is an MFC-based object derived from the CEdit class. The CRTFEditCtrl control fills the void left when Microsoft was unable to complete a proper MFC RichText edit control management class. To be fair, Microsoft could not create this class until the RichText edit control was officially released—this happened with the release of Windows 95.

The CRTFEditCtrl class offers both basic functions (such as Create()) and functions that are specific to the RichText edit control, including character attribute management functions. The next sections of this chapter are a reference to the inputs, outputs, and purpose of the CRTFEditCtrl member functions.

The *CRTFEditCtrl* Members

There are 16 member functions in the CRTFEditCtrl class. Of these, the constructor and destructor are not normally used by programmers. There are several member functions that are intended to be called by other CRTFEditCtrl member functions only. And there are three callback functions that are outside the class definition, for the simple reason that a callback function cannot be a class member function.

If you derive a new class based on the CRTFEditCtrl, you should make sure that if you override the Create() function that your code creates a window with the correct class name.

Create(DWORD dwStyle, const RECT& rect, CWnd* pParentWnd, UINT nID)

The `Create()` member function takes four parameters, all of which are required. The `Create()` function is used to create a RichText edit control window. The function prototype for `Create()` is

```
BOOL Create(
    DWORD dwStyle,
    const RECT& rect,
    CWnd* pParentWnd,
    UINT nID)
```

Where:

> *dwStyle* is the window's style. The RichText edit control styles were described in Table 22.1.

> *rect* is a RECT structure that contains the coordinates for the RichText edit control's window.

> *pParentWnd* is the parent window's CWnd.

> *nID* is the window's ID. This ID is like a dialog box control's ID.

The return value is the return from `CWnd::Create()`, which indicates the success of the `Create()` function. A non-zero value indicates success. You should check the return value to ensure that the window was actually created.

The `Create()` function returns a non-zero value if the window was created successfully, or zero if the `Create()` function fails for any reason. The CWnd data variable members will be filled in as appropriate (m_hWnd for example).

The following code shows that `CRTFEditCtrl::Create()` calls the `CWnd::Create()` function to create the window. The window style is defined with the character constant `T("RichEdit")`, while the styles, location and size, and parent window's CWnd are passed to `Create()`.

```
BOOL CRTFEditCtrl::Create(DWORD dwStyle, const RECT& rect, CWnd* pParentWnd,
    UINT nID)
{
    return CWnd::Create(_T("RichEdit"), NULL, dwStyle, rect, pParentWnd, nID);
}
```

You can add whatever other code to the `Create()` function that you feel is necessary; however, in most situations you will find that the preceding simple function is all that is required.

GetCharAttribute(DWORD dwMask, DWORD dwEffects)

The GetCharAttribute() member function takes two parameters, both of which are required. This function is used to determine whether the characters have the specified attribute. The function prototype for GetCharAttribute() is

```
int GetCharAttribute(
    DWORD dwMask,
    DWORD dwEffects)
```

Where:

> dwMask is a mask value that indicates which effects are desired. Any of the mask values indicated in Table 22.3 may be used (use an OR to separate multiple mask values).

> dwEffects is the effect for which you are checking. The effect value may be one of the values indicated in Table 22.4.

The GetCharAttribute() function returns one of the following values. These identifiers are defined in the CRTFEditCtrl header file.

- CHAR_ATTRIB_YES—All the characters have the attribute(s) specified.
- CHAR_ATTRIB_NO—None of the characters have the attribute(s) specified.
- CHAR_ATTRIB_WAFFLE—Some, but not all, of the characters have the attribute(s) specified.

The code for GetCharAttribute() is shown in the following listing:

```
int CRTFEditCtrl::GetCharAttribute(DWORD dwMask, DWORD dwEffects)
{
    CHARFORMAT CharacterFormat;

    SetFocus();
    ::SendMessage(m_hWnd, EM_GETCHARFORMAT, TRUE, (LPARAM)&CharacterFormat);

    if (CharacterFormat.dwMask & dwMask)
    {
        if (CharacterFormat.dwEffects & dwEffects)
        {
            return (CHAR_ATTRIB_YES);
        }
        else
        {
            return (CHAR_ATTRIB_NO);
        }
    }
    else
    {
        return (CHAR_ATTRIB_WAFFLE);
    }
}
```

The call to SetFocus() is used to return focus to the RichText edit control. This was done so that dialog box controls that are used to set character attributes would return focus to the RichText edit control and not leave focus to the character-setting dialog box control.

Table 22.3 shows the `dwMask` parameter values that are supported by the RichText edit control.

Table 22.3. The values for the `dwMask` parameter.

Parameter	Description
CFM_BOLD	Specifies that the bold effect is valid
CFM_COLOR	Specifies that the text color (`crTextColor`) member and the `CFE_AUTOCOLOR` effect are valid
CFM_FACE	Specifies that the typeface name (`szFaceName`) member is valid
CFM_ITALIC	Specifies that the italic effect is valid
CFM_OFFSET	Specifies that the `yOffset` member is valid
CFM_PROTECTED	Specifies that the protected effect is valid
CFM_SIZE	Specifies that the `yHeight` member is valid
CFM_STRIKEOUT	Specifies that the strikeout effect is valid
CFM_UNDERLINE	Specifies that the underline effect is valid

Table 22.4 shows the `dwEffects` parameter values that are supported by the RichText edit control.

Table 22.4. The values for the `dwEffects` parameter.

Attribute	Description
CFE_AUTOCOLOR	The text color is returned, using `crTextColor`.
CFE_BOLD	Characters are bold.
CFE_ITALIC	Characters are italic.
CFE_STRIKEOUT	Characters are struck out.
CFE_UNDERLINE	Characters are underlined.
CFE_PROTECTED	The characters are write protected. If the user makes any attempt to change these characters, an EN_PROTECTED notification message will result.

Also see `ChangeCharAttribute()` in the next section for information about changing the attributes of characters.

ChangeCharAttribute(DWORD dwMask, DWORD dwEffects)

The ChangeCharAttribute() member function takes two parameters, both of which are required. This function will change the attributes of the characters in the current selection. The function prototype for ChangeCharAttribute() is

```
ChangeCharAttribute(
    DWORD dwMask,
    DWORD dwEffects)
```

Where:

> dwMask is a mask value that indicates which effects are desired. Any of the mask values indicated in Table 22.3 may be used (use an OR to separate multiple mask values).

> dwEffects is the effect for which you are checking. The effect value may be one of the values indicated in Table 22.4.

This function has no return value. The code for ChangeCharAttribute() is shown in the following listing:

```
void CRTFEditCtrl::ChangeCharAttribute(DWORD dwMask, DWORD dwEffects)
{
    CHARFORMAT CharacterFormat;

    CharacterFormat.cbSize = sizeof(CharacterFormat);

    SetFocus();
    ::SendMessage(m_hWnd, EM_GETCHARFORMAT, TRUE, (LPARAM)&CharacterFormat);

    // Tell the RTF control which attribute to change.
    CharacterFormat.dwMask      = dwMask;

    // Flip the bits
    CharacterFormat.dwEffects   ^= dwEffects;

    // Set the new attribute(s):
    ::SendMessage(m_hWnd, EM_SETCHARFORMAT, SCF_SELECTION,
        (LPARAM)&CharacterFormat);
}
```

The call to SetFocus() is used to return focus to the RichText edit control. This was done so that dialog box controls which are used to set character attributes would return focus to the RichText edit control and not leave focus to the character-setting dialog box control.

Also see GetCharAttribute() in the previous section for information about how to retrieve character attributes.

ChangeSizeAttribute(int iPointChange)

The ChangeSizeAttribute() member function takes one parameter. The function prototype for ChangeSizeAttribute() is

```
void ChangeSizeAttribute(
    int iPointChange)
```

Where:

iPointChange is the amount to change the size of the characters. Use a negative value to make the characters smaller.

This function has no return value. The code for `ChangeSizeAttribute()` is shown in the following listing:

```
void CRTFEditCtrl::ChangeSizeAttribute(int iPointChange)
{
    CHARFORMAT CharacterFormat;

    CharacterFormat.cbSize = sizeof(CHARFORMAT);

    CharacterFormat.cbSize = sizeof(CharacterFormat);

    SetFocus();
    if (::SendMessage(m_hWnd, EM_GETCHARFORMAT, TRUE,
        (LPARAM)&CharacterFormat) == 0)
    {
        TRACE("EM_GETCHARFORMAT failed\n");
    }

    CharacterFormat.dwMask      = CFM_SIZE;

    if (((CharacterFormat.yHeight + 20*iPointChange) <= (128*20))  &&
        ((CharacterFormat.yHeight + 20*iPointChange) >= (6*20)))
    {
        CharacterFormat.yHeight += 20*iPointChange;
    }

    if (::SendMessage(
        m_hWnd, EM_SETCHARFORMAT, SCF_SELECTION,
        (LPARAM)&CharacterFormat) == 0)
    {
        TRACE("EM_SETCHARFORMAT failed\n");
    }
}
```

The call to `SetFocus()` is used to return focus to the RichText edit control. This was done so that dialog box controls which are used to set character attributes would return focus to the RichText edit control and not leave focus to the character-setting dialog box control.

There are minimum and maximum values for character sizes, as the listing shows.

ChangeFont()

The `ChangeFont()` member function takes no parameters. It will display the common dialog box for fonts, which the user can use to alter the font and the font's attributes. The function prototype for `ChangeFont()` is

```
void ChangeFont()
```

This function has no return value and no parameters. The code for `ChangeFont()` is shown in the following listing:

```
void CRTFEditCtrl::ChangeFont()
{// No parameters!
    CHARFORMAT CharacterFormat;
    CHOOSEFONT ChooseFontStruct;
    LOGFONT    lf;
    HDC        hDC;

    CharacterFormat.cbSize = sizeof(CharacterFormat);

    ::SendMessage(m_hWnd, EM_GETCHARFORMAT, TRUE, (LPARAM)&CharacterFormat);

    // Fill in the CHOOSEFONT structure for the font common fialog

    ZeroMemory(&ChooseFontStruct, sizeof(CHOOSEFONT));
    ZeroMemory(&lf, sizeof(LOGFONT));

    hDC = ::GetDC(GetParent()->m_hWnd); // Need a screen DC, use the parent's DC

    // The RTF Edit control measures in twips, but LOGFONT measures
    // in logical units (here, pixels) so we must convert.
    //    1 point == 20 twips
    //    1 inch  == 72 points
    //      ==> 1 inch  == 1440 twips

    lf.lfHeight = MulDiv(CharacterFormat.yHeight,
        GetDeviceCaps(hDC, LOGPIXELSY), -1440);

    // Done with this
    ::ReleaseDC(GetParent()->m_hWnd, hDC);

    // Set up the rest of the logfont structure according to the
    // information retrieved from the EM_GETCHARFORMAT message

    if (CharacterFormat.dwEffects & CFE_BOLD)
        lf.lfWeight = FW_BOLD;
    else
        lf.lfWeight = FW_NORMAL;

    lf.lfItalic = (BOOL)(CharacterFormat.dwEffects & CFE_ITALIC);
    lf.lfUnderline = (BOOL)(CharacterFormat.dwEffects & CFE_UNDERLINE);
    lf.lfCharSet = ANSI_CHARSET;
    lf.lfQuality = DEFAULT_QUALITY;
    lf.lfPitchAndFamily = CharacterFormat.bPitchAndFamily;
    lstrcpy(lf.lfFaceName, CharacterFormat.szFaceName);

    // Fire up the common dialog.

    ChooseFontStruct.lStructSize = sizeof(ChooseFontStruct);
    ChooseFontStruct.hwndOwner = GetParent()->m_hWnd;

    ChooseFontStruct.hDC = GetCurrentPrinterDC();

    ChooseFontStruct.lpLogFont = &lf;
    ChooseFontStruct.Flags = CF_BOTH | CF_SCALABLEONLY | CF_WYSIWYG
        | CF_NOVECTORFONTS | CF_INITTOLOGFONTSTRUCT;
    ChooseFontStruct.rgbColors = RGB(0,0,0);
```

```
ChooseFontStruct.nFontType = 0;

if (ChooseFont(&ChooseFontStruct))
{
    // Set the dwMask parameter to tell the
    // RTF Edit control to pay attention to the font format:
    CharacterFormat.dwMask = CFM_BOLD | CFM_FACE | CFM_ITALIC |
        CFM_OFFSET | CFM_SIZE | CFM_UNDERLINE;

    // ChooseFont returns the new point size in
    // tenths of a point so we can multiply by 2
    // to get twips for the richedit control.

    CharacterFormat.yHeight = 2 * ChooseFontStruct.iPointSize;

    CharacterFormat.dwEffects = 0;

    if (lf.lfWeight >= FW_BOLD)
        CharacterFormat.dwEffects |= CFE_BOLD;

    if (lf.lfItalic)
        CharacterFormat.dwEffects |= CFE_ITALIC;

    if (lf.lfUnderline)
        CharacterFormat.dwEffects |= CFE_UNDERLINE;

    CharacterFormat.bPitchAndFamily = lf.lfPitchAndFamily;

    lstrcpy(CharacterFormat.szFaceName, lf.lfFaceName);

    // Set the new formatting to the RTF control:
    ::SendMessage(m_hWnd, EM_SETCHARFORMAT, SCF_SELECTION,
        (LPARAM)&CharacterFormat);

}

if (ChooseFontStruct.hDC)
    DeleteDC(ChooseFontStruct.hDC);
}
```

This function works by getting the font for the current selection and passing the font information to the fonts common dialog box.

GetFileName(LPSTR szFileName, BOOL bOpen)

The GetFileName() member function requires two parameters. The function prototype for GetFileName() is

```
private: BOOL GetFileName(
    LPSTR szFileName,
    BOOL bOpen)
```

Where:

> szFileName is the filename for the user's document. This field is both input and output.

bOpen is a flag that tells GetFileName() whether the file is being used for input or output.

This function returns TRUE if a valid filename is returned. The code for GetFileName() is shown in the following listing:

```
BOOL CRTFEditCtrl::GetFileName(LPSTR szFileName, BOOL bOpen)
{
    OPENFILENAME OpenFileName;

    OpenFileName.lStructSize        = sizeof(OPENFILENAME);
    OpenFileName.hwndOwner          = (HWND)m_hWnd;
    OpenFileName.hInstance          = NULL;
    OpenFileName.lpstrFilter        = "RTF Files (*.RTF)\0*.RTF\0";
    OpenFileName.lpstrCustomFilter  = (LPSTR)NULL;
    OpenFileName.nMaxCustFilter     = 0L;
    OpenFileName.nFilterIndex       = 1L;
    OpenFileName.lpstrFile          = szFileName;
    OpenFileName.nMaxFile           = 256;
    OpenFileName.lpstrFileTitle     = NULL;
    OpenFileName.nMaxFileTitle      = 0;
    OpenFileName.lpstrInitialDir    = NULL;
    OpenFileName.lpstrTitle         = (LPSTR)NULL;
    OpenFileName.Flags              = OFN_HIDEREADONLY | OFN_PATHMUSTEXIST;
    OpenFileName.nFileOffset        = 0;
    OpenFileName.nFileExtension     = 0;
    OpenFileName.lpstrDefExt        = (LPSTR)"RTF";
    OpenFileName.lCustData          = 0L;
    OpenFileName.lpfnHook           = 0L;  // Zero eliminates compiler warnings
    OpenFileName.lpTemplateName     = (LPSTR)NULL;

    if (bOpen)
    {
        return GetOpenFileName (&OpenFileName);
    }
    else
    {
        return GetSaveFileName(&OpenFileName);
    }
}
```

The call to SetFocus() is used to return focus to the RichText edit control. This was done so that dialog box controls which are used to set character attributes would return focus to the RichText edit control and not leave focus to the character-setting dialog box control.

A call to either GetOpenFileName() or GetSaveFileName() is made depending on the value of the bOpen parameter.

Save()

The Save() member function takes no parameters. The function prototype for Save() is

```
BOOL Save()
```

This function returns TRUE if the save was successful. This function will call the GetFileName() function (see the preceding section) to get a filename if the document has no filename assigned to it.

```
BOOL CRTFEditCtrl::Save()
{
    HFILE          hFile;  // File handle
    OFSTRUCT       OpenFileName;     // open file strucuture
    EDITSTREAM     es;     // The EDITSTREAM structure

    if(m_szFileName[0] || GetFileName(m_szFileName, FALSE))
    {// Open the file, erasing previous contents
        hFile = OpenFile(m_szFileName, &OpenFileName, OF_CREATE);

        // Set up the EDITSTREAM structure
        es.dwCookie    = (DWORD)hFile;  // our file handle
        es.dwError     = 0;             // No error
        es.pfnCallback = (EDITSTREAMCALLBACK)SaveCallback;  // Use callback

        // save the file using the callback:
        ::SendMessage(m_hWnd, EM_STREAMOUT, SF_RTF, (LPARAM)&es);

        // Close the file when done.
        _lclose(hFile);

//        clear dirty bit flag and return!
        ::SendMessage(m_hWnd, EM_SETMODIFY, FALSE, 0);
        return TRUE;
    }
    return FALSE;
}
```

The call to SetFocus() is used to return focus to the RichText edit control. This was done so that dialog box controls which are used to set character attributes would return focus to the RichText edit control and not leave focus to the character-setting dialog box control.

This function uses the SaveCallback() function to do the actual output to the file. The SaveCallback() function is documented later in the chapter.

SaveAs()

The SaveAs() member function takes no parameters. The function prototype for SaveAs() is

```
BOOL SaveAs()
```

This function returns TRUE if the save was successful. This function will first clear the current document filename, and then call the Save() function (see the preceding section), to do the actual save.

```
BOOL CRTFEditCtrl::SaveAs()
{
    m_szFileName[0] = '\0';
    return(Save());
}
```

Open()

The Open() member function takes no parameters. The function prototype for Open() is

```
BOOL Open()
```

This function returns TRUE if the file is opened and read by the RichText edit control. The listing for Open() is shown in the following listing:

```
BOOL  CRTFEditCtrl::Open()
{
    HFILE        hFile;  // File handle
    OFSTRUCT     OpenFileName;       // open file strucuture
    EDITSTREAM   es;     // The EDITSTREAM structure

// Get a filename to get the document from

    if(GetFileName(m_szFileName, TRUE))
    {
    // Open the file, read mode:
        hFile = OpenFile(m_szFileName, &OpenFileName, OF_READ);

        if (hFile)
        {
            // Set up the EDITSTREAM structure
            es.dwCookie   = (DWORD)hFile; // our file handle
            es.dwError    = 0;            // No errors
            es.pfnCallback = OpenCallback; // Use callback

            // Get the file using the callback:
            ::SendMessage(m_hWnd, EM_STREAMIN, SF_RTF, (LPARAM)&es);

            // Close the file when done.
            _lclose(hFile);
        }

//       clear dirty bit flag and return!
        ::SendMessage(m_hWnd, EM_SETMODIFY, FALSE, 0);
        return TRUE;

    }
    return FALSE;
}
```

The filename of the document that was opened is saved for the user in the member variable m_szFileName.

CheckForDirtyContents()

The CheckForDirtyContents() member function takes no parameters. The function prototype for CheckForDirtyContents() is

```
BOOL CheckForDirtyContents()
```

This function will return TRUE unless the user selects the Cancel button in the prompting dialog box. The code for CheckForDirtyContents() is shown in the following listing:

```
BOOL CRTFEditCtrl::CheckForDirtyContents()
{
    char szMsg[512];
    int  iRetVal;

    // Check dirty bit
    if (::SendMessage(m_hWnd, EM_GETMODIFY, 0, 0L))
    {
        if (*m_szFileName)
        {
            wsprintf(szMsg, "Save the current document \"%s\"?", m_szFileName);
        }
        else
        {
            lstrcpy(szMsg, "Save the current untitled document?");
        }

        // Get the user's response
        iRetVal = AfxMessageBox(szMsg, MB_YESNOCANCEL | MB_ICONQUESTION);

        switch (iRetVal)
        {
            case IDYES:
                Save();
                return TRUE;
                break;

            case IDNO:
                return TRUE;
                break;

            case IDCANCEL:
                return FALSE;
                break;
        }
    }

    return TRUE;
}
```

The application will check the RichText edit control to see if the document has changed. If there have been no changes, there is no need to prompt the user to save the document. However, if the document has changed, then the application must prompt the user as to whether to save the document, and the document is saved using the Save() member function.

Print()

The Print() member function takes no parameters. The function prototype for Print() is

```
VOID Print()
```

This function has no return value. The code for `Print()` is shown in the following listing:

```cpp
void CRTFEditCtrl::Print()
{
    HDC          hPrinterDC;     // DC for printer
    FORMATRANGE  fr;             // Page to print
    DOCINFO      di;             // For the Escape API
    LONG         lTextLength;    // Length of document
    LONG         lTextPrinted;   // Amount of document printed

    // Get a printer DC

    if (*m_szPrinter ||
        SelectPrinter(m_szPrinter, GetParent()->m_hWnd, &m_dmDriverExtra))
    {
        hPrinterDC =
            GetPrinterDC(m_szPrinter, m_dmDriverExtra, GetParent()->m_hWnd);

        if (!hPrinterDC)
        {
            AfxMessageBox("Printer CreateDC call Failed", MB_OK);
            return;
        }
    }
    else
    {
        AfxMessageBox("No printer was selected", MB_OK);
        return;
    }

    // we now have our printer DC, now print the document
    // First, do the page size setup

    fr.hdc = fr.hdcTarget = hPrinterDC;

    // We will use a 6x9" printing area (for ease of use!)
    fr.rc.left   = fr.rc.top = 0;
    fr.rc.right  = 6*1440;  // 6" wide
    fr.rc.bottom = 9*1440;  // 9" down
    fr.rcPage    = fr.rc;

    // Print the entire document
    fr.chrg.cpMin = 0;
    fr.chrg.cpMax = -1;

    // do real setup
    di.cbSize = sizeof(DOCINFO);

    if (*m_szFileName)
    {
        di.lpszDocName = m_szFileName;
    }
    else
    {
        di.lpszDocName = "(Untitled)";
    }
```

```
        di.lpszOutput = NULL;

        // Set the printer's DC to MM_TEXT

        SetMapMode(hPrinterDC, MM_TEXT);

        StartDoc(hPrinterDC, &di);
        StartPage(hPrinterDC);

        // Get number of characters in our document
        lTextLength = ::SendMessage(m_hWnd, WM_GETTEXTLENGTH, 0, 0);

        do // Row, row, row your boat: Print, print, print your page:
        {
        // Print a page, where the return (lTextPrinted)
        // is the index of the next character (on next page)
            lTextPrinted =
                ::SendMessage(m_hWnd, EM_FORMATRANGE, TRUE, (LPARAM)&fr);

        // More to print?
        // if so, then start a new page
            if (lTextPrinted < lTextLength)
            {
                EndPage(hPrinterDC);
                StartPage(hPrinterDC);

                // Reset what to print to exclude the already printed portion
                fr.chrg.cpMin = lTextPrinted;
                fr.chrg.cpMax = -1;
            }
        }
        while (lTextPrinted < lTextLength); // Till all done!

        // Reset our RTF control to be normal
        ::SendMessage(m_hWnd, EM_FORMATRANGE, TRUE, (LPARAM)NULL);

        // Eject the paper
        EndPage(hPrinterDC);
        EndDoc(hPrinterDC);

        // Die, DC, DIE!
        DeleteDC(hPrinterDC);
}
```

The Print() function is used to print the RichText edit control's contents, formatted correctly for the currently selected printer. The Print() function is able to manage multiple page documents; however, this version of Print() does not enable the page parameters such as margins, to be set.

NOTE

A useful addition to the CRTFEditCtrl class would be a page setup dialog box.

SelectPrinter(LPSTR szPrinter, HWND hWndParent, UINT FAR *pdmDriverExtra)

The `SelectPrinter()` private member function takes three parameters. The function prototype for `SelectPrinter()` is

```
private: BOOL SelectPrinter(
    LPSTR szPrinter,
    HWND  hWndParent,
    UINT  FAR *pdmDriverExtra)
```

Where:

szPrinter is a pointer to a string that will contain the name of the current printer.

hWndParent is the parent window's HWND.

pdmDriverExtra is a pointer to an integer variable that will hold the printer extra value.

This function returns a BOOL, either TRUE if the function is successful, or FALSE if the function fails. The code for `SelectPrinter()` is shown in the following listing:

```
BOOL CRTFEditCtrl::SelectPrinter
    (LPSTR szPrinter, HWND  hWndParent, UINT  FAR *pdmDriverExtra)
{
    PRINTDLG    pd;         // From commdlg.h
    LPDEVMODE   lpDevMode;  // From print.h
    HANDLE      hDevMode;

    ZeroMemory(&pd, sizeof(pd));

/* Initialize the necessary pd structure members. */

    pd.lStructSize = sizeof(PRINTDLG);
    pd.hwndOwner = hWndParent;
    pd.Flags = PD_PRINTSETUP;

/* Get the info we need */

    if (!PrintDlg(&pd))
    {
        return (0);
    }

    hDevMode = pd.hDevMode;

    if (hDevMode)
      {
        lpDevMode = (LPDEVMODE)GlobalLock(hDevMode);

        *pdmDriverExtra = lpDevMode->dmDriverExtra;

        lstrcpy(m_szPrinter, (LPCSTR)lpDevMode->dmDeviceName);

        GlobalUnlock(hDevMode);
        GlobalFree(hDevMode);
```

```
        return (TRUE);
    }
    else
    {
        *pdmDriverExtra = 0;
        return (FALSE);
    }
}
```

This function can fail, but failure is unusual—`SelectPrinter()` can fail if the user has no printer defined. The `SelectPrinter()` function calls the `PrintDlg()` common dialog box function. This function is normally called only by `CRTFEditCtrl` member functions.

GetPrinterDC(LPSTR szPrinter, HWND hWndParent, UINT FAR *pdmDriverExtra)

The `GetPrinterDC()` member function takes one parameter. The function prototype for `GetPrinterDC()` is:

```
private: HDC GetPrinterDC(
    LPSTR szPrinter,
    HWND  hWndParent,
    UINT  FAR *pdmDriverExtra)
```

Where:

> `szPrinter` is a pointer to a string that contains the name of the currently selected printer.
>
> `hWndParent` is the RichText edit control's parent `HWND`.
>
> `pdmDriverExtra` is a pointer to the storage location (32-bit integer) that will be used to hold the printer `DriverExtra` bytes.

This function returns either a valid `HDC` or `NULL` if the function fails. The code for `GetPrinterDC()` is shown in the following listing:

```
HDC CRTFEditCtrl::GetPrinterDC(LPSTR szPrinter, UINT  dmDriverExtra,
    HWND   hWndParent)

{
    PRINTDLG    pd;
    LPDEVMODE   lpDevMode;
    HANDLE      hDevMode;

    hDevMode = GlobalAlloc(GHND, sizeof(DEVMODE)+(LONG)dmDriverExtra);
    if (!hDevMode)
        return ((HDC)0);

    lpDevMode = (LPDEVMODE)GlobalLock(hDevMode);

    lstrcpy((LPSTR)lpDevMode->dmDeviceName, m_szPrinter);
    lpDevMode->dmSize = sizeof(DEVMODE);
    lpDevMode->dmSpecVersion = 0x030A;
```

```
lpDevMode->dmDriverExtra = dmDriverExtra;

GlobalUnlock(hDevMode);

ZeroMemory(&pd, sizeof(pd));

/* Initialize the necessary pd structure members. */

pd.lStructSize = sizeof(PRINTDLG);
pd.hwndOwner = hWndParent;
pd.Flags = PD_RETURNDC ¦ PD_ENABLEPRINTHOOK;
pd.hDevMode = hDevMode;
pd.lpfnPrintHook = (LPPRINTHOOKPROC)GetDCHook;

if (!PrintDlg(&pd))
{
    return (0);
}

GlobalFree(hDevMode);

return (pd.hDC);
}
```

This function calls the `PrintDlg()` function to get the `HDC` for the current printer.

NOTE

The `GetPrinterDC()` function calls `PrintDlg()` to get the printer `HDC`. Normally, `PrintDlg()` displays a dialog box for the user to select a printer. However, by having the application use a callback function to press the OK button before the dialog box is even displayed, the user never sees the Select Printer dialog box. The callback function's listing is

```
BOOL CALLBACK GetDCHook (HWND hDlg, UINT msg, WPARAM wParam, LPARAM lParam)
{
    switch (msg)
    {
        case WM_INITDIALOG:
            PostMessage (hDlg, WM_COMMAND, IDOK, 0L);
            return FALSE;
            break;

        default:
            return FALSE;
            break;
    }
}
```

NewDocument()

The NewDocument() member function takes no parameter. The function prototype for NewDocument() is

```
VOID NewDocument()
```

This function has no return value. The code for NewDocument() is shown in the following listing:

```
void    CRTFEditCtrl::NewDocument()
{
    CHARRANGE    cr;

    m_szFileName[0] = '0';

    cr.cpMin = 0;
    cr.cpMax = -1;

//    Zap RTF's contents:

    ::SendMessage(m_hWnd, WM_SETREDRAW, FALSE, 0);
    ::SendMessage(m_hWnd, EM_EXSETSEL, 0, (LPARAM)&cr);
    ::SendMessage(m_hWnd, WM_SETREDRAW, TRUE, 0);
    ::SendMessage(m_hWnd, EM_REPLACESEL, 0, (LPARAM)"");

// Clear the dirty bit
    ::SendMessage(m_hWnd, EM_SETMODIFY, FALSE, 0);
}
```

The NewDocument() function first clears the current document's filename. Then the current document is deleted and the document modified flag is cleared.

SetupPrinter()

The SetupPrinter() member function takes no parameters. The function prototype for SetupPrinter() is

```
VOID SetupPrinter()
```

This function has no return value. The code for SetupPrinter() is shown in the following listing:

```
void CRTFEditCtrl::SetupPrinter()
{
    SelectPrinter(m_szPrinter, GetParent()->m_hWnd, &m_dmDriverExtra);
}
```

SetupPrinter() simply calls the SelectPrinter() member function to display the setup printer common dialog box.

CRTFEditCtrl Unveiled

This section shows the complete listings for the CRTFEditCtrl class. The source file (RTFEDITC.CPP) is shown in Listing 22.3, and the header file (RTFEDITC.H) is shown in Listing 22.4.

Listing 22.3. The CRTFEditCtrl source RTFEDITC.CPP file.

```cpp
// rtfeditc.cpp : implementation file
//

#include "stdafx.h"
#include "Dummy.h"
// #include "rtfeditc.h" // Move to DUMMY.H!

#ifdef _DEBUG
#undef THIS_FILE
static char BASED_CODE THIS_FILE[] = __FILE__;
#endif

/////////////////////////////////////////////////////////////////////////////
// CRTFEditCtrl

CRTFEditCtrl::CRTFEditCtrl()
{
    // Microsoft will eventually fold the RTF edit control
    // into the Win32 Common Controls library. Until this
    // happens it is going to be necessary to load the RICHED32.DLL
    // library to use the RTF edit control.

    m_hRTFLib = LoadLibrary("RICHED32.DLL");
    if (!m_hRTFLib)
    {// This may not be an error once the RTF edit ctrl is in W32CC lib.
        AfxMessageBox("Could not load the RICHEDIT library");
    }

    ZeroMemory(&m_szFileName, sizeof(m_szFileName));
    ZeroMemory(&m_szPrinter, sizeof(m_szPrinter));
    m_dmDriverExtra = 0;
}

CRTFEditCtrl::~CRTFEditCtrl()
{
    // Microsoft will eventually fold the RTF edit control
    // into the Win32 Common Controls library. Until this
    // happens it is going to be necessary to load
    // and then free the RICHED32.DLL library to use the
    // RTF edit control.

    if (m_hRTFLib)
    {
        FreeLibrary((HINSTANCE)m_hRTFLib);
        m_hRTFLib = NULL;
    }
}
```

```
BEGIN_MESSAGE_MAP(CRTFEditCtrl, CEdit)
    //{{AFX_MSG_MAP(CRTFEditCtrl)
        // NOTE - the ClassWizard will add and remove mapping macros here.
    //}}AFX_MSG_MAP
END_MESSAGE_MAP()


BOOL CRTFEditCtrl::Create(DWORD dwStyle, const RECT& rect, CWnd* pParentWnd,
    UINT nID)
{
    return CWnd::Create(_T("RichEdit"), NULL, dwStyle, rect, pParentWnd, nID);
}

int CRTFEditCtrl::GetCharAttribute(DWORD dwMask, DWORD dwEffects)
{
    CHARFORMAT CharacterFormat;

    SetFocus();
    ::SendMessage(m_hWnd, EM_GETCHARFORMAT, TRUE, (LPARAM)&CharacterFormat);

    if (CharacterFormat.dwMask & dwMask)
    {
        if (CharacterFormat.dwEffects & dwEffects)
        {
            return (CHAR_ATTRIB_YES);
        }
        else
        {
            return (CHAR_ATTRIB_NO);
        }
    }
    else
    {
        return (CHAR_ATTRIB_WAFFLE);
    }
}

void CRTFEditCtrl::ChangeCharAttribute(DWORD dwMask, DWORD dwEffects)
{
    CHARFORMAT CharacterFormat;

    CharacterFormat.cbSize = sizeof(CharacterFormat);

    SetFocus();
    ::SendMessage(m_hWnd, EM_GETCHARFORMAT, TRUE, (LPARAM)&CharacterFormat);

    // Tell the RTF control which attribute to change.
    CharacterFormat.dwMask      = dwMask;

    // Flip the bits
    CharacterFormat.dwEffects  ^= dwEffects;

    // Set the new attribute(s):
    ::SendMessage(m_hWnd, EM_SETCHARFORMAT, SCF_SELECTION,
        (LPARAM)&CharacterFormat);
}
```

continues

Listing 22.3. continued

```
void CRTFEditCtrl::ChangeSizeAttribute(int iPointChange)
{
    CHARFORMAT CharacterFormat;

    CharacterFormat.cbSize = sizeof(CHARFORMAT);

    CharacterFormat.cbSize = sizeof(CharacterFormat);

    SetFocus();
    if (::SendMessage(m_hWnd, EM_GETCHARFORMAT, TRUE,
        (LPARAM)&CharacterFormat) == 0)
    {
        TRACE("EM_GETCHARFORMAT failed\n");
    }

    CharacterFormat.dwMask      = CFM_SIZE;

    if (((CharacterFormat.yHeight + 20*iPointChange) <= (128*20))  &&
        ((CharacterFormat.yHeight + 20*iPointChange) >= (6*20)))
    {
        CharacterFormat.yHeight += 20*iPointChange;
    }

    if (::SendMessage(
        m_hWnd, EM_SETCHARFORMAT, SCF_SELECTION,
        (LPARAM)&CharacterFormat) == 0)
    {
        TRACE("EM_SETCHARFORMAT failed\n");
    }
}

static HANDLE hDevNames = NULL;
static HANDLE hDevMode = NULL;

HDC GetCurrentPrinterDC(void)
{
    HDC hdc = NULL;

    if (hDevNames)
    {
        LPDEVNAMES lpdn = (LPDEVNAMES)GlobalLock(hDevNames);
        LPDEVMODE lpdm = NULL;

        if (hDevMode)
            lpdm = (LPDEVMODE)GlobalLock(hDevMode);

        hdc = CreateDC((LPSTR)lpdn + lpdn->wDriverOffset,
            (LPSTR)lpdn + lpdn->wDeviceOffset,
            (LPSTR)lpdn + lpdn->wOutputOffset, lpdm);
    }
    else
    {
        PRINTDLG pd = {0};

        if (hDevMode)
            GlobalFree(hDevMode);
```

```
            pd.lStructSize = sizeof(pd);
            pd.hwndOwner   = NULL;
            pd.Flags = PD_RETURNDEFAULT | PD_RETURNDC;

            if (PrintDlg(&pd))
            {
                hDevMode = pd.hDevMode;
                hDevNames = pd.hDevNames;
                hdc = pd.hDC;
            }
        }

        return hdc;
}

void CRTFEditCtrl::ChangeFont()
{// No parameters!
        CHARFORMAT CharacterFormat;
        CHOOSEFONT ChooseFontStruct;
        LOGFONT    lf;
        HDC        hDC;

        CharacterFormat.cbSize = sizeof(CharacterFormat);

        ::SendMessage(m_hWnd, EM_GETCHARFORMAT, TRUE, (LPARAM)&CharacterFormat);

        // Fill in the CHOOSEFONT structure for the font common dialog

        ZeroMemory(&ChooseFontStruct, sizeof(CHOOSEFONT));
        ZeroMemory(&lf, sizeof(LOGFONT));

        hDC = ::GetDC(GetParent()->m_hWnd); // Need a screen DC, use the parent's DC

        // The RTF Edit control measures in twips, but LOGFONT measures
        // in logical units (here, pixels) so we must convert.
        //   1 point == 20 twips
        //   1 inch  == 72 points
        //     ==> 1 inch  == 1440 twips

        lf.lfHeight = MulDiv(CharacterFormat.yHeight,
            GetDeviceCaps(hDC, LOGPIXELSY), -1440);

        // Done with this
        ::ReleaseDC(GetParent()->m_hWnd, hDC);

        // Set up the rest of the logfont structure according to the
        // information retrieved from the EM_GETCHARFORMAT message

        if (CharacterFormat.dwEffects & CFE_BOLD)
            lf.lfWeight = FW_BOLD;
        else
            lf.lfWeight = FW_NORMAL;

        lf.lfItalic = (BOOL)(CharacterFormat.dwEffects & CFE_ITALIC);
        lf.lfUnderline = (BOOL)(CharacterFormat.dwEffects & CFE_UNDERLINE);
        lf.lfCharSet = ANSI_CHARSET;
        lf.lfQuality = DEFAULT_QUALITY;
        lf.lfPitchAndFamily = CharacterFormat.bPitchAndFamily;
```

continues

Listing 22.3. continued

```
    lstrcpy(lf.lfFaceName, CharacterFormat.szFaceName);

    // Fire up the common dialog.

    ChooseFontStruct.lStructSize = sizeof(ChooseFontStruct);
    ChooseFontStruct.hwndOwner = GetParent()->m_hWnd;

    ChooseFontStruct.hDC = GetCurrentPrinterDC();

    ChooseFontStruct.lpLogFont = &lf;
    ChooseFontStruct.Flags = CF_BOTH | CF_SCALABLEONLY | CF_WYSIWYG
        | CF_NOVECTORFONTS | CF_INITTOLOGFONTSTRUCT;
    ChooseFontStruct.rgbColors = RGB(0,0,0);
    ChooseFontStruct.nFontType = 0;

    if (ChooseFont(&ChooseFontStruct))
    {
        // Set the dwMask parameter to tell the
        // RTF Edit control to pay attention to the font format:
        CharacterFormat.dwMask = CFM_BOLD | CFM_FACE | CFM_ITALIC |
            CFM_OFFSET | CFM_SIZE | CFM_UNDERLINE;

        // ChooseFont returns the new point size in
        // tenths of a point so so we can multiply by 2
        // to get twips for the richedit control.

        CharacterFormat.yHeight = 2 * ChooseFontStruct.iPointSize;

        CharacterFormat.dwEffects = 0;

        if (lf.lfWeight >= FW_BOLD)
            CharacterFormat.dwEffects |= CFE_BOLD;

        if (lf.lfItalic)
            CharacterFormat.dwEffects |= CFE_ITALIC;

        if (lf.lfUnderline)
            CharacterFormat.dwEffects |= CFE_UNDERLINE;

        CharacterFormat.bPitchAndFamily = lf.lfPitchAndFamily;

        lstrcpy(CharacterFormat.szFaceName, lf.lfFaceName);

        // Set the new formatting to the RTF control:
        ::SendMessage(m_hWnd, EM_SETCHARFORMAT, SCF_SELECTION,
            (LPARAM)&CharacterFormat);
    }

    if (ChooseFontStruct.hDC)
        DeleteDC(ChooseFontStruct.hDC);
}


BOOL CRTFEditCtrl::GetFileName(LPSTR szFileName, BOOL bOpen)
{
    OPENFILENAME OpenFileName;
```

```
        OpenFileName.lStructSize       = sizeof(OPENFILENAME);
        OpenFileName.hwndOwner         = (HWND)m_hWnd;
        OpenFileName.hInstance         = NULL;
        OpenFileName.lpstrFilter       = "RTF Files (*.RTF)\0*.RTF\0";
        OpenFileName.lpstrCustomFilter = (LPSTR)NULL;
        OpenFileName.nMaxCustFilter    = 0L;
        OpenFileName.nFilterIndex      = 1L;
        OpenFileName.lpstrFile         = szFileName;
        OpenFileName.nMaxFile          = 256;
        OpenFileName.lpstrFileTitle    = NULL;
        OpenFileName.nMaxFileTitle     = 0;
        OpenFileName.lpstrInitialDir   = NULL;
        OpenFileName.lpstrTitle        = (LPSTR)NULL;
        OpenFileName.Flags             = OFN_HIDEREADONLY | OFN_PATHMUSTEXIST;
        OpenFileName.nFileOffset       = 0;
        OpenFileName.nFileExtension    = 0;
        OpenFileName.lpstrDefExt       = (LPSTR)"RTF";
        OpenFileName.lCustData         = 0L;
        OpenFileName.lpfnHook          = 0L;  // Zero eliminates compiler warnings
        OpenFileName.lpTemplateName    = (LPSTR)NULL;

        if (bOpen)
        {
            return GetOpenFileName (&OpenFileName);
        }
        else
        {
            return GetSaveFileName(&OpenFileName);
        }
}

DWORD CALLBACK SaveCallback
        (DWORD dwCookie, LPCSTR pbBuff, LONG cb, LONG *pcb)
{
        _lwrite((HFILE)dwCookie, pbBuff, cb);
        return(0);
}

BOOL CRTFEditCtrl::SaveAs()
{
        m_szFileName[0] = '\0';
        return(Save());
}

BOOL CRTFEditCtrl::Save()
{
        HFILE        hFile;  // File handle
        OFSTRUCT     OpenFileName;       // open file structure
        EDITSTREAM   es;     // The EDITSTREAM structure

        if(m_szFileName[0] || GetFileName(m_szFileName, FALSE))
        {// Open the file, erasing previous contents
            hFile = OpenFile(m_szFileName, &OpenFileName, OF_CREATE);

            // Set up the EDITSTREAM structure
            es.dwCookie    = (DWORD)hFile; // our file handle
            es.dwError     = 0;            // No error
            es.pfnCallback = (EDITSTREAMCALLBACK)SaveCallback;  // Use callback
```

continues

Listing 22.3. continued

```
                // save the file using the callback:
                ::SendMessage(m_hWnd, EM_STREAMOUT, SF_RTF, (LPARAM)&es);

                // Close the file when done.
                _lclose(hFile);

//          clear dirty bit flag and return!
                ::SendMessage(m_hWnd, EM_SETMODIFY, FALSE, 0);
                return TRUE;
        }

    return FALSE;
}

DWORD CALLBACK OpenCallback
    (DWORD dwCookie, LPBYTE pbBuff, LONG cb, LONG *pcb)
{
// Read as much data as allowed in the cb variable
    *pcb = _lread((HFILE)dwCookie, pbBuff, cb);

    if(*pcb < cb)
    {// If done, say:
        return (0);    // All done!
    }

    return *pcb;  // Otherwise say: There is more to read!
}

BOOL  CRTFEditCtrl::Open()
{
    HFILE       hFile;  // File handle
    OFSTRUCT    OpenFileName;     // open file structure
    EDITSTREAM  es;     // The EDITSTREAM structure

// Get a filename to get the document from

    if(GetFileName(m_szFileName, TRUE))
    {
    // Open the file, read mode:
        hFile = OpenFile(m_szFileName, &OpenFileName, OF_READ);

        if (hFile)
        {
            // Set up the EDITSTREAM structure
            es.dwCookie    = (DWORD)hFile; // our file handle
            es.dwError     = 0;            // No errors
            es.pfnCallback = OpenCallback; // Use callback

            // Get the file using the callback:
            ::SendMessage(m_hWnd, EM_STREAMIN, SF_RTF, (LPARAM)&es);

            // Close the file when done.
            _lclose(hFile);
        }

//          clear dirty bit flag and return!
```

```
            ::SendMessage(m_hWnd, EM_SETMODIFY, FALSE, 0);
            return TRUE;

    }
    return FALSE;
}

BOOL CRTFEditCtrl::CheckForDirtyContents()
{
    char szMsg[512];
    int  iRetVal;

    // Check dirty bit
    if (::SendMessage(m_hWnd, EM_GETMODIFY, 0, 0L))
    {
        if (*m_szFileName)
        {
            wsprintf(szMsg, "Save the current document \"%s\"?", m_szFileName);
        }
        else
        {
            lstrcpy(szMsg, "Save the current untitled document?");
        }

        // Get the user's response
        iRetVal = AfxMessageBox(szMsg, MB_YESNOCANCEL | MB_ICONQUESTION);

        switch (iRetVal)
        {
            case IDYES:
                Save();
                return TRUE;
                break;

            case IDNO:
                return TRUE;
                break;

            case IDCANCEL:
                return FALSE;
                break;
        }
    }

    return TRUE;
}

void CRTFEditCtrl::Print()
{
    HDC          hPrinterDC;   // DC for printer
    FORMATRANGE  fr;           // Page to print
    DOCINFO      di;           // For the Escape API
    LONG         lTextLength;  // Length of document
    LONG         lTextPrinted; // Amount of document printed

    // Get a printer DC

    if (*m_szPrinter ||
```

continues

Listing 22.3. continued

```
        SelectPrinter(m_szPrinter, GetParent()->m_hWnd, &m_dmDriverExtra))
    {
        hPrinterDC =
            GetPrinterDC(m_szPrinter, m_dmDriverExtra, GetParent()->m_hWnd);

        if (!hPrinterDC)
        {
            AfxMessageBox("Printer CreateDC call Failed", MB_OK);
            return;
        }
    }
    else
    {
        AfxMessageBox("No printer was selected", MB_OK);
        return;
    }

    // we now have our printer DC, now print the document
    // First, do the page size setup

    fr.hdc = fr.hdcTarget = hPrinterDC;

    // We will use a 6x9" printing area (for ease of use!)
    fr.rc.left   = fr.rc.top = 0;
    fr.rc.right  = 6*1440;  // 6" wide
    fr.rc.bottom = 9*1440;  // 9" down
    fr.rcPage    = fr.rc;

    // Print the entire document
    fr.chrg.cpMin = 0;
    fr.chrg.cpMax = -1;

    // do real setup
    di.cbSize = sizeof(DOCINFO);

    if (*m_szFileName)
    {
        di.lpszDocName = m_szFileName;
    }
    else
    {
        di.lpszDocName = "(Untitled)";
    }

    di.lpszOutput = NULL;

    // Set the printer's DC to MM_TEXT

    SetMapMode(hPrinterDC, MM_TEXT);

    StartDoc(hPrinterDC, &di);
    StartPage(hPrinterDC);

    // Get number of characters in our document
    lTextLength = ::SendMessage(m_hWnd, WM_GETTEXTLENGTH, 0, 0);

    do // Row, row, row your boat: Print, print, print your page:
```

```
    {
    // Print a page, where the return (lTextPrinted)
    // is the index of the next character (on next page)
        lTextPrinted =
            ::SendMessage(m_hWnd, EM_FORMATRANGE, TRUE, (LPARAM)&fr);

    // More to print?
    // if so, then start a new page
        if (lTextPrinted < lTextLength)
        {
            EndPage(hPrinterDC);
            StartPage(hPrinterDC);

            // Reset what to print to exclude the already printed portion
            fr.chrg.cpMin = lTextPrinted;
            fr.chrg.cpMax = -1;
        }
    }
    while (lTextPrinted < lTextLength); // Till all done!

    // Reset our RTF control to be normal
    ::SendMessage(m_hWnd, EM_FORMATRANGE, TRUE, (LPARAM)NULL);

    // Eject the paper
    EndPage(hPrinterDC);
    EndDoc(hPrinterDC);

    // Die, DC, DIE!
    DeleteDC(hPrinterDC);
}


HDC CRTFEditCtrl::GetPrinterDC(LPSTR szPrinter,
    UINT   dmDriverExtra, HWND  hWndParent)
{
    PRINTDLG    pd;
    LPDEVMODE   lpDevMode;
    HANDLE      hDevMode;

    hDevMode = GlobalAlloc(GHND, sizeof(DEVMODE)+(LONG)dmDriverExtra);
    if (!hDevMode)
        return ((HDC)0);

    lpDevMode = (LPDEVMODE)GlobalLock(hDevMode);

    lstrcpy((LPSTR)lpDevMode->dmDeviceName, m_szPrinter);
    lpDevMode->dmSize = sizeof(DEVMODE);
    lpDevMode->dmSpecVersion = 0x030A;
    lpDevMode->dmDriverExtra = dmDriverExtra;

    GlobalUnlock(hDevMode);

    ZeroMemory(&pd, sizeof(pd));

    /* Initialize the necessary pd structure members. */

    pd.lStructSize = sizeof(PRINTDLG);
    pd.hwndOwner = hWndParent;
```

continues

Listing 22.3. continued

```
    pd.Flags = PD_RETURNDC | PD_ENABLEPRINTHOOK;
    pd.hDevMode = hDevMode;
    pd.lpfnPrintHook = (LPPRINTHOOKPROC)GetDCHook;

    if (!PrintDlg(&pd))
    {
        return (0);
    }

    GlobalFree(hDevMode);

    return (pd.hDC);
}

void CRTFEditCtrl::SetupPrinter()
{
    SelectPrinter(m_szPrinter, GetParent()->m_hWnd, &m_dmDriverExtra);
}

BOOL CRTFEditCtrl::SelectPrinter
    (LPSTR szPrinter, HWND  hWndParent, UINT  FAR *pdmDriverExtra)
{
    PRINTDLG    pd;          // From commdlg.h
    LPDEVMODE   lpDevMode;   // From print.h
    HANDLE      hDevMode;

    ZeroMemory(&pd, sizeof(pd));

/* Initialize the necessary pd structure members. */

    pd.lStructSize = sizeof(PRINTDLG);
    pd.hwndOwner = hWndParent;
    pd.Flags = PD_PRINTSETUP;

/* Get the info we need */

    if (!PrintDlg(&pd))
    {
        return (0);
    }

    hDevMode = pd.hDevMode;

    if (hDevMode)
      {
        lpDevMode = (LPDEVMODE)GlobalLock(hDevMode);

        *pdmDriverExtra = lpDevMode->dmDriverExtra;

        lstrcpy(m_szPrinter, (LPCSTR)lpDevMode->dmDeviceName);

        GlobalUnlock(hDevMode);
        GlobalFree(hDevMode);

        return (TRUE);
    }
    else
```

```
        {
            *pdmDriverExtra = 0;
            return (FALSE);
        }
    }

/****************************************************************

    Shamelessly borrowed from some bright programmer from Microsoft:

    (This is the slickest way to do this that I've ever seen!)

    The GetDCHook function is the dialog procedure for the
    print common dialog. This function's sole purpose in life is
    to press the OK button instantly. This causes the dialog to never
    appear, yet we can get a printer DC back from it.

    ****************************************************************/

BOOL CALLBACK GetDCHook (HWND hDlg, UINT msg, WPARAM wParam, LPARAM lParam)
{
    switch (msg)
    {
        case WM_INITDIALOG:
            PostMessage (hDlg, WM_COMMAND, IDOK, 0L);
             return FALSE;
            break;

        default:
            return FALSE;
            break;
    }
}

void    CRTFEditCtrl::NewDocument()
{
    CHARRANGE    cr;

    m_szFileName[0] = '0';

    cr.cpMin = 0;
    cr.cpMax = -1;

//  Zap RTF's contents:

    ::SendMessage(m_hWnd, WM_SETREDRAW, FALSE, 0);
    ::SendMessage(m_hWnd, EM_EXSETSEL, 0, (LPARAM)&cr);
    ::SendMessage(m_hWnd, WM_SETREDRAW, TRUE, 0);
    ::SendMessage(m_hWnd, EM_REPLACESEL, 0, (LPARAM)"");

// Clear the dirty bit
    ::SendMessage(m_hWnd, EM_SETMODIFY, FALSE, 0);
}

/////////////////////////////////////////////////////////////////////////////
// CRTFEditCtrl message handlers
```

722

The header file for the `CRTFEditCtrl` class is shown in Listing 22.4.

Listing 22.4. The `CRTFEditCtrl` header file, RTFEDITC.H.

```
// rtfeditc.h : header file
//

/////////////////////////////////////////////////////////////////////////
// CRTFEditCtrl window

// Some handy defines (from MSFT's example of RTF control):

#include "richedit.h"

#define CHAR_ATTRIB_YES 0
#define CHAR_ATTRIB_NO 1
#define CHAR_ATTRIB_WAFFLE 2


class CRTFEditCtrl : public CEdit
{
// Construction
public:
    CRTFEditCtrl();

// Attributes
public:

    HANDLE    m_hRTFLib;
    char      m_szFileName[256];
    char      m_szPrinter[256];
    UINT      m_dmDriverExtra;
// Operations
public:

// Overrides
    // ClassWizard generated virtual function overrides
    //{{AFX_VIRTUAL(CRTFEditCtrl)
    //}}AFX_VIRTUAL

// Implementation
public:
    virtual ~CRTFEditCtrl();

    virtual BOOL Create(DWORD dwStyle, const RECT& rect, CWnd* pParentWnd,
        UINT nID);

    virtual int  GetCharAttribute(DWORD dwMask, DWORD dwEffects);
    virtual void ChangeCharAttribute(DWORD dwMask, DWORD dwEffects);
    virtual void ChangeSizeAttribute(int iPointChange);
    virtual void ChangeFont();
    virtual BOOL Save();
    virtual BOOL SaveAs();
    virtual BOOL Open();
    virtual BOOL CheckForDirtyContents();
    virtual void Print();
    virtual void NewDocument();
```

```
        virtual void SetupPrinter();

private:

        virtual BOOL GetFileName(LPSTR szFileName, BOOL bOpen);
        virtual BOOL SelectPrinter
            (LPSTR szPrinter, HWND  hWndParent, UINT  FAR *pdmDriverExtra);
        virtual HDC  GetPrinterDC
            (LPSTR szPrinter, UINT  dmDriverExtra, HWND  hWndParent);

        // Generated message map functions
protected:
        //{{AFX_MSG(CRTFEditCtrl)
            // NOTE - the ClassWizard will add and remove member functions here.
        //}}AFX_MSG

        DECLARE_MESSAGE_MAP()
};

//////////////////////////////////////////////////////////////////////////

// The following cannot be member functions as they are callbacks or
// used in some other code.

HDC GetCurrentPrinterDC(void);

DWORD CALLBACK SaveCallback
    (DWORD dwUserData, LPCSTR pbBuff, LONG cb, LONG *pcb);

DWORD CALLBACK OpenCallback
    (DWORD dwUserData, LPBYTE pbBuff, LONG cb, LONG *pcb);

BOOL CALLBACK GetDCHook
    (HWND hDlg, UINT msg, WPARAM wParam, LPARAM lParam);
```

The CRTFEditCtrl class source files are also found as part of the DUMMY sample application, which can be found on the CD-ROM.

What Could Be Added?

Right now you may be thinking that I've done it all. Actually, the CRTFEditCtrl class was created with a few days effort, and represents a rather minimal implementation of the RichText edit control by an MFC-based class.

If you intend to use the CRTFEditCtrl classes in your application, you should add more support to this class. The following lists some areas that could use improvement:

- Margins, both in the RichText edit control itself and for the printed output. The RichText edit control is WYSIWYG, which should make this feature easy to implement.

- Text colors. The text in a RichText edit control may have different colors. For those users who have color printers, this can be an important feature to support.

■ Support for initialization, from a resource stored in the owning application.

■ More and improved error handling and recovery. Each function should check for all possible errors and recover (as best as possible) from these errors.

You probably will come up with other areas that could be improved as well.

OLE Support

Do you want your RichText edit control to support OLE? Because OLE is a major keyword in Windows 95 application development, an OLE RichText edit control would be a major asset. What do you have to do to enable OLE in your RichText edit control? Nothing; it is already done!

The Animation Control

An Animation control enables an application to display certain types of animation (AVI) files (usually called an AVI clip) in a window. The AVI file must meet certain criteria (see the following list) to be used with the Animation control. For the remainder of this chapter, I'll refer to this control as the Animation control.

For an AVI file to be used with the Animation control, it must meet the following criteria:

■ The AVI file must be a silent AVI. No sound track is allowed.

■ The AVI file must be either uncompressed, or compressed using the Run Length Encoded (RLE) compression technique. Other compression techniques are not supported.

■ The AVI must be either a file or an application resource.

At the time this book was written, Visual C++ 2.1 did not enable direct creation of animation resources. To create an Animation resource you must follow these steps:

1. Create a new type of resource called AVI.

2. Visual C++ will create an initial resource under AVI and open a binary edit window (see Figure 22.3). You could use the keyboard to enter an AVI file's contents, but that would be rather time-consuming. Instead, go to step 3.

FIGURE 22.3.

An AVI resource in DUMMY.RC.

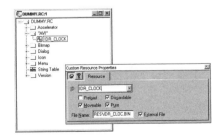

3. Rename the new resource to a logical name (I used IDR_CLOCK in my program).

4. Open the new AVI resource by double-clicking the resource.

5. Open the AVI file that you intend to use as your resource. In my example program, the AVI file is called CLOCK.AVI. This file will also be opened in the binary mode, as shown in Figure 22.4.

FIGURE 22.4.

The CLOCK.AVI file opened in Visual C++.

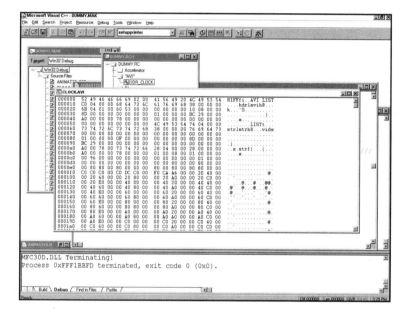

6. Select the entire contents of the AVI file by positioning the cursor at the first byte in the file and pressing Ctrl+Shift+End. Then copy the file's contents to the clipboard by pressing Ctrl+C.

7. In the AVI resource edit window, copy the clipboard's contents using Ctrl+V.

8. The new AVI resource will now contain the contents of your AVI file. You can then open the AVI resource with a call to CAnimateCtrl::Open() as shown here:

```
m_AnimateCtrl.Open(IDR_CLOCK);
```

Having your AVI clips as resources makes managing the application easier, because there will not be a separate AVI file for each animation effect. However, when AVI clips are resources it is much more difficult to use a different AVI clip without more extensive programming. Generally, however, most applications will want to include their AVI clips as application resources.

Figure 22.5 shows an Animation control in a dialog box. This example is from the sample program and shows a typical implementation of the Animation control in a dialog box.

FIGURE 22.5.

*An Animation control
shown in a dialog box.*

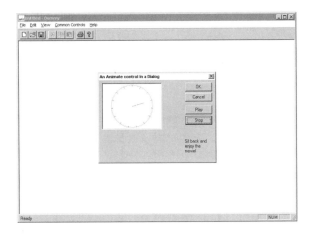

When your application uses a CAnimateCtrl class object, your application will need to do a
minimum amount of management of the Animation control. The application must open
the AVI clip that will be displayed, and may optionally start the playback of the AVI. An
Animation control has a few special attributes, which are described in Table 22.5. In
addition to these special attributes, the Animation control also supports the standard
attributes for dialog box controls.

Table 18.5. The Animation control's special attributes.

Attribute	Description
Center	The actual window that is created will be centered in the window defined by either the dialog box template or the RECT structure passed to the Create() function.
Transparent	The background of the Animation control will be transparent, instead of being the background color that was specified by the AVI file.
Autoplay	The AVI clip will automatically play once the Animation control has been created and made visible to the user. Once Autoplay has started, the AVI clip will repeat automatically until it is explicitly ended.

After you have added the Animation control to a dialog box, you can use ClassWizard to
bind a CAnimateCtrl object to your Animation control. This CAnimateCtrl object is your
interface with the Animation control.

Implementing a *CAnimateCtrl* Animation Control

If you are using an Animation control in a dialog box, you can use ClassWizard to bind a `CAnimateCtrl` object to the control. If you are implementing an Animation control in a window that is not a dialog box, then you need to call the `CAnimateCtrl::Create()` function to create the Animation control. You might find a use for an Animation control in a normal window, or perhaps as part of a toolbar.

Figure 22.6 shows our dialog box (in Visual C++'s resource editor) with the properties for the Animation control shown. You can easily set these properties for Animation controls that are in dialog boxes using the resource editor. When the Animation control is in a window other than a dialog box, then the properties are set when the Animation control is created.

FIGURE 22.6.

The Animation control and its properties in Visual C++'s resource editor.

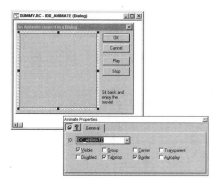

If you look at Figure 22.6, you will see that I've added two new buttons, a Play button and a Stop button. The handlers for these two buttons simply call the `CAnimateCtrl::Play()` and the `CAnimateCtrl::Stop()` functions.

Listing 22.5 is the code that manages our Animate sample dialog box. The basis for this code was developed using ClassWizard, and then modified to add the features that were necessary. The code that was manually added is shown in bold in this listing.

Listing 22.5. The ANIMATED.CPP file.

```
// animated.cpp : implementation file
//

#include "stdafx.h"
#include "Dummy.h"
#include "animated.h"
```

continues

Listing 22.5. continued

```
#ifdef _DEBUG
#undef THIS_FILE
static char BASED_CODE THIS_FILE[] = __FILE__;
#endif

/////////////////////////////////////////////////////////////////////////////
// CAnimateDlg dialog


CAnimateDlg::CAnimateDlg(CWnd* pParent /*=NULL*/)
    : CDialog(CAnimateDlg::IDD, pParent)
{
    //{{AFX_DATA_INIT(CAnimateDlg)
    //}}AFX_DATA_INIT
}


void CAnimateDlg::DoDataExchange(CDataExchange* pDX)
{
    CDialog::DoDataExchange(pDX);
    //{{AFX_DATA_MAP(CAnimateDlg)
    DDX_Control(pDX, IDC_ANIMATE, m_AnimateCtrl);
    //}}AFX_DATA_MAP
}


BEGIN_MESSAGE_MAP(CAnimateDlg, CDialog)
    //{{AFX_MSG_MAP(CAnimateDlg)
    ON_BN_CLICKED(IDC_PLAY, OnPlay)
    ON_BN_CLICKED(IDC_STOP, OnStop)
    //}}AFX_MSG_MAP
END_MESSAGE_MAP()


/////////////////////////////////////////////////////////////////////////////
// CAnimateDlg message handlers

BOOL CAnimateDlg::OnInitDialog()
{
    CDialog::OnInitDialog();

    // TODO: Add extra initialization here

//      m_AnimateCtrl.Open("CLOCK.AVI");
    m_AnimateCtrl.Open(IDR_CLOCK);


    return TRUE;  // return TRUE unless you set the focus to a control
                  // EXCEPTION: OCX Property Pages should return FALSE
}

void CAnimateDlg::OnPlay()
{
    // TODO: Add your control notification handler code here

    m_AnimateCtrl.Play(0, (UINT)-1, 1);
}
```

```
void CAnimateDlg::OnStop()
{
    // TODO: Add your control notification handler code here

    m_AnimateCtrl.Stop();
}
```

Listing 22.6 is the ANIMATED.H header file that accompanies the ANIMATED.CPP file shown in Listing 22.5. The ANIMATED.H file was modified only by ClassWizard; no manual changes were necessary.

Listing 22.6. The ANIMATED.H file.

```
// animated.h : header file
//

/////////////////////////////////////////////////////////////////////////
// CAnimateDlg dialog

class CAnimateDlg : public CDialog
{
// Construction
public:
    CAnimateDlg(CWnd* pParent = NULL);   // standard constructor

// Dialog Data
    //{{AFX_DATA(CAnimateDlg)
    enum { IDD = IDD_ANIMATE };
    CAnimateCtrl    m_AnimateCtrl;
    //}}AFX_DATA


// Overrides
    // ClassWizard generated virtual function overrides
    //{{AFX_VIRTUAL(CAnimateDlg)
    protected:
    virtual void DoDataExchange(CDataExchange* pDX);   // DDX/DDV support
    //}}AFX_VIRTUAL

// Implementation
protected:

    // Generated message map functions
    //{{AFX_MSG(CAnimateDlg)
    virtual BOOL OnInitDialog();
    afx_msg void OnPlay();
    afx_msg void OnStop();
    //}}AFX_MSG
    DECLARE_MESSAGE_MAP()
};
```

The *CAnimateCtrl* Class in a Dialog Box

As stated earlier, you would usually bind your `CAnimateCtrl` object to an Animation control using ClassWizard. Once you have bound the `CAnimateCtrl` object, you can then initialize your Animation control in the `OnInitDialog()` function.

Generally, you will want to load an ANI clip (either from a resource or an ANI file) and often the animation will be started at this time. You can usually use the Autoplay attribute (see Table 22.5) to start an animation at creation time.

The following code listing shows the line (in bold) that initializes our Animation control. I've added to this listing an optional function call (`m_AnimateCtrl.Play(0, (UINT)-1, 1)`) to start the animation immediately.

```
BOOL CAnimateDlg::OnInitDialog()
{
    CDialog::OnInitDialog();

    // TODO: Add extra initialization here

// The first example of Open()  will open an
// AVI file:

//    m_AnimateCtrl.Open("CLOCK.AVI");

// The second example of Open()  will open an
// AVI resource:

    m_AnimateCtrl.Open(IDR_CLOCK);

// Start playing the AVI clip, with frame zero,
// to the end of the clip. Play it one time only:

    m_AnimateCtrl.Play(0, (UINT)-1, 1);

    return TRUE;  // return TRUE unless you set the focus to a control
                  // EXCEPTION: OCX Property Pages should return FALSE
}
```

Creating *CAnimateCtrl* Objects in Nondialog Windows

To create a `CAnimateCtrl` object in a window that is not a dialog box, you can call `CAnimateCtrl::Create()`. The `CAnimateCtrl::Create()` function takes four parameters: a style (only the standard dialog box control styles are supported by an Animation control), a `RECT` structure specifying the Animation control's location and size, a pointer to the parent window, and the control ID.

```
CAnimateCtrl::Create(
    WS_CHILD ¦ WS_VISIBLE ¦ WS_BORDER ¦ WS_TABSTOP ¦ ACS_AUTOPLAY,
    rect, this, 0);
```

There are many situations in which a programmer might want to create an Animation control in a nondialog window. Using `CAnimateCtrl::Create()` is an easy way to create an Animation control.

Options for the window styles of an Animation control are listed in Table 22.6. None of these options are mandatory.

Table 22.6. The `CAnimateCtrl::Create()` options.

Attribute	Description
ACS_CENTER	The actual window created will be centered in the window defined by either the dialog box template or the `rect` structure passed to the `Create()` function.
ACS_TRANSPARENT	The background of the Animation control will be transparent rather than the background color that was specified by the AVI file.
ACS_AUTOPLAY	The AVI clip will automatically play once the Animation control has been created and made visible to the user. Once Autoplay has started, the AVI clip will repeat automatically until explicitly ended.

CAnimateCtrl Interaction

The `CAnimateCtrl` object enables you to play, seek, and stop the animation. The Animation control does not have any facility to return the current frame, nor is there a method to determine the size, or number of frames, of the AVI file.

NOTE

Once an Animation control has been stopped, you must restart it from a known point. There is no way to determine the currently stopped frame.

WARNING

Animation controls only support AVI clips of 65,535 frames. At 20 frames per second, this limits your AVI clip to about 55 minutes in length.

Using the *CAnimateCtrl* Animate Object

The CAnimateCtrl Animate object takes no input from the user, and is only capable of providing output (the AVI clip). You can create start and stop buttons for the users, but the usefulness of such controls is questionable. For more advanced animation techniques, it would be best if you used the MCIWnd class window instead.

The *CAnimateCtrl* Animate Input

You can initialize the CAnimateCtrl Animation control using the CAnimateCtrl::Open() member function. This function takes either the filename for an AVI file, or the resource identifier for an AVI resource.

An example of how to create an AVI resource was provided earlier in the section "The Animation Control."

Summary

This chapter showed you two different Win32 Common Controls, as outlined in the following list. You also learned about a class for the RichText edit control.

- The RichText edit control provides a way for applications to present an edit window that supports RichText. This window can provide the majority of the application's user interface (such as the Windows 95 application, WordPad), or it can simply be a control in a dialog box, as our sample application shows.

- Microsoft has not yet created an MFC class object for the RichText edit control. This chapter presents a simple MFC CEdit based class (called CRTFEditCtrl) that you can use while you wait for Microsoft to create the RichText edit control's MFC interface.

- The CAnimateCtrl is the MFC interface with the Animation control. The Animation control offers the user visual, animated feedback.

VI

PART

OLE Programming

OLE for the
First-Timer

23

*by Lawrence
Harris*

IN THIS CHAPTER

With the release of Windows 95, OLE not only becomes part of the Windows operating system, it plays a major role in the operating system. OLE is used by the Windows 95 shell, the briefcase, and other components of Windows 95. When reading through the SDK for Windows 95, you might have decided not to implement some of the new features of Windows 95 because they require OLE. Don't despair. It isn't difficult to add OLE functionality to your applications. In the next several chapters, OLE programming will be demonstrated so that you can start to incorporate OLE into your applications. Also, don't worry if you're not using Microsoft's Foundation Class or Borland's OWL, because the implementation of OLE I discuss doesn't require these class libraries. Before I get into the programming of OLE, I will provide you with a brief look at the history of OLE.

In the early versions of Windows, before OLE, if you had a spreadsheet to include in a word processing document, you typically had to export the data from the spreadsheet, import the data into the word processor, and then reformat the data once it was in the word processor. If you were lucky, the two applications supported cut-and-paste operations; instead of an explicit export-import operation, you could cut-and-paste the information from the Clipboard. If the spreadsheet data changed, the process of transferring the data had to be redone. This was an extreme waste of time and energy.

When OLE 1 appeared in Windows 3.1, the previous example became easier in applications that used OLE. Instead of using export-import or cut-paste operations, you were given the additional options of linking and embedding objects. You could now link your spreadsheet to your word processing document so that whenever the spreadsheet changed, the document would reflect the changes. In addition, from the word processing document, you could click the spreadsheet, and the spreadsheet application would automatically start, allowing you to edit the spreadsheet data. When you finished making changes, you could select File Update, the spreadsheet closed, and the word processing document had the new data.

OLE 2 is the next logical step in the progression of this technique. In OLE 1 when you clicked the spreadsheet in a word processing document, the spreadsheet application started as a separate application in a separate window. OLE 2 introduces the concept of in-place editing (also known as visual editing). The spreadsheet application still starts up as before, but instead of working in a different window, the spreadsheet seems to merge with the word processing application. The word processing application's menus change to reflect the spreadsheet's menus, and even the toolbars change, but you are still in your word processing application. The two applications appear to merge—with the word processor getting spreadsheet functionality. As a user, you do not need to switch between applications to revise data. You can work from the application best suited for the majority of your task and use the features of the other application within the primary application.

OLE 2 needed to reimplement much of OLE 1 in order to gain additional functionality and performance. For example, OLE 1 was built upon Dynamic Data Exchange (DDE). DDE basically uses window messages and callbacks to pass information back and forth. Because window messages were used (at that time), DDE was restricted to a single machine: That is, it was not designed in a multiuser or network environment (although recently, Windows for

Workgroups, Windows NT, and Windows 95 have added network DDE support). The 16-bit implementation of OLE 2 is not built on DDE, but instead is built on Lightweight Remote Procedure Calls (LRPC). LRPC is similar to its UNIX counterpart, RPC (Remote Procedure Call), in that it allows applications to pass information. Unlike RPC, LRPC is limited to passing information to applications within the same machine (RPC can pass information between applications in the same machine, different machines, or machines with unlike architecture). Distributed OLE is another version of OLE that uses RPC instead of LRPC in which objects can actually cross machine boundaries. The 32-bit implementation of OLE 2 does not use LRPC, but instead it uses Local Procedure Calls (LPC). LPC does not use window messages, but instead it uses an efficient private messaging scheme (using shared memory and bypassing the Windows message queue). LPCs are so efficient that NT uses LPCs to handle communications between the Win32 subsystem and many of the User32 calls in your application.

OLE Architecture

In order for OLE to accomplish its functionality, many building block objects were used. OLE contains new objects for concepts such as marshalling (which handles the communication between processes and relies on LRPC, LPC, or RPC), structured storages (which handle saving documents that contain other documents), and monikers (which handle reconnecting linked data). Each of these concepts are needed for OLE 2 to perform its job. In addition, OLE introduces the concept of automation, which is not required for linking and embedding in the traditional sense. Automation can be thought of as the way a user can use your application within a user-defined macro language. An OLE Automation server can be controlled by any OLE Automation controller. Table 23.1 shows a few OLE Automation servers and controller applications.

Table 23.1. OLE Automation server and controller applications.

Product	OLE Automation Server	OLE Automation Controller
Visual Basic	No	Yes
Excel 5	Yes	Yes
Word 6	Yes	No
MS Project 4	Yes	Yes
MS Access 2	No	Yes
Visio 3	Yes	No

You might have noticed that both Excel 5 and Project 4 are an OLE Automation server and an OLE Automation controller; not only can they control other applications, but other applications can control them. This type of client-server (or server-client) relationship exists throughout OLE. Every OLE object is either a client or a server, or both.

In OLE Automation every object is either a client or a server of another object. In the opening example, the word processing application invoked the spreadsheet application (the word processor is the client, the spreadsheet is the server). OLE basic objects follow this same relationship. As you will see as you read this book, all of the higher-level OLE objects rely on the lower-level OLE objects to perform various operations for them.

Although I will go over the details of OLE architecture in next few chapters, I will now give you a brief tour of the major OLE building blocks and OLE terminology.

Objects

An OLE object is anything that can have a computer representation. An OLE object may be a word processing document, a spreadsheet, a cell within a spreadsheet, a video clip, or even an application. This differs from the standard interpretation of an object in which an object is data that includes functions and procedures to manipulate the data. In C++ an object is further restricted to a single machine: The C++ object cannot span machine boundaries. OLE objects do not have this restriction. If OLE only supports objects within a single machine, it is not a restriction of OLE, but of its current implementation. A version of OLE called Distributed OLE, which has already been demonstrated at various trade shows, allows objects to cross CPU boundaries transparently. In order words, when you ask for an object, the provider of the object might not necessarily reside on your machine, but from your point of view, the object is local.

Interfaces

An interface is a method by which related functions for an object can be accessed. An interface is actually a pointer to the set of related functions. In C++, if you have a pointer, you have access to any function the object publicly exposes. In OLE, if you have a pointer to an interface for an object, you only have access to the functions the interface supports, not necessarily to all the public functions of the object. OLE objects usually have multiple interfaces, with each interface having functions relevant only to that interface. For example, if an object has five interfaces, each of those interfaces has functions that are only appropriate for that interface (an object might have a math interface with functions for addition and subtraction, and a spelling interface with spelling-related functions).

Structured Storage

Structured storage is OLE's equivalent of DOS. Structured storage supports many of DOS's "objects" such as files and directories. Structured storage also supports many of the aspects of DOS's functionality such as the moving and copying of files. In addition, structured storage does not imply that the data is stored only on disk. Just as a DOS file can reside on a

RAM disk, a floppy disk, or even a CD-ROM, structured storage can reside in any of these places as well as others. To enable DOS to use other storage mediums such as an optical floppy or a network drive, a device driver is usually required. Similarly, structured storage has methods that allow non-native devices to be supported. A compound document is a specific implementation of structured storage in which an object or objects are stored within a storage (file).

OLE Automation

Automation is a set of interfaces that typically allows an application to be an OLE object However, automation is not restricted to just applications; it can also be a DLL. OLE Automation allows an application to be externally programmed or customized through a set of predefined rules. For example, this allows a Visual Basic application to control Excel, and makes it appear that Excel is part of the Visual Basic application. An OLE Automation controller is an application that uses or controls an automation object (server).

Uniform Data Transfer

Uniform Data Transfer is a set of interfaces that allow data to be exchanged from the server to the client. Uniform Data Transfer is OLE's equivalent of DDE and the Clipboard's cut-and-paste functionality all rolled into one. Uniform Data Transfer supports notification when data has changed, as well as negotiation for the format in which the data will be transferred. In addition, Uniform Data Transfer supports the possibility that the actual data is not transferred, but a handle to the data is. For example, instead of passing 20 MB of data in RAM through the Clipboard, a server object can pass a handle to the data so that the client can get the data (or just part of the data) itself. This saves the server from reading all the data and passing it to the client, and the client from processing all the data itself. It also saves the end user from waiting in front of the PC for the transfer to complete.

Linking and Embedding

OLE is traditionally known for linking and embedding. Linking and embedding allows a client object (which can be another application) to tie to a server object. The tie can either be linked, in which the actual data resides outside of a compound document, or embedded, in which the actual data resides within a compound document. OLE 2 uses monikers (which are objects that identify the source for linked data) to gain access to the linked data.

Part of linking and embedding is OLE 2's ability to perform in-place activation. In OLE 1, when you double-click on a linked or embedded object, the server of the object (such as Excel) started and you were placed in the server application. OLE 2 allows in-place activation so that the two applications appear to the user as one application. In-place activation merges the relevant parts of the server's application (such as menu items and toolbars) into the client while the user is working on the embedded object. For example, if you have an

Excel 5 spreadsheet embedded in your Word 6 document (see Figure 23.1), when you click
the spreadsheet within the document, Word's menu and toolbar are transformed into
Excel's menu and toolbar (see Figure 23.2). Then, when you click a nonspreadsheet part of
your document, your menu changes back into Word's menu. When you double-click the
linked object, the application is started as in OLE 1, as a separate window (see Figure 23.3).

FIGURE 23.1.

*Word document with
an embedded
spreadsheet and a
linked chart.*

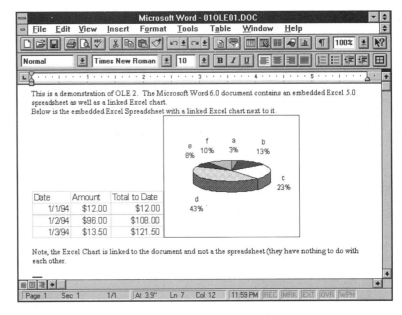

FIGURE 23.2.

*Word document after
double-clicking the
embedded spreadsheet.*

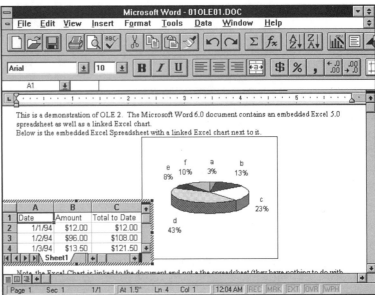

FIGURE 23.3.

Word document after double-clicking the linked chart.

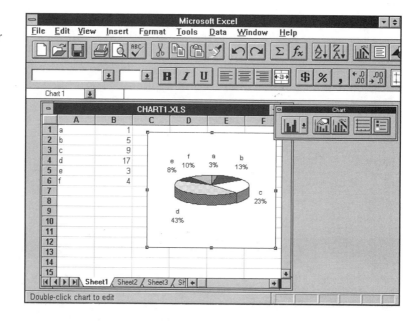

In OLE terms, the action previously described (double-clicking to activate the spreadsheet) is called outside-in activation. For outside-in activation, the server of the object is not activated (Excel is not started) until the user double-clicks the object. Inside-out activation requires that the client object activates the server object whenever it is visible. Basically, because the server object is already active for inside-out objects, the server gains control on a single-click.

As you can see, the OLE architecture is rich, and linking and embedding is only a part of the overall structure.

OLE Initialization

Every OLE application requires simple initialization to be called before anything within OLE can be performed. For Windows 3.1, OLE internally uses PostMessage to get messages from one application to another. Because the traffic can be high, most OLE programs increase the default queue size from 8 to 96 (as recommended by Microsoft). Windows 95 and Windows NT dynamically change the queue size; therefore, there is no need to change the message queue size (although the message queue size should be changed if your application can run under Win32s). Increased message queue size is only required if one application will interface with objects in another application. If an application will not interface with external objects, there is no need to increase the queue size.

An application that increases its queue size must perform this task before any messages are in the queue or else the messages can be lost. In order to guarantee that this is done, call

`SetMessageQueue` before any other call that creates a window. In addition, never assume that the call to `SetMessageQueue` will succeed (`SetMessageQueue` returns a zero if the function fails). If `SetMessageQueue` fails, you have no message queue. You should continue to call `SetMessageQueue` with smaller values until it succeeds. In Listing 23.1 (which is code fragment), it is not assumed that `SetMessageQueue` will ever succeed, so the function returns `FALSE` if the `SetMessageQueue` fails. If this function returns `FALSE`, you must terminate your application because you have no message queue.

Listing 23.1. The `SetMessageQueue` code fragment.

```
int     iMsgQueSize = 96;
while ((SetMessageQueue(iMsgQueSize) == 0) && (iMsgQueSize>0))
 iMsgQueSize -= 8;
if (iMsgQueSize <= 0)
return FALSE;
```

> **NOTE**
>
> Check the return value of `SetMessageQueue`. If a zero is returned, you have no message queue and Windows will not be able to process messages. You must call `SetMessageQueue` with progressively lower values until success (a positive value) is returned, or you must exit the program.
>
> Don't call `SetMessageQueue` with a value larger than 120 because it will return success; however, no queue is actually created.

In addition to changing the message queue size (if necessary), OLE itself must be initialized. To initialize the 16-bit version of OLE, a call must first be made to `OLEBuildVersion`. This call returns the OLE build number. The build number is not the OLE version, thus you do not compare this value to 2.02, for example. In the OLE header file OLE2VER.H (the 2 is the version number of OLE) are two constants, `rmm` and `rup`, that contain the major and minor build version numbers, respectively. You must never use a version of the OLE DLL that returns a major version number (`rmm`) that does not agree with your compiled version number. You should only use a version of the OLE DLL that returns a minor version number greater than or equal to your compiled version number. If you use a minor version number DLL that is less than your compiled minor version number, you should take caution not to use any features that are not included in the release. When writing a 32-bit application, you are not required to call `OLEBuildVersion`.

Finally, `OleInitialize` must be called (see Listing 23.2). `OleInitialize` takes one parameter. In the 16-bit implementation of OLE the parameter is either a pointer to an `IMalloc` interface (which handles memory allocation) or `NULL`, to use the default memory allocation. In the 32-bit implementation of OLE the parameter to `OleInitialize` must be `NULL`, because the 32-bit implementation does not support user-specified memory allocation. Once all the initialization has taken place, the rest of the OLE API can be used. When your application has completed its use of OLE, you must call `OleUninitialize`. This will free the OLE 2 library as well as the memory it was using. `OleInitialize` and `OleUninitialize` must be a matched set; in other words, for every successful `OleInitialize` call there must be a corresponding `OleUninitialize` call.

Another set of APIs (discussed in Chapter 24, "Component Object Model (COM)"), `CoInitialize` and `CoUninitialize`, could be used instead of `OleInitialize` and `OleUninitialize` if only a subset of OLE is used (the component Object and compound File subset of OLE). Because `OleInitialize` internally calls `CoInitialize`, I prefer to use `OleInitialize` in all cases rather than deciding which initialization routine to use. In addition, if you use `CoInitialize` in your application, and then add additional OLE functionality to your application, you will most likely need to change `CoInitialize` to `OleInitialize`. `OleUninitialize` calls `CoUninitialize` internally as well.

Listing 23.2 shows a code fragment of an application that uses OLE. The complete code is shown in Chapter 24.

Listing 23.2. Implementation of `OleInitialize` and `OleUninitialize`.

```
int CALLBACK WinMain(
        HINSTANCE hInstance,
        HINSTANCE hPrevInstance,
        LPSTR /* lpCmdLine */,
        int nCmdShow)
{

        MSG msg;
        HACCEL hAccelTable;

        //Under Windows 95 and Windows NT you do not need
        //to change the message queue
        //size as the queue will change dynamically.
        //Under Win32s and Win16 the message queue size
        //must be changed to work
        //with many OLE APIs
        //Since changing the queue size under Windows 95 and
        //Windows NT is not harmful
        //the queue size will be changed in all cases.
        //
        int     iMsgQueueSize = 96;
        while   ((SetMessageQueue(iMsgQueueSize) == 0)
        ➥ && (iMsgQueueSize>0))
            iMsgQueueSize -= 8;
        if (iMsgQueueSize <= 0)
            return FALSE;

//In Win32 hPrevInstance is always NULL regardless of
//whether a previous instance
//is running. If we want to determine
```

continues

Listing 23.2. continued

```
//if a previous instance is running
//we'll look for a window which we create
//
//If we find a previous instance,
//we terminate the current instance and
//bring focus to the previous instance
//
        HWND    hWndPreviousInstance;

        if ((hWndPreviousInstance = FindWindow(szAppName,NULL)) != NULL){
            ShowWindow(hWndPreviousInstance,SW_SHOW);
            return (FALSE);
        }

        if (!hPrevInstance) {         // Other instances of app running?
            if (!InitApplication(hInstance)) {
        ➡ // Initialize shared things
                return (FALSE);       // Exits if unable to initialize
            }
        }

        /* Perform initializations that apply to a specific instance */

        if (!InitInstance(hInstance, nCmdShow)) {
                return (FALSE);
        }

        HRESULT hResult;
        IUnknown *punk;
        IShellLink *pShellLink;
        IPersistFile *pFile;

        TCHAR   szError[100];

        //Initialize OLE
        hResult = ::OleInitialize(NULL);
        if (FAILED(hResult)){
            HResultToString(hResult,szError);
            MessageBox(NULL,szError,"OleInitialize",MB_OK);
            return (FALSE);
        }
. ADDITIONAL CODE is added in Chapter 24, Component Object Model
        .
        hAccelTable = LoadAccelerators (hInstance,
                                    MAKEINTRESOURCE(IDR_PMOLE));

        /* Acquire and dispatch messages until
            a WM_QUIT message is received. */

        while (GetMessage(&msg, // message structure
            NULL,   // handle of window receiving the message
            0,      // lowest message to examine
            0))     // highest message to examine
        {
```

```
        if (!TranslateAccelerator (msg.hwnd, hAccelTable, &msg)) {
                TranslateMessage(&msg);
                ➥ // Translates virtual key codes
                DispatchMessage(&msg);
                ➥ // Dispatches message to window
        }
    }

    //Uninitialize OLE
    ::OleUninitialize();
return (msg.wParam); // Returns the value from PostQuitMessage
}
```

Listing 23.2 shows a generic 32-bit application's WinMain implementation with OLE initialization code added. First, the message queue size is changed to handle 96 entries. Remember that if your application is going to run on Win32s, you need to change the message queue size. However, if your application will only run under Windows 95 or Windows NT 3.5, you don't need to change the message queue size (it changes dynamically in Windows 95 and Windows NT 3.5). If the application could not successfully change the message queue size, the application terminates by returning FALSE. The application must terminate if the message queue size is not successfully changed because the application no longer has a message queue.

After application and instance initialization has been performed (such as registering window classes), OLE is initialized by calling OleInitialize. OleInitialize, like almost all OLE API calls, returns HRESULT. HRESULT under the 16-bit implementation of Windows is a handle to a result code, while under the 32-bit implementation of Windows, HRESULT is the actual result code. With the HRESULT returned by OleInitialize, you can determine whether the initialization succeeded or failed by using the macros SUCCEEDED(hresult) or FAILED(hresult). Although it is possible to check for success by comparing the returned HRESULT to S_OK (which means the initialization was successful), you should get in the habit of using the macros SUCCEEDED or FAILED, because in OLE there are a number of APIs that return various success codes.

If OleInitialize fails, the application calls HResultToString. HResultToString is not an OLE API, but is a routine I frequently use to debug my OLE applications. HResultToString simply converts HRESULT, which is a number, to an equivalent ASCII string. For example, if OleInitialize returns S_OK, the returned value would be 0L. HResultToString would convert 0L to S_OK.

Finally, once the application is about to terminate, OleUninitialize is called. Once OleUninitialize has been called, the application can terminate. In Chapter 24, you will build on the information discussed in this chapter and complete a simple OLE application.

An important aspect of OLE as implemented in Windows 95 and Windows NT 3.5 is that OLE requires the use of Unicode (a two-byte implementation of character sets). Under NT, using Unicode is not a problem because NT supports Unicode applications. Under Windows 95, using Unicode is unusual because Windows 95 does not support Unicode. Here is the problem: Because the 32-bit implementation of OLE requires Unicode, how can you write applications that will work under Windows 95 and Windows NT and OLE? To satisfy the requirements of each of the environments, you should consider making your application a 32-bit ANSI application and perform translations from ANSI to Unicode when calling an OLE API. Listing 23.3 shows a portion of the header file COMMON.H, which handles the differences between Unicode applications and non-Unicode applications.

Listing 23.3. Unicode header routines from COMMON.H.

```
#define WideToAnsi(szInput, szOutput, cbOutputSize) WideCharToMultiByte(CP_ACP,\
                                                    WC_SEPCHARS, \
                                                    szInput, \
                                                    -1, \
                                                    szOutput, \
                                                    cbOutputSize, \
                                                    NULL, \
                                                    NULL)

#define AnsiToWide(szInput, szOutput, cbOutputSize) MultiByteToWideChar(CP_ACP,\
MB_PRECOMPOSED, \
                                                    szInput, \
                                                    -1, \
                                                    szOutput,        \
                                                    cbOutputSize)

OLECHAR *AnsiToUnicode(TCHAR *szInput);
OLECHAR *AnsiToUnicode256(TCHAR *szInput);

//AnsiToOlechar will translate an ANSI string
//to an Unicode string if UNICODE
//is not defined. If UNICODE is defined,
//the input is assumed to already be in
//Unicode and no translation is performed.
//If you explicitly wish to translate
//an ANSI string into Unicode regardless
//you can use AnsiToUnicode or AnsiToUnicode256
//
#ifdef UNICODE
        #define AnsiToOlechar(x)     (x)
#else
        #define AnsiToOlechar(x)     (AnsiToUnicode256(x))
#endif
```

The most important part of Listing 23.3 is the last five lines. When COMMON.H is included in a Unicode application, AnsiToOlechar simply passes the parameter with no translation (the string is most likely already Unicode in a Unicode application). When COMMON.H is included in a non-Unicode application, AnsiToOlechar calls a function, called AnsiToUnicode256, which translates an ANSI string to a Unicode string. Listing 23.4 shows the implementation of AnsiToUnicode256.

Listing 23.4. Unicode translation routines from COMMON.CPP.

```
//The routine AnsiToUnicode converts an ANSI string into an OLECHAR
//An OLECHAR is a UNICODE string under Win32 and is a char under Win16
//A TCHAR is not a UNICODE string unless UNICODE is defined during the
//compilation of the application
//Also Windows 95 and Win32s do not support Unicode, however the OLE libraries
//for the Win32 platform requires Unicode
//
OLECHAR *AnsiToUnicode(TCHAR *szInput)
{
    //uiInputLength is the number of characters (not the number of bytes) of
    //szInput. 1 is added to the length to include the NUL terminator.
    //
    //If you need the number of bytes use: (uiInputLength * sizeof(TCHAR))
    //
    unsigned int uiInputLength = lstrlen(szInput)+1;

    //Since the follow code performs a 'new' the caller is expected to 'delete'
    //the OLECHAR which is returned
    //
    OLECHAR *pRet = new OLECHAR(uiInputLength);

    //'new' failed so there's no point in going on
    if (pRet == NULL)
        return pRet;

    //If you want to try to ensure that szInput is not Unicode, you
    //can call IsTextUnicode (before AnsiToWide)
    //which returns either TRUE (szInput is probably Unicode)
    //or FALSE (szInput is
    //probably not Unicode).
    //IsTextUnicode performs statistical tests on the input
    //string so it may not always return the correct answer
    //
    //AnsiToWide is a macro defined in Common.h
    //which simply calls MultiByteToWideChar
    //with the necessary parameters.
    //MultiByteToWideChar is actually the Window API
    //which performs the conversion.
    //
    AnsiToWide(szInput,pRet,uiInputLength);
    return pRet;
}

//The routine AnsiToUnicode256 converts
//an ANSI string into an OLECHAR
//An OLECHAR is a UNICODE string under Win32
//and is a char under Win16
//This routine differs from AnsiToUnicode
//in that you don't delete the
//returned string. In addition, this routine
//has a limit of 256 characters.
//
OLECHAR         AnsiToUnicodeReturn[256];

OLECHAR *AnsiToUnicode256(TCHAR *szInput)
{
```

continues

Listing 23.4. continued

```
//uiInputLength is the number of characters (not the number of bytes) of
//szInput. 1 is added to the length to include the NUL terminator.
//
//If you need the number of bytes use: (uiInputLength * sizeof(TCHAR))
//
unsigned int uiInputLength = lstrlen(szInput)+1;

//This routine supports a maximum size of 256, if you need a larger
//translation, use AnsiToUnicode instead
//
if (uiInputLength >= 256)
        return NULL;

OLECHAR *pRet = AnsiToUnicodeReturn;

//If you want to try to ensure that szInput is not Unicode, you
//can call IsTextUnicode (before AnsiToWide)
//which returns either TRUE (szInput is probably Unicode)
//or FALSE (szInput is
//probably not Unicode).
//IsTextUnicode performs statistical tests on the input
//string so it may not always return the correct answer
//
//AnsiToWide is a macro defined in Common.h
//which simply calls MultiByteToWideChar
//with the necessary parameters.
//MultiByteToWideChar is actually the Window API
//which performs the conversion.
//
AnsiToWide(szInput,pRet,uiInputLength);
return pRet;
}
```

In Listing 23.4 there are two routines that can be used to translate ANSI strings to Unicode strings. The first routine, AnsiToUnicode, is a general-purpose routine that accepts a string and converts it to Unicode. The main drawback in using AnsiToUnicode is that any string returned by AnsiToUnicode must be freed (by using delete) by your application. In most situations, when you convert an ANSI string to a Unicode string, the ANSI string will be 256 characters or less. If your ANSI string is 256 characters or less, you can use AnsiToUnicode256. AnsiToUnicode256 uses a static area to return the Unicode string so that the returned result can be used directly as a parameter in an OLE function call. Because AnsiToUnicode256 uses a single static area to return the Unicode string, you must use the returned result before calling AnsiToUnicode256 again, or else the original result will be lost.

Multithreaded OLE

Windows 95 applications differ from 16-bit applications, because Windows 95 supports multithreaded applications. In the 16-bit world, applications always ran in a single thread. In Windows 95 an application can be written so that it is multithreaded (appearing to do a number of things at the same time within one application). Windows NT also supports multithreaded applications; however, in Windows NT, multiple threads may run on multiple CPUs within the same machine. To accommodate multithreaded applications, the concept of an "apartment model" has been created.

In the 16-bit implementation of OLE, an OLE object lived in a single thread. OLE is first initialized (using `OleInitialize` or `CoInitialize`) and then the OLE object is created. In the "apartment model," the concept of initializing OLE and then creating an object in a single thread is known as a "single apartment." Windows 95 expands on the "single apartment" concept by allowing multithreaded applications to create multiple "apartments" with the restrictions that a thread, which will use OLE, initializes OLE and creates an object within a thread and that an object must reside in a single thread. In other words, if you create (or use) an OLE object in thread *X*, all OLE interactions for that OLE object must occur in thread *X*. You can create a different object in thread *Y;* however all OLE interactions for the object created in thread *Y* must occur in thread *Y.*

In order to write a multithreaded OLE application, the "apartment model" has a few rules that must be observed as well as making sure that all OLE interactions for a particular object occur in the single thread. The following list contains the rules that must be followed.

- Each thread with an OLE object must have a message queue.
- Objects created in a DLL that support the "apartment model" must be aware that they may be called from multiple threads within a single application and be expected to create the object in the application thread which requested the object to be created.
- The registration database entries for objects created in a DLL that support the "apartment model" must have the entry `ThreadingModel=Apartment`. This is discussed further in Chapter 24.

Differences Between Windows 95 OLE and 16-Bit Windows OLE

If you read articles or books on OLE, you will find that the 16-bit implementation of OLE is different from the OLE implementation in Windows 95 in a number of areas. For example, the Windows 95 (and Windows NT 3.51) implementation of OLE supports multithreaded OLE applications. Because multithreading in the 16-bit version of Windows was not possible, there was no reason to support multithreading in OLE. Although Windows NT 3.5 supported multithreaded applications, Windows NT 3.5 does not support multithreaded OLE applications. As discussed in the previous section "Multithreaded OLE," Windows 95 and Windows NT 3.51 both support OLE in multiple threads.

In the 16-bit version of Windows, OLE used window messages to exchange information between OLE applications (these window messages are known as Lightweight Remote Procedure Calls or LRPC). The 32-bit implementation of OLE uses Local Procedure Calls (also known as LPC) to exchange information between OLE applications on the same machine. Local Procedure Calls are private, nonpublished methods used to exchange data. Local Procedure Calls do not use the Windows message queue. This is one of the reasons why OLE applications running on Windows 95 or Windows NT 3.5 (but not Win32s) do not require your application to change the message queue size for OLE applications. The other reason is that Windows 95 and Windows NT 3.5 can dynamically change the message queue size.

Sixteen-bit Windows applications (and Win32s) must call `OLEBuildVersion` to obtain the version number OLE. Windows 95 and Windows NT 3.5 do not require a call to `OLEBuildVersion`.

Windows 95 and Windows NT 3.5 both require parameters that are passed as strings to be Unicode strings. Sixteen-bit Windows applications require parameters that are passed as strings to be ANSI strings.

Previous implementations of OLE (16- and 32-bit versions) came with a sample directory that contained the OLEUI, which contained OLE-specific common dialog boxes. Windows 95 has these common dialog boxes built into OLEDLG.DLL. To use these common dialog boxes, your applications need to include OLEDLG.H and link with OLEDLG.LIB.

The 16-bit implementation of OLE allowed applications to have application-specific memory allocation for OLE by calling `OleInitialize` with an `IMalloc` interface pointer. The 32-bit implementation of OLE does not allow applications to specify memory allocations for OLE's use.

Windows 95 (and Windows NT 3.51) support a new root storage type known as "simple storage." Simple storages are discussed in Chapter 25, "Window Objects and Compound Documents."

Summary

OLE plays a major role in Windows 95, and you will find OLE mentioned throughout this book. If you previously used OLE on Windows 3.1, you will find that OLE has changed in Windows 95. In Windows 95, `OleBuildVersion` is no longer required, the OLE common dialog boxes are part of the operating system, and OLE now supports multithreaded applications. If you are new to OLE, you will find that OLE supports automation which allows an application to control another application, and OLE includes a file system that is akin to DOS.

Component Object Model (COM)

24

by Lawrence Harris

IN THIS CHAPTER

The Component Object Model, also known as COM, is a specification for how objects communicate with each other. In its simplest form, COM is a contract for binary compatibility among OLE objects.

Interfaces

An *interface* is nothing more than a pointer to an object. An interface does not directly point to the object, but actually points to a virtual function table (see Figure 24.1). This virtual function table only contains the methods (functions and procedures) related to that particular interface. Every OLE object typically has multiple interfaces, each with a specialty. For example, an object might contain a file interface, a printing interface, and a calculation interface. Functions or procedures within the file interface can be used to read, write, or delete a file. The printing interface can have functions or procedures to write the printout heading, printout footer, and printout body. The calculation interface can be used to multiply, divide, add, and subtract.

FIGURE 24.1.
OLE object interfaces.

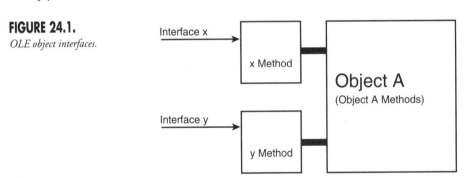

One way to conceptualize an interface is to imagine your PC as an OLE object. DOS can be thought of as an interface, which handles your I/O methods. Windows is another interface, which handles your screen methods and requires your DOS methods. Your PC might also have private methods and interfaces that are not exposed, such as some of the ROM BIOS routines. Your first problem is how to discover all the interfaces an object might have. You cannot, for example, query your PC to find out what interfaces it supports—you must know what interfaces it supports. OLE, however, enables you to query an object to discover what specific interfaces the object supports by using IUnknown.

IUnknown

In order to find out if an object supports a particular interface in OLE, you can simply ask the object, do you support *x*? If the object supports *x*, the object responds yes; otherwise, the object responds no. If the object responds that it does support a particular interface, the question becomes, how do you get the interface (because all interfaces are pointers)? OLE solves this problem by not responding yes, but instead returning the requested interface pointer (or an error code if it does not support the interface). The interface you would question is called IUnknown. IUnknown is required for every object. IUnknown is also required for every interface. If you look at Figure 24.2, you will notice that the object has an IUnknown (which is at the top of the object). This IUnknown is the object's main IUnknown and is normally drawn on the top of the object. This IUnknown typically knows about all the interfaces an object exposes (aggregation supports a technique in which the main IUnknown does not know all of the interfaces that are publicly exposed). If you then examine the two interfaces to the right of the object, you will notice that each of them has an IUnknown as the first part of their virtual table. If you were to further examine IUnknown, you would see that it has three methods: QueryInterface, AddRef, and Release.

FIGURE 24.2.

An object's IUnknown interface.

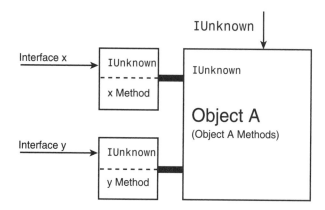

QueryInterface

Now that you understand that an interface is just a pointer to a function table within the object, how do you get the interface you want? Using the IUnknown interface, you call the method QueryInterface. QueryInterface is required to be implemented in every implementation of every interface. QueryInterface enables you to ask the question, do you support interface *x*? The function then returns the interface if the object does support the interface in question. Here is the actual syntax for QueryInterface:

```
HRESULT IUnknown::QueryInterface(REFIID riid, LPVOID FAR *ppvObj);
```

In this example riid is the interface ID (IID) of the interface in question (more on this a little later), and ppvObj is a pointer to the interface if the requested riid is supported. ppvObj is NULL if the interface is not supported. If the requested riid is not supported (ppvObj is NULL), what is the HRESULT being returned? An HRESULT is a handle to a result, just as HWND is a handle to a window. The HRESULT, as currently defined, is the following:

Bits	Field	Description
31	Severity field	Returns 0 if the function succeeded; otherwise, returns 1 if the function failed or an error has occurred.
20–30	Context field	Reserved for future use. Its value should not be assumed to be 0.
16–19	Facility field	Allocated only by Microsoft. This field indicates to which error group an error belongs. Here are the currently valid facilities:
0–15	Code field	Describes the error or status that occurred, based on the facility (see the OLE `include` files for the currently supported codes). The code field does not necessarily indicate an error code. It may actually pass additional information on success; therefore, do not assume that an error has occurred if the code field is not 0. The severity field indicates whether an error has occurred.

Constant	Error Type	Value
FACILITY_NULL	Common	0
FACILITY_RPC	RPC error	1
FACILITY_DISPATCH	IDispatch	2
FACILITY_STORAGE	Storage error	3
FACILITY_ITF	Interface error	4

Currently, all code constants are defined in the following format:

*<Facility>*_*<Severity>*_*<Reason>*, where, if the facility is FACILITY_NULL, then *<Facility>*_ is dropped. Examples are E_UNEXPECTED (FACILITY_NULL), STG_S_CONVERTED (FACILITY_STORAGE and success), and DISP_E_MEMBERNOTFOUND (FACILITY_DISPATCH).

Now, refer back to QueryInterface in the earlier example. QueryInterface returns an HRESULT. If the requested interface is not supported, QueryInterface returns E_NOINTERFACE, and if the interface is supported, QueryInterface returns S_OK. Functions that return an HRESULT can either succeed or fail, both for a particular reason. The HRESULT provides information indicating success or failure. On a failure, the HRESULT also provides a reason for the failure. The following example illustrates how errors are handled:

```
HRESULT hresult = x->QueryInterface(IID_ICLASSFACTORY, ppv);
 if (SUCCEEDED(hresult)) {
   // do success stuff
 } else {
   // do failed stuff
 }
```

The macro SUCCEEDED is defined in SCODE.H (part of the OLE SDK) and returns TRUE if bit 31 (severity field) is 0. Otherwise, SUCCEEDED returns FALSE. SCODE.H also has another macro, called FAILED, which returns TRUE if bit 31 is 1. Otherwise, FAILED returns FALSE.

AddRef and Release

AddRef is the next required method of IUnknown. AddRef is used to maintain a reference count on an object. A *reference count* is used to determine when an object should be destroyed. One of the main rules of OLE programming is that when an interface is given out, it remains valid until the object is destroyed. Objects typically (although not always) are destroyed when there are no more references to that object. An object increments its reference count whenever AddRef is called, and decrements its reference count whenever Release is called. When the reference count for an object reaches 0, that is, when Release is called and it decrements the reference count to 0, the Release method can destroy the object.

The following are the declarations for AddRef and Release:

```
ULONG IUnknown::AddRef(void);
ULONG IUnknown::Release(void);
```

The return from both AddRef and Release is the current number of outstanding references to the object. If Release returns 0, the object was destroyed. OLE 2 requires Release to return 0 if the object was destroyed, but other implementations of OLE might not return or require 0. Therefore, do not test for 0 to see if an object was destroyed. Also, because AddRef and Release both return an unsigned long, your object must be able to handle 2<31>−1 outstanding interface references.

The value returned by AddRef and Release is the current number of outstanding references to the object. If you need to know the number of references an object has and you already have an interface pointer to the object, you can call AddRef, immediately followed by Release. The value returned by Release is the current number of references to the object. If you use the value returned by AddRef, it will be off by one; you want the number of references to the object, not including the reference you just made by calling AddRef. Microsoft does not recommend that you use the values returned by AddRef or Release for any purpose other than debugging.

Whenever you release an interface pointer, you should first test to see if the interface pointer is NULL. If the interface pointer is NULL, do not call Release (because you don't have an interface pointer), and if the interface pointer is not NULL, call Release and then null out the pointer after calling Release. You will find that this technique will keep you out of trouble because calling Release on a NULL pointer will cause a program error.

IUnknown Implementation

Most IUnknown implementations look very similar to each other. Listing 24.1 contains a typical implementation of IUnknown. QueryInterface will list all the interfaces the object exposes. Listing 24.1 shows the implementation of IUnknown.

Listing 24.1. The Implementation of *IUnknown*.

```
STDMETHODIMP
COleWpuObject::QueryInterface(REFIID riid, void FAR* FAR* ppv)
{
        if (riid == IID_IUnknown)
                *ppv = this;
         else {
                *ppv = NULL;
                return ResultFromScode(E_NOINTERFACE);
        }

        AddRef();
        return NOERROR;
}

STDMETHODIMP_(ULONG)COleWpuObject::AddRef()
{
        return ++m_refs;
}

STDMETHODIMP_(ULONG)COleWpuObject::Release()
{
        if(--m_refs == 0)
        {
          delete this;
          return 0;
        }
        return m_refs;
}
```

In this example, the QueryInterface only supports the IUnknown interface; therefore, it returns a pointer to itself in ppv whenever it is asked for the IUnknown interface. QueryInterface then calls AddRef to let the object know that it has given out an interface, and returns NOERROR. If any other interface is requested, ppv contains a NULL and E_NOINTERFACE is returned. In this case, AddRef is not called because the object did not return an interface (it returned NULL).

Next, AddRef is defined. In your implementation AddRef merely increments a reference counter and returns the current reference count. Finally, Release is implemented. Release looks to see if the reference count is becoming 0 and if it is the object to be deleted. If the reference count is not 0, the current value of the reference count is returned.

Depending on the complexity of the object, additional code may be implemented in QueryInterface, AddRef, and Release to perform additional functions. Objects that are more complex may require the implementation of Release to perform additional cleanup (such as deleting memory allocated by the object).

GUID

GUID (Global Unique Interface ID, pronounced "GOO-ID") is a 128-bit number represented in string form by 32 hex digits. A CLSID (class ID) is used to uniquely identify an object. A CLSID is a GUID. An IID (interface ID), which uniquely identifies an interface, is also a GUID. An example of a CLSID is {00021A00-0000-0000-C000-000000000046}, which is used by Visio. An example of an IID is {00000000-0000-0000-C000-000000000046}, which belongs to IUnknown. When CLSIDs and IIDs are visually represented, they are enclosed in curly braces {}, and are in the following format: Eight hexdigits, dash, four hexdigits, dash, four hexdigits, dash, four hexdigits, dash, and 12 hexdigits, with all the hexdigits in uppercase.

IClassFactory

Now that you have learned about IUnknown, here is the next question: How is an object created? One way you can create an object is to use the *class factory interface* (IClassFactory). IClassFactory creates instances of the object class. The class factory interface requires you to implement five methods: Three for IUnknown, which is required for every interface, and two for the class factory itself, CreateInstance and LockServer.

CreateInstance is called to create an instance of an object. CreateInstance can almost be thought of as the OLE equivalent of C++'s new. The main conceptual difference between C++'s new and CreateInstance is that new allocates memory in the caller's process space for the object (if you call new on an object), whereas CreateInstance creates the object in the object server's process space. For example, if you have the interface pointer to a class factory within Excel, you create an object within Excel's process space (LRPC takes care of passing the interface and data between your application and Excel). If the object server is implemented in a DLL, the object is created in your process space (LRPC and LPC are not involved). The following is the syntax for CreateInstance:

```
HRESULT IClassFactory::CreateInstance(LPUNKNOWN pUnkOut,
➡REFIID riid, LPVOID FAR *ppvObj);
```

In this example, pUnkOut is NULL unless the object is being created as part of an aggregate object. If pUnkOut is not NULL, it is an interface pointer to the controlling IUnknown interface. riid is the interface ID (IID) of the interface you want from the newly created object. ppvObj is an interface pointer to the interface if the requested IID is supported. ppvObj is NULL if the interface is not supported.

LockServer is used to keep the server in memory. Keeping the server in memory can make the creation of additional instances of the object faster — the server is already in memory and you don't need to start it again. Large applications, such as Microsoft Excel or Microsoft Word, may take several seconds to reload the entire executable, which is slower than if Windows just needed to swap in the needed portion of the server (Excel or Word, for example). LockServer keeps the server in memory regardless of whether the server is currently maintaining any objects.

Interfaces Revisited

Previously, I stated that an interface is merely a pointer to an object through a virtual table. C++ programmers are familiar with virtual tables because this technique is used to access C++ class objects. You might have assumed that OLE actually used the C++ class to implement OLE; however, OLE actually uses the C++ struct in its OLE implementation. For non-Borland users interface is defined as this:

```
#define  interface struct FAR
```

while for Borland users it's defined as this:

```
#define  interface struct huge
```

Declaring a class/struct as huge in Borland C++ makes the virtual table pointer a far pointer, which is required for OLE.

OLE actually creates an interface by using the C++ form of 'struct' (which is different than the C form of 'struct'). A typical OLE interface (for non-Borland users) appears in Listing 24.2.

Listing 24.2. A non-Borland implementation of IClassFactory.

```
struct FAR IClassFactory : public IUnknown
{
 virtual HRESULT STDMETHODCALLTYPE QueryInterface(
        IID FAR& riid,
        LPVOID FAR* ppvObj) = 0;
 virtual HRESULT STDMETHODCALLTYPE AddRef(void) = 0;
 virtual HRESULT STDMETHODCALLTYPE Release(void) = 0;
 virtual HRESULT STDMETHODCALLTYPE CreateInstance(
        LPUNKNOWN pUnkOuter,
        IID FAR& riid,
        LPVOID FAR* ppvObject) = 0;
 virtual HRESULT STDMETHODCALLTYPE LockServer(
        BOOL fLock)=0;
 };
```

In C++, this form of 'struct' is similar to 'class' except that by default the members are public. The keyword virtual and the trailing = 0 make each function a pure virtual function, which is the C++ equivalent of an abstract class/struct. Because the class/struct has pure virtual functions, it cannot be instantiated. And because these are pure virtual functions, when you derive from this class/struct, you need to fully define all the members in the base class. Because all OLE interfaces use IUnknown, you can now see why IUnknown is required to be implemented in every interface. It is not optional. The compiler will force you to define the members of IUnknown because the IUnknown methods are defined as pure virtual functions. In fact, the first three entries in the virtual table for every OLE interface are QueryInterface, AddRef, and Release.

When you create a single OLE object, you are actually creating one or more C++ objects, depending on the number of interfaces your OLE object supports. Typically, for each interface your OLE object supports, you will be creating one C++ object.

Marshaling

Although a complete discussion on marshaling is beyond the scope of this book, a brief discussion is in order for you to at least understand the concept.

Marshaling in OLE is the act of making an interface available from an object server to an object client. When an OLE automation client talks to an automation server, for example, the client requests the IUnknown interface in order to obtain the IDispatch interface. The only problem is that the IUnknown interface is a pointer, which is in the address space of the server. In order to provide this pointer to the client, OLE "packaged" the IUnknown interface to pass the pointer to the client. The client in turn "unpackaged" the data to obtain the pointer. The act of "packaging" the data for transfer is referred to as marshaling, while the act of "unpackaging" the data is called *unmarshaling*.

In order to "package" the data, OLE normally relies on a technique called Lightweight Remote Procedure Calls (LRPC) under the 16-bit implementation of Windows and Local Procedure Calls (LPC) under the 32-bit implementation of Windows. The LRPC mechanism, as currently implemented in OLE, uses the Windows PostMessage to send data from the automation server to the automation client. In fact, you need to set the message queue to 96 in Win16 applications because the message queue is large enough to handle all the PostMessages generated by the OLE marshaling methods. LRPC differs from the more traditional Remote Procedure Calls (RPC) in that LRPC only supports communication between processes on the same machine, whereas RPC supports communication between processes on the same or different machines.

Marshaling is only required for OLE objects that are implemented in executables. DLL objects do not require marshaling because they run in the process space of the requesting application. Since DLL objects do not require marshaling, they tend to run faster than their EXE counterparts. An advantage EXE objects have is that it doesn't matter whether the server application is a 16-bit server or a 32-bit server.

Another advantage in the implementation of marshaling is that objects do not need to reside on the same machine. When the server is one type of machine, and the client is on another type of machine, OLE uses RPC to perform the data transfer. In this case, the two machines do not even have to be the same processor types (one can be an Intel machine and the other could be a DEC Alpha, for example). At this time, however, marshaling across CPU boundaries is only provided by Distributed OLE.

Currently, all interfaces defined by OLE provide marshaling except `IEnumUnknown`. This allows all interfaces defined by OLE to be marshaled across process boundaries. At this time the fact that `IEnumUnknown` does not provide marshaling is a known bug in OLE 2.01.

The Component Object Model (COM) is the infrastructure for OLE. COM is not only a set of standards for the implementation of objects, but it is also a set of APIs to facilitate the implementation of these standards.

The COM includes the following:

- Interfaces that implement `IUnknown`
- An `IMalloc` interface, which allows OLE to easily use custom memory management
- Enumeration, which is a standard used to iterate through a group of items
- Marshaling, which is a technique used to pass interfaces between processes

IShellLink

To demonstrate a simple OLE application I will show you how to create an application that uses an interface used by Windows 95, `IShellLink`. If you have used Windows 95, you might be familiar with a shortcut. A *shortcut* is simply a small file that points to another file. A shortcut is typically used to place an icon on the desktop (where the shortcut will appear in the desktop directory) and to point to the application that is run whenever the icon is selected. A shortcut is created by using `IShellLink`. Listing 24.3 shows a simple application which uses `IShellLink`.

Listing 24.3. Implementation of `IShellLink`.

```
int CALLBACK WinMain(
        HINSTANCE hInstance,
        HINSTANCE hPrevInstance,
        LPSTR /* lpCmdLine */,
        int nCmdShow)
{

        MSG msg;
        HACCEL hAccelTable;

        //Under Windows 95 and Windows NT you do
        //not need to change the message queue
        //size as the queue will change dynamically.
        //Under Win32s and Win16 the message queue size
```

```
       //must be changed to work
       //with many OLE APIs
       //Since changing the queue size under Windows 95
       //and Windows NT is not harmful
       //the queue size will be changed in all cases.
       //
       int     iMsgQueueSize = 96;
       while   ((SetMessageQueue(iMsgQueueSize) == 0)
       ➥ && (iMsgQueueSize>0))
           iMsgQueueSize -= 8;
       if (iMsgQueueSize <= 0)
           return FALSE;

//In Win32 hPrevInstance is always NULL
//regardless of whether a previous instance
//is running. If we want to determine
//if a previous instance is running
//we'll look for a window which we create
//
//If we find a previous instance,
//we terminate the current instance and
//bring focus to the previous instance
//
       HWND    hWndPreviousInstance;

       if ((hWndPreviousInstance =
       ➥ FindWindow(szAppName,NULL)) != NULL){
           ShowWindow(hWndPreviousInstance,SW_SHOW);
           return (FALSE);
       }

       if (!hPrevInstance) { // Other instances of app running?
           if (!InitApplication(hInstance)) { // Initialize shared things
               return (FALSE); // Exits if unable to initialize
           }
       }

       /* Perform initializations that apply to a specific instance */

       if (!InitInstance(hInstance, nCmdShow)) {
               return (FALSE);
       }

       HRESULT hResult;
       IUnknown *punk;
       IShellLink *pShellLink;
       IPersistFile *pFile;

       TCHAR   szError[100];

       //Initialize OLE
       hResult = ::OleInitialize(NULL);
       if (FAILED(hResult)){
           HResultToString(hResult,szError);
           MessageBox(NULL,szError,"OleInitialize",MB_OK);
           return (FALSE);
       }
```

continues

Listing 24.3. continued

```
//Try to obtain an IShellLink object
hResult = ::CoCreateInstance(CLSID_ShellLink,
                NULL,
                CLSCTX_SERVER,
                IID_IUnknown,
                (void **)&punk);
if (FAILED(hResult)){
    HResultToString(hResult,szError);
    MessageBox(NULL,szError,"CoCreateInstance",MB_OK);
    ::OleUninitialize();
    return (FALSE);
} else {
    //Get the IShellLink interface
    hResult = punk->QueryInterface(IID_IShellLink,
                                   (void **)&pShellLink);

    if (FAILED(hResult)){
        HResultToString(hResult,szError);
        MessageBox(NULL,szError,"IShellLink",MB_OK);
        punk->Release();
        ::OleUninitialize();
        return (FALSE);
    }

    TCHAR    szPathName[MAX_PATH];
    TCHAR    szPName[MAX_PATH];
    TCHAR    szWorking[MAX_PATH];

    //Setup the info to create a link
    GetModuleFileName(hInstance,
                    szPathName,
                    sizeof(szPathName)/sizeof(TCHAR));
    splitpath(szPathName,szWorking,szPName,NULL,NULL);
    lstrcat(szWorking,szPName);
    pShellLink->SetPath(szPathName);
    pShellLink->SetWorkingDirectory(szWorking);
    pShellLink->SetDescription("My DeScRiPtIoN");

    //Get the IPersistFile interface to create the link
    hResult = punk->QueryInterface(IID_IPersistFile,
                                   (void **)&pFile);
    if (FAILED(hResult)){
        HResultToString(hResult,szError);
        MessageBox(NULL,szError,"IPersistFile",MB_OK);
    } else {
        DWORD cb;
        TCHAR szDesktop[MAX_PATH], szStartMenu[MAX_PATH];
        TCHAR szTemp[MAX_PATH];
        HKEY hKey, hKey1, hKey2, hKey3, hKey4, hKey5;

        //Find out the directories to store the links
        ::RegOpenKeyEx(HKEY_CURRENT_USER,
                    "Software",0, KEY_ALL_ACCESS,&hKey);
        ::RegOpenKeyEx(hKey,"Microsoft",0,
                    KEY_ALL_ACCESS,&hKey1);
        ::RegOpenKeyEx(hKey1,"Windows",0,
                    KEY_ALL_ACCESS,&hKey2);
```

```
            ::RegOpenKeyEx(hKey2,"CurrentVersion",0,
                            KEY_ALL_ACCESS, &hKey3);
            ::RegOpenKeyEx(hKey3,"Explorer",0,
                            KEY_ALL_ACCESS, &hKey4);
            ::RegOpenKeyEx(hKey4,"Shell Folders",0,
                            KEY_ALL_ACCESS, &hKey5);
            cb = sizeof(szDesktop);
            ::RegQueryValueEx(hKey5,"Desktop",
                            NULL,NULL,
                            (LPBYTE)szDesktop,&cb);
            cb = sizeof(szStartMenu);
            ::RegQueryValueEx(hKey5, "Start Menu",
                            NULL, NULL,
                            (LPBYTE)szStartMenu,&cb);

            //Places the shortcut on the Programs menu
            lstrcpy(szTemp,szStartMenu);
            lstrcat(szTemp,"\\programs\\tst.lnk");
            hResult = pFile->Save(AnsiToOleChar(szTemp),FALSE);
            HResultToString(hResult,szError);
            MessageBox(NULL,szError,"IPersistFile->Save",MB_OK);

            //Places the shortcut directly onto the Start menu
            lstrcpy(szTemp,szStartMenu);
            lstrcat(szTemp,"\\tst.lnk");
            hResult = pFile->Save(AnsiToOleChar(szTemp),FALSE);
            HResultToString(hResult,szError);
            MessageBox(NULL,szError,"IPersistFile->Save",MB_OK);

            //Places the shortcut directly onto the user's desktop
            lstrcpy(szTemp,szDesktop);
            lstrcat(szTemp,"\\tst.lnk");
            hResult = pFile->Save(AnsiToOleChar(szTemp),FALSE);
            HResultToString(hResult,szError);
            MessageBox(NULL,szError,"IPersistFile->Save",MB_OK);
        }

    //Release the obtained interfaces
    if (pFile != NULL){
        pFile->Release();
        pFile = NULL;
    }

    if (pShellLink != NULL){
        pShellLink->Release();
        pShellLink = NULL;
    }

    if (punk != NULL){
        punk->Release();
        punk = NULL;
    }
}

hAccelTable = LoadAccelerators (hInstance,
                                MAKEINTRESOURCE(IDR_PMOLE));

/* Acquire and dispatch messages until a
```

continues

Listing 24.3. continued

```
        WM_QUIT message is received. */

    while (GetMessage(&msg, // message structure
        NULL,    // handle of window receiving the message
        0,       // lowest message to examine
        0))      // highest message to examine
    {
            if (!TranslateAccelerator (msg.hwnd,
                                        hAccelTable, &msg)) {
                    TranslateMessage(&msg);
                    ➡ // Translates virtual key codes
                    DispatchMessage(&msg);
                    ➡ // Dispatches message to window
            }
    }

    //Uninitialize OLE
    ::OleUninitialize();
    return (msg.wParam); // Returns the value from PostQuitMessage
}
```

The first part of the application changes the message queue size to 96. Once this has been accomplished, initialize OLE by calling OleInitialize (disregarding the calls to InitInstance and InitApplication). Once OLE has been initialized, a new IShellLink is obtained by calling CoCreateInstance, which requests the object CLSID_ShellLink. If the object is successfully created, CoCreateInstance returns the IUnknown interface to the object. Once the IUnknown interface is obtained, the application then calls QueryInterface to obtain the IShellLink interface.

After an application has obtained the IShellLink interface, it can use the interface to create a shortcut. In the sample application, the application creates three shortcuts. The application first calls GetModuleFileName to obtain its own filename and path, and then calls _splitpath to separate the filename from the path. Once the filename and path is obtained, the application calls the SetPath member of IShellLink to set its path and name. The application then calls SetWorkingDirectory to set its working directory. SetDescription is called to set the description field for the shortcut.

After you have set the application specific information for a shortcut, you need to write the information to disk. The interface used by IShellLink to write information to disk is IPersistFile (see Chapter 25, "Window Objects and Compound Documents"). To obtain the IPersistFile interface pointer, the application uses the IUnknown interface pointer (which was obtained from CoCreateInstance) and calls QueryInterface to request a pointer to the IPersistFile interface. Once you have a pointer to the IPersistFile interface, you need to decide where to store the shortcut. For example, to have the shortcut become a part of the Programs menu, you need to obtain the directory in which entries for the Programs menu are written. To obtain this directory, the sample application uses the registration database to obtain directory information. Once it obtains the directory information it needs, the application creates a shortcut, called TST.LNK, by calling the `Save` member of `IPersistFile` to write the shortcut file. The application then creates an entry on the Start menu and an icon on your desktop for the shortcut file.

After all the shortcuts have been created, the application releases the `IPersistFile` interface pointer and then releases the `IShellLink` interface pointer. Finally, the application releases the `IUnknown` interface pointer and calls `OleUninitialize`.

NOTE

To delete the shortcuts created by this application, use the Start menu Find option. Select "Files or Folders" and enter TST.LNK. Then select "Find Now." When the three entries appear, you can select each entry and then press the delete key to remove the entry.

Also, although this application demonstrates how to create shortcuts on the desktop and on the Start and Programs menu, you should not arbitrarily create these items for the user. For the proper use of shortcuts for installation applications, you should refer to the section "Application Setup Guides" in the Windows 95 Guide to Programming help file.

Summary

The Component Object Model (COM) is a specification dictating the communication between OLE objects. The interface that is used to determine the capabilities of an object is `IUnknown`. In addition, OLE objects are created by calling the `IClassFactory` interface for an object.

Finally, Windows 95 has an `IShellLink` interface that is used to create shortcuts. For the proper use of 'shortcuts' for installation applications, you should refer to the "Application Setup Guides" section in the Windows 95 Guide to Programming help file.

Window Objects and Compound Documents

25

by Lawrence Harris

Window objects and compound documents are two implementations of OLE based on the Component Object Model discussed in Chapter 24, "Component Object Model (COM)." In this chapter you will learn the differences between a C++ object and a Window object, and then create an OLE container that uses compound documents. In Chapter 26, "Visual Editing," you will change your container to support visual editing; in Chapter 27, "Drag and Drop," you will add drag/drop support; and in Chapter 28, "OLE Automation," you will add OLE automation support.

Window Objects

In Chapter 24, I discussed the Component Object Model. It is, as you learned, a specification. Objects that follow the Component Object Model specification are called *Window Objects*. A Window Object is independent of any implementation language, although C++ is currently the easiest language in which to develop Window Objects. Window Objects must not be confused with C++ objects, however. Window Objects are always accessed via interfaces, and each interface has a minimum of three methods (`QueryInterface`, `AddRef`, and `Release`), whereas C++ objects are accessed via their member functions (with a minimum of two member functions, the constructor and destructor). C++ objects are not easily accessed using non-C++ applications; in fact, an object created in one vendor's C++ compiler is not easily accessible by an application created using another's (because of name mangling). Window Objects, on the other hand, can be accessed by many different languages, and an object created using one vendor's C++ compiler can be accessed by an application created in another's. Window Objects can also be accessed easily by applications created in Visual Basic or Visual Basic for Applications.

Compound Documents

A *compound document* can be thought of as a collection of Window Objects. Window Objects are implemented in applications or dynamic link libraries called *servers* and are manipulated by applications called *containers*. It is possible, however, to implement a Window Object in a container that includes server functionality; it is also possible to manipulate objects using OLE Automation (discussed in Chapter 28). Compound documents are typically stored in *structured storage*, which is OLE's equivalent to a file system. To see how compound documents work, let's take a look at container applications.

Containers

If you have used Microsoft Word 6, Microsoft Excel 5, or WordPad (which is included in Windows 95), you have used an OLE container. A *container* is simply an application that is capable of holding one or more Window Objects. A container minimally needs to support

`IOleClientSite`, `IAdviseSink`, and `IStorage` interfaces. Let's quickly take a look at each of these interfaces.

IOleClientSite

Every OLE container must support the `IOleClientSite` interface. `IOleClientSite` is used by servers to obtain information from or provide information to containers. `IOleClientSite` has six methods (in addition to `AddRef`, `Release`, and `QueryInterface`), as indicated in Table 25.1.

Table 25.1. `IOleClientSite` **methods.**

Method	Description
SaveObject	Called by an object when the user selects File Exit or Update from the object server's application. The container then saves the object into a compound document.
GetMoniker	Called by an object when the object needs the container's moniker to support linking.
GetContainer	Called when the object requires the container's `IOleContainer` interface to support linking.
ShowObject	Called when the object wants the container to make the object fully visible. The container might need to scroll the document in order to make the object fully visible, or might need to restore a document if the document is currently minimized.
OnShowWindow	Called when an object wants to inform a container whether the object is becoming visible or invisible. If an object is visible, the container needs to display the object hatched; otherwise the object is displayed without hatching.
RequestNewObjectLayout	Called by OLE controls to tell a container that the OLE control needs more or less display room.

Every time a new object is inserted in a container, the container must provide to the object a new `IOleClientSite` interface pointer (for that object's exclusive use). The object then uses the `IOleClientSite` interface pointer that was provided by the container to communicate with the container.

IAdviseSink

IAdviseSink is another interface that is required to be implemented by a container. IAdviseSink is used by a container to receive notification from an object when the object changes. For example, when an object's data changes, OnDataChange is called, whereas when an object's view changes, OnViewChange is notified. The reason that there is separate notification for data and view changes is because a view change does not necessarily cause a data change (and vice versa). For example, if you zoom an object (causing the object to become larger), the data for the object does not change, just the physical appearance of the object. Table 25.2 shows the six methods (not including AddRef, Release, and QueryInterface) for IAdviseSink.

Table 25.2. IAdviseSink methods.

Method	Description
OnDataChange	Notification that the object's data has changed. You can ignore this notification or implement it as you see fit.
OnViewChange	Notification that the object's view has changed; this does not necessarily mean, however, that the object's data has changed. dwAspect is the aspect that has changed, whereas lindex is the piece of the view that has changed and is always -1 (in OLE 2.01). You should redraw your object (if it is visible) when you receive this notification.
OnRename	Notification that the object has been renamed. It can be ignored for containers because it is used to inform an OLE link object that the object's name or its container's name has changed. You will not receive this notification if you use SetOleStdSetupAdvises.
OnSave	Notification that the object has been saved. It can be ignored (not implemented) by containers because the container is typically the application that saves the object.
OnClose	Notification that the object is no longer in the running state (the object has closed). A container normally ignores this notification.
OnLinkSrcChange	Only valid for IAdviseSink2; is used to manage link source change notification. It is not implemented in a container unless the container supports links, in which case the container should use pmk as the new link source's moniker.

> **NOTE**
>
> Although Microsoft states that you can ignore the OnClose method, I have discovered that it should be implemented and an Advise notification registered so that you receive this notification. When your application receives this notification, your application must release any interfaces to the object being closed, because some ill-behaved applications will actually terminate even though there are references to the object. If you don't want to implement this method, you should call CoLockObjectExternal to force OLE to keep the object in memory until you release it (and call CoLockObjectExternal again to release the external lock). We will discuss CoLockObjectExternal in Chapter 27 because CoLockObjectExternal is used by drop targets.

When a container obtains an interface pointer for an object it is about to insert, it sets up an advise sink on the object. The object then notifies the container whenever a change is made to the object.

IStorage

IStorage and IStream are the interfaces to storages and streams, which are most closely akin to the directories and files in DOS (where IStorage is similar to a directory and IStream is similar to a file). Also, just as DOS has the concepts of root directory (such as C:\) and subdirectory (such as C:\DOS), OLE has the concepts of root storage (similar to root directory) and storage (similar to subdirectory). Collectively, IStorage and IStream are known as *structured storage* (which was briefly discussed in Chapter 23, "OLE for the First-Timer").

OLE's structured storage parallels the DOS file system in that streams exist in storages, and storages exist in root storages (just as xyz.abc exists in subdirectory def and subdirectory def is off of the root directory C:\, for example). Currently a root storage has an additional property in that it is a file in the Windows file system. In other words, when you create a root storage, you will be able to find it using the Windows 95 explorer application and it will appear as a traditional file. OLE's structured storage also parallels DOS in the operations that can be performed. For example, in DOS you can copy a file from one directory to another, or copy one directory into another. OLE's structured storage enables you to copy a stream from one storage to another, and copy a storage (and its contents) to another storage. Table 25.3 lists the methods that are part of the IStorage interface.

Table 25.3. IStorage methods.

Method	Description
Commit	Similar to the runtime API fflush when used on a root storage (in direct or transacted mode). See the text following the table on the discussion of the behavior for non-root storages.
CopyTo	Copies a storage to another storage.
CreateStorage	Creates a substorage (similar to a subdirectory) in the current storage.
CreateStream	Creates a stream (similar to a file) in the current storage.
DestroyElement	Deletes the named item (either a storage or a stream) from the storage.
EnumElements	Provides an IEnumSTATSTG that can then be used to enumerate through the streams and storages (at the current level) of the storage.
MoveElementTo	Copies or moves a substorage or a stream to another storage.
OpenStorage	Opens an existing substorage.
OpenStream	Opens an existing stream.
RenameElement	Renames either a substorage or a stream.
Revert	Discards all changes that have not yet been committed. This method also discards any changes that have been committed in a substorage, but have not yet been committed at the current level.
SetClass	Assigns a class ID to the storage.
SetElementTimes	Enables you to set or change the creation, access, and modification times of the named substorage or stream.
SetStateBits	Although this method enables you to set the state bits in a storage, there are currently no defined state bits, so this method should not be used.
Stat	Returns a STATSTG that contains information such as the current name, size, and creation, access, and modification times of the current storage (similar to the _stat runtime API).

Glancing at the table, notice that IStorage has methods called CopyTo, MoveElementTo, DestroyElement, and RenameElement. These methods are equivalent in concept to DOS's Copy, Move, Delete and Rename commands. As compound documents can be thought of as files, it makes sense that a container would require structured storage support in order to read and write OLE objects to and from storage.

Rich Edit Control

Creating OLE containers can be difficult without tools such as Microsoft's AppWizard or Borland's AppExpert, but with Windows 95 you can make a simple container using a *Rich Text Format* edit control (also known as an *rich edit control*). The rich edit control is similar to an edit control except that it supports formatted text (such as bold characters and underlines) and can be used as the foundation of an OLE container with the control's OLE support. Although the rich edit control is discussed in Chapter 22, "The RichText Control and the Animation Control," we will take a brief look at the control here and then implement an OLE container using the control.

Using the rich edit control can make the creation of certain OLE containers (which need the functionality of the control) easier to implement because the rich edit control has some OLE capabilities. The rich edit control is not an OLE container in a box, however. It does require the application using the control to perform a fair amount of work. To use the rich edit control, a container application is required to support two interfaces that are specific to rich edit controls, `IRichEditOle` and `IRichEditOleCallback`.

IRichEditOle

`IRichEditOle` is exposed by the rich edit control so that the container application can obtain information from the rich edit control on the objects the control currently has. In addition, `IRichEditOle` is used by the container application to insert objects into the rich edit control. To obtain a pointer to the control's `IRichEditOle` interface, the application sends the message `EM_GETOLEINTERFACE` to the rich edit control. In response to this message, the rich edit control returns a pointer to its `IRichEditOle` interface.

> **NOTE**
>
> To use `IRichEditOle`, your application must include the `richole.h` header file. Table 25.4 shows the methods that are implemented by the `IRichEditOle` interface.

Table 25.4. `IRichEditOle` methods.

Method	*Description*
`GetClientSite`	Returns an `IOleClientSite` interface pointer. The `IOleClientSite` interface pointer is then given to an object that is about to be inserted into the rich edit control. For every object that is inserted into the rich edit control, your application needs to obtain a new `IOleClientSite` interface pointer using `GetClientSite`.

continues

774

Table 25.4. continued

Method	Description
GetObjectCount	Returns the number of objects currently in the rich edit control.
GetLinkCount	Returns the number of linked objects in the rich edit control.
GetObject	Returns information about an object that the rich edit control currently contains. Using this method, an application can also obtain an object's IOleObject or IStorage from the object or the IOleClientSite interface pointer that the container provided to the object.
InsertObject	Used to insert a new object into the rich edit control.
ConvertObject	Tells the rich edit control to convert an object to another type of object (such as converting a metafile to a bitmap).
ActivateAs	Tells OLE to treat an object of a particular class as an object of a different class.
SetHostNames	Used by objects to obtain the name of the container application and the name of the document into which the object is inserted.
SetLinkAvailable	Used by the container to inform the rich edit control if a link could be established with a linked object.
SetDvaspect	Changes the aspect that is used to draw the object.
HandsOffStorage	Used by a container when the container is about to save its data.
SaveCompleted	Used by a container when the container has finished saving its data. HandsOffStorage is called when the container is about to perform a save operation, whereas SaveCompleted is used when the container has completed the save operation.
InPlaceDeactivate	Used by a container that supports in-place activation.
ContextSensitiveHelp	Tells the rich edit control whether the control should enter or exit context-sensitive help mode.
GetClipboardData	Used to provide data to the Clipboard from the rich edit control.
ImportDataObject	Used to import data from the Clipboard into the rich edit control.

IRichEditOleCallback

IRichEditOleCallback is an interface that is created by the container application and provided to the rich edit control. The rich edit control then uses IRichEditOleCallback to obtain information from the container (remember that IRichEditOle was used by the container to obtain information from the control). The container application is required to implement IRichEditOleCallback and provide a pointer to the interface by sending the control the message EM_SETOLECALLBACK with the address of the pointer to the container's IRichEditOleCallback interface. Table 25.5 lists the methods that are part of the IRichEditOleCallback interface.

> **NOTE**
>
> The help file included with the M8 beta release states that one should send the message EM_SETOLEINTERFACE to the control. EM_SETOLEINTERFACE is not defined by any header included with the beta release; the actual message should be EM_SETOLECALLBACK.

Table 25.5. IRichEditOleCallback **methods.**

Method	Description
GetNewStorage	Provides an IStorage interface that can be used by the rich edit control to support adding new objects from the Clipboard or from stream input. A new substorage is provided by the container application every time the rich edit calls GetNewStorage (a substorage is a storage that is contained within a root storage).
GetInPlaceContext	Used to provide the rich edit control an IOleInPlaceFrame and an IOleInPlaceUIWindow interface pointers for use if the container supports in-place activation.
ShowContainerUI	Tells the container whether the container should display the container's user interface for in-place activation support.
QueryInsertObject	Called by the rich edit control to determine whether an object that is being pasted or read from the input stream can be inserted into the control.
DeleteObject	Notifies the container application that the rich edit control is about to delete an object.
QueryAcceptData	Called by the rich edit control to determine whether the data on the Clipboard (or about to be dragged into the control) can be pasted or dragged into the control.

continues

Table 25.5. continued

Method	Description
ContextSensitiveHelp	Tells the container application whether to transition into or out of context-sensitive help mode.
GetClipboardData	Enables the container application to provide its own formats to place data onto the Clipboard instead of the formats that the rich edit control supports.
GetDragDropEffect	Enables the container application to override the default behavior and displays used during a drag/drop operation.
GetContextMenu	Used by the rich edit control to obtain the context menu that is to be used in response to the user using the right mouse button.

Putting It Together

Now that we have briefly gone over the OLE interfaces required for an OLE container and have looked at the OLE interfaces used by the rich edit control, let's create a container using the rich edit control. Listing 25.1 shows a simple class definition that can be used for the rich edit control.

Listing 25.1. CRTFControl class header.

```
//
//CRTFControl
//Class Rich Text Format Control
//
//@doc
//
//@module crtfcon.h | Header for CRTFControl class
//
//
#ifndef __CRTFCONTROL_H__
#define __CRTFCONTROL_H__

#ifndef _RICHEDIT_
#include <richedit.h>
#include <richole.h>
#endif

#ifndef    _CRICHEDITOLECALLBACK_H__
#include    "crichbck.h"
#endif

//@class CRTFControl class for RichEdit controls
//
class  CRTFControl
```

```
{
//@access Public Members
//
public:

    //@cmember Constructor
    CRTFControl();

    //@cmember Destructor
    virtual ~CRTFControl();

//Character Format
    //@cmember Gets the character format of the default for the control or
    //the current selection
    DWORD GetCharFormat(BOOL fSelection, CHARFORMAT FAR *lpCFmt);
    //@cmember Gets the paragraph format
    DWORD GetParaFormat(PARAFORMAT FAR *lpPFmt);
    //@cmember Retrieves the formatting rectangle of the control
    void GetRect(LPRECT lpRect);
    //@cmember Sets the background color
    COLORREF SetBkgndColor(BOOL fUseSysColor, COLORREF cRef);
    //@cmember Sets the character format of the default for the control or
    //the current selection
    BOOL SetCharFormat(UINT uFlags, CHARFORMAT FAR *lpCFmt);
    //@cmember Sets the paragraph format
    BOOL SetParaFormat(PARAFORMAT FAR *lpPFmt);
    //@cmember Sets the formatting rectangle
    void SetRect(LPRECT lpRect);

//Selection and Hit Testing
    //@cmember Retrieves the character and line position
    //of the character closest to
    //the provided point
    LONG CharFromPos(POINT pt, int *iCharNo, int *iLineNo);
    //@cmember  Retrieves the start and end of the current selection
    void ExGetSel(CHARRANGE FAR *lpCRange);
    //@cmember Sets the start and end for a selection range
    LONG ExSetSel(CHARRANGE FAR *lpCRange);
    //@cmember Retrieves the line number of the first visible line
    LONG GetFirstVisibleLine(void);
    //@cmember Gets the current selection.
    //The start and end values are 32bit values
    void GetSel(LPDWORD lpdwStart, LPDWORD lpdwEnd);
    //@cmember Sets or hides the current selection
    void HideSelection(BOOL fHide, BOOL fChangeStyle);
    //@cmember Returns the selection type of the current selection
    LONG SelectionType(void);
    //@cmember Sets the current selection range.
    //The start and end values are 32bit values
    void SetSel(INT nStart, INT nEnd);

//Text Operations
    //@cmember Sets the upper limit of text for the control
    void ExLimitText(DWORD dwMax);
    //@cmember Finds the text in the control
    LONG FindText(int iFlag, FINDTEXT FAR *pFindText);
```

continues

Listing 25.1. continued

```
    //@cmember Gets the current upper limit of text for the control
    LONG GetLimitText(void);
    //@cmember Retrieves the selection text
    LONG GetSelText(LPSTR pszText);
    //@cmember Retrieves a range of characters from the control
    LONG GetTextRange(TEXTRANGE FAR* pTextRange);
    //@cmember Replace the current selection with new text
    void ReplaceSel(LPCTSTR pszText);
    //@cmember Sets the upper limit of text for a control
    //(up to 32K for single or 64K for multi)
    void SetLimitText(LONG lLimit);

//Word and Line Breaks
    //@cmember Returns the line number for the character position number
    LONG ExLineFromChar(DWORD dwCharPos);
    //@cmember Finds the next word break
    LONG FindWordBreak(UINT code, DWORD dwStart);
    //@cmember Obtains the address of the current word break procedure
    EDITWORDBREAKPROC FAR*GetWordBreakProc(void);
    //@cmember Sets the address of a word break procedure
    void SetWordBreakProc(EDITWORDBREAKPROC *pProc);

//Lines and Scrolling
    //@cmember Copies a line of text into a buffer
    LONG GetLine(LONG lLine, TCHAR *szBuffer);
    //@cmember Obtains the number of lines in the control
    LONG GetLineCount(void);
    //@cmember Retrieves the current position of the control's scroll bar
    LONG GetThumb(void);
    //@cmember Retrieves the line number for the character
    //position number (the character pos value
    //is a word)
    LONG GetLineFromChar(LONG lCh);
    //@cmember Retrieves the character position from a line number
    LONG LineIndex(LONG lLine);

//Editing Operations
    //@cmember Determines whether the control can paste the provided format
    BOOL CanPaste(UINT uFormat);
    //@cmember Determines whether the control can perform an undo operation
    BOOL CanUndo(void);
    //@cmember Emptys the contents of the controls undo buffer
    void EmptyUndoBuffer(void);
    //@cmember Tells the control to perform a paste from the specified format
    void PasteSpecial(UINT uFormat);
    //@cmember Tells the control to undo the last operation
    BOOL Undo(void);
    //@cmember Tells the control to paste from the clipboard
    void Paste(void);
    //@cmember Tells the control to cut the selection data to the clipboard
    void Cut(void);
    //@cmember Tells the control to copy the selection data to the clipboard
    void Copy(void);

//Streams
    //@cmember Tells the control to read the data from the
```

```
        //stream in the provided format
        LONG StreamIn(UINT uFormat, EDITSTREAM FAR *pStream);
        //@cmember Tells the control to read the RTF data from the stream
        LONG StreamIn(EDITSTREAM FAR *pStream);
        //@cmember Tells the control to write the data to the
        //stream in the provided format
        LONG StreamOut(UINT uFormat, EDITSTREAM FAR *pStream);
        //@cmember Tells the control to write the data to the
        //stream in RTF format
LONG StreamOut(EDITSTREAM FAR *pStream);

//Printing
        //@cmember Displays a portion of the control
        BOOL DisplayBand(LPRECT lpRect);
        //@cmember Formats a range of the control for the specified device
        LONG FormatRange(FORMATRANGE FAR *lpFmtRng);
        //@cmember Sets the target device and line width
        BOOL SetTargetDevice(HDC hDCTarget, INT cxLineWidth);

//Bottomless Rich Edit Controls
        //@cmember Tells the control to tell its parent
        //an EN_REQUESTRESIZE notification

        void RequestSize(void);

//OLE Interfaces
        //@cmember Obtains the IRichEditOle interface pointer from the control
        void GetOleInterface(IRichEditOle FAR **pIRichEditOle);
        //@cmember Sets the IRichEditOleCallback interface pointer for the control
        void SetOleCallback(CRichEditOleCallback FAR *pRichEditOleCallback);

//Miscellaneous
        //@cmember Retrieve the event mask (notifications)
        DWORD GetEventMask(void);
        //@cmember Returns whether the controls contents have been modified
        BOOL GetModify(void);
        //@cmember Returns whether the controls contents have
        //been modified since the last save
        BOOL IsDirty(void);
        //@cmember Sets the event masks
        //(the notification which the control should tell the parent about)
DWORD SetEventMask(DWORD dwMask);
        //@cmember Sets the control's modify flag
        void SetModify(BOOL bFlag);
        //@cmember Changes the Read-only flag for the control
        BOOL SetReadOnly(BOOL bFlag);

//Routines which help in the use of the control
//
        //@cmember Enables the control to support OLE
        BOOL EnableOle(void);
        //@cmember Determines whether the control currently supports OLE
        BOOL IsOleEnabled(void);
        //@cmember Obtains the HWND of the control
        HWND GetHwnd(void);
        //@cmember HWND|Create|HWND hParent,
        //HINSTANCE hInstance, ULONG ulControlID,
```

continues

Listing 25.1. continued

```
    //int x, int y, int iheight, int iwidth,
    //DWORD dwStyle, LPCTSTR lpstrTitle ¦
    //Creates the RichEdit control
    HWND Create(HWND hParent,
                        HINSTANCE hInstance,
                        ULONG ulControlID = 1000,
                        int x = CW_USEDEFAULT,
                        int y = CW_USEDEFAULT,
                        int iheight = CW_USEDEFAULT,
                        int iwidth = CW_USEDEFAULT,
                        DWORD dwStyle = WS_CHILD ¦
                        WS_VISIBLE ¦ES_MULTILINE ¦
                        WS_VSCROLL ¦ ES_AUTOVSCROLL ¦ ES_NOHIDESEL ¦
                        ES_SAVESEL ¦ ES_SUNKEN,
                        LPCTSTR lpstrTitle = NULL);
    //@cmember Returns the IOleClientSite interface pointer from the control
    HRESULT GetClientSite(IOleClientSite FAR * FAR*pIOleClientSite);
    //@cmember Returns a new substorage
    HRESULT CreateSubStorage(IStorage FAR * FAR*pIStorage);
    //@cmember Inserts an object into the control
    HRESULT InsertObject(REOBJECT FAR *prObject);
    //@cmember Sets the controls root storage
    void SetRootStorage(IStorage FAR *pIStorage)
        {m_pIRichEditOleCallback->SetRootStorage(pIStorage);}

//@access Private Members
//
private:
    //@cmember Sends a command to the RichEdit control
    LRESULT SendRTF(UINT uMsg,WPARAM wParam = 0, LPARAM lParam = 0);
    //@cmember Changes the m_bOleEnabled flag
    BOOL SetEnableOle(BOOL bEnable);
    //@cmember Helper member to enable OLE for the RichEdit control
    void EnableOleHelper(void);

    //@cmember Window handle of the RichEdit control
    HWND m_hWndRichControl;
    //@cmember OLE enabled flag (for the control)
    BOOL m_bOleEnabled;
    //@cmember IRichEditOle interface pointer for the control
    IRichEditOle FAR *m_pIRichEditOle;
    //@cmember IRichEditOleCallback interface pointer for the control
    CRichEditOleCallback FAR *m_pIRichEditOleCallback;

#ifdef __USE_LOADRICH__
    //@cmember Used to store the HINSTANCE if
    //LoadLibrary is used to install the control.
    //Only used if we have to use LoadLibrary instead
    //of InitCommonControls
    HINSTANCE  m_hRichInstance;

#endif
};
```

```
//Include inlines
//
#include "crtfcon.inl"
#endif
```

The class CRTFControl from Listing 25.1 makes using the rich edit control a little easier to use. For example, to communicate with the rich edit control, you need to send messages to the control. The CRTFControl class handles sending the appropriate message to the rich edit control, depending on what you want to do. It also has the functionality to use the rich edit control with OLE. The member functions EnableOle and EnableOleHelper perform some of the work needed to enable the rich edit control to be used as an OLE container. Listing 25.2 shows the implementation of EnableOle and EnableOleHelper.

Listing 25.2. Implementation of EnableOle and EnableOleHelper.

```
//EnableOLE is used to allow an RTF control to access OLE objects
//EnableOLE can be called before or after creating the control (with Create)
//At the current time, once EnableOle is called you cannot disable OLE at
//another time without deleting the CRTFControl object and creating a new one.
//
BOOL CRTFControl::EnableOle(void)
{
HRESULT hResult = ::OleInitialize(NULL);
    if (FAILED(hResult)){
#ifdef _DEBUG
        TCHAR szError[100];
        HResultToString(hResult,szError);
        MessageBox(NULL,szError,TEXT("OleInitialize"),MB_OK);
#endif
        return (FALSE);
    }
    SetEnableOle(TRUE);

    if (IsWindow(m_hWndRichControl)){
        EnableOleHelper();
    }
    return (TRUE);
}

//EnableOleHelper is a routine which creates the callback which the RTF control
//needs for OLE. The reason a helper function was needed is that EnableOle and
//Create both call the helper function.
//EnableOle calls the helper function if the RTF control was already created
//If the RTF control was not yet created, EnableOleHelper will be called by
//Create, after Create creates the control
//
void CRTFControl::EnableOleHelper(void)
{
    m_pIRichEditOleCallback =
      (CRichEditOleCallback *)new CRichEditOleCallback;
    GetOleInterface(&m_pIRichEditOle);
    SetOleCallback(m_pIRichEditOleCallback);
}
```

EnableOle is a simple function that initializes OLE by calling OleInitialize and then sets an internal flag so that the user knows that OLE has been initialized. EnableOle then checks to see if the rich edit control window has already been created (by calling IsWindow). If the rich edit control has not yet been created, EnableOle simply returns. After the rich edit control has been created (by calling the create member), EnableOleHelper is automatically called. If the rich edit control has already been created then, EnableOle automatically calls EnableOleHelper. EnableOleHelper creates an IRichEditOleCallback interface and gives the interface to the rich edit control. In addition, EnableOleHelper obtains the IRichEditOle interface pointer from the rich edit control for later use.

Typical containers can either create a new document when the user selects File | New from the menu, or the user can open an existing document by selecting File | Open. When the user selects File | New, your application needs to create a new document. Listing 25.3 shows how a new document can be created.

Listing 25.3. File | New handler.

```
BOOL CContainDoc::DocView_OnFileNew()
{
    if (m_pRootStorage != NULL)
        m_pRootStorage->Release();

    HRESULT hResult = StgCreateDocfile(NULL,STGM_TRANSACTED |
                    STGM_READWRITE | STGM_DELETEONRELEASE |
                    STGM_SHARE_EXCLUSIVE,0,&m_pRootStorage);

    if (hResult != NOERROR) {
        return FALSE;
    }

    m_pRTFControl->SetRootStorage(m_pRootStorage);
    return TRUE;
}
```

When you create a new document, the OLE API StgCreateDocfile is used to obtain a pointer to an IStorage interface. The most interesting aspect of calling StgCreateDocfile is that your application does not yet know the name of the document, so you pass a NULL as the first parameter to StgCreateDocfile (which is the filename parameter). StgCreateDocfile automatically generates a name for the storage. You might also notice that StgCreateDocfile is called with the STGM_DELETEONRELEASE flag, indicating that when all references to the interface have been released, the document should automatically be deleted. Thus you have created a temporary file. After you have called Release on the IStorage interface pointer, your document is automatically deleted. Why have you created a document that has a system-defined name and will automatically be deleted when you release it? Because in order to insert an object into a rich edit control, you need to provide the control (and the object) an IStorage interface pointer. To give the rich edit control your

IStorage interface pointer, you call SetRootStorage (which is implemented in your rich edit control class), which simply stores the IStorage interface pointer.

After you have created a root storage (or if File | Open was selected, you have opened an existing root storage), you can insert an object. Listing 25.4 shows the logic used when the user selects Insert | Object from the menu.

Listing 25.4. Partial implementation of Insert | Object.

```
void CContainDoc::DocView_OnInsertObject(void)
{
    TCHAR     szFile[260];        //If you use a value greater than 260,
                                  //the Insert Object dialog will not come up.
    HRESULT   hResult;

    memset(&szFile,0,sizeof(szFile)/sizeof(TCHAR));

    OLEUIINSERTOBJECT  OleUIInsertObj;

    //You must null out OleUIInsertObject or else
    //the Dialog box will not come up
    memset(&OleUIInsertObj, 0, sizeof(OleUIInsertObj));

    OleUIInsertObj.cbStruct   = sizeof(OleUIInsertObj);
    OleUIInsertObj.hWndOwner  = m_hWndView;
    OleUIInsertObj.lpszCaption = NULL;
    OleUIInsertObj.lpfnHook   = NULL;
    OleUIInsertObj.lCustData  = NULL;
    OleUIInsertObj.hInstance  = NULL;
    OleUIInsertObj.lpszTemplate = NULL;
    OleUIInsertObj.hResource  = NULL;
    OleUIInsertObj.lpszFile   = szFile;
    OleUIInsertObj.cchFile    = sizeof(szFile)/sizeof(TCHAR);

    //We want the OleUIInsertObject to do all the work of creating the object
    //for us.  Why should we re-invent the wheel?
    OleUIInsertObj.dwFlags    = IOF_SELECTCREATENEW |
                                IOF_CREATENEWOBJECT | IOF_CREATEFILEOBJECT |
                                IOF_CREATELINKOBJECT;
    OleUIInsertObj.iid        = IID_IOleObject;

    OleUIInsertObj.oleRender     = OLERENDER_DRAW;

    hResult = m_pRTFControl->GetClientSite(&OleUIInsertObj.lpIOleClientSite);
    if (hResult != S_OK)
        return;

    OleUIInsertObj.lpFormatEtc = NULL;
    OleUIInsertObj.lpIStorage  = NULL;
    OleUIInsertObj.ppvObj      = NULL;
    hResult = m_pRTFControl->CreateSubStorage(&OleUIInsertObj.lpIStorage);
    IOleObject *m_pIOleObject;

    OleUIInsertObj.ppvObj = (LPVOID *)&m_pIOleObject;
```

continues

Listing 25.4. continued

```
//Set cursor to hourglass
HCURSOR hCursorOld = SetCursor(LoadCursor(NULL,IDC_WAIT));
UINT uiRet = OleUIInsertObject(&OleUIInsertObj);
SetCursor(hCursorOld);

if (uiRet == OLEUI_SUCCESS){

    REOBJECT   rObject;

    rObject.cbStruct = sizeof(REOBJECT);
    rObject.cp       = -1;
    rObject.clsid    = OleUIInsertObj.clsid;
    rObject.poleobj  = m_pIOleObject;
    rObject.pstg     = OleUIInsertObj.lpIStorage;
    rObject.polesite = OleUIInsertObj.lpIOleClientSite;
    rObject.sizel.cx = 0;
    rObject.sizel.cy = 0;
    rObject.dvaspect = (OleUIInsertObj.dwFlags &
➥ IOF_CHECKDISPLAYASICON)?
                                DVASPECT_ICON : DVASPECT_CONTENT;
            rObject.dwFlags      = REO_RESIZABLE ¦ REO_BLANK;
            rObject.dwUser       = 0;

            m_pRTFControl->InsertObject(&rObject);
    }
}
```

When a user selects Insert | Object from a container's menu, he or she expects to see an Insert Object dialog box (see Figure 25.1). Fortunately, Windows 95 includes the Insert Object dialog box as part of OLE (the previous version of OLE included the dialog box as part of the sample code delivered with the OLE SDK).

FIGURE 25.1.

Standard Insert Object dialog box.

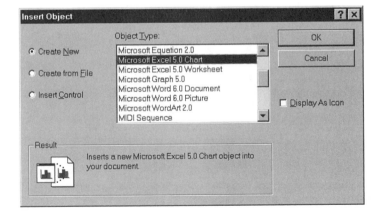

The Insert Object dialog box used by calling OleUIInsertObject with a structure of type OLEUIINSERTOBJECT. OLEUIINSERTOBJECT requires a number of fields to be filled in, but here we will look at just a few of the fields. First, the OLEUIINSERTOBJECT structure must be initialized to zero; otherwise the dialog box will not come up. In addition, the field cbStruct must be set to the size of the structure (using sizeof(OleUIInsertObj) to obtain the size). The field hWndOwner is set to the window handle of the parent to the dialog box (according to Microsoft, this field should not be NULL, although the documentation does not state what happens if it is NULL). lpszFile is assigned to a buffer to store a filename (if the user selects link to file), while cchFile is set to the size of the buffer. The size of the buffer cannot exceed 260; if it does, the Insert Object dialog box does not come up.

The dwFlags field is probably the most interesting field in the OLEUIINSERTOBJECT structure. Depending on how you set dwFlags, OleUIInsertObject will do various things. The Insert Object dialog box has support for inserting objects, inserting compound documents for links, and inserting OLE controls (although in beta 8, the logic for displaying available OLE controls appears not to work). The Insert Object dialog box also has the capability to create the object based on the user's selection. When OleUIInsertObject is used to create the object, the OLEUIINSERTOBJECT structure requires you to fill in a few more parameters. When OleUIInsertObject creates the object, the object returns an interface pointer, the iid field, which is used to determine what interface should be obtained. For this example, you will obtain the IOleObject interface because IOleObject is required to be implemented by all servers. In addition, when OleUIInsertObject creates an object, the object needs the container to provide an IOleClientSite interface pointer and an IStorage interface pointer. To obtain an IOleClientSite interface pointer, you call GetClientSite, which obtains an IOleClientSite interface pointer for the object. OLE requires that a unique IOleClientSite interface pointer is provided to every object, and the rich edit control handles creating and managing a unique IOleClientSite interface pointer (the rich edit control makes an IOleClientSite interface pointer available by calling GetClientSite on the IRichEditOle interface). In addition, every object needs to be stored in a unique substorage in your root storage. The IStorage interface pointer for the substorage can be obtained by calling CreateSubStorage, which is a member function in your CRTFControl class (the rich edit control itself does not provide this functionality).

Finally, you can call OleUIInsertObject to display the dialog box and obtain the object. When the object has been obtained, OleUIInsertObject returns OLEUI_SUCCESS. Now that your container has the object, you need to give the object to the rich edit control. The rich edit control expects the object to be inserted by calling InsertObject (which is a member of IRichEditOle). Your object is finally inserted into the container.

The actual implementation of using the rich edit control requires a few more support functions, such as being able to read from and write to a compound document. Look at the source code that is included on the disc that accompanies this book to see the full implementation (the full source is several hundred lines of code). In addition, the source handles the fact that OLE as implemented on Windows 95 requires some parameters to be in UNICODE, although most applications are written for ANSI. In addition, the source is fully documented and a help file (FUNCTION.HLP) has been created that contains all of the classes and member functions used to create the container application. The classes have been written so that you should be able to include them into your C++ applications (they have been created so that they are compiler-independent).

Summary

A Window Object is simply an OLE object that adheres to the Component Object Model. A compound document is a structured storage that can contain Window Objects. A container is an application that can read from and write to compound documents.

In this chapter I also discussed how to use the rich edit control as a container, specifically using the OLE interfaces IRichEditOle and IRichEditOleCallback.

Visual Editing

26

by Lawrence Harris

IN THIS CHAPTER

From the user's point of view, visual editing can be one of the most useful parts of OLE; from a programmer's point of view, visual editing is one of the most difficult aspects of OLE programming. In this chapter, I'll discuss what visual editing is and then convert the container application from Chapter 25, "Window Objects and Compound Documents," to support visual editing.

In-Place Activation

When the container was created in Chapter 25, whenever an object was placed into the container, the object's application became visible in a separate window, just as if the server's application had been launched. When an object and container support in-place activation, the visual effects are different. Let's look at an example using Word 6, Excel 5, and Visio 3.0. Figure 26.1 shows a Word document that has two embedded objects: a Visio diagram on the left and an Excel 5 graph on the right.

FIGURE 26.1.

A Word document with an embedded Visio drawing and an Excel graph.

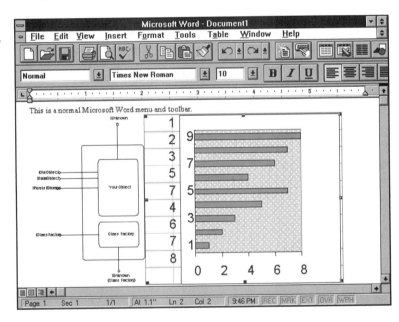

From Figure 26.1, you can see that the normal Word menu appears. If you double-click on the Visio diagram, the screen shown in Figure 26.2 appears.

Notice that when the Visio drawing is active, the Word menu and toolbar changes to the Visio menu and Visio toolbar. In addition, Visio activates a floating toolbox, which contains additional tools that Visio supports. Notice the hatched window around the Visio drawing to show you that the Visio drawing is active. You can now work on the Visio drawing as if you were actually in Visio. If you then double-click the Excel graph, the screen shown in Figure 26.3 appears.

FIGURE 26.2.

A Word document with the Visio drawing activated.

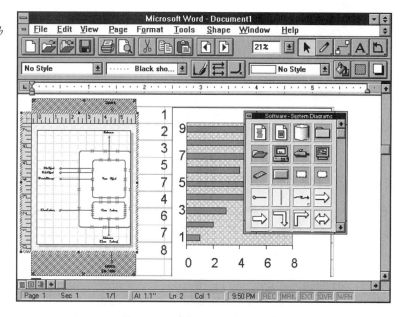

FIGURE 26.3.

A Word document with the Excel graph activated.

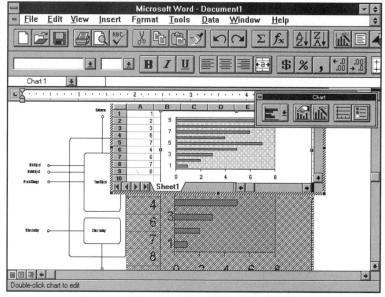

Notice that when Excel is activated, the menu changes once again, but this time it changes from a Visio menu to an Excel menu. Notice also that the floating toolbox for Visio disappears, and Excel displays a floating toolbox for Excel graphs. In-place activation shows the menu and tools that correspond to the object that is currently active. In Figure 26.1, the Word document is the active object, so the user interface reflects Word. In Figure 26.2,

Visio is active, so the user interface reflects Visio. In Figure 26.3, Excel Graph is active, so the user interface reflects Excel. The user does not know or care that other programs are running; the user is still in Word, and Word appears to have adopted the functionality of the other applications.

Originally, Microsoft called the behavior of visual editing *in-place activation*. In fact, when you look at the interfaces required to support visual editing, you see that they are called in-place activation. Rumor has it that the marketing folks added their two cents and changed the name from in-place activation to *visual editing* because visual editing describes from the user's point of view what is occurring. You can use whichever term you prefer. (I usually use the term *in-place activation* because the interfaces also use it.)

MFC, OWL, OCF, and Visual Editing

Currently, various class libraries are available for Windows programming, with Microsoft Foundation Class and Borland's OWL and OCF being two of the most popular. When you add OLE support for applications, the class library upon which your application is dependent doesn't usually affect how the OLE support is added. In other words, if you currently have an application written in MFC and you decide to add OLE support by adding interfaces and methods directly into your application (without using the MFC support OLE), there is no problem. When you decide to support visual editing, however, you should use the class library's support for OLE (instead of just adding the required interface pointers). This is because visual editing has many non-OLE requirements. For example, in the earlier discussion of how Word's menu and Visio's menu merged, you learned that OLE only handles part of the menu merging. Your container application must make the pieces of the menu that should be merged available for OLE to merge. In addition, much of the work for visual editing occurs in your application's frame window. Your frame window needs to handle much of the menu negotiation, toolbar space negotiation, and window space negotiation. Unless you know how your class library accommodates these items, I strongly recommend that visual editing applications (containers and servers) should be created using the same class library (if any) as the rest of the application. Also, although Borland's OCF class library for OLE enables you to integrate it into existing MFC applications, adding OCF to an MFC application is not easy. Finally, MFC changes with each release of Visual C++, and you have no guarantee that the new version of MFC will work with OCF. Because MFC supports OLE directly, I don't recommend mixing MFC with OCF.

Visual Editing Interfaces For Containers

For a container to support visual editing (in-place activation), a container needs to implement a few more interfaces in addition to IOleClientSite, IAdviseSink, and IStorage. A container needs to support IOleInPlaceFrame, IOleInPlaceSite, and—optionally—IOleInPlaceUIWindow. Although the rich edit control used in your container handles some of the methods required, you need to do some of the work yourself, so let's look at each of the interfaces.

IOleWindow Interface

IOleWindow is the base interface for IOleInPlaceFrame, IOleInPlaceSite, and IOleInPlaceUIWindow, so let's discuss this interface first. IOleWindow is a common interface that provides information to either the container or the object for in-place activation. IOleWindow only has two methods (besides the three methods for IUnknown, which IOleWindow is derived from): ContextSensitiveHelp and GetWindow (see Table 26.1).

Table 26.1. `IOleWindow` methods.

Method	Description
ContextSensitiveHelp	Specifies whether to enter context-sensitive help mode.
GetWindow	Returns the window handle for the frame, document, parent, or in-place object, depending on the class derived from IOleWindow.

IOleInPlaceUIWindow Interface

The IOleInPlaceUIWindow interface is implemented by containers so that an in-place active object can negotiate border space. Border space is the area in which an in-place active object can place toolbars in the container's window. IOleInPlaceUIWindow has four methods in addition to the two methods from IOleWindow (which IOleInPlaceUIWindow is derived from) and the three methods from IUnknown (which IOleWindow is derived from). Table 26.2 lists the IOleInPlaceUIWindow methods.

Table 26.2. `IOleInPlaceUIWindow` methods.

Method	Description
GetBorder	The object calls this method to obtain a rectangle from the container, in which the object can display any toolbars that the object needs to display.
RequestBorderSpace	This method allows the object to tell the container how much space the object needs for the object's toolbars. The container does not necessarily need to approve giving the object the requested space.

continues

Table 26.2. continued

Method	Description
SetBorderSpace	After negotiation of border space using RequestBorderSpace, the object can tell the container that it will use none, some, or all of the available border space. In addition, the object can tell the container not to display the container's toolbars.
SetActiveObject	This method gives the container an interface (IOleInPlaceActiveObject) to the active object and provides a user-displayable name for the object. An object must call this method before calling IOleInPlaceFrame::SetMenu, because SetMenu requires the IOleInPlaceActiveObject interface provided by this method.

IOleInPlaceFrame Interface

The methods specific to the IOleInPlaceFrame interface handle menus, status bar information, modeless dialog boxes, and keyboard accelerators for in-place activation. In addition, because IOleInPlaceFrame is derived from IOleInPlaceUIWindow, IOleInPlaceFrame also handles border negotiation. IOleInPlaceFrame is required to be exposed in every container that can support in-place activation. Table 26.3 lists the methods specific to IOleInPlaceFrame.

Table 26.3. IOleInPlaceFrame methods.

Method	Description
EnableModeless	Enables or disables modeless dialog boxes.
InsertMenus	Allows a container to add its menus from the frame.
RemovesMenus	Allows a container to remove its menus from the frame.
SetMenu	Installs the composite menu into the container.
SetStatusText	Allows the active object to add text to the container's status bar.
TranslateAccelerator	Allows the object to translate accelerator keys, which are intended for the container application.

IOleInPlaceSite Interface

IOleInPlaceSite manages the in-place activation at the object level (as opposed to the border/document level of IOleInPlaceUIWindow, and the menu/frame level of IOleInPlaceFrame). IOleInPlaceSite is required to be implemented and exposed in every container that supports in-place activation. Table 26.4 shows the methods that are specific to IOleInPlaceSite (not including IOleWindow or IUnknown).

Table 26.4. IOleInPlaceSite **methods.**

Method	Description
CanInPlaceActivate	The object calls this method to determine whether the container can activate the object in-place.
DeactivateAndUndo	The object calls this method when the object wants the container to remove the in-place activation for the object, deactivate the object, and undo the object (to the state and data the container previously had for the object).
DiscardUndoState	When an object calls this method, the container is to discard any undo information the container might have for the object.
GetWindowContext	This method allows the object to obtain the IOleInPlaceFrame and IOleInPlaceUIWindow interfaces and provides the object with information on where the object can display itself in the container.
OnInPlaceActivate	This method notifies the container that an object is activating in-place.
OnInPlaceDeactivate	This method notifies the container that an object is no longer in-place active.
OnPosRectChanged	This method notifies the container that the size of the in-place activated object has changed. The object does not resize itself, however, until the container calls IOleInPlaceObject::SetObjectRects.
OnUIDeactivate	This method tells the container to reinstall the container's user interface (toolbars).
Scroll	This method tells the container to scroll the object a specific number of pixels.

Implementing a RichEdit In-Place Active Container

Using the rich edit control, the container can support in-place activation; however, there is a fair amount of work that your application needs to implement. In fact, other than the container support that the rich edit control provided in Chapter 25, the rich edit control only implements the IOleInPlaceSite interface itself. Because in-place activation requires the IOleInPlaceFrame interface and optionally the IOleInPlaceUIWindow interface, in addition to IOleInPlaceSite, you need to add support for IOleInPlaceFrame and IOleInPlaceUIWindow. Supporting these two interfaces requires a fair amount of work, so let's take a look at the highlights for their support. (The full source, which includes the implementation of all the methods, is included on the source disc provided with this book.)

Since we are using the rich edit control as the container, I decided to expose IOleInPlaceUIWindow and IOleInPlaceFrame from the IRichEditOleCallback interface. Because, in this example, IOleInPlaceFrame and IOleInPlaceUIWindow cannot exist without IRichEditOleCallback, IRichEditOleCallback should handle the reference count and QueryInterface for IOleInPlaceUIWindow and IOleInPlaceFrame. In addition, IOleInPlaceUIWindow is only required to be implemented as a separate interface when it is possible for the frame to be a separate application from the document. The condition of the frame being a separate application from the document occurs in containers that are also servers. For example, you might insert an OLE object into Microsoft Excel; Microsoft Excel would be considered the container. You might then decide to insert the Microsoft Excel spreadsheet into Microsoft Word. Microsoft Excel is then acting as a server to Microsoft Word, but as a container to your OLE object. From the OLE object's point of view, Microsoft Excel is the document that the object is inserted into, and Microsoft Word is the frame that is to be used for in-place activation. In the container example, there is no reason to implement IOleInPlaceUIWindow as a separate interface (however, the listing includes it for illustrative purposes). Listing 26.1 shows the IUnknown methods for the IRichEditOleCallback, IOleInPlaceUIWindow, and IOleInPlaceFrame.

Listing 26.1. IUnknown **methods for** IRichEditOleCallback, IOleInPlaceUIWindow, **and** IOleInPlaceFrame.

```
STDMETHODIMP CRichEditOleCallback::QueryInterface(REFIID riid, LPVOID FAR* ppvObj)
{
    if (riid == IID_IUnknown)
        *ppvObj = this;
    else if (riid == IID_IOleInPlaceFrame)
        *ppvObj = m_pIOleInPlaceFrame;
    else if (riid == IID_IOleInPlaceUIWindow)
        *ppvObj = m_pIOleInPlaceUIWindow;
    else{
        *ppvObj = NULL;
        }
```

```
      if (*ppvObj != NULL){
       ((LPUNKNOWN)(*ppvObj))->AddRef();
       return NOERROR;
      }

//If for some reason our constructor did not create the requested interface
//don't pass the NULL interface without telling the caller that we don't support
//the requested interface.
    return ResultFromScode(E_NOINTERFACE);
}

//@mfunc Addref processing. Increment private counter of references.
//@rdesc The current number of references to the object
//
STDMETHODIMP_(ULONG) CRichEditOleCallback::AddRef(void)
{
    return ++m_refs;
}

//@mfunc Release processing. Decrement private reference count.
//If reference count is zero, then delete the object.
//@rdesc The current number of references to the object
//
STDMETHODIMP_(ULONG) CRichEditOleCallback::Release(void)
{
   if(--m_refs == 0){
    if (m_pIOleInPlaceActiveObject != NULL){
        m_pIOleInPlaceActiveObject->Release();
        m_pIOleInPlaceActiveObject = NULL;
    }

    if (m_pIOleInPlaceUIWindow != NULL){
        delete m_pIOleInPlaceUIWindow;
        m_pIOleInPlaceUIWindow = NULL;        //Defensive programming
    }
    if (m_pIOleInPlaceFrame != NULL){
        delete m_pIOleInPlaceFrame;
        m_pIOleInPlaceFrame = NULL;           //Defensive programming
    }
    //And now we can delete this object
    delete this;
   }

   return m_refs;
}
STDMETHODIMP CIOleInPlaceFrame::QueryInterface(REFIID riid, LPVOID FAR* ppvObj)
{
    //If the callers requests IOleWindow, give them the IOleWindow
      for IOleInPlaceFrame,
    //otherwise delegate the call to CRichEditOleCallback
    //
    if (riid == IID_IOleWindow){
        *ppvObj = this;
        ((LPUNKNOWN)(*ppvObj))->AddRef();
        return NOERROR;
    }

    return m_pCRichEditOleCallback->QueryInterface(riid, ppvObj);
```

continues

Listing 26.1. continued

```
}

//@mfunc Addref processing. Increment private counter of references.
//@rdesc The current number of references to the object
//
STDMETHODIMP_(ULONG) CIOleInPlaceFrame::AddRef(void)
{
    return m_pCRichEditOleCallback->AddRef();
}

//@mfunc Release processing. Decrement private reference count.
//If reference count is zero, then delete the object.
//@rdesc The current number of references to the object
//
STDMETHODIMP_(ULONG) CIOleInPlaceFrame::Release(void)
{
    return m_pCRichEditOleCallback->Release();
}
STDMETHODIMP CIOleInPlaceUIWindow::QueryInterface(REFIID riid,
                                                  LPVOID FAR* ppvObj)
{
    //If the callers requests IOleWindow, give them the
    //IOleWindow for IOleInPlaceUIWindow,
    //otherwise delegate the call to CRichEditOleCallback
    //
    if (riid == IID_IOleWindow){
        *ppvObj = this;
        ((LPUNKNOWN)(*ppvObj))->AddRef();
        return NOERROR;
    }

    return m_pCRichEditOleCallback->QueryInterface(riid, ppvObj);
}

//@mfunc Addref processing. Increment private counter of references.
//@rdesc The current number of references to the object
//
STDMETHODIMP_(ULONG) CIOleInPlaceUIWindow::AddRef(void)
{
    return m_pCRichEditOleCallback->AddRef();
}
```

Listing 26.1 shows that the IUnknown methods for IOleInPlaceUIWindow and
IOleInPlaceFrame delegate the AddRef and Release methods to CRichEditOleCallback. In
addition, IOleInPlaceUIWindow and IOleInPlaceFrame delegate QueryInterface to
CRichEditOleCallback, except for the IOleWindow interface. The reason IOleWindow is not
delegated is that IOleInPlaceFrame and IOleInPlaceUIWindow both have IOleWindow. So,
depending on whether the QueryInterface request comes from the IOleInPlaceFrame
interface or the IOleInPlaceUIWindow interface, the correct IOleWindow needs to be returned.

To handle in-place activation, you need to first determine what menu the user will see for the container when an object is activated in-place. The container application must only display the menu items that are appropriate for the container as a whole. The container application generally supplies File and Window menu items, and it might supply additional items that relate to the container or document as a whole. The object supplies Edit and Help menu items, and it might supply additional items that relate specifically to the object. Listing 26.2 shows the implementation of InsertMenus, which handles the menu negotiation for the container.

Listing 26.2. The implementation of InsertMenus.

```
STDMETHODIMP CIOleInPlaceFrame::InsertMenus(HMENU hmenuShared,
                                LPOLEMENUGROUPWIDTHS lpMenuWidths)
{
   HMENU hMenuFile = GetSubMenu(hMenuViewWindow,0);
   AppendMenu(hmenuShared, MF_BYPOSITION | MF_POPUP,
           (UINT)hMenuFile,"&File");
   AppendMenu(hmenuShared, MF_BYPOSITION | MF_POPUP,
           (UINT)hMenuViewWindowWindow,"&Window");
         lpMenuWidths->width[0] = 1;
         lpMenuWidths->width[2] = 0;
         lpMenuWidths->width[4] = 1;

   return NOERROR;
}
```

In your implementation of InsertMenus, you first obtain the menu handle of the container's File menu by calling GetSubMenu(hMenuViewWindow,0). The menu handle for the File menu item is then added to the shared menu by using the Windows API AppendMenu. Next, the menu handle for the Window menu item is added to the shared menu. Finally, tell OLE that you have added two menu items: The first menu item belongs in the beginning of the menu (File should be the first item, so setting lpMenuWidths->width[0] = 1 tells OLE that the first menu in the shared menu belongs in the beginning of the menu line); the second item belongs at the end of the menu. OLE then constructs the appropriate shared menu from the information that the container provides and the information that the object provides, and it calls the SetMenu method from IOleInPlaceFrame so that the container can display the shared menu. Listing 26.3 shows the implementation of SetMenu.

Listing 26.3. SetMenu implementation.

```
STDMETHODIMP CIOleInPlaceFrame::SetMenu(HMENU hmenuShared,
           HOLEMENU holemenu, HWND hWndActiveObject)
{
   HMENU hMenu = hMenuViewWindow;
```

continues

Listing 26.3. continued

```
    if (holemenu)
        hMenu = hmenuShared;

    // call the windows api, not this method
    ::SetMenu (hWndFrameWindow, hMenu);

    OleSetMenuDescriptor(holemenu, hWndFrameWindow, hWndActiveObject, this,
                        m_pCRichEditOleCallback->m_pIOleInPlaceActiveObject);

    return NOERROR;
}
```

After you have implemented the menu negotiation items, you need to implement border space negotiation. Border space negotiation involves returning to the in-place active object the amount of space that the in-place active object can use to display any toolbars that the object might have. The code to support border space negotiation is complex and affects large portions of the application, so the full listing is included on the source disc that accompanies this book. The reasons for the complexity of border space negotiation are shown in the following list:

- The container needs to tell the object how much space is available in the document for the in-place active object's toolbars.

- The container needs to remove any toolbars that belong to the container when it is told to by OLE. (This also means that when the container is calculating the available border space, the container should include the space that is taken by the container's toolbars, which will be removed.)

- When an in-place active object tells the container how much space the in-place active object's toolbars will take, the container needs to move any document windows so that the document windows do not overlap with the toolbars.

- When the in-place active object is no longer active, the container application must restore its own toolbars and might need to move document windows to reflect the new size of the client area.

When the border space negotiation routines have been completed, IOleInPlaceUIWindow and IOleInPlaceFrame are complete, but the rich edit control still needs to be made aware of these interfaces. IRichEditOleCallback has a method called GetInPlaceContext, which is used to provide the interfaces to the rich edit control. Listing 26.4 shows the implementation of GetInPlaceContext.

Listing 26.4 Implementation of GetInPlaceContext.

```
STDMETHODIMP CRichEditOleCallback::GetInPlaceContext(
        LPOLEINPLACEFRAME FAR *lplpFrame,
        LPOLEINPLACEUIWINDOW FAR * lplpDoc,
        LPOLEINPLACEFRAMEINFO lpFrameInfo)
```

```
{
    HRESULT hResult = NOERROR;

    *lplpFrame = NULL;
    *lplpDoc   = NULL;

    //Assign the IOleInPlaceFrame if possible
    if (lplpFrame != NULL){
        *lplpFrame = (LPOLEINPLACEFRAME)m_pIOleInPlaceFrame;
        m_pIOleInPlaceFrame->AddRef();
    } else
        hResult = E_INVALIDARG;

    //Assign the IOleInPlaceUIWindow if possible
    if (lplpDoc != NULL)
        *lplpDoc   = (LPOLEINPLACEUIWINDOW)m_pIOleInPlaceUIWindow;
    else
        hResult = E_INVALIDARG;

    if (lpFrameInfo != NULL){
        if (lpFrameInfo->cb < sizeof(OLEINPLACEFRAMEINFO))
            hResult = E_INVALIDARG;
        else {
            lpFrameInfo->fMDIApp = TRUE;      //This is an MDI container
            lpFrameInfo->hwndFrame = hWndFrameWindow;
            //The frame window handle
lpFrameInfo->haccel     = NULL;
            lpFrameInfo->cAccelEntries = 0;
        }
    } else
        hResult = E_INVALIDARG;

    return hResult;
}
```

Drag and Drop

27

by Lawrence Harris

If you are an active Windows user, you might have noticed that you often cut or copy information from one application and then paste the information into another application or into a different location in the same application. The operations of cut and copy involve selecting the information you want, placing the information onto the Clipboard using the Cut or Copy command, moving to the other application, selecting a location, and selecting Paste. If you perform this series of operations often enough, you probably want an easier and faster way to accomplish the same result. This is where OLE Drag and Drop steps in. With this feature, you can select the information you want and then, with the left mouse button still down, drag it to the application or location where you want the data to go, and release the left mouse button to drop the data. This operation makes cutting or copying data from one place to another rather easy (if you are comfortable with using a mouse) but has one major problem: both applications need to support OLE Drag and Drop. So how do you support OLE Drag and Drop? This chapter will show you how easy it is to do. In fact, if you compiled your container application from Chapter 25, "Window Objects and Compound Documents," you might have noticed that the container already supports OLE Drag and Drop, because the rich edit control automatically supports this feature when you enable the control for OLE support.

Drag and Drop

As discussed in the introduction to this chapter, *drag and drop* is the process of selecting an object from one application or document and (with the left mouse button still down) dragging the object to another application or to another document in the same application. When you reach the destination, you release the left mouse button and the object is "dropped" into the destination application. In OLE terms, the source application/document is called the *drop source* and the destination application/document is called the *drop target*. To create a drop source, you need to implement a new interface called IDropSource, and to create a drop target you need to implement another interface called IDropTarget. Let's look at each of them individually.

IDropSource

As mentioned, the IDropSource interface needs to be implemented in order for your application to become a drop source. This interface has a few unusual characteristics about which you should be aware. First, it does not require you to implement IDropTarget. If for some reason your application can only be a drop source and not a drop target, you need to implement only IDropSource. Servers typically will only implement IDropSource and not IDropTarget because servers typically only provide data and don't accept it.

Another interesting characteristic is that an application normally creates IDropSource when a drag operation is about to begin, and deletes it when the operation has been completed. Most of your other objects have been created when the application or document was already created.

The final characteristic concerning IDropSource is that it always has an associated IDataObject. The associated IDataObject is created when the IDropSource is created, and it is deleted at the same time as IDropSource. Why does IDropSource have its own IDataObject? Just as with any data you place on the Clipboard, that object is not supposed to change during the drag-and-drop operation. To ensure that the data does not change during the drag-and-drop operation, you create a static IDataObject just as you did when you placed data onto the Clipboard. Why don't you use the same IDataObject that you created for the Clipboard? Because if you did, you would destroy any data that the Clipboard's IDataObject was holding.

The implementation for IDropSource is rather trivial. In fact, the hardest piece of coding (and it's not all that hard) is determining when to start the drag operation. Remember, a drag operation is started when the user clicks the left mouse button and then drags the mouse (while still holding down the left mouse button). Your instinct might be to start the drag operation when the left mouse button is pressed down. You shouldn't do this, however, because the user might just be selecting an object, and you don't want to create the IDropSource and IDataObject interfaces unnecessarily (it slows down the system). You might then decide to create the interfaces when the mouse moves while the left mouse button is down. This also wouldn't be a good thing because the user might have moved the mouse slightly (just enough so that Windows registers a mouse move), but the user doesn't notice that the mouse actually moved. The user could also be selecting a number of objects (such as when you select words with MS Word). So what do you do?

To determine the start of a drag operation, you first set a flag when the application receives the message that the left mouse button is down. At this time you also set a timer. If the mouse does not move significantly over a period of *x* milliseconds (use DD_DEFDRAGDELAY as a default value), you know the user wants to perform a drag so the application can create the interfaces. A second method is if the left mouse button is down and the mouse has moved a certain number of pixels (use DD_DEFDRAGMINDIST as a default value). When the application has determined that the drag operation should be started, the application needs to create an IDropSource and an IDataObject. The IDataObject should be created in the same manner as that created for the Clipboard because a static IDataObject is needed. After you have these two items, call DoDragDrop, which will perform much of the work for a drag/drop source. DoDragDrop will not return until the drag-and-drop operation has been completed or canceled.

IDropSource has two methods (in addition to the IUnknown methods). The first method is QueryContinueDrag.

DoDragDrop is basically a tight-loop that calls QueryContinueDrag and GiveFeedback as conditions change. QueryContinueDrag enables the drag/drop source application to determine whether the drag-and-drop operation can continue. If QueryContinueDrag returns DRAGDROP_S_CANCEL, DoDragDrop assumes the user has canceled the current drag-and-drop operation. If QueryContinueDrag returns DRAGDROP_S_DROP, DoDragDrop assumes the user has decided to drop the data, whereas returning NOERROR means that he or she is still dragging-and-dropping.

If you have ever played with drag and drop, you might have noticed that your cursor changes its appearance depending on whether you can drop an object into the window over which your mouse is currently positioned. The cursor will also change its appearance depending on whether you are performing a move operation or a copy operation. DoDragDrop calls IDropSource::GiveFeedback, which is responsible for changing the cursor to the appropriate cursor for the current operation (just select a cursor and then call SetCursor). If you want OLE to handle the cursor selection (which is best unless you have some reason to change the default behavior), your GiveFeedback implementation should be the same as Listing 27.1.

Listing 27.1. `GiveFeedback` implementation.

```
STDMETHODIMP CIDropSource::GiveFeedback (DWORD /* dwEffect */)
{
    return ResultFromScode(DRAGDROP_S_USEDEFAULTCURSORS);
}
```

As you can see, you simply return DRAGDROP_S_USEDEFAULTCURSORS, which causes OLE to use its default cursor for the current operation.

IDropTarget

IDropTarget is slightly more complex to implement than is IDropSource, yet is still fairly easy to implement if your application already supports Paste. In fact, as you will shortly see, when you drop an object on a target, you will call the same routines that are used to implement Paste.

RegisterDragDrop

Before you can create a drop area, you need to tell OLE which of your application's windows can be a drop target. This does not mean, however, that an object can be dropped anywhere within the window (although in our example program it does); it just means that somewhere in this window is a *possible* drop target. I say "possible" drop target because you might decide that the data the user wants to drop is not appropriate for your window (if you try to insert an object that the application doesn't support being pasted, for example). See Listing 27.2.

Listing 27.2. Registering Drag and Drop.

```
m_pIDropTarget->AddRef();
CoLockObjectExternal((LPUNKNOWN)m_pIDropTarget,TRUE,FALSE);
RegisterDragDrop(m_hWndView, (LPDROPTARGET)m_pIDropTarget);
```

CoLockObjectExternal

Because of the way OLE works internally, you must always call `CoLockObjectExternal` on your `IDropTarget` interface when you call `RegisterDragDrop` (and again when you call `RevokeDragDrop`, as you will see shortly). `CoLockObjectExternal` places what is known in OLE terms as a *strong* lock on the object. In an experiment, I did not call `CoLockObjectExternal` and the first drag-and-drop operation on a window was fine; however, all subsequent drag-and-drop operations to the window failed. I checked the object's reference counts and they were fine. As far as my application was concerned, my `IDropTarget` object existed and appeared functional. For some reason, however, OLE did not work with the `IDropTarget` in my application until I put back `CoLockObjectExternal`. It appears that the *weak* locks (`AddRef/Release`) were not enough for `IDropTarget` to consistently work. Until a strong or OLE lock is placed on `IDropTarget`, it will not consistently work. `CoLockObjectExternal` has the following syntax:

```
HRESULT CoLockObjectExternal(LPUNKNOWN pUnk, BOOL fLock, BOOL
fLastUnlockReleases);
```

pUnk—The object to be locked

fLock—if TRUE the object is locked

   —if FALSE the object is unlocked

fLastLockReleases— Specifies whether the lock is the last reference to the object that is to keep the object alive

To create a strong lock on an OLE object, simply call `CoLockObjectExternal` as follows:

```
CoLockObjectExternal(obj, TRUE, FALSE);
```

To unlock an object that you have previously placed a strong lock on, call the following:

```
CoLockObjectExternal(obj, FALSE, TRUE);
```

> **NOTE**
>
> Remember to call `CoLockObjectExternal(obj, TRUE, FALSE)` to lock your `IDropTarget` object.
>
> Call `CoLockObjectExternal(obj, FALSE, TRUE)` when you are finished with your `IDropTarget` object.

RevokeDragDrop

Before you destroy your window, you need to revoke drag and drop. To do this, simply call `RevokeDragDrop` with the same window handle you used to `RegisterDragDrop`. You also need to call `CoLockObjectExternal` to remove the strong lock you placed on the object when you registered drag and drop. Listing 27.3 shows the implementation of revoking drag and drop.

Listing 27.3. Revoking Drag and Drop.

```
RevokeDragDrop(m_hWndView);

CoLockObjectExternal((LPUNKNOWN)m_pIDropTarget,FALSE,TRUE);
m_pIDropTarget->Release();
```

The window handle used for `RevokeDragDrop` must be the same window that was used in `RegisterDragDrop` and must still be a valid window handle. In other words, you need to call `RevokeDragDrop` before you destroy your window!

When you have registered your application for drag and drop, you don't need to do anything special. When your window becomes a possible drop target, your `IDropTarget::DragEnter` method (for the window that is about to become a drop target) will be called (see Listing 27.4 for a minimal implementation).

Listing 27.4. `IDropTarget::DragEnter` implementation.

```
STDMETHODIMP CIDropTarget::DragEnter (LPDATAOBJECT pDataObj,
                                      DWORD grfKeyState,
                                      POINTL pointl,
                                      LPDWORD pdwEffect)
{
    *pdwEffect = FindDragDropEffect(grfKeyState, pointl);
    return NOERROR;
}
```

When `DragEnter` is called, your object is being told that a drag-and-drop operation is underway and that the mouse has just entered your window. You are passed an `IDataObject` so that you can determine whether the data this object contains can be dropped into your application. You are also told whether (at the current time) this is a move operation or a copy operation. Your `DragEnter` routine can determine whether it supports the requested operation (and in most cases the target does care whether the user wants a move or a copy).

When your application has been notified that it is a potential drop target (from `IDropTarget::DragEnter`), the `IDropTarget::DragOver` method will be called as the mouse moves across a drop target window. The `DragOver` routine should change the cursor to reflect whether the current mouse location is a possible drop site. In your application, the whole window is a drop site, so the implementation is extremely simple (see Listing 27.5).

Listing 27.5. `IDropTarget::DragOver` **implementation.**

```
STDMETHODIMP CIDropTarget::DragOver    (DWORD grfKeyState,
                                        POINTL pointl,
                                        LPDWORD pdwEffect)
{
    *pdwEffect = FindDragDropEffect(grfKeyState, pointl);
    return NOERROR;
}
```

One important item to note is that *DragOver* does not receive the *IDataObject* interface when it is called. If you need the *IDataObject* interface (to determine whether a particular drop site can accept the data on the Clipboard), you need to save the *IDataObject* that you received in *DragEnter*.

When the mouse has moved outside your window without performing a drop, your `DragLeave` method is called. `DragLeave` should perform any necessary cleanup, which might include releasing the `IDataObject` you obtained from `DragEnter` (if you performed an `AddRef` in `DragEnter` so that you could keep the `IDataObject`). Listing 27.6 shows the minimal implementation, which just returns `NOERROR`.

Listing 27.6. `IDropTarget::DragLeave` **implementation.**

```
STDMETHODIMP CIDropTarget::DragLeave (void)
{
    return NOERROR;
}
```

If the user decides to drop the object that is being dragged into your window, `IDropTarget::Drop` will be called with the current mouse position in screen coordinates, along with the `IDataObject` (so unless you need the `IDataObject` in `DragOver`, you don't need to save it from `DragEnter`). Listing 27.7 shows this implementation.

Listing 27.7. `IDropTarget::Drop` implementation.

```
STDMETHODIMP CIDropTarget::Drop (LPDATAOBJECT pIDataObject,
                                 DWORD grfKeyState,
                                 POINTL pointl,
                                 LPDWORD pdwEffect)
{
    pIDataObject->AddRef();

    *pdwEffect = FindDragDropEffect(grfKeyState, pointl);

    if (m_pContainDoc->m_pOleSiteObject)
        delete m_pContainDoc->m_pOleSiteObject;
    m_pContainDoc->m_pOleSiteObject = new COleSiteObject(m_pContainDoc);
    FORMATETC fmtetc;
    fmtetc.cfFormat = NULL;
    fmtetc.ptd = NULL;
    fmtetc.lindex = -1;
    fmtetc.dwAspect = DVASPECT_CONTENT;
    fmtetc.tymed = TYMED_NULL;
    m_pContainDoc->m_pOleSiteObject->AddSiteFromData(m_pContainDoc,
                                                     pIDataObject,
                                                     &fmtetc);

    pIDataObject->Release();

    DragLeave();
    return NOERROR;
}
```

This implementation of Drop simply creates a new `COleSiteObject` and then calls `AddSiteFromData`, which is similar to the implementation of Paste in an OLE application. The major difference is that in Paste the application received the `FORMATETC` from an internal lists of `FORMATETC`s that the application's object could accept. In an implementation of drop, you create a `FORMATETC` that only has `dwAspect` as `DVASPECT_CONTENT`. In your implementation of Drop, `dwAspect` should be obtained from the `ObjectDescriptor`, which can be obtained *from* `IDataObject->GetData`.

In all of the methods you implemented for `IDropTarget`, you might have noticed that your application called `FindDragDropEffect`. `FindDragDropEffect` is a helper function and is not part of OLE, which returns whether a move, copy or link is being requested for the Drag/Drop operation. Listing 27.8 shows an implementation of `FindDragDropEffect`.

Listing 27.8. `IDropTarget::FindDragDropEffect` implementation.

```
DWORD    CIDropTarget::FindDragDropEffect(DWORD grfKeyState, POINTL /* pointl */)
{
        DWORD    dwRet;

        //          no modifier -- DROPEFFECT_MOVE or source default
        //          SHIFT       -- DROPEFFECT_MOVE
        //          CTRL        -- DROPEFFECT_COPY
        //          CTRL-SHIFT  -- DROPEFFECT_LINK
```

```
    dwRet = OleStdGetDropEffect(grfKeyState);
    if (dwRet == 0)
        dwRet = DROPEFFECT_COPY;

    return dwRet;
}
```

As you can see in this implementation of FindDragDropEffect, you call a routine in OLEUI named OleStdGetDropEffect to determine whether a move, a copy, or a link is in process. Unfortunately, OleStdGetDropEffect can also return a 0, which means "use the default effect." In your application, the default is copy, so you will return DROPEFFECT_COPY. Your application will most likely implement a different version of FindDragDropEffect. Notably, your implementation doesn't care where the cursor is currently (you ignore point1, which is the current mouse/cursor position). In your application, you might decide that in certain places within your window a drop is not possible, so you need to look at point1 to determine whether a drop operation can occur at the current location.

Summary

The steps to implement a Drop Source are as follows:

1. Select a condition that will cause a drop operation to start. This will typically be when the left mouse button is down for a certain period of time (DD_DEFDRAGDELAY in milliseconds), or if the left mouse button is down and the mouse is moved a certain distance (DD_DEFDRAGMINDIST in pixels).

2. When the drop operation has been started, create your IDropSource and your IDataObject and call DoDragDrop. DoDragDrop will not return until the drag-and-drop operation has been completed or canceled.

3. Implement IDropSource::QueryContinue. This method determines whether the drag-and-drop operation should continue. In most situations you will want to implement this method as provided in Listing 27.9.

4. Implement IDropSource::GiveFeedback. This method determines what visual effect (cursor) should be displayed for the drag-and-drop operation based on the current mouse location, application, and which key is pressed (if any). In most situations you will want to implement this method as provided in Listing 27.10.

5. Perform any necessary cleanup when DoDragDrop returns. This might involve deleting any objects or data created for the drag-and-drop operation. You might also need to delete the selected object if a move operation was selected.

The steps to implement a Drop Target are as follows:

1. For every window that can be a drop target, implement IDropTarget.

2. For every window that can be a drop target, call CoLockObjectExternal and then call RegisterDragDrop.

3. Implement IDropTarget::DragEnter. This routine should check the IDataObject, which it receives to determine whether the format provided by the drag/drop source is supported by the IDataObject.

4. Implement IDropTarget::DragOver. This routine should do any necessary work (usually user-interface changes) that is required as the mouse moves across a drop target.

5. Implement IDropTarget::DragLeave. This routine performs any necessary cleanup that is required when the mouse has left a drop target.

6. Implement IDropTarget::Drop. This routine handles receiving of the data/object when a drop operation occurs.

OLE Automation

28

by Lawrence Harris

IN THIS CHAPTER

OLE automation is one of the easiest pieces of OLE to implement. OLE automation allows one program to use the features of another program. You may be familiar with the Macro Recorder included in Windows. This program saves a series of keystrokes or mouse movements and then replays them at a later time. This is great if you always want the same series of input to occur, but it is essentially one way: You cannot change the macro based on what is occurring. Also you cannot change the input without recreating the macro. OLE automation changes this by letting you write such a macro, for example, in any language that can be an OLE automation controller. Because you choose the language, you can write an intelligent macro that can change its behavior depending on the results it receives. In addition, you can write a program in a language, such as C++, that can also be the controlling application. This means that if your application needs to do limited word processing, for example, you could write a small program that controls Microsoft Word for Windows 6.0. In this application, you can get input data from anywhere you want, perform a series of actions, and then have your application create a Word document. You can even have your application mail or fax the created document automatically. You don't have to reinvent the wheel—you can use existing features from existing applications. Typically, object-oriented programming is about code reusability, but now you have achieved application reusability. OLE automation basically allows the integration of applications. Because you can take existing applications and customize them for your needs, you don't start coding from scratch. If you write automation servers, other programmers might integrate your applications into their applications. This means that your application might be purchased for purposes you have not even imaged.

So how do you make an OLE automation server? It's easier than you might think. I will use the rich edit control-based container application created in Chapter 25, "Window Objects and Compound Documents," for my example. First, you need to think of your application as an OLE object. In fact, many people refer to OLE automation servers as OLE automation objects. This means that you need to create an `IUnknown` interface and an `IClassFactory` interface for your object. In addition, you need to use `IDispatch` as an interface for OLE automation.

IClassFactory

`IClassFactory`, as I discussed in Chapter 24, "Component Object Model (COM)," creates an OLE object. OLE automation applications require a class factory because an application is essentially an object, and as with any other object, a method is needed to create it. As with all class factories, the class includes `QueryInterface`, `AddRef`, `Release`, `CreateInstance`, and `LockServer`. The final method, `Create`, is not required for a class factory, but I use this method to create the sample class factory. `Create` is not exposed to the outside world; it is just a helper function that helps create a class factory. Listing 28.1 shows the sample implementation of `IClassFactory`.

Listing 28.1. The sample `IClassFactory` implementation.

```
//@mfunc QueryInterface for the class factory.
//Only returns interface pointers
//to IUnknown (for the class factory) and IClassFactory.
//@rdesc NOERROR on success, otherwise returns
//E_NOINTERFACE if an interface was
//requested which is not supported by the class factory
STDMETHODIMP CAutoRtnsClassFactory::QueryInterface(REFIID riid,
                                                  void FAR* FAR* ppv)
{

    if ((riid == IID_IUnknown) || (riid == IID_IClassFactory)){
        *ppv = this;
        ++m_refs;
        return NOERROR;
        }
    *ppv = NULL;
    return ResultFromScode(E_NOINTERFACE);
}


//@mfunc Increments the reference count for the class factory.
//@rdesc Returns the number of references currently
//outstanding on the class factory
STDMETHODIMP_(unsigned long) CAutoRtnsClassFactory::AddRef(void)
{
    return ++m_refs;
}


//@mfunc Decrements the reference count for the class factory.
// When there are no
//outstanding references on the class factory,
//the class factory will be deleted.
//<nl>If LockServer is implemented then the class factory
// must only be deleted if
//the number of outstanding references is zero and
// the server is not locked.
//@rdesc Returns the number of references currently
//outstanding on the class factory
STDMETHODIMP_(unsigned long) CAutoRtnsClassFactory::Release(void)
{
    if (--m_refs == 0){
        delete this;
        return 0;
    }
    return m_refs;
}


//@mfunc Instantiates an AutoRtnsObject.
//@rdesc HRESULT error code.
STDMETHODIMP CAutoRtnsClassFactory::CreateInstance(IUnknown FAR*
➡/* punkOuter */,
             REFIID iid,
             void FAR* FAR* ppv)
{
        HRESULT hresult;
        CAutoRtnsObject FAR* pAutoRtnsObject;
```

continues

Listing 28.1. continued

```
        if ((pAutoRtnsObject = CAutoRtnsObject::Create(m_hWnd)) == NULL){
            *ppv = NULL;
            return ResultFromScode(E_OUTOFMEMORY);
        }
        hresult = pAutoRtnsObject->QueryInterface(iid, ppv);
        pAutoRtnsObject->Release();
        return hresult;
}

//@mfunc Locks or unlocks the class factory. Currently unimplemented.
//@rdesc Returns NOERROR.
STDMETHODIMP CAutoRtnsClassFactory::LockServer(BOOL /* flock */)
{
    return NOERROR;
}


//@mfunc Helper static routine to create the class factory object.
//@rdesc Returns a pointer to the newly created class factory interface.
IClassFactory FAR* CAutoRtnsClassFactory::Create(HWND hWnd)
{
    CAutoRtnsClassFactory FAR* pCF;

    if ((pCF = new FAR CAutoRtnsClassFactory()) == NULL)
        return NULL;
    pCF->m_hWnd = hWnd;
    pCF->AddRef();
    return pCF;
}
```

The Create method is used to create the sample class factory object. Create firsts performs a new to create a new class factory object and then calls AddRef to increment the reference count. It then returns the new interface. This is why it must call AddRef, because AddRef must be called before returning any interface pointer. Next, there are the implementations of QueryInterface, AddRef and Release, all of which have a standard implementation (for a class factory). CreateInstance creates the sample application object, while LockServer has no implementation: It always returns NOERROR. This implementation is fairly standard, and your implementation will most likely be very similar.

IDispatch

Once the ClassFactory has been implemented, you need to implement the IDispatch interface. IDispatch is the interface that exposes OLE automation servers to OLE automation controllers. IDispatch requires the implementation of the methods (in addition to the three required for IUnknown) shown in Table 28.1.

Table 28.1. The `IDispatch` methods.

Method	Description
`Invoke`	Allows an external program to tell your application what to do
`GetIDsofNames`	Changes a name to an ID (`Invoke` requires an ID, not a name)
`GetTypeInfo`	Returns the names of the methods and properties that can be invoked
`GetTypeInfoCount`	Returns the number of type information interfaces an object provides

Fortunately, OLE provides a default implementation of `IDispatch`. By calling the `CreateStdDispatch` function, the OLE libraries create an `IDispatch` interface for your use. Listing 28.2 shows the implementation of `CAutoRtnsObject`, with `CreateStdDispatch` called in the `Create` method.

Listing 28.2. Implementation of `CAutoRtnsObject`.

```
//@mfunc Constructor for the automation object
//@rdesc None
CAutoRtnsObject::CAutoRtnsObject()
{
    //Initialize the reference count
    m_refs = 0;

    //Initialize the IDispatch interface pointer
    //and ITypeInfo interface pointer
    m_disp_interface = NULL;
    m_typeinfo_interface = NULL;

    //Initialize typical automation variables
    m_bIsVisible = FALSE;

    //Initialize application specific variables (if any)

}

//@mfunc QueryInterface for the automation class.
//@rdesc NOERROR on success, otherwise returns E_NOINTERFACE if an interface was
//requested that is not supported by the object
STDMETHODIMP CAutoRtnsObject::QueryInterface(REFIID riid, void FAR* FAR* ppv)
{
    //They want an interface pointer to our object or to IUnknown
    if ((riid == IID_IUnknown) ¦¦ (riid == IID_IContApp))
        *ppv = this;
    //They want an interface pointer to our IDispatch
    else if ((riid == IID_IDispatch) ¦¦ (riid == IID_DContApp))
        return m_disp_interface->QueryInterface(IID_IDispatch,ppv);
    //They want an interface pointer to our ITypeInfo
    else if (riid == IID_ITypeInfo)
        return m_typeinfo_interface->QueryInterface(IID_ITypeInfo,ppv);
```

continues

Listing 28.2. continued

```
//Whatever they want we don't support so return E_NOINTERFACE
    else {
        *ppv = NULL;
        return ResultFromScode(E_NOINTERFACE);
    }

    //Don't forget to increment the reference count before
    //returning an interface pointer
    AddRef();

    //All was well so return NOERROR
    return NOERROR;
}

//@mfunc Increments the reference count for the object.
//@rdesc Returns the number of references currently outstanding on the object
STDMETHODIMP_(ULONG)CAutoRtnsObject::AddRef()
{
    return ++m_refs;
}

//@mfunc Decrements the reference count for the object. When there are no
//outstanding references on the object, the object will be deleted.
//@rdesc Returns the number of references currently outstanding
STDMETHODIMP_(ULONG)CAutoRtnsObject::Release()
{
    if(--m_refs == 0){
      //We're going to delete the object so release the
      //reference to the dispatch interface if we have one
      if (m_disp_interface != NULL)
        m_disp_interface->Release();
      //Also release the reference to the typeinfo interface if we have one
      if (m_typeinfo_interface != NULL)
        m_typeinfo_interface->Release();
      //Now we can delete the object
      delete this;
      //And terminate the program (if appropriate)
      PostQuitMessage(0);
      return 0;
    }

    //Reference count not zero so return the number of outstanding references
    return m_refs;
}

//@mfunc Helper static routine to create the object.
//@rdesc Returns a pointer to the newly created object.
CAutoRtnsObject FAR* CAutoRtnsObject::Create(HWND hWnd)
{
    CAutoRtnsObject FAR* pAutoRtnsObject;

    //Try to create the object, but if we can't then return NULL
    if ((pAutoRtnsObject = new FAR CAutoRtnsObject()) ==
        (CAutoRtnsObject FAR*)NULL)
            return (CAutoRtnsObject FAR*)NULL;
```

```
    //The object was created so increment the reference count
    pAutoRtnsObject->AddRef();

    //And save the handle of the application's main window
    pAutoRtnsObject->m_hWnd = hWnd;

    ITypeLib  FAR* ptlib;
    ITypeInfo FAR* ptinfo;

    //Load the type library which might be in the executable or a separate file
    HRESULT hresult = LoadRegTypeLib(CLSID_ContAppTypLib,1,0,0x0409, &ptlib);
    if (hresult != NOERROR){
        //The type library is not in the executable so check for a separate file
        if ((hresult = LoadTypeLib(AnsiToOlechar("CONTAPP.TLB"),&ptlib))
            != NOERROR){
            //No type library so fail
            return NULL;
        }
    }

    //Get the ITypeInfo interface pointer
    hresult = ptlib->GetTypeInfoOfGuid(IID_IContApp, &ptinfo);
    if (hresult != NOERROR)
        return NULL;

    //Save the ITypeInfo interface pointer
    pAutoRtnsObject->m_typeinfo_interface = ptinfo;
    ptinfo->AddRef();   // Because we assigned it to another variable

    //Create an standard IDispatch interface pointer
    hresult = CreateStdDispatch(pAutoRtnsObject,
                                pAutoRtnsObject,ptinfo,
                                &pAutoRtnsObject->m_disp_interface);
    ptinfo->Release();
    ptlib->Release();   // Because we don't need ptlib anymore


    if (hresult != NOERROR)
        return NULL;

    return pAutoRtnsObject;
}
```

CAutoRtnsObject is the object created from the class factory. CAutoRtnsObject follows the common object model and has an IUnknown with the QueryInterface, AddRef, and Release methods. The QueryInterface method returns the object's IUnknown interface pointer, an IDispatch interface pointer, or an ITypeInfo interface pointer. ITypeInfo is discussed in the next section "ITypeLib and ITypeInfo."

The AddRef method is standard and increments the sample object's reference counter; however, Release is a little different. Instead of simply deleting the object when the reference count is zero, Release first releases a reference to the IDispatch and ITypeInfo interface pointers. As discussed in Chapter 24, any interface pointers you obtain must be released in order for your application to terminate properly and for all libraries to be freed. Also, if you don't properly free references, then other applications might still reside in your application after you terminate; that is, if you have an interface pointer to an object in another application. Because I obtain an `IDispatch` interface pointer and an `ITypeInfo` interface pointer in the sample application, I need to release them before the object is destroyed. The `Release` method also calls `PostQuitMessage` to terminate the application. If your application only runs multiple instances of the application, OLE creates multiple instances, and each instance can terminate when `CAutoRtnsObject` is destroyed. If your application does not support multiple instances, you need to determine under what conditions your application can terminate.

The `Create` method is where all of the work gets done in the creation of the sample object. The `Create` method is a static function, and it first creates a `CAutoRtnsObject` C++ object. Upon successful creation of the C++ object, `Create` obtains an interface pointer to `ITypeLib` in order to obtain an interface pointer to `ITypeInfo` (`ITypeLib` and `ITypeInfo` are discussed in the next section). Once the interface pointer to `ITypeInfo` is obtained, `CreateStdDispatch` can be called to obtain an interface pointer to a standard OLE-created implementation of `IDispatch`. These are all the interfaces the sample OLE object needs.

ITypeLib and ITypeInfo

Automation servers can be created in two ways. In the OLE 2 beta, the only way to create an automation server is to create a series of structures that contain information on all the methods, parameters, and interfaces an automation server supports. Creating the structures is tedious and can be prone to error. Microsoft has developed another way to create the same information—type libraries. *Type libraries* are not just the information previously provided in the structures, but rather a whole wealth of information. Because these libraries contain extensive information about automation servers, Microsoft has also created a new language to work with this information—object description language or ODL.

In addition, OLE defines the `ITypeLib` and `ITypeInfo` interfaces for accessing type information. `ITypeLib` provides information about a type library, while `ITypeInfo` provides information contained in the type library. Think of `ITypeLib` as accessing the description of the information contained in the library (the card catalog in a real library) and think of `ITypeInfo` as accessing the information about the objects.

The Registry Database

When another application requests your application to create an object, OLE needs to know the name of your application so that your application can be launched. OLE finds the information needed to launch your application in the registration database, which is integrated into Windows 95. Listing 28.3 shows the routines used to add and remove information for the automation server in the registry database.

Listing 28.3. Registry routines.

```c
static  void    AddRegKeysHelper(char *iszSubKey, char *iszValue)
{
    static  char    szValue[200];
    static  char    szSubKey[100];

    strcpy(szSubKey,iszSubKey);
    strcpy(szValue,iszValue);
    RegSetValue(HKEY_CLASSES_ROOT, szSubKey, REG_SZ, szValue, sizeof(szValue));
}

void    AddRegKeys(void)
{
    HKEY    hKey;
    static  char    szCLSID[] = "CLSID";
    char    szAppString[_MAX_PATH + 20];
    char    szTypString[_MAX_PATH + 20];
    char    szTempString[_MAX_PATH + 20];

    hKey = NULL;

    strcpy(szAppString,CONTAPPAppObject.szModuleFullName);
    strcat(szAppString," /Automation");

    char    szDrv[_MAX_DRIVE];
    char    szDir[_MAX_DIR];
    char    szFname[_MAX_FNAME];

    _splitpath(CONTAPPAppObject.szModuleFullName,szDrv,szDir,szFname,NULL);
    strcpy(szTypString,szDrv);
    strcat(szTypString,szDir);
    strcat(szTypString,szFname);
    strcat(szTypString,".TLB");

    RegOpenKey(HKEY_CLASSES_ROOT, szCLSID, &hKey);

        //Registers the extension
        AddRegKeysHelper(".CTA","ContApp.Document");
        strcpy(szTempString,CONTAPPAppObject.szModuleFullName);
        strcat(szTempString," %1");
        AddRegKeysHelper("ContApp.Document\\shell\\open\\command",szTempString);
        AddRegKeysHelper("ContApp.Document\\shell\\open\\ddeexce",
    ➥ "[open(\"%1\")]");

    //Registration for automation
    AddRegKeysHelper("ContApp.Application","WPU Container Application");
    AddRegKeysHelper("ContApp.Application\\Clsid",
            "{0002A43F-0000-0000-C000-000000000046}");

    AddRegKeysHelper("ContApp.Application.1","WPU Container Application");
    AddRegKeysHelper("ContApp.Application.1\\Clsid",
            "{0002A43F-0000-0000-C000-000000000046}");

    AddRegKeysHelper("CLSID\\{0002A43F-0000-0000-C000-000000000046}",
                "WPU Container Application");
    AddRegKeysHelper("CLSID\\{0002A43F-0000-0000-C000-000000000046}\\ProgId",
                "ContApp.Application.1");
```

continues

Listing 28.3. continued

```
    AddRegKeysHelper(
 "CLSID\\{0002A43F-0000-0000-C000-000000000046}\\VersionIndependentProgID",
                   "ContApp.Application");
    AddRegKeysHelper(
 "CLSID\\{0002A43F-0000-0000-C000-000000000046}\\LocalServer32",
                   szAppString);
    AddRegKeysHelper("TypeLib\\{0002A43C-0000-0000-C000-000000000046}","");
    AddRegKeysHelper("TypeLib\\{0002A43C-0000-0000-C000-000000000046}\\1.0",
                   "WPU Container Application Type Library");
    AddRegKeysHelper(
 "TypeLib\\{0002A43C-0000-0000-C000-000000000046}\\1.0\\HELPDIR",
                   "");
    AddRegKeysHelper(
 "TypeLib\\{0002A43C-0000-0000-C000-000000000046}\\1.0\\409\\win32",
                   szTypString);
    AddRegKeysHelper("Interface\\{0002A43E-0000-0000-C000-000000000046}",
                   "_DContApp");
    AddRegKeysHelper(
 "Interface\\{0002A43E-0000-0000-C000-000000000046}\\ProxyStubClsid",
                   "{00020420-0000-0000-C000-000000000046}");
    AddRegKeysHelper(
 "Interface\\{0002A43E-0000-0000-C000-000000000046}\\NumMethod",
                   "7");
    AddRegKeysHelper(
 "Interface\\{0002A43E-0000-0000-C000-000000000046}\\BaseInterface",
                   "{00020420-0000-0000-C000-000000000046}");

    RegCloseKey(hKey);
}

void    DeleteRegKeys(void)
{
    HKEY    hKey;
    static char    szCLSID[] = "CLSID";

    hKey = NULL;

    RegOpenKey(HKEY_CLASSES_ROOT, szCLSID, &hKey);

    RegDeleteKey(HKEY_CLASSES_ROOT,"ContApp.Application");
    RegDeleteKey(HKEY_CLASSES_ROOT,"ContApp.Application\\Clsid");

    RegDeleteKey(HKEY_CLASSES_ROOT,"ContApp.Application.1");
    RegDeleteKey(HKEY_CLASSES_ROOT,"ContApp.Application.1\\Clsid");

    RegDeleteKey(HKEY_CLASSES_ROOT,
 "CLSID\\{0002A43F-0000-0000-C000-000000000046}");
    RegDeleteKey(HKEY_CLASSES_ROOT,
 "CLSID\\{0002A43F-0000-0000-C000-000000000046}\\ProgId");
    RegDeleteKey(HKEY_CLASSES_ROOT,
 "CLSID\\{0002A43F-0000-0000-C000-000000000046}\\VersionIndependentProgID");
    RegDeleteKey(HKEY_CLASSES_ROOT,
 "CLSID\\{0002A43F-0000-0000-C000-000000000046}\\LocalServer32");
    RegDeleteKey(HKEY_CLASSES_ROOT,
 "TypeLib\\{0002A43C-0000-0000-C000-000000000046}");
    RegDeleteKey(HKEY_CLASSES_ROOT,
 "TypeLib\\{0002A43C-0000-0000-C000-000000000046}\\1.0");
    RegDeleteKey(HKEY_CLASSES_ROOT,
```

```
    "TypeLib\\{0002A43C-0000-0000-C000-000000000046}\\1.0\\HELPDIR");
      RegDeleteKey(HKEY_CLASSES_ROOT,
    "TypeLib\\{0002A43C-0000-0000-C000-000000000046}\\1.0\\409\\win32");
      RegDeleteKey(HKEY_CLASSES_ROOT,
    "Interface\\{0002A43E-0000-0000-C000-000000000046}");
      RegDeleteKey(HKEY_CLASSES_ROOT,
    "Interface\\{0002A43E-0000-0000-C000-000000000046}\\ProxyStubClsid");
      RegDeleteKey(HKEY_CLASSES_ROOT,
    "Interface\\{0002A43E-0000-0000-C000-000000000046}\\NumMethod");
      RegDeleteKey(HKEY_CLASSES_ROOT,
    "Interface\\{0002A43E-0000-0000-C000-000000000046}\\BaseInterface");

      RegCloseKey(hKey);
}
```

AddRegKeysHelper is a routine that is simply a wrapper around the Windows API
RegSetValue. All the work of adding the information to the registry database is performed by
AddRegKeys. First, AddRegKeys obtains the full name (including path) of an application.
AddRegKeys then appends "/Automation" to the end of the full name. "/Automation" is a
command line option for the sample application. It indicates that the application is
launched as an OLE automation server instead of being launched by the user. Next,
AddRegKeys adds three entries to the database for non-OLE purposes. The .CTA extension
and the two shell entries are registered so that Windows 95 will associate CTA with the
sample application. If a user double-clicks on a file with a .CTA extension from Explorer,
for example, Windows 95 will launch the sample application. In addition, because the
sample application supports Send, the mail application will launch the sample application
when asked to open a CTA file. Finally, the rest of AppRegKeys adds the example's OLE
automation registration information into the registry database. DeleteRegKeys is the third
routine and simply deletes all the entries added by AppRegKeys.

Command Line Options

The sample application now has a routine for adding entries to the registration database and
for deleting entries. OLE standards dictate that an application must operate as an automation server if it is launched with the "/Automation" switch on the command line (see the
"/Automation" switch on the local server entry in the registration database). Listing 28.4 is
the implementation of ParseCmdLine, which parses "/Automation," "/RegServer,"
"/UnRegServer," and "/Embedded" from the command line.

NOTE

If you intended to process other application-defined options on the command line or
filenames from the command line, you might need to change how this routine is
implemented.

Listing 28.4. The implementation of `ParseCmdLine`.

```c
BOOL ParseCmdLine(TCHAR FAR*szCmdLine, BOOL FAR *pbDoAutomation,
                                       BOOL FAR *pbDoEmbedded,
                                       BOOL FAR *pbDoRegister,
                                       BOOL FAR *pbDoUnRegister)
{
        BOOL    bDidOption    = FALSE;
        BOOL    bDoAutomation = FALSE;
        BOOL    bDoEmbedded   = FALSE;
        BOOL    bDoRegister   = FALSE;
        BOOL    bDoUnRegister = FALSE;

        while (*szCmdLine != 0){
        if (*szCmdLine == '-' || *szCmdLine == '/'){
            if (_fstrnicmp(szCmdLine+1,"automation",10) == 0){
                szCmdLine += 11;
                bDoAutomation = TRUE;
                bDidOption = TRUE;
            }
            else if (_fstrnicmp(szCmdLine+1,"embedded",8) == 0){
                szCmdLine +=9;
                bDoEmbedded = TRUE;
                bDidOption = TRUE;
            }
            else if (_fstrnicmp(szCmdLine+1,"regserver",9) == 0){
                szCmdLine +=10;
                bDoRegister = TRUE;
                bDidOption = TRUE;
            }
            else if (_fstrnicmp(szCmdLine+1,"unregserver",11) == 0){
                szCmdLine += 12;
                bDoUnRegister = TRUE;
                bDidOption = TRUE;
            }
        }
        szCmdLine++;
    }

    if (pbDoAutomation != NULL)
        *pbDoAutomation = bDoAutomation;
    if (pbDoEmbedded != NULL)
        *pbDoAutomation = bDoEmbedded;
    if (pbDoRegister != NULL)
        *pbDoRegister = bDoRegister;
    if (pbDoUnRegister != NULL)
        *pbDoUnRegister = bDoUnRegister;

    return bDidOption;
}
```

"/Automation" indicates that the sample application is launched as an automation server. The sample application uses "/RegServer" to register itself whenever it runs. "/UnRegServer" calls the `DeleteRegKeys` routines, which remove entries of an application in the registry database. In *OLE Control Specifications*, Microsoft recommends that you use "/RegServer" and "/UnRegServer" to register and unregister OLE controls; therefore, for consistency, I use these options in the sample application. Finally, "/Embedded" is not used in the sample application, because it is received by applications that are OLE-embedded object servers.

Launching an OLE Automation Server

When "/Automation" is parsed from the command line, the sample application is launched as an OLE automation server. When the sample application is launched as an OLE automation server, OLE asks for the IClassFactory interface so that CAutoRtnsObject can be created from the class factory. To create the class factory, the sample application calls CAutoRtnsClassFactory::Create. Once the class factory is created, the OLE API CoRegisterClassObject is called to provide OLE with an interface pointer to the example's class factory. Listing 28.5 is an excerpt that shows how CoRegisterClassObject is called.

Listing 28.5. Creating an automation object.

```
gpAutoRtnsClassFactory = CAutoRtnsClassFactory::Create(hWnd);
    if (gpAutoRtnsClassFactory != NULL){
        HRESULT hresult = CoRegisterClassObject(CLSID_ContAppObject,
                                    gpAutoRtnsClassFactory,
                                    CLSCTX_LOCAL_SERVER,
                                    REGCLS_SINGLEUSE,
                                    &gdwAutoRtnsClassFactory);
    }
```

CoRegisterClassObject is called with the parameter REGCLS_SINGLEUSE, which tells OLE that a new copy of the sample application must be launched whenever another application requests an object supported by the sample application. If "single use" is not specified, then once a single instance of the sample application is running, OLE automatically calls the example's class factory to create a new object whenever another application requests the CAutoRtnsObject.

Properties and Methods

All the changes have been made to support the creation of an OLE automation object and the sample application has been recompiled; however, the sample automation server still does nothing. You can launch the sample automation server from an automation controller, such as Visual Basic or Excel, but the actions for the sample automation server have not yet been defined. OLE automation supports methods and properties as the means for an OLE automation controller, such as Visual Basic or Excel, to interact with an OLE automation server.

Properties are the logical equivalent of *variables* in C++. Some properties allow their values to be both set and retrieved, while other properties allow their values to be either set or retrieved. For example, the sample container application has a property called Visible. The value of Visible can be retrieved. Visible tells the caller whether the container application is currently visible or hidden. The Visible property also allows the caller to set its value, making the container application either visible or hidden. Listing 28.6 shows the implementation of the Visible property.

Listing 28.6. The implementation of the Visible property.

```
STDMETHODIMP_(void) CAutoRtnsObject::put_Visible(VARIANT_BOOL bFlag)
{
    if (bFlag == m_bIsVisible)
            return;
    m_bIsVisible = bFlag;
    if (m_bIsVisible)
        ShowWindow(m_hWnd,SW_NORMAL);
    else
        ShowWindow(m_hWnd,SW_HIDE);
    UpdateWindow(m_hWnd);
}

STDMETHODIMP_(VARIANT_BOOL)CAutoRtnsObject::get_Visible()
{
    return (VARIANT_BOOL)m_bIsVisible;
}
```

If a property's value can be changed by an automation controller, the property has a put routine. In Listing 28.6, put_Visible is the put routine for the Visible property. The put_Visible routine accepts one parameter, either TRUE or FALSE, and determines whether the parameter being passed is different than the current state of the property. If the state is the same, the routine simply returns—the property is already set to the requested value. If the parameter is not the same as the current state, the parameter is saved, and the application window is either displayed or hidden, depending on the value of the parameter.

If a property's value can be retrieved by an automation controller, the property has a get routine. In Listing 28.6, get_Visible is the get routine for the Visible property. The get_Visible routine simply returns the value of the visible property.

Properties do not need to have both a put and get method. Some properties may be write-only; other properties may be read-only. Listing 28.7 shows three examples of a read-only property (write-only properties are rarely used).

Listing 28.7. Three sample read-only properties.

```
STDMETHODIMP_(BSTR)CAutoRtnsObject::get_Name()
{
    return SysAllocString(AnsiToOlechar("ContApp"));
```

```
}

STDMETHODIMP_(BSTR)CAutoRtnsObject::get_FullName()
{
    return SysAllocString(AnsiToOlechar(CONTAPPAppObject.szModuleFullName));
}

STDMETHODIMP_(BSTR)CAutoRtnsObject::get_Path()
{
    char    szDrv[_MAX_DRIVE];
    char    szDir[_MAX_DIR];
    char    szPathString[_MAX_PATH];

    _splitpath(CONTAPPAppObject.szModuleFullName,szDrv,szDir,NULL,NULL);
    strcpy(szPathString,szDrv);
    strcat(szPathString,szDir);

    return SysAllocString(AnsiToOlechar(szPathString));
}
```

The Name property obtains the name of the application, which for the sample application is
ContApp. The FullName property obtains the full name of the application and includes the
path for the executable. The Path property obtains the current path of the application. Each
of these three properties returns strings. In OLE automation, strings are type BSTR (binary
string). A binary string is not the same as a character area. A binary string contains a length
followed by character data without a NULL termination. In addition, under Windows 95 and
Windows NT 3.5*x*, BSTR is a Unicode string. AnsiToOlechar, which is from COMMON.H,
converts an ANSI string to a Unicode string, whereas SysAllocString, which is part of
OLE, creates a binary string from a Unicode string.

Finally, OLE automation servers have methods in addition to properties. A *method* is the
equivalent of a *function call*. A method can accept parameters from the calling program
although it is not necessary for a method to have parameters. Listing 28.8 shows an implementation of the Quit method.

Listing 28.8. A sample implementation of the Quit method.

```
STDMETHODIMP_(void)CAutoRtnsObject::Quit()
{
    PostQuitMessage(0);
}
```

The Quit method takes no parameters and returns no value—it simply terminates the
automation server application.

Once you have determined what methods and properties your application will support,
you need to create an ODL (object description language) file, which, when compiled, will
become the application's type library. Listing 28.9 shows the ODL for the sample container
application.

Listing 28.9. The ODL file for `ContApp`.

```
[uuid(0002A43C-0000-0000-C000-000000000046)]

library ContApp {
   importlib("stdole.tlb");

   [odl, uuid(0002A43D-0000-0000-C000-000000000046),
       helpstring("ContApp Automation")]
   interface _IContApp : IUnknown
   {
    [id(2), propget] long GetFirstVisibleLine();
    [id(3), propget] long GetLineCount();
    [id(1), propput] void Visible([in] boolean bflag);
    [id(1), propget] boolean Visible();
    [id(0), propget] BSTR Name();
    [id(4), propget] BSTR FullName();
    [id(5), propget] BSTR Path();
    void Quit();
   };
   [uuid(0002A43E-0000-0000-C000-000000000046)]
   dispinterface _DContApp{
       interface _IContApp;
   }
   [uuid(0002A43F-0000-0000-C000-000000000046)]
       coclass ContApp {
       dispinterface _DContApp;
       interface      _IContApp;
   }
};
```

You will notice by looking at Listing 28.9 that Visible has two entries: one that has a propput entry and another that has a propget entry. When the ODL file is compiled, Mktyplib converts the propput entry to put_Visible, whereas the propget entry is converted to get_Visible. Mktyplib recognizes that Quit does not have a propput or a propget entry and assumes that Quit is a method.

Summary

OLE Automation is a functionality that can be added to applications to allow other applications to control your application, or for your application to control other applications. Using OLE Automation you can use applications as building blocks, where each application performs a specific function; OLE Automation will tie the applications together to perform one unified task.

OLE as a DDE Replacement

by Lawrence Harris

29

IN THIS CHAPTER

Over the past year I have often heard the question, "How can OLE replace DDE?" The answer actually depends on what is meant by *replace*. Many who ask this question want OLE applications and DDE applications to exchange data with each other. Unless an OLE application supports DDE or a DDE application supports OLE, the two applications will not be able to exchange data with each other through OLE or DDE. If by the word *replace* it is meant that OLE and DDE have similar functionality, then the answer is yes: OLE and DDE do share similar functionality, although DDE's functionality is a subset of OLE's functionality. Throughout this chapter I will show you how OLE can be used as a replacement for DDE's functionality.

DDE Versus OLE

Dynamic data exchange (DDE) is a message-based protocol used to exchange data between applications. DDE can be used to exchange data within a single application as well. DDE consists of specific Windows messages as well as a set of rules to be used when one application receives a specific DDE message from another application. Initially, DDE could only exchange data between applications on the same machine; however, with the introduction of Windows for Workgroups, DDE can now exchange data between applications on different machines. Windows NT and Windows 95 also support the exchange of data between different machines using DDE.

OLE was initially a protocol used to exchange data between applications; OLE 1 used DDE as the mechanism to facilitate the exchange of data. When OLE 2 was introduced for the 16-bit implementation of Windows, OLE no longer used DDE as the underlying communication mechanism. Instead, OLE used its own private messaging mechanism based on lightweight remote procedure calls or LRPC. OLE 2 is not simply a method for communication between applications (also known as interprocess communications), but is a whole environment in which data exchange is a piece of OLE. When OLE 2 was introduced for Windows NT, OLE was no longer based on LRPC but instead was based on local procedure calls or LPC, a private messaging mechanism built into Windows NT.

Here is one comparison that can be made of DDE and OLE: The nine functions provided by the nine messages supported by DDE are equivalent to the two interfaces supported by OLE. Table 29.1 shows the DDE messages and the functionally equivalent OLE interfaces.

Table 29.1. DDE messages and the equivalent OLE implementations.

DDE Message	OLE Implementation	Description
WM_DDE_ACK	IDataObject	Notification that the message has been received
WM_DDE_ADVISE	IDataObject	Starts notification
WM_DDE_DATA	IDataObject	Notification of data change

DDE Message	OLE Implementation	Description
WM_DDE_EXECUTE	IDispatch	Runs a command at the server
WM_DDE_INITIATE	IDataObject or IDispatch	Starts a conversation
WM_DDE_POKE	IDataObject	Updates server or IDispatch data
WM_DDE_REQUEST	IDataObject	Data request
WM_DDE_TERMINATE	IDataObject	End of a conversation
WM_DDE_UNADVISE	IDataObject	Stops notification

Table 29.1 is an oversimplification of the functional equivalencies of DDE and OLE. For example, WM_DDE_INITIATE is not exactly equivalent to IDataObject or IDispatch; however, in OLE, you first need to start the server using the appropriate OLE API. Once the OLE server has been started, your application will ultimately obtain either IDataObject or IDispatch. Actually, in OLE, you can use another interface to exchange data, or you can create your own interface; however, in most applications, either IDataObject or IDispatch is used to exchange data. Because IDispatch was discussed in Chapter 28, "OLE Automation," the rest of this chapter concentrates on IDataObject.

IDataObject

IDataObject is the heart and soul of OLE's ability to exchange data between applications. It provides mechanisms similar to DDE and the Clipboard data transfer. When DDE applications exchange data, DDE allocates a block of global memory and basically passes a handle to the global memory from one application to another application. Although passing a memory handle is fast, it is not necessarily an efficient way to pass data between applications. Imagine that one application wants to pass a large amount of data (a picture, for example) from one application to another. If the source application has the picture already in memory, then passing the global memory handle from the source application to the client application is efficient. However, if the source application does not have the picture in memory but rather on disk, then the source application needs to first read in the picture and then pass the memory handle. If the picture is large (10 MB, for example), then Windows can write the picture to its virtual memory (on disk) as the source application reads the data, creating a duplicate image and causing the picture to double in size (the original picture plus the virtual memory picture). Using OLE and IDataObject, the source and client applications can simply exchange the file on disk instead of using the global memory handle. Exchanging the file prevents the source application from reading the data into memory and prevents Windows from creating a virtual memory of the picture. The IDataObject interface allows the source application and client application to negotiate to determine the best medium for data exchange.

IDataObject also allows the source and client applications to negotiate the format of the data exchange. A client application can ask the source application if it supports rich format text (RTF), for example. If the source doesn't support rich format text, the client application can request the data in text format. IDataObject has methods that allow for a client to request data in a particular format using predefined methods. DDE, on the other hand, has no direct method a client can use to request a particular format. When using DDE, the client application must know how to request a particular format from a particular server; the mechanism used to request a format varies from application to application.

DDE also has mechanisms used to request data change notification. This allows a client application either to be notified when the data in the server changes or to allow the server to send the data whenever the data changes. IDataObject also supports a similar data change notification. However, the IDispatch interface currently has no mechanism for data change notification.

IDataObject owes much of its flexibility for using different types of data and storage formats to the FORMATETC and STGMEDIUM structures. Before examining the members of IDataObject, I provide a brief look at the FORMATETC and STGMEDIUM structures.

FORMATETC

FORMATETC is used by IDataObject to inform the server and the data consumer of the possible formats available for a piece of data. Using an array of FORMATETC structures, a data consumer can query a data server to find out what formats are supported, select a format, and request the data in the selected format. Table 29.2 shows the fields in the FORMATETC structure.

Table 29.2. The FORMATETC structure elements.

Field	Type	Description
cfFormat	CLIPFORMAT	Indicates the particular Clipboard format of interest. This can be one of the standard Clipboard formats or it can be a unique, application-registered format.
ptd	DVTARGETDEVICE	Indicates the target device for which the data is composed. This is actually a pointer to a DVTARGETDEVICE structure (ptd stands for pointer, target, device), which tells an application if the data is currently rendered for a screen or printer or for another device. This field is typically only used if a piece of data is rendered in a device-specific format. In many cases, this field is null, indicating that the information is not rendered for any particular device.

Field	Type	Description
dwAspect	DWORD	Provides different views or aspects of an object, such as a thumbnail or an icon. When data is provided with a lower detail than is actually available, the data is usually referred to as a *thumbnail.* If it does not make sense to be provided the data as a thumbnail, a client can request the data as an icon. Both methods provide a way for the user to look at a piece of data without waiting for all the details. For example, it does not make sense to display a WAV (sound) file as a thumbnail; therefore, an application can display the WAV file as an icon. The dwAspect field indicates whether the data is presented in its entirety (by using DVASPECT_CONTENT), as a thumbnail (by using DVASPECT_THUMBNAIL), or as an icon (using DVASPECT_ICON). In addition, dwAspect can be DVASPECT_DOCPRINT if the data is fully formatted for a printer (with headers and footers, and so on).
lindex	LONG	The lindex field indicates the page or pages of a document. If dwAspect is set to DVASPECT_THUMBNAIL or DVASPECT_ICON, the lindex value is ignored. If dwAspect is set to DVASPECT_CONTENT, the lindex value must be -1 to indicate that the whole document is passed. In a future version of OLE, if the value of dwAspect is DVASPECT_DOCPRINT, the lindex value will indicate the piece of the document being passed. Currently this field must be -1.
tymed	DWORD	The tymed field indicates the type of medium (tymed stands for type medium) used to pass the data. One of the problems that many transfer mechanisms have is that data can only be transferred using global memory. OLE does not suffer from this restriction. Within OLE, data can be transferred using global memory or a file. This type of flexibility can have tremendous benefits. If for example, you wish to transfer a 10 MB file, you don't have to use global memory; instead, you can use a file. This can dramatically improve performance, because the server application can just pass the file handle to the

continues

Table 29.2. continued

Field	Type	Description
		consumer application; it does not need to read all the data and then pass the data into memory while the consumer application writes the data. In OLE, a file can be a regular file (based on the file system of the application), or it could be an OLE structure storage, which includes storages and streams. The possible values are discussed in the next section.

STGMEDIUM

The STGMEDIUM structure (STGMEDIUM stands for storage medium) informs OLE how to use or release the data described by FORMATETC. Table 29.3 lists the fields within the STGMEDIUM structure.

Table 29.3. The STGMEDIUM structure elements.

Field	Type	Description
tymed	DWORD	As previously described in FORMATETC, tymed describes the type of medium used. The possible values are discussed in the pUnkForRelease section.
hBitmap*	HBITMAP	tymed==TYMED_GDI hBitmap is a handle to a bitmap. This field is part of a union.
hMetafilePict*	HMETAFILEPICT	tymed==TYMED_MFPICT hMetafilePict is a handle to a metafile. This field is part of a union.
hEnhMetafilePict*	HENHMETAFILEPICT	tymed ==TYMED_ENHMF hEnhMetafilePict is a handle to an enhanced metafile. This field is part of a union.
hGlobal*	HGLOBAL	tymed== TYMED_HGLOBAL hGlobal is a handle to global memory. This field is part of a union.

Field	Type	Description
lpszFileName*	LPWSTR	tymed==TYMED_FILE lpszFileName is the name of the file that contains the data. This field is part of a union.
pStg*	IStorage FAR*	tymed ==TYMED_ISTORAGE pStg is a pointer to an IStorage interface. This field is part of a union.
pStm*	IStream FAR*	tymed ==TYMED_ISTREAM pStm is a pointer to an IStream interface. This field is part of a union.
pUnkForRelease		This field indicates how tymed is released and who is responsible for releasing the data. If this field is not set to NULL, the receiver of the data is required to release the data. Table 29.4 lists the method to delete the various tymed fields.

*These field names are members of a union. For compilers that do not support nameless unions, such as Borland, the union name is *u*; otherwise, the union has no name. For example, to access pStm on a compiler that does not support nameless unions, you use the syntax "*<VariableName>*.u.pStm". Otherwise, use "*<VariableName>*.pStm".

Table 29.4. Releasing a type medium.

Tymed	Field in Union	Meaning	Release
TYMED_HGLOBAL	hGlobal	Global memory	GlobalFree memory (pUnkForRelease is NULL)
TYMED_FILE	lpszFileName	Disk file	lpszFileName disk file is deleted. pIMalloc ->Free(lpszFile Name) to free the filename string (pUnkForRelease is NULL)
TYMED_ISTORAGE	pStg	Storage	pStg->Release()

continues

Table 29.4. continued

Tymed	Field in Union	Meaning	Release
TYMED_ISTREAM	pStm	Stream	pStm->Release()
TYMED_GDI	hBitmap	GDI	DeleteObject (pUnkForRelease is NULL)
TYMED_MFPICT	hMetafilePict	Metafile	DeleteMetaFile (pUnkForRelease is NULL)
TYMED_ ENHMFPICT	hEnhMetafile Pict	Enhanced metafile	DeleteMetaFile (pUnkForRelease is NULL)
TYMED_NULL	Undefined	Not initialized	Undefined

Armed with this information on FORMATETC and STGMEDIUM, you are now ready to take a look at the members of IDataObject.

EnumFormatEtc

EnumFormatEtc returns an IEnumFORMATETC interface pointer to the caller. Using the IEnumFORMATETC interface pointer, the caller can determine what formats are supported by the IDataObject. IEnumFORMATETC is known as an enumerator; in OLE, enumerators have predefined methods. An interface that is an enumerator supports the following methods: Next, Skip, Reset, and Clone. These methods allow your application to step through (in this case) all the formats IDataObject supports.

GetCanonicalFormatEtc

GetCanonicalFormatEtc returns to the caller an equivalent FORMATETC structure on output based on the FORMATETC structure provided on input. If GetCanonicalFormatEtc returns the exact same FORMATETC structure on output, then GetCanonicalFormatEtc returns a NULL FORMATETC and a return code of DATA_S_SAMEFORMATETC. GetCanonicalFormatEtc is typically used to minimize the number of formats a caller obtains from an IDataObject.

GetData

GetData is used to obtain data from IDataObject in a specific format (based on FORMATETC) and in a specific medium (based on STGMEDIUM). When GetData is called, IDataObject is responsible for creating the data on the medium requested by the caller.

GetDataHere

GetDataHere is used to obtain data from IDataObject in a specific format (based on a FORMATETC) and in a specific medium (based on a STGMEDIUM). GetDataHere differs from GetData in that when GetDataHere is called, the caller provides the medium to use. For example, if GetDataHere is called, and the desired medium is global memory, then the caller is responsible for allocating the memory and providing a handle to the memory for IDataObject. If GetData is called, and the desired medium is global memory, the IDataObject is responsible for allocating memory, placing the data into memory, and then returning the handle to the allocated data to the caller.

QueryGetData

Using QueryGetData, the caller can determine whether IDataObject supports a particular FORMATETC. QueryGetData differs from EnumFormatEtc in two ways. First, QueryGetData is called with FORMATETC and will return whether or not the GetData method supports the particular format, whereas EnumFormatEtc will return an IEnumFORMATETC interface pointer of all the formats supported. Second, QueryGetData only tells the caller whether the particular format is supported by the GetData method, whereas EnumFormatEtc can be used to obtain the formats supported by GetData or SetData.

SetData

SetData is called to provide data to IDataObject. Any data IDataObject previously has is discarded, and only the new data is retained.

DAdvise

DAdvise is used to tell the server that a consumer wishes to receive notification. The consumer calls DAdvise to inform the server of the FORMATETC structure to use to send notification, the type of notification to send, and the IAdviseSink interface to use to send the information. The consumer needs to implement an IAdviseSink interface in order to receive the data.

Because the consumer specifies the FORMATETC structure, the server might not be able to comply with the request. If the server does not support the requested format, it will return DATA_E_FORMATETC; otherwise, it will establish a connection and return a connection number. The consumer uses this connection number to terminate the request.

The consumer is also responsible for stating the type of notification it wishes to receive. If it passes ADVF_NODATA, the consumer is requesting a warm link—the server will notify the consumer that the data has changed but will not actually pass the data. The consumer is then responsible for requesting the data when the data is needed. Unfortunately, the consumer cannot just use GetData to receive the data. OLE does not support making synchronous calls within asynchronous methods; in other words, under certain conditions, the consumer cannot call GetData while processing the notification. If the server is implemented as a local server (an EXE), the consumer cannot make a request to the server for the data because of the way LRPC is implemented. If the server is a DLL, this restriction does not apply. DLL servers do not use LRPC to talk with their consumers.

Although a consumer might have requested ADVF_NODATA, the server may actually ignore this flag and still return data with the notification. It is the responsibility of the consumer to make sure that the tymed field returned upon notification is equal to TYMED_NULL. This indicates that the server is just sending a notification. If the tymed field is not TYMED_NULL, then the server returned the data, and the consumer can use the data. However, the data must be copied by the consumer, because the data is only valid during the call.

If the consumer sends ADVF_PRIMEFIRST, the server will send data and notification immediately instead of waiting for the data to change.

ADVF_ONLYONCE requests that the server breaks the connection after sending one notification. If this flag is combined with ADVF_PRIMEFIRST, the connection is broken as soon as the data has been sent to the consumer, not waiting for the data to change.

ADVF_DATAONSTOP requests that the server sends the actual data when the connection is about to shut down. This flag only makes sense with ADVF_NODATA because the other flags actually send the data; therefore, the consumer already has the data. Because ADVF_NODATA implies that the consumer does not have the data (just notification), ADVF_DATAONSTOP forces the server connection to remain intact until the consumer has the data (except when a GPF error or any other program error occurs).

If multiple consumers attach to a single server, the server is responsible for managing the connections. Fortunately, OLE provides a method so that you don't have to manage the connections yourself (that is, unless you want to). OLE provides an interface called IDataAdviseHolder whose responsibility is to manage connections. To create an IDataAdviseHolder interface, you simply call the OLE API CreateDataAdviseHolder, which will return to you an IDataAdviseHolder interface. This interface can then be used by your implementation of DAdvise. Once you have an interface to IDataAdvise, you simply call its Advise whenever you receive a DAdvise on your IDataObject. The implementation of DAdvise can be as little as three lines of code.

DUnadvise

DUnadvise informs IDataObject that the caller no longer wants the previous notification.

EnumDAdvise

EnumDAdvise returns an IEnumSTATDATA interface pointer, which allows the caller to obtain an enumerator of all the notification requests on IDataObject. An enumerator supports the Next, Skip, Reset, and Clone methods.

When to Implement DDE Versus OLE

In general, when writing a new application, you should implement OLE. In fact, if you want the Microsoft Windows logo, you must implement OLE. DDE should only be implemented if your application needs to communicate with an application that supports DDE and does not yet support OLE. When upgrading an existing application, you should add support for OLE. If your application already supports DDE, you can keep the DDE support, however, you might want to wean your existing users off your DDE interface and prepare them for OLE support.

Installation programs have typically used DDE to communicate with the Program Manager when adding a new application to the Program Manager. Although you can continue to install your applications this way, Microsoft recommends that you don't. Instead, Microsoft recommends you use the IShellLink interface, which is demonstrated in Chapter 24, "Component Object Model (COM)."

IDataAdviseHolder

OLE has an interface called IDataAdviseHolder that is used to make the implementation of notification in IDataObject very easy. The IDataAdviseHolder is responsible for keeping track of all notification connections for IDataObject. IDataAdviseHolder implements all the notification methods (Advise, Unadvise, and EnumAdvise) so that IDataObject can just pass requests directly to IDataAdviseHolder. In addition, IDataAdviseHolder implements an additional method: SendOnDataChange.

SendOnDataChange

When data has changed in an object, IDataObject sends notification to any objects that have previously registered using DAdvise. IDataObject then sends the notification and data to the object's IAdviseSink::OnDataChange method (this is part of the consumer). Because the IDataObject is not managing the connections, IDataObject doesn't know to which objects to send the notification and data, or even what to send, because responsibility for notification is given to IDataAdviseHolder. To solve this problem, IDataAdviseHolder has a method called SendOnDataChange that is responsible for sending the notification and data to all the appropriate consumers.

IAdviseSink

IAdviseSink is used by the consumer of a notification. The consumer first obtains the IDataObject interface of the server and then makes a request to the DAdvise method. When the data is available from the server, the server returns the information to the consumer's IAdviseSink (specifically to the OnDataChange method). IAdviseSink also has four other methods—OnViewChange, OnRename, OnSave, and OnClose)—which can all be null routines. These methods are typically used when implementing an application that supports compound documents.

OnDataChange

The OnDataChange method receives the notification or data (or both) when a server object's data changes, and the consumer has a notification on the object. When performing DAdvise with notification, the consumer passes to the server the IAdviseSink interface. When the server can honor the consumer's request (when data changes or prime first), the server returns the requested data or notification to the OnDataChange method in IAdviseSink. The consumer then can check the FORMATETC and STGMEDIUM structures to ensure that the medium and format are as requested. Specifically, if the consumer requests only notification (ADVF_NODATA), the server may honor the request and just pass notification. The consumer should check the STGMEDIUM structure's tymed field to see if the field is TYMED_NULL. If the field is TYMED_NULL, then there is a notification; otherwise, the actual data is passed and the tymed field indicates the type of medium on which the data is passed.

As you can see, because of OLE's uniform data transfer model, implementing notification can be fairly easy. When IDataObject is implemented to support functionality, such as a Clipboard transfer or general data transfer, notification support is virtually free. OLE's notification offers much of the functionality provided by DDE with much less code.

Summary

As you can see, OLE is not a direct replacement of DDE. Although OLE and DDE have similar functionality, an OLE application cannot exchange data with a DDE application and vice versa. In order for two applications to exchange data, both applications need to support DDE or both applications need to support OLE. As previously mentioned, if you have an existing application that supports DDE, you should consider adding OLE support. When writing new applications, consider adding only OLE support.

OLE Control
Development Kit

30

*by Lawrence
Harris*

IN THIS CHAPTER

Before you can learn about OLE controls, you first need to read a brief description of Visual Basic controls.

Visual Basic Controls

When Visual Basic first came out, it supported Visual Basic Custom Controls. A Visual Basic Custom Control (or VBX) is the equivalent of a Windows custom control, except VBXs were designed specifically to work in the Visual Basic environment.

A Visual Basic Custom Control has routines for altering the behavior or visual aspects of the control by using properties. For example, you can change the font that a control uses by changing the `FontName` and `FontSize` properties. You can change the size of a control by changing the `Height` and `Width` properties. Visual Basic Custom Controls also support notification through events. For example, a button has a `Click` event, which tells your application that the button has been clicked, enabling the application to perform whatever action is appropriate.

OLE Controls

The key statement about VBXs is that they were designed to work in Visual Basic. Although Microsoft supports Visual Basic Custom Controls in Visual C++, Visual C++ needs to emulate some of the functionality of Visual Basic in order to get VBXs to work. (Borland C++ 4.X also supports Visual Basic Custom Controls.) In addition, VBXs are written for a 16-bit environment. If you have ever delved into the internals of VBXs, you might have noticed that many of the pointers are near pointers, which makes VBXs nonportable to 32-bit environments such as NT (Borland C++ supports 16-bit VBXs in 32-bit applications). In order to port VBXs to 32-bit environments, Microsoft would need to re-architect VBXs (because NT has no concept of near or far pointers).

Instead of re-architecting VBXs, Microsoft created OLE controls. OLE controls were written to give controls portability between 16- and 32-bit environments. OLE controls do not depend on the Visual Basic architecture, and because OLE is being ported to various non-Intel machines, OLE controls could also inherit this portability. (OLE is currently available for Intel, MIPS, DEC Alpha, and Apple Macintosh environments, and will be available shortly for the PowerPC.)

OLE controls support three different types of properties: ambient, control, and extended control. An *ambient* property is a property that concerns the environment of the container and is given by the container to the custom control. A container gives a control information such as the default font, background and foreground color, and whether the control is being used in design mode rather than runtime mode. Controls typically need this information before they are initially displayed so that they do the right thing when they first appear.

A *control* property is specific information that a control needs, such as background and foreground color and the font. This information might be different from the ambient property information that is provided by the container. For example, if a container states that the ambient property of the container is cyan background with a black foreground, the custom control might elect to display itself on a white background with a red foreground. The control's property would contain this information. An *extended control* property is information that a container provides to each control. An example of an extended control property is Cancel or Default, which inform the control of whether it is the container's cancel button or default button. In addition, the container informs the control of whether the control is visible (by setting the control's Visible property), the control's name (by setting the control's Name property), or the window handle of the document that the control is on (by setting the control's Parent property).

OLE Control Interfaces

At first glance, an OLE control might appear to be an OLE in-process server (with in-place activation). However, an OLE control is more than an in-process server. An in-process server with in-place activation contains the interfaces as indicated in Table 30.1.

Table 30.1. OLE interfaces for in-place activated servers.

Interface	*Meaning*
IDataObject	An interface for data transfer.
IOleCache	An interface to cache various presentations.
IOleInPlaceActiveObject	An interface for an in-place active object to communicate with frames and document windows.
IOleInPlaceObject	An interface for activating and deactivating in-place objects.
IOleObject	An interface for compound document management.
IPersist	Root interface for IPersistStorage (as well as for IPersistStream and IPersistFile). This interface is always implemented for IPersistStorage but not always exposed.
IPersistStorage	An interface for compound document storage.
IUnknown	Required interface for all OLE COM objects.
IViewObject	An interface for drawing an object.
IViewObject2	An alternate interface for drawing an object.

An OLE control supports all the interfaces in Table 30.1, plus a few additional interfaces. An OLE control is conceptually an in-process server that supports in-place activation and OLE automation. If you understand how to create an in-process server that supports in-place activation and OLE automation, you have the foundation for OLE controls. So what makes OLE controls special or different? The difference between an OLE control and an in-process server is in the OLE automation methods that are defined for an OLE control, and support for the `IOleControl`, `IConnectionPoint`, and the `IConnectionPointContainer` interface. The `IOleControl` interface is used to translate keyboard mnemonics. The problem with using `IOleInPlaceActiveObject` is that `IOleInPlaceActiveObject` works for the object that currently has focus, which is not necessarily the OLE control. `IOleControl` was added to handle the keyboard mnemonics translation issues.

`IConnectionPoint` and `IConnectionPointContainer` are used by an OLE control to communicate event information between the container and the control. Note that `IConnectionPoint` is not available through the control's `QueryInterface`. Your application first needs to obtain the `IConnectionPointContainer` interface and then call `FindConnectionPoint`, which returns the `IConnectionPoint` interface pointer. When a container has the `IConnectionPoint` interface, the container calls the `IConnectionPoint` advise method and gives the advise method the container's `IDispatch` interface, on which the container wishes to receive event notification from the OLE control.

Why Should You Create OLE Controls?

When I first learned about OLE controls, I wondered why I would want to implement an OLE control when I could achieve the same functionality using OLE automation. In addition, Visual Basic and Visual Basic for Applications support OLE automation, but currently the only application that supports OLE controls is Microsoft Access 2.0. So why implement an OLE control? First, look at what OLE automation provides. OLE automation enables another application to control your automation server, but your server cannot be embedded into your container application. If you want the server to draw directly into your container, you need to support in-place activation. When you have supported in-place activation, what's the difference between your application and an OLE control?

A major advantage that an OLE control has is licensing support. For example, when you sell your OLE control, you don't need to make separate versions for developers and end users. Using methods provided in the OLE control architecture, an OLE control can determine whether it is running in a development environment or in an end user environment (a similar concept is supported by VBXs). This means that a developer can purchase your OLE control, incorporate the OLE control into his or her application, and then distribute the application. The end user of the application that includes the OLE control will not be able to use your OLE control for development without obtaining a development license. If you don't allow your OLE control to be freely distributed (a runtime license is required), your

OLE control is also able to tell whether a valid license is on the end user's machine, and it will refuse to run if no license is found. If you create an application that supports automation instead of an OLE control, you need to figure out how to implement the licensing yourself.

OLE controls are also more standardized in their programming interface than is your automation application. An OLE control has a set of standard methods and properties that enable developers using your OLE control to quickly understand how to use your OLE control. For example, OLE controls have a standard font property so that the OLE control's font can easily be changed. OLE controls also have property sheets so that an OLE control can be customized without programming (similar to VBXs).

If OLE controls are so great, why would you ever implement an in-process server that supports automation? I always implement an in-process server that supports automation if the functionality of the server is complex. An OLE control is usually a very simple server that performs a very specific specialized task. For example, I would not implement a word processor such as Microsoft Word as an OLE control. Microsoft Word is a complex application that can perform a number of different tasks. I also would not implement an OLE control if the server can be a container and the application can be run as a stand-alone program. For example, Visio is not normally used as a server; it is normally used as a stand-alone application.

Using the CDK

The OLE Control Development Kit is currently distributed with Microsoft Visual C++. The OLE Control Development Kit installs the necessary files to write Microsoft Foundation Class applications using a ControlWizard. The ControlWizard is an application that asks a series of questions and then generates the appropriate skeleton OLE control source. It is possible to develop OLE controls without the CDK by obtaining the OLE control header files and libraries from either the Microsoft Windows Objects Forum on CompuServe (Go WinObjects) or on the Internet from ftp.microsoft.com.

1. Start the ControlWizard, which is located on the Tools Menu within Visual C++. If it isn't on your menu, the Control Development Kit has not yet been successfully installed on your machine.
2. Enter the name and location of the OLE control to be created.
3. Select Project Options.
4. Decide whether you want Context Sensitive Help, External Makefile, Source Comments, and/or License Validation.
5. Select OK.
6. Select Control Options.

7. The dialog box will contain the following choices that can be selected (in combination, if desired): Activate when visible, Show in Insert Object dialog box, Invisible at runtime, Simple Frame, About box, Subclass Windows control, Use VBX control as template.

8. After you have selected the control option or options you require, select OK.

9. Select Controls if multiple OLE controls will be supported.

10. Select OK from the ControlWizard, and then select Create. The source for a skeleton OLE control will be generated. You can then customize the generated source to perform the desired functionality.

11. When you have made the customization necessary for your control and you have successfully compiled the control, you need to register the control. From Visual C++, select Tools and then Register Control. Your control is now available for use.

12. To test your control, select Tools and Test Container from Visual C++. When the Test Container has been launched, you can select Edit and then Insert OLE Control from the Test Container's menu (if you selected Show in Insert Dialog Box when creating your control). The control can now be inserted and tested.

Using the steps just mentioned, you can create a rudimentary OLE control that will display a bitmap. The following steps indicate what needs to be entered:

1. Start the Control Wizard.

2. Enter the name as CTLBMP, and enter the location for the OLE control.

3. Select Project Options.

4. Select License Validation.

5. Select OK.

6. Select Control Options.

7. Select Activate when visible, Show in Insert Object dialog box, Simple Frame, and About box.

8. Select OK.

9. Select OK from the ControlWizard, and then select Create. The source for a skeleton OLE control will be generated.

10. Compile the application. The compilation should be successful. When the compilation is successful, select Tools from the Visual C++ menu and then select Register Control.

11. After the control is registered, select Tools from the Visual C++ menu and then select Test Container. From the test container, you should now be able to insert the newly created control, which simply draws a circle.

NOTE

If you selected support for license validation, you must copy the same directory (which will be "*controlname*.lic," where *controlname* is the name of the ocx) as the ocx file. If you do not copy the license validation file, you will not be able to insert the control.

12. Exit the test container application and return to Visual C++. Using the ClassWizard, you can now add some properties to the control.

13. From ClassWizard, select the OLE Automation tab (at the top of the dialog box). If `CCtlBmpCrl` is not displayed as the class name, select `CCtlBmpCrl` from the Class Name drop-down list box.

14. Press the Add Property button, which will bring up the Add Property dialog box. In the External Name drop-down control, select `BackColor`. This property allows your control to obtain the container's ambient background color, and also allows the user of the control to change the background color for the control. Select OK to return to the OLE Automation dialog box.

15. Once again, press the Add Property button to bring up the Add Property dialog box. This time, press Get/Set Methods in the Implementation group box. In the External Name edit control, type `FileName`, select `BSTR` in the Type drop-down control, and then select OK. ClassWizard now creates the `GetFileName` and `SetFileName` methods.

16. Press the Add Property button again. From the Add Property dialog box, press Get/Set Method. In the External Name edit control, type `GraphicsMode`. In the Type drop-down control, select Short. Erase the entry that the ClassWizard shows in the Set Function edit control, and then select OK. ClassWizard now creates a read-only property, which you will use to return the current graphics image type.

17. Select OK in ClassWizard to be returned to the Visual C++ edit mode.

18. In ctlbmctl.cpp, add the following line:

```
#include "cgraphic.h"
```

In ctlbmctl.cpp, change the Draw method to the following:

```
void CCtlbmpCtrl::OnDraw(
        CDC* pdc, const CRect& rcBounds, const CRect& rcInvalid)
{
    if (m_GraphicsFile.GraphicsType() != eUnknown)
        m_GraphicsFile.DrawGraphics(pdc, rcBounds);
    else {
        CBrush   bkBrush(TranslateColor(GetBackColor()));
        pdc->FillRect(rcBounds, &bkBrush);
    }
}
```

19. Change the generated `GetFileName`, `SetFileName`, and `GetGraphicsMode` properties to appear as follows:

```
BSTR CCtlbmpCtrl::GetFileName()
{
    CString s = m_GraphicsFile.GetFileName();
    return s.AllocSysString();
}

void CCtlbmpCtrl::SetFileName(LPCTSTR lpszNewValue)
{
    m_GraphicsFile.SetFileName(lpszNewValue);
    SetModifiedFlag();
    InvalidateControl();
}

short CCtlbmpCtrl::GetGraphicsMode()
{
    return m_GraphicsFile.GraphicsType();
}
```

20. At the beginning of the ctlbmctl.h header file, add the following:

```
#ifndef    cgraphic_h__
#include "cgraphic.h"
#endif
```

21. In the public section of the `CCtlbmpCtrl` class (in ctlbmctl.h), add the following line:

```
CGraphicsFile    m_GraphicsFile;
```

22. Create the text/code file, which contains the following lines:

```
#ifndef __cgraphic_h__
#define __cgraphic_h__

enum  eGraphicsType { eUnknown=0,eBmp=1, eGif=2, eJpg=3};

class CGraphicsFile
{
public:
    CGraphicsFile(void);
    ~CGraphicsFile(void);
    eGraphicsType    GraphicsType(void);
    CString    GetFileName(void);
    BOOL    SetFileName(LPCSTR strFileName);
    void    DrawGraphics(CDC FAR *pdc, const CRect& rcBounds);
protected:
    void    SetGraphicsType(eGraphicsType GraphicsTyp);
    void    DrawBmp(CDC FAR *pdc, const CRect& rcBounds);
    void    DrawJpg(CDC FAR *pdc, const CRect& rcBounds);
    void    DrawGif(CDC FAR *pdc, const CRect& rcBounds);
    BOOL    IsBmp(void);
    BOOL    IsJpg(void);
    BOOL    IsGif(void);
    BOOL    ReadBmp(CString strFileName);
    BOOL    ReadJpg(CString strFileName);
    BOOL    ReadGif(CString strFileName);
private:
    eGraphicsType    m_eGraphicsType;
    CString          m_strFileName;
```

```
        CBitmap     FAR         *m_pBitmap;
        char FAR        *m_pBitmapArray;
        PBITMAPINFO        m_pBitmapInfo;
        HFILE            m_hFile;
};

    #endif
```

23. Save the file as cgraphic.h.

24. Create a text/code file that has the following lines:

```
#include    "stdafx.h"
#include    "cgraphic.h"

CGraphicsFile::CGraphicsFile(void)
{
    m_strFileName.Empty();
    m_pBitmap = NULL;
    m_pBitmapArray = NULL;
    m_pBitmapInfo = NULL;
    SetGraphicsType(eUnknown);
}

CGraphicsFile::~CGraphicsFile(void)
{
    if (GraphicsType() != eUnknown){
        SetGraphicsType(eUnknown);
    }

    if (m_pBitmapArray != NULL)
        delete m_pBitmapArray;
    if (m_pBitmapInfo != NULL)
        delete m_pBitmapInfo;
    if (m_pBitmap != NULL)
        delete m_pBitmap;
}

eGraphicsType    CGraphicsFile::GraphicsType(void)
{
    return    m_eGraphicsType;
}

void    CGraphicsFile::SetGraphicsType(eGraphicsType GraphicsTyp)
{
    m_eGraphicsType = GraphicsTyp;
}

CString    CGraphicsFile::GetFileName(void)
{
    return    m_strFileName;
}

BOOL    CGraphicsFile::SetFileName(LPCSTR strFileName)
{
    BOOL    bRet = FALSE;

    m_strFileName.Empty();
```

```
        if (GraphicsType() != eUnknown){
            SetGraphicsType(eUnknown);
        }

        m_hFile = _lopen(strFileName,OF_READ);
        if (m_hFile == HFILE_ERROR){
            return bRet;
        }
        if (IsBmp()){
            SetGraphicsType(eBmp);
        } else if (IsJpg()){
            SetGraphicsType(eJpg);
        } else if (IsGif()){
            SetGraphicsType(eGif);
        }

        if (GraphicsType() != eUnknown){
            _llseek(m_hFile,0,0);
            BOOL    bNoError = FALSE;

            switch (GraphicsType()){
            case eBmp:
                bNoError = ReadBmp(strFileName);
                break;
            case eJpg:
                bNoError = ReadJpg(strFileName);
                break;
            case eGif:
                bNoError = ReadGif(strFileName);
                break;
            default:
                break;
            }
            if (bNoError == TRUE){
                m_strFileName = strFileName;
                bRet = TRUE;
            } else {
                SetGraphicsType(eUnknown);
            }

        }
        _lclose(m_hFile);
        return bRet;
}

void    CGraphicsFile::DrawGraphics(CDC FAR *pdc, const CRect& rcBounds)
{
    switch (GraphicsType()){
    case eBmp:
        DrawBmp(pdc, rcBounds);
        break;
    case eJpg:
        DrawJpg(pdc, rcBounds);
        break;
    case eGif:
        DrawGif(pdc, rcBounds);
        break;
    default:
        break;
```

```
        }
}

void    CGraphicsFile::DrawBmp(CDC FAR *pdc, const CRect& rcBounds)
{

    StretchDIBits(pdc->m_hDC,
            rcBounds.left,rcBounds.top,rcBounds.Width(),rcBounds.Height(),
                0,0,(int)m_pBitmapInfo->bmiHeader.biWidth,
                            (int)m_pBitmapInfo->bmiHeader.biHeight,
                            m_pBitmapArray,m_pBitmapInfo,DIB_RGB_COLORS,
                            SRCCOPY);

}

void    CGraphicsFile::DrawJpg(CDC FAR *pdc, const CRect& rcBounds)
{
}

void    CGraphicsFile::DrawGif(CDC FAR *pdc, const CRect& rcBounds)
{
}

BOOL    CGraphicsFile::IsBmp(void)
{
    char    Buf[2];
    _lread(m_hFile,Buf,2);
    if ((Buf[0] == 'B') && (Buf[1] == 'M'))
        return TRUE;
    else
        return FALSE;
}

BOOL    CGraphicsFile::IsJpg(void)
{
    return FALSE;
}
BOOL    CGraphicsFile::IsGif(void)
{
    return FALSE;
}

BOOL    CGraphicsFile::ReadBmp(CString strFileName)
{
    BOOL    bRet = FALSE;
    union BitmapFileHeader{
            BITMAPFILEHEADER    fileHeader;
            char    buffer[sizeof(BITMAPFILEHEADER)];
    } BitmapFileHeader;

    union BitmapInfoHeader {
            BITMAPINFOHEADER    infoHeader;
            char    buffer[sizeof(BITMAPINFOHEADER)];
    } BitmapInfoHeader;

    //Read the file header
    if (_lread(m_hFile,BitmapFileHeader.buffer,sizeof(BITMAPFILEHEADER)) !=
        sizeof(BITMAPFILEHEADER))
        return bRet;
```

```
            //Next comes the info header
            if (_lread(m_hFile,BitmapInfoHeader.buffer,sizeof(BITMAPINFOHEADER)) !=
                sizeof(BITMAPINFOHEADER))
                return bRet;

        UINT    uiColorArraySize = 1;

            if (BitmapInfoHeader.infoHeader.biClrUsed != 0)
                uiColorArraySize = (UINT)BitmapInfoHeader.infoHeader.biClrUsed;
            else
                uiColorArraySize << BitmapInfoHeader.infoHeader.biBitCount;

            uiColorArraySize *= sizeof(RGBQUAD);

            if (m_pBitmapInfo != NULL)
                delete m_pBitmapInfo;

            m_pBitmapInfo = (PBITMAPINFO)new char[sizeof(BITMAPINFOHEADER) +
            ➥uiColorArraySize];

            //Assign BitmapHeaderInfo information

#define     InfoFieldCopy(x)    m_pBitmapInfo->bmiHeader.x =
        ➥BitmapInfoHeader.infoHeader.x;

            m_pBitmapInfo->bmiHeader.biSize            = sizeof(BITMAPINFOHEADER);

        InfoFieldCopy(biWidth);
        InfoFieldCopy(biHeight);
        InfoFieldCopy(biPlanes);
        InfoFieldCopy(biBitCount);
        InfoFieldCopy(biCompression);
        InfoFieldCopy(biSizeImage);
        InfoFieldCopy(biXPelsPerMeter);
        InfoFieldCopy(biYPelsPerMeter);
        InfoFieldCopy(biClrUsed);
        InfoFieldCopy(biClrImportant);
#undef InfoFieldCopy

        _lread(m_hFile,m_pBitmapInfo->bmiColors,uiColorArraySize);
        if (m_pBitmapArray != NULL)
            delete m_pBitmapArray;

        m_pBitmapArray = new char[BitmapFileHeader.fileHeader.bfSize -
    BitmapFileHeader.fileHeader.bfOffBits + 5];

        _llseek(m_hFile,BitmapFileHeader.fileHeader.bfOffBits,0);
        _lread(m_hFile,m_pBitmapArray,(UINT)(BitmapFileHeader.fileHeader.bfSize
        ➥  - BitmapFileHeader.fileHeader.bfOffBits + 1));

    return TRUE;
    }

    BOOL CGraphicsFile::ReadJpg(CString strFileName)
    {
        BOOL bRet = FALSE;
        return bRet;
```

```
}
BOOL CGraphicsFile::ReadGif(CString strFileName)
{
    BOOL bRet = FALSE;
    return bRet;
}
```

25. Save the file as cgraphic.cpp and add the file to the project. Recompile the application.

26. Copy ctlbmp.lic to the objd32 directory (or whatever directory you compiled your OLE control to). You can now use the OLE test container to test your bitmap control.

The control currently only works with bitmaps (with GIF and JPEG support stubbed out). Support for GIFs and JPEGs is left as an exercise for the reader.

Creating an OLE control does not necessarily add complexity to your application, especially when using the ControlWizard. As more products support OLE controls, you might see the same explosive growth in the OLE control industry as occurred in the VBX industry or the Windows custom control industry.

Introduction to Converting a VBX to an OLE Control

So far in this chapter, I've discussed what an OLE control is and how an OLE control can be created. But what do you do if you have an existing VBX and want to convert it to an OLE control? In this section, I'll discuss how to convert a VBX into an OLE control, as well as some of the issues that might occur during your conversion process. Before looking at how to convert a VBX, let's discuss some of the pros and cons of a VBX versus an OLE control.

VBX and OLE Control Comparison

You might have read in the press that OLE controls are the future and you should start creating OLE controls. Although OLE controls are the migration path that Microsoft is recommending, are OLE controls always the right way to go? The answer is *maybe*. Unfortunately, there are no hard and fast rules on when to implement an OLE control or keep your existing VBX, but there are some issues that need to be considered. The most important consideration is who will use your OLE control. VBXs can currently be used by a number of applications and development environments such as Watcom's PowerBuilder, BlueSky's WindowsMaker Professional, and Borland's Delphi. C++ compiler vendors, including Microsoft and Borland, also support VBXs, and of course Microsoft's Visual Basic supports VBXs. But who supports OLE controls? Currently, Microsoft Access supports OLE controls, and the next generation of Microsoft Visual Basic is expected to support OLE controls. So if you want your control to work with Microsoft Access (which does not support VBXs) or with a future version of Visual Basic, you can consider converting to an OLE control. If your target audience is using another package, you might need to postpone the conversion until the package supports OLE controls. In addition, if you are using VBXs in a custom application, converting the VBX to an OLE control will also require you to convert your custom application to support OLE controls. Unless you are willing to convert your custom application to become an OLE container, you might not want to convert your VBX to an OLE control.

One reason you might want to convert your VBX to an OLE control is that VBXs are strictly 16 bits and OLE controls are either 16 bits or 32 bits. There are ways of using a 16-bit VBX in a 32-bit application, but unless you are using a development environment such as Borland C++ 4.5x, using a VBX in a 32-bit application can be difficult. OLE controls can be written as 16-bit controls or 32-bit controls, and it is expected that OLE controls will also be able to be used in non-Intel environments that support OLE, thus increasing the portability of your control. At the current time, however, you need to create a separate control for every environment you want to support. But if you write your control with portability in mind, you should be able to easily compile your control for the desired environment.

Converting a VBX to an OLE Control

After you have made the decision to convert a VBX to an OLE control, you need to decide how this conversion should be done. At the present time, there are three options for creating your OLE control: without using Microsoft's ControlWizard or Symantec's AppExpress, using the ControlWizard or AppExpress, or using the ControlWizard's VBX conversion facility. You might think that you should always use the ControlWizard's VBX conversion facility, but the VBX conversion facility cannot be used under certain circumstances, and in other circumstances the conversion facility is more trouble than it is worth. Let's take a look at the ControlWizard and how it can create an OLE control.

Examine the VBX to Be Converted

Before you can convert a VBX, you need to examine the VBX to determine whether the ControlWizard can use the VBX. The ControlWizard requires that the VBX supports the `VBGetModelInfo` function; otherwise, the ControlWizard will crash when it tries to create your OLE control. If your VBX does not support `VBGetModelInfo`, add the code in Listing 30.1 to support `VBGetModelInfo`.

Listing 30.1. `VBGetModelInfo`.

```
MODEL modelApp_Vbx =
    {
    VB_VERSION,            // Use VB100_VERSION for VC compatible VBXs
```

```
    0,                          // MODEL flags
    (PCTLPROC)AppCtlProc,       // Control procedure
    CS_VREDRAW | CS_HREDRAW,    // Class style
    0L,                         // Default Windows style
    sizeof(AppStruct),          // Size of AppStruct structure
    IDBMP_APPBMP,               // Palette bitmap ID
    "APPCTLCLASS",              // Default control name
    "APPCLASS",                 // Visual Basic class name
    NULL,                       // Parent class name
    App_Properties_Vb1,         // Property information table
    App_Events_Vb1,             // Event information table
    IPROP_APP_DEF_PROP,         // Default property
    IEVENT_APP_DEF_EVENT        // Default event
    };

LPMODEL modelListAppName[] = {
&modelAppName,NULL
};

MODELINFO modelInfoAppName = {
VB_VERSION, modelListAppName
};

LPMODELINFO FAR PASCAL _export VBGetModelInfo(USHORT usVersionNo)
{
    return &modelInfoAppName;
}
```

When you have added support for VBGetModelInfo into your VBX, you can use
ControlWizard to generate an OLE control template based on the VBX.

ControlWizard and ClassWizard

In the section "OLE Controls," earlier in this chapter, I showed how the ControlWizard
can be used to generate an OLE control from scratch. When you want to generate an OLE
control based on an existing VBX, all the procedures previously discussed are still performed, with one addition: in Control Options, you select Use VBX Control as Template,
and then select the VBX to use. When the ControlWizard generates your OLE control
source code, the source code includes some of the properties and events that the VBX
supported. The ControlWizard doesn't generate template code for the DragDrop event or
DragOver event. In addition, the ControlWizard doesn't generate template code for the
DragIcon, DragMode, Height, Index, Left, Name, Tag, Top, Visible, or Width properties. The
ControlWizard generates code for functionality that does not exist in your VBX as well. For
example, if your VBX has read-only or write-only properties, the ControlWizard generates
Get and Set functions; you need to delete the property using the ClassWizard and add the
property with support for only the Get or Set function manually. The ControlWizard is
used to generate a template OLE control, whereas the ClassWizard is used to change the
generated code.

Depending on the VBX being converted, the ControlWizard might generate code to handle fonts and pictures. For example, if your VBX displays bitmaps, icons, or metafiles, the ControlWizard generates code to use `CPictureHolder`, which is an OLE control MFC class that helps an OLE control display a picture. If your VBX supports the `font` property, the ControlWizard generates support for the `font` property within the OLE control.

If you don't use the ControlWizard to convert the VBX, the required work is slightly more complex. Assuming that you still use the ControlWizard to generate a skeleton OLE control, you would use the ClassWizard to add methods and properties to your control. You can use stock properties or custom properties, and you can create `Get` and `Set` functions. (However, if you use a VBX as a template, you need to delete any function that only has a `Get` or `Set` function, because the ControlWizard generates both functions automatically.) If you don't use the ControlWizard, you can also change the data types that are being passed to or returned from the OLE control. VBXs support only a handful of data types, whereas OLE and OLE controls support many more data types. When the ControlWizard converts a VBX, the ControlWizard selects the data type that closely matches the data type used by the VBX. You might determine that one of the OLE data types better fits the function or method and want to change the data type. To change the data type, you need to delete the function or method using the ClassWizard, and then add the desired function or method back with the new data type using the ClassWizard.

Converting the VBX Source Code

After you have created a skeleton OLE control, you will want to port the source code from your VBX to the OLE control. Unfortunately, the source code port is not straightforward. If your original VBX is written using Microsoft Foundation Class (MFC), you will probably have little difficulty porting the source. However, if you have written your VBX using any other method, you will have a great deal of work ahead. For example, if you wrote your VBX in Pascal, you need to convert the source to C++ using MFC. If you used Borland C++ and OWL, you also need to port the source to use native Windows APIs and C++ or fully convert the source to MFC. If you have written your VBX using C, you can probably use most of the source as it is, although you might want to consider switching to MFC. The bottom line is that no matter how your original VBX was written, when you use the ControlWizard your OLE control is an MFC application.

Summary

The introduction of OLE controls gives developers the ability to develop Visual Basic–like controls for either 16-bit or 32-bit Windows environments. In addition, because OLE is portable to non–Intel-based machines, OLE controls can be recompiled and used on a Macintosh, DEC Alpha, MIPS, and the PowerPC.

Providing File Viewers for the Windows 95 Explorer

31

by Lawrence Harris

In Windows 95, OLE plays an important role in the shell. In previous versions of Windows, the shell was accessed via a few APIs or DDE. Previously, the shell was usually the Program Manager, although you could substitute other applications to be the primary user interface. Windows 95 includes a shell that is significantly different from the Program Manager's user interface. In Windows 95, the shell has a Macintosh or OS/2 look and feel. The primary access method for the shell has also changed from DDE and APIs to OLE interfaces. In this chapter, we'll take a look at some of the features of the shell and how the shell can be extended to support additional functionality using OLE.

The Shell and OLE

Pre-Windows 95 users are probably most familiar with the Program Manager, which the users typically used as their initial interaction with Windows. Users also typically used File Manager to copy and delete files within Windows. Although Program Manager and File Manager are available in Windows 95, Windows 95 also has a new environment that is called the Shell. The Windows 95 Shell incorporates the functionality of Program Manager and File Manager and adds some functionality of its own.

Pre-Windows 95, the typical interaction with Program Manager was performed by setup programs to install program icons within Program Manager by using DDE. The functionality of Program Manager could not be extended. File Manager, on the other hand, could be extended to a limited degree, by adding tools in the form of a DLL. Windows 95 changes the rules by allowing applications to extend the functionality of the Shell by using OLE interfaces. In Windows 95, when an object is selected (the object can be a file, directory, disk, or computer) and the right mouse button is clicked, a context-sensitive menu appears that has the functionality that can be performed on this object. Operations such as Open, Copy, Delete, Print, Send, and Properties are typical operations that can be performed. Using OLE, you have the ability to add additional functionality that can be performed. Some files also have a Quick View option on the context menu, which enables you to look at the contents of a file without using the application that created the file. For example, if you select Quick View on a BMP (bitmap) file, you see the bitmap on the screen. If you want to manipulate the bitmap, you need to run Paintbrush (or some other application that can edit a bitmap).

OLE *InProc* Server

In Windows 95 (and a future release of Windows NT), Shell Extensions and File Viewers are written as OLE in-process servers. An in-process server in OLE is essentially an OLE object that is implemented completely in a DLL. An in-process server differs from an in-process handler (which is also implemented as a DLL) in that an in-process server can completely handle the implementation of an OLE object; whereas an in-process handler can only handle some of the implementation of an OLE object and defers requests that it cannot handle to a local server (which is an executable or EXE implementation). Because the implementation of the Shell Extensions and File Viewers are in an in-process server, let's take a look at how an in-process server is implemented.

In the 16-bit implementation of Windows, when you create an application that is a DLL, the DLL always had a LibMain to initialize the DLL, and a WEP that handled the termination of the DLL (if you used a class library, the implementation of LibMain and WEP may have been part of the class library). In the 32-bit implementation of Windows, DLLs have a single entry and exit routine called DllMain. It is important to realize that DllMain is called whenever an application loads or unloads your DLL and is also called whenever a thread loads or unloads your DLL. DllMain requires three parameters: an HINSTANCE, which is the instance that is calling your DLL; a DWORD, which is a flag we will explain shortly; and an LPVOID, which is always NULL. The flag that is passed to DllMain is the key in determining how DllMain is being called. The flag can be DLL_PROCESS_ATTACH, DLL_PROCESS_DETACH, DLL_THREAD_ATTACH, or DLL_THREAD_DETACH. If a process or a thread loads a DLL, then either DLL_PROCESS_ATTACH or DLL_THREAD_ATTACH would be passed to your DLL; and if a process or thread unloads your DLL, then DLL_PROCESS_DETACH or DLL_THREAD_DETACH would be passed. You can consider DLL_PROCESS_ATTACH and DLL_THREAD_ATTACH similar to calling LibMain and DLL_PROCESS_DETACH and DLL_THREAD_DETACH similar to calling WEP. The key difference between DLL_x_ATTACH and LibMain is that LibMain is called only once when your DLL is loaded in memory, whereas DllMain is called every time a process or thread loads your DLL. Similarly, DLL_x_DETACH and WEP differ in that DllMain is called whenever a process or thread unloads your DLL, whereas the WEP is called only when the last application unloads your DLL. Listing 31.1 shows an implementation of DllMain for a shell extension/file viewer in-process server.

Listing 31.1. DllMain implementation.

```
extern "C" BOOL APIENTRY
DllMain(HINSTANCE hInstance, DWORD dwReason, LPVOID lpReserved)
{
  //Save the instance for later use
  if (dwReason == DLL_PROCESS_ATTACH) {
    g_hInstanceDll = hInstance;
  }

  return 1;  //Return a 1 if all is well
}
```

Once your DLL has been initialized for the current instance, OLE will call DllGetClassObject to obtain the class factory for the object that the caller requested (although other interfaces could be requested, DllGetClassObject is almost always called, requesting the IClassFactory interface). The sample application supports three different objects: shell extension, drag/drop shell extension, and file viewer. Listing 31.2 shows how to implement DllGetClassObject to support multiple objects.

Listing 31.2. `DllGetClassObject` **implementation.**

```
//@func DllGetClassObject is called by OLE to request the creation of an object
//@rdesc NOERROR indicates no error, otherwise an HRESULT indicating
//the error is returned
STDAPI DllGetClassObject(REFCLSID rclsid, REFIID riid, LPVOID *ppvOut)
{
  //In OLE we are supposed to release any interface pointers before
  //assigning a new value to it, so look at the interface pointer
  //and determine if it is already assigned.
  //Because many applications pass uninitialized interface pointers
  //our implementation is in a try/catch so that uninitialized interface
  //pointers will be initialized by the catch.
#ifdef USE_TRY
  try{
    if (*ppvOut != NULL){
      ((LPUNKNOWN)(*ppvOut))->Release();
      *ppvOut = NULL;
    }
  }
  catch(...){
    *ppvOut = NULL;
  }
#else
  *ppvOut = NULL;
#endif

  //Look for either a request for CLSID_WPUShellExtension object
  //or a CLSID_WPU_FileViewer object and create the appropriate
  //class factory
    if (IsEqualIID(rclsid, CLSID_WPUShellExtension)){
        CWPUShellExtensionClassFactory *pcf = new CWPUShellExtensionClassFactory;

        return pcf->QueryInterface(riid, ppvOut);
    }else if (IsEqualIID(rclsid, CLSID_WPUShellExtensionDragDrop)){
        CWPUShellExtensionDragDropClassFactory *pcf = new
        ➥CWPUShellExtensionDragDropClassFactory;

        return pcf->QueryInterface(riid, ppvOut);
    }else if (IsEqualIID(rclsid, CLSID_WPUFileViewer)){
        CWPUFileViewerClassFactory *pcf = new CWPUFileViewerClassFactory;

        return pcf->QueryInterface(riid, ppvOut);
    }

  //The request for an object which is not supported, so tell the
  //call that the requested class is not available.
    return CLASS_E_CLASSNOTAVAILABLE;
}
```

From Listing 31.2 you can see that there are three separate objects with three separate class IDs all being handled by a single `DllGetClassObject`. It is not necessary to implement all three objects into the same in-process server; you can create three separate in-process servers. It is also not required to implement all three objects; you can implement just the objects you require.

Registration

In order for the Shell to use your object you need to make some entries into the registration database. Shell extensions can be on a per file type (using the file extension) basis or can apply to folders, directories, drives, or everything. For example, if you want the context menu for all C++ programs to have entries to bring up an editor, preprocess the file, or compile the file, you would have entries in the registration database for .cpp and .cxx, which would be on a file type basis. If you wanted a context menu for folders, directories, drives, or printers, you would have entries under Folder, Directory, Drives, or Printers, respectively. Finally, if you wanted a context menu for everything, you would have entries under *.

To add entries into the registration database, you could manually enter the required information using RegEdit, which is supplied with Windows 95; however, this is not feasible if you are writing applications that will be used by end users. The traditional method to add entries into the registration database is to create a registration file, which is a text file with the information that will be merged (or imported) into the registration database. The problem with using a registration file is that your in-process server must be in a directory that is in your path, or the registration database must explicitly have the path of where the in-process server is located.

A third method that can be used to enter registration information into the registration database is for the in-process server to be able to register itself. OLE controls support self-registration through the implementation of DllRegisterServer. When an application calls DllRegisterServer, the server enters all the registration information into the registration database itself. To implement a self-registering server, the sample application uses a C++ object called CWPURegistry, which handles the details of entering information into the registration database. Listing 31.3 shows the class definition of CWPURegistry, and Listing 31.4 shows the implementation.

Listing 31.3. CWPURegistry **object definition.**

```
//@class Registry class
class  CWPURegistry
{
//@access Private
private:
  //@cmember Key for access by Class ID
  HKEY  m_hKeyClsID;
  //@cmember const CLSID
  TCHAR  m_szconstCLSID[6];
  //@cmember Current CLSID to use
  CLSID  m_clsid;
  //@cmember Current CLSID to use as a string
  TCHAR  m_szCLSID[40];
//@access Public
public:
```

continues

Listing 31.3. continued

```
//@cmember Constructor
CWPURegistry();
//@cmember Destructor
~CWPURegistry();
//@cmember Adds a key and value under the requested key
void AddRegKeysHelper(HKEY hKey,TCHAR *iszSubKey, TCHAR *iszValue);
//@cmember Adds a key and value under the root
void AddRegKeysHelper(TCHAR *iszSubKey, TCHAR *iszValue)
   {AddRegKeysHelper(HKEY_CLASSES_ROOT,iszSubKey, iszValue);}
//@cmember Adds a CLSID
void AddClsIDSubkey(TCHAR *szSubkey, TCHAR *iszValue)
    {AddRegKeysHelper(m_hKeyClsID,szSubkey, iszValue);}
//@cmember Adds the necessary InProc registry information
void AddInProcRegKeys(TCHAR *szModuleFullName, TCHAR *szDesc,
                      BOOL bThreadApt=FALSE);
//@cmember Adds entries into the registry for the requested extension
void AddExtensionRegKeys(TCHAR *szModuleFullName, TCHAR *szDesc,
➥TCHAR *szExt);
//@cmember Adds entries into the registry for a shell handler
void AddShellHandlersRegKeys(TCHAR *szModuleFullName,
                             TCHAR *szDesc, UINT uiFlags);
//@cmember Adds entries into the registry for a drag/drop handler
void AddDragDropHandlersRegKeys(TCHAR *szModuleFullName,
                                TCHAR *szDesc, UINT uiFlags);
//@cmember Adds entries into the registry for a file viewer
void AddFileViewerExtensionRegKeys(TCHAR *szExt, TCHAR *szExtDesc,
                                   TCHAR *szDesc, UINT uiFlags);
//@cmember Used to set the current class ID for this object
void SetClsID(CLSID clsid, TCHAR *szDesc);
};
```

Listing 31.4. CWPURegistry object implementation.

```
CWPURegistry::CWPURegistry()
{
  lstrcpy(m_szconstCLSID,"CLSID");
  m_hKeyClsID = NULL;
  lstrcpy(m_szCLSID,"");
}

CWPURegistry::~CWPURegistry()
{
  if (m_hKeyClsID != NULL){
    RegCloseKey(m_hKeyClsID);
    m_hKeyClsID = NULL;
  }
}

void  CWPURegistry::SetClsID(CLSID clsid, TCHAR *szDesc)
{
    LPOLESTR  pszCLSID;
    DWORD     dwDisposition;
    HKEY      hKey;
```

```
    m_clsid = clsid;
    StringFromCLSID(m_clsid,&pszCLSID);
    WideToAnsi(pszCLSID,m_szCLSID,sizeof(m_szCLSID));
    OLEMemFree(pszCLSID);
      RegOpenKeyEx(HKEY_CLASSES_ROOT, m_szconstCLSID, NULL,
        KEY_ALL_ACCESS,&m_hKeyClsID);
    RegCreateKeyEx(m_hKeyClsID,m_szCLSID,0,NULL,REG_OPTION_NON_VOLATILE,
            KEY_ALL_ACCESS,NULL,&hKey,&dwDisposition);
    RegSetValueEx(hKey,NULL,NULL,REG_SZ,(CONST BYTE *)szDesc, lstrlen(szDesc));
    RegOpenKeyEx(hKey,m_szCLSID,NULL,KEY_ALL_ACCESS, &m_hKeyClsID);
    RegCloseKey(hKey);
}

void    CWPURegistry::AddRegKeysHelper(HKEY hKey, TCHAR *iszSubKey,
                                       TCHAR *iszValue)
{
    TCHAR    szValue[200];
    TCHAR    szSubKey[100];
  HKEY  hKey1;
  DWORD  dwDisposition;

    lstrcpy(szSubKey,iszSubKey);
    lstrcpy(szValue,iszValue);
  RegCreateKeyEx(hKey,szSubKey,0,NULL,REG_OPTION_NON_VOLATILE,
KEY_ALL_ACCESS,NULL,
    &hKey1,&dwDisposition);
    RegSetValueEx(hKey1, NULL,NULL,REG_SZ,(CONST BYTE *)szValue,
 sizeof(szValue));
  RegCloseKey(hKey1);
}


void  CWPURegistry::AddInProcRegKeys(TCHAR *szModuleFullName, TCHAR *szDesc,
 BOOL bThreadApt)
{
#ifdef  _DEBUG
    if (lstrlen(m_szCLSID) == 0){
        MessageBox(NULL,"You must call CWPURegistry::SetCLSID first",
            "CWPURegistry::AddInProcRegKeys",MB_OK);
        return;
    }
#endif
    HKEY  hKey;
      RegOpenKeyEx(m_hKeyClsID,m_szCLSID, NULL, KEY_ALL_ACCESS,&hKey);
    AddRegKeysHelper(hKey,"InProcServer32",szModuleFullName);
    if (bThreadApt == TRUE){
      HKEY  hKey1;
      RegOpenKeyEx(hKey,"InProcServer32",NULL,KEY_ALL_ACCESS,&hKey1);
        RegSetValueEx(hKey1, "ThreadingModel",NULL,REG_SZ,
(CONST BYTE *)"Apartment", 10);
      RegCloseKey(hKey1);
    }
    RegCloseKey(hKey);

}

void  CWPURegistry::AddExtensionRegKeys(TCHAR *szModuleFullName,
TCHAR *szDesc, TCHAR *szExt)
```

continues

Listing 31.4. continued

```c
{
  TCHAR  szFname[_MAX_PATH];
    _splitpath(szModuleFullName,NULL,NULL,szFname,NULL);

  AddRegKeysHelper(HKEY_CLASSES_ROOT,szExt,szFname);
  AddRegKeysHelper(HKEY_CLASSES_ROOT,szFname,szDesc);
}

void  CWPURegistry::AddShellHandlersRegKeys(TCHAR *szModuleFullName,
 TCHAR *szDesc, UINT uiFlags)
{
  TCHAR  szFname[_MAX_PATH];
    _splitpath(szModuleFullName,NULL,NULL,szFname,NULL);

  AddRegKeysHelper(HKEY_CLASSES_ROOT,szFname,szDesc);
  HKEY  hKey,hKey1, hKey2;
  DWORD  dwDisposition;
  RegCreateKeyEx(HKEY_CLASSES_ROOT,szFname,0,NULL,REG_OPTION_NON_VOLATILE,
        KEY_ALL_ACCESS,NULL,&hKey,&dwDisposition);
  RegSetValueEx(hKey,NULL,NULL,REG_SZ,(CONST BYTE *)szDesc, lstrlen(szDesc));
  RegCreateKeyEx(hKey,"shellex",0,NULL,REG_OPTION_NON_VOLATILE,
        KEY_ALL_ACCESS,NULL,&hKey1,&dwDisposition);
  RegCreateKeyEx(hKey1,"ContextMenuHandlers",0,NULL,REG_OPTION_NON_VOLATILE,
        KEY_ALL_ACCESS,NULL,&hKey2,&dwDisposition);
  AddRegKeysHelper(hKey2,m_szCLSID,"");
  RegCloseKey(hKey2);
  RegCreateKeyEx(hKey1,"PropertySheetHandlers",0,NULL,REG_OPTION_NON_VOLATILE,
        KEY_ALL_ACCESS,NULL,&hKey2,&dwDisposition);
  AddRegKeysHelper(hKey2,m_szCLSID,"");
  RegCloseKey(hKey2);
  RegCreateKeyEx(hKey1,"IconHandler",0,NULL,REG_OPTION_NON_VOLATILE,
        KEY_ALL_ACCESS,NULL,&hKey2,&dwDisposition);
  RegSetValueEx(hKey2,NULL,NULL,REG_SZ,(CONST BYTE *)m_szCLSID,
lstrlen(m_szCLSID));
  RegCloseKey(hKey2);
  RegCloseKey(hKey1);
  RegCreateKeyEx(hKey,"DefaultIcon",0,NULL,REG_OPTION_NON_VOLATILE,
        KEY_ALL_ACCESS,NULL,&hKey1,&dwDisposition);
  RegSetValueEx(hKey1,NULL,NULL,REG_SZ,(CONST BYTE *)"%1",3);
  RegCloseKey(hKey);

  RegCreateKeyEx(HKEY_CLASSES_ROOT,"Directory",0,NULL,REG_OPTION_NON_VOLATILE,
        KEY_ALL_ACCESS,NULL,&hKey,&dwDisposition);
  RegSetValueEx(hKey,NULL,NULL,REG_SZ,(CONST BYTE *)"Directory",10);
  RegCreateKeyEx(hKey,"shellex",0,NULL,REG_OPTION_NON_VOLATILE,
        KEY_ALL_ACCESS,NULL,&hKey1,&dwDisposition);
  RegCreateKeyEx(hKey1,"CopyHookHandlers",0,NULL,REG_OPTION_NON_VOLATILE,
        KEY_ALL_ACCESS,NULL,&hKey2,&dwDisposition);
  AddRegKeysHelper(hKey2,szFname,m_szCLSID);
  RegCloseKey(hKey2);
  RegCloseKey(hKey1);
  RegCloseKey(hKey);

}

void  CWPURegistry::AddDragDropHandlersRegKeys(TCHAR *szModuleFullName,
 TCHAR *szDesc, UINT uiFlags)
```

```
{
  TCHAR   szFname[_MAX_PATH];
    _splitpath(szModuleFullName,NULL,NULL,szFname,NULL);

  HKEY  hKey,hKey1, hKey2;
  DWORD  dwDisposition;

  RegCreateKeyEx(HKEY_CLASSES_ROOT,"Folder",0,NULL,REG_OPTION_NON_VOLATILE,
          KEY_ALL_ACCESS,NULL,&hKey,&dwDisposition);
  RegSetValueEx(hKey,NULL,NULL,REG_SZ,(CONST BYTE *)"Folder",7);
  RegCreateKeyEx(hKey,"shellex",0,NULL,REG_OPTION_NON_VOLATILE,
          KEY_ALL_ACCESS,NULL,&hKey1,&dwDisposition);
  RegCreateKeyEx(hKey1,"DragDropHandlers",0,NULL,REG_OPTION_NON_VOLATILE,
          KEY_ALL_ACCESS,NULL,&hKey2,&dwDisposition);
  AddRegKeysHelper(hKey2,szFname,m_szCLSID);
  RegCloseKey(hKey2);
  RegCloseKey(hKey1);
  RegCloseKey(hKey);

}

void  CWPURegistry::AddFileViewerExtensionRegKeys(TCHAR *szExt,
 TCHAR *szExtDesc, TCHAR *szDesc, UINT uiFlags)
{
  HKEY  hKey,hKey1, hKey2;
  DWORD  dwDisposition;

  RegCreateKeyEx(HKEY_CLASSES_ROOT,"QuickView",0,NULL,REG_OPTION_NON_VOLATILE,
          KEY_ALL_ACCESS,NULL,&hKey,&dwDisposition);
  RegCreateKeyEx(hKey,szExt,0,NULL,REG_OPTION_NON_VOLATILE,
          KEY_ALL_ACCESS,NULL,&hKey1,&dwDisposition);
  RegSetValueEx(hKey1,NULL,NULL,REG_SZ,(CONST BYTE *)szExtDesc,
lstrlen(szExtDesc));
  RegCreateKeyEx(hKey1,m_szCLSID,0,NULL,REG_OPTION_NON_VOLATILE,
          KEY_ALL_ACCESS,NULL,&hKey2,&dwDisposition);
  RegSetValueEx(hKey2,NULL,NULL,REG_SZ,(CONST BYTE *)szDesc,
lstrlen(szDesc));
  RegCloseKey(hKey2);
  RegCloseKey(hKey1);
  RegCloseKey(hKey);

}
```

Table 31.1. Registration database entries.

Purpose	Registration Entry
Extension	HKEY_CLASSES_ROOT\.**ext**=**InProcessServerName**
InProc Server	HKEY_CLASSES_ROOT\CLSID**objectClsID**\InProc Server32=**InProcessServerExecutablePathAndName**
Context Menu	HKEY_CLASSES_ROOT**InProcessServerName**\shell ex\ContextMenuHandlers=**ShExtClsID**

continues

Table 31.1. continued

Purpose	Registration Entry
Property Sheet	`HKEY_CLASSES_ROOT\InProcessServerName\shell` `ex\PropertySheetHandlers=`**`ShExtClsID`**
Copy Hook	`HKEY_CLASSES_ROOT\Directory\shellex\CopyHook` `Handlers=`**`ShExtClsID`**

Icon Handler	`HKEY_CLASSES_ROOT\InProcessServerName\shellex`
	`\IconHandler=`**`ShExtClsID`**
	`HKEY_CLASSES_ROOT\InProcessServerName\DefaultIcon=%1`
	
	`HKEY_CLASSES_ROOT\Folder\shellex\DragDrop`
	`Handlers=`**`DDHClsID`**

File Viewer	`HKEY_CLASSES_ROOT\QuickView\`**`.ext\FVClsID`** where: `.ext` is the file extension to be registered. `InProcessServerName` is what the in-process server will be named in the registration database. `objectClsID` is the class ID of the object whose server is being registered. `InProcessServerExecutablePathAndName` is the executable name of the in-process server. `ShExtClsID` is the class ID of the shell extension object. `DDHClsID` is the class ID of the drag-drop shell extension object. `FVClsID` is the class ID of the file viewer object.

Based on the information from Table 31.1, the registration database entries can be made. Listing 31.5 illustrates how `DllRegisterServer` utilizes the `CWPURegistry` object to add entries for the shell extensions and file viewer objects.

Listing 31.5. `DllRegisterServer` implementation.

```
//@func DllRegisterServer is used to add registration
//information into the registration database
//@rdesc NOERROR is always returned
STDAPI DllRegisterServer(void)
```

```
{
  TCHAR  szPath[_MAX_PATH];
  GetModuleFileName(g_hInstanceDll,szPath,_MAX_PATH);
  CWPURegistry  registry;

  //Shell extension entries (non-DragDrop)
  registry.SetClsID(CLSID_WPUShellExtension,"WPU Shell Extension");
  registry.AddInProcRegKeys(szPath,"WPU Shell Extension",TRUE);
  registry.AddExtensionRegKeys(szPath,"WPU Shell Extension",".dll");
  registry.AddExtensionRegKeys(szPath,"WPU Shell Extension",".ocx");
  registry.AddShellHandlersRegKeys(szPath,"WPU Shell Extension",0);

  //Drag drop entries
  registry.SetClsID(CLSID_WPUShellExtensionDragDrop,"WPU Drag Drop");
  registry.AddInProcRegKeys(szPath,"WPU Drag Drop",TRUE);
  registry.AddDragDropHandlersRegKeys(szPath,"WPU Drag Drop",0);

  //File viewer entries
  registry.SetClsID(CLSID_WPUFileViewer,"WPU File Viewer");
  registry.AddInProcRegKeys(szPath,"WPU File Viewer",TRUE);
  registry.AddFileViewerExtensionRegKeys(".ocx","OLE Control",
"WPU File Viewer",0);
  registry.AddFileViewerExtensionRegKeys(".dll","Dynamic Link Library",
"WPU File Viewer",0);

  return NOERROR;
}
```

Shell Extensions

In the previous section we looked at the registration information required for shell extensions; however, we have not yet implemented a shell extension. If you right-click on a DLL or OCX, you will get a context menu similar to Figure 31.1. Also, if you look at the icon for a DLL or OCX, you will notice that it is the default Windows icon. In the example that follows, we will implement a shell extension that enables you to register and unregister self-registering DLLs and OCXs. The shell extension will also show different icons depending on whether the DLL or OCX supports self-registration (in which case the icon appears in red), the DLL or OCX is 16 bit (in which case the icon appears in magenta), or the DLL or OCX is 32 bit (in which case the icon appears in cyan). The extension will also demonstrate how to add menu entries to support drag and drop and how to add a property sheet and copy hook. Before we can start implementing the shell extension-specific OLE interfaces, we first need to implement a class factory.

FIGURE 31.1.

A context menu.

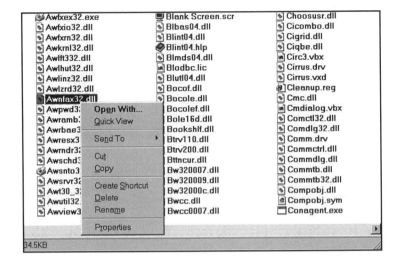

Class Factories

In OLE, a class factory is used to instantiate an object, and because shell extensions are OLE in-process servers, they also require the implementation of a class factory. Our sample program actually creates three objects: an object for the shell extensions without drag-drop support, an object for drag-drop support, and an object for the file viewer. Each of the three objects requires a separate class factory, although the implementation of each of the class factories is similar. Listing 31.6 shows the implementation of the shell extension (without drag-drop support) class factory.

Listing 31.6. Shell extension class factory.

```
CWPUShellExtensionClassFactory::CWPU  ShellExtensionClassFactory()
{
  m_refs = 0;

  //Increment the DLL object usage count
  g_refsDll++;
}

CWPUShellExtensionClassFactory::~CWPUShellExtensionClassFactory()
{
  //Decrement the DLL object usage count
  g_refsDll--;
}

STDMETHODIMP CWPUShellExtensionClassFactory::QueryInterface(REFIID riid,
                                                LPVOID FAR *ppv)
{
#ifdef USE_TRY
  try{
    if (*ppv != NULL){
      ((LPUNKNOWN)(*ppv))->Release();
```

```
      *ppv = NULL;
    }
  }
  catch(...){
    *ppv = NULL;
  }
#else
  *ppv = NULL;
#endif

    if (IsEqualIID(riid, IID_IUnknown) || IsEqualIID(riid, IID_IClassFactory)){
        *ppv = (LPCLASSFACTORY)this;

        AddRef();

        return NOERROR;
    }

    return E_NOINTERFACE;
}

STDMETHODIMP_(ULONG) CWPUShellExtensionClassFactory::AddRef()
{
    return ++m_refs;
}

STDMETHODIMP_(ULONG) CWPUShellExtensionClassFactory::Release()
{
  if (--m_refs == 0){

    delete this;
  }

    return m_refs;
}

STDMETHODIMP
 CWPUShellExtensionClassFactory::CreateInstance(LPUNKNOWN pUnkOuter,
                                                REFIID riid,
                                                LPVOID *ppvObj)
{
    *ppvObj = NULL;

    if (pUnkOuter)
      return CLASS_E_NOAGGREGATION;

  CWPUShellExtensionObject *pShellExtensionObject =
  ➥new CWPUShellExtensionObject();

    if (pShellExtensionObject == NULL)
      return E_OUTOFMEMORY;

  return pShellExtensionObject->QueryInterface(riid, ppvObj);
}


STDMETHODIMP CWPUShellExtensionClassFactory::LockServer(BOOL fLock)
{
```

continues

Listing 31.6. continued

```
  if (fLock == TRUE)
    g_refsDll++;
  else
    g_refsDll--;

    return NOERROR;
}
```

The difference between the class factories is in the implementation of the CreateInstance method. Each of the CreateInstance implementations creates the object that is specific for itself. You may be wondering why we couldn't just use one object and one class factory. The reason is because implementation of a drag-drop handler uses some of the same interfaces as the context menu, and the implementation of the interfaces is different depending on whether it is for a context menu or drag-drop handler. The file viewer also uses an interface that is used by the context menu, so it also needs to be separate. It would be possible to combine the file viewer object with the drag-drop handler; however, because their overall functionality is so dissimilar (as we will see shortly), it makes more sense to keep the file viewer separate.

IShellExtInit

IShellExtInit is an interface that is used by context menus, property sheets, and drag-drop handlers. The shell will use the IShellExtInit interface to give your object a target folder (for drag-drop handlers only), and IDataObject to obtain the objects that are currently selected (such as files, folders, drives, and so on) and a registration key. These values must be saved for later use because other interfaces will require this information. The shell may call IShellExtInit multiple times, and you only need to retain the information for the last invocation. IShellExtInit only has one method (besides the methods required for IUnknown), and Listing 31.7 shows the implementation that our example will use.

Listing 31.7. IShellExtInit implementation.

```
STDMETHODIMP CWPUShellExtensionObject::Initialize(LPCITEMIDLIST pidFolder,
    LPDATAOBJECT lpDataObject, HKEY hKeyProgID)
{
#ifdef USE_TRY
 try{
#endif
  //See if the caller provided an IDataObject
  if (lpDataObject != NULL){
    //The caller supplied an IDataObject, but are we currently
    //saving one?
    if (m_pIDataObject != NULL){
      //Release the saved pointer
      m_pIDataObject->Release();
      m_pIDataObject = NULL;
```

```
    }
    //Save the pointer provided by the caller
    m_pIDataObject = lpDataObject;
    //and increment the reference count since we're keeping the pointer
    lpDataObject->AddRef();
  }

  return NOERROR;
#ifdef USE_TRY
  }
  catch(...){
   m_pIDataObject = NULL;
   //Invalid pointer for IDataObject so fail
   return E_POINTER;
  }
#endif
}
```

The sample application only uses the IDataObject interface pointer, so Initialize only saves the IDataObject interface pointer. From Listing 31.7 you will see that the interface pointer is saved into m_pIDataObject. If m_pIDataObject is not NULL, Release is called before the new value is stored. If Release was not called, the reference count for the previously held IDataObject interface pointer would never be decremented and the object would never be freed.

Although not required for the implementation of IShellExtInit, you may consider implementing two additional methods, which I have called GetNumOfObjects and GetObjectName. Listing 31.8 shows the implementation of these two methods.

Listing 31.8. IShellExtInit helper functions.

```
//@mfunc GetNumOfObjects is used to determine the number of objects which
//are available from the IDataObject provided by IShellExtInit::Initialize
//This function is a helper function and not required for the implementation
//of shell extensions
//@rdesc Number of objects available or zero if no objects or no IDataObject
UINT CWPUShellExtensionObject::GetNumOfObjects(void)
{
    FORMATETC fmte = {CF_HDROP,
                      (DVTARGETDEVICE FAR *)NULL,
                      DVASPECT_CONTENT,
                      -1,
                      TYMED_HGLOBAL
                     };
    STGMEDIUM medium;
    HRESULT hResult = 0;
    UINT uiNumOfFilesSelected = 0;

    //If there is no IDataObject don't attempt to obtain any data
    if (m_pIDataObject)
       hResult = m_pIDataObject->GetData(&fmte, &medium);
```

continues

Listing 31.8. continued

```
    //If we obtained data from the IDataObject, find out how much is out there
    if (SUCCEEDED(hResult)){
      uiNumOfFilesSelected = 0;
      //Use DragQueryFile to determine the number of entries
        if (medium.hGlobal)
            uiNumOfFilesSelected = DragQueryFile((HDROP)medium.hGlobal,
                (UINT)-1, 0, 0);
    }
  return uiNumOfFilesSelected;
}

//@mfunc GetObjectName obtains the name of the object based on
//a zero-based index.
//@parm UINT¦uiObjectIndex¦The zero-based index of the desired object.
// uiObjectIndex must
//be less than the value provided by GetNumOfObjects
//@parm TCHAR *¦szObjectName¦The name of the object (file)
//will be returned here.
//You should allocate _MAX_PATH as the size of szObjectName
//@rdesc szObjectName is returned the name of the object.
void CWPUShellExtensionObject::GetObjectName(UINT uiObjectIndex,
                                               TCHAR *szObjectName)
{
    FORMATETC fmte = {CF_HDROP,
                    (DVTARGETDEVICE FAR *)NULL,
                     DVASPECT_CONTENT,
                     -1,
                     TYMED_HGLOBAL
                    };
    STGMEDIUM medium;
    HRESULT hResult = 0;

    //Empty the return string
    lstrcpy(szObjectName,"");

    //Obtain the data if we have an IDataObject
    if (m_pIDataObject)
      hResult = m_pIDataObject->GetData(&fmte, &medium);
    else
      return;

    //If we could obtain the data, then ask for the specific item the
    //caller is interested in
    if (SUCCEEDED(hResult)){
      TCHAR szFileName[_MAX_PATH];

      //Use DragQueryFile to obtain the desired object name
      DragQueryFile((HDROP)medium.hGlobal,
                              uiObjectIndex,
                              szFileName,
                              sizeof(szFileName));
        //Try to copy the data into the caller provided buffer
#ifdef USE_TRY
    try{
#endif
        lstrcpy(szObjectName,szFileName);
#ifdef USE_TRY
```

```
      }
      //Not enough room in user supplied buffer
      catch(...){
        lstrcpy(szObjectName,"");
      }
#endif
    }
}
```

`GetNumOfObjects` is used to obtain the number of objects (files, directories, and so on) that the `IDataObject` has. `GetObjectName` is used to obtain a specific object from the `IDataObject`. `GetObjectName` is called with an index number that indicates the object you are interested in. The index numbers fall into the range of zero through the number returned by `GetNumOfObject -1`. By using `GetNumOfObjects` and `GetObjectName` your application can iterate through the list of file names, folders, and so on, that the user currently has selected.

Context Menu

As previously mentioned, a context menu appears when you right-click on an object. Using the shell extensions, you can customize the context menu. In our sample program, for example, when you right-click on a DLL or an OCX, two custom entries are added to the context menu, `Register` and `Unregister`. If you select `Register`, the sample shell extension will call `DllRegisterServer` (if the DLL or OCX supports `DllRegisterServer` and the DLL or OCX is a 32-bit DLL or OCX), whereas `Unregister` calls `DllUnregisterServer`. If you are writing OLE in-process servers or OLE controls, `Register` and `Unregister` will aid in your application development because `Register` can be used instead of merging your registration information into RegEdit, and `Unregister` has no RegEdit equivalent other than manually deleting the entries for the DLL or OCX. Context menus require the implementation of two interfaces, `IShellExtInit`, which was discussed previously, and `IContextMenu`.

`IContextMenu` has three methods (besides the methods required for `IUnknown`): `QueryContextMenu`, `InvokeCommand`, and `GetCommandString`. The shell will call `QueryContextMenu` so that your shell extension can add items to the context menu. `InvokeCommand` is called by the shell when the user selects a menu entry that your shell extension added in `QueryContextMenu`. Finally, `GetCommandString` is used by the shell to display help text on the status line of the shell for your menu entries. Listing 31.9 shows the example's implementation of `IContextMenu`.

Listing 31.9. `IContextMenu` implementation.

```
STDMETHODIMP CWPUShellExtensionObject::QueryContextMenu(HMENU hMenu,
                                                        UINT uiIndexMenu,
                                                        UINT uiCmdFirst,
                                                        UINT uiCmdLast,
                                                        UINT uiFlags)
```

continues

Listing 31.9. continued

```
{
  UINT uiCmdID = uiCmdFirst;

  //See if there are enough IDs to add our menu items
  if (uiCmdFirst+2 > uiCmdLast)
    return (MAKE_SCODE(SEVERITY_ERROR,FACILITY_NULL, 0));

  //Add our menu items
  InsertMenu(hMenu,uiIndexMenu++,MF_STRING | MF_BYPOSITION,
             uiCmdID++,"&Register");
  InsertMenu(hMenu,uiIndexMenu++,MF_STRING | MF_BYPOSITION,
             uiCmdID++,"&UnRegister");
  return ResultFromScode(MAKE_SCODE(SEVERITY_SUCCESS,FACILITY_NULL,(USHORT)2));
}

//@mfunc InvokeCommand is part of IContextMenu and is called by the shell when
//the user selects one of the items which was added by this handler
//@parm LPCMINVOKECOMMANDINFO|lpInvokeCmdInfo|A pointer to a structure which
//contains information which was passed by the shell for the use of the handler
//@rdesc Either NOERROR or the HRESULT of the error that occurred
STDMETHODIMP CWPUShellExtensionObject::InvokeCommand(LPCMINVOKECOMMANDINFO
lpInvokeCmdInfo)
{
  //Determine which menu item of the handler's was selected and call the
  //appropriate routine
  switch (LOWORD(lpInvokeCmdInfo->lpVerb)){
  case 0:
  case 1:
    //Our two commands can be processed by the same function
    ParseNames(LOWORD(lpInvokeCmdInfo->lpVerb));
    break;
  default:
    //Should never happen
    MessageBox(lpInvokeCmdInfo->hwnd,
               "Invalid request",
               "IContextMenu::InvokeCommand",MB_OK);
    break;
  }

  return NOERROR;
}

//@mfunc GetCommandString member of IContextMenu which
//returns the help string
//to be displayed when the user has one of the
//context menu items highlighted
//@parm UINT|uiCmd|The command which is currently highlighted
//@parm UINT|uiFlags|GCS_HELPTEXT, GCS_VALIDATE or GCS_VERB
//@parm UINT FAR *|uiReserved|Always NULL
//@parm LPSTR|pszName|The help text or information on return
//@parm UINT|uiMax|The maximum size of pszName
//@rdesc The HRESULT result code
STDMETHODIMP  CWPUShellExtensionObject::GetCommandString(UINT uiCmd,
                                                         UINT uiFlags,
                                                         UINT FAR *uiReserved,
                                                         LPSTR pszName,
```

```
                                         UINT uiMax)
{
#ifdef USE_TRY
 try{
#endif
  switch (uiCmd){
  //Help text for Register
  case 0:
    lstrcpyn(pszName,"Register a control or object",uiMax);
    break;
  //Help text for Unregister
  case 1:
    lstrcpyn(pszName,"Unregister a control or object",uiMax);
    break;
  //Help text for expected request
  default:
    lstrcpyn(pszName,"Unsupported request",uiMax);
    break;
  }
#ifdef USE_TRY
 }
 catch(...){
  lstrcpy(pszName,"");
 }
#endif
  return NOERROR;
}
```

QueryContextMenu has five parameters: hMenu, uiIndexMenu, uiCmdFirst, uiCmdLast, and uiFlags. hMenu is the menu handle, provided by the shell, that you can add your menu entries to. uiIndexMenu is a zero-based index indicating where you should add your first menu item. uiCmdFirst is the minimum value you can specify for your menu identifier, and uiCmdLast is the maximum value you can specify for your menu identifier. uiFlag for context menus will be CMF_NORMAL, indicating that your handler can add menu items to the context menu.

InvokeCommand has one parameter, lpInvokeCmdInfo, which is a pointer to a structure of type CMINVOKECMDINFO. Table 31.2 shows the elements in CMINVOKECMDINFO.

Table 31.2. CMINVOKECMDINFO structure.

Name	Type	Description
cbSize	DWORD	Size of CMINVOKECMDINFO structure.
fMask	DWORD	CMIC_MASK_HOTKEY indicates the dwHotKey entry is valid.
		CMIC_MASK_ICON indicates the hIcon entry is valid.

continues

Table 31.2. continued

Name	Type	Description
		CMIC_MASK_FLAG_NO_UI indicates that the system should not display user interface elements such as error messages.
hwnd	HWND	Window handle of the window that owns the context menu.
lpVerb	LPCSTR	If the high-order word is zero, then the low-order word is the zero-based menu identifier offset of the command the user selected. If the high-order word is not zero, then lpVerb is the address of a command string.
lpParameters	LPCSTR	This is always NULL in shell extensions.
lpDirectory	LPCSTR	This is always NULL in shell extensions.
nShow	int	The nCmdShow parameter that is used by ShowWindow. If the command displays a window or executes an application, this value should be used when calling ShowWindow.
dwHotKey	DWORD	The hotkey to assign to an application that is activated by this command.
hIcon	HANDLE	The icon to use for the application executed by this command.

The sample shell extension uses lpVerb to tell the shell extension which command the user selected and hwnd to display an error message box if the shell passes an unexpected value of lpVerb.

GetCommandString is normally called by the shell to obtain the status line help text for menu entries created by your shell extension. Table 31.3 shows the five parameters for GetCommandString.

Table 31.3. `GetCommandString` **parameters.**

Name	Type	Description
uiCmd	UINT	Zero-based menu identifier offset of the command the user currently has highlighted.
uiFlags	UINT	GCS_HELPTEXT—the shell is requesting the status line help text.
		GCS_VALIDATE—used by the shell to validate that the requested menu item exists.
		GCS_VERB—used by the shell to request a language-independent command string.
uiReserved	UINT FAR *	Always NULL.
pszName	LPSTR	Address of a string that receives the status line help text.
uiMax	UINT	Maximum size available in pszName.

Once `IShellExtInit` and `IContextMenu` have been implemented, you can register your in-process server for context menu support.

Drag-Drop Shell Extension

When a user selects a folder and drags it to another location using the right mouse button, a context menu is displayed. The context menu that is displayed is the drag-drop context menu. When implemented, the drag-drop object is normally a different OLE object from the previously discussed OLE object because the drag-drop handler also uses `IShellExtInit` and `IContextMenu`. However, the context menu that you will display will normally have different menu commands from the shell extension context menu. Listing 31.10 shows an implementation of `CWPUShellExtensionDragDropObject`.

Listing 31.10. Drag-drop object implementation.

```
//@mfunc The constructor for CWPUShellExtensionDragDropObject
//which simply handles
//initialization and incrementing the global lock count
CWPUShellExtensionDragDropObject::CWPUShellExtensionDragDropObject(void)
{
  m_refs = 0;
  m_pIDataObject = NULL;

  //Increment the DLL object usage count
  g_refsDll++;
```

continues

Listing 31.10. continued

```
}

//@mfunc The constructor for CWPUShellExtensionDragDropObject
//which releases any held
//interfaces and decrements the global lock count
CWPUShellExtensionDragDropObject::~CWPUShellExtensionDragDropObject(void)
{
  if (m_pIDataObject != NULL){
    m_pIDataObject->Release();
    m_pIDataObject = NULL;
  }

  //Decrement the DLL object usage count
  g_refsDll--;
}

//@mfunc QueryInterface for CWPUShellExtensionDragDropObject.
//It will return the requested
//interface pointer if the object supports the interface, otherwise it will
//return NULL
//@parm REFIID|riid|Desired interface
//@parm LPVOID FAR *|ppv|A pointer to the requested interface or NULL
//@rdesc An HRESULT of the error that occurred
STDMETHODIMP CWPUShellExtensionDragDropObject::QueryInterface(REFIID riid,
                                                LPVOID FAR *ppv)

{
#ifdef USE_TRY
  try{
    if (*ppv != NULL){
      ((LPUNKNOWN)(*ppv))->Release();
      *ppv = NULL;
    }
  }
  catch(...){
    *ppv = NULL;
  }
#else
  *ppv = NULL;
#endif

    if (IsEqualIID(riid, IID_IUnknown) ||
      IsEqualIID(riid, IID_IShellExtInit))
    *ppv = (LPSHELLEXTINIT)this;
  else if (IsEqualIID(riid, IID_IContextMenu))
      *ppv = (LPCONTEXTMENU)this;
    else
      return E_NOINTERFACE;

    AddRef();

    return NOERROR;
}

//@mfunc Increments the reference count for the
//CWPUShellExtensionDragDropObject
STDMETHODIMP_(ULONG) CWPUShellExtensionDragDropObject::AddRef()
{
```

```
          return ++m_refs;
}

//@mfunc Decrements the reference count for the
//CWPUShellExtensionDragDropObject and
//destroys the object if the count reaches zero.
STDMETHODIMP_(ULONG) CWPUShellExtensionDragDropObject::Release()
{
   if (--m_refs == 0){
     delete this;
   }

     return m_refs;
}

//IShellExtInit member
//@mfunc Initialize is required for IShellExtInit which is one of the base
//classes of CWPUShellExtensionDragDropObject.
//Initialize is called by the shell
//to provide folder, key and an IDataObject for context menus,
//property sheets and
//drag drop handlers
//@parm LPCITEMIDLIST¦pidFolder¦The target folder for
//drag drop menu extensions
//@parm LPDATAOBJECT¦lpDataObject¦The IDataObject which is
//used to obtain a list
//of the selected objects
//@parm HKEY¦hKeyProgID¦Registry key for the folder or file
//@rdesc A
STDMETHODIMP
 CWPUShellExtensionDragDropObject::Initialize(LPCITEMIDLIST pidFolder,
               LPDATAOBJECT lpDataObject, HKEY hKeyProgID)
{
#ifdef USE_TRY
 try{
#endif
   //See if the caller provided an IDataObject
   if (lpDataObject != NULL){
     //The caller supplied an IDataObject, but are we currently
     //saving one?
     if (m_pIDataObject != NULL){
       //Release the saved pointer
       m_pIDataObject->Release();
       m_pIDataObject = NULL;
     }
     //Save the pointer provided by the caller
     m_pIDataObject = lpDataObject;
     //and increment the reference count since we're keeping the pointer
     lpDataObject->AddRef();
   }

   return NOERROR;
#ifdef USE_TRY
 }
 catch(...){
  m_pIDataObject = NULL;
  //Invalid pointer for IDataObject so fail
  return E_POINTER;
```

continues

Listing 31.10. continued

```
 }
#endif
}

//IContextMenu members
//@mfunc QueryContextMenu is part of IContextMenu and is called by the shell
//so that handlers can add items to the context menu
//@parm HMENU¦hMenu¦A handle to the context menu where items can be added
//@parm UINT¦uiIndexMenu¦Zero based position of where to insert the first
//item on the menu (by the handler)
//@parm UINT¦uiCmdFirst¦Minimum menu item ID
//@parm UINT¦uiCmdLast¦Maximum menu item ID
//@parm UINT¦uiFlags¦CMF_DEFAULTONLY, CMF_EXPLORER, CMF_NORMAL, CMF_VERBSONLY
//@rdesc use MAKE_SCODE(code, facility, num) where code is SEVERITY_SUCCESS or
//SEVERITY_ERROR, facility is FACILITY_NULL and num is the number of menu
//items added (if SEVERITY_SUCCESS).
STDMETHODIMP  CWPUShellExtensionDragDropObject::QueryContextMenu(HMENU hMenu,
                UINT uiIndexMenu,
                UINT uiCmdFirst,
                UINT uiCmdLast,
                UINT uiFlags)
{
  UINT  uiCmdID = uiCmdFirst;

  //See if there are enough IDs to add our menu items
  if (uiCmdFirst+3 > uiCmdLast)
    return (MAKE_SCODE(SEVERITY_ERROR,FACILITY_NULL, 0));

  //Add our menu items
  InsertMenu(hMenu,uiIndexMenu++,MF_STRING |
  ➥MF_BYPOSITION,uiCmdID++,"Drag 1");
  InsertMenu(hMenu,uiIndexMenu++,MF_STRING |
  ➥MF_BYPOSITION,uiCmdID++,"Drop 2");
  InsertMenu(hMenu,uiIndexMenu++,MF_STRING |
  ➥MF_BYPOSITION,uiCmdID++,"Drag/Drop 3");
 return ResultFromScode(MAKE_SCODE(SEVERITY_SUCCESS,FACILITY_NULL,(USHORT)3));
}

//@mfunc InvokeCommand is part of IContextMenu and is
//called by the shell when
//the user selects one of the items which was added
//by this handler
//@parm LPCMINVOKECOMMANDINFO¦lpInvokeCmdInfo¦A pointer
//to a structure which contains
//information which was passed by the shell for the use of the handler
//@rdesc Either NOERROR or the HRESULT of the error that occurred
STDMETHODIMP
CWPUShellExtensionDragDropObject::InvokeCommand(LPCMINVOKECOMMANDINFO
➥lpInvokeCmdInfo)
{
  //Determine which menu item of the handler's was selected
  //and call the appropriate
  //routine
  switch (LOWORD(lpInvokeCmdInfo->lpVerb)){
  case 0:
```

```
    case 1:
    case 2:
      //Each of the cmds currently performs no actions
      break;
    default:
      //Should never happen
      MessageBox(lpInvokeCmdInfo->hwnd,"Invalid request",
  "IContextMenu::InvokeCommand",MB_OK);
      break;
    }

    return NOERROR;
}


//@mfunc GetCommandString member of IContextMenu which returns the help string
//to be displayed when the user has one of the context menu items highlighted
//@parm UINT|uiCmd|The command which is currently highlighted
//@parm UINT|uiFlags|GCS_HELPTEXT, GCS_VALIDATE or GCS_VERB
//@parm UINT FAR *|uiReserved|Always NULL
//@parm LPSTR|pszName|The help text or information on return
//@parm UINT|uiMax|The maximum size of pszName
//@rdesc The HRESULT result code
STDMETHODIMP   CWPUShellExtensionDragDropObject::GetCommandString(UINT uiCmd,
                 UINT uiFlags,
                 UINT FAR *uiReserved, LPSTR pszName,
                 UINT   uiMax)
{
#ifdef USE_TRY
 try{
#endif
  switch (uiCmd){
  //Help text for Drag 1
  case 0:
    lstrcpyn(pszName,"Drag 1 Stuff",uiMax);
    break;
  //Help text for Drop 2
  case 1:
    lstrcpyn(pszName,"Drop 2 Stuff",uiMax);
    break;
  //Help text for Drag/Drop 3
  case 2:
    lstrcpyn(pszName,"Drag/Drop 3 Stuff",uiMax);
    break;
  //Help text for unexpected request
  default:
    lstrcpyn(pszName,"Unsupported request",uiMax);
    break;
  }
#ifdef USE_TRY
 }
 catch(...){
  lstrcpy(pszName,"");
}
#endif
  return   NOERROR;
}
```

Property Sheets

When the user selects an object such as a file or folder and clicks the right mouse button, a context menu appears. The last entry on the context menu is Properties, which will display a property page (or pages) that gives information about the object. For example, if you select Properties for a shortcut item, the shell will display a property page that has two pages: General, which shows information about a shortcut DOS file (such as when it was created and last modified and its attributes), and a Shortcut page, which enables you to change the link information. Using the property sheet shell extension, you can add your own pages to any property sheet.

To implement a property sheet shell extension, you need to implement two OLE interfaces, IShellExtInit (which was discussed previously) and IShellPropSheetExt. IShellPropSheetExt has two methods, ReplacePage and AddPages. ReplacePage is only used to replace a property page for a control panel object, so your shell extension implementation will normally just return E_FAIL, indicating that your handler does not support ReplacePage. AddPages is used to add one or more property pages for the shell and has two parameters as described in Table 31.4.

Table 31.4. AddPages parameters.

Name	Type	Description
lpfnAddPage	LPFNADDPROPSHEETPAGE	Pointer to the shell's AddPropSheetPage routine.
lParam	LPARAM	The lParam that is to be passed to lpfnAddPage.

When the shell calls AddPages, the shell gives your handler the address to the shell's AddPropSheetPage function. When you call the shell's AddPropSheetPage function, you need to give it two parameters; the first parameter is handle to a PropSheetPage, and the second parameter is an LPARAM that was provided by the shell when the shell called your handler's AddPages method. The handle to the PropSheetPage is created by creating a property sheet using CreatePropertySheetPage. Listing 31.11 shows the implementation of IPropertySheetExt.

Listing 31.11. IPropertySheetExt implementation.

```
STDMETHODIMP
CWPUShellExtensionObject::AddPages(LPFNADDPROPSHEETPAGE lpfnAddPage,
                                   LPARAM lParam)
{
  PROPSHEETPAGE psp;
  HPROPSHEETPAGE hpage;
```

```
    CWPUShellExtensionObject *pCurrentShellExtensionObject = this;

    //Set up property page info
    psp.dwSize      = sizeof(psp);
    psp.dwFlags     = PSP_USEREFPARENT ¦ PSP_USETITLE;
    psp.hInstance   = g_hInstanceDll;
    psp.pszTemplate = MAKEINTRESOURCE(IDD_WPUPROP);
    psp.hIcon       = 0;
    psp.pszTitle    = "Registration Ability";
    psp.pfnDlgProc  = WPUShellExtensionObjectPropertySheetDlgProc;
    psp.lParam      = (LPARAM)pCurrentShellExtensionObject;
    psp.pfnCallback = NULL;
    psp.pcRefParent = &g_refsDll;

    //Create the page
    hpage = CreatePropertySheetPage(&psp);

    //If the page was created, add the page to the Property
    if (hpage){
      if (!lpfnAddPage(hpage, lParam))
        DestroyPropertySheetPage(hpage);
    }

    return NOERROR;
}


//@mfunc ReplacePage is a member of IShellPropSheetExt and
//is for control panel pages
//@parm UINT¦uiPageID¦Page to replace
//@parm LPFNADDPROPSHEETPAGE¦lpfnReplaceWith¦Property page handler address
//@parm LPARAM¦lParam¦lParam to pass to the Property page handler address
//@rdesc An HRESULT of the error code (or success) is returned
STDMETHODIMP CWPUShellExtensionObject::ReplacePage(UINT uiPageID,
                               LPFNADDPROPSHEETPAGE lpfnReplaceWith,
                               LPARAM lParam)
{
    //We don't need this function for our purposes so just fail
    return E_FAIL;
}


//@func BOOL¦WPUShellExtensionObjectPropertySheetDlgProc¦The callback procedure
//which our property page will use.
//@parm HWND¦hDlg¦Handle of the dialog box which has the property page
//@parm UINT¦uiMsg¦Message
//@parm WPARAM¦wParam¦WPARAM of call
//@parm LPARAM¦lParam¦LPARAM of call
//@rdesc Return TRUE if we processed the message,
//otherwise return FALSE in most cases
//Some notification messages such PSN_APPLY, PSN_KILLACTIVE
//and PSN_SETACTIVE should always return TRUE
BOOL CALLBACK WPUShellExtensionObjectPropertySheetDlgProc(HWND hDlg,
                               UINT uiMsg,
                               WPARAM wParam,
                               LPARAM lParam)
{
  LPPROPSHEETPAGE psp;
  CWPUShellExtensionObject *pCurrentShellExtensionObject;
```

continues

Listing 31.11. continued

```c
if (uiMsg != WM_INITDIALOG)
  psp = (LPPROPSHEETPAGE)GetWindowLong(hDlg, DWL_USER);

switch (uiMsg){
//Our page is being initialized
case WM_INITDIALOG:
  SetWindowLong(hDlg, DWL_USER, lParam);
  psp = (LPPROPSHEETPAGE)lParam;
  pCurrentShellExtensionObject = (CWPUShellExtensionObject *)psp->lParam;
  SetDlgItemText(hDlg,IDC_REGINFO,"Registration information can go here");
  break;
case WM_DESTROY:
  break;
case WM_COMMAND:
  break;
//Handle notifications
case WM_NOTIFY:
  switch (((NMHDR FAR *)lParam)->code){
  //The user selected OK or APPLY so we need to apply any changes
  //from our page. The example current does nothing
  case PSN_APPLY:
    SetWindowLong(hDlg, DWL_MSGRESULT,0);
    //Set the return code to any value you require
    return TRUE;  //Always return TRUE
  //The user needs help
  case PSN_HELP:
    break;
  //Can we give up focus?
  case PSN_KILLACTIVE:
    SetWindowLong(hDlg, DWL_MSGRESULT,FALSE);
    return TRUE;
  //The user selected Cancel, can they cancel?
  case PSN_QUERYCANCEL:
    return FALSE;    //Return TRUE if user cannot select cancel
  //Cancel is being processed so lose all changes
  case PSN_RESET:
    break;
  //We are about to receive focus, do we want the focus?
  //We can change the SetWindowLong, 0 value to a page we want focus to
  //go to if we don't want to be displayed
  case PSN_SETACTIVE:
    SetWindowLong(hDlg, DWL_MSGRESULT,0);  //Accepts activation of page
    return TRUE;
  default:
    break;
  }
  break;
default:
  return FALSE;
}

return TRUE;
}
```

When you implement a property sheet, the property sheet also requires a dialog procedure. Listing 31.11 shows a sample dialog procedure that can be used for property sheets. There are two points that you need to be aware of when implementing a dialog procedure for property sheets. First, the shell will send you various notifications through a WM_NOTIFY message. Listing 31.11 shows the various messages that the shell will send your dialog procedure in terms of notifications. The second point is that the shell can also pass information between your AddPages implementation and your dialog procedure. In Listing 31.11, the AddPages implementation fills in a PROPSHEETPAGE structure in order to create your property sheet. The field lParam can be assigned any pointer or any value that can be passed as an LPARAM. The shell will pass the value of this field to your dialog procedure as the lParam in the WM_INITDIALOG message.

Copy Hooks

A copy hook handler is called by the shell whenever a request is made to copy, move, delete, or rename a folder. A copy hook handler is extremely easy to implement because the handler does not perform the requested operation; it only gives the shell approval on whether the operation should be performed. Because the copy hook handler only gives approval, the OLE interface for the copy hook is trivial; it is a single method called CopyCallback. CopyCallback has seven parameters as described in Table 31.5.

Table 31.5. CopyCallback **parameters.**

Name	Type	Description
hWnd	HWND	Parent window that the handler can use to display messages.
wFunc	INT	FO_COPY—a copy request from szSrcFile to szDestFile.
		FO_DELETE—a delete request of szSrcFile.
		FO_MOVE—a move request from szSrcFile to szDestFile.
		FO_RENAME—a rename request of szSrcFile.
		PO_DELETE—a delete request of the szSrcFile printer.
		PO_PORTCHANGE—a printer port change request. szSrcFile contains a list of printer names followed by ports, and szDestFile contains a list of printer names followed by the new ports.

continues

Table 31.5. continued

Name	Type	Description
		PO_RENAME—a printer rename request of the szSrcFile printer.
		PO_REN_PORT—a combination of PO_PORTCHANGE and PO_RENAME.
wFlags	UINT	Flags that are used to control the operation of your copy handler. See the latest documentation for the possible values and meanings. During the beta period, some possible flags were not implemented.
szSrcFile	LPCSTR	Source name.
dwSrcAttrib	DWORD	Source attributes.
szDestFile	LPCSTR	Destination name.
dwDestAttrib	DWORD	Destination attributes.

You should be aware that for the Windows 95 beta, ICopyHook is the base class definition for a copy hook handler, and IID_IShellCopyHook is the class ID for the interface (in other words, derive your object from ICopyHook, but use IID_IShellCopyHook in your QueryInterface implementation).

During the beta period it appears that copy hook handlers are only loaded by the shell when the shell first comes up. In order to test a copy hook handler, add the required entries for your handler into the registration database, then terminate Explorer by using a tool such as PVIEW95. Once Explorer has been terminated, left double-click on the desktop, which will bring up the task menu, and select Run Application. Type in explorer; Explorer will then read the registration database and use your newly installed copy hook. Instead of terminating and restarting Explorer, you could also restart Windows; however, I have found that terminating Explorer is much faster than terminating Windows.

Icon Handler

The icon handler shell extension may be one of the most interesting parts of the shell extension but also could cause the most amount of trouble. The icon handler enables your shell extension to decide what icon should be displayed for a particular file or folder. In the sample program provided with this book, the icon handler will display 16-bit DLLs and OCXs in magenta, 32-bit DLLs and OCXs that do not support OLE self-registration in cyan, and 32-bit DLLs and OCXs that do support OLE self-registration in red, thereby giving you visual cues about the DLL or OCX. The way this particular shell extension can cause trouble is that, in the case of the sample application, there are many DLLs in the

Win95\System directory, and the sample application loads each one to determine whether the DLL or OCX is 16- or 32-bit and supports self-registration. All of this loading and unloading can take time. Depending on how you implement your icon handler, you could bring the system to a screeching halt.

Icon handlers are fairly easy to implement and require three interfaces: IPersist, IPersistFile, and IExtractIcon. IPersist is a standard OLE interface that only has one method, GetClassID, which for icon handlers simply returns E_FAIL. The reason IPersist needs to be implemented is because the icon handler needs to implement IPersistFile, and IPersist is the base class (along with IUnknown) for IPersistFile. The implementation of IPersistFile is also fairly easy, although IPersistFile has five methods: GetCurFile, IsDirty, Save, SaveCompleted, and Load. GetCurFile, Save, and SaveCompleted simply return E_FAIL for icon handlers because the shell will not call these methods. IsDirty returns S_FALSE because icon handlers only read files; they do not write files (because the save methods are not implemented). This leaves Load as the only method that requires some work. The shell will call Load for every file or folder that needs to be displayed and is supported by your icon handler (based on the registration information). In the implementation of Load, your handler receives a file or folder name and then decides what icon it should display for this file or folder. Listing 31.12 shows a sample implementation of IPersist and IPersistFile.

Listing 31.12. `IPersist` and `IPersistFile` implementation.

```
//IPersist member
//@mfunc GetClassID(LPCLSID pClsID)
STDMETHODIMP CWPUShellExtensionObject::GetClassID(LPCLSID pClsID)
{
  return E_FAIL;
}


//IPersistFile members
//@mfunc GetCurFile is a member of IPersistFile and returns the absolute pathname
//of the current file
STDMETHODIMP CWPUShellExtensionObject::GetCurFile(LPOLESTR *ppszFileName)
{
  return E_FAIL;
}

//@mfunc IPersistFile::IsDirty is a member of IPersistFile and
//returns whether the
//file has been changed since the last save (or open)
//@rdesc Return S_OK if the object has changed, and S_FALSE if the object has
//not changed
STDMETHODIMP CWPUShellExtensionObject::IsDirty(void)
{
  return S_FALSE;
}

//@mfunc IPersistFile::Load is a member of IPersistFile and opens and
//'reads' the requested file
```

continues

Listing 31.12. continued

```
STDMETHODIMP CWPUShellExtensionObject::Load(LPCOLESTR pszFileName,
 DWORD dwMode)
{
  TCHAR sz[_MAX_PATH];
  HINSTANCE hInstance;
  typedef ULONG (FAR PASCAL *pfnDllRegisterServer)(void);
  pfnDllRegisterServer lpfnDllRegisterServer;

  WideToAnsi(pszFileName,sz,sizeof(sz));
  m_iIconToUse = 0;

  TCHAR sz1[_MAX_PATH], sz2[_MAX_PATH];
  _splitpath(sz,NULL,NULL,sz1,sz2);

  lstrcat(sz1,sz2);

  //The following DLL(s) crash when loaded and queried
  if (lstrcmpi(sz1,TEXT("MFCO30UD.DLL")) == 0)
    return NOERROR;
  if (lstrcmpi(sz1,TEXT("MFCO30U.DLL")) == 0)
    return NOERROR;
  if (lstrcmpi(sz1,TEXT("MFC30UD.DLL")) == 0)
    return NOERROR;
  if (lstrcmpi(sz1,TEXT("MFC30U.DLL")) == 0)
    return NOERROR;
  if (lstrcmpi(sz1,TEXT("MFCN30UD.DLL")) == 0)
    return NOERROR;
  if (lstrcmpi(sz1,TEXT("MFCN30U.DLL")) == 0)
    return NOERROR;
  if (lstrcmpi(sz1,TEXT("OC30UD.DLL")) == 0)
    return NOERROR;
  if (lstrcmpi(sz1,TEXT("OC30D.DLL")) == 0)
    return NOERROR;
  if (lstrcmpi(sz1,TEXT("OC30U.DLL")) == 0)
    return NOERROR;
  if (lstrcmpi(sz1,TEXT("WNDTOOLS.DLL")) == 0)
    return NOERROR;

#ifdef USE_TRY
  try{
#endif
  hInstance = LoadLibrary(sz);
#ifdef USE_TRY
  }
  catch(...){
  hInstance = NULL;
  }
#endif

  if (hInstance != NULL){
    lpfnDllRegisterServer =
      (pfnDllRegisterServer)GetProcAddress(hInstance,"DllRegisterServer");
    if (lpfnDllRegisterServer != NULL)
      m_iIconToUse = 1;
    FreeLibrary(hInstance);
  } else
    m_iIconToUse = 2;
```

```
  return NOERROR;
}

//@mfunc IPersistFile::Save is a member of IPersistFile and
//saves the current file
STDMETHODIMP CWPUShellExtensionObject::Save(LPCOLESTR pszFileName,
BOOL bRemember)
{
  return E_FAIL;
}
//@mfunc IPersistFile::SaveCompleted is a member of
//IPersistFile and allows the
//application to write to the file again (after being in an
//NoScribble state
//from a Save)
STDMETHODIMP CWPUShellExtensionObject::SaveCompleted(LPCOLESTR pszFileName)
{
  return E_FAIL;
}
```

If you are a 16-bit OLE programmer, you may have noticed that IPersistFile is implemented differently in 32-bit OLE than in 16-bit OLE. The reason is that 32-bit OLE uses Unicode for strings, whereas 16-bit OLE uses ANSI for strings. In addition, Windows 95 normally uses ANSI strings; however, strings in OLE are Unicode, so the Load routine needs to convert the Unicode filename to an ANSI filename. This is accomplished by calling WideToAnsi, which is a macro included with the sample source (in the header file common.h).

IExtractIcon is the final interface that needs to be implemented for an icon handler. IExtractIcon has two methods, Extract and GetIconLocation. In most cases, Extract simply returns S_FALSE, because Extract is used by the shell to obtain an icon when an icon is not implemented in a DLL or executable. When it returns S_FALSE, Extract is indicating to the shell that the shell can obtain the icon itself. GetIconLocation is used by the shell to obtain the name of the file that contains the desired icon, and your handler would also tell the shell whether the icon applies to all files of this type (based on file extension, by returning GIL_PERCLASS to the shell), or whether every file of this particular type may require a different icon (by returning GIL_PERINSTANCE). Listing 31.13 shows the sample implementation of IExtractIcon.

Listing 31.13. IExtractIcon **implementation.**

```
//IExtractIcon members
//@mfunc Extract  is a member of IExtractIcon and used to extract an icon from
//a file on behalf of the shell when the icon is not in a DLL or EXE
STDMETHODIMP CWPUShellExtensionObject::Extract(LPCSTR pszFile,
UINT uiIconIndex, HICON FAR *phIconLarge,
HICON FAR *phIconSmall, UINT uiIconSize)
```

continues

Listing 31.13. continued

```
{
  return S_FALSE;      //Tells the shell to get the icon itself
}

//@mfunc GetIconLocation is a member of IExtractIcon and tells the shell where
//to locate the desired icon
//@parm UINT¦uiFlags¦GIL_FORSHELL or GIL_OPENICON
//@parm LPSTR¦szIconFile¦Name of icon file
//@parm UINT¦cchMax¦Max. size of szIconFile
//@parm int FAR *¦piIndex¦Index of entry in icon file
//@parm UINT FAR *¦puiFlags¦GIL_DONTCACHE, GIL_NOTFILENAME, GIL_PERCLASS,
// GIL_PERINSTANCE,
//GIL_SIMULATEDOC
//@rdesc Return NOERROR if OK, or S_FALSE to use the default icon
STDMETHODIMP CWPUShellExtensionObject::GetIconLocation(UINT uiFlags,
LPSTR szIconFile, UINT cchMax, int FAR *piIndex, UINT FAR *puiFlags)
{
  GetModuleFileName(g_hInstanceDll,szIconFile,cchMax);
  *piIndex  = m_iIconToUse;
  *puiFlags = GIL_PERINSTANCE;
  return NOERROR;
}
```

File Viewers

Windows 95 has a feature that is called a File Viewer, or a Quick View (which is how it appears on a context menu). A file viewer is an application that enables the user to look at a particular file without being able to edit the file. A file viewer can enable a user to look at a file that the user may not have the application to. For example, by using a file viewer that comes with Windows 95, a user who does not own Microsoft Word can view a Microsoft Word document. The file viewer is also known on the menu as Quick View because a Quick View application should not have the same overhead as the actual application (because they can only display files and not modify them). A file viewer is an OLE object that implements two main interfaces, IPersistFile and IFileViewer (in addition to IPersist, which is required for IPersistFile, and IUnknown, which is always required).

QuickView

When a user selects Quick View from a context menu, Windows 95 (more specifically, the Explorer application) launches an application called QuickView. Using the selected file, QuickView tries to determine the type of file that is selected so that it can run the appropriate file viewer. QuickView first determines whether the selected file is an OLE compound file, and if the file is a compound file, QuickView uses the class ID that is embedded in the compound file to determine the correct file viewer. If the file is not a compound file, QuickView uses the registration database to determine the file type. QuickView and OLE have the capability to register a file pattern and associate it with a particular class ID. For example, if a file always has LMH in bytes 3,4, and 5, and ABCD98123 as the last nine bytes of the file, you can add entries into the registration database (under the FileType subkey) to express that particular pattern. If QuickView finds that your file matches the registered pattern, QuickView will use the file server that is associated with the defined pattern. If QuickView still cannot determine the file viewer to use, QuickView will look up the file extension (if any) and see what file viewer is associated with that particular extension. If it still cannot determine the viewer to use, QuickView gives up.

Once QuickView has determined which file viewer to use, QuickView launches the file viewer that is implemented as an OLE 32-bit in-process server. Because the viewer is an in-process server, when the server is loaded, the server's DllMain method calls the server's DllGetClassObject method to obtain the class factory for the file viewer. Once an interface pointer to the file viewer's class factory has been obtained, QuickView then creates the file viewer object. So far all of this is fairly standard and is similar to the implementation of shell extensions. QuickView has one additional requirement, however, in that QuickView requires that your server support references to multiple class objects; in other words, QuickView may cause *n* number of your file viewer object to exist simultaneously. Recall that g_refsDll is a global variable that we use to determine whether our server can be unloaded from memory. Because multiple instances may access this global variable simultaneously and Windows 95 supports multithreaded OLE applications, it is possible for two threads to try to access and change g_refsDll, possibly corrupting its value. In order to protect g_refsDll, you should not perform g_refsDll++ or g_refsDll--; instead you should use InterlockedIncrement and InterlockedDecrement to change the value of g_refsDll. InterlockedIncrement and InterlockedDecrement protect multiple threads from simultaneously changing the value of a variable, thus eliminating the possibility of corrupting that variable (by multiple simultaneous access).

Once QuickView has obtained the class factory for the file viewer object and instantiated the file viewer, QuickView then obtains (by using QueryInterface) the interface pointer to the file viewer's IPersistFile.

IPersist and IPersistFile

We discussed IPersist and IPersistFile when we discussed icon handlers earlier in this chapter. QuickView obtains an interface pointer to the file viewer's IPersistFile and calls the Load method. When QuickView calls Load, QuickView passes the filename that the user has selected, and the Load method can then read in the user-selected file. Some Microsoft documentation states that in addition to the Load method, QuickView will call IPersist::GetClassID and IPersistFile::GetCurFile, although I have not seen this occur. To be on the safe side, implement IPersist::GetClassID so that it returns the class ID of your file viewer, and implement IPersistFile::GetCurFile to return the filename that was passed to IPersistFile::Load. After calling IPersistFile::Load, QuickView then obtains and calls the file viewer's IFileViewer interface.

IFileViewer

IFileViewer has three methods: ShowInitialize, Show, and PrintTo. When QuickView obtains an interface pointer to IFileViewer, QuickView calls the ShowInitialize method and then calls the Show method. QuickView calls ShowInitialize so that your file viewer can perform any actions that are required of your file viewer and that might fail. ShowInitialize must register any window classes your file viewer will use and then create any windows that your file viewer will use but not display the windows. Depending on your file viewer, ShowInitialize must do additional work; as previously mentioned, ShowInitialize must perform any function that might fail. Once ShowInitialize has returned to QuickView, QuickView calls Show. Show is required to never fail and always return NOERROR. In addition, Show must have a message loop that includes calling GetMessage, TranslateMessage, and DispatchMessage, as well as ShowWindow. Show is also required to process messages just as if it were a stand-alone Windows application. Show may also be required to use a pre-existing window as supplied by QuickView. In file viewer terms, the currently displayed window is considered a pinned window, and Show may tell your file viewer to use the pinned window. If all of this sounds complicated, that's because it is. When you finally implement all that is needed for a file viewer, you will discover that you have implemented a stripped-down version of your application and added the capability to display your information in your own window or in a provided window.

Summary

Because OLE is starting to integrate more tightly into the Windows environment, some of the new functionality in Windows 95 requires OLE. Using OLE, you can expand the Explorer application in ways that the original programmers never imagined. In addition, with the viewer capabilities in Windows 95, you can continually add support for new file types, and the functionality from the user's point of view remains consistent.

VII

PART

Windows 95 Networking and Communications

Programming for Windows 95 in a Network Environment

32

by Timothy Parker

IN THIS CHAPTER

Windows 95 incorporates a number of important changes to the network programming when compared to earlier Windows versions. The network architecture of Windows 95 is considerably different from earlier versions, which has led to several changes in the manner in which applications are coded for networks. Also, the use of 32-bit APIs has made network programming a different process.

This chapter looks at the changes you can expect when dealing with network application programming. The chapter begins with a look at the Windows 95 architecture itself and shows how it is refined from earlier Windows systems. Then, you can look at the Windows 95 API itself.

Windows 95 Network Architecture

Up until now, Windows for Workgroups 3.11 and Windows NT have been the Windows networking environments, and their architecture has been similar to each other. Windows 95 refines the network architecture for better performance and reliability, as well as to cater to the demands of different network requirements. Because Windows 95 supports many different network protocols in 16- and 32-bit Virtual Mode Driver (VxD) versions, the architecture must provide the flexibility to accommodate a number of structures.

The Windows 95 architecture is layered, and has a rough correlation to the OSI Reference Model, although several layers are merged together. The Windows 95 network layered architecture is known as Microsoft's Windows Open Services Architecture (WOSA). WOSA was developed to enable applications to work with several different network types, and it includes a set of interfaces designed to enable the coexistence of several network components. The basic concepts of the layered WOSA design of Windows 95 are shown in Figure 32.1.

FIGURE 32.1.

The Windows 95 WOSA networking software architecture.

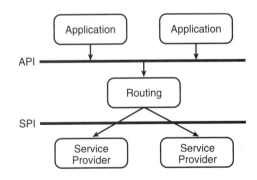

The WOSA architecture relies on the API layer, a routing module, the SPI layer, and underlying service providers to provide network functionality. WOSA uses the Service Provider Interface (SPI) to enable the operating system to interact with components of the network, which are more formally called Service Providers.

The Application Programming Interface (API) is independent of the hardware. The API is usually service-dependent, so it must interact with the proper drivers in the lower layer.

The Windows 95 architecture is much more complicated than the WOSA architecture would lead you to believe. The networking software components of Windows 95 are shown in their respective layers in Figure 32.2. Although the Windows 95 architecture retains the basics of the WOSA architecture, you will see that the actual components are more complicated. Many of the network components will be familiar from earlier versions of Windows or other operating systems and communications protocols.

FIGURE 32.2.

The components of the Windows 95 networking software architecture.

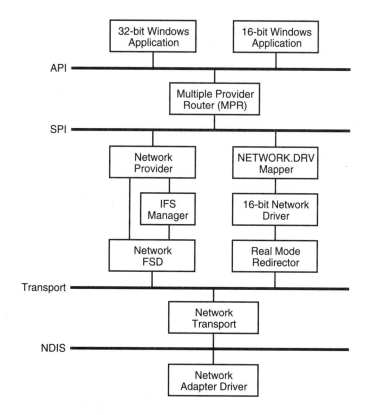

Look at each layer in the Windows 95 architecture in a little more detail so that you better understand the function of each component.

- ■ API: This is the standard Win32 API (the same as Windows NT). The API handles remote file operations and remote resources (printers and other devices). The Win32 APIs are used for programming applications.

- ■ Multiple Provider Router (MPR): The MPR routes all network operations for Windows 95; it also implements network functions common to all network types. Win32 APIs communicate directly with the MPR, although some might be routed straight through, bypassing the MPR. The MPR is a 32-bit protected mode DLL.

- ■ Network Provider: The network provider implements the network service provider interface. Only the MPR can communicate with the network provider. The network provider is a 32-bit protected mode DLL.

- ■ IFS Manager: The IFS Manager routes file system requests to the proper file system driver (FSD). The IFS Manager can be called directly by network providers.

- ■ Network File System Driver (FSD): The FSD implements the particular remote file system characteristics. The FSD can be used by the IFS Manager when the file system of the local and remote machines match. The FSD is a 32-bit protected mode VxD.

- ■ Network Transport: The network transport is a VxD that implements the device-specific network transport protocol. Multiple network transports can be active at one time. The network FSD interfaces with the network transport, usually with a one-to-one mapping, although that is not necessarily the case.

- ■ Network Driver Interface Specification (NDIS): A vendor-independent software specification that defines interactions between the network transport and device driver. Windows 95 supports both 32-bit and 16-bit NDIS versions.

- ■ Network Adapter Driver: The network adapter driver VxD controls the actual network hardware device. NDIS communicates with the driver, which sends packets over the network. Windows 95 uses Media Access Control (MAC) drivers.

A few of the architecture components are worth a closer look to explain their functionality.

Multiple Protocol Support

One of the key features of Windows 95 is the inclusion of support for multiple concurrent protocols. Several protocol drivers are included with Windows 95. The new default protocol is NetWare's IPX/SPX, which reflects the dominance of Novell's network operating system. Also included are NetBIOS and NetBEUI drivers, and a complete 32-bit VxD for TCP/IP. All of these drivers are Plug and Play enabled, allowing dynamic loading and unloading.

The NetWare IPX/SPX driver is faster than Novell's own driver, and it includes support for packet burst mode. The Microsoft IPX/SPX driver has an added Windows Sockets (WinSock) interface.

A full range of TCP/IP utilities is included with the TCP/IP driver. Also added is support for both Domain Naming Service (DNS) and Windows Internet Naming Service (WINS, first introduced in Windows NT). Dynamic Host Configuration Protocol (DHCP) enables a machine to query a DHCP server for an IP address, minimizing installation and configuration problems for new devices.

NDIS 3.1 and Multiple Protocol Support

One of the strong points of Windows 95 is its support for multiple protocols. This support is gained through the Network Driver Interface Specification (NDIS), which is a superset of the NDIS used in Windows for Workgroups and Windows NT. The version of NDIS included with Windows 95 is Version 3.1, which adds Plug and Play enhancements and new minidrivers.

The Plug and Play capability is added to the Protocol Manager and the Media Access Control (MAC) layer. It lets network drivers dynamically load and unload. The minidriver (which is binary-compatible with the minidriver models used in Windows NT 3.5) decreases the amount of code that must be written to support a network adapter. It does this by dividing the NDIS into a single component for the network adapter, ignoring the rest of the code that is provided as part of the Windows 95 architecture. The minidriver is common to all protocols.

The NDIS 3.1 driver has three parts to it: the protocol itself (which can be implemented by third-party vendors) and protocol manager, the MAC or mini-port, and the mini-port wrapper. The NDIS protocol manager loads and unloads protocols as needed.

Beneath the protocol manager is the MAC and mini-port. The MAC and mini-port system is designed to enable several MACs or mini-ports to be loaded at the same time to support multiple protocols. Because Windows 95 is usually used on an Intel architecture, the mini-port wrapper is a very small application, which sits below the mini-port to act as a mapper for Win32 APIs.

The Network Provider Interface and Concurrent Network Servers

Windows 95 enables support for many network servers concurrently. This is an improvement over Windows for Workgroups 3.11, which only enabled its own network and one additional network. The server support of Windows 95 is provided by the Network Provider Interface (NPI).

The NPI is situated between the application and network layers so that applications have no dependence on the two components (in other words, an application can be written without considering the NPI directly). For example, a user interface can look and behave exactly the same way, regardless of the network layer contents, and vice versa.

The NPI provides a single API for all applications, which call it through the Multiple Provider Router (MPR). All requests sent through NPI are then forwarded to one or more of the network service providers in use, depending on the call. To help vendors of network products, Microsoft has released the specifications of the interface in the hope that the features of the 32-bit system will be incorporated into drivers.

Installable File System Interface

The Installable File System Manager (IFS) has a different role with Windows 95 than it had with earlier versions such as Windows for Workgroups. Earlier versions of IFS managed only a single file system that depended on the operating system. The IFS of Windows for Workgroups handled DOS file systems only, for example. The IFS of Windows 95 handles multiple file systems and supports loadable drivers for file systems that Windows 95 knows nothing about.

Windows 95 has extended the support for DOS through the VDOS driver loaded by the IFS. Additional drivers included with Windows 95 are a CD-ROM file system, a Microsoft NetWare protocol driver, and Microsoft network clients.

Windows 95 Network API

Windows 95 includes a new Windows Network (also called WNet) application programming interface that enables developers to access network resources without worrying about the network software or architecture. Designed to be a high-level API, WNet provides several functions that are similar to standard Windows API functions, such as file selection.

Because most Windows 95 applications will not be involved in the development of software protocols but simply need access to network resources, WNet provides a relatively easy method to provide those features. We can look at the key areas of interest to application programmers in the API in more detail.

The important structure and function prototypes used by WNet are in the file WINNETWK.H, which usually resides in the directory MSTOOLS\H.

NETRESOURCE Structure

The center point of the WNet API is the NETRESOURCE structure defined within WINNETWK.H. This structure is shown here:

```
typedef struct  _NETRESOURCEA {
    DWORD     dwScope;
    DWORD     dwType;
    DWORD     dwDisplayType;
    DWORD     dwUsage;
    LPSTR     lpLocalName;
    LPSTR     lpRemoteName;
    LPSTR     lpComment ;
    LPSTR     lpProvider;
}NETRESOURCEA, *LPNETRESOURCEA;
typedef struct  _NETRESOURCEW {
    DWORD     dwScope;
    DWORD     dwType;
    DWORD     dwDisplayType;
    DWORD     dwUsage;
```

```
    LPWSTR    lpLocalName;
    LPWSTR    lpRemoteName;
    LPWSTR    lpComment ;
    LPWSTR    lpProvider;
}NETRESOURCEW, *LPNETRESOURCEW;
```

The NETRESOURCE structure is commonly used, although not all of the fields are applicable for all protocols. As you can see, there are two NETRESOURCE structures included in the WINNETWK.H file. The fields in the structure and their valid values are as follows:

- dwScope: A dword specifying the scope of the operation. Valid values are RESOURCE_CONNECTED (the currently connected resource), RESOURCE_GLOBALNET (all resources on the network), and RESOURCE_REMEMBERED (persistent connection).

- dwType: A dword for the resource type. Valid values are RESOURCETYPE_ANY (any resources), RESOURCETYPE_DISK (disk resources), and RESOURCETYPE_PRINT (a printer resource).

- dwDisplayType: A dword defining how objects are displayed to the user in a dialog box. There are definitions for several values, including domains, servers, share points, and a generic "don't care."

- dwUsage: A dword defining how the network resource is used. Valid values include RESOURCEUSAGE_CONNECTABLE (connectable resource) and RESOURCEUSAGE_CONTAINER (contains resources).

- lpLocalName: A pointer to a string that contains the name of the local device. This is an optional field.

- lpRemoteName: A pointer to a string that contains the name of the remote resource. This is optional.

- lpComment: A pointer to a string that represents a comment. Usually this field is filled by the provider.

- lpProvider: A pointer to a string that holds the name of the provider that owns the resource.

AddConnection: Network Resource Entry Point

The entry point for attaching network resources to the local machine is WNetAddConnection. There are two WNetAddConnection structures to deal with. The first is WNetAddConnection2, which should be used for most applications. The following is the WNetAddConnection2 code:

```
DWORD APIENTRY
WNetAddConnection2A(
    LPNETRESOURCEA lpNetResource,
    LPCSTR          lpPassword,
    LPCSTR          lpUserName,
    DWORD           dwFlags
    );
```

```
DWORD APIENTRY
WNetAddConnection2W(
    LPNETRESOURCEW  lpNetResource,
    LPCWSTR         lpPassword,
    LPCWSTR         lpUserName,
    DWORD           dwFlags
    );
```

The fields in WNetAddConnection2 are a pointer to the NetResource structure containing the remote resource name, a local device to be redirected, an optional pointer to the name of the network provider, and the type of resource. The lpPassword pointer is to a password string, if one is necessary to access the resource. If the pointer's value is NULL, no password is used. The lpUserName field is a pointer to the current user name. Finally, dwFlags is a set of flags indicating some behavioral aspects of the connection. A value of NULL means that no information about the connection is saved. A value of CONNECT_UPDATE_PROFILE with a local name not NULL means that details of a successful connection should be stored in the user's profile. If this happens, the connection is reestablished every time the user logs in (in other words, the connection is persistent).

The WNetAddConnection2 entry point is accompanied by another entry point called WNetAddConnection, which is provided for backward compatibility to older Windows versions. The following is the code for WNetAddConnection:

```
DWORD APIENTRY
WNetAddConnectionA(
    LPCSTR  lpRemoteName,
    LPCSTR  lpPassword,
    LPCSTR  lpLocalName
    );
DWORD APIENTRY
WNetAddConnectionW(
    LPCWSTR  lpRemoteName,
    LPCWSTR  lpPassword,
    LPCWSTR  lpLocalName
    );
```

The lpRemoteName field is the name of the network device, and lpPassword is a pointer to the password string to access the remote resource. lpLocalName is the name of the local device that is redirected.

WNetCancelConnection: Breaking a Connection

WNetCancelConnection2 breaks connections to network resources. As with WNetAddConnection, there are two versions: one for Windows 95 use and one for backward compatibility with older Windows versions. The following shows the Windows 95 WNetCancelConnection2 code:

```
DWORD APIENTRY
WNetCancelConnection2A(
    LPCSTR  lpName,
    DWORD   dwFlags,
    BOOL    fForce
```

```
        );
DWORD APIENTRY
WNetCancelConnection2W(
    LPCWSTR lpName,
    DWORD   dwFlags,
    BOOL    fForce
    );
```

The function includes parameters for a pointer to the name of the resource to be disconnected, a dword of flags similar to the flags in WNetAddConnection, and a Boolean flag that
indicates whether to force the disconnection. If the fForce flag is true, the disconnection is
performed regardless of open files and processes underway. If the flag is false, the disconnection is not forced if files or processes are open. If the dwFlags dword has the value
CONNECT_UPDATE_PROFILE, when the disconnection is made the connection is removed from
the user's profile.

For backward compatibility, the function WNetCancelConnection is also available within the
Windows 95 API. Its code looks like the following:

```
DWORD APIENTRY
WNetCancelConnectionA(
    LPCSTR lpName,
    BOOL   fForce
    );
DWORD APIENTRY
WNetCancelConnectionW(
    LPCWSTR lpName,
    BOOL    fForce
    );
```

The WNetCancelConnection function requires a pointer to the name of the connection and a
Boolean flag. With this function, the connection entry is always removed from the user's
profile with no capability to retain it.

WNetGetConnection: Retrieving the Remote Resource Name

The name of a remote resource attached to the local system can be retrieved with the
WNetGetConnection function. The following is the code for WNetGetConnection:

```
DWORD APIENTRY
WNetGetConnectionA(
    LPCSTR lpLocalName,
    LPSTR  lpRemoteName,
    LPDWORD lpnLength
    );
DWORD APIENTRY
WNetGetConnectionW(
    LPCWSTR lpLocalName,
    LPWSTR  lpRemoteName,
    LPDWORD lpnLength
    );
```

The `lpLocalName` field is the local name of the resource, and `lpRemoteName` is a buffer for the name of the remote resource. The `lpnLength` field is a pointer to a `dword` specifying the length of the buffer. When buffer overflow occurs, the current value in the buffer is replaced with the required buffer size and the function fails.

Enum Functions: Getting Resource Lists

If you need to obtain a list of the resources available through the network, a set of entry points must be used. The process starts with the function `WNetOpenEnum`, which looks like the following:

```
DWORD APIENTRY
WNetOpenEnumA(
        DWORD         dwScope,
        DWORD         dwType,
        DWORD         dwUsage,
        LPNETRESOURCEA lpNetResource,
        LPHANDLE      lphEnum
        );
DWORD APIENTRY
WNetOpenEnumW(
        DWORD         dwScope,
        DWORD         dwType,
        DWORD         dwUsage,
        LPNETRESOURCEW lpNetResource,
        LPHANDLE      lphEnum
        );
```

The `WNetOpenEnum` fields specify the scope of the resource search, the type of network resources to look for, the type of usage, a pointer to the `NetResource` structure that specifies the network container to search, and a pointer to the enumeration handle, which is filled in and used by subsequent calls. The pointer to the `NetResource` structure involves network containers, which are network objects that hold resources. A container can be within other containers.

After the enumerator handle has been provided, the next function to use is `WNetEnumResource`, which retrieves the contents of the network container specified in `WNetOpenEnum`. Entries in the network container are returned in an array of `NETRESOURCE` structures. The code for `WNetEnumResource` looks like the following:

```
DWORD APIENTRY
WNetEnumResourceA(
        HANDLE  hEnum,
        LPDWORD lpcCount,
        LPVOID  lpBuffer,
        LPDWORD lpBufferSize
        );
DWORD APIENTRY
WNetEnumResourceW(
        HANDLE  hEnum,
        LPDWORD lpcCount,
        LPVOID  lpBuffer,
```

```
    LPDWORD lpBufferSize
    );
```

WNetEnumResource has fields for the enumeration handle (which can be passed from WNetOpenEnum), a pointer to a dword holding the number of entries to be returned, a pointer to a buffer, and a dword specifying the size of the buffer. To get as many entries as possible in the NETRESOURCE array, set the number of entries to -1. The buffer size will be replaced by the required buffer size and the function will fail in case of overflow.

Finally, you should terminate the enumeration process using the WNetCloseEnum function. Its code looks like the following:

```
DWORD APIENTRY
WNetCloseEnum(
    HANDLE  hEnum
    );
```

The only argument WNetCloseEnum needs is the enumeration handle from WNetOpenEnum.

User Dialog Boxes for Connecting and Disconnecting Resources

The WNet interface can be used to present the user with dialog boxes to select network resources. To connect to a resource, use the WNetConnectionDialog function.

```
DWORD APIENTRY
WNetConnectionDialog(
    HWND   hwnd,
    DWORD  dwType
    );
```

WNetConnectionDialog requires a window handle (a reference to a window) and a dword that specifies the type of resource for which to browse. If the user makes a valid selection from the dialog box, the connection is established and the function returns successfully.

You can use a similar disconnection dialog box to disconnect a resource. The WNetDisconnectDialog function does this.

```
DWORD APIENTRY
WNetDisconnectDialog(
    HWND   hwnd,
    DWORD  dwType
    );
```

The WNetDisconnectDialog function requires the same parameters as WNetConnectionDialog. When WNetDisconnectDialog is called, it displays a dialog box that shows all the connected resources. After the user selects a resource, the resource is disconnected and the function returns.

WNetGetUser: User Names

To obtain the name of the current default user or the name of the user associated with a network connection, use the WNetGetUser function.

```
DWORD APIENTRY
WNetGetUserA(
    LPCSTR    lpName,
    LPSTR     lpUserName,
    LPDWORD   lpnLength
    );
DWORD APIENTRY
WNetGetUserW(
    LPCWSTR   lpName,
    LPWSTR    lpUserName,
    LPDWORD   lpnLength
    );
```

The WNetGetUser function fields include a pointer to a string with the local device name or the network name (if NULL, the user of the current process is returned), a pointer to a buffer to receive the name of the owner, and a pointer to a dword holding the buffer size. As before, if the buffer is too small, the required size is returned and the function fails.

Error Handling

You program network error handling in much the same way as you program other Windows 95 error handling. Use the WNetGetLastError function.

```
DWORD APIENTRY
WNetGetLastErrorA(
    LPDWORD    lpError,
    LPSTR      lpErrorBuf,
    DWORD      nErrorBufSize,
    LPSTR      lpNameBuf,
    DWORD      nNameBufSize
    );
DWORD APIENTRY
WNetGetLastErrorW(
    LPDWORD    lpError,
    LPWSTR     lpErrorBuf,
    DWORD      nErrorBufSize,
    LPWSTR     lpNameBuf,
    DWORD      nNameBufSize
    );
```

The WNetGetLastError function comprises a pointer to a dword for the provider-specific network error code, a pointer to a buffer to receive the text description of the error, a dword with the size of the buffer (messages are truncated if the buffer is too small), a pointer to a buffer for the name of the network provider, and a dword for the size of that buffer (again with truncation if the buffer is too small).

WinSock API

The Windows Sockets (WinSock) API is available. For those not familiar with the UCB TCP/IP Sockets system, a *socket* is a unique connection on one machine that has an identification consisting of the IP address and a port number. Two sockets are required for a connection, and each end has the socket number of the other. Communication between the two ends is with respect to the socket number, because one end must send a message containing the socket number of the other (and vice versa). WinSock differs from WNet in the type of abstraction involved. WinSock's abstraction is of the connection, whereas WNet abstracts the resources.

Due to the popularity of socket programming in the UNIX environment, there is a lot of existing code—including many utilities and toolsets—available for the socket programmer. Windows 95 provides both 16- and 32-bit WinSock versions, and either can be used. Of course, 32-bit VxDs are preferable for new applications.

Two communications methods are available with sockets: connection-based (TCP, or Transmission Control Protocol) and connectionless (UDP, or User Datagram Protocol). These are often referred to as *streams* and *datagram*, respectively, reflecting their behavior. Streams are much more reliable as communications are acknowledged, but they do need connections to be established and maintained.

All entry points for WinSock are prefixed with WSA or WSAAsync, the latter for asynchronous entry points. The primary structures used in WinSock programming are defined in the file WINSOCK.H, which is usually in the directory MSTOOLS/H.

Initializing and Closing Sockets

You must call WSAStartup to initialize the data structures, even when a socket is already established or the DLL is loaded. The WSAStartup call looks like this:

```
int PASCAL FAR WSAStartup(WORD wVersionRequired, LPWSADATA lpWSAData);
```

The WSAStartup function initializes the socket's DLL, checks the version numbers for compatibility, and increments a counter that tracks the DLL usage. Because there are several versions of UCB Sockets in current use, version checking is recommended. Some systems limit the number of sockets available, hence the DLL counter.

To close a socket, use the WSACleanup function. This is a simple function that decrements the DLL counters and unloads the DLL if it is not needed anymore. The function looks like the following:

```
int PASCAL FAR WSACleanup(void);
```

WSAData and sockaddr

The key structure of socket programming is WSAData, which is completed and returned by the WSAStartup entry point. The WSAData structure contains versioning and capability information for the sockets. WSAData has the following format:

```
typedef struct WSAData {
        WORD                    wVersion;
```

```
      WORD                    wHighVersion;
      char                    szDescription[WSADESCRIPTION_LEN+1];
      char                    szSystemStatus[WSASYS_STATUS_LEN+1];
      unsigned short          iMaxSockets;
      unsigned short          iMaxUdpDg;
      char FAR *              lpVendorInfo;
} WSADATA;
```

The fields include some vendor-specific information that is provided with the protocols. The fields include version numbers (two words), descriptions and status fields, the number of maximum sockets allowed, UDP-specific parameters, and vendor information, as the field titles suggest.

The sockaddr structure is used to define socket addresses. The structure looks like this:

```
struct sockaddr {
      u_short sa_family;
      char    sa_data[14];
};
```

There must be one socket address for each end of the connection. The first field in sockaddr defines the protocol used, because sockets can be used with many protocols other than TCP/IP. Based on the protocol code, the rest of the sockaddr data field can be interpreted (it differs with each protocol). The data field can be up to 14 bytes long. In its usual form, the family code is set to Internet addressing (TCP/IP protocols), in which case the data consists of two bytes for the TCP or UDP port number and four bytes for the IP address. The rest of the field is padded with zeros.

The most common sockaddr formats are embedded in the WINSOCK.H file. For example, the Internet layout just mentioned is shown as sockaddr_in.

```
/* Socket address, internet style */
struct sockaddr_in {
      short   sin_family;
      u_short sin_port;
      struct  in_addr sin_addr;
      char    sin_zero[8];
};
```

NOTE

For more information on TCP/IP, sockets, and related issues, see *Teach Yourself TCP/ IP in 14 Days* from Sams Publishing.

Host Information

To obtain information about host systems, a number of structures are provided. The hostent structure contains information about the host, including the text name, aliases, and one or more addresses where the machine can be reached. The structure is

```
struct  hostent {
        char    FAR * h_name;
        char    FAR * FAR * h_aliases;
        short   h_addrtype;
        short   h_length;
        char    FAR * FAR * h_addr_list;
};
```

WinSock provides a function for obtaining the machine name on which the application is running. This function simply returns the machine name.

```
int PASCAL FAR gethostname (char FAR * name, int namelen);
```

To obtain information about the protocol running on the host system, you can use the protoent function. It looks like the following:

```
 struct  protoent {
        char    FAR * p_name;
        char    FAR * FAR * p_aliases;
        short   p_proto;
};
```

The fields in protoent include the protocol name as a text string, zero or more aliases, and the protocol ID number.

The network identification can be obtained with the netent function, which has the following structure:

```
struct  netent {
        char    FAR * n_name;
        char    FAR * FAR * n_aliases;
        short   n_addrtype;
        u_long  n_net;
};
```

The fields include the name of the network, zero or more aliases, the network address type, and the network number. The netent structure assumes that the network number can fit into 32 bits.

The services available to the host can be determined with the servent function. That function's structure is

```
struct  servent {
        char    FAR * s_name;
        char    FAR * FAR * s_aliases;
        short   s_port;
        char    FAR * s_proto;
};
```

The fields are the name of the service, zero or more aliases, the service's port number, and the protocol to use with that service.

If a remote machine's address is known by the application, you can use the gethostbyaddr function to determine the machine's name. This involves a pointer to the hostent structure.

```
struct hostent FAR * PASCAL FAR gethostbyaddr(const char FAR * addr,
                                              int len, int type);
```

The function requires a pointer to the address, the length of the address, and the address type.

Alternatively, if the host name is known by the application and the address is required, you can use the gethostbyname function.

```
struct hostent FAR * PASCAL FAR gethostbyname(const char FAR * name);
```

This function returns a pointer to a hostent structure.

Servers can be reached in much the same manner. Sockets can be established to a server in the same manner as to another machine. To get server names based on the address, use the getservbyname function.

```
struct servent FAR * PASCAL FAR getservbyname(const char FAR * name,
                                              const char FAR * proto);
```

This returns a completed servent structure.

The getservbyport function can get a server name based on the port number.

```
struct servent FAR * PASCAL FAR getservbyport(int port, const char FAR * proto);
```

There are also functions that enable you to get the protoent structure using either the protocol name or number.

```
struct protoent FAR * PASCAL FAR getprotobynumber(int proto);
struct protoent FAR * PASCAL FAR getprotobyname(const char FAR * name);
```

Byte Order and IP Address Conversions

Byte ordering is difficult to do with sockets. To help programmers, WinSock uses the Network Byte Order and Host Byte Order. *Network Byte Order* is the order in which bytes are transmitted over the network. This order is called *big-endian* because the most significant byte is first. *Host Byte Order* is the order of the local machine. WinSock uses these two conventions to make communicating across platforms easier for applications. There is no overhead involved in using the byte ordering functions, so their use is recommended.

The macros that perform byte order conversions are named using acronyms. The macros include versions for short (16-bit) and long (32-bit) conversions. The macros are these:

- ▪ u_long PASCAL FAR htonl (u_long hostlong); for host-to-network long
- ▪ u_short PASCAL FAR htons (u_short hostshort); for host-to-network short
- ▪ u_long PASCAL FAR ntohl (u_long netlong); for network-to-host long
- ▪ u_short PASCAL FAR ntohs (u_short netshort); for network-to-host short

IP address conversion to a string and vice versa are provided by two macros.

The following macro converts the IP address from a string to a `long`:

```
unsigned long PASCAL FAR inet_addr (const char FAR * cp);
```

The following macro converts the `long` to a string:

```
char FAR * PASCAL FAR inet_ntoa (struct in_addr in);
```

In both cases, the IP address must be provided in network byte order.

Sending and Receiving Data

The full process for using sockets in a network application is too lengthy to explain here, but the basic process can be mentioned. Before data can be sent or received, a socket must be created and acknowledged. A socket is allocated using the following function:

```
SOCKET PASCAL FAR socket (int af, int type, int protocol);
```

The socket function returns a socket handle, a unique integer that identifies the socket. After the socket is created, it can be bound to the port. This is done with the `bind` function.

```
int PASCAL FAR bind (SOCKET s, const struct sockaddr FAR *addr, int namelen);
```

A bind to a port does not have to be performed on the client, only on the server machine. The server must then enter listening mode for traffic on that port. This is done with the `listen` function.

```
int PASCAL FAR listen (SOCKET s, int backlog);
```

The client can use the `connect` function to create the connection to the socket. If `connect` is not called, the system will bind to an internally assigned address. The `connect` function looks like the following:

```
int PASCAL FAR connect (SOCKET s, const struct sockaddr FAR *name, int namelen);
```

Data is sent and received with the `send` and `recv` functions.

```
int PASCAL FAR send (SOCKET s, const char FAR * buf, int len, int flags);
int PASCAL FAR recv (SOCKET s, char FAR * buf, int len, int flags);
```

After all data has been sent, the `closesocket` function terminates the connections.

```
int PASCAL FAR closesocket (SOCKET s);
```

Error Handling

Errors with WinSock applications are based on threads, so an error reporting call must be in the same thread as the error to be successful. Most WinSock functions return an error code when failure occurs. To get more information about an error, you can call the WNet function `WSAGetLastError`. This can be done through the following function:

```
int PASCAL FAR WSAGetLastError(void);
```

You can also set the last error code with the following function:

```
void PASCAL FAR WSASetLastError(int iError);
```

You should use the WSASetLastError function with care to avoid wiping out any important information.

Summary

Windows 95 provides both the WNet and WinSock interfaces for programming, making it versatile and customizable for each application. Windows 95's inherent improvements in network architecture make the operating system's overall programming interface simpler and easier to work with.

Although you've only been able to learn the basics of the Windows 95 network programming tool set, you should be able to construct networked applications by using the functions, coupled with documentation in the .H files. Of course, documentation is readily available with the development kits.

Remote Procedure Calls (RPC)

33

by Orin Eman

One of the features of Windows NT that is also in Windows 95 is the support for Remote Procedure Calls, commonly abbreviated as RPC. This is based on the Distributed Computing Environment (DCE), which is used in many client/server applications that run under UNIX. In fact, with a little care, you can write applications that can communicate easily between Windows 95, Windows NT, and UNIX. I won't be covering this interoperability here, but for an excellent treatment of the subject, see *Distributing Applications Across DCE and Windows NT,* Ward Rosenberry and Jim Teague, O'Reilly & Associates, Inc., 1993.

What Is a Remote Procedure Call?

A *remote procedure call* is a method of Inter-Process Communication (IPC) that can communicate between processes either on the same machine, across a local area network, or with TCP/IP and wide area networks anywhere in the world. A major advantage of an RPC is that the communication looks just like a regular procedure call. The RPC libraries take care of passing parameters to the procedure in the remote process, constructing packets, and dealing with different network protocols, different structure alignments, and even big- and little-endian machines.

How Does It Work?

When the client machine makes a procedure call that has been defined as a remote procedure, it actually calls a stub procedure on the client machine. This procedure along with a set of system libraries takes care of formatting the parameters of the procedure into a standard form, then transmitting them across the network to the remote server machine. On the server machine, another set of system libraries along with a different stub procedure converts the parameters into the form expected by the procedure on the server machine, then the stub procedure calls the real procedure. When the procedure returns on the server machine, the whole process operates in reverse to pass any results back to the client.

Where Might RPC Be Used?

RPC might be used in the following cases:

- Client/server applications where the server application runs on a separate machine.
- Communicating between processes in different address spaces on the same machine. This is not so relevant to Windows 95, but on Windows NT, it can be very useful for communicating between a Win32 process and 16-bit DLLs that provide services to old 16-bit Windows applications. This is one way of fulfilling Microsoft's Win95 logo requirement that Win95 programs also run under Windows NT.

- Distributed processing where many machines cooperate to share the processing requirements of large, CPU-intensive tasks.

- Communication with DCE-compliant applications running under different operating systems.

Defining a Remote Procedure Call Interface

A remote procedure interface is specified in an Interface Definition Language (IDL) and Application Configuration File (ACF) that are compiled by the MIDL (which stands for Microsoft IDL) compiler. These files specify the procedures and parameters for a set of remote procedure calls. The MIDL compiler produces a set of C source and header files. These files contain the code that interfaces with a set of system DLLs that do the actual work of transferring the calls/data across the network, or just to a different process on the same computer. The interface definition looks a lot like normal C procedure definitions.

Bindings

Before jumping into a simple interface definition, we need to discuss bindings. A *binding* is a collection of information that enables the RPC libraries on the client machine to send a remote procedure call to the correct server. A binding is usually passed around in the form of a binding handle, which hides the actual information. Bindings can be built from the ground up from such information as a machine name, an interface definition, and an endpoint; they can be read from a special database called a name service; or you can let the libraries take care of it all automatically (assuming it doesn't matter which server you call).

It is also possible to explicitly define which server a particular remote procedure call is sent to by adding an extra parameter as the procedure's first parameter, which contains the binding handle for the server the call is to go to.

The following example will use implicit binding, in which a global variable will be used to contain the binding handle and all remote procedure calls will use the binding handle in the global variable.

A NOTE ON THE WIN32 SDK EXAMPLES

The Microsoft examples on the latest Win32 SDK don't work under Windows 95 "out of the box." This is because they are set up to use named pipes to communicate. Unfortunately, Windows 95 only supports named pipe clients, not servers, so the server can't create its pipe, gets an exception, and dies. You can, however, specify the protocol to be used as command line flags to the example, but then you also have to specify the endpoint and network address. It gets complicated. For example, using the TCP/IP protocol, you could use 127.0.0.1 for the network address (the local machine), but what would you use for the endpoint? Well, the sample code on one particular run used 1030, but it used a special call to get a unique endpoint. If you were to use 1030 blindly, it might clash with some other server and at best, just cause an exception in the SDK sample applications.

A Sample Interface Definition

Here is part of the IDL file for the sample application:

```
[
 uuid(34b391b0-445b-11ce-ace7-00608c34cc67),
 version(1.0),
 pointer_default(ref)
]
interface RPCExDef
{
/*
Get the machine name
*/
short __cdecl
MachineName([out,string] char         return_string[30]);

}
```

The first section specifies the uuid for the interface (refer to the sidebar "Universal Unique Identifiers (UUIDs)"), its version, the type of pointers being used, and the name of the interface.

The second section specifies the procedures in this interface. In this case, we only have one procedure defined, MachineName(), which uses the C calling convention, returns a short integer, and takes one parameter, an array of characters. The [out, string] indicates that the array is to be treated as a string, and data is transferred *out* of the procedure, from the server to the client, so the RPC libraries only need to send the data one way. (The keyword in indicates that data is transferred from the client to the server.) Note that the __cdecl is a Microsoft extension—you have to use the /c_ext flag with the Microsoft MIDL compiler.

Here is the ACF file:

```
[
implicit_handle (handle_t RPCExHandle)
]
interface RPCExDef
{
}
```

This code defines the type of binding the interface will use. In this case, it is using implicit binding with a handle contained in the variable, RPCExHandle. Later in the chapter, we will see how to use this handle to indicate the server we are using.

UNIVERSAL UNIQUE IDENTIFIERS (UUIDS)

A UUID is a unique number used to identify an RPC interface. By unique it means there is no other RPC interface in the world using this number. If you have a network card in your machine, you can use the uuidgen program to generate as many UUIDs as you desire; the program uses the network card's unique address along with the current date and time to generate the UUID. If you don't have a network card, there is a very slim possibility that the UUID won't be unique.

Pointer Types

Pointers cause special problems for the stub procedures and libraries that implement a remote procedure call. For example, you can actually define a procedure in an interface that takes a pointer to a linked list! The stub procedure and libraries must follow this list and send every entry across to the server, allocate storage on the server for each list entry, then link the list up correctly before calling the procedure on the server. When the server procedure returns, the stub procedure then sends all the entries back and the client stub procedure puts the new data back in the original data structures. Confused? In order to simplify life where possible and to save time and space, there are three types of pointers that can be used in a remote procedure call: reference, unique, and full.

Reference pointers are the simplest pointers that can be used with a remote procedure call. The MachineName() procedure in the sample code uses a reference pointer. A reference pointer cannot be null; indeed, the stub procedure doesn't test for null, and you would likely get some form of exception if you tried to pass null as a reference pointer. It cannot change during a call so it always points to the same storage. Data returned from the remote procedure overwrites the existing data. A reference pointer cannot have any aliases; no other pointer used by the remote procedure can point to the same data. This eliminates any kind of circularly linked list, and the non-null provision eliminates a null-terminated linked list.

Unique pointers allow null pointers, so you could theoretically pass a singly linked list, or even tree data structures. A unique pointer can also change value during the call and change to and from null. There are special rules on memory allocation that are covered in the RPC help. The other restrictions of reference pointers still apply, so you will have no circular or doubly linked lists.

With *full pointers*, anything goes! You can have more than one pointer pointing to the same address, so doubly linked lists are possible. Obviously, such support in the procedure stubs and libraries is very complicated and time-consuming. It is best to use reference pointers wherever possible.

Creating a Server

First, I want to make a note on the sample code. I'm not going to present a useful application here—rather, a framework that can be used to create your own application. I have usually found I had to go through several examples in the SDK to get the information to create the framework here. In this example, I am putting the server code in a DLL. This allows both the client and the server to run in the same application.

Protocol Sequences

Before we start to create the server, we have to decide how the libraries will talk over the network to the client. A *protocol sequence* is used to define this. Sample protocol sequences are described in Table 33.1.

Table 33.1. Protocol sequences.

Protocol Sequence Name	*Description*
ncacn_np	Named pipes—very efficient if the server runs on Windows NT; cannot be used if the server is to run on Windows 95.
ncacn_nb_nb	NETBEUI over NETBIOS—In my experience, this has been a little slower than named pipes when using a Windows NT server. Note that this will only work on a local network because NETBEUI cannot be routed.
ncacn_ip_tcp	TCP/IP—useful if you want to interoperate with non-Microsoft DCE servers, or if you need to communicate with a client or server that isn't on the local network.

This is not a complete list. There are also IPX/SPX protocol sequences available if you are using Novell networks, and for interprocess communication between processes on the same Windows NT machine, there is ncalrpc.

I'm going to use ncacn_ip_tcp in the example, but I'll also present code to use all available protocol sequences.

Endpoints Again

We have a choice of either letting the RPC libraries pick an endpoint for us, or specifying it ourselves. If we are able to use named pipes, specifying it ourselves is easy. The endpoint is the name of the pipe the server will use; for example, \pipe\ApplicationName would be a good name to use. For TCP/IP, the endpoint is the port TCP/IP will use. In this case, the endpoint must be unique on the server; it must not be the same as any other server or application using TCP/IP on any server. For this reason, I'm going to let the libraries pick the endpoint for me.

Registering the Server Interface

The first thing we do to create the server is register its interface with the RPC libraries. This is done with the `RpcServerRegisterIf()` call. The interface is defined by a handle that is created when the IDL file is compiled. The handle name is composed of the interface name, the version number of the interface, a c for a client interface, an s for a server interface, and the string `ifspec`. The handles for the sample application are:

```
RPCExDef_v1_0_c_ifspec and
RPCExDef_v1_0_s_ifspec
```

`RPCExDef` is the name of the interface and is short for RPC Example Definition. I have defined the variables `ServerIfSpec` and `ClientIfSpec` in the header files to hide these rather unwieldy names, as follows:

```
#define ServerIfSpec RPCExDef_v1_0_s_ifspec
#define ClientIfSpec RPCExDef_v1_0_c_ifspec
```

Now we are ready to register the interface:

```
/*
Register the interface:
*/
RpcStatus = RpcServerRegisterIf(ServerIfSpec, 0, 0);

if ( RpcStatus != RPC_S_OK )
    {
    MessageBox(0, "Unable to register Server Interface",
               "RPC Example", MB_OK);
    return FALSE;
    }
```

Nothing fancy. This code registers the server interface defined by the handle `ServerIfSpec` with the RPC libraries. This example just displays a message box on failure. The rest of the server sample also displays a message box on failure, but I'm going to omit the failure code here.

Having registered the interface, we now need to tell the libraries which protocol sequences we want to use. The following shows code for using just one (TCP/IP) or all the sequences that are available.

Registering a Server with the Locator

After a server has registered its interface, it must register its information with the Locator. The Locator is a database of bindings that clients use in order to find a server. The database contains an entry string that identifies the particular server and the bindings associated with that string. This information stays in the Locator's database until it is "unexported" or the Locator is restarted. The information is put in the Locator's database with the `RpcNsBindingExport()` call as follows:

```
/* Get the actual bindings that were created */
RpcServerInqBindings(&bindingVector);

/* Add the Server's computer name to the server entry string
   which will be put in the Locator's database */
unsigned char serverEntry[256] = "/.:/ServerType/"
DWORD oldlen = strlen((char *)serverEntry);
DWORD newlen = 256 - oldlen;
// The following will put the computer name immediately
// after the "/d:/ServerType/" in the server entry array.
// newlen is the number of characters left in the array
// available for the computer name.
GetComputerName((char *)serverEntry + oldlen, &newlen);

RpcStatus = RpcNsBindingExport(
             RPC_C_NS_SYNTAX_DEFAULT,// name syntax type
             serverEntry,         // nsi entry name
             ServerIfSpec,
             BindingVector,       // set in previous call
             0);                  // UUID vector
```

It is important to note the addition of the machine name to the server entry string. If this is not done, then deleting the information from the Locator will not work as expected. When one server deletes its entry, all the entries for this interface specification get deleted, and you end up running servers with no entry in the Locator's database.

It is also quite possible for the Locator to contain old, stale information (although this usually means that the server that put the information there crashed). To handle this case, Microsoft recommends that you see if the `serverEntry` string already exists in the Locator's database and if so, to re-use it (code to get servers from the Locator is given later). This avoids having more than one entry for the same server machine. If there is more than one entry, then it is likely that a client will pick the wrong entry and be unable to communicate with the server (attempts to call procedures on the server raise exceptions).

The second parameter here is `0`. This means that any server using the given interface specification will be found. For example, if "Server1" puts in an entry, say `/.:/TestService/Server1` and "Server2" puts in `/.:/TestService/Server2`, both will be found.

Creating a Client

Now I'll discuss how the client is created. The most difficult part is finding the server, so I'll start with that.

Finding the Server

If it doesn't matter which server runs our remote procedure calls, we can use the
auto_handle handle type in the ACF file and not worry about finding a server or bindings.
The code generated by MIDL along with the RPC libraries takes care of finding a server and
calling it. But what happens when the libraries can't find a server? An exception will be
generated. If you are using auto handles, you have to put exception handling blocks around
your remote procedure calls to handle the case where a server can't be found.

Most of the Microsoft SDK examples compose a binding from the basics: a network
address, a protocol sequence, and an endpoint.

```
status = RpcStringBindingCompose(pszUuid,
                                 pszProtocolSequence,
                                 pszNetworkAddress,
                                 pszEndpoint,
                                 pszOptions,
                                 &pszStringBinding);

status = RpcBindingFromStringBinding(pszStringBinding,
                                     &IfHandle);
```

The details aren't important, but it should be noted that the parameters passed to
RpcStringBindingCompose() are either hard-wired into the application or passed in as
parameters when the program is run.

Once the binding is created with RpcBindingFromStringBinding(), the SDK examples then
make their Remote Procedure Calls; for example, in the 'hello' example, it simply makes a
call to HelloProc(). The example also uses an RpcTryExcept block to catch errors from the
RPC libraries. Catching errors in this manner is necessary because the return value from the
procedure is the return value from the procedure on the remote machine!

So, we have an example of how to make a remote procedure call from one computer to
another, if we know the name of the other computer. Obviously, this isn't too useful if the
user is always required to enter the name of the remote computer. We need a way of finding
a server. Microsoft provides a service called the Locator with Windows NT. This is basically
a database that contains a list of servers and the information required to connect to them.
Unfortunately, the Locator only runs on Windows NT because it uses named pipes to
communicate and only client-side named pipes are supported under Windows 95 (fortunately, only Windows NT Workstation is required, not the Advanced Server). It is also
possible to use a DCE name server if you have one available (this would usually be the case
only if you wanted to interoperate with DCE applications running under a different
operating system, such as UNIX).

Whether using the Microsoft Locator or the DCE Name Service, it is necessary to point some entries in the registry to the machine running the Locator or Name Service.

The entries are under the key `HKEY_LOCAL_MACHINE\SOFTWARE\Microsoft\Rpc\NameService` and are as follows:

```
DefaultSyntax           "3"
Endpoint                "\pipe\locator"
NetworkAddress          "\\<Machine>"
Protocol                "ncacn_np"
ServerNetworkAddress    "\\<Machine>"
```

`<Machine>` is the name of the computer the Locator is running on.

With the current version of Windows 95, you will have to use the RegEdit program to add these entries, and you might find that you need to add the `NameService` key. There might eventually be a way to do this through the control panel.

With this set up, we can make calls to the Locator using the `RpcNsXXX()` calls. These are actually RPC calls themselves! They use RPC calls to communicate with the Locator.

The following code fragments come from the RPC sample application function, `CRPCExampleView::OnRpcListservers()`, which is called from the RPC/List Servers menu item.

The process of reading servers from the name server is started by calling `RpcNsBindingImportBegin()`. This starts up a conversation with the name server. The parameter `RPC_C_NS_SYNTAX_DEFAULT` causes it to use the default syntax defined in the registry. The second parameter is null in order to pick up all the entries in the name server for this type of server. Note that this is different from the Win32 SDK example that specifies the entry string. See the discussion on exporting the server's information to the name server for an explanation of the problems that occur if all servers were to use the same entry name.

```
RPC_STATUS RPC_ENTRY    RPCStatus;
RPC_NS_HANDLE           ImportContext;
RPCStatus = RpcNsBindingImportBegin(RPC_C_NS_SYNTAX_DEFAULT,
                        0,
                        ClientIfSpec,
                        0,
                        &ImportContext);

switch ( RPCStatus )
    {
// Success
case RPC_S_OK:
    break;

// No servers there
case RPC_S_ENTRY_NOT_FOUND:
    DisplayMessage("No entries found");
    return;
```

```
default:
    DisplayMessage("RpcNsBindingImportBegin failed");
    return;
    }
```

Note that there is a separate error returned if there are no servers found in the name server's database. It is also possible to get `RPC_S_NAME_SERVICE_UNAVAILABLE`. One would hope that the computer running the Locator would stay available and that this would be a rare error!

Now we go through the entries in the name server's database using the `RpcNsBindingImportNext()` call. Each call to this will return the next entry in the list of entries for this interface. It returns `RPC_S_OK` as long as it finds entries. It is almost certain that at this point, there are entries to be found.

```
while ( RpcNsBindingImportNext(ImportContext, &RPCExHandle)
                                            == RPC_S_OK )
    {
    unsigned char    *StringBinding;
    RPCStatus = RpcBindingToStringBinding(RPCExHandle,
                                        &StringBinding);
    if ( RPCStatus != RPC_S_OK )
        {
        DisplayMessage("RpcBindingToStringBinding Failed");
        continue;
        }

    unsigned char *name;
    RpcNsBindingInqEntryName(RPCExHandle,
                        RPC_C_NS_SYNTAX_DEFAULT, &name);
    if ( RPCStatus != RPC_S_OK )
        {
        DisplayMessage("RpcNsBindingInqEntryName Failed");
        continue;
        }
```

For each server entry we find, this sample code converts the binding into a string binding using `RpcBindingToStringBinding()` and reads the entry name from the name server using `RpcNsBindingInqEntryName()`. This is merely so the sample application can display the entry name and binding. It wouldn't be necessary in a real application.

There is no guarantee that server we found in the name server database is still alive, so we make a simple remote procedure call to the server to check on its health. This could be any simple call to the server. In this example, the call merely returns the server's computer name. The name returned will match that in the entry name. If the server is no longer alive, then the `MachineName()` call will raise an exception, so an `RpcTryExcept` block is required here.

```
RpcTryExcept
    {
    DisplayMessage("About to make RPC to check server...");

    unsigned char mch[30];
    MachineName(mch);
```

```
            DisplayMessage("...success, computer name is:");
            DisplayMessage((char *)mch);
            }
        RpcExcept(1)
            {
            char buf[80];
            unsigned long ulCode = RpcExceptionCode();
            sprintf(buf, "RPC Runtime raised exception 0x%xl\r\n",
                    ulCode);
            DisplayMessage(buf);
            }
        RpcEndExcept
```

At this point, for the purposes of this example, we have finished with this server and its binding information, so we free the binding handle and string binding. A real application would probably fill in a list of available servers for the user to choose from.

```
RPCStatus = RpcBindingFree(&RPCExHandle);
if ( RPCStatus )
    {
    char buf[80];
    sprintf(buf, "RpcBindingFree returned 0x%x", RPCStatus);
    DisplayMessage(buf);
    }

RpcStringFree(&StringBinding);
```

Finally, having found all the available servers, RpcNsBindingImportDone() is used to clean up the conversation with the name service.

```
RpcNsBindingImportDone(&ImportContext);
```

Creating Windows on Behalf of an RPC Client

An RPC server cannot create a window on behalf of a client because an RPC is executed in one of a pool of threads created by the server. Once a call is completed, the thread dies. On the death of the thread, any window handle it had created becomes useless! So the following doesn't work:

```
hWnd = (HWND)RPCCall1();
...
RPCCall2(hWnd);


Server code

WORD RPCCall1()
{
...
return (DWORD)CreateWindow(...);
}
```

```
VOID RPCCall2(DWORD hWnd)
{
    HWND hWnd32 = (HWND)hWnd;
    someData = GetWindowWord(hWnd32, GWWOFFSET);
}
```

The GetWindowWord will always fail because the thread that created it has died.

Fortunately, for the case of the client and server running on the same machine, the
Microsoft RPC implementation has a method of achieving the same effect. The window is
created in the client application by means of a callback. Normally, RPC is one way: The
client makes a call to the server, then the server processes the call and returns to the client. A
callback is a call from the server to the client. Such a callback can only be made while the
server is processing a call from the client. Using a callback, the sample code becomes:

```
hWnd = (HWND)RPCCall1();
...
RPCCall2(hWnd);

DWORD RPCCallback()
{
return (DWORD)CreateWindow(...);
}


Server code

WORD RPCCall1()
{
...
return (DWORD)RPCCallback();
}

VOID RPCCall2(DWORD hWnd)
{
    HWND hWnd32 = (HWND)hWnd;
    someData = GetWindowWord(hWnd32, GWWOFFSET);
}
```

In this case, the client code calls RPCCall1(). This is turned into a call to RPCCall1() in the
server code, which eventually calls RPCCallback(). RPCCall1() returns to the client code with
an indication that it is doing a callback, not returning from the original call. The client
function RPCCallback() is called and creates the window. The window handle is eventually
passed back to the client via the server call RPCCall1(). Because this window was created in
the context of the client application, it is not affected by the death of the server thread that
executed RPCCall1(); therefore, it is still valid when RPCCall2() is called.

The preceding example is rather artificial, but it illustrates the problems associated with
RPC calls and window creation.

Summary

Remote procedure calls are very powerful tools in achieving interprocess communication between processes on the same machine and between processes on separate machines. In the case of separate machines, using the appropriate wide area network technology, the machines may be on opposite sides of the country or even opposite sides of the world!

A remote procedure call looks exactly like a call to a normal procedure, so once you get a client and server set up, it is incredibly easy to use. It is the setup of the clients and servers that is tricky, particularly finding the correct server. A service known as the Microsoft Locator (which runs under Windows NT) is used to enable clients and servers to find each other. It is a database that contains a list of servers, their bindings, and a string that the server can be identified by.

A remote procedure call can use many networking protocols—TCP/IP, NETBIOS, IPX/SPX—and all the details of data transfer across the protocol are hidden. Only the protocol sequence needs be known. Unfortunately, Windows 95 doesn't support the easiest protocol to use, named pipes, for RPC servers. Windows NT does provide named pipe server support, so it is possible to run a server on a Windows NT machine and a client on a Windows 95 machine.

Microsoft's RPC implementation can also interoperate with DCE (Distributed Computing Environment), enabling clients or servers to run under completely different operating systems. Because of this, a decision to use RPCs certainly doesn't tie a client or server to Windows 95 or Windows NT. In fact, there are client-only libraries available for DOS and Windows 3.1, so there is an incredible amount of interoperability available.

I suggest careful study of the examples in the Win32 SDK to fill in the details. I hope this introduction will answer the questions that come up when you're first using RPCs.

WinSock

34

by Lawrence Harris

IN THIS CHAPTER

Starting with Windows NT and Windows for Workgroups 3.11, Microsoft made WinSock available so that Windows applications could communicate using Transmission Control Protocol/Internet Protocol (TCP/IP). This chapter highlights some of the features of WinSock as implemented in Windows 95.

Overview

WinSock was developed by several vendors to standardize the implementation of TCP/IP in the Windows environment. Under Windows 3.1, WinSock is implemented by various vendors such as Distinct, FTP Software, and Netmanage (to name a few). Windows NT includes WinSock as part of its native operating system, while Windows for Workgroups 3.11 has WinSock as an add-on obtained directly from Microsoft (or from Microsoft Forums on CompuServe). In Windows 95, Microsoft includes WinSock as part of the native operating system, making TCP/IP communications available to all Win32-based and Win16-based applications. Before I discuss WinSock, I will give you a brief look at TCP/IP.

TCP/IP

TCP/IP refers to a network specification (or protocol) developed for the Department of Defense in the 1980s to connect (or network) the machines for various experimental research projects used by the Advanced Research Projects Agency or ARPA. TCP/IP also describes a subset of the network protocol (or TCP) for the Department of Defense.

The Internet Protocol (or IP) is a low-level protocol used to receive and transmit data. User Data Protocol (or UDP) is a layer that sits above IP and provides checksums for data packets (also known as datagrams) and port numbers. A port number is a 16-bit integer used to define a user process. UDP is typically used to broadcast data to a number of processes simultaneously when it is not important for the sending process to know whether the data has been successfully received by all the receiving processes.

Transmission Control Protocol (or TCP) is a layer that sits above IP and provides a reliable data transmission mechanism. TCP also supports checksums and port numbers. TCP is used when the sending process must know if the receiving process successfully received the data sent. Figure 34.1 shows the relationship between IP, TCP, and UDP.

An Internet address (also known as an IP address) is a 32-bit number that uniquely defines a network connection. It is possible for a computer to have multiple IP addresses. For example, if a PC has multiple network adapter cards, the PC can have multiple IP addresses. It is possible for a PC with multiple network adapter cards to have a single IP address, but only one of the network adapter cards can then be used for IP, UDP, or TCP. The other network adapter cards can be used for other network protocols (such as NetBIOS or Novell's IPX protocol). As an aside, it is also possible for a single network card to support multiple protocols and it is also possible (although difficult) for a single network card to

support multiple IP addresses. An IP address is typically represented in decimal format as
a.b.c.d (128.3.100.2, for example).

FIGURE 34.1.

*The relationship between
IP, TCP, and UDP.*

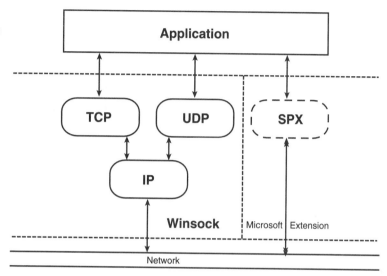

A *socket* is one half of the communication to the network. Whenever you want to communicate using TCP or UDP, your application needs to create a socket. A socket can be thought
of as a telephone, and unless there is more than one telephone on the network, your application cannot communicate. There is a special condition for a socket, however. If a PC creates
multiple sockets, it is possible for a PC to talk to itself. Many UNIX programs use this
ability for InterProcess Communication (or IPC). When a conversation occurs solely in a
single machine, the data for the conversation is transmitted via memory instead of through
the network adapter card if the IP address is the same for both sides of the conversation. If,
at a later time, the two applications are moved to two separate PCs, the applications do not
need to change. Just change the IP address used, and the conversation occurs though the
network adapter card instead of in memory.

WinSock API

The WinSock API incorporates many of the APIs to which UNIX TCP/IP programmers are
accustomed. It also includes a number of new APIs to specifically deal with the issues that
occur in the Windows environment (specifically restrictions within Windows 16, the
environment the WinSock specification originally supported). For example, in UNIX many
server applications can create a socket, and once a client application attaches to the server
application, the server application will spawn a process to handle the client application.
However, under the 16-bit versions of Windows the server application cannot spawn
another process to handle the client application because the socket handle (which is created
when the server and client connect) cannot be passed to the spawned application.

Another problem that WinSock needed to address involved issues that occurred due to blocking operations. *Blocking operations* are API calls that do not return until the requested task has been completed (or has failed). In the 16-bit versions of Windows a blocking operation could cause the PC application to stop responding during the execution of the API. The user cannot move any of the windows in the blocked application. Also, under Windows 3.1 or Windows for Workgroups 3.11 it is also possible that the PC will not be usable during the blocked operation.

WinSock supports a series of APIs whose prefix is WSA (which stands for WinSock Asynchronous). The WSA APIs solve the problems caused by using blocking sockets because the WSA APIs are asynchronous. This means that when you call a WSA API, the API returns immediately. Once the asynchronous call has completed, a message will be posted to your application's message queue to inform your application of the completion of the API.

I will now provide a quick look at the WinSock API. This is not a complete description of WinSock (or TCP/IP), but rather some of the highlights of WinSock. But, before I dive into the WinSock API, a brief discussion of the class library is in order.

The examples in this chapter use the CWinSock class library (the source is included with this book). The CWinSock class library is a very thin envelope around the WinSock API. In fact, most of the CWinSock member functions simply call the equivalent WinSock API. The best time to use the CWinSock class library over the native WinSock API is when your application is compiled with debugging mode enabled. The CWinSock class library contains a number of macros and APIs to help you debug your WinSock application. In addition, the CWinSock class library checks the error condition returned by every WinSock API and reports any errors found.

The CWinSock class library also contains member functions that make WinSock a little easier to use. For example, many of the WinSock APIs require a socket as one of the parameters to the API. CWinSock defaults to an internally stored and maintained socket (m_sockCurrentSocket) that can be used if a socket is not provided in the API. In addition, CWinSock has default parameters used when formal parameters are not present. The default parameters typically handle most cases for a particular API, making your application a little easier to program. Finally, CWinSock has a member function, called StringError, that converts the current WinSock error into a string (WinSock returns an error number).

Initialization of WinSock

Programs initialize WinSock by calling WSAStartup. If you are creating a socket in a thread, the thread also needs to initialize WinSock. Listing 34.1 shows the constructor for the CWinSock class library that calls WSAStartup.

Listing 34.1. The CWinSock constructor.

```
//CWinSock Constructor
//Initializes WinSock
//Your application should check m_eCurrentSocketState
//If m_eCurrentSocketState == eSocketUninitialized then WinSock
//                could not be initialized
//                           == eWSStarted then WinSock was started
//                but does not support the requested version
//                           == eWSInitialized then all is well
//
//If you compile with WS_USE_ REGISTERED_MSGS then the
//constructor will also register
//the window messages, otherwise the constants in csock.h will be used
//
CWinSock::CWinSock(UINT uMajorVersion, UINT uMinorVersion)
{
      WORD    wVersionRequested;
      int     err;

   //Since we currently have no socket, mark the CurrentSocket as Invalid
   //and the current state as Uninitialized
   m_sockCurrentSocket = INVALID_SOCKET;
   m_eCurrentSocketState = eSocketUninitialized;

   //When asked to create a socket we will default to AF_INET for the family
   //and INADDR_ANY for the address
   m_SockAddrIn.sin_family = AF_INET;
   m_SockAddrIn.sin_addr.s_addr = INADDR_ANY;

   #ifdef WS_USE_REGISTERED_MSGS
   //If we wanted to used Registered Windows messages instead of constants
   //we would add the code here
   if (m_bRegisteredWinSockMsgs == FALSE){
      m_uWSA_READ    = RegisterWindowMessage("WSA_READ");
      m_uWSA_WRITE   = RegisterWindowMessage("WSA_WRITE");
      m_uWSA_ACCEPT  = RegisterWindowMessage("WSA_ACCEPT");
      m_uWSA_CONNECT = RegisterWindowMessage("WSA_CONNECT");
      m_uWSA_CLOSE   = RegisterWindowMessage("WSA_CLOSE");
      m_uWSA_OOB     = RegisterWindowMessage("WSA_OOB");
      m_bRegisteredWinSockMsgs = TRUE;
   }
   #endif

      wVersionRequested = MAKEWORD(uMajorVersion,uMinorVersion);

   err = WSAStartup(wVersionRequested, &m_wsaData);
   if (err != 0){
      PrintError();
      return;
   }

   //Although we don't know if we can use this version yet,
   //set m_eCurrentSocketState to eWSStarted so that our destructor will
   //call WSACleanup

   m_eCurrentSocketState = eWSStarted;
```

continues

Listing 34.1. continued

```
//LoByte is the Major version number and the HiByte is the minor
if (LOBYTE(m_wsaData.wVersion) != uMajorVersion ||
    HIBYTE(m_wsaData.wVersion) != uMinorVersion){
    return;
}

if (LOBYTE(wVersionRequested) < uMajorVersion ||
    (LOBYTE(wVersionRequested) == uMajorVersion &&
    HIBYTE(wVersionRequested) < uMinorVersion)){
    return;
}
m_wsaData.wVersion = MAKEWORD(uMajorVersion,uMinorVersion);
    m_wsaData.wHighVersion = MAKEWORD(uMajorVersion,uMinorVersion);

    m_eCurrentSocketState = eWSInitialized;

    m_ulCWinSockInitialized++;
}
```

WSAStartup returns the structure of WSADATA, stored in CWinSock in m_wsaData. Listing 34.2 shows the definition of the WSADATA structure in WINSOCK.H.

Listing 34.2. The WSADATA structure in WINSOCK.H.

```
typedef struct WSAData {
        WORD                    wVersion;
        WORD                    wHighVersion;
        char                    szDescription[WSADESCRIPTION_LEN+1];
        char                    szSystemStatus[WSASYS_STATUS_LEN+1];
        unsigned short          iMaxSockets;
        unsigned short          iMaxUdpDg;
        char FAR *              lpVendorInfo;
} WSADATA;
```

In addition to version number information, WSADATA returns szDescription, which contains vendor information. szSystemStatus contains vendor-specific system status information. iMaxSockets indicates the maximum number of sockets a process may open. iMaxUdpDg contains the maximum size of the datagram received or sent. lpVendorInfo is a pointer to a vendor-specific data structure, which may contain additional vendor specific information. When using WinSock Version 1.1, szDescription, szSystemStatus, iMaxSockets, iMaxUdpDg, and lpVendorInfo should be used with care, if used at all. WinSock Version 2.0 will change the way this information is obtained. The section titled "The Future of WinSock" highlights some of the changes expected in WinSock Version 2.0. Table 34.1 shows the values for WSADATA in Windows 95.

Table 34.1. WSADATA **fields and values in Windows 95.**

Field	Value in Windows 95
szDescription	Microsoft Windows Sockets Version 1.1.
szSystemStatus	Running Windows 95
iMaxSockets	256
iMaxUdpDg	65467
lpVendorInfo	? (value is unknown)

Although Windows 95 returns 256 for iMaxSockets (the maximum number of sockets opened by a process), this does not mean an application can actually open 256 sockets. In fact, to open more than 64 sockets, you must recompile your application with FD_SETSIZE set to the number of sockets your application requires. FD_SETSIZE is defined to default to 64.

Termination of WinSock

When an application has finished with WinSock, the application must call WSACleanup. In fact, WSACleanup must be called for every successful call to WSAStartup. In the CWinSock class library, WSACleanup is automatically called by the CWinSock destructor (see Listing 34.3).

Listing 34.3. The CWinSock **destructor.**

```
//CWinSock destructor
//Closes the socket if the socket is open
//Calls WSACleanup if WinSock was successfully started
//
CWinSock::~CWinSock()
{
    //Close the socket if it's open
    if (m_eCurrentSocketState == eSocketOpened)
        closesocket();

    //If WinSock was initialized we need to call WSACleanup
    if (m_eCurrentSocketState != eSocketUninitialized)
        WSACleanup();

    //Decrement our counter
    if (m_ulCWinSockInitialized > 0)
        m_ulCWinSockInitialized—;
}
```

When the destructor for CWinSock is called, the state of the object is first determined by examining m_eCurrentSocketState. If the current state is eSocketOpened (meaning a socket is currently opened), the socket is closed by calling the WinSock API closesocket (see the section "Terminating a Conversation"). If the object was successfully initialized and WSAStartup was successfully called, then the value for m_eCurrentSocketState is something other than eSocketUninitialized. If the state is not uninitialized, then WSACleanup is called.

Creating a Socket

To create a socket (client-side and server-side sockets are created the same way), you simply call socket(AF_INET, SOCK_STREAM, INADDR_ANY). In some WinSock documentation you might see the socket call as socket(PF_INET,SOCK_STREAM,0). In WINSOCK.H (the include file for WinSock), PF_INET is defined as AF_INET, and INADDR_ANY is defined as 0; therefore, the two socket calls are equivalent. Listing 34.4 shows the implementation of CWinSock::socket.

Listing 34.4. CWinSock socket implementation.

```
SOCKET CWinSock::socket(int af, int type, int protocol)
{
#ifdef _WS_VERBOSE_API
            WS_TRACE0("CWinSock::socket\n");
#endif
            SOCKET sock = ::socket(af,type,protocol);
            m_iLastError = ::GetLastError();
            if (sock == INVALID_SOCKET){
                    WS_TRACE0("socket error:");
                    PrintError(m_iLastError);
            } else {
                    m_sockCurrentSocket = sock;
                    m_eCurrentSocketState = eSocketOpened;
            }
            return sock;
}
```

The first parameter to the socket API is the address family, AF_INET, or Address Family InterNET for TCP/IP. The Windows 95 and Windows NT implementations also support AF_IPX, used for SPX support.

The second parameter to the socket API is the socket type. The socket type can be SOCK_STREAM (for TCP), SOCK_DGRAM (for UDP), or SOCK_SEQPACKET (for SPX).

The third parameter to the socket API is the protocol family. The protocol family can be 0 or INADDR_ANY; both mean the protocol family is determined by the address family (the first parameter). If the protocol family is not 0 or INADDR_ANY, then it must be either IP_PROTOTCP for TCP/IP or NS_PROTOSPX for SPX. The protocol family and address family parameters must be consistent; you cannot select NS_PROTOSPX for the protocol family (which is for SPX) and AF_INET for the address family (which is for TCP/IP). At the current time there isn't a reason why the protocol family should be set to any value other than INADDR_ANY.

Establishing a Conversation

Over the past few years you might have heard the term *client-server*. A client is an application that needs information and a server is an application that provides information (to the client). WinSock has a similar concept in which a client is an application that requests to establish a conversation (with a server), and a server is an application waiting to establish a conversation. It is extremely important to understand that the client-server relationship in WinSock only affects how a conversation is established. Once the conversation is established, there is no difference between the client and the server at the TCP/IP level.

It is also important to remember that the client-server relationship is at the socket level. For example, an application can establish a conversation and the same application can also listen for a conversation. In fact, the client and the server can be in the same application (although it would be a bit strange for an application to communicate with itself using sockets).

Listening for a Connection

As I have just discussed, in a client-server relationship a client tries to establish a connection with a server. In order for a client to establish a connection with a server, the server must be willing to accept the connection. Before the server can listen for a connection, the server needs to bind to a socket. *Binding* is the process in which a socket is assigned to an address/port. This is accomplished with the bind API. The socket created in Listing 34.4 (using socket) does not have an address/port number associated with it. Listing 34.5 shows a sample implementation of the bind API. The bind API requires three parameters: the socket to use, the address/port to use, and the size of structure used to pass the address/port information.

Listing 34.5. A sample implementation of the bind API for CWinSock.

```
int CWinSock::bind(SOCKET s, const struct sockaddr FAR *name, int namelen)
{
#ifdef _WS_VERBOSE_API
            WS_TRACE0("CWinSock::bind\n");
#endif
            int iBind = ::bind(s, name, namelen);
            m_iLastError = ::GetLastError();
            if (iBind == SOCKET_ERROR){
                WS_TRACE0("bind error:");
                PrintError(m_iLastError);
            }
            return iBind;
}
```

> **TIP**
>
> getsockname can be used to find what address/port has been assigned to a socket. When calling getsockname(struct sockaddr *sa, int *size_sa), make sure you initialize size_sa to the size of (sockaddr) or else you will receive an error indicating that there is a parameter error.

In Listing 34.5 the address/port information is passed in a structure of type sockaddr. It is possible to bind a socket without specifying either an address or a port number, or both, but typically you will want to bind to a specific address and port number.

After you have bound your socket to a specific address and port number, your server is ready to listen for a connection. The code fragment in Listing 34.6 shows how to listen for a connection.

Listing 34.6. Code fragment used to listen for a connection.

```
        m_local_sin.sin_family = AF_INET;
        PHOSTENT phe;

        if (strServer == NULL){
                DWORD  dwSize;
                char   szBuff[128];

                dwSize = sizeof(szBuff);
                gethostname(szBuff, dwSize);
                phe = gethostbyname(szBuff);
        } else {
                phe = gethostbyname(strServer);
        }

        if (phe == NULL){
                WS_TRACE0("WaitForClient: GetHostByName Error-");
                PrintError();
                return;
        }
memcpy((char FAR*)&m_local_sin.sin_addr,phe->h_addr,phe->h_length);
        m_local_sin.sin_port = htons(usPortNo);

        int err = bind((struct sockaddr FAR*)&m_local_sin, sizeof(m_local_sin));
        if (err == SOCKET_ERROR){
                WS_TRACE0("WaitForClient: Bind error-");
                PrintError();
                return;
        }

    int SetOpVal = 1;
    setsockopt(SOL_SOCKET, SO_DONTLINGER,&SetOpVal,sizeof(SetOpVal));
    setsockopt(SOL_SOCKET, SO_KEEPALIVE, &SetOpVal, sizeof(SetOpVal));

    #ifdef _WS_VERBOSE
        WS_TRACE0("WaitForClient: About to listen\n");
```

```
#endif

err = listen(GetMaxSockets());
if (err < 0){
    WS_TRACE0("WaitForClient: Listen error- ");
    PrintError();
    return;
}
```

Listing 34.6 first shows how to bind a socket to a particular address/port number. The code attempts to obtain the name of the server passed in strServer, or it obtains the name of the current machine if strServer is NULL. Once a name has been determined, the code attempts to convert the name into an address by calling gethostbyname. If gethostbyname is successful, then the code assigns the newly discovered address and the requested port number to the socket and binds the socket to this address. Finally, listen is called so that the server can listen for connection requests from client applications. Currently in Windows 95, a socket can queue up to five requests for a connection to a particular socket from client applications.

Blocking Acceptance of a Connection

Calling listen on a socket does not fully establish a conversation between a client and server; the server still has additional work to perform before a conversation can be started. If a server application is ready to establish a conversation on a listening socket, the server application needs to perform an accept API when a client connection request arrives. In WinSock there are two ways a server can *accept* a client connection: using a blocking call or using a nonblocking call.

A *blocking call* is a call that does not return until it has completed. Under the 16-bit implementation of WinSock, blocking calls put the current process to sleep until the blocking operation (also known as a synchronous operation) has completed. This can cause a number of problems, including Windows locking up completely. The problem is that the blocking operation causes the process to sleep until the blocking operation has completed. Because the process is asleep, it is no longer processing its message queue. If a message arrives for the sleeping application, it is not processed until the application resumes processing. Here is a simple example.

Assume that you have two applications on the same PC: a server that wants to receive data, and a client that wants to send data. A server may issue a blocking receive, and the server application will go to sleep until the client sends the server some data. If the client immediately sends the data, all is well. The server will wake up and process the data. The problem occurs if the server receives a window message after issuing the receive, and the client application needs to process a window message before it can send data to the server. When this happens, under the 16-bit implementation of Windows, the window message for the server is in front of the message queue. The client application cannot receive its window message until after the server processes its window message, and the server cannot process its window message until the client sends the data. This is a deadlock situation.

Under the 32-bit implementation of Windows, blocking sockets are less of an issue for a number of reasons. First, under the 32-bit implementation of Windows, a blocking operation only places the thread that issued the blocking operation to sleep. Second, under the 32-bit implementation of Windows, each process (application) has its own message queue; therefore, the example indicated in the previous paragraph can never occur.

If blocking sockets are such a problem, why use them at all? The answer is simple: Blocking sockets are typically easier to code than nonblocking sockets. Nonblocking sockets require an application to take extra care when a block of memory is given to WinSock. For example, when you are sending data on a blocking socket, you can delete or change the data immediately after the send API returns, because WinSock has already sent the data. On a nonblocking socket, you cannot delete or change the data until the send operation completes. The send operation is not considered complete until you receive notification from WinSock that the operation is complete (not when the send API returns). This requires your application to perform data management. For applications that perform multiple operations that could block, this additional management can cause significant coding.

Listing 34.7 shows a sample blocking implementation of the accept API. The accept API requires three parameters: the socket to use (the socket used in the sample bind operation), an address (used to return the address information of the client), and the size of the address structure.

Listing 34.7. A sample implementation of the accept API for CWinSock.

```
SOCKET    CWinSock::accept(SOCKET s, struct sockaddr FAR *addr, int FAR *addrlen)
{
#ifdef _WS_VERBOSE_API
      WS_TRACE0("CWinSock::accept\n");
#endif
      SOCKET    sockRet = ::accept(s, addr,addrlen);
      m_iLastError = ::GetLastError();
      if (sockRet == INVALID_SOCKET){
          WS_TRACE0("accept error:");
          PrintError(m_iLastError);
      }
      return sockRet;
}
```

Nonblocking Acceptance of a Connection

Although accept can be used in blocking mode, Microsoft recommends that applications perform nonblocking operations whenever possible. Listing 34.8 shows a sample nonblocking implementation of accept.

Listing 34.8. Code fragment for a nonblocking accept API.

```
if (IsWindow(m_hWndServer))
    WSAAsyncSelect(m_hWndServer, WSA_EVENT, FD_ACCEPT);
```

As you can see from Listing 34.8, the non-blocking form of accept calls WSAAsyncSelect, and passes it a window handle, a window notification message, and FD_ACCEPT, indicating that notification is to be given when a client is trying to connect with the server. When a client attempts to connect with the server, WinSock will issue a window message (in this example, Windows will send a WSA_EVENT) to the window indicated in WSAAsyncSelect. Once the window receives notification, the accept API is called. The accept API will not block because a connection request is waiting for it.

Blocking Connection to a Server

When a client wishes to establish a connection with a server, the client uses the connect API. The connect API is similar to the bind API that a server uses, except in connect, the client indicates the desired address and port number used to establish a conversation. Listing 34.9 shows the code fragment for the blocking version of the connect API.

Listing 34.9. Code fragment for a blocking connection.

```
dest_sin.sin_family = AF_INET;

PHOSTENT phe;

if (strServerName == NULL){
    DWORD     dwSize;
    char      szBuff[128];

        dwSize = sizeof(szBuff);
        gethostname(szBuff, dwSize);

        phe = gethostbyname(szBuff);
} else {
    phe = gethostbyname(strServerName);
}

if (phe == NULL){
        WS_TRACE0("ConnectToServer: GetHostByName error-");
    PrintError();
        return;
}

memcpy((char FAR*)&(dest_sin.sin_addr), phe->h_addr,phe->h_length);
dest_sin.sin_port = htons(usPortNo);
//or
//PSERVENT pse = getservrbyname(szBuff,"tcp");
//if (pse == NULL)
// return;
```

continues

Listing 34.9. continued

```
//dest_sin.sin_port = pse->s_port;

int SetOpVal = 1;
setsockopt(SOL_SOCKET, SO_DONTLINGER,&SetOpVal,sizeof(SetOpVal));
setsockopt(SOL_SOCKET, SO_KEEPALIVE, &SetOpVal,sizeof(SetOpVal));

int err = connect((PSOCKADDR)&dest_sin, sizeof(dest_sin));
if (err < 0){
        WS_TRACE0("ConnectToServer: connect error-");
     PrintError();
     return;
}
```

Listing 34.9 shows how to call connect with the address and port number of the server application. The code attempts to obtain the name of the server that is passed in strServerName; otherwise, it obtains the name of the current machine if strServerName is NULL. Once a name has been determined, the code will attempt to convert the name into an address by calling gethostbyname. If gethostbyname is successful, then the code assigns the newly discovered address and the requested port number to the socket that uses the information to establish a connection. The connect API does not return until either a connection is established or an error occurs.

Nonblocking Connection to a Server

On a server, when performing a nonblocking accept, you call WSAAsyncSelect. When you receive notification that a client is trying to establish a connection, you call accept. The nonblocking connect API does not work in a similar manner. To use the nonblocking version of connect, you call WSAAsyncSelect using FD_CONNECT (instead of FD_ACCEPT) as shown in Listing 34.10. Once WSAAsyncSelect is called, you then use the connect code from Listing 34.9. Once the connection has been established or an error occurs, you receive notification.

Remember, unlike the accept API, the connect API sends you notification when the connect operation has completed, whereas the accept API sends you notification when an accept operation can be performed without blocking.

Listing 34.10. Code fragment for a nonblocking connection.

```
if (IsWindow(m_hWndServer))
    WSAAsyncSelect(m_hWndServer, WSA_EVENT, FD_CONNECT);
```

In the next section you will see other flags that can be used in WSAAsyncSelect besides FD_CONNECT and FD_ACCEPT. You need to be aware that each time you call WSAAsyncSelect, you only receive notification based on the current WSAAsyncSelect flags. Thus, if you call

WSAAsyncSelect first with FD_ACCEPT and then immediately by FD_CONNECT, the only notification you will receive is FD_CONNECT. In the sample code included with the book, you will see that the client application calls WSAAsyncSelect with FD_CONNECT ¦ FD_READ ¦ FD_WRITE ¦ FD_CLOSE. This is done during the connect processing so that the application can receive all notifications once a connection is established.

Transferring Data

Once the server and client applications have established a conversation, they can send and receive data. In the following sections you will see how data is sent and received using WinSock.

Sending Data

When the client application or the server application wishes to make data available to the other side, the data provider uses the send API to send the data to the data consumer (the recipient of the data). As with many of the WinSock APIs, the send API can either be a blocking call or a nonblocking call, depending on whether WSAAsyncSelect was previously called with the FD_WRITE flag. When discussing the connect API, I mentioned that I typically call WSAAsyncSelect with FD_CONNECT ¦ FD_READ ¦ FD_WRITE ¦ FD_CLOSE. Once a connection has been completed, the application that issued WSAAsyncSelect with the flags is immediately notified that a send can be performed (FD_WRITE notification is received). The FD_WRITE notification tells an application that it can issue send. An application can continue to issue send APIs until a send API returns WSAEWOULDBLOCK. This indicates that the last send was not performed because it would cause the application (or thread) to block. Once the system is available again, the application receives FD_WRITE notification. Notice that you do not necessarily receive an FD_WRITE for every send you issue. You only receive FD_WRITE notification when you first connect and after every send call that could block the system. Listing 34.11 shows the CWinSock implementation of the send API.

Listing 34.11. The CWinSock implementation of the send API.

```
int CWinSock::send(SOCKET s, LPCSTR buf, int len, int flags)
{
#ifdef _WS_VERBOSE_API
        WS_TRACE0("CWinSock::send\n");
#endif
        int isend = ::send(s,buf,len,flags);
        m_iLastError = ::GetLastError();
        if (isend == SOCKET_ERROR){
            WS_TRACE0("send error:");
            PrintError(m_iLastError);
        }
        return isend;
}
```

In Listing 34.11 you can see that the send API takes four parameters. The first parameter is the socket used to send the data. The socket must be a previously bound and connected socket; otherwise, send will return the error WSAEINVAL, which indicates that the socket is not yet bound. It is also possible to receive a number of different errors such as WSAENOTSOCK, which indicates that the socket parameter indicates memory that is not a socket, or WSAENOTCONN, which indicates that the socket is not connected.

The second parameter of the send API is a pointer to the data you want to send. Although it is beyond the scope of this chapter to go into them in depth, there are a few issues you need to be aware of concerning the data you send. When you send data using TCP/IP, the data is delivered to the data consumer in the same format provided by the data provider. Although this might not sound like a big deal, it can cause you a lot of grief if you don't understand the implications.

Thirty-two–bit applications under Windows 95 (and Windows NT) use four-byte integers, and 16-bit applications use two-byte integers. Thus, if your 16-bit application sends an integer and a 32-bit application expects an integer, the two applications need to decide at application design time how big an integer is to be. Typically, the two applications may instead decide to send either a WORD, which is 2 bytes under both platforms, or a DWORD, which is 4 bytes, to avoid this problem. In addition, suppose that one application is running on one PC while the second application is running on a different PC. If the two computers use the same CPU type (for example, both computers use Intel-based CPUs), the data is internally represented in the same format.

When creating an application that uses the WinSock send API, you should be aware that send only returns an error if the data cannot reach the TCP/IP layer of the data consumer application. The application that issues the send is not notified when the data consumer receives the data. Thus, unless your application implements it own application-level protocol, the data provider only knows that the data sent has been successfully delivered to the TCP/IP layer of the data consumer. The data provider doesn't know when the data consumer reads the data from the TCP/IP buffer.

Although I discuss the receive API in the next section, you need to be aware that the data sent is not delimited; in other words, if the data provider issues a send of five bytes of data and then issues a send of ten bytes of data, the data consumer sees fifteen bytes of data. The data consumer is not made aware (from TCP/IP) that the data was sent as five bytes and ten bytes. If your application requires the data consumer to be message oriented, then your application will need to implement an application-level protocol.

Blocking and Nonblocking Calls

When a socket is created, the socket is created as a blocking socket. A blocking socket will not return control to the current process in the 16-bit implementation of Windows and in Win32s, or to the current thread in the 32-bit implementation of Windows until the requested command is completed or returns an error. In WinSock there are two ways to make a blocking socket into a nonblocking socket: using WSAAsyncSelect or using ioctlsocket. I have previously discussed using WSAAsyncSelect for nonblocking operations. WSAAsyncSelect automatically makes a blocking socket into a nonblocking socket for all operations; in other words, when WSAAsyncSelect is issued using FD_CONNECT in our sample application, the socket is made into a nonblocking socket for all operations, but the sample application will only receive notification on a connect.

In WinSock, ioctlsocket(socket, FIONBIO, &x) can be used to make a socket blocking or nonblocking. If x (which is an unsigned long) is a nonzero value, then the socket is made a nonblocking socket; if x is zero, then the socket is made a blocking socket if the socket was previously made nonblocking using ioctlsocket. If a socket was previously made nonblocking using WSAAsyncSelect, then you must call WSAAsyncSelect(socket, hWnd, 0,0) first, and then you call ioctlsocket to make the socket blocking.

In general, if you are converting a UNIX application into a Windows application, your UNIX application might call ioctl to make a socket into a nonblocking socket. When the application is converted to WinSock, you need to change ioctl to ioctlsocket. If you are writing a new application or want to receive notification of events in an application you have converted, you should use WSAAsyncSelect. In the section titled "WinSock for UNIX Programmers," I go over additional issues concerning the UNIX environment.

Receiving Data

When a data provider sends data to the data consumer, the consumer needs to receive the data. The data consumer uses the recv API to receive data from the data provider. The data consumer doesn't need to issue a recv API before the data provider sends the data, and any data that a provider sends will be buffered by TCP/IP until the data consumer takes the data. The amount of data buffered by TCP/IP is typically between 4 KB and 16 KB, depending on the WinSock implementation. When a data consumer issues a recv API, the data in the TCP/IP buffer will be transferred to the area indicated in the recv API call. If no data is available, the recv API will either not return until data is available (if the socket is a blocking socket) or will return WSAEWOULDBLOCK, indicating that the call will block. Listing 34.12 shows the CWinSock class library wrapper to the recv API.

Listing 34.12. The CWinSock implementation of the recv API.

```
int CWinSock::recv(SOCKET s, LPTSTR buf, int len, int flags)
{
#ifdef _WS_VERBOSE_API
        WS_TRACE0("CWinSock::recv\n");
#endif
        int irecv = ::recv(s,buf,len,flags);
        m_iLastError = ::GetLastError();
```

continues

Listing 34.12. continued

```
        if (irecv == SOCKET_ERROR){
            WS_TRACE0("recv error:");
            PrintError(m_iLastError);
        }
        return irecv;
}
```

The recv API has four parameters. The first parameter is the socket from which the data is retrieved, the second parameter is the area in which the data is placed, and the third parameter is the size of the data area. The final parameter is a flag. The flag can be 0, MSG_PEEK, or MSG_OOB. MSG_PEEK | MSG_OOB is also valid. MSG_PEEK means that the data should be copied to the data area provided by the recv API, but the data should not be removed from the TCP/IP; thus, the next recv call will retrieve the same data. MSG_OOB is used to retrieve out-of-band data. Briefly, when a data provider sends data to a data consumer, the data consumer receives the data in the same order the data provider sends the data. If the data provider has data for the data consumer to see immediately (regardless of whether the data consumer still has data in the TCP/IP buffer to process), the data provider can mark the data as out-of-band data.

Terminating a Conversation

When the data consumer or the data provider no longer wishes to maintain a conversation, either side (the consumer or provider) can call closesocket to terminate the conversation. closesocket releases any data, resources, and queues maintained by the socket; thus, when closesocket completes, any data remaining in the socket might be lost. Listing 34.13 is the implementation of CWinSock::closesocket.

Listing 34.13. The CWinSock implementation of the closesocket API.

```
int CWinSock::closesocket(SOCKET s)
{
#ifdef _WS_VERBOSE_API
        WS_TRACE0("CWinSock::closesocket\n");
#endif
        int iclose = ::closesocket(s);
        m_iLastError = ::GetLastError();
        if (iclose == SOCKET_ERROR){
            WS_TRACE0("closesocket error:");
            PrintError(m_iLastError);
        } else {
            m_eCurrentSocketState = eSocketClosed;
        }
        return iclose;
}
```

When a socket should no longer allow sends or receives (or both), an application can call the shutdown API. The shutdown API differs from the closesocket API in that the socket is still a valid socket; however, the socket no longer allows sends or receives (or both). Listing 34.14 shows the CWinSock class library wrapper for the shutdown API.

Listing 34.14. The CWinSock implementation of the shutdown API.

```
int CWinSock::shutdown(SOCKET s, int how)
{
#ifdef _WS_VERBOSE_API
        WS_TRACE0("CWinSock::shutdown\n");
#endif
        int ishutdown = ::shutdown(s,how);
        m_iLastError = ::GetLastError();
        if (ishutdown == SOCKET_ERROR){
            WS_TRACE0("shutdown error:");
            PrintError(m_iLastError);
        } else {
            m_eCurrentSocketState = eSocketClosed;
        }
        return ishutdown;
}
```

The shutdown API requires two parameters: the socket affected and a flag to indicate the operation or operations no longer permitted on the socket. If the flag is set to 0, then receives are no longer permitted on the socket. 1 indicates that sends are no longer permitted, and 2 indicates that both sends and receives are no longer allowed. Once you use the shutdown API to stop sends or receives (or both) on a socket, the operation cannot be reversed. In other words, to re-enable sends after you have shut them down on a socket, you must call closesocket to close the socket and then re-establish the connection.

WinSock Used for Interprocess Communications

Under Windows NT, applications can create named-pipes for transferring data between applications. Windows 95 has support for named-pipes; however, Windows 95 applications can only be a client application, and Windows 95 applications cannot create a named-pipe. When an application needs to transfer data between applications in a Windows 95 environment, you might want to consider using WinSock. WinSock supports many of the concepts supported by named-pipes, but WinSock does not support any of the security features of named-pipes. In WinSock, if you require that only certain applications (or users) have access to a server WinSock application, you need to program the security you require into the client and server applications.

Windows 95 Implementation of WinSock

The Windows 95 implementation of WinSock has the following features that are not part of the WinSock specification:

- WSOCK32.DLL is the 32-bit implementation, and WINSOCK.DLL is the 16-bit implementation.
- SPX is supported as a transport in addition to TCP/IP.
- MSG_PARTIAL is used as support for sending partial messages.
- WSARecvEx is the recv API used to receive partial messages.

WinSock for Windows 3.1 Programmers

If you are currently using WinSock under Windows 3.1 or Windows 3.11, you need to be aware of several potential differences in the Windows 95 implementation of WinSock. Here is a list of specific items:

- The 16-bit version of the WinSock DLL is called WINSOCK.DLL, and the 32-bit version is called WSOCK32.DLL.
- When compiling your application, 16-bit applications must use the WINSOCK.LIB library, and 32-bit applications must use WSOCK32.LIB.
- Because Windows 3.1 does not support multithreaded applications, your application cannot use threads to prevent the blocking issues.
- Although Windows 95 and Windows NT support multithreaded applications, Win32s does not. Therefore, you might want to make your application use nonblocking calls to ensure compatibility in all the 32-bit environments.
- WSARecvEx is not available under Windows 3.1 and Win32s.
- SPX support is not available under Windows 3.1.
- Because Microsoft did not provide WinSock under Windows 3.1 (although they did provide a version for Windows for Workgroups 3.11), you should check with your WinSock vendor for any other differences in the implementations of WinSock.

WinSock for UNIX Programmers

Although WinSock is similar to the Berkeley sockets used in UNIX, you need to be aware of several issues and differences. Here is a list of specific items:

- When using the 16-bit implementation of WinSock, you should use blocking sockets with care. When a socket is blocked, it is possible that no other processing will occur on the PC in Windows for Workgroups 3.11. Under Windows 95 the blocking socket can prevent other 16-bit and 32-bit applications from running.

- Many UNIX programmers are accustomed to spawning a new process to handle multiple sockets. Under Windows 95 and Windows NT you should consider creating threads instead of processes. The creation of threads typically takes less CPU overhead than the creation of processes.

- When using the 32-bit version of WinSock, you should decide if your application should run under Win32s (32-bit applications can run under Windows 3.1 using Win32s). If your application can run under Win32s, then you cannot use threads.

- Many UNIX programmers are accustomed to using the C library functions, such as read and write, to communicate with a socket. This is supported under the 32-bit version of WinSock but might not be portable to other implementations of WinSock (from other vendors) or other compilers (besides Microsoft).

- UNIX applications that use the select API need to be changed because the information used by the select API is no longer stored in a bitmask under WinSock.

- Applications that use errno to determine errors under UNIX need to use WSAGetLastError under WinSock. In addition, although the UNIX error codes are valid under WinSock, the WinSock standards recommend you use the WinSock error codes instead (the WinSock error codes are prefixed with WSA).

- UNIX applications use close to close sockets. The equivalent function under WinSock is closesocket.

- UNIX applications use ioctl to change or obtain low-level socket information. The equivalent function under WinSock is ioctlsocket.

- WinSock applications need to call WSAStartup to initialize WinSock and WSACleanup to terminate WinSock (in an application, process, or thread). There are no equivalent requirements under UNIX.

The Future of WinSock

Sometime during 1995 or early 1996, WinSock 2.0 will be made available. WinSock 2.0 will have a number of enhancements over WinSock 1.1. Therefore, you might want to consider some the changes in your current design.

In WinSock 1.1, the vendor that supplied the WinSock DLL was also responsible for providing the implementation of TCP/IP. In Windows 95 and Windows NT, Microsoft provides the WinSock DLL and TCP/IP implementation. FTP, Netmanage, Distinct, Microsoft, and others provide the WinSock DLL and TCP/IP implementation under the 16-bit version of Windows. Under WinSock 2.0, the vendor that provides the WinSock DLL will not necessarily be the same vendor to supply the TCP/IP implementation. In fact, WinSock 2.0 was changed so that one vendor (most probably Microsoft under Windows 95 and Windows NT) would supply the WinSock DLL, and other vendors could provide the transport (see Figure 34.2). The *transport* is the communications layer, such as TCP/IP or SPX (Novell). WinSock 2.0 will be able to support multiple transports. A PC application will be able to enumerate the transports available on a particular PC and determine which transport to use.

FIGURE 34.2.

A WinSock 2.0 overview.

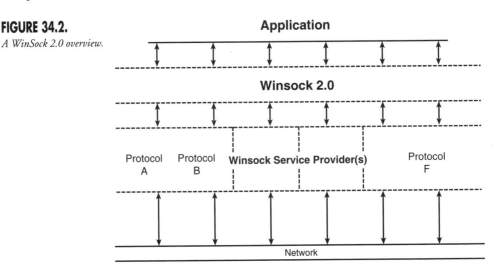

WinSock 2.0 has a number of new APIs that make using WinSock easier. For example, WinSock 2.0 has two new functions: WSASend and WSARecv. These functions are similar to send and recv in WinSock 1.1. The major difference is that WSASend and WSARecv do not return immediately. Once the requested operations are completed, WSASend and WSARecv call a user-specified routine to indicate that the requested task has been done.

You can get the latest version of the WinSock specification from sunsite.unc.edu/winsock/winsock-2.0 on the Internet.

Summary

WinSock provides Windows applications a common API to communicate using TCP/IP, in addition to other supported network protocols. WinSock makes it possible to port UNIX applications that use TCP/IP, although some changes will be required in the ported application. WinSock also provides to Windows applications a simple method to perform interprocess communication in addition to providing communications between machines.

Microsoft Exchange
for the Programmer

IN THIS CHAPTER

Since the introduction of Microsoft Windows for Workgroups Version 3.10 in 1992, every new Microsoft operating system has included a workgroup version of Microsoft Mail. This decision has helped make Microsoft Mail the most popular LAN e-mail system, with over five million users to date.

As time progressed, Microsoft became increasingly aware of the need for a true client-server mail system to serve the needs of the enterprise. The design and function of the full product, Exchange Server (as yet to be released), is beyond the scope of this book. However, Microsoft's decision to include Exchange Client software in Windows 95 in place of MS Mail makes Exchange Server a subject that every Windows 95 programmer needs to know.

This chapter covers the following topics:

- Microsoft Exchange Client
- Exchange and online services
- Microsoft Fax
- Microsoft Exchange in an MS Mail environment
- Microsoft Exchange Server

Whither Messaging...

Most programmers are familiar with the traditional role of messaging—electronic mail. However, messaging has moved far beyond mere e-mail: Messaging now plays the role of "real enough time" network transport, moving information packets from a program running on one computer to a remote computer in a very cost-efficient manner.

Messaging forms the heart of *workgroup computing*—a form of computing in which the emphasis is on many people working together. Workgroup functionality can be as simple as making it possible for a user to send a document to someone else, or as complex as making it possible for an application to collect data on multiple computers and then send the data to an aggregator application on another computer, which processes the data and sends reports to the appropriate people.

What Is Microsoft Exchange?

Microsoft Exchange is several things, depending on who you are. To the end user, Exchange is the Inbox on the Windows 95 desktop. To the corporate IS department, Exchange might be Exchange Server running on a Windows NT server. To an application programmer, Exchange might be Simple MAPI, while to a systems programmer, it might be the OLE-based MAPI 1.0 API.

All of these views are what Microsoft Exchange is—a powerful, client-server messaging platform capable of supporting an enterprise as easily as it supports small workgroups.

Exchange is an open platform, which uses the WOSA standard Messaging API (MAPI) to provide the programmatic interface to and among its various components.

This book is about Windows 95 programming, and as a result, any discussion of MS Exchange is really about the component that comes in the box with Windows 95—Exchange Client. Windows 95 does not include the server component of Exchange and therefore depends on using a transport, such as the older MS Mail transport, the Internet, or a transport provider that carries mail across online services.

Microsoft Exchange Server

Microsoft Exchange Server is, as of this writing, being beta tested. It consists of a number of Windows NT services that implement a true client-server messaging system. Microsoft Exchange Server is designed for messaging "beyond the enterprise," through the use of connectors and gateways to other mail systems, including X.400 and SMTP.

Conceptually, servers in a Microsoft Exchange server system are grouped into *sites*, and sites are grouped into an enterprise. All servers within a single site are required to have permanent network connections to each other and to use RPC connections to exchange directory information.

Intersite communication can take place over a variety of methods, including RPC, X.400, or the MS Mail connector over X.25, LAN, asynchronous connections, or RAS.

Microsoft Exchange Server uses an X.500-compatible directory service and provides the following features:

- *Public folders*, the cornerstone of Microsoft Exchange Server, allow users to place messages, documents, and forms in an area where they can be accessed by other users within the site. With public folders, the actual data can be stored on any server, and the user can be attached to any server.

- Public folder access is controlled by Windows NT security, which allows only certain people to create public folders or to read messages in a public folder.

- Microsoft Exchange Server uses *replication* to copy new and updated directory information, public folder addresses and data, distribution lists, and addresses of users of foreign mail systems. This enables the automatic distribution of data throughout the enterprise.

Interoperability with Microsoft Mail 3.x

Microsoft Exchange Client can use Microsoft Mail 3.2 post offices (including workgroup post offices) as its transport and store. In addition, because Microsoft Exchange uses RAS connections rather than depending upon the special MS Remote Mail Client for Windows, it is much more flexible than the previous alternatives.

Remote access service, called *Dial-Up Networking* in Windows 95, enables remote users to access a LAN as though they were attached to the LAN. This means that users can access anything on the LAN, including mail, from outside of the office.

Windows 95 Microsoft Exchange Client also offers support for 16-bit extensions, custom message types, and handlers designed for use with MS Mail 3.x for Windows. In fact, Exchange Client reads MSMAIL.INI and attempts to implement as many of the entries from the [Custom Menus], [Custom Commands], and [Custom Messages] sections of MSMAIL.INI as possible.

From the 16-bit application program point of view, Microsoft Exchange is completely compatible with MS Mail 3.x—mail-enabled and mail-aware applications written to run with the MS Mail clients should be fully functional on Windows 95 with Exchange Client.

Exchange and Developers

As trade barriers fall and we move towards a global economy, communication with all parts of the world becomes very important. In the past, communication between computers and the applications running on them has been accomplished through real-time methods—by accessing a common database or through direct communication protocols, such as RPC or APPC. The only alternative to using real-time methods has been to send files through a store-and-forward type of system, often as electronic mail attachments, and then to process them manually.

The incorporation of a fully functional messaging system within the Windows operating system changes the picture significantly. Now, programmers are not limited to creating code that writes out files for the user to mail to a remote location for processing. Instead, they can use the messaging API to create applications that work with real-enough time methods and that automatically communicate with counterpart applications, possibly on the other side of the globe.

Microsoft, in fact, has been adding messaging features into virtually all of their products since 1993 and has been evangelizing the use of real-enough time programming techniques through their developer broadcasts as well as in their code samples (Workgroup Templates, for example). In fact, applications that receive the "Designed for Windows 95" logo are required to support a minimal level of messaging functionality.

There are many opportunities for developers to create extensions to Microsoft Exchange. For example, programmers can create service providers that talk to other messaging systems, such as pagers or voice mail, or they can create client extensions that add custom functionality to the user interface of Microsoft Exchange.

Exchange Client extensions can include command extensions, event extensions, property sheet extensions, and advanced criteria extensions.

Command extensions add new commands (or replace existing commands) on Exchange Client's menus and toolbars. This functionality is equivalent to placing entries in the [Custom Commands] and [Custom Menus] sections of the MSMAIL.INI file in MS Mail 3.x.

Event extensions are special handlers for specific events that take place within Microsoft Exchange: For example, the reception of a message in the user's inbox might trigger an event extension that looks for a particular message type and then decrypts the contents. This functionality is roughly equivalent to placing entries in the [Custom Messages] section of the MSMAIL.INI file in MS Mail 3.x.

Property sheet extensions allow you to add customer property sheets to information stores, folders, and messages. A typical use of property sheet extensions is to set the properties of a message that is a member of a custom message type that you created. There is no direct equivalent in MS Mail 3.x.

Advanced criteria extensions allow you to create dialog boxes that prompt for advanced search criteria when the user is searching for messages in an information store. There is no direct equivalent in MS Mail 3.x.

An Overview of MS Exchange

Microsoft Exchange Client is not installed on Windows 95 by default. The user must choose to install it either by making the appropriate choice while running Windows 95 Setup or by using Add/Remove Software from the Windows 95 Control Panel.

Universal Inbox

For the end user, the single most compelling reason to move to Microsoft Exchange is the Universal Inbox. Finally, users don't have to use different mail clients to access mail coming from a variety of sources—without using a central server with gateways.

Figure 35.1 shows the Microsoft Exchange Inbox. It consists of two panes: The left pane contains a tree view of the folder hierarchy, and the right pane shows the contents of the currently open folder. Notice the icons that look like envelopes; they indicate that the messages are regular mail messages. Programmers can choose which icons are displayed for a particular message type. For example, if you've developed a voice mail application that mails recorded voice mail to the user, you might want to use an icon that looks like a telephone.

The paper clip indicates that the message has an attachment. Attachments can be files, OLE objects, or any kind of data that makes sense to an application. For example, you can write a form in Visual Basic that creates a mail message containing a SQL query. On another machine, you can have another VB application that monitors an Exchange mailbox, retrieves the message, and uses ODBC to hand the query off to SQLServer. SQLServer performs the query and mails it back to the original user as an attachment using its built-in messaging capabilities.

FIGURE 35.1.

The Microsoft Exchange Inbox.

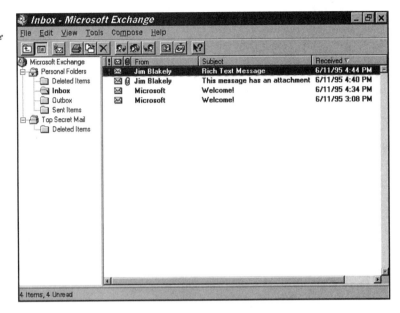

Rich Text

Messages in Microsoft Exchange are rich text formatted by default (see Figure 35.2). This enables users to express themselves more creatively. It also means that Exchange applications can format reports or other documents and send them back to the user as regular messages rather as than attachments.

FIGURE 35.2.

Rich Text in a message.

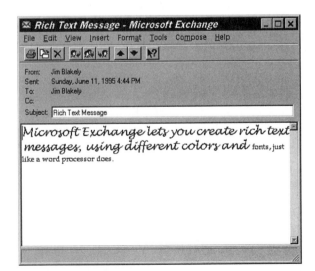

Service Providers

The back-end functions of Microsoft Exchange are implemented as MAPI service providers. Exchange defines three types of possible service providers: stores, transports, and address books. The Windows 95 version of Exchange Client includes one store provider, several transport providers, and a single address book provider.

Stores

Stores, as the name implies, are responsible for the persistent storage of messages. The store provider that comes with Windows 95 creates a *personal information store* (PST file) in the C:\EXCHANGE directory by default.

Exchange Server adds a store provider that accesses the message database on the servers using a client-server method. This minimizes the amount of data that needs to be stored on local machines. Developers might write a store provider to access messages that reside in some form of storage on a foreign mail system or in some form of proprietary database.

Address Books

Address book providers are responsible for providing address and distribution list management. The standard personal address book that comes with Windows 95 allows the user to create address book entries and personal distribution lists.

Address book providers can also access other sources of address information: PIMs, network directory services such as Novell's NDS or Exchange Server's directory service, or even foreign mail systems' directory services such as X.500 or PROFs.

Transports

A transport provider is responsible for carrying messages from one mail system to another. The Windows 95 version of Microsoft Exchange Client includes several transports:

- MSSFS—Microsoft Mail 3.x post offices
- COMPUSERVE—The CompuServe Information Service
- MSN—The Microsoft Network
- FAX—Microsoft Fax

In addition, Microsoft Exchange Server includes a transport that accesses the server. Also, an Internet POP3-compliant transport is available with Microsoft Plus! for Windows 95.

MSSFS Transport

The MSSFS, or Microsoft Mail transport, can carry messages to and from a Microsoft Mail post office. MSSFS is the transport most commonly used with the Windows 95 version of Microsoft Exchange Client, because it supports LAN-based e-mail with other users of Windows (including Windows for Workgroups and Windows NT) as well as users of MS-DOS and users on any foreign mail system that might have a gateway to the post office.

Configuring the Microsoft Mail provider is done by choosing Tools->Services... and then double-clicking Microsoft Mail, which brings up the dialog box in Figure 35.3.

FIGURE 35.3.

Configuring an MS Mail connection.

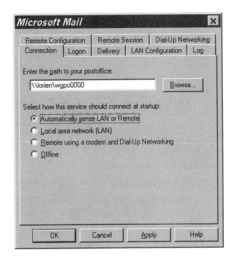

As previously mentioned, Exchange Client is capable of connecting to the MS Mail post office through a normal LAN connection or by dialing in using Dial-Up Networking. The options on this dialog box tab let you decide whether the service should connect through the LAN only or through a modem only (remote), or whether it should try to autosense the appropriate method or just start up offline. In addition, you tell the service where the post office is located by typing a UNC filename in the edit box.

Figure 35.4 shows the tab where you configure the Dial-Up Networking parameters. You need to specify which of the Dial-Up Networking connections the service should use, whether it should retry if the connection fails for any reason (such as a busy signal), and whether it should bring up a confirmation dialog box before deciding to connect remotely.

Figure 35.5 shows the Remote Configuration tab. It is identical in function to the LAN Configuration tab, except that the options in this tab only apply when the computer is connected to the post office through Dial-Up Networking.

FIGURE 35.4.

Configuring MS Mail with Dial-Up Networking.

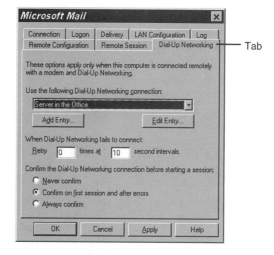

Tab

FIGURE 35.5.

Configuring remote mail options.

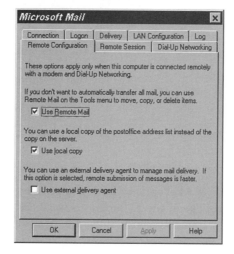

The two most useful options are Use Remote Mail and Use Local Copy. The Use Remote Mail option, instead of automatically transferring all messages from the post office when the connection is made, allows the user to transfer the message headers first and then to pick and choose the messages for transfer. This enables the user to avoid transferring messages with large attachments, which would take a long time over the relatively slow dial-up connections.

Similarly, the Use Local Copy option lets the user avoid the overhead of downloading a copy of the post office address list when using it. There is a corresponding Download Address Lists menu item in Tools->Microsoft Mail Tools that transfers the current list to the computer.

Figure 35.6 shows the Delivery tab, which configures options that affect the delivery of mail messages. Several options are important here. First, both incoming and outgoing mail deliveries have checkboxes. The user might be dialing in remotely from overseas and only wants to send a message without retrieving any messages. The user can disable outgoing mail delivery simply by clearing the checkbox.

FIGURE 35.6.

Configuring Delivery options.

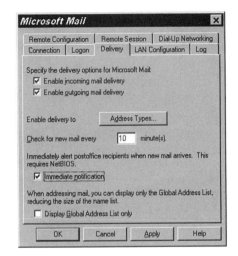

The Enable Delivery To Address Types... option is important if mail gateways are installed on the post office, because a given address type, such as SMTP, might be deliverable by several different transport providers. This option and similar options in other service providers allow you to control which provider actually gets used.

The Check For New Mail option controls how often the service looks at the user's mailbag on the post office to see if any mail messages were received. Like the corresponding option under MS Mail 3.x, this option should be adjusted when mail delivery is slow.

The Immediate Notification option is only effective if it is checked on all computers that exchange messages with each other. When it is checked, the sender notifies the recipient through NETBIOS; new messages are received faster than the poll time set in the previous option.

Finally, the MS Mail global address list (GAL) makes the task of finding the person to send mail to easier. A GAL is optionally created as the last part of an MS Mail directory synchronization.

CompuServe

The CompuServe transport allows the sending and receiving of mail messages to and from the CompuServe Information Service. Configuration is relatively simple—you actually only need to know your CompuServe account number, password, and the telephone number and type of the node you use to connect to CompuServe.

The CompuServe transport can be configured to dial in automatically and check for mail on a regular basis.

The Microsoft Network

The Microsoft Network (MSN) is Microsoft's online service. Not only does it support sending mail to MSN members, but it also supports sending mail to Internet users. One distinguishing feature of this transport is its capability to embed shortcuts to files and features on the service.

The MSN transport is a bit different in its configuration. Instead of configuring the account name and phone numbers through the service properties as you do with the CompuServe transport, the MSN transport brings up the regular MSN login procedure. You can configure options such as whether to stay logged on after checking for new mail. However, you cannot configure the MSN transport to poll at regular intervals.

Microsoft Fax

The Microsoft Fax service gives you the ability to send and receive faxes—both regular Group 3 noneditable faxes and editable faxes that travel across the fax connection—in their original format, which appear as attachments in the inbox. The protocol used to transfer editable faxes was formerly known as At Work Fax.

For the developer, Microsoft Fax enables your application to fax directly whatever printed output it generates. You can create a basic fax by using MAPI to create a mail message with the fax number as the address in the following form:

```
[FAX:user@+1 (234) 555-1298]
```

Internet Mail

Internet service providers normally give every user with a POP mailbox. POP stands for post office protocol and refers to an Internet standard. As of this writing, Microsoft is going to provide a transport capable of sending and receiving mail through a POP mailbox with the Microsoft Plus! collection of add-on software for Windows 95.

Profiles

A Microsoft Exchange profile is a collection of services being used at any particular time. Using different profiles, different client programs can access Exchange at the same time, and any given computer can have multiple Exchange profiles on it.

Profiles and Multiple Users

One reason to set up multiple profiles is that a computer might have multiple users on it. In this instance, at minimum, you need to have separate personal information stores so that one user's mail does not get mixed up with another user's mail.

Multiple Instances of a Service

Sometimes you need to have multiple instances of a given service on the computer, but the service itself only permits a single copy. A typical example is when you have more than one CompuServe account. In order for Microsoft Exchange to access both accounts and to retrieve the mail waiting in both accounts, you have to create two separate Exchange profiles and add separate copies of the CompuServe transport service to each one.

Fortunately, you can include the same Personal Address Book store and Personal Information store in each of the profiles so that the messages end up going to the same place.

Profiles for Multiple Locations

Another reason for using multiple profiles is for handling different messaging needs based on where you are. In Figure 35.7, two profiles are set up on the machine: the default MS Exchange Settings profile, which contains services appropriate to normal use in the office, and the Internet Mail Only profile, which contains the Internet Mail service that the user has configured to use a dial-up connection on the road.

FIGURE 35.7.

Multiple stores in a profile.

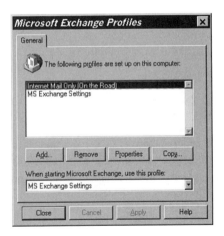

In Figure 35.8, a second instance, Top Secret Mail, of the Personal Information store is shown. It is added using the dialog box shown in Figure 35.9 and is used to store secret messages; therefore, criteria is put on it. First, the Best Encryption option is selected, which ensures that the messages in the file remains secret unless the user has the password. Second, the Remember Password box was *not* checked when the store was created, meaning that every time Exchange is opened using this profile, the password prompt shown in Figure 35.10 appears for an added measure of security. (The Save This Password In Your Password List option can be used to have Windows automatically supply the password.)

FIGURE 35.8.

A profile with two stores.

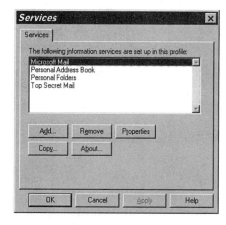

FIGURE 35.9.

Configuring a message store.

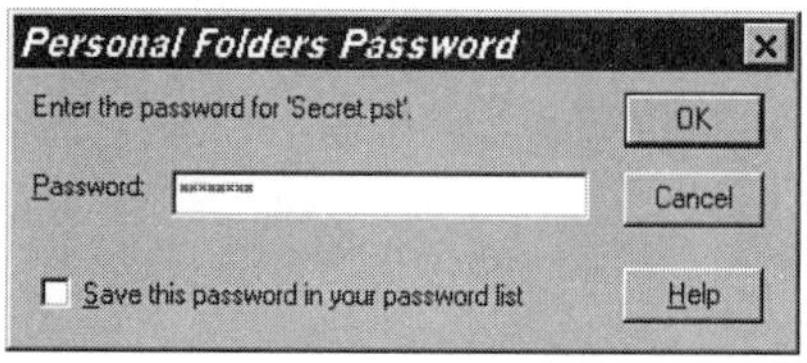

FIGURE 35.10.

Entering a store password.

Schedule+

Microsoft includes Schedule+ 1.0, a basic group scheduling program, free with Windows for Workgroups, giving companies a good reason to upgrade to Windows for Workgroups.

Unfortunately, Microsoft decided not to include Schedule+ 7.0 in the Windows 95 package, deciding instead to move it into the Office 95 package (as well as Exchange Server). Schedule+ 1.0 works under Windows 95 as long as the old version of MS Mail is left in place, which means losing out on the advantages of Microsoft Exchange.

There are, however, compelling reasons for users to switch to Schedule+ 7.0. First, virtually every aspect of the program has been improved. Second, and more important from the developer's point of view, Schedule+ 7.0 is a full OLE application, which makes accessing and modifying information about appointments, tasks, and contacts stored in the Schedule+ 7.0 database easy to do from Visual Basic.

Summary

This chapter is an overview of Microsoft Exchange as implemented in Windows 95. For more information on programming for Exchange, see Chapter 36, "The Messaging System—Extended MAPI."

The Messaging System—Extended MAPI

36

by John J. Kottler

> *"Transport of the mails, transport of the human voice, transport of flickering pictures—in this century as in others our highest accomplishments still have the single aim of bringing men together."*
>
> —Antoine de Saint-Exupéry (1900-1944)

The Newest Transport

For centuries, people have striven to communicate better. In the age of information, this need to communicate has perhaps never been more evident. Technology has offered many advances in communication over the past decades and now the computer promises to be another example of communication enhanced by technology.

Because of the ever-increasing use of computer systems, communicating between systems has become logical. A primary example of how people communicate via computer systems is by electronic mail (e-mail). This method of communicating has blossomed heartily throughout the past few years and is becoming the communication method of choice for many people and organizations. In addition, with the tremendous growth in online services and the Internet, it is possible for typical users to communicate with people halfway around the world, with tremendous response time.

The world of computer communications is growing vast, and so is the task of managing and working with the medium. Windows 95 attempts to aid computer users by providing several key technologies for electronic communications as a core set of tools in the operating system. With Windows 95, it will become possible to handle electronic communications as diverse as e-mail, forms, faxes, and online services in one common environment. Also, if you have never been exposed to e-mail, you will have ample opportunity with Windows 95 to experiment with this new form of communication. The operating system includes a client for viewing mail messages (discussed in Chapter 35, "Microsoft Exchange for the Programmer"), capabilities for creating and maintaining electronic "post offices," and a complete Messaging Application Programming Interface (MAPI) for programs to interact with the messaging system.

This chapter offers an overview of Extended MAPI and demonstrates how to send and read e-mail messages in an individual message store. The Extended MAPI system is a very complex system, and talking about the system in its entirety is beyond the scope of this book. Instead, this chapter introduces you to the basic concepts to help you develop more complex systems of your own.

A Quick History of MAPI

The messaging system included with Windows 95 is very complex, and you need to become familiar with it before venturing into the world of MAPI programming. To begin your tour, first get acquainted with the older application programming interface: MAPI.

MAPI was originally designed to give application developers the ability to link into the Microsoft messaging system. With MAPI, it was suddenly possible for developers to easily create applications that were messaging-enabled or messaging-aware. With the older version of MAPI, which is now referred to as Simple MAPI, a developer could include code to log on and off of the messaging system, create messages, read messages in the inbox, and perform other simple tasks such as work with the messaging system's address book. It is possible with Simple MAPI to add a Send option to an application's menu that would create a new message and send it, using parameters generated automatically from the application or from user interaction and standard MAPI dialog boxes. It was also possible to develop applications that extended the capabilities of a common MAPI client interface such as Microsoft Mail 3.x.

However, developers and users alike who used Simple MAPI soon found the limitations of such an interface. Simple MAPI lacked capabilities such as spanning the hierarchy of message folders, creating data tables for advanced manipulation of messages, or even supporting rich-text formatting options like those found in word processors. Simple MAPI and the messaging system also lacked support for other ways in which people could receive messages such as by faxes, the Internet, and other online services. Often, users had to use several separate applications to receive incoming messages—one for checking e-mail, another for receiving faxes, and multiple applications for examining mail from online services. In addition, the telephone is a source of incoming messages. Therefore, the messaging system's capabilities were expanded to overcome the need for separate applications to check all forms of communication. Extended MAPI is an open architecture, as you will see shortly, and it supports the capability to add additional data types such as voice or video. Now the reality of checking in one place for all messages is possible. (For information on handling telephony, refer to Chapter 37, "TAPI.")

Extended MAPI, or MAPI 1.0, is the newest incarnation of the messaging application programming interface. With Extended MAPI, a user can now have multiple message stores for keeping messages, an expandable interface for adding new features, and a common client and programming interface for handling vastly different message types. Extended MAPI also adds support to facilitate forms routing and workflow technologies.

Extended MAPI Quick Tour

The new messaging system that is included with Windows 95 is more complex than previous versions. To understand it, let's examine an overview of the system. It is important to understand the hierarchy of this system and some of the relevant terminology.

To begin touring the messaging system, you must first start it. Invoking the messaging system in Extended MAPI enables the user to choose from a list of *profiles*. A profile is simply a list of different message services and their associated properties. For example, you can create a standard profile called MS Exchange Settings that contains information services such as Microsoft Fax, Microsoft Mail, Microsoft Network, and CompuServe Mail. See Figure 36.1 for an example listing from a profile. If the user chooses a profile with services such as those shown in Figure 36.1 as the default profile or picks it when he or she starts an Extended MAPI application, the profile acts on messages from the fax system, e-mail, CompuServe mail, and the Microsoft Network.

FIGURE 36.1.

This is an example of an Extended MAPI profile's properties. Each service listed can contain specific properties for that service.

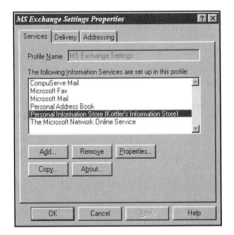

The use of profiles demonstrates the expandability of the messaging system in Windows 95. As mentioned earlier, the telephone is an additional source of messages. To receive these voice messages in the mail system, it would be possible for a telecommunications company to write an information service that could be added to the default profile list. This service provider software could actually link into the telecommunications system and convert a voice mail message into an audio wave file. The service could then create a message in your message store with an attachment that plays that voice mail message.

In order to use the messaging system, you must log on to the system. Logging on to the system establishes your personal connection to your unique set of messages. This uniqueness is determined by both your logon ID and password. When you log on to the system, you work in a MAPI session. Every application call your program makes to MAPI works within the current session. In addition, some applications "share" sessions. For example, Microsoft Mail and Schedule+ both share the same mail session to avoid forcing the user to log on several times. Figure 36.2 shows the standard logon dialog box.

FIGURE 36.2.

The standard logon dialog box may be used with your applications.

A *session* is the connection between a messaging-aware application and your personal message space in the messaging system. Extended MAPI organizes information into message *stores.* A store holds your personal messages and folders, as well as additional information about each. These stores are then typically accessed by a client such as Exchange that presents, maintains, and submits the messages. It is quite possible for a person to have multiple message stores. For example, a user might have one that is used when they dial in with a modem, and a second that is used when he or she connects to a network.

The next level deeper into the system is a *folder.* A typical user will use the messaging system to send, receive, and delete messages. To avoid confusion, messages are automatically sorted into their respective Outbox, Inbox, and Deleted Items folders. An additional folder, Sent Items, enables the user to access messages that were recently queued for submission in the message system. A user can also create and delete folders at will, as well as copy messages into other folders. Figure 36.3 shows a typical Extended MAPI client that displays folders and messages.

FIGURE 36.3.

Microsoft Exchange displays the hierarchy of message stores and folders in the left window pane, and messages in the right.

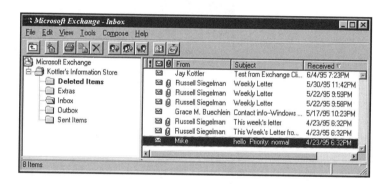

Finally, a series of *messages* resides inside a folder. A message typically contains information about the author of the message, the recipients of the message (TO, CC, and BCC), a subject line, and a rich-text field for the message content. A message can also contain one or more file attachments that are either true files or OLE objects that link to other applications or data files. See Figure 36.4 for a sample message as displayed in Microsoft Exchange.

It would be pointless to have a messaging system that could not communicate with others. Therefore, the messaging system must have a method for creating, maintaining, and selecting names that identify addresses to route messages. The messaging system uses an *address book* to maintain this information. The address book is an entity that is unique to each individual user, but is not an entity of the message store. Extended MAPI provides methods to access and alter the contents of your personal address book. Just as people may have multiple message stores, they may have multiple address books. For example, because certain recipients may have access to one service but not another, a user may have a network address book of users in his or her organization on a LAN and a second address book with users on the Microsoft Network. See Figure 36.5 for an example of the address book.

FIGURE 36.4.

This is a sample message that was automatically generated from a program included with this book and discussed in this chapter.

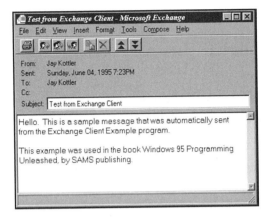

FIGURE 36.5.

This sample address book has four different lists that show names.

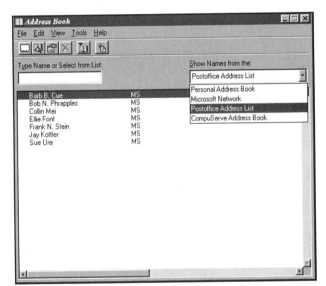

Extended MAPI Programming in Windows 95

Now that you have the basics covered, let's begin examining the actual programming interface. Extended MAPI acts as a translator between calls your application makes and the actual processes necessary in the messaging system to perform the function you want. The benefit of this design is that the Extended MAPI can shield the applications developer from the technicalities of the messaging system, such as which information service to use and how to connect to each one. This way, for instance, Extended MAPI will handle the actual processes of sending an Internet mail message versus a Microsoft mail message while all the developer needs to know is how to send a message to a recipient.

In this chapter, you will learn how to use Extended MAPI to do basic messaging functions such as log on to the messaging system, open the message store and appropriate folders, read message properties, compose new messages, use the address book, and log off the system.

Initializing Extended MAPI

Before it even uses one Extended MAPI feature, the messaging-aware application must first initialize Extended MAPI. A single MAPIIntialize function call is necessary to enable use of the Extended MAPI toolset. The definition for this function is

```
STDAPI MAPIInitialize (LPVOID lpvReserved)
```

lpvReserved is a reserved parameter and must be zero.

If the function successfully starts the Extended MAPI system, then a value of S_OK is returned. Otherwise, S_FALSE is returned if a problem was encountered.

Logging Onto the Message System

Once the Extended MAPI system has been initialized, the first step in creating a messaging-aware application is to log on to the messaging system using the MAPILogon function. This function is used in both Simple MAPI and Extended MAPI. Logging onto the message system returns a pointer to the MAPI session. The pointer to the session is necessary for using additional Extended MAPI functions. This pointer actually points to a C++ interface, on which several methods may be invoked. The logon function also starts the default message store and address book. The definition of MAPILogon is

```
ULONG (FAR PASCAL MAPILogon) (ULONG ulUIParam,
                              LPTSTR lpszProfileName,
                              LPTSTR lpszPassword,
                              FLAGS flFlags,
                              ULONG ulReserved,
                              LPLHANDLE lplhSession)
```

The following list identifies and describes each of the parameters MAPILogon expects.

   ulUIParam   Specifies the parent window handle of the calling application. If a zero is passed as this parameter, no parent window is indicated.

   lpszProfileName   As discussed earlier, there may be several profiles available to each user. You may specify the name of a profile as this parameter—MS Exchange Settings, for example—or pass in NULL. When you pass NULL as this parameter, Extended MAPI will present a dialog box in which you can choose the profile you wish to use. (See Figure 36.6.)

FIGURE 36.6.

The Choose Profile dialog box appears when you set the lpszProfileName *parameter to* NULL *in the* MAPILogon *function.*

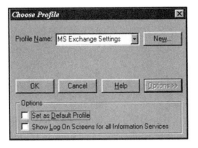

lpszPassword   To enable a user to log onto the messaging system without being required to enter the password manually, your application may pass the correct password directly to the messaging system and avoid the logon window. If you do this, make sure that you somehow maintain the integrity of the password in your application using encryption or other means. If NULL is passed into this parameter, the user must type the correct password before logging onto the system.

flFlags   You may specify certain conditions by passing one of the flags listed in Table 36.1 into this parameter.

Table 36.1. Valid flags to use with the MAPILogon function.

MAPI_ALLOW_OTHERS	Indicates a shared session. This will enable several messaging-aware applications to access the messaging system without having to log on more than once.
MAPI_EXPLICIT_PROFILE	If you wish to log on using the default profile, use this flag. This flag instructs the messaging subsystem to use the default profile name as lpszProfileName.
MAPI_EXTENDED	Specifies that the return value of this function should be an HRESULT rather than a ULONG and that no stores should be started automatically.
MAPI_FORCE_DOWNLOAD	Attempts to download all messages before returning. Otherwise, message downloads are conducted in the background after the MAPILogon call.
MAPI_LOGON_UI	Enables the logon dialog box shown in Figure 36.2. If this flag is not set and the user does not log on correctly, MAPILogon will return an error.
MAPI_NEW_SESSION	Explicitly asks the messaging system to create a new session rather than sharing any open sessions. If this flag is not set, the default is to attempt to share the MAPI session.

`MAPI_NO_MAIL`	This disables the receiving or transmitting of new messages. This flag could be used by applications that need to just browse the messaging system or do other maintenance.
`MAPI_NT_SERVICE`	This flag is only used if the client logging on is using Windows NT.
`MAPI_PASSWORD_UI`	Setting this flag instructs the messaging system to display a dialog box for entering a password only. This prevents other entry items usually found in the dialog box presented by `MAPI_LOGON_UI` from being displayed. A messaging-aware application should use only one of these two flags, not both.
`MAPI_SERVICE_UI_ALWAYS`	Specifying this will cause the messaging system to display a configuration interface for each Information Service in a profile. This dialog box appears after a profile has been selected, but before the user logs on.
`MAPI_SIMPLE_DEFAULT`	Combines the `MAPI_LOGON_UI`, `MAPI_FORCE_DOWNLOAD`, and `MAPI_ALLOW_OTHERS` flags.
`MAPI_SIMPLE_EXPLICIT`	Combines the `MAPI_NEW_SESSION`, `MAPI_FORCE_DOWNLOAD`, and `MAPI_EXPLICIT_PROFILE` flags.
`MAPI_USE_DEFAULT`	Uses the default profile when a user logs onto the system.

`ulReserved` The `ulReserved` parameter is reserved for future use. Therefore, you must pass zero into this parameter.

`lplhSession` The handle to the current message session must be saved. You may pass an output variable of the type `LPMAPISESSION`. This handle will be accessed as a pointer to the session object in other Extended MAPI calls.

`MAPILogon` then returns a result that indicates either a successful logon (`SUCCESS_SUCCESS`) or one of the following 14 error conditions:

`MAPI_E_ACCESS_DENIED` The user does not have appropriate access to log onto the messaging system.

`MAPI_E_AMBIGUOUS_RECIPIENT` The user name used for logging onto the system is invalid.

`MAPI_E_DISK_FULL` The disk is full and any necessary temporary files cannot be created.

`MAPI_E_FAILONEPROVIDER` A provider in the profile failed to initialize.

`MAPI_E_FAILURE` A non-specific error has occurred.

`MAPI_E_INSUFFICIENT_MEMORY` There is not enough memory available to continue.

`MAPI_E_LOGIN_FAILURE` The logon process was unsuccessful. This could be because the user signed on incorrectly or because default information in the `MAPILogon` function was incorrect.

`MAPI_E_NETWORK_FAILURE` The network that the messaging system works with has failed.

`MAPI_E_NOT_SUPPORTED` The operation is not supported by the messaging system.

`MAPI_E_STRING_TOO_LONG` A string passed into this function is longer than the maximum string length allowed.

`MAPI_E_TOO_MANY_SESSIONS` Too many other MAPI sessions are open at one time.

`MAPI_E_UNCONFIGURED` A service provider in the profile has not been properly configured.

`MAPI_E_USER_ABORT` The user canceled the logon process.

`MAPI_E_USER_CANCEL` The user canceled the logon process.

The code in Listing 36.1 demonstrates how to obtain the session handle of a MAPI session.

Listing 36.1. Code for logging onto the message system and obtaining a pointer to that session.

```
// Global pointer to the Extended MAPI Session
LPMAPISESSIONlpSession = NULL;

void CExchangeView::OnMailLogon()
{
   ULONG ulUIParam = (ULONG)(void *)m_hWnd;

   if (lpSession)
   {
      MessageBox("You're already logged on, logoff first.",
               "ERROR", MB_OK);
      return;
   }

   // Logon and get the handle to the MAPISession.
   if(FAILED(MAPILogon(ulUIParam, NULL, NULL, MAPI_LOGON_UI,
                     0, (LPLHANDLE) &lpSession)))
   {
      MessageBox("Cannot logon to the Message System.", "ERROR", MB_OK);
      return;
   }
}
```

MAPI Object Interfaces

After the logon has successfully completed, your application obtains a pointer to a C++ interface for the session, known as an `IMAPISession` object. An interface is typically identified by a capital I before the interface name. However, in your applications the interface will be identified by a pointer that you establish. For instance, in the logon example in Listing 36.1, the pointer `lpSession` identifies the `IMAPISession` interface. All session methods will then be called using this pointer.

There are several methods that may be called from the `IMAPISession` object. Table 36.2 depicts just a sample of the methods that are used in this chapter.

Table 36.2. A few of the many methods available in the `IMAPISession` interface.

`GetMsgStoresTable`	Retrieves a MAPI table that describes each message store available in the currently logged-on profile.
`OpenMsgStore`	Opens a specified message store and returns a pointer to that store's interface. The resulting `IMSGStore` object then contains additional methods for acting on the message store.
`OpenAddressBook`	Establishes a pointer to the address book interface, `IAddrBook`. Like any MAPI interface, `IAddrBook` then contains methods that are specific to address book manipulation.
`Logoff`	Discontinues use of an Extended MAPI session and logs the user off.

It is important to understand that there are multiple interfaces available in Extended MAPI. There also exist hierarchies for these Extended MAPI methods, just as there are hierarchies of message stores and folders in the messaging system. Figure 36.7 shows a sample of such a hierarchy tree that exists under the `IMAPISession` interface.

FIGURE 36.7.

The `IMAPISession` interface contains a hierarchy tree that must be traversed to read or send messages.

```
IMAPISession
     |
  IMsgStore
     |
  IMAPIFolder
     |
   IMessage
```

Therefore, to work with messages your application must first establish a MAPI session and then traverse the hierarchy tree to connect to the appropriate message store, folder, and eventually, message. It is important to note that this is not the only hierarchy tree that exists in Extended MAPI. Because most of your work in this chapter deals with handling e-mail messages, I will avoid the explanation of additional interfaces such as those used for forms and workflow, message store providers, or transport providers. Remember that there are various methods and properties that may be applied to each interface along the hierarchy path. Some of these methods and properties are unique to each interface, and others are shared.

MAPI, the Database

Before we continue examining the process of opening a message store, it is important to define the use of MAPI tables. Although it may not seem apparent at first, the messaging system is a large database system. True, there are extensions to the system that are necessary for communications, but the underlying stores of messages, addresses, and additional information are comparable to a series of databases. Therefore, it is only logical that Extended MAPI supports a table interface with numerous methods.

An example MAPI table would be the table of message stores. In this table, information about the different message stores available is kept. Each different store is represented by a row in the table; the properties for that store, such as the store's name and identification, make up the columns of the table.

Programs can use the `IMAPITable` interface to examine and modify these tables of message information dynamically. Just as with the `MAPISession` interface, your program must establish a pointer that will point to a MAPI table. There are several tables, and some are associated directly with another MAPI object. For instance, to get a listing of available information stores, the `GetMsgStoresTable` method is available from the `IMAPISession` interface.

Once the pointer to a table interface has been established, several table methods are available. Table 36.3 lists the few that are examined in this chapter.

Table 36.3. A few of the methods used in the `IMAPITable` interface.

`SetColumns`	MAPI tables contain many columns of information. To restrict what is returned to your application, use the `SetColumns` method to retrieve only columns you need.
`GetRowCount`	Retrieves the total number of rows in the MAPI table.
`SeekRow`	Moves to a specific row in the table.
`QueryRows`	Actually retrieves one or more rows of data from the table into a MAPI table structure variable in your application.

You will see shortly how to use tables to open message stores and folders, as well as retrieve information about messages in the messaging system.

Using the Message Store Table

According to the hierarchy tree depicted in Figure 36.7, the next step after obtaining a pointer to the session interface is to open a message store. As discussed earlier, there may be multiple message stores for the profile a user logs onto. Fortunately, Extended MAPI tables store additional property information about each object in the system. Therefore, it is possible to find a message object with a property indicating the default message store.

To open a default message store, your program must obtain the MAPI table that contains the list of stores. Then the rows from that table are to be searched, using a loop in your application. The application must scan the default property column for a TRUE value. Once that row has been found, that store's entry ID must be used to open the message store. The entry ID is a binary identifier in Extended MAPI that is uniquely assigned to each individual MAPI object, including message stores, folders, and messages.

The first method, `GetMsgStoresTable`, is needed to obtain a pointer to the MAPI table of message stores.

```
HRESULT GetMsgStoresTable(ULONG ulFlags, LPMAPITABLE FAR * lpTable)
```

> `ulFlags`   A single flag, `MAPI_UNICODE`, may be set with this parameter. Passing `MAPI_UNICODE` into this parameter instructs the messaging system to return UNICODE strings.
>
> `lpTable`   An output variable declared as a MAPI table structure. This is the pointer to the table object, on which additional methods will be called.

`GetMsgStoresTable` will return a status of the following type:

> `S_OK`   The method executed successfully.
> `MAPI_E_BAD_CHARWIDTH`   The UNICODE option has been enabled, but UNICODE strings were not used in the method.
> `MAPI_E_CALL_FAILED`   A non-specific error occurred.
> `MAPI_E_INVALID_OBJECT`   The table object is invalid because it was either released or modified since the method was called.
> `MAPI_E_INVALID_PARAMETER`   A parameter passed to the method is invalid.
> `MAPI_E_NO_SUPPORT`   The method is not supported by the messaging system or a provider.
> `MAPI_E_NOT_ENOUGH_MEMORY`   There is not enough memory to complete this method.
> `MAPI_E_UNKNOWN_FLAGS`   An invalid flag was passed to this method.

After the table object pointer has been determined, you need to restrict the amount of information that will be returned to your program. To do this, you need to use the `SetColumns` method of the table object.

```
HRESULT SetColumns(LPSPropTagArray lpPropTagArray, ULONG ulFlags)
```

lpPropTagArray   This parameter specifies the actual properties that are to be returned from the table. Each property specifies the appropriate column in the table to return. The actual array can be created using the following syntax:

```
const static SizedSPropTagArray(2,columns) =
{
    2,
        {
            PR_DEFAULT_STORE,
            PR_ENTRYID
        }
};
```

The function `SizedPropTagArray` creates an appropriate property tag array of the size specified in the first parameter and references that array by the variable in the second parameter. The declaration of property tags must then follow, first indicating the total number of properties, and then the appropriate property IDs, as specified in the MAPI SDK.

ulFlags   Several flags may be passed to specify options for the `SetColumns` method. See Table 36.4 for a complete listing of these options.

Table 36.4. Valid flags that may used for the `SetColumns` method.

TBL_ASYNC	Does not actually set retrieval columns until the request to return data is initiated.
TBL_BATCH	Returns immediately after beginning the `SetColumns` method.
TBL_NOWAIT	Forces an immediate return from `SetColumns`, regardless of other settings.

`SetColumns` will return one of the following conditions:

S_OK   `SetColumns` executed successfully.

MAPI_E_BUSY   Another process is busy and should be stopped first or be allowed to complete.

MAPI_E_CALL_FAILED   The call failed for a non-specific reason.

MAPI_E_INVALID_PARAMETER   An invalid parameter was passed to this method.

MAPI_E_NO_SUPPORT   Either the messaging system or a provider does not support this method.

MAPI_E_NOT_ENOUGH_MEMORY   There is not enough memory to complete this action.

MAPI_E_UNKNOWN_FLAGS   An invalid flag was specified.

In order to scan through the list of message stores available, you need to determine the total number of message stores that are available in the system. To do this, you will need to call the `GetRowCount` method, which is part of the table object.

```
HRESULT GetRowCount(ULONG ulFlags, ULONG FAR * lpulCount)
```

ulFlags   This is a reserved parameter and must be zero.

lpulCount   This parameter returns the total number of rows in the MAPI table.

As usual, this method returns the status of the call.

S_OK   The method executed successfully.

MAPI_E_BUSY   Another process is busy and should be stopped first or be allowed to complete.

MAPI_E_CALL_FAILED   The call failed for a non-specific reason.

MAPI_E_INVALID_PARAMETER   An invalid parameter was passed to this method.

MAPI_E_NO_SUPPORT   Either the messaging system or a provider does not support this method.

MAPI_E_NOT_ENOUGH_MEMORY   There is not enough memory to complete this action.

MAPI_E_UNKNOWN_FLAGS   An invalid flag was specified.

MAPI_W_APPROX_COUNT   An approximate row count was returned because the exact count could not be determined.

Now you are ready to begin extracting row information from the table. To do this, use the QueryRows method that is available to the table object.

```
HRESULT QueryRows(LONG lRowCount, ULONG ulFlags, LPSRowSet FAR * lppRows)
```

lRowCount   This parameter specifies the number of rows to return at a time.

ulFlags   TBL_NOADVANCE is the one flag that you may set for QueryRows. If this flag is enabled, the position is not advanced and the first position, relative to the current position in the table before the call, is returned.

lppRows   Specifies the variable that will hold the information returned from the table. This variable must be of the type SRowSet, which is discussed later in the chapter.

Again, the status of the call will be returned. Notice that some of these return values are unique to QueryRows.

S_OK   The method executed successfully.

MAPI_E_CALL_FAILED   The call failed for some non-specific reason.

MAPI_E_INVALID_BOOKMARK   A bookmark is invalid because it no longer exists or exists beyond the range of result rows.

MAPI_E_INVALID_PARAMETER   One of the parameters passed to the method is invalid.

MAPI_E_NO_SUPPORT   The method is not supported by either the messaging system or a provider.

MAPI_E_NOT_ENOUGH_MEMORY   There is not enough memory to complete this action.

MAPI_E_UNKNOWN_FLAGS   An invalid flag was specified.

MAPI_W_POSITION_CHANGED   The bookmark is not currently at the same position at which it was last.

Understanding Table Structures

The QueryRows call returns a predetermined number of rows of information from the table to a structure that holds this information. This structure, SRowSet, is quite complex, and you need an overview of it before attempting to understand the messaging system further.

Because a hierarchy is so important to the messaging system, you should not be surprised that the SRowSet is made up of a hierarchy of data types. Figure 36.8 depicts the relationship of several data types within SRowSet.

FIGURE 36.8.

Hierarchy of data types used in MAPI tables.

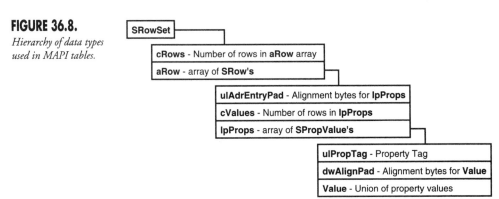

Although the structure depicted in Figure 36.8 appears daunting, the actual process of setting and retrieving property values from the table structure is fairly straightforward. Let's first review the structure of information in a table.

As mentioned earlier, there are many tables for different MAPI objects in the messaging system. In our example, we want to examine the message store table in order to determine the default message store. In this case, the message store table would consist of a series of rows and columns; each row represents a message store and each column represents the properties of each individual message store. Table 36.5 shows a sample of what a message store table might look like.

Table 36.5. A sample of what a message store table object might contain.

PR_PROVIDER_DISPLAY	PR_DISPLAY_NAME	PR_DEFAULT_STORE
Microsoft Mail	My Information Store	TRUE
Microsoft Mail	Second Info Store	FALSE
Microsoft Fax	Just the Fax	FALSE

Assume for a moment that the data in Table 36.5 is valid. Therefore, the messaging system should have one profile with three message stores labeled My Information Store, Second Info Store, and Just the Fax. To retrieve this table, you could use the following lines of code:

```
LPSRowSet lpRows = NULL;
const static SizedSPropTagArray(3, columns)=
    {3,{ PR_PROVIDER_DISPLAY, PR_DISPLAY_NAME, PR_DEFAULT_STORE }};

// Assuming we already have the pointer to the session, open the
// Message Stores Table for access.
lpSession->GetMsgStoresTable(0, &lpTable);

// Instruct the system to return only the provider and display names
// and the default flag.
hResult = lpTable->SetColumns((LPSPropTagArray)&columns, 0);

// Let's just retrieve two rows for an example.
lpTable->QueryRows(2, 0, &lpRows);
```

Now that lpRows holds two rows from the table, how do we analyze lpRows? To understand the data structure thoroughly, let's examine an example where we want to retrieve the display name of the second message store in the table.

According to Figure 36.8, our lpRows structure should contain an array of aRows. The number of elements in the array aRows is the same number of rows you asked the messaging system to return when QueryRows was called. Remember, all C and C++ arrays begin with zero unless otherwise specified. Therefore, if you wanted to evaluate information stored in the second row returned from the table, you would begin building the following C++ syntax:

```
// This is the second row of the table, since arrays begin with
// zero index.
lpRows->aRow[1]
```

The next data structure depicted in Figure 36.8 shows that lpProps is an element of aRows. lpProps is also an array structure, where the number of elements in the array is the number of columns that were asked to be returned from the MAPI table with the SetColumns method. Again, array indices begin at zero. Now you can add the following to the preceding C++ code to retrieve the second column of the second row:

```
lpRows->aRow[1].lpProps[1]
```

Now the code will bring you to the structure that contains the actual data. Adding Value to the end of your code will enable access to the actual data found at the current row and column.

```
lpRows->aRow[1].lpProps[1].Value
```

In Figure 36.8, you may notice that Value is a union of properties. In reality, there are multiple data types for each piece of data in the table. Just as there are numeric and alphanumeric data types in databases, Extended MAPI enjoys over two dozen data types specific to MAPI tables. The information we are interested in returning in this example is in a string format, LPSZ to be exact. Therefore, example code to display the string in the table at row two, column two, in a message box would be

```
MessageBox(lpRows->aRow[1].lpProps[1].Value.LPSZ, "RESULT", MB_OK);
```

Be forewarned, some of the Value data types are arrays or structures of their own. For instance, the bin data type is a structure with two members: cb and lpb. You will see how the binary data type is used to store the entry ID of a message store in a moment, when you open the message store.

Opening the Message Store

You are finally ready to open the message store. A messaging-aware application may wish to present valid message stores in a list or other GUI interface, or may wish to simply use the default message store. This chapter examines opening the default message store, because this introduces fundamental techniques.

To open the default message store, you must first search through the message store table for the entry ID of the default store. Using Figure 36.8 as a guide, notice that the lpProps array (properties of data at a particular row and column) contains a member ulPropTag. To determine the default message store, you can construct code that loops through the total number of rows (message stores) of a message store table and reads each one line by line. The code can then check the ulPropTag of each row to see if the current row is marked as PR_DEFAULT_STORE.

```
static SizedSPropTagArray(2, columns) =
    {2,{ PR_DEFAULT_STORE, PR_ENTRYID }};

lpSession->GetMsgStoresTable(0, &lpTable);

// Now that the store table has been created, we need to find the
// DEFAULT message store.  We'll search through the list for a
// DEFAULT property tag by querying the MAPI table, pulling only
// the PR_DEFAULT_STORE and PR_ENTRYID columns.
hResult = lpTable->SetColumns((LPSPropTagArray)&columns, 0);

hResult = lpTable->GetRowCount(0, lpulRowCount);

for (ulIndex=0; ulIndex<(ULONG)lpulRowCount; ulIndex++){

    // Retrieve only one row at a time.
    // Only one row (aRow[0]) is returned from the table.
    lpTable->QueryRows(1, 0, &lpRows);

    // Examine the ulPropTag of the 1st column (PR_DEFAULT_STORE)
    // to see if it exists.  If it does, then the currently selected
    // row is the default row (message store) so stop checking.
```

```
    if(lpRows->aRow[0].lpProps[0].ulPropTag == PR_DEFAULT_STORE)
        break;

    lpRows = NULL;
}
```

Now that you have the current default message store, which is indicated by the current row in the message store table, you can open it. To open it, you must use the OpenMsgStore method.

```
HRESULT OpenMsgStore(ULONG ulUIParam,
                     ULONG cbEntryID,
                     LPENTRYID lpEntryID,
                     LPCIID lpInterface,
                     ULONG ulFlags,
                     LPMDB FAR * lppMDB)
```

ulUIParam   Specifies the parent window handle of the calling application. If a zero is passed as this parameter, no parent window is indicated.

cbEntryID   The length in bytes of the entry ID for the message store to be opened.

lpEntryID   A pointer to the entry ID for the message store to be opened. This parameter may not be NULL.

lpInterface   If you wish to use an interface other than the standard, you may specify it with this parameter. Passing NULL will instruct the messaging system to use the default interface.

ulFlags   There are four flags that may be used to determine the behavior of OpenMsgStore. Valid flags are listed in Table 36.6.

Table 36.6. The OpenMsgStore parameter will accept these flags.

MAPI_BEST_ACCESS	Opens the message store with the user's typical read and write privileges.
MAPI_DEFERRED_ERRORS	Causes the OpenMsgStore message to succeed, even if the message store cannot be opened. Later calls may then be used to return error codes.
MDB_NO_DIALOG	Restricts logon dialog boxes from appearing.
MDB_WRITE	Attempts to open the message store with write privileges.

lppMDB   An output parameter that points to the opened message store object. This pointer will be necessary for additional methods to be used on the message store.

As usual, the status of the call is returned. Some error codes are unique to the OpenMsgStore method.

S_OK   The method was executed successfully.

MAPI_E_CALL_FAILED   The method failed to execute for some non-specific reason.

MAPI_E_EXTENDED_ERROR   An undefined error has occurred. GetLastError should be used on the object to determine the exact error specified by the service provider.

MAPI_E_INVALID_ENTRYID   The entry ID specified is invalid.

MAPI_E_INVALID_OBJECT   The object has been released or modified since the method was called.

MAPI_E_INVALID_PARAMETER   A parameter passed to the method is invalid.

MAPI_E_NO_ACCESS   The user has insufficient rights to use this method.

MAPI_E_NO_SUPPORT   Either the messaging system or a service provider does not support this method.

MAPI_E_NOT_ENOUGH_MEMORY   There is not enough memory to complete this action.

MAPI_E_UNKNOWN_FLAGS   An invalid flag was specified.

MAPI_W_ERRORS_RETURNED   The call was successful, but a property could not be accessed.

As you may notice, the OpenMsgStore method expects the length of the entry ID as well as the pointer to the entry ID for a message store in order to open it. Fortunately, the message store table that you queried earlier retrieved the PR_ENTRY_ID column. This table column holds the entry ID structure for each row (or message) store in the table. The PR_ENTRY_ID column formats the data to an SBinary type, which conveniently holds both the length and pointer of the entry ID.

The following sample code finishes the process to open a default message store:

```
// Now open the default message store. Notice lpProps[1] in the
// OpenMsgStore call. The lpProps array holds the results that we
// asked for when we set the columns for retrieval above (SetColumns).
// So the first spot in the array (lpProps[0]) has the info on if the
// current row (aRow[0]) is a default store and the second spot
// (lpProps[1]) holds the entry ID for the default store.
lpSession->OpenMsgStore(ulUIParam,
                        lpRows->aRow[0].lpProps[1].Value.bin.cb,
                        (LPENTRYID)lpRows->aRow[0].lpProps[1].Value.bin.lpb,
                        NULL,
                        MDB_WRITE,
                        &lpStore);
```

Opening Folders

The inside of a message store is the heart of the MAPI message system, messages, and folders. However, to work with most messages, a basic understanding of folders is necessary. For instance, to compose outgoing messages, the application must be able to compose a new message in the Outbox folder. To read new messages, access to the Inbox is required. The following sections examine how to access these two types of folders in a message store.

Planting Trees

Before you begin searching through the message store for the Outbox and Inbox folders, you must guarantee that the current message store has these default folders. This verification may be performed with the `HrValidateIPMSubtree` function. The `HrValidateIPMSubtree` function verifies that the standard Interpersonal Message (IPM) folders—IPM root, Deleted Items, and Finders—are available to the message store. If not, this function will create the default tree.

```
STDAPI HrValidateIPMSubtree(LPMDB lpMDB,
                            ULONG ulFlags,
                            ULONG FAR *lpcValues,
                            LPSPropValue FAR *lppProps,
                            LPMAPIERROR FAR *lppMapiError)
```

`lpMDB`   This is an input parameter that is a pointer to the message store on which you wish to validate the tree structure.

`ulFlags`   The two flags listed in Table 36.7 are available to control the behavior of this function.

Table 36.7. Valid flags for the `HrValidateIPMSubtree` function.

`MAPI_FORCE_CREATE`	If a folder has valid properties, it may be verified before creation. This flag enforces this rule.
`MAPI_FULL_IPM_TREE`	Although the function call without this flag enabled creates the basic IPM structure, you must enable this flag to add Inbox, Outbox, and Sent Mail folders, as well as Common Views.

`lpcValues`   This parameter accepts the number of properties that will be copied into the `lppProps` array after the call has completed.

`lppProps`   An output parameter pointing to an array of properties for the folders. All of the properties below are returned when the `MAPI_FULL_IPM_TREE` flag is used. Without this flag set, every property below is returned except: `PR_IPM_OUTBOX_ENTRYID`, `PR_IPM_SENTMAIL_ENTRYID`, and `PR_COMMON_VIEWS_ENTRYID`.

`PR_IPM_SUBTREE_ENTRYID`

`PR_IPM_WASTEBASKET_ENTRYID`

`PR_IPM_OUTBOX_ENTRYID`

`PR_IPM_SENTMAIL_ENTRYID`

`PR_VIEWS_ENTRYID`

`PR_COMMON_VIEWS_ENTRYID`

`PR_FINDER_ENTRYID`

lppMapiError   An output pointer to a MAPI error structure for additional error information.

The HrValidateIPMSubtree function will return one of the following codes, depending on the result.

S_OK   The call was executed successfully.

MAPI_E_INVALID_PARAMETER   An invalid parameter was passed to the method.

MAPI_E_NOT_ENOUGH_MEMORY   There is not enough memory to complete this action.

MAPI_E_UNKNOWN_FLAGS   An invalid flag was specified.

Getting the Outbox, Sent Mail, and Wastebasket

Once an application has guaranteed that the correct IPM structure is available with the HrValidateIPMSubtree function, it is possible to obtain the entry ID for the Outbox, Sent Mail, and Wastebasket folders. As shown earlier, the HrValidateIPMSubtree function returns an array of properties for each folder. These properties include PR_IPM_OUTBOX_ENTRYID, PR_IPM_SENTMAIL_ENTRYID, and PR_IPM_WASTEBASKET_ENTRYID.

To find the appropriate entry ID for one of these special IPM folders, you must loop through all of the properties returned from HrValidateIPMSubtree. Each property's ulPropTag must be compared to find a match for the folder you wish to open. The following source code demonstrates how to use this process to find the Outbox folder.

```
hResult = HrValidateIPMSubtree(lpStore, MAPI_FULL_IPM_TREE,
                          &ulPropCount, &pProps, NULL);
BOOL found = FALSE;

for (i=0; i<ulPropCount; i++){
    if (pProps[i].ulPropTag == PR_IPM_OUTBOX_ENTRYID){
        found = TRUE;
        break;
    }
}
```

This sample code will scan through the list of folders available and stop the search when the outbox has been found. The entry ID information for the outbox may then be obtained by examining the property value's (SPropValue) data structure for the property array. For example, the following two lines demonstrate how to access the length of the entry ID and the actual entry ID pointer, based on the results of the previous code.

```
pProps[i].Value.bin.cb
pProps[i].Value.bin.lpb
```

Getting the Inbox

Retrieving the entry ID of an inbox is a little different. Although there is a placeholder in the properties returned from HrValidateIPMSubtree for an inbox, a separate message store method is available that returns the correct information directly.

The `GetReceiveFolder` method is a member of the message store object. The first parameter of this method prompts for a message class. These message classes are strings that help the messaging system identify and act upon messages based on their type. For instance, IPM.NOTE is the typical message class used to identify standard e-mail messages. There are additional classes such as IPM.FAX or IPM.PHONE and more can be added in the future. It is important to remember to include these message classes when retrieving the entry ID of an inbox or composing new messages. Later in the chapter you will see how the message class is important to new messages and how to set this property.

```
HRESULT GetReceiveFolder(LPTSTR lpszMessageClass,
                         ULONG ulFlags,
                         ULONG FAR * lpcbEntryID,
                         LPENTRYID FAR * lppEntryID,
                         LPTSTR FAR * lppszExplicitClass)
```

   `lpszMessageClass`   This is a string that identifies the message class type to use for the inbox. A value of NULL uses the default inbox folder for the message store.

   `ulFlags`   You may choose to use Unicode strings with this method. If so, make sure you set this flag to MAPI_UNICODE.

   `lpcbEntryID`   This is an output parameter that holds the length of `lppEntryID` in bytes. This parameter, in conjunction with the `lppEntryID` parameter, is essential to opening the inbox folder.

   `lppEntryID`   The returned value in this parameter is the actual entry ID for the inbox folder.

   `lpszExplicitClass`   The returned value of this parameter is a string identifying a class name. This is the name of the message class that uses the inbox folder returned in `lppEntryID`, as that class's receive folder. Passing a NULL into this parameter indicates that no such class name should be returned.

The following return codes are generated from `GetReceiveFolder`:

   `S_OK`   The method executed successfully.
   `MAPI_E_BAD_CHARWIDTH`   Unicode was specified but not used with Unicode strings.
   `MAPI_E_CALL_FAILED`   The call failed for some non-specific reason.
   `MAPI_E_INVALID_ENTRYID`   An invalid entry ID was specified.
   `MAPI_E_INVALID_PARAMETER`   An invalid parameter was passed to this method.
   `MAPI_E_NO_SUPPORT`   Either the messaging system or a service provider does not support this method.
   `MAPI_E_NOT_ENOUGH_MEMORY`   There is not enough memory to complete this action.
   `MAPI_E_UNKNOWN_FLAGS`   An invalid flag was specified.

This line of code demonstrates how to use the `GetReceiveFolder` method:

```
// Get the IPM Inbox folder with no flags and hold the entry ID
// and the length of the entry ID in their respective variables.
hResult = lpStore->GetReceiveFolder("IPM", 0, &cbEIDSize, &pEID, NULL);
```

Opening a Folder

Once the appropriate folder has been found and its appropriate entry ID has been determined, it may be opened for further work. To do this, Extended MAPI provides the OpenEntry method. Although in this example you will be using OpenEntry to open a folder, it is a common method that may be applied to other objects such as messages or the address book. The actual method you will be using to open a folder is associated with the message store object.

```
HRESULT OpenEntry(ULONG cbEntryID,
                  LPENTRYID lpEntryID,
                  LPCIID lpInterface,
                  ULONG ulFlags,
                  ULONG FAR * lpulObjType,
                  LPUNKNOWN FAR * lppUnk)
```

cbEntryID   This is the length of the entry ID for the folder in bytes. This value is returned as a parameter in the GetReceiveFolder function and may be extracted from the SPropValue data structure for other IPM-related folders such as the outbox, as shown earlier.

lpEntryID   This parameter is the actual entry ID that uniquely identifies the folder object that OpenEntry is attempting to open.

lpInterface   If NULL is passed into this parameter, the standard interface is used for the return information. Another interface identifier pointer may be passed into this parameter as well.

ulFlags   As with most methods, the OpenEntry method enables special flags to control its functionality. Table 36.8 lists the available flags.

Table 36.8. Flags that may be used with the OpenEntry method.

MAPI_BEST_ACCESS	Opens the message store with the user's typical read and write privileges.
MAPI_DEFERRED_ERRORS	Causes the OpenMsgStore message to succeed, even if the message store cannot be opened. Later calls may then be used to return error codes.
MAPI_MODIFY	The default mode for the interface returned by OpenEntry is read-only. You must specify this flag to enable modification to the interface.

lpulObjType   Returns the type of object that was opened via the OpenEntry method.

lppUnk   This parameter returns a pointer to the actual opened object. For instance, when opening a folder object based on its entry ID, the opened folder object is returned to the variable in this parameter. This pointer variable may then be used for additional methods to be performed on the open folder object.

This method would not be complete without returning a status code.

S_OK   The method was executed successfully.

MAPI_E_CALL_FAILED   The method failed to execute for some non-specific reason.

MAPI_E_INTERFACE_NOT_SUPPORTED   The object does not support this interface.

MAPI_E_INVALID_ENTRYID   An invalid entry ID was specified.

MAPI_E_INVALID_OBJECT   An object was released or modified since the method was called.

MAPI_E_INVALID_PARAMETER   A parameter passed to the method is invalid.

MAPI_E_NO_ACCESS   The user has insufficient privileges to use this method.

MAPI_E_SUBMITTED   The message has been submitted.

MAPI_E_NO_SUPPORT   Either the messaging system or a service provider does not support this method.

MAPI_E_NOT_ENOUGH_MEMORY   There is not enough memory to complete this action.

MAPI_E_NOT_FOUND   The object specified is invalid.

In the next sections, you will see how to use OpenEntry to open both the Inbox and Outbox folders.

Reading the Inbox

Now that the GetReceiveFolder and OpenEntry methods have been explained, you can use them together to open the Inbox and read mail messages stored there. For this example, we will open the inbox and obtain a MAPI table that holds the contents of that folder. We then scan through the table information to retrieve and display the subjects for all messages in the default inbox.

Doing this requires the knowledge of another method that retrieves the contents information of an object. GetContentsTable is very similar to other table methods such as the GetMsgStoresTable method you learned earlier. In fact, the GetContentsTable method expects the same parameters and returns the same type of table structure as GetMsgStoresTable. The difference is that GetContentsTable returns information about everything in a particular object, not just the message store. As you explore Extended MAPI further, you will notice that there are several methods available to retrieve additional information tables. Remember that although each of these methods returns different sets of data, they often accept the same type of parameters and return a table structure that must be analyzed as discussed earlier in the section "Understanding Table Structures."

Therefore, let's examine the source code necessary to open an IPM inbox and display the subjects of all messages in that folder.

```
LPMAPITABLE pInboxTable;
const static SizedSPropTagArray(2, sptMailProps)=
    {2, { PR_ENTRYID, PR_SUBJECT }};

HrValidateIPMSubtree(lpStore, MAPI_FULL_IPM_TREE,
                     &ulPropCount, &pProps, NULL);

hResult = lpStore->GetReceiveFolder("IPM", 0, &cbEIDSize, &pEID, NULL);
hResult = lpStore->OpenEntry(cbEIDSize, (LPENTRYID)pEID, NULL,
                        MAPI_MODIFY ¦ MAPI_DEFERRED_ERRORS,
                        &ulObjType, (LPUNKNOWN *)&lpFolder);

hResult = lpFolder->GetContentsTable(0, &pInboxTable);

// We only need to read the subjects, so pull entry ID and subject
// of each message.
hResult = pInboxTable->SetColumns((LPSPropTagArray)&sptMailProps, 0);
hResult = pInboxTable->GetRowCount(0, &ulRowCount);

// Make sure we're at the beginning of the table.
hResult = pInboxTable->SeekRow(BOOKMARK_BEGINNING, 0, NULL);

for (i=0; i<ulRowCount; i++){
    hResult = pInboxTable->QueryRows(1, 0, &pRows);
    wsprintf(MsgHeader,"Message #%lu Subject", i+1);
    MessageBox(pRows->aRow[0].lpProps[1].Value.LPSZ, MsgHeader, MB_OK);
}
```

Composing a New Message

Besides reading message information and navigating folders, it is important to be able to create and send new MAPI messages. This will be a popular function of Windows 95 application software as more applications become messaging-aware. Sending a message requires the following key steps:

- Opening the default message store
- Opening the Outbox folder
- Creating a new message
- Setting attributes on the message, including attachments
- Choosing recipients
- Submitting the message for delivery

The sample code that follows executes these exact steps to create a new message. However, before you examine the sample code, review two additional methods: the folder object's CreateMessage method and the message object's SubmitMessage method. The SubmitMessage method belongs to the message object that is created and returned by the CreateMessage object.

```
HRESULT CreateMessage(LPCIID lpInterface, ULONG ulFlags, LPMESSAGE FAR *
➥lppMessage)
```

lpInterface   This is a reserved parameter and must be NULL.

ulFlags   Once again, this method can use two flags to determine its behavior. MAPI_ASSOCIATED instructs the method to return an Associated Entries table instead of the standard MAPI table. This table typically contains information regarding forms and views in the messaging system. The second flag, MAPI_DEFERRED_ERRORS, enables the method to succeed so that a later call can expose the error.

lppMessage   The final return parameter is a pointer to the new message object that is created. This object pointer will then be used in subsequent method calls and property changes.

As usual, this method returns one of the following results, based on the success of the call.

S_OK   The call was successful.

MAPI_E_CALL_FAILED   The call failed for some non-specific reason.

MAPI_E_INTERFACE_NOT_SUPPORTED   An interface is not supported for the object specified.

MAPI_E_INVALID_OBJECT   An object has been modified or released since the method was called.

MAPI_E_INVALID_PARAMETER   An invalid parameter was passed to the method.

MAPI_E_NO_ACCESS   The user has insufficient privileges to use this method.

MAPI_E_NO_SUPPORT   Either the messaging system or a service provider does not support this method.

MAPI_E_NOT_ENOUGH_MEMORY   There is not enough memory to complete this action.

MAPI_E_UNKNOWN_FLAGS   An invalid flag was specified.

After a new message has been created and any necessary properties have been modified, the messaging system must be instructed to take the newly formed message and send it out. This is accomplished with the SubmitMessage message object method.

HRESULT SubmitMessage(ULONG ulFlags)

ulFlags   This flag can be set to FORCE_SUBMIT, which instructs the messaging system to submit the message, although it may not be sent immediately.

Return codes include the following:

S_OK   The message was successfully submitted.

MAPI_E_CALL_FAILED   The call failed for some non-specific reason.

MAPI_E_INVALID_PARAMETER   A parameter passed to the method is invalid.

MAPI_E_NO_RECIPIENTS   No recipients were specified to receive the new message.

MAPI_E_NO_SUPPORT   Either the messaging system or a service provider does not support this method.

MAPI_E_NOT_ENOUGH_MEMORY   There is not enough memory to complete this action.

MAPI_E_NON_STANDARD   Submission of a message will take longer than typically necessary. This is a warning of such a condition.

MAPI_E_UNKNOWN_FLAGS   An invalid flag was specified.

Changing New Message Properties

Sometimes the default MAPI client interface for composing and sending messages is sufficient for a messaging-aware application. However, there are times when setting these properties automatically is necessary or convenient. Setting message properties such as the message body, subject, or recipients may be accomplished using SPropValue data structures like those used in MAPI tables. Thankfully, the syntax for accessing the property structure is shortened because message properties do not require the SRowSet and SRow structures necessary in MAPI tables.

For this chapter, let's automatically insert a subject into the message and a few simple lines of text into the main body of the message. It is important to notice that this example will insert standard text into the message body for simplicity, yet the Extended MAPI system fully supports rich-text data.

To set a property, the ulPropTag element of the SPropValue structure must be set to the appropriate property type you wish to change. These types are the same property names as those used with the SetColumn statements to extract property information from a table. For example, the following code would be used to set the property type as PR_SUBJECT.

```
spvProp.ulPropTag = PR_SUBJECT;
```

Now additional assignments can be made to modify the subject property of the message object. In this case, the subject of a message is a string. Therefore, you would now set the LPSZ property value.

```
spvProp.Value.LPSZ = (LPSTR)"This is the message subject";
```

Now that you have updated the property structure, you must instruct the message object to use these new settings. You can use the HrSetOneProp function to set a single object property. This function can be used with multiple MAPI object types, but in this example you will use it with a message object. The HrSetOneProp function is defined as

```
STDAPI HrSetOneProp (LPMAPIPROP pmp, LPSPropValue pprop)
```

> pmp   This parameter points to a MAPIPROP (MAPI Properties) interface or one that is derived from this interface. When setting message properties, it would be correct to cast the pointer of the MAPI message object as MAPIPROP.
>
> pprop   This parameter points to the SPropValue structure that holds the modified properties to be committed.

This function returns one of the following result codes, indicating its success or failure.

> S_OK   The function was successful.
> MAPI_E_INVALID_PARAMETER   A parameter passed to the function is invalid.
> MAPI_E_INVALID_TYPE   The property type specified is invalid.
> MAPI_E_NOT_FOUND   The object specified does not exist.

To commit the changes made to the subject line of a message, you must add the following line after you set the property values:

```
hResult = HrSetOneProp((LPMAPIPROP)lpMessage, &spvProp);
```

This process can be repeated to set another message object property, such as the body text of the message.

```
spvProp.ulPropTag = PR_BODY;
spvProp.Value.LPSZ = (LPSTR)"This is the body of the message.";
hResult = HrSetOneProp((LPMAPIPROP)lpMessage, &spvProp);
```

Although these are optional properties to set on a message, there is one property that is important to remember to set any time a new message is composed. It is the PR_MESSAGE_CLASS property. This property contains a string that is the message class name that identifies the new message's type. If you fail to set this property accordingly, messages may be misunderstood by a messaging client program. For example, Exchange will display the new messages created in the outbox with question marks on top of the envelope icon for the message. This indicates that Exchange is not sure what type the new message is and therefore cannot determine the appropriate icon to display. The following example details how to set the PR_MESSAGE_CLASS property:

```
spvProp.ulPropTag = PR_MESSAGE_CLASS;
spvProp.Value.LPSZ = (LPSTR)"IPM.NOTE";
hResult = HrSetOneProp((LPMAPIPROP)lpMessage, &spvProp);
```

Using the Address Book

The address book interface, like the message store, contains a hierarchical structure of information. It is quite complex, capable of displaying multiple address books based on multiple information service provider types, as well as robust maintenance commands and address book-specific tables.

Before using any methods of the address book, a messaging-aware application must first retrieve a pointer to an open address book object using the OpenAddressBook method that is available to the session object.

```
HRESULT OpenAddressBook(ULONG ulUIParam,
                        LPCIID lpInterface,
                        ULONG ulFlags,
                        LPADRBOOK FAR * lppAdrBook)
```

ulUIParam   Specifies the parent window handle of the calling application. If a zero is passed as this parameter, no parent window is indicated.

lpInterface   If you wish to use an interface other than the standard, you may specify it with this parameter. Passing NULL will instruct the messaging system to use the default interface.

ulFlags   AB_NO_DIALOG prevents the address book from displaying dialog boxes that may be invoked.

lppAdrBook   This output parameter returns a pointer to the address book object. This pointer should be maintained for additional method calls and property manipulation on the address book.

OpenAddressBook can return one of the following values:

S_OK   The method executed successfully.

MAPI_E_CALL_FAILED   The call failed for some non-specific reason.

MAPI_E_EXTENDED_ERROR   An undefined error has occurred. GetLastError should be used on the object to determine the exact error specified by the service provider.

MAPI_E_INVALID_OBJECT   The object specified is invalid.

MAPI_E_INVALID_PARAMETER   A parameter passed to this method is invalid.

MAPI_E_NO_SUPPORT   Either the messaging system or a service provider does not support this method.

MAPI_E_NOT_ENOUGH_MEMORY   There is not enough memory to complete this action.

MAPI_E_UNKNOWN_FLAGS   A specified flag is invalid.

The following code is an example of this method in action:

```
lpSession->OpenAddressBook((ULONG)(void *)m_hWnd, NULL, 0, &lpAdrBook);
```

Address Book Properties

The address book object is now available, so it is possible to display the address book and use it. However, before displaying the interface, it is crucial to set particular properties for the address book that control its appearance and additional functionality. These properties are stored in the ADRPARM address book data structure.

The ADRPARM structure contains 18 elements that may be set to affect the overall display and use of the address book. The following are the properties for the address book:

ULONG cbABContEntryID   Size of the entry ID, in bytes, of the ID passed in as lpABContEntryID.

LPENTRYID lpABContEntryID   This is the entry ID of a specific address book container. Passing in NULL to this property will cause the address book to use a custom recipient provider.

ULONG ulFlags   Table 36.9 shows valid flags that you can use when you are working with the address book.

Table 36.9. A list of valid flags to use in the ADRPARM structure.

AB_RESOLVE	Forces names picked in the address list to be verified and resolved if necessary.
AB_SELECTONLY	Enabling this flag will remove items in the address book dialog box that are related to creating new addresses or typing in addresses.
ADDRESS_ONE	Instructs the address book to enable the user to pick only one recipient from the address list.
DIALOG_MODAL	Makes the address book dialog box modal.
DIALOG_OPTIONS	Displays the Send Options button in the address book dialog box.
DIALOG_SDI	Makes the address book dialog box modeless.

LPFNABHOOKPROC lpfnHook   If an application needs to process the messages sent to the address book, a pointer to the callback function may be passed in as this property.

ULONG ulTemplateOwner   If a dialog box template is to be used, this is the hInstance of that dialog box.

LPTSTR lpTemplateName   When the client application wishes to use its own dialog resource instead of the standard dialogs provided with the address book, this property must specify that dialog resource's name.

LPFNABSDI lpfnABSDI   If the DIALOG_SDI flag is set in the ulFlags property, then lpfnABSDI points to a function in the client application that will be used to process the Windows message loop.

LPFNDISMISS lpfnDismiss   If the DIALOG_SDI flag is used, then lpfnDismiss is the address of a callback function in the client application that is executed when the dialog box is dismissed.

LPVOID lpvDismissContext   If the DIALOG_SDI flag is used, this property points to the context information that was passed in when the Address method of the address book object was called. This context is used in conjunction with the lpfnDismiss property for dismissing dialog boxes.

LPTSTR lpszCaption   This is the string that specifies the caption to use on the window of the address book.

LPTSTR lpszNewEntryTitle   This is the actual text prompt used in the dialog box to ask the user to pick recipients from the dialog box.

LPTSTR lpszDestWellsTitle   Above the typical TO, CC, and BCC wells that appear on the right side of the standard address book, there is room for a line of instruction. This line may be set with the lpszDestWellsTitle property.

`ULONG cDestFields`   This property indicates the number of recipient wells to display. The value assigned to this property may be 0 through 3. Zero indicates that there are no wells and that the address book is to be opened for browsing purposes only. A 1 indicates just the TO well, 2 indicates both the TO and CC wells, and 3 indicates the TO, CC, and BCC wells.

`ULONG nDestFieldFocus`   This property specifies the well to receive focus initially when the address book is displayed. Its value may range between 0 and 2, where 0 specifies the TO well, 1 indicates the CC well, and 2 is the BCC well.

`LPTSTR FAR *lppszDestTitles`   In order to set multiple titles, this property expects a string array (`LPSTR`) defined as large as the number of wells displayed in the dialog box. This array structure will then contain the text used to title the TO, CC, and BCC buttons. The index for each element in the array may range from 0 to 2, where 0 specifies the TO button's text, 1 indicates the CC button's text, and 2 indicates the BCC button's text.

`ULONG FAR *lpulDestComps`   Like `lppszDestTitles`, this property expects an array in order to set multiple values at once. The values set in this array configure the three well types. Typically, the wells appear in the top to bottom order TO, CC, and BCC. The well types are determined by the values passed into this property of the address book. Again, the index for each element ranges from 0 to 2, where 0 indicates the first well and 2 indicates the third well. Each element of the array may then be set to an appropriate type such as `MAPI_TO`, `MAPI_CC`, or `MAPI_BCC`.

`LPSRestriction lpContRestriction`   This is a pointer to a structure (`SRestriction`) that restricts the address book container.

`LPSRestriction lpHierRestriction`   This pointer is similar to `lpContRestriction`, except that it restricts the hierarchy of the address book.

Invoking the Address Book

After each of these properties have been set accordingly, the address book object's `Address` method may be invoked to display the address book.

```
HRESULT Address(ULONG FAR * lpulUIParam,
            LPADRPARM lpAdrParms,
            LPADRLIST FAR * lppAdrList)
```

`lpulUIParam`   Specifies the parent window handle of the calling application. If a zero is passed as this parameter, no parent window is indicated.

`lpAdrParms`   This is the pointer to the `ADRPARM` structure, which contains properties that specify the nature of the address book.

`lppAdrList`   This is an output parameter that receives a pointer to an address list structure. It contains the recipients chosen by a user using the address book.

The `Address` method returns a result of the call.

`S_OK`   The method executed successfully.
`MAPI_E_CALL_FAILED`   The call failed for some non-specific reason.
`MAPI_E_INVALID_PARAMETER`   A parameter passed to this method is invalid.
`MAPI_E_NO_SUPPORT`   Either the messaging system or a service provider does not support this method.
`MAPI_E_NOT_ENOUGH_MEMORY`   There is not enough memory to complete this action.

Setting the Recipients for a Message

When a new message is composed, you can pass into the recipient list of the new message the recipient list specified in the `lppAdrList` parameter of the `Address` method. To do this, you need the new message object's `ModifyRecipients` method. Then the address list returned by the `Address` method is passed as the second parameter in `ModifyRecipients`.

`HRESULT ModifyRecipients(ULONG ulFlags, LPADRLIST lpMods)`

ulFlags   Several flags may be passed into this method to determine options for the method, as shown in Table 36.10.

Table 36.10. Flags used with the `ModifyRecipients` method.

`MODRECIP_ADD`	Adds the recipients from the address list to the current message.
`MODRECIP_MODIFY`	Modifies the properties of a recipient entry in the current message.
`MODRECIP_REMOVE`	Removes recipients from the current message's address list.

lpMods   A pointer to the list of recipients. You can add to or delete from this list, or modify the current address list for a message.

`ModifyRecipients` returns a single status code, just as every method outlined in this chapter.

`S_OK`   The method executed successfully.
`MAPI_E_CALL_FAILED`   The call failed for some non-specific reason.
`MAPI_E_INVALID_OBJECT`   An object is invalid because it was either released or modified since the method was called.
`MAPI_E_INVALID_PARAMETER`   A parameter passed to this method is invalid.
`MAPI_E_NO_SUPPORT`   Either the messaging system or a service provider does not support this method.
`MAPI_E_NOT_ENOUGH_MEMORY`   There is not enough memory available to complete this action.
`MAPI_E_NOT_FOUND`   The object specified is invalid.
`MAPI_E_UNKNOWN_FLAGS`   An invalid flag was passed to this method.

All Together Now

Let's take a look at some sample code that puts together everything you've learned. This code will open and display the address book and set the recipient list for the message from the address book. Figure 36.9 shows the appearance of the address book, based on the properties set.

```
lpSession->OpenAddressBook((ULONG)(void *)m_hWnd, NULL, 0, &lpAdrBook);

rglpszDestTitles[0]            = "MY To";
rglpszDestTitles[1]            = "MY Cc";
rgulDestComps[0]               = MAPI_TO;
rgulDestComps[1]               = MAPI_CC;

adrparm.cbABContEntryID        = 0;
adrparm.lpABContEntryID        = NULL;
adrparm.ulFlags                = DIALOG_MODAL;
adrparm.lpReserved             = NULL;
adrparm.ulHelpContext          = 0;
adrparm.lpszHelpFileName       = NULL;
adrparm.lpfnABSDI              = NULL;
adrparm.lpfnDismiss            = NULL;
adrparm.lpvDismissContext      = NULL;
adrparm.lpszCaption            = "Address Book - lpszCaption";
adrparm.lpszNewEntryTitle      = "In this example only -
                                     lpszNewEntryTitle";
adrparm.lpszDestWellsTitle     = "Pick - lpszDestWellsTitle";
adrparm.cDestFields            = 2;
adrparm.nDestFieldFocus        = 0;
adrparm.lppszDestTitles        = rglpszDestTitles;
adrparm.lpulDestComps          = rgulDestComps;
adrparm.lpContRestriction      = NULL;
adrparm.lpHierRestriction      = NULL;

hResult = lpAdrBook->Address(&ulUIParam, &adrparm, &lpadrlist)
hResult = lpMessage->ModifyRecipients(MODRECIP_ADD, lpadrlist);
```

FIGURE 36.9.

Snapshot of the address book (left window) and a new entry dialog (right window) with the appropriate properties used in the sample code.

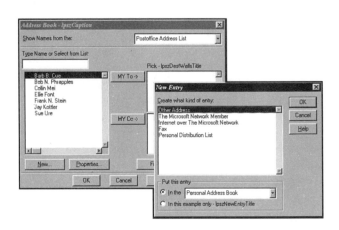

FinishedMsg

This chapter touched only the surface of Extended MAPI. The system is vastly complex, with additional forms and views capabilities, Exchange client extensions, information service provider interfaces, and OLE Automation support for applications such as Visual Basic or VBA. It would be impossible to cover the entire depth of Extended MAPI with the detail it deserves in a single chapter. But now you should be familiar with the fundamentals of Extended MAPI and hopefully can begin exploring the further depths of the messaging system on your own.

TAPI

37

by James Thayer

IN THIS CHAPTER

Computer telephony integration (CTI) combines two technologies: computers and telecommunications. These technologies have become very important to the way we conduct business in the 1990s. Broadly stated, the idea is to use computers to assist and improve the way we communicate.

Familiar examples of computer-telephony integration are data communication and fax programs. Other examples that are becoming more prevalent are personal information managers, which enable you to makes a call by clicking on a name; contact managers, which use caller ID information to provide information on a caller automatically; call control software, which make the advanced features of PBXs and Centrex easier to use; and information managers, which give the user access to incoming e-mail, faxes, and voice mail, all in one place. The final example exists in Windows 95 already—the InBox.

Chapter Scope

This chapter gives you a basic understanding of the concepts and techniques for producing telephony applications using the Telephony API and concentrates primarily on the information needed to create and tear down telephone calls. Advanced calling features and phone devices are only mentioned briefly. Also included in this chapter are some of the tips and pitfalls I have learned the hard way.

This chapter does not include everything there is to know about TAPI. A lot of information was winnowed for the sake of brevity and clarity. For complete information, please refer to the *TAPI Reference Manual* included with the TAPI SDK 1.0 and with the Windows 95 SDK.

What Is TAPI?

The world of telecommunications is filled with a tremendous variety of hardware and systems. There is the standard telephone service most of us have in our homes, known in the industry as POTS (plain old telephone service.) There are advanced calling features, such as conference calling, made available through PBXs and Centrex. There are analog systems where the switching information is handled by sending tones along the same pathway as the voice, and there are digital systems that use a separate pathway for switching information. Finally, there is the integrated services digital network (ISDN), which promises to provide high-speed data communications for the masses. The variations are almost endless. Just collecting the standards, documents, and interface specifications is a daunting task. Designing a program that takes into account all of the differences can be a most difficult undertaking.

Recognizing a need to ease the burden on application developers, Microsoft and Intel teamed up to create the Windows Telephony API (TAPI), which provides a uniform interface to the applications programmer and allows an application to operate with a wide variety of telecommunication systems without change.

TAPI was originally released for the Windows 3.1 platform, but it was not widely supported. However, with the advent of new telephony hardware and the release of Windows 95, there has been renewed interest in TAPI. A version of TAPI for Windows NT has been announced but does not exist as of this writing.

TAPI Architecture

Figure 37.1 shows how this piece of magic was pulled off. At the bottom, connecting TAPI to the actual telephone hardware is a TAPI *service provider* (TSP), the glue that binds the actual hardware to TAPI. Typically, TSPs are provided by the hardware vendor. A service provider called UNIMODEM, which is designed to work with AT command set modems, is provided with Windows 95.

FIGURE 37.1.
TAPI block diagram.

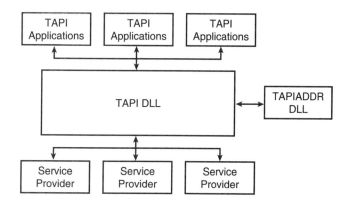

TIP

A very handy service provider to have is the Economical Service Provider (ESP). This service provider is purely software and doesn't actually connect to any telephone hardware. ESP provides an interface that allows the user to mimic almost any capability or feature supported by TAPI and allows programmers to test features of their applications without having to purchase or lease expensive telephone switches.

The middle layer, TAPI.DLL, supplies service provider management and information routing between the service providers and the applications. Multiple service providers and applications can coexist simultaneously; TAPI ensures that they coexist peacefully.

The TAPI DLLs are 16-bit DLLs; 16-bit applications can call the TAPI.DLL directly, whereas 32-bit applications, such as those written for Windows 95, use a thunking layer called TAPI32.DLL.

An adjunct to TAPI is TAPIADDR, which can ease the formatting of complete telephone numbers. TAPIADDR handles the details of taking a simple telephone number and converting it to a dialable format, which may include access code, area or city code, country code, as well as credit or calling card information.

Some Definitions

At this point, it will be helpful to define a few terms of the trade. Telephony people live in an alternate universe, and as a result, their language differs from normal human beings.

A *line* refers to a physical telephone line—what you plug into your telephone. The location at the end of the line is called the *station*.

An *address* is a telephone number. An address determines where the call is going; it is analogous to the street address of a house or building, which helps you find where you are going. It is important to note that although lines and addresses are often related on a one-to-one basis, this relationship is not guaranteed. An example of multiple addresses per line is *distinctive ringing*, where multiple addresses (telephone numbers) map to a single telephone line; each address causes the telephone to ring using a different ringing pattern.

> **TIP**
>
> If the distinction between an address and a line doesn't seem clear to you, cheer up. You are not alone. The differences between a line and an address can be blurred, particularly on PBXs. One manufacturer might treat a given configuration as several lines with one address each. Another manufacturer might treat the same configuration as one line with many addresses. As long as your application can deal with multiple lines and multiple addresses per line, it will be able to cope. The real trick is to hide the confusion from the user.

A *line device* is any physical device, such as a modem or ISDN card, that connects a computer to a telephone line or lines. A line device does not necessarily have to exist on the same computer on which the application is running. A PBX, for instance, might be connected to the computer through a local area network.

A *phone device* is any local device that can be used to control a call and sometimes to display information about the call. Usually this refers to telephone handsets and speakerphones but can also refer to other devices such as caller ID adjuncts and headsets.

A *terminal* is something at the end of a line. It can be a phone device (speakerphone, handset, etc.), or it can be a modem, fax card, or even a sound card installed in a computer. Some line devices have the capability to switch between several different terminals.

A *call* is the state that exists when two line devices are connected together by a telephone network. The *calling party* is the end that places the call, and the *called party* is the end that answers the call.

A *PBX*, or *private branch exchange*, is a privately owned telephone switch that provides switching within a building or set of buildings. Companies often use PBXs instead of providing individual telephone lines for all of their employees. A *trunk* is the connection between the PBX and the telephone company. Centrex is similar to a PBX in the sense that it gives the user a lot of the same features, but the switching equipment is owned by the telephone company and it is situated within the telephone company's facilities.

When preparing to place a call, the line is taken *offhook*, and when the call is ended, the line is put back *onhook*. These terms refer to the time when a telephone handset would literally hang on a hook. The device that senses when the handset is picked up is called a *hookswitch*. Operating the hookswitch rapidly is called a *flashhook* (or *flash* for short). *Flashhook* is the old-fashioned way of controlling a telephone.

Pulse dialing refers to the "clicky-click" dialing used by rotary-dial phones; the telephone number is transferred by current pulses. In *tone* dialing, special tones are used to send the number. Each digit or tone corresponds to the combination of two frequencies. Tone dialing is also know as Dual Tone Multi-Frequency (DTMF) dialing.

Ringback is a buzzing sound, which indicates to the caller that the phone is ringing at the other end of the line.

Callback, not to be confused with ringback, refers to a feature that can be invoked when a busy number is reached. When the busy line hangs up, the original caller is "called back." A similar feature is called "camp-on." To the typical user, the features are identical because the feature is invoked in a similar manner and the result is the same. To a telephony person, however, the two features are unrelated because they are implemented in different ways.

The *media mode* is the type of call. Typical media modes are voice, fax, and data. A *media stream* is the actual information flowing on the telephone connection. Table 37.9 gives a list of the media modes supported by TAPI.

Assisted TAPI

Assisted TAPI is a very easy way for a developer to provide limited telephony service to an application. Assisted TAPI does nothing more than dial a telephone number. Any program that provides a means of calling a DLL function can use Assisted TAPI. Many word processors, for instance, provide this capability in their macro language. It's not too hard for a clever programmer to write a macro that searches for a telephone number in a document and then dials the number. For example, you can use the following function:

```
LONG lErrCode =  tapiRequestMakeCall( lpszAddress,
                                      lpszAppname,
```

1002

```
                        lpszName,
                        lpszComment);
```

The number to dial is pointed to by `lpszAddress`. `lpszAppname` is the name of the application making the request. `lpszName` is the name of the person being called, and `lpszComment` is an optional comment. The only required parameter is `lpszAddress`. A null pointer may be passed in the place of any of the other parameters. `tapiRequestMakeCall()` returns a zero if the function is successful or an error code if the function fails. Table 37.1 lists the possible error codes.

Table 37.1. Assisted TAPI error codes.

Error Code	Meaning
TAPIERR_NOREQUESTRECIPIENT	No recipient application is available to handle the request.
TAPIERR_REQUESTQUEUEFULL	There is no room for any further call requests in the request queue.
TAPIERR_INVALDESTADDRESS	The specified address is not a valid address or is too long.
TAPIERR_INVALPOINTER	A pointer does not reference a valid memory location.

The program T_ASSIST.EXE, included on the CD-ROM, demonstrates a no frills Assisted TAPI application. The important part of the program is contained in the following lines—a telephone number is retrieved from an edit box and a call is made using that number:

```
char tele_str[TAPIMAXDESTADDRESSSIZE];

    // Grab the number from the edit box and dial it.
    GetDlgItemText( IDC_EDIT1, tele_str, sizeof(tele_str) );

    LONG lErrCode = tapiRequestMakeCall( tele_str,
                                         "T_ASSIST.EXE",
                                         NULL, NULL );
```

TAPI Concepts

Before I begin an exploration of the full Telephony API, it is useful to cover some of the concepts that permeate TAPI.

Device IDs

Device IDs are assigned to each device sequentially starting at zero; thus, if there are four line devices installed, the device IDs that correspond to those devices are 0, 1, 2, and 3.

Handles

TAPI uses handles to refer to every important class of object. There are handles for the application, for line devices, for addresses, for phone devices, and for calls. There are three kinds of call handles used: a generic call handle, a call handle used for consultation calls, and a call handle used for conference calls. It is very easy to get confused about which handle you should use. When in doubt, check the *TAPI Reference Manual.*

In TAPI, all handles are 32 bits long. (Pointers and simple data types are also 32 bits long.) This was done so that Windows 3.1 to Windows 95 porting problems would be minimized.

Variable-Length Data Structures

Most of the complex data types TAPI uses are in the form of variable-length data structures. The organization of these structures is shown in Figure 37.2. The first three fields, dwTotalSize, dwNeededSize, and dwUsedSize, are always the same. Following these fields are the fixed-length fields. This section of the structure is always the same length for a given structure type. In the last part are the variable-length fields. Typically the length ranges from 0 to 300 bytes—the potential exists for structures that are thousands of bytes long.

FIGURE 37.2.

A variable-length data structure.

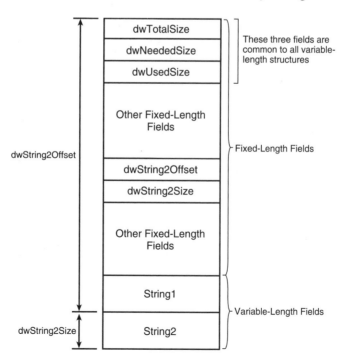

Information stored in the variable portion of the structure is always referenced in the fixed-length portion of the structure by an offset and a size. The offset tells, in bytes, where the variable-length data lies relative to the *beginning* of the data structure. The size, as one might expect, is the number of bytes that the variable-length data takes up. The size includes the null terminator at the end of the string.

> **WARNING**
>
> Most variable-length data are ASCII strings. TAPI, however, is fully capable of using DBCS and UNICODE strings. Therefore, the size of a variable-length data field may or may not correspond to the number of characters in the string. You can determine whether ASCII, DBCS, or UNICODE is used by checking the dwStringFormat fields in the LINEDEVCAPS and PHONECAPS structures. (See the section "Service Provider Capabilities.")

Memory for these structures is always allocated by the application. The application won't always know how big the data structure needs to be. That's where the first three fields come in. Before passing the structure to TAPI, the application fills in the dwTotalSize field with the size of the buffer.

TAPI verifies that the structure is at least big enough to hold the fixed-length part of the structure and then fills in the fixed-sized fields. Then the variable items are filled in. TAPI fills in variable items until there is no more room. TAPI then fills in the dwNeededSize field with the amount of space needed to get all of the data. The dwUsedSize field is filled in with the amount of space TAPI actually used.

When the application gets the structure back, it should check the dwNeededSize and dwUsedSize fields. If they are equal, then TAPI was able to find space for all of the variable-length data. If dwUsedSize is less than dwNeededSize, then an item of interest may not be present. The application can check the corresponding offset and size fields to see if the desired variable length data is present. If those fields are set to zero, then the application must allocate a larger buffer and try again. The following code fragment demonstrates this process:

```
LONG LineDev::GetProviderString( CString& StringRef,
                                 HLINEAPP appHandle )
{
    //Allocate space and assign to structure pointer.
    LONG lErrCode;
    BOOL done = FALSE;
    LPBYTE buffer = new BYTE[BIG_BUFF];
    LPLINEDEVCAPS lpDevCaps = (LPLINEDEVCAPS)buffer;
```

```
// Set dwTotalSize and make the call.
lpDevCaps->dwTotalSize = sizeof(BYTE)*BIG_BUFF;
while( !done )
{
    lErrCode = lineGetDevCaps( appHandle,
                              _lineID,
                              _APIVersion,
                              0, //Extensions not used.
                              lpDevCaps );
    // And now, check the results, if the call didn't fail...
    if( lErrCode == 0 )
    {
        // Check to see if the structure was large enough.
        if( lpDevCaps->dwUsedSize == lpDevCaps->dwNeededSize )
        {
            // If it was big enough, then copy the string.
            // and return.
            if( lpDevCaps->dwProviderInfoSize != 0 )
            {
                StringRef = (LPCSTR)(buffer +
                    LOWORD(lpDevCaps->dwProviderInfoOffset));
            }
            else   // If no string, then return an error.
                lErrCode = APPERR_NOSTRING;
            done = TRUE;
        }
        else
        {
            // If too small, then allocate a new
            // buffer and try again.
            DWORD newsize = lpDevCaps->dwNeededSize;
            delete[] buffer;
            buffer = new BYTE[newsize];
        }
    }
    else
        // If we got an error, then just return the errorcode
        done = TRUE;
    }
}
delete[] buffer;
return lErrCode;
}
```

TAPI Messages

TAPI messages, like Windows messages, are used as a signal to the application that certain asynchronous events have occurred. TAPI messages, however, are not handled by the normal Windows messaging process. Instead, when the application initializes, it can register a callback function with TAPI. TAPI calls this function whenever an asynchronous event occurs. There is one callback function to handle line device messages and one callback function to handle phone device messages.

A callback function is declared as follows:

```
VOID FAR PASCAL CallbackFunc( dwDevice,
                              dwMsg,
                              dwCallbackInstance,
                              dwParam1,
                              dwParam2,
                              dwParam3)
```

dwDevice is the handle of a device, application, or call. dwMsg is the message type. dwCallbackInstance is filled with a value supplied by the programmer when the line is opened. TAPI does not use this value for anything, and the programmer is free to use this parameter in any manner. The meaning of dwParam1, dwParam2, and dwParam3 are specific to each message type. Here is an example of a TAPI message callback function:

```
void LineDev::LineCallback( DWORD dwDevice, DWORD dwMsg,
                            DWORD dwCallbackInstance,
                            DWORD dwParam1, DWORD dwParam2,
                            DWORD dwParam3  )
{
    // Retrieve the "this" pointer for the address object.
    LineDev* lpLine = (LineDev*)dwCallbackInstance;

    // Handle each message based upon the message type.
    switch( dwMsg )
    {
        case LINE_CALLSTATE:
            lpLine->CallStateMsgHandler( (hCall)dwDevice,
                                         dwParam1,
                                         dwParam2 );
            break;

        <other TAPI message cases>
    }
}
```

TIP

For C++ programmers, if you want the callback function to be a member function of a class, you must declare the function as static in your class declaration. You must do this because TAPI does not supply a this pointer when it calls these functions. You can supply a this pointer when you open the line with lineOpen() as the dwCallbackInstance parameter. TAPI gives you the pointer back as the dwCallbackInstance parameter of the message, as shown in the previous code fragment.

Table 37.2 lists some of the TAPI message types. I delve into the details of some of these messages in subsequent sections.

Table 37.2. Selected TAPI message types.

Message	Meaning
Line Device Messages	
LINE_ADDRESSSTATE	Status of an address has changed
LINE_CALLINFO	Information about a call has changed
LINE_CALLSTATE	Status of a call has changed
LINE_CLOSE	Specified line device has been forcibly closed
LINE_GATHERDIGITS	Digit-gathering request has terminated
LINE_GENERATE	Digit or tone generation request has been completed
LINE_LINEDEVSTATE	Line device status has changed
LINE_MONITORDIGITS	Digit was detected
LINE_MONITORMEDIA	Media mode has changed
LINE_MONITORTONE	Tone has been detected
LINE_REPLY	Asynchronous line function request has been completed
LINE_REQUEST	Another application has made an Assisted TAPI request
Phone Device Messages	
PHONE_BUTTON	Button has been pressed
PHONE_CLOSE	Specified phone device has been forcibly closed
PHONE_REPLY	Asynchronous phone function request has been completed
PHONE_STATE	Phone device status has changed

TAPI Function Calls

There are two types of function calls used by TAPI: synchronous and asynchronous. *Synchronous* functions perform actions and return results immediately. Synchronous functions are used to perform initialization, retrieve status and device capabilities, and to allocate TAPI resources. The return value of a synchronous function is always zero if the function is successful and a negative number if the function fails. Here is an example of a synchronous function:

```
LONG LineAddress::GetNumRings()
{
    // Retrieve the number of rings and return.
```

```
DWORD numRings;
LONG lErrCode = lineGetNumRings( lineDev->GetHandle(),
                                 _addressID,
                                 &numRings );

if( lErrCode == 0 )
   return (LONG)numRings;
else
   return lErrCode;
}
```

Asynchronous functions initiate an action and return before the requested action is completed. The requested action may take some time to complete, and it is important not to block other tasks from running during this time. Asynchronous functions are used when the application controls the telephony hardware.

An asynchronous function returns a negative value if TAPI immediately determines that there is some reason the action cannot go forward. Otherwise, the function returns a nonzero, positive request ID. Here is an example of an asynchronous function:

```
LONG LineAddress::Hold()
{
   LONG lReplyCode = lineHold( _callHandle );

   // If no error, then save the reply handle.
   if( lReplyCode > 0 )
   {
      _requestID = lReplyCode;
      _requestType = REPTYPE_hold;
   }
   return lReplyCode;
}
```

For the sample code in this chapter, the following convention is used: Synchronous functions assign their return value to lErrCode, and asynchronous functions assign their return value to lReplyCode.

When the action has been completed, TAPI sends a LINE_REPLY message or a PHONE_REPLY message, depending on whether a line action or a phone action was initiated. LINE_REPLY is shown in Table 37.3. PHONE_REPLY has an identical structure.

Table 37.3. LINE_REPLY **messages.**

Parameter	Meaning
dwDevice	Not used.
dwParam1	This parameter corresponds to the reply code returned by the asynchronous function call.
dwParam2	Error code (zero if successful, negative if an error occurred).
dwParam3	Not used.

Table 37.4 contains the some of the more common error codes returned by TAPI functions.

Table 37.4. Selected TAPI error codes.

Error Code	Meaning
Line Device Error Codes	
LINEERR_ADDRESS_BLOCKED	The specified address cannot be dialed from this location.
LINEERR_ALLOCATED	A required resource (a serial port, for example) has already been allocated to another process.
LINEERR_BADDEVICEID	The specified device ID is out of range.
LINEERR_CALLUNAVAIL	No call appearances are currently available at this address.
LINEERR_DIALBILLING	The wait-for-billing tone $ is not supported by the service provider. (See Table 37.14.)
LINEERR_DIALTONE	The wait-for-dial tone W is not supported by service provider.
LINEERR_DIALPROMPT	The wait-for-prompt ? is not supported by service provider.
LINEERR_DIALQUIET	The wait-for-silence @ is not supported by the service provider.
LINEERR_INCOMPATIBLEAPIVERSION	The specified version number is incompatible.
LINEERR_INUSE	The specified line is already in use.
LINEERR_INVALADDRESS	The specified address contains invalid characters.
LINEERR_INVALADDRESSID	The specified address is out of range.
LINEERR_INVALAPPHANDLE	The specified application handle is invalid.
LINEERR_INVALCOUNTRYCODE	The specified country code is invalid.
LINEERR_INVALCALLHANDLE	The specified call handle is invalid.
LINEERR_INVALCALLSTATE	The specified call is not in the proper call state for the requested action.
LINEERR_INVALLINEHANDLE	The specified line handle is invalid.
LINEERR_INVALMEDIAMODE	The specified media mode is invalid.
LINEERR_INVALPARAM	A parameter has been determined to be invalid.

continues

Table 37.4. continued

Error Code	Meaning
Line Device Error Codes	
LINEERR_INVALPOINTER	A pointer does not reference a valid memory location.
LINEERR_NODRIVER	The service provider found one of its components missing.
LINEERR_NOMEM	Not enough memory for the requested action.
LINEERR_NOTOWNER	The requested action has been rejected because the application does not own this call.
LINEERR_OPERATIONFAILED	The request failed for unspecified reasons.
LINEERR_OPERATIONUNAVAIL	The request is not supported by the service provider.
LINEERR_RESOURCEUNAVAIL	Insufficient resources to complete the request.
LINEERR_STRUCTURETOOSMALL	The specified structure is too small to contain the fixed-length data.
LINEERR_TARGETNOTFOUND	The target of a handoff was not found.
LINEERR_TARGETSELF	The application invoking the handoff is the target.
LINEERR_UNINITIALIZED	TAPI has not yet been initialized.
Phone Device Error Codes	
PHONEERR_INVALPHONEHANDLE	The specified phone handle is invalid.
PHONEERR_NOTOWNER	The requested action has been rejected because the application does not own this device.
PHONEERR_INVALPHONESTATE	The phone device is not in the proper phone state for the requested action.
PHONEERR_INVALPOINTER	A pointer does not reference a valid memory location.
PHONEERR_OPERATIONUNAVAIL	This request is not supported by the service provider.
PHONEERR_NOMEM	Not enough memory for the requested action.

Error Code	Meaning
Phone Device Error Codes	
PHONEERR_RESOURCEUNAVAIL	Insufficient resources to complete the request.
PHONEERR_UNINITIALIZED	TAPI has not yet been initialized.
PHONEERR_STRUCTURETOOSMALL	The specified structure is too small to contain the fixed-length data.
PHONEERR_OPERATIONFAILED	The request failed for unspecified reasons.
PHONEERR_INVALHOOKSWITCHDEV	The specified hook switch device is invalid.

Call Information

When a call is in progress, there are many pieces of information associated with that call. TAPI keeps track of this information and provides a mechanism to get it. Here is a function you will see in coming examples:

```
LONG lErrCode = lineGetCallInfo( hCall, lpCallInfo );
```

The handle associated with the call is hCall. lpCallInfo is a pointer to a LINECALLINFO structure. Some of the more important fields of the LINECALLINFO structure are shown in Table 37.5. Most of the information needed to do call logging can be found in this structure.

Table 37.5. Selected LINECALLINFO structure fields.

Field	Meaning
hLine	Specifies the line handle associated with the call.
dwLineDeviceID	The ID of the line device associated with the call.
dwAddressID	The ID of the address associated with the call.
dwMediaMode	The media mode of the call (see Table 37.9 for a list of media modes).
dwCallParamFlags	Miscellaneous flags related to the call (refer to Table 37.15 for further information).

continues

Table 37.5. continued

Field	Meaning
dwCallStates	Specifies the call states of which the application might be notified for the call (see Table 37.17).
dwOrigin	Specifies the origin of the call. The call origin will specified by one of the following values:
LINECALLORIGIN_OUTBOUND	An outbound call.
LINECALLORIGIN_INTERNAL	Internal inbound call (from the same PBX, for instance).
LINECALLORIGIN_EXTERNAL	External inbound call.
LINECALLORIGIN_UNKNOWN	The origin is unknown but might become known later.
LINECALLORIGIN_UNAVAIL	The origin is unknown and will never become known.
LINECALLORIGIN_CONFERENCE	The call handle is for a conference call.
dwReason	The reason for the call occurring. The reason will be one of the following values:
LINECALLREASON_DIRECT	A direct call.
LINECALLREASON_FWDBUSY	The call was forwarded after reaching a busy number.
LINECALLREASON_FWDNOANSWER	The call was forwarded after no one answered the original number.
LINECALLREASON_FWDUNCOND	The call was forwarded unconditionally.
LINECALLREASON_CALLCOMPLETION	The call is the result of an automatic callback or camp-on.
LINECALLREASON_TRANSFER	The call was transferred.
LINECALLREASON_UNKNOWN	The reason is unknown but might become known later.
LINECALLREASON_UNAVAIL	The reason is unknown and will never become known.
dwCallerIDFlags	Provides information about the caller ID fields. The information that is provided is specified by one or more of the following flags:

Field	Meaning
`LINECALLPARTYID_BLOCKED`	The caller ID information would have been available but was blocked by the calling party.
`LINECALLPARTYID_OUTOFAREA`	The caller ID is not available because the call is from outside of the area.
`LINECALLPARTYID_NAME`	The name of the calling party is available.
`LINECALLPARTYID_ADDRESS`	The number of the calling party is available.
`LINECALLPARTYID_PARTIAL`	The caller ID information is valid but only part of the number is available.
`LINECALLPARTYID_UNKNOWN`	The caller ID information is unknown but might become known later.
`LINECALLPARTYID_UNAVAIL`	The caller ID information is unknown and will never be known.
`dwCallerIDOffset`	The offset of the caller ID number.
`dwCallerIDSize`	The size of the caller ID number.
`dwCallerIDNameOffset`	The offset of the caller ID name.
`dwCallerIDNameSize`	The size of the caller ID name.

When information in this structure changes, TAPI sends a `LINE_CALLINFO` message to the application to let it know what information has changed. Table 37.6 shows the structure of this message. The `LINECALLINFO` constants, which indicate which information has changed, are shown in Table 37.7.

Table 37.6. Parameters for the `LINE_CALLINFO` message.

Parameter	Meaning
`dwDevice`	`hCall` is the handle for this call.
`dwParam1`	Specifies which call information has changed (see Table 37.7).
`dwParam2`	Unused.
`dwParam3`	Unused.

Table 37.7. Selected `LINECALLINFOSTATE_` **constants.**

Constant	Meaning
`LINECALLINFOSTATE_MEDIAMODE`	The media mode of the call has changed (see Table 37.9).
`LINECALLINFOSTATE_CALLID`	This is a unique identification given to the call by a switch or service provider. It should not be confused with caller ID.
`LINECALLINFOSTATE_REASON`	The reason for the call has changed (see Table 37.5).
`LINECALLINFOSTATE_ORIGIN`	The origin information has changed.
`LINECALLINFOSTATE_CALLERID`	The caller ID information has changed.
`LINECALLINFOSTATE_CALLEDID`	The called party identification has changed.
`LINECALLINFOSTATE_MONITORMODES`	One of the monitoring modes (digit, tone, or media) has changed.

Line Devices

TAPI deals with line devices and phone devices separately. From here until the end of the chapter, I concentrate almost exclusively on line devices.

Initializing TAPI

Before TAPI can be used to make calls, it must first be initialized. There are three steps to this process:

1. Initialize TAPI.DLL.

2. Negotiate the version of TAPI used.

3. Open the line or lines used.

The first step is to initialize the line device side of TAPI using the `lineInitialize()` function (see the following code fragment), which tells TAPI that the application exists. In return, you get an application handle, and you find out from TAPI how many line devices are currently installed. If there is more than one service provider installed, you get the total number of lines and not just the number from a single service provider.

```
lErrCode = lineInitialize( lphLineApp,
                           hInstance,
                           lpfnCallback,
                           lpszAppName,
                           lpdwNumDevs );
```

TAPI fills in `lphLineApp` with a line application handle. `hInstance` is the instance handle of the application or DLL. `lpfnCallback` is a pointer to a callback routine that is defined for handling line messages. `lpszAppName` points to the name of the application. If this parameter is `NULL`, the application's file name is used. TAPI returns the number of installed line devices in `lpdwNumDevs`.

The next step is to negotiate the version of TAPI that you are going to use (see the following code fragment). *Each line device is negotiated separately.* The application provides the highest and lowest version numbers that it is willing to use. TAPI checks this range against the service provider for the line devices to determine the version to use. The version chosen is the highest version in the overlap between the application's acceptable range and the service provider's acceptable range. If there is no overlap then the function fails.

```
lErrCode = lineNegotiateAPIVersion( hLineApp,
                                    dwDeviceID,
                                    dwAPILowVersion,
                                    dwAPIHighVersion,
                                    lpdwAPIVersion,
                                    lpExtensionID );
```

`hLineApp` is the line application handle returned in the `lineInitialize()` function. `dwDeviceID` specifies the line device for which you are negotiating the version.

`dwAPILowVersion` and `dwAPIHighVersion` set the acceptable range of versions that the application supports. The high order word is the major version number and the low order word is the minor version number. Thus, TAPI Version 1.4 is represented, in hexadecimal, as 00010004. `lpdwAPIVersion` is filled in with the negotiated API version.

The last parameter is a pointer to a structure of type `LINEEXTENSIONID`. If the service provider supports any extensions, this structure is filled with the IDs of these extensions. The structure is filled with zeros if no extensions are supported. If the application is not going to make use of any extensions, this structure can be ignored.

WARNING

As of this writing, there are only two versions of TAPI. The first is Version 1.3, which was released for Windows 3.1 as the TAPI SDK 1.0. The second version, 1.4, is the one that is shipping with Windows 95. Version 1.4 corrects some oversights in Version 1.3 and is therefore not entirely backwards compatible. At this time, Microsoft has announced that it will not be releasing an updated version of TAPI for Windows 3.1. Because of this, any application developer who wants to have a single executable for both Windows 3.1 and Windows 95 needs to become aware of the differences and to write code that makes use of the negotiated API version to account for these differences.

There is a similar negotiation that can take place to negotiate the extension version. The *extension version* is used to determine the version of any service provider extensions. So far, there are very few extensions that have been publicly documented. If the application is not going to make use of these extensions, this negotiation can be ignored.

The last step in the initialization process is to open one or more line devices. This lets TAPI know which lines an application uses and how these lines are used. Here is the function:

```
lErrCode = lineOpen( hLineApp,
                     dwDeviceID,
                     lphLine,
                     dwAPIVersion,
                     dwExtVersion,
                     dwCallbackInstance,
                     dwPrivileges,
                     dwMediaModes,
                     lpCallParams );
```

The line application handle is in `hLineApp`. `dwDevice` can be a particular device ID, or it can have the value `LINEMAPPER`. In the latter case, TAPI uses the information contained in the structure `lpCallParams` to locate a compatible line device. If the `LINEMAPPER` feature is not used, then the `lpCallParams` parameter can be `NULL`. (See Table 37.15 for further information about call parameters.)

The negotiated API version and extension version are passed in `dwAPIVersion` and `dwExtVersion`, respectively. If the application does not use any extensions, then zero can be passed for the latter parameter.

The `dwCallbackInstance` value is passed back to the application with every TAPI message. TAPI makes no use of this information, therefore the programmer is free to use this for any purpose.

`dwPrivileges` specifies which privileges the application wants for the line device. Table 37.8 shows the privilege flags. There can be more than one privilege flag set.

Table 37.8. Call privilege flags.

Flag	Meaning
LINECALLPRIVILEGE_NONE	The application only makes outbound calls.
LINECALLPRIVILEGE_MONITOR	The application wants to monitor inbound and outbound calls.
LINECALLPRIVILEGE_OWNER	The application wants to own inbound calls of the types specified in `dwMediaModes`. (See Table 37.9.)

dwMediaModes specifies which media types the application wants to be responsible for on an inbound call. LINEMEDIAMODE_UNKNOWN is used when the service provider cannot determine what media mode the call is. In this case, it is up to the application that agrees to handle this type of call to make the determination about what to do with the call. Table 37.9 shows the media modes defined by TAPI. Only the first four values are widely supported.

Table 37.9. Media modes.

Media Mode	Meaning
LINEMEDIAMODE_UNKNOWN	Unknown media type.
LINEMEDIAMODE_INTERACTIVEVOICE	Human to human voice call.
LINEMEDIAMODE_AUTOMATEDVOICE	Human to answering machine voice call.
LINEMEDIAMODE_DATAMODEM	Data modem call.
LINEMEDIAMODE_G3FAX	Group 3 fax call (the common fax protocol that most of us use).
LINEMEDIAMODE_G4FAX	Group 4 fax call (a newfangled digital fax protocol that is not widely used yet).
LINEMEDIAMODE_DIGITALDATA	Digital data call.
LINEMEDIAMODE_TDD	Telephony devices for the deaf (TDD) call.
LINEMEDIAMODE_TELETEX	Teletex call.
LINEMEDIAMODE_VIDEOTEX	Videotex call.
LINEMEDIAMODE_TELEX	Telex call.
LINEMEDIAMODE_MIXED	ISDN mixed mode call.
LINEMEDIAMODE_ADSI	Analog data services interface (ADSI) call.

WARNING

Most service providers can support outbound and inbound voice calls. The UNIMODEM service provider that comes with Windows 95 can support inbound and outbound data and fax calls, but it cannot support inbound voice calls. Therefore, the lineOpen() function fails if you specify LINECALLPRIVILEGE_OWNER along with LINEMEDIAMODE_INTERACTIVEVOICE. Ownership is not required when making a call.

> **NOTE**
>
> Several TAPI hardware devices are accessed through serial ports. This is typical for the voice-fax-modem cards that are now shipping. When you open the line with `LINECALLPRIVILEGE_OWNER`, the serial port is allocated to the service provider. The service provider needs to have control of the serial port if there is an incoming call. This causes a problem if the user wants to use a fax program that doesn't know about TAPI, because the fax program cannot use the serial port. The user can tell TAPI to close the line, but then TAPI cannot handle incoming calls. Unfortunately, there is not much that can be done about this until the fax program vendors and the terminal program vendors are TAPI-aware.

TAPI Shutdown

Once you have figured out how to start up TAPI, it is useful to know how to shut it down again. It's really quite easy. Call `lineClose()` for every line that is open and then call `lineShutdown()`. Here is an example:

```
LONG lErrCode = lineClose( hLine );

LONG lErrCode = lineShutdown( hLineApp );
```

`hLine` is the line handle that you obtain when you open a line. `hLineApp` is the application handle you obtain when you initialize TAPI.DLL.

Closing a line when there is an existing call may or may not cause the call to be dropped. If the call will be dropped, it is a good idea to put up a warning for the user prior to closing the line. You can determine if the call will be dropped by examining the `dwDevCapFlags` field of the `LINEDEVCAPS` structure for the `LINEDEVCAPFLAGS_CLOSEDROP` bit. (Refer to the section titled "Service Provider Capabilities" for more information on `LINEDEVCAPS`.)

The following code fragment demonstrates how to close a line prior to shutting down TAPI. Note that it checks the line device capabilities to see if an in-progress call will be hung up by closing the line. Under this circumstance, a warning is presented to the user along with the opportunity to stop the procedure.

```
LONG LineDev::Close()
{
    LONG lErrCode = 0;

    // If there is a call in progress,
    // Check to see if we need to warn the user.
    if( CallInProgress() )
    {
        // If there is a call in progress, check to
        // see if it will be dropped if we continue
        LINEDEVCAPS lineDevCaps;
        lineDevCaps.dwTotalSize = sizeof(LINEDEVCAPS);
```

```
        lErrCode = lineGetDevCaps( _lineApp->GetAppHandle(),
                                    _lineNum,
                                    _lineApp->GetApiVersion(),
                                    _lineApp->GetExtVersion(),
                                    &lineDevCaps );
        if( lErrCode == 0 )
        {
            if( lineDevCaps->dwDevCapFlags
                & LINEDEVCAPFLAGS_CLOSEDROP )
            {
                // If the user says "Don't Drop", then
                // abort the function.
                if( AfxMessageBox( CALLDROPMSG,
                                   MB_YESNO ¦ MB_ICONQUESTION )
                    == IDNO )
                {
                    lErrCode = APPERR_USERABORT;
                }
            }
        }
    }
    // If we made it this far with a zero error code, then
    // close the line
    if( lErrCode == 0 )
        lErrCode = lineClose( _lineHandle );
    return lErrCode;
}
```

Service Provider Capabilities

It is now time to look at line device capabilities. Not every line device supports every
possible telephone feature. Furthermore, as you might expect, in a world where everyone is
free to develop their own standards, features that are conceptually identical are often
implemented in different ways. The service provider shields an application from some of
this, but it is not possible to shield the application from all possible differences. The keys to
survival in this situation are the line device capabilities and the related address capabilities.
Here are the function calls to retrieve this information:

```
LONG lErrCode = lineGetDevCaps( hLineApp, dwDevice,
                                dwAPIVersion, dwExtVersion,
                                lpLineDevCaps );

LONG lErrCode = lineGetAddrCaps( hLineApp,
                                 dwDevice, dwAddressID,
                                 dwAPIVersion, dwExtVersion,
                                 lpAddressCaps );
```

Most of the parameters are already familiar, but there are a few new ones. dwAddressID
specifies which address to look at. The number of addresses a line supports are retrieved by
the lineGetDevCaps() function. Address IDs are numbered sequentially starting at zero,
same as with the line device IDs. TAPI fills in the LINEDEVCAPS structure pointed to by
lpLineDevCaps. Likewise, lpAddressCaps points to a LINEADDRESSCAPS structure. Tables
37.10 and 37.11 show some of the important fields of these structures.

Table 37.10. Selected LINEDEVCAPS structure fields.

dwProviderInfoOffset	Offset of the service provider information string
dwProviderInfoSize	Size of the service provider information string
dwStringFormat	Can be one of the following:
STRINGFORMAT_ASCII	ASCII strings
STRINGFORMAT_DBCS	Double byte character strings
STRINGFORMAT_UNICODE	Unicode strings
dwNumAddresses	Number of addresses for this line
dwMediaModes	Media modes supported (see Table 37.9)
dwGenerateDigitModes	Digit type flags
LINEDIGITMODE_PULSE	Generates rotary/pulse sequences
LINEDIGITMODE_DTMF	Generates tone sequences
dwMonitorDigitModes	Digit type flags
LINEDIGITMODE_PULSE	Monitors rotary/pulse sequences
LINEDIGITMODE_DTMF	Monitors tone sequences
dwDevCapFlags	Miscellaneous device capability flags
LINEDEVCAPFLAGS_CLOSEDROP	Closing line will drop calls
LINEDEVCAPFLAGS_DIALBILLING	$ dial modifier supported
LINEDEVCAPFLAGS_DIALQUIET	@ dial modifier supported
LINEDEVCAPFLAGS_DIALTONE	W dial modifier supported

Table 37.11. Selected LINEADDRESSCAPS structure fields.

dwCallStates	The call states supported by the service provider (see Table 37.17)
dwLineAddrCapFlags	Miscellaneous address capability flags
LINEADDRCAPFLAGS_SECURE	The call waiting signal can be blocked
LINEADDRCAPFLAGS_BLOCKIDDEFAULT	The caller ID information is blocked by default
LINEADDRCAPFLAGS_BLOCKIDOVERRIDE	Caller ID blocking can be overridden
LINEADDRCAPFLAGS_PARTIALDIAL	Partial dialing is available
dwCallFeatures	The calling features supported (see Table 37.18)

A utility, T_PROBE.EXE, is included on the CD-ROM that can be used to determine the supported capabilities of all installed service providers. It does not report 100% of all service provider capabilities, but it is easily modified to add anything not currently reported.

Telephone Numbers

TAPI defines two forms of telephone number formats. The first form is referred to as *canonical*, a universal form of the telephone number that contains no information about the source of the call. The other format is the *dialable* format—the number actually used to dial the telephone. It may or may not contain access codes, country codes, area codes, city codes, and credit card numbers. The format is specific to the source of the telephone call.

The canonical form is designed for ease of conversion to the dialable form. All that is required is information on the caller's country, area or city code, access code, and credit card number. The dialable number can change when the user flies across the country, for instance, but the canonical number will not change. For this reason, the TAPI designers recommend that you use the canonical form for numbers stored in databases and address books.

The canonical form is a null-terminated ASCII string. Its structure is shown in Table 37.12. The format of the canonical number string is as shown here:

`+CountryCode`**SPACE**`(AreaCode)`**SPACE**`Number¦SubAddress^Name`**CRLF**

Table 37.12. Canonical address format.

Field	Meaning
+	(ASCII hex 2B) Indicates that this is a canonical number as opposed to a dialable number.
`CountryCode`	One or more digits (0–9). Indicates the country of the number.
SPACE	(ASCII hex 20) Used to delimit the end of the country code (and the area code as well).
`(AreaCode)`	One or more digits (0–9) preceded by a left parenthesis (ASCII hex 28) and followed by a right parenthesis (ASCII hex 29). This field is optional. If the field is left out, then the space following it is also left out. This is usually referred to as the *city code* for telephone numbers not in the U.S. or Canada.

continues

Table 37.12. continued

Field	Meaning
Number	One or more digits (0–9). This is the subscriber number. Other formatting characters may be included, such as hyphen (ASCII hex 2D), dot (ASCII hex 2E), or space (ASCII hex 20). The following dialing-control characters should not be included: A a B b C c D d P p T t W w * # ! , @ $? ; It may not contain a circumflex (ASCII hex 5E), a solid vertical bar (ASCII hex 7C), a carriage return (ASCII hex 0D), or line feed (ASCII hex 0A).
¦SubAddress	One or more digits (0–9) preceded by a solid vertical bar (ASCII hex 7C). This is used for ISDN subaddressing. This field is optional.
^Name	One or more ASCII characters preceded by a circumflex (ASCII hex 5E) and delimited by either carriage return–line feed or NULL (ASCII hex 00). This field is optional.
CRLF	Carriage return–line feed (ASCII hex 0D 0A). This field is optional and indicates that another canonical number will follow immediately. This form can be used when the service provider is capable of dialing multiple numbers simultaneously (referred to as *inverse multiplexing*).

For example, the canonical format of the number to dial for 800 directory assistance (in the US) is **+1 (800) 555-1212**.

TIP

Although the area code can be left out of the canonical format, it is not recommended. If the area code is present, you—or TAPI if using `lineTranslateAddress()`—can determine whether the number is local or from another area by comparing it to the local area code. Without the area code, you have no clue as to whether the number is local. If people never moved their computers, this might be acceptable (no area code means local number). But in an age where the laptop computer is commonplace and business travelers change cities hourly, not knowing whether a telephone number is local just isn't good enough.

The dialable format is the full telephone number with everything that it needs to access a telephone line, to dial the number, and (potentially) to pay for the call. It is a null-terminated ASCII string. The format of the dialable number string is shown here:

```
DialableNumber¦Subaddress^NameCRLF
```

The fields of its structure are shown in Table 37.13 and the definition of the characters is shown in Table 37.14.

Table 37.13. Dialable address format.

Field	Meaning
`DialableNumber`	Digits and modifiers as shown in Table 37.14. The string is delimited by a circumflex (ASCII hex 5E), a solid vertical bar (ASCII hex 7C), a carriage return–line feed, or the end of the string.
`¦SubAddress`	One or more digits (0–9) preceded by a solid vertical bar (ASCII hex 7C). This can contain a subaddress. During dialing, this can be passed to the remote party. This field is optional.
`^Name`	One or more ASCII characters preceded by a circumflex (ASCII hex 5E) and delimited by either carriage return–line feed or by NULL (ASCII hex 00). During dialing, this can be passed to the remote party. This field is optional.
`CRLF`	The carriage return–line feed (ASCII hex 0D 0A). This field is optional and denotes that another canonical number will follow immediately. This form can be used when the service provider is capable of dialing multiple numbers simultaneously (referred to as *inverse multiplexing*).

Table 37.14. Dialable number digit definitions.

Dialing Character	Meaning
`0-9, A-D,`	ASCII characters corresponding to dialable * and # digits.
`!`	Hookflash (1/2 second onhook followed by 1/2 second offhook).
`P p`	Digits following are to be pulse dialed.
`T t`	Digits following are to be DTMF (tone) dialed.

continues

Table 37.14. continued

Dialing Character	Meaning
,	A pause (the duration is device dependent but typically is two seconds by default).
W w	Wait for dial tone before proceeding.
@	Wait for quiet answer before proceeding. This is used when the rest of the number must be dialed after the far end has been answered. The service provider waits for at least one ringback tone detection followed by a long period of silence (typically around seven seconds).
$	Wait for billing signal. This is used when the service provider must wait for the "bong" sound, which signals that the system is ready to accept credit card information.
?	Display a user prompt before continuing.
;	Indicates that the number is incomplete and that further dialing information will follow. In other words, dialing is not yet complete. This symbol may only occur as the last character of the dialable number.

Of the modifiers listed in Table 37.14, only @, $, and W are not supported by every service provider. The application can either pass the number to the service provider, which will return an error if any unsupported modifiers are found, or it can check the dwLineDevCapFlags field of the LINEDEVCAPS structure (see Table 37.10) and filter out unsupported modifiers prior to dialing. The ? modifier is always rejected by the service provider. The application must check for it and divide up the number.

TAPI provides the following function for converting a canonical address into a dialable address:

```
LONG lErrCode = lineTranslateAddress( hLineApp,
                                      dwDeviceID,
                                      dwAPIVersion,
                                      lpszAddressIn,
                                      dwCard,
                                      dwTranslateOptions,
                                      lpTranslateOutput );
```

The first three parameters are the familiar application handle, the line device ID, and the negotiated API version. lpszAddressIn points to the address to be converted. This can either be a canonical or dialable address. Only canonical addresses are converted. Dialable addresses return untouched. dwCard is the ID of a credit card returned from TELEPHON.INI. This field is ignored unless the LINETRANSLATEOPTION_CARDOVERRIDE bit of the dwTranslateOptions parameter is set. There are no other flags defined for dwTranslateOptions. lpTranslateOutput is a pointer to a buffer of type LINETRANSLATEOUTPUT.

In the LINETRANSLATEOUTPUT structure, the dialable address is a variable-length string found with the dwDialableStringOffset and dwDialableSize fields. There is also a displayable string that can be found using dwDisplayableOffset and dwDisplayableSize. The displayable string is similar to the dialable string, except that credit card numbers are hidden.

Although convenient, it is not a requirement to use lineTranslateAddress(). Several applications do not use it, either because they store their numbers in some form other than the canonical form, or because they handle address formatting issues that lineTranslateAddress() does not cover.

Dialing the Phone

At long last, the preliminaries are over. Now it's time to turn to the most basic of all telephony features: placing an outgoing call. Although placing an outgoing call is somewhat more complex than the Assisted TAPI case, it's still not very complicated. Here is the function that does it:

```
LONG lReplyCode = lineMakeCall( hLine,
                                lphCall,
                                lpszDestAddress,
                                dwCountryCode,
                                lpCallParams);
```

The line handle, hLine, is obtained when the line is opened. lphCall is a pointer to a call handle, which TAPI fills in for you once the call is placed.

WARNING

The location referenced by lphCall is not filled in until after the call has been successfully initiated. Examining this location immediately after lineMakeCall() returns will, almost certainly, yield an incorrect value. You cannot count on the call handle being valid until you receive the corresponding LINE_REPLY message from TAPI.

---

lpszDestAddress is a string that contains the dialable address. dwCountryCode can be used by the service provider to adjust for the different call progress tones (ringback, busy, etc.) used in other countries. Not all service providers have this capability. If dwCountryCode is set to zero, then the default (which usually means the tones used in the United States) is used.

lpCallParams can be NULL (in which case, defaults are used) or can point to a LINECALLPARAMS structure (see Table 37.15). NULL is usually sufficient. If this structure is used, the proper procedure is to fill the structure with zeros and then fill in the fields that are important to the call being placed.

Table 37.15. Selected LINECALLPARAMS structure fields.

Field	Meaning
dwTotalSize	Filled in with the structure's size
dwMediaMode	Media mode (see Table 37.9)
dwCallParamFlags	Miscellaneous call setup flags
LINECALLPARAMFLAGS_SECURE	Call-waiting signal blocking
LINECALLPARAMFLAGS_IDLE	Call gets an idle call appearance
LINECALLPARAMFLAGS_BLOCKID	Blocks transmission of caller ID
LINECALLPARAMFLAGS_ORIGOFFHOOK	Phone should be taken offhook

> **TIP**
>
> It is a good idea to set LINECALLPARAMFLAGS_ORIGOFFHOOK anytime the call is placed in a "hands free" or speakerphone mode. Most service providers just ignore this bit and automatically take the line offhook. However, there are a few service providers that will not take the line offhook for a hands-free call unless this bit is set.

Here is one more dialing function that deserves mention:

```
LONG lReplyCode = lineDial( hCall,
                            lpszDestAddress,
                            dwCountryCode );
```

This function is used in cases where the address supplied to the lineMakeCall() function is incomplete. hCall is the call handle generated by the lineMakeCall() function. lpszDestAddress is the continuation of the dial string. As with lineMakeCall(), dwCountryCode is the destination country code.

The following code fragment demonstrates the process of formatting a number and making a call:

```
LONG LineAddr::MakeCall( const CString& TeleNum,
                         const CString& TeleName,
                         const HLINE lineHandle,
                         const HLINEAPP appHandle,
                         const DWORD lineID,
                         const DWORD apiVersion )
{
    LONG lReplyCode;
```

```
    _tapiDlg->UpdateCLID( TeleNum, TeleName );
    LPBYTE buffer = new BYTE[BIG_BUFF];
    LPLINETRANSLATEOUTPUT lpTransOut = (LPLINETRANSLATEOUTPUT)buffer;
    lpTransOut->dwTotalSize = sizeof(BYTE)*BIG_BUFF;
    lReplyCode = lineTranslateAddress( appHandle,
                                       lineID,
                                       apiVersion,
                                       TeleNum,
                                       0, 0,   // Use default card
                                       lpTransOut );
    if( lReplyCode != 0 )
       return lReplyCode;   // Bail out if translate error.

    // Grab the things we want.
    DWORD countryCode = lpTransOut->dwDestCountry;
    CString dialnum = (LPCSTR)buffer
                      + lpTransOut->dwDialableStringOffset;

    // Set up the call parameters buffer
    LPLINECALLPARAMS lpCallParams = (LPLINECALLPARAMS)buffer;

    // Clear the buffer and then start filling it in.
    memset( buffer, 0, sizeof(BYTE)*BIG_BUFF );
    lpCallParams->dwTotalSize = sizeof(BYTE)*BIG_BUFF;
    lpCallParams->dwMediaMode = LINEMEDIAMODE_INTERACTIVEVOICE;
    lpCallParams->dwAddressMode = LINEADDRESSMODE_DIALABLEADDR;
    lpCallParams->dwCallParamFlags = LINECALLPARAMFLAGS_IDLE
                                   | LINECALLPARAMFLAGS_ORIGOFFHOOK;

    // Add some variable-length stuff to the end.
    DWORD offset = sizeof(LINECALLPARAMS);
    lpCallParams->dwCalledPartyOffset = offset;
    lpCallParams->dwCalledPartySize = TeleName.GetLength()+1;
    lstrcpy( (LPSTR)(buffer + offset), TeleName );

    offset += lpCallParams->dwCalledPartySize;
    lpCallParams->dwOrigAddressOffset = offset;
    lpCallParams->dwOrigAddressSize = TeleNum.GetLength()+1;
    lstrcpy( (LPSTR)(buffer + offset), TeleNum );

    // Finally, place the call.
    lReplyCode = lineMakeCall( lineHandle,
                               &_callHandle,
                               dialnum,
                               0,
                               lpCallParams );
    return lReplyCode;
}
```

Call Status Monitoring

Once the call is dialed, there is a new problem to solve: you need to know what kind of
progress the call is making. Are you getting the ringback signal? Did the call connect? Did
you get a busy signal? When you make a call the old-fashioned way, you use your ears to tell
you these things. Computers don't have ears, but there is a way for the computer to tell you
what it is "hearing."

One of the messages that TAPI sends you contains call state information. This, appropriately enough, is the LINE_CALLSTATE message. It is sent any time the call changes status. Table 37.16 shows the format of the LINE_CALLSTATE message.

Table 37.16. Parameters for the LINE_CALLSTATE message.

Parameter	Meaning
dwDevice	hCall is the handle for this call.
dwParam1	Specifies the new call state, one of the LINECALLSTATE_ values shown in Table 37.17.
dwParam2	In most cases, this parameter is not used. Where used, the meaning is dependent upon the call state in dwParam1. These cases are noted in Table 37.17.
dwParam3	This parameter will be zero if the application's call privilege has not changed. If the application's call privilege has changed, it will either be LINECALLPRIVILEGE_MONITOR or LINECALLPRIVILEGE_OWNER.

Not every service provider is capable of detecting every possible call state change. The application must use lineGetAddressCaps() to determine the list of call states the service provider reports. Table 37.17 shows the list of call states supported by TAPI.

Table 37.17. Selected TAPI call state constants.

Constant	Meaning
LINECALLSTATE_IDLE	The call just went idle. It no longer exists.
LINECALLSTATE_OFFERING	A new call is being offered. Usually, this means an incoming call.
LINECALLSTATE_ACCEPTED	A new call has been accepted. This alerts any other applications that may be monitoring that the current owner has accepted responsibility for the call.
LINECALLSTATE_DIALTONE	A dial tone has been detected. The dwParam2 of this message has the following meanings:
LINEDIALTONEMODE_NORMAL	The normal, continuous dial tone.
LINEDIALTONEMODE_SPECIAL	A special dial tone used to signal some unspecified condition. Often used for voice mail waiting.

Constant	Meaning
LINEDIALTONEMODE_INTERNAL	An internal dial tone (such as one that might be generated by a PBX).
LINEDIALTONEMODE_EXTERNAL	The telephone company dial tone.
LINEDIALTONEMODE_UNKNOWN	The dial tone's type is unknown, but it might be known later.
LINEDIALTONEMODE_UNAVAIL	The dial tone's type will never be known.
LINECALLSTATE_DIALING	Address information is being transferred to the telephone switch.
LINECALLSTATE_RINGBACK	Ringback signals have been detected.
LINECALLSTATE_BUSY	The call could not be completed because of one of the following conditions (dwParam2 values):
LINEBUSYMODE_STATION	The person you are trying to reach is already using the phone. This is the busy signal that you usually hear.
LINEBUSYMODE_TRUNK	All circuits are busy. You can tell this from a normal busy signal because the cadence is faster. Hence it is sometimes referred to as "fast busy." (This happens a lot on Mother's Day.)
LINEBUSYMODE_UNKNOWN	The line is busy. You don't know why, but you might find out later.
LINEBUSYMODE_UNAVAIL	The line is busy, and you'll never know why.
LINECALLSTATE_CONNECTED	The call has been successfully established.
LINECALLSTATE_PROCEEDING	The call has been dialed and is proceeding through the switch.
LINECALLSTATE_ONHOLD	The call has been placed on hold.
LINECALLSTATE_CONFERENCED	The call is part of a multiparty conference call.
LINECALLSTATE_DISCONNECT	The far end of the call has hung up or has been disconnected. The following reasons for the disconnect are found in dwParam2:
LINEDISCONNECTMODE_NORMAL	The remote user hung up the phone.

continues

Table 37.17. continued

Constant	Meaning
LINEDISCONNECTMODE_UNKNOWN	The reason for the disconnect is unknown, but it might become known later.
LINEDISCONNECTMODE_UNAVAIL	The reason for the disconnect will never be known.
LINEDISCONNECTMODE_REJECT	The remote user rejected the call.
LINEDISCONNECTMODE_PICKUP	The call was picked up from another location.
LINEDISCONNECTMODE_FORWARDED	The call was forwarded by the switch.
LINEDISCONNECTMODE_BUSY	The call disconnected because of a busy result.
LINEDISCONNECTMODE_NOANSWER	The call was not answered.
LINEDISCONNECTMODE_BADADDRESS	The destination address was bad.
LINEDISCONNECTMODE_UNREACHABLE	The destination was not reachable.
LINEDISCONNECTMODE_CONGESTION	The telephone network was congested.

Most of the time, the only action that needs to be taken in response to a call state message is to update the part of the application that displays the call status. But sometimes, as is shown in the following code, there are further actions that need to taken. The example shown here demonstrates the deallocation of call handles when the call ends (goes idle).

```
void LineDev::CallStateMessageHandler( HCALL hCall,
                                       DWORD dwCallState,
                                       DWORD dwCallMode )
{
    // First call GetCallInfo to find out what address
    // we are using.
    LINECALLINFO callInfo;
    callInfo.dwTotalSize = sizeof(LINECALLINFO);
    if( lineGetCallInfo( hCall, &callInfo ) != 0 )
        return;        // Bail out if function failed.

    // Use the address ID as an array index...
    int addr_idx = callInfo.dwAddressID;

    // Now deal with the call state
    switch( dwCallState )
    {
        case LINECALLSTATE_IDLE:
            // A call just went idle, deallocate the call handle
            // and NULL out our record of it.
            _lineAddr[addr_idx]->DeallocateCall();
            break;
```

```
        <other LINECALLSTATE_ cases>
    }
    // Update the display...
    _tapiDlg->->UpdateMessage( "LINE_CALLSTATE", dwCallState );
}
```

If there is a need to get the call state immediately without waiting for the next
LINE_CALLSTATE message, the call state can be obtained by calling this:

```
LONG lErrCode = lineGetStatus( hCall, lpCallStatus );
```

hCall is the handle for the call. lpCallStatus is a pointer to a LINECALLSTATUS structure. The
call state can be found in the dwCallState field. For those call states that have different
modes (this corresponds to dwParam2 of the LINE_CALLSTATE message), the mode can be
found in the dwCallStateMode field. The call privilege information that corresponds to
dwParam3 of the LINE_CALLSTATE message can be found in the dwCallPrivilege field.

There is another field that can be found in both the LINEADDRESSCAPS structure and the
LINECALLSTATUS structure. This field is dwCallFeatures. The difference in meaning between
the two structures is subtle but quite important. In LINEADDRESSCAPS, the presence of a
feature means that the service provider has this feature. In LINECALLSTATUS, the presence of a
feature means that it can be used at this time. The importance is that sometimes you want
to know if a service provider has a feature and sometimes you want to know if the feature
can be used. A list of the features TAPI supports is in Table 37.18.

Table 37.18. Selected TAPI call feature constants.

Constant	Meaning
LINECALLFEATURE_ACCEPT	Accept a call
LINECALLFEATURE_ADDTOCONF	Add to a conference call
LINECALLFEATURE_ANSWER	Answer a call
LINECALLFEATURE_BLINDTRANSFER	Transfer a call without speaking to the third party
LINECALLFEATURE_COMPLETECALL	Complete an automatic callback or camp-on
LINECALLFEATURE_COMPLETETRANSFER	Complete a call transfer
LINECALLFEATURE_DIAL	Finish dialing a partial address
LINECALLFEATURE_DROP	Hang up the phone
LINECALLFEATURE_GENERATEDIGITS	Send digits (usually DTMF)
LINECALLFEATURE_HOLD	Go on hold
LINECALLFEATURE_MONITORDIGITS	Monitor digits (usually DTMF)
LINECALLFEATURE_PREPAREADDCONF	Prepare to add a call to a conference

continues

Table 37.18. continued

Constant	Meaning
LINECALLFEATURE_REMOVEFROMCONF	Remove a call from a conference
LINECALLFEATURE_SETTERMINAL	Transfer the call from one terminal to another (from a speakerphone to a handset, for example)
LINECALLFEATURE_SETUPCONF	Set up a conference call
LINECALLFEATURE_SETUPTRANSFER	Set up a call transfer
LINECALLFEATURE_SWAPHOLD	Swap a call that is on hold with one that is not on hold (call-waiting)
LINECALLFEATURE_UNHOLD	Go off hold

Each of the LINECALLFEATURE_XXXX constants has a corresponding lineXXXX() function.

Ending a Telephone Call

Ending a telephone call is quite simple. You hang up (another reference to the old switchhook) or, to use the industry vernacular, you "drop the line." Here is the function that performs this:

```
LONG lErrCode = lineDrop( hCall,
                          lpUserUserInfo,
                          dwSize );
```

The first parameter is the ever present call handle. The other two parameters, lpUserUserInfo and dwSize, are rarely used but deserve a bit of explanation. Some service providers, notably those that support ISDN, have the capability of sending data along with the call. This information is then displayed for the party at the other end of the line. lpUserUserInfo points to a string that should be sent as part of the disconnection process, and dwSize contains the length of that string. If this feature is not used, lpUserUserInfo can be set to NULL. dwSize is ignored in this case.

Once the call is dropped, the call state goes to LINECALLSTATE_IDLE. At this point, the application should deallocate the call handle so that TAPI can reuse it. (If this is not done, TAPI eventually runs out of call handles.) A code fragment that demonstrates this can be found in the previous section.

NOTE

Some line devices (modems, for example) were not really designed to handle voice telephone calls. When lineDrop() is called, the service provider clears the call from

TAPI. However, if the user has the handset offhook, there is no mechanism in the hardware that can force the call to actually be dropped. The call continues until the user hangs up the phone. This can be much longer than the time logged by the application. People who need to bill for time spent on the phone (lawyers, for instance) will find this "feature" rather annoying. Many of the voice-fax-modem cards currently available suffer from this flaw.

Some service providers have the ability to detect a "far end disconnect." To put it another way, the service provider can detect that the other party has ended the call. When this occurs, the call makes a transition to the LINECALLSTATE_DISCONNECT state. The application can react to this by notifying the user or by automatically dropping the line (or both). The following code fragment presents a message to the user that the call has been disconnected and then, if the user requests it, drops the call.

```
void LineDev::CallStateMessageHandler( HCALL hCall,
                                       DWORD dwCallState,
                                       DWORD dwCallMode )
{
    // Handle the call state transition.
    switch( dwCallState )
    {
        case LINECALLSTATE_DISCONNECT:
            // The call was disconnected, tell the user.
            if( AfxMessageBox( "Call was disconnected.\r\nHang up?",
                               MB_YESNO | MB_ICONQUESTION )
                == IDYES )
            {
                lineDrop( hCall, NULL, 0);
            }
            break;

        <other LINECALLSTATE_ cases>
    }
}
```

Answering Incoming Calls

Once they are connected, incoming calls are pretty much the same as outgoing calls. There can be a few differences in the treatment of some of the advanced features (conference calling, for example). For the most part, the real difference lies in what happens before the call starts.

When a call comes in, the service provider notifies TAPI. TAPI, in turn, notifies one of the applications (there can be more than one TAPI application running at one time) with the LINE_CALLSTATE message. The initial state is LINECALLSTATE_OFFERING. The application that gets notified is the one that opened the line with LINECALLPRIVILEGES_OWNER for the call's media type.

TIP

Some service providers send `LINECALLSTATE_OFFERING` when the user picks up the telephone handset in preparation for making an outbound call. In order to recognize this situation, call `lineGetCallInfo()` and examine the `dwOrigin` field of the `LINECALLINFO` structure. If the `LINECALLORIGIN_OUTBOUND` bit is set, then the call is outbound and the application should act accordingly.

The application that gets notification of the call is registered as `LINE_PRIVILEGEOWNER` for a particular set of media modes. Applications that handle fax calls register using `LINEMEDIAMODE_G3FAX`, and those that handle voice calls register as the owner for `LINEMEDIAMODE_INTERACTIVEVOICE`. A list of media modes can be found in Table 37.9.

Here a small problem arises. On a standard telephone line (those that most people have), there is no way to determine the type of the incoming call before it is answered. In this case, the media mode assigned to the call is `LINEMEDIAMODE_UNKNOWN`, and the application that registered as the owner for unknown media modes gets the call. I discuss how the application can deal with this situation later in this chapter, but for now, I just cover the simple mechanics of answering a call.

When the call is offered to the application, the first thing the application should do is to call

```
LONG lReplyCode = lineAccept( hCall, lpUserUserInfo, dwSize );
```

The parameters are the same ones found in the `lineDrop()` function. The call handle is allocated automatically by TAPI and is returned as part of the `LINE_CALLSTATE` message. When dialing out, the application asks TAPI to allocate one through `lineMakeCall()`. When the call is accepted, all of the other applications are notified.

NOTE

Most service providers (or other TAPI applications) don't care whether `lineAccept()` is called. In fact, some don't even support the call. A check of `LINECALLFEATURES_` (refer to Table 37.18) is worthwhile before calling `lineAccept()`. It is for the few service providers that do require `lineAccept()` that the effort is made at all.

The call is answered with the following function, which uses the same parameters as `lineAccept()`:

```
LONG lReplyCode = lineAnswer( hCall, lpUserUserInfo, dwSize );
```

Upon successful completion of this function, the call is connected. The following code executes when a call comes in:

```
void LineDev::CallStateMessageHandler( HCALL hCall,
                                       DWORD dwCallState,
                                       DWORD dwCallMode )
{
    // First call GetCallInfo to find out what address
    // we are using.
    LONG lErrCode, lReplyCode;
    LINECALLINFO callInfo;
    callInfo.dwTotalSize = sizeof( LINECALLINFO );
    if( lineGetCallInfo( hCall, &callInfo ) != 0 )
        return;          // Bail out if function failed.

    int addr_idx = callInfo.dwAddressID;

    // Now deal with the call state
    switch( dwCallState )
    {
        // A call is being offered to us, try to answer it.
        case LINECALLSTATE_OFFERING:
            // Is this a media mode that care about?
            if( !(callInfo.dwMediaMode &
                (LINEMEDIAMODE_UNKNOWN
                 | LINEMEDIAMODE_INTERACTIVEVOICE)) )

                // If not, we can leave right now.
                break;

                // Try to see if we can become the owner
                // of this call.
                lErrCode = lineSetCallPrivilege(hCall,
                            LINECALLPRIVILEGE_OWNER);
                tapiDlg->UpdateFuncs( "lineSetCallPrivilege",
                            lErrCode );
                if( lErrCode != 0 )
                    break;

                // Check the address capabilities to find out if we
                // can accept the call.
                if( _lineAddr[addr_idx]->GetCallFeatures()
                    & LINECALLFEATURE_ACCEPT )
                {
                    _lineAddr[addr_idx]->Accept( hCall );
                }
                < At this point, the program should take steps to
                  notify the user of the incoming call, by
                  creating noise and/or by popping up a dialog
                  on the users screen. >

                break;

        <other LINECALLSTATE_ cases>
    }
    // Update the display...
    _tapiDlg->Update( dwCallState );
}
```

Media Modes and Handoffs

As was mentioned previously, often the service provider is unable to determine what the media mode of the call is until after the call has been answered. Hopefully, in this case, there is an application that has bravely volunteered to handle unknown media mode calls by using the lineOpen() function. Here is the way to deal with situation.

The first step can (and should) actually take place prior to accepting the call. The application tells TAPI to notify it of any media mode changes by using the following function:

```
LONG lErrCode = lineMonitorMedia( hCall, dwMediaModes );
```

As usual, hCall is the call handle. dwMediaModes is a one or more of the media mode constants shown in Table 37.9 (except for LINEMEDIAMODE_UNKNOWN, which wouldn't make any sense in this case). TAPI only notifies the application for the modes specified in the dwMediaModes parameter.

When the media mode does change, TAPI sends a LINE_MONITORMEDIA message to the application. The format of this message is shown in Table 37.19.

Table 37.19. Parameters for the LINE_MONITORMEDIA message.

Parameter	Meaning
dwDevice	hCall is the handle for this call.
dwParam1	Specifies the new media mode. It's one of the LINEMEDIAMODE_ values shown in Table 37.9.
dwParam2	Unused.
dwParam3	Unused.

An application can also detect the media mode by making a call to lineGetCallInfo() to determine the current media mode. (Refer to Table 37.5.) The field to examine is dwMediaMode.

Sometimes, it is the application that determines the media mode. This can happen, for example, if the user presses the Receive Fax button. To do this, the application calls

```
LONG lErrCode = lineSetMediaMode( hCall, dwMediaMode );
```

where hCall is the call handle and dwMediaMode is the new media mode.

Once an application has discovered what the media mode is, it might not be prepared to handle the media mode. When this happens, the application needs to hand off the call to an application that can handle the media mode. There are two variations of a handoff. The first is called the *directed handoff*. In this kind of handoff, the application specifies the name of the new application to get the call. This type of handoff is intended for use with a suite of call-processing software—each program knows the capabilities of the others. The other type of handoff is called a *media mode handoff*. The application can use this type of handoff when it doesn't know which application should handle the call. The choice is left for TAPI to decide. Here is a single function that handles both cases:

```
LONG lErrCode = lineHandoff( hCall, lpszFileName, dwMediaMode);
```

hCall is, of course, the call handle. For a directed handoff, lpszFileName contains the name of the program to receive the call. This name should *not* include the path of the program. If the handoff is a media mode handoff, then lpszFileName is to be set to NULL. dwMediaMode specifies the media mode by using one of the LINEMEDIAMODE_ constants (see Table 37.9) for a media mode handoff. If lpszFileName is not NULL, then dwMediaMode is ignored. The lineHandoff() function does not change the mode. The media mode of the call must be changed prior to making the function call, either by the service provider or by the application calling the lineSetMediaMode() function.

When the handoff has been successfully completed, the application should deallocate its call handle using lineDeallocateCall(). There are times when the handoff fails because there is no other application that can handle the specified media mode. In this case, there is not much that can be done except to tell the user and to drop the call.

Caller ID

Caller ID, also known as calling line identification (CLID), is a feature that really shows the benefits of combining computers and telephones. Contact management software can use this information to bring up the relevant contact history for the person calling even before the phone is answered. Voice mail software can route recorded messages into different folders based on the name of the caller.

TAPI makes caller ID a piece of cake. When the service provider gets the caller ID information, it sends a LINE_CALLINFO message (see Table 37.6). dwParam1 has the LINECALLINFOSTATE _CALLERID bit set. When the application detects this situation, then it can retrieve the LINECALLINFO structure by calling lineGetCallInfo(). At this point, it is a simple matter for the application to read the caller ID information from the structure. The following code demonstrates this procedure:

```
void LineDev::CallInfoMessageHandler( HCALL hCall,
                                      DWORD dwCallInfoState )
{
// Get a large call info structure since we'll
    // need all of the information.
    LPBYTE buffer = new BYTE[BIG_BUFF];
    LPCALLINFO lpCallInfo = (LPCALLINFO)buffer;

    // Set dwTotalSize and make the call.
    lpCallInfo->dwTotalSize = sizeof(BYTE)*BIG_BUFF;
    if( lineGetCallInfo( hCall, lpCallInfo ) != 0 )
        return;        // Bail out if function failed.
```

```
    // Now deal with whatever has changed. A switch
    // statement is not used since several things may
    // changed at the same time.
    CString callIDNum;
    CString callIDName;

// If we got caller ID information, then read it out.
    if( state & LINECALLINFOSTATE_CALLERID )
    {
        // Was the call blocked or out of area?
        if( lpCallInfo->dwCallerIDFlags
            & LINECALLPARTYID_BLOCKED )
        {
            callIDNum = "Caller ID Blocked";
        }
        if( lpCallInfo->dwCallerIDFlags
            & LINECALLPARTYID_OUTOFAREA )
        {
            callIDNum = "Out of Area Call";
        }

        // Get the number if it exists.
        if( lpCallInfo->dwCallerIDSize > 0 )
        {
            callIDNum = (LPCSTR)(buffer
                    + lpCallInfo->dwCallerIDOffset );
        }

        // Get the name if it exists.
        if( lpCallInfo->dwCallerIDNameSize > 0 )
        {
            callIDName = (LPCSTR)(buffer
                    + lpCallInfo->dwCallerIDNameOffset );
        }
    __tapiDlg->UpdateCLID( callIDNum, callIDName );
    }
    < check for other LINECALLINFOSTATE_ changes>
}
```

Handling Assisted TAPI Requests

The beginning of this chapter discusses the method of using Assisted TAPI to make a call. Nothing is mentioned, however, about how this works. As it happens, TAPI doesn't do much more than broker the request. TAPI applications can, if appropriate, register to handle these requests. The application that handles the request now has complete control over the call. Figure 37.3 shows the path that an Assisted TAPI request takes in making a call.

If there is no TAPI application running, the TAPI DLL examines the TELEPHON.INI file to find the name of a likely request handler. By default, this application is the Dialer applet that comes with Windows 95. If you want to change this, you need to modify the [HandoffPriorities] section of TELEPHON.INI so that RequestMakeCall= is set to your application.

FIGURE 37.3.
*Assisted TAPI request
handling.*

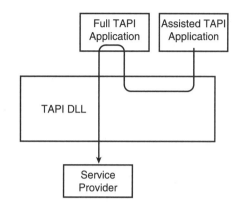

To register as an Assisted TAPI request handler, the application calls

```
LONG lErrCode = lineRegisterRequestRecipient
                ( hLineApp,
                  dwRegistrationInstance,
                  dwRequestMode,
                  bEnable );
```

hLineApp is the line application handle returned from lineInitialize(). The
dwRegistrationInstance is passed back to the application when it receives a LINE_REQUEST
message. The application is free to set this to any value it chooses. TAPI does not make any
use of this information. dwRequestMode should be set to LINEREQUESTMODE_MAKECALL. bEnable
is set to TRUE when the application registers and is set to FALSE when it unregisters.

> **WARNING**
>
> The TAPI SDK 1.0 mentions another request mode, LINEREQUESTMODE_MEDIACALL. Use
> of this request mode is discouraged because it will not be supported in future versions
> of TAPI.

When an Assisted TAPI request is made, TAPI sends a LINE_REQUEST message to all applications that have registered to handle Assisted TAPI requests. Table 37.20 shows the format of
this message.

Table 37.20. Parameters for the LINE_REQUEST message.

Parameter	Meaning
dwDevice	Not Used
dwParam1	Specifies the request mode (LINEREQUESTMODE_MAKECALL)
dwParam2	Unused
dwParam3	Unused

When an application receives this request, it calls

```
LONG lErrcode = lineGetRequest( hLineApp,
                                dwRequestMode,
                                lpRequestBuffer );
```

to get the information needed to place the call. `hLineApp` is the application handle. `dwRequestMode` is sent to `LINEREQUESTMODE_MAKECALL`. `lpRequestBuffer` is a pointer to a buffer that contains the needed information. With this information, the application can place the call using `lineMakeCall()`. Table 37.21 shows the structure of this buffer. The fields of this buffer correspond to the parameters used in the `tapiMakeCall()` function.

Table 37.21. The `LINEREQMAKECALL` structure.

`szDestAddress[]`	A null-terminated ASCII string containing the destination address (telephone number). This number may be canonical or dialable.
`szAppName[]`	A null-terminated ASCII string containing the name of the application that made the call.
`szCalledParty[]`	A null-terminated ASCII string containing the name of the party being called.
`szComment[]`	A null-terminated ASCII string containing a comment.

Phone Devices

TAPI also provides a complete API for interfacing with the telephone devices that sit on the user's desk. The functions provided allow the application to sense the hookswitch state, to sense button presses, and to display information on the phone device's display.

So far, service provider vendors have not seen fit to support phone devices to any large extent. Therefore, these functions are only be covered briefly in this chapter. The mechanics are essentially the same as those used for line devices. The reader who is familiar with programming for line devices will have no trouble coping with the phone device functions.

The initialization and shutdown processes are similar to the ones for line devices except that you use `phoneInitialize()`, `phoneNegotiateAPIVersion()`, `phoneOpen()`, `phoneClose()`, and `phoneShutdown()`. The `phoneGetDevCaps()` and `phoneGetStatus()` functions are used to retrieve device capabilities and status, respectively.

Information about the phone device's buttons can be retrieved with the `phoneGetButtonInfo()` function, and information about the buttons can set with the corresponding `phoneSetButtonInfo()` function. Likewise, the contents of a display (check the PHONECAPS structure to see if the phone device has one) can be retrieved with the phoneGetDisplay() function, and the contents of the display can be changed with the phoneSetDisplay() function.

The two most useful PHONE_ messages TAPI sends are PHONE_BUTTON and PHONE_STATUS. The former notifies the application that a button has been pressed. The latter is sent when the phone device's status has changed. The application can use this message, for instance, to detect when a handset was picked up and when the handset was replaced. In order to get PHONE_STATUS messages, the application needs to call phoneSetStatusMessages() in order to tell TAPI what messages it wants to receive.

> **NOTE**
>
> There are times when you need to coordinate the actions of a phone device with the actions of a line device. For example, detecting a handset being placed onhook can be a reason to drop a call. (Some service providers coordinate this "under the hood" so that the application doesn't need to worry about it.) Unfortunately, TAPI has no formal method of relating a line device with a phone device. One method that might work is to use the lineGetID() and phoneGetID() functions. With luck, the service provider vendor has seen fit to use the same device-naming scheme. If so, the line and phone devices can be correlated.

About the Included Software

There are three programs, along with their original source files, included on the CD-ROM. They were created using Microsoft's Visual C++ 2.0 compiler and MFC 3.0 framework. They are compiled as 32-bit Windows 95 applications. These programs were written to be fully backward compatible with Visual C++ 1.5 and MFC 2.5 so that they can be compiled as 16-bit Win 3.1 applications. (Use the large model.) The techniques used in these programs should also convert easily to Borland's OWL 2 framework.

T_ASSIST.EXE is a no-frills demonstration of Assisted TAPI.

T_PROBE.EXE is a utility that can be used to discover the device capabilities of any installed TAPI service provider.

T_DEMO.EXE is a demonstration application for the full Telephony API. It is intended to show how the TAPI portions of a telephony application can be written. T_DEMO.EXE for the sake of clarity is missing several features—notably an address book and call log, both of which should be considered essential to any "real" TAPI application.

Summary

Telephony API provides a rich tool kit to develop telephony applications. It provides a consistent methodology for coping with the diverse world of telephony systems. The mechanisms in TAPI handle almost any situation. However, it is the responsibility of the application to check if the features it needs are supported by the installed hardware and to decide how it will deal with unsupported features. By the same token, the application doesn't need to support every feature that the installed hardware supports. It only needs to support those features that are important to its own functionality. By keeping these things in mind, the programmer can create applications that will run without change on disparate telephone systems.

INDEX

Programming Windows 95 Unleashed

X-Y-Z

Add to Your Sams Library Today with the Best Books for Programming, Operating Systems, and New Technologies

The easiest way to order is to pick up the phone and call

1-800-428-5331

between 9:00 a.m. and 5:00 p.m. EST.
For faster service please have your credit card available.

ISBN	Quantity	Description of Item	Unit Cost	Total Cost
0-672-30593-3		Develop a Professional Visual C++ Application in 21 Days (Book/CD)	$35.00	
0-672-30493-7		What Every Visual C++ Programmer Should Know	$29.99	
0-672-30568-2		Teach Yourself OLE Programming in 21 Days	$39.99	
0-672-30594-1		Programming WinSock (Book/Disk)	$35.00	
0-672-30703-0		Programming Plug and Play (Book/Disk)	$39.99	
0-672-30549-6		Teach Yourself TCP/IP in 14 Days	$29.99	
0-672-30236-5		Windows Programmer's Guide to DLLs and Memory Management (Book/Disk)	$34.95	
0-672-30295-0		Moving into Windows NT Programming	$39.95	
0-672-30338-8		Inside Windows File Formats (Book/Disk)	$29.95	
0-672-30299-3		Uncharted Windows Programming (Book/Disk)	$34.95	
0-672-30239-x		Windows Developer's Guide to Application Design (Book/Disk)	$34.95	
0-672-30602-6		Programming Windows 95 Unleashed	$49.99	
❏ 3 ½" Disk		Shipping and Handling: See information below.		
❏ 5 ¼" Disk		TOTAL		

Shipping and Handling: $4.00 for the first book, and $1.75 for each additional book. Floppy disk: add $1.75 for shipping and handling. If you need to have it NOW, we can ship product to you in 24 hours for an additional charge of approximately $18.00, and you will receive your item overnight or in two days. Overseas shipping and handling adds $2.00 per book and $8.00 for up to three disks. Prices subject to change. Call for availability and pricing information on latest editions.

201 W. 103rd Street, Indianapolis, Indiana 46290

1-800-428-5331 — Orders   1-800-835-3202 — FAX   1-800-858-7674 — Customer Service

Book ISBN 0-672-30602-6

PLUG YOURSELF INTO...

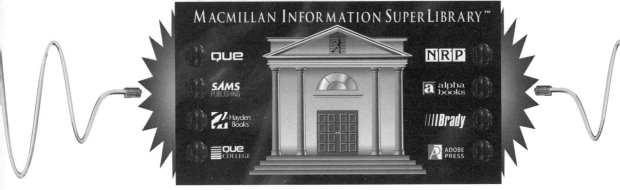

THE MACMILLAN INFORMATION SUPERLIBRARY™

Free information and vast computer resources from the world's leading computer book publisher—online!

FIND THE BOOKS THAT ARE RIGHT FOR YOU!

A complete online catalog, plus sample chapters and tables of contents give you an in-depth look at *all* of our books, including hard-to-find titles. It's the best way to find the books you need!

- STAY INFORMED with the latest computer industry news through our online newsletter, press releases, and customized Information SuperLibrary Reports.

- GET FAST ANSWERS to your questions about MCP books and software.

- VISIT our online bookstore for the latest information and editions!

- COMMUNICATE with our expert authors through e-mail and conferences.

- DOWNLOAD SOFTWARE from the immense MCP library:
    - Source code and files from MCP books
    - The best shareware, freeware, and demos

- DISCOVER HOT SPOTS on other parts of the Internet.

- WIN BOOKS in ongoing contests and giveaways!

TO PLUG INTO MCP: ➡ WORLD WIDE WEB: **http://www.mcp.com**

GOPHER: gopher.mcp.com

FTP: ftp.mcp.com

CD-ROM
Installation
Instructions

The Companion CD-ROM

The included disc contains new 32-bit Windows 95 applications, source code from the book, and much more. The CD-ROM is designed to be explored using a "Guide to the CD-ROM" program (\CDGUIDE\CDGUIDE.EXE).

Instructions for Windows 95 Users

If Windows 95 is installed on your computer and if you have the AutoPlay feature enabled, the Guide program starts automatically whenever you insert the disc into your CD-ROM drive.

Instructions for Windows 3.x Users

If you are running Windows 3.1 or if you have the Windows 95 AutoPlay feature disabled, you should run INSTALL.EXE from the root directory of the CD-ROM. INSTALL creates a Program Manager group named "Programming Windows 95" and also a directory on your hard drive named \WPU. When INSTALL ends, the "Guide to the CD-ROM" program starts automatically. An icon in the Programming Windows 95 group enables you to restart the Guide program without re-running INSTALL.

The "Guide to the CD-ROM" program requires at least 256 colors. For best results, set your monitor to display between 256 and 64,000 colors. A screen resolution of 640×480 pixels is also recommended. If necessary, adjust your monitor settings before using the CD-ROM.